Lecture Notes in Artificial Intelligence   13015

Subseries of Lecture Notes in Computer Science

More information about this subseries at http://www.springer.com/series/1244

Xin-Jun Liu · Zhenguo Nie · Jingjun Yu ·
Fugui Xie · Rui Song (Eds.)

Intelligent Robotics
and Applications

14th International Conference, ICIRA 2021
Yantai, China, October 22–25, 2021
Proceedings, Part III

 Springer

Editors
Xin-Jun Liu
Tsinghua University
Beijing, China

Zhenguo Nie
Tsinghua University
Beijing, China

Jingjun Yu
Beihang University
Beijing, China

Fugui Xie
Tsinghua University
Beijing, China

Rui Song
Shandong University
Shandong, China

ISSN 0302-9743   ISSN 1611-3349 (electronic)
Lecture Notes in Artificial Intelligence
ISBN 978-3-030-89133-6   ISBN 978-3-030-89134-3 (eBook)
https://doi.org/10.1007/978-3-030-89134-3

LNCS Sublibrary: SL7 – Artificial Intelligence

This Springer imprint is published by the registered company Springer Nature Switzerland AG
The registered company address is: Gewerbestrasse 11, 6330 Cham, Switzerland

Preface

With the theme "Make Robots Infinitely Possible", the 14th International Conference on Intelligent Robotics and Applications (ICIRA 2021) was held in Yantai, China, during October 22–25, 2021, and designed to encourage advancement in the field of robotics, automation, mechatronics, and applications. The ICIRA series aims to promote top-level research and globalize quality research in general, making discussions and presentations more internationally competitive and focusing on the latest outstanding achievements, future trends, and demands.

ICIRA 2021 was organized by Tsinghua University, co-organized by Beihang University, Shandong University, YEDA, Yantai University, and IFToMM China-Beijing, undertaken by the Tsingke+ Research Institute, and technically co-sponsored by Springer. On this occasion, three distinguished plenary speakers and 10 keynote speakers delivered their outstanding research works in various fields of robotics. Participants gave a total of 186 oral presentations and 115 poster presentations, enjoying this excellent opportunity to share their latest research findings.

The ICIRA 2021 proceedings cover over 17 research topics, with a total of 299 papers selected for publication in four volumes of Springer's Lecture Note in Artificial Intelligence. Here we would like to express our sincere appreciation to all the authors, participants, and distinguished plenary and keynote speakers. Special thanks are also extended to all members of the Organizing Committee, all reviewers for peer review, all staff of the conference affairs group, and all volunteers for their diligent work.

October 2021

Xin-Jun Liu
Zhenguo Nie
Jingjun Yu
Fugui Xie
Rui Song

Organization

Honorary Chair

Youlun Xiong   Huazhong University of Science and Technology, China

General Chair

Xin-Jun Liu   Tsinghua University, China

General Co-chairs

Rui Song   Shandong University, China
Zengguang Hou   Institute of Automation, CAS, China
Qinchuan Li   Zhejiang Sci-Tech University, China
Qinning Wang   Peking University, China
Huichan Zhao   Tsinghua University, China
Jangmyung Lee   Pusan National University, South Korea

Program Chair

Jingjun Yu   Beihang University, China

Program Co-chairs

Xin Ma   Shandong University, China
Fugui Xie   Tsinghua University, China
Wenguang Yang   Yantai University, China
Bo Tao   Huazhong University of Science and Technology, China
Xuguang Lan   Xi'an Jiatong University, China
Naoyuki Kubota   Tokyo Metropolitan University, Japan
Ling Zhao   Yantai YEDA, China

Publication Chair

Zhenguo Nie   Tsinghua University, China

Award Chair

Limin Zhu   Shanghai Jiao Tong University, China

Advisory Committee

Jorge Angeles	McGill University, Canada
Jianda Han	Shenyang Institute of Automation, CAS, China
Guobiao Wang	National Natural Science Foundation of China, China
Tamio Arai	University of Tokyo, Japan
Qiang Huang	Beijing Institute of Technology, China
Tianmiao Wang	Beihang University, China
Hegao Cai	Harbin Institute of Technology, China
Oussama Khatib	Stanford University, USA
Tianran Wang	Shenyang Institute of Automation, CAS, China
Tianyou Chai	Northeastern University, China
Yinan Lai	National Natural Science Foundation of China, China
Yuechao Wang	Shenyang Institute of Automation, CAS, China
Jie Chen	Tianjin University, China
Jangmyung Lee	Pusan National University, South Korea
Bogdan M. Wilamowski	Auburn University, USA
Jiansheng Dai	King's College London, UK
Zhongqin Lin	Shanghai Jiao Tong University, China
Ming Xie	Nanyang Technical University, Singapore
Zongquan Deng	Harbin Institute of Technology, China
Hong Liu	Harbin Institute of Technology, China
Yangsheng Xu	The Chinese University of Hong Kong, China
Han Ding	Huazhong University of Science and Technology, China
Honghai Liu	Harbin Institute of Technology, China
Huayong Yang	Zhejiang University, China
Xilun Ding	Beihang University, China
Shugen Ma	Ritsumeikan University, Japan
Jie Zhao	Harbin Institute of Technology, China
Baoyan Duan	Xidian University, China
Daokui Qu	SIASUN, China
Nanning Zheng	Xi'an Jiatong University, China
Xisheng Feng	Shenyang Institute of Automation, CAS, China
Min Tan	Institute of Automation, CAS, China
Xiangyang Zhu	Shanghai Jiao Tong University, China
Toshio Fukuda	Nagoya University, Japan
Kevin Warwick	Coventry University, UK

Contents – Part III

Machine Intelligence for Human Motion Analytics

Human-Robot Interaction for Service Robots

Novel Mechanisms, Robots and Applications

Robotic Machining

An Intelligent Path Generation Method of Robotic Grinding for Large Forging Parts

Shouxin Yan, Qilong Wang, Pengfei Su, and Wei Wang$^{(\boxtimes)}$

School of Mechanical Engineering and Automation, Beihang University, Beijing 100191, China
wangwei701@buaa.edu.cn

Abstract. Large forging parts widely adopted in oil rigs, wind mills, large vessels and other complex equipment often carry random forging defects such as parting lines, burrs and high islands, which are traditionally removed through manual grinding by skilled operators. These random defects pose a big challenge to researchers interested in large forging parts grinding path generation by a CAD/CAM system. This paper proposes a new path generation method based on intelligent defect recognition of robotic grinding for large forging parts. A point cloud is first constructed of random defects on the surfaces of the to-be-ground parts from the unmatched points that emerge from the matching of the point clouds captured by a laser camera from the parts against those from the standard parts, a process employing both a random sample consensus algorithm and a modified iterative closest point algorithm. Then, the grinding path generation strategy is established by sorting the random defects according to a law of area on the fitting surface and robotic grinding motion programs are generated by transferring the coordinates of the random defects from the laser camera frame into the robot base frame. Finally, robotic grinding tests are conducted to verify the identification accuracy of the proposed new method. Results of the tests indicate that the method has accurately identified all random defects on a 10-m long forging part and intelligently generated subsequent robotic grinding paths according to the identified random feature categories. This study therefore provides an intelligent tool for finishing large forging parts.

Keywords: Large forging part · Defect identification · Robotic grinding · Path generation

1 Introduction

Large forging parts are the fundamental components used in many heavy equipment, and their manufacturing methods are a major indicator of the service performance of large complex equipment [1]. One key consideration for the grinding of such large parts is the removal of parting lines, flashes, oxide skins, higher islands and other random defects on the surface after forging [2]. Manual grinding, which remains an unavoidable choice in forging workshops, is highly demanding yet with low efficiency [3]: The identification

---

S. Yan, Q. Wang—Authors with equal contributions.

© Springer Nature Switzerland AG 2021
X.-J. Liu et al. (Eds.): ICIRA 2021, LNAI 13015, pp. 3–13, 2021.
https://doi.org/10.1007/978-3-030-89134-3_1

and location of random defects by vision and haptic perception and subsequent decisions on grinding strategies and grinding paths depend largely on the years-long grinding experience of grinding operators. Currently traditional CNC and teaching robot programming methods have been applied to generate economical grinding paths on very large surfaces, but with low efficiency in removing the randomly distributed large forging defects, as is shown by Fig. 1, which presents a 10-m long forging part in an oil rig before grinding, after manual grinding and its CAD model respectively. Therefore, the main technical challenge in a robotic grinding task for large forging parts is how to integrate effective human grinding skills into robotic identification of random defects and generation of grinding paths specifically suited to them, instead of performing uniform grinding paths on the whole large part.

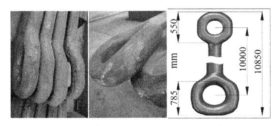

Fig. 1. A typical large forging part: before grinding, after manual grinding, and its CAD model

Recognition of local features, a key technique in robot-oriented intelligent manufacturing, has attracted much research interest in recent years. Xiao et al. processed the point cloud slices for the analysis of surface geometric features in identifying the blade local wear area after repairing with an additive manufacturing method [4]. Deng et al. applied the hand-eye monocular recognition system in building a global map of the workpiece, and an ellipse detection algorithm in identifying its local features [5]. Their research has proved processing point clouds an effective research tool for identifying local features on large complex parts, but the existing recognition methods ineffective in locating random defects on large forging parts with low texture and no irregular geometric contours, which instead can be quickly accomplished by experienced manual operators. We therefore hypothesize that a point cloud matching technique can be employed to compare the to-be-ground forging part with a standard golden part from manual grinding, and human grinding skills thus generalized for the identification of random defects can then be transferred into a robot controller.

Recent research has also directed at grinding path generation, another key factor in robotic manufacturing Ma et al. applied feature points selected on the surface of the workpiece model to the synchronous generation of a B-spline curve and the position coordinates and contact directions on the grinding path [6]. Based on the contact kinematics, Wang et al. proposed a targeted path generation strategy according to the curvature of the workpiece, effectively improving the robotic grinding quality [7]. Lv et al. proposed a path generation method based on the material removal profile model, which took the elastic deformation of the tool and the workpiece into account, resulting in improved accuracy of robotic grinding [8]. Considering the deformation of the contact wheel caused by belt tension, Wang et al. established an improved grinding stress distribution model to predict the grinding depth [9]. The above-mentioned methods all require accurate CAD models of workpieces, which however often fail to cover significant inconsistency in the actual shapes of forging parts, therefore incapable of generating the desired grinding paths. The path generation methods involved are often flawed, making no distinction between areas with and those without obvious defects, lacking in intelligent decision-making about defect types and distribution, and consequently unable to generate grinding paths specifically suited to the defects. This indiscriminate grinding pattern usually leads to high cost and low processing efficiency. We therefore speculate on the idea of intelligent feature classification decision for better performance of CAD models in robotic path grinding generation.

In summary, based on the point cloud registration technology, this paper proposes a feature extraction method to establish a point cloud for low-texture and irregular defects on a large forging part. Then the pose information extracted from the resulted point cloud will be applied in a CAD/CAM system to directly generate robot grinding paths, without reconstructing a part model out of the point cloud data. Afterwards, a feature classification decision will be introduced to generate the corresponding grinding paths for random forging defects, aimed to lower the time cost of large forging parts grinding. This paper is structured as follows: After the introduction and literature review in Sect. 1, Sect. 2 presents the main methods involved in the present study, including algorithm overview, feature recognition method, and path generation method. The grinding tests conducted to verify the validity of the proposed method are reported in Sect. 3, and Sect. 4 will provide a brief summary of the conclusions from the study.

2   Methods

2.1   Algorithm Overview

This paper proposes a new frame for random features recognition and robotic grinding paths generation for large forging parts. An overview of the methods is shown in Fig. 2, including Step 1. random features recognition based on point cloud, and Step 2. robot grinding path generation.

With 3D capturing devices, the point clouds of large forging parts can be captured. Meanwhile, the geometric information is presented in point cloud data.

For the direct robot grinding path generation method without surface reconstruction from the point cloud, a modified ICP (Iterative Closest Point) algorithm based on KD-tree search is invented to match the point cloud captured from a forging part with that from the standard part's point cloud. The purpose is to extract random defect features, which are to be classified by their dimensions to select path generation strategies. And the robot grinding motion programs will be subsequently generated.

2.2   Recognition of Random Features Based on Point Clouds

In order to extract the relevant random forging features, target point cloud M and the standard point cloud N need to be matched. Where the point clouds do not match suggests

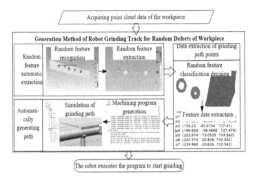

Fig. 2. Algorithm overview

the location of defect features. In this study, Fast Point Feature Histograms (FPFH) is adopted as the point cloud match parameters. The algorithm flowchart of random features recognition is shown in Fig. 3.

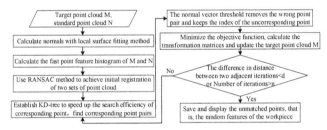

Fig. 3. Flowchart for random defect recognition

Point cloud registration is the core step of the algorithm, which can be divided into two stages, initial matching and fine matching to correct the initial matrix. Initial matching aims to achieve the initial estimation of the conversion matrix between two point clouds. The initial matching is performed by the RANSAC algorithm.

In fine point cloud matching, the modified ICP incorporating KD-tree search with the traditional ICP algorithm can significantly cut the computing cost of the traditional ICP algorithm [10]. In this study, the software is developed in QT environment to implement the above algorithm, and the result of defects feature extraction from a large forging part is shown in Fig. 4.

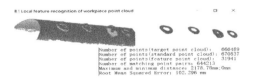

Fig. 4. Feature recognition result

The target point cloud M includes 666,489 points, and the standard point cloud N has 670,837 points. It takes 19 s to execute the recognition algorithm on M and N, and the number of matched point pairs are 31,941. The results show that the algorithm has identified the higher island features information, and output the coordinates of the unmatched points, which will be used in generating grinding paths.

2.3 Generation Method of Robotic Grinding Paths

The extracted random defect point cloud in the previous section contains a large number of disordered point information, and random defects have to be sorted out before generating grinding paths. Without reconstructing the 3D point cloud, the grinding paths are generated based on the unmatched point cloud data. The corresponding path generation strategy depends the size of the unmatched point cloud. The generation method of robotic grinding path includes the following key steps: (1) Random defect classification based on the size of the point cloud; (2) Positions and orientations of path points; (3) The grinding path generation and robot program updating. The flowchart is shown in Fig. 5.

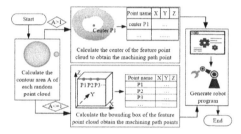

Fig. 5. Flowchart of intelligent path generation for robotic grinding

Classification of Random Defects Based on Point Cloud Area. Grinding tools meet with the workpiece in line or surface contact. Belt grinding is adopted in this study. According to Hertz contact formula, the actual contact area between the elastic contact wheel and the rigid part is modeled as an ellipse. The robotic grinding path strategy depends on the ratio between the defect size and the contact area. If the defect area is less than the actual contact area between the tool and the part, the defects can be ground by one PTP path. If the defect size is greater than the actual contact area, a continuous grinding path needs to be designed, and sometimes the grinding path has to repeat itself in some cycles, as shown in Fig. 6(a).

The actual contact area between the grinding tool and the workpiece is expressed as

$$S_g = \pi ab \tag{1}$$

where a and b are the semi-major and semi-minor axis of the contact ellipse. b can be approximated by $b = \beta a$, where β is the non-circular section constant. According to Hertz contact formula, the contact area can be

$$S_g = \pi \beta \left(3FR/4E^*\right)^{2/3} \tag{2}$$

Where F is the contact force, E is the elastic modulus and R is the contact radius. The defect area S can be obtained by processing the defect point cloud through the open source toolkit (Visualization Toolkit) VTK. Take $A = Sg/S$ as the sorting criterion. When $A \geqslant 1$, the defect is seen as a small area defect, which otherwise is a large one. The results after classification are shown in Fig. 6(b).

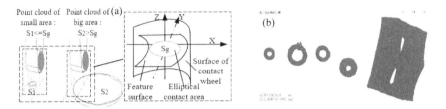

Sketch of random defect area and contact area   Results of Random defect classification

Fig. 6. Random defect classification

Robot Path Point Positioning and Method Disorientation. Based on the defect classification, the corresponding grinding path is generated. It is necessary to obtain the path points and determine the normal vector of the grinding tool with respect to the workpiece. For small-area defects, it is enough to extract the center coordinate of the point cloud as the robot path point. The path point for small area is shown in Fig. 7(a).

For large random defects with multi-path points but not regular geometric contours, a bounding box calculation method is used to generate the grinding path. The large defect path points are shown in Fig. 7(b). First, the bounding box AABB of the large defect is calculated. Then, perpendicular to the grinding direction, divide the bounding box equally by $\eta(\eta = 0.3 -9)$ times of the actual processing width W, and set each node on the edge as the path point. Finally make the contact normal vector of the grinding tool coincide with the normal vector of the center point of the bounding box. In this way the contact direction of the robot grinding path is determined.

Robot Program Generation Strategy. The robot grinding path includes not only the grinding path, but also the necessary cut-in and cut-out path, and passes of robot grinding path. As shown in Fig. 8(a), for small area defects, the single grinding path is generated. Suppose $p_{i,k} = (x_i, y_i, z_i)$ (where i is the index of centers, k is the number of the program segment) is the center of a small area random feature. Grinding direction is along the X-axis, and the radius of the contact wheel is r. According to the tool tangential in and out principle during grinding, define the path correction starting point $p_{i,k-1}$ and correction end point $p_{i,k+1}$

$$P_{i,k-1} = (x_i - r, y_i, z_i), P_{i,k+1} = (x_i + r, y_i, z_i) \tag{3}$$

The k-th grinding path passes through the center $p_{i,k}$ from the starting point $p_{i,k-1}$ to the end $p_{i,k+1}$. The transition path between different path segments is generated according to the path from $p_{i-1,k+1}$ to $p_{i+1,k-1}$. According to the value of the center z_i and the single

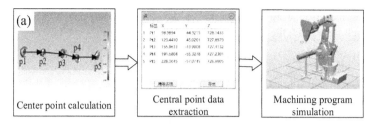

Path point data extraction for Small random defects

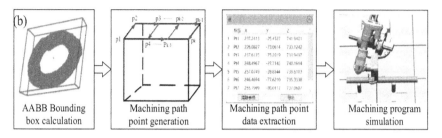

Path point data extraction for Large random defects

Fig. 7. Via point data extraction for Random defects on large forging parts

grinding depth, the pass number of the defect grinding is determined. Suppose the single grinding depth is h, usually obtained by test grinding. The pass number C_i of each path segment is

$$C_i = ceil(z_i/h) \tag{4}$$

where ceil (*) is the rounding up function. After each pass, the C_i value of all path segments is checked. When C_i of one path segment is reduced to 0, the path segment is deleted from the program and the robot program is updated. Program running until all the C_i is 0.

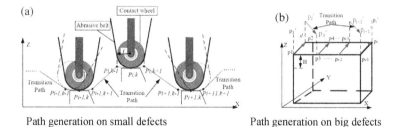

Path generation on small defects   Path generation on big defects

Fig. 8. Grinding path generation.

Next the continuous grinding path can be generated. Constrained by processing consistency in path segments, grinding large defects is carried out in the same direction.

The grinding direction from p_{i-1} to p_i keeps the same in each pass. Assume the tool height of each pass as H, the via point P_i' as

$$P_i' = (x_i, y_i, z_i + H) \tag{5}$$

Similar to the small defect, after determining the continuous path, the pass number needs to be generated. Rewrite z_i in formula (4) as the side length Z_i in the Z-axis direction of the bounding box, and then determine the pass number to complete the defect grinding. When Z_i is zero, the grinding program ends. In this study, the QT developing environment is used to implement the above algorithm, and then generate the RAPID program. After importing it into the robot simulation software RobotStudio, the simulation result is shown in Fig. 9.

Simulation of grinding path for small defects

Simulation of grinding path for large defects

Fig. 9. Simulations of grinding path generation.

3   Experiments

The robot platform is composed of an ABB IRB6660 industrial robot, a binocular vision scanner, a large forging part, fixtures and a computer control system, as shown in Fig. 10. The random defects are simulated by intendedly placing random fasteners on the part. A robot offline programming software is developed based on the QT platform, where all the algorithms in this study are assembled. The sample contains 4 small "defects" and 1 large "defect". All features are recognized, and then 12 robot path points are generated, including 4 small-area feature centers and 8 large defect feature bounding box nodes. Their coordinates transformed into the robot base frame are shown in Table 1.

To verify the algorithm proposed in this paper, a comparative experiment is conducted with respect to the conventional point cloud reconstruction method. Take a cylindrical

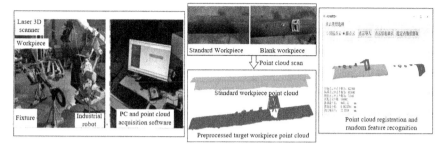

Fig. 10. Experiment platform and point cloud acquisition

Table 1. Point coordinates with respect to robot base frame

point name	X	Y	Z
Ceter p1	104.709	−46.7918	728.272
...	...	...	...
Ceter p4	199.628	− 58.3608	727.479
P5	222.574	−73.0525	733.342
...	...	...	...
p12	274.756	−73.0525	733.342

part with a length of 1000mm and a diameter of 150mm as an example. When the point cloud reconstruction method is used, it needs the steps of point cloud preprocessing, point cloud packaging, grid filling and smoothing, and set nearly ten parameters such as the size of non-connected items, the sensitivity of isolated points in vitro, and the maximum number of edge holes. Then the reconstructed model is imported into the offline programming software to generate a machining path covering all the workpieces. Firstly, this complex process cannot be automatically completed by the computer software, but requires multiple manual interventions. The path generation takes about 30 min. In contrast, the new method proposed in this paper to generate the grinding path is finished in three steps only: point cloud registration, feature extraction and classification, and path generation. Only two parameters, the normal vector threshold and the area threshold, need to be preset. Especially, the entire process can be completed automatically by software, and the time consumed for path generation is about 8 min.

Secondly, because the point cloud reconstruction method does not make random feature classification decisions, the length of the generated grinding path is about 4,300 mm to cover the entire workpiece, as shown in Fig. 11(b). Assuming the robot is move at the speed of 50 mm/s, and the total time for grinding is about 2 min. Comparatively, the new method is incorporated with random feature classification decisions, so the generated path length is only about 2000 mm, as shown in Fig. 11(a), and grinding time only need 40 s at the same robot speed. The robotic grinding test is shown in Fig. 12.

The experimental results show that the method proposed in this paper has greatly reduced the load of path generation and parameter settings. The path generation efficiency is increased by about 4 times. Furthermore, it is completed automatically without any manual intervention. The last point is, due to the introduction of feature classification decisions, the grinding paths are generated according to defect feature types. The intelligent method greatly reduces the complexity of the robot path and shortens the grinding time by 50%. If the size of the workpiece and random features increase, the efficiency will be further improved.

(a)
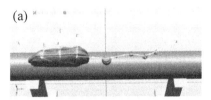

Paths generated without random classification decisions;

(b)
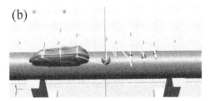

Paths generated with random classification decisions;

Fig. 11. Path simulation

Fig. 12. Robotic grinding for a large forging part

4 Conclusions

In the present study, an intelligent grinding path generation method based on random defects identification has been proposed to realize robotic grinding for large forging parts.

Validation experiments have shown that this method can accurately identify random defects on the surfaces of large forging parts, resulting in a significant 50% increase in grinding efficiency. Conclusions of the study are summarized as follows:

(1) The adoption of point cloud registration technology for random defects identification of forging parts successfully tackled the challenge of low-texture and irregular features identification, significantly improving identification accuracy.
(2) The direct application of point cloud to robot grinding path generation yielded calculation efficiency more than five times that of the existing complex point cloud reconstruction method. Its intelligent one-click operation suggests remarkable engineering significance.
(3) The designed classification decision method of random defects and the appropriate path generation strategy for random defect types of different areas greatly simplified the generated path, which promises shortened forging parts finishing cycle and lower energy consumption.
(4) The robotic tool created by the proposed method provides an effective alternative to manual grinding, which is expected to greatly reduce the work intensity of large forging part finishing.

References

1. Kafle, A., Shrestha, P.L., Chitrakar, S., et al.: A review on casting technology with the prospects on its application for hydro turbines. J. Phys. Conf. Ser. **1608** (2020)
2. Prabhakar, A., Papanikolaou, M., Salonitis, K., Jolly, M., et al.: Minimising defect formation in sand casting of sheet lead: a DoE approach. Metals-Open Access Metall. J. **10**(2), 252 (2020)
3. Zhang, M., Chen, T., Tan, Y., et al.: An adaptive grinding method for precision-cast blades with geometric deviation. Int. J. Adv. Manuf. Technol. (3) (2020)
4. Xiao, W., Liu, G., Zhao, G.: Generating the tool path directly with point cloud for aero-engine blades repair. Proc. Inst. Mech. Eng. **235**(5) (2021)
5. Di, D., Polden, J., Dong, J., et al.: Sensor guided robot path generation for surface repair tasks on a large scale buoyancy module. IEEE/ASME Trans. Mechatron. **23**(2), 636–645 (2018)
6. Ma, K., Han, L., Sun, X., et al.: A path planning method of robotic belt grinding for workpieces with complex surfaces. IEEE/ASME Trans. Mechatron. **PP**(99), 1 (2020)
7. Wang, W., Yun, C.: A path planning method for robotic belt surface grinding. Chin. J. Aeronaut. **24**(004), 520–526 (2011)
8. Lv, Y., Peng, Z., Qu, C., et al.: An adaptive trajectory planning algorithm for robotic belt grinding of blade leading and trailing edges based on material removal profile model. Robot. Comput.-Integr. Manuf. **66**, 101987 (2020)
9. Wang, W., Liu, F., et al.: Prediction of depth of cut for robotic belt grinding. Int. J. Adv. Manuf. Technol. **91**(1–4), 699–708 (2017)
10. Li, S., Wang, J., Liang, Z., et al.: Tree point clouds registration using an improved ICP algorithm based on kd-tree. In: IGARSS 2016–2016 IEEE International Geoscience and Remote Sensing Symposium. IEEE (2016)

Research and Analysis on Energy Consumption of Underwater Hexapod Robot Based on Typical Gait

Xiufeng Ma[1,2,3,4], Qifeng Zhang[2,3,4(✉)], Yingzhe Sun[2,3,4,5], and Ning Wang[2,3,4,6]

[1] College of Information Science and Engineering, Northeastern University,
Shenyang 110819, China
`maxiufeng@sia.cn`
[2] State Key Laboratory of Robotics, Shenyang Institute of Automation,
Chinese Academy of Sciences, Shenyang 110016, China
`{zqf,sunyingzhe,wangning1}@sia.cn`
[3] Institutes for Robotics and Intelligent Manufacturing, Chinese Academy of Sciences,
Shenyang 110169, China
[4] Key Laboratory of Marine Robotics, Liaoning Province, Shenyang 110169, China
[5] University of Chinese Academy of Sciences, Beijing 100049, China
[6] School of Mechanical Engineering and Automation, Northeastern University,
Shenyang 110819, China

Abstract. The energy consumption status of underwater hexapod robot has reference significance for long-time operation, energy power system design and global path planning. The purpose of this paper is to analyze the motion energy consumption of the underwater hexapod robot walking in the seabed environment. Based on the principle of kinematics, a typical gait is designed for the hexapod robot proposed in this paper, and a detailed dynamic model of the underwater hexapod robot in underwater motion is attempted to be established. Therefore, a foot force distribution method is proposed and combined with the dynamics model, and the energy consumption model of the robot in this gait is deduced and constructed, with the mobile energy consumption rate as the evaluation index. The effects of different water flow velocity, adjusting gait parameters and changing rotation angular velocity on the energy consumption of the robot are studied. Finally, the simulation results and low-energy motion are given to illustrate the effectiveness of the above methods, which provides the basis for the design of physical prototype and energy based path planning.

Keywords: Underwater hexapod robot · Gait · Dynamics · Foot force distribution · Energy consumption

1 Introduction

The ocean occupies a large part of the total area of the earth, and different kinds of underwater robots are created. The foot robot is one of them. Compared with the traditional underwater robot driven by propeller or crawler, the foot robot is more suitable for off-shore areas or uneven terrain, so there is a hexapod robot with better adaptability to the environment to complete underwater exploration and operation tasks. It is also used in offshore oil, cable laying, and Environmental geomorphology acquisition, military and other fields [1–4]. However, the leg driven foot robot has the characteristics of low load to weight ratio and low energy consumption efficiency [5]. For the underwater robot applied in the seabed environment, whether it is powered by cable or battery, energy consumption is a major challenge for the long-term work of the robot system, the energy consumption of robot in periodic motion with specific gait plays a key role in power supply system design and motion path planning.

The influencing factors of energy consumption of underwater hexapod robot are: robot structure parameters, gait parameters, environmental effects and so on. In the past few decades, many researchers have done research on the energy consumption and motion of multi-foot robot. R. kurazume [6] has carried out experimental research on the energy efficiency of multi-foot walking robot. M. F. Silva [7] has analyzed the relationship between the power consumption of multi-foot system and the motion parameters. Based on the simplified model of underwater hexapod robot, Kar et al. [8] analyzed the energy consumption from the aspects of structure parameters, friction coefficient and gait duty cycle, combined with the instantaneous joint torque and joint angular velocity data. According to the model of underwater hexapod robot, Marhefka and Orin analyzed the average power consumption of straight-line walking with wave gait [9]. Based on the optimal foot force distribution, Roy and Pratihar [10] studied the influence of walking parameters on the motion energy consumption of underwater hexapod robot, Kelasidi et al. [11] compared and analyzed the energy efficiency of underwater snake like robot and ROV, and simulated the total energy consumption and transportation cost of them. Most of the work mentioned above focuses on the land robot moving along a straight line. At present, there is no analysis on the motion energy consumption of building the underwater hexapod robot model walking in the seabed environment using typical gait. Finally, the power consumption curves under different water flow speeds and changing gait parameters are obtained.

2   Configuration and Walking Gait of Robot

2.1   Configuration of Robot

As shown in Fig. 1, the underwater hexapod robot configuration considered in this study is composed of body and six legs, each leg has the same structure, and consists of three rotating joints and three connecting rods driven by three DC motors and wave reducer. Three joints are root joint along the axis of z axis, hip joint and knee joint parallel to y axis. Among them, coordinate system {B} represents the fixed coordinate system of the center of the body, the coordinate system {G} represents the fixed coordinate system on the ground, and the z axis points to the negative direction of gravity.

Taking the single leg as an example, the kinematics analysis is carried out, and the single leg D-H coordinate system of the underwater hexapod robot is established. As shown in Fig. 2, the root joint coordinate system is taken as the reference coordinate system, and the kinematics equation of the underwater hexapod robot takes the joint angle as the independent variable to establish the spatial position of the foot end E point in the reference coordinate system.

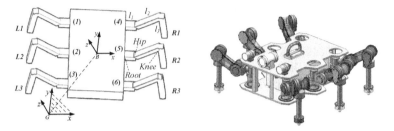

Fig. 1. Configuration of underwater hexapod robot.

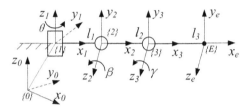

Fig. 2. Single leg D-H coordinate system.

The forward kinematics is obtained by using the transformation formula of continuous rotation between joints.

$$_E^0\mathbf{T} = {}_1^0\mathbf{T}_2^1\mathbf{T}_3^2\mathbf{T}_E^3\mathbf{T} \tag{1}$$

Where the right side of Eq. (1) is formed by the rotation and translation transformation matrix from the root joint to the end of the leg.

2.2 Walking Gaits of Robot

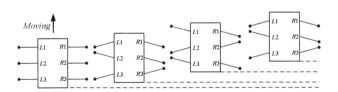

Fig. 3. Three gait of robot.

Gait research was initially carried out by zoologists, and McGhee systematically gave a series of description methods about gait [12]. In many walking gait, the typical triangle gait mode of continuous leg movement is adopted. Because this walking mode takes into account both speed and stability, the six legs are divided into two groups, the first group (G1) L1, R2, L3, the second group (G2) R1, L2, R3. The two groups of legs alternately perform swing and support to achieve movement. Figure 3 is straight and fixed-point rotation modes respectively. The walking mode of the robot is generated by sine function with parameters, and the specific parameters are described in Table 1. Among them, the walking speed can be changed by modifying the swing time, waiting time or step size to improve the stability.

Table 1. Gait parameters.

Number	Parameter	Description
1	Swing time (Tss)	Leg swing time/leg support time
2	Waiting time (Tw)	Swing and support interval
3	Movement Period (Tc)	Tc = Tss + Tw
4	Step length (B)	Leg swing length
5	Step high (H)	Leg swing height

3 Dynamic Model of Robot

3.1 One Leg Dynamic Model

For each leg of the underwater hexapod robot, it exerts force on the body in the process of motion, as shown in Fig. 4a). In order to derive the dynamic equation including hydrodynamic term and determine the change of joint torque in the motion period, Newton Euler equation system is used to derive a dynamic expression, which can be written in the form of vector matrix given below.

$$\tau = \mathbf{M}\ddot{\theta} + \mathbf{C}_E + \mathbf{C}_O + \mathbf{H} + \mathbf{J}^T\mathbf{F}_E + \mathbf{D}_L \tag{2}$$

Among them, $\mathbf{M}$ is the mass matrix of the leg, $\mathbf{C}_E$ is the centrifugal force term, $\mathbf{C}_O$ is the Coriolis force term, $\mathbf{H}$ is the net buoyancy term, $\mathbf{F}_E$ is the contact force between the end of the leg and the ground, $\mathbf{J}$ is the Jacobian matrix of the leg mechanism, $\mathbf{D}_L$ is the hydrodynamic term, which is obtained by Morrison formula and hydrodynamic simulation parameter identification method [13], and the hydrodynamic term composed of hydrodynamic moment and inertia moment is obtained, while the foot contact force term is calculated by dynamics and force distribution method.

3.2 Body Dynamic Model

The underwater environment is more complex than the land environment. The foot robot walking underwater will also be affected by buoyancy and water flow. The force of the underwater hexapod robot is shown in Fig. 4b). For the sake of simplicity, only one foot force component is drawn in the figure.

The vertical projection of the body is in the X-Y plane, and the coordinate system $\{O_i\}$ is the fixed coordinate system of the root joint, which can be obtained by the offset of the fixed coordinate system $\{B\}$ in the center of the body. The three force components at the end of the supporting foot are represented by the $\{O_i\}$ coordinate system with f_{xi}, f_{yi} and f_{zi} respectively. The typical triangular gait is used as the gait mode of the robot, and the number of supporting legs varies between 3 and 6 during the movement, $\mathbf{F} = [Fx\ Fy\ Fz]^T$ is the resultant force vector of the robot body, $\mathbf{T} = [Tx\ Ty\ Tz]^T$ is the resultant moment vector of the robot body, which is the result of gravity, self-motion and external environment water flow acting on the robot body. The equilibrium equation of force and moment is expressed as:

$$\mathbf{BL} + \mathbf{H} = \mathbf{0} \tag{3}$$

where

$$\mathbf{B} = \begin{bmatrix} \mathbf{I} & \mathbf{I} & \dots & \mathbf{I} \\ \mathbf{A}_1 & \mathbf{A}_2 & \dots & \mathbf{A}_n \end{bmatrix} \quad \mathbf{A}_i = \begin{bmatrix} 0 & -z_i & y_i \\ z_i & 0 & -x_i \\ -y_i & x_i & 0 \end{bmatrix},$$

$$\mathbf{L} = \begin{bmatrix} f_{x1}\ f_{x1}\ f_{z1} & \dots & f_{xn}\ f_{yn}\ f_{zn} \end{bmatrix}^T \quad \mathbf{H} = \begin{bmatrix} \mathbf{F}^T & \mathbf{T}^T \end{bmatrix}^T$$

where the size of coefficient matrix B varies with the number of support legs, and when $n = 3$, $\mathbf{B} \in R^{6 \times 9}$, when $n = 6$, $\mathbf{B} \in R^{6 \times 18}$, $\mathbf{I} \in R^{3 \times 3}$ is the identity matrix, $\mathbf{A}_i \in R^{3 \times 3}$ is an antisymmetric matrix composed of the position of the end of the support leg, the position, (x_i, y_i, z_i) is expressed in the body coordinate system $\{B\}$, $\mathbf{L} \in R^{9 \times 1}$ or $\mathbf{L} \in R^{18 \times 1}$ is the column vector formed by the foot contact force of the supporting leg, $\mathbf{H} \in R^{6 \times 1}$ is a column vector composed of the resultant force and moment of the body. On the premise that $\mathbf{B}$ and $\mathbf{H}$ are known, the result is not unique for the above Eq. (3), that is, there are multiple solutions for the contact force at the foot end, and for the underwater hexapod robot how to determine the specific force at the foot end, a method of force distribution at the foot end of the supporting leg is proposed as an additional constraint, which is also limited by the maximum driving capacity of the joint.

3.3 Contact Force Distribution

In the process of using the typical triangle gait, the robot has at least three legs to support and at most six legs to support. The z-component of the support leg directly affects the pitch angle, roll angle and height of the body, and ensures that the center projection point of the body falls in the polygon surrounded by the contact point of the support leg. The components in X and Y directions are used for crawling, dealing with the forward and lateral flow forces, and providing the body with rotational torque during rotation.

For the Z-direction force distribution, using the lever balance principle, the sum of Z-direction force components of the left supporting leg of the forward direction body is defined as f_{zl}, and the right is f_{zr}. These two resultant forces should be balanced with the gravity of the whole robot. The mass center of the robot body is regarded as the

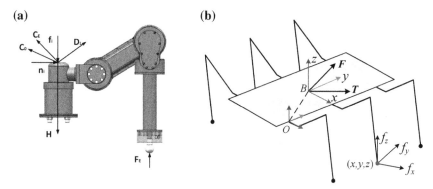

Fig. 4. a) Force diagram of single leg. b) Force acting on robot.

fulcrum, and the sum of x values of the supporting leg and the ground contact point in the body fixed coordinate system is regarded as the force arm, The forces on the left and right sides are equivalent to the fuselage to form an equivalent lever, as shown in Fig. 8. At the same time, the following formula of foot end force distribution on both sides of the fuselage is obtained, in which the true and false Boolean flag indicates whether the corresponding leg is in the supporting state.

$$\begin{cases} f_{zl} \cdot l_l = f_{zr} \cdot l_r \\ f_{zl} + f_{zr} = F_G \end{cases} \Rightarrow \begin{cases} f_{zl} = \frac{F_G \cdot l_r}{l_l + l_r} \\ f_{zr} = \frac{F_G \cdot l_l}{l_l + l_r} \end{cases} \tag{4}$$

where

$$f_{zl} = \sum_{i=1}^{3} (flag_{li} \cdot f_{zli}) \quad l_l = \sum_{i=1}^{3} (flag_{li} \cdot |x_{li}|)$$

$$f_{zr} = \sum_{i=1}^{3} (flag_{ri} \cdot f_{zrj}) \quad l_r = \sum_{i=1}^{3} (flag_{ri} \cdot |x_{ri}|)$$

The above method is also suitable for the foot end force distribution of the supporting leg on the same side of the fuselage. At this time, the number of legs in the sup-porting state at the same time can be 1, 2 or 3.

1. When there is a supporting leg on the same side, all the vertical force components are borne by the leg, as shown in Fig. 5a), where $f_{zr2} = f_{zr}$.
2. The two supporting legs on the same side provide the resultant force f_{zl} in the vertical direction, and use the principle of equivalent lever to realize the full force distribution, as shown in Fig. 5a) and Fig. 6b). The equivalent fulcrum (resultant force action point) is the intersection of the extension line of the line connecting the contact point of the right support leg and the projection point of the body center of mass on the X-Y plane and the line connecting the left support leg, which changes with the movement of the support leg. In the formula, the equivalent arm $l_i = |y_{li} + y_{rj}|$ is calculated by the position information of the supporting leg.

$$\begin{cases} f_{zl1} \cdot l_1 = f_{zl3} \cdot l_3 \\ f_{zl1} + f_{zl3} = f_{zl} \end{cases} \Rightarrow \begin{cases} f_{zl1} = \frac{f_{zl} \cdot l_3}{l_1 + l_3} \\ f_{zl3} = \frac{f_{zl} \cdot l_1}{l_1 + l_3} \end{cases} \tag{5}$$

3. As shown in Fig. 6c), the force distribution at the foot end cannot be achieved only by using the above methods. Additional constraints should be added to the underwater hexapod robot to realize the calculation and solution.

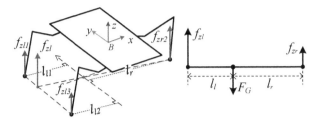

Fig. 5. a) Force distribution of robot b) equivalent lever of robot.

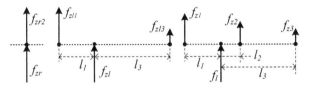

Fig. 6. Force distribution of a) one supporting leg b) two supporting legs c) three supporting legs on the same side.

During the movement of the robot, the force in the X-Y plane is not only the tangential force, but also the resistance of the water flow to the body and the resistance moment of the water flow to the body. The lever balance method is also applicable to the forward and lateral forces on the body. When the robot rotates around the Z axis and receives the resultant moment, the force distribution at the foot end of the supporting leg is completed by the following method, as shown in Fig. 7.

$$f_{ti} \cdot l_{ti} = F_{TZ} \left/ \sum_{j=1}^{6} 1 \cdot flag_j \right. \tag{6}$$

where

$$f_{ti} = \sqrt{f_{txi}^2 + f_{tyi}^2} \quad f_{txi} = (f_{ti} \cdot -y_i)/l_{ti} \quad f_{tyi} = (f_{ti} \cdot x_i)/l_{ti} \quad l_{ti} = \sqrt{x_i^2 + y_i^2}$$

Secondly, to ensure that the foot end of the supporting leg does not slide, the following formula should be satisfied.

$$\sqrt{f_{xi}^2 + f_{yi}^2} \leq \eta \cdot f_{zi} \ (i = 1, 2, 3, \ldots, 6) \tag{7}$$

where η is the static friction coefficient of the contact surface.

Finally, considering the limitation of the maximum driving torque of the leg electric joint, Eq. (8) should be satisfied for any given leg.

$$\left| \mathbf{J}^{\mathrm{T}} [f_x \ f_y \ f_z]^{\mathrm{T}} \right| \leq \tau_{max} \tag{8}$$

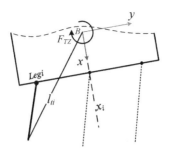

Fig. 7. Force distribution of robot's sum moment at foot end.

4   Energy Consumption Model

The total energy consumed by the underwater hexapod robot is the sum of the energy required by each driving joint, μ is used to evaluate the total energy consumption per unit weight of the robot moving unit distance or rotating unit angle. In the aspect of robot gait performance evaluation, besides stability index, energy consumption is also an important index. Through the previous kinematics and dynamics correlation analysis, the driving torque and angular velocity of each rotating joint can be easily obtained, which provides the basis for the analysis of robot energy consumption. The energy consumption of an underwater hexapod robot is related to its mass, gait (including forward and rotational gait) and water flow. According to the dynamic equation of the robot, the joint driving torque τ_i ($i = 1, 2, 3$) of the leg is related to the angular acceleration, angular velocity, foot contact force of each joint and the structural parameters of the robot model. At time t, when the output torque of a driving joint i is $\tau_i(t)$ and the rotational angular velocity of the joint is $\omega_i(t)$, the driving power consumed by the joint is:

$$P_i(t) = \tau_i(t) \cdot \omega_i(t) = \tau_i(t) \cdot \dot{q}_i(t) \tag{9}$$

where $\dot{q}_i(t)$ is another expression of angular velocity of driving joint. The total energy consumed by the 18 driving joints of the underwater hexapod robot in a typical gait time is as follows:

$$E = \sum_{i=1}^{18} E_i = \sum_{i=1}^{18} \left(\int_0^T |P_i(t)| dt \right) \tag{10}$$

μ is used as the evaluation index of mobile energy consumption of underwater hexapod robot, The smaller the value of μ, the higher the efficiency of mobile energy consumption.

$$\mu = \frac{E}{mgS} \tag{11}$$

where E is the total energy consumed in the process of motion, m is the mass of the underwater robot, g is the acceleration of gravity, S is the moving distance of the body in the process of motion, and the moving speed of the robot is expressed by the ratio of the moving distance S and the moving time T.

5   Modeling and Simulation Results

The simplified conditions for the model are: the body and each leg are homogeneous rigid bodies, ignoring joint friction and other energy consuming equipment on the robot except legs.

The three-dimensional solid model of the underwater hexapod robot includes the body, six three joint legs, ground and environmental forces. The robot shows six degrees of freedom in space. The body dimensions of the three-dimensional model of the underwater hexapod robot are 800 mm in length, 500 mm in width and 150 mm in height, and rotation constraints are established at the joints.

CFD hydrodynamic simulation is carried out for the underwater hexapod robot to obtain the force of water on the robot in different directions and velocities, as shown in Fig. 8.

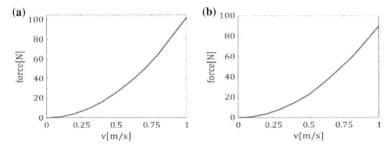

Fig. 8.   a) Forward facing flow and force. b) Lateral flow and forces of the robot.

Before the simulation analysis, the virtual prototype model is checked to make the joint angle, angular velocity and angular acceleration change smoothly during the use of the designed gait. Before the dynamic simulation, the static analysis of the foot force distribution module is carried out to ensure the correctness. Figure 9a) shows the movement trajectory of the body and foot end when the step is used in a typical gait.

By changing the step parameters of the robot gait, the forward motion speed of the robot is changed from 0.1 m/s (step size is 100 mm) to 0.2 m/s (step size is 200 mm), and the water flow speed is changed from 0.1 m/s to 1 m/s. The simulation results are shown in Fig. 9b), which shows the change of energy consumption rate μ with the relative water velocity v of the robot. The results show that: μ increases with the increase of the robot's step length, and for a fixed step length, μ increases with the increase of the relative water velocity of the robot. In terms of underwater walking, small step length has better energy consumption performance.

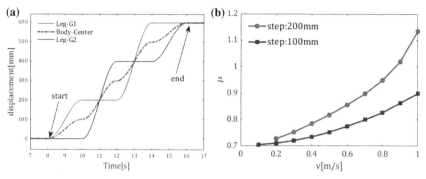

Fig. 9. a) Movement of body center and foot end in Y direction. b) Curve of forward speed and energy consumption rate.

6 Conclusion

In this paper, based on the principle of contact force distribution at the end of the foot, the dynamics and energy consumption model of the underwater hexapod robot is established, and the energy consumption data curve of the robot walking in the underwater environment is obtained. The energy consumption is taken as the evaluation index of the robot motion. Through a series of simulation experiments, under the conditions of different water flow and different motion parameters, the energy consumption of the robot is calculated. The relationship between the mobile energy consumption rate and the mobile speed of the underwater hexapod robot is established. The results show that the mobile energy consumption rate increases with the increase of step length and water flow speed, and increases with the increase of speed for a fixed step length. When the speed is the same, it is more energy-saving to use smaller step length than larger step length.

Acknowledgment. This work was supported by the Liaoning Province youth top talent project [Grant No. XLYC1807174] and the Independent projects of the State Key Laboratory [Grant No. 2019-Z08].

References

1. Greiner, H., Shectman, A., Won, C., Elsley, R., Beith, P.: Autonomous legged underwater vehicles for near land warfare. In: Symposium on Autonomous Underwater Vehicle Technology, pp. 41–48. IEEE (1996)
2. Tanaka, T., Sakai, H., Akizono, J.: Design concept of a prototype amphibious walking robot for automated shoreline survey work. In: MTTS/IEEE TECHNO-OCEAN 2004, OCEANS 2004, pp. 834–839. IEEE (2004)
3. Davliakos, I., Roditis, I., Lika, K., Breki, Ch.-M., Papadopoulos, E.: Design, development, and control of a tough electrohydraulic hexapod robot for subsea operations. Adv. Robot. **32**(9), 477–499 (2018)
4. Yoo, S., Jun, B.H., Shim, H., Park, J.Y., Baek, H., Kim, B., et al.: Preliminary water tank test of a multi-legged underwater robot for seabed explorations. Oceans. IEEE (2016)

5. Song, S.M., Waldron, K.J.: Machines That Walk: The Adaptive Suspension Vehicle. The MIT Press, Cambridge (1989)
6. Kurazume, R., Byong-Won, A., Ohta, K., et al.: Experimental study on energy efficiency for quadruped walking vehicles. In: IEEE/RSJ International Conference on Intelligent Robots & Systems. IEEE (2003)
7. Silva, M.F., Machado, J., Lopes, A.M.: Performance analysis of multi-legged systems. In: IEEE International Conference on Robotics & Automation, pp. 2234–2239. IEEE (2002)
8. Kar, D.C., Issac, K.K., Jayarajan, K.: Minimum energy force distribution for a walking robot. J. Field Robot. **18**(2), 47–54 (2015)
9. Marhefka, D.W., Orin, D.E.: Gait planning for energy efficiency in walking machines. In: Robotics and Automation, pp. 474–480. IEEE (1997)
10. Roy, S.S., Pratihar, D.K.: Dynamic modeling and energy consumption analysis of crab walking of a six-legged robot. In: 2011 IEEE Conference Technologies for Practical Robot Applications (TePRA), pp. 82–87. IEEE (2011)
11. Kelasidi, E., Pettersen, K.Y., Gravdahl, J.T.: Energy efficiency of underwater robots. In: 10th IFAC Conference on Manoeuvring and Control of Marine Craft, vol. 48, no. 16, pp. 152–159 (2015)
12. McGhee, R.B.: Some finite state aspects of legged locomotion. Math. Biosci. **2**(1–2), 67–84 (1968)
13. Wang, K.P.: Mechanical Modeling and Simulation of Underwater Hexapod Mobile System. Harbin University of Technology, Harbin (2018)

Bearing Fault Diagnosis Based on Attentional Multi-scale CNN

Shuai Yang[1], Yan Liu[1], Xincheng Tian[1(✉)], and Lixin Ma[2]

1 Shandong University, Jinan 250014, China
yeah-1997@mail.sdu.edu.cn
2 CODESYS Software System (Beijing) Co., Ltd., Beijing, China

Abstract. Bearing is an indispensable component of industrial production equipment. The health status of bearing affects the production efficiency of equipment, so it is necessary to detect the health status of bearing in real time. In this paper, a multi-scale feature fusion convolutional neural network with attention mechanism (AMMNet) is proposed for bearing fault diagnosis. Firstly, different scale shallow features of the input signal are extracted by parallel convolutional layers with different kernel sizes. Then, the shallow features are sent to the feature fusion module based on channel attention mechanism. After that, the fused features are fed to the deep feature extractor. Finally, the bearing fault type is identified by the classifier. We introduce a novel dropout mechanism to the input signal to improve the generalization ability of the network. Experiments show that the proposed method has high stability and generalization ability. It can not only achieve high average accuracy in fixed load environment, but also has higher recognition accuracy and better stability than some intelligent algorithms in variable load conditions.

Keywords: Bearing fault diagnosis · Feature fusion · Attention mechanism · Convolutional neural network

1 Introduction

Bearing fault diagnosis plays an important role in production and manufacturing. Bearing fault will affect the normal operation of rotating machinery and cause the loss of life and property. Accurate bearing fault diagnosis method has always been the research frontier [10,11]. The health status of bearings is usually monitored by various sensors installed near the motor, among which the analysis of vibration signal is the most important approach to identify the health status of bearings [19].

Researchers have put forward many effective methods for bearing fault diagnosis. Some methods are to select representative features through the transformation of vibration signal, and then process the features to get the fault

Supported by the National Natural Science Foundation of China under Grant U20A20201 and the Shandong Provincial Key Research and Development Program under Grant 2019JZZY010441.

X.-J. Liu et al. (Eds.): ICIRA 2021, LNAI 13015, pp. 25–36, 2021.
https://doi.org/10.1007/978-3-030-89134-3_3

type. Cocconcelli et al. [3] utilized the features obtained by short-time Fourier trans-form (STFT) as an indicator of bearing damage. Sharma et al. [14] used continuous wavelet transform and modern algebraic function to make a lookup table. With the help of the lookup table, one can figure out the type of fault. This method is very simple and gives out magnificent result. Zhang et al. [18] proposed a new method to extract the early fault characteristics of bearings based on wavelet packet transform (WPT) and the time-delay correlation demodulation analysis. Wang et al. [17] used the graph Fourier transform (GFT) to extract the graph spectrum domain feature as fault feature set combines with the C4.5 classification algorithm to identify the fault of the rolling bearing. Experiments show that GFT features are suitable for fault diagnosis in railway background. These methods mentioned above need to extract the features of the signal manually, which has a great subjectivity, and the better fault diagnosis results can't be achieved without the features extracted by expert experience.

With the successful application of deep learning in image classification [9] and image segmentation [1,13], researchers have proposed some bearing fault diagnosis methods based on deep neural network. Zhang et al. [20] used convolution neural network to train the original vibration signal directly. The results show that when there are enough training samples, this method can achieve high recognition rate and stability. Chen et al. [2] proposed a bearing detection method based on multi-scale CNN and LSTM model. Experiments show that this method not only has high accuracy, but also can achieve good performance in noise environment. Liang et al. [11] proposed a parallel convolutional neural network with feature fusion ability. In this method, convolution neural network is used to extract time domain features, and continuous wavelet transform is used to extract time-frequency domain features. In the merged layer, the time-frequency features are fused together with the time-domain features as inputs to the final classifier. Wang et al. [16] proposed a multi-scale neural network including one-dimensional and two-dimensional convolution channels. In the feature extraction stage, the two CNNs are independent of each other. The features extracted by the two CNNs are fused in the classification stage, and then used for the final classification. Experimental results show that the accuracy of this network is higher than that of 2D CNN and 1D CNN. Jia et al. [6] used the signal after fast Fourier transform as the input, and applied pre-training and fine-tune steps to train five layers of DNN for bearing fault identification.

In this research, we proposed a convolutional neural network based on feature fusion and attention mechanism for bearing fault diagnosis. The traditional CNN adopts a fixed size of convolutional kernel to extract features, which may lead to the loss of some information. Inspired by the idea of continuous wavelet transform (CWT), we use the convolution kernel of different sizes to simulate the scaling factor in CWT to extract the features of different frequencies of signals. Similar to [22], a channel attention based module is designed for the fusion of different scale features. In order to handle the over-fitting problem of the model, we introduce a novel dropout [15] mechanism to the signals input to the different convolutional layers. The proposed network is compared with other intelligent algorithms under variable load conditions, and results are analyzed in depth.

2   Theoretical Background

2.1   Convolutional Neural Network

Convolutional Layer. Convolutional layer is the core of convolutional neural network, and its main function is feature extraction. One dimension convolutional layer is used in this paper. Let C be the channel number of the input to the convolutional layer, and O be the channel number of the output of the convolutional layer. The output of the j-th channel of the convolutional layer can be obtained as.

$$Y_j = \sum_{i=1}^{C} w_j^i \star X_i + b_j \qquad (1)$$

Where X_i indicates the i-th channel of the input, $\star$ is the valid cross-correlation operator, w_j and b_j indicate the weight and bias of the j-th convolutional kernel respectively.

Pooling Layer. Pooling layer is an effective down sampling method, which can effectively reduce the parameters of convolutional neural network and reduce the over fitting of the model. In this paper, the maximum value of local feature region is selected as output by max-pooling. Let C be the number of input signal channels. P_j^c indicates the j-th neuron of the c-th output channel, and H_i^c indicates the i-th neuron of the c-th input channel. Max-pooling can be described as the following formula.

$$P_j^c = \max_{2(j-1)+1 \leq i \leq 2j} H_i^c \qquad (2)$$

2.2   Squeeze and Excitation Block

Hu et al. [4] designed squeeze and excitation block (SEBlock), and proved that SEBlock can significantly improve the performance of the existing state of the art CNNs with a slight computational cost. The contents of the dotted box in Fig. 2 show the structure of SEBlock. SEBlock mainly includes two parts: squeeze and excitation. This article deals with one-dimensional vibration signals and the Squeeze operation can be described as.

$$z_c = F_{sq}(u_c) = \frac{1}{L} \sum_{i=1}^{L} u_c(i) \qquad (3)$$

Where z_c indicates the channel description descriptor of channel c, L indicates the length of channel c signal, and u_c indicates the input signal of channel c.

Excitation first obtains the scaling factors of the channels through two fully connected layers. It can be described as follows.

$$s = F_{ex}(z, W) = \sigma(W_2 \delta(W_1 z)) \tag{4}$$

Where $W_1 \in R^{\frac{C}{r} \times C}$, δ represents the ReLU [12] function, $W_2 \in R^{C \times \frac{C}{r}}$, σ represents the sigmoid function, and r represents the reduction ratio (in this paper, $r = 16$). The output of SEBlock can be expressed as.

$$\widetilde{x}_c = F_{scale}(u_c, s_c) = s_c u_c \tag{5}$$

Where $F_{scale}(u_c, s_c)$ represents the channel level multiplication of the scaling factor s_c and the characteristic graph u_c.

3   Proposed Network

Figure 1 shows the overall structure of AMMNet. It consists of three main modules: multi-shallow-level feature extractor, deep-level feature extractor and classifier.

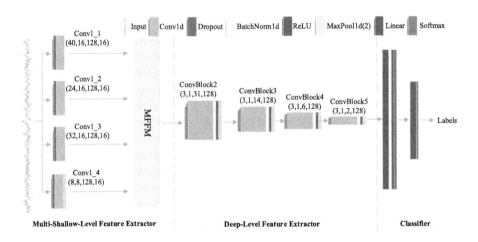

Fig. 1. The overall structure of AMMNet. The numbers in brackets in the figure represent: conv kernel size, stride size, output feature map size, output channels.

The multi-shallow-level feature extractor consists of four convolutional modules with different kernel sizes and a multi-level feature fusion module (MFFM). In order to improve the generalization ability of the network, we introduce dropout mechanism to the input signal. Zhang et al. [21] proved that for the input convolutional layer, the larger convolutional kernel has stronger anti-interference ability than the smaller convolutional kernel. In order to ensure that the interference degree in the receptive field of different convolutional modules is basically the same, the dropout rate of signals input to different convolutional modules is proportional to the convolutional kernel size. For signals input to Conv1_1 – Conv1_4, the dropout rates are 0.15, 0.09, 0.12 and 0.03 respectively.

Conv1_1 has large kernels that can extract low-frequency features of the signal. The medium-sized convolutional kernels of Conv1_2 and Conv1_3 are implemented to extract medium-frequency signal features. Conv1_4 has a small receptive field and is responsible for extracting high-frequency features of the signal. The max-pooling layer in Conv1_4 is used to adjust the size of the feature map to facilitate the fusion of features of different scales. The structure of the multi-scale feature fusion module (MFFM) is shown in Fig. 2. MFFM first splices the input feature maps along the channel direction. Then SEBlock assigns different weights to the features of each channel. Channels that are helpful for fault identification will be given larger weights, while the insignificant characteristic channels will be suppressed. Finally, the fused shallow level features are fed into the deep feature extractor after the operations of batch normalization (BN) [5] layer, ReLU activation function and max-pooling layer.

The deep-level feature extractor is composed of four consecutive convolutional modules. Each convolutional module is composed of convolutional layer, BN layer, ReLU activation function and max-pooling layer. The deep feature extractor further transforms the features to obtain high-level representative features. BN layers in the network are implemented to accelerate the training process. Classifier is composed of two fully connected layers. Dropout is introduced in the last fully connected layer, and the dropout rate is 0.3. The softmax function is implemented to output the probabilities of different fault types.

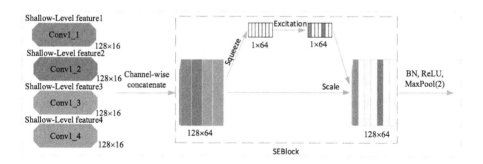

Fig. 2. Multi-scale feature fusion module.

4 Experiment

4.1 Dataset and Implementation Details

Dataset. The bearing failure dataset comes from Case Western Reserve University bearing data center (http://csegroups.case.edu/bearingdatacenter). Data of many bearing fault diagnosis methods are based on this dataset [2,11,20]. We select the drive end accelerometer data with a sampling frequency of 12kHz to train and verify the model. The length of each sample is 2048 [21]. There are four datasets D0–D3, and the motor loads of the D0–D3 datasets are 0HP–3HP respectively. Each dataset contains three fault locations: inner race (IR), ball (B), and six o'clock on the outer ring (OR). The fault diameter of each fault location includes three sizes: 0.007 in., 0.014 in. and 0.021 in.. With the bearing data under normal conditions, there are 10 $(3 \times 3 + 1)$ types of failures in each dataset. Figure 3 shows the data augmentation method of this article and the principle of dividing the training set and test set. We use the sliding sampling method to obtain samples, and the sliding interval is 200. The number of training set and testing set is about 2:1. In order to prevent information leakage caused by sliding sampling, the training set and the testing set are not randomly extracted from the total samples. In this paper, the training set comes from the top 67% of the data, and the test set is the bottom 33% of the data. There is no overlapping data between training set and testing set due to sliding sampling. In order to facilitate the training of the neural network, the obtained samples were all processed by min-max normalization. Table 1 shows the details of the partitioning of the dataset.

Table 1. Fault datasets details.

Labels	Fault location	Size (in)	Dataset D0 no. (0HP)		Dataset D1 no. (1HP)		Dataset D2 no. (2HP)		Dataset D3 no. (3HP)	
–	–	–	Train	Test	Train	Test	Train	Test	Train	Test
0	None	–	385	185	385	185	385	185	385	185
1	IR	0.007	385	185	385	185	385	185	385	185
2	B	0.007	385	185	385	185	385	185	385	185
3	OR	0.007	385	185	385	185	385	185	385	185
4	IR	0.014	385	185	385	185	385	185	385	185
5	B	0.014	385	185	385	185	385	185	385	185
6	OR	0.014	385	185	385	185	385	185	385	185
7	IR	0.021	385	185	385	185	385	185	385	185
8	B	0.021	385	185	385	185	385	185	385	185
9	OR	0.021	385	185	385	185	385	185	385	185

Implementation Details AMMNet is developed with PyTorch. Adam [8] optimization algorithm is used to update the network weights with an exponential learning rate (base rate is 0.001, decay is 0.95), and the cross entropy function is used as the loss function. Keskar et al. [7] proved that using small batch size data to train the network can obtain stronger generalization ability. Therefore, the batch size of the network training in this paper is selected as 16. A total of 30 epochs were trained for the network. In order to reduce the contingency of recognition results, we trained AMMNet 10 times independently on each dataset.

Fig. 3. Schematic diagram of sample division.

4.2   Fault Identification Results

Results Under Fixed Load Conditions Figure 4 shows the training set accuracy rate and test set accuracy rate of 10 trainings of AMMNet when the load is respectively 0HP–3HP. The results show that the accuracy of the training set and the test set can reach more than 99% and 98% under different loads. Table 2 shows the average and standard deviation of the accuracy of AMMNet for 10 trainings under different load conditions. It can be observed that the standard deviation of the recognition accuracy of the model is relatively small, indicating that the model has strong stability.

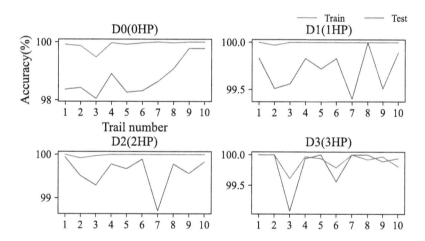

Fig. 4. The accuracy of AMMNet under different load conditions.

Table 2. The average and standard deviation of the accuracy of AMMNet under different loads.

	D0 (0HP)	D1 (1HP)	D2 (2HP)	D3 (3HP)
Training (%)	99.91 ± 0.15	99.99 ± 0.01	99.98 ± 0.02	99.90 ± 0.12
Testing (%)	98.76 ± 0.58	99.70 ± 0.19	99.59 ± 0.35	99.84 ± 0.28

Noting that the accuracy of the training set did not reach 100%. This is because dropout is introduced into the input signal. Each training sample randomly misses a part of the value, which is equivalent to each training sample with different interference. For this reason, the neural network needs to constantly adjust the parameters, thus the accuracy of the training set does not reach 100%. It will be proved later that the introduction of dropout mechanism to the input signal is helpful to improve the generalization ability of the model. Overall, AMMNet can accurately identify various types of faults under different loads.

Results Under Variable Load Conditions. In order to test the generalization ability of AMMNet, we designed a variable load prediction experiment. Variable load prediction means that the model is trained on the training set of one of the datasets and then predicts the test sets of the other three datasets respectively. For example, $D0 \rightarrow D1$ represents the network is training on the training set of dataset D0 and testing performance on the test set of dataset D1. Several other fault diagnosis methods including WDCNN [21], SVM, KNN are used to compare with the network in this article. WDCNN adopts the traditional CNN structure in cascade form, and directly inputs the normalized vibration signal during training. When using SVM and KNN, we first carry out the Fast Fourier Transform (FFT) on the vibration signal. Since the Fourier coefficients are symmetric, we use the first 1024 coefficients of each sample. These methods were also independently trained 10 times on each dataset.

Table 3. Result of different methods under variable load conditions

	WDCNN	FFT–SVM	FFT–KNN	AMMNet
$D0 \rightarrow D1$	97.59 ± 1.29	66.42 ± 0.31	86.40 ± 1.90	$\mathbf{97.92 \pm 0.85}$
$D0 \rightarrow D2$	95.35 ± 2.15	69.15 ± 3.58	80.01 ± 0.67	$\mathbf{97.91 \pm 0.70}$
$D0 \rightarrow D3$	89.52 ± 3.10	56.74 ± 3.23	78.74 ± 1.81	$\mathbf{96.30 \pm 1.68}$
$D1 \rightarrow D0$	97.32 ± 1.20	62.91 ± 0.73	90.92 ± 0.94	$\mathbf{98.14 \pm 0.45}$
$D1 \rightarrow D2$	$\mathbf{99.63 \pm 0.45}$	66.78 ± 0.45	83.19 ± 1.03	99.28 ± 0.34
$D1 \rightarrow D3$	93.48 ± 2.01	60.37 ± 0.71	67.75 ± 0.79	$\mathbf{97.18 \pm 1.00}$
$D2 \rightarrow D0$	92.35 ± 2.50	64.35 ± 2.15	79.46 ± 0.11	$\mathbf{92.46 \pm 2.78}$
$D2 \rightarrow D1$	91.75 ± 2.01	63.94 ± 2.45	86.94 ± 0.22	$\mathbf{92.87 \pm 1.33}$
$D2 \rightarrow D3$	97.99 ± 0.98	69.35 ± 0.33	79.62 ± 1.15	$\mathbf{98.23 \pm 0.93}$
$D3 \rightarrow D0$	79.51 ± 3.32	65.46 ± 1.52	72.07 ± 1.03	$\mathbf{88.58 \pm 0.78}$
$D3 \rightarrow D1$	81.54 ± 2.62	56.55 ± 1.23	77.21 ± 1.16	$\mathbf{88.70 \pm 0.62}$
$D3 \rightarrow D2$	92.52 ± 2.57	60.93 ± 0.28	79.38 ± 0.16	$\mathbf{96.03 \pm 2.54}$
Average	92.38	63.58	80.14	$\mathbf{95.3}$

Table 3 shows the average identification accuracy and standard deviation of these methods in different scenarios, and trends of the average accuracy in the variable load conditions are shown in Fig. 5. As can be seen from Table 3, AMMNet has the highest recognition rate in almost all variable load scenarios.

Only in the D1 → D2 scene, the accuracy is slightly lower than that of WDCNN, but it still achieves more than 99% recognition accuracy.

Besides, the average recognition rate of AMMNet under various variable load scenarios is 95.3%, which is nearly 3% higher than WDCNN, 30% higher than SVM and 15% higher than KNN. It can be seen from Fig. 5 that the recognition accuracy of the four methods fluctuates in the scenes of variable load, while the fluctuation of AMMNet is the smallest. WDCNN showed a significant decrease in the recognition rate under D3 → D0 and D3 → D1 scenarios, while AMMNet still achieved an accuracy rate of more than 88% in these two scenarios. The main difference between WDCNN and AMMNet is that WDCNN uses fixed-size convolutional kernels to extract shallow signal features, while AMMNet adopts the multi-scale feature fusion and input signal dropout strategy. The results in above two scenarios prove the effectiveness of the strategy in this paper. From the above analysis, it can be concluded that the AMMNet model proposed in this paper has stronger generalization ability and better adaptability in variable load conditions compared with other intelligent algorithms.

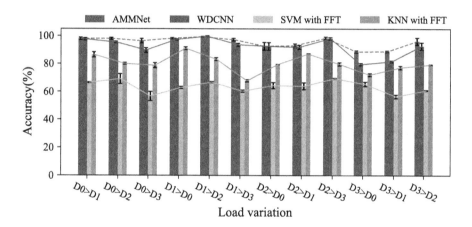

Fig. 5. The trend of average recognition accuracy of different methods.

In addition, we trained an AMMNet model without dropout for the input signal, called AMMNetWD for short. Similarly, the model was independently trained 10 times on each dataset. Figure 6 shows the average recognition accuracy of AMMNet and AMMNetWD in the scenes of variable load. It can be observed that AMMNet and AMMNetWD have similar trends in recognition accuracy. But there are still some important differences. As shown in the box diagram in Fig. 6, AMMNet has higher average recognition accuracy and smaller variance in different scenarios compared with AMMNetWD model, which proves that the introduction of dropout into the input signal can effectively improve the generalization ability and stability of the model.

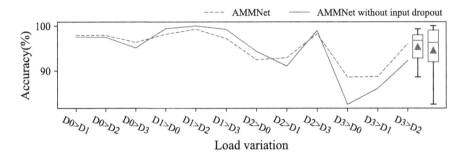

Fig. 6. Schematic diagram of the variation trend of the average classification accuracy of the two models under different load scenarios. The triangle in the box chart indicates the mean value of the average classification accuracy under different scenarios.

5 Conclusion

In this paper, a multi feature fusion convolutional neural network with channel attention mechanism is proposed for bearing fault diagnosis. The network adopts parallel multi convolutional layers with different kernel sizes to extract features, and fuses features based on channel attention mechanism. By introducing dropout mechanism into the input signal, the generalization ability of the model is effectively improved. The performance of the proposed network is tested in fixed load environments and multiple variable load environments. Experimental results show that the proposed network not only achieves high recognition accuracy in the fixed load scenarios, but also achieves higher average recognition rate and more stable performance than other intelligent algorithms in the variable load scenarios.

References

1. Badrinarayanan, V., Kendall, A., Cipolla, R.: SegNet: a deep convolutional encoder-decoder architecture for image segmentation. IEEE Trans. Pattern Anal. Mach. Intell. **39**(12), 2481–2495 (2017)
2. Chen, X., Zhang, B., Gao, D.: Bearing fault diagnosis base on multi-scale CNN and LSTM model. J. Intell. Manuf. 1–17 (2020)
3. Cocconcelli, M., Zimroz, R., Rubini, R., Bartelmus, W.: STFT based approach for ball bearing fault detection in a varying speed motor. In: Fakhfakh, T., Bartelmus, W., Chaari, F., Zimroz, R., Haddar, M. (eds.) Condition Monitoring of Machinery in Non-Stationary Operations, pp. 41–50. Springer, Heidelberg (2012). https://doi.org/10.1007/978-3-642-28768-8_5
4. Hu, J., Shen, L., Sun, G.: Squeeze-and-excitation networks. In: Proceedings of the IEEE Conference on Computer Vision and Pattern Recognition, pp. 7132–7141 (2018)
5. Ioffe, S., Szegedy, C.: Batch normalization: accelerating deep network training by reducing internal covariate shift. In: International Conference on Machine Learning, pp. 448–456. PMLR (2015)

6. Jia, F., Lei, Y., Lin, J., Zhou, X., Lu, N.: Deep neural networks: a promising tool for fault characteristic mining and intelligent diagnosis of rotating machinery with massive data. Mech. Syst. Signal Process. **72**, 303–315 (2016)

7. Keskar, N.S., Mudigere, D., Nocedal, J., Smelyanskiy, M., Tang, P.T.P.: On large-batch training for deep learning: generalization gap and sharp minima. arXiv preprint arXiv:1609.04836 (2016)

8. Kingma, D.P., Ba, J.: Adam: a method for stochastic optimization. arXiv preprint arXiv:1412.6980 (2014)

9. Krizhevsky, A., Sutskever, I., Hinton, G.E.: ImageNet classification with deep convolutional neural networks. In: Advances in Neural Information Processing Systems, vol. 25, pp. 1097–1105 (2012)

10. Li, H., Lian, X., Guo, C., Zhao, P.: Investigation on early fault classification for rolling element bearing based on the optimal frequency band determination. J. Intell. Manuf. **26**(1), 189–198 (2013). https://doi.org/10.1007/s10845-013-0772-8

11. Liang, M., Cao, P., Tang, J.: Rolling bearing fault diagnosis based on feature fusion with parallel convolutional neural network. Int. J. Adv. Manuf. Technol. (1), 819–831 (2020). https://doi.org/10.1007/s00170-020-06401-8

12. Nair, V., Hinton, G.E.: Rectified linear units improve restricted Boltzmann machines. In: ICML (2010)

13. Ronneberger, O., Fischer, P., Brox, T.: U-Net: convolutional networks for biomedical image segmentation. In: Navab, N., Hornegger, J., Wells, W.M., Frangi, A.F. (eds.) MICCAI 2015. LNCS, vol. 9351, pp. 234–241. Springer, Cham (2015). https://doi.org/10.1007/978-3-319-24574-4_28

14. Sharma, R., Kumar, A., Kankar, P.K.: Ball bearing fault diagnosis using continuous wavelet transforms with modern algebraic function. In: Babu, B.V., et al. (eds.) Proceedings of the Second International Conference on Soft Computing for Problem Solving (SocProS 2012), December 28-30, 2012. AISC, vol. 236, pp. 313–322. Springer, New Delhi (2014). https://doi.org/10.1007/978-81-322-1602-5_35

15. Srivastava, N., Hinton, G., Krizhevsky, A., Sutskever, I., Salakhutdinov, R.: Dropout: a simple way to prevent neural networks from overfitting. J. Mach. Learn. Res. **15**(1), 1929–1958 (2014)

16. Wang, D., Guo, Q., Song, Y., Gao, S., Li, Y.: Application of multiscale learning neural network based on CNN in bearing fault diagnosis. J. Signal Process. Syst. **91**(10), 1205–1217 (2019)

17. Wang, Y., Qin, Y., Zhao, X., Zhang, S., Cheng, X.: Bearing fault diagnosis method based on graph Fourier transform and C4.5 decision tree. In: Qin, Y., Jia, L., Liu, B., Liu, Z., Diao, L., An, M. (eds.) EITRT 2019. LNEE, vol. 639, pp. 697–705. Springer, Singapore (2020). https://doi.org/10.1007/978-981-15-2866-8_66

18. Zhang, C., et al.: Rolling element bearing fault diagnosis based on the wavelet packet transform and time-delay correlation demodulation analysis. In: Ball, A., Gelman, L., Rao, B.K.N. (eds.) Advances in Asset Management and Condition Monitoring. SIST, vol. 166, pp. 1195–1203. Springer, Cham (2020). https://doi.org/10.1007/978-3-030-57745-2_98

19. Zhang, S., Zhang, S., Wang, B., Habetler, T.G.: Deep learning algorithms for bearing fault diagnosticsx–a comprehensive review. IEEE Access **8**, 29857–29881 (2020)

20. Zhang, W., Peng, G., Li, C.: Rolling element bearings fault intelligent diagnosis based on convolutional neural networks using raw sensing signal. In: Advances in Intelligent Information Hiding and Multimedia Signal Processing. SIST, vol. 64, pp. 77–84. Springer, Cham (2017). https://doi.org/10.1007/978-3-319-50212-0_10

21. Zhang, W., Peng, G., Li, C., Chen, Y., Zhang, Z.: A new deep learning model for fault diagnosis with good anti-noise and domain adaptation ability on raw vibration signals. Sensors **17**(2), 425 (2017)
22. Zhao, Q., et al.: M2Det: a single-shot object detector based on multi-level feature pyramid network. In: Proceedings of the AAAI Conference on Artificial Intelligence, vol. 33, pp. 9259–9266 (2019)

Robot Hand-Eye Calibration Method Based on Intermediate Measurement System

Qi Zhang, Wei Tian$^{(\boxtimes)}$, Junshan Hu, Pengcheng Li, and Chao Wu

Nanjing University of Aeronautics and Astronautics, Nanjing, China
`tw_nj@nuaa.edu.cn`

Abstract. Aiming at the problem of low accuracy of industrial robot hand-eye calibration, a robot hand-eye calibration method based on an intermediate measurement system is proposed. The checkerboard calibration board with the marker points pasted is photographed by the camera, and the coordinates of the marker points in the checkerboard calibration board coordinate system are calculated according to the principle of cross-ratio invariance, and the coordinate system matrix between the C-Track optical dynamic tracking system and the industrial robot is established. The transformation relationship finally obtains the closed-loop coordinate system matrix transformation equation with the marker point, the checkerboard calibration board and the C-Track optical dynamic tracking system as the intermediate measurement system, thereby avoiding the introduction of the mobile industrial robot manipulator in the traditional hand-eye calibration process Kinematic error. The experimental results show that the translation error in the hand-eye relationship matrix is 0.6 mm, and the rotation error is 0.3°. Compared with the traditional hand-eye calibration method, this method improves the accuracy of hand-eye calibration, simplifies the hand-eye calibration process, and meets the needs of actual processing and production.

Keywords: Industrial robot · Hand-eye calibration · Calibration board · Cross-ratio invariance · Kinematic error

1 Introduction

The combination of visual measurement system and industrial robots forms an industrial robot system with environmental perception capabilities, which improves the automation and intelligent operation level of industrial robots, and is of great significance for achieving high-quality and high-efficiency aircraft assembly [1, 2]. According to the position relationship between the visual measurement system and the industrial robot, it can be divided into eye-in-hand and eye-to-hand [3, 4]. The visual measurement system is installed outside of the robot arm and does not move with the robot arm, called eye-to-hand. The vision measurement system is installed at the end of the robotic arm and moves with the robotic arm, which is called eye-in-hand. To accurately transfer the visual measurement data to the industrial robot system, it is necessary to accurately calculate the relative position relationship between the industrial robot flange coordinate

© Springer Nature Switzerland AG 2021
X.-J. Liu et al. (Eds.): ICIRA 2021, LNAI 13015, pp. 37–47, 2021.
https://doi.org/10.1007/978-3-030-89134-3_4

system and the visual sensor coordinate system [5], that is hand-eye calibration. The traditional hand-eye calibration method was proposed by Tsai [6]. First, the camera is fixed on the robotic arm and moves with the robotic arm. The calibration board is placed in the camera's field of view, and the position is fixed. By controlling the industrial robot to transform to different poses, the camera observes the calibration board and uses the plane calibration method to obtain the pose transformation relationship between the camera coordinate system and the calibration board coordinate system, and then combines the industrial robot flange and the robot base in the industrial robot control panel. The pose transformation relationship of the coordinate system is established and solved by the matrix equation, and the hand-eye calibration transformation matrix is obtained. For the problem of solving equations, many people have proposed different mathematical methods. Zhang [7] proposed a method of redistributing the corresponding weights according to the measurement data error; Heller [8] and Li [9] proposed a global optimization method; Chou [10] proposed a quaternion-based singular value decomposition method; Hu [11] proposed a nonlinear optimization method for simultaneous camera and hand-eye relationship calibration; Chen [12] and Wang [13] respectively proposed using Kalman filter realizes the recursive estimation of translation vector and the robot hand-eye calibration method based on unscented Kalman filter; Park [14] proposed a global optimization method based on branch and bound method based on the angle projection error as the optimization model. In order to establish a homogeneous equation, the above methods need to move the manipulator many times, resulting in the final hand-eye calibration result being affected by the positioning error and return error of the industrial robot. At the same time, the position and posture changes of the mobile manipulator need to be as large as possible to ensure that the equation is solved. In order to avoid the above problems, Bi [15] and Liu [16] respectively proposed hand-eye calibration methods based on a three-coordinate measuring instrument and a laser tracker. The transformation relationship between the robot end tool, flange and camera was established through the three-coordinate measuring instrument. It establishes a hand-eye relationship with the method of direct measurement using a laser tracker, but the above methods all require the design of an end effector, which does not have universal applicability.

In response to the above problems, this article establishes an intermediate measurement system through marker points, checkerboard calibration boards and C-Track optical dynamic tracking system. The intermediate measurement system is used to directly establish the closed-loop coordinate system matrix transformation relationship with the robot flange coordinate system and the camera coordinate system. Solve the hand-eye calibration matrix by constructing a homogeneous equation. There is no need to move the industrial robot manipulator during the calibration process, thus avoiding the influence of the kinematic error of the manipulator. The experimental results show that the method in this paper has the advantages of high calibration accuracy, simple operation process, and wide application range.

2   Analysis of the Principle of Hand-Eye Calibration

The traditional hand-eye calibration process needs to move the robot arm to change the pose, but there are kinematic errors in the robot arm movement process, resulting in errors in the conversion matrix from the flange coordinate system to the robot base coordinate system, which affects the final hand-eye calibration accuracy. In order to avoid the introduction of kinematic errors due to the transformation of the robot arm's pose, the marker point, the checkerboard calibration board and the C-Track optical dynamic tracking system are used to establish an intermediate measurement system, as shown in Fig. 1. Establish a checkerboard calibration-board frame ({CCF}) on the checkerboard calibration board; establish a C-Track optical dynamic tracking system coordinate system on the C-Track optical dynamic tracking system ({CDF}); establish a camera frame ({CF}) on the camera; establish a base frame ({BF}) on the industrial robot; establish a flange frame ({FF}) on the industrial robot flange; establish a marker point frame ({MF}) on the marker point. When the manipulator is in the initial pose state, calculate the transformation matrix between the intermediate measurement system and the camera coordinate system and the robot base coordinate system, and finally get the matrix equation about the hand-eye relationship.

$$\mathrm{_{CCF}^{CF}}T\,\mathrm{_{MF}^{CCF}}T\,\mathrm{_{MF}^{CDF}}T^{-1}\,\mathrm{_{BF}^{CDF}}T\,\mathrm{_{FF}^{BF}}T\,\mathrm{_{CF}^{FF}}T = E \tag{1}$$

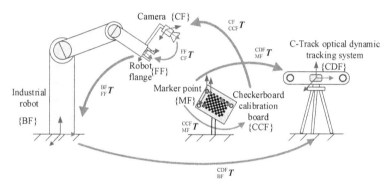

Fig. 1. Schematic diagram of hand-eye calibration based on intermediate measurement system

3   The Center Coordinate of the Marker Point in the Calibration Board Coordinate System

As shown in Fig. 2 (a), paste three marker points on the checkerboard calibration board, denoted as M_1', M_2' and M_3', which correspond to the marker points in the image as M_1, M_2 and M_3 respectively. In order to calculate the homogeneous transformation matrix between the coordinate system {MF} composed of three marker points and the coordinate system {CCF}, it is necessary to calculate the coordinate value of the marker point center in the {CCF} coordinate system.

3.1   Image Preprocessing

The checkerboard calibration board with marker points is photographed by the camera to obtain the original image. By adjusting the brightness and contrast of the image, the characteristics of the marker point are more obvious, which is beneficial to the subsequent edge extraction of the marker point. The result of image preprocessing is shown in Fig. 2 (b).

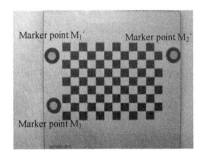 

(a) Actual position relationship   (b) Preprocessed image

Fig. 2. Checkerboard calibration board and marker points

3.2 Calculate the Coordinates of the Center of the Marker Point in the Pixel Coordinate System

In order to reduce the amount of data and time of image processing, and improve the accuracy of marker point center extraction, the image marker point ROI area is cropped in Fig. 2 (b) to obtain the image of interest containing the marker point area. The cropping result is shown in Fig. 3 (a). The Canny edge detection operator is used to perform edge detection on the marker point image, and the edge contour of the marker point is obtained. The result is shown in Fig. 3 (b).

 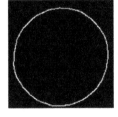

(a) Marker point ROI area   (b) Marker point edge detection

Fig. 3. Marker point image processing

Theoretically, the image of the plane circle in the camera image in the space is an ellipse. Based on this, the ellipse detection is performed on the edge contour of the marker point and the center of the ellipse is obtained. First, perform the binarization process on Fig. 3 (b). Suppose all pixels in the image whose gray value is not zero are n and denoted as $[u_i, v_i]$. Calculate the distance between all pixels of the image (u, v) to n pixels $[u_i, v_i]$.

$$D(u, v) = \sum_{i=1}^{n} \sqrt{(u - u_i)^2 + (v - v_i)^2} \tag{2}$$

When $D(u, v)$ takes the minimum value, the position of the corresponding pixel point is the position of the center of the ellipse, and the coordinates of the center of the marker point in the pixel coordinate system are calculated according to the boundary value of the clipping of the ROI area.

3.3 Calculate the Coordinates of the Marker Point in the Coordinate System {CCF}

The principle is shown in Fig. 4. Knowing the coordinates of the center of the three marker points in the pixel coordinate system, a linear equation is constructed through the marker points M_1 and M_2.

$$y = a_1 x + b_1 \tag{3}$$

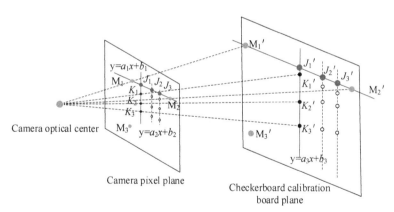

Fig. 4. Schematic diagram of the coordinate solution of the marker point in the coordinate system {CCF}

Use OpenCV to call the sub-pixel corner detection operator to calculate the coordinates of all corners on the checkerboard calibration board in the pixel coordinate system. At the same time, the corner coordinates of all corners on the checkerboard calibration board in the coordinate system {CCF} can be get. Extract the coordinates of the first column of corner points in the pixel coordinate system and construct a linear equation according to the principle of least squares.

$$y = a_2 x + b_2 \tag{4}$$

Calculate the intersection point of Eqs. 3 and 4, get intersection point $J_1(u_1, v_1)$. Knowing the coordinates of intersection J_1 in the pixel coordinate system, the three adjacent corner points $K_1\left(u_{K_1}, v_{K_1}\right), K_2'\left(X_{K_2'}, Y_{K_2'}\right), K_3'\left(X_{K_3'}, Y_{K_3'}\right)$ in the column where intersection J_1 is located, and the corner coordinates of the corresponding corner points in the coordinate system {CCF} can be obtained $K_1'\left(X_{K_1'}, Y_{K_1'}\right), K_2'\left(X_{K_2'}, Y_{K_2'}\right)$, and $K_3'\left(X_{K_3'}, Y_{K_3'}\right)$.

Suppose the intersection point J_1 corresponds to the point under the coordinate system {CCF} as $J_1'(X_1, Y_1)$. According to the principle of invariance of the intersection ratio, the equation is as follows:

$$\frac{X_{K_1'} - X_1}{X_{K_2'} - X_{K_1'}} : \frac{X_{K_3'} - X_1}{X_{K_3'} - X_{K_1'}} = \frac{u_{K_2} - u_1}{u_{K_2} - u_{K_1}} : \frac{u_{K_3} - u_1}{u_{K_3} - u_{K_1}} \tag{5}$$

Solving Eq. 5 can get the abscissa X_1 of intersection J_1'. The corner points $K_1'\left(X_{K_1'}, Y_{K_1'}\right), K_2'\left(X_{K_2'}, Y_{K_2'}\right)$, and $K_3'\left(X_{K_3'}, Y_{K_3'}\right)$ are used to construct a linear equation according to the principle of least squares.

$$y = a_3 x + b_3 \tag{6}$$

Put $x = X_1$ into the Eq. 6, and solve for Y_1. In the same way, the Eq. 3 can be solved to fit the intersection points J_2 and J_3 of the linear equation with the corner points in the second column and the third column respectively. Solve the coordinates of intersection points J_2' and J_3' corresponding to intersection points J_2 and J_3 in the coordinate system {CCF}.

Since the marker point M_1 and the intersection points J_1, J_2, and J_3 are on the same linear equation, the coordinates of the marker point M_1' in the coordinate system {CCF} can be obtained according to the principle of the invariance of the intersection ratio. In the same way, the coordinates of marker points M_2' and M_3' in the coordinate system {CCF} can be obtained. So far, the coordinates of the three marker points under the calibration board coordinate system are all calculated.

4 Homogeneous Transformation Matrix Between Coordinate Systems

4.1 Homogeneous Transformation Matrix $_{\mathrm{MF}}^{\mathrm{CCF}} T$

As shown in Fig. 5, establish the checkerboard calibration board coordinate system {CCF} and the marker point coordinate system {CCF}. Take the coordinate system {CCF} as the world coordinate system, the homogeneous equation between the coordinate system {MF} and the coordinate system {CCF} is:

$$\left[X_{\mathrm{CCF}} \; Y_{\mathrm{CCF}} \; Z_{\mathrm{CCF}} \; 1 \right]^{\mathrm{T}} = {}_{\mathrm{MF}}^{\mathrm{CCF}} T \left[X_{\mathrm{MF}} \; Y_{\mathrm{MF}} \; Z_{\mathrm{MF}} \; 1 \right]^{\mathrm{T}} \tag{7}$$

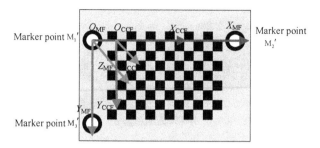

Fig. 5. Coordinate system {CCF} and {MF} established

4.2 Homogeneous Transformation Matrix $_{\text{FF}}^{\text{BF}}T$

As shown in Fig. 6, establish the robot flange coordinate system {FF} and the robot base coordinate system {BF}. Take the coordinate system {BF} as the world coordinate system, the homogeneous equation between the coordinate system {FF} and the coordinate system {BF} is:

$$\begin{bmatrix} X_{\text{BF}} & Y_{\text{BF}} & Z_{\text{BF}} & 1 \end{bmatrix}^{\text{T}} = {}_{\text{FF}}^{\text{BF}}T \begin{bmatrix} X_{\text{FF}} & Y_{\text{FF}} & Z_{\text{FF}} & 1 \end{bmatrix}^{\text{T}} \tag{8}$$

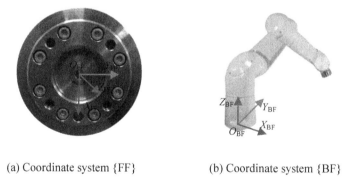

(a) Coordinate system {FF}   (b) Coordinate system {BF}

Fig. 6. Coordinate system {FF} and {BF} established

4.3 Homogeneous Transformation Matrix $_{\text{CCF}}^{\text{CF}}T$

As shown in Fig. 7, establish the camera coordinate system {CF}. Take the coordinate system {CF} as the world coordinate system, the homogeneous equation between the coordinate system {CCF} and the coordinate system {CF} is:

$$\begin{bmatrix} X_{\text{CF}} & Y_{\text{CF}} & Z_{\text{CF}} & 1 \end{bmatrix}^{\text{T}} = {}_{\text{CCF}}^{\text{CF}}T \begin{bmatrix} X_{\text{CCF}} & Y_{\text{CCF}} & Z_{\text{CCF}} & 1 \end{bmatrix}^{\text{T}} \tag{9}$$

Fig. 7. Coordinate system {CF} established

4.4 Homogeneous Transformation Matrix $_{\mathrm{MF}}^{\mathrm{CDF}}T$

As shown in Fig. 8, establish a C-Track coordinate system {CDF}. Take the coordinate system {CDF} as the world coordinate system, the homogeneous equation between the coordinate system {MF} and the coordinate system {CDF} is:

$$\left[X_{\mathrm{CDF}}\ Y_{\mathrm{CDF}}\ Z_{\mathrm{CDF}}\ 1\right]^{\mathrm{T}} = {}_{\mathrm{MF}}^{\mathrm{CDF}}T\left[X_{\mathrm{MF}}\ Y_{\mathrm{MF}}\ Z_{\mathrm{MF}}\ 1\right]^{\mathrm{T}} \tag{10}$$

Fig. 8. Coordinate system {CDF} established

4.5 Homogeneous Transformation Matrix $_{\mathrm{BF}}^{\mathrm{CDF}}T$

In order to calculate $_{\mathrm{BF}}^{\mathrm{CDF}}T$, it is necessary to use the coordinate system {CDF} as the world coordinate system to establish the robot base coordinate system {BF}. Take the coordinate system {CDF} as the world coordinate system, the homogeneous equation between the coordinate system {BF} and the coordinate system {CDF} is:

$$\left[X_{\mathrm{CDF}}\ Y_{\mathrm{CDF}}\ Z_{\mathrm{CDF}}\ 1\right]^{\mathrm{T}} = {}_{\mathrm{BF}}^{\mathrm{CDF}}T\left[X_{\mathrm{BF}}\ Y_{\mathrm{BF}}\ Z_{\mathrm{BF}}\ 1\right]^{\mathrm{T}} \tag{11}$$

5   Experiment and Discussion

5.1   Experiment Platform

In order to verify the accuracy of the method in this paper, a hand-eye calibration experiment platform was built, as shown in Fig. 9. The industrial robot selects the TX90 robot of STAUBLI company, the repeat positioning accuracy is ±0.03 mm, and the angular resolution of each axis is less than 0.000183°. The camera selects the EXG50 model camera of Baumer company, the camera resolution is 2592×1944 pixels, and the pixel size is $2.2~\mu m \times 2.2~\mu m$, the focal length of the lens is 8 mm. The C-Track optical dynamic tracking system of CREAFORM company is selected, and the measurement accuracy can reach 0.025 mm. The checkerboard calibration board pasted with marker points is fixed in the field of view of the camera and the field of view of the C-Track optical dynamic tracking system, the camera and the robot flange are fixedly connected through the connecting plate.

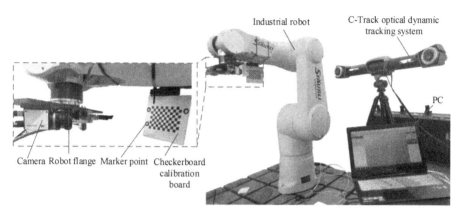

Fig. 9. Hand-eye calibration experiment platform

5.2 Results and Discussion

In order to verify the reliability and accuracy of the method in this paper, the method in this paper is compared with the traditional hand-eye calibration method that establishes and solves the matrix equation by a mobile manipulator, and 50 sets of independent hand-eye calibration experiment are carried out respectively. Since the absolute true value of the hand-eye relationship cannot be known, the average value of the hand-eye calibration experimental results is taken as the true value for comparison and analysis, as shown in Fig. 10. It can be drawn from the figure that the relative error of hand-eye relationship translation obtained according to the traditional hand-eye calibration method is within ± 1.2 mm, the relative error of rotation is within $\pm 0.7°$, and the relative error of hand-eye relationship translation obtained according to the hand-eye calibration method of this paper within the range of ± 0.6 mm, the relative error of rotation is within the range of $\pm 0.3°$.

The error of the hand-eye calibration experiment is analyzed, as shown in Table 1. Compared with the traditional hand-eye calibration method, the hand-eye relationship matrix obtained according to the hand-eye calibration method in this paper reduces the average translation relative error by 46.2%, the maximum translation relative error by 55.5%, the average rotation relative error by 62.2%, and the maximum rotation relative error by 60.2%, which proves that the method proposed in this paper has higher calibration accuracy and better stability.

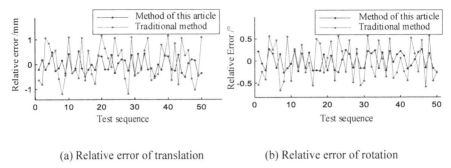

(a) Relative error of translation   (b) Relative error of rotation

Fig. 10. Experimental results

Table 1. Experimental error analysis

Parameter	Average translation relative error/mm	Maximum translation relative error/mm	Average rotation relative error/°	Maximum rotation relative error/°
Traditional method	0.520	1.196	0.450	0.665
Method of this article	0.280	0.532	0.170	0.265

6 Conclusion

A brief analysis of the traditional hand-eye calibration method, a hand-eye calibration method with marker points, checkerboard calibration board and C-Track optical dynamic tracking system as the intermediate measurement system is proposed, which improves the accuracy of hand-eye calibration and simplifies the hand-eye calibration process.

The marker point, the checkerboard calibration board, the C-Track optical dynamic tracking system, the industrial robot, the robot flange and the camera coordinate system were established respectively, and the homogeneous transformation matrix between each coordinate system was analyzed and calculated. The method of extracting the marker point center and using the principle of cross-ratio invariance to calculate the position of the marker point in the coordinate system of the checkerboard calibration board are introduced.

The experimental results show that the relative error of translation of the hand-eye relationship obtained according to the hand-eye calibration method of this paper is within ±0.6 mm, and the relative error of rotation is within ±0.3°. Compared with the experimental results of the traditional hand-eye calibration method, the average translation relative error is reduced by 46.2%, the maximum translation relative error is reduced by 55.5%, the average rotation relative error is reduced by 62.2%, the maximum rotation relative error is reduced by 60.2%.

References

1. Cao, T.Y., Cai, H.Y., Fang, D.M., Liu, C.: Robot vision system for keyframe global map establishment and robot localization based on graphic content matching. Opt. Precis. Eng. **25**(08), 2221–2232 (2017)
2. Lin, Y.M., Lv, N.G., Lou, X.P., Dong, M.L.: Robot vison system for 3D reconstruction in low texture environment. Opt. Precis. Eng. **23**(02), 540–549 (2015)
3. Andreff, N., Horaud, R., Espiau, B.: Robot hand-eye calibration using structure-from-motion. Int. J. Robot. Res. **20**(3), 228–248 (2001)
4. Malm, H., Heyden, A.: A new approach to hand-eye calibration. In: 15th International Conference on, Pattern Recognition (2000)
5. Yang, S.R., Yin, S.B., Ren, Y.J., Zhu, J.G., Ye, S.H.: Improvement of calibration method for robotic flexible visual measurement systems. Opt. Precis. Eng. **22**(12), 3239–3246 (2014)
6. Tsai, R.Y., Lenz, R.K.: A new technique for fully autonomous and efficient 3D robotics hand/eye calibration. Robot. Autom. **5**(3), 345–358 (1989)
7. Zhang, T., Ye, J.Y., Liu, X.G.: Weighted hand-eye calibration algorithm for robot grinding. J. Mech. Eng. **54**(17), 142–148 (2018)
8. Heller, J., Havlena, M., Pajdla, T.: A branch-and-bound algorithm for globally optimal hand-eye calibration. In: 2012 IEEE Conference on Computer Vision and Pattern Recognition (CVPR). IEEE (2012)
9. Li, W., Lv, N.G., Dong, M.L., Lou, X.P.: Simultaneous robot-world/hand-eye calibration dual quaternion. Robot **40**(03), 301–308 (2018)
10. Chou, J.C.K., Kamel, M.: Finding the position and orientation of a sensor on a robot manipulator using quaternions. Int. J. Robot. Res. **10**(3), 240–254 (1991)
11. Hu, J.-S., Chang, Y.-J.: Automatic calibration of hand–eye–workspace and camera using hand-mounted line laser. IEEE/ASME Trans. Mechatron. **18**(6), 1778–1786 (2013)
12. Chen, T.F., Wang, Y., Chen, Y.Q., Wu, X., Ma, Z.: An online hand-eye calibration approach based on cascaded filter. J. Southeast Univ. **43**(S1), 138–142 (2013)
13. Wang, J.C., Wang, T.M., Yang, Y., Hu, L.: Robot hand-eye calibration using unscented Kalman filtering. Robot **33**(05), 621–627 (2011)
14. Park, Y., Choi, Y., Seo, Y.: Globally optimal camera-and-rotation-sensor calibration with a branch-and-bound algorithm. Appl. Opt. **56**(12), 3462 (2017)
15. Bi, D.X., Wang, X.L., Liu, Z.F., Wang, X.M.: New method for robot tool and camera pose calibration. Chin. J. Sci. Instrum. **40**(01), 101–108 (2019)
16. Liu, C.J., Duan, Y., Wang, Y., Ye, S.H.: Study on the field calibration technology of robot flexible coordinate measurement system. J. Mech. Eng. **46**(18), 1–6 (2010)

Review on Energy Consumption Optimization Methods of Typical Discrete Manufacturing Equipment

Ming Yao[1,2], Zhufeng Shao[1,2(✉)], and Yanling Zhao[3]

[1] State Key Laboratory of Tribology and Institute of Manufacturing
Engineering, Tsinghua University, Beijing 100084, China
shaozf@mail.tsinghua.edu.cn
[2] Beijing Key Lab of Precision/Ultra-precision Manufacturing Equipments and Control,
Tsinghua University, Beijing 100084, China
[3] Instrumentation Technology and Economy Institute, Beijing 100055, China

Abstract. With China's commitments on "carbon peak" and "carbon neutral", energy consumption optimization for discrete manufacturing has become an important hot issue. By reviewing and analyzing related researches on energy consumption of typical discrete manufacturing equipment such as machine tools and industrial robots, this paper summarizes energy consumption optimization methods for the discrete manufacturing, especially focusing on the promising intelligent optimization technology. The intelligent optimization for multi parameters in complex and variable working conditions is the trends of the energy consumption, which requires the combination of software and hardware.

Keywords: Discrete manufacturing · Energy consumption optimization · Machine tool · Industrial robot · Intelligent algorithm

1 Introduction

The global manufacturing industry is a big contributor to greenhouse gas emissions and energy consumption, consuming 33% of the total energy and accounting for 38% of direct or indirect CO_2 emissions [1], which has become the focus of energy conservation and emission reduction. Facing the demand of global sustainable development, the research related to reducing energy consumption in manufacturing industry has gradually become a hot spot, and low-carbon manufacturing has attracted more and more attention [2].

As core equipment of the discrete manufacturing system, machine tools and industrial robots are the main energy consumers. At the same time, a large number of survey statistics show that the energy utilization of machine tool and industrial robot is low [3]. Research on energy consumption optimization for typical equipment, is of great significance for improving the energy utilization efficiency of discrete manufacturing and fulfilling China's commitment of "carbon peak" and "carbon neutral". This article will focus on the energy consumption optimization of machine tools and industrial robots, discuss the existing researches, and explore potential research directions in the future.

X.-J. Liu et al. (Eds.): ICIRA 2021, LNAI 13015, pp. 48–58, 2021.
https://doi.org/10.1007/978-3-030-89134-3_5

2   Typical Equipment Energy Consumption Optimization Method

Machine tools and industrial robots are the main body of energy consumption in discrete manufacturing [4]. The energy consumption optimization methods of these two typical equipment can be divided into three categories: hardware approaches, software approaches and hybrid approaches, as shown in Fig. 1.

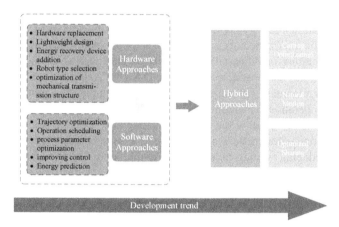

Fig. 1. Development of the energy consumption optimization

2.1   Hardware Approaches

The hardware approaches to lower the energy consumption is mainly concentrated in the design and manufacturing stage of the equipment [5]. Common solutions include adopting lightweight design and adding energy recovery units.

Industrial robot hardware solutions include methods such as lightweight design [6, 7], adding energy recovery units [8] and robot type selection [9]. The lightweight design of industrial robot mainly adopts the methods of sub-component redesign, optimization and replacement. Using more efficient or lighter components to reduce weight and arm inertia, so the robot movement consumes less energy, which is the main hardware optimization method.

The hardware optimization methods of machine tools mainly include the use of high-efficiency components, optimization of mechanical transmission structure, lightweight design, adding energy recovery units and reducing auxiliary system energy consumption [10]. The use of high-efficiency components is mainly to reduce the energy consumption of the system by using high-efficiency drive components. For the lightweight design of machine tools, researchers have proposed three types of lightweight design methods: structural lightweight design, material lightweight design and system lightweight design [11].

Hardware approaches can reduce the energy consumption of equipment. But it is mainly applicable to the design phase of the equipment. At the same time, it's hardware changes are relatively large, and the modification cost is relatively high [5]. For equipment that has already been put into the production cycle, more consideration should be given to software solutions.

2.2 Software Approaches

Software approach can reduce the energy consumption without making a lot of hardware modifications. Compared with the hardware approach, it has the advantages of low cost and good applicability. Energy optimization methods at software level generally involve parameter modification, trajectory optimization and operation scheduling.

Software solutions for industrial robots can be divided into two categories: trajectory optimization [12, 13] and operation scheduling [14, 15]. Trajectory optimization refers to the trajectory planning with minimum energy consumption to complete the same task, while the operation scheduling generally considers the time scale and sequence arrangement of the robot cell or the robot production line.

Software optimization methods for machine tools mainly include process parameter optimization, reducing waiting time and improving control. Optimization of process parameters, including tool paths, minimum machine tool standby time and scheduling, etc. Using the constructed energy consumption model to optimize the process parameters can reduce the energy consumption of the machine tool and does not require major hardware transformation [16].

The software method does not need to modify or redesign hardware, which is an ideal solution to reduce energy consumption for equipment that is already in the mature production cycle. However, due to the high dimension of the relevant parameters of the discrete manufacturing equipment and the complex working conditions, the optimization algorithm is difficult to achieve global optimization and rapid planning, and fail to meet the actual production needs.

2.3 Hybrid Approaches

The hybrid energy consumption optimization method is a comprehensive optimization scheme that takes into account both hardware and software approaches. Scholars have proposed various optimization methods.

As for industrial robots, literature [17] divides hybrid approaches into two categories: natural motion [18] and optimized sharing [19]. Natural motion transforms the hardware system by adding elastic elements to the actuator, and carries out corresponding motion planning accordingly. Optimal sharing is to comprehensively consider the impact of motion optimization, energy storage and sharing devices on the energy consumption of the robot, so as to jointly optimize the energy consumption of the robot.

The hybrid energy consumption optimization method of machine tools is focusing on the cutting process, which is the effective and kernel action. Since the energy consumption of cutting process is attributed to the cutting load in the process, the energy consumption of machine tools can be reduced by optimizing the cutting parameters and using advanced cutting technologies, such as using high-efficiency lubrication systems [20] and auxiliary processing technology [21].

The hybrid optimization method can comprehensively consider the constraints of hardware and software to optimize energy consumption of the equipment, which has the best optimization result. However, because it is necessary to modify the equipment at both the hardware and software levels at the same time, the hybrid optimization method is complex and difficult, and the robustness and stability in the actual production environment are not desirable.

In addition to hybrid approaches, the optimization technology based on intelligent algorithm has also emerged in recent years, which has achieved good results in dealing with complex nonlinear energy consumption modeling and prediction problems. The intelligent energy consumption optimization method is introduced in the following.

3 Intelligent Optimization Method

Energy consumption modeling and forecasting are the key to optimization. However, the energy consumption modeling and prediction of manufacturing equipment is a highly nonlinear problem with many influencing factors, and traditional mathematical modeling methods are difficult to solve well. In recent years, intelligent algorithms have been developing rapidly and show advantages in dealing with nonlinear problems, which have achieved good results in the energy consumption modeling and prediction of industrial robots and machine tools.

3.1 Industrial Robots

The intelligent optimization method on energy consumption of industrial robots is to realize data-driven optimization, and the existing research will be discussed below.

Researches on energy consumption optimization of industrial robots mainly focused on the trajectory optimization with intelligent algorithms such as genetic algorithm and cloning algorithm. For example, Biswas A et al. [22] used a genetic algorithm to determine the trajectory that minimizes energy consumption when studying the collision-free trajectory planning problem of a 3 DOFs space manipulator. Because dynamic models are difficult to discover the precise relation-ship between robot motion parameters and energy consumption, algorithms such as neural network have been applied to the energy consumption optimization of industrial robots. Yin S et al. [23] proposed a trajectory planning method that combines artificial neural network (ANN) with evolution-based/swarm intelligent algorithms. The model after neural network training can provide a fitness function for evolutionary algorithms, and provide powerful optimization capabilities on achieving energy efficiency goals.

Different from the traditional energy consumption modeling that takes the dynamic behavior of industrial robots as the main research object, Zhang M et al. [24] proposed a data-driven energy consumption optimization method, using back propagation neural network (BPNN) to accurately reveal the quantitative relationship between operating parameters and energy consumption, and used genetic algorithms to optimize the parameters. In addition, some scholars apply BPNN to the energy consumption prediction of the articulated manipulator under unknown angular displacement and load [25]. Apart from neural network, Efimov A et al. [26] applied the neuro-fuzzy inference system to the energy consumption prediction of industrial robots to provide support for finding the trajectory with the least energy consumption in the robot workspace.

At present, there are few studies on intelligent energy consumption optimization of industrial robots, and the actual application in industrial field is relatively few. Therefore, it needs more further studies.

3.2 Machine Tools

The energy consumption of machine tools is a multi-component and multi-level system problem. There are many energy-consuming components with the characteristics of multi-source energy consumption [27]. During the operation of the machine tool, there are various energy interactions and mutual influences among various components, which makes the research on energy consumption optimization more complicated. This also brings great difficulties to the energy consumption modeling, prediction and optimization of machine tools.

Table 1. Machine learning algorithms for machine tool energy consumption optimization.

Algorithm	Literature	Year
Neural Network	Xie D et al. [28]	2012
	Garg A et al. [31]	2015
	Kant G et al. [29]	2015
	Li L et al. [34]	2015
	Ak R et al. [35]	2015
	Long Z et al. [32]	2018
	Shin et al. [33]	2018
	Shin S J et al. [37]	2019
	CHEN Shiping et al. [36]	2020
Support Vector Machine	Chen W W et al. [40]	2014
Ensemble Learning	Ak R et al. [35]	2015
	Liu Z et al. [42]	2018
	Chen T et al. [43]	2019
	CHEN Shiping et al. [36]	2020
Transfer Learning	Shin S J et al. [37]	2019
	Chaoyang Zhang et al. [38]	2020
k-Nearest Neighbor	Ak R et al. [35]	2015
	Komoto H et al. [41]	2020
Gaussian Process Regression	Bhinge R et al. [44, 45]	2015, 2017
Deep Learning	Y He et al. [39]	2020

At present, most researches based on machine learning algorithms include at least three types of input data: spindle speed, feed rate and depth of cut. Table 1 lists the common machine learning algorithms in the research on energy consumption optimization of machine tools. It can be seen that many researches are based on neural network models.

Neural Network. BPNN is an artificial neural network based on error back propagation algorithm. Xie D et al. [28] built the cutting parameters-based energy consumption model for machine tool with BPNN, and used genetic algorithms to optimize the cutting parameters. The energy consumption prediction accuracy reached 92%. In order to choose the optimal processing parameters, Kant G et al. [29] used ANN to establish a prediction model for the milling process, with an average relative error of 1.50%. The relevant data set can be found in literature [30]. In addition, Garg A et al. [31] added a variety of intelligent algorithms such as ANN, Bayesian models and genetic algorithms to the energy consumption modeling of machine tools. Long Z et al. [32] proposed a method for predicting energy consumption using Elman neural network. These energy consumption optimization researches have achieved good results.

The above studies only considered relatively simple working conditions, and established a coarse-grained model for the cutting process of machine tools, which is not for actual manufacturing. In response to the above problems, Shin et al. [33] used ANN to propose a predictive modeling method based on historical data of machine tool operation, and created multiple fine-grained power consumption prediction models, which are suitable for predicting energy consumption of machine tools under different processes. Professor Fei L from Chongqing University also carried out researches on the application of BPNN in energy consumption optimization, and proposed a multi-objective optimization method based on neural network to optimize cutting parameters [34].

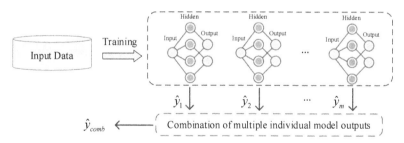

Fig. 2. Basic scheme of neural network ensemble [35]

Some scholars found that the generalization performance of a single neural network model in actual applications is not good for the energy consumption optimization. Therefore, they introduced ensemble learning into energy consumption optimization. Through the combination of multiple learners, ensemble learning can often obtain more significantly superior generalization performance than a single learner. By using neural network as the basic learner, they built a neural network ensemble learning model to predict machine tool energy consumption [35], which is shown in Fig. 2. Then, CHEN

Shiping et al. [36] integrated BPNN through the Adaboost algorithm to obtain a strong predictor, which improved the prediction accuracy for the CNC machine tool.

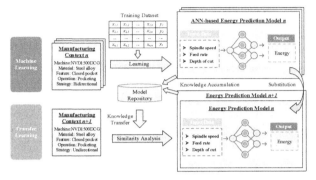

Fig. 3. Transfer learning in machine tool energy consumption prediction [37]

In addition, another important reason that affects the generalization of intelligent algorithms is lack of data and insufficient sample data quality in the complex cutting environment. Transfer learning can reuse a pre-trained model in another task, and can be used to solve the above problems. Shin S J et al. [37] proposed a self-learning factory mechanism based on transfer learning, as shown in Fig. 3. When the training data set exists, the energy consumption prediction model is established based on ANN. When the training data set is not available, the transfer learning algorithm creates an alternative model by transferring the learned knowledge. Using this method, the energy consumption can be reduced by 9.70%. In addition, some scholars have established a machine tool energy saving decision-making method that integrates deep belief networks and transfer learning [38], which reduces the energy consumption of waiting process.

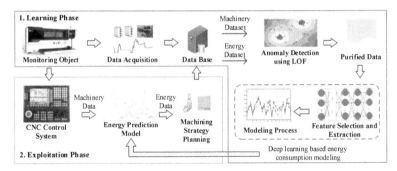

Fig. 4. General framework of the energy prediction method based on deep learning [39]

The existing data-driven researches mainly focus on the use of manual feature learning methods, which are low in efficiency and poor in generalization. To solve this problem, Yan He et al. [39] proposed a data-driven energy prediction method, which used deep learning to extract sensitive energy consumption features from raw data in an unsupervised manner, and developed and extracted them in a supervised manner, as shown in Fig. 4. The results show that it can improve the energy prediction performance, which is superior to the traditional method in terms of effectiveness and versatility.

The unique advantage of deep learning is that it can spend little effort and expert knowledge to extract energy consumption characteristics, which has great potential in practical applications. But the shortcomings are higher requirements for computing resources, longer model training time and the risk of overfitting.

Other Machine Learning Algorithms. In addition to neural network, other machine learning algorithms such as support vector machine and k-nearest neighbor algorithm have also been used in the research of machine tool energy optimization.

Support Vector Machine (SVM). SVM can solve practical problems such as small samples, nonlinearity and local minima. Some scholars verified the feasibility of energy consumption prediction methods based on SVM [40]. However, SVM cannot handle the complex nonlinear relationship between the cutting parameters of the machine tool well, and the effect in the application of the energy consumption optimization of the machine tool is not as good as the neural network. Therefore, SVM has not received much attention in the following research.

K Nearest Neighbor (KNN). KNN is a non-parametric machine learning algorithm in which the value of each sample can be represented by its nearest K neighboring values. Some scholars have applied the KNN algorithm, and proposed a behavioral model that characterizes the five-axis machining center during the finishing process of the test piece. This behavior model predicts the behavior and energy consumption in the finishing process from multiple technological perspectives such as production, processing and cutting [41], and can accurately predict the energy usage of machine tools.

Ensemble Learning Based on Tree Model. Except from using neural network as the basic learner, a number of scholars construct an ensemble learning model based on the tree model. Liu Z et al. [42] proposed a cutting energy prediction model based on a tree-based gradient boosting method, which improved the prediction accuracy of milling energy and provided a new method for energy optimization in the milling process. Later, Chen T et al. [43] conducted related research and proposed a milling energy consumption prediction model based on the gradient advance regression tree algorithm, which achieved the prediction accuracy of 94%.

Gaussian Process Regression. Gaussian process regression is also a non-parametric machine learning algorithm. The team of Professor Bhinge R from the University of California has been studying the application of this algorithm to the energy optimization of machine tools. They used gaussian process regression to establish an energy prediction model for CNC machine tools and modeled the complex relationship between processing parameters and energy consumption. The accuracy of the total predicted energy is above 95% [44]. Moreover, they also extended the energy prediction model to multiple process parameters and operations for process planning to optimize the energy efficiency of the machining process [45].

4 Conclusions

In this paper, the energy consumption optimization of two typical equipment of discrete manufacturing system is reviewed. Firstly, it summarizes the energy consumption optimization methods of machine tools and industrial robots, which are divided into three categories: hardware approaches, software approaches and hybrid approaches. Then, it focuses on the data-driven intelligent optimization technology on the energy consumption, summarizes the existing researches and analyzes their application effects. Conclusions are drawn as follows.

1. Hybrid optimization method of energy consumption. At present, most researches focus on a single level, hardware or software. However, the overall energy consumption optimization combining hardware and software deserves further attention. In addition, many researches only focus on single device without considering factors such as the environment in which the device is located. The hybrid energy consumption optimization technology that integrates multiple factors such as environment and production requirements is a worth direction.
2. Self-learning, adaptive real-time energy consumption optimization. Discrete manufacturing production tasks continue change. It is a new challenge that how to adapt quickly to the working conditions, learn independently and make real-time response in the face of unfamiliar tasks and uncertainty of production data. In the future, the latest artificial intelligence technologies such as transfer learning will be adopted to improve self-learning capabilities. According to different environments and tasks, it can independently select the most suitable energy consumption plan in real time.
3. Intelligent optimization technology that considers multiple parameters and complex working conditions. The equipment energy consumption process is highly nonlinear, while the discrete manufacturing system is random and dynamic in production process with many influencing factors. Therefore, pure mathematical models and traditional machine learning methods are difficult to accurately model the energy consumption process of the manufacturing system and its equipment. Instead, it is the key to solving the above problems that combining deep learning to learn deep-level feature representations and research energy consumption modeling and prediction.

Acknowledgement. This work is supported by the National Key R&D Program of China (Grant No. 2020YFB1710700).

References

1. Wang, J.: A survey on energy efficient discrete manufacturing system. J. Mech. Eng. (2013)
2. Duflou, J.R., Sutherland, J.W., Dornfeld, D., et al.: Towards energy and resource efficient manufacturing: a processes and systems approach. CIRP Ann. Manuf. Technol. **61**(2), 587–609 (2012)

3. Fei, L.: Content architecture and future trends of energy efficiency research on machining systems. J. Mech. Eng. **49**(19), 87 (2013)
4. Zhao, G.Y., Liu, Z.Y., He, Y., et al.: Energy consumption in machining: Classification, prediction, and reduction strategy. Energy **133**(Aug 15), 142–157 (2017)
5. Hou, Q., Yang, D., Guo, S.: Review on energy consumption optimization methods of industrial robots. Comput. Eng. Appl. **54**(22), 1–9 (2018)
6. Albuschäffer, A., Haddadin, S., Ott, C., et al.: The DLR lightweight robot: design and control concepts for robots in human environments. Ind. Robot **34**(5), 376–385 (2007)
7. Aziz, M., Zanibek, M., Elsayed, A., et al.: Design and analysis of a proposed light weight three DOF planar industrial manipulator. In: 2016 IEEE Industry Applications Society Annual Meeting. IEEE (2016)
8. Gale, S., Eielsen, A.A., Gravdahl, J.T.: Modelling and simulation of a flywheel based energy storage system for an industrial manipulator. In: IEEE International Conference on Industrial Technology. IEEE (2015)
9. Li, Y., Bone, G.M.: Are parallel manipulators more energy efficient? In: Proceedings of 2001 IEEE International Symposium on Computational Intelligence in Robotics and Automation. IEEE (2001)
10. Yue-Jiang, W.U., He-Jian, O.U., Zhang, C.: Review and application of energy consumption model for cutting machine. J. New Ind. (2016)
11. Kroll, L., Blau, P., Wabner, M., et al.: Lightweight components for energy-efficient machine tools. CIRP J. Manuf. Sci. Technol. **4**(2), 148–160 (2011)
12. Liu, S., Wang, Y., et al.: Energy-efficient trajectory planning for an industrial robot using a multi-objective optimisation approach. Procedia Manuf. **25**, 517–525 (2018)
13. Wang, Q., Cheng, X., et al.: Inverse solution optimization and research on Trajectory Planning of cleaning manipulator for insulator. In: IOP Conference Series: Materials Science and Engineering, vol. 493, no. 1, pp. 12060–12060 (2019)
14. Pellicciari, M., Berselli, G., Leali, F., et al.: A method for reducing the energy consumption of pick-and-place industrial robots. Mechatronics **23**(3), 326–334 (2013)
15. Brossog, M., Bornschlegl, M., Franke, J.: Reducing the energy consumption of industrial robots in manufacturing systems. Int. J. Adv. Manuf. Technol. **78**(5–8), 1315–1328 (2015)
16. Yoon, H.S., Kim, E.S., Kim, M.S., et al.: Towards greener machine tools – a review on energy saving strategies and technologies. Renew. Sustain. Energy Rev. (2015)
17. Giovanni, C., Erich, W., Renato, V.: A review on energy-saving optimization methods for robotic and automatic systems. Robotics **6**(4), 39 (2017)
18. Iwamura, M., Imafuku, S., Kawamoto, T., Schiehlen, W.: Design and control of an energy-saving robot using storage elements and reaction wheels. In: Font-Llagunes, J.M. (ed.) Multibody Dynamics. CMAS, vol. 42, pp. 277–297. Springer, Cham (2016). https://doi.org/10.1007/978-3-319-30614-8_13
19. Boscariol, P., Richiedei, D.: Energy-efficient design of multipoint trajectories for Cartesian robots. Int. J. Adv. Manuf. Technol. (2019)
20. Reddy, N.S.K., Nouari, M., Yang, M.: Development of electrostatic solid lubrication system for improvement in machining process performance. Int. J. Mach. Tools Manuf. **50**(9), 789–797 (2010). https://doi.org/10.1016/j.ijmachtools.2010.05.007
21. Germain, G., et al.: Comprehension of chip formation in laser assisted machining. Int. J. Mach. Tools Manuf. **51**(3), 230–238 (2011). https://doi.org/10.1016/j.ijmachtools.2010.11.006
22. Biswas, A., Deekshatulu, B.L., Roy, S.S.: Energy Optimal Trajectory Planning of a Robotic Manipulator Using Genetic Algorithm. American Institute of Physics (2010)
23. Yin, S., Ji, W., et al.: A machine learning based energy efficient trajectory planning approach for industrial robots. In: The 52nd CIRP Conference on Manufacturing Systems (2019)
24. Zhang, M., Yan, J.: A data-driven method for optimizing the energy consumption of industrial robots. J. Cleaner Prod. **285** (2020)

25. Ding, Y., Zhu, X., Sun, X., et al.: Soft sensor simulation of minimum energy consumption of joint manipulator drive system based on improved BP neural network. In: Journal of Physics: Conference Series, vol. 1626, no. 1, p. 012020 (16pp) (2020)
26. Efimov, A., Gorkavyy, M., Gorkavyy, A.: Predicting power consumption of robotic complex based on neuro-fuzzy system. In: 2020 International Conference on Industrial Engineering, Applications and Manufacturing (ICIEAM) (2020)
27. Wang, Q.: Mathematical model of multi-source energy flows for CNC machine tools. J. Mech. Eng. 49(7), 5 (2013)
28. Xie, D., Chen, G.R., Wang, F., et al.: Modeling of CNC machine tool energy consumption and optimization study based on neural network and genetic algorithm. Appl. Mech. Mater. 195–196, 770–776 (2012)
29. Kant, G., Sangwan, K.S.: Predictive modelling for energy consumption in machining using artificial neural network. Procedia CIRP 37, 205–210 (2015)
30. Yan, J., Lin, L.: Multi-objective optimization of milling parameters - the trade-offs between energy, production rate and cutting quality. J. Clean. Prod. 52, 462–471 (2013)
31. Garg, A., Lam, J., Gao, L.: Energy conservation in manufacturing operations: modelling the milling process by a new complexity-based evolutionary approach. J. Cleaner Prod. 108(DEC.1PT.A), 34–45 (2015)
32. Long, Z., Zhang, J., Fan, Q., et al.: Energy prediction for rotating ultrasonic machining based on neural network model. In: 2018 IEEE International Conference on Information and Automation (ICIA). IEEE (2018)
33. Shin, S.-J., et al.: Standard data-based predictive modeling for power consumption in turning machining. Sustainability 10(3), 598 (2018)
34. Li, L., Fei, L., et al.: Multi-objective optimization of cutting parameters in sculptured parts machining based on neural network. J. Intell. Manuf. 26(5) (2015)
35. Ak, R., Helu, M.M., Rachuri, S.: Ensemble neural network model for predicting the energy consumption of a milling machine. In: ASME International Design Engineering Technical Conferences & Computers & Information in Engineering Conference (2015)
36. Chen, S., Xie, J., Luo, X.: Study on material cutting energy consumption prediction of CNC machine tool based on BP-Adaboost algorithm. Green Manuf. 12, 20–24 (2020)
37. Shin, S.J., Kim, Y.M., Meilanitasari, P.: A holonic-based self-learning mechanism for energy-predictive planning in machining processes. Processes 7(10), 739 (2019)
38. Zhang, C., Ji, W., Peng, W.: Decision-making method for energy-saving control of CNC machine tools based on transfer learning. China Mech. Eng. 31(23), 2855 (2020)
39. He, Y., Wu, P., Li, Y., et al.: A generic energy prediction model of machine tools using deep learning algorithms. Appl. Energy 275, 115402 (2020)
40. Chen, W.W., Zhang, H., et al.: Research on CNC machine tool cutting energy consumption prediction based on support vector machine. Mach. Des. Manuf. (2014)
41. Komoto, H., Herrera, G., Herwan, J.: An evolvable model of machine tool behavior applied to energy usage prediction. CIRP Ann. Manuf. Technol. 69(1) (2020)
42. Liu, Z., Guo, Y.: A hybrid approach to integrate machine learning and process mechanics for the prediction of specific cutting energy. CIRP Ann. Manuf. Technol. (2018). S0007850618300155
43. Chen, T., Shang, H., Bi, Q.: A prediction method of five-axis machine tool energy consumption with GBRT algorithm. In: International Conference on Mechatronics System and Robots (2019)
44. Bhinge, R., Biswas, N., Dornfeld, D., et al.: An intelligent machine monitoring system for energy prediction using a Gaussian Process regression. In: 2014 IEEE International Conference on Big Data (Big Data). IEEE (2015)
45. Rachuri, S., Bhinge, R., et al.: Toward a generalized energy prediction model for machine tools. J. Manuf. Sci. Eng. Trans. ASME (2017)

Medical Robot

Development and Control of a CT Fluoroscopy Guided Lung Puncture Robot

Rui He[1], Hao Wen[1], Changsheng Li[1] , Xiangqian Chen[2], Xiaogang Chen[2], Xiaowei Mao[1], and Xing-guang Duan[1(✉)]

[1] Beijing Institute of Technology, Beijing 100081, China
duanstar@bit.edu.cn
[2] True Health (Beijing) Medical Technology Co., Ltd., Beijing 100086, China

Abstract. Puncture surgery is an effective method for tumor diagnosis and treatment. Traditional manual puncture surgery guided by CT has the shortcomings of invisible tumor target, low puncture accuracy and complications. CT fluoroscopy scanning can obtain almost real-time refreshed CT images, which can help surgeons to puncture in the visibility of the tumor target and puncture needle. However, surgeons suffer from radiation harm and their flexibility and stability of the needle manipulation are greatly reduced. The puncture robot can replace surgeons in radiation and improved the accuracy of the surgery. In this paper, the puncture robot is introduced into the CT fluoroscopy guided lung puncture surgery procedure. The manual puncture surgery procedure is researched first and the requirements and design principles of robot are proposed. A 6-Degreee-Of-Freedom (DOF) puncture robot which can be controlled remotely is developed. The Remote Center Motion (RCM) control of the robot is studied to achieve the puncture angle adjustment under CT fluoroscopy. The developed robot system and puncture surgery scheme combine visibility, accuracy, safety and are of high clinical application value.

Keywords: CT fluoroscopy · Puncture robot · Remote center motion

1 Introduction

In recent years, the incidence rate of lung cancer is very high and is growing rapidly in Chinese population. According to the latest statistics of China National Cancer Center, there were about 3.929 million new cases of malignant tumors in 2015, in which lung cancer accounted for about 20% and the incidence rate ranked first. During the COVID-19 pandemic, more people are screened for the new coronavirus by CT scans and accidentally find small pulmonary nodules, which may eventually develop into lung cancers. To improve the diagnosis and treatment effect of lung cancer is of great significance.

CT guided percutaneous lung puncture is an effective minimally invasive method for diagnosis and treatment [1]. Surgeons need to use a needle to hit the target inside the lung percutaneously, establishing a percutaneous access. For a small pulmonary nodule, a biopsy needle is subsequently inserted into the access to extract the diseased tissue

© Springer Nature Switzerland AG 2021
X.-J. Liu et al. (Eds.): ICIRA 2021, LNAI 13015, pp. 61–70, 2021.
https://doi.org/10.1007/978-3-030-89134-3_6

for diagnosis. For a tumor diagnosed, an ablation needle is inserted and the tumor is carbonized and eliminated by heat. In order to find the exact location of the target in the lung, the patient need to screen a preoperative CT scan. Surgeons choose the target on the CT images, plan the puncture path, find the corresponding position and puncture angle on the patient with the anatomy knowledge and clinical experience, and then puncture the needle to the target.

CT images help surgeons to see inside of the patient's lung. However, CT images are static and CT scans produce radiation, which is harmful to the human body. Therefore, surgeons have to puncture intermittently [2]. After a certain depth of puncture, surgeons leave the CT room where the patient is scanned to avoid radiation. The position and angle of the puncture needle are observed and assessed on CT images. Then, with CT off, surgeons adjust the position and angle of the puncture needle on the patient. Operations above are repeated until the puncture needle hits the target. The entire procedure cannot be seen in real-time and the puncture accuracy is quite limited. Complications such as pneumothorax, bleeding occur. Actually, static CT images cannot truly represent the lung state. Soft tissue will move and deform under the influence of respiration and puncture force, which greatly increases the difficulty of surgery and reduces the accuracy of puncture. For small pulmonary nodules, inaccurate puncture positions will directly lead to false-negative diagnosis and surgery failure.

Thanks to the development of CT technology, CT images have achieved a better real-time performance. Using Cone Beam CT (CBCT) or CT fluoroscopy, the tumor target and the puncture needle can both be seen in nearly real-time [3, 4]. Blood vessels and trachea can show up clearly. Theoretically, surgeons can watch almost real-time refreshed CT images, adjust the needle to aim at the target and puncture until it hits the target. Meanwhile, complications are assessed. The problem that soft tissue moves and deforms is perfectly solved and the puncture accuracy is significantly improved. However, manipulating the puncture needle while the CT is scanning, surgeons will suffer more radiation, especially their hands holding the puncture needle which are directly exposed to the slip-ring of the CT machine. Surgeons can only do a limited number of surgeries every year to prevent the accumulated radiation dose. Clinically, surgeons use a long-handle clamp to hold the puncture needle, operating the puncture needle outside the slip-ring of the CT machine to avoid radiation. However, the flexibility and stability of needle manipulation are greatly reduced.

Robots are considered as effective helpers for human, working in dangerous or special environment. In the case of lung puncture surgery, robots can be exposed to the slip-ring of the CT machine, replacing surgeons, to manipulate the puncture needle. With the combination of a puncture robot and CT fluoroscopy, lung puncture surgeries can be practically achieved under the guidance of nearly real-time CT fluoroscopy images. Advantages of the puncture robot also include its more precise and stable operation [5, 6]. Manipulation of the puncture needle can be more accurate and uncertain factors such as surgeons' fatigue and shake are eliminated. In addition, after the registration of the robot and CT images, the robot can automatically find the puncture path on the patient corresponding to the one planned on CT images, which is more accurate than that found by surgeons with the anatomy knowledge and clinical experience. However, puncture surgeries still need to be monitored and controlled by reliable surgeons to ensure the absolute safety of patients. Under the guidance of CT fluoroscopy real-time images, surgeons control the robot to manipulate the needle. An excellent surgery solution with visibility, accuracy and safety for lung puncture is formed.

This paper focuses on the development and control of a puncture robot guided by CT fluoroscopy. Although there are numerous researches on similar robot systems, practicability and versatility of the system are important factors considered. With these design principles, manual lung puncture procedure guided by CT fluoroscopy is analyzed and the puncture robot is introduced changing as limited steps as possible. A puncture robot is developed. The puncture path on the patient is found by adjusting the needle position and the puncture angle with the robot under the real-time CT scans. To adjust the puncture angle, the robot is controlled to move around the RCM (Remote Center Motion) point. Thanks to its unique structure, the RCM control method is quite simple and effective. Advantages of the robot system are concluded and the further research is proposed.

2 Related Work

The surgical robot has become a research hotspot in the field of healthcare and robotics. For lung or soft tissue puncture surgeries, many researches have focused on CT fluoroscopy guided puncture robot systems [7–9]. Many of them have been validated technically and used in clinical animal or human experiments. Some excellent robots have obtained FDA certifications and have been commercialized. However, from the perspective of technical research, we pay more attention to their robot surgery schemes, development and control solutions, and the surgery effects robots can provide. Some mature products and representative puncture robots are reviewed as followed.

Acubot [10–13] is one of the earliest CT fluoroscopy guided lung puncture robots developed at the Johns Hopkins University. Acubot is mainly composed of a linear motion platform with 3 orthogonal axes, a 7-DOF passive arm and a RCM mechanism. The robot is stably installed on the CT bed and scanned with the patient. The robot registration is realized by scanning a Z-frame bracket fixed on the end effector or by using the laser line of the CT. Then, the robot automatically moves to the puncture path on the patient. Surgeons control the robot with a control box to puncture and adjust the puncture angle under the guidance of CT fluoroscopy images. The shortcomings of Acubot include that customized table adapters are needed to adapt to CT beds with different sizes and the 7-DOF passive arm has to be placed so that the puncture path is within its workspace. The CT registration scheme also needs to be improved. The Z-frame bracket is relatively large to provide high registration accuracy, however reducing the workspace inside the CT hole. When the laser line of the CT is used, the needle shaft needs to be manually moved to reflect the laser light.

Innomotion [14, 15] is a commercial puncture robot with a similar design to the Acubot. The robot is installed on the CT bed through a semicircular slide. The robot has 5 DOF, i.e., 3 linear motion DOF in the direction of 3 orthogonal axes and a RCM mechanism at the end effector. The robot can be fixed on the semicircular slide with the angle of $0°$, $\pm 35°$, $\pm 67°$, which can meet the need of puncturing in different parts of the patient with different angles. The robot registration is realized by scanning the marker balls fixed on the end effector. The most important character of the robot is that it is made of non-metallic materials, which almost does not produce artifacts on CT images. The advantage of the puncture robot installed on the CT bed is that the robot registration is easier because the robot and the CT bed move together and share the same coordinate system. However, the robot takes up too much patient space and workspace inside the CT hole, which brings inconvenience to the surgeons in anesthesia, skin incision and other operations. And, table adapters are necessary for different robots and CT beds.

Robospy [16] is a puncture robot that can be mounted on the patient body, which is smaller and lighter. The robot has 4 DOF including a 2-DOF spherical RCM mechanism and a 2-DOF needle-holding mechanism. Actually, it is more an electronically controlled RCM mechanism than a robot. Before puncturing, surgeons first need to use the metal grids and the laser line of CT to determine the needle entry point on the patient's skin. Then, the robot is attached to the patient so that its RCM point is coincidence with the entry point. The robot is scanned with the patient and only the puncture angle is adjusted under the guidance of CT fluoroscopy images. Attached to the patient, Robospy can move with the patient's respiration and unpredictable movement. This ensures the safety of the patient during the puncture. However, for a patient in the lateral position which frequently appears in clinical practice, the robot may not be firmly attached, which leads to unstable puncture operation and affects the puncture accuracy. The base of the robot needs to be customized according to the shape of different parts of the body to fit the patient's skin.

Xact [17] is also a patient-mounted puncture robot. The robot base is tied to the patient. Similar to the Robospy, it is composed of a needle posture adjustment mechanism and a needle insertion mechanism. The robot registration is realized by scanning the metal strip layout on the robot. The difference compared with the Robospy is that both the needle entry point and the puncture angle can be adjusted under the guidance of CT fluoroscopy images. Besides, the puncture force of the puncture needle can be monitored and recorded. When the puncture force exceeds the preset value, the needle insertion mechanism is disabled to ensure the safety of the patient. The patient-mounted puncture robot, compared with the CT bed installed ones, leaves more access to patients and working space for surgeons. However, it can only move the needle in a small range and is mainly used to adjust the puncture angle. Thus, before puncturing, the robot has to be manually placed near the puncture path on the patient. Problems still exist when puncturing in a lateral position, for the robot may remain unstable on the patient whether it is attached or tied.

Zerobot [18, 19] is a puncture robot installed on the ground beside the CT bed developed at the Okayama University. It consists of 3 linear motion DOF in the direction of 3 orthogonal axes and 2 rotation DOF. To find the puncture path on the patient, positioning of the needle by the robot is realized by manual teleoperation. The planned puncture path on the CT images is indicated by the laser light, and the surgeon controls the robot to place the needle so that the needle shaft is coincidence with the laser light. During the puncturing process, the CT fluoroscopy can be off intermittently to reduce the radiation does. Zerobot has been verified by animal and human biopsy test, animal ablation test and the system accuracy reaches 1.6mm. The robot installed on the ground, like the industrial robot, has better stability and higher absolute position accuracy. It does not have any direct mechanical connection with the CT equipment so the versatility of the robot is improved. However, certain skills are necessary to achieve the robot registration. CT fluoroscopy images and the laser light are combined and flexibly used in clinical practice.

3   CT Fluoroscopy Guided Puncture Procedure

The CT fluoroscopy guided manual puncture procedure is illustrated in Fig. 1. The steps with orange background indicate that CT or CT fluoroscopy scan is needed. The patient is first scanned by spiral CT and the surgery is designed based on the CT images and the 3D reconstruction images. The target point is found and the puncture path is usually designed on only one CT image. Then, metal grids are attached to the patient skin near the target. The patient moves with the CT bed until the target moves into the field of view of the CT fluoroscopy, which is usually automatically completed by the CT machine according to the Z coordinate value of the CT bed. Next, the patient is scanned by the CT fluoroscopy to obtain images with metal grids. Surgeons find the needle entry point on the patient, corresponding to the entry point on the image, by counting the metal grids and using the laser line of the CT machine. After the entry point is determined, disinfection and local anesthesia are carried out around and skin incision needs to be done to make it easier to puncture inside the body. Finally, the surgeon holds the needle with a long-handle clamp and places the needle tip at the entry point. Under the guidance of CT fluoroscopy real-time images, the puncture angle is adjusted while puncturing until the target is hit.

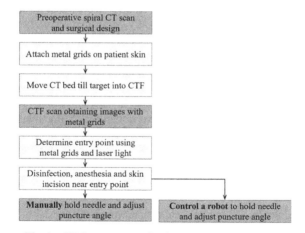

Fig. 1. CT fluoroscopy guided lung puncture procedure

In clinical practice, the surgical design is made by surgeons. Using the metal grids and the laser line of the CT machine, it is easy to find the needle entry point on the patient's skin. Disinfection, anesthesia and skin incision, which are personalized for every patient, have to be operated by the surgeon at the current stage. The step in which the robot can really help and replace the surgeon is the final one. Robots can hold the needle instead of the surgeons to protect against radiation. Robots can hold the needle more stably, adjusting the needle angle and puncturing with higher accuracy.

Therefore, we propose a CT fluoroscopy guided robot puncture procedure. As shown in Fig. 1, the existing steps before the puncture operation is unchanged. In the final step, the robot holds the puncture needle instead of the surgeon. The surgeon controls the robot to place the needle tip at the entry point, and controls the robot to adjust the puncture angle while puncturing with the guidance of the CT fluoroscopy.

4   Development of the Puncture Robot

In the CT fluoroscopy guided robot puncture procedure, the robot needs to place the needle tip at the entry point on the patient's skin and adjust the puncture angle. In terms of motion ability, the end effector of the robot should be able to move linearly in 3D cartesian space in a large range, and has 2 DOF to adjust the puncture angle. The motion of the robot should be able to be controlled remotely to help surgeons avoid radiation. The end effector needs to be scanned by CT fluoroscopy, so it must be made of non-metallic materials to avoid artifacts. In addition to meeting the functional requirements, we hope to integrate the robot as a general medical device into the existing CT machine and operating room environment without any form of changes to them. Therefore, the scheme that the robot is installed on the ground beside the CT bed is a good choice. Considering all these factors, we obtain the design principles of the robot:

- At least 6 DOF are needed to realize the space translation, puncture angle adjustment and puncture actuation.
- The motion of each DOF can be independently controlled remotely by the surgeon.
- The end effector must be non-metallic in material to avoid artifact interference to CT images.
- The robot is used as a relatively independent module, without changing the existing equipment and environment.

The puncture robot we developed is shown in the Fig. 2. It is mainly composed of a puncture robot arm and a control box. Surgeons can control the motion of the robot arm by pushing the buttons on the control box. Emergency stop buttons are designed on both modules. When any one of the buttons is pressed, the motion of the robot arm stops immediately. Surgeons can take charge of the operation at any time in case of an accident.

The robot arm consists of 3 orthogonal linear motion DOF and 2 orthogonal rotational motion DOF. The linear motion is used to move the position of the needle tip. The linear motion pattern is similar to that of the CT bed along the Z axis and the coordinate system of the robot arm is consistent with that of the CT image. Surgeons can intuitively control the robot to move the needle towards left or right or along any one of the coordinate axes. The motion of the 2 rotational DOF is divided into 2 modes functionally, named non-RCM mode and RCM mode. In the non-RCM mode, the end effector can independently move around the two rotation axes, which can adjust the needle to an estimated initial puncture angle. In RCM mode, the 5 DOF of the robot arm move together to ensure the

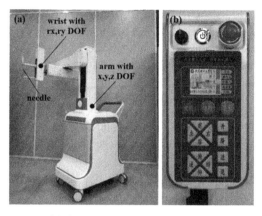

Fig. 2. CT fluoroscopy guided puncture robot, the robot arm (a) and the control box (b)

puncture needle moves around the RCM point, that is, the entry point on the patient's skin. When adjusting the puncture angle, RCM motion can avoid the transverse tear of skin tissues and the bending deformation of the puncture needle.

The control box is designed with an enable button to active the whole robot system. Surgeons need to operate with both hands, one hand to active the robot, the other hand to press the function button to control the motion of the robot arm, which can prevent the surgeon from mis-operation. The speed adjustment button can adjust the motion speed and the puncture speed of the robot arm.

5   RCM Control of the Puncture Robot

When the robot adjusts the puncture angle, it needs to make sure that the needle entry point on the patient's skin does not move to avoid the transverse tear of skin tissues and the bending deformation of the puncture needle. This can be achieved by RCM motion control of the robot. There are generally two ways to achieve the RCM motion. One is to use the specially designed RCM mechanism. The other is to solve the robot kinematics, which is adopted in this paper. Thanks to the specially designed structure of the robot, the RCM control method is quite simple and effective.

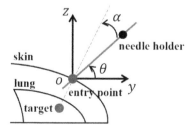

Fig. 3. RCM motion control in plane of the puncture path

The puncture path is usually designed in only one CT image. To achieve the RCM motion in the plane, one rotational DOF and two linear DOF of the robot need to move cooperatively. The angle increment of the rotational DOF and the position increment of the wrist in space are solved. As expected trajectories, they are sent to the robot for execution.

As shown in Fig. 3, a coordinate system is established by taking the needle entry point as the origin. The initial angle between the needle and the y-axis θ, the distance between the needle holding point and the entry point l is already known. When the needle needs to rotate a certain angle α, according to the geometric relationship, the increments of the three DOF can be obtained:

$$\begin{cases} \Delta z = l(\sin(\theta + \alpha) - \sin(\theta)) \\ \Delta y = l(\cos(\theta + \alpha) - \cos(\theta)) \\ \quad\quad \Delta rx = \alpha \end{cases} \tag{1}$$

To achieve the RCM motion in 3D space, the 5 DOF of the robot need to act cooperatively. The initial wrist position P_0 in the entry point coordinate system is already known. When the needle needs to rotate a certain angle α in the direction of rx, and β in the direction of ry, according to the rigid transformations, the new wrist position P can be obtained:

$$P = R_x R_y P \tag{2}$$

where $R_x = \begin{bmatrix} 1 & 0 & 0 \\ 0 & \cos(\alpha) & -\sin(\alpha) \\ 0 & \sin(\alpha) & \cos(\alpha) \end{bmatrix}$ and $R_y = \begin{bmatrix} \cos(\beta) & 0 & \sin(\beta) \\ 0 & 1 & 0 \\ -\sin(\beta) & 0 & \cos(\beta) \end{bmatrix}$, which are basic rotation transformations. The position increment of the wrist in space are solved and sent to the robot for execution.

Figure 4 shows the RCM motion control simulation in 3D Cartesian space. Figure 4(a), 4(b) and 4(c) represent the motions in the direction of rx, ry and in 3D space respectively. The trajectories of the wrist of the robot arm are shown in the red curves. The trajectory of the wrist is an arc in a plane and a helix in the space. The entry point on the patient's skin, i.e., the needle tip in the Fig. 4, remains still, which confirms the validity and efficiency of the RCM control method.

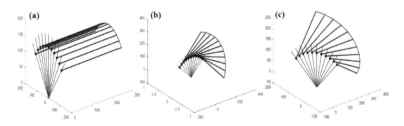

Fig. 4. RCM motion control in 3D cartesian space, motion in plane (a) and (b), in space (c)

6 Conclusion

Advantages of the puncture robot include its more precise and stable operation. Manipulation of the puncture needle can be more accurate and uncertain factors such as surgeons' fatigue and shake are eliminated. The benefit of using the CT fluoroscopy is the tumor target and the puncture needle can both be seen in nearly real time. We combine them both. The CT fluoroscopy guided manual lung puncture procedures are researched. On this basis, the requirements and design principles of robot are proposed. The developed puncture robot system and puncture surgery scheme can meet the requirements of visibility, accuracy and safety of the surgery. The RCM control method of the robot is proposed and the simulation proves its validity and efficiency. The puncture robot system and the control method are quite simple and effective, which have high clinical application value. Future research will be mainly to carry out the CT fluoroscopy guided robot puncture experiments to verify the effect of the robot in clinical practice. The CT fluoroscopy guided puncture robot will make a great breakthrough in the field of healthcare and robotics.

Acknowledgement. This research is supported by the National Key R&D Program of China (Grant No. 2019YFC0118000) & National Natural Science Foundation of China (Grant No. U2013209).

References

1. Taylor, A.J., Xu, S., Wood, B.J., et al.: Origami lesion-targeting device for CT-guided interventions. J. Imaging **5**(2), 23 (2019)
2. Arnolli, M.M., Buijze, M., Franken, M., et al.: System for CT-guided needle placement in the thorax and abdomen: a design for clinical acceptability, applicability and usability. Int. J. Med. Robot. Comput. Assisted Surg. **14**, e1877 (2017)
3. Rotolo, N., Floridi, C., Imperatori, A., et al.: Comparison of cone-beam CT-guided and CT fluoroscopy-guided transthoracic needle biopsy of lung nodules. Eur. Radiol. **26**(2), 381–389 (2016)
4. Iguchi, T., Hiraki, T., Matsui, Y., et al.: CT Fluoroscopy-guided renal tumour cutting needle biopsy: retrospective evaluation of diagnostic yield, safety, and risk factors for diagnostic failure. Eur. Radiol. **28**, 283–290 (2018)
5. Perez, R.E., Schwaitzberg, S.D.: Robotic surgery: finding value in 2019 and beyond. Ann. Laparosc. Endosc. Surg. **4**, 51 (2019)
6. Tacher, V., de Baere, T.: Robotic assistance in interventional radiology: dream or reality? Eur. Radiol. **30**(2), 925–926 (2020)
7. Kettenbach, J., Kronreif, G.: Robotic systems for percutaneous needle-guided interventions. Minim. Invasive Ther. Allied Technol. **24**(1), 45–53 (2015)
8. Arnolli, M.M., Hanumara, N.C., Franken, M., et al.: An overview of systems for CT-and MRI-guided percutaneous needle placement in the thorax and abdomen. Int. J. Med. Robot. Comput. Assisted Surg. **11**(4), 458–475 (2015)
9. Kulkarni, P., Sikander, S., Biswas, P., et al.: Review of robotic needle guide systems for percutaneous intervention. Ann. Biomed. Eng. **47**(12), 2489–2513 (2019)
10. Stoianovici, D., Cleary, K., Patriciu, A., et al.: Acubot: a robot for radiological interventions. IEEE Trans. Robot. Autom. **19**(5), 927–930 (2003)

11. Cleary, K., Zigmund, B., Banovac, F., et al.: Robotically assisted lung biopsy under CT fluoroscopy: lung cancer screening and phantom study. Int. Congr. Ser. **1281**, 740–745 (2005)
12. Xu, S., Fichtinger, G., Taylor, R.H., et al.: CT fluoroscopy-guided robotically-assisted lung biopsy. Proc. SPIE Int. Soc. Opt. Eng. **6141**(1), 4–20 (2006)
13. Patriciu, A., Awad, M., Solomon, S.B., et al.: Robotic assisted radio-frequency ablation of liver tumors-randomized patient study. Med. Image Comput. Comput. Assist. Interv. **8**(Pt 2), 526–533 (2005)
14. Melzer, A., Gutmann, B., Remmele, T., et al.: INNOMOTION for percutaneous image-guided interventions: principles and evaluation of this MR- and CT-compatible robotic system. IEEE Eng. Med. Biol. Mag. **27**(3), 66–73 (2007)
15. Wiewiorski, M., Valderrabano, V., Kretzschmar, M., et al.: CT-guided robotically-assisted infiltration of foot and ankle joints. Minim. Invasive Ther. Allied Technol. **18**(5), 291–296 (2009)
16. Walsh, C.J., Hanumara, N.C., Slocum, A.H., et al.: A Patient-mounted, telerobotic tool for CT-guided percutaneous interventions. J. Med. Devices **2**(1), 121–136 (2008)
17. Ben-David, E., Shochat, M., Roth, I., et al.: Evaluation of a CT-guided robotic system for precise percutaneous needle insertion. J. Vasc. Interv. Radiol. **29**(10), 1440–1446 (2018)
18. Takao, H., Tetsushi, K., Takayuki, M., et al.: Zerobot$^@$: a remote-controlled robot for needle insertion in CT-guided interventional radiology developed at Okayama University. Acta Med. Okayama **72**(6), 539–546 (2018)
19. Hiraki, T., Kamegawa, T., Matsuno, T., et al.: Robotically driven CT-guided needle insertion: preliminary results in phantom and animal experiments. Radiology **258**(2), 454–461 (2017)

Unmarked External Breathing Motion Tracking Based on B-spline Elastic Registration

Huixian Peng[1,2], Lei Deng[1], Zeyang Xia[1], Yaoqin Xie[1], and Jing Xiong[1(✉)]

[1] Shenzhen Institute of Advanced Technology, Chinese Academy of Sciences,
Shenzhen 518055, China
jing.xiong@siat.ac.cn
[2] School of Mechatronic Engineering and Automation, Foshan University,
Foshan 528255, China

Abstract. In robotic radiosurgery, tracking and modeling of breathing motion is crucial for accurate treatment planning while dealing with tumor inside the thoracic or abdominal cavity, because patient respiration can induce considerable external and internal motion in the thoracic and abdominal regions. Currently, methods for characterizing respiration motion mainly focused on sparse point markers placed on the surface of chest. However, limited number of markers failed to encode the comprehensive features of respiratory motion. Besides, the markers can make partial occlusion during the operation. In this work, a novel method for respiratory motion characterization based on RGB-D camera and B-spline elastic registration is proposed. Images taken from depth camera are used for modeling of abdomen surface during respiration, while B-spline elastic registration technique is applied to restrain the measuring area into an anatomically consistent region during the treatment. In addition, an elastic dynamic motion simulator is designed to test our proposed method. Finally, the feasibility of the method and the device is verified by error analysis and shape comparison.

Keywords: Respiratory motion · B-spline elastic registration · RGB-D camera · Surface modeling

1 Introduction

Radiotherapy is widely used in cancer treatment, because of its constantly improved precision. However, in the process of radiotherapy, there are still remaining uncertain factors resulting in unexpected treatment errors. In the chest and abdomen radiotherapy, the anatomical movement and deformation

Supported by National Natural Science Foundation of China (62073309, 61773365, U2013205 and 61811540033), and Shenzhen Science and Technology Program (JCYJ20200109114812361).

X.-J. Liu et al. (Eds.): ICIRA 2021, LNAI 13015, pp. 71–81, 2021.
https://doi.org/10.1007/978-3-030-89134-3_7

caused by respiratory movement will largely affect the normal implementation of radiotherapy plan [10]. Because of respiration, tumors in abdominal and chest can move nearly 35 mm [3]. Thus, the accurate tacking of treatment target is essential for correctly adjusting the radiation beam in accordance with the target motion to ensure high-precision radiotherapy.

Several traditional methods, such as breath holding, respiratory gating [9, 11] and forced shallow breathing with abdominal compression [6], were used to deal with respiratory motion. However, these techniques have some limitations and defects, such as long intervention time, short operative treatment time, and patients' discomfort. Therefore, the real-time tumor tracking methods have raised increased interests, one of those is mainly based on modeling the relationship between internal target and skin surface displacement. Normally, devices are applied to measure the respiratory motion of the skin surface in real-time, which connects a physical device to a patient like marker placed on the patient's surface or an apparatus worn by the patient. For example, the CyberKnife treatment system used three laser sources to record the motion of skin surface in its respiratory tracking system; Ernst et al. [4] proposed a method wherein a shirt with multiple printed markers tracks the respiratory motion using the Kinect v2 device. Alnowami et al. proposed a probability density estimation method, and employed the Codamotion infrared marker-based tracking system to acquire the chest wall motion [1, 2]. Wijenayake et al. used stereo cameras to calculate the three-dimensional coordinates of markers, and proposed a motion estimation method based on coded visual markers to predict respiratory motion [12]. However, due to insufficient information of respiratory signals by a limited number of IR markers, there is inevitable accumulation error of targeting in the abdominal region. Moreover, the placement of marker points will block part of the treatment area.

In this paper, a breathing motion modeling system based on commercial RGB-D camera is proposed, which is adapted to trace and record a patient's breathing pattern in a marker-less way. To test the proposed workflow, a respiratory motion simulator is designed. By controlling the patient-specific input signals, the device can simulate the human abdominal breathing motion via motor driven elastic surface deformation so that the anthropomorphic breathing motion can be obtained from the device. First, a certain number of markers are employed to enhance the precision of depth information collection for the RGB-D camera, but these markers are only needed in the process of modeling. After the model is established, it can track any area of the abdomen without markers. Next, the data is analyzed to obtain the images that represent the peak and trough periods of respiration. Finally, the overall motion in the abdomen is modeled by a free-form deformation (FFD) based on B-splines [5, 7, 8]. The motion of the abdomen during the non-respiratory peak and trough is described by interpolation method.

2   Design of Abdominal Breathing Simulator

2.1   Structure Design

The abdominal breathing simulator, consisting of a driving device, an acrylic box, four sponges and a piece of latex film with markers on its surface, is developed for the simulation of abdominal motion caused by respiration (Fig. 1a). The driving device is an independently controlled vertical platform build in CIRS Dynamic Thorax Simulator (Fig. 1b), which can be programmed by CIRS motion control software to move up and down. However, the device can only move rigidly and simulating the breathing motion of a certain point on the abdominal surface. In order to characterize the breathing motion of the entire abdomen surface, an elastic covering is added, which is supported by an acrylic box with size close to the adult abdomen. The height of the acrylic box will be lower than the lowest height of the driving platform (Fig. 1c). So that fix four sponges with a thickness of 1mm between the driving platform and the latex film can be fixed, where the number of sponges can be added or subtracted according to the shape of human abdomen.

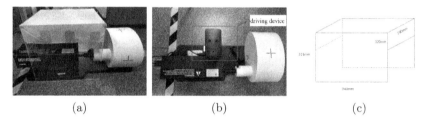

(a)   (b)   (c)

Fig. 1. (a) Abdominal breathing simulator; (b) Driver device; (c) Dimensions of acrylic box.

2.2   Motion Control

For the dynamic breathing simulation, after importing the patient-specific breathing curve into the CIRS motion control software, the driving device can control the vertical platform motion accurately enough to ensure the real displacement is closely the same with the programmed. When carrying extra load i.e. the tension induced by the deformation of the elastic film, the control accuracy is barely affected according to the former verification experiments. Also, the platform can exert force on the sponge and latex film above, causing the deformation of the sponge and latex film, which visually mimic the morphological states of human abdomen. The overall motion amplitude and period can be easily adjusted by the control software. Although only the convex only shape with single peak can be created, the phantom design was successful because it catches the main motion feature of the abdomen surface under breathing motion. As shown in the Figure, Fig. 2a and Fig. 2b respectively simulate the abdominal state of a real person during inspiration and expiration.

(a)   (b)

Fig. 2. (a) Simulate the abdominal state during inspiratory process; (b) Simulate the abdominal state during expiratory process.

3   Design of Tracking Method

3.1   Image Preprocessing

In this paper, a statistical model is constructed based on the motion data of markers representing abdominal motion under respiratory motion. First, the depth image and the corresponding RGB image of the abdomen area are obtained. Then K-nearest neighbor method is applied to fill the gap in the depth image, and then S-G (Savitzky-Golay) filter is used to denoise the depth image. All marks are localized via processing the RGB image. Global binary threshold algorithm (Otsu's method) followed by contour detection and ellipse fitting is applied to identify the center coordinates of each marker accurately in each frame. Corresponding depth value in the depth image are also recorded. The markers are used to track the motion associated with a specific location on the body and monitor the depth change as it moves across the frame.

3.2   Tracking Method

The motion data of markers are averaged and smoothed, to obtain a curve that can represent the abdominal motion frequency under respiratory motion. Then, the number of frames corresponding to the curve in the rising phase and the falling phase of each cycle are counted and averaged. Accordingly, two categories of RGB images belonging to the peak or valley phase are sorted out and unified into two gray level images by frame-wise and channel-wise averaging, during which the abnormal breathing cycle are excluded as outliers. Thus, two feature images that represents the whole abdominal motion during human inhalation and exhalation is acquired.

After obtaining the required gray image, the deformable registration method based on B-spline is applied to make a respiratory motion model. Because, the abdominal motion is nonrigid in general, elastic image registration is necessary for modeling the dense motion vector fields. The optimal transformation facilitates mapping any point in the dynamic image sequence at one time into its corresponding point in the reference image accurately.

The basic idea of FFD is to deform an object by manipulating an underlying mesh of control points. The resulting deformation controls the shape of the 3-D object and produces a smooth and continuous transformation. Based on the B-spline FFD model, the coordinates of each pixel in the image after moving are calculated, and decompose the movement of the pixels in the image into X and Y directions, then locate the X and Y coordinates respectively.

For any pixel (x, y), the coordinate position (relative to the pixel grid) after cubic B-splines elastic deformation can be expressed as

$$T(x,y) = \sum_{l=0}^{3} \sum_{m=0}^{3} B_l(u) B_m(v) \phi_{i+l,j+m}, \tag{1}$$

where $i = \lfloor x/n_x \rfloor - 1, j = \lfloor y/n_y \rfloor - 1, u = x/n_x - \lfloor x/n_x \rfloor, v = y/n_y - \lfloor y/n_y \rfloor$, and B_l represents the lth basis function of the B-spline

$$\begin{cases} B_0(u) = (1-u)^3/6 \\ B_1(u) = (3u^3 - 6u^2 + 4)/6 \\ B_2(u) = (-3u^3 + 3u^2 + 3u + 1)/6 \\ B_3(u) = u^3/6 \end{cases} \tag{2}$$

The control points act as parameters of the B-spline FFD and the degree of nonrigid deformation which can be modeled depends essentially on the resolution of the mesh of control points. The Φ is used to represent the grid composed of $n_x \times n_y$ control points $\phi_{i,j}(0 \le j < n_x, 0 \le j < n_y)$, and the spacing between each control point is δ.

According to Eq. (1), the optimal solution is obtained ϕ. The main idea is to search for the minimum space transformation position of similarity measure E_{ssd}, which is denoted as

$$E_{ssd} = \frac{1}{N} \sum (I_1(T(x,y)) - I_2(x,y))^2, \tag{3}$$

where N is the total number of pixels in the image registration area, I_1 and I_2 represent the gray function of the reference image and the image to be registered in the two-dimensional space. When these two images match the best, the metric value E_{ssd} reaches minimum.

3.3   Model Optimization

Because the respiratory motion is not strictly periodic, there will be some abnormalities. In order to increase the robustness of the model to deal with the abnormal case, an adaptive link in the model is added. Through the analysis of historical waveform data, the abnormal situation is divided into two cases:

low peak and high valley, for which two models are established. The discrimination of anomalies is out of an empirical criterion. In the case of RGB-D camera tracking anatomic points in real-time, by analyzing the depth information of the initial position of anatomic points, the model can get the index of frames corresponding to the two abnormal situations, and then switch the corresponding model. This method has strengths compared with previous models, which is model parameters trained adaptively by inputting the corresponding images in all abnormal cases. In addition, for improving the tracking accuracy of the model, a self-calibration link in the model is added. The calibration system is modeled as follows:

$$F_{t+1} = (Z_t - F_t) + f_{t+1}, \tag{4}$$

where F_{t+1} and f_{t+1} denote the position frames corresponding to the peaks or valleys output by the model and the uncorrected model at time $t+1$, respectively. And Z_t represents the position frames corresponding to the peaks or valleys output by the initial position of the anatomical point collected by the camera at time t.

4   Experiments and Results

4.1   Data Acquisition

Fig. 3. RGB-D camera is placed nearly 73 cm above the breathing simulation. (Color figure online)

The technology is mainly based on real-time data acquisition by the depth camera (PERCOPIO FM851-GI-E1). The system is designed to track specific pixels from the depth image and record the depth values over time. During the laboratory level experiments, the abdominal breathing simulator is used as the object of data acquisition, 11 yellow non-reflective markers are randomly attached on the surface of the abdomen, and the RGB-D camera is placed nearly 73 cm above the abdomen, as shown in Fig. 3. The number of markers can be greater than or less than 11. Increasing in marker numbers improves amount of acquired abdominal motion information but aggravates the computational burden at the same

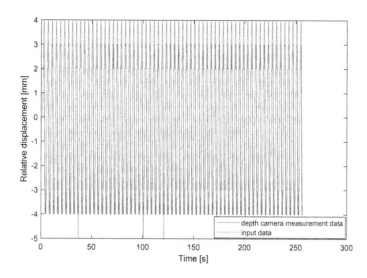

Fig. 4. Experimental results of RGB-D camera accuracy evaluation.

time. The optimum number of markers can balance the modal accuracy and the amount of calculation. Then, the image is acquired and processed according to the method in Sect. 3.1 to acquire the motion data of 11 markers. The data is only used for model building and testing. After the model is built, no markers are needed in the tracking phase.

4.2 Camera Error Test

The motion accuracy of the driving platform in Fig. 2 is ±0.1 mm, so the platform can be used to evaluate the stability and measurement accuracy of the depth camera. Input signal to CRIS control platform is a sinusoidal curve with amplitude as ±4 mm, period as 4 s. At the same time, the motion distance of the platform is measured by using a depth camera. The experimental results are shown in Fig. 4, in which the measurement error of the camera is about 1 mm. In the nearly four minutes of the measurement, the data curve measured by the camera does not appear abnormal fluctuations, indicating that the camera has a good stability.

4.3 Abdominal Breathing Simulator Test

To verify the usefulness of the abdominal breathing simulator. First, the simulated abdominal surface is visualized to observe the shape. As shown in Fig. 5, the device simulates three states of the human body: inhalation, the transition from inspiration exhalation, breathing to inspiration, and exhalation. It can be intuitively observed from the figure that the changes in the volume and area of the abdomen simulated in the three states are mimic to that of human. Secondly, the depth values of 11 pixels in a period are extracted from the simulated abdominal surface. Figure 6 shows that the change of the depth values of the extracted points shows high correlation with patient breathing motion pattern. Finally, the data of the human abdominal surface in two states of inspiration and respiration are extracted. In Fig. 7, compared with the inspiratory and expiratory states simulated by the abdominal breathing simulator, the morphological changes of the two states are very close. Thus, the usefulness and feasibility of the abdominal breathing simulation device proposed in this paper are illustrated.

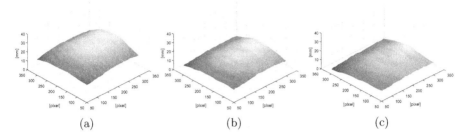

(a)   (b)   (c)

Fig. 5. The device simulates three states of the human body: (a) inhalation, (b) transition between inhalation and exhalation, (c) exhalation.

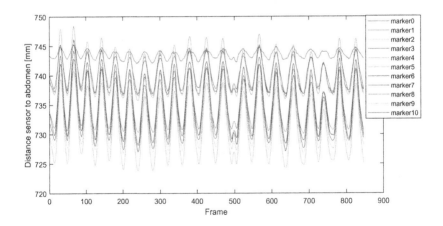

Fig. 6. The depth values of 11 pixels in a period of time.

4.4   Model Method Validation

To make the quantitative comparison, 11 markers randomly distributed on the surface of the abdomen are selected. The center coordinates of each point mark

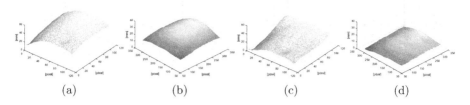

(a)   (b)   (c)   (d)

Fig. 7. Comparison of the shape of abdominal breathing simulator and human in the state of inspiration and expiration.

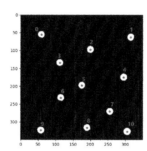

Fig. 8. Center positioning result of marker.

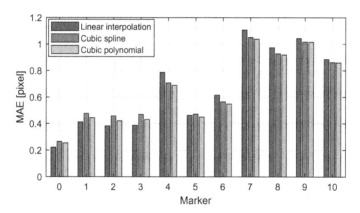

Fig. 9. Histogram of mean absolute error (MAE) of three interpolation methods.

are accurately determined in each frame (Fig. 8), and the relative displacement data of 11 markers on the abdominal surface during a period of breathing motion are obtained. The tracking error of the model is also evaluated based on the data measured by the image segmentation method. Equation 5 is used to calculate the motion error.

$$MAE = \frac{1}{N} \sum_{i=1}^{n} \left| \sqrt{x_i^2 + y_i^2} - \sqrt{X_i^2 + Y_i^2} \right| \tag{5}$$

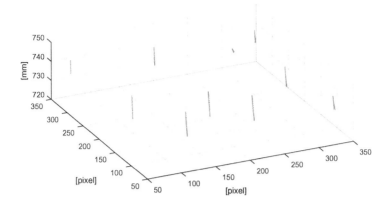

Fig. 10. Trajectory of all markers. The purple dotted line represents the predicted marker trajectory, and the green dotted line represents the real marker trajectory. (Color figure online)

The (X_i, Y_i) represents the coordinates of the markers in i^{th} frame, and (x_i, y_i) denotes the marker coordinates predicted by the model in i^{th} frame.

Linear interpolation, cubic spline interpolation, and cubic polynomial interpolation are separately used in the model. The motion errors calculated by the three interpolation methods are shown in Fig. 9. As can be seen from Fig. 9, except that the average absolute error of marker 7 and marker 9 is more than one pixel, the error of other mark points is less than one pixel. For marked points 4~10, the error of the cubic polynomial interpolation method is lower than the other two interpolation methods. For the marked points 0~3, the error of linear interpolation is lower and the results improved. In general, the cubic polynomial interpolation outperforms the others with the manually fine-tuned parameters.

Finally, in order to see the tracking effect more intuitively, this paper visualizes all the marked tracking curves. As shown in Fig. 10, The purple dotted line represents the predicted marker trajectory, and the green dotted line represents the real marker trajectory. The purple dotted line tracks the motion trend that complies well with the green dotted line, which shows the feasibility and accuracy of the proposed model.

5   Conclusion

In this study, a non-contact, non-invasive, and real-time breathing motion measurement technology is introduced. During the real-time tracking, the model does not require any markers or other devices on the human abdominal surface. Compared with the previous methods of tracking the abdominal target area using limited markers, our method of state-to-state image registration can achieve better results. In addition, through the accurate tracking verification of multiple marked points on the abdomen, this paper realizes the tracking from multiple points to surface, which can predict the position of any point on the abdominal surface. In future, in order to improve the tracking accuracy, we will further optimize the model by increasing the adaptability of the model. At the same time, we will optimize the representation method of abdominal surface state, and strive to provide more abundant and accurate information for respiratory tracking of radiosurgery robots.

References

1. Alnowam, M.R., Lewis, E., Wells, K., Guy, M.: Respiratory motion modelling and prediction using probability density estimation. In: IEEE Nuclear Science Symposium & Medical Imaging Conference, pp. 2465–2469. IEEE (2010)
2. Alnowami, M., Lewis, E., Wells, K., Guy, M.: Inter-and intra-subject variation of abdominal vs. thoracic respiratory motion using kernel density estimation. In: IEEE Nuclear Science Symposium & Medical Imaging Conference, pp. 2921–2924. IEEE (2010)
3. Barnes, E.A., Murray, B.R., Robinson, D.M., Underwood, L.J., Hanson, J., Roa, W.H.: Dosimetric evaluation of lung tumor immobilization using breath hold at deep inspiration. Int. J. Radiat. Oncol.* Biol.* Phys. **50**(4), 1091–1098 (2001)
4. Ernst, F., Saß, P.: Respiratory motion tracking using Microsoft's Kinect V2 camera. Curr. Dir. Biomed. Eng. **1**(1), 192–195 (2015)
5. Holden, M.: A review of geometric transformations for nonrigid body registration. IEEE Trans. Med. Imaging **27**(1), 111–128 (2007)
6. Keall, P.J., et al.: The management of respiratory motion in radiation oncology report of AAPM task group 76 a. Med. Phys. **33**(10), 3874–3900 (2006)
7. Lee, S., Wolberg, G., Chwa, K.Y., Shin, S.Y.: Image metamorphosis with scattered feature constraints. IEEE Trans. Vis. Comput. Graph. **2**(4), 337–354 (1996)
8. Lee, S., Wolberg, G., Shin, S.Y.: Scattered data interpolation with multilevel b-splines. IEEE Trans. Vis. Comput. Graph. **3**(3), 228–244 (1997)
9. Mageras, G.S., et al.: Fluoroscopic evaluation of diaphragmatic motion reduction with a respiratory gated radiotherapy system. J. Appl. Clin. Med. Phys. **2**(4), 191–200 (2001)
10. Ozhasoglu, C., Murphy, M.J.: Issues in respiratory motion compensation during external-beam radiotherapy. Int. J. Radiat. Oncol.* Biol.* Phys. **52**(5), 1389–1399 (2002)
11. Vedam, S., Keall, P., Kini, V., Mohan, R.: Determining parameters for respiration-gated radiotherapy. Med. Phys. **28**(10), 2139–2146 (2001)
12. Wijenayake, U., Park, S.Y.: Respiratory motion estimation using visual coded markers for radiotherapy. In: Proceedings of the 29th Annual ACM Symposium on Applied Computing, pp. 1751–1752 (2014)

Design, Development, and Preliminary Experimental Analysis of a Novel Robotic Laparoscope with Continuum Mechanism

Shiyang Bao, Zhengyu Wang$^{(\boxtimes)}$, Xun Wei, Can Zhou, Guangming Liu, and Ping Zhao

School of Mechanical Engineering, Hefei University of Technology, Hefei 230009, China
wangzhengyu_hfut@hfut.edu.cn

Abstract. In order to improve and realize an intelligent robot-assisted laparoscopic system, a novel flexible end-effector is developed for the laparoscopic robot. This paper presents the design, development, and preliminary experimental analysis of a novel robotic laparoscope with continuum mechanism. The Mechanical structure design of this flexible laparoscope is mainly based on the two-degree of freedom continuum mechanism, cable-pulley driven system, elastic connection element and miniature linear servo actuators. The continuum mechanism is designed with 10 mm external diameter and 80 mm length. The driving cable is chosen as a kind 0.45 mm external diameter. The finite element analyses, kinematics and workspace analyses are studied for the continuum mechanism. The experimental prototype of this flexible robotic laparoscope is established through 3D Printing. Preliminary experimental results show the feasibility and effectiveness of the robotic laparoscope with continuum mechanism.

Keywords: Robotic laparoscope · Cable-driven · Continuum mechanism · Kinematics · Experiment

1 Introduction

Robot assisted minimally invasive surgery has been widely used in gynecology, abdominal cavity and other fields because of its advantages of small trauma and short recovery time [1]. Among them, laparoscopy plays a real-time role in robot assisted minimally invasive surgery, and its flexibility will have an important impact on the surgical effect. Therefore, flexible endoscope is proposed and further developed [2]. In the traditional use of laparoscopy, the rigid part of the endoscope is inside the human body, and the surgeon needs to control the handle of the endoscope outside the trocar. If the viewing angle of the endoscope need to be changed, the whole rigid endoscope needs to move, which takes up a lot of space and may even touch other areas of the body. It can be seen that the advantage of flexible laparoscopy is that it takes up less space and can

Supported by the National Natural Science Foundation of China (Grant No. 51805129), and The Fundamental Research Funds for the Central Universities (Grant No. JZ2019HGTB0078, PA2021KCPY0046).

© Springer Nature Switzerland AG 2021
X.-J. Liu et al. (Eds.): ICIRA 2021, LNAI 13015, pp. 82–92, 2021.
https://doi.org/10.1007/978-3-030-89134-3_8

move flexibly only depending on the end flexible joint [3]. Flexible bending joints are usually realized in the form of continuum mechanism, generally including integrated skeleton, multi skeleton structure and nested skeleton structure [4–7], among which the cable-driving is more common [8, 9].

In addition, the tube body of traditional endoscope is rigid, and the contact with the body surface is also rigid. Once an accident occurs during the operation, the secondary injury to the wound of the patient is great and irreversible. Because the endoscope robot doesn't need to bear more force in the process of assisted surgery, and considering the safety factors, a buffer joint can be introduced for the flexible endoscope. This idea comes from the flexible joints of the rehabilitation robot [10–12]. By giving the rigid endoscope tube flexibility, it can not only meet the basic function of flexible capture of surgical images, but also have a certain ability to resist the risk of surgical accidents.

The main contributions of this paper are that a novel laparoscope was made and its feasibility was preliminarily verified. In this paper, a flexible laparoscope is introduced. It is different from the traditional laparoscope, and its camera is installed on the end of the continuum mechanism, which can be driven by four cables to achieve any direction of bending in space. Considering the safety factors, a series elastic element is innovatively introduced to provide flexibility for the rigid pipe body. When unexpected conditions occur during the operation, the elastic connection element has the function of buffering and absorbing energy, greatly reducing the secondary injury to the surface wound of the patient.

2 Structure Design

The flexible laparoscope is shown in Fig. 1, of which the main body is made of resin material by 3D printing. In order to facilitate the installation, a nested structure is adopted. The design retains a mechanical interface, which can be connected with a six-dimensional force sensor or Franka robotic arm. The intelligent robot-assisted laparoscopic system consists of manipulator, upper computer, optical capture system and robotic laparoscope.

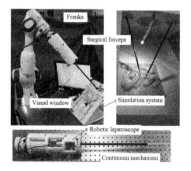

Fig. 1. Intelligent robot-assisted laparoscopic system.

2.1 Overall Design

The main body of the flexible laparoscope is divided into three parts, the actuator module, the tensioning mechanism, the elastic connection element and the continuum mechanism, as shown in Fig. 2.

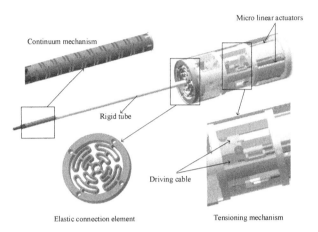

Fig. 2. Overall mechanism.

The actuator module is four micro servo linear actuators, and the actuator output shaft is connected with four cables. The tensioning mechanism has four groups of the same guide wheel structure, as shown in Fig. 2. The four groups of cables are guided to the continuum structure, as shown in Fig. 3.

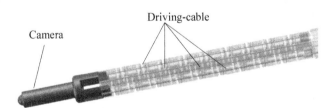

Fig. 3. Driving method of continuum mechanism.

The guide wheel can move to adjust the tension of the cable. The elastic connection element is made of high elastic material by 3D printing, with a radius of 50 mm and a thickness of 10 mm. The round hole in the middle is used to install the rigid pipe, and the four groups of hollow structures can be deformed under force to provide flexibility for the rigid pipe. The continuum structure is manufactured by 3D printing, and the material is a highly elastic nylon material with a radius of 5 mm and a height of 80 mm. Four groups of through holes are arranged in the axial direction, and round grooves are arranged in the radial direction. The groove height is 1 mm, and the groove spacing is 1 mm. There is a groove for every 90-degree staggered angle, and the four grooves are a group. The continuum mechanism is provided with nine groups of grooves, and can be bent after the force is applied, as shown in Fig. 4. Under the stretching of the cable, the flexible continuum joint can bend in any direction in space, meeting the requirements of the flexible laparoscope to capture images.

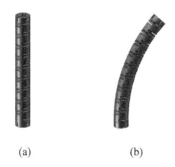

(a)   (b)

Fig. 4. Continuum structure. (a) Initial state. (b) Bending state.

2.2 Finite Element Analysis

The elastic connection element is elastically deformed by passive force, and the continuum structure is elastically deformed by active force. Therefore, finite element analysis is used to simulate the force and deformation of key components to obtain a structure, which satisfies the function.

First, the force simulation analysis of the continuum structure is carried out, and a bending movement is applied at the end of the continuum mechanism, which causes the continuum mechanism to bend and deform, as shown in Fig. 5. Under the action of the

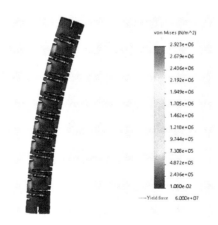

Fig. 5. Finite element analysis of continuum mechanism.

bending movement, the maximum stress of bending deformation is located at the round slot, and it is much smaller than the yield stress.

Next, the single round slot of the continuum mechanism is analyzed in the limit state. In the limit state, when the round groove is forced to close, it is the maximum deformation position. At this time, if the maximum stress still does not exceed the yield value, that is, the material structure is reasonably selected and designed, and no fracture will occur, as shown in Fig. 6.

Fig. 6. Finite element analysis of single round slot.

Due to the amplification of the fulcrum, much elasticity and large stiffness coefficient are needed. When the rigid pipe body is subjected to force or impact, energy will be buffered and absorbed. The outer ring of the elastic connection element is set to be fixed, the inner ring applies force and moment, and the finite element analysis is performed,

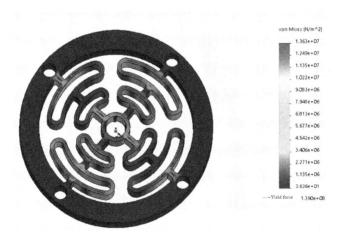

Fig. 7. Finite element analysis of elastic connection element.

as shown in Fig. 7. The four groups of hollow structures can undergo slight elastic deformation when subjected to force, and the maximum stress is much smaller than the safe stress value, providing a certain degree of flexibility for the rigid tube.

3   Kinematic Analysis

Kinematic analysis of continuum structure is to deduce the mapping relationship among driving space, joint space and operation space. The constant curvature method is adopted in the kinematic modeling of flexible continuum mechanism. The bending shape of the continuum mechanism is approximately equivalent to an arc, and the length of the continuum mechanism is L, the definitions of coordinate system and joint variables are shown in Fig. 8. Taking the center of the near end face of the continuum mechanism as the origin, the base coordinate system $X_0 Y_0 Z_0$ of the continuum mechanism is established, where Z_0 along the axis of the continuum mechanism, X_0 points from the origin to the first cable, Y_0 is determined by the right-handed coordinate system. Then, the corresponding coordinate system $X_1 Y_1 Z_1$ is established at the end of the continuum mechanism. when the continuum mechanism is bent, the bending angle is θ_1, and the rotation angle is φ_1 with $X_0 Z_0$ plane.

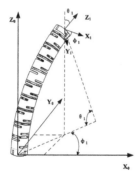

Fig. 8. Definition of the coordinate system and joint variables.

First the $X_0 Y_0 Z_0$ coordinate system translates and then rotate φ_1 around Z, then rotate θ_1 around Y, finally rotate $-\varphi_1$ around Z, $X_1 Y_1 Z_1$ coordinate system can be got. The transformation matrix based on the above change process is as follows:

$$T = \text{Trans}[\frac{L}{\theta_1} \cos \varphi_1 (1 - \cos \theta_1), \frac{L}{\theta_1} \sin \varphi_1 (1 - \cos \theta_1), \frac{L}{\theta_1} \sin \theta_1] * Rot(z, \varphi_1) * Rot(y, \theta_1) * Rot(z, -\varphi_1)$$

(1)

Then, the joint variables need to be mapped to the driving variables of four cables. By analyzing the spatial geometric relationship, the following conclusions can be obtained:

$$\Delta L_1 = -\Delta L_3 = r\theta_1 \cos \varphi_1$$

(2)

$$\Delta L_2 = -\Delta L_4 = -r\theta_1 \sin \varphi_1$$

(3)

$$\varphi_1 = \arctan(\frac{\Delta L_2}{\Delta L_1}) \qquad (4)$$

$$\theta_1 = \arctan(\frac{\Delta L_1}{r \cos \varphi_1}) \qquad (5)$$

The bending angle of continuum mechanism is θ_1. The rotation angle is φ_1. r is the dividing circle radius of the cable, ΔL_i is the length variation of the i_{th} cable.

Through the above mapping relationship, the kinematic simulation analysis can be obtained, as shown in Fig. 9.

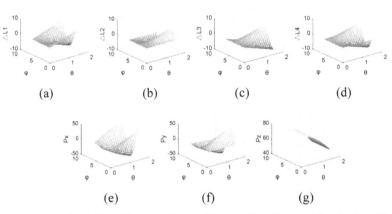

(a)   (b)   (c)   (d)

(e)   (f)   (g)

Fig. 9. Kinematics simulation. (a) ΔL_1 with φ and θ. (b) ΔL_2 with φ and θ. (c) ΔL_3 with φ and θ. (d) ΔL_4 with φ and θ. (e) Position P_x with φ and θ. (f) Position P_y with φ and θ. (g) Position P_z with φ and θ.

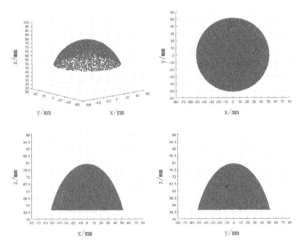

Fig. 10. Theoretical working space.

The theoretical workspace of continuum structure is shown by Monte Carlo, where θ is $(0, \pi/2)$, φ is $(0, 2\pi)$, as shown in Fig. 10.

4 Preliminary Experiments and Analyses

In this section, the kinematics model of flexible laparoscope is tested through experiments, and the experimental platform is built, as shown in Fig. 11. PC is the upper computer to control through software. The optical target is installed at the front end of the continuum joint and other positions of the experimental platform. The spatial pose of the optical target relative to the world coordinate system can be obtained by the optical vision capture system, which is used to test the kinematic model.

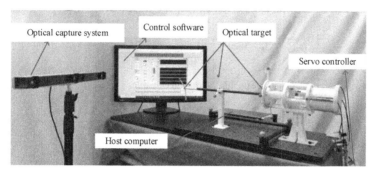

Fig. 11. Experimental platform.

By giving the sine wave signal to the linear actuator, the cable is driven to make the continuum mechanism bending, as shown in Fig. 12.

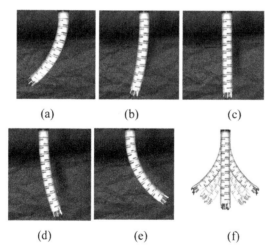

Fig. 12. Bending state of continuum mechanism. (a) State 1. (b) State 2. (c) State 3. (d) State 4. (e) State 5. (f) Process of bending.

The driver 1 and 3 are distributed in the horizontal plane, and driven by sinusoidal signal with specific frequency, as shown in Fig. 13. The position and attitude changes in the direction of 1-DoF are shown in Fig. 14.

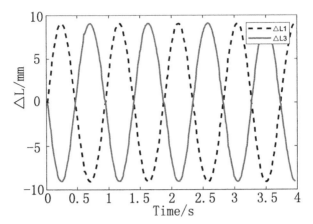

Fig. 13. Variation of cable.

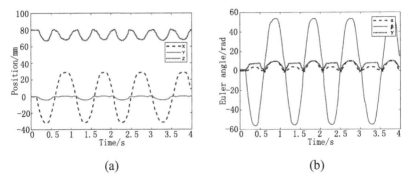

(a)   (b)

Fig. 14. Pose-curve. (a) Space coordinate. (b) Euler angle.

The driver 2 and 4 are distributed in the vertical plane, and the driver 1, 2, 3 and 4 are driven by sine and cosine signals of another frequency, as shown in Fig. 15. The position and attitude changes in any direction of space are shown in Fig. 16.

There is a certain gap between the actual kinematic model and the constant curvature theoretical model. The main reasons are as follows: The actual deformation of continuum mechanism is not a standard arc; There is hysteresis effect in the tension process of cable, and the more obvious the hysteresis effect is when the speed is slower, and there is jitter when the continuum mechanism changes direction; In actual bending, there is strong coupling effect between four cables.

The control accuracy can be improved by the following aspects: The error model of constant curvature model can be established, the error parameters are identified, and the theoretical model is modified; The relevant performance models of cables, such as hysteresis model and friction model, can be introduced for compensation; Find out the corresponding relationship between input and output for control by learning method.

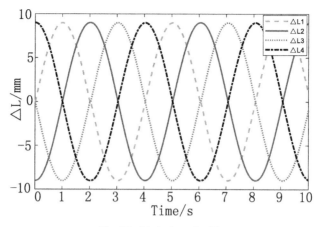

Fig. 15. Variation of cable.

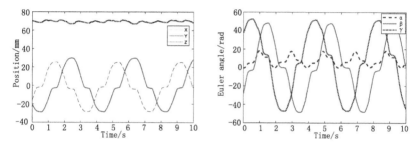

Fig. 16. Pose-curve. (a) Space coordinate. (b) Euler angle

5 Conclusions

This paper presented a study on the mechanical design, development, realization, and preliminary experimental analysis of a novel two-degree of freedom flexible laparoscope with continuum mechanism for the intelligent robot-assisted laparoscopic system. The continuum mechanism, cable-pulley driven system, elastic connection element and miniature linear servo actuators were used on the mechanical structure design of this flexible laparoscope. Meanwhile, the finite element analyses, kinematics and workspace analyses of the continuum mechanism, were studied for improving the structural performance. The mechanical parts of the experimental prototype were established through 3D Printing method. The feasibility and effectiveness were verified by the preliminary experimental results of the robotic laparoscope with continuum mechanism. Future work will focus on the error compensation, kinematics decoupling and high precision tracking control.

References

1. Maeso, S., Reza, M., Mayol, J., et al.: Efficacy of the Da Vinci surgical system in abdominal surgery compared with that of laparoscopy: a systematic review and meta-analysis. Ann. Surg. **252**(2), 254–262 (2010)
2. Li, Z., et al.: Design of a novel flexible endoscope—cardioscope. Mech. Robot **8**(5), 51014 (2016)
3. Simaan, N., Taylor, R., Flint, P.: A dexterous system for laryngeal surgery. In: 2004 IEEE International Conference on Robotics and Automation (ICRA). IEEE (2004)
4. Ma, J., Sefati, S., Taylor, R., et al.: An active steering hand-held robotic system for minimally invasive orthopaedic surgery using a continuum manipulator. IEEE Robot. Autom. Lett. 3059634 (2021). https://doi.org/10.1109/LRA.2021
5. Li, W., Song, C., Li, Z.: An accelerated recurrent neural network for visual servo control of a robotic flexible endoscope with joint limit constraint. IEEE Trans. Industr. Electron. **67**(12), 10787–10797 (2020)
6. Morimoto, T., Okamura, A.: Design of 3-D printed concentric tube robots. IEEE Trans. Rob. **32**(6), 1419–1430 (2016)
7. Qi, P., Qiu, C., Liu, H., et al.: A novel continuum manipulator design using serially connected double-layer planar springs. IEEE/ASME Trans. Mechatron. **21**(3), 1281–1292 (2016)
8. Frazelle, C., Kapadia, A., Walker, I.: A haptic continuum interface for the teleoperation of extensible continuum manipulators. IEEE Robot. Autom. Lett. **5**(2), 1875–1882 (2020)
9. Wang, Z., Zi, B., Wang, D., et al.: External force self-sensing based on cable-tension disturbance observer for surgical robot end-effector. IEEE Sens. J. **19**(3), 5274–5284 (2019)
10. Calanca, A., Muradore, R., et al.: Impedance control of series elastic actuators: passivity and acceleration-based control. Mechatronics **47**, 37–48 (2017)
11. Xiang, L., Pan, Y., Gong, C., et al.: Adaptive human-robot interaction control for robots driven by series elastic actuators. IEEE Trans. Rob. **33**(1), 169–182 (2017)
12. Lagoda, C., Schouten, A.C., Stienen, A., et al.: Design of an electric series elastic actuated joint for robotic gait rehabilitation training. In: 2010 3rd IEEE RAS and EMBS International Conference on Biomedical Robotics and Biomechatronics (BioRob). IEEE (2010)

A Self-evolution Hybrid Robot for Dental Implant Surgery

Yuan Feng[1], Min Chen[1], BaoXin Tao[2], ShiGang Wang[1], JinQiu Mo[1], YiQun Wu[2], and QingHua Liang[1(✉)]

[1] School of Mechanical Engineering, Shanghai Jiao Tong University, Dongchuan Road 800, Minhang District, Shanghai 200240, China
qhliang@sjtu.edu.cn
[2] Department of Second Dental Center, Shanghai Ninth People's Hospital, College of Stomatology, School of Medicine, National Clinical Research Center for Oral Disease, Shanghai Key Laboratory of Stomatology and Shanghai Research Institute of Stomatology, Shanghai Jiao Tong University, 639, Zhizaoju Road, Shanghai 200011, China

Abstract. Dental implant surgery is an effective method for remediating the loss of teeth. A novel custom-built hybrid robot, combining the advantages of serial manipulator and parallel manipulator, was proposed for assisting the dental implant surgery. The hybrid robot is comprised of 3 DOF translation joints, 2 DOF revolute joints and a Stewart manipulator. The translation joints are used for initial position adjustment, making the Stewart manipulator near the target position. The revolute joints are used for assisting the Stewart manipulator in initial orientation adjustment. The procedure of robot-assisted dental implant surgery is designed and described. Considering the limited workspace of Stewart manipulator, we set minimizing the joint displacement of the Stewart manipulator as the optimization objective to find an optimal joint configuration during initial orientation adjustment. In order to find the optimal joint configuration quickly, neural network is used to map the relationship between the target orientation and the optimal joint configuration. In addition, a self-evolution strategy is proposed for optimizing the learning model continuously. And the effectiveness of the strategy is validated in the phantom experiment.

Keywords: Robot-assisted dental implant surgery · Hybrid robot · Neural network · Self-evolution strategy

1 Introduction

Dental implant surgery has been recognized as a standard of care for remediating the loss of teeth [1]. The operation process involves in drilling a cavity and

This work was supported by grants from National Key R & D Program of China (2017YFB1302901).

placing an implant in the jawbone. The pose accuracy of drilling the cavity could influence the implant placement, which will increase the success rate of operation [2]. However, due to the possibility of human error, it is difficult to drill a cavity accurately.

Dental implant robot system was developed to satisfy the requirement of high precision for operation. Sun et al. [3] proposed an image-guided robot system for dental implant. The system comprises of a Coordinate Measurement Machine and a commercial 6 DOF serial robot Mitsubishi. A two-step registration is proposed to transform the planned implant insertion into robot target pose, guiding the robot perform the operation accurately. Cao. [4] used surgical navigation system for guiding an UR robot for zygomatic implant placement. With the help of surgical navigation system, the movement of patient can be tracked constantly, and the robot can adjust the target pose in real time. Phantom experiments were performed and it shows that compared with manual operation, robot can improve the pose accuracy of the cavity. J Li [5] design a compact serial robot based on tendon-sheath transmission, by which the actuators could be placed away from the manipulator. The robot adopted teleoperation technology, which allows the surgeon control the robot by a haptic device. Although the robot could relief burdens of surgeon, the accuracy of the cavity can only be guaranteed through the experience of doctors. Yomi [6] developed by Neocis company, is the first commercially available robot system for dental implant. It is a 6 DOF serial cooperative robot. After registration, the Surgeon can drag the robot to the target pose according to the visual guidance. Once the robot in the right orientation and position, it can guide the surgeon complete the drilling operation.

However, the structure of the above robots is all serial manipulator. Although the manipulator possesses large workspace, it has low stiffness, which may lead large deviation from the planned trajectory in the case of high feed force. Compared to serial manipulator, parallel robot has high stiffness and precision. While its workspace is limited, sometimes operation may not be completed.

In this study, we combine the advantages of parallel robot and serial robot, designing a novel hybrid robot system. The hybrid robot is composed of parallel manipulator and serial manipulator. The parallel manipulator is responsible for drilling the cavity due to its high stiffness. The serial manipulator is responsible for enlarging the workspace of parallel manipulator, assisting it in adjusting the pose of drill bit. In addition, we propose a self-evolution strategy to coordinate the motion relationship between serial and parallel manipulator.

2   Structure Design of the Robot

2.1   Structure Scheme

The structure scheme of the hybrid robot is shown in Fig. 1. The parallel manipulator is a 6 DOF Stewart platform, which could adjust the position and orientation of the end-effector. The serial manipulator is composed of three translation joints for assisting the Stewart manipulator in position adjustment, two revolute joints for assisting the Stewart manipulator in orientation adjustment.

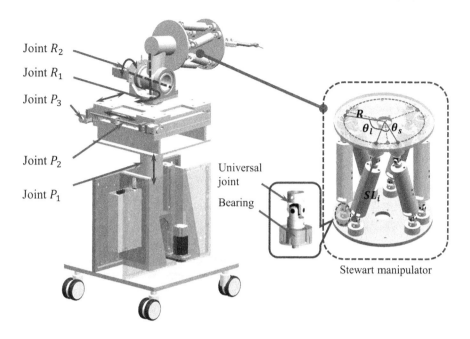

Joint R_2

Joint R_1

Joint P_3

Joint P_2

Joint P_1

Universal joint

Bearing

Stewart manipulator

Fig. 1. Structure of the hybrid robot.

The three translation joints are actuated by three screw modules. The axes of the three translation joints are perpendicular to each other and decoupled, which could simplify the control. The first joint P_1 provides linear motion perpendicular to the ground. The motion range of P_1 joint is 0 to 200 mm, which determines overall height of the robot from 1220–1420 mm. Joint P_2 and joint P_3 provide planner motion, and the motion range of them is $-100 - 100$ mm, which is satisfied with the requirement of position workspace. The two rotation joints adopted gear drive, and the motion range of them is $-10° - 10°$. Joint R_1 is also used to switch between the initial state and the working state of the robot.

The Stewart manipulator is comprised of a moving platform, a fixed platform, and six prismatic joint. The base and the moving platform are connected by the prismatic joint by two equivalent sphere(S) joints. It is noticed that the equivalent sphere joint is composed of a universal joint and two angular contact bearings, increasing the loading capability, as Fig. 1 shows. The radius R of moving platform and fixed platform is the same, both of which is 190 mm. The equivalent sphere(S) joints are evenly distributed. The angle θ_s is 30° and θ_l is 90°. The motion of the moving platform is generated by the six prismatic joints, which could be denoted by SL_i (i = 1, 2, ..., 6). The motion range of the prismatic joint is 199.85–238.85 mm, and the initial position is 219.35 mm.

2.2 Working Principle

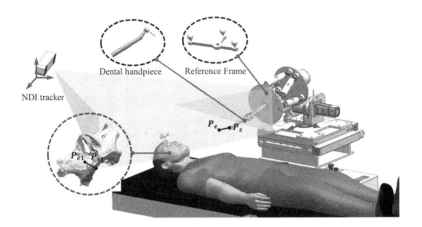

Fig. 2. The working diagram of the robot.

The working principle is illustrated in Fig. 2. The hybrid robot is under the guidance of surgical navigation system. Robot and patient are attached to the passive optical frame. Through the optical tracking device (NDI, Northern Digital Inc.), the pose of robot and patient could be detected real time. Before robot operation, the planned drilling trajectory and the drill bit are transformed to robot base coordinate and denoted by two vectors $P_{s1}P_{e1}$, $P_{s}P_{e}$ respectively. P_{e} represents the tip of drill bit and P_{s} represents a point in the axis of drill bit. The length of $P_{s}P_{e}$ is equal to the length of drill bit.

The robot operation has three steps:

(1) Initial orientation adjustment. The hybrid robot adjusts the orientation of drill bit $P_{s}P_{e}$ parallel with the planned trajectory $P_{s1}P_{e1}$
(2) Initial position adjustment. In order to ensure the safety motion of robot from the outside of oral cavity to the planned trajectory, physical human-robot interaction (PHRI) is applied. the surgeon drags the handpiece through PHRI to make the position of drill bit P_{s} near the start position P_{s1}
(3) Stewart manipulator precise adjustment and cavity preparation. The parallel manipulator adjusts the drill bit to the start point, and performs the cavity preparation after surgeon confirm.

3   Self-evolution Strategy for Orientation Adjustment

3.1 Analysis of Orientation Adjustment

During initial orientation adjustment, two revolute joints and Stewart manipulator are involved. The orientation of drill bit with respect to base coordinates could be determined by Eq. 1:

$$\boldsymbol{X}_{dv} = \boldsymbol{f}\left(\theta_1, \theta_2\right) \boldsymbol{F}(x, y, z, \alpha, \beta, \gamma) * \boldsymbol{P}_s \boldsymbol{P}_e \tag{1}$$

According to Eq. 1, given a target vector $\boldsymbol{X}_{dv}$, the computation of variable $\boldsymbol{X} = (\theta_1, \theta_2, x, y, z, \alpha, \beta, \gamma)$ belongs to solving the underdetermined equations, which means there are infinite solutions. As Fig. 3 shows, different joint configurations correspond to the same orientation of the drill bit.

Considering the limited joint range of Stewart manipulator, if the joints approach the limit position after orientation adjustment, the Stewart manipulator may not complete the surgical operation. Therefore, among the infinite solutions, it is essential to find the proper solution that minimum the joint displacement. The problem may be solved by optimal algorithm, which could be presented as Eq. 2:

$$\begin{aligned} \min \| &\boldsymbol{F}_I(x, y, z, u, v, w) - \boldsymbol{SP}_{\text{init}} \| \\ \text{s.t.} \ \ \boldsymbol{X}_{dv} = \ &\boldsymbol{F}_I\left(\theta_1, \theta_2, x, y, z, \alpha, \beta, \gamma\right) * \boldsymbol{P}_s \boldsymbol{P}_e \\ &\theta_{\min} \le \theta \le \theta_{\max} \\ &\boldsymbol{SL}_{\min} \le \boldsymbol{SL}_i \le \boldsymbol{SL}_{\max} \end{aligned} \tag{2}$$

Fig. 3. Multiple solution for the same orientation.

After given the aim orientation, the optimal algorithm, for example genetic algorithm, could search in the joint space to find an optimal solution, minimizing the joint displacement. However, those algorithms are easily trapped in local minimum. In addition, the initial random solutions are often difficult to meet the constraints, which increase the exploration time.

Actually, from the Eq. 1, it could be found that once the variables (θ_1, θ_2) are determined, the pose of the Stewart manipulator is unique. Besides, if the distance between $\boldsymbol{\theta}_i = (\theta_{1i}, \theta_{2i})$ and $\boldsymbol{\theta}_{i+1} = (\theta_{1i+1}, \theta_{2i+1})$ is close, the corresponding joint displacement of Stewart manipulator is similar. Therefore, the revolute joint variables $\boldsymbol{\theta}_i$ could be discretized and the global optimal solution could be derived by grid search in the variables space. However, grid search method often takes a lot of time, which is not suitable for robot control during surgery operation. An efficient solution is establishing a mapping function from the aim orientation to the global optimal joints space.

Neural networks were capable of learning complex functions, which led to their use in applications including pattern recognition, function approximation, data fitting, and control of dynamic systems [7]. The multilayer perception neural network includes input layer, hidden layers, and output layer. In this study, the input is the desire orientation of drill bit X_{dv} The output is the corresponding global optimal joint variable θ_{op}. For feed forward, the output of the neurons are given by Eq. 3. According to the existing input and output data, it could learn the mapping function by updating the weights w_{ij} through backpropagation algorithm, as Eq. 4 shows.

$$\theta_{\text{out}} = \varphi \left(\sum_j W_j \varphi \left(\sum_k W_k \varphi \right) \cdots \varphi \left(\sum_i W_i X_{dv} \right) \right) \tag{3}$$

$$w_{ij} = w_{ij} + \frac{\partial \Delta E}{w_{ij}} \tag{4}$$

where $\phi(\cdot)$ is the activation function, ΔE is the RMSE, which could be represented by:

$$\Delta E = \frac{1}{2} \left(\theta_{\text{out}} - \theta_{\text{op}} \right)^2 \tag{5}$$

After the neural network has been trained, it could be used for giving an approximate value for a new sample. However, the architecture of neural network is hard to design, requiring a lot of expert knowledge and taking ample time [8].

Haifengjin [9] had proposed an efficient neural architecture search method auto-keras, which is based on network morphism guided by Bayesian optimization. The method turns out to be better than other automated machine learning methods for regression [10]. There are five steps for searching the optimal model:

(1) Initial the neural network according to the type of input data and output data.
(2) Train the generated neural network on GPU and evaluate the performance on the dataset.
(3) According to the trained model and its performance, update the surrogate model.
(4) The updated surrogate model generates new neural network by optimizing the acquisition function.
(5) The program returns to the second steps to train the new neural network and start the loop, until the stop criterion met.

In this study, we applied the method in our robot system as a self-evolution strategy for orientation adjustment. The algorithm flow is shown in Fig. 4.

Firstly, on the premise that the robot base coordinate system coincides with the human body coordinate system, we simulate the orientation of the drill bit in the robot base coordinate system. And then the corresponding optimal joint configuration is computed by grid search. Those values are added to the dataset and used for searching the first-generation neural network. Secondly,

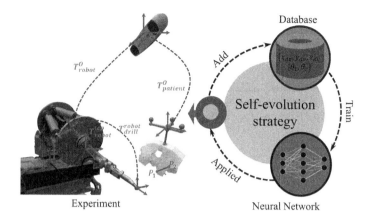

Fig. 4. Self-evolution strategy for orientation adjustment

we set up the phantom experiment as Fig. 4 shows. The robot is guided under the navigation system [11]. The orientation of the drill bit in the robot base coordinate could be derived by Eq. 6 and Eq. 7.

$$X_{dv}^{\text{robot}} = \left(T_{\text{robot}}^0\right)^{-1} T_{\text{patient}}^o \, P_1 P_2 \tag{6}$$

$$X_{dv}^{\text{base}} = T_{\text{tcp}}^{\text{base}} \, T_{\text{robot}}^{\text{tcp}} \, X_{dv}^{\text{robot}} \tag{7}$$

where $P_1 P_2$ represents the planned trajectory in the patient coordinate.

The trained neural network is applied in orientation adjustment during experiment. The robot system will record the experiment process. Finally, according to the recorded orientation of the drill bit, the global optimal joint configurations are computed. And the new values are added to the dataset, which are used for finding a better neural network model. Compared with traditional machine learning applied in robot kinematic [12–14], the self-evolution strategy could constantly explore more optimized learning model with the increase of data.

3.2 Experiment and Result

The orientation of the drill bit could be determined by the angle θ_s within $\pm 10°$ between the drill bit and the sagittal plane, θ_p within $70° \sim 90°$ between the drill bit and the jaw plane. Therefore, we could simulate the target orientation by selecting reasonable angle pairs (θ_s, θ_p) randomly and transforming the angle pairs to coordinate vectors according to geometry relationship. After getting the target orientation, the corresponding optimal joint configuration are found by grid search. In this study, 1910 target orientations are simulated, and the variables (θ_1, θ_2) are dispersed to a grid with 0.1° step size for grid search. The simulated dataset is divided into two subsets $(subd_1, subd_2)$ with the ratio 5:4. $subd_1$ is used for searching the first-generation neural network model. $subd_2$ are used for updating the trained neural network model to indicate the necessary of self-evolution. For each subset, the ratio of training dataset to testing dataset is 4:1. Besides, we performed phantom experiments, and drilled 24 cavities to test the effectiveness of the self-evolution model.

During the training process, the input and output of the neural network are target orientation and optimal joint configuration respectively. The Relu activation function was used in the hidden layers. And the loss function is RMSE (root mean square error), as Eq. 5 shows. The exploration parameters are shown in Table 1.

Table 1. Exploration parameters

Parameter	Value
Number of layers	1, 2, 3, 4, 5
Number of neurons	16, 32, 64, 128, 256, 512, 1024
Dropout	0, 0.25, 0.5
Optimizer	Adam, SGD, Adam with weight decay
Learning rate	0.1, 0.01, 0.001, 0.0001

The first-generation neural network is shown in Fig. 5(a). The number of hidden layers is four layers. The number of neurons in the hidden layer is 64, 64, 256, 1024 respectively. The network weight is updated by Adam (adaptive moment estimation) optimization algorithm, and learning rate is set 0.001. Figure 5(b) shows the last-generation neural network. The number of hidden layers is four layers and the number of neurons in each layer is 64,64,64,64,128. During training, Adam is also used for updating the weight, and the learning rate is set 0.001. Figure 5(c)–(d) show the comparison of the error distribution between the first-generation neural network and the last-generation neural network. For the first joint variable, the most of the errors are concentrated around 0.192 for the first-generation neural network and 0.086 for the last-generation neural network. For the second joint variable, the most of the errors are concentrated around 0.713 for the first-generation neural network and 0.07 for the last-generation neural network. The result indicates that the last-generation after self-evolution has a better performance on predicting the joint configuration. Figure 5(e)–(f) shows the performance of the two neural network model in the phantom experiment. The error of the last-generation neural network is smaller than that of the first-generation neural network. The average error of the θ_1 is 0.42 for the first-generation model and 0.16 for the last-generation model. The average error of the θ_2 is 1.07 for the first-generation model and 0.38 for the last-generation model. The experiment shows that if the structure of the neural network isn't changed with the increase of the amount of data, the performance of the neural network on the new data is likely to be worse. It validates the effectiveness of self-evolution strategy.

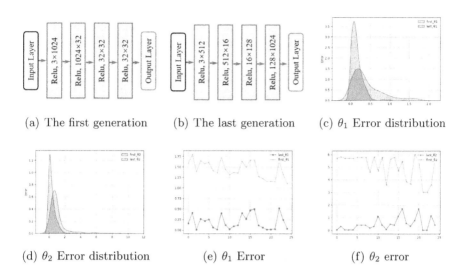

(a) The first generation   (b) The last generation   (c) θ_1 Error distribution

(d) θ_2 Error distribution   (e) θ_1 Error   (f) θ_2 error

Fig. 5. Experiment result

4   Conclusion

In this study, we developed a novel hybrid robot dedicated to dental implant. The hybrid robot consists of three translation joints, two revolute joints and a Stewart parallel manipulator. The Stewart manipulator is used for surgical operation considering the stiffness requirement of the robot. The three translation joints and two revolute joints are used to enlarge the workspace of Stewart manipulator. The corresponding operation flow for robot-assisted dental implant surgery is designed and could be divided into three steps: initial orientation adjustment, initial position adjustment and Stewart manipulator to complete surgical operation. During initial orientation adjustment, a neural network is used for finding the optimal joint configuration rapidly after given the target orientation. Besides, the neural network is updated by self-evolution strategy, which could learn the mapping relationship between the target orientation and the optimal joint configuration better and better. We manufactured the robot prototype, and integrated the robot system with the surgical navigation system to perform the phantom experiment. The phantom experiment validated the correctness of the robot kinematic model and the effectiveness of the self-evolution strategy.

References

1. Sun, X., Yoon, Y., Li, J., McKenzie, F.D.: Automated image-guided surgery for common and complex dental implants. J. Med. Eng. Technol. **38**(5), 251–259 (2014)
2. Wu, Y., Wang, F., Fan, S., Chow, K.F.: Robotics in dental implantology. Oral Maxillofacial Surg. Clin. North America **31**(3), 513–518 (2019)

3. Sun, X., Mckenzie, F.D., Bawab, S., Li, J., Yoon, Y., Huang, J.K.: Automated dental implantation using image-guided robotics: registration results. Int. J. Comput. Assist. Radiol. Surg. **6**(5), 627–634 (2011). https://doi.org/10.1007/s11548-010-0543-3

4. Cao, Z., et al.: Pilot study of a surgical robot system for zygomatic implant placement. Med. Eng. Phys. **75**, 72–78 (2020)

5. Li, J., et al.: A compact dental robotic system using soft bracing technique. IEEE Robot. Autom. Lett. **4**(2), 1271–1278 (2019)

6. Bolding, S.L., Reebye, U.N.: Accuracy of haptic robotic guidance of dental implant surgery for completely edentulous arches. J. Prosthet. Dent. (2021)

7. Köker, R., Öz, C., Çakar, T., Ekiz, H.: A study of neural network based inverse kinematics solution for a three-joint robot. Robot. Auton. Syst. **49**(3), 227–234 (2004). Patterns and Autonomous Control

8. Leiva-Aravena, E., Leiva, E., Zamorano, V., Rojas, C., Regan, J.M.: Neural architecture search with reinforcement learning. Science of the Total Environment (2019)

9. Jin, H., Song, Q., Hu, X.: Auto-Keras: an efficient neural architecture search system. In: Proceedings of the 25th ACM SIGKDD International Conference on Knowledge Discovery & Data Mining, pp. 1946–1956 (2019)

10. Truong, A., Walters, A., Goodsitt, J., Hines, K., Bruss, C.B., Farivar, R.: Towards automated machine learning: Evaluation and comparison of AutoML approaches and tools. In: 2019 IEEE 31st International Conference on Tools with Artificial Intelligence (ICTAI), pp. 1471–1479 (2019)

11. Chen, X., Ye, M., Lin, Y., Wu, Y., Wang, C.: Image guided oral implantology and its application in the placement of zygoma implants. Comput. Methods Programs Biomed. **93**(2), 162–173 (2009)

12. Limtrakul, S., Arnonkijpanich, B.: Supervised learning based on the self-organizing maps for forward kinematic modeling of Stewart platform. Neural Comput. Appl. **31**(2), 619–635 (2019). https://doi.org/10.1007/s00521-017-3095-4

13. Gao, R.: Inverse kinematics solution of robotics based on neural network algorithms. J. Ambient. Intell. Humaniz. Comput. **11**(12), 6199–6209 (2020). https://doi.org/10.1007/s12652-020-01815-4

14. Jiménez-López, E., de la Mora-Pulido, D.S., Reyes-Ávila, L.A., de la Mora-Pulido, R.S., Melendez-Campos, J., López-Martínez, A.A.: Modeling of inverse kinematic of 3-DOF robot, using unit quaternions and artificial neural network. Robotica **39**, 1230–1250 (2021)

Design and Optimization of a Novel Intramedullary Robot for Limb Lengthening

ShiKeat Lee[1,2], Zhenguo Nie[1,2(✉)], Handing Xu[1,3], Kai Hu[4], Zhao Gong[1,2], Qizhi Meng[1,2], Fugui Xie[1,2], and Xin-Jun Liu[1,2]

[1] The State Key Laboratory of Tribology, Department of Mechanical Engineering, Tsinghua University, Beijing 100084, China
zhenguonie@tsinghua.edu.cn
[2] Beijing Key Lab of Precision/Ultra-precision Manufacturing Equipments and Control, Tsinghua University, Beijing 100084, China
[3] School of Mechatronical Engineering, Beijing Institute of Technology, Beijing 100084, China
[4] Jiangsu Key Lab of Special Robot Technology, Hohai University, Changzhou, Jiangshu 213022, China

Abstract. Limb length discrepancy is a crucial problem that can seriously affect the life quality and likely leads to other diseases. Free from extracorporal surgery, the intramedullary limb-lengthening treatment has become increasingly popular in recent years as a method of long-bone distraction osteogenesis. To overcome the mechanical and electromagnetic problems caused by the medical device miniaturization, this paper presents a study on the design and optimization of a novel Intramedullary Robot for Limb Lengthening (IR4LL) with robust mechanical stiffness and surplus electromagnetic driving force. A solenoid-driven design with a large reduction ratio is proposed and analyzed. Based on the experimental and simulation results, IR4LL is proven to be safe and reliable for limb-lengthening operations, which can significantly reduce lifestyle disruption and medical complications during and after the treatment.

Keywords: Limb length discrepancy · Limb lengthening · IR4LL · Design and optimization

1 Introduction

Limb length discrepancy (LLD) is a crucial problem among clinicians because it can be caused by either congenital or acquired conditions, such as osteomyelitis, tumour, etc. [1]. In the 1980s, the Ilizarov fixator invented by Professor Gavriil A. Ilizarov unquestionable set off a revolution on limb lengthening and deformity correction [2]. However, the drawbacks of the Ilizarov fixator are long-term exposure causing inconvenience and uncomfortable, and some complication such as pin site infection, ankylosis, etc. [3–5].

© Springer Nature Switzerland AG 2021
X.-J. Liu et al. (Eds.): ICIRA 2021, LNAI 13015, pp. 103–112, 2021.
https://doi.org/10.1007/978-3-030-89134-3_10

In order to shorten treatment duration and reduce patient's pain, implantable lengthening nail (ILN) [6] is proposed which can be implanted into a human body. The first public ILN is from Bliskunov which used a rotational motion machine for elongation [7]. In 1991, Baumgart and Betz invented an autonomous ILN with a receiver embedded under the skin to recept the movement instruction signal [8,9]. However, the signal might fail because the tiny thread that connects with ILN may fracture during daily activities.

In 2001, Food and Drug Administration (FDA) approve an Intramedullary Skeletal Kinetic Distractor (ISKD) from an Orthofix company and is delisted from the market due to over-distract and unable to control its distracion rate [10–12]. Although a magnetic drive ILN called Phenix which is invented by Arnaud Soubieran achieved good clinical result, but it is less reported around the world [13].

The latest and most successful ILN, PRECICE, is approved by FDA in 2011 and updated later to PRECICE 2(P2) in 2013. The main difference between PRECICE(P1) and P2 are welding and seamless connection and higher bending strength [6,12] which is proven later that P1 has a fracture at welding part on clinical result [11]. Although P2 has huge success in limb lengthening, there are some defects that need to be solved such as temporarily slowing down or stopping distraction and 1cm shortening at the regenerated bone during consolidation phase [14].

In this paper, Intramedullary Robot for Limb Lengthening (IR4LL) is aiming to carry out structural optimization [22] solving fracture issues and insufficient power when lengthening that often happens in ILN. Later on, the static structural and modal of IR4LL during the gait cycle, and magnetic field intensity for driving the IR4LL power mechanism is analyzed. It proves that IR4LL is well-designed and giving outstanding results.

2   IR4LL Design and Method

IR4LL is an apparatus based on the principle proposed by Ilizarov which considered two parts: a motion device that is implanted into a human body for lengthening the bone (Intramedullary Robot (IR)) and a driving device that provides torque for the motion device (magnetic drive) as Fig. 1 shown. Bone screws are used to fix IR in the bone cavity, where the distal part of the bone is lengthened together with IR's elongation part when torque is provided to the threaded rod which achieved the purpose of limb lengthening. In this paper, two devices are designed and their mechanisms are introduced.

2.1   IR Design

The IR consists of four main parts, including the proximal part, middle part, distal part and elongation part. The components of IR are mainly manufactured by stainless steel which have high strength and good biocompatibility [15]. The proximal part, middle part and distal part are designed in different thicknesses

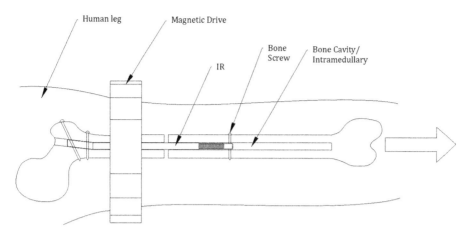

Fig. 1. The schematic figure of Intramedullary Robot for Limb Lengthening (IR4LL)

according to the forces acting on them during the human walking gait cycle. They are attached tightly through interference fit while the elongation part can move smoothly in the distal part track. As Fig. 2 shows, the proximal part and elongation part have screw holes arranged in conventional patterns which can fix the device tightly in the bone cavity.

The drive system of IR consists of a permanent magnet, a reducer, a threaded rod and an elongation part. When the permanent magnet is driven by the outer magnetic field and starts to rotate, the torque from the permanent magnet is amplified by reducer and transfers to the threaded rod. An elongation part and threaded rod which are threaded connection will do spiral motion meaning elongate as the driving torque is given. The distal part of the bone starts to lengthen as the elongation part is moving due to the existence of bone screws.

Stress and Modal. LLD is a corrective surgery that needs the ILN long term implanted in the human limb bone cavity. Therefore, safety and comfortability is the main concern for the patient. In order to ensure the IR will not break during the walking gait cycle after it is implanted, the maximum stress of the IR must not exceed the tensile strength of the material. Moreover, modal analysis is required to determine the dynamic behaviour of the system in the forms of natural frequencies, damping factors and mode shapes. Therefore, the natural frequency of IR must be much larger than the walking gait cycle frequency to avoid resonant damage.

2.2 Magnetic Drive Design

The IR magnetic drive consists of a group of stator core module, steel cable and winding coils as Fig. 3 shown. The stator core module has two nylon protective

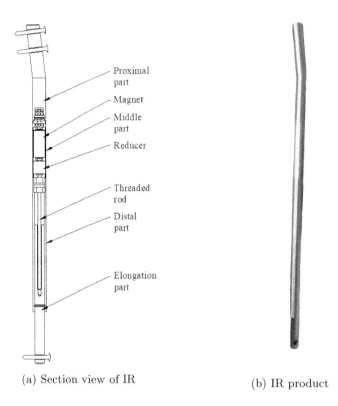

(a) Section view of IR   (b) IR product

Fig. 2. The schematic figure of IR

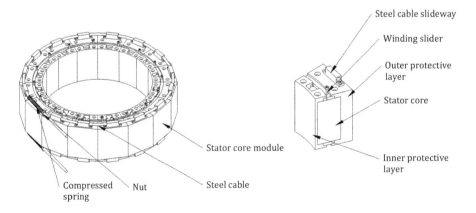

Fig. 3. IR Magnetic drive and its stator core module

layers on both inner diameter and outer diameter to prevent a direct contact on the stator core which is manufactured by silicon steel sheet. A steel cable slideway is fixed on the outer diameter while the winding slider is slid into the gap between the outer and inner protective layer. A group of the stator core module is connected in series to form a circular magnetic field generator that can be put on by the patient. A compressed spring and a nut are used at the end of the steel cable for adjusting the space between the stator core module. The purpose of the winding slider is to adjust the total diameter of the winding when the magnetic drive's diameter change.

Lifting Torque and Supplying Torque. Based on the combination of IR's permanent magnet and the magnetic drive, we can assume that it is similar to a permanent magnet brushless DC motor (PMBLDC) model. Supplying torque is contributed by the magnetic drive and acts as an input of the drive system while lifting torque is the output of the drive system to overcome the load. The lifting torque required for the threaded rod during limb lengthening can be calculated as:

$$T = \frac{Fd_m}{2}\left(\frac{l + \pi\mu d_m}{\pi d_m - \mu l}\right) \tag{1}$$

where F is the load, d_m is the mean thread diameter, μ is the coefficient of friction for thread, l is the screw's lead.

Apart from decreasing the lifting torque, increasing the magnetic field intensity of the magnetic drive can also increase the supplying torque. In this paper, we are using the PMBLDC motor principle to control the permanent magnet in IR in order to follow the stator magnetic field rotates synchronously. The total torque of the PMBLDC motor may be described with the relations [17]

$$T = 2PB_g I_s n_s LR_{si} \tag{2}$$

where P is the number of poles, B_g is the air gap flux density in the middle 120° of a pole, I_s is the DC source current, n_s is the number of turns in slot, L is the active length of the motor and R_{si} is the stator inner radius. Based on Eq. 2 given above, increasing the source current or number of turns in the PMBLDC motor is an effective way to increase its total torque.

3   Analysis and Simulation

In this section, finite element analysis which has a wide range of applications in mechanical design and manufacturing [21] is used in IR4LL to ensure the structure of IR is not breakable during the human walking gait cycle and the rotating magnetic field formed by the magnetic drive are sufficient for limb lengthening. The design specifications of IR is shown in Table 1:

3.1   Analysis and Simulation of Mechanical Stiffness

Static Structural and Modal Analysis. In order to avoid IR breakage after it is implanted into the bone cavity, 3 different directions of forces (frontal force, lateral force and axial force) during the walking gait cycle [16, 20] must not

Table 1. IR design specifications

Material	Maximum diameter	Maximum allowable elongation	Threaded rod specification	Reduction ratio
SS316L	12.5 mm	80 mm	M4	50

exceed the material's tensile strength. In this paper, we assume IR is implanted for femur lengthening and the walking gait cycle of a 100 Kg body weight patient is decomposed into 6 steps.

Table 2. The average frontal, lateral and axial force acting on the femur and the minimum, maximum and average stress on IR during walking gait cycle

Steps	1	2	3	4	5	6
Frontal force (N)	119.7	119.7	119.7	119.7	359.1	119.7
Lateral force (N)	−91.8	−198.9	−91.8	−91.8	0	0
Axial force (N)	499.52	854.83	1128.38	769.35	0	512.9
Minimum stress (MPa)	1.806e−3	3.124e−3	4.075e−3	2.779e−3	4.659e−3	1.823e−3
Maximum stress (MPa)	330.2	486.89	344.12	335.78	550.51	266.07
Average stress (MPa)	57.132	88.828	62.684	59.389	128.26	46.247

The load from Table 2 is applied on the screw hole of the elongation part while fixed support is applied on the screw holes of the proximal part. According to the result shown in Table 2 and Fig. 4, the Von Mises Stress is mainly taking part at the middle part of IR which is around 550.5 MPa at the 5th step. The maximum stress is smaller than its yield strength (946 MPa), but it is not encouraged to use it while doing intense activities such as running. The base frequency given in modal analysis is 213.55 Hz which is larger than the walking gait cycle (shown in Table 3).

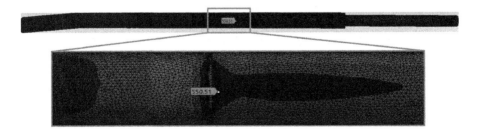

Fig. 4. Von Mises stress simulation shows that the maximum value occurs at IR's middle part

Table 3. The first 8 mode of natural frequency

Mode	1	2	3	4	5	6	7	8
Frequency (Hz)	213.55	213.56	1274.1	1274.2	2232.8	3809.4	3810.8	4558.6

3.2 Analysis and Simulation of Electromagnetic Driving

Lifting Torque. In order to calculate the lifting torque required for the
threaded rod, the load acting on IR during lengthening is our main concern.
According to Zhang et al. [18], the distraction rate of ILN is 0.5 to 1.32 mm/day
and the force is related to the body mass of the patient during the distraction
period [19]. Therefore, the assumption of the lifting torque is given in Table 4.

Table 4. Assumption for the lifting torque

Distraction rate	Distraction period	Forces in relation to the body mass at the end of the distraction period	Coefficient of friction
1 mm/day	80 days	9.5 N/Kg	0.15

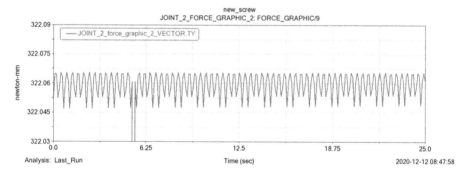

Fig. 5. The result of lifting torque simulation

Based on the result shown in Fig. 5, we can approximate the minimum torque
required for the linear motion is 325 Nmm. According to Table 1, the reduction
ratio of the reducer is 50 which gives the final lifting torque will be at least 6.5
Nmm.

Supplying Torque. The proposed magnetic drive which is similar to PMBLDC
model has 2 magnet poles and a stator core that has three-phase six salient poles.
The design specifications of the magnetic drive and IR's PM are shown in Table 5
where the material of PM and stator core are NdFe35 and M27_29G respectively.

Table 5. Stator core and rotor core design specifications

Stator dimension			
Outer diameter	Inner diameter	Length	Stacking factor
250 mm	200 mm	40 mm	0.95
Stator winding			
Conductors per slot	Number of strands	Wire wrap	Wire diameter
75	1	0.2 mm	1.829 mm
Rotor dimension			
Outer diameter	Inner diameter	Length	Embrace
11 mm	3 mm	25 mm	1

Although PMBLDC motor's current source is DC current, its commutation can be implemented in software using a microcontroller, or may alternatively implemented using analog or digital circuits. The commutation sequence of PMBLDC motor is one winding energized positive, one winding energized negative and one winding non-energized. In this paper, the maximum current of the magnetic drive is restricted to below 10 A because the allowable current for 1.829 mm diameter wire is 10.368 A. From Fig. 6, the average supplying torque of the magnetic drive is 8.6 Nmm which is larger than the minimum lifting torque 6.5 Nmm.

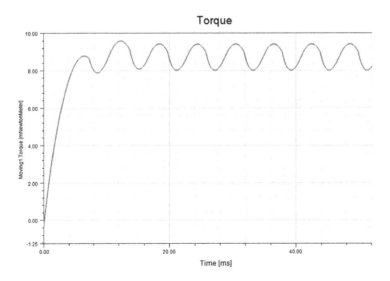

Fig. 6. Average supplying torque of magnetic drive

4   Conclusion and Future Work

In this article, we have successfully designed an ILN named IR4LL which is aimed to solve LLD disease that has been troubling clinicians. The IR which is implanted into the bone cavity is driving by the magnetic flux formed from the magnetic drive. The rotating magnetic field rotates the PM inside IR to transfer the rotational motion to linear motion that can lengthen the bone. Either increasing the source current or number of turns in the magnetic drive enhances the supplying torque while increasing the reduction ratio in the reducer lessens the lifting torque required. As further work, IR4LL will be manufactured and the animal experiment will be carried out to prove it is effective in solving the LLD problem.

Acknowledgement. This work is supported by National Natural Science Foundation of China under Grant 52175237, and National Key R&D Program of China under Grant 2019YFA0706701.

References

1. Bowen, S., Hengsheng, S.: Research progress of fully implantable intramedullary lengthening nail. Chin. J. Orthop. **39**(1), 58–64 (2019). https://doi.org/10.3760/cma.j.issn.0253-2352.2019.01.009
2. Birch, J.G.: A brief history of limb lengthening. J. Pediatric Orthop. **37**(Suppl 2), S1–S8 (2017). https://doi.org/10.1097/BPO.0000000000001021
3. Fragomen, A.T., Miller, A.O., Brause, B.D., Goldman, V., Rozbruch, S.R.: Prophylactic postoperative antibiotics may not reduce pin site infections after external fixation. HSS J. ® **13**(2), 165–170 (2016). https://doi.org/10.1007/s11420-016-9539-z
4. Bhave, A., Shabtai, L., Woelber, E., et al.: Muscle strength and knee range of motion after femoral lengthening. Acta Orthop. **88**(2), 179–184 (2017). https://doi.org/10.1080/17453674.2016.1262678
5. Kazmers, N.H., Fragomen, A.T., Rozbruch, S.R.: Prevention of pin site infection in external fixation: a review of the literature. Strateg. Trauma Limb Reconstr. **11**(2), 75–85 (2016). https://doi.org/10.1007/s11751-016-0256-4
6. Paley, D.: PRECICE intramedullary limb lengthening system. Expert Rev. Med. Dev. **12**(3), 231–249 (2015). https://doi.org/10.1586/17434440.2015.1005604
7. Birch, J.G.: A brief history of limb lengthening. J. Pediatr. Thop. **37**(Suppl 2), S1-8 (2017). https://doi.org/10.1097/BPO.0000000000001021
8. Black, S.R., Kwon, M.S., Cherkashin, A.M., et al.: Lengthening in congenital femoral deficiency: a comparison of circular external fixation and a motorized intramedullary nail. J. Bone Joint Surg. Am. **97**(17), 1432–1440 (2015). https://doi.org/10.2106/JBJS.N.00932
9. Accadbled, F., Pailhé, R., Cavaignac, E., et al.: Bone lengthening using the Fitbone(®) motorized intramedullary nail: the first experience in France. Orthop. Traumatol. Surg. Res. **102**(2), 217–222 (2016). https://doi.org/10.1016/j.otsr.2015.10.011
10. Lee, D.H., Ryu, K.J., Song, H.R., Han, S.-H.: Complications of the intramedullary skeletal kinetic distractor (ISKD) in distraction osteogenesis. Clin. Orthop. Relat. Res.® **472**(12), 3852–3859 (2014). https://doi.org/10.1007/s11999-014-3547-4

11. Schiedel, F.M., Vogt, B., Tretow, H.L., et al.: How precise is the PRECICE compared to the ISKD in intramedullary limb lengthening? Reliability and safety in 26 procedures. Acta Orthop. **85**(3), 293–298 (2014). https://doi.org/10.3109/17453674.2014.913955

12. Paley, D., Harris, M., Debiparshad, K., et al.: Limb lengthening by implantable limb lengthening devices. Tech. Orthop. **29**(2), 72–85 (2014). https://doi.org/10.1097/BTO.0000000000000072

13. Thaller, P.H., Fürmetz, J., Wolf, F., et al.: Limb lengthening with fully implantable magnetically actuated mechanical nails (PHENIX®)- preliminary results. Injury **45**(Suppl 1), S60-65 (2014). https://doi.org/10.1016/j.injury.2013.10.029

14. Nasto, L.A., et al.: Clinical results and complication rates of lower limb lengthening in paediatric patients using the PRECICE 2 intramedullary magnetic nail: a multicentre study. J. Pediatric Orthop. B **29**(6), 611–617 (2020). https://doi.org/10.1097/BPB.0000000000000651

15. Manam, N.S., et al.: Study of corrosion in biocompatible metals for implants: a review. J. Alloys Compd. **701**, 698–715 (2017). https://doi.org/10.1016/j.jallcom.2017.01.196

16. Duda, G.N., Schneider, E., Chao, E.Y.: Internal forces and moments in the femur during walking. J. Biomech. **30**(9), 933–941 (1997). https://doi.org/10.1016/S0021-9290(97)00057-2

17. Carunaiselvane, C., Jeevananthan, S.: Generalized procedure for BLDC motor design and substantiation in MagNet 7.1.1 software. In: 2012 International Conference on Computing, Electronics and Electrical Technologies (ICCEET), pp. 18–25. IEEE (2012). https://doi.org/10.1109/ICCEET.2012.6203783

18. Zhang, J., Zhang, Y., Wang, C., et al.: Research progress of intramedullary lengthening nail technology. Zhongguo xiu fu chong jian wai ke za zhi **35**(5), 642–647 (2021). https://doi.org/10.7507/1002-1892.202012084

19. Lauterburg, M.T., Exner, G.U., Jacob, H.A.: Forces involved in lower limb lengthening: an in vivo biomechanical study. J. Orthop. Res. **24**(9), 1815–1822 (2006). https://doi.org/10.1002/jor.20217

20. Schneider, E., Michel, M.C., Genge, M., et al.: Loads acting in an intramedullary nail during fracture healing in the human femur. J. Biomech. **34**(7), 849–857 (2001). https://doi.org/10.1016/S0021-9290(01)00037-9

21. Nie, Z., Wang, G., Wang, L., et al.: A coupled thermomechanical modeling method for predicting grinding residual stress based on randomly distributed abrasive grains. J. Manuf. Sci. Eng. **141**(8), 081005 (2019). https://doi.org/10.1115/1.4043799

22. Nie, Z., Jung, S., Kara, L.B., et al.: Optimization of part consolidation for minimum production costs and time using additive manufacturing. J. Mech. Design, **142**(7) (1990, 2020). https://doi.org/10.1115/1.4045106

Camera Pose Estimation Based on Feature Extraction and Description for Robotic Gastrointestinal Endoscopy

Yuwei Xu[1,2], Lijuan Feng[3], Zeyang Xia[1,2], and Jing Xiong[1,2(✉)]

[1] Shenzhen Institute of Advanced Technology, Chinese Academy of Sciences, Shenzhen, China
jing.xiong@siat.ac.cn
[2] University of Chinese Academy of Sciences, Beijing, China
[3] Department of Gastroenterology, Shenzhen University General Hospital, Shenzhen, China

Abstract. The application of robotics in gastrointestinal endoscopy has gained more and more attention over the past decade. The localization and navigation of the robotic gastrointestinal endoscopy is very important in robot-assisted gastrointestinal examination and surgery. The camera pose of the robotic gastrointestinal endoscopy can be estimated directly from the image sequence. However, due to the texture-less nature and strong specular reflections of the digestive tract surface, it is hard to detect enough keypoints to estimate the camera pose when using the traditional handcrafted method. In this paper, we propose an end-to-end CNN-based network to deal with this problem. Our network is trained in a self-supervised manner, and the network plays two roles, a dense feature descriptor and a feature detector simultaneously. The network takes the image sequence as input, and the featured keypoints and their corresponding descriptors as outputs. We demonstrate our algorithm on images captured in stomach phantom. The experimental results show that our method can effectively detect and describe the featured keypoints in challenging conditions.

Keywords: Robotic gastrointestinal endoscopy · Localization · Convolutional neural network · Feature detector · Feature descriptor

1 Introduction

Gastrointestinal endoscopy is the most important procedure in minimally invasive surgical interventions and lesion diagnosis [1]. The camera pose of the robotic gastrointestinal endoscopy provides the doctor with information on the position and orientation of the endoscopy, which can serve for minimally invasive surgery. The pose estimation of the robotic gastrointestinal endoscopy may rely on additional locators such as the magnetic locator [2], or estimate the pose of the robotic gastrointestinal endoscopy from image

Supported by National Key R&D Program of China (2019YFB1311503), National Natural Science Foundation of China (62073309, 61773365 and 61811540033) and Shenzhen Sci-ence and Technology Program (JCYJ20210324115606018).

© Springer Nature Switzerland AG 2021
X.-J. Liu et al. (Eds.): ICIRA 2021, LNAI 13015, pp. 113–122, 2021.
https://doi.org/10.1007/978-3-030-89134-3_11

sequence directly [3]. Additional locators require to attach additional accessories to the endoscopy and also increase the cost, and estimate the pose from image sequence directly requires only a gastrointestinal endoscopy and routine operations. The direct pose estimation with image sequence needs to detect and match the feature points of different image frames.

Feature detection and description is the fundamental computer vision problem, and it is widely use in pose estimation [4], object detection [5], Structure-from-Motion [6] and 3D reconstruction [7, 8]. Traditional handcrafted descriptors like the famous SIFT [9], SURF [10], ORB [11] follow the detect-then-describe process, which first apply a feature detector to detect a set of keypoints, then provide image patches extracted around the keypoints to describe them with a multidimensional vector. Bergen et al. used the Scale Invariant Feature Transform (SIFT) to detect keypoints in every endoscopy video frame and match the keypoints between frames based on their similarity, then performed the task of image mosaicking [12]. To detect keypoints on digestive tract surface is a challenging task due to the texture-less characteristic of the digestive tract surface. In order to detect enough feature points, Dual et al. used an active vision based endoscope which launched laser spots to the organ surface, and detected the laser dots as feature points to reconstruct organ [13, 14], Widya et al. through spreading indigo carmine dye on the stomach surface and capture images with chromo-endoscopy to increase the number of feature points, which can deal with texture-less area and avoid the Structure-from-Motion algorithm fail [7]. Classical feature based methods (e.g. SIFT, SURF) are often inoperative for images with weak texture, so optical flow-based solution always be a candidate [15, 16], Trinh et al. proposed a variation optical flow method to deal with the texture-less images captured by gastrointestinal endoscopy and implemented image mosaicking [15]. Phan et al. introduced a dense optical flow-based solution and reconstructed the organ surface [16]. Although the optical flow-based methods can deal with some challenging conditions, it suffered from the fact that they have a high computational complexity, especially the dense optical flow methods, which cannot be used in scenarios that required real-time performance.

In recent years, with the development and success of deep learning method in the field of natural image research, researchers have turned to the Convolutional Neural Network (CNN) based methods for feature detection and description in the field of natural image. Recently, more and more learning based feature detection and description methods appear [17–21]. Different from traditional approaches which are mostly driven by researcher's expertise, learning based approaches are driven by data. Match-Net [17], used a Siamese network to detect feature representation, and a metric network for measuring similarity of feature pairs. PN-Net [18], proposed a Convolutional Neural Network based descriptor to improve matching performance, and introduced a softPN loss to optimize the distances of patch triplets. L2-Net [19], introduced a network for learning the discriminative patch descriptor and used L2 distance for measuring the similarity of descriptors. D2-Net [20], introduced a path that jointly detect and describe the local features, the network is a detector and a descriptor simultaneously. He et al. proposed an Average Precision loss for optimizing the performance of descriptor matching [22].

In this paper, we focus on extracting and describing feature points in digestive endoscopy images, then we estimate the pose of the gastrointestinal endoscopy based on feature matching. We train our network in a self-supervised manner, and follow the path of detect-and-describe proposed by D2-Net. For descriptor matching, we follow the similar optimal path in He's research [22]. Revaud et al. proposed a feature description method, referred to as R2D2, which was the state-of-the-art descriptor on the natural image dataset (e.g. HPatches dataset). And we have done the comparative experiment with R2D2 on ours dataset.

2   Method

The goal of our method is to extract and describe feature points in gastrointestinal endoscopy images, which is a challenging task for traditional methods due to the weak texture nature of the digestive tract surface. To do so, we propose to train a Convolutional Neural Network, which predicts three outputs for an image I with size $H \times W \times C$. The first output is a tensor $F \in R^{H \times W \times D}$, which is a dense set of descriptors correspond to every pixel in the image. The second output is a ranking map $R \in [0, 1]$ with size $\times W$, which indicates the reliability of the feature points. The third one is a heatmap $Q \in [0, 1]$ with the size same as ranking map.

2.1   Feature Detection and Camera Pose Estimation

Feature points detection and description is the fundamental task in camera pose estimation. Due to the fact that the images taken from stomach phantom or in-vivo with weak texture and the state-of-the-art traditional method (*e.g., SIFT, ORB*) can't extract enough feature points for estimating the pose, and we train a Convolutional Neural Network to deal with this problem.

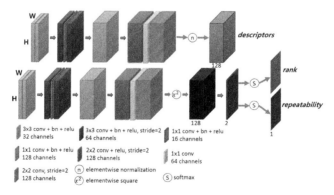

Fig. 1. Architecture of the network

The network architecture is depicted in Fig. 1. The backbone is similar to L2-Net [19], and we expand the L2-Net to two pipelines, one for learning descriptors and another for learning the feature points. The pipeline for learning feature points has two branches, one for learning repeatability, another for learning ranking of every feature point. Compared to L2-Net, we add a 1×1 convolutional layer after third convolutional layer, and we replace the sixth layer with a 1×1 convolutional layer, besides, we expand the last 8×8 convolutional layer to three convolutional layers, two 2×2 convolutional layers, and one 1×1 convolutional layer between two 2×2 convolutional layers. The 1×1 convolutional kernel can flexibly adjust the depth of the feature map, so it can easily reduce parameters and due to the 1×1 convolutional kernel fuse each pixel's information by channel, so it can retain more details. Our experimental results show that these modifications can significantly reduce the parameters and the network training speed is faster than that in R2D2 [21], we spend about 6 min per epoch when training the network, and get a better matching accuracy on our dataset.

To detect the feature points, the repeatability and reliability of the feature points are critical, and we follow the path in D2-Net [20], which jointly learning detector and descriptor. To learn the repeatability, we need to find the overlapping region between the input images. Let I_1 and I_2 be the image pair which captured in the same scene, and $S \in R^{H \times W \times 2}$ be the ground-truth of I_1 and I_2, S can be estimated with optical flow method [23] and interpolate to the size of I_1 or I_2. Let R_1 and R_2 be the repeatability map for I_1 and I_2 respectively, and R_2^S is the heatmap from image I_2 warped by S. The goal is to maximize the similarity between R_1 and R_2^S, we evaluate the similarity over many patches, the patches denoted as $P = \{p\}$, which contains $N \times N$ patches, and the similarity loss is defined as:

$$L_{sim} = 1 - \frac{1}{|P|} \sum_{p \in P} sim(R_1[p], R_2^S[p]) \tag{1}$$

where $R_1[p]$ denotes the $N \times N$ patch p extracted from I_1, and the same with $R_2^S[p]$. According to R2D2 [21], when R_1 and R_2^S are constant, the L_{sim} can be minimized. To avoid that, we follow the method in R2D2, and using a *peaky* loss to maximize the local peakiness of the repeatability map:

$$L_{peaky} = 1 - \frac{1}{|P|} \sum_{p \in P} \left(\underset{(i,j) \in p}{max} R_{ij} - \underset{(i,j) \in p}{mean} R_{ij} \right) \tag{2}$$

finally, the repeatability loss can be denoted as the weighted sum of the similarity loss and peaky loss:

$$L_{rep} = L_{sim}(I_1, I_2, H) + \alpha(L_{peaky}(I_1) + L_{peaky}(I_2)) \tag{3}$$

To learn the reliability, we need to extract local descriptors D and need to predict a confidence value $X_{ij} \in [0, 1]$ for each pixel's descriptor $D_{ij} \in R^D$. We compute the descriptors in I_1 and I_2 with CNN, that is apply a CNN on the input image I to obtain a tensor $T \in R^{H \times W \times C}$, where $H \times W$ is the resolution of the feature map, and C is the number of channel, in our work, C = 128. The descriptor matching can be seen as a ranking optimization problem, that is for two images I_1 and I_2, each descriptor from I_1 matches all descriptors in I_2, and computing the distance between them, then ranking all matches according to their distance. We follow the method of Average Precision (AP) [22] to optimize the descriptor matching, which similar to R2D2. For each descriptor d (from I_1) in batch B, we maximize the AP and compute the average over the batch.

$$L_{AP} = \frac{1}{B} \sum_{d=1}^{B} L_{AP}(d) L_{AP}(d) = 1 - AP(d) \tag{4}$$

After detecting the feature points and their descriptors, we can estimate the camera pose from image sequence. We first need to estimate the *Essential Matrix* E according to image matching. According to the geometric relationship (see Fig. 2) between keypoints and their scenic points, we can obtain the geometric constraint of any point pair:

$$\left(X'\right)^T K^{-T} E K^{-1} X = 0 \tag{5}$$

where K is the camera intrinsic, X and X' are pixels in image I_1 and I_2 respectively. And we can compute the relative rotation and translation between I_1 and I_2 from *Essential Matrix* E with SVD algorithm.

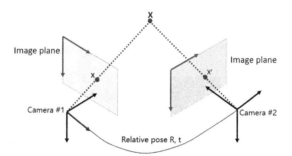

Fig. 2. Two-view geometry

2.2 Training Details

Training Data. Our training data is captured by Olympus GIF-HQ290 gastroscopy. The number of images for training are 4873 and we use random crop and random scale to achieve the purpose of data augmentation and prevent overfitting due to the small dataset. The images are cropped to 1058×900 and de-distortion using the lib *OPENCV*.

Training Parameters. We using the Adam optimizer with learning rate of 0.0001, the batch size is 8, and the weight decay is 0.0005.

3 Experimental Result

The main motivation of our work is to develop a feature detection and description method that can deal with challenging conditions. We evaluate our approach on the images captured by a gastrointestinal endoscopy and perform feature points detection and description with a CNN network. And we estimate the pose of the robotic gastrointestinal endoscopy based on the image matching.

3.1 Feature Detection

We evaluated the performance of feature detection in stomach phantom images captured by a gastrointestinal endoscopy, we selected the images with weak texture, motion blur, and the images without these phenomena. From the experimental results we found that our method could extract enough feature points even if on texture-less images or the images with motion blur when compared to the traditional algorithm like SIFT and ORB. When we evaluated the methods on the general images, that was the images no motion blur and with rich texture, the results shown that our method and traditional ones have a similar performance in terms of the number of keypoints. The results shown that the learning-based method were more robust when deal with the challenging conditions (Fig. 3).

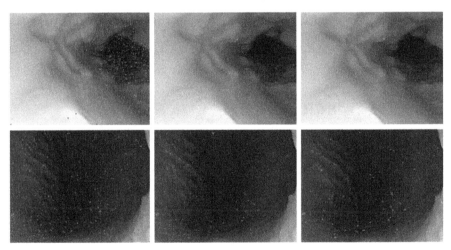

Fig. 3. Comparison of the feature extraction with different methods. Method: Ours (left), SIFT (middle), ORB (right). The results show that our method is more robust on the texture-less images.

We have evaluated the number of feature points extracted by different methods. The results are shown in Table 1.

Table 1. Evaluation on the feature extraction of stomach phantom dataset

Dataset	Method	Feature points
1368 images	SIFT [24]	1435K
	ORB [11]	612K
	Ours	**2736K**

3.2 Image Matching

We also evaluated the performance of our method on image matching. We used the k-Nearest Neighbor (KNN) algorithm to match the feature points based on their corresponding descriptors, and used the method proposed by Lowe [25] to select the robust matching at different ratios. The results (see Fig. 4 and Table 2) show that the descriptors are competitive. We used the mean matching accuracy (MMA) which proposed in Schmid's study [26] to evaluate the image matching accuracy, and the results are shown in Table 2.

Table 2. The MMA of different methods with different ratios

Method	MMA	
	Ratio = 0.8	Ratio = 0.85
R2D2 [21]	0.411	0.605
Ours	**0.454**	**0.642**

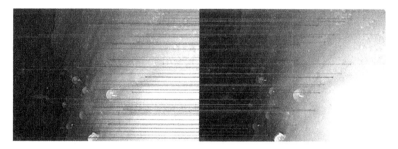

Fig. 4. Image matching

We have performed the comparative experiment on our method and the method in Revaud's research [21], Our network has fewer parameters, the number of parameters is only 1/3 of the Revaud's (615 KB vs 1905 KB) but get a better result (Fig. 5).

3.3 Camera Pose Estimation

We have estimated the pose of the gastrointestinal endoscopy based on the image matching, we selected a continuous image sequence (744 images) that could extract enough feature points by SIFT [9] algorithm. And we took the trajectory estimated by SIFT [9] as our baseline. The result shown that the two trajectories were consistent (Fig. 6).

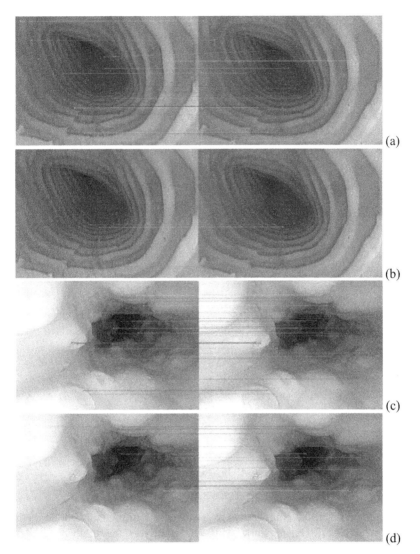

Fig. 5. Image matching comparison with different methods. (a) and (c) are the results of our method, (b) and (d) are the results of Revaud's method (R2D2 [21]). The results show that in the case of extracting the same number of feature points, the descriptors obtained by our method are better than that of Revaud's (R2D2 [21]), and get a better matching performance.

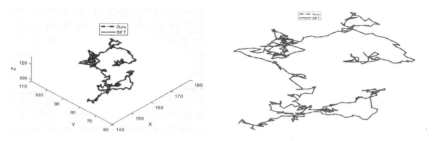

Fig. 6. The trajectory estimated by SIFT and our method. left: original view, right: enlarged view

4   Conclusion

In this paper, a novel learning-based approach for feature extraction on gastrointestinal endoscopy images is proposed, which can serve in the visual localization for the robotic gastrointestinal endoscopy. The network follows the path of detect-and-describe and performs feature extraction and description simultaneously. In contrast to traditional feature detection approaches, our method is more robust to the challenging conditions. Our network is trained in a self-supervision manner, which does not need to spend a lot of time and effort to label the data. And the network can successfully extract and describe feature points. Moreover, we estimate the pose of gastrointestinal endoscopy based on image matching, and we take the trajectory estimated by SIFT as the baseline, the results show that our method can correctly estimate the camera pose.

There are some works using CNN as a feature extractor on natural images. In the future, we will compare our method with other deep learning methods on endoscopic images and improve the accuracy of the image matching.

References

1. Bernhardt, S., Abi-Nahed, J., Abugharbieh, R.: Robust dense endoscopic stereo reconstruction for minimally invasive surgery. In: Menze, B.H., Langs, G., Lu, L., Montillo, A., Tu, Z., Criminisi, A. (eds.) MCV 2012. LNCS, vol. 7766, pp. 254–262. Springer, Heidelberg (2013). https://doi.org/10.1007/978-3-642-36620-8_25
2. Qian, Y., Bai, T., Li, J., et al.: Magnetic-guided capsule endoscopy in the diagnosis of gastrointestinal diseases in minors. Gastroenterol. Res. Pract. **2**, 1–8 (2018)
3. Ozyoruk, K.B., et al.: EndoSLAM dataset and an unsupervised monocular visual odometry and depth estimation approach for endoscopic videos: Endo-SfMLearner (2020)
4. Kundu, J.N., Rahul, M.V., Aditya Ganeshan, R., Babu, V.: Object pose estimation from monocular image using multi-view keypoint correspondence. In: Leal-Taixé, L., Roth, S. (eds.) ECCV 2018. LNCS, vol. 11131, pp. 298–313. Springer, Cham (2019). https://doi.org/10.1007/978-3-030-11015-4_23
5. Ren, S.H.K., Girshick, R.: Faster R-CNN: towards real-time object detection with region proposal networks. IEEE Trans. Pattern Anal. Mach. Intell. **39**(6), 1137–1149 (2017)
6. Pentek, Q., Hein, S., Miernik, A., et al.: Image-based 3D surface approximation of the bladder using structure-from-motion for enhanced cystoscopy based on phantom data. Biomed. Tech. (Berl) **63**(4), 461–466 (2018)

7. Widya, A., Monno, Y., Okutomi, M., Suzuki, S., Gotoda, T., Miki, K.: Whole stomach 3D reconstruction and frame localization from monocular endoscope video. IEEE J. Transl. Eng. Health Med. **7**, 1–10 (2019)
8. Widy, A., Monno, Y., Okutomi, M., et al.: Stomach 3D reconstruction based on virtual chromoendoscopic image generation. In: International Conference of the IEEE Engineering in Medicine and Biology Society (EMBC). IEEE (2020)
9. Lowe, D.G.: Distinctive image features from scaleinvariant keypoints. Int. J. Comput. Vis. **20**(2) (2004)
10. Bay, H., Ess, A., Tuytelaars, T.: Speeded-up robust features. Comput. Vis. Image Underst. **110**(3), 404–417 (2008)
11. Rublee, E., Rabaud, V., Konolige, K., Bradski, G.: ORB: an efficient alternative to SIFT or SURF. In: IEEE International Conference on Computer Vision. IEEE (2011)
12. Bergen, T., Wittenberg, T., Munzenmayer, C., et al.: A graph-based approach for local and global panorama imaging in cystoscopy. In: SPIE, vol. 8671, no. 1–7 (2013)
13. Achrafben-Hamadou, D.C, Soussen, C., et al.: A novel 3D surface construction approach: application to three-dimensional endoscopic data. In: IEEE International Conference on Image Processing (ICIP). IEEE (2010)
14. Daul, C., et al.: From 2D towards 3D cartography of hollow organs. In: Electrical Engineering Computing Science and Automatic Control (CCE). IEEE (2010)
15. Trinh, D.H., Daul, C., Blondel, W., et al.: Mosaicing of images with few textures and strong illumination changes: application to gastroscopic scenes. In: International Conference on Image Processing (ICIP), pp. 1263–1267. IEEE (2018)
16. Phan, T., Trinh, D., Lamarque, D., et al.: Dense optical flow for the reconstruction of weakly textured and structured surfaces: application to endoscopy. In: IEEE International Conference on Image Processing. IEEE (2019)
17. Han, X., Leung, T., Jia, Y., Sukthankar, R., Berg, A.C.: MatchNet: unifying feature and metric learning for patch-based matching. In: Computer Vision & Pattern Recognition. IEEE (2015)
18. Balntas, V., Johns, E., Tang, L., Mikolajczyk, K.: PN-Net: conjoined triple deep network for learning local image descriptors (2016)
19. Tian, Y., Fan, B., Wu, F.: L2-Net: deep learning of discriminative patch descriptor in Euclidean space. In: IEEE Conference on Computer Vision and Pattern Recognition (CVPR). IEEE (2017)
20. Dusmanu, M., et al.: D2-Net: a trainable CNN for joint description and detection of local features. In: IEEE/CVF Conference on Computer Vision and Pattern Recognition (CVPR). IEEE (2019)
21. Revaud, J., et al.: R2D2: repeatable and reliable detector and descriptor (2019)
22. He, K., Lu, Y., Sclaroff, S.: Local descriptors optimized for average precision. In: IEEE/CVF Conference on Computer Vision and Pattern Recognition. IEEE (2018)
23. Revaud, J., Weinzaepfel, P., Harchaoui, Z., Schmid, C.: EpicFlow: edge-preserving interpolation of correspondences for optical flow. In: Computer Vision & Pattern Recognition. IEEE (2015)
24. Lowe, D.G.: Distinctive image features from scale-invariant keypoints. Int. J. Comput. Vis. **60**(2), 91–110 (2004). https://doi.org/10.1023/B:VISI.0000029664.99615.94
25. Brown, M., Lowe, D.G.: Automatic panoramic image stitching using invariant features. Int. J. Comput. Vis. **74**(1), 59–73 (2006)
26. Mikolajczyk, K., Schmid, C.: A performance evaluation of local descriptors. IEEE Trans. Pattern Anal. Mach. Intell. **27**(10), 1615–1630 (2005)

A Nature-Inspired Algorithm to Adaptively Safe Navigation of a Covid-19 Disinfection Robot

Tingjun Lei[1], Timothy Sellers[1], Shahram Rahimi[2], Shi Cheng[3], and Chaomin Luo[1(✉)]

[1] Department of Electrical and Computer Engineering, Mississippi State University, Mississippi State, MS 39762, USA
`Chaomin.Luo@ece.msstate.edu`
[2] Department of Computer Science and Engineering, Mississippi State University, Mississippi State, MS 39762, USA
[3] School of Computer Science, Shaanxi Normal University, Xi'an 710119, China

Abstract. Autonomous mobile robots have been extensively used in medical services. During the Covid-19 pandemic, ultraviolet type-C irradiation (UV-C) disinfection robots and spray disinfection robots have been deployed in hospitals and other public open spaces. However, adaptively safe navigation of disinfection robots and spray disinfection robots have not been adequately studied. In this paper, an adaptively safe navigation model of Covid-19 disinfection robots is proposed using a nature-inspired method, cuckoo search algorithm (CSA). A Covid-19 disinfection robot is adaptively navigated to decelerate in the vicinity of objects and obstacles thus it can sufficiently spray and illuminate around objects, which assures objects to be fully disinfected against SARS-CoV-2. In addition, the path smoothing scheme based on the $\mathcal{B}$-spline curve is integrated with adaptive-speed navigation to generate a safer and smoother trajectory at a reasonable distance from the obstacle. Simulation and comparative studies prove the effectiveness of the proposed model, which can plan a reasonable and short trajectory with obstacle avoidance, and show better performance than other meta-heuristic optimization techniques.

Keywords: Covid-19 disinfection robot · Adaptive speed navigation · Path planning · Cuckoo search algorithm · Speed modulation

1 Introduction

Nowadays, mobile robots have been broadly used in many fields, such as medical services, material transportation, household services and exploration. Ultraviolet type-C irradiation (UV-C) disinfection robots and spray disinfection robots have been commonly deployed in hospitals and other public areas [1,2]. Robot path planning and navigation problems can be addressed by defining a path with obstacle avoidance from the robot's starting position to its target position according to certain evaluation criteria in the environment with obstacles.

X.-J. Liu et al. (Eds.): ICIRA 2021, LNAI 13015, pp. 123–134, 2021.
https://doi.org/10.1007/978-3-030-89134-3_12

To maximize the effect of UV-C irradiation disinfection and spray disinfection, Covid-19 disinfection robots are expected to autonomously adjust their speed to decelerate in the vicinity of obstacles, avoid collisions with obstacles, and accelerate in open areas. Many well-established methods have been proposed to resolve robot the navigation issue, such as sampling-based algorithm [3,12], graph-based method [4], learning-based model [5,12], neural networks [6,7], firework algorithm [8], ant colony optimization [9,14], particle swarm optimization [10], genetic algorithms [11], etc.

Chintam *et al.* [3] proposed a sampling-based algorithm framework that extends the rapidly exploring random tree (RRT) algorithm to plan trajectories with obstacle avoidance for mobile robots. A graph theory-based model has been proposed in [4], which decomposes the robot workspace into maps with multiple morphological layer sets so that the self-reconfigurable robot can be successfully navigated to perform a complete coverage task. Moussa *et al.* [5] proposed a learning-based real-time path planning model with virtual magnetic fields. Based on the bio-inspired neural network approach, Yang and Luo [6] proposed an efficient real-time robot coverage path planning model, which enables autonomous robots to avoid obstacles in dynamic environments. Then, Luo *et al.* [7] evolved the neural network approach to real-time multiple mobile intelligent agents formation and navigation.

Based on the optimization and search capabilities of evolutionary algorithms, researchers have recently explored many evolutionary computation approaches to solve robot path planning and navigation problems. For instance, a hybrid fireworks algorithm based on LIDAR-based local navigation algorithm was proposed in [8], which is able to plan reasonable and short trajectories in unstructured environments with obstacle avoidance. Lei *et al.* [9] proposed an ant colony optimization (ACO) combined with a graph representation model to navigate the robot under kinematics constraints. In [10], a couple of improved particle swarm optimization (PSO) algorithms are proposed to resolve local optima issues in basic PSO, which can successfully navigate the autonomous mobile robots in complex environments. Sarkar *et al.* [11] proposed a domain knowledge-based genetic algorithm integrated four operators based on the domain knowledge to search a trajectory with obstacle avoidance from the starting point to single or multiple goals. Some researchers integrate two or three algorithms together for the algorithm of robot navigation. Wang *et al.* [12] developed a novel learning enabled path planning approach Neural RRT*, which combines the convolutional neural network with the sampling-based algorithm RRT*. In [13], a two-layer algorithm based on ACO and tabu search is proposed, which uses a hierarchical and partitioned navigation method for coverage path planning. Chen *et al.* [14] suggested a hybrid structure, ACO-APF, which integrates the ant colony optimization (ACO) mechanism with the artificial potential field (APF) algorithm for unmanned surface vehicles path planning. Luo *et al.* proposed a hybrid approach that integrates the bio-inspired neural network model and a heuristic algorithm for intelligent mobile robot motion planning in an unknown environment.

There are merely a few studies on UV-C disinfection robot navigation. Onsite disinfection robot evaluation has been performed to measure doses of UV-C radiation. Although genetic algorithms (GA) and an adjustable artificial potential field (APF) as path planners were able to maximize the delivered UV-C dose. They can only traverse at a constant speed without considering the vicinity of objects [1]. Conroy *et al.* [2] proposed a waypoint-based Dijkstra path planner for ultraviolet light irradiation Covid-19 disinfection robot using traveling salesman problem (TSP). However, this navigation method fails to effectively cover entire field with a variety of paces. Overall, the above methods consider no robot speed in path planning. In real-world applications, intelligent mobile robots assume to move at variable speeds based on environmental information. The Covid-19 disinfection robot traverses at low speed in the vicinity of obstacles to adequately spray and illuminate around objects, while for efficiency, it should move at high speed in open areas.

An adaptive speed navigation approach of an autonomous Covid-19 disinfection robot in adaptive environment scenarios are developed in cooperation with a cuckoo search algorithm (CSA) in this paper. The smooth and safe trajectory is planned with more reasonable distance away from the obstacles by the proposed segmented cubic $\mathcal{B}$-spline curve-based smoothing paradigm. This paper is organized as follows. Adaptive speed navigation based on cuckoo search algorithms is proposed in Sect. 2. In Sect. 3, a smoothing scheme based on segmented cubic $\mathcal{B}$-spline curve is considered to generate safe and smooth trajectories away from obstacles. An adaptive speed approach is applied to decrease the odometry error and safely navigate the robots in the turning. Afterward, the simulation and comparative studies of cuckoo search algorithm path planning of the Covid-19 disinfection robot in various environments are described in Sect. 4. Finally, important properties of the proposed model are concluded and future work is directed in Sect. 5.

2 Developed Path Planning Algorithm for Disinfection

An improved cuckoo search method is integrated with a local search approach to perform disinfection robot navigation. Utilized the grid representation of the map, the weight of the adjacency matrix between each grid is updated according to environmental information to generate the shortest path.

2.1 Environment Modeling

To achieve a high degree of robustness and autonomy in mobile Covid-19 disinfection robot navigation, environment modeling or map construction enables autonomous robots to generate trajectories with obstacle avoidance. In this paper, we consider 2D navigation in an environment with various obstacles. The grid map is composed of equal sized grid cells. The path planning becomes more accurate as the number of grids in the map increases; nevertheless, as the number of grids increases, the path planning takes more computational efforts. Thus, the grid of the map required for optimal path planning is defined by actual requirements. The environment is modeled as a matrix where element 0 represents open areas and element 1 represents obstacles. Each obstacle or dangerous region is represented as one or more grids, which is expanded based on the grid map as illustrated in Fig. 1. The trajectory is defined as the initial point $\mathcal{S}$, target point $\mathcal{T}$ and n waypoints between them.

$$\mathcal{P} = [\mathcal{S}, wp_1, wp_2, \ldots, wp_n, \mathcal{T}] \tag{1}$$

Each point is defined by its coordinates (x, y) of the grid, and the center of the grid pixel is regarded as the specific point. The sum of the Euclidean distance between two adjacent points on the trajectory is the length of the path:

$$L(\mathcal{P}) = \sum_{i=0}^{n} \sqrt{\left(x_{wp_{i+1}} - x_{wp_i}\right)^2 + \left(y_{wp_{i+1}} - y_{wp_i}\right)^2} \tag{2}$$

where x_{wp_0} denotes the initial point, and $x_{wp_{n+1}}$ depicts the goal.

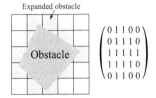

Fig. 1. Grid-based map comprising of grids, each with free or occupied states

2.2   Cuckoo Search Algorithm

The Cuckoo Search algorithm (CSA) is a meta-heuristic swarm-based search algorithm inspired by the breeding behavior of the cuckoos in combination with the Lévy flight phenomenon in some birds and fruit flies [16]. The common cuckoo is an obligate brood parasite; it does not build its own nest, but lays its eggs in the nest of other species, leaving the host bird to take care of its eggs. For simplicity in describing the breeding behavior of cuckoo species, it could be conceptualized as some rules (please refer to [16]).

The Lévy flight pattern can be observed when some animals move and forage normally, accompanied by short-term movements in random directions. The Lévy flight process is essentially a model of random walk that has a power-law step length distribution with a heavy tail [16]. Let N be the population size, which represents the number of search agents in the workspace. Let D be the dimension of the variable, which denotes the number of desired waypoints to be generated in the workspace. A Lévy flight is achieved in Eq. (3) to create a new solution $Q^i(\tau + 1)$.

$$Q^i(\tau + 1) = Q^i(\tau) + \alpha \oplus \text{Lévy}(\mu) \tag{3}$$

where $Q^i(\tau)$ represents the position of the i-th nest at the τ-th iteration, and $Q^i(\tau + 1)$ is the new nest generated by Lévy flight. The $\oplus$ denotes dot product. α is a parameter defined in Eq. (4):

$$\alpha = \alpha_0 \times \left(Q^i(\tau) - Q_{\text{best}} \right) \tag{4}$$

where Q_{best} denotes the global best solution. α_0 is the scale factor, generally taking $\alpha_0 = 0.01$. Lévy denotes the process of the Lévy flight, which could be defined as

$$\text{Lévy}(\mu) = \frac{\eta}{|v|^{\frac{1}{\mu}}} \tag{5}$$

where η and v follow the normal distribution.

$$\eta \sim N\left(0, \sigma_\eta^2\right), \quad v \sim N\left(0, \sigma_v^2\right), \quad \sigma_v = 1$$

$$\sigma_\eta = \left(\frac{\Gamma(1+\mu) \times \sin\left(\frac{\pi \times \mu}{2}\right)}{\Gamma\left(\frac{1+\mu}{2}\right) \times \mu \times 2^{\frac{\mu-1}{2}}} \right)^{\frac{1}{\mu}} \tag{6}$$

where $\mu = 1.5$, Γ denotes the Gamma function. In summary, we can combine the above equations to obtain the final expression of Lévy flight exploitation random walk as follows:

$$Q^i(\tau + 1) = Q^i(\tau) + \alpha_0 \frac{\eta}{|v|^{\frac{1}{\mu}}} \left(Q^i(\tau) - Q_{\text{best}} \right) \tag{7}$$

In the exploration process, there should be a certain rate of random generation of new solutions, which ensures that the system will not fall into a local optimal state and provide fine diversity and exploratory properties in the entire search space. The probability p_a is introduced to abandon the worst nests and construct the new ones at new positions in light of Eq. (8).

$$Q^i(\tau + 1) = \begin{cases} Q^i(\tau) + r\left(Q^j(\tau) - Q^k(\tau)\right), & p < p_a \\ Q^i(\tau), & p \geq p_a \end{cases} \tag{8}$$

where r and p are random variables uniformly distributed over [0,1]; p_a is a parameter that tunes the exploration and the exploitation of CSA ($0 \leq p_a \leq 1$); τ is current iteration number; $Q^j(\tau)$ and $Q^k(\tau)$ are the two randomly selected nest locations in the τ-th iteration.

2.3   Cuckoo Search Algorithm for Robot Path Planning

A trajectory to avoid obstacles while seeking the shortest distance to reduce energy consumption and improve efficiency should be formed. In this paper, we take advantage of the fast convergence characteristics of the CSA, combined with the local search process to rapidly search the shortest trajectory in the simplified grid map. Among them, the first step to find the optimal trajectory is to eliminate the infeasible trajectory with obstacle collision. In order to improve the performance of finding the best trajectory through the CSA algorithm, we first gradually construct a trajectory based on the random points generated by the algorithm (all in free space, outside the obstacle).

Dijkstra's algorithm is utilized to find the shortest trajectory in the graph. The trajectory is established from the starting point S, and the next path point is selected from the points randomly generated by N. For selected points, the same process will be performed until the final goal is reached. When the connecting line passes through obstacles, we set it as an infeasible solution. By setting the distance between impassable nodes to infinite, the feasible solution is obtained, thereby generating the shortest trajectory. The advantage of the local search process used is that it can filter out the infeasibility between nodes, and the optimized path points obtained by the CSA algorithm can quickly generate the final trajectory. Through the algorithm of CSA, we obtain the waypoints in the map. Set the number D as the number of the generated waypoints, which is also the number of dimensions in the CSA algorithm. However, at the same time, it will consume more running time. Take advantage of local search based on Dijkstra's algorithm, our improved CSA algorithm can obtain a collision-free path accurately and efficiently. The algorithm of the CSA is identified in Algorithm 1.

Algorithm 1: Pseudo-code of Cuckoo Search Algorithm (CSA)

Parameter Initialization
Initialize the size of population N, the probability of replacing p_a, maximum iteration time T_{max}
Population Initialization
Provide N initial solutions in the workspace
Initialize the solution generated by Dijkstra Algorithm in the workspace
Evaluate the fitness value for all initial nodes
for $\tau = 1 : T_{max}$ **do**
    for $i = 1 : N$ **do**
        Generate new solution $Q^i(\tau + 1)$ via Lévy flight based on Eq. (7);
        Evaluate its fitness value $f(P^i(t + 1))$;
        if $f(Q^i(\tau + 1)) < f(Q^i(\tau))$ **then**
            | Replace $Q^i(\tau)$ by the new solution $Q^i(\tau + 1)$;
        end
    end
    Replace the worst nodes with a probability p_a with new ones in light of Eq. (8);
    Maintain the best solutions;
    Rank the solutions and find the current best;
end
Return the best solution and optimal fitness value;

---

3 Path Smoother with Adaptive Speed Robot Navigation

3.1 Segmented Cubic $\mathcal{B}$-spline Path Smoother

The smoothing scheme is utilized to smooth the trajectory in the vicinity of the turning point near the obstacles [17]. Unlike the traditional $\mathcal{B}$-spline curve, the segmented $\mathcal{B}$-spline curve merely smooths the trajectory at each corner separately. At the same time, the smoothed trajectory achieves continuous curvature to ensure that the disinfection robot reaches a precise trajectory and a smooth steering command for the robots. Therefore, a segmented cubic $\mathcal{B}$-spline curve is proposed to smooth the path.

A $\mathcal{B}$-spline curve can be represented by fundamental functions $\mathcal{N}_{i,k}(u)$, control points $\mathcal{P}_i$ and degree $(k-1)$, the equation is defined as

$$C(u) = \sum_{i=1}^{n+1} \mathcal{N}_{i,k}(u)\mathcal{P}_i \tag{9}$$

where $\mathcal{P}_i = [\mathcal{P}_{ix}, \mathcal{P}_{iy}]$ are the (n + 1) control points and a knot vector u. $\mathcal{N}_{i,k}(u)$ are the fundamental functions defined recursively:

$$\mathcal{N}_{i,k}(u) = \frac{(u - x_i)}{x_{i+k-1} - x_i}\mathcal{N}_{i,k-1}(u) + \frac{(x_{i+k} - u)}{x_{i+k} - x_{i+1}}\mathcal{N}_{i+1,k-1}(u) \tag{10}$$

$$\mathcal{N}_{i,k}(u) = \begin{cases} 1, \ u_i \le u \le u_{i+1} \\ 0, \quad \text{otherwise} \end{cases} ; u \in [0,1] \tag{11}$$

where with the limitation condition of the $0/0 = 0$ for $k = 1$. The illustration of the G^2 $\mathcal{B}$-spline curve is shown in Fig. 2.

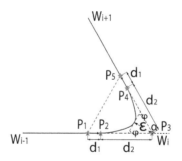

Fig. 2. Illustration of the G^2 $\mathcal{B}$-spline curve

To adapt to the parameterization difference, in the curve smoothing process, we use geometric continuity to evaluate the trajectory smoothness. G^2 continuity is a curve smoothing criteria based on the disinfection robot's kinematic. It can make an identical curvature vector and tangent unit at the intersection of two consecutive segments, avoiding the discontinuity of normal acceleration and result in a safe trajectory. Higher levels of continuity require more calculation resources, and the cubic $\mathcal{B}$-spline curve we utilized in this paper is due to the lowest degree of G^2 continuity. To make our smoothing method not affect the overall path trajectory, we insert a $\mathcal{B}$-spline curve into the existing straight trajectory and realize the continuity of G^2. In the smoothing process, the control points $\mathcal{P}_i$ of of $\mathcal{B}$-spline curve relative to the path point W_i is defined as

$$\mathcal{P}_1 = W_i - (1+c)d_2 u_{i-1}$$
$$\mathcal{P}_2 = W_i - d_2 u_{i-1}$$
$$\mathcal{P}_3 = W_i \qquad\qquad (12)$$
$$\mathcal{P}_4 = W_i + d_2 u_i$$
$$\mathcal{P}_5 = W_i + (1+c)d_2 u_i$$

where c is smoothing length ratio $c = d_1/d_2$, u_{i-1} is the unit vector of line $W_{i-1}W_i$ and v_i is the unit vector of line $W_i W_{i+1}$. The sum of d_1 and d_2 is the smoothing length. $\phi = \alpha/2$ is half of the corner angle. If knot vector $[0,0,0,0,0.5,1,1,1,1]$ is defined, the smoothing error distance ε and the maximum curvature K_{max} of smooth trajectory may be obtained analytically as

$$\varepsilon = \frac{d_2 \sin(\varphi)}{2} \qquad\qquad (13)$$

$$K_{\max} = \frac{4\sin(\varphi)}{3d_2 \cos^2(\varphi)} \qquad\qquad (14)$$

From (13) and (14), the smoothing error distance ε is defined by the existing maximum curvature K_{max} provided by the disinfection robots:

$$\varepsilon = \frac{d_2 \sin(\varphi)}{2} \qquad\qquad (15)$$

3.2   Adaptive Speed Navigation

Adaptive speed navigation is designed to drive the disinfection robot at variable speeds to adapt to the surrounding environments. When the robot is approaching obstacles, especially when making a turn, it is better for the robot to slow down for precise navigation to avoid an accumulation of odometry errors due to instrument errors. In our model, the disinfection robot moves at a faster speed in an open area and slowly moves near an obstacle. Once the obstacle area (such

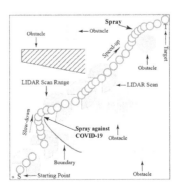

Fig. 3. Illustration of adaptive speed robot navigation

as the red border of the obstacle) is sensed by on-board LIDAR, the disinfection robot will decrement its speed near the obstacle (see Fig. 3). In the global path planning, when the robot enters the turning path generated by the path smoother, it starts to decelerate. The deceleration point adjusted during the turn is $\mathcal{P}_1$ in Fig. 2, and it continues to return to the original speed at $\mathcal{P}_5$.

4   Simulation and Comparative Studies

In order to validate our developed real-time adaptive speed-based CSA model, we compare our CSA method with other typical algorithms, multiple maps are used to carry out the simulation and comparative studies of the Covid-19 disinfection robot navigation.

Table 1. Comparison of trajectory length and number of turns

Methods	Minimum length	Increase of length (%)	Number of turns	Difference of turns (%)
Proposed CSA model	27.6709	———	5	———
SA-PSO [10]	28.7831	3.86	9	44.44
NLI-PSO [10]	30.3623	8.86	10	50.00
Basic PSO [10]	32.0153	13.57	13	61.53

4.1   Comparison of Our Adaptive Speed Algorithm with PSO Model

The developed cuckoo search algorithm associated with adaptive speed path smoother is used to compare with PSO algorithm, nonlinear inertia weight PSO (NLI-PSO) and simulated annealing PSO (SA-PSO) approaches, respectively. As we are aware, Nie *et al.* [10] suggested a hybrid PSO method to solve the issue of robot motion planning. However, their model has not yet considered the tuning curve and speed modulation in need of intelligent robot navigation systems. In this section, a comparative study is conducted to validate the effectiveness of the developed algorithm. The minimum trajectory length and number of turns of our model and others are compared as follows. The test scenario is based on Fig. 6 of [10], which is shown in Fig. 4 in this paper. The size of the workspace with a grid map is 20×20. The trajectory length generated by the proposed CSA model is 27.6709. The computed trajectory lengths for the trajectories in [10] and the produced values were 32.0153, 30.3623 and 28.7831 by PSO, nonlinear inertia weight PSO and simulated annealing PSO algorithms, respectively. The developed CSA algorithm found 13.57% less than PSO, 8.86% less than NLI-PSO and 3.86% less than SA-PSO, respectively. The number of turns of the developed CSA algorithm is 61.53% better than basic PSO, 50.00% less than NLI-PSO and 44.44% less than SA-PSO, respectively (Table 1). Then the segmented cubic $\mathcal{B}$-spline path smoother is used to the proposed CSA model. The different smooth trajectory obtained based on the constraints of the robot is illustrated in Fig. 5. The adaptive speed navigation is performed to slow down the robot in the dark red area as shown in Fig. 5.

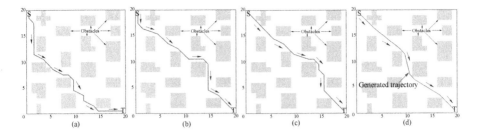

Fig. 4. Illustration of a variety of methods of navigation. (a) Basic PSO model [10]; (b) Nonlinear inertia weight PSO model (NLI-PSO) [10]; (c) Simulated annealing PSO model (SA-PSO) [10]; (d) The proposed CSA model.

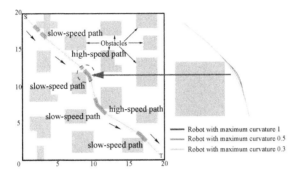

Fig. 5. Simulation results of the adaptive speed navigation with different robot tuning curvature constraint based on segmented cubic $\mathcal{B}$-spline path smoother. The light green represents the high speed areas whereas dark red represents the slow down areas. (Color figure online)

4.2   Comparison of the Proposed Adaptive Speed Model with Various Algorithms

We then apply the proposed model to room-like test scenarios. The shorter trajectory is generated by our CSA model in comparison with other commonly used path planning algorithms, Probabilistic Road Map (PRM), Rapidly exploring Random Tree* (RRT*) and Q-learning approaches as shown in Fig. 6(a). The path distance generated by our CSA model is 4.04% less than the PRM model, 5.97% less than the RRT* and 8.42% less than the Q-learning method, respectively. The number of turns of developed CSA approach is 15.38% better than the PRM, 76.08% less than RRT* and 8.33% less than Q-learning method, respectively. In Table 2, we observe that our model outperforms others in terms of path length and number of turns. We have the significant feature of adaptive speed navigation. In the vicinity of obstacles, the disinfection robots operate at a slow speed to adapt environment with the placement of obstacles, while the robot operates at high speed in free space as shown in Fig. 6(b).

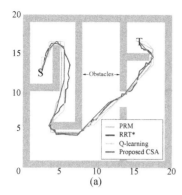 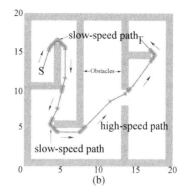

(a)   (b)

Fig. 6. (a) Comparison of disinfection robot navigation with various models. (b) Result of the adaptive speed navigation based on segmented cubic $\mathcal{B}$-spline path smoother.

Table 2. Comparison of trajectory length and number of turns

Methods	Minimum length	Increase of length	Number of turns	Difference of turns
Proposed CSA model	37.8997	———	11	———
PRM	39.4963	4.04%	13	15.38%
RRT*	40.3049	5.97%	46	76.08%
Q-learning	41.3848	8.42%	12	8.33%

5 Conclusion

In this paper, we have developed an efficient adaptive speed CSA algorithm. The proposed method combines a cuckoo search algorithm with a local search method based on a 2D grid-based map. For the process of approaching obstacles and turning, the smoothing scheme in light of segmented cubic $\mathcal{B}$-spline curve integrated with the method of adaptive speed navigation, so that the Covid-19 disinfection robot can plan a safer and smoother trajectory at a reasonable distance from objects and obstacles while safely and adaptively navigating the autonomous Covid-19 disinfection robot. Simulation and comparative studies have proved the efficiency and robustness of the developed CSA method.

References

1. Tiseni, L., Chiaradia, D., Gabardi, M., Solazzi, M., Leonardis, D., Frisoli, A.: UV-C mobile robots with optimized path planning: algorithm design and on-field measurements to improve surface disinfection against SARS-CoV-2. IEEE Robot. Autom. Mag. **28**(1), 59–70 (2021)
2. Conroy, J., et al.: Robot development and path planning for indoor ultraviolet light disinfection. arXiv preprint arXiv:2104.02913 (2021)
3. Chintam, P., Luo, C., Liu, L.: Advised RRT*: an optimal sampling space enabled bi-directional RRT*. Technical report, IEEE Robotics and Automation Letters (RA-L) (submitted)

4. Cheng, K.P., Mohan, R.E., Nhan, N.H.K., Le, A.V.: Graph theory-based approach to accomplish complete coverage path planning tasks for reconfigurable robots. IEEE Access **7**, 94642–94657 (2019)
5. Moussa, M., Beltrame, G.: Real-time path planning with virtual magnetic fields. IEEE Robot. Autom. Lett. **6**(2), 3279–3286 (2021)
6. Yang, S.X., Luo, C.: A neural network approach to complete coverage path planning. IEEE Trans. Syst. Man Cybern. Part B **34**(1), 718–725 (2004)
7. Luo, C., Yang, S.X., Li, X., Meng, M.Q.-H.: Neural dynamics driven complete area coverage navigation through cooperation of multiple mobile robots. IEEE Trans. Industr. Electron. **64**(1), 750–760 (2017)
8. Lei, T., Luo, C., Ball, J.E., Bi, Z.: A hybrid fireworks algorithm to navigation and mapping. In: Handbook of Research on Fireworks Algorithms and Swarm Intelligence, pp. 213–232. IGI Global (2019)
9. Lei, T., Luo, C., Ball, J.E., Rahimi, S.: A graph-based ant-like approach to optimal path planning. In: 2020 IEEE Congress on Evolutionary Computation, vol. 1, no. 6 (2020)
10. Nie, Z., Yang, X., Gao, S., Zheng, Y., Wang, J., Wang, Z.: Research on autonomous moving robot path planning based on improved particle swarm optimization. In: 2016 IEEE Congress on Evolutionary Computation, CEC, pp. 2532–2536 (2016)
11. Sarkar, R., Barman, D., Chowdhury, N.: Domain knowledge based genetic algorithms for mobile robot path planning having single and multiple targets. J. King Saud Univ. Comput. Inf. Sci. (2020)
12. Wang, J., Chi, W., Li, C., Wang, C., Meng, M.Q.-H.: Neural RRT*: learning-based optimal path planning. IEEE Trans. Autom. Sci. Eng. **17**(4), 1748–1758 (2020)
13. Wang, J., Chen, J., Cheng, S., Xie, Y.: Double heuristic optimization based on hierarchical partitioning for coverage path planning of robot mowers. In: 12th International Conference on Computational Intelligence and Security, pp. 186–189 (2016)
14. Chen, Y., Bai, G., Zhan, Y., Hu, X., Liu, J.: Path planning and obstacle avoiding of the USV based on improved ACO-APF hybrid algorithm with adaptive early-warning. IEEE Access **9**, 40728–40742 (2021)
15. Luo, C., Yang, S.X., Krishnan, M., Paulik, M.: An effective vector-driven biologically motivated neural network algorithm to real-time autonomous robot navigation. In: IEEE International Conference on Robotics and Automation, pp. 4094–4099 (2014)
16. Yang, X.S., Deb, S.: Cuckoo search via Lévy flights. In: 2009 World Congress on Nature and Biologically Inspired Computing (NaBIC), pp. 210–214 (2009)
17. Farin, G., Rein, G., Sapidis, N., Worsey, A.J.: Fairing cubic B-spline curves. Comput. Aided Geom. Des. **4**(1–2), 91–103 (1987)
18. Huang, Y., Wang, P., Yuan, M., Jiang, M.: Path planning of mobile robots based on logarithmic function adaptive artificial fish swarm algorithm. In: 2017 36th Chinese Control Conference (CCC), pp. 4819–4823 (2017)

A Master-Slave Robotic System for Transurethral Surgery

Guo Zheng, Xingwei Zhao, Teru Chen, and Bo Tao[✉]

School of Mechanical Science and Engineering, Huazhong University of Science and Technology, Wuhan 430074, China
taobo@mail.hust.edu.cn

Abstract. Transurethral prostatectomy surgical robot is the frontier field in surgical robot, which combines the traditional Transurethral Resection Prostate (TURP) and burgeoning Robot-assisted Minimally Invasive Surgery (RMIS). It can overcome the existing problems and effectively improve the efficiency and treatment of operation. In this regard, a master-slave robotic system is proposed to assist the surgeon to complete the transurethral surgery better in this paper. The Touch Haptic Device is employed to serve as master device, and an active algorithm based on the serial 6 DOFs robot is developed to realize Remote Center of Motion (RCM) which is the basic requirement of minimally invasive surgery. A series of vitro experiments are conducted to test the validity of the system and assess the trajectory accuracy of excision. The experiments results expresses that the accuracy is below 0.6 mm which satisfies the requirements of transurethral surgery.

Keywords: Surgical robot · Master-slave robotic system · Motion planning · RCM algorithm

1 Introduction

Transurethral Resection Prostate (TURP) and Transurethral Resection of Bladder Tumor (TURBT) are the classic transurethral surgery in clinic, which are internationally recognized as the gold standard for the treatment of Benign Prostatic Hyperplasia (BPH) and Non-muscle Invasive Bladder Cancer (NMIBC) [1]. However, TURP and TURBT still face the following problems: 1) The operation space is small and the operation skill level requirement is high; 2) Narrow vision and poor visibility bring extra mental burden to doctors; 3) Physical shaking of the doctor's hand will increase the risk of intraoperative bleeding; 4) The doctor will be contaminated by splashing blood and urine when operating on the affected side. In addition, in order to reduce the complications and shorten the operation time, the surgery request proficient surgical skills and rich operation experience for doctors, which means the period for training is a long time. The prognosis of the operation depends heavily on the doctor's personal operation level [2]. These problems all bring difficulties and challenges to transurethral surgery.

© Springer Nature Switzerland AG 2021
X.-J. Liu et al. (Eds.): ICIRA 2021, LNAI 13015, pp. 135–144, 2021.
https://doi.org/10.1007/978-3-030-89134-3_13

With the development of medical surgical robot technology, Robot-assisted Minimally Invasive Surgery (RMIS) provides feasible solutions to these problems. The research of transurethral prostatectomy surgical robot, which combines RMIS and TURP, has been carried out for decades. Early Davis et al. [3] attempt BPH surgery by transurethral surgical robot. The robot employs common series manipulator which is controlled by computer instruction and the resectoscope is attached to the end of robot. However, limited to the development of robot technology, the robot just stayed in the early prototype. de Badajoz et al. [4] reported a master-slave robot system to control a commercial rigid resectoscope. Goldman et al. [5] introduced an inside dexterous continuum arm with access channels for the parallel deployment of surgical instruments which adopts master-slave control mode and successfully carried out in vivo experiments on pigs. Hendrick et al. [6] proposed a multi-arm, hand-held robotic system which provides the surgeon with two concentric tube manipulators that can aim the laser and manipulate tissue simultaneously, and successfully completed vitro cadaveric experiments in 2016. Sun Y H et al. [7] presented a transurethral surgical robot based on flexible continuum manipulator. Wang et al. [8] developed a master-slave robotic system for transurethral resection which is composed by a user console and a slave robot. the slave robot performs the surgery conveniently by means of surgical vision and intuitive human-robot interaction interface provided by the console and they finished the prostatectomy experiments in living pigs and upgraded the system later.

In spite of the research of transurethral prostatectomy surgical robot started early, the related achievements are not rich. There are still some shortcomings in the dexterity and accuracy of transurethral prostatectomy surgical robot. Prostatectomy requires that the position error of the manipulator end should be less than 1 mm, the operation end error should be less than 0.6 mm and the delay of operation should be below 330 ms [2]. Motivated by the objective of increasing dexterity and accuracy of the surgery, this paper presents a mater-slave robotic system for BPH surgery, which uses flexible interactive equipment with high precision and active RCM algorithm.

2 System Overview

The proposed master-slave robotic system is displayed in Fig. 1 (a) The robot is set on the fixed platform, which consists of a commercial resectoscope, an endoscope, a 6 DOFs (degrees of freedom) serial robot arm, and an end-effector to hold and control the resectoscope. The master devices include a laptop workstation to receive, process and send data and display the view of resectoscope end from endoscope, a Touch Haptic Device as the interactive device to control the resectoscope. The endoscope and the resectoscope are assembled together. The resectoscope is fixed with the end of the robot through support frame of the end-effector and the central axis of the resectoscope and z axis of the robot end coordinate system are coaxial. The Touch Haptic Device is employed

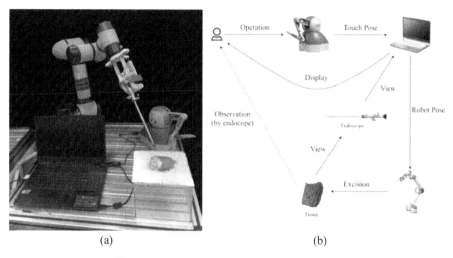

Fig. 1. (a) System overview; (b) Control scheme.

to control the motion of the robot arm and execute the cutting operation remotely. The pose data from the Touch Haptic Device is processed by the workstation to obtain the desired pose of the resectoscope, and then is sent to the robot arm to execute. The control scheme is shown in Fig. 1 (b).

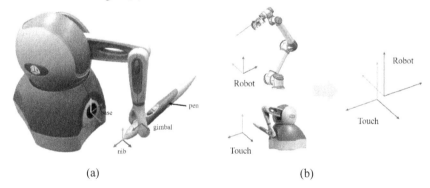

Fig. 2. (a) The Touch Haptic Device and its coordinate systems; (b) The coordinate system of Touch and robot. (red, green and blue arrows are X, Y, Z axes respectively) (Color figure online)

3   Acquisition of Target Trajectory from TOUCH

3.1   Acquisition of Nib Coordinates

The Touch Haptic Device is shown in Fig. 2 (a). Touch provides a variety of interfaces for obtaining the descriptions of the gimbal coordinate system, which includes positions, angles and pose matrix etc. However, it is more convenient to control robot with the nib, since it is more suitable for people's usage habits. But coordinates of nib aren't given directly. So coordinates of nib need to be calculated in the other way.

Matrix T is used to describe the transformation between the gimbal coordinate system and the Touch base coordinate system, which can be arranged as:

$$T = T_{gimbal}^{base} = \begin{bmatrix} n_g & o_g & a_g & p_g \\ 0 & 0 & 0 & 1 \end{bmatrix}. \tag{1}$$

Where, n_g, o_g, a_g represent the direction vector of X, Y, Z axes of the gimbal coordinate system in the Touch base coordinate respectively. p_g is the origin position of the gimbal coordinate system.

Actually, the position instead of the direction of the nib coordinate is required, hence it is uninfluential for the nib coordinate system to share the same direction with the base coordinate system. Then the description of nib in the base can be written as

$$T_{nib}^{base} = \begin{bmatrix} n_n & o_n & a_n & p_n \\ 0 & 0 & 0 & 1 \end{bmatrix}. \tag{2}$$

Where $n_n = n_g, o_n = o_g, a_n = a_g$. p_n is the coordinates of nib, and it is noticed that the origin of nib coordinate system is on the Z-axis of the gimbal coordinate system, which means:

$$p_n = p_g + d * (-a_g) \tag{3}$$

If nib is fixed, gimbal will move on the sphere with the center nib and radius d. Move pen arbitrarily and acquire a couple of p and a, which is able to get the fitted value of d using the least square method.

3.2 Map of Pose

After obtaining the nib coordinates p_n, it needs to be mapped into the robot work coordinate system. To achieve that, the rotation relationship between the Touch base coordinate system and the robot work coordinate is needed, which can be described as rotation matrix R_{Robot}^{Touch}. In the same space, the pose of the two coordinate systems is shown in Fig. 2 (b). According to the corresponding relation of rotation matrix, it can be given directly:

$$R_{Robot}^{Touch} = \begin{bmatrix} 0 & -1 & 0 \\ 0 & 0 & 1 \\ -1 & 0 & 0 \end{bmatrix} \tag{4}$$

It is noticed that the zero point of the Touch base coordinate system needs a corresponding point in the robot work coordinate system as the start point of robot, which is names as p_{R0} and is given according to the actual need of operate.

Each time the nib coordinates p_n is obtained, add them to the starting point as the target point p_t after multiplying R_t^n and a scaling factor k which is used to ensure the scope of operate. In other words, the target point p_t will be expressed as:

$$p_t = p_{R0} + kR_{Robot}^{Touch}p_n \tag{5}$$

where p_t is the target point in the robot work coordinate system, p_{R0} is the starting point, and k is the scaling factor.

Through the formula (3), the way to obtain the target point is figured out. However, in addition to the coordinate degrees of freedom, the resectoscope also needs to rotate around the central axis. The Touch Haptic Device directly provides the software interface for developers to obtain the rotation angle of pen, so we map it as the rotation angle of the resectoscope after multiplying a scaling factor η. The relationship can be described as:

$$\theta_t = \eta\theta_n \tag{6}$$

where θ_t is the target rotation angle of the resectoscope, θ_n is the rotation angle of pen, and η is the scaling factor.

4   Active Control Algorithm for Remote Center of Motion

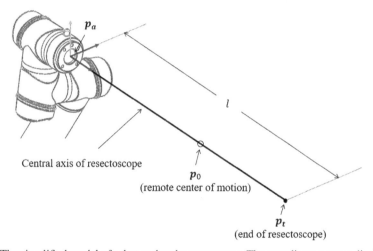

Fig. 3. The simplified model of robot end and resectoscope. The coordinate system displayed in figure is the robot end coordinate system.

Remote Center of Motion (RCM) is the basic requirement of minimally invasive surgery, which also applies to transurethral surgery. In this paper, the active control algorithm is adopted to realize the motion.

The simplified model of robot end and resectoscope are indicated in Fig. 3. It is noticed that the coordinates in this section are all described in the robot work coordinate system. In order to realize the active RCM motion, the length between the end of robot arm and the end of the resectoscope (i.e., l), which can be obtained by actual measurement, and the coordinates of remote motion center (i.e., p_0), which is given by the actual need is both required. Based on p_t, p_0, l, the pose of the robot can be Derived.

The end of the robot arm, the remote motion center and the target point are in the same line. So there is:

$$\frac{p_t - p_0}{\|p_t - p_0\|} = \frac{p_0 - p_a}{\|p_0 - p_a\|}. \tag{7}$$

Accordingly, l can be expressed as:

$$l = \|p_t - p_a\| = \|p_t - p_0\| + \|p_0 - p_a\|. \tag{8}$$

Thus:

$$\|p_0 - p_a\| = l - \|p_t - p_0\|. \tag{9}$$

Substituting (9) into (7) leads to:

$$\frac{p_t - p_0}{\|p_t - p_0\|} = \frac{p_0 - p_a}{l - \|p_t - p_0\|}. \tag{10}$$

It can be rearranged as:

$$p_a = p_t - \frac{p_t - p_0}{\|p_t - p_0\|} * l. \tag{11}$$

Where p_a is the coordinates of the end of the robot arm, p_t is the coordinates of the target point, p_0 is the coordinates of remote motion center, and l is the length between the end of robot arm and the end of resectoscope. In fact, p_a is just the coordinates of the origin of the robot arm end coordinate system.

In order to control the robot, the pose of the end of the robot is also needed, which is represented by rotation matrix R. Furthermore, R describe the rotation relationship between the robot work coordinate system and the robot end coordinate system. It doesn't matter whether determining the direction of the X and Y axes of the end because the resectoscope and the Z-axis of the end are coaxial, which means it only affects the angle of the sixth axis and it is appropriate to take θ_t directly as the angle of the sixth axis after getting the angle of each joint of the robot arm to eliminate its impact. R can be obtained by the equivalent rotation axis. the Z-axis of the end can be written as:

$$v_{z-end}^{work} = \frac{p_t - p_0}{\|p_t - p_0\|}. \tag{12}$$

The Z-axis of the RWCS can be written as:

$$v_{z-work}^{work} = [0, 0, 1]^T. \tag{13}$$

So the equivalent rotation axis is:

$$k' = v_{z-end}^{work} \times v_{z-work}^{work} = [k_x', k_y', k_z']^T. \tag{14}$$

Since (13) and properties of cross product, $k_z = 0$, and normalize k' so there is:

$$k = v_{z-end}^{work} \times v_{z-work}^{work} = [k_x, k_y, 0]^T. \tag{15}$$

Where $k_x = k_x'/\|k'\|$, $k_y = k_y'/\|k'\|$. And the equivalent rotation angles is:

$$\alpha = \cos\langle v_{z-end}^{work}, v_{z-work}^{work}\rangle. \tag{16}$$

According to the transformation relationship between the equivalent rotation axis and the rotation matrix, we have:

$$R = R(k, \alpha) = \begin{bmatrix} k_x k_x Ver\alpha + c\alpha & k_x k_y Ver\alpha & k_y s\alpha \\ k_x k_y Ver\alpha & k_y k_y Ver\alpha + c\alpha & -k_x s\alpha \\ -k_y s\alpha & k_x s\alpha & c\alpha \end{bmatrix} \tag{17}$$

Where $c\alpha = \cos\alpha$, $Ver\alpha = 1 - \cos\alpha$, $s\alpha = \sin\alpha$.

After obtaining p_a and R, the end homogeneous transformation matrix T can be expressed as:

$$T = \begin{bmatrix} R & p_a \\ 0 & 1 \end{bmatrix}. \tag{18}$$

Based on T, each joint angles of the robot arm can be calculated, which means:

$$q = k^{-1}(T). \tag{19}$$

Where $q = [\theta_1, \theta_2, \theta_3, \theta_4, \theta_5, \theta_6]$, which are the angles corresponding to six joint angles. T is the end homogeneous transformation matrix. Last, replace θ_6 with θ_t, we have:

$$q_t = [\theta_1, \theta_2, \theta_3, \theta_4, \theta_5, \theta_t] \tag{20}$$

q_t is what the results needed to control the robot, which can be sent to the robot directly to execute. When inputting continuous target points and target rotation angles, the algorithm can calculate continuous six axis angles to realize active RCM.

5 Experiments

This paper uses experiments to verify the validity of the system and provides the assessment of the trajectory accuracy of excision in the cutting experiments on pork tissue. It is noticed that the position and pose of the robot end can be acquired from the software interface of the robot and the validity which means whether the remote center is existed and the resectoscope does move around the center can be confirmed from that. In the simulation, operator controls the robot to move along a specific track, and meanwhile poses and positions of robot end are recorded. Combined the constant length of resectoscope, the actual resectoscope track can be calculated point by pretty point and the consequence is displayed in Fig. 4. As the figure indicates, the remote center is actually existed and is close to the theoretical remote center, and the calculated track of resectoscope is nearly coincident to target track, which proves the RCM algorithm meets expectation of system and the robotic system is viable.

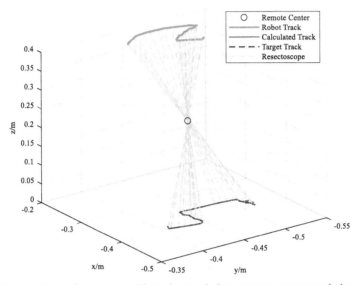

Fig. 4. The trajectory of each part. There is an obvious remote center and the calculated resectoscope track is coincident to the target track.

An experiment was also conducted to assess the trajectory accuracy in excision. In the vitro simulated excision experiments, operator controls the robot to cut the pork tissue with the view provided by the endoscope attached to the resectoscope and the track data are recorded meanwhile. On account of the cutting track is the object of analysis, trajectory data unrelated to excision are removed. The track data and the effects after excision are displayed in Fig. 5. There are three tracks, which includes two line-like and one annular score and numbered as No.1, 2, 3. Because the number of collected points of target trajectory is not consistent with that of actual trajectory, there is no way to get the error point by point. Instead based on the target trajectory point, the nearest actual point is searched and their Euclidean distance is calculated as the error, which can be described as:

$$e_i = \min_{j=1...n} \left(dist\left(t_i, a_j\right)\right)(i = 1 \ldots m, m < n) \tag{21}$$

Where t_i, e_i is coordinates and error of the target point numbered i respectively. a_j is coordinates of the resectoscope end point numbered j. m and n is the number of target points and end points of resectoscope. By this way, the error of each target point can be calculated in turn. The errors of each score are indicated in Fig. 6. The errors of trajectory No.1 and No.3 are not above 0.6 mm, and the errors of trajectory are not above 0.5 mm. The accuracy of excision satisfies the requirements of transurethral surgery.

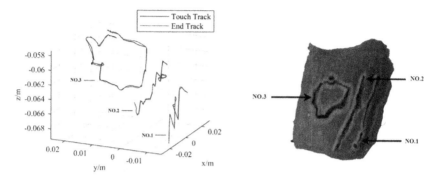

Fig. 5. Touch track (*i.e.,* target track), end track of resectoscope and the effects after excision. The recorded trajectory is coincident to actual effects of excision.

Fig. 6. The errors of three tracks. The errors of each track are no more than 0.6 mm, which completely satisfies the requirements of transurethral surgery.

Additionally, the delay of the operate system is simply assessed. The system delay mainly comes from two parts and one is robot motion delay, the other is program running delay. The motion delay of robot depends on maximum acceleration of robot and the program running delay is below 50ms according to experimental measurement, which meet the requirements of surgery.

6 Conclusion

This paper has proposed a master-slave robotic system to assist the surgeon to complete the transurethral surgery better and surgeon can handle the robot to complete excision with the surgical view provided by the endoscope. In order to make the operation more convenient and flexible, the Touch Haptic Device is employed to serve as the master device. The nib coordinates which the system uses as reference of resectoscope end, aren't provided by the Touch directly so the method to obtain the nib coordinates and map it to the robot work space is presented as well.

Matching with the interactive device, an active control algorithm to realize RCM motion based on the serial 6 DOFs robot arm is developed. The algorithm can calculate the pose of robot by length and target rotation angles of resectoscope, coordinates of target point and remote center. The pose is then executed by the robot to realize the RCM motion. A series of experiments are carried out to verify the validity of system and assess accuracy and delay of trajectories. The results indicate that the system is viable and the accuracy and delay satisfies the requirements of transurethral surgery.

The mater-slave robotic system has great application value in the field of transurethral prostatectomy surgical robot, which can assist surgeons to overcome a couple of problems such as narrow vision and poor visibility etc. and complete the surgery with better treatment. Additionally, other issues such as higher accuracy in excision and lower delay of operation should be taken into account in future research.

References

1. Yanqun, N., Zhangqun, Y., Guang, S.: Guidelines for the Diagnosis and Treatment of Urological Diseases in China. People's Medical Publishing House, Beijing (2014)
2. Sun, Z., Wang, T., Wang, J., Zhang, X.: Advances and key techniques of transurethral surgical robot. Robot **42**(06), 716–733 (2020)
3. Davies, B.L., et al.: A surgeon robot prostatectomy–a laboratory evaluation. J. Med. Eng. Technol. **13**(6), 273–277 (1989)
4. Sánchez de Badajoz Chamorro, E., Jiménez Garrido, A., García Vacas, F., et al.: Nuevo brazo maestro para la resección transuretral mediante robot. Archivos Españoles de Urología, **55**(10), 1247–1250 (2002)
5. Goldman, R.E., et al.: Design and performance evaluation of a minimally invasive telerobotic platform for transurethral surveillance and intervention. IEEE Trans. Bio-Med. Eng. **60**(4), 918–925 (2013)
6. Hendrick, R.J., Herrell, S.D., Webster, R.J.: A multi-arm hand-held robotic system for transurethral laser prostate surgery. In: 2014 IEEE International Conference on Robotics and Automation (ICRA), pp. 2850–2855. IEEE (2014)
7. Sun, Y.H., Xu, K., Zhao, J.R., et al.: Transurethral surgical robot and control system, China: CN106510848A. 2017-03-22
8. Wang, J., Zhao, J., Ji, X., Zhang, X., Li, H.: A surgical robotic system for transurethral resection. In: Lhotska, L., Sukupova, L., Lacković, I., Ibbott, G.S. (eds.) World Congress on Medical Physics and Biomedical Engineering 2018, pp. 711–716. Springer Singapore, Singapore (2019). https://doi.org/10.1007/978-981-10-9023-3_129

Analysis of Dynamic Friction and Elongation Characteristics of the Tendon Sheath System

Tao Zhang[1] ⬤, Mingyue Liu[1], Yanqiang Lei[2,3], Fuxin Du[1,2,3](✉), Rui Song[2,3], and YiBin Li[2,3]

[1] School of Mechanical Engineering, Shandong University, Jinan, China
dufuxin@sdu.edu.cn
[2] School of Control Science and Engineering, Shandong University, Jinan, China
[3] Engineering Research Center of Intelligent Unmanned System, Ministry of Education, Jinan, China

Abstract. The manipulator system of the robot for natural orifice transluminal endoscopic surgery (NOTES) consists of two parts: The tendon sheath system and the continuum manipulator. The continuum manipulator is connected with the driving element by the tendon sheath system. However, the continuum manipulator is so small that a tiny error in the position of the tendon which drives the continuum manipulator can cause a huge change in its shape. This is contradictory to the characteristics of high friction loss and high position error of the tendon sheath system. Therefore, it is necessary to analyze the nonlinear friction force of the tendon sheath system and construct its elongation model. In this paper, the Stribeck friction model and Hooke's law were used to study the hysteresis characteristics of the driving tendon. And a novel friction model is proposed which can accurately describe the tension distribution and elongation of the driving tendon in the sheath at different velocities. The simulation results show that the friction and the position error during the reciprocating motion of the tendon sheath system can be accurately described by the proposed friction model.

Keywords: Surgical robot · Tendon sheath system · Nonlinear friction · Hysteresis

1 Introduction

In the course of clinical operation, the size of the wound is closely related to the patient's postoperative recovery and the occurrence of surgical complications. To minimize surgical wounds and ensure the patient's safety, minimally invasive surgery has been greatly

This work was supported in part by The National Key Research and Development Program of China under Grant 2018YFB1307700, in part by the China Postdoctoral Science Foundation funded project under Grant 2019M662346, in part by the Fundamental Research Funds for the Central Universities, in part by the Intelligent Robots and Systems High-precision Innovation Center Open Fund under Grant 2019IRS06, and in part by postdoctoral innovation project of Shandong Province under Grant 238226.

X.-J. Liu et al. (Eds.): ICIRA 2021, LNAI 13015, pp. 145–154, 2021.
https://doi.org/10.1007/978-3-030-89134-3_14

developed, and the Da Vinci surgical robot used in laparoscopic surgery has already been commercially available. However, in contrast, the robot used in NOTES has not been applied in clinical practice due to its serious motion errors.

To adapt to the internal environment of the human body, the robot for NOTES is driven by a tendon sheath system. However, it has many disadvantages such as serious tension loss and difficulty in the position control, which will seriously affect the accuracy of the surgical robot [1–3]. Wenjun Xu et al. [4] have studied the influence of transmission error of the tendon sheath system on the position error of continuum robots. Moreover, in practical application, the size of the actuator is so small that a tiny error of the driving tendon can cause a great impact on the motion precision of the actuator [5–7]. Therefore, to compensate the transmission error of it, establishing a friction model and elongation model of the tendon sheath system is of great significance. Zheng Wang et al. [8] split the tendon sheath system into infinitesimal segments and assumed that the curvature of each segment was constant. Then the friction of the whole system was obtained by integrating the friction of each segment. And they also proposed that the friction of a tendon sheath system is only related to its total bending angle.

However, the friction models above do not take velocity into account. To investigate the factors affecting the nonlinear friction characteristics of the tendon sheath system, Dangyang Chen et al. [9] designed a series of experiments aiming at the tendon sheath system, and systematically studied the influence of motion speed, total bending angle, friction coefficient, the stiffness of the tendon and the stiffness of the sheath on the nonlinear friction force. But they did not have a specific formula to describe these properties. T.N. Do et al. [10] proposed a velocity-dependent friction model using the lumped-mass method. However, as the non-uniform elongation of the tendon is closely related to its tension distribution [11], the lumped-mass method makes it unable to represent it. Therefore, a velocity correlation model which can construct the distribution of friction force needs to be established.

To solve the above problems, this paper will carry out work from the following aspects: In the second section, based on the Stribeck friction model, a novel friction model, and a novel elongation model of the tendon sheath system are established. In the third section, the parameters of the friction model are identified by experiments, and the transmission characteristics of driving force at different speeds are simulated and analyzed. The fourth section summarizes the research content of this paper.

2 Dynamic Model of the Tendon Sheath System

Since the friction between the tendon and sheath is not only affected by the cumulative bending angle but also affected by the relative speed, the Coulomb friction model cannot accurately describe the friction characteristics of the tendon sheath system. Besides, as the elongation of the tendon varies when it is in different shapes, once its shape changes, the elongation model based on the lumped-mass method needs to re-identify its parameters, which is impossible. So it is necessary to use the infinitesimal method to model the friction characteristics.

As shown in Fig. 1, the input tension is T_{in}, the input displacement is L_{in}, the output tension is T_{out} and the output displacement is L_{out}. And there must be $T_{out} < T_{in}$ and $L_{out} < L_{in}$, due to the existence of friction.

The mechanical model of the tendon system is as follows:

$$\begin{cases} T_{in} = T_{out} + F_f \\ L_1 = L_2 + \Delta L \end{cases} \tag{1}$$

Where F_f and ΔL are the total friction and the position error of the tendon sheath system, respectively.

T_{out}, L_{out}

T_{in}, L_{in}

Fig. 1. Schematic diagram of the tendon sheath system

2.1 Friction Modeling

As shown in Fig. 2, an infinitesimal section of the tendon sheath system is analyzed:

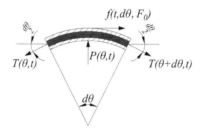

$f(t,d\theta, F_0)$

$T(\theta,t)$ $P(\theta,t)$ $T(\theta+d\theta,t)$

$d\theta$

Fig. 2. Analysis of an infinitesimal section

The equations of forces are as follows:

$$\begin{cases} T(\theta, t) \cos\left(\frac{d\theta}{2}\right) - \mathrm{sgn}(v)F_f(v) = T(\theta + d\theta, t) \cos\left(\frac{d\theta}{2}\right) \\ F_f(v) = F_c + (F_s - F_c) \exp\left[-(v/v_s)^\delta\right] + F_v v \end{cases} \tag{2}$$

Where $T(\theta, t)$ is the tension of the tendon section with the cumulative bending angle θ at time t, v is the relative velocity between the tendon and the sheath, $sgn(v)$ is a sign function with a value of 1 when v is positive and -1 when v is negative, $d\theta$ is the bending angle of the infinitesimal section, $F_f(v)$ is the Stribeck friction of the infinitesimal section,

F_s and F_c are the static friction and Coulomb friction of the segment, respectively, v_s is the Stribeck velocity and δ is a constant parameter of the Stribeck model, which can be 1 or 2. For the convenience of integration, the static friction force F_s and Coulomb friction force F_c are respectively expressed as functions of positive pressure, F_v is the coefficient of viscous friction, and v is the velocity of the tendon. It is assumed that the viscous friction is uniformly distributed on the whole silk sheath mechanism, then:

$$\begin{cases} F_s = \mu_1 P(\theta,t) = 2\mu_1 T(\theta,t)\sin\left(\dfrac{d\theta}{2}\right) \\ F_c = \mu_2 P(\theta,t) = 2\mu_2 T(\theta,t)\sin\left(\dfrac{d\theta}{2}\right) \end{cases} \tag{3}$$

Where μ_1 and μ_2 are the static friction coefficient and the Coulomb coefficient of friction, separately. As $d\theta$ approaches to 0, the following transformation can be performed:

$$\begin{cases} \sin\left(\frac{d\theta}{2}\right) = \frac{d\theta}{2} \\ \cos\left(\frac{d\theta}{2}\right) = 1 \end{cases} \tag{4}$$

Substitute Eq. 3 and Eq. 4 into Eq. 2, it can be simplified as follows:

$$dT(\theta,t) = T(\theta+d\theta,t) - T(\theta,t)$$
$$= -\,\mathrm{sgn}(v)T(\theta,t)d\theta\left[\mu_2 + (\mu_1-\mu_2)\exp\left(-\left(\frac{v}{v_s}\right)^\delta\right)\right] - \mathrm{sgn}(v)\frac{F_v v d\theta}{\Theta} \tag{5}$$

Solve the above differential equation, we can get:

$$T(\theta,t) = T_{in}\exp\left\{-\mathrm{sgn}(v)\theta\left[\mu_2 + (\mu_1-\mu_2)\exp\left(-\left(\frac{v}{v_s}\right)^\delta\right)\right]\right\}$$
$$-\left(\frac{\mathrm{sgn}(x)F_v v}{\Theta}\right)\Big/\left(\mu_2 + (\mu_1-\mu_2)\exp\left(-\left(\frac{v}{v_s}\right)^\delta\right)\right) \tag{6}$$

According to Eq. 6, if the speed remains constant, the output force and the input force show a linear relationship, and the magnitude of the output force and the output force is related to the direction of the driving speed.

2.2 Elongation Modeling

As the elongation of each segment of the tendon is different when the tension is different, to accurately describe the position error of the tendon sheath system, it is necessary to use the infinitesimal method to describe the distribution law of tension in the tendon. Based on the above friction model, the elongation of the tendon can be obtained as follows:

$$\frac{d\delta l(\theta, t)}{dl} = \frac{1}{EA} T(\theta, t) \tag{7}$$

Where E and A are the elastic moduli and cross-sectional area of the tendon respectively, and $\Delta L\ (\theta, t)$ is the elongation of the tendon.

It can be seen from Eq. 7 that the elongation is related to the tension of the tendon. However, there is always pre-tension in the tendon sheath system before work, so the tendon also has pre-elongation, which should be subtracted when calculating the position error. Note that the pretension of the tendon is T_0, then:

$$\frac{d\delta l(\theta, t)}{dl} = \frac{1}{EA} (T(\theta, t) - T_0(\theta, t)) \tag{8}$$

Considering that the radius of the tendon sheath system is $R(\theta, t)$, then $dl = R(\theta, t)d\theta$. Substituting into Eq. 8, we can get:

$$\delta l = \int_0^\Phi \frac{R(\theta, t)}{EA} (T(\theta, t) - T_0(\theta, t)) d\theta \tag{9}$$

3   Simulation and Experimental Verification

To simulate the tendon sheath system, the first step is to identify the parameters through experiments. The structure of the experimental device is shown in Fig. 3.

The driving motor (*Maxon DCX 19S*) is used to provide driving force, the ball screw (*HIWIN* 0802) is used to convert the rotary motion output by the driving motor into linear motion, force sensor 1 is used to measure the input force, force sensor 2 is used to measure the output force, and the load device is used to provide a constant load.

The parameters which are needed to identify mainly include the static friction coefficient μ_1, the dynamic friction coefficient μ_2, the viscous friction coefficient F_v, and the Stribeck velocity v_s. In order to accurately identify these parameters, the output load is designed to keep a constant value of 6 N·m, and the input velocity varies from 0.5 mm/s to 15 mm/s, respectively. The value of friction is obtained by the tension difference between the two tension sensors. The experimental results are shown in Fig. 4.

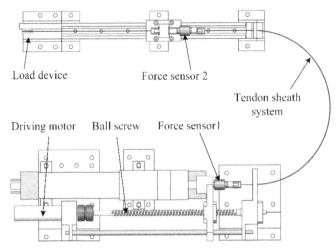

(a) Model of the experimental device

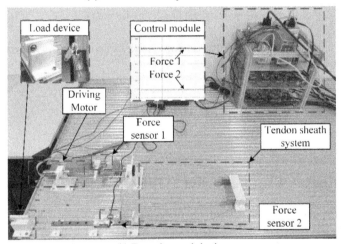

(b) Experimental device

Fig. 3. Diagram of the experimental device

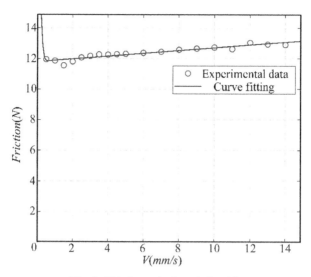

Fig. 4. Friction-velocity relationship

The least square method was used to identify the above parameters, and the friction parameters of the tendon sheath system were obtained as Table 1.

Table 1. Friction parameters

	μ_1	μ_2	v_s	F_v
Value	0.4766	0.3458	0.2143	0.0336

Based on the above parameters, the friction estimation errors of the proposed model and that of the Coulomb friction model are analyzed, which are shown in Fig. 5. The result illustrates that the Coulomb model can accurately predict the friction at low speed. However, the higher the speed is, the larger the estimation error is. On the contrary, the corresponding error for the new friction model maintains a low level despite the change of velocity.

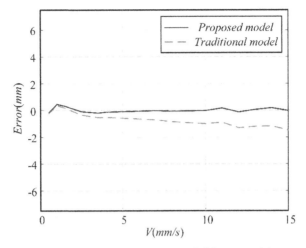

Fig. 5. Friction estimation error of different models

When the velocity is constant, the tension distribution and the elongation of the tendon (It is a stainless steel wire with a diameter of 0.4 mm, $E = 199$ GPa) can be obtained based on the proposed friction model and elongation model as shown in Fig. 6.

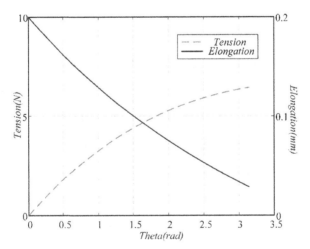

Fig. 6. The tension of the driving wire at different sections

Figure 6 shows that compared with the lumped-mass model, the proposed model can describe the tension distribution and elastic elongation of the tendon on different cross-sections, laying a foundation for error compensation of the tendon sheath system.

Under the preload of 2 N, $v_1 = 10$ mm/s, $v_2 = 15$ mm/s and $v_3 = 20$ mm/s are selected to simulate the friction characteristics of the tendon sheath system in a reciprocating motion. And the results are shown in Fig. 6.

Figure 7 shows that during a reciprocating motion, the working state of the tendon sheath system can be divided into four stages: a. The input force starts to rise from the preloading force, but the output tension of the driving wire remains constant. b. The input force continues to rise, and its change can affect the tension at the output end, at this point, the output force and the input force show a linear relationship. c. The input force begins to decrease, but the output force does not change due to the effect of friction. d. The input force continues to decrease, and the relationship between the input force and the output force is still linear. However, the ratio of the two is different in the first stages and the fourth stages, which shows the asymmetry of reciprocating motion. And it also shows that with the increase of the velocity, the friction of the tendon sheath system increases, too.

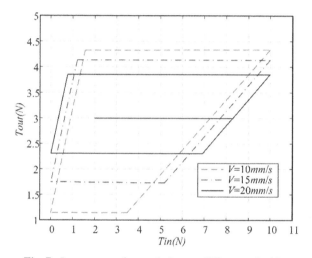

Fig. 7. Input-output force relations at different velocities

4   Conclusion

To compensate the force error caused by serious nonlinear friction in the tendon sheath system, and improve the accuracy of the robot for NOTES, a novel friction model and elongation model considering the effect of velocity was proposed in this paper, and the friction parameter identification was carried out. Furthermore, the simulation results of the friction model at different speeds show that the proposed friction model can describe the dynamic characteristics of the tendon sheath system. In future work, we will consider the error compensation strategy of the double tendons cooperative control, and further, analyze the coupling relationship between the tendon sheath system and the external environment.

Acknowledgment. Fundamental Research Funds for the Central Universities.

References

1. Wu, Q., Wang, X., Chen, B., et al.: Modeling, online identification, and compensation control of single tendon sheath system with time-varying configuration Mech. Syst. Signal Process. **130**(56), 73 (2019)
2. Lei, Y., Li, Y., Song, R., et al.: Development of a novel deployable arm for natural orifice transluminal endoscopic surgery. Int. J. Med. Robot. Comput. Assist. Surg. **17**(3), e2232 (2021)
3. Simaan, N., Xu, K., Wei, W., et al.: Design and integration of a telerobotic system for minimally invasive surgery of the throat. Int. J. Robot. Res. **28**(9), 1134–1153 (2009)
4. Xu, W., Poon, C.C.Y., Yam, Y., et al.: Motion compensated controller for a tendon-sheath-driven flexible endoscopic robot. Int. J. Med. Robot. Comput. Assist. Surg. **13**(1), e1747 (2017)
5. Lu, J., Du, F., Li, Y., et al.: A novel inverse kinematics algorithm using the Kepler oval for continuum robots. Appl. Math. Model. **93**, 206–225 (2021)
6. Lu, J., Du, F., Yang, F., et al.: Kinematic modeling of a class of n-tendon continuum manipulators. Adv. Robot. **34**(19), 1254–1271 (2020)
7. Lu, J., Du, F., Zhang, T., et al.: An efficient inverse kinematics algorithm for continuum robot with a translational base. In: 2020 IEEE/ASME International Conference on Advanced Intelligent Mechatronics (AIM), pp. 1754–1759. IEEE (2020)
8. Wang, Z., Sun, Z., Phee, S.J.: Haptic feedback and control of a flexible surgical endoscopic robot. Comput. Methods Programs Biomed. **112**(2), 260–271 (2013)
9. Chen, D., Yun, Y., Deshpande, A.D.: Experimental characterization of Bowden cable friction. In: 2014 IEEE international Conference on Robotics and Automation (ICRA), pp. 5927–5933. IEEE (2014)
10. Do, T.N., Tjahjowidodo, T., Lau, M.W.S., et al.: Hysteresis modeling and position control of tendon-sheath mechanism in flexible endoscopic systems. Mechatronics **24**(1), 12–22 (2014)
11. Sun, Z., Wang, Z., Phee, S.J.: Elongation modeling and compensation for the flexible tendon—sheath system. IEEE/ASME Trans. Mechatron. **19**(4), 1243–1250 (2013)

A Tactile Sensor with Contact Angle Compensation for Robotic Palpation of Tissue Hardness

Yingxuan Zhang[1], Yan Hong[1], Chengjun Zhu[2], and Feng Ju[1(✉)]

[1] College of Mechanical and Electrical Engineering, Nanjing University of Aeronautics and Astronautics, Nanjing 210016, China
juf@nuaa.edu.cn
[2] Department of Oncology, Jiangsu Province Hospital, Nanjing 210029, China

Abstract. At present, robot-assisted minimally invasive surgery (RAMIS) has increasingly become the mainstream of operation. In the case of intraoperative tumor palpation with tactile hardness sensors, most existing solutions need to place the sensor normal to the tissue surface. But this requirement cannot always be met due to the limitation of the robot's degree of freedoms and the limited operating space, which causes error in the detected hardness. This paper proposes a piezoelectric tactile sensor that can detect the hardness A even under non-normal contact conditions based on two resonant frequencies (f_{RN} and f_{RT}) measured in two detection modes - normal and tangential. Since the contact angle θ has opposite effects on the two resonant frequencies, by solving two equations $f_N(A, \theta) = f_{RN}$ and $f_T(A, \theta) = f_{RT}$, the effect of the contact angle can be eliminated to obtain the compensated hardness. This can improve the accuracy and reliability of tumor palpation in RAMIS.

Keywords: Tactile sensor · Piezoelectric · Hardness detection · Contact angle compensation · Robot-assisted minimally invasive surgery

1 Introduction

In the current process of RAMIS, since surgeons cannot directly touch tumors and other lesions with their hands, they cannot accurately detect tumors through palpation and identify their boundaries. Therefore, it is necessary for surgical robots to have tactile sensing ability [1].

Existing tactile sensors detect the hardness of tissues mainly by pressing the tissue to deform. Due to the large force, it is likely to cause damage to the tissue. Such sensors often use piezoresistive [2], strain gauges [3], capacitors [4], FBGs [5] as sensitive components. The sensitivity of the first two is relatively low. Capacitive sensors usually have a narrow sensitivity range. FBG sensors need complex signal processing devices and is difficult to integrate into the end of a flexible surgical instrument. There are also tactile sensors based on the dynamic vibration of piezoelectric transducers, which have high sensitivity and only need to lightly contact the tissue for hardness detection [6].

© Springer Nature Switzerland AG 2021
X.-J. Liu et al. (Eds.): ICIRA 2021, LNAI 13015, pp. 155–164, 2021.
https://doi.org/10.1007/978-3-030-89134-3_15

However, the piezoelectric sensor needs to be placed normal to the tissue surface during detection [7]. In actual surgery, this normal contact requirement cannot always be met due to the limitation of the degree of freedom of the robot and the limited operating space. As a result, the detected hardness will be affected by the contact angle.

This paper proposes a tactile sensor that can detect the hardness of tissue accurately by eliminating the effect of contact angle. First, the structure and two detection modes of the sensor, the principle of compensated hardness and contact angle detection are introduced. Then the proposed sensor and methodology are verified through simulation and experimental studies.

2 Design of the Tactile Sensor

The sensor uses piezoelectric material as the sensitive element, its unique configuration allows it to have two detection modes - the normal mode and the tangential mode.

2.1 Structure of the Tactile Sensor

As shown in Fig. 1, two vertically parallel lead-zirconate-titanate (PZT) bimorphs are fixed at the end of the instrument. They are connected to a V-shape connection with a spherical tip. This structure greatly reduces the overall size of the sensor compared to the traditional cantilever piezoelectric sensors [6]. So it is suitable for RAMIS such as transurethral and transnasal surgeries.

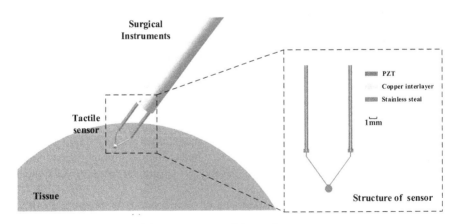

Fig. 1. Structure of the tactile sensor

2.2 Detection Principles

Principle of Two Detection Modes
The sensor can change the direction of detection by applying different AC voltages to the electrodes, as shown in Fig. 2. Two vibration directions (normal and tangential) can be produced by switching the two circuits.

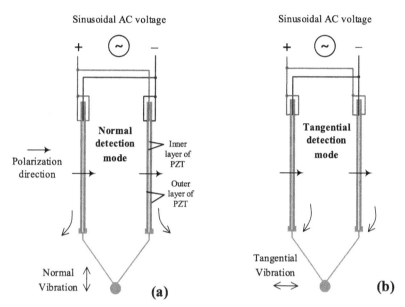

Fig. 2. Detection modes and their circuits. (a) Normal detection mode. (b) Tangential detection mode.

In the normal mode, opposite sinusoidal AC voltages are applied to two piezo bimorphs which have the same polarization direction, as shown in Fig. 2 (a). Because of the inverse piezoelectric effect, the two PZT bimorphs vibrate in the different directions, and lead to the up-down vibration of the tip. It can be used to detect the hardness of tissue in the normal direction. In the tangential mode, same sinusoidal AC voltages are applied to two PZT bimorphs, as shown in Fig. 2 (b). They vibrate in the same directions, and lead to the left-right vibration of the tip. It can be used to detect the hardness of tissue in the tangential direction.

Analysis of Hardness Deviation Under Non-normal Contact Conditions
The hardness can be detected in a certain mode alone when the contact angle θ is $0°$, ensuring the hardness is accurate. It can be obtained by measuring the resonant frequency of sensor when it is in contact with sample, since the resonant frequency of the sensor is positively related to hardness [8]. If θ is not equal to $0°$, as shown in Fig. 3, the hardness detection will have deviation caused by contact angle.

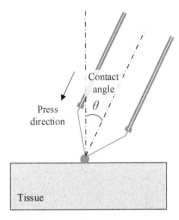

Fig. 3. Schematic diagram of contact angle

When the contact angle θ is not $0°$, the contact model is shown in Fig. 4. A static force F in the θ direction is applied to the sensor to make the tip come into contact with the sample. In Fig. 4 (a), a sinusoidal AC voltage is applied to drive the sensor in the normal detection mode, and the generated harmonic force $aF_0(t)$ is in the θ direction (vibration direction). The function relating the normal resonant frequency f_{RN} to the sample hardness A and the contact area S_N is shown in Eq. 1. In Fig. 4(b), the sensor is driven in the tangential detection mode, and the generated harmonic force $aF_0(t)$ is in the direction of vibration. The function relating the tangential resonant frequency f_{RT} to the hardness A and the contact area S_T is shown in Eq. 2.

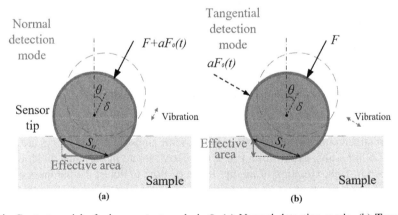

Fig. 4. Contact model of when contact angle is θ. (a) Normal detection mode. (b) Tangential detection mode. (δ is the indentation depth)

$$f_{RN} = (A, S_N) \propto CA\sqrt{S_N}/\left(\pi^{1.5}\omega LZ_1\left(1 - v_x^2\right)\right) \tag{1}$$

$$f_{RT} = (A, S_T) \propto CA\sqrt{S_T} / \left(\pi^{1.5} \omega L Z_1 (1 - v_x)(1 + v_x/2) \right) \tag{2}$$

$$S_N = \left(S_{st} + S_{dyN} \right) cos\theta \tag{3}$$

$$S_T = S_{st} sin\theta + S_{dyT} cos\theta \tag{4}$$

where the f_{RN} and f_{RT} are the resonant frequencies of normal and tangential detection mode, C is a constant number, A is the hardness of the sample, S_N and S_T are the effective contact area between the tip and the sample in normal and tangential detection mode, ω is the angular frequency, L is the length of PZT, Z_1 is the equivalent impedance of sensor, v_x is the Poisson's ratio, S_{st} is the contact area caused by static force, S_{dyN} (much less than S_{st}) is the contact area caused by up-down vibration, S_{dyT} (much less than S_{st}) is the contact area caused by left-right vibration, and θ is the contact angle.

Obviously, the resonant frequency f_R is positively related to the hardness A, negatively related to the contact angle θ in normal detection mode, and is positively related to θ in the tangential detection mode when θ is in the interval $[0°, 90°]$.

Calculation of Compensated Hardness and Contact Angle
A calibration process is needed before using the sensor.

The resonant frequency f_{RN} in the normal detection mode and the resonant frequency f_{RT} in the tangential detection mode are detected for multiple samples of known hardness at multiple known contact angles. Calibration functions $f_N(A, \theta) = f_{RN}$ and $f_T(A, \theta) = f_{RT}$ can be obtained in the two detection modes respectively. With these two functions, the compensated hardness and contact angle of an unknown sample can be detected by measuring the resonant frequencies f_{RN} and f_{RT} in two modes, and solve for A and θ with function $f_N(A, \theta) = f_{RN}$ and $f_T(A, \theta) = f_{RT}$. This process is shown in Fig. 5.

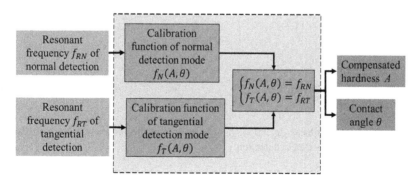

Fig. 5. Detection of compensated hardness and contact angle.

3   Simulation Studies

Hardness detection is simulated by using one detection mode alone when the contact angle is $0°$. Compensated hardness and contact angle detection are simulated by using two detection mode together.

3.1   Simulation of Hardness Detection When θ is $0°$

Five silicone samples are used, with the hardness values of 33A, 40, 49A, 61A and 67A in the unit of Shore A. The materials of sensor are set the same as shown in Fig. 1. And the normal and tangential detection mode are wired as shown in Fig. 2 (a) and (b) respectively. The indentation depth is at a constant value of 0.2–0.5 times the diameter of the tip. And the direction is normal to the surface of sample. Finite element (FE) harmonic response analysis is carried out, and the model is shown in Fig. 6 (a) and simulation results are shown in Fig. 6 (b) and (c).

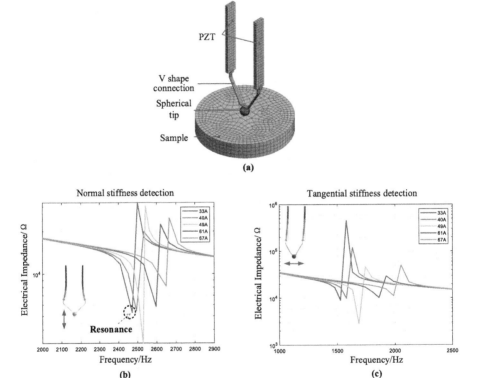

Fig. 6. Simulation of hardness detection. (a) FE sensor-sample model. (b) Normal hardness detection. (c) Tangential hardness detection.

The resonant frequency corresponds to the frequency of the local minimum in the impedance curve. As shown in Fig. 6 (b) and (c), the resonant frequency is positively related to the sample's hardness.

3.2   Simulation of Compensated Hardness and Contact Angle Detection

In order to detect the compensated hardness and contact angle, the functions $f_N (A, \theta) = f_{RN}$ and $f_T (A, \theta)$ corresponding to the two modes must be calibrated first. The same five samples as above are used, the contact angles tested are set to $0°$, $15°$, $30°$ and $45°$.

First, the normal detection mode is chosen by applying the same voltage as shown in Fig. 2(a). The indentation depth is controlled to 0.25 mm. The FE harmonic response analysis is carried out. A series of resonance frequencies and the corresponding hardness and contact angle can be obtained by testing the sample and the contact angle one by one. These data are used to fit a binary quadratic function $f_N(A, \theta) = f_{RN}$, as shown in Eq. (5) and plotted in Fig. 7(a). Then the detection mode is changed to the tangential detection mode, and the above steps are repeated to obtain the function $f_T(A, \theta) = f_{RT}$, as shown in Eq. (6) and plotted in Fig. 7(b).

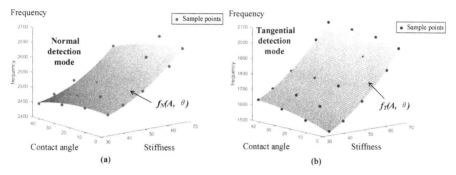

Fig. 7. Simulation result of two mode detection (resonant frequency- hardness- contact angle functions). (a) Function fitted in normal mode. (b) Function fitted in tangential mode.

$$f_{RN} = f_N(A, \theta) = 2489.58 + 0.09A^2 - 0.03\theta^2 - 3.59A + 1.51\theta - 0.03A\theta \quad (5)$$

$$f_{RT} = f_T(A, \theta) = 1430.53 + 0.16A^2 - 0.04\theta^2 - 2.57A + 4.73\theta - 0.02A\theta \quad (6)$$

As shown in Fig. 7 (a), the resonant frequency is positively related to the hardness of samples and is negatively related to the contact angle in the normal detection mode. As shown in Fig. 7 (b), the resonant frequency is positively related to the hardness and the contact angle in the tangential detection mode. When resonant frequencies of two modes are obtained, the compensated hardness and contact angle corresponding to them can be calculated by solving Eq. (5) and (6).

4   Experimental Studies

Based on simulation studies, an experiment of compensated hardness and contact angle detection is performed. A piezoelectric tactile sensor is fabricated. Two pieces of SYT16–1.6–0.55–1 (PANT Piezo) type piezo bimorphs are used. The V-shape connection and the tip are made of stainless steel. The diameter of the tip is 1.5 mm. As shown in Fig. 8, the sensor is mounted on the fixture. Motorized linear stage and rotary stage are used to control the up and down displacement and the contact angle of sensor. NI compactRIO-9045 which is connected to a host computer, is used to generate, acquire and process signals. Then the resonant frequency can be extracted and displayed on the host computer.

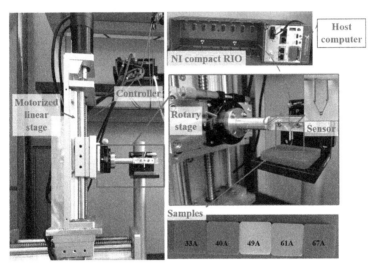

Fig. 8. Experiment settings.

Five silicone samples are used, with the hardness values of 33A, 40, 49A, 61A and 67A, which is the same as simulation settings. The contact angles tested are set to 0°, 15°, 30° and 45°.

First, the normal detection mode is chosen by applying the same voltage as shown in Fig. 2(a). The motorized linear stage is controlled to slowly move down to contact the sample, and the indentation depth is kept at 0.75 mm. Then the normal mode resonant frequency f_{RN} can be obtained on the host computer. A series of resonance frequencies and the corresponding hardness and contact angle can be obtained by testing the sample and the contact angle one by one. These data are used to fit a binary quadratic function $f_N(A, \theta) = f_{RN}$, as shown in Eq. (7) and plotted in Fig. 9 (a). Then the detection mode is changed to the tangential detection mode, and the above steps are repeated to obtain the function $f_T(A, \theta) = f_{RT}$, as shown in Eq. (8) and plotted in Fig. 9 (b).

$$f_{RN} = f_N(A, \theta) = 3884.93 + 1.33A^2 - 0.06\theta^2 - 94.63A - 13.17\theta + 0.48A\theta \quad (7)$$

$$f_{RT} = f_T(A, \theta) = 2966.83 + 0.45A^2 + 0.04\theta^2 - 22.73A + 6.65\theta - 0.28A\theta \quad (8)$$

As shown in Fig. 9(a), the resonant frequency is positively related to the hardness of samples and is negatively related to the contact angle in the normal detection mode. As shown in Fig. 9(b), the resonant frequency is positively related to the hardness and the contact angle in the tangential detection mode. When resonant frequencies of two modes are obtained, the compensated hardness and contact angle corresponding to them

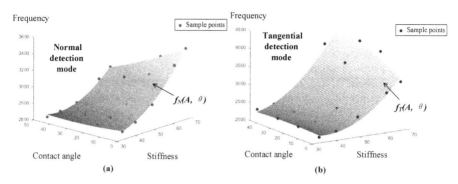

Fig. 9. Experiment result of two mode detection (resonant frequency- hardness- contact angle functions). (a) Function fitted in normal mode. (b) Function fitted in tangential mode.

can be calculated by solving Eq. (7) and (8). It can be seen that the experimental results are consistent with the simulation results.

5   Conclusions

The proposed tactile sensor can detect the hardness of the measured tissue with only a negligible contact force. It has two detection modes, which can be used to detect the hardness and compensate for the effect of the contact angle. In the normal detection mode, its resonant frequency is positively related to the hardness of samples and negatively related to the contact angle. In the tangential detection mode, its resonant frequency is positively related to the hardness and the contact angle. Based on this, two different functions of resonant frequency-hardness-contact angle can be obtained. Samples with known hardness values are used to calibrate the two functions. Then the compensated hardness of an unknown sample can be obtained by solving the two functions after measuring the resonant frequencies in the two detection modes. It is utilized to eliminate the effect of the contact angle on the hardness measurement to improve the detect accuracy. The requirement of normal contact in traditional tactile sensing systems can be avoided, and facilitates more convenient and accurate tumor detection and identification.

Acknowledgements. This work is supported by National Natural Science Foundation of China (No. 61973335 and No. 62111530151) and Natural Science Foundation of Jiangsu Province under Grant BK20191272.

References

1. Bandari, N., Dargahi, J., Packirisamy, M.: Tactile sensors for minimally invasive surgery: a review of the state-of-the-art, applications, and perspectives. IEEE Access **8**, 7682–7708 (2020)
2. Chi, C., Sun, X., Xue, N., Li, T., Liu, C.: Recent progress in technologies for tactile sensors. Sensors **18**(4), 948 (2018)

3. Li, L., Yu, B., Yang, C., Vagdargi, P., Srivatsan, R.A., Choset, H.: Development of an inexpensive tri-axial force sensor for minimally invasive surgery. In: 2017 IEEE/RSJ International Conference on Intelligent Robots and Systems (IROS), Vancouver, BC, pp. 906–913 (2017)
4. Nagatomo, T., Miki, N.: Three-axis capacitive force sensor with liquid metal electrodes for endoscopic palpation. Micro Nano Lett. **12**, 564–568 (2017)
5. Li, T., Pan, A., Ren, H.: Reaction force mapping by 3-axis tactile sensing with arbitrary angles for tissue hard-inclusion localization. IEEE Trans. Biomed. Eng. **68**(1), 26–35 (2021)
6. Ju, F., Yun, Y.H., Zhang, Z.: A variable-impedance tactile sensor with online performance tuning for tissue hardness palpation in robot-assisted minimally invasive surgery. In: 2018 40th Annual International Conference of the IEEE Engineering in Medicine and Biology Society (EMBC), Honolulu, HI, pp. 2142–2145 (2018)
7. Goldman, R.E., Bajo, A., Simaan, N.: Algorithms for autonomous exploration and estimation in compliant environments. Robotics **31**, 71–87 (2012)
8. Zhang, Y., Ju, F., Wei, X., Wang, D., Wang, Y.: A piezoelectric tactile sensor for tissue stiffness detection with arbitrary contact angle. Sensors **20**, 6607 (2020)

A Robotic Endoscopic Injection Needle with Integrated Tactile Sensor for Intraoperative Autonomous Tumor Localization

Yan Hong[1], Yingxuan Zhang[1], Chengjun Zhu[2], and Feng Ju[1(✉)]

[1] College of Mechanical and Electrical Engineering, Nanjing University of Aeronautics and Astronautics, Nanjing 210016, China
juf@nuaa.edu.cn
[2] Department of Oncology, Jiangsu Province Hospital, Nanjing 210029, China

Abstract. En bloc resection of tumor is a minimally invasive surgical method for removing tumors precisely and completely at one time. It can decrease the risk of recurrence and tumor spread after surgery. However, it requires surgeons to accurately locate the tumor and its boundary. In minimally invasive surgery (MIS), surgeons cannot directly palpate cancerous areas to obtain tactile information. Therefore, a tactile sensor that can be integrated onto surgical instruments is highly demanded. This paper proposes a tactile sensor integrated onto an injection needle for robotic endoscopes. The tactile sensor is based on the principle of piezoelectric effect and can detect the hardness of tissues by changes of resonant frequency. In addition, an autonomous palpation algorithm is developed to accurately localize the tumor and identify its boundaries.

Keywords: Tactile sensor · Tumor palpation · Robotic endoscope · Autonomous tumor localization · Injection needle

1 Introduction

En bloc resection is a kind of minimally invasive surgical method to remove a tumor at one time. This method can effectively decrease the possibility of postoperative recurrence. It lifts the tumor by injecting sodium hyaluronate, and then completely separates it from healthy tissue by an electrosurgical knife [1]. It requires surgeons to accurately locate the tumor and its boundary. If the location of the tumor cannot be accurately detected, surgeons may possibly remove healthy tissues as tumors. It maybe causes massive bleeding and endangers the lives of patients. However, the surgeon cannot directly palpate the cancerous area with hands. Therefore, it is necessary to design a tactile sensor to assist surgeons in acquiring the location of the tumor. Up to now, tactile sensors based on various principles have been developed.

© Springer Nature Switzerland AG 2021
X.-J. Liu et al. (Eds.): ICIRA 2021, LNAI 13015, pp. 165–176, 2021.
https://doi.org/10.1007/978-3-030-89134-3_16

Zareinia et al. [2] developed a force-sensing bipolar forceps based on piezoresistive principle for quantifying the force between surgical instruments and tissues in microsurgery. In a recent study, Sharma et al. [3] developed a biopsy needle integrated with a piezoelectric sensor that can detect changes of tissue hardness. Kim et al. [4] proposed a novel perceptual surgical forceps consisting of two compact capacitive sensors located on two jaws of the forceps. It provides the surgeon with force and torque information. Tanaka et al. [5] proposed a tactile sensor based on acoustic reflection. By measuring the change of acoustic wave amplitude in the pipe, the sensor can obtain the deformation when contacting with the tissue. In recent years, fiber Bragg grating (FBG) has been widely used in tactile sensors. Li et al. [6] proposed a triaxial tactile sensor based on FBG for surface reactivity mapping, recognition and localization of tissue hard inclusion. However, all tactile sensors mentioned above require a force large enough to squeeze the tissue to generate a significant deformation for measurement, which may cause damage to living tissues. In [7, 8], a piezoelectric sensor was proposed to detect the hardness of tissue through the change of its resonant frequency when contacting with the tissue. In this way, the deformation of tissue can be reduced and tissue damage can be avoided. However, the integration of this sensor with existing surgical instruments remains a problem to solve.

The paper proposes a tactile sensor which can be easily integrated onto a robotic endoscopic injection needle. It can detect tissue hardness by the change of resonant frequency. A boundary recognition algorithm is proposed for accurately detecting the tumor location and its boundary, which is suitable for en bloc tumor resection. Section 2 introduces the structure and working principle of the sensor. Section 3 verifies the detection performance of the sensor through a series of simulation studies. Section 4 presents the principle of boundary recognition algorithm and its simulation results.

2 Design of the Tactile Sensor

2.1 Structure of the Tactile Sensor

The structure of the tactile sensor is shown in Fig. 1. It consists of a PZT (Pbbased Lanthanumdoped Zirconate Titanates) patch and a small stainless steel tip. One end of the PZT patch is fixed on the needle sheath. The tip is fixed on the other end of the PZT and contacts with the injection needle. This configuration adds the tactile sensing capability to the disposable injection needle without affecting its medical functions. In the tactile sensing mode, the tip of the injection needle is controlled by the robotic endoscope (e.g. a continuum robot) to contact with the tissue. Then the hardness of tissue is sensed by the PZT patch based on the following principle.

2.2 Hardness Sensing Principle

Due to the inverse piezoelectric effect, as shown in Fig. 2(a), when an AC voltage is applied to the electrode of a Y-axis polarized PZT patch, periodic expansion and contraction movements will occur in the X-axis. As a result, the tip of the injection

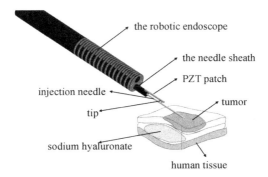

Fig. 1. Structure of the tactile sensor and the application in en bloc tumor resection.

needle will be excited to vibrate in the Y-axis. According to the equivalent circuit model in Fig. 2(b), the electrical impedance Z_e of the PZT patch can be expressed as:

$$Z_e = \frac{\left(L_1 C_1 \omega^2 - 1\right) - j(R_1 C_1 \omega)}{\left(R_1 C_1 C_0 \omega^2\right) + \left[L_1 C_0 C_1 \omega^3 - \omega(C_1 + C_0)\right]} = |Ze(\omega)| \angle \theta(\omega) \tag{1}$$

where C_0 is the electrical capacitance, R_1 is the mechanical dissipation, L_1 is the mechanical mass, C_1 is the mechanical compliance, and ω is the frequency [9]. When the sensor is excited at its resonant frequency ω_R, the amplitude of its electrical impedance $|Ze(\omega)|$ reaches a local minimum which can be used to extract the ω_R (Fig. 2(c)). When the sensor is in contact with the tissue, its resonant frequency will change due to the change of the mechanical compliance C_1 (related to the hardness of the tissue). Therefore, tissue hardness can be measured from the resonant frequency of the sensor.

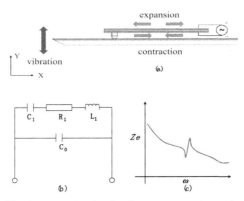

Fig. 2. (a) Principle of hardness sensing by simultaneous actuation and sensing capability of the sensor. (b) Equivalent circuit. (c) Electrical impedance - frequency curve.

3   Simulation Studies

3.1   Static Simulation for Verifying Whether the Sensor Damages Tissue

A finite element model of the sensor is built for simulation. The dimensions and materials are listed in Table 1.

Table 1. Dimensions and materials of the FE model

Component	Dimensions	Material
Piezo bimorph upper layer	$10 \times 0.7 \times 0.15$ mm	PZT-5A
Piezo bimorph substrate	$10 \times 0.7 \times 0.15$ mm	Brass
Piezo bimorph lower layer	$10 \times 0.7 \times 0.15$ mm	PZT-5A
Tip	Diameter 0.6 mm	Stainless steel
Injection needle	Diameter 0.75 mm	Stainless steel
Needle sheath	Diameter 2.4 mm	Stainless steel
Sample	$10 \times 10 \times 3$ mm	Silicone

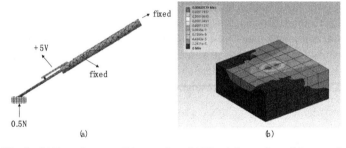

Fig. 3. (a) Boundary condition setting. (b) The deformation of the sample

For the boundary conditions, we fixed the upper end of the injection needle and the upper end of the needle sheath. At the same time, we applied a voltage of 5 V on the upper layer of the PZT patch for driving the PZT. Simultaneously, the contact between the tip and the injection needle is set to bonding, and the boundary condition between the injection needle and the sample is also set to bonding. In addition, in order to make the sensor better contact with the tissue model, a force of 0.5 N was applied to the sample (shown in Fig. 3(a)). The maximum deformation of the sensor is 0.2 mm, so it will not damage the tissue when detecting the hardness (shown in Fig. 3(b)).

3.2   Harmonic Response Simulation of Tissue Hardness Detection

Since the paper mainly studies the relationship between the sensor's resonant frequency and the hardness of the tissue, five tissue models with different elastic modulus are set for simulation, shown in Table 2.

For each tissue model, a 5 V swept sinusoidal voltage signal with a frequency range of 900–2300 Hz was applied to the two electrodes of the PZT patch in the sensor to drive the PZT patch to vibrate and its electrical impedance curve was recorded.

Table 2. Sample number and hardness

Sample number	Hardness (MPa)
1	0.157
2	0.228
3	0.414
4	0.6
5	0.883

The electrical impedance curves corresponding to different tissue models are shown in Fig. 4. The frequency corresponding to the lowest part of the curve is the resonant frequency of the sensor. It can be seen from the figure that the resonant frequency of the sensor changes when it is in contact with tissues with different elastic modulus. The bigger the elastic modulus, the higher the resonant frequency. It can be seen that the sensor has the function of identifying tissues with different hardness.

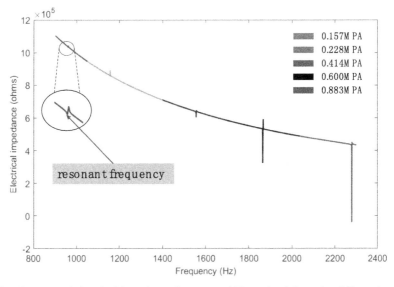

Fig. 4. The curve of electrical impedance-frequency shifts to the right under different hardness.

3.3 Sensor Performance Simulation Under Different Contact Angles

Disposable injection needles for endoscopes cannot ensure that the tip of the needle fits closely with the tissue due to the limited field of view during MIS. Therefore, we need to consider the impact of different contact angles on sensor performance.

We set up 5 tissue samples with different hardness, including one normal tissue and four high-hardness tissues as tumors. The hardness of the tissue samples is shown in Table 3 below. The elastic modulus of normal tissue refers to the hardness of muscle tissue. The elastic modulus of the tumors is 5–15 times that of normal tissue. In order to compare with the simulation results of the above structure, we also designed another structure to perform the same simulation as shown in Fig. 5(a), which directly adheres the PZT patch on the injection needle.

The changes of contact angle can be divided into two types, one is 'front', which will increase the contact angle between the injection needle and the tissue sample (+); the other is 'back', which will decrease the contact angle between the injection needle and the tissue sample (−). We set up seven contact models with contact angles of −15°, −10°, −5°, 0°, 5°, 10°, and 15°, shown in Fig. 6(a–c). The simulation results are shown in Fig. 7 and Fig. 8.

Table 3. Sample number and hardness

Sample number	Hardness (MPa)
1	0.045
2	0.157
3	0.228
4	0.414
5	0.6

(a)   (b)

Fig. 5. (a) Structure A. (b) Structure B.

From Fig. 7, we can see that compared with structure B, structure A is more easily affected by the change of contact angle. Then, in order to better show the performance difference between the two structures, we can calculate the frequency change ratio (R) according to the following equation:

$$R = \frac{f_r^\alpha - f_r^0}{f_r^\alpha} \tag{2}$$

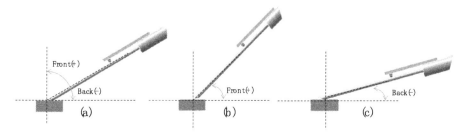

Fig. 6. (a) Ideal contact model. (b) 'front' contact model. (c) 'back' contact model

Where f_r^α refers to the resonant frequency of the sensor under different contact angles and f_r^0 refers to the resonant frequency of the sensor at $0°$ contact angle. The results are shown in Fig. 8.

It can be seen that the structure A is greatly affected by the contact angle, and the frequency change rate is 15% to 30%. It is not conducive for the sensor to recognize tissues of different hardness. As shown in Fig. 8(b), the frequency change rate of the structure B is 3% to 7%. It is much smaller than the structure A, which shows that the structure designed in the paper has a certain improvement effect in dealing with the impact of different contact angles on the performance of the sensor. At the same time, we found that under the same angle of change of the two changing methods, the change of resonant frequency is similar, and the error can be ignored.

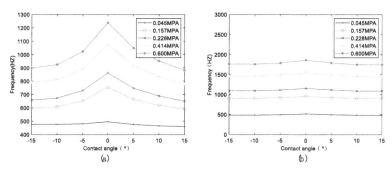

Fig. 7. (a) Contact angle-frequency curve of structure A. (b) Contact angle-frequency curve of structure B.

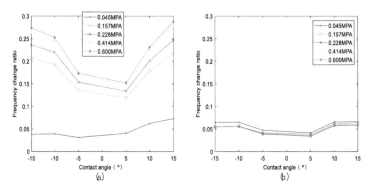

Fig. 8. (a) Frequency change ratio of structure A. (b) Frequency change ratio of structure B.

4   Intraoperative Autonomous Tumor Boundary Recognition

A tumor boundary recognition algorithm is proposed to use the above developed tactile sensor for robotic autonomous tumor localization and boundary identification.

4.1   The Boundary Recognition Function

The boundary recognition function is used to select the point to detect. After enough points have been detected, the final hardness distribution map can be obtained and the boundary is clear enough to guide tumor resection. The boundary recognition function is based on two strategies: exploration and exploitation. The functions of these two strategies are:

$$\mathbf{x}_t = \arg\max_{\mathbf{x}\in T}(\sigma_{t-1}(\mathbf{x})) \tag{3}$$

$$\mathbf{x}_t = \arg\max_{\mathbf{x}\in T}(\mu_{t-1}(\mathbf{x})) \tag{4}$$

$\mu(x)$ is the average of the predicted output. $\sigma^2(x)$ is the variance of the predicted output. The exploration function aims at exploring unknown areas and the exploitation function aims at exploiting areas of interest. Combining (3) and (4), the tumor boundary recognition function is:

$$\mathbf{x}_t = \arg\max_{\mathbf{x}\in T}((1-\theta)*\sigma_{t-1}(\mathbf{x}) - \theta*|\mu_{t-1}(\mathbf{x}) - h_{t-1}|) \tag{5}$$

where θ is a weight coefficient, h_{t-1} represents the hardness on the tumor boundary.

4.2 Simulation Process

A virtual sample with surface discretization is divided into three regions according to its hardness: tumor interior, tumor boundary and normal tissue. The shape of tumor is set as a circle. The number of sampling point is $N = 100$. The input is point coordinate and hardness; the algorithm uses the known information to calculate the next optimal point to detect; the output is the hardness distribution map of target area. The F_1 score [10] is used to evaluate the quality of recognition:

$$F_1 = 2 \times \frac{Precision \times Recall}{Precision + Recall} \in [0, 1] \tag{6}$$

By adjusting θ, obtaining the maximum F_1 value, and the θ at this time is substituted into the algorithm.

Flow diagram of the tumor boundary recognition algorithm is shown in Fig. 9.

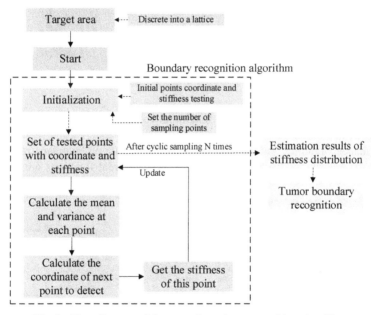

Fig. 9. Flow diagram of the tumor boundary recognition algorithm.

4.3 Results and Discussion

Set θ around 0.5 (= 0.4, 0.5, 0.6, 0.7) to balance exploration and exploitation. The corresponding F_1 score is shown in Fig. 10.

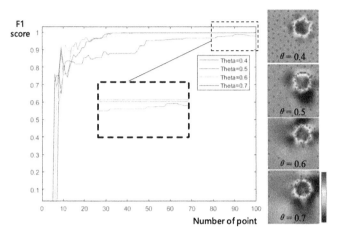

Fig. 10. F1 score corresponding to different θ.

Obviously, the F_1 score obtained 1 (maximum value) when $\theta = 0.5$. So $\theta = 0.5$ is used in the next simulation.

Two shapes of tumor sample are used to test the tumor boundary recognition algorithm. The hardness distribution maps of three different functions are shown in Fig. 11.

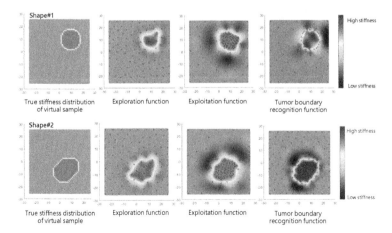

Fig. 11. Tumor recognition result.

It can be seen from Fig. 11 that the boundary of tumor can be clearly recognized using the tumor boundary recognition function. The exploration function can't maintain sampling points around the tumor. The exploitation function can find tumor and sample around it easily but can't recognize the boundary clearly.

5 Conclusions

This paper presents a tactile sensor integrated onto an endoscopic injection needle and a tumor boundary palpation algorithm. The tactile sensor is based on piezoelectric effect, which can effectively detect the hardness of tissue. Moreover, the performance of the sensor is less affected by the contact angle between the needle sheath and the tissue. In addition, a tumor boundary recognition algorithm is applied to estimate tissue hardness distribution. Compared with existing tumor detection algorithms, the simulation results show that the boundary recognition algorithm can accurately detect the location and shape of tumor in tissue samples, which is better than the exploration strategy and the exploitation strategy.

Acknowledgements. This work is supported by National Natural Science Foundation of China (No. 61973335 and No. 62111530151), Natural Science Foundation of Jiangsu Province (BK20191272) and Postgraduate Research & Practice Innovation Program of Jiangsu Province (SJCX21_0096).

References

1. Morizane, S., Honda, M., Ueki, M., Masumori, N., Fujimiya, M., Takenaka, A.: New technique of transurethral en bloc resection of bladder tumor with a flexible cystoscope and endoscopic submucosal dissection devices for the gastrointestinal tract. Int. J. Urol. **27**, 268–269 (2020). https://doi.org/10.1111/iju.14169
2. Zareinia, K., et al.: A force-sensing bipolar forceps to quantify tool-tissue interaction forces in microsurgery. IEEE/ASME Trans. Mechatron. **21**(5), 2365–2377 (2016)
3. Sharma, S., Aguilera, R., Rao, J., Gimzewski, J.K.: Piezoelectric needle sensor reveals mechanical heterogeneity in human thyroid tissue lesions. Sci. Rep. **9**(1), 9282 (2019)
4. Kim, U., Kim, Y.B., So, J., Seok, D.-Y., Choi, H.R.: Sensorized surgical forceps for robotic–assisted minimally invasive surgery. IEEE Trans. Ind. Electron. **65**(12), 9604–9613 (2018)
5. Tanaka, Y., Fukuda, T., Fujiwara, M., et al.: Tactile sensor using acoustic reflection for lump detection in laparoscopic surgery. Int. J. Comput. Assist. Radiol. Surg. **10**(2), 183–193 (2014)
6. Li, T., Pan, A., Ren, H.: Reaction force mapping by 3-axis tactile sensing with arbitrary angles for tissue hard-inclusion localization. IEEE Trans. Biomed. Eng. **68**, 26–35 (2020)
7. Ju, F.: A piezoelectric tactile sensor and human-inspired tactile exploration strategy for lump palpation in tele-operative robotic minimally invasive surgery. In: Proceedings of the 2019 IEEE International Conference on Robotics and Biomimetics (ROBIO), Dali, China, 6–8 December 2019, pp. 223–228 (2019)
8. Uribe, D.O., Schoukens, J., Stroop, R.: Improved tactile resonance sensor for robotic assisted surgery. Mech. Syst. Signal Process. **99**, 600–610 (2018)

9. Ju, F., Wang, Y., Zhang, Z., et al.: A miniature piezoelectric spiral tactile sensor for tissue hardness palpation with catheter robot in minimally invasive surgery. Smart Mater. Struct. **28**, 025033 (2019)

10. Yun, Y., Ju, F., Zhang, Y., et al.: Palpation-based multi-tumor detection method considering moving distance for robot-assisted minimally invasive surgery. In: 2020 42nd Annual International Conference of the IEEE Engineering in Medicine & Biology Society (EMBC), Montreal, QC, Canada, pp. 4899–4902 (2020). https://doi.org/10.1109/EMBC44109.2020.9176127

Vision-Based Pointing Estimation and Evaluation in Toddlers for Autism Screening

Haibo Qin[1], Zhiyong Wang[1], Jingjing Liu[1], Qiong Xu[2], Huiping Li[2], Xiu Xu[2(✉)], and Honghai Liu[1,3(✉)]

[1] State Key Laboratory of Mechanical System and Vibration, Shanghai Jiao Tong University, Shanghai, China
[2] Department of Child Health Care, Children's Hospital of Fudan University, Shanghai, China
duanstar@bit.edu.cn
[3] State Key Laboratory of Robotics and System, Harbin Institute of Technology, Shenzhen, China

Abstract. Early screening of autism spectrum disorder is essential since early intervention can enhance the functional social behavior of autistic children. Among the behavior characteristics of autism, pointing is strongly related to human communicative interaction and cognitive development. To improve the efficiency and accuracy of autism screening, this paper presents a novel vision-based evaluation method for pointing behavior in the screening scenario: expressing needs with pointing (ENP). During the protocol process, a series of features such as hand position, gesture, the pointing direction can be detected, and the pointing behavior can be assessed by the evaluation method. In order to verify the effectiveness of the protocol and evaluation method, 19 toddlers (8 ASD toddlers and 11 non-ASD toddlers) between the ages of 16 and 32 months participate in this study. The accuracy of the automatic evaluation method for pointing behavior is 17/19. It shows that the ENP protocol and the proposed method based on computer vision are feasible in the early screening of autism.

Keywords: Autistic early screening · Pointing direction estimation · Index finger pointing

1 Introduction

Autism spectrum disorder (ASD) is a neurodevelopmental syndrome characterized by impairments in social reciprocity and communication, restricted and stereotyped patterns of behaviors and interests [1]. At present, the research [2] has shown that early diagnosis and intervention can enhance a child's long-term outcome. The Autism Diagnostic Observation Schedule (ADOS) and Autism Diagnostic Interview (ADI) are two standard interviews guiding the diagnostic

© Springer Nature Switzerland AG 2021
X.-J. Liu et al. (Eds.): ICIRA 2021, LNAI 13015, pp. 177–185, 2021.
https://doi.org/10.1007/978-3-030-89134-3_17

and screening process [3]. Traditional ASD screening requires experienced clinicians to observe children's behaviors and takes a long time. With the rapid development of artificial intelligence, many technological ways are applied for autism screening. Wang et al. [4] proposed a new ASD screening protocol and built a multi-sensor computer vision platform. The experimental results showed that the accuracy of ASD classification reached 92.7%. Liu et al. [5] proposed a response-to-instruction protocol and an evaluation method that achieves 95%. Moreover, because toddlers with autism are lack verbal communication skills, it is crucial to express their needs through non-verbal language. Cook et al. [6] proposed a non-intrusive action analysis method based on skeleton key-point recognition to distinguish typical and atypical behaviors of ASD children.

Remarkable differences have been found between typically developing (TD) children and ASD children in pointing gestures for a communicative purpose, especially when children share attention and interests in some objects or events [7]. The ability to expressing needs with pointing has been evaluated in both ADOS and ADI. Therefore, it is essential to detect the behavior of pointing with the index finger for autism screening.

We propose a vision-based pointing estimation and evaluation method for the protocol expressing needs with pointing (ENP) [8]. In this protocol, the ability to use pointing to express needs can be evaluated automatically. The main contributions of the paper are summarized as follows:

1. A novel vision-based pointing direction estimation method has been proposed in natural and unconstrained settings.
2. An evaluation method of pointing combined with the hand movement trend for autism screening is proposed.
3. A children hand database named TASD (The ASD database) [8] is enriched.

2   Protocol and Method

2.1   Protocol

Scenario and Equipment. A platform is designed to evaluate the activity of toddlers for ASD screening, as shown in Fig. 1. In a 4 m × 2.5 m room, the clinician and child sit face to face on two chairs. A 0.6 m × 0.6 m × 0.6 m table is placed between the clinician and the child. Also, a bottle of bubble water is provided to attract the attention of the child. One RGB camera (Logitech BRIO C1000e) is placed 1.0 m above the table to record the video information of the evaluation process.

Protocol Procedure. The detailed procedure of ENP protocol is listed as follows.

1. The child is invited to sit down, and the clinician plays with him to familiarize him with the surroundings.

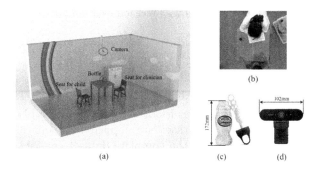

Fig. 1. (a) Presentation of the experimental platform. (b) Top view by an RGB camera. (c) Bubble water bottle for attracting child's attention. (d) RGB camera for recording the video.

2. The clinician takes out a bottle of bubble water and blows a few bubbles to attract the child's attention.
3. The clinician stops blowing bubbles, tightens the bubble water bottle and sets the bottle on the table out of the child's reach. The child is observed whether he makes an action to express that he wishes to continue blowing bubbles.

2.2   Method

The automatic detection and evaluation algorithm has four parts, object detection, gesture recognition, pointing direction estimation and pointing evaluation. Figure 2 shows the general process of the whole evaluation method.

Object Detection. Images captured by the RGB camera are used to detect the child's hands and the bottle of bubble water. At first, a hand and bottle cap dataset in the ENP scenario is created to detect the child's hands and bottle. The dataset has about 3600 images recorded by an RGB camera, Logitech BRIO. The location of the child's hands and a bottle cap is annotated. The dataset is shuffled to be divided into three parts: 80% for training, 16% for test and 4% for evaluation. You Only Look Once v3 (YOLO v3) [9] model is the preliminary model for object detection because of its high accuracy and speed.

The YOLO v3 model is pretrained by the VOC2007 dataset [10] before training our dataset. Before being input into the neural network, the image is resized into 416×416. The network is trained for 100 epochs with a batch size of 6 and 6 types of anchors. Among the 100 epochs, the first 50 epochs freeze all layers except the last layer trained by Adam optimizer with a learning rate of 1.0×10^{-3}. The last 50 epochs unfreeze all layers using Adam optimizer with a learning rate of 1.0×10^{-4} (Table 1).

Hand Gesture Recognition. In this paper, children's hand gestures are divided into index finger pointing, palm pointing with five fingers and other

Table 1. Mean average precision over 0.5 IOU.

Object class	Bottle cap	Child's hand	All classes
AP@0.5IOU (%)	98.57	95.71	97.14

gestures. For children's gesture recognition, we build a dataset of children's gestures. The hand images of the dataset are clipped from our hand detection dataset. After data augmentation, the complete dataset consists of more than 4000 hand images of three gestures. The dataset is shuffled to be split into two parts: training and test with a ratio of 4:1.

In this paper, the ResNet-18 [11] neural network is used for children's hand gesture recognition. The hand gesture dataset is taken to train the ResNet-18. At first, all the hand images are resized to 32×32 to ensure the same size. The network is trained using SGD optimizer with a starting learning rate of 0.1, a momentum of 0.9, a weight decay of 5.0×10^{-4} and a batch size of 64. After 50 epochs of training, the accuracy of the three classes is up to 98%.

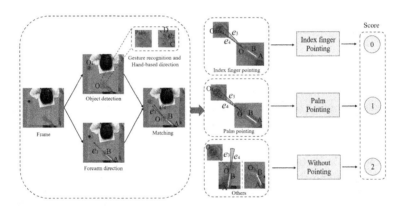

Fig. 2. Overview of the pointing detection and evaluation method. First, the children's hand and the bubble cap are obtained via object detection algorithm. The image of the child's hand area is used for gesture recognition. According to the child's gestures, pointing-related points C, D can be obtained and hand-based direction e_2 can be calculated. At the same time, the frame is used to detect the elbow A and wrist B points of children, and then the forearm direction e_1 is obtained. Vectors e_3 and e_4 are generated through translating the starting points of e_1 and e_2 to point O. The sector area Z_2 is formed by e_3 and e_4. If the pointing area Z_2 intersects the bubble water area Z_1, it indicates that the pointing behavior has occurred. Pointing behavior can be divided into three situations and each situation corresponds to a score.

Pointing Direction Estimation. Index finger pointing and palm pointing are gestures to express needs or show attention, but the latter is not firm or direct. In the protocol, the pointing direction of these two gestures will be estimated. At present, there is no consensus on the definition of pointing direction. In order not to omit children's pointing behavior, we expand children's pointing area as a sector region rather than a line. The two boundaries of the sector are determined by forearm direction and hand-based pointing direction.

The forearm direction e_1 is defined as the vector from elbow joint A to wrist joint B. The two skeleton key points are detected by OpenPose [12]. OpenPose is a real-time multi-person keypoint detection library for the body, face and hands. In this paper, we use OpenPose to detect the key points, including wrist and elbow.

Hand-based pointing direction e_2 is a direction estimation method based on the pose of the hand. A two-stage method is proposed to estimate the hand-based pointing direction. The first stage is to predict the pointing-related hand key points. The pointing direction is calculated according to the key point coordinates in the second stage. The pointing-related key points are start point C and end point D. Different hand gestures have different pointing-related hand key points in Fig. 3. The vector from start point C to end point D is the hand-based pointing direction e_2.

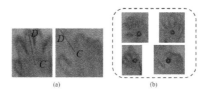

Fig. 3. (a) Presentation of the pointing direction dataset. (b) Result of hand key points detection by AlexNet. The blue circle represents the start point C and the red circle represents the end point D. (Color figure online)

On the basis of the gesture classification dataset, the new pointing direction dataset has about 3000 hand images. It contains two types of gestures, palm pointing and index finger pointing. Each image is annotated with pointing start and end point coordinates based on its gesture type. The dataset is shuffled to be split into three parts: training, test, evaluation with a ratio of 8:1:1. In this section, the AlexNet [13] network model is used for pointing-related key point prediction. First, the images are resized into 224×224. Then the AlexNet has been trained using Adam optimizer with a learning rate of 0.1, batch size of 8 and MSE loss. After 50 epochs training, the average angle error is $4.70°$.

Pointing Evaluation. First, O and O_1 point are the center of the bottle cap box and child's hand, respectively. As shown in the shaded area Z_1, the circle is drawn with the center coordinate of the bottle cap, and the radius r with the distance between the center and the apex of the box. Second, points A and B are the children's elbow and wrist key points detected by OpenPose. The ray e_1 is generated by A pointing to B. At the same time, the ray e_2 is generated by the start point C and end point D of the pointing-related key points in Fig. 4(a).

Then, ray e_1 and ray e_2 are translated to the starting point O to generate ray e_3 and ray e_4 in Fig. 4(b). The ray e_3 and ray e_4 are the two boundaries of hand pointing zone Z_2 in Fig. 4(c). Finally, all rays emitted from point O in the sector area Z_2 form a directed ray cluster. Pointing gestures are evaluated by judging whether the hand pointing ray cluster and the circular area intersect.

Figure 4(d) shows the angle between ray e_3 and horizontal direction ON is θ_1 and the angle between ray e_4 and horizontal direction ON is θ_2. With point O as the starting point, the vectors a and b are the two tangents of the circular area Z_1. The angle between a and b with horizontal direction ON is φ_1 and φ_2. At the same time, $\varphi_1 > \varphi_2$ is satisfied.

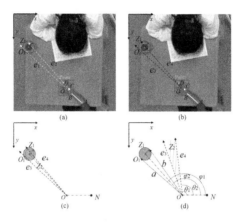

Fig. 4. Pointing direction and evaluation criteria. (a) Presentation of forearm direction e_1 and hand-based direction e_2. (b) Vectors e_3 and e_4 are generated through translating the starting points of e_1 and e_2 to point O. (c) The basis of pointing behavior evaluation. (d) The details of pointing behavior evaluation.

If the following inequality holds, it indicates rays in the directional cluster directed at the bottle.

$$\begin{cases} \max(\theta_1, \theta_2) > \varphi_2 \\ \min(\theta_1, \theta_2) < \varphi_1 \end{cases} \tag{1}$$

Palm pointing and index finger pointing express needs in different degrees. Therefore, we take other evaluation methods for the two pointing behaviors.

During the test, if there are more than m consecutive frames, the index finger pointing relationship is satisfied, and the child is regarded as pointing at the bottle of bubble water. In this paper, m is equal to 6 empirically. Because palm gesture is common and does not always express needs in most cases. Based on the consecutive frame number judgment and introducing the direction and distance of children's hand movement, a palm pointing evaluation method combined with movement trend is proposed. The specific process is as follows in Algorithm 1. In this paper, the number of continuous frames, $k = 10$, and the critical value of correlation coefficient $R_0 = 0.443$ are determined empirically when statistical significance is equal to 0.20.

Algorithm 1. Palm pointing evaluation method

Input:

    Date sequence of three groups:

    The set of bottle box center coordinate for n frames, $B = [O_1^{(1)}, O_1^{(2)}, \ldots, O_1^{(t)}, \ldots, O_1^{(n)}]$;

    The set of child's hand center coordinate, $H = [(O_l^{(1)}, O_r^{(1)}), (O_l^{(2)}, O_r^{(2)}), \ldots, (O_l^{(n)}, O_r^{(n)})]$;

    The set of pointing judgment $J = [(b_l^{(1)}, b_r^{(1)}), (b_l^{(2)}, b_r^{(2)}), \ldots, (b_l^{(n)}, b_r^{(n)})]$;

    h represents right hand, r or left hand, l.

    f_t is the projection of the movement direction onto the target direction.

    Threshold: correlation coefficient R_0, continuous frames, k;

Output:

    Palm pointing evaluation result, T; Correlation coefficient, $R_{\max}$;

1: $T \leftarrow 0$, $R \leftarrow 0$, $R_{\max} \leftarrow 0$, $L = [0, 1, 2, \ldots, k - 1]$;

2: **for** $i = 1$ to $n - k + 1$ **do**

3:     **if** The values of $[b_h^{(i)}, b_h^{(i+1)}, \ldots, b_h^{(i+k-1)}]$ are all 1 **then**

4:         **for** $m = i$ to $i + k - 2$ **do**

5:             $f_t = < \overrightarrow{O_h^{(t)} O_1^{(t)}}, \overrightarrow{O_h^{(t)} O_h^{(t+1)}} >$

6:         **end for**

7:         $F \leftarrow [0, f_i, f_{i+1}, \ldots, f_{i+k-2}]$

8:         R is equal to the correlation between F and L.

9:         **if** $R > R_0$ **then**

10:           $T = 1$

11:           **if** $R > R_{\max}$ **then**

12:              $R_{\max} = R$

13:           **end if**

14:         **end if**

15:     **end if**

16: **end for**

17: **return** T, $R_{\max}$;

---

3 Experiments and Results

3.1 Experiments

The experiment was carried out in the children's hospital of Fudan University. Nineteen toddlers between 16 and 32 months of age participate in the experiments to validate the ENP protocol. Among these 19 participants, 8 children with ASD, 11 non-ASD children are assessed via the ENP protocol. In the experimental scenario we constructed, a professional clinician and children will implement ENP protocol. The whole process is recorded by a RGB camera. The experiments have passed the ethical review, and we pledged not to disclose any personal information about the subjects. After the experiments, clinicians need to make assessments and judgments as to the ground truth of our automatic evaluation method.

3.2 Results

Table 2 presents the two group of children and their experiment ground truth and results in the ENP protocol. Compared to ASD children, it can be clearly found that non-ASD children can mainly use index finger pointing or palm pointing to express their needs. However, only 2 of 8 ASD children can use palm pointing, 6 of 8 ASD children do not show the ability to express needs using pointing gestures. It also indicates that ASD children cannot use pointing gestures to express needs in non-verbal scenarios.

Comparing results with ground truth, our evaluation method achieves 17/19. This accuracy suggests that most pointing behaviors can be detected and evaluated correctly. But there are still two children whose test results do not match the actual evaluation results. For the bad situation of child B in non-ASD, the child does point with his index finger. From the top view, his gesture was more like a transition from the palm pointing to the index finger pointing with his middle finger straight. For the child D with ASD, when he pointed to the bubble, his hand did not move directly against the bubble but at a relatively large Angle. This makes the motion coefficient R_{max} small resulting in ignoring the pointing behavior. So, the accuracy of hand gesture recognition and pointing behavior evaluation method need to be further improved in future.

Table 2. The result of ENP evaluation system.

Subs	TD											ASD							
	A	B	C	D	E	F	G	H	I	J	K	A	B	C	D	E	F	G	H
GT	1	0	2	1	0	0	1	2	1	1	1	2	2	1	1	2	2	2	2
Result	1	2	2	1	0	0	1	2	1	1	1	2	2	1	2	2	2	2	2
R_{max}	0.58	0	0	0.69	0	0	0.54	0	0.83	0.65	0.63	0	0	0.8	0	0	0	0	0

Through the above analysis, although there are still some failure cases in using the vision-based method to detect pointing gestures, it is feasible from the perspective of detection accuracy. The expressing need with pointing protocol can evaluate the non-verbal communication ability of children in the early screening of ASD, which can reduce the requirements for the high experience of clinicians and give a more objective evaluation.

4   Conclusion

We proposed a novel vision-based pointing estimation and evaluation method to evaluate children's non-verbal ability in the expressing need with pointing (ENP) scenario. To validate the protocol and evaluation method, we recruited 19 toddlers between 16 and 32 months of age for the experiment. Results suggested that the accuracy of the automatic evaluation system is 17/19. This illustrates that pointing behavior expressing needs is evaluated accurately. With the increasing demand for autism screening, this method is expected to be widely used. Our future work will focus on introducing the gaze direction of the child to the protocol to detect the children's attention in the protocol.

References

1. Bailey, A., et al.: A clinicopathological study of autism. Brain J. Neurol. **121**(5), 889–905 (1998)
2. Eikeseth, S.: Outcome of comprehensive psycho-educational interventions for young children with autism. Res. Dev. Disabil. **30**(1), 158–178 (2009)
3. Geschwind, D.H.: Advances in autism. Annu. Rev. Med. **60**, 367–380 (2009)
4. Wang, Z., Liu, J., He, K., Xu, Q., Xu, X., Liu, H.: Screening early children with autism spectrum disorder via response-to-name protocol. IEEE Trans. Industr. Inf. **17**, 587–595 (2019)
5. Liu, J., et al.: Early screening of autism in toddlers via response-to-instructions protocol. IEEE Trans. Cybern. (2020)
6. Cook, A., Mandal, B., Berry, D., Johnson, M.: Towards automatic screening of typical and atypical behaviors in children with autism. arXiv preprint arXiv:1907.12537 (2019)
7. Carpenter, M., Pennington, B.F., Rogers, S.J.: Interrelations among social-cognitive skills in young children with autism. J. Autism Dev. Disord. **32**(2), 91–106 (2002)
8. Wang, Z., Xu, K., Liu, H.: Screening early children with autism spectrum disorder via expressing needs with index finger pointing. In: Proceedings of the 13th International Conference on Distributed Smart Cameras, pp. 1–6 (2019)
9. Redmon, J., Farhadi, A.: Yolov3: an incremental improvement. arXiv preprint arXiv:1804.02767 (2018)
10. Everingham, M., Van Gool, L., Williams, C.K.I., Winn, J., Zisserman, A.: The PASCAL visual object classes challenge 2007 (VOC 2007) results. http://www.pascal-network.org/challenges/VOC/voc2007/workshop/index.html
11. Szegedy, C., Ioffe, S., Vanhoucke, V., Alemi, A.A.: Inception-v4, inception-resnet and the impact of residual connections on learning. In: Thirty-First AAAI Conference on Artificial Intelligence (2017)
12. Cao, Z., Simon, T., Wei, S.-E., Sheikh, Y.: Realtime multi-person 2D pose estimation using part affinity fields. In: Proceedings of the IEEE Conference on Computer Vision and Pattern Recognition, pp. 7291–7299 (2017)
13. Krizhevsky, A., Sutskever, I., Hinton, G.E.: ImageNet classification with deep convolutional neural networks. In: Advances in Neural Information Processing Systems, pp. 1097–1105 (2012)

Machine Intelligence for Human Motion Analytics

Multi-Person Absolute 3D Pose and Shape Estimation from Video

Kaifu Zhang[1,2], Yihui Li[1,2], Yisheng Guan[1,2(✉)], and Ning Xi[1,2]

[1] Biomimetic and Intelligent Robotics Lab (BIRL),
Guangdong University of Technology, Guangzhou 510006, China
ysguan@gdut.edu.cn
[2] Department of Industrial and Manufacturing Systems Engineering,
The University of Hong Kong, Pok Fu Lam, HK SAR, China
xining@hku.hk

Abstract. It is a challenging problem to recover the 3D absolute pose and shape of multiple person from video because of the inherent depth, scale and motion blur in the video. To solve this ambiguity, we need to aggregate temporal information, relationship between people and environmental factors, etc. Although many methods have made progress in 3D pose estimation, most of them can not produce accurate and natural motion sequences with absolute scale. In this paper, we propose a new framework, which is composed of human tracking, root-related human mesh estimation and root depth estimation model, adopts temporal network architecture, self-attention mechanism and adversarial training. The experiments show that the method has achieved good performance in in-the-wild datasets.

Keywords: Human pose estimation · Root depth estimation

1 Introduction

In recent years, monocular 3D human pose estimation has broad application prospects in the fields of augmented reality, human-robot interaction, and video analysis. This paper aims to solve the problem of how to use temporal information to accurately estimate the absolute 3D pose and shape of each person at the same time from the monocular RGB multi-person interactive video. Unlike the single-person 3D pose estimation problem that focuses on recovering relative to the root (that is, the 3D position of the key points of the human body relative to the pelvis), the task described here also needs to recover the 3D translation of each person in the camera coordinate system and the shape of the human body.

Existing video pose and shape estimation methods usually cannot get accurate predictions. Previous work [9,23] combined indoor 3D datasets with videos having 2D real or pseudo real keypoint annotations. However, this has several limitations: Indoor 3D datasets have limitations in the number of objects, range of motion, and image complexity; The number of videos marked with real 2D

© Springer Nature Switzerland AG 2021
X.-J. Liu et al. (Eds.): ICIRA 2021, LNAI 13015, pp. 189–200, 2021.
https://doi.org/10.1007/978-3-030-89134-3_18

Fig. 1. We propose a framework to estimate absolute 3D pose and shape of multiple people from video. The figure visualizes the result of our model on an image sequence. The proposed independent dual-branches design allows to estimate SMPL parameters and absolute root depth, respectively.

poses is still not enough to train deep networks, etc. We believe that accurate estimation of the global position of the human body requires focusing on depth-related cues on the entire image, such as the size of the human body, occlusion and the layout of the scene. For 3D human relative pose and shape estimation, the output of our method is based on the pose and shape parameters of SMPL human model [12], learning human motion pattern from video sequences, and then reasonable human motion is generated based on AMASS [13]. Specifically, we balance the two unpaired information sources by training a sequence-based generative adversarial network (GAN) [4]. For the absolute root depth estimation, we regress the root depth of human body in the form of a root depth map using a three-stage Hourglass network. Then the root depth map, relative 3D pose and human body shape parameters are used to recover the absolute 3D pose and shape. The output rersult is shown in Fig. 1. Importantly, on the challenging 3D pose estimation datasets 3DPW [25], Human3.6M [6], and MuPoTS-3D [17], the experimental results show that our framework has significant advantages over the single-frame method. This clearly demonstrates the benefits of using video in 3D pose and shape estimation.

In summary, the main contributions of this paper are:

- A combining attention mechanism and adversarial training method top-down framework for multi-person 3D pose estimation is adopted. By using depth-related cues in the entire image, the absolute 3D position and shape of multi-person can be reliably estimated.
- We have quantitatively compared different temporal model structures for 3D human motion estimation, and we have achieved good results on the main 3D pose estimation dataset.

2   Related Work

2.1   3D Pose and Shape Estimation from a Single Image

Recently, many works trained deep neural networks that can directly regress the parameters of the SMPL human body model from pixel images. For example, due to the lack of in-the-wild datasets with 3D annotations, some methods [8, 24] use weak supervision signals obtained from 2D keypoint reprojection loss. Kolotooros et al. [10] combine regression-based and optimization-based methods in a collaborative manner by using SMPLify in the training loop. In each step of training, a specific deep network [8] is used to initialize the SMPLify optimization method to fit the body model to the 2D joint points, and get an improved fitting result that can be used to supervise the network model. Kolotooros et al. [11] used graph convolutional networks to directly return the positions of the vertex of the human body template. Although the human body is output from a single image, these methods can get unstable results when applied to video.

2.2   3D Pose and Shape Estimation from Video

Recently, some deep learning methods for estimating human pose from videos only focus on joint position. Several of these methods [3, 20] use two-stage method to "lift" the 2D coordinates of key points to 3D coordinates. In contrast, Mehta et al. [16] used the end-to-end method to directly regress the 3D joint position. However, it did not perform well in-the-wild dataset 3DPW [25] and MPI-INF-3DHP [15]. Recently, several methods extend SMPLify to compute consistent body shape and smooth motion sequences, and recover SMPL pose and shape parameters from videos. Among them, Arnab et al. [1] show that internet video data annotated with their SMPLify version can help improve human motion recovery when used for fine-tuning. Kanazawa et al. [9] learned the human kinematics model by predicting past and future image frames. They also show that internet videos annotated with 2D keypoint detectors can reduce the need for in-the-wild 3D pose tags.

3   Approach

The goal of our system is to recover 3D coordinates of human root and SMPL human model parameters [12]. To solve this problem, we built a framework consisting of Tracking Model, Pose and Shape Model and Root Depth Model, as show in Fig. 2. The Tracking Model detects the human body bounding box sequence of each person from video. Pose and Shape Model takes the cropped human body image from the Tracking Model as input and estimates the SMPL model parameters $(\hat{\theta}_t, \hat{\beta})$ of human body. The Root Depth Model takes the entire video sequence as input and estimates the 3D coordinates $p_t^{cam} = (x_{root}, y_{root}, z_{root}^{cam})$ of the root of the human body relative to the center of the camera, in which x_{root} and y_{root} are pixel coordinates in the image space

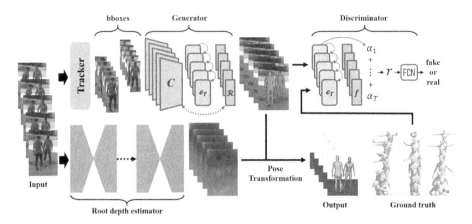

Fig. 2. Proposed independent dual-branches framework. The temporal generator estimates SMPL body model parameters for each frame of video sequence, which is trained together with a temporal discriminator. The root depth estimator outputs absolute human root coordinate using a multi-stage Hourglass network.

and z_{root}^{cam} is an absolute depth value. Finally, $\hat{\theta}_t$ is converted to $\hat{\theta}_t^{cam}$ by adding z_{root}^{cam}. Then, the final absolute 3D pose $\hat{\theta}_t^{cam}$ is obtained through a simple back projection.

3.1   Tracking Model

We use FairMOT [26] as the tracking framework. The one-shot tracker FairMOT consists of two parts. The first part is the backbone network, which inputs video images to the encoder-decoder network to extract high-resolution feature maps (step size = 4). The second part is two homogeneous branch networks, which are used to track the target position and extract the ID feature respectively, and use the feature of the predicted target center to track. Compared with other trackers and detection areas, it has achieved very good performance on the publicly available human tracking dataset. Due to its high performance and publicly available code, we use FairMOT as the human body tracking model in our entire framework.

3.2   Pose and Shape Model

The overall framework of this model is shown in Fig. 2. Given a T length cropped single-person video input $V = \{F_t\}_{t=1}^T$, we use a pre-trained CNN C to extract the features of each frame. We train a temporal encoder e_T and output latent variables containing information about past and future frames. Then, Regressor R regress these features to the parameters $\hat{\Theta}$ of the SMPL model at each time step. We call this model as generator $\mathcal{G}$. Then, the output $\hat{\Theta}$ of $\mathcal{G}$ and the sample $\hat{\Theta}_{real}$ of AMASS are input to a motion discriminator $\mathcal{D}$ to distinguish between fake and real examples.

The Parameter Representation of SMPL. We use a gender-neutral SMPL model [12] to represent the 3D mesh of human body. The model parameter is Θ, which is consisted of the pose parameter $\theta \in \mathbb{R}^{72}$ and the shape parameter $\beta \in \mathbb{R}^{10}$. The pose parameters include the rotation of whole human body and the relative rotation of 23 joints in axis-angle format, and the shape parameters are the first 10 linear coefficients of a PCA shape space.

Model Design. The intuitive explanation of using recurrent architecture is that the information of future frames can benefit from past frames. This is useful when a person's 3D pose is ambiguous or part of the body is occluded in a given frame. In this way, the information of the past frame can help solve and constrain the pose estimation.

Using a temporal encoder e_T as a generator $\mathcal{G}$, given a frame sequence $\{F_1, \cdots, F_T\}$, outputs the pose and shape parameters corresponding to each frame. A seque nce of T frames are input to the convolutional network C, which acts as a feature extractor and outputs a vector $C_i \in \mathbb{R}^{2048}$ for each frame $C(F_1), \cdots, C(F_T)$. Based on the previous frames, they are then input to the Gated Recursive Unit (GRU) layer [2] e_T, which generates a latent feature vector e_i for each frame: $e(C_1), \cdots, e(C_T)$. Then, e_i is input to the T regressor, which is the same as [8]. The regressor is initialized with the mean pose $\bar{\Theta}$, and takes the current parameter Θ_k and the feature e_i as input in each iteration k. We use 6D continuous rotation notation [10] instead of axis-angles. In general, the loss of the generator is composed of four kinds of loss (when these losses are available), the total loss of $\mathcal{G}$ is:

$$L_G = L_{2D} + L_{3D} + L_\theta + L_\beta + L_d \tag{1}$$

The calculation formula for each item is:

$$L_{2D} = \sum_1^T \|x_t - \hat{x}_t\|_2 \tag{2}$$

$$L_{3D} = \sum_1^T \left\|X_t - \hat{X}_t\right\|_2 \tag{3}$$

$$L_\theta = \sum_1^T \left\|\theta_t - \hat{\theta}_t\right\|_2 \tag{4}$$

$$L_\beta = \left\|\beta - \hat{\beta}\right\|_2 \tag{5}$$

The loss L_d will be explained in the following content.

Since the constraints of a single image are not sufficient to explain the pose sequence, multiple imprecise poses may be considered reasonable when the temporal continuity of motion is ignored. In order to alleviate this problem, we use a motion discriminator $\mathcal{D}$ to determine whether the generated pose sequence corresponds to the real sequence. The output of the generator $\hat{\Theta}$ is used as the input of the GRU model e_M, which estimates the latent state h_i at each time step i, where $h_i = e_M(\hat{\Theta}_i)$. To gather the hidden states $[h_i, \ldots, h_T]$, we use the self-attention mechanism. Finally, a linear layer predicts a value between $[0, 1]$, which represents the probability that $\hat{\Theta}$ belongs to a possible human motion sequence. The adversarial loss term backpropagated to $\mathcal{G}$ is:

$$L_d = \mathbb{E}_{\Theta \sim p_{\mathcal{G}}}[(\mathcal{D}(\hat{\Theta}) - 1)^2] \tag{6}$$

and the loss function of $\mathcal{D}$ is:

$$L_{\mathcal{D}} = \mathbb{E}_{\Theta \sim p_{\mathcal{G}}}[\mathcal{D}(\hat{\Theta})^2] + \mathbb{E}_{\Theta \sim p_{real}}[(\mathcal{D}(\Theta) - 1)^2] \tag{7}$$

Where p_{real} is the real motion sequence from the AMASS data set, and $p_{\mathcal{G}}$ is the generated motion sequence. Since $\mathcal{D}$ is trained according to real posture, it can also learn reasonable human motion rules.

The recurrent network updates its hidden state as it processes the input sequentially. Therefore, the final hidden state saves the information summary in the sequence. We use the self-attention mechanism to amplify the contribution of key frames in the final representation, instead of using hard-choice pooling of the final hidden state h_t or the hidden state feature space of the entire sequence. By using the attention mechanism, the representation r of the input sequence is a learned convex combination of hidden states. The weight is learned by the multi-layer perceptron ϕ, and then using softmax to normalize to get a probability distribution. Formally:

$$r = \sum_1^N \frac{e^{\phi(h_i)}}{\sum_{t=1}^N e^{\phi(h_t)}} h_i \tag{8}$$

3.3   Root Depth Model

Since the number of people in the input video is unknown, we use a root depth map to represent the absolute depth of all human bodies in the video frames. The pixel values of the depth map are the human skeleton root joints absolute depths and the 2D position are their root position in image. During training, we only supervise the value of the root position. As shown in Fig. 2, we use three-stage hourglass [19] as the root depth model, and only requires 3D pose (rather than full depth map) as supervision, which makes our algorithm's complexity and Training data is very advantageous.

It is worth noting that the scale and depth of visual perception objects depend on the size of the field of view (FoV), that is, the ratio of the image size to the focal length. If two images are obtained with different FoVs, the same person at the same depth accounts for different proportions, and it is possible for the neural network to output different depth values, which may mislead the depth information Learning. Therefore, we normalize the root depth according to the size of FoV, as shown below:

$$\tilde{z} = z \frac{w}{f} \tag{9}$$

Among them, $\tilde{z}$ is the normalized depth, z is the original depth, f and w are the focal length and the image width, respectively, in pixels. In general, the loss of the Root Depth Model is:

$$L_z = \sum_1^M \|\tilde{z}_i - \tilde{z}_i^*\|_1 \tag{10}$$

where $H(x_i^{root}, y_i^{root})$ is the root gepth map.

3.4   Training Procedure

Pose and Shape Model consists of generator $\mathcal{G}$ and motion discriminator $\mathcal{D}$, as shown in the Fig. 2. The backbone network of the generator is a pre-trained ResNet-50 network [5], which is used to extract the features of a single frame image and output $f_i \in \mathbb{R}^{2048}$, and the parameters of ResNet-50 are not updated. We use $T = 16$ as the sequence length, and the minimum batch size is 32. The neck network contains 3 layers of GRUs with a hidden size of 1024, and the head network is a linear projection layer. Then use the pre-trained SMPL regressor [10] to estimate the pose and shape parameters, and output $\hat{\Theta} \in \mathbb{R}^{85}$, including the pose, shape and camera parameters. The motion discriminator consists of 3 layers of hidden GRU with a size of 1024 and a self-attention layer in turns. For the self-attention layer, we use 3 MLP layers, each with 1024 neurons, the probability of dropout is 0.2, and the activation function is tanh. The final linear layer predicts a true or false probability for each sample.

The Root Depth Model output the root depth map which has only one channel. Each output branch contains only two convolutional layers. We adopted multi-scale intermediate supervision to.

We use Adam optimizer [32] with a learning rate of $5 \times 10^{-5}, 1 \times 10^{-4}, 2 \times 10^{-4}$ for the $\mathcal{G}$, $\mathcal{D}$, and Root Depth Model, respectively. In the loss function, we use different weight coefficients for each term. The weight coefficients of L_{2D} and L_{3D} are respectively $\omega_{2D} = 280$ and $\omega_{3D} = 310$, and the weight coefficients of L_θ and L_β are respectively $\omega_\beta = 0.06$ and $\omega_{theta} = 65$. We set the anti loss term L_d of the supervisor as $\omega_d = 2.2$.

4   Experiments

4.1   Datasets and Evaluation

According to the characteristics of our model framework, we used a batch of training sets that mixed 2D and 3D data during training. InstaVariety [8] is a pseudo ground-truth dataset annotated by a 2D keypoint detector. For 3D annotations, we used 3D joint annotations in Human3.6M [6], MuCo-3DHP and MuPoTS-3D [17]. AMASS [13] is used for adversarial training to obtain real samples. We also use the 3DPW [14] training set for ablation experiments to prove the strength of our model in-the-wild environment. Compared with the previous methods that do not use 3DPW for training, the results without 3DPW are also fairly compared.

We evaluated on 3DPW, Human3.6M and MuPoTS-3D. We report the results with and without the 3DPW training set for direct comparison with previous work. The evaluation criteria reported in this paper are PA-MPJPE, MPJPE, PVE, 3DPCK, Acceleration error (Accel) and AP_{25}, and compared with some previous methods.

4.2   Comparison to State-of-the-Art-Results

In Table 1, we compare our root-relative pose and shape model with some previous methods. The previous methods did not use 3DPW as the training set, but we want to prove that using 3DPW for training helps improve the actual performance of our model. The model in Table 1 uses the pre-trained HMR [10] as the feature extractor. It can be seen from the results in the table that although the performance of our model is slightly worse than that of the state-of-the-art method in the Human3.6M data set, the performance in the challenging in-the-wild dataset 3DPW is better than previous methods. Please note that Human3.6M is an indoor data set with a limited number of subjects and minimal background changes, while 3DPW contains challenging outdoor environment videos. These results verify our hypothesis that the development of human kinematics is very important for improving pose and shape estimation in videos.

Table 1. Benchmark of state-of-the-art models on 3DPW, Human3.6M and MuPoTS-3D datasets. we compare the results of recent state-of-the-art models on three different datasets. Ours(w-3DPW) is our proposed framework trained on datasets whitch included 3DPW. Ours, on the other hand, trained without 3DPW training set.

	3DPW		Human3.6M		MuPoTS-3D
	$PA-MPJPE\downarrow$	$PVE\downarrow$	$PA-MPJPE\downarrow$	$MPJPE\downarrow$	$PCK_{rel}\uparrow$
Doersch. [3]	75.5	–	–	–	–
Kolotouros. [10]	59.9	117.1	41.7	–	–
Kanazawa. [7]	77.1	–	56.8	88.4	–
Kanazawa. [8]	72.8	139.6	57.2	–	–
Moon. [18]	–	–	**34.7**	**54.8**	80.5
Rogez. [22]	–	–	–	–	71.0
Mehta. [16]	–	–	–	–	65.5
Ours	63.5	121.8	42.8	64.9	78.5
Ours(w-3DPW)	**57.8**	**115.6**	36.6	69.4	**82.6**

Table 2 shows that the performance of our Root Depth Model on the Human3.6M dataset based on protocol 2 outperforms the previous methods. In addition, the Root Depth Model can be designed independently, thus providing design flexibility for different modules. In contrast, the Baseline method requires 2D and 3D prediction of root location, which leads to a lack of generalizability.

4.3   Ablation Analysis

Table 3 shows the performance of the model with and without motion discriminator $\mathcal{D}$. First, we use the original HMR model proposed in [7] as a feature extractor ($\mathcal{G}^*$). Once we add the generator $\mathcal{G}$, due to lack of sufficient video

Table 2. MRPE comparisons between previous root depth estimation models and ours on the Human3.6M dataset. $MRPE_x$, $MRPE_y$, and $MRPE_z$ represent the mean of the errors in the x, y, and z axes, respectively.

Methods	$MRPE_x\downarrow$	$MRPE_y\downarrow$	$MRPE_z\downarrow$	$MRPE\downarrow$
Baseline [15,21]	270.6	30.2	30.9	263.7
Moon. [18]	**122.7**	**26.1**	25.7	109.9
Ours	123.1	27.9	25.3	110.6
Ours (w-3DPW)	122.8	27.4	**24.2**	**108.3**

training data, we got slightly worse but smoother results than other model. Then, using $\mathcal{D}$ helps to improve the performance of $\mathcal{G}^*$ while still producing smoother predictions. When we use the pre-trained HMR in [10] ($\mathcal{G}$), we observe similar enhancements when using $\mathcal{D}$ or only using $\mathcal{D}$.

Table 3. Ablation experiments with generator $\mathcal{G}$ and discriminator $\mathcal{D}$

Model	$PA-MPJPE\downarrow$	$MPJPE\downarrow$	$Accel\downarrow$
Kolotouros. [9]	61.3	103.5	30.2
Only $\mathcal{G}^*$	76.9	127.1	29.3
$\mathcal{G}^* + \mathcal{D}$	73.4	117.6	28.8
Only $\mathcal{G}$	58.2	91.4	29
$\mathcal{G} + \mathcal{D}$	**53.3**	**84.2**	**25.4**

As shown in Table 4, compared with the static pooling, the dynamic characteristic aggregation in $\mathcal{D}$ has a significant improvement in the final result. The self-attention mechanism enables $\mathcal{D}$ to learn how the previous and next frames are related to each other temporally, instead of hardly focusing on their feature. In most cases, using the self-attention mechanism will produce better results.

Table 4. Ablation experiments on structure of attention

Model	$PA-MPJPE\downarrow$	$MPJPE\downarrow$
D - concat	55.9	88
D - attention [2 layers,512 nodes]	54.7	86.5
D - attention [2 layers,1024 nodes]	53.6	83.8
D - attention [3 layers,512 nodes]	55.3	87.8
D - attention [3 layers,1024 nodes]	**52.8**	**83.2**

Table 5 shows the impact of different structural designs on the accuracy of human root depth estimation: 1) If depth normalization is not performed, the

Table 5. Ablation experiments on structure of human root depth estimation model

Design	$AP_{25}\uparrow$	$AUC\uparrow$	$3DPCK_{abs}\uparrow$
No Depth Normalization	5.7	39.1	9.3
No Multi-scale Supervision	29.5	**39.8**	36.2
One-stage Model	27.1	39.6	34.9
Full Model	**30.9**	**39.8**	**38.7**

performance of the model will be severely degraded. As we discussed in the previous chapter, normalizing the depth value by the FoV size can make training easier. 2) Multi-scale supervision is beneficial. 3) Multi-backbone networks have better performance than single-backbone networks.

5   Conclusions

Our framework includes human body tracking, 3D single person root-related pose and shape estimation, and 3D body absolute root positioning, from which the absolute 3D pose and shape of multiple people can be reconstructed. The accuracy of the proposed model is basically better than that of the previous 3D multi-person pose estimation methods. The experiment proves the performance and generalization ability of the model in 3D pose and shape estimation in-the-wild multi-person scene.

References

1. Arnab, A., Doersch, C., Zisserman, A.: Exploiting temporal context for 3D human pose estimation in the wild. In: Proceedings of the IEEE/CVF Conference on Computer Vision and Pattern Recognition, pp. 3395–3404 (2019)
2. Dabral, R., Mundhada, A., Kusupati, U., Afaque, S., Jain, A.: Structure-aware and temporally coherent 3D human pose estimation. arXiv preprint arXiv:1711.09250 **3**(4), 6 (2017)
3. Doersch, C., Zisserman, A.: Sim2Real transfer learning for 3D human pose estimation: motion to the rescue. arXiv preprint arXiv:1907.02499 (2019)
4. Grauman, K., Shakhnarovich, G., Darrell, T.: Inferring 3D structure with a statistical image-based shape model. In: ICCV, vol. 3, p. 641 (2003)
5. He, K., Zhang, X., Ren, S., Sun, J.: Identity mappings in deep residual networks. In: Leibe, B., Matas, J., Sebe, N., Welling, M. (eds.) ECCV 2016. LNCS, vol. 9908, pp. 630–645. Springer, Cham (2016). https://doi.org/10.1007/978-3-319-46493-0_38
6. Ionescu, C., Papava, D., Olaru, V., Sminchisescu, C.: Human3.6M: large scale datasets and predictive methods for 3D human sensing in natural environments. IEEE Trans. pattern Anal. Mach. Intell. **36**(7), 1325–1339 (2013)
7. Kanazawa, A., Black, M.J., Jacobs, D.W., Malik, J.: End-to-end recovery of human shape and pose. In: Proceedings of the IEEE Conference on Computer Vision and Pattern Recognition, pp. 7122–7131 (2018)

8. Kanazawa, A., Zhang, J.Y., Felsen, P., Malik, J.: Learning 3D human dynamics from video. In: Proceedings of the IEEE/CVF Conference on Computer Vision and Pattern Recognition, pp. 5614–5623 (2019)
9. Kay, W., et al.: The kinetics human action video dataset. arXiv preprint arXiv:1705.06950 (2017)
10. Kolotouros, N., Pavlakos, G., Black, M.J., Daniilidis, K.: Learning to reconstruct 3D human pose and shape via model-fitting in the loop. In: Proceedings of the IEEE/CVF International Conference on Computer Vision, pp. 2252–2261 (2019)
11. Kolotouros, N., Pavlakos, G., Daniilidis, K.: Convolutional mesh regression for single-image human shape reconstruction. In: Proceedings of the IEEE/CVF Conference on Computer Vision and Pattern Recognition, pp. 4501–4510 (2019)
12. Loper, M., Mahmood, N., Romero, J., Pons-Moll, G., Black, M.J.: SMPL: a skinned multi-person linear model. ACM Trans. Graph. (TOG) **34**(6), 1–16 (2015)
13. Mahmood, N., Ghorbani, N., Troje, N.F., Pons-Moll, G., Black, M.J.: AMASS: archive of motion capture as surface shapes. In: Proceedings of the IEEE/CVF International Conference on Computer Vision, pp. 5442–5451 (2019)
14. von Marcard, T., Henschel, R., Black, M.J., Rosenhahn, B., Pons-Moll, G.: Recovering accurate 3D human pose in the wild using IMUs and a moving camera. In: Proceedings of the European Conference on Computer Vision (ECCV), pp. 601–617 (2018)
15. Mehta, D., et al.: Monocular 3D human pose estimation in the wild using improved CNN supervision. In: 2017 international conference on 3D vision (3DV), pp. 506–516. IEEE (2017)
16. Mehta, D., et al.: XNect: real-time multi-person 3D human pose estimation with a single RGB camera. arXiv preprint arXiv:1907.00837 (2019)
17. Mehta, D., et al.: Single-shot multi-person 3D pose estimation from monocular RGB. In: 2018 International Conference on 3D Vision (3DV), pp. 120–130. IEEE (2018)
18. Moon, G., Chang, J.Y., Lee, K.M.: Camera distance-aware top-down approach for 3D multi-person pose estimation from a single RGB image. In: Proceedings of the IEEE/CVF International Conference on Computer Vision, pp. 10133–10142 (2019)
19. Newell, A., Yang, K., Deng, J.: Stacked hourglass networks for human pose estimation. In: Leibe, B., Matas, J., Sebe, N., Welling, M. (eds.) ECCV 2016. LNCS, vol. 9912, pp. 483–499. Springer, Cham (2016). https://doi.org/10.1007/978-3-319-46484-8_29
20. Pavlakos, G., Zhu, L., Zhou, X., Daniilidis, K.: Learning to estimate 3D human pose and shape from a single color image. In: Proceedings of the IEEE Conference on Computer Vision and Pattern Recognition, pp. 459–468 (2018)
21. Rogez, G., Weinzaepfel, P., Schmid, C.: LCR-Net: localization-classification-regression for human pose. In: Proceedings of the IEEE Conference on Computer Vision and Pattern Recognition, pp. 3433–3441 (2017)
22. Rogez, G., Weinzaepfel, P., Schmid, C.: LCR-Net++: multi-person 2D and 3D pose detection in natural images. IEEE Trans. Pattern Anal. Mach. Intell. **42**(5), 1146–1161 (2019)
23. Sapp, B., Taskar, B.: MODEC: multimodal decomposable models for human pose estimation. In: Proceedings of the IEEE Conference on Computer Vision and Pattern Recognition, pp. 3674–3681 (2013)
24. Sun, Y., Ye, Y., Liu, W., Gao, W., Fu, Y., Mei, T.: Human mesh recovery from monocular images via a skeleton-disentangled representation. In: Proceedings of the IEEE/CVF International Conference on Computer Vision, pp. 5349–5358 (2019)

25. Varol, G., et al.: BodyNet: volumetric inference of 3D human body shapes. In: Proceedings of the European Conference on Computer Vision (ECCV), pp. 20–36 (2018)
26. Zhang, Y., Wang, C., Wang, X., Zeng, W., Liu, W.: FairMOT: on the fairness of detection and re-identification in multiple object tracking. arXiv e-prints pp. arXiv-2004 (2020)

Effects of Wrist Configuration and Finger Combination on Translational Range of Bimanual Precision Manipulation

Yuan Liu[(✉)], Qian Cheng, Wenjie Wang, and Dong Ming

Tianjin University, Tianjin 300072, China
ryanliu@tju.edu.cn

Abstract. Bimanual manipulation is an essential ability in daily human lives, enhancing the one-hand functionality and grasping tolerance ability. The present work focuses on the effects of wrist and finger factors on bimanual precision manipulation abilities regarding the range of workspace and translational distance. Ten participants were asked to bimanually manipulate object under 12 situations, paired with three wrist configurations and four finger combinations. The results show that the wrist configurations and the finger combinations have significant effects on the translational range. Specifically, the involvement of the wrists significantly improves the workspace range of the object by increasing the translational distance in each axis direction. Among them, the growth rate of the translation distance of the sagittal axis and vertical axis is significantly higher than that of the frontal axis. Compared with the other three finger combinations, the translational distances on the frontal axis and vertical axis of the two indexes combination are increased significantly and similarly, suggesting that for bimanual manipulation, the index finger result in an increase in performance. The study has many applications, including developing two-handed robot and novel human augment equipment.

Keywords: Bimanual · Precision manipulation · Translational range

1 Introduction

The human hand has up to 24 degrees of freedoms (DOFs), which gives it great agility, and two hands have double DOFs. Besides, we are able to manipulate and move objects using two hands with great precision and security, which is one of the hallmarks of human talent [1]. Bimanual manipulation is an essential ability in daily human lives. Most daily activities require a degree of coordination between two hands, such as sewing, opening a bottle, playing musical instruments, preparing and eating food, using the screwdriver and electric drill, etc. [2]. Two hands have evolved into a highly complex system whose powerful motor functions and talent are still unknown.

In this study, we focused on the most dexterous movement of bimanual manipulation – bimanual precision manipulation, which involves movement using the fingertips of both hands to move objects without changing the point of contact (Fig. 1). Specifically,

© Springer Nature Switzerland AG 2021
X.-J. Liu et al. (Eds.): ICIRA 2021, LNAI 13015, pp. 201–212, 2021.
https://doi.org/10.1007/978-3-030-89134-3_19

we look at the reachable translational range of the object being manipulated in different hand situations, including the range of the workspace and the translational distance of the coordinate axes. This operational capability dramatically increases the one-hand dexterity functionality and grasping tolerance ability. Thus, bimanual precision manipulation is helpful in small space, expanding the range of movement while improving the accuracy of manipulation [3].

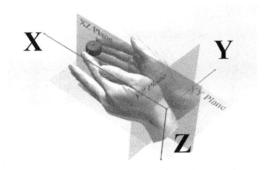

Fig. 1. The reachable range of bimanual precision manipulation (take the combination of two index fingers, for example). According to the reference point for calculating the volume and visualization of the translational distance, a new coordinate system is established.

Previous studies on bimanual manipulation have focused on bimanual coupling effects [4, 5] and handedness, including competitive advantage and priority characteristics of two hands. Instead of collecting and analyzing hand movements, they did a qualitative analysis to generalize behavioral patterns [6, 7]. Other studies considered the wide range movements with the arms rather than bimanual manipulation with a hand-centric consideration [8]. Only Yao et al. selected the task of watch maintenance to study bimanual precision manipulation [9]. They used surface force and kinematics indicators to evaluate coordination patterns and inverse optimization methods to infer optimal criteria. The significant difference is that this paper focuses on the translational range for hand-centric bimanual precision manipulation.

In the research of one-handed precision manipulation, reachable range and its influencing factors are often concerned. Quantitative analysis metrics typically include the volume of the workspace and translational distance of the axes. Previous studies focused on the influencing factors for one-handed precision manipulation, such as the number of fingers, the size of the object [10], and the way of grasping. For example, Bullock et al. showed that different participating fingers significantly influence single-handed object grasping and dexterous manipulation [11]. In addition, some studies have shown that wrist posture plays an essential role in the range of motion and strength of our finger application [12]. Still, few studies have considered the influence of the wrist factor on precision manipulation. Therefore, to focus on the motor ability of human hands, this research selected two factors, wrist configuration and finger combination, that may affect the bimanual precision manipulation ability to verify and analyze their influence rules on the reachable translational range of bimanual precision manipulation.

Knowledge of the bimanual precision manipulation translational range can be applied to many domains. For example, in rehabilitation, the bimanual manipulation information can help standardize the hand rehabilitation data [13]. In microsurgery, it can provide doctors with precise training guidelines to improve their surgery level [14]. Finally, in robotics, it can serve as the anthropomorphic control of dual-arm and dual-hand [15], and the results can be applied to the design of the drive configuration [16].

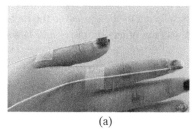
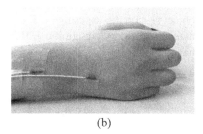

(a)   (b)

Fig. 2. Sensor paste position. Take the right hand, for example, and attach them to the two hands symmetrically. (a) Shows the marker position of fingernails, and the sensor records the motion data of fingertips. (b) Is the marker sticking position of the back of the hand and the arm.

The organization of the whole paper is as follows: Sect. 2 introduces the research methods, Sect. 3 presents the results, and Sect. 4 discusses the results and applications. Finally, Sect. 5 summarizes the whole paper.

2   Methods

2.1   Participants

Ten participants who completed the experiment were recruited from the local university. They were 20–24 years old, with seven female and three male participants. Their hands ranged in length from 16.5 to 19.1 cm, with an average length of 17.7 cm. The experimental setup required right-handed participants, and any participants with previous severe hand or wrist injuries were excluded. The university's IRB approved the study, and all participants were informed and agreed in advance.

2.2   Equipment

A trakSTAR magnetic tracking system (Ascension Technologies, Burlington, VT) with a medium-range transmitter (MRT) and eight MODEL-180 2 mm diameter sensors were used. Each system provides 6 DOF data at the configured, recommended sampling rate of 80 Hz. The positional accuracy of the system is 1.4 mm RMS, and the angular accuracy is 0.5° RMS.

The eight sensors were fixed on the human body using 3M double-sided tape and medical pressure-sensitive tape to reduce the involuntary rotation of the sensor's long axis during the experiment. The positions of sensors are symmetrical. As shown in Fig. 2, four sensors were pasted on the fingertips of the thumb and index finger respectively to record the motion data of the fingertips. The other four sensors are pasted on the back of the hands and the arms as coordinate reference points. In addition, another sensor is fixed to the center of the object using a set screw to record position information.

The object to be manipulated is a 3D-printed cylindrical with rounded corners. The material is plastic, which can avoid interfering with the magnetic field. There are four diameters of the object, respectively 3.32, 3.52, 3.66 or 3.86 cm (Fig. 3). The diameter is determined according to the hand length of the participants to exclude the influence of the object size on the experiment. The diameter was selected as the closest to the target diameter specified by equation $d = 0.2 L$, where d was the object diameter and L was the hand length.

d =3.32 cm   d =3.52 cm   d =3.66 cm   d =3.86 cm

Fig. 3. The pointed object used for manipulation in this study. The object size was scaled according to participant hand length.

A liquid crystal display (LCD) was placed one meter in front of the testbed to provide visual feedback (Fig. 4a). The three projections of the new coordinate system, as shown in Fig. 4b, are displayed on the screen. During each trial, participants were asked to visually map out the extensive range possible and fill in the area. This method can help participants to detect the limit of workspace and find the maximum range of movement.

2.3 Procedure

Some preparatory work was done before the experiment. First, the participants were shown photos of the experimental paradigm and explained the whole process in detail according to the pictures. Then, participants were told to manipulate the object under different experimental conditions and ensure that the initial contact point was in the lower half of each finger pad without slippage of the contact point of the fixed screw. During the experiment, this constraint was enforced, and the experimenter observed the participants in real-time ensure that they understood the instructions and did not violate the rule.

The experimental scene is shown in Fig. 4a. There were three types of wrist configurations throughout the experiment: 1) the wrists are appressed without rotating (ANR), 2) the wrists are appressed and rotatable (AR), 3) free state (FREE). In addition, there were four different finger combinations: left thumb and right thumb (TT), left thumb and right index (TI), left index and right thumb (IT), left index and right index (II). Participants had to manipulate objects in 12 different situations (Three wrist configurations are paired with four finger combinations).

In ANR, the wrist could not rotate, the participants' forearms and hands were placed on the table, and the little finger and the side of the hand were fixed on the table, unable to lift and move, limiting the DOFs of wrists. In ANR and AR, a motion strap was used to help participants keep their wrists appressed. When the wrists are FREE, it just needs to immobilize the participant's forearm, avoiding hand motion constraint by other supporting methods (Fig. 5). According to the above three wrist configurations, we can obtain the effects of wrists participation and distance between the wrists on the bimanual precision manipulation.

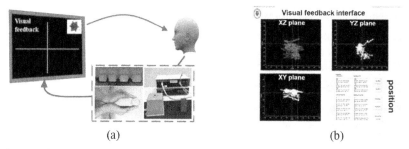

(a)   (b)

Fig. 4. (a) Is the experiment scene. Participants manipulate the object as required, while a screen in front of them provides visual feedback to help them explore the maximum workspace. (b) Is visual feedback of three views of the translational range traced out is provided on display.

The trial order is random. Each trial takes 90 s and is repeated three times under each situation. After each trial, there was a rest period of 30 s. Overall, the experiment lasted about 70 min, including the time it took the experimenter to switch between different conditions.

2.4 Data Processing

Normalization

We expect that most of the effects will scale with the size of the hand. Therefore, all data were normalized to keep measurements intuitive and exclude the influence of hand length, according to the median 17.7 cm of all participants' hand length. The individual reachable range points for a given participant i are scaled according to

$$\left(x', y', z'\right) = \left(\frac{\bar{l}}{l_{hi}}x, \frac{\bar{l}}{l_{hi}}y, \frac{\bar{l}}{l_{hi}}z\right) \tag{1}$$

where $\bar{l}$ is the median hand length, l_{hi} is the given participant's hand length. The desired effect is to view all data as if it came from a participant with a median 17.7 cm hand length while keeping the data in units that are easier to understand intuitively.

Workspace Range Quantification

Sensors were fitted on each participant's arms as a reference point for the volume of the workspace (Fig. 2b). Although the participants were required to keep the arm from moving, it could not be avoided entirely. Using the arm's sensors as a reference point can reduce the error caused by arm movement.

The sensors can collect the 3D coordinate data of the hand and the moving object at each sampling moment. The 3D coordinate data of the object is subtracted from the coordinate data of the reference at each moment, and the obtained data is used to calculate the object workspace volume.

The convex hull is a computational geometric concept often used to calculate three-dimensional irregular point sets. It uses convex polygon boundaries to classify points into convex hulls in 3D spaces. Then the volume of the three-dimensional body surrounded by the edge is calculated as the workspace volume. For convex hull calculation, the MATLAB convhull solver was used. This tool is based on the Qhull algorithm developed by Barber et al. [17].

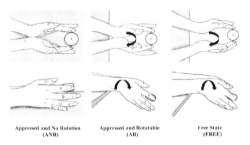

Appressed and No Rotation
(ANR)

Appressed and Rotatable
(AR)

Free State
(FREE)

Fig. 5. Three types of wrist configurations (take the combination of two index fingers, for example). In any case, the arm is immobile.

Coordinate System Establishment

We establish a new coordinate system according to the arm and hand reference point (Fig. 1). Reference point to two arms the midpoint at the initial coordinates of the origin, the halfway point of the two-initial coordinate of hand datum to X-axis direction (sagittal axis), the right arm datum of the initial coordinates of Y-axis direction (frontal axis), transmitters of vertical downward direction for the Z-axis are the direction (vertical axis). As Fig. 1 is shown, the three planes of the new coordinate system are parallel to the three anatomical planes of the human body.

Statistics Analysis

After the gaussian test, it is found that the distribution of relevant data in this experiment does not meet the normality, so the non-parametric analysis method is adopted in this study. The differences between the wrist configuration (ANR/AR/FREE) and the finger combination (TT/TI/IT/II) in the workspace range and the translation distance on the coordinate axes were studied by the Friedman rank-sum test. Statistical significance was set at $p < 0.05$. SPSS (IBM V.23) was used to run statistical analysis.

3 Results

The influence of wrist configuration and finger combination on the accessible workspace range of the object is shown in Table 1. The mean volumes in all situations ranged from 158.77 to 1752.43 cm^3, with the difference volumes up to ten times. Friedman's rank test results show that both wrist configuration and finger combination significantly affect the workspace range of bimanual precision manipulation ($p < 0.001$, $p < 0.001$).

The influence of wrist factors on workspace range under different finger combinations is shown in Fig. 6a. Paired comparison of the wrist factors shows that the ANR range is significantly smaller than those of AR and FREE ($p < 0.001$, $p < 0.001$). In the same finger combination, the average volume of the workspace with the wrist movement is about five times that of the workspace without the wrist. On the other hand, there is no significant difference in the volume of FREE and AR as a whole ($p = 0.85$).

Table 1. The data of the object workspace.

	Object Workspace(cm^3) (M ± SD)			p value	
	ANR	AR	FREE	Wrist	Finger
TT	169.29 ± 97.27	893.17 ± 680.98	967.19 ± 806.38	**<0.001**	**<0.001**
TI	207.73 ± 113.28	1099.48 ± 1019.88	1351.35 ± 1115.47		
IT	262.19 ± 180.51	1065.76 ± 846.51	1284.35 ± 890.70		
II	320.65 ± 180.27	1632.71 ± 1230.69	1709.86 ± 1263.87		

Significant differences ($p < 0.05$) for the Friedman's rank test results are indicated in bold.

The effect of changing different finger combinations on the workspace range is shown in Fig. 6b. The paired comparison results show a significant difference between the workspace range in II combination and TT, TI and IT combinations ($p < 0.001$, $p < 0.001$, $p = 0.008$). Thus, in bimanual precision manipulation, a larger workspace can be obtained with the cooperation of two indexes.

To more intuitively analyze the law and mechanism of the influence of wrist factor and finger factor on the translational range, we also observed the translational distance of the object in the three coordinate axes (the new coordinate system) (Fig. 7c). Specifically, we used a common outlier detection method, which identifies and removes points in each direction that is more than three standard deviations from the mean and then calculates the distance of the points in each direction.

The influence of the wrist factor on the translational distance is shown in Fig. 7a and Table 2. Similar to the results in the workspace ranges, the wrist factor significantly affects the translational distance of all three axes ($p < 0.001$, $p < 0.001$, $p < 0.001$). The distances are significantly increased when the wrists are involved. We use growth rates to quantify the extent to which the translational distance has grown. The results show that when the wrists are involved, the growth rates in the X and Z direction are significantly higher than that in the Y direction, generally more than twice ($p < 0.001$) (Table 2).

The effect of changing the finger combinations on the translational distance is shown in Fig. 7b. The finger factor has no significant effect on the translational distance of the X-axis ($p = 0.26$). In contrast, the finger combination significantly affected the translational distance of the Y and Z-axis ($p < 0.001$). Under the same wrist configuration, the Y and Z-axis translational distance in II is significantly larger than in the other three combinations ($p < 0.001$). The result of the growth rate shows that the growth rate of the Y-axis is significantly higher than that of the Z-axis for the TT to II combination. Under TI and IT combinations, there is no significant difference in the growth rate between the Y-axis and Z-axis (Table 3).

4 Discussion

In this paper, the influence of the wrist factor and the finger factor on the reachable translational range of bimanual precision manipulation was analyzed quantitatively. In general, wrist configurations and finger combinations significantly affect the workspace range and translational distance of the coordinate axes for bimanual precision manipulation.

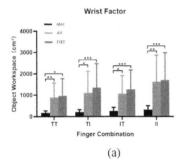
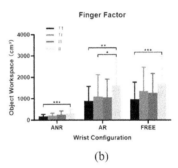

(a)   (b)

Fig. 6. The mean value trend of wrist and finger factors on workspace volume. (a) The volume of the workspace in ANR is much lower than that in AR and FREE ($p < 0.001$) and there is no significant difference between AR and FREE ($p = 0.85$). (b) The workspace volume of II is significantly larger than that of TT, TI and IT ($p < 0.001, p < 0.001, p < 0.001$).

The results for the different wrist configurations show a significant five-fold increase in workspace volume when the wrists are involved. One reason for the results is that the involvement of the wrists increases the DOFs of bimanual precision manipulation, and the abduction and flexion of the wrists significantly expand the range of motion. In addition, previous studies have shown that wrist posture also plays an important role in the range and strength of fingers motion [12]. Thus, when wrist movement is limited, participants cannot ensure without hindering the free movement of the fingers.

The study of the translational distance of the coordinate axes shows that when the wrists are involved, the range of motion on each axis increased significantly. The results suggest that the movement of wrists increases the workspace range, increasing the translational distance along each axis. Specifically, when the wrists are involved, the X and Z-axis translational distance growth rate is significantly higher than that of the Y-axis.

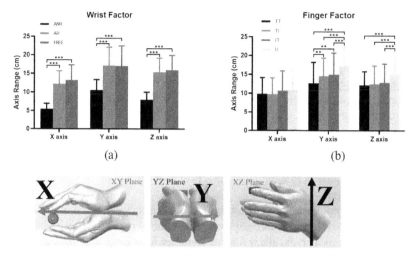

Fig. 7. The mean value trend of wrist and finger factors on translational distance. (a) The translational distance on each axis in ANR is much lower than that in AR and FREE on each axis ($p <$ 0.001) (b) The translational distance of II is significantly larger than that of TT, TI and IT on Y- and Z-axis ($p < 0.001, p < 0.001$). (c) Is a schematic diagram of the three axes.

Table 2. The growth rate of the translational distance when the wrists are involved.

	Growth rate (M ± SD)			p value		
	X axis	Y axis	Z axis	X-Y	X-Z	Y-Z
ANR-AR	1.33 ± 0.76	0.69 ± 0.55	1.03 ± 0.70	*<0.001*	*0.539*	*0.002*
ANR-Free	1.50 ± 0.80	0.66 ± 0.52	1.12 ± 0.77	*<0.001*	*0.133*	*0.002*

Table 3. The growth rate of the translational distance in II combination.

	Growth Rate (M ± SD)		p value
	Y axis	Z axis	
TT-II	0.45 ± 0.26	0.22 ± 0.27	*0.002*
TI-II	0.20 ± 0.12	0.21 ± 0.14	*0.544*
IT-II	0.20 ± 0.19	0.18 ± 0.20	*0.959*

One probable cause is that the degree of freedom of wrist abduction plays a more important role in the performance of finger function. When wrists abduction and finger movement are carried out simultaneously, and the increase in the range caused by wrist movement, the range of fingertip movement relative to the palm is also increased.

The mean value of the workspace volume shows that the order of the workspace range for the same wrist configuration is: TT < TI < IT < II. This seems to be a general trend. However, only the II has a statistically significant difference in the workspace range compared with the other three combinations. Specifically, the II significantly increases the accessible workspace range for bimanual precision manipulation. It is possible that the II combination has a better counterpoint and has stronger control over the object. Another probable cause is that the index fingers are longer and move synchronously to make the range larger.

Thumbs are physiologically better suited to the coordination of the other fingers of one hand, so the two thumbs work even worse in bimanual precision manipulation. The coordination degree is also excellent for the asymmetric finger configurations (TI, IT), and the manipulation is more stable than the TT combination. However, the ranges of their workspaces are significantly smaller than that of the II. It is possible that the thumb itself has a short structure and cannot reach some areas within reach of the index finger. As a result, the index finger movement compensates for the movement of the thumb, and its motion range is reduced.

The results show that the finger combination has no significant effect on the translational distance of the X-axis but has a significant effect on the Y and Z-axis. The translational distance of II in the Y and Z-axis is significantly larger than that of TT, TI and IT. This result indicates that the index finger's abduction-adduction and swinging motion ability are fully exerted when the two index fingers cooperate. However, the flexion of the index finger is affected by the operating object, and its contact property is easy to change. The motion is reduced to maintain the stability of the object.

Knowledge of the bimanual precision manipulation translational range can be applied to many domains of robotics. Most of the existing supernumerary robotic limbs (SRL) were designed for subjective purposes and lacked objective kinematic data to support them. For instance, some SRLs cooperate with the whole hand, only play a fixed and supporting role to compensate for grasping in several activities of daily living (ADLs) without dexterity [18]. The results of this paper can provide the basis for the design and actuation configuration of SRL. For example, it is necessary to add the degree of freedom of the wrist into the design of the SRL, which can significantly improve its movement ability. In addition, the structural design of SRL finger should also refer to the human finger. If dexterous manipulation is the goal orientation, the external finger structure should be designed to imitate the index finger. The length should be similar to that of the matching finger to maximize the movement ability of the hand and the external limb, enhancing agility.

5 Conclusion

In this paper, the factors of finger and wrist that may affect the reachable translational range of bimanual precision manipulation are analyzed. The workspace volume and the translational distance of each coordinate axis are used as quantitative indexes to find the influence rules of these two factors. The results show that the wrist configurations and the finger combinations have significant effects on the maximum reachable workspace range and the translational distance of the coordinate axis. The involvement of the wrists significantly increases the workspace range for bimanual precision manipulation, and the translational distance on each axis is increased considerably. When the two index fingers cooperate, the workspace range is significantly larger than that of the other three finger combinations, and the translational distance of the Y and Z-axis is significantly increased.

Acknowledgement. This work was supported in part by the National Natural Science Foundation of China (51905375), the China Post-doctoral Science Foundation Funded Project (2019M651033), Foundation of State Key Laboratory of Robotics and System (HIT) (SKLRS-2019-KF-06), and Peiyang Elite Scholar Program of Tianjin University (2020XRG-0023).

References

1. Babik, I., Michel, G.F.: Development of role-differentiated bimanual manipulation in infancy: Part 3. Its relation to the development of bimanual object acquisition and bimanual non-differentiated manipulation. Dev. Psychobiol. **58**(2), 268–277 (2016)
2. Swinnen, S.P., Wenderoth, N.: Two hands, one brain: cognitive neuroscience of bimanual skill. Trends Cogn. Sci. **8**(1), 18–25 (2004)
3. Nemec, B., Likar, N., Gams, A., Ude, A.: Bimanual human robot cooperation with adaptive stiffness control. In: Asfour, T., et al. (eds.) IEEE International Conference on Humanoid Robots, pp. 607–613 (2016)
4. Duque, J., et al.: Monitoring coordination during bimanual movements: where is the mastermind? J. Cogn. Neurosci. **22**(3), 526–542 (2010)
5. Squeri, V., Sciutti, A., Gori, M., Masia, L., Sandini, G., Konczak, J.: Two hands, one perception: how bimanual haptic information is combined by the brain. J. Neurophysiol. **107**(2), 544–550 (2012)
6. Babik, I., Michel, G.F.: Development of role-differentiated bimanual manipulation in infancy: Part 1. The emergence of the skill. Dev. Psychobiol. **58**(2), 243–256 (2016)
7. Serrien, D.J., O'Regan, L.: The development of motor planning strategies in children. Eur. J. Dev. Psychol. **18**(1), 1–17 (2021)
8. van der Wel, R.P., Rosenbaum, D.A.: Bimanual grasp planning reflects changing rather than fixed constraint dominance. Exp. Brain Res. **205**(3), 351–362 (2010)
9. Yao, K., Billard, A.: An inverse optimization approach to understand human acquisition of kinematic coordination in bimanual fine manipulation tasks. Biol. Cybern. **114**(1), 63–82 (2020). https://doi.org/10.1007/s00422-019-00814-9
10. Bullock, I.M., Feix, T., Dollar, A.M.: Human precision manipulation workspace: effects of object size and number of fingers. In: Annual International Conference of the IEEE Engineering in Medicine and Biology Society, no. 2694-0604, pp. 5768–5772 (2015)
11. Feix, T., Bullock, I.M., Gloumakov, Y., Dollar, A.M.: Effect of number of digits on human precision manipulation workspaces. IEEE Trans. Haptics **14**(1), 68–82 (2021)
12. Hallbeck, M.S.: Flexion and extension forces generated by wrist- dedicated muscles over the range of motion. Appl. Ergon. **25**(6), 379–385 (1994)
13. Bullock, I.M., Feix, T., Dollar, A.M.: Workspace shape and characteristics for human two- and three-fingered precision manipulation. IEEE Trans. Biomed. Eng. **62**(9), 2196–2207 (2015)

14. Guan, Y., Yokoi, K., Zhang, X.: Numerical methods for reachable space generation of humanoid robots. Int. J. Robot. Res. **27**(8), 935–950 (2008)
15. Liarokapis, M.V., Artemiadis, P.K., Kyriakopoulos, K.J.: Quantifying anthropomorphism of robot hands. In: IEEE International Conference on Robotics and Automation, pp. 2041–2046 (2013)
16. Rodriguez-Garavito, C.H., Camacho-Munoz, G., Alvarez-Martinez, D., Cardenas, K.V., Rojas, D.M., Grimaldos, A.: 3D object pose estimation for robotic packing applications. Commun. Comput. Inf. Sci. **916**, 453–463 (2018)
17. Bradford Barber, C., Dobkin, D.P., Huhdanpaa, H.: The quickhull algorithm for convex hulls. ACM Trans. Math. Softw. **22**(4), 469–483 (1996)
18. Hussain, I., Spagnoletti, G., Salvietti, G., Prattichizzo, D.: Toward wearable supernumerary robotic fingers to compensate missing grasping abilities in hemiparetic upper limb. Int. J. Robot. Res. **36**(13–14), 1414–1436 (2017)

Robustness of Combined sEMG and Ultrasound Modalities Against Muscle Fatigue in Force Estimation

Jia Zeng[1], Yu Zhou[1], Yicheng Yang[1], Zenglin Xu[2], Hongwei Zhang[3],
and Honghai Liu[1,3(✉)]

[1] State Key Laboratory of Mechanical System and Vibration,
Shanghai Jiao Tong University, Shanghai, China
`honghai.liu@icloud.com`
[2] School of Computer Science, Harbin Institute of Technology, Shenzhen, China
[3] State Key Laboratory of Robotics and System, Harbin Institute of Technology,
Shenzhen, China

Abstract. It is evident that surface electromyography (sEMG) based prosthesis is constrained due to sensitivity to muscle fatigue. This paper investigated the muscle fatigue robustness for sEMG, ultrasound and the fusion sEMG/ultrasound signals towards the proportional force prediction. The linear regression model is developed, and evaluated on the non-fatigue state and fatigue state. Seven able-bodied subjects participated in the experiment to validate the model. The results demonstrate that sEMG outperforms ultrasound in force estimation accuracy, but ultrasound is more robust against muscle fatigue than sEMG. Furthermore, the fusion sEMG/ultrasound signal shows comparable force prediction accuracy to sEMG and better muscle fatigue robustness than sEMG. The fusion sEMG/ultrasound modality overcomes the defect of sEMG modality, making it a promising modality for the long-term use of prosthetic force control.

Keywords: sEMG · A-mode ultrasound · Force estimation · Muscle fatigue

1 Introduction

Neural prosthetic hand is a typical human-machine interface application, which is promising in the rehabilitation of amputee. Though pattern recognition based prosthesis has made great success over the past few years [1,2], the clinical applicability of it is limited. There remains many significant challenges in bio-signal controlled prosthetic hands, one of which is the simultaneous and proportional force estimation. It is a challenging task to establish a force prediction model with strong anti-interference ability and robustness based on bio-signal.

Surface electromyography (sEMG) is a popular neuromuscular interface [3–5]. Due to reflecting the activation degree of muscle contraction, sEMG signal is

© Springer Nature Switzerland AG 2021
X.-J. Liu et al. (Eds.): ICIRA 2021, LNAI 13015, pp. 213–221, 2021.
https://doi.org/10.1007/978-3-030-89134-3_20

usually used in force estimation [6–8]. Choi et al. [9] applied ANN algorithm to estimate pinch force by sEMG and achieved a promising result with NRMSE of 0.081 ± 0.023. Cao et al. [10] adopted extreme learning machine (ELM) to predict hand grip force by sEMG signals from forearm muscles, and the achieved root mean squared error (RMSE) and correlation coefficient were 1.165 ± 0.475 and 0.991 ± 0.007 respectively. Though the aforementioned studies have obtained high accuracy, the problem with them is not taking the non-stationary property of sEMG into consideration. SEMG signal is susceptible to muscle fatigue, electrode displacement and sweating, which limits its long-term use. Electrode displacement and sweating can be avoided by strictly controlling the external environment, but muscle fatigue is inevitable.

Ultrasound signal is another biosensing method. The principle of ultrasound generation is that the ultrasound probe sends ultrasound pulses into human tissue and the pulses will be reflected at tissue interface. These reflected echoes can be used to detect the morphological changes in muscle deformation. As reported by [11], there is a linear relationship between finger force and spatial first-order features extracted from ultrasound images of the forearm. Although the research of human-machine interface based on B-mode ultrasound image has made great progress [12,13], the B-mode ultrasound device is bulky and not portable. In contrast, A-mode ultrasound apparatus [14] is more realistic to be wearable and embedded into prosthetic hands. Zhou et al. [15] utilized A-model ultrasound to predict finger movement and obtained excellent accuracy. Yang et al. [16] successfully applied A-mode ultrasound signal to predict grasp force with average $NRMSE$ of 0.102 ± 0.037 and R^2 of 0.905 ± 0.057. The aforementioned studied proved that force regression accuracy on A-mode ultrasound signal was acceptable. However, whether A-mode ultrasound based force estimation is robust against muscle fatigue remains uncertain.

In order to further improve the performance of human-machine interface, multi-modality fusion has gradually become a research trend. Guo et al. [17] developed a hybrid EMG/NIRS sensor system, and recognition performance were improved. Leeb et al. [18] developed the multimodal fusion approach of EEG and EMG, which yielded accurate and more stable performance even in muscle fatigue condition. Inspired by these work, this paper explores the difference between sEMG and ultrasound signals in force regression accuracy and fatigue robustness, and investigates the fusion of sEMG and ultrasound modality. It is expected that their combination can exert the complementary advantages of muscle morphology information and electrophysiological information, breaking through the bottleneck of single modality and attaining both high accuracy and robustness against muscle fatigue.

2   Muscle Fatigue Robustness Evaluation

2.1   Subjects

Seven healthy subjects (referred as S1–S7, 23–29 years old, six males, one female) without any neuromuscular diseases history were recruited to participate in this experiment. The maximum voluntary contraction (MVC) of each subject was measured for experiment configuration.

2.2   Experimental Apparatus

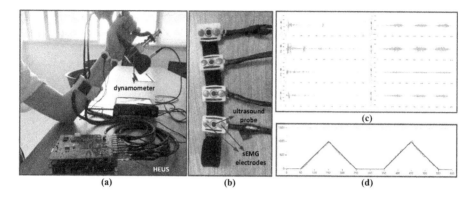

Fig. 1. The overview of experimental platform: (a) The employed signal acquisition apparatus, including hybrid sEMG/A-mode ultrasound system (HEUS) and hand grip dynamometer; (b) The exhibition of four-channel sensor arm band, each small module is embedded with a pair of sEMG electrodes and an ultrasound probe; (c) The real-time acquisition of ultrasound signals (left side) and sEMG signals (right side); (d) The curve of the actual hand grip force (green line) collected by dynamometer and an estimated force (red line).

A portable hybrid sEMG/A-mode ultrasound system was employed in this study. The detail of this hardware system can be seen from [14]. The system is capable of simultaneously acquiring four channels of sEMG signals and A-mode ultrasound signals. Owing to the four-channel sensor arm band shown in Fig. 1(b), these two signals can be collected in the same position, which makes comparasion of sEMG signals and ultrasound signals impartial and meaningful. Hand grip dynamometer (G100, Biometrics Ltd., UK) was applied to evaluate the MVC of subjects and record the hand grip force when exacting contraction. It should be noticed that the sample rate of sEMG, ultrasound and force sensors 1000 Hz, 10 Hz, 1000 Hz respectively.

2.3   Experimental Protocols

During the experiment, the subjects were asked to sit in front of a PC screen with their elbow laid comfortably on the desk. The four sensor modules in the arm band were placed on four muscles: flexor digitorum superficialis (FDS), flexor carpi ulnaris (FCU), extensor carpi ulnaris (ECU) and extensor digitorum (ED). The subjects hold the grip dynamometer with their dominant hand.

Firstly, the subject gave the most strength to grasp the dynamometer for 10 s, the average force between 2.5 s and 7.5 s was defined as his MVC. The experiment configuration in the following stage varied between subjects according to the MVC.

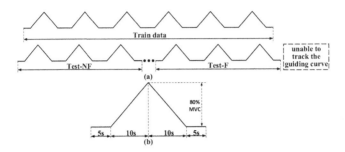

Fig. 2. The demonstration of the experimental protocols: (a) The demonstration of indicative force curve on the computer screen for the whole trial (15–20 repetitions), (b) the indicative force curve of one repetition.

Secondly, after evaluating the MVC, the subject was instructed to exert grip force in the shape of triangular curve. As present in Fig. 1(d), there was a moving green line indicating the real-time grip force and the subject was asked to precisely control their grip force to track the red line of triangular curve. The subject was asked to output 15 to 25 repetitions of triangular wave force according to the instructions on the screen. The number of repetitions varies according to each person's fatigue resistance. Each repetition lasted 30 s. In the first 5 seconds and the last 5 seconds, the subject rested. Between 5 seconds and 15 seconds, the subject's grip strength was slowly increased from 0 to 80% MVC, and between 15 seconds and 25 seconds, the subject's grip strength was slowly reduced from 80% MVC to 0. The indicative force curve of one repetition is shown in Fig. 2(b). The subjects repeated the repetitions until he felt intense muscle fatigue and his grip force was not sufficient to track the indicator force curve on the screen. Whether the highest point of the force curve in one repetition was less than 70% of MVC was regarded as a sign of muscle fatigue. The procedure repeated 3 trials, with an enough time rest between each trial in order to allow muscles to recover from fatigue.

In each trial, during the first six repetitions, the subject's muscles were considered to be in non-fatigue state. The data collected from first six repetitions were used as the training set. The muscle status of the following three repetitions was considered to be similar to that of the first six repetitions and can also be considered as non-fatigue state. The data collected from this three repetitions were used as the testing data on non-fatigue state (referred as Test-NF). The last three repetitions before the subject's grip strength is insufficient to track the screen's indicator force curve were designated as fatigue state. The data collected from this three repetitions were used as the testing data on fatigue state (referred as Test-F). The illustration of split method for selecting the training data, Test-NF, Test-F is shown in Fig. 2(a).

2.4   Signal Processing and Feature Extraction

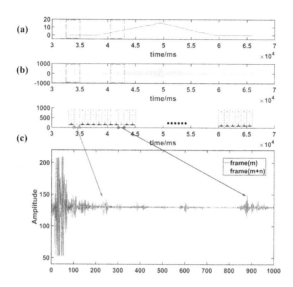

Fig. 3. The process of signal alignment and preprocessing on sEMG, ultrasound and force signals: (a) force signal and its slide window, (b) sEMG signal and its slide window, (c) original A-mode ultrasound signal.

Firstly, samples needed to be separated and extracted from the original sEMG, ultrasound and force signals. The process of signal alignment and preprocessing on sEMG, ultrasound and force signals are shown in Fig. 3. Since the sampling rate of sEMG signal 1000 Hz and the frame rate of ultrasound signal is 10 frames per second, ultrasound and sEMG signals need to be unified and aligned. The sliding window and step of sEMG was set to 250 ms and 100 ms respectively, consequently, the sEMG samples is separated 10 times per second by slide window. Through this approach the matching of the ultrasound samples and sEMG samples is achieved. In addition, the same sliding window operation is performed on the force signal to maintain the same samples number. Concretely, Fig. 3(a) and Fig. 3(b) represent the force signal curve and sEMG signal curve respectively. Force signals and sEMG signals are one-dimensional time series signals. Different from them, ultrasound signals can be regarded as one-dimensional images, which are updated every 100 ms. Figure 3(c) displays several different frames of ultrasound signals and zooms in on two of the frames.

For sEMG samples, TD-AR6 feature is employed in this paper. TD-AR6 feature is a combination between four time domain features (mean absolute value (MAV), waveform length (WL), zero crossing number (ZC), and slop sign changes (SSC)) and 6th order AR coefficient of autoregressive model (AR6). For ultrasound, each frame is composed of 1000 sample dots. The first 20 dots and last 20 dots were discarded as they contains no meaningful information. The raw ultrasound signals are processed by time gain compensation, band-pass filtering, envelope detection, and log compression [16]. Then the processed ultrasound signals are divided into 48 segmentations. The MSD [16] feature, which represented mean value and standard deviation, is extracted from each segmentation of ultrasound signals. The TD-AR6 features and MSD features across all channels are regarded as sEMG features and ultrasound features respectively. The stacked features of these two signals are used as fusion features of sEMG and ultrasound.

2.5   Linear Regression Model

This article applied linear regression (LR) model to hand grip force by the features of bio-signals. The ability of the sEMG/ultrasound signal features to characterize the grip strength was evaluated through the force estimation accuracy. The LR model is defined as Eq. 1:

$$\hat{y}_i = \hat{x}_i^T (X^T X)^{-1} X^T y \tag{1}$$

where y means labels of train data, and $\hat{x}_i$, $\hat{y}_i$ represent feature vector and predicted label of test data respectively. The train dataset is represented as a matrix X of size $m * (n + 1)$, and m, n represent number of train samples and feature dimension respectively. Each row of the matrix X represents an instance and each column represents a feature.

2.6   Evaluation Metrics

The aforementioned regression models were employed to estimate the exerted hand grip force. The normalized root-mean-square error ($NRMSE$) were applied to quantify the force estimation precision, which were defined as

$$NRMSE = \frac{\sqrt{\sum_{i=1}^{m}(y_i - \widetilde{y}_i)^2 / m}}{y_{max} - y_{min}} \tag{2}$$

where m means the total number of test samples and y_i, $\widetilde{y}$, y_{max}, y_{min} represent predicted force, actual force, maximum of actual force, minimum of actual force respectively. The $NRMSE$ of non-fatigue state and fatigue state are compared to evaluate the robustness to muscle fatigue.

3   Results

3.1   Force Estimation Performance and Robustness Evaluation

The accuracies of different modalities (separate sEMG, separate ultrasound and combined sEMG/ultrasound) for hand grip force estimation are investigated in

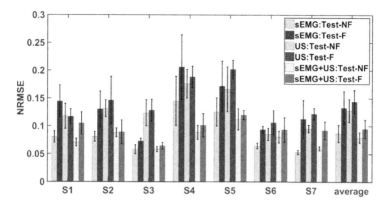

Fig. 4. The comparison of hand grip force estimation accuracy on Test-NF and Test-F across different modalities (separate sEMG, separate ultrasound and combined sEMG/ultrasound). Error bars represents the standard deviation.

this study. The statistical results are shown in Fig. 4. The symbol Test-NF and Test-F represent testing on non-fatigue state and fatigue state respectively. Considering force estimation accuracy on Test-NF, separate sEMG signal always outperforms separate ultrasound signal, and there is little difference between accuracies of combined sEMG/ultrasound signal and separate sEMG signal. The average NRMSE of sEMG, ultrasound, fusion sEMG/ultrasound are 0.0869, 0.1280, and 0.0798. However, as for force estimation accuracy on Test-F, $NRMSE$ of separate sEMG signals fell to 0.1321, and $NRMSE$ of separate ultrasound signals and combined sEMG/ultrasound signals are 0.1445 and 0.0949. The force estimation accuracy on Test-F of combined sEMG/ultrasound signal outperforms that of separate sEMG signal. The declines of these three modalities are 0.0452 (52.01%), 0.0165 (12.89%), and 0.0151 (18.92%). It shows that the robustness of ultrasound and combined sEMG/ultrasound are better than that of separate sEMG.

Based on the analysis of the results in Fig. 4, it can be concluded that the force estimation precision of the sEMG signal under non-fatigue state is excellent, but once the muscle fatigue induced, the precision decreases significantly, which indicates that there is a strong correlation between sEMG signals and force, but sEMG signals are very sensitive to muscle fatigue. Although ultrasound signal is not as accurate as sEMG signal in force estimation, it is more robust to muscle fatigue than sEMG signal. As for combined sEMG/ultrasound signal, under non-fatigue condition, the force prediction accuracy of the combined signals is comparable to that of the sEMG signal, and when muscle fatigue occurred, the accuracy of the combined signal is significantly better than separate sEMG signal. These results demonstrate the superior performance of the combined sEMG/ultrasound signals in both force prediction accuracy and robustness against muscle fatigue. Figure 5 shows a typical force estimation result, from which sEMG modality's sensitivity to muscle fatigue, fusion sEMG/ultrasound

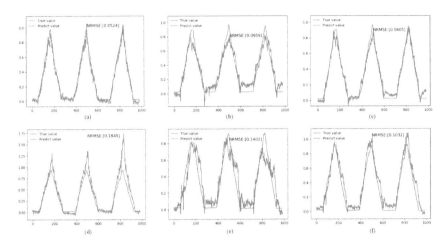

Fig. 5. Typical demonstrations of force estimation result: (a) non-fatigue state with sEMG feature; (b) non-fatigue state with ultrasound feature; (c) non-fatigue state with fusion sEMG and ultrasound features; (d) fatigue state with sEMG feature; (e) fatigue state with ultrasound feature; (f) fatigue state with fusion sEMG and ultrasound features.

modality's excellent precision and enhanced fatigue robustness can be clearly demonstrated.

4   Conclusion

In a conclusion, this paper validates that the force estimation accuracy of sEMG signal is superior, but sEMG signal is susceptible to muscle fatigue. Although the force estimation accuracy of the ultrasound signal cannot be compared with the sEMG signal, its robustness against muscle fatigue can make up for the short board of the sEMG signal. The fusion sEMG and ultrasound signals have the characteristics of high force prediction accuracy and excellent fatigue robustness.

References

1. Zhang, X., et al.: On design and implementation of neural-machine interface for artificial legs. IEEE Trans. Ind. Inf. **8**(2), 418–429 (2012)
2. Al-Timemy, A., Bugmann, G., Escudero, J., Outram, N.: Classification of finger movements for the dexterous hand prosthesis control with surface electromyography. IEEE J. Biomed. Health Inform. **17**(3), 608–618 (2013)
3. Chu, J., Moon, I., Mun, M.: A real-time EMG pattern recognition system based on linear-nonlinear feature projection for a multifunction myoelectric hand. IEEE Trans. Biomed. Eng. **53**(11), 2232–2239 (2006)
4. Young, A., Smith, L., Rouse, E., Hargrove, L.: Classification of simultaneous movements using surface EMG pattern recognition. IEEE Trans. Biomed. Eng. **60**(5), 1250–1258 (2013)

5. Zeng J., Zhou Y., Yang Y., Wang J., Liu H.: Feature fusion of sEMG and ultrasound signals in hand gesture recognition. In: 2020 IEEE International Conference on Systems, Man, and Cybernetics (SMC), pp. 3911–3916. IEEE (2020)
6. Zhou, Yu., Liu, J., Zeng, J., Li, K., Liu, H.: Bio-signal based elbow angle and torque simultaneous prediction during isokinetic contraction. SCIENCE CHINA Technol. Sci. **62**(1), 21–30 (2018). https://doi.org/10.1007/s11431-018-9354-5
7. Liu, M., Herzog, W., Savelberg, H.: Dynamic muscle force predictions from EMG: an artificial neural network approach. J. Electromyogr. Kinesiol. **9**(6), 391–400 (1999)
8. Zeng J., Zhou Y., Yang Y., Liu H.: Hand grip force enhancer based on sEMG-triggered functional electrical stimulation. In: 2019 IEEE 9th Annual International Conference on CYBER Technology in Automation, Control, and Intelligent Systems (CYBER), pp. 231–236. IEEE (2019)
9. Changmok, C., et al.: Real-time pinch force estimation by surface electromyography using an artificial neural network. Med. Eng. Phys. **32**(5), 429–436 (2010)
10. Cao, H., Sun, S., Zhang, K.: Modified EMG-based handgrip force prediction using extreme learning machine. Soft. Comput. **21**(2), 491–500 (2015). https://doi.org/10.1007/s00500-015-1800-8
11. Sierra González, D. and Castellini, C.: A realistic implementation of ultrasound imaging as a human-machine interface for upper-limb amputees. Front. Neurorobotics **7**(17) (2013)
12. Shi, J., Guo, J., Hu, S., Zheng, Y.: Recognition of finger flexion motion from ultrasound image: a feasibility study. Ultrasound Med. Biol. **38**(10), 1695–1704 (2012)
13. Claudio, C., Georg, P., Emanuel, Z.: Using ultrasound images of the forearm to predict finger positions. IEEE Trans. Neural Syst. Rehabil. Eng. **20**(6), 788–797 (2012)
14. Xia, W., et al.: Toward portable hybrid surface electromyography/a-mode ultrasound sensing for human-machine interface. IEEE Sens. J. **19**(13), 5219–5228 (2019)
15. Zhou, Y., et al.: Voluntary and fes-induced finger movement estimation using muscle deformation features. IEEE Trans. Ind. Electron. **67**(5), 4002–4012 (2019)
16. Yang, X., et al.: A proportional pattern recognition control scheme for wearable a-mode ultrasound sensing. IEEE Trans. Ind. Electron. **67**(1), 800–808 (2019)
17. Guo, W., et al.: Development of a multi-channel compact-size wireless hybrid sEMG/NIRS sensor system for prosthetic manipulation. IEEE Sens. J. **16**(2), 447–456 (2016)
18. Robert L., et al.: A hybrid brain-computer interface based on the fusion of electroencephalographic and electromyographic activities. J. Neural Eng. **8**(2) (2011)

An Abnormal Behavior Recognition Method Based on Fusion Features

Gang Yu[(✉)], Jia Liu, and Chang Zhang

Harbin Institute of Technology, Shenzhen, Shenzhen 518055, China
gangyu@hit.edu.cn

Abstract. The human action recognition technology has developed rapidly in recent years. The technologies of RNN and 3D convolution based on posture information and video frame information respectively have achieved high accuracy using various data sets, however, both of them have shortcomings in the field of abnormal behavior recognition. The definition of abnormal behavior needs to consider not only the action type simply, but also the environmental information comprehensively, so there are limitations in using RNN only based on posture information. Due to the input characteristics, action recognition technology based on 3D convolution is more related to environmental information and group behavior information, it cannot locate the action time accurately. This paper proposed an abnormal behavior recognition framework based on P3D and LSTM. The framework used pre-trained P3D to extract environmental features, and adopted pre-trained LSTM to extract individual action features to help system for time positioning, finally apply ranking model to classify abnormal behaviors after combining environmental features with action features. When training LSTM model, a regression network was added to enhance its time positioning ability. The experiment showed that the proposed framework based on P3D and LSTM has a greater improvement in the recognition accuracy and time positioning than only using 3D convolution technology or LSTM technology, and can accurately recognize abnormal behaviors.

Keywords: Abnormal behavior recognition · LSTM · 3D convolution · Action feature extraction · Time positioning

1 Introduction

Video understanding is a very popular and challenging research direction in the field of computer vision. The task of action recognition is simply to classify the given segmented video clips according to the human behavior. Before the emergence of deep learning, the best algorithm was IDT [1–3], and the following work was basically to make optimization on the basis of IDT methods. With the popularity of deep learning, there were many methods proposed to solve this problem, including two streams [4–6], 3D convolution [7–9] and so on. Although behavior recognition has been studied for many years, it is still in the testing stage based on laboratory data set, and has not reached the practical and industrial level. Therefore, there is still no good solution for this task at present, video

© Springer Nature Switzerland AG 2021
X.-J. Liu et al. (Eds.): ICIRA 2021, LNAI 13015, pp. 222–232, 2021.
https://doi.org/10.1007/978-3-030-89134-3_21

classification has one more temporal dimension which has not been well dealt with in the computer field. With the rapid development of posture detection technology [10, 11], researchers thought that RNN based on human posture information in video can be used to classify behaviors because human posture contains more advanced semantic information as compared with video signals. The RNN behavior classification technology based on posture information or video coding information [12–15] had achieved good results in behavior recognition relying on the powerful ability to process time series. In addition, the literatures [16–18] also proposed improvement measures in terms of spatial positioning, temporal positioning, and boundary matching of actions.

However, abnormal behavior recognition is still one of the most challenging problems in computer vision [19–21], which is quite different from general behavior recognition tasks. Firstly, it is difficult to define a clear boundary between normal behavior and abnormal behavior so that the types of abnormal behaviors are also difficult to define due to the complexity of actions. To solve this problem, researchers have tried to use limited application scenarios to study specific abnormal events [22–24], and to reduce the dependence of algorithms on events by defining a normal behavior pattern [25, 26], but these methods are obviously not universal. Besides, it is not feasible to identify the action types without the environment, due to a lot of information contained in real environment.

In order to deal with the above issues, this paper proposed a new framework of abnormal behavior recognition method, which used the pre-trained 3D convolution neural network to extract the video environment features, apply a LSTM model including attention mechanism to extract the action features in the posture information, then fuse the environmental features and action features together and input them into a Multi-instance Learning (MIL) model. The method can complete the classification of abnormal behavior of human objects in video after training the MIL model by UCF crime data set. A regression network was used to train the time positioning ability of LSTM model in the process of pre-training. The experimental results showed that the method used in this paper has good performance and the main contributions of this paper are as follows:

A new framework for abnormal behavior recognition was proposed which considered both the overall environment characteristics and human posture features. After sufficient data training, the framework can be applied to different environments and accurately identify abnormal behaviors.

A method was presented to improve the time positioning ability of the system. The deep LSTM network trained by this method can assist 3D convolution in time positioning with high accuracy.

A benchmark was designed to measure the accuracy of time positioning which proved the proposed method has better performance.

2 Approach

In this chapter, the abnormal behavior recognition method is introduced.

2.1 Overall Network Architecture

The network architecture used in this paper is shown in Fig. 1. The pre-trained 3D convolution is used to extract the environment features by inputting 16 consecutive frames of images, and apply the pre-trained deep LSTM model to extract the action features by inputting extracted posture information (joint point coordinates) from the images. As our purpose is to judge whether the behaviors were abnormal or not, there is no need for specific action classification, so the two features are fused into a classification network. This network can finally output a prediction value, which is the probability value of the abnormal behaviors. Details of the architecture are described in the following sections.

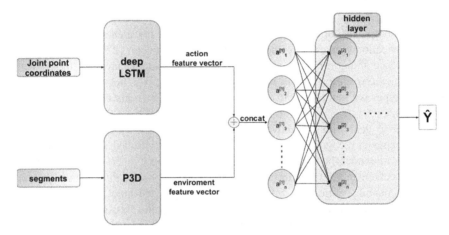

Fig. 1. Overall network architecture.

2.2 Environment Feature Extraction

Whether a person's behavior belongs to abnormal behavior needs to consider the environment comprehensively, and the same behavior may belong to different categories in different environments. Because of the continuity of human actions, it is necessary to extract the information of multiple images to judge a person's behavior, instead of determining the behavior patterns according to the information of a single image. Therefore, it is necessary to extract the environmental information from the start time to the end time of the action. Traditional 2D convolution does not have this function, so 3D convolution is needed to extract the information of continuous video frames.

The pre-trained P3D [27] neural network with a fully connected neural network for action classification is used as the backbone.

The 16 consecutive frames are used as a clip of inputs, the ability of action classification is trained on the sports1M, which is a multiple classification action recognition data set. The softmax loss function is shown as the following:

$$L(y, \hat{y}) = -\sum_{j=1}^{m} y_j \log \hat{y}_j \qquad (1)$$

where y is the groundtruth value, $\hat{y}$ is the predicted value, and m is the number of action types divided in the dataset.

After several rounds of iterations, the top 5 accuracy reached 83.7%, which is lower than the two-stream method [6]. This showed that although P3D can extract the environment information of continuous video frames quickly, the accuracy of motion classification needs to be improved.

Based on this, the full connection layer for classification is discarded and the pre-trained P3D is used to extract a 2048 dimensional feature vector as the environment feature.

2.3 Action Feature Extraction

Behavior recognition based on 3D convolution relied too much on background and appearance features, but lacked of modeling of the action itself. Human postures contain high-level semantic information of human behaviors, which is similar to the environment features. The extraction of human action features also needs to consider the information of multiple consecutive images, so it is necessary to extract the temporal features of posture information.

In this paper, LSTM with attention mechanism was used to extract the features of joint point coordinates, and the kinematics data set of Mask RCNN [28] was used to extract human posture features as the training data of LSTM. The posture features of each person were represented by pixel coordinates of 15 joint points.

Meanwhile, the environmental information extracted before was observed to be inaccurate in the time domain, which meant that the P3D neural network cannot capture the start and end of the action well, and there was a lag in the recognition. This is because the training data used in pre-training P3D marked every 16 frames of images as a clip. Only the action type was marked in each input, while the start time of the action was not marked. Simultaneously, due to the reason that P3D network needs to consider the overall environment and is lack of enough attention to the key human targets, which leads to the insensitivity of P3D to clips with a small number of positive samples, however, these clips with less positive samples are more likely to contain the start time of the action. The change of the attitude information is more obvious than that of the environmental information, which can locate the start time of the action more accurately.

In order to extract the feature of the action and accurately locate the start time of the action, a regression network was used to train the time positioning ability of LSTM.

As shown in Fig. 2, the output of LSTM is divided into two channels, one of which passes through the full connection layer and softmax layer, and outputs a label for action classification. The other channel outputs a confidence value after passing through the regression network, which represents the confidence value of the start or end of the action.

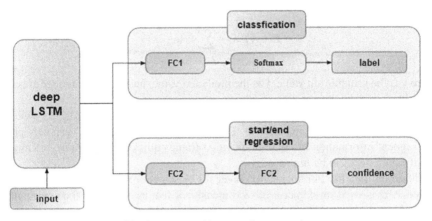

Fig. 2. LSTM with regression network

In order to train the regression task, the training data set is manually labeled. Taking the start frame and the end frame as the center, its normal distribution is calculated, and the maximum value of normal distribution value on each frame is taken as marked value.

$$S_k(p) = \frac{1}{\sqrt{2\pi}\sigma} \exp(-\frac{\|p - x_k\|_2^2}{\sigma^2}) \tag{2}$$

$$S(p) = \max S_k(p) \tag{3}$$

where $S_k(p)$ represents the distribution value of the normal distribution with the k start frame (or end frame) of x_k as the center; $S(p)$ is the maximum value at point P in the normal distribution of K, which is the groundtruth value. Each frame of the video can get a marked value by this method, and the closer to the start or end frame of the action, the larger the groundtruth value.

The network loss function is composed of two parts, one of which is softmax classification loss L1 that can be obtained using formula (1).

The other part is the return loss L2.

$$L_2 = \left\| S(p) - \hat{S}(p) \right\|_2^2 \tag{4}$$

where $\hat{S}(p)$ is the regression prediction value at the frame number p. The total loss is obtained by the weighted sum of two parts.

$$L = \alpha L_1 + \beta L_2 \tag{5}$$

Many experiments showed that when α and β were taken as 0.5, better results can be obtained.

Fully connected layer and regression network for classification were discarded, and 1024 dimension feature vectors output by LSTM layer were used as action features.

2.4 Training

After extracting the environment features and action features, the two group of features were connected and input into a fully connected neural network to predict the behavior types. In this paper, the data set of UCF crime [29] was used for training, which covered almost all typical abnormal behaviors including fighting, robbery, and vandalism. This data set contains a total of 1900 video sequences, which are generally abnormal behaviors. 90% of the video sequences in the data set are used as training samples (Fig. 3).

Fighting   Robbery   Vandalism

Fig. 3. Examples of anomalous event from the UCF-Crime dataset

It can been seen from Fig. 1 that the parameters of P3D and deep LSTM were fixed in the process of training, and only the weights of hidden layer can be updated. A posture detection was done on the dataset image, and the coordinates of each human joint point were took as the input of the pre-trained LSTM neural network. Different from the traditional deep learning method that each sample corresponds to a label, MIL was used for training in order to better extract the temporal characteristics of video. The specific steps of the method were as follows: when there is no abnormal behavior in the video with 16 frames, it is marked as negative sample, otherwise, as long as one abnormal behavior appears, it is marked as positive sample. Basically similar to the training method proposed in reference [29], a neural network of MIL was used to score each segment. The segment (potentially abnormal sample) with the highest score from the positive samples, and the segment with the highest score from the negative samples were used to train the model parameters of MIL by hinge-loss, which is shown as follows:

$$L(\beta_a, \beta_n) = \max(0.1 - \max_{i \in \beta_a} y_a^i + \max_{j \in \beta_n} y_n^j) \qquad (6)$$

where β_a and β_n represent positive sample and negative samples respectively; y_a^i and y_n^j represent corresponding predicted scores. The boundary between positive and negative samples can be more obvious by using this loss function. In this method, environment feature vector with 2048 dimensions and action feature vector with 1024 dimensions were extracted. The action feature vector can not only improve the recognition accuracy, but also help the system for time positioning, and better identify the start and end time of abnormal behaviors.

3 Experiment

In order to verify the effectiveness of the proposed method, it was compared with both the existing methods for behavior recognition, and the method proposed in the literature [29] for time positioning accuracy. Moreover, a traditional neural network similar to the structure as shown in the Fig. 1 was retrained, the difference is that this network used the ordinary LSTM action classification network to extract the action features. The LSTM with regression network proposed in Sect. 2 is compared with this network to verify if it improves the time positioning ability of the system.

3.1 Data

In order to ensure the validity of the experimental results, all the methods used in the experiment are trained with UCF crime data set.

The data set used for verification was collected from the internet including video monitoring, movie clips, etc. This data set contains a variety of abnormal behaviors defined in UCF crime, and has a great diversity in the collection of actions, including changes in human body proportion, background, light and shooting angle and so on.

3.2 Comparison of Behavior Recognition Accuracy

Since 3D convolution and LSTM based on posture information were used to extract features in this paper, our method was firstly compared with those using 3D convolution or LSTM based on posture information respectively. In order to verify the performance of the proposed method, it was compared with the accuracy of the current behavior recognition methods, the results are shown in Table 1.

Table 1. Comparison of classification accuracy.

Methods	Accuracy
Binary classifier	50.0
C3D [29]	67.9
RAPN [14]	64.4
Two-Stream [6]	78.6
R-C3D [30]	81.6
Ours	82.2

It was found from Table 1 that the accuracy of our behavior recognition method has been greatly improved. In Ref. [30], two 3D convolution neural networks with the similar structure to the networks in this paper were used to extract environment features and motion optical flow features respectively, which is one of the most advanced behavior recognition methods. It can be seen that our method is also slightly better than R-C3D in the accuracy of abnormal behavior recognition. Figure 4 showed the ROC curve comparison between our method and various methods in Table 1, where our method was represented by purple curve. It was found that the recognition accuracy of our method is the highest among these methods.

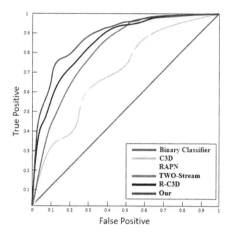

Fig. 4. ROC curve

3.3 Comparison of Time Positioning Accuracy

Since this paper adopted a method similar to that in the literature [29], in order to verify that the LSTM with regression network proposed in this paper improved the time positioning ability of 3D convolution, a comparative study for the accuracy of time positioning was performed. The identical training method was used to train the methods for comparison under the same condition. The start time of each person's action was marked, and the accuracy score of time positioning for a sample was defined by the following formula:

$$Score = \frac{1}{2m}(\left|B_s - \hat{B}_s\right| + \left|B_e - \hat{B}_e\right|) \tag{7}$$

where B_s represents the bag number at the start of the action, B_e represents the bag number at the end of the action, $\hat{B}_s$ represents the bag number when the system output value exceeds 0.5, and $\hat{B}_e$ represents the bag number when the system output value drops to less than 0.5. The score can be used to measure the accuracy of the system's time positioning and the lower score meant higher accuracy of time positioning.

The mean value of time positioning accuracy score of m samples is calculated as the final result, which is shown in Table 2. It can be seen that our approach of using LSTM with regression network has the highest time positioning accuracy, which indicates that the regression network enhances the extraction ability of LSTM for the time domain features of actions.

Table 2. Score comparison of time positioning accuracy

Methods	Score
C3D [29]	1.43
R-C3D [30]	0.77
P3D + LSTM without regression network	0.91
Ours	0.24

4 Conclusion

This paper proposed a framework of 3D convolution+ LSTM for abnormal behavior recognition, and put forward a method to train the time positioning ability of deep LSTM. The experimental results showed that the framework has good performance in the accuracy of behavior recognition and time positioning, and the structure of LSTM with regression network proposed in the paper improved the time positioning ability of the system. The framework can be applied to security video in many occasions, and can identify most abnormal behaviors that may lead to dangerous consequences, so it has a broad application prospects.

References

1. Wang, H., Kläser, A., Schmid, C., Liu, C.L.: Action recognition by dense trajectories, In: Proceedings of the IEEE International Conference on Computer Vision, pp. 3551–3558 (2011)
2. Wang, H., Kläser, A., Schmid, C., Liu, C.L.: Dense trajectories and motion boundary descriptors for action recognition. Int. J. Comput. Vision **103**(1), 60–79 (2013)
3. Wang, H., Schmid, C.: Action recognition with improved trajectories. In: Proceedings of the IEEE International Conference on Computer Vision, pp. 3551–3558 (2013)
4. Simonyan, K., Zisserman, A.: Two-stream convolutional networks for action recognition in videos. arXiv preprint arXiv:1406.2199 (2014)
5. Feichtenhofer, C., Pinz, A., Zisserman, A.: Convolutional two-stream network fusion for video action recognition (2016).https://doi.org/10.1109/CVPR.2016.213
6. Wang, L., et al.: Temporal segment networks: towards good practices for deep action recognition. In: Leibe, B., Matas, J., Sebe, N., Welling, M. (eds.) ECCV 2016. LNCS, vol. 9912, pp. 20–36. Springer, Cham (2016). https://doi.org/10.1007/978-3-319-46484-8_2
7. Tran, D., Bourdev, L., Fergus, R., Torresani, L., Paluri, M.: Learning spatiotemporal features with 3D convolutional networks. In: Proceedings of the IEEE International Conference on Computer Vision, pp. 4489–4497 (2015)
8. Yousefzadeh, R., Van Gool, L.: Temporal 3Dd convnets: new architecture and transfer learning for video classification. arXiv preprint arXiv:1711.08200 (2017)
9. Shou, Z., Chan, J., Zareian, A., Miyazawa, K., Chang, S.F.: CDC: convolutional-de-convolutional networks for precise temporal action localization in untrimmed videos. In: Proceedings of the IEEE Conference on Computer Vision and Pattern Recognition, pp. 5734–5743 (2017)
10. Newell, A., Yang, K., Deng, J.: Stacked hourglass networks for human pose estimation. In: Leibe, B., Matas, J., Sebe, N., Welling, M. (eds.) ECCV 2016. LNCS, vol. 9912, pp. 483–499. Springer, Cham (2016). https://doi.org/10.1007/978-3-319-46484-8_29

11. Cao, Z., Simon, T., Wei, S.E., Sheikh, Y.: Realtime multi-person 2D pose estimation using part affinity fields. IEEE Trans. Pattern Anal. Mach. Intell. **43**(1), 172–186 (2017)
12. Du, W., Wang, Y., Qiao, Y.: RPAN: an end-to-end recurrent pose-attention network for action recognition in videos. In: Proceedings of the IEEE International Conference on Computer Vision, pp. 3725–3734 (2017)
13. Ng, J.Y.H., Hausknecht, M., Vijayanarasimhan, S., Vinyals, O., Monga, R., Toderici, G.: Beyond short snippets: deep networks for video classification. In: Proceedings of the IEEE Conference on Computer Vision and Pattern Recognition, pp. 4694–4702 (2015)
14. Song, S., Lan, C., Xing, J., Zeng, W., Liu, J.: An end-to-end spatio-temporal attention model for human action recognition from skeleton data. In: Proceedings of the AAAI Conference on Artificial Intelligence, vol. 31, no. 1 (2017)
15. Zhu, W., et al.: Co-occurrence feature learning for skeleton based action recognition using regularized deep LSTM networks. In: Proceedings of the AAAI Conference on Artificial Intelligence, vol. 30, no. 1 (2016)
16. Zeng, R., et al.: Graph convolutional networks for temporal action localization. In: Proceedings of the IEEE/CVF International Conference on Computer Vision, pp. 7094–7103 (2019)
17. DIba, A., Sharma, V., Van Gool, L., Stiefelhagen, R.: DynamoNet: dynamic action and motion network. In: Proceedings of the IEEE/CVF International Conference on Computer Vision, pp. 6192–6201 (2019)
18. Lin, T., Liu, X., Li, X., Ding, E., Wen, S.: BMN: boundary-matching network for temporal action proposal generation. In: Proceedings of the IEEE/CVF International Conference on Computer Vision, pp. 3889–3898 (2019)
19. Basharat, A., Gritai, A., Shah, M.: Learning object motion patterns for anomaly detection and improved object detection. In: 2008 IEEE Conference on Computer Vision and Pattern Recognition, pp. 1–8 (2008)
20. Wu, S., Moore, B.E., Shah, M.: Chaotic invariants of lagrangian particle trajectories for anomaly detection in crowded scenes. In: 2010 IEEE Computer Society Conference on Computer Vision and Pattern Recognition, pp. 2054–2060 (2010)
21. Xu, D., Ricci, E., Yan, Y., Song, J., Sebe, N.: Learning deep representations of appearance and motion for anomalous event detection. arXiv preprint arXiv:1510.01553 (2015)
22. Mohammadi, S., Perina, A., Kiani, H., Murino, V.: Angry crowds: detecting violent events in videos. In: Leibe, B., Matas, J., Sebe, N., Welling, M. (eds.) ECCV 2016. LNCS, vol. 9911, pp. 3–18. Springer, Cham (2016). https://doi.org/10.1007/978-3-319-46478-7_1
23. Karpathy, A., Toderici, G., Shetty, S., Leung, T., Sukthankar, R., Li, F.F.: Large-scale video classification with convolutional neural networks. In: Proceedings of the IEEE Conference on Computer Vision and Pattern Recognition, pp. 1725–1732 (2014)
24. Sultani, W., Choi, J.Y.: Abnormal traffic detection using intelligent driver model. In: 2010 20th International Conference on Pattern Recognition, pp. 324–327 (2010)
25. Lu, C., Shi, J., Jia, J.: Abnormal event detection at 150 FPS in MATLAB. In: Proceedings of the IEEE International Conference on Computer Vision, pp. 2720–2727 (2013)
26. Zhao, B., Fei-Fei, L., Xing, E.P.: Online detection of unusual events in videos via dynamic sparse coding. In: CVPR 2011, pp. 3313–3320 (2011)
27. Qiu, Z., Yao, T., Mei, T.: Learning spatio-temporal representation with pseudo-3D residual networks. In: Proceedings of the IEEE International Conference on Computer Vision, pp. 5533–5541 (2017)
28. He, K., Gkioxari, G., Dollar, P., Girshick, R.: Mask R-CNN. In: Proceedings of the IEEE International Conference on Computer Vision, pp. 2961–2969 (2017)

29. Sultani, W., Chen, C., Shah, M.: Real-world anomaly detection in surveillance videos. In: Proceedings of the IEEE Conference on Computer Vision and Pattern Recognition, pp. 6479–6488 (2018)
30. Xu, H., Das, A., Saenko, K.: Two-stream region convolutional 3D network for temporal activity detection. IEEE Trans. Pattern Anal. Mach. Intell. **41**(10), 2319–2332 (2019)

Human-Robot Interaction for Service Robots

A Dynamic Head Gesture Recognition Method for Real-Time Human-Computer Interaction

Jialong Xie[1], Botao Zhang[1(✉)], Sergey A. Chepinskiy[2],
and Anton A. Zhilenkov[3]

[1] School of Automation, Hangzhou Dianzi University, Hangzhou, Zhejiang, China
`billow@hdu.edu.cn`
[2] Faculty of Control Systems and Robotics, ITMO University,
St. Petersburg, Russia
[3] Institute of Hydrodynamics and Control Processes, Saint-Petersburg State Marine
Technical University, Saint Petersburg, Russia

Abstract. In human-computer interaction, head gestures play a significant role in improving smoothness and naturality. However, existing head gesture recognition algorithms have disadvantages in accuracy and generalization ability. To deal with these problems, this paper addresses a two-stream dynamic head gesture recognition method with the SlowFast pathway called 3DSFI (3D SlowFast Inception). The SlowFast pathway is designed to reduce parameters and computational costs. Meanwhile, its two-stream structure can efficiently capture motion features in videos and dense optical flows. Besides, Inception blocks of InceptionV3 are expanded by the 3D convolutional kernel into space-time and serve as a feature extractor. Finally, 3DSFI is applied to a robot Pepper in order to evaluate realistic performance. Experimental results show that the proposed method has higher accuracy and better generalization performance than the classical C3D (Convolutional 3D) and I3D (Inflated 3D ConvNet) methods.

Keywords: Human-computer interaction · Computer vision · Deep learning · Dynamic head gesture recognition

1 Introduction

In the past, HCI (Human-Computer Interaction) heavily depended on physical contacts, such as keyboard, joystick, mouse and touchpad. Nowadays, it has gradually evolved into some more natural and comfortable ways [1]. In human interactions, there is not only verbal information but also several non-verbal

This work is supported by the Key Research and Development Project of Zhejiang Province (Grant No. 2019C04018) and the Ministry of Science and Higher Education of the Russian Federation as part of World-class Research Center program: Advanced Digital Technologies (contract No. 075-15-2020-903 dated 16.11.2020).

X.-J. Liu et al. (Eds.): ICIRA 2021, LNAI 13015, pp. 235–245, 2021.
https://doi.org/10.1007/978-3-030-89134-3_22

information [2]. In particular, the head gesture is one of the most common inter-active ways among humans and has been regarded as an auxiliary language in daily communication. Head gestures have been utilized to control wheelchairs, manipulators and robots as well as improve the interactive experience apart from conveying the expression of emotion for some disabled people [3]. In virtual reality, the experience of players will be improved greatly by the head gesture. Moreover, head gesture recognition is an excellent testing tool for fatigue driving in surveillance recognition.

Nowadays, the majority of researchers focus on static head gestures [4]. How-ever, the static head gesture omits abundant motion information and has limita-tions in application scenarios. In particular, the head gesture is the continuous motion on the sequential time series [5], its recognition exists many difficulties including small amplitude, the difference of frequency for different people and whether people wear a mask on faces. Rudigkeit et al. [6] adopted a 9-axis IMU to measure Euler degrees of head motions and controlled a manipulator. Its average classification rate achieved $93.56\% \pm 4.96\%$. Jackowski et al. [7] utilized the FSM-9 sensor to collect head motion and designed commands to operate a robot. Its average accuracy achieved 81.825%. A major disadvantage of the head-mounted device is that it requires wearing at least one sensor that must attach or strap on the head which is not convenient.

Specially, Various service robots with cameras are widely placed in public. That means the vision-based method of head gesture recognition is easier to generalize and be accepted. However, it is difficult to extract motion features from images or videos. MVM (Multi-View Model) and HMM (Hidden Markov Model) were combined to extract action features from video frames in [5], which got 88.1% accuracy for "nods" and "shake". Suni et al. [4] employed artificial fea-tures to detect faces and eyes, and then, those features were fed to SVM (Support Vector Machine). Its accuracy is 91.1%. Whereas recent vision-based methods usually have disadvantages in recognition accuracy and generalization ability, its accuracy cannot meet the requirements of HCI. Until now, 3DCNN (3D Convo-lutional Neural Network) is still attractive for researchers in action recognition, because its recognition rate has advantages comparing with other methods such as artificial feature extraction, LSTM and CNN. The classical 3DCNN models with high accuracy do not consider the parameters and computational costs for an onboard microcomputer. But the trade-off between computation and accu-racy is extremely essential for the application.

The focus of this paper is to propose a low-computation head gesture method for HCI. Therefore, 3DSFI is proposed by combining the 3D convolutional kernel and the two-stream structure. The proposed method is inspired by the Incep-tionV3, the SlowFast pathway and the 3D convolutional kernel. First, Inception modules are widely used in image ConvNet design, which are light in terms of its network parameters. Second, the 3D convolution kernel and the SlowFast pathway can extract both temporal and spatial features. In summary, the main contributions of this paper are as follow:

- A lightweight two-stream module termed SFstem is combined to efficiently extract the spatiotemporal feature from videos;
- The Inception blocks of InceptionV3 are expanded into the space-time by the 3D convolutional kernel for extracting the fusion features;
- The proposed method 3DSFI is deployed and verified on a real robotic platform.

2 Dynamic Head Gesture Recognition Method Based on 3DSFI

2.1 Problem Setup

Our intent is to recognize the class y of a head gesture video $\mathbf{x}$, and head gestures contain Y category action. First, the data preprocessing function $P : \mathbf{x} \to \mathbf{x}^k$ is designed to normalize the video. A head gesture video $\mathbf{x}$ with T frames is uniformly sampled into K frame. Note that for different videos, their length T is different. Besides, the starting frame of the video is randomly selected from a video $\mathbf{x}^{(K)}$, meanwhile, k frames data $\mathbf{x}^{(k)}$ that are fed into the feature extractor is successively taken behind the starting frame.

Given N training videos $\{\mathbf{x}_i, y_i\}_{i=1}^N$, the normalized video $\mathbf{x}_i^{(k)}$ is obtained by data preprocessing function P, and then we would like to design a feature extraction function $F : \mathbf{x}_i^{(k)} \to \tilde{y}_i$, where $\tilde{y} \in Y$ is the label of a head gesture. Finally, parameters of F will be learned and optimized according to the cost function $L : \{y, \tilde{y}\} \to \varepsilon$, where ε is the value of cost.

2.2 Spatiotemporal Feature Extractor

Convolutional neural network (CNN) is a crucial approach in image recognition. Many researchers proved that CNN had great advantages over hand-crafted features in generalization ability and accuracy in terms of shadow, illumination, and viewing angle [8]. However, 2DCNN is not suitable for videos, its accuracy is insufficient for HCI.

To simultaneously capture both the temporal and spatial features in the video, 3DCNN architecture was presented in [9]. The 3D convolution operation is given by Eq. 1.

$$v_{ij}^{xyz} = ReLU\left(b_{ij} + \sum_m \sum_{p=0}^{P_i-1} \sum_{q=0}^{Q_i-1} \sum_{r=0}^{R_i-1} w_{ijm}^{pqr} v_{(i-1)m}^{(x+p)(y+q)(z+r)}\right), \qquad (1)$$

where v_{ij}^{xyz} is the value of the jth feature map in the ith layer at the position (x, y, z), $ReLU(\cdot)$ is the activation function, b_{ij} is the bias, w_{ijm}^{pqr} is the $(p, q, r)th$ value of the kernel connected to the mth feature map in the previous layer.

C3D network based on the 3D convolutional kernel was proposed in [10] and has been regarded as an efficient, simple and generic motion feature extractor due to its strong representation ability for spatio-temporal features. To further improve the performance of action recognition, Carreira et al. [11] introduced the I3D model and the two-stream I3D, but the two-stream I3D needs a large number of GPUs for parameter training and the I3D cannot satisfy the accuracy requirement. Therefore, there still exist some limitations in the computational cost for generic networks.

Inception is an efficient deep neural network architecture [8], it not only gains a lower error in the ILSVRC-2014 challenge but also reduces 12 times parameters than AlexNet. Thus Inception blocks of InceptionV3 are utilized by the 3D convolutional kernel into 3D spatiotemporal domain. Besides, the SlowFast presented by Feichtenhofer [12] is extremely lightweight by decreasing the channel capacity. Thus, the Slow pathway and the Fast pathway are employed to reduce the computational cost.

2.3   Feature Extraction and Fusion

In this paper, a two-stream structure named SFstem block is designed to capture features in videos and optical flows, the structure is given by Fig. 1. The RGB feature extraction channel adopts the slow pathway. RGB images contain rich visual features. Besides, the optical flow is applied as another input of the feature extractor, which is computed by Farnebäck algorithm [13]. The Fast pathway is designed to rapidly capture motion features in optical flows, its characteristics include higher temporal rate and lightweight parameters. The two-stream network is composed of the Slow pathway and the Fast pathway, which are fused by lateral connections. The connection operation is given as Eq. 2.

$$Z = x^S_{t,i,j,d} + \text{reshape}\left(x^F_{t',i',j',d'}\right), \tag{2}$$

where $x^S_{t,i,j,d}$ and $x^F_{t',i',j',d'}$ are the feature map of the Slow and Fast pathway respectively, t is the temporal dimension, i and j are spatial dimension, d is the number of channels, reshape$(\cdot)$ denotes the dimension adjustment operation.

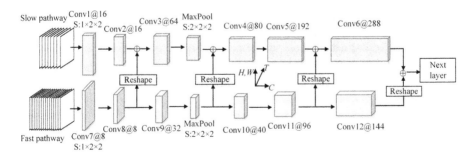

Fig. 1. SFstem block. This block is divided into the Slow pathway and the Fast pathway. The Slow pathway can fully extract spatiotemporal features in RGB videos. Meanwhile, the Fast pathway can rapidly extract the motion feature in the optical flow.

The size of data that is fed into the Slow pathway is $8 \times 112 \times 112 \times 3$, another is $16 \times 112 \times 112 \times 3$. S is the stride of convolution and pooling in Fig. 1. The stride of Conv1 and Conv7 is $1 \times 2 \times 2$, the rest is $1 \times 1 \times 1$. The Slow pathway is responsible for focusing on the spatial feature, meanwhile, the fast pathway captures more temporal features.

2.4 3DSFI Network Architecture

To effectively capture as many motion features as possible in RGB videos and dense optical flows, Inception blocks of InceptionV3, a popular 2D image architecture, are expanded into the space-time by the 3D convolutional kernel, which gives our network the capability to extract simultaneously both temporal and spatial features. The strategy of expanding the time domain is that every spatial 3×3 convolution in the inception block is extended to a $3 \times 3 \times 3$ spatiotemporal convolution, as shown in Fig. 2, where the stride of all Conv and Pool is 1.

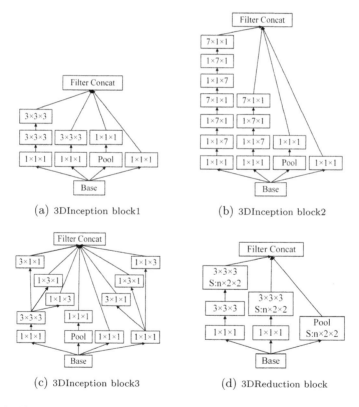

Fig. 2. The block of 3DSFI. The 3DInception block1, block2 and block3 are designed to increase the width and depth of the network. 3DReduction block is capable of adjusting the scale of the feature map.

3DInception block can efficiently capture features because of its wide range of width and depth. To reduce the computational costs of the network, the size of the feature map has to be decreased appropriately. Therefore, 3DReduction blocks are introduced to reduce the grid-size of spatial dimension instead of direct MaxPool or AvgPool operation, as shown in Fig. 2(d), where n is the scale of the temporal dimension.

The feature extractor named 3DSFI is proposed by connecting the above all of the blocks, it involves 1 SFstem block, 3 Inception block1, 5 Inception block2, 2 Inception block3, 2 Reduction block, 1 AvgPool and 1 fully connected layer, as shown in Fig. 3. The stride size of the first Reduction block is set to 1 in time axes for capturing more motion features. Besides, AvgPool is adopted to replace the fully connected layer for reducing training parameters. Finally, a Softmax classifier is employed.

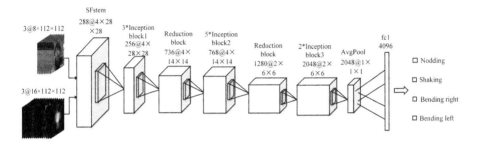

Fig. 3. 3DSFI network architecture. The overall architecture is composed of SFstem,3 Inception block1, 2 Reduction block, 5 Inception block2, 2 Inception block3, AvgPool and fully connected layer.

3   Experiments and Results

This section shows the comparison of the performance of several methods: C3D, I3D, 3DSFI and state-of-the-art methods, and then a head gesture dataset is built to train and test the above methods. Besides, the proposed method is applied to a real-life service robot called Pepper for verification.

3.1   Experimental Dataset

In this work, videos of the head gesture, containing nodding, shaking, bending left and bending right, are collected. The gathering environment involves different lighting, angle, background and person while keeping the camera still. Meanwhile, all videos are divided into training and validation sets. Test1 that the participant different from the training set and the validation set is constructed to verify the generalization ability of the network, the difference in test2 is that all participants wear masks. Finally, data enhancement is utilized to expand the number of datasets. The final dataset is listed in Table 1.

Table 1. The Dataset of the Head Gesture. The participants of test1 are different with training and validation, ones in test2 wear face masks.

Categories	Training	Validation	Test1	Test2
Nodding	724	208	96	80
Shaking	732	204	108	80
Bending left	656	204	112	80
Bending right	796	260	103	80

Algorithm 1 shows the pseudocode of data preprocessing. In this experiment, K is 32 and k is 16. Therefore, every video contains 32 frames and holds 2s in total, its resolution is 640×360. When data are fed into the network, its size will be center cropped to 112×112, and starting frame will be randomly selected from the 1st to 16th frame.

Algorithm 1. Algorithm for data preprocessing.

Input: Videos $\mathbf{x}_i, i = 1, ..., N$; K; k;
Output: Preprocessed videos , $\mathbf{x}_i^{(k)}, i = 1, ..., N$;
1: **for** $i = 1$ to N **do**
2:     Compute the length T of video $\mathbf{x}_i$;
3:     m $\leftarrow \frac{T}{K}$
4:     **for** $j = 1$ to T **do**
5:         **if** j % m $== 0$ **then**
6:             $\mathbf{x}_i^{(K)} \leftarrow \mathbf{x}_i^j$
7:         **end if**
8:     **end for**
9:     Randomly select index s of the starting frame from 1 to $T - k$;
10:     **for** $j = s$ to $s + k$ **do**
11:         $\mathbf{x}_i^{(k)} \leftarrow \mathbf{x}_i^{(K)j}$
12:     **end for**
13:     Normalize the size of $\mathbf{x}_i^{(k)}$
14: **end for**
15: **return** $\mathbf{x}_i^{(k)}$;

3.2 Models Training and Verification

Experimental conditions are as follow: Operating system is Windows 10 64-bit, 16 GB RAM, CPU is a 6-core 2.90 GHz Intel i5-10400, and GPU is a NVIDIA GeForce GTX2070 Super. Adam optimizer is adopted to train iteratively 2000 times with a batch size of 15. Its initial learning rate is set to 0.0001. Each batch is selected randomly from datasets. In addition, C3D and I3D employ only RGB video for training and their hyperparameters are the same as the above.

All methods are trained on head gesture datasets. The variation of accuracy and loss is shown in Fig. 4 for the validation set during training. Table 2 shows the results of comparison with the accuracy and complexity for three methods. The table reports the validation accuracy, test accuracy, parameters, multiply-add operations (FLOPs), time consumption per batch. In comparison, the proposed method provides significantly higher accuracy on test1 and test2. I3D has great advantages in the parameters, FLOPs and time consumption, but it sacrifices the generalization ability to some extent. C3D has a better performance than I3D due to its enormous parameters, but its FLOPs and time consumption have to make huge concessions and the curve of the loss and accuracy is fluctuant. Besides, the accuracy of state-of-the-art methods is listed in Table 3. Results show that our method is able to surpass the performance of all algorithms. The proposed method obtains a good accuracy to complexity trade-off and shows a great generalization performance.

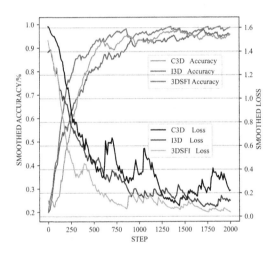

Fig. 4. The variation of accuracy and loss on the validation set.

Table 2. Comparison with Classical Method on Head Gesture Datasets. The accuracy, parameter, FLOPs and time consumption of serval methods are compared.

Methods	Validation	Test1	Test2	Param	FLOPs	Time consumption
C3D	95.43%	95.22%	90.62%	78M	491M	69 ms
I3D	94.64%	90.45%	86.57%	12M	71M	10 ms
3DSFI	**96.92%**	**96.42%**	**95.94%**	**46M**	**296M**	**30 ms**

Table 3. The accuracy comparison of the state-of-the-art methods.

Equipment	Method	Category	Accuracy
Head-mounted sensor	FSM-9 [7]	4	81.80%
	IMU + DTW [14]	4	85.68%
	myAHRS + SVM [15]	4	98.42%
	GY-87 + HGR-RF [16]	6	99.17%
Camera	MS-ConvLSTM [17]	4	73.25%
	MVM + HMM [5]	2	88.10%
	Eye Detection + SVM [4]	3	91.10%
	SVM [18]	2	92.00%
	C3D	4	95.22%
	I3D	4	90.54%
	3DSFI	**4**	**96.42%**

3.3 Application

In this work, 3DSFI is applied to a Pepper robot for validating actual performance. Pepper, a humanoid service robot, is used in serving retail, finance, public service and many other industries. The head gesture recognition will give it more effective interaction capabilities.

The proposed method is developed based on ROS (Robot Operating System) which is a powerful developer tool and open source. The interaction strategy is as follows: When a head gesture is identified, Pepper will perform the same motion as the head. Pepper and the interactive interface are given as Fig. 5. The camera with 640 × 480 resolution is selected in front of its head. The interactive interface consists of the robot's view, the live screen of HCI, simulation in Rviz, robot's response and window of head gesture recognition.

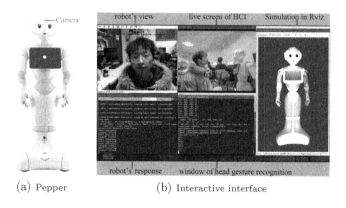

(a) Pepper   (b) Interactive interface

Fig. 5. The deployment of 3DSFI on Pepper.

The experimental result is shown in Fig. 6. When the user shakes his head, as shown in Fig. 6(a), Pepper with the 3DSFI algorithm accurately identifies the motion and meanwhile shakes its head to respond, as shown in Fig. 6(b). Experimental results indicate the proposed method is capable of efficiently deploying on the service robot and its interaction capability is improved.

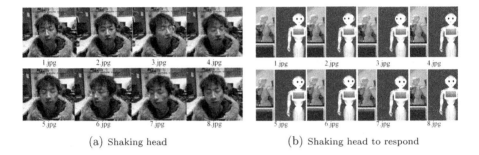

(a) Shaking head   (b) Shaking head to respond

Fig. 6. Actual interaction display of shaking head

4   Conclusion

A two-stream dynamic head gesture recognition method termed 3DSFI is presented in this paper. The two-stream structure with SFstem module is capable of reducing parameters and computational costs, meanwhile, it can efficiently capture motion features in videos and dense optical flows. The proposed method has distinct advantages over the classical C3D and I3D methods for accuracy and generalization performance. Moreover, the successful deployment of 3DSFI on Pepper demonstrated its effectiveness and practicality.

References

1. Ng, P.C., De Silva, L.C.: Head gestures recognition. In: Proceedings of the 2001 International Conference on Image Processing, vol. 3, pp. 266–269. IEEE, Thessaloniki (2001)
2. Fujie, S., Ejiri, Y., Nakajima, K., Matsusaka, Y., Kobayashi, T.: A conversation robot using head gesture recognition as para-linguistic information. In: Proceedings of the RO-MAN 2004. 13th IEEE International Workshop on Robot and Human Interactive Communication, pp. 159–164. IEEE, Kurashiki (2004)
3. Solea, R., Margarit, A., Cernega, D., Serbencu, A.: Head movement control of powered wheelchair. In: Proceedings of the 2019 23rd International Conference on System Theory, Control and Computing, pp. 632–637. IEEE, Sinaia (2019)
4. Suni, S.S., Gopakumar, K.: A real time decision support system using head nod and shake. In: Proceedings of the 2016 International Conference on Circuit, Power and Computing Technologies, pp. 1–5. IEEE, Nagercoil (2016)

5. Lu, P., Zhang, M., Zhu, X., Wang, Y.: Head nod and shake recognition based on multi-view model and hidden Markov model. In: Proceedings of International Conference on Computer Graphics, Imaging and Visualization, pp. 61–64. IEEE, Beijing (2005)
6. Rudigkeit, N., Gebhard, M., Graser, A.: An analytical approach for head gesture recognition with motion sensors. In: Proceedings of the 2015 9th International Conference on Sensing Technology, pp. 1–6. IEEE, Auckland (2015)
7. Jackowski, A., Gebhard, M., Gräser, A.: A novel head gesture based interface for hands-free control of a robot. In: Proceedings of the 2016 IEEE International Symposium on Medical Measurements and Applications, pp. 1–6. IEEE, Benevento (2016)
8. Pak, M., Kim, S.: A review of deep learning in image recognition. In: Proceedings of the 2017 4th International Conference on Computer Applications and Information Processing Technology, pp. 1–3. IEEE, Kuta Bali (2017)
9. Ji, S., Xu, W., Yang, M., Yu, K.: 3D convolutional neural networks for human action recognition. IEEE Trans. Pattern Anal. Mach. Intell. **35**(1), 221–231 (2013)
10. Tran, D., Bourdev, L., Fergus, R., Torresani, L., Paluri, M.: Learning spatiotemporal features with 3D convolutional networks. In: Proceedings of the 2015 IEEE International Conference on Computer Vision, pp. 4489–4497. IEEE, Santiago (2015)
11. Carreira, J., Zisserman, A.: Quo vadis, action recognition? A new model and the kinetics dataset. In: Proceedings of the 2017 IEEE Conference on Computer Vision and Pattern Recognition, pp. 4724–4733. IEEE, Honolulu (2017)
12. Feichtenhofer, C., Fan, H., Malik, J., He, K.: SlowFast networks for video recognition. In: 2019 IEEE/CVF International Conference on Computer Vision, pp. 6201–6210. IEEE, Seoul (2019)
13. Farnebäck, G.: Two-frame motion estimation based on polynomial expansion. In: Bigun, J., Gustavsson, T. (eds.) SCIA 2003. LNCS, vol. 2749, pp. 363–370. Springer, Heidelberg (2003). https://doi.org/10.1007/3-540-45103-X_50
14. Mavuş, U., Sezer, V.: Head gesture recognition via dynamic time warping and threshold optimization. In: 2017 IEEE Conference on Cognitive and Computational Aspects of Situation Management, pp. 1–7. IEEE, Savannah (2017)
15. Haseeb, M.A., Kyrarini, M., Jiang, S., Ristic-Durrant, D., Gräser, A.: Head gesture-based control for assistive robots. In: 11th ACM International Conference on PErvasive Technologies Related to Assistive Environments, pp. 379–383. ACM, Corfu (2018)
16. Wu, C., Yang, H., Chen, Y., Ensa, B., Ren, Y., Tseng, Y.: Applying machine learning to head gesture recognition using wearables. In: 2017 IEEE 8th International Conference on Awareness Science and Technology, pp. 436–440. IEEE, Taichung (2017)
17. Sharma, M., Ahmetovic, D., Jeni, L.A., Kitani, K.M.: Recognizing visual signatures of spontaneous head gestures. In: 2018 IEEE Winter Conference on Applications of Computer Vision, pp. 400–408. IEEE, Lake Tahoe (2018)
18. Numanoglu, T., Erzin, E., Yemezy, Y., Sezginy, M.T.: Head nod detection in dyadic conversations. In: 27th Signal Processing and Communications Applications Conference. SIU 2019, pp. 1–4. Institute of Electrical and Electronics Engineers Inc., Sivas (2019)

Research on Passive Energy-Regulated Bionic Shell for Lateral Fall Recovery Behavior of Large Quadruped Robots

Xiang Zeng[1], Wenchuan Jia[1(⊠)], Shugen Ma[1,2], Xin Luo[3], Yi Sun[1], Jianjun Yuan[1], and Yu Zhang[1]

[1] School of Mechatronic Engineering and Automation,
Shanghai University, Shanghai 200444, People's Republic of China
lovvchris@shu.edu.cn
[2] Department of Robotics, Ritsumeikan University, Kusatsu, Shiga 525-8577, Japan
[3] School of Mechanical Science and Engineering, Huazhong University of Science and Technology, Wuhan 430074, People's Republic of China

Abstract. The lateral fall of a quadruped robot is difficult to avoid. However, there are few studies on the fall recovery of quadruped robots, especially that with large size and weight. One of the important reasons originates from the driving capability of robot joints. This paper analyzes the fall recovery behavior of several animals in nature, and designs a bionic shell structure. Then the working mechanism and critical conditions of the shell have been studied in detail. The shell that with the ability of regulating the energy changes of the robot when rolling, can make the quadruped robot withstand large impacts and avoid tipping. Based on the compliant movement generated by the arc-shaped contour of the bionic shell, the demand for the explosive joint driving force can be greatly reduced. These inherent advantages of the mechanism of the shell make it suitable for the lateral fall recovery of a large quadruped robot. The effectiveness of the mechanism is verified by simulation. Moreover, the performance of the bionic shell is discussed, for different factors including impacts, terrains and structures.

Keywords: Bionic shell · Fall self-recovery · Passive energy-regulated

1 Introduction

A variety of legged robots, which have motion mechanism similar to that of special animals, can achieve more dynamic and suitable actions to better adapt to the terrain through the imitation of the real motion behaviors of the animals, have once again become a hot topic in the field of robotics in the past decade.

Although many different types of methods [1–3] have been studied to improve the stability of legged dynamic walking, which is the core task of legged motion control, it is still unavoidable for robots to fall, mainly due to the complexity of movement behavior [4] and unpredictable external disturbance. No matter what causes the robot to fall, for

© Springer Nature Switzerland AG 2021
X.-J. Liu et al. (Eds.): ICIRA 2021, LNAI 13015, pp. 246–257, 2021.
https://doi.org/10.1007/978-3-030-89134-3_23

the legged robot challenges complex tasks, how to stand up by itself will immediately be the highest priority task or even become the only current task once it falls.

The research and application of quadruped robots have been in the forefront of legged robots, and quadruped robots with high load capacity have begun to perform actual tasks [5], so we focus on the fall recovery behavior of the similar large quadruped robot.

A fallen quadruped robot can self-recover from prone posture to standing posture by motion planning [6]. But for quadruped robots, lateral fall is more likely to occur. When a small or medium-sized quadruped robot falls sideways, it can still recover with human intervention or instantaneous explosive force provided by hip joints, as implemented in *HyQ*, *RHex*, locust-inspired robot and flea-inspired robot [7–10]. However, for a large quadruped robot, due to its weight, size and limited joint torque, it is difficult to recover like those small robots. Therefore, how to complete self-recovery of this type of robot has become a realistic problem, which is also the biggest motivation of this paper.

Although this task is very important and practical, the current methods of traditional gait analysis and motion stability research on legged robots rarely involve falling and recovery behavior. One of the important reasons is that the driving ability of the joints is limited, that is, the legged robot prototype designed for achieving rhythmic gait with low energy consumption cannot meet the power required for fall recovery behavior.

It is a natural idea to use other body parts such as spine, torso, and arms to actively provide additional power, and to combine leg movements to achieve self-recovery. Besides four legs, the *CENTAURO* robot also has two 7-DOFs arms and a 1-DOF torso, which can help the robot return to its original posture after it falls [11]. Juan et al. proposed a fall recovery strategy for the robot [12]. A recovery of humanoid robot from supine and prone posture to standing posture under the cooperation of the arms and the torso are discussed in [13, 14].

Nevertheless, the above methods are not suitable for most quadruped robots, which do not have other motion units except the legs. It is necessary to design a simple and economical mechanism to implement self-recovery for them. Perhaps it is a good choice to learn from the fall recovery behaviors of animals in nature. Figure 1 shows the fall recovery process of four species. After falling, the elephants and horses use their backs as supports and then adjust the center of mass (CoM) quickly to a critical position with their waist, abdomen and limbs, as shown in phase I, where the boundary of arc-shaped contour contacts with the ground. Then relying on inertia and limb actions to cross the critical position and transition to the prone or semi-standing posture, as shown in phase II. And finally, adjusting posture to stabilize the CoM, as shown in phase III. For geochelones [15] and ladybugs [16] with hemispherical back, they utilize the inertia generated by limbs to a critical position, and then completing recovery through the power provided by legs, neck or wings. In above recovery process, phase I and II are the key phases, which determine whether the animals can complete the fall recovery from. The fall recovery behaviors of the animals and the body structure just provide an excellent reference for the fall recovery of the robot.

Previously, many researchers have combined robots with circular structures. When a quadrotor with a hemispherical protection structure falls over, it can recover to a safe posture that can take off, by virtue of the compliant motion of the structure and external force from the rotating arm [17]. When the ball-leg hybrid robot [18, 19] lateral falls in quadruped form, adjusting the limb actions would generate compliant movement, which can assist it to complete the fall recovery. Some mechanisms inspired by insect wings can also assist small robot to implement fall recovery. The cockroach-inspired robot [20] and *JumoRoACH* [21] control the expansion and contraction of the bionic wings through an additional drive unit to realize self-recovery after tipping over.

As the size of the quadruped robot increases, its weight increases exponentially. Those self-righting methods that suitable for small and medium-sized robot may not be suitable for the large one. As mentioned in the above literatures, the arc-shaped structure can effectively save power. Therefore, giving full play to the role of the arc-shaped structure in the process of later fall recovery is an effective approach to solve the problem of self-recovery of the large quadruped robot. In this paper, we design a bionic shell with an arc-shaped profile, and the quadruped robot installed with the bionic shell is shown in Fig. 2. With the compliant movement along the arc-shaped contour, the requirement for joint driving force during the fall recovery process is reduced, and the energy can be passively adjusted.

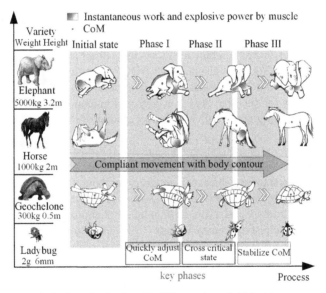

Fig. 1. Fall recovery behavior of animals with different sizes. Initial state represents fall posture. They use their backs as supports and then adjust the CoM quickly to a critical position with the muscle power, in phase I. In phase II, with the compliant movement of body contour and limb movements, cross the critical state of CoM. In phase III, adjusting the posture to stabilize CoM. The phase I and II are key phases, which determine whether they can complete the recovery. The red area represents the instantaneous work and explosive power by muscle, and the shade indicates the magnitude of value.

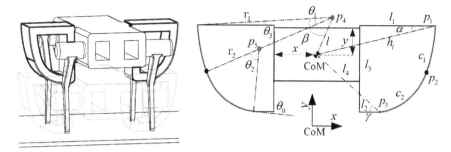

Fig. 2. Left: The installation diagram of the bionic shell, and the shadow represents the prone posture. Right: The shape and parameters of the shell.

2 Recovery Mechanism

2.1 Structure Design of the Bionic Shell

In order to avoid tipping over and implement lateral fall recovery, after our exploration and practice, we adopt the following principles for the shell design.

(1) In the whole recovery process, the robot rolls along with the profile of the shell. There is only the mutual transformation of energy consumption such as gravitational potential energy, kinetic energy and friction loss of the body, and the body posture is adjusted by the passive change of potential energy.

(2) The contour of the bionic shell contains a smooth curve, whose curvature can be adjusted to regulate the potential energy change.

(3) In the shape design of the bionic shell, the height of CoM of the robot should keep changing monotonously during the compliant motion of the robot, which can avoid possible local energy traps effectively.

(4) When the speed of robot is 0, it resumes motion with the effect of gravity moment.

(5) When the robot is in a prone posture, only the bionic shell provides support.

(6) The top of the shell is basically flat with the robot body which differ in *LS3* [22], that provides a large platform for fixing a robotic arm, similar to *spot mini* [23].

Based on the above principles, the structure of the bionic shell is designed, whose profile is a trapezoid with curve side, as shown in Fig. 2. And the curve composed of two tangent arcs, which can not only increase the arc-length of the curve but also reduce the width of bionic shell. The centers of the two arcs and the boundary of the curve satisfy $y_{p_4} \geq y_{p_1}$ and $|x_{p_3}| > |x_{p_5}|$, which can meet the monotonous change of the height of CoM during the working process. The CoM is below three straight lines, where the radiuses of the arcs at p_1, p_2, p_3 lie respectively, which can meet the fourth criterion. Designing an angle θ_0 can not only shorten l_1 but also reduce the impact from the third collision. To simplify analysis and calculation, the initial contact point with ground is designed as the tangent position of two arcs. The work mechanism of this shell is described in next subsection.

2.2 Recovery Behavior

When the quadruped robot falls sideways, its movement process with the effect of the bionic shell is shown in Fig. 3. There are several different possibilities in the movement process. Behavior I is the preferred design way, where the robot can implement self-recovery. At the end of Behavior II, the robot tips over and the mission failed. In the Behavior III, the robot would fall into static stable states, requiring the intervention of the joint driving torque to resume movement. Among them, the Behavior I, an ideal recovery process, is designed and analyzed in this paper. Behavior II and III need to be avoided by analyzing the critical states which are specifically discussed in Sect. 3.

In Behavior I, the robot receives a large impact on the left side, then collides with the ground for the first time. The next moment, it continues to move along the profile of the bionic shell with the effect of inertia, and then reaches the limit state, where the velocity of the robot is 0 and the position of CoM is get to the left of p_1. This process corresponding to A–D in Fig. 3 is defined as the falling process, and the kinetic energy of the robot converts into collision loss, potential energy and friction loss. Afterward, with the effect of the gravity moment, the robot moves along arc c_1, and then the second collision occurs. This belong to a part of recovery process, corresponding to D–F, where the potential energy of robot converts into kinetic energy and friction loss. After one or more collisions, the kinetic energy becomes 0, and the robot is statically stable on the ground. At the moment, the position of CoM is get to left of p_2. Ultimately, after retracting the legs and shanks, it moves along the arc c_2 with the effect of gravity moment, and then rotates around p_3, completing fall recovery. This is other part of recovery process, corresponding to F–H, where the potential energy is converted into kinetic energy and friction loss, and in the end of the process, the third collision occurs.

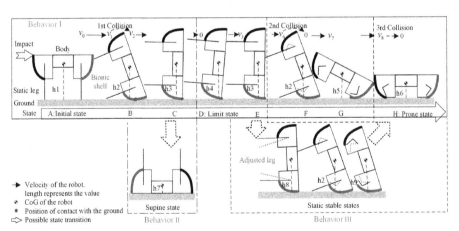

Fig. 3. The lateral fall recovery process of the quadruped robot. It includes three possible behaviors, represented by different line types. In behavior I, A–D belong to the fall process, and D–H belong to the recovery process. The robot only needs to retract the legs, which is indicated by the red dot to recover to the prone state during the whole process. And there are three collisions in B, F, H. Behavior II is the worst result. There would be some static stable states, in which requiring the intervention of actuated joints to resume movement in Behavior III.

The bionic shell proposed in this paper has the several advantages in action process:

- When the robot falls sideways, it can effectively reduce the possibility of the robot tipping over;
- Only relying on its own structural properties to produce conformed actions, without the intervention of the control system, can implement the recovery;
- Significantly reducing the work done by the actuated joint, the requirements for the joint power (especially the maximum torque) and the overall energy consumption during the self-recovery;
- It can effectively protect the robot in the case of a sudden fall of the robot.

3   Critical States Analysis

During the self-recovery process described in last section, there are some important critical states would determine the subsequent behavior of the robot and whether it can successfully complete the task. This section focuses on the analysis of the critical states.

3.1   Analysis of the State D

When the robot rolls along c_1 to the boundary, its velocity is not 0 and rotates around point p_1 until it decelerates to 0, that is, the kinetic energy is all converted into collision loss, friction loss, and potential energy. To prevent the robot from tipping over, the projection of the CoM on the ground is get to the left of p_1. The limit height of the CoM can be obtained by the geometric relationship

$$h_l^2 = (l_1 + x)^2 + y^2 \tag{1}$$

where h_l is the distance between the CoM and p_1, l_1 represents the top width of the shell, and x, y are the distances between CoM and the boundary of the robot body.

The height of CoM at state D can be obtained by the energy conservation formula

$$mgh_4 = 1/2mv_2^2 + mgh_2 \tag{2}$$

where h_4 is the height of CoM at state D, m is total mass of the robot and the bionic shell, v_2 is the velocity of the robot after the collision, h_2 represents the height of CoM at state B, which is given by $h_2 = r_1 - l\cos(\beta - \theta_1)$.

When $h_4 < h_l$ is satisfied, robot would not tip over.

3.2   Analysis of the State F

The robot moves along c_1 from p_1 to p_2, reaching state F. In this process, due to some reasons (e.g. uneven terrain), the robot maybe unable to reach state F when only with the effect of the gravity moment, so it is necessary to determine whether it needs the intervention of the joint driving force. The instantaneous velocity in this state is

$$V_6 = \sqrt{2E_{k6}/m} \tag{3}$$

$$E_{k6} = 1/2mv_2^2 - 2f\,\bar{c}_1 \tag{4}$$

where E_{k6} is the kinetic energy at the moment before the second collision, f represents the friction force between the robot and ground, and $\bar{c}_1$ is the arc-length of c_1.

When $V_6 \geq 0$ is satisfied, the robot can completely pass through c_1 only with the effect of gravity moment. In addition, it could be as close to 0 as possible for reducing the impact from the second collision.

3.3 Analysis of the State G

Here, we mainly analyze whether the robot can move adaptively from state F to G. At state F, adjusting the limb movements would reduce the support point for robot, and make it move to p_3 along c_2 with the effect of the gravity moment. The instantaneous velocity in this state is

$$V_7 = \sqrt{2E_{k7}/m} \tag{5}$$

$$E_{k7} = mg(h_2 - h_5) - f\,\bar{c}_2 \tag{6}$$

where E_{k7} is the kinetic energy of robot at state G, $\bar{c}_2$ is the arc-length of c_2, h_5 represents the height of CoM at state G, calculated by $h_5 = l_4 \cos(\gamma + \theta_0)$.

When $V_7 \geq 0$, the robot can completely pass through c_2 only with the effect of the gravity moment. And the closer V_7 is to 0, the smaller impact from the third collision.

Through analyzing the above three critical states, it is found that the performance of the bionic shell can be enhanced by adjusting the structural parameters. Each bionic shell corresponds to an impact threshold. only when the impact exceeds the threshold, the robot would reach the supine state, which is difficult to recover. Increasing h_l will enhance the anti-tipping ability of the robot and the effect of the bionic shell on c_1. However, as h_l increases, l_1 and the mass of shell would increase. The robot maybe unable to pass through some narrow space areas with l_1 increases. By reducing the difference between h_1 and h_2, the impact from the first collision can be reduced. Reducing the difference between h_2 and h_4 or increasing $\bar{c}_1$ can reduce the impact from the second collision. To reduce the impact from the third collision, we can increase $\bar{c}_2$ or reduce the difference between h_2 and h_6. h_1 and h_6 are properties of the robot and determined by the quadruped robot. The adjustments of the height of CoM at other positions and the arc-length of the profile curve can be completed by adjusting the width and the radius of the bionic shell. In fact, we adjust l_1 and r_1. And the specific adjustment methods need to comprehensively consider the performance of the bionic shell during the transition between the above-mentioned critical states.

4   Simulation

Simulation is used to validate the effectiveness of the bionic shell and its mechanism proposed in this paper. In the simulation, it is found that no matter what posture the quadruped robot falls sideways, the bionic shell would land first and provide support for it. So we focus on the analysis and discussion of the effect of the recovery behavior after state B for different terrains, impacts and structural parameters of the bionic shell. Combined with the preliminary analysis, we assume that the robot moves along the curve with as the starting point.

4.1 Basic Function Validation

An 8020N impact is applied on the side of a standing quadruped robot weighs 430 kg to make it falls sideways, then it follows the profile of the bionic shell and reaches the state F. And then retracting the legs and shanks at 6s to recover to prone state. The simulation time is set to 8 s, and the shell parameters are: $l_1 = 0.6$ m, $l_2 = 0.18$ m, $l_3 = 0.7$ m, $r_1 = 1.352$ m, $r_2 = 0.404$ m. The above process is simulated in Adams, and the result is shown in Fig. 4(a), which corresponds to Behavior I in Fig. 3. During the process, the potential energy, kinetic energy and friction loss are mutual converted continuously and monotonously. There are some sudden changes in kinetic energy at 2.85 s, 4.5 s, and 6.96 s, which are caused by the three collisions marked in Fig. 3. Eventually, the robot recovers to the prone state and the potential energy is constant.

4.2 Terrain and Impact Adjustment

Adjusting the friction coefficient, stiffness coefficient and damping ratio in the Coulomb friction model can simulate different terrains and floor materials. This subsection focuses on the influence of friction coefficient, and sets the stiffness coefficient and damping ratio to constant. Due to the collisions, the material of the shell is set to steel with higher stiffness. And the range of friction coefficient of steel is 0.2–0.6.

In state B, setting the initial horizontal speed of the robot to 1.5 m/s, without vertical speed, and adjusting the friction coefficient to 0.2, 0.4, 0.6 respectively. The results are shown in Fig. 4(b). When the friction coefficient is 0.4 or 0.6, the energy curves basically overlap. Moreover, when the friction coefficient is 0.2, the robot slips, and part of the energy is lost, causing the peak value of potential energy to be lower than the value obtained by pure rolling of the robot when the friction coefficient is larger. When no sliding, the friction coefficient has little effect on the energy curve during the movement.

Different impacts cause different velocities of the robot and the subsequent self-recovery behavior. And the different impacts are simulated by adjusting the initial velocity in state B. The energy curves ($\mu = 0.5$) of the self-recovery process with different initial velocities are shown in Fig. 4(c). When the horizontal speed is 1.69 m/s and the vertical speed is 0, the robot tips over, which caused by the excessive initial velocity. Therefore, the critical horizontal speed of the bionic shell, without vertical speed, is 1.68 m/s–1.69 m/s. After falling, the vertical speed of the robot comes from the impact or elastic deformation caused by the collision. To keep the bionic shell contacting with the ground at all times, the vertical speed of the robot would not be great, so it is set to 0.05 m/s in the simulation to analyze whether its presence would affect the tipping. Obviously, with a constant horizontal speed, as the vertical speed increases, the height of CoM has little change. So it has little effect on the function of the shell.

4.3 Parameter Adjustment of the Bionic Shell

As mentioned in theoretical analysis, adjusting the parameters of the bionic shell would improve the potential energy regulation ability, impact resistance and tipping resistance of robot. As shown in Fig. 4(d), under the same initial conditions, when r_1 is reduced, the peak height of CoM and the impact from the second and third collision are reduced. And the working time of the bionic shell is shortened, which can effectively enhance the efficiency of the shell. Notice that r_1 is corresponding to a critical value. When it is less than the critical value, the robot would tip over and be difficult to recover.

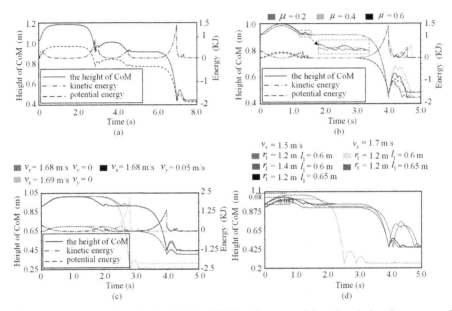

Fig. 4. Simulation results. (a) The height of CoM and energy of the robot during the process of the lateral fall recovery. (b) The height of CoM and energy of the robot during the self-recovery process when the initial speed of the robot is 1.5 m/s, and with different friction coefficients. The dashed box is a partial enlarged view. (c) Simulation results with different initial velocities, when $\mu = 0.5$. (d) The height of CoM obtained by adjusting the parameters of the shell. Increasing l_1 has little effect on the peak height of CoM.

Obviously, only increasing the width of the bionic shell would slightly reduce the change in potential energy, which shows that the effect of the c_1 is slightly enhanced. But it also increases the difference between h_5 and h_6, which subsequently increases the impact from the third collision. Comparing the two curves with the initial speed of 1.7 m/s in Fig. 4(d), it can be found that increasing l_1 could effectively enhance the capability of anti-tipping and impact resistance of the robot. With adjustment of l_1, r_1 and r_2 would change accordingly, and the ability of the bionic shell in other phases would be affected. Therefore, l_1 and r_1 need to be balanced in the design process. Considering the benefits after adjusting the parameters, we prefer to adjust r_1.

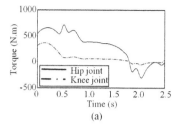 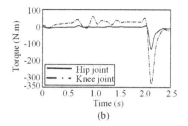

Fig. 5. Torque requirements during active and passive recovery. (a) Active recovery. (b) Passive recovery.

4.4 Active Recovery

When a large quadruped robot without bionic shell falls sideways, a huge instantaneous torque is required for re-standing, which is as about three times as required for standing normally, in Fig. 5(a). For a quadruped robot equipped with bionic shells, in Fig. 5(b), the maximum torque required for passive recovery is only half of that for a quadruped robot without a shell, and it can be reduced by reducing the mass of shell. The bionic shell provides a very practical mechanism for realizing the lateral fall recovery.

5   Discussion

When the positional relationships are uncertain, there would be some static stable states during the recovery process, as shown in Behavior II, that is, when the velocity of the robot decreases to 0, the CoM is in the support area. In this situation, the robot needs the assistance of joint driving force to recover. To have a better self-recovery effect, we restrict the relationships between the CoM and the centers of arcs of the bionic shell.

The recovery behavior proposed in this paper has a high similarity with the elephant. As shown in Fig. 6(a), after lateral fall, it would like to transform the kinetic energy into potential energy with the compliant movement; then continue to move until the legs contact with the ground with the effect of inertia; and then recover to prone state with the assistance of limbs; and finally resume standing by adjusting legs. In addition to shape and behavior, the force exerted by elephants during the recovery process could be studied to implement the active recovery (include active force) of the robot.

In nature, animals with different sizes can recover from the lateral fall state by the compliant movement. After studying their recovery behavior, shape and exertion process, various quadruped robots equipped with the bionic shell can also complete the self-recovery. As shown in Fig. 6(b), all the robots with different scale factors could recover to the prone state after being subjected to a proportional impact.

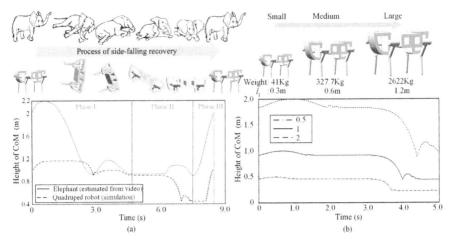

Fig. 6. (a) Lateral fall self-recovery process and the height curves of CoM. The data of elephant comes from a rough estimation of the public video and the data of quadruped robot obtained by simulation. (b) The height of CoM in different sizes. The scale factor equals to 1 represents the original size, equals to 0.5 represents half of the original size, and equals to 2 is twice of the original size.

6 Conclusion

Based on the analysis of the fall recovery behavior of several kinds of animals with arc-shaped bodies in nature, this paper designs a bionic shell suitable for the lateral fall recovery of a large quadruped robot. When the quadruped robot falls sideways without tipping over, the shell can implement the self-recovery by planning and adjusting the potential energy conversion process in advance, as well as effectively improve the ability of anti-tipping and impact resistance. And the bionic shell has good terrain adaptability, when μ is in range of 0.2–0.6, it can always complete the recovery task successfully. Furthermore, the working process of the bionic shell mainly relies on the compliant movement with the arc-shaped contour, not only doesn't require the intervention of a complex control system, but also greatly reduces the peak value of the required instantaneous force of the joint and the total energy consumption. This bionic shell is also suitable for small or medium-sized quadruped robots. The hyperlink of one summary video is https://v.youku.com, with the access password *2021*.

References

1. Sugihara, T., Yamamoto, T.: Foot-guided agile control of a biped robot through ZMP manipulation. In: 2017 IEEE/RSJ International Conference on Intelligent Robots and Systems, Vancouver, pp. 4546–4551 (2017)
2. Poulakakis, I.: Spring loaded inverted pendulum embedding: extensions toward the control of compliant running robots. In: 2010 IEEE International Conference on Robotics and Automation, Anchorage, pp. 5219–5224 (2010)

3. Winkler, A., Havoutis, I., Bazeille, S., et al.: Path planning with force-based foothold adaptation and virtual model control for torque controlled quadruped robots. In: 2014 IEEE International Conference on Robotics and Automation, Hong Kong, pp. 6476–6482 (2014)
4. Dickinson, M.H., Farley, C.T., Full, R.J., et al.: How animals move: an integrative view. Science **288**(5463), 100–106 (2000)
5. Raibert, M., Blankespoor, K., Nelson, G., et al.: BigDog, the rough-terrain quadruped robot. In: IFAC Proceedings, pp.10822–10825 (2008)
6. Yang, J., Jia, W., Sun, Y., et al.: Mechanical design of a compact and dexterous quadruped robot. In: 2017 IEEE International Conference on Mechatronics and Automation (ICMA 2017), Takamatsu, pp. 1450–1456 (2017)
7. Claudio, S., Jake, G., Bilal, R., et al.: Design overview of the hydraulic quadruped robots HyQ2Max and HyQ2Centaur. In: The Fourteenth Scandinavian International Conference on Fluid Power, Tampere, pp. 20–22 (2015)
8. Saranli, U., Alfred, A., Daniel, E.: Model-based dynamic self-righting maneuvers for a hexapedal robot. Int. J. Robot. Res. **23**, 903–918 (2004)
9. Chen, K., Chen, D., Zhang, Z., et al.: Jumping robot with initial body posture adjustment and a self-righting mechanism. Int. J. Adv. Robot. Syst. **13**, 127–135 (2016)
10. Noh, M., Kim, S.W., An, S., et al.: Flea-inspired catapult mechanism for miniature jumping robots. IEEE Trans. Rob. **28**(5), 1007–1018 (2012)
11. Kashiri, N., Baccelliere, L., Muratore, L., et al.: CENTAURO: a hybrid locomotion and high power resilient manipulation platform. IEEE Robot. Autom. Lett. **4**, 1595–1602 (2019)
12. Castano, J.A., Zhou, C., Tsagarakis, N.: Design a fall recovery strategy for a wheel-legged quadruped robot using stability feature space. In: 2019 IEEE International Conference on Robotics and Biomimetics (ROBIO 2019), Dali, pp. 41–46 (2019)
13. Kanehiro, F., Kaneko, K., Fujiwara, K., et al.: The first humanoid robot that has the same size as a human and that can lie down and get up. In: 2003 IEEE International Conference on Robotics and Automation (ICRA 2003), Taipei, pp. 1633–1639 (2003)
14. Stückler, J., Schwenk, J., Behnke, S.: Getting back on two feet: reliable standing-up routines for a humanoid robot. In: Proceedings of the 9th International Conference on Intelligent Autonomous Systems, Tokyo, pp. 676–685 (2006)
15. Ruhr, I.M., Rose, K.A.R., Sellers, W.I., et al.: Turning turtle: scaling relationships and self-righting ability in Chelydra serpentina. Proc. R. Soc. B **288**(1946), 20210213 (2021)
16. Zhang, J., Li, J., Li, C., et al.: Self-righting physiology of the ladybird beetle Coccinella septempunctata on surfaces with variable roughness. J. Insect Physiol. **130**, 104202–104211 (2021)
17. Peng, J., Song, G., Qiao, G., et al.: A self-recovery mechanism for quadrotors. In: 2014 IEEE International Conference on Robotics and Biomimetics, Bali, pp. 1531–1536 (2014)
18. Huang, Z., Jia, W., Sun, Y., et al.: Design and analysis of a transformable spherical robot for multi-mode locomotion. In: 2017 IEEE International Conference on Mechatronics and Automation, Takamatsu, pp. 1469–1473 (2017)
19. Nemoto, T., Mohan, R.E., Iwase, M.: Rolling locomotion control of a biologically inspired quadruped robot based on energy compensation. Robotics 1–10 (2015)
20. Xuan, Q., Li, C.: Coordinated appendages accumulate more energy to self-right on the ground. IEEE Robot. Autom. Lett. **5**(4), 6137–6144 (2020)
21. Jung, G.P., Casarez, C.S., Baek, S.-M., et al.: JumpRoACH: a trajectory-adjustable integrated jumping-crawling robot. IEEE/ASME Trans. Mechatron. **24**(3), 947–958 (2019)
22. Michael, K.: Meet Boston dynamics' LS3 - the latest robotic war machine. Tedxuwollongong Talk 2012 (2012)
23. Niquille, S.C.: Regarding the pain of SpotMini: or what a robot's struggle to learn reveals about the built environment. Archit. Des. **89**(1), 84–91 (2019)

Research on Adaptive Control in Complex Terrain for Quadruped Robot

Peng Xu, Lei Jiang, Qichang Yao, Ruina Dang, Yunfeng Jiang, Boyang Xing, Wei Xu, Yufei Liu, and Bo Su[✉]

China North Vehicle Research Institute, Beijing 100072, China
bosu@noveri.com.cn

Abstract. In order to improve the locomotion ability of quadruped robot under the uneven terrain, an adaptive control method of quadruped robot is proposed in this paper. Firstly, by introducing into the threshold of terrain elevation and calculating irregularity information to detect whether the foothold area is safe. Secondly, according to the key points and size information of the virtual obstacle, re-plan the swing trajectory and foothold of the swing leg online. Thirdly, the body balance control strategy is used to achieve obstacle crossing by integrating the ground plane estimation and force allocation optimization. Finally, this proposed method is tested in Vortex simulation environment, and the experiment verifies the effectiveness.

Keywords: Quadruped robot · Uneven terrain · Adaptive control · Balance control

1 Introduction

At present, quadruped robots are developing towards intelligence. More and more domestic and foreign research institutions are carrying out in-depth research. In view of the high mobility and adaptability of typical animals such as cheetahs, goats, wolves and dogs, these robots will play an important role in military, space exploration, safety and explosion protection, injury rescue and other areas.

For the adaptive control of quadruped robot under complex terrain, research institutes at home and abroad have successively carried out research on dynamic stability control and autonomous locomotion. Raibert established the inverted pendulum control model based on the virtual leg. The stable locomotion of the quadruped robot "BigDog" under the complex terrain was achieved [1], and the quadruped robot "LS3" was developed which used for carrying out tasks of transportation and leader tracking under outdoor environment [2]. The quadruped robot "SpotMini" could achieve the stable locomotion in the indoor stairs based on perception sensors with the autonomous dynamic gait [3]. The biped robot "Atlas" was developed which used airborne radar etc. to recognize obstacles such as logs and steps with re-planning the foothold, and achieved the crossing of logs and steps [4]. The quadruped robot "Cheetah" developed by MIT, used the planning of the height force and the method of stability control to achieve the stable

© Springer Nature Switzerland AG 2021
X.-J. Liu et al. (Eds.): ICIRA 2021, LNAI 13015, pp. 258–268, 2021.
https://doi.org/10.1007/978-3-030-89134-3_24

locomotion [5–7], afterwards, the crossing of regular obstacles was achieved by the dynamic adjustment of the jump trajectory based on the feature recognition [8]. The quadruped robot "StarlETH" was developed by ETH with the virtual force control to achieve the compliant and stable locomotion [9]. Based on the control method, combined with the autonomous perception system, the quadruped robot "AnyMal" could achieve autonomous locomotion under complex terrain [10]. Recently, the team adopted a deep reinforcement learning method to achieve the fast and efficient locomotion and self-recovery behavior [11, 12]. The quadruped robot "HyQ" developed by Italian Institute of Technology adopted the control method of linear inverted pendulum to realize the stable locomotion [13–15]. The quadruped robot "Scalf" developed by Shandong University adopted static walk gait to achieve obstacle crossing of continuous steps [16].

Based on the above, at present, Boston Dynamic had carried out research on the adaptive dynamic obstacle crossing, however, technical details of the planning method are not yet available. MIT "Cheetah" achieved the autonomous dynamic planning of jumping gait under regular obstacles with distinctive color features. Except that, less researches have been carried out. This paper is aimed to realize dynamic autonomous planning of trot gait for quadruped robot, which will be of great significance for quadruped robots to perform tasks efficiently in complex terrain.

In order to verify the feasibility of this control method, firstly, the safe foothold area of foothold for the robot is detected. Secondly, the swing trajectory and foothold position of swing leg are re-planned, also, the model of body posture control in obstacle-crossing environment is established, and the simulation environment of typical working conditions is built. The control method is validated with trot gait. Lastly, the work is summarized and prospected.

2 Detection of Foothold Area

Based on airborne radar and stereo camera, the surrounding environment is identified and modeled, and the elevation map of terrain is established. In order to reduce the blind area of terrain recognition, the installation and layout of the sensing module will be configured, and the recognition area of the sensing module to the environment will be widened, as shown in Fig. 1.

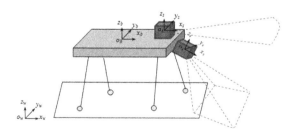

Fig. 1. Layout of the system

According to the elevation and irregularity of the terrain, it can be determined whether it is a safe area to choose the foothold. The irregularity of the terrain can be described by the standard deviation of elevation. The number of meshes selected and the search direction can be set according to the locomotion direction.

When the robot crosses a step obstacle, it can be determined whether it is a safe area to choose the foothold with the irregularity. Setting the threshold of irregularity σ^*, if $\sigma \leq \sigma^*$, the area is considered to be a safe area. If the new foothold is in the safe area, the new foothold can be re-planned by the following adaptive method from the next chapter. If the new foothold is not in the safe area, the foot will remain in the original safe foot area, and the body will move in the original direction accordingly, so that the step obstacle grid of the robot can be adapted, as shown in Fig. 2.

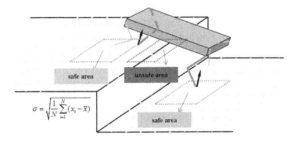

Fig. 2. Adaptation of steps

When the robot crosses the trenches, it can be determined whether it is a safe area to choose the foothold with the irregularity and the elevation. Setting the threshold of irregularity σ^* and elevation x^*, if $\sigma \leq \sigma^*$ and $x \geq x^*$, the area is considered to be a safe area. If the new foothold is in the safe area, the new foothold can be re-planned by the following adaptive method from the next chapter. If the new foothold is not in the safe area, the foot will remain in the original safe foot area, and the body will move in the original direction accordingly, so that the trenches grid of the robot can be adapted, as shown in Fig. 3.

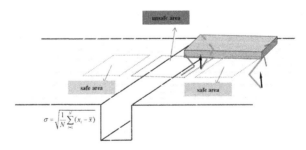

Fig. 3. Adaptation of trenches

3   Behavior Re-planning

For larger obstacles, virtual envelopes of corresponding sizes are established based on perceptual information, and then the swing trajectory and foothold are re-planned. By changing the locomotion rhythm, according to the robot size and maximum capacity of rhythmic behavior, as well as the size of obstacles, obstacles are selectively crossed and landed on the surface of obstacles through dynamic adjustment. The swing trajectory, the lifting height and the foothold of the swing leg can realize the gait adjustment and active smoothness control of the robot in complex terrain.

When there is no perception module, the robot relies on the own-sensors information to achieve the stability of the body. The rhythmic locomotion could be achieved according to the operator's inputs, if the obstacle size is in the normal rhythmic locomotion range of the robot, the robot can pass through the terrain without changing the rhythmic behavior. The normal locomotion rhythm is described by the spring inverted pendulum model as follows:

$$x_f = k_x v + k_a (v - v_d) \tag{1}$$

Where, x_f is the foothold position of swing leg, m; v_d is the input velocity from the user, m/s; v is actual speed of the robot, m/s; k_x and k_a are controller coefficients, s.

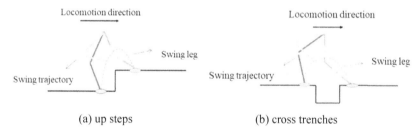

(a) up steps   (b) cross trenches

Fig. 4. Typical obstacles behavior

As shown as Fig. 4, when encountering larger obstacles, if the robot maintains its original rhythmic locomotion behavior, it may lead to collision between the robot and obstacles, at this time, the robot will not pass through the obstacles, or even will cause the instability to damage the robot. Therefore, in this case, on one hand, choosing to bypass obstacles, on the other hand, can cross obstacles. In order to improve the performance and efficiency, according to the size and rhythmic behavior of the robot itself, and the size of obstacles, the obstacles can be selectively crossed. At this time, the swing trajectory and foothold need to be changed. The step trajectory design is shown in Fig. 5.

The swing trajectory is planned by spline. Five key points are involved in the trajectory $p_1 \sim p_5$. Where, p_1 is the starting point, p_5 is the end point, p_3 is the highest point, p_2 and p_4 are the midpoint. h_0 is the swing height, l_0 is the swing length.

By setting the swing height, swing length and the key points, the planning of the swing trajectory can be realized. The swing height and length are related to the information of obstacles.

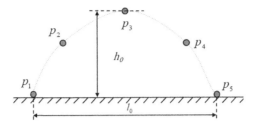

Fig. 5. Swing trajectory

As shown in the Fig. 6, according to the recognition of obstacles by perception module, the size of obstacles can be identified. The height of obstacles is H and the length of obstacles is L. In the case, the original rhythmic locomotion will be hindered by obstacles. Therefore, the swing trajectory should be adjusted according to the information of obstacles.

While choosing to cross the step with the small step, setting the stride threshold δ ($\delta \leq 1$), if $(L + 2\Delta H)/l \leq \delta$, where, ΔH is distance between actual obstacle and virtual obstacle. According to the corner information of obstacle, adjust the key point position of swing trajectory. In order to maintain the flexibility of the swing trajectory, the height of the stride also needs to be adjusted, the adjusted height is h_1, p_2 will be adjusted according to the height of the obstacle Δh. The position of foothold can be adjusted according to the length of the obstacle.

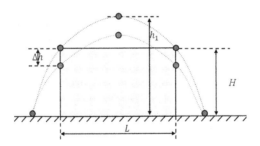

Fig. 6. Obstacles detection and re-planning of swing trajectories

In order to ensure the safety of the robot crossing obstacles, a virtual obstacle is established based on the original size of the identified obstacle. According to the size and the corner position of the virtual obstacle, the swing trajectory is re-planned, and the trajectory is as shown in Fig. 7, where, h_2 is the new swing height.

When the size of the obstacle exceeds the given threshold, in order to ensure that the robot could cross through the obstacle, firstly, the swing trajectory needs to adjust the key points according to the corner of the virtual obstacle, and the end position of the contact point also needs to be adjusted accordingly, which could be decided by the safe foothold area presented in the first chapter. The swing height is adjusted according to the change of swing length. The adjusted height is h, as shown in Fig. 8.

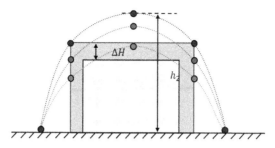

Fig. 7. Virtual obstacle and re-planning of swing trajectory

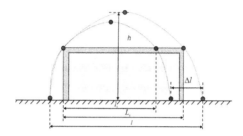

Fig. 8. Re-planning the swing trajectory with the length of the obstacle

Where, Δl is the change of foothold, m; l is the new swing length, m; l_1 is the corner length corresponding to the approximate symmetric virtual key point, m; L_v is the length of the virtual obstacle, m.

Aiming at the obstacle with the bigger size step or continuous obstacle, the foot should be placed on the surface of the obstacle. The height of the foothold needs to be adjusted, and the vertical and horizontal positions of the key corners need to be adjusted smoothly, as shown in Fig. 9.

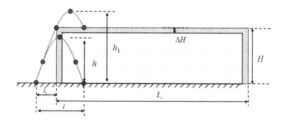

Fig. 9. Re-planning of the swing trajectory with the bigger obstacle

The new height of foothold is the height H of virtual obstacle, and the key safe corner position are adjusted to $p_1 = (l_1, H)$, which could be decided by the safe foothold area and ΔH. If the foothold area is in the safe area, the swing length will remain, and the position of foothold coincides with the third key point.

When crossing the trench, it is also necessary to adjust the foothold position of the swing trajectory. According to the size of trench, a virtual obstacle is established.

According to the size and the corner position of the virtual obstacle, the safe distance and safe swing length are set based the safe foothold area, and the swing trajectory is re-planned as shown in Fig. 10.

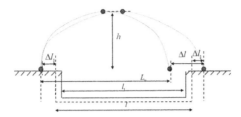

Fig. 10. Re-planning of the swing trajectory according the trench

Where, Δl_1 is safe distance, m; l is the length of virtual obstacle, m; l_1 is the length of actual obstacle, m; L_v is the swing length before adjustment, m; h is the swing height, m; Δl is the change of the foothold, m; Δl is decided according to the safe area of foothold, ΔH and Δl_1, m.

4   Balance Control

The attitude of the terrain is measured by multi-sensor information fusion using the position of contact points. Set the position of the contact point relative to the body to be $p_m = (x_m, y_m, z_m)^T$, the position of the contact point relative to the world coordinate is $p = (x, y, z)^T$.

$$\begin{bmatrix} p \\ 1 \end{bmatrix} = T_R \begin{bmatrix} p_m \\ 1 \end{bmatrix} \tag{2}$$

Where, T_R is the transform matrix. Set the initial position to $p_0 = (x_0, y_0, z_0)^T$, and the origin of the world coordinate coincides with the origin of the body. Define the normal vector of the plane as $n = (A, B, C)$.

$$n(p - p_0) = 0 \tag{3}$$

Assume that $C = -1$, and the normal vector is $n = (A, B, -1)$.

$$z = Ax + By + H \tag{4}$$

Where, $H = -Ax_0 - By_0 + z_0$.

The four position of the contact point including the positions of two stance legs and the last two positions of the swing legs touch down are selected to solve the normal vector of the supporting plane. According to the normal vector, the attitude angles of the terrain, including roll angle and pitch angle, are solved.

When the robot crosses the obstacle, it is necessary to adjust the posture according the terrain. Because the position and force of the contact point have changed, and the size of the obstacle exceeds the swing range of the normal rhythmic motion, if the robot maintains the original posture, the robot will be unstable.

In view of the irregularity of the terrain, the position and posture of the robot need to adapt to the change of terrain. According to the six-dimensional state information of the robot, which includes three translational positions, velocities and accelerations of the robot, as well as three orientations, angular velocities and angular accelerations of the robot, and the characteristics of virtual components, six-dimensional state information of the platform is measured based multi-sensor information, the characteristics of virtual components depend on the dynamics of robot and the control response. Based on the stiffness and damping coefficients of the model, the virtual servo model of the robot is established by input of stiffness, damping coefficients and desired body position and posture, as shown in Fig. 11.

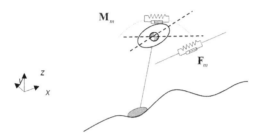

Fig. 11. Virtual model of the robot

According to the characteristics of virtual components, a virtual model with spring and damping is established. The translation virtual model is established to support the body and provide the required traction, and the orientation virtual model is also established to control the attitude of the body, which could maintain excellent flexibility and stability. Based on the virtual model of the robot, it can be obtained:

$$\begin{bmatrix} M_m \\ F_m \end{bmatrix} = -k_p(q - q_d) - k_v(\dot{q} - \dot{q}_d) + k_{vff}\dot{q}_d + k_{aff}\ddot{q}_d + [0, 0, 0, mg]^T \quad (5)$$

Where, M_m and F_m are virtual forces vector of body; k_p and k_v the positive definite gain and differential coefficient matrix respectively; k_{vff} is the velocity feedforward coefficient matrix; k_{aff} is the acceleration feedforward coefficient matrix; q and q_d is for actual and desired posture vector of body respectively; $\dot{q}$ and $\dot{q}_d$ is for actual and desired velocity vector of body respectively; $\ddot{q}_d$ is the desired acceleration vector of body; m is the mass of the robot, kg; g is the gravity acceleration, m/s^2.

Establishing objective optimization function F(x). By setting constraints, we could solve the solution with the minimum of the objective function.

$$\min \mathbf{F}(x) = (\mathbf{A}x - \mathbf{b})^T \mathbf{S}(\mathbf{A}x - \mathbf{b}) + \alpha x^T \mathbf{W} x + \beta \|\mathbf{F}_d - \mathbf{F}_d^*\| \quad (6)$$

Where, S is weighted matrix, W is semi-positive definite symmetric matrix, α and β are factors. $\mathbf{F}_d$ and $\mathbf{F}_d^*$ are current foot desired force and last foot desired force, A is map matrix between foot forces and virtual forces, B is virtual forces vector.

The constraints are as follows:

$$F_{l,i}^n \geq F_{min}^n \tag{7}$$

$$\mu F_{l,i}^n \geq F_{l,i}^t \tag{8}$$

Where, $F_{l,i}^n$ is normal force vector for the i-th contact point, N; $F_{l,i}^t$ is tangential force vector for the i-th contact point, N; F_{min}^n is the minimum normal force, N; μ is the friction coefficient.

According to the higher level controller, desired locomotion behavior will be generated in the corresponding stance or swing phase, which contains desired foot position and desired force. The joint control can be realized by compliance controller, which maps to the joint through leg inverse kinematics and jacobian matrix.

$$\boldsymbol{u}(t) = -\boldsymbol{k}_{p\theta}(\boldsymbol{\theta} - \boldsymbol{\theta}_d) - \boldsymbol{k}_{v\theta}\left(\dot{\boldsymbol{\theta}} - \dot{\boldsymbol{\theta}}_d\right) + \boldsymbol{\tau}_{ff} \tag{9}$$

Where, $k_{p\theta}$ and $k_{v\theta}$ are the stiffness and damping coefficient matrix respectively, θ_d and θ are desired joint angle respectively, $\dot{\theta}_d$ and $\dot{\theta}$ is desired and actual joint angular velocity vector respectively, $\tau_{ff} = -J^T F_d$ is the feedforward joint torque vector, F_d is desired foot force vector, J is leg jacobian matrix, u(t) is the control input vector of the actuator.

The joint controller will adjust the foot force to achieve the posture balance. The controllers comprises of a typical joint stiffness and damping controller through joint position and velocity, which ensures the tracking of joint force and position.

5   Experiment

Building a dynamic simulation environment of terrain and robot based on multi-rigid-body dynamics engine Vortex, the weight of the robot is 135 kg, the walking height is 0.8 m, standing height is 0.72 m, as shown in Fig. 12.

The obstacle-crossing performance of the robot is tested by building a simulation environment. By building typical obstacle-crossing conditions and global map grid map, we re-plan the locomotion behavior of the robot. In the simulation system, the height of the step is set to 30 cm, the width of step is set to 30 cm in turn.

Figure 13a shows that the attitude of the robot changes during the obstacle-crossing process, but the robot restores the balance quickly. Define x as the forward direction of the robot, and z as the height direction. During the step crossing process, x and z position of the foot relative to the center of mass of the robot occur obvious changes, as shown as Fig. 13b and Fig. 13c, and z force is used for controlling the body height and attitude as shown as Fig. 13d. During the trench crossing process, x position of the foot changes obviously, as shown as Fig. 13b.

The method could also been used for climbing the stairs, as shown as Fig. 14.

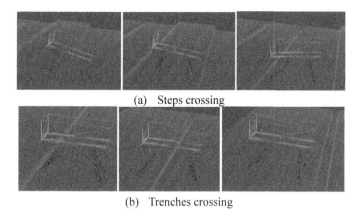

(a)   Steps crossing

(b)   Trenches crossing

Fig. 12. Quadruped robot and terrain elevation dynamics system

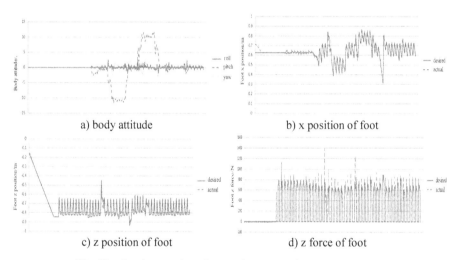

a) body attitude

b) x position of foot

c) z position of foot

d) z force of foot

Fig. 13. Continuous obstacle-crossing curve of a quadruped robot

Fig. 14. Quadruped robot climbs the stairs

6   Conclusion

In this paper, an autonomous dynamic adaptive model under typical working conditions such as steps and trenches is established, which verifies the effectiveness of the method. And the stairs could also been adapted. Next work, we will use this method to adapt the irregular terrains and various locomotion gaits.

Acknowledgements. This work was supported in part by National Natural Science Foundation of China (Grant No. 91748211).

References

1. Raibert, M., Blankespoor, K., Nelson, G., et al.: Bigdog, the rough-terrain quadruped robot. In: Proceedings of the 17th World Congress, pp. 10822–10825 (2008)
2. Boston Dynamics. LS3 – Legged Squad Support Systems (2013). http://www.bostondyn amics.com
3. Boston Dynamics. SpotMini–Good Things Come in Small Packages (2017). http://www.bos tondynamics.com
4. Boston Dynamics. Atlas–The World's Most Dynamic Humanoid (2018). http://www.boston dynamics.com
5. Seok, S., Wang, A., Chuah, M.Y.M., et al.: Design principles for energy-efficient legged locomotion and implementation on the MIT Cheetah robot. IEEE/ASME Trans. Mechatron. **20**(3), 117–1129 (2015)
6. Hyun, D.J., Seok, S., Lee, J., et al.: High speed trot-running: Implementation of a hierarchical controller using proprioceptive impedance control on the MIT Cheetah. Int. J. Robot. Res. **33**(11), 1417–1445 (2014)
7. Sprowitz, A., Tuleu, A., Vespignani, M., et al.: Towards dynamic trot gait locomotion: design, control, and experiments with Cheetah-cub, a compliant quadruped robot. Int. J. Robot. Res. **32**, 932–950 (2013)
8. Park, H.W., Wensing, P.M., Kim, S.: High-speed bounding with the MIT Cheetah 2: control design and experiments. Int. J. Robot. Res. **36**(2), 167–192 (2017)
9. Gehring, C., Coros, S., Hutter, M., et al.: Control of dynamic gaits for a quadrupedal robot. In: International Conference on Robotics and Automation, pp. 3287–3292 (2013)
10. Hutter, M., Gehring, C., Jud, D., et al.: Anymal-a highly mobile and dynamic quadrupedal robot. In: 2016 IEEE/RSJ International Conference on Intelligent Robots and Systems (IROS), pp. 38–44 (2016)
11. Hwangbo, J., Lee, J., Dosovitskiy, A., et al.: Learning agile and dynamic motor skills for legged robots. Sci. Robot. **4**(26) (2019)
12. Lee, J., Hwangbo, J., Hutter, M.: Robust recovery controller for a quadrupedal robot using deep reinforcement learning. ArXiv preprint arXiv (2019)
13. Semini, C., Tsagarakis, N.G., Guglielmino, E., Focchi, M., Cannella, F., Caldwell, D.G.: Design of HyQ – a hydraulically and electrically actuated quadruped robot. Proc. Inst. Mech. Eng. Part I: J. Syst. Control Eng. **225**(6), 831–849 (2011)
14. Semini, C., et al.: Towards versatile legged robots through active impedance control. Int. J. Robot. Res. **34**(7), 1003–1020 (2015)
15. Ugurlu, B., Havoutis, I., Semini, C., et al.: Dynamic trot-walking with the hydraulic quadruped robot—HyQ: analytical trajectory generation and active compliance control. In: Intelligent Robots and Systems, pp. 6044–6051 (2013)
16. Li, Y., Li, B., Rong, X., et al.: Mechanical design and gait planning of a hydraulically actuated quadruped bionic robot. J. Shandong Univ. (Eng. Sci.) **41**(05), 32–45 (2011)

An Intuitive Interaction System Using Laser Spot for Daily Household Tasks Operation Autonomous

Yaxin Liu, Shouqiang Li, Wendong Zhang, Yan Liu, and Ming Zhong$^{(\boxtimes)}$

Industrial Research Institute of Robotics and Intelligent Equipment, Harbin Institute of Technology (Weihai), Weihai 264209, Shandong, China
`zhongming@hit.edu.cn`

Abstract. The Wheelchair Mounted Robotic Arm (WMRA) can help the elderly and handicapped to complete some household tasks independently, while due to the mobility of these people are limited, they cannot complete household tasks easily through the interactions that need frequent operations such as using handles. If the tasks are completed automatically and users only need to send commands by gestures or EEG. The user will lose involvement and adaptability to the environment. In this paper, we propose a method named laser intuitive interaction, it can analyze the user's intention by identifying the semantic information of the laser and assemble actions to complete unstructured tasks. Firstly, the household tasks are summarized base on the International Classification of Functionality, Disability and Health (ICF) and the laser semantics are designed according to the daily household tasks; Secondly, the method of laser semantic detection base on SVM is discussed; Finally, the information of the laser semantic and the action of the robotic arm are integrated into the ROS. The results of the experiment on daily household tasks show that the accuracy of laser semantic detection is above 92%, the number and time of laser interaction are 33% and 75% of the handle interaction.

Keywords: Human-computer interaction · Laser interaction · WMRA

1 Introduction

Nowadays, the population of our country is in the stage of accelerating aging. The large and increasing number of disabled, semi-disabled elderly and handicapped people bring a heavy burden to family and social care services. WMRA is an effective means to improve the quality of life and reduce nursing pressure which can help the disabled to complete some household tasks independently.

In recent years, in order to facilitate the manipulation of robots by users of different levels of disability, many novel human-computer interfaces have emerged and are used in WMRA, such as gestures, chin, shoulders, head, neck, eye movements, brain electricity and so on. Currently, the interaction methods of WMRA can be divided into the following three categories.

© Springer Nature Switzerland AG 2021
X.-J. Liu et al. (Eds.): ICIRA 2021, LNAI 13015, pp. 269–280, 2021.
https://doi.org/10.1007/978-3-030-89134-3_25

Manual Control. The intention is mapped to the basic instructions to control the manipulator. For example, the assistive robot FRIEND IV [1] uses the chin joystick, handle and head control panel to control the mouse to select the command buttons on the screen, frequent limb operations are required to adjust the grasping posture of the gripper.

Autonomous Control. The output command of the human-computer interface is mapped to the switch to carry out the tasks in a fixed scene. For example, KERAS II [2] presets 12 mission scenarios such as picking up objects, eating, drinking and so on. When the robot receives the name of the task, it will carry out the corresponding tasks autonomously. However, "As the ability to operate autonomously increases, the user's sense of engagement diminishes and they feel they have lost it" [3]. Moreover, limited by the number of interface command modes, the number and content of autonomous tasks are limited, making it difficult to adapt to an unstructured environment.

Semi-autonomous Control. In the process of executing tasks automatically, the control can be released to the user when the user request or the system fail to operate. Then the user can control the system through the human-computer interface manually. For example, the WMRA [4] designed by Purdue University can recognize the object automatically and move to the vicinity of the object quickly in the task of object grabbing. Then the user can manipulate the robotic arm manually to adjust to the best grasping posture through the gesture interface. However, the difficult parts such as grasping and placing are still operated manually.

The results of survey for disabled users show that [5] they hope the interaction interface use less language or physical movements, they eager to use the remaining limbs to participate in tasks, they hope the WMRA can work in an unstructured environment.

According to the comparison above, it is clear that the existing mode of interaction of WMRA cannot meet the needs of users. This paper proposes a minimalist method of interaction. We use laser spot to select objects, use the semantics of laser spot as clues to convey intentions and assemble actions according to the user's intentions. This paper mainly focuses on the design and detection technology of laser semantics, and integrates the laser semantic and control program of robotic arm into ROS. The method we propose can improve user's self-care ability, promote the practical usage of WMRA, and relieve the nursing pressure of huge special groups.

2 Related Work

Researchers have applied the method of laser guidance in many fields such as large-screen interaction, medical treatment, robot navigation and so on.

Fukuda et al. [6] used laser spot to guide the direction of the electric wheel-chair and bypassed obstacles successfully; Widodo et al. [7] selected the buttons on large-screen by laser spot to control the movement of the robot for the people with limited mobility; Kemp [8] proposed a human-computer interaction interface that used a laser spot to navigate the EL_E robot. It allowed humans to select the three-dimensional position in the world and communicate with the mobile robot intuitively. The robot can pick up the object selected by the laser spot; Nguyen et al. [9] improved Kemp's work and according to the behavior of the laser spot and context environment to complete the object picking and placement. It can pick up the designated object from the floor or table, hand the object to the designated person, place the object on the designated table, turn to the designated position, and touch the designated position with its manipulator; Guigui Liu et al. [10] assisted in grasping by the blue laser guidance which can locate any object in the field of the view of the binocular camera; Boston State University [11] combined with the technology of the object captured automatically realized grasping objects locked by the laser spot autonomous in an unstructured environment. Dennis et al. [12] used a laser spot to teach the virtual boundary to the mobile robot so that it can navigate according to the user's wishes.

The combination of laser guidance and robot applications has become a new inter-active trend in the control of robot motion and grasping. However, the robots can only operate some simple tasks. The interaction by laser spot is an intuitive and convenient way. Because there is no need for a specific interface and any movable part of the user can use the laser pointer. There is no heavy burden on the body when equipped with a laser pointing device, and users can also participate in the process of task performing. In the laser semantic intuitive interaction system, the user selects the object and performs some laser semantics, the WMRA selects and executes actions autonomously, assembles the tasks according to the user's intention through minimalist guidance to complete unstructured tasks.

3   Laser Semantic Design

First, we summarize seven daily household tasks of the disabled according to the "International Classification on Function, Disability and Health" (ICF) which made the tasks we summarized cover most requirements of the disabled. And then the objects and actions involved in each task are summarized, which is shown in Table 1.

Table 1. The statistics of daily household tasks and the objects

Task	The objects and actions involved
Eating	Bowl, Plate, Spoon, Desk, Towel; Scooping, Grabbing, Wiping, Moving to the specified location, Putting down;
Drinking	Cup, Desk; Grabbing, Moving to the specified location, Putting down;
Brushing teeth	Toothbrush, Cup, Towel, Desk; Grabbing, Wiping, Moving to the specified location, Putting down;
Wiping face	Towel, Desk; Grabbing, Wiping, Moving to the specified location, Putting down;
Making a call	Cellphone, Desk; Grabbing, Moving to the specified location, Pressing, Putting down;

(*continued*)

Table 1. (*continued*)

Task	The objects and actions involved
Shaving	Shaver, Desk; Grabbing, Moving to the specified location, Pressing, Putting down;
Using household appliances	Various household appliances; Pressing;

According to Table 1, this paper designs two basic laser semantics: laser spot short selection and laser spot holding-on selection. The practical applications of laser semantics are the combination of the two basic laser semantics. The division of the two kinds of laser semantics is based on the time the laser spot stays at the same point. When the time is less than three seconds, means the laser spot short selection; Otherwise, means the laser spot holding-on selection. The whole laser semantics we design are shown in Table 2. The letter T means there is an object in the gripper and F means there is no object in the gripper.

Table 2. The table of the laser semantic

The behavior of laser spot	Laser semantics
The laser spot short selects the object once	Hold the object in the gripper and scoop it into the object pointed by the laser spot (T) Grasp the object selected by the laser spot (F)
The laser spot short selects the desk once	Place the object in the position pointed by the laser spot (T)
The laser spot short selects the object twice	Hold the object in the gripper and dumping it into the object selected by the laser spot (T) Push the object selected by the laser spot (F)
The laser spot short selects the desk twice	Loosen the gripper (T) Reset the manipulator (F)
The laser spot holding-on select object	Hold the object in the gripper and stir in the object selected by the laser spot (T) Grab the object selected and bring it to the mouth (F)
The laser spot holding-on select desk	Wipe the desk (T) Cancel last operation (F)
The laser spot short selects the object (desk) and holding-on select object (desk)	Bring the object in the gripper to the mouth (T) Push the position selected by the laser spot (F)

4   The Recognition of Context Information of Laser Semantic

4.1   The Recognition of Laser Spot

The premise for detecting the laser semantic is detecting the laser spot accurately. This paper chooses the YOLO v3 algorithm, whose speed of detection is fast currently. To improve the accuracy of laser spot detection, we collect about 900 photos containing laser spots in different lighting and different daily home scenes. We perform augmentation operations on images such as random dim, random rotation, and random addition of salt and pepper noise to the collected photos.

4.2   The Detection of the Position of the Laser Spot and the Object Selected

To make the manipulator grasp the object selected by the laser spot, it is necessary to detect the position of the object in the world coordinate. Therefore, this paper calibrates the internal and external parameters of the RGB-D camera used in the experiment. Then the pixel coordinate and world coordinate of the laser spot and object can be unified to the camera coordinate and the object selected by the laser spot can be obtained through comparison. The process of the detecting the position of the object selected by the laser spot is shown in Fig. 1.

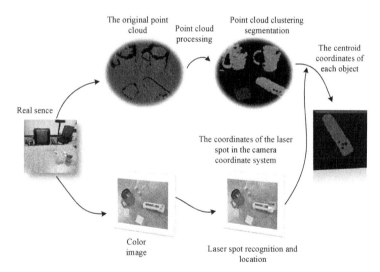

Fig. 1. The process of object position detection selected by the laser spot

The pixel coordinates of the laser spot and each object are obtained through the color camera, and the object selected by the laser spot can be obtained through comparison. The pixel coordinate of the object selected is transformed into the camera coordinate. The centroid coordinates of point cloud of each object can be obtained through the depth camera, and the centroid coordinates of the object selected can be obtained by comparing the centroid coordinates of all the objects with the coordinates of the object selected in camera coordinate. The point cloud of this object can be obtained by point cloud clustering segmentation. The world coordinate of the object selected is sent to the robot arm for the manipulator to reach the object and perform the task of grasping.

4.3 The Detection of the Laser Semantics

Considering the unstable hands of the disabled, if the laser semantics are detected by calculating the time of the laser turning on and off, the system will mistakenly recognize the laser semantics when the user's hand shake. Thus, we detect the laser semantics based on the Support Vector Machine (SVM) algorithm and the samples of hand shaking are added to the training set to improve the accuracy of detection. The negative samples are added to improve the robustness of the system.

First, training sets are collected to train the SVM. In this process, we use the method in Sect. 4.1 to detect the laser points in each frame of the image. If the image of current frame detects the laser spot, it stores a 1 into a predefined 26-dimensional array; Otherwise, it stores a 0. Different 0,1 sequences represent different laser semantics. In the experiment, 100 groups of training sets are annotated to train the SVM classifier. The training sets can be expressed as $\{(x^{(1)}, y^{(1)}), (x^{(2)}, y^{(2)}) \ldots \ldots (x^{(m)}, y^{(m)})\}$, where $x^{(i)}$ is the 26-dimensional training set, $y^{(i)}$ is the label of the training sets.

The cost function of SVM is minimized using mathematic method such as gradient descent in the process of training the model. The cost function of SVM can be expressed as

$$J(\theta) = \min_{\theta} C \left[\sum_{i=1}^{m} y^{(i)} \cos t_1(\theta^T x^{(i)}) + (1 - y^{(i)}) \cos t_0(\theta^T x^{(i)}) \right] + \frac{1}{2} \sum_{j=1}^{n} \theta_j^2 \quad (1)$$

When the formula C is large enough, to minimize the cost function, the following conditions must meet

$$\sum_{i=1}^{m} y^{(i)} \cos t_1(\theta^T x^{(i)}) + (1 - y^{(i)}) \cos t_0(\theta^T x^{(i)}) = 0 \quad (2)$$

At this time, we can optimize the cost function as

$$J(\theta) = \min_{\theta} \sum_{j=1}^{n} \theta_j^2 \quad (3)$$

$$s.t. \begin{cases} \theta^T x^{(i)} \geq 1, y^{(i)} = 1 \\ \theta^T x^{(i)} < 1, y^{(i)} = 0 \end{cases}$$

Where C is the regularization factor constant, m is the number of training samples, n is the number of features, θ is the weight.

Consider our datasets are high-dimensional and non-linear, this paper uses the Gauss Kernel function to construct new features and train the samples. The features of the new structure are

$$f_i = similarity(x, l^{(i)}) = \exp(-\frac{\|x - l^{(i)}\|^2}{2\sigma^2}) = \exp(-\frac{\sum_{j=1}^{n} (x_j - l_j^{(i)})^2}{2\sigma^2}) \quad (4)$$

For the training samples, construct the following features

$$f^{(i)} = \begin{bmatrix} f_0^{(i)} = 1 \\ f_2^{(i)} = similarity(x^{(i)}, l^{(1)}) \\ \cdots \cdots \\ f_i^{(i)} = similarity(x^{(i)}, l^{(i)}) = 1 \\ \cdots \cdots \\ f_m^{(i)} = similarity(x^{(i)}, l^{(m)}) \end{bmatrix} \tag{5}$$

Where $l^{(1)} = x^{(1)}, l^{(2)} = x^{(2)}, \ldots \ldots l^{(m)} = x^{(m)}$. Then the model can be trained with these new features to predict the laser semantics.

In the process of detection, we send a 26-dimensiona array filled with 0,1 to the SVM classification to predict the laser semantic. We initialize this array after each detection to wait for a next signal.

5 The Execution and Assembly of Actions

In order to establish the connection between laser semantics and the actions of manipulator, we integrate the visual system and control system of manipulator into the ROS.

The manipulator can grasp objects by calling the software package of object autonomous grasping. The purpose of this paper is to verify the laser semantic interaction system we proposed can guide the manipulator to grasp the object we selected and carry out some daily household tasks. Therefore, we store the grasping pose of each object separately and attach to a label of category.

In the process of carrying out household tasks, the manipulator continues to publish the information of the opening size through the node, the analysis system of laser semantic subscribes to the topic and determines whether there is an object in the gripper through the opening information of the gripper.

6 Experiment

In order to evaluate the performance of the laser intuitive interactive system, this paper designed some experiments on the premise of simulating the daily home environment. We evaluate the accuracy of laser semantic recognition, calculate the number and the time of interactions when using laser spot and handle to carry out the tasks of drinking, dumping, eating, and wiping the desktop.

6.1 Laser Semantic Detection Experiment

This paper designs the experiments to detect the laser semantics and the position of laser spots and objects. Firstly, in order to verify the influence of the proficiency of operation, we select three members of research group (A, B, C) and three members of non-research group (D, E, F) as volunteers and record the results of the experiment. The experiment is carried out 50 times in total, and each time the laser semantics are executed randomly according to Table 1. When the system detects the laser semantics and the position of the object and the laser spot successfully, it is deemed as success. The results are shown in Table 3. Secondly, we detect the accuracy of each laser semantic and the result is shown in Table 4.

Table 3. The results of detection of laser semantic carried out by different people

Volunteers	The number of successes	The number of failures	The rate of successes
A	47	3	94%
B	48	2	96%
C	48	2	96%
D	39	11	78%
E	37	13	74%
F	41	9	82%

Table 4. The results of detection of every laser semantics

Laser semantics	The number of successes	The number of failures	The rate of successes
Short selection once	50	0	100%
Short selection twice	48	2	96%
holding-on selection	49	1	98%
Short selection once + Holding-on selection	46	4	92%

The result of laser semantic detection as shown in Table 4, we find that the success rate of the non-research group is lower than that of the research group. Because they cannot control the time between two selections and they can't easily distinguish the length of time between laser spot short selection and holding-on selection. The success rate of them improving quickly in the progress of the experiment. It means that non-specialists can master our system through a short period of training.

The result in Table 4 shows that the accuracy of detection of the composite laser semantic is lower than that of single semantics. There is a misidentification phenomenon such as laser spot short selection twice can sometimes be misidentified as once holding-on selection and the most misidentification occurs with reflective or transparent household objects. Thus, when using our system for daily household tasks, try to choose opaque objects and try not in the environment of strong light.

6.2   Daily Household Tasks Execution Experiment

According to the preset laser semantics, we carry out the experiments of drinking, dumping and wiping the desktop. The process of the experiments of drinking (left) and dumping (right) is shown in Fig. 2. Firstly, when we select the cup (bottle or any other objects) once using the laser spot, the manipulator will grasp the cup and wait for the next command; then if we select the desktop twice using the laser spot, the manipulator will send the cup to the mouth of the user; if we select the cup twice, the manipulator will dump the object in the gripper into the cup.

In order to verify the superiority of our method, we calculate the number and the time of interactions when using laser spot and handle to carry out the tasks of drinking, dumping, eating, and wiping the desktop. In the experiment of calculating the number of interactions, the reset point of the manipulator is considered as the starting and ending position of interaction. The result is shown in Table 5. Taking eating as an example, the process of interaction using laser spot is as follows: short selecting spoon, short selecting bowl, short and holding-on selecting desk, short selecting desk, short selecting desk twice. The process of interaction using the handle is as follows: moving the manipulator to near the spoon, adjusting the posture of the wrist, adjusting the position of the claw, grabbing, lifting up, moving the spoon near the bowl, adjusting the posture of scooping, adjusting the position of the claw, scooping, lifting up, moving to the mouth, moving near the specified position on the desktop, adjusting the position of the claw, loosening the claw, resetting the manipulator.

Fig. 2. The process of drinking and dumping in clutter environment

Table 5. The comparison of the numbers of interaction between laser and handle

Mode of interaction	Eating	Drinking	Dumping	Wiping
Interaction using laser spot	5	4	4	4
Interaction using handle	15	10	13	14

The result from Table 5 shows that the number of laser interactions is about 33% of the number of handle interactions, and the more complex the task is, the more obvious the advantage of laser interaction is. When performing the task, the laser interaction only needs to use the laser to select the corresponding object, and the operation is simple and can be completed with one hand. However, handle interaction requires adjustment of grasping position and pose and other complex body operations frequently, which is obviously not easy to use and requires the assistance of both hands.

In the experiment of compare the time of interaction between laser and handle, this paper selects 6 volunteers who master the two methods of interaction skillfully. Every experiment is carried out in a cluttered daily household environment without direct sunlight but direct light. This paper carries out the tasks of eating, drinking, dumping, and wiping desktop. Each task is performed 50 times and the average time is calculated. The result is shown in Table 6 and Table 7.

Table 6. The time of interaction using laser (s)

Volunteers	Eating	Drinking	Dumping	Wiping
A	75.9	70.2	56.3	54.6
B	75.1	72.3	56.7	54.4
C	75.3	71.7	55.3	56.7
D	74.8	70.3	55.1	54.5
E	75.4	72.4	55.6	53.9
F	74.9	70.8	55.7	53.4

Table 7. The time of interaction using handle (s)

Volunteers	Eating	Drinking	Dumping	Wiping
A	101.7	75.5	75.2	85.6
B	103.5	74.8	74.7	85.3
C	102.8	74.9	74.6	84.5
D	102.4	76.2	74.1	84.7
E	103.6	75.3	73.9	84.2
F	101.9	74.6	75.2	83.9

The result from Table 6 and Table 7 show that the time of completing daily household tasks based on laser interaction is about 75% of the time of handle interaction. In other words, daily household tasks can be completed faster by the method of laser interaction. Besides, the operation of laser interaction is simple and the burden of limbs is small.

The experiments of daily household tasks show that our system can use the laser spot to complete household tasks. The users only need to use the laser spot to select the object they want to use and our system can accomplish the corresponding tasks according to the corresponding laser semantics. The elderly and the disabled can complete daily household tasks easily and quickly using laser spot; They can participate in daily household tasks, and our system can grasp different objects in the different home environments to complete daily household tasks.

7 Conclusion

In this paper, we proposed a method of laser intuitive interaction and design two kinds of laser semantics based on the time of the laser spot to select the object. First, the YOLO v3 algorithm was used to detect the laser points. Then, the laser semantics are detected based on SVM algorithm, and the detection accuracy is more than 92%. Finally, the laser semantic detection system is integrated with the manipulator control system, and the feasibility of our laser intuitive interaction system is verified by experiments. The number of laser interactions is about 33% of the number of handle interactions, the time of completing daily household tasks based on laser interaction is about 75% of the time of handle interaction. It means that laser intuitive interaction system proposed in this paper has the characteristics of easy to operate, strong interaction between users and can adapt to the unstructured environment. It can improve user's acceptance and self-care ability, promote the practical use of WMRA and relieve the nursing pressure of huge special groups. It has great economic value and social benefits. The video of our experiment can be found at the following website: https://www.jianguoyun.com/p/DYr za2kQsKr9BRi7y_cD.

Acknowledgment. This work is supported by the National Key R&D Program of China (Grant No. 2018YFB1309400), the Key R&D Program of Shandong Province (Grant No. 2016GGX101013), and the University Common Construction Project of Weihai (Grant No. 2016DXGJMS04).

References

1. Graser, A., Heyer, T., Fotoohi, L.: A supportive friend at work: robotic workplace assistance for the disabled. Robot. Autom. Mag. **20**(4), 148–159 (2013)
2. Bien, Z., Chung, M.J., Chang, P.H.: Integration of a rehabilitation robotic system (KARES II) with human-friendly man-machine interaction units. Auton. Robot. **16**(2), 165–191 (2004)
3. Quintero, C.P., Ramirez, O., Jägersand, M.: VIBI: assistive vision-based interface for robot manipulation. In: Proceedings IEEE International Conference on Robotics & Automation, pp. 4458–4463. IEEE, Seattle (2015)
4. Jiang, H., Wachs, J.P., Duerstock, B.S.: Integrated vision-based robotic arm interface for operators with upper limb mobility impairments. In: IEEE International Conference on Rehabilitation Robotics, pp.1–6. IEEE, Seattle (2013)
5. Philipp, B., Gionata, S., Ramazan, U.: A human-robot interaction perspective on assistive and rehabilitation robotics. Front. Neurorobot. **11**, 24 (2017)
6. Minato, Y., Tsujimura, T., Izumi, K.: Sign-at-ease: Robot navigation system operated by connoted shapes drawn with laser beam. In: SICE Annual Conference 2011, pp. 2158–2163. IEEE, Tokyo (2011)
7. Fukuda, Y., Kurihara, Y., Kobayashi, K.: Development of electric wheelchair interface based on laser pointer. In: 2009 ICCAS-SICE, pp. 1148–1151. IEEE, Fukuoka (2009)

8. Kemp, C.C., Anderson, C.D., Nguyen, H.: A point-and-click interface for the real world: Laser designation of objects for mobile manipulation. In: Amsterdam: Human-Robot Interaction (HRI), pp.241–248. IEEE, Amsterdam (2008)
9. Hai, N., Jain, A., Anderson, C.: A clickable world: behavior selection through pointing and context for mobile manipulation. In: 2008 IEEE/RSJ International Conference on Intelligent Robots and Systems, pp. 787–793. IEEE, Nice (2008)
10. Liu, G.G., Fan, B.H., Wang, C.J.: Application of binocular vision in positioning system of senior and disable people aid's manipulator. Microcomput. Appl. **035**(013), 45–47,50 (2016)
11. Chavez, F., Alcala, R.: Evolutionary learning of a laser pointer detection fuzzy system for an environment control system. In: 2011 IEEE International Conference on Fuzzy Systems (FUZZ-IEEE 2011), pp. 256–263. IEEE, Taipei (2011)
12. Sprute, D., Tnnies, K.D., Koenig, M.: This far, no further: introducing virtual borders to mobile robots using a laser pointer. In: 2019 Third IEEE International Conference on Robotic Computing (IRC), pp. 403–408. IEEE, Naples (2019)

Design of a Novel Wheelchair-Exoskeleton Robot for Human Multi-mobility Assist

Hexi Gong[1,2], Zhibin Song[1,2(✉)], and Paolo Dario[1,3,4]

[1] School of Mechanical Engineering, Tianjin University, Tianjin, China
songzhibin@tju.edu.cn
[2] Key Laboratory of Mechanism Theory and Equipment Design of the Ministry of Education, Centre for Advanced Mechanisms and Robotics, Tianjin University, Tianjin, China
[3] The BioRobotics Institute, Scuola Superiore Sant'Anna, Pisa, Italy
[4] Department of Excellence in Robotics and AI, Scuola Superiore Sant'Anna, Pisa, Italy

Abstract. Lower limb exoskeleton robots are able to provide walking assist and training for paraplegic and hemiplegic patients and elder people with lower limb motor dysfunction. However the lower limb exoskeleton robot can't support the patient to move for a long time and distance, because the patient needs to consume a lot of energy to maintain balance. As a traditional movement assist device, wheelchairs can guarantee the balance for patients during their moving, however most of them can only allow patients sit to use them, and can not provide walking assist and training, which induces bedsore and muscle atrophy. In this paper, a novel movement assist robot combining the advantages of wheelchair and exoskeleton is proposed and designed, which can assist patients to sit, stand and walk. The novel structure and mechanisms are proposed to implement three mobility assist and their transfer movement. Then the kinematics analysis of the transfer process from sitting to stance is analyzed. The coupling relationship between rotation speed of each joint of exoskeleton and the forward and upward speed of the device are calculated. Finally, the trunk speed of walking process in a gait cycle is analyzed, and the simulation is completed in ADAMS software, which verifies the effectiveness of the proposed method.

Keywords: Wheelchair-exoskeleton · Movement assist · Kinematics

1 Introduction

The aggravation of the aging of the population leads to the increase of the population of cerebral apoplexy, and the patients with cerebral apoplexy are often accompanied by paraplegia, hemiplegia, cerebral infarction and other symptoms, resulting in the loss of lower limb motor ability [1, 2]. In addition, traffic accidents, natural disasters and other factors can also lead to human limb and nerve damage, and then make people disabled.

© Springer Nature Switzerland AG 2021
X.-J. Liu et al. (Eds.): ICIRA 2021, LNAI 13015, pp. 281–292, 2021.
https://doi.org/10.1007/978-3-030-89134-3_26

Long term walking inconvenience causes great psychological distress to patients. Therefore, it is a critical challenge in China and many developed countries to help patients and elder people stand and regain walking ability [3, 4].

As a new technology, lower limb exoskeleton robot can meet the rehabilitation needs of patients, help patients to stand and walk [5]. Some lower limb exoskeleton robots includes mobile exoskeleton robot and treadmill exoskeleton robot [6]. Lokomat is a typical representative of treadmill type exoskeleton robot [7], which is jointly developed by HOCOMA medical equipment company of Switzerland and ETH of Zurich. The Lokomat robot can provide feedback for patients through virtual reality technology, so as to achieve the training goal. The device can train according to the range of patients' personal ability, and provide different gait patterns and training programs. The angle of hip joint and knee joint can also be adjusted separately during training to meet the specific needs of patients. Lokomat can also adjust the speed and weight support ratio of robot to achieve the best treatment intensity [8]. Another device with similar functions is the Autoambulator developed by HAWLTHSOUTH in the United States. However, this kind of treadmill exoskeleton robot is bulky in structure, and it can't make patients obtain the feeling of walking on the real ground. The representatives of mobile exoskeleton robots are HAL, Esko, Rewalk etc. [10–12], which are light in structure and can make patients walk on the real road, but patients often need to hold crutches to keep balance, which will consume a lot of energy of patients and the balance is not guaranteed well. In addition, these two kinds of exoskeleton robots can't realize the state transition from sitting to stance and the function of sitting for resting after walking training.

Wheelchair has a very long history and it provide a simple and comfortable platform for people with lower limb dysfunction. However, long time seat can induce bedsore and muscle atrophy, therefore, few wheelchairs with standing support have been developed via mechanisms to solve this problem [13]. However, there is no wheelchair can help people to train walking mobility as the exoskeleton does.

Therefore, our contribution is to propose a new mobility assist strategy for people with lower limb motor dysfunction via combing wheelchair and exoskeleton to implement comfortable sitting, walking assist with adjustable suspension, guaranteeing balance and transit from sitting to standing without caregiver's help.

2 Design Methodology of the Wheelchair-Exoskeleton Robot

2.1 The Basic Principle and Its Structure Design

To combine the wheelchair and exoskeleton is a big challenge in mechanical and mechanism design. It is need to consider the different configuration of mechanical structure for different mobility. For example, seat plate should be laid down horizontally at sitting state and packed up at walking state without disturbance on legs. Figure 1 shows the overall model of the wheelchair-exoskeleton device (sitting state). The whole device mainly includes three parts: the lifting mechanism, the seat plate and the exoskeleton. The main function of the lifting device is to realize the state transition of patients from sitting to stance. The device relies on the stepping motor to drive the ball screw (Fig. 2(b)) to move, driving the side plate to move up and down. The seat plate (Fig. 2(a)) provides rest support for patients after walking training and realizes the function of sitting posture.

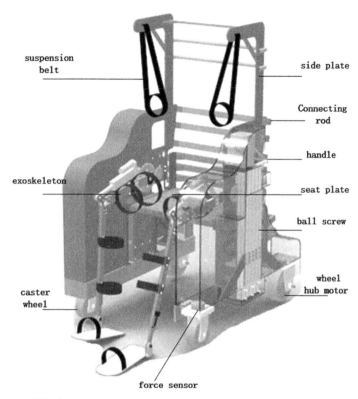

Fig. 1. Overall model of wheelchair-exoskeleton (sitting state)

The rollers at the front end of the base plate are inserted into the grooves of the left and right supports, and slide in the grooves. The rod fixedly connected with the side plate drives the seat plate to move up and down with the side plate, realizing that when the patient sits down, the seat plate is placed flat to provide support for the patient. When the patient stands up, the seat plate is folded up, which does not interfere with the patient's walking. Exoskeleton is a device to help patients with rehabilitation walking training and recover their motor ability, as shown in Fig. 2(c). The hip joint of the exoskeleton is connected with the side plate, so the degree of freedom of the exoskeleton is three degrees of freedom in the sagittal plane. The hip joint and knee joint are active, and the ankle joint is passive. The hip joint of the exoskeleton is driven by a servo motor installed on the side plate, and the knee joint is driven by the linear motor installed above the thigh bar.

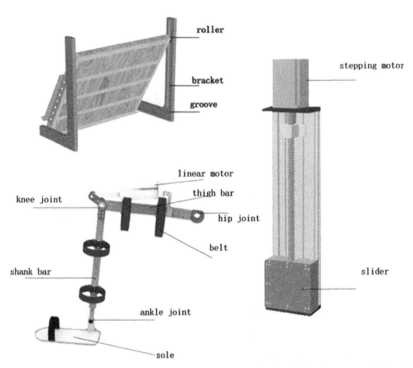

Fig. 2. Main parts of wheelchair-exoskeleton. (a) seat plate. (b) lead screw guide rail. (c) exoskeleton

In addition, the whole wheelchair-exoskeleton device also includes two wheel hub motors to drive the device forward and backward, and two caster wheels to realize the steering of the device. Each side of the caster wheel and wheel hub motor is equipped with a force sensor, a total of 4 force sensors, which are used to detect the pressure values of the left and right sides during walking process, identifying the movement intention and judge which moment of the gait cycle the patient is in.

The principle of the process from sitting to stance: the stepping motor drives the ball screw to rotate, and the ball screw drives the side plate fixed with the slide block of the ball screw to rise. The patient holds the handle on the side plate with his hands, and at the same time, the suspension belt fixed on the side plate pulls the patient upward, so that the patient can complete the transformation from sitting to stance. In this process, the hub motor is also required to drive the whole device to move forward accordingly, realizing the forward movement of the patient's center of gravity and body. Figure 3 shows the model diagram of the whole wheelchair-exoskeleton device after stance.

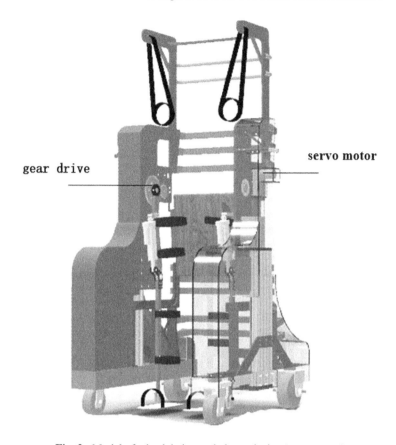

gear drive

servo motor

Fig. 3. Model of wheelchair-exoskeleton device (stance state)

2.2 The Selection of the Motor and the Velocity Analysis of the Joint of Exoskeleton in the Process from Sitting to Stance

The process from sitting to stance is coupled by multiple movements, including the upward movement of the ball screw guide, the forward movement of the whole device, the rotation of the thigh rod around the hip joint, the rotation of the shank rod around the knee joint, and the rotation of the shank rod around the ankle joint. The sole does not move in this process, which can be regarded as a frame. The stepping motor, the hub motor, the servo motor and the linear motor cooperate to realize this movement. The motors that play a major role in the whole movement is the stepper motor. In order to make the movement be performed smoothly, the stepper motor accelerate first, then up to a constant speed, and finally decelerate to zero. Considering the sitting up time of general patients and the height of shoulder rise, the movement process is taken for 8 s for safe, and the movement distance of the slider of the ball screw is 400 mm. At the same time, according to the performance of the stepping motor (the maximum speed under the peak torque is 400 rpm), the formula of the stepping motor speed is given as follows.

$$
v_y = \begin{cases} \frac{200}{3}\sin(\frac{\pi-2}{2}t) & t \in (0, \frac{\pi}{\pi-2}) \\ \frac{200}{3} & t \in (\frac{\pi}{\pi-2}, \frac{7\pi-16}{\pi-2}) \\ \frac{200}{3}\sin(\frac{\pi-2}{2}t) & t \in (\frac{7\pi-16}{\pi-2}, 8) \end{cases}
\tag{1}
$$

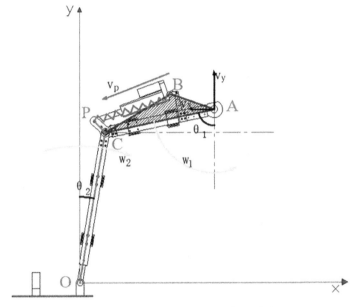

Fig. 4. Movement diagram of the process from sitting to stance

The motion diagram of the whole process is shown in Fig. 4, in which the coordinates are established, $O(0, 0)$, $A(x_A, y_A)$, $C(x_C, y_C)$, $P(x_P, y_P)$. According to the geometric relationship, the position coordinates can be got as follows:

$$
\begin{pmatrix} x_C \\ y_C \end{pmatrix} = \begin{pmatrix} L_2 & 0 \\ 0 & L_2 \end{pmatrix} \cdot \begin{pmatrix} \sin\theta_2(t) \\ \cos\theta_2(t) \end{pmatrix}
\tag{2}
$$

$$
\begin{pmatrix} x_A \\ y_A \end{pmatrix} = \begin{pmatrix} \sin\theta_1(t) & \sin\theta_2(t) \\ \cos\theta_1(t) & \cos\theta_2(t) \end{pmatrix} \cdot \begin{pmatrix} L_1 \\ L_2 \end{pmatrix}
\tag{3}
$$

$$
\begin{pmatrix} x_P \\ y_P \end{pmatrix} = \begin{pmatrix} L_{OP} & 0 \\ 0 & L_{OP} \end{pmatrix} \cdot \begin{pmatrix} \cos(\theta_0 - \theta_2(t)) \\ \sin(\theta_0 - \theta_2(t)) \end{pmatrix}
\tag{4}
$$

$\theta_1(t)$ is the angle between the thigh bar and the y-axis, $\theta_2(t)$ is the rotation angle of the shank rod around the ankle joint. At the initial time, the angle (θ_0) between OP and x-axis is 94.535°, the angle (β) between BC and x-axis is 18.201°, angle ($\alpha(t)$) between thigh bar and x-axis can be expressed as follows.

$$
\alpha(t) = \theta_1(t) + \beta
\tag{5}
$$

Distance (L_2) between OC is 535 mm, distance (L_1) between AC is 535 mm, rod CP and rod OC are fixed together, they rotate around O together, the distance (L_{OP}) between OP is 569.1 mm, distance (L_{BC}) between BC is 272.116 mm. The moving distance ($s(t)$) of the linear motor can be expressed as follows.

$$s(t) = \sqrt{(L_{BC} \cdot \cos(\alpha(t)) + L_2 \cdot \sin\theta_2(t) - x_P)^2 + (L_{BC} \cdot \sin(\alpha(t)) + L_2 \cdot \cos\theta_2(t) - y_P)^2} \tag{6}$$

Differentiating the position and angle, the following equations are got as follows:

$$\begin{pmatrix} L_1 \cdot \cos\theta_1(t) & L_2 \cdot \cos\theta_2(t) \\ -L_1 \cdot \sin\theta_1(t) & -L_2 \cdot \sin\theta_2(t) \end{pmatrix} \cdot \begin{pmatrix} \dot{\theta}_1(t) \\ \dot{\theta}_2(t) \end{pmatrix} = \begin{pmatrix} v_x \\ v_y \end{pmatrix} \tag{7}$$

$$v_P = \dot{s}(t) \tag{8}$$

The system has two degrees of freedom, so it needs the input of two motors, the speed of ball screw is given in the above content. The angle of rotation of the hip joint is considered as $\pi/2$. In order to ensure the stability of the servo motor, the angular velocity of hip joint (servo motor velocity) is given as follows.

$$\theta_1(t) = -\frac{\pi^2}{32} \sin(\frac{\pi}{8}t) \tag{9}$$

According to the previous formula (6), (7), (8), $\theta_2(t)$, $\dot{\theta}_2(t)$, v_x and $v_P(t)$ can be figured out. The function image is shown in Fig. 5.

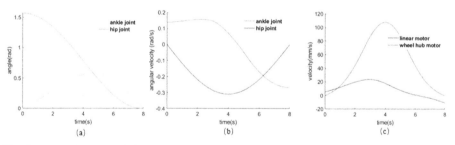

Fig. 5. (a) angle curve of hip joint and ankle joint. (b) angular velocity curve of hip joint and ankle joint. (c) wheel motor speed and linear motor speed

It can be seen from the figure that in the whole movement process, the speed of each motor is relatively stable without large fluctuation, which is consistent with our expected results.

3 Analysis of Trunk Velocity in Gait Cycle

Gait cycle of human walking is divided into stance state and swing state, as shown in Fig. 6.

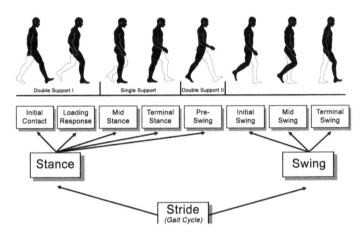

Fig. 6. A gait cycle of human walking

The stance state refers to the period when the lower limb contacts the ground and support gravity, and the swing state refers to the period between the foot leaving the ground and stepping forward to land again. Because the left and right legs are symmetrical with a certain phase difference, to calculate the forward speed of the trunk in a gait cycle, the right leg is taken as the research object, and calculate the forward speed of the trunk in the stance state (half a cycle), then transform the calculation results through the cycle to get the speed of a cycle. As the hip joint of the exoskeleton is connected with the whole device, the speed of the trunk is equal to that of the hip joint.

During the stance state, the process can be divided into three stages: heel support, whole sole support and forefoot support. The foot can be equivalent to a triangle, so the movement can be regarded as the process of rotating around the two vertices of the triangle and fixing the bottom edge. The specific motion model is shown in Fig. 7.

In (a) stage, the triangle vertex A can be regarded as a fixed point, and the basic coordinate system is established on point A. According to the homogeneous coordinate transformation of robotics, the homogeneous transformation matrix from point A to ankle joint can be obtained as follows.

$$T_0^1 = \begin{pmatrix} \cos\theta_4 & -\sin\theta_4 & 0 & a_1 \cdot \cos\theta_4 \\ \sin\theta_4 & \cos\theta_4 & 0 & a1 \cdot \sin\theta_4 \\ 0 & 0 & 1 & 0 \\ 0 & 0 & 0 & 1 \end{pmatrix} \tag{10}$$

Where θ_4 is obtained by geometric relation, expressed as follows.

$$\theta_4 = \theta_3 + \theta_0 - \theta_2 + \theta_1 \tag{11}$$

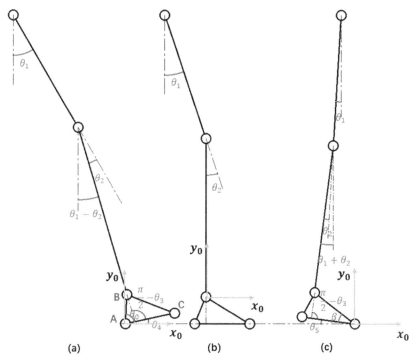

Fig. 7. Motion model in support state. (a) heel support. (b) whole sole support. (c) forefoot support.

Where θ_0 is an inner angle of the triangle, θ_1 is the hip angle, θ_2 is the knee angle, θ_3 is the ankle angle.

Similarly, the homogeneous transformation matrix of ankle joint to knee joint and knee joint to hip joint can be got according to the same method, as follows.

$$T_1^2 = \begin{pmatrix} \sin(\theta_3 + \theta_0) & -\cos(\theta_3 + \theta_0) & 0 & L_2 \cdot \sin(\theta_3 + \theta_0) \\ \cos(\theta_3 + \theta_0) & \sin(\theta_3 + \theta_0) & 0 & L_2 \cdot \cos(\theta_3 + \theta_0) \\ 0 & 0 & 1 & 0 \\ 0 & 0 & 0 & 1 \end{pmatrix} \tag{12}$$

$$T_2^3 = \begin{pmatrix} \cos(\theta_2 - \theta_1) & -\sin(\theta_2 - \theta_1) & 0 & L_2 \cdot \cos\theta_2 \\ \sin(\theta_2 - \theta_1) & \cos(\theta_2 - \theta_1) & 0 & L_2 \cdot \sin\theta_2 \\ 0 & 0 & 1 & 0 \\ 0 & 0 & 0 & 1 \end{pmatrix} \tag{13}$$

So the homogeneous transformation matrix from A to hip joint is got.

$$T_0^3 = T_0^1 \cdot T_1^2 \cdot T_2^3 \tag{14}$$

Finally, the position coordinates of the hip joint can be calculated as follows.

$$\begin{cases} x_{pa} = -L_1 \cdot \sin\theta_1 + L_2 \cdot \sin(\theta_2 - \theta_1) + a_1 \cdot \cos(\theta_3 + \theta_0 - \theta_2 + \theta_1) \\ y_{pa} = L_1 \cdot \cos\theta_1 + L_2 \cdot \cos(\theta_2 - \theta_1) + a_1 \cdot \sin(\theta_3 + \theta_0 - \theta_2 + \theta_1) \end{cases} \tag{15}$$

Take differentiation to position, the expression of hip joint velocity can be got as follows.

$$\begin{pmatrix} v_x \\ v_y \end{pmatrix} = \begin{pmatrix} \dot{x}_{pa} \\ \dot{y}_{pa} \end{pmatrix} = J \cdot \begin{pmatrix} \dot{\theta}_1 \\ \dot{\theta}_2 \\ \dot{\theta}_3 \end{pmatrix} \tag{16}$$

Where J is the Jacobian matrix of joint angular velocity.

Using the same analysis method, the hip position coordinates of (b) state and (c) state are got, which are (x_{Pb}, y_{Pb}) and (x_{Pc}, x_{Pc}).

$$\begin{cases} x_{pb} = -L_1 \cdot \sin\theta_1 + L_2 \cdot \sin(\theta_2 - \theta_1) \\ y_{pb} = L_1 \cdot \cos\theta_1 + L_2 \cdot \cos(\theta_2 - \theta_1) \end{cases} \tag{17}$$

$$\begin{cases} x_{pc} = L_1 \cdot \sin\theta_1 + L_2 \cdot \sin(\theta_1 + \theta_2) - a_1 \cdot \cos(\theta_3 + \theta_0 - \theta_2 + \theta_1) \\ y_{pc} = L_1 \cdot \cos\theta_1 + L_2 \cdot \cos(\theta_1 + \theta_2) + a_1 \cdot \sin(\theta_3 + \theta_0 - \theta_2 + \theta_1) \end{cases} \tag{18}$$

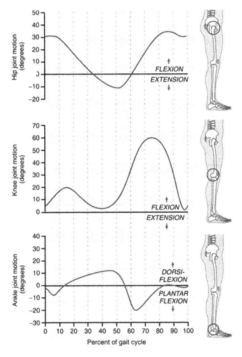

Fig. 8. Curve of joint angle in gait cycle

Calculate the expression of velocity according to the position coordinate and the total time of the whole gait cycle is 12%, 20% and 18% respectively in the phase (a), (b) and (c).

According to the data of clinical gait database (CGA), the time of one gait cycle of the patient walking process is selected as 1.2 s, and the curve of each joint angle is shown in Fig. 8.

Using a polynomial equation to fit the joint angle curve, and the polynomial equation is brought into Eq. (16) to get the hip joint speed during walking (half gait cycle).

4 Simulation

In order to verify the accuracy of the trunk velocity calculated previously, the 3D model of exoskeleton established by SolidWorks is introduced into ADAMS software, as shown in Fig. 9(a).

In ADAMS, we set the constraint conditions of joints, and make the joint angle meet the angle curve fitted by polynomial, and the speed curve of trunk is shown in Fig. 9(b).

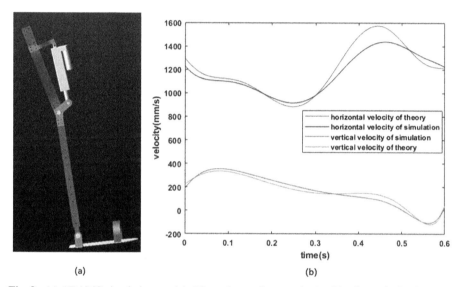

(a)   (b)

Fig. 9. (a) ADAMS simulation model. (b) trunk speed curve obtained by theoretical calculation and simulation

From the results of the curve, it can be seen that the speed trend of the simulation is consistent with that of the theoretical calculation, which can verify the efficacy of the theoretical analysis. But there are some errors in the two curves. Analysis of the causes of errors, summed up in the following two points.

a. Each person's walking habits (including step length, walking speed, etc.) and body characteristic parameters (thigh length, leg length, etc.) are different, so the joint angle curve is different.
b. There are some errors in fitting the joint angle curve with polynomial equation.

5 Conclusion and Future Work

Considering the advantages and disadvantages of exoskeleton and wheelchair, this paper proposed a design method of wheelchair-exoskeleton robot which combines their own advantages. The new design is innovative, which overcomes the limitations of exoskeleton and wheelchair, and can realize the three functions of sitting, stance and walking, so as to meet the rehabilitation needs of patients. This paper also analyzed the speed of the joint in the process from sitting to stance, and planned and designed the speed of each motor. Finally, this paper analyzed the trunk speed of a gait cycle during walking and complete the simulation verification in ADAMS software.

In the future, the prototype will be completed and the proposed method in this paper will be tested in the physical experiments.

Acknowledgement. This research is supported by the Natural Science Foundation of China (Project No. 51775367, 51975401).

References

1. Zhang, Y., Liu, H., Zhou, L., et al.: Applying Tai Chi as a rehabilitation program for stroke patients in the recovery phase: study protocol for a randomized controlled trial. Trials **15**(1), 484 (2014)
2. Scivoletto, G., Morganti, B., Molinari, M.: Early versus delayed inpatient spinal cord injury rehabilitation: an Italian study. Arch. Phys. Med. Rehabil. **86**(3), 512–516 (2005)
3. Rossi, P.W., Forer, S., Wiechers, D.: Effective rehabilitation for patients with stroke: analysis of entry, functional gain, and discharge to community. J. Neurorehabil. Neural Repair **11**(1), 27–33 (1997)
4. Lu, R., Li, Z., Su, C.Y., et al.: Development and learning control of a human limb with a rehabilitation exoskeleton. IEEE Trans. Ind. Electron. **61**(7), 3776–3785 (2014)
5. George, H.T., Zemon, D.H., Donielle, C.: Robotic-assisted, body-weight–supported treadmill training in individuals following motor incomplete spinal cord injury. Phys. Ther. (1), 1 (2005)
6. Colombo, G., Joerg, M., Schreier, R., et al.: Treadmill training of paraplegic patients using a robotic orthosis. J. Rehabil. Res. Dev. **37**(6), 693–700 (2000)
7. MacWilliams, B.A., Armstrong, P.F.: Clinical applications of plantar pressure measurement in pediatric orthopedics. In: Pediatric Gait, A New Millennium in Clinical Care & Motion Analysis Technology. IEEE (2000)
8. Colombo, G., Wirz, M., Dietz, V.: Driven gait orthosis for improvement of locomotor training in paraplegic patients. Spinal Cord **39**(5), 252–255 (2001)
9. Hussain, S., Sheng, Q.X., Liu, G.: Robot assisted treadmill training: Mechanisms and training strategies. Med. Eng. Phys. **33**(5), 527–533 (2011)
10. Peshkin, M., Brown, D.A., Santos-Munne, J.J., et al.: KineAssist: a robotic overground gait and balance training device. In: 2005 9th International Conference on Rehabilitation Robotics, ICORR 2005. IEEE (2005)
11. Tsukahara, A., Hasegawa, Y., et al.: Restoration of gait for spinal cord injury patients using HAL with intention estimator for preferable swing speed. IEEE Trans. Neural Syst. Rehabil. Eng. **23**(2), 308–318 (2014)
12. Zoss, A.B., Kazerooni, H., Chu, A.: Biomechanical design of the berkeley lower extremity exoskeleton (BLEEX). IEEE ASME Trans. Mechatron. **11**, 128–138 (2006)
13. Song, Z., Tian, C., Dai, J.S.: Mechanism design and analysis of a proposed wheelchair-exoskeleton hybrid robot for assisting human movement. Mech. Sci. **10**(1), 11–24 (2019)

Gaze Based Implicit Intention Inference with Historical Information of Visual Attention for Human-Robot Interaction

Yujie Nie and Xin Ma[✉]

School of Control Science and Engineering, Shandong
University, Jinan 250061, People's Republic of China
maxin@sdu.edu.cn

Abstract. Human-robot interaction (HRI) is the key capability for assistive robots to provide support for the elders and impaired in daily activities. Implicit intention understanding is a challenge problem for natural and intuitive HRI. In this paper, an implicit intention inference framework based on gaze behavior is proposed. First, support vector machine classifier is used to classify human's gaze behavior as intentional and unintentional visual behavior. Then, a Naive Bayes model based on implicit intention inference is presented with taking historical visual attention into accounts. The advantage of this model is that the human's implicit intention could be inferred based on his/her gaze at multiple objects by dealing with the historical information of visual behavior. Finally, experiments are conducted in a scenario of "home care in the kitchen". People are free to look at one or more objects among 14 kinds of objects provided in experiment. With the proposed model, four kinds of intentions could be inferred based on people's historical gaze on objects. The experiment results validate that the proposed model, which considers the historical information of visual behavior, outperforms the previous gaze-based intention inference methods.

Keywords: Implicit intention recognition · Gaze behavior · Human-robot interaction

1 Introduction

With the aging of the population, the need of assistance in diary life for the elderly has increased substantially. Assistive robots have been increasingly accepted to care for the elderly and disabled [1]. Assistive robots can recognize people's everyday demands and perform auxiliary actions by sensing and processing sensory information. The emergence of assistive robots presents the possibility of improving the quality of life and personal independence of elderly people [2]. To increase acceptance of assistive robots by the elderly, robots should be able to communicate with the elderly smoothly. Researches on different communicating modalities have been carried out, including speech [3, 4], gestures [5, 6], wearable sensor [7, 8] and multimodal fusion [9]. These works simplify the process of interaction to some extent, but the effect is not satisfactory for a

© Springer Nature Switzerland AG 2021
X.-J. Liu et al. (Eds.): ICIRA 2021, LNAI 13015, pp. 293–303, 2021.
https://doi.org/10.1007/978-3-030-89134-3_27

smooth cooperation. An important factor is that the robots lack understanding of people's inner thoughts [10]. To achieve a natural and convenient human-robot interaction, it's necessary that robots recognize user's intention automatically.

Human intention understanding is significant for human-robot interaction. In many cases, intention recognition is an appropriate solution for a robot to be aware of the current situation, therefore, a robot can understand the human's real intention and provide reasonable assistance [11]. Expression of intention can be explicit or implicit based on researches into human intention in the fields of psychology and cognitive science. Generally, humans express their intention explicitly through facial expressions, speech, and hand gesture [12]. Works [10–15] have been performed on these modalities. Speech and gesture can promote the understanding of intention. However, these methods require explicit service requests generated by users. But not all of the elderly and impaired with disability have clear expression and behavioral ability. And facial expressions express willingness, not specific intentions. These imperfections may lead to deterioration of service quality. Some researches attempt to recognize people's implicit intention using Electro Encephalogram (EEG) [16–18], Electrooculogram (EOG) [19, 20] and Electromyogram (EMG) [21, 22]. However, these methods require users to wear complex instruments and devices, which may undermine the acceptance of assistive technologies by users.

Eye movement is considered to have a close connection with people's inner thoughts [23], which doesn't need people's extra efforts. People's eye gaze reveals their purposes and future actions by indicating their direction of attention [24]. Empirical evidence has shown that gaze cues indicate action intent and lead flowing motor actions [25]. Furthermore, the objects that are focused upon reflect a person's certain desires [26]. Deictic gaze toward an object, for instance, may signal the person's interest in the object [27]. For example, people usually fixated on the tap, soap, and paper towels in sequence to achieve a hand-washing task, before they guided hands to pick up objects [28]. This kind of gaze is purposeful and affects subsequent planning. Therefore, understanding and following gaze clues is essential for recognizing human intentions [29].

Previous works have focused on the position or direction of gaze to infer intention, Gajwani [30] used the left or right motion of eyes to control the wheelchair to move to desired direction. Ishii [31] estimated people's conversational engagement with salespeople based on gaze direction. Some works quantified how gaze patterns may indicate a person's intention. Jang [12] classified visual intention as informational intention and navigational intention based on the eyeball movement patterns and pupil size variation. Huang [29] trained an SVM classifier using four gaze patterns (number of glances, duration of first glance, total duration of glances, and whether a particular ingredient was most recently glanced at) to predict the intended target of a client's request for ingredients. These works provided essential implications for using gaze feature to intention understanding.

On the basis of these works, Li [26] detected intentional gaze and calculated the probability of intention for each object that users have looked at.They take the intention with maximum probability value as inferred intention using a naïve Bayes classifier. They inferred 4 kinds of intention (Prepare a cup of coffee; Prepare breakfast; Take medicine; Wash a washable target) mainly based on a dominant object. They achieved a result of 75% accuracy rate. This work simplifies HRI by recognizing human intention based on visual behavior. However, this approach does not consider the effect that the previously viewed objects have on the current intention. While previously viewed objects play an important role in predicting intentions in real life. Therefore, using historical visual information to infer people's implicit intention becomes necessary and feasible.

Inspired by above works, in this paper, we take into consideration the effect of historical visual objects on current intention. We introduce an intention recognition framework based on historical visual attention for implicit intention recognition. The number of focused objects is uncertain during inference process, which is in line with the way that people express their intention. Experiments prove that our method improves the accuracy of intention recognition.

2   Gaze Based Intention Inference Framework

This section describes the proposed framework in detail. Figure 1 shows the block diagram of proposed framework for recognizing human implicit intention based on gazed objects. The framework mainly consists of three parts. Firstly, Eye tracker is used to extract human eyeball movement features, which are fixation length, fixation count, gaze interval and gaze speed. Then, Support vector machine (SVM) [32] classifier is used to classify gaze behaviors as intentional gaze and unintentional gaze based on the features obtained by eye tracker. Finally, the naïve Bayes method is used to infer human intention based on historical visual objects. The following sections introduce each component in detail.

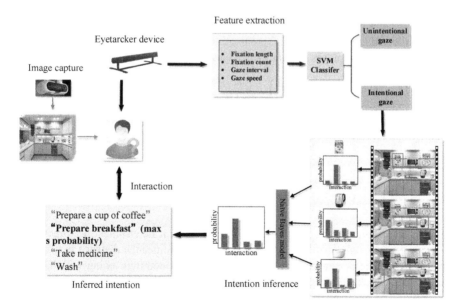

Fig. 1. Structure of gaze-based intention recognition

2.1 Intentional Visual Attention Detection

Support vector machine (SVM) is a binary classification model defined in the eigenspace. This paper uses SVM to classify user's gaze data into two categories: intentional gaze and unintentional gaze.

For gaze model, we utilize fixation length, fixation count, gaze interval and gaze speed as gaze features. Intentional visual attention and unintentional visual attention show different eye fixation characteristics in visualization stage [29]. In the process of intentional visual attention, people's fixation length stays longer and their attention is more concentrated than that of unintentional visual attention. During the transition from unintentional gaze to intentional gaze, the number of fixations on object will be significantly more than the number of unintentional glances. Eye tracker detects an eye movement when a person's gaze fixation on a specific area exceeds a threshold (for example, 60 ms). A single gaze behavior begins when people begins to gaze at a specific target, and ends when people begins to gaze at another target. The change of the target area is demonstrated by 2-d position coordinates (x, y) collected by eye tracker.

For each gaze behavior, we calculate the fixation length, which is, the difference between the start time and the end time of each fixation. For each target region, we collect the total number of times that the user has looked at and take these number of times as fixation count. To accommodate blinking (less than 60 ms), we combine the fixation length if the target is fixed before and after blinking. Our gaze model forms as the following. For each object O_j, we have four gaze features: $f_j^l, f_j^c, f_j^{val}, f_j^s$ and a label y_j. Where O_j is the j_{th} kind of object, f_j^l is the fixation length on object O_j in the past 60 s, f_j^c is the number of times that people gaze at object O_j, f_j^{val} is the average time interval of gazing at the object O_j and f_j^s is the speed of eye movement. Label y_j indicates whether or not there is an intentional gaze.

The collected gaze characteristics are fixation count and fixation length. The training sample set contains m pieces of data, which can be described as:

$$D = \{f = \left(f_j^l, f_j^c, f_j^{val}, f_j^s\right), y_j | f_j^l, f_j^c, f_j^{val}, f_j^s \in R, j = 1, 2, \ldots, m\} \tag{1}$$

The classification problem can be described as finding the parameters ω and b to make the classification interval of different categories maximum, which is:

$$\min_{\omega, b} \frac{1}{2} ||\omega||^2$$

$$s.t. y_j(\omega^T f_j + b) \geq 1, j = 1, 2, \ldots, m \tag{2}$$

In which $\omega = (\omega_1; \omega_2; \ldots; \omega_d)$ is the normal vector, it determines the direction of the hyperplane; b is the displacement term which determines the distance between the hyperplane and the origin. ω and b parameters are obtained by training with datasets. The datasets which satisfy Eq. (3) are considered to be intentional gaze, the rest are considered to be unintentional gaze.

$$\omega^T f_j + b > 0 \tag{3}$$

2.2 Intention Inference

Objects of visual attention indicate user's implicit desire. We quantify how objects imply people's intention using naïve Bayes model. Furthermore, we analyze effects that the historical visual objects have on current intention. We use naive Bayes method based on independent condition to infer intentions based on objects that users are interested in.

In this paper, visual attention refers to the intentional gaze of users when observing different areas, each area represents different object respectively. We design an interactive interface to collect object-intention data to analyze correlation between object and intention. We choose 4 kinds of intention and 14 kinds of objects which are similar to [26]. Participants are free to look at objects displayed on the interface to achieve a certain intention. We obtain multiple sets of intention - object pairs (I_i, O_j). I_i is the i_{th} kind of intention and O_j is the j_{th} kind of object. According to Bayes' formula (4), we figure out probability distributions which indicate how an object represents a certain intention with probability value.

$$P(I_i|O_j) = \frac{P(I_i, O_j)}{P(O_j)} \quad (4)$$

Where $P(O_j)$ is the probability of appearance of object O_j, $P(I_i, O_j)$ is the probability of simultaneous appearance of O_j and I_i.

We take the probability distributions of object and intention above as priori knowledge to infer user's intention. The intention inference is based on the sequence of viewed objects in the process of intention expression. Formally, we describe intention recognition problem as a tuple: $T = (I_i, O)$. In which I_i is the i_{th} kind of intention, $O = (O_1, O_2, O_3, \ldots, O_j)$ represents the possible sequences of viewed objects. We can describe the problem as estimating the probability of each intention I_i: $P(I_i|O_1, O_2, \ldots, O_j)$. We assume that every time the observed O_j achieves its intention probability, it has no impact on the appearance of next object O_{j+1}, which means that the appearance probability of O_j is not affected by the appearance of O_{j-1}. With this assumption, we can calculate as follows:

$$P(I_i|O) = \frac{P(I_i)P(O|I_i)}{P(O)} = \frac{P(I_i)}{P(O)} \prod_{j=1}^{d} P(O_j|I_i) \quad (5)$$

By analyzing visual objects, the conditional probability of each intent can be calculated. The intention with highest probability is considered as the inferred intention. The formula is expressed as the following:

$$\hat{I} = \mathrm{argmax}_{I_i \in I} P(I_i) \prod_{j=1}^{d} P(O_j|I_i) \quad (6)$$

Where d is the length of the sequence of intentional historical visual objects, I is the collection of intentions to be recognized, $\hat{I}$ is the result of possible intention.

3   Experiments on Intention Inference

3.1   Experiment Environment

We validated the proposed intention understanding framework in a home care kitchen scenario. Participants look at a scene picture on screen which is fed back from an assistive robot. Tobbi eyetracker 5 tracks the location of user's gaze and records fixation length, fixation count, gaze interval and gaze speed. In the process of intention expression, we assumed that the assistive robot provides a stable kitchen scene image for the user. The goal of experiments is to infer user's intention based on user's gazed objects.

3.2   Data Collection

For intentional gaze detection, we invite 20 volunteers between the ages of 22 and 28, who are graduate students in our laboratory. They are required to look at the image of a kitchen scene and find a certain object according to hints on screen. They browse the screen of kitchen scene and press the button when they find the suggestive object to indicate the presence of visual attention on the current target area. Tobii Eyetracker 5 record the location that volunteers have seen in this progress. The system will automatically change the prompt object and a total of 950 sets of data were collected.

For intention inference, we divided the interactive interface of kitchen scene into 14 target areas as shown in Fig. 2. Volunteers were required to look at the interactive interface of the kitchen scene. According to the prompting intention of the interactive interface, they searched for the objects which could imply the intention from kitchen image and press the button to indicate the presence of visual attention in current target area. The system will automatically change the prompt intention. In the end, data were collected including 4 kinds of intention and 14 kinds of objects in a kitchen scene.

Fig. 2. Kitchen scene image

Volunteers were free to choose their intentions and objects. A total of 1110 groups of data were collected, each group of data was recorded as $(I_i: O_1, O_2, \ldots, O_j)$. Eight hundred sets of data were used for training, and the rest are used for testing. The format of the collected data is shown in Table 1.

Table 1. Datasets of intention-object pairs

Intention	Object
Prepare a cup of coffee (Pre.Cof)	Cup, Coffee pot, Milk, Kettle, Spoon…
Prepare breakfast (Pre.Brf)	Bowl, Oatmeal, Spaghetti, Microwave oven…
Take Medicine (TK.Med)	Medicine container, Cup, Spoon…
Wash	Tap, Cleaning, sponge, Dishwashing liquid, Washable object…

3.3 Experimental Results and Analysis

Performance of Intentional Gaze Detection
A total of 950 sets of training data were collected for SVM classifier training, of which 680 sets are positive training data and 270 sets are negative training data. The overall training success rate was 90.37%, which means that, among the visual attention produced by the participants, 90.37% was recognized successfully. More detailed training performance is shown as Table 2.

Table 2. SVM classifier for attention detection performance

	Classified as positive	Classified as negative
Positive training data	95.63%	4.37%
Negative training data	23.05%	76.95%

Performance of Intention Inference Based on Gazed Objects
We collected 1110 pairs of datasets, 800 pairs are used for training data and the rest 310 pairs of datasets are used for testing data. We get the probability distributions of which each object is inferred to be a certain kind of intention of four kinds of intention. The detailed probability distributions are shown in Fig. 3. The probability distribution shows how strongly an object is associated with an intention. A larger probability value represents a larger correlation strength.

As we can see in Fig. 3, although everyone expresses their intention in a different way, in most cases, they have several of same objects in their choices. For example, in expressing the intention "Prepare breakfast", most participants would choose "bowl", "oatmeal" and "spaghetti". Based on probability distribution in Fig. 3, we infer the intention based on a single object, and the detailed inference performance is illustrated as a confusion matrix shown in Fig. 4(a).

As shown in Fig. 4(a), the horizontal axis is the target intention and the vertical axis is the inferred intention. The correctness for each type of intention and overall correctness is summarized at the bottom row. As shown, the overall correctness rate is 80.1%, the

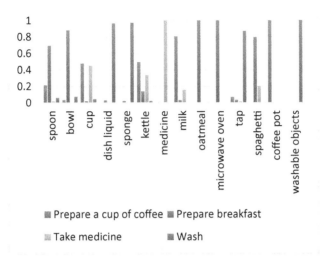

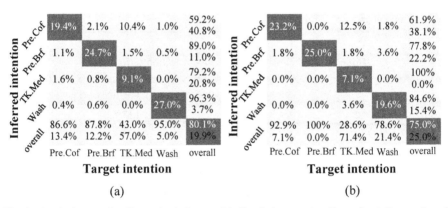

Fig. 3. Intention probability distributions based on a single object

Fig. 4. Confusion matrix of intention inference (a): Confusion matrix of intention inference based on single object; (b) Confusion matrix of intention inference based on dominant object.

intention "Prepare a cup of coffee" was inferred correctly in 86.6% of the cases, and "Prepare breakfast" was inferred correctly in 87.8% of the case. "Take medicine" was inferred correctly 43.0%. "Wash" was inferred correctly in 95.0% of the cases.

Figure 4(b) shows the confusion matrix of intention inference based on dominant objects in [26]. They achieve a higher correctness rate in intention "Prepare a cup of coffee" and the intention "Prepare breakfast", but a lower correctness rate in intention "Take medicine" and "Wash". The correctness rate of intention "Take medicine" is 28.6%, which is lower than the error rate. The overall correctness rate is 75.0%, which is 5.1% lower than the overall correctness rate we achieved in Fig. 4(a).

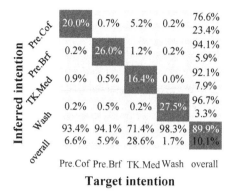

Fig. 5. Confusion matrix of intention inference based on historical visual objects

The inference performance based on historical visual objects is shown as a confusion matrix shown in Fig. 5. We recorded objects that users have seen during the progress of expressing intention, 300 of testing datasets are collected to validate the performance.

As shown in Fig. 5, the overall correctness rate is 89.91%, which is 9.8% higher than the correctness rate of intention inference based on a single object in Fig. 4(a) and 14.9% higher than the correctness rate of intention inference based on dominate object in Fig. 4(b). As shown, the intention "Prepare a cup of coffee" was inferred correctly in 93.4%, and "Prepare breakfast" was inferred correctly in 94.1%. "Wash" was inferred correctly in 98.3%, and "Take medicine" was inferred correctly 71.4%. Compared with the accuracy of intention prediction based on a single object in Fig. 4, the accuracy of intention prediction based on historical visual objects is higher, which proves that our method has a better performance.

4 Conclusion

In this paper, we infer human intention based on historical visual objects. Gaze data based on a single object is used to build probability distributions over four kinds of intentions, which are then used as priori knowledge in intention inference based on all objects that users have looked at. Experiments demonstrated that intention recognition based on historical visual objects significantly improved the accuracy of the inferences when compared with single object-based approaches. However, the results also show that improvements can be made. In particular, the objects that are viewed earlier have different degrees of impact on intention. As such, assigning weights to all the viewed objects in order would be useful. In future work, we will also explore how other modalities indicate intention, such as gestures, or a combination of gaze and gestures.

Acknowledgement. This work was supported in part by the National Key Research and Development Plan of China under Grant 2018YFB1305803 and the Key Development Program for Basic Research of Shandong Province under Grant ZR2019ZD07.

References

1. Louie, W.Y.G., McColl, D., Nejat, G.: Acceptance and attitudes toward a human-like socially assistive robot by older adults. Assist. Technol. **26**(3), 140–150 (2014)
2. Trick, S., Koert, D., Peters, J.: Multimodal uncertainty reduction for intention recognition in human-robot interaction. arXiv preprint arXiv:1907.02426 (2019)
3. Bingol, M.C., Aydogmus, O.: Performing predefined tasks using the human–robot interaction on speech recognition for an industrial robot. Eng. Appl. Artif. Intell. **95**, 103903 (2020)
4. Pleshkova, S., Bekiarski, A.: Algorithm for motion management by interaction between mobile robot and human. In: 2019 II International Conference on High Technology for Sustainable Development (HiTech), pp. 1–4. IEEE (2019)
5. Droeschel, D., Stückler, J., Behnke, S.: Learning to interpret pointing gestures with a time-of-flight camera. In: Proceedings of the 6th International Conference on Human-Robot Interaction, pp. 481–488 (2011)
6. Canal, G., Escalera, S., Angulo, C.: A real-time human-robot interaction system based on gestures for assistive scenarios. Comput. Vis. Image Underst. **149**, 65–77 (2016)
7. Sheng, W., Du, J., Cheng, Q.: Robot semantic mapping through human activity recognition: a wearable sensing and computing approach. Robot. Auton. Syst. **68**, 47–58 (2015)
8. Zhu, C., Sheng, W.: Wearable sensor-based hand gesture and daily activity recognition for robot-assisted living. IEEE Trans. Syst. Man Cybern.-Part A: Syst. Hum. **41**(3), 569–573 (2011)
9. Rodomagoulakis, I., Kardaris, N., Pitsikalis, V.: Multimodal human action recognition in assistive human-robot interaction. In: 2016 IEEE International Conference on Acoustics, Speech and Signal Processing (ICASSP), pp. 2702–2706. IEEE (2016)
10. Chen, L., Zhou, M., Wu, M.: Three-layer weighted fuzzy support vector regression for emotional intention understanding in human–robot interaction. IEEE Trans. Fuzzy Syst. **26**(5), 2524–2538 (2018)
11. Yang, J.Y., Kwon, O.H., Lim, C.S., Kwon, D.S.: Human-robot interaction-based intention sharing of assistant robot for elderly people. In: Lee, S., Cho, H., Yoon, K.J., Lee, J. (eds.) Intelligent Autonomous Systems 12. AISC, vol. 194. pp. 283–291. Springer, Heidelberg. (2013). https://doi.org/10.1007/978-3-642-33932-5_27
12. Jang, Y.M., Mallipeddi, R., Lee, S., et al.: Human intention recognition based on eyeball movement pattern and pupil size variation. Neurocomputing **128**, 421–432 (2014)
13. Mi, J., Tang, S., Deng, Z.: Object affordance based multimodal fusion for natural human-robot interaction. Cogn. Syst. Res. **54**, 128–137 (2019)
14. Feng, Y., Chen, L., Wanjuan, S.U.: Gesture intention understanding based on depth and RGB data. In: 2018 37th Chinese Control Conference (CCC), pp. 9556–9559. IEEE (2018)
15. Chen, L., Feng, Y., Maram, M.A.: Multi-SVM based Dempster-Shafer theory for gesture intention understanding using sparse coding feature. Appl. Soft Comput. **85**, 105787 (2019)
16. Park, S.M., Ko, K.E., Park, J.A.: study on hybrid model of HMMs and GMMs for mirror neuron system modeling using EEG signals. In: 2011 IEEE International Conference on Fuzzy Systems (FUZZ-IEEE 2011), pp. 2752–2755. IEEE (2011)
17. Kang, J.S., Park, U., Gonuguntla, V.: Human implicit intent recognition based on the phase synchrony of EEG signals. Pattern Recogn. Lett. **66**, 144–152 (2015)
18. Choi, J., Lee, S.J., Kim, S.J.: Detecting voluntary gait initiation/termination intention using EEG. In: 2018 6th International Conference on Brain-Computer Interface (BCI), pp. 1–3. IEEE (2018)
19. Ahsan, M.R., Ibrahimy, M.I., Khalifa, O.O.: EMG signal classification for human computer interaction: a review. Eur. J. Sci. Res. **33**(3), 480–501 (2009)

20. Li, T., Yang, J., Bai, D.: A new directional intention identification approach for intelligent wheelchair based on fusion of EOG signal and eye movement signal. In: 2018 IEEE International Conference on Intelligence and Safety for Robotics (ISR), pp. 470–474. IEEE (2018)

21. Sy, A.C., Bugtai, N.T.: Velocity and acceleration induced response to bicep EMG signal threshold for motion intention detection. In: 2014 International Conference on Humanoid, Nanotechnology, Information Technology, Communication and Control, Environment and Management (HNICEM), pp. 1–6. IEEE (2014)

22. Fernandes, P.N., Figueredo, J., Moreira, L.: EMG-based motion intention recognition for controlling a powered knee orthosis. In: 2019 IEEE International Conference on Autonomous Robot Systems and Competitions (ICARSC), pp. 1–6. IEEE (2019)

23. Mennie, N., Hayhoe, M., Sullivan, B.: Look-ahead fixations: anticipatory eye movements in natural tasks. Exp. Brain Res. **179**(3), 427–442 (2007)

24. Admoni, H., Srinivasa, S.: Predicting user intent through eye gaze for shared autonomy. In: 2016 AAAI Fall Symposium Series (2016)

25. Land, M., Mennie, N., Rusted, J.: The roles of vision and eye movements in the control of activities of daily living. Perception **28**(11), 1311–1328 (1999)

26. Li, S., Zhang, X.: Implicit intention communication in human–robot interaction through visual behavior studies. IEEE Trans. Hum.-Mach. Syst. **47**(4), 437–448 (2017)

27. Meyer, A.S., Sleiderink, A.M., Levelt, W.J.M.: Viewing and naming objects: eye movements during noun phrase production. Cognition **66**(2), B25–B33 (1998)

28. Pelz, J.B., Canosa, R.: Oculomotor behavior and perceptual strategies in complex tasks. Vision. Res. **41**(25–26), 3587–3596 (2001)

29. Huang, C.M., Andrist, S., Sauppé, A.: Using gaze patterns to predict task intent in collaboration. Front. Psychol. **6**, 1049 (2015)

30. Gajwani, P.S., Chhabria, S.A.: Eye motion tracking for wheelchair control. Int. J. Inf. Technol. **2**(2), 185–187 (2010)

31. Ishii, R., Ooko, R., Nakano, Y.I.: Effectiveness of gaze-based engagement estimation in conversational agents. In: Nakano, Y., Conati, C., Bader, T. (eds.) Eye Gaze in Intelligent User Interfaces, pp. 85–110. Springer, London (2013). https://doi.org/10.1007/978-1-4471-4784-8_6

32. Cortes, C., Vapnik, V.: Support vector machine. Mach. Learn. **20**(3), 273–297 (1995)

Online Object-Oriented Semantic Mapping in Triger Classification Environment

Wanlei Li, Yujing Chen, Haixiang Zhou, Minghui Hua, and Yunjiang Lou$^{(\boxtimes)}$

Harbin Institute of Technology, Shenzhen 518055, China
louyj@hit.edu.cn

Abstract. Creating and maintaining an accurate representation of the environment is an essential capability for every mobile robot. Especially, semantic information plays an important role in mobile robot navigation and other operations. Some scholars are studying different forms of expression of the environment, including geometric, semantic and other forms. In this paper, we present a semantic mapping framework. Our system is capable of online mapping and object updating given object detections from RGB-D data. The map can provides 2D representations, the locations and labels of the mapped objects. To undo wrong data association, we perform a judgment whether to intersect when updating object shapes. Furthermore, we maintain a merge step to deal with part of object detections and keep the map updated. Our mapping system is highly accurate and efficient. We evaluated our approach in the simulated triger classification environments using turtlebot3 robot. As the experimental results demonstrate, our system is able to generate maps that are close to the simulated environment.

Keywords: Object detection · Semantic map · Triger classification

1 Introduction

Maps play the key role in the robotics application, and the foundation of navigation. While geometrical map representation such as occupied grid maps is an established researched topic, the maps including semantic information attract the attention of researchers [1]. In mobile robotics, the most common way to represent spatial information about the environment is through maps, which differ in precision and complexity depending on the application. If only navigation capabilities are required, 2D occupancy grid maps are the most common for indoor robots as they are usually sufficient for planar navigation [2]. These maps represent the environment as a fixed size grid where each cell describes

This work was supported partially by the National Key Research and Development Program of China (2020YFB1313900), and partially by the Shezhen Science and Technology Program (No. JCYJ20180508152226630).

X.-J. Liu et al. (Eds.): ICIRA 2021, LNAI 13015, pp. 304–313, 2021.
https://doi.org/10.1007/978-3-030-89134-3_28

the occupancy probability of the area it represents [3]. Especially, in the triger classification environment to finish the rescure task, a proper environment understanding is necessary to not only effective navigate but also interact reasonably with the wounded and the world.

At the disaster environment, triage is an important part in the whole rescue work. All the wounded need to judged the injury and choosed different treatment plans according to different situations. Due to the inconvenient transportation at the disaster site, there is a lack of medical staff at the scene. Thus, we can use mobile robots to complete some tasks such as triger classification. Mobile robot can fastly and effectively play the role of medical workes. But, the premise is that robot will understand the environment. Not only the obstacles, bus also the wounded information in the triage sites are necessary. So, a semantic map is very important and we need the accurate semantic map to accomplish the triage task, navigation and other related task.

To produce accurate semantic maps for navigation, recent research concentrates on object-based SLAM algorithms or exact representation of the entities in the environment [4]. However, the interest of maps with focus on just the objects has increased noticeably. One of the main reasons is the usefulness of concrete object instances, which can be accessed more easily in an object-based approach. However, the map complexity is higher, because they provide a 3D object reconstruction together with the position in the map [5]. While the 3D information is redundant for navigation tasks and need additional computing resources [6].

In this work, we introduce a mapping algorithm that generate polygonal semantic maps from RGB-D image. Apart from the 3D point cloud describing the object and its semantic type, also the 2D shape in form of a polygon is stored. This allows the robot to increase or decrease the dimension of information according to the current task and the information is reduced to the relevant parts [7]. A map representation that provides several object information such as the object label, and the 2D polygon shape in the corresponding position of wounded.

In the rest of this paper, we first introduce detection of objects, depth image preprocessing, map generation algorithm in our system. Then we do the experiment in the simulated environment to verify the feasibility and practic ability of the system. Finally, we discuss the results and summarize the system proposed in this paper.

2 Method

In this section, we describe the pipeline of our system. A semantic map is an entity that consists of N semantic objects P. Each object P_i contain several features such as the name of object, the location of object, the 2D shape polygon and so on. The first part of our framework is point cloud preprocessing. Second, the shape generation algorithm is runed to make 2D polygon shape. Then, each segmented part is assigned to an detected object in the RGB image. Finally, our system generate semantic mapping including detected objects. Figure 1 shows an overview of our system. The individual steps are described in detail in the following.

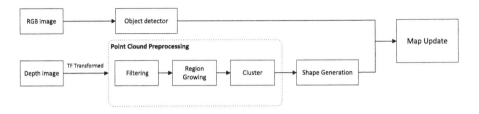

Fig. 1. Overview of our system

2.1   Detection of Objects

Target detection is the current research hotspot and many open source can obtained. You only look once (YOLO) is a state-of-the-art, real-time object detection system. The pre-trained model of the convolutional neural network is able to detect pre-trained classes including the data set from VOC and COCO [8]. The wounded and rescuer are the major components in the disaster environment. The above data set contain the needed class, so, the pre-trained model meets the requirement.

For each detection, the algorithm accept the RGB image from the camera and provides the object type and a mask around it [9]. But, there are some false detection sometimes, because the part of the wounded show in the view of the camera and the pre-trained set contain other type objects. The wrong detection results may lead to wrong segmentation and display wrong results on the map. For example, the people is detected as chairs or other classes in our environment. Because, when the part of the wounded show in the field of the camera, the detector identify the other similar objects. As show in the Fig. 2. In our approach, we add a precondition to remove the false detected class. Thus, we can improve the accuracy of semantic map. In the future work, we can use the self-made casualty data set or pedestrian data set for training if needed.

2.2   Depth Image Preprocessing

The key step of the semantic mapping is the depth image preprocessing. However, the essence of it is processing the point cloud. So, we adapt the PCL library as the library function [10]. The point-cloud from the depth image is showed in Fig. 4(a). An important step is the transformation of coordinates about the map frame and the camera frame before the possible point cloud operations are executed. The flow of the calculation process is showed in the Fig. 3.

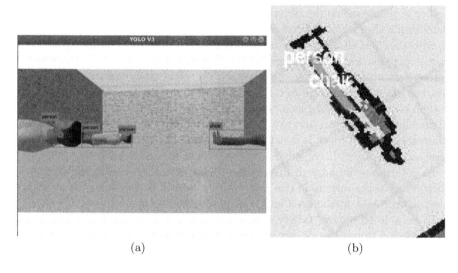

(a)   (b)

Fig. 2. (a) False detection of human (b) wrong representation on the map

In the first step, our system removes the ground. At next step, we apply region growing segmentation on the point cloud [11]. Because, it can be noticed in Fig. 2 that the detected masks can sometimes include parts of the background. For this reason, the detected pixels are transferred to corresponding points in the point-cloud generated from the depth image, and the background is removed by using the segmentation algorithm. Before this, we need calculate the normal vector of the point cloud. Then, we apply the Euclidean cluster extraction of PCL. In our environment, there is a low probability to have small object. So, it is easier for the algorithm to find larger clusters, due to more continuous information. After the preprocessing, we store the generated clusters to combine them with the bounding boxes of the object detector.

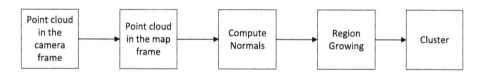

Fig. 3. Process of calculation

2.3   2D Pology Shape Generation

To determine the area of the object on the map, the point-cloud clusters of the above section is projected on the $x - y$ plane. Given the bounding box of each object and the generated clusters, our system assigns the best fitting cluster to each bounding box. To do so, it first determines the cluster that has the highest number of points inside the object bounding box. Afterwards, the corresponding points inside the box are stored as the object point cloud. To generate the initial 2D object shape, all 3D points of the object point cloud are projected onto the 2D $x - y$ plane and the convex hull of the remaining points is computed to express it as a polygon. The area is passed on to the map generate. Figure 4(b) show the 2D polygon shape of the detected wounded on the map.

If an object is identified as a possible fit for the new area, the area is added to the area list of the object and the existence probability of the object is increased. Otherwise, a new object is created. If the existence probability exceeds a set threshold, the object is considered as the part of the map.

To determine the area to display for the object, the average centroid of all collected areas is computed. The area whose centroid is closest to the average is chosen as the best fitting area and is displayed on the map.

To be able to remove falsely detected objects, the existence probability has to be reduced in case an object is not detected. For this purpose, the visibility area of the camera is used: for each object in the map within the visibility area of a sensor measurement which has not received new evidence, the existence probability is reduced. The visibility area is determined by projecting the complete camera point-cloud to the x-y plane of the map frame and then computing the convex hull. An example of this visibility area is shown in purple in Fig. 4(b).

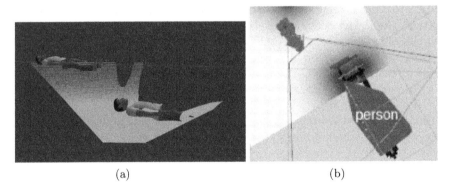

(a)   (b)

Fig. 4. (a) Point cloud representation (b) polygon representation

2.4   Map Generation

The map generator accept the area from shape generator. Then, we need to determine whether to insert a new object or update an existing p_i when handle a new detection [4]. When detecting a area of the object overlapping with a detected region. We make use of an R-tree structure to deal with this situation [12], then the two regions can be combined. The update process the consists of one of the following two cases.

New Object. In the first case, the initial polygon has no intersection with any already mapped object, therefore our system create a new semantic object and show it on the map.

Intersection with Existing Semantic Objects. In the second case, the point clouds of all overlapping semantic objects are combined together with the newly found object to create a single semantic object. The criterion for judging whether two areas intersect is determined by computing the Jaccard index [1]. The Jaccard index between areas A and B is computed as

$$J(A, B) = \frac{|A \cap B|}{|A \cup B|} \tag{1}$$

If the index exceeds a set threshold, the areas are assumed to belong to the same object. If an object is identified as a possible fit for the new area, the area is added to the area list of the object and the existence probability of the object is increased [4]. Otherwise, a new object is created. If the existence probability exceeds a set threshold, the object is considered part of the map. We hereby filter the combined point cloud with down sampling to get evenly point cloud. Then, the polygon of the corresponding combined objects is updated.

To determine the area to display for the object, the average centroid of all collected areas is computed. The area whose centroid is closest to the average is chosen as the best fitting area and is displayed on the map.

Merge Existing Semantic Objects on the Map. In our simulated environment, the wounded are major component and there are no small objects. Therefore, the area of polygon can not be small. It is possible that in the update process two regions do not intersect but are adjacent judging by the procedure. The actual physical meaning corresponding to it is that the two wounded are closed. This can not happened in our environment, because the wounded are placed nearby, but they can not too closed for providing convenience for triging and treating. So, our system compute the distance between areas A and B. The equation is defined as:

$$DIS(A, B) = A.cent - B.cent \tag{2}$$

The $DIS(A, B)$ is computed the geometric distance of the centre of A and B in the $x - y$ plane. If the distance less than a set threshold, the areas are assumed to belong to one object. Figure 5 show the mapping of the wounded with and without the object merge. Without the object merge one person is divided into several persons and this is obviously unreasonable. With the object merge, objects are accurately displayed on the map and have clean boundaries.

(a)   (b)

Fig. 5. (a) Without merge of objects (b) With merge of objects

3 Experiments

For the experiments, we evaluated the capabilities of the semantic mapping algorithm by generating map in the simulated environment that builted by ourselves.
Firstly, we introduce the hardware platform of robot and sensors. Secondly, we
show the experiment. Then, we demonstrate the semantic map produced by our
method. Next, we will explain the experimental conditions in detail.

Platforms. For the simulation, a simulated turtlebot3 was used. The robot
is equipped with laser scanners to provide obstacle detection. The base can be
moved in any direction. Spherical joints also allow for 360° rotations without
moving the robot. Additionally, the robot contains Kinect RGB-D camera that
fixed at a height of 0.5 m. For the conducted mapping experiments, as it provided
the most complete view of the environment in front of the robot. And the robot
equipped with laser to sense the surrounding environment to avoid safety issues.

For object detection, a ROS package for YOLO V3 [13] was implemented.
YOLO V3 offers real-time instance segmentation for images. No training of
the network was performed. Instead, the pre-trained base model trained on the
COCO dataset [14] was used.

The semantic mapping requires a localization on an existing occupancy map.
The occupancy maps of the environments were generated before the experiments
from odometry and laser scan data using off-the-shelf Gmapping [3] and the
Monte Carlo localizer [15].

Environment. By consulting the literature, the tirger classification of the disaster environment should be set up in the open field. Because, on the one hand,
the site should protect the casualty from secondary injury, on the other hand, the
site should have the peculiarity of commodiously transport the wounded. The
simulated environment is a flat ground with multiple wounded. Figure 6 show
the builted simulation environment. The eight wounded were placed side by side
on the ground, with four wounded in each row. Each of them is separated by a
certain distance in order to reflect the real environment.

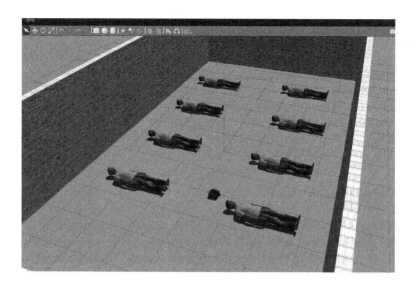

Fig. 6. The simulated environment

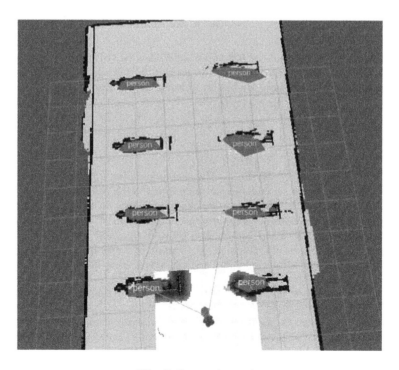

Fig. 7. Semantic result

Simulation Results. To show the performance of our system, we carried out the experiment in the simulated environment. The minimal Jaccard index for areas to be considered evidence for the same object was set to 0.1. And the value of $DIS(A, B)$ is set to 0.35. The robot generates a semantic map by traversing the triger environment. As show in the Fig. 7, our algorithm can detected the all wounded and show them on the map. The accuracy of the results is 100%. And, the 2D polygon shape can accurately reflect the location of the wounded on the map. Comparing the experimental results with the true value, our system can complete the semantic mapping work which label the numbers and positions of the wounded. It can provide convenience for the triger of the robots.

4   Conclusion

In this paper, we presented an online semantic mapping approach that creates polygonal semantic maps from RGB-D camera images. Our approach differs from previous work in the way the created map is segmented multiple objects in the environment. In the disaster environment, the wounded is the major objects. We do not need to classify multiple objects. So, we propose the algorithm to handle the special situation. In the mapping process, our intersection with existing semantic objects and object merge steps ensures that object point assignments can be undone to deal with wrong data processing. We demonstrated the efficacy of our approach in the triger classification environment. The results proved the effectiveness of the method.

For future work, we plan to use other geometry to express the shape of the human body and build a map manager to store different maps. Furthermore, we intend to use the information of objects to build an accurate map. We intend to use semantic information to navigate.

References

1. Zaenker, T., Verdoja, F., Kyrki, V.: Hypermap mapping framework and its application to autonomous semantic exploration, pp. 133–139 (2020)
2. Rosinol, A., Abate, M., Chang, Y., Carlone, L.: Kimera: an open-source library for real-time metric-semantic localization and mapping. In 2020 IEEE International Conference on Robotics and Automation (ICRA), pp. 1689–1696. IEEE (2020)
3. Grisetti, G., Stachniss, C., Burgard, W.: Improved techniques for grid mapping with Rao-Blackwellized particle filters. IEEE Trans. Rob. **23**(1), 34–46 (2007)
4. Dengler, N., Zaenker, T., Verdoja, F., Bennewitz, M.: Online object-oriented semantic mapping and map updating with modular representations. arXiv preprint arXiv:2011.06895 (2020)
5. Hermans, A., Floros, G., Leibe, B.: Dense 3D semantic mapping of indoor scenes from RGB-D images. In: 2014 IEEE International Conference on Robotics and Automation (ICRA), pp. 2631–2638. IEEE (2014)
6. Nakajima, Y., Saito, H.: Efficient object-oriented semantic mapping with object detector. IEEE Access **7**, 3206–3213 (2019)

7. Foux, G., Heymann, M., Bruckstein, A.: Two-dimensional robot navigation among unknown stationary polygonal obstacles. IEEE Trans. Robot. Autom. **9**(1), 96–102 (1993)
8. Grinvald, M., et al.: Volumetric instance-aware semantic mapping and 3D object discovery. IEEE Robot. Autom. Lett. **4**(3), 3037–3044 (2019)
9. Mozos, O.M., Mizutani, H., Kurazume, R., Hasegawa, T.: Categorization of indoor places using the kinect sensor. Sensors **12**(5), 6695–6711 (2012)
10. Rusu, R.B., Cousins, S.: 3D is here: Point cloud library (PCL). In: 2011 IEEE International Conference on Robotics and Automation, pp. 1–4. IEEE (2011)
11. Liu, Z., Chen, D., von Wichert, G.: 2D semantic mapping on occupancy grids. In: ROBOTIK 2012; 7th German Conference on Robotics, pp. 1–6. VDE (2012)
12. Guttman, A.: R-trees: a dynamic index structure for spatial searching. In: Proceedings of the 1984 ACM SIGMOD International Conference on Management of Data, pp. 47–57 (1984)
13. Redmon, J., Farhadi, A.: YOLOv3: an incremental improvement (2018)
14. Lin, T.-Y., et al.: Microsoft COCO: common objects in context. In: Fleet, D., Pajdla, T., Schiele, B., Tuytelaars, T. (eds.) ECCV 2014. LNCS, vol. 8693, pp. 740–755. Springer, Cham (2014). https://doi.org/10.1007/978-3-319-10602-1_48
15. Fox, D., Burgard, W., Dellaert, F., Thrun, S.: Monte Carlo localization: efficient position estimation for mobile robots. In: AAAI/IAAI 1999, pp. 343–349:2–2 (1999)

Research on Virtual Training System for Intelligent Upper Limb Prosthesis with Bidirectional Neural Channels

Yawen Hu, Li Jiang[✉], and Bin Yang

State Key Laboratory of Robotics and System,
Harbin Institute of Technology, Harbin 150001, China
jiangli01@hit.edu.cn

Abstract. The training is very important for the application of electromyography (EMG) prosthesis. Because the traditional training with physical prostheses is inefficient and boring, the virtual training system, which has natural advantages in terms of intuitiveness and interactivity, is more widely used. In this study, a virtual training system for intelligent upper limb prosthesis with bidirectional neural channels has been developed. The training system features motion and sensation neural interaction, which is realized by an EMG control module and sense feedback module based on vibration stimulation. A Human-machine closed-loop interaction training based on the virtual system is studied. The experiments are carried out, and the effectiveness of the virtual system in shortening the training time and improving the operation ability of prosthesis has been verified.

Keywords: Intelligent prosthesis · Virtual training system · Neural control · Perception

1 Introduction

Advanced myoelectric prosthesis can provide multi-DOF intuitive control and it is expected to integrate sense feedback [1], while complex training is essential for effective operation [2]. In traditional training, patients need to wear physical prosthesis, which is costly and boring. Virtual reality uses computer to simulate 3-D virtual world and human senses to make users feel immersive [3]. In recent years, it is widely used in the simulation of medical and military training. The application of virtual reality in prosthetic training can not only overcome the limitations of environment and equipment but also greatly increase the enthusiasm and initiative of patients.

The most famous virtual training system is Virtual Integration Environment [4] (VIE), which is developed by APL Laboratory of Johns Hopkins University in the second phase of DARPA Revolutionizing Prosthetics program, as shown in Fig. 1. VIE uses the modular prosthesis and Delta3D as the simulation engine to rebuild the function of the modular prosthesis in the virtual environment. But limited by the performance of rendering engine and graphics processor at that time, VIE needs three desktop computers to form a parallel architecture to ensure the real-time performance of the system. Compared

© Springer Nature Switzerland AG 2021
X.-J. Liu et al. (Eds.): ICIRA 2021, LNAI 13015, pp. 314–323, 2021.
https://doi.org/10.1007/978-3-030-89134-3_29

with VIE, Virtual Reality Environment [5] (VRE) of Brown University in the United States, adopts human bone skin technology (Fig. 2), and has configurable parameters on the interface. With the development of computer hardware, head mounted display is also used in virtual training system. Chau B [6] uses HTC vive head mounted display to add interactive scenes in daily life in virtual training, and the amputation end positioning is more accurate. Ortiz Catalan [7] and others applies augmented reality (AR) technology to the training platform, and connect the virtual hand to the end of the patient's stump.

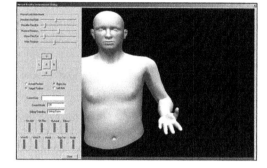

Fig. 1. A precision grip in VIE [4].

Fig. 2. VRE from front [5].

At present, most virtual rehabilitation systems, including VIE, focus on the forward control channel, but few systems can provide haptic feedback to amputee to form a closed-loop control. The ability of two-way information interaction and control is one of the core characteristics of intelligent prosthetic [8], and the perception ability is also a research hotspot in the field of intelligent prosthetic. Compared with visual feedback, the prosthetic practice with haptic feedback can make the control effect more accurate and natural, as well as enhance the immersion of virtual training system and improve the user experience. Additionally, most of the virtual training systems only have a virtual prosthetic hand or wrist, which cannot completely meet the needs of patients with upper arm amputation.

The virtual training system established in this paper includes not only multi-DOF prosthetic hand with the finger driven independently, but also a 7-DOF anthropomorphic prosthetic arm, and we consider the cooperative operation of arm and hand. We design a two way neural interaction module of motion and sensation, which is composed of a multi-mode neural control submodule based on EMG and a sense feedback submodule to form a control loop and realize the interconnection between the prosthesis and the human nervous system. As a closed-loop interactive training platform, the system has significant effectiveness and superiority for the design debugging, control algorithm verification and optimization in the development process of prosthesis.

2 Overall Description of the Virtual Training System

The training system consists of 3 function units: virtual reality software subsystem, neural control subsystem and sense feedback subsystem. Virtual reality software subsystem provides reasonable human-computer interaction interface and realistic virtual reality environment. It integrates EMG control method and sense feedback strategy, including automatic demonstration mode and control training mode. Neural control subsystem is mainly responsible for the acquisition and decoding of human EMG signal. After filtering and amplification, the data acquisition equipment performs A/D conversion and inputs it to the system. The sense feedback subsystem feeds back torque and joint angle in the process of virtual operation to the user through vibration stimulation. The overall architecture of the system is described in Fig. 3.

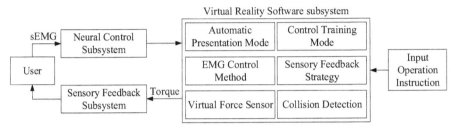

Fig. 3. Framework of the intelligent upper limb prosthesis training system with bidirectional neural channel.

3   Design of the Virtual Training System

3.1   Upper Limb Prosthetic Model

In order to make patients have a better immersion [9], our virtual training system uses the data of the actual prosthesis 3D model to build a virtual scene. The virtual prosthesis is composed of HIT-V [10] hand and 7-DOF arm as shown in Fig. 4. HIT-V has five fingers and 11 active joints. Except thumb, the other four fingers are modular prosthetic finger with two knuckles. Thumb has a pronation/abduction joint in addition. The size of HIT-V is slightly smaller than that of normal male hands. The prosthetic arm consists of wrist, elbow and shoulder. The wrist joint and shoulder joint have 3-DOF of pitch, lateral swing and rotation, and the elbow joint has 1-DOF of bending.

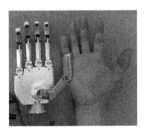

Fig. 4. HIT-V hand compared with a normal male hand [11].

The virtual prosthesis used in our system is the shell of 3D upper-limb prosthetic model, that is, only the prosthetic shell and the necessary rotating shaft are retained. So that the system has better execution efficiency and virtual visual effect. Through SolidWorks 3D modeling, read by Open Inventor, the virtual prosthesis display window is shown in Fig. 5.

Fig. 5. Virtual prosthetic demonstration window.

3.2   Software Subsystem

As shown in Fig. 6, the system interface includes virtual scene demonstration window, control interface and menu bar. In the virtual scene demonstration window, users can zoom in or out to focus on particular joints as well as change the perspective. The control interface is the main operation platform of the software, in which there are various indicators and results display options. The menu bar contains operation commands, such as files, views, etc.

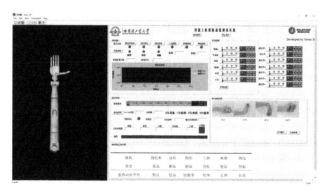

Fig. 6. Human-computer interaction interface.

Automatic Presentation Mode. Automatic presentation mode has been designed to help users get familiar with the system. This mode is used to demonstrate the position and rotation range of the joint, various virtual objects and the correct grasping operations. In this mode, users learn the control information mainly through observation.

"Auto Demo" and "Stop Demo" buttons are used to control the demo process. When "Auto Demo" is selected, the system state will be initialized, that is, the virtual prosthesis will be restored to its initial posture, the angle slider and other controls in the control interface are initialized, as well as the signal acquisition channel, signal duration and other edit box controls are set to zero. Then, the virtual prosthesis demonstrates 6 operations which is already set up in the system.

Control Training Mode. Control training mode is used to realize the function of myoelectric prosthetic training, including multi-mode neural control and sense feedback. In the process of collecting EMG, firstly, the function named "SignalInput" is called to input the information of the data acquisition card. Then, the "Channel" edit boxes display the value of EMG in real time, and the waveform of flexion signal and extensor signal are drawn with iPlot, as shown in Fig. 7. The classification results of EMG in the classifier are displayed in the "Classification Results" edit box, the corresponding control indicator is activated. The "Signal Duration" edit box displays the time of EMG. The movement speed of virtual prosthesis can be adjusted by the speed slider in the interactive interface.

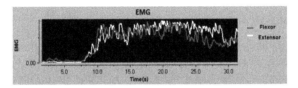

Fig. 7. Virtual EMG oscilloscope.

When virtual prosthesis collides with the virtual object, the torque sensor displays the contact torque value of the fingertip. The rectangular indicator light is activated. The serial port of communication is opened. The torque information is mapped into the control information of the feedback component. The lower computer drives the micro vibration motor and feeds back the contact information to the user.

3.3 Neural Control Subsystem

The training system in this paper uses surface electromyography (SEMG) as the input control signal, and adopts the control method based on finite state machine proposed in reference [12]. After the SEMG of a pair of flexion/extensor muscles of the radial wrist are collected, the action intention is obtained after classification and decoding, and 6 typical grasp modes with the frequency of more than 80% [13] in daily life can be controlled.

Two DJ-03 electrodes are attached to the muscle abdomen of flexor carpi radialis and extensor longus with appropriate pressure. By controlling the states of the forearm muscles, EMG can be categorized into 4 classes: rest, extension, flexion, and clench. Figure 8 shows the hand movement and its EMG. The flexion signal waveform is represented by dotted line, and the extensor signal waveform is represented by solid line.

By setting the long-term action threshold, the above four signals are divided into short extension, short flexion, short clench, long extension, long flexion, long clench and rest. Then the control state and operation of prosthesis are selected according to the seven signals. The coding control process is shown in the Fig. 9.

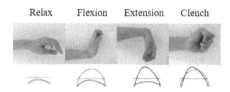

Fig. 8. Four kinds of EMG corresponding to hand movements.

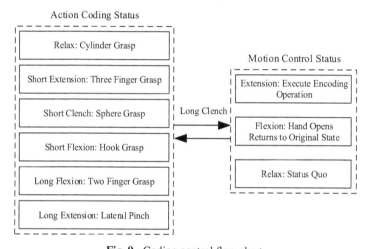

Fig. 9. Coding control flow chart.

3.4 Sense Feedback Subsystem

Calculation of Virtual Force. Contact force is important to force control in prosthetic grasping. In this paper, the spring-damping model is used as the contact force model of virtual environment. Compared with the commonly used pure stiffness model, this method reflects the contact force between finger and object more comprehensively, and is suitable for more characteristic objects.

When solving the virtual contact force, it is necessary to determine the deformation of the virtual object after contact. When the knuckle of the virtual prosthetic hand contacts with the surface of the virtual object, the surface of the virtual object will be deformed. When the balance is reached, the position of the knuckle of the virtual prosthetic hand relative to the surface of the virtual object is offset, which is recorded as the collision depth Δx.

The mechanical properties of virtual objects can be obtained by the following:

$$f = K\Delta x + B\Delta \dot{x} \tag{1}$$

Where f is virtual contact force, Δx is deformation variable, K is the stiffness coefficient, and B is the damping coefficient.

Figure 10 is a schematic diagram of the contact force, which is used to calculate the contact force between the knuckle and the virtual object. Point A represents the initial position of the knuckle contact point, and its coordinate is (x_1, y_1, z_1). Point B represents the position of the knuckle contact point after moving, and its coordinate is (x_2, y_2, z_2).

The surface of virtual object

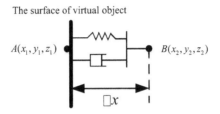

Fig. 10. Contact force diagram.

The distance between point A and point B is the shape variable, expressed by Δx. x_t is the actual position and x_e is the initial contact position. So $\Delta x = x_t - x_e$.

According to Hooke's law, the contact force F is as following:

$$F = K\Delta x + B\Delta \dot{x} \tag{2}$$

Sense Feedback. The function of two-way information interaction and control is one of the core characteristics of intelligent prosthesis, and perception is the hotspot in the field of prosthesis now. The survey shows that the prosthesis with sense feedback can effectively improve the performance of prosthesis. To serve the actual prosthesis, the virtual training system should also have sense feedback system.

We use the vibration tactile feedback, which is relatively simple and easy to implement. The average value of contact force is selected as the feedback information. According to the experimental data of physical prosthesis, the fingertip force of HIT-V ranges from 0 N to 6.5 N [10]. After testing, the duty cycle is 10% when the vibration can be felt, and the duty cycle exceeds 70% when the vibration intensity is not obvious. So we choose 10%– 70% as the output space of duty cycle and map the contact force received from the training system to this space.

4 Experiments

4.1 Human-Machine Closed-Loop Interactive Experiment

Human- machine closed-loop interactive (HMCLI) experiment is carried out by using the virtual training system. In this paper, we set up two training methods: traditional training and HMCLI training. By comparing the coding success rate and operation coding time of different training methods when reaching the same index, we can verify the effectiveness of the system in the process of training patients to use EMG prosthesis.

Subjects. Six healthy male subjects, aged between 24 and 30, were recruited in this study. All subjects had no experience in EMG control and had not used the system before. They all signed the informed consent. The six subjects were divided into two groups for traditional training and HMCLI training.

The Process of the Experiments. Traditional method is to use the physical prosthesis for training. The subjects judge whether the coding is correct by observing. In HMCLI training, the subjects can not only adjust according to waveform, classification results and duration of the two channel EMG displayed on the interactive interface, but also feel the contact information through vibration feedback to compare the difference between the actual result and the expected result.

After learning the EMG control coding method, 6 grasp commands appear randomly for 5 times, and the subjects need to complete each command within 10 s. The success rate of coding will be tested every 15 min. They have some time to rest each round. Each subject trains for 90 min. The succeed operation time and the coding time will be recorded. The process of training is as shown in Fig. 11.

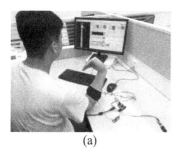 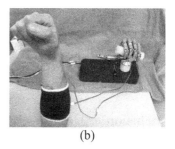
(a)   (b)

Fig. 11. The training process of subjects. (a) HMCLI experiment. (b) Traditional experiment.

The success rate of coding and succeed operation time are used as evaluation indexes, and the success rate of coding P is defined as following:

$$P = \frac{n}{N} \times 100\% \tag{3}$$

Where N is the number of detection, n is the number of correct operation. The succeed operation time is defined as: starting from the subject clear grasp command to the correct grasp of the virtual prosthesis.

Results and Discussion. Figure 12 shows the average success rate of coding of the two groups. It can be seen from the figure that the rate of HMCLI training is significantly higher than that of the traditional training in the same time. After training, the average rate of success of traditional training is 73.3%, while the rate of interactive training is 92.2%, which basically meets the training requirements.

Figure 13 shows the average coding time of the two groups. According to the figure, the time of HMCLI training is significantly less than that of traditional training, with the most significant difference at the initial stage. After 90 min training, the average coding time of traditional training and HMCLI training are 5.5 s and 4.8 s respectively. It indicates that within same time, the subjects used HMCLI training are more proficient in the control of prosthesis.

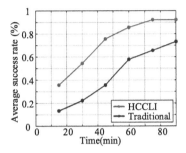 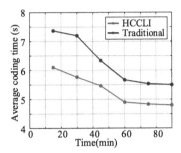

Fig. 12. Average success rate of coding.   **Fig. 13.** Average coding time.

The results also show that the coding success rate is negatively correlated with the complexity of gesture code. For example, in the traditional training, the success rate of cylinder grasp which can be chosen by default is the highest, up to 96.21%. However, the rate of lateral pinch is low. Therefore, optimizing coding algorithm is also an effective way to improve the training effect. It takes a lot of time to evaluate a new algorithm. By using HMCLI training, the time of this link can be significantly shortened. So the algorithm developers can better focus on the design and implementation of the algorithm, so as to speed up the research process of physical prosthetic control.

5   Conclusion

To solve the problems of low efficiency in the training of using EMG prosthesis, we use virtual reality technology to establish an intelligent upper limb prosthesis training system with motor-sensory bidirectional neural channel. Firstly, we analyze the kinematics of the arm hand system to control the motion of the upper limb prosthesis. Then 3 functional units are designed to realize the training function of the system. Virtual reality software subsystem includes automatic demonstration mode and control training mode. The neural control subsystem collects EMG signals to obtain human operation intention to control the virtual prosthesis. The sense feedback subsystem feeds back torque to the user through vibration stimulation. In addition, we establish a HMCLI platform based on the system, and conduct a comparative experiment of training effect. This paper analyzes the function of the system and proves the effectiveness of the system in shortening training time and improving the operation ability of amputees.

Acknowledgments. This work was supported in part by the National Natural Science Foundation of China (No. 91948302 and No. 51875120).

References

1. Dhillon, G.S., Horch, K.W.: Direct neural sense feedback and control of a prosthetic arm. IEEE Trans. Neural Syst. Rehabil. Eng. **13**(4), 468–472 (2015)
2. Perry, B.N., Armiger, R.S., Yu, K.E., et al.: Virtual integration environment as an advanced prosthetic limb training platform. Front. Neurol. **9**, 785 (2018)
3. Wang, C.W., Gao, W., Wang, X.R.: The theory, implementation and application of virtual reality technology. Tsinghua university, Beijing (1996)
4. Armiger, R.S., Tenore, F.V., Bishop, W.E., et al.: A real-time virtual integration environment for neuroprosthetics and rehabilitation. J. Hopkins APL Tech. Dig. **30**(3), 198–206 (2011)
5. Linda, R., Katherine, E., Lieberman, K.S., Charies, K.: Using virtual reality environment to facilitate training with advanced upper-limb prosthesis. J. Rehabil. Res. Dev. **48**(6), 707–718 (2011)
6. Chau, B., Phelan, I., Ta, P., et al.: Immersive virtual reality therapy with myoelectric control for treatment-resistant phantom limb pain: case report. Innov. Clin. Neurosci. **14**(7–8), 3–7 (2017)
7. Ortiz, C.M.: Phantom motor execution facilitated by machine learning and augmented reality as treatment for phantom limb pain: a single group, clinical trial in patients with chronic intractable phantom limb pain. Lancet **388**(10062), 2885 (2016)
8. Johannes, M.S., Bigelow, J.D., Burck, J.M., et al.: An overview of the developmental process for the modular prosthetic limb. J. Hopkins APL Tech. Dig. **30**(3), 207–216 (2011)
9. Hsiu, H., Ulrich, R., Shu, L.: Investigating learners' attitudes toward virtual reality learning environments: based on a constructivist approach. Comput. Educ. **55**, 1171–1182 (2010)
10. Gu, Y., Yang, D., Huang, Q., et al.: Robust EMG pattern recognition in the presence of confounding factors: features, classifiers and adaptive learning. Expert Syst. Appl. **96**, 208–217 (2018)
11. Zeng, B., Fan, S., Jiang, L., Liu, H.: Design and experiment of a modular multisensory hand for prosthetic applications. Ind. Robot: Int. J. **44**(1), 104–113 (2017)
12. Yang, D., Jiang, L., Zhang, X., Liu, H.: Simultaneous estimation of 2-DOF wrist movements based on constrained non-negative matrix factorization and Hadamard product. Elsevier Ltd. (2020)
13. Taylor, C.L., Schwarz, R.J.: The anatomy and mechanics of the human hand. Artif. Limbs **2**, 22–35 (1955)

Real Time Volume Measurement of Logistics Cartons Through 3D Point Cloud Segmentation

Wu Yan[1], Chen Xu[1], Hongmin Wu[1(✉)], Shuai Li[2,3], and Xuefeng Zhou[1]

[1] Guangdong Key Laboratory of Modern Control Technology, Institute of Intelligent Manufacturing, Guangdong Academy of Sciences, Guangzhou, China
`hm.wu@giim.ac.cn`
[2] School of Engineering, Swansea University, Swansea, UK
[3] Foshan Tri-Co Intelligent Robot Technology Co., Ltd., Foshan, China

Abstract. Vision-based measurement has been studied extensively in recent decades for its potential applications in robotics. However, there still remain challenges when we aim at a fast and robust detecting system even in the presence of damaged cartons. This paper implements a non-contact volume measurement system based on point cloud geometric properties of objects for logistics parcels, which recognizes and measures different types of objects or even deformed cartons in various scenarios. Our proposed method is robust to handle the different sizes of objects using the same system. Experimental verification is performed with different cartons on the conveyor belt, results indicate that our proposed system with error percentage in volume is 5.92% with an affordable 3D camera (ASUS Xtion Pro Live).

Keywords: Volume measurement · 3D vision · PointCloud segmentation

1 Introduction

Logistics packaging is playing a significant role in modern manufacturing and warehousing, the combination of weight and volume define the freight costs of packages. Parameters used for size measurement ranged from length to area, perimeter, width, and heights on the purpose of sorting and grading, and species classification. Volume estimation is a common problem in the industry which is often time-consuming, complex, and usually performed by human operators.

This work is supported by the GDAS' Project of Thousand doctors (postdoctors) Introduction (Grant NO. 2020GDASYL-20200103127), Key Areas R&D Program of Guangdong Province (Grant NO. 2020B090925001), Basic and Applied Basic Research Project of Guangzhou City (Grant NO. 202002030237), Key Technology Research Project of Foshan City (Grant NO. 1920001001148), Innovation and Entrepreneurship Team Project of Foshan City (Grant NO. 2018IT100173).

X.-J. Liu et al. (Eds.): ICIRA 2021, LNAI 13015, pp. 324–335, 2021.
https://doi.org/10.1007/978-3-030-89134-3_30

Non-contact, and fast size measurement system of packaging parts is important to them. This reduces production and operation costs by not only decreasing the manual labor that would otherwise be needed for inspection but also reducing the number of defects that could be missed due to human errors. Different methods are used to get volume data based on vision.

Direct Geometric Method: There have been several recent attempts to automatically estimate size or volume using a distance sensor. In [13], the authors use a fixed set-up, depth data are acquired for different views of the object, following with the geometric computation to get the target size. However, there exist some shortcomings in these methods such as slow response time of measurements and great error by dynamic measurement.

2D-3D Correspondence: In order to detect the exact location of the targets in the images, computer vision methods such as corner detect and Hough Transform have been introduced. Volumnect [4] gets the rectangle corner pixel point then use the camera intrinsic parameter to get the 3D information. The others first use some artificial or markers which with before-hand known length as a reference in the same view of targets, then the pixel and physical length ratio under this resolution could be computed. Lastly, by using the conversion relationship between the pixel length and physical ratio, the size of them can then be obtained. However, drawbacks are obvious that the camera must be calibrated beforehand and the edge detection result is easy to be affected by light conditions. For the second method, their works only for the fixed depth-of-field situation, can't measure different types of objects at the same time, large errors will be imported when the target is big and out of the focus, the contour will be a blur and hard to detect.

Bounding Box: Because of the conveyor belt is moving, there is a relative motion between the image capture system, many literature works concerning the dimension measurement using the laser scan or LIDAR [6]. The laser has obvious features and easy for the algorithm to find line or contour shapes. The bounding box is imported to compute a convex hull on the point cloud then use the bounding box length and width as the target shape parameters [1]. However, the convex hull is noise sensitive, the estimated volume will drastically be changed even with a single outlier point. As for deep learning methods, in [12], the authors use deep learning to predict the 3D bounding box size around the target. These methods require expert knowledge, significant human labor, and a complex setup.

Calculus Methods: Literature [3] uses attached marker on a rotary plate to merge multiple views and then using the sum of voxel box as the volume representation. While [5] use the slice of every scanning, the sum of each meta-element's volume under laser curve is taken as the target size.

Deep Learning: More recent deep learning architectures have performed detection and pose estimation on RGB or 3D data. In [9], the authors use CNN method on 3D View synthesis and propose a VolumeNet architecture for point completion, after getting the mesh, the volume is then computed. [10] use deep learning method to detecting edge and object boundaries in natural images. Recently, FS-Net [2] use deep learning method to get target pose. For both or end-to-end methods, the gap between the data and real scenes still needs to be improved, especially for logistic packages with complex and irregular shapes. Besides, these algorithms require a large amount of computation, which will take a lot of time for data collection, network training and affect the user experience in practice.

To achieve real time 3D vision-based measurement solutions or ensuring robustness even in the presence of damaged packages, the proposed systems have to involve two main modules: segmentation and size measurement. In this paper, we propose a fast volume measurement method based on 3D Vision which can get different objects length data in real-time even with the deformed parcels. A plane segmentation and line feature extractor are integrated to generate a precise length and volume estimation. Hereafter, the manuscript is divided into five main parts. The remainder of this paper is organized as follows. Section 2 describes the plane segmentation and line feature extractor of the target. In Sect. 3, the experimental results are shown to verify the performance of the proposed method. Section 4 summarizes the contribution of this paper.

2   Volume Measurement

2.1   Filter Based ROI and Plane Segmentation

Here we use a commercial depth camera (ASUS Xtion Pro Live) to get point cloud, usually, the sensors will save the noise infinite point or the point missing depth value to not a number (NaN) data that need to be removed or converted. The prepossessing section is introduced to handle this problem and then followed with a voxelized grid approach to down-sampling the input point cloud stream for reducing the number of points to accelerate the processing part. Besides, we will perform a filtering along a specified dimension to get ROI area - that is, cut off values that are either inside or outside a given user range (here mainly along the camera optical axis). Followed with the ROI point cloud, to get the package's length, width, and height information, we proposed RANSAC plane model segmentation method to obtain the cloud fitting to the plane model. An advantage of RANSAC is its ability to do a robust estimation of the model parameters, i.e., it can estimate the parameters with a high degree of accuracy even when a significant number of outliers are present in the dataset. To avoid the disadvantage of RANSAC that there is no upper bound on the time it takes to compute these parameters. When the number of iterations computed is limited the solution obtained may not be optimal, and it may not even be one that fits the data in a good way. Here we specify the "distance threshold" in our point cloud data, which determines how close a point must be to the model in order to be considered an inlier to terminate RANSAC iteration. After RANSAC segmentation, the parameters of space plane cloud get (in $ax + by + cz + d = 0$ form) and if we plot in 3D space, it as shown in Fig. 1, the left and right are two different types to shown the processed point cloud. The left one is the segmented plane of the target (using different colors for visualization) and the right one is the contour of these planes. Because of the occlusion of the carton along the optical axis, the back of carton lacks of depth information(the spot of black color in the left image), therefore there are some holes in the biggest plane.

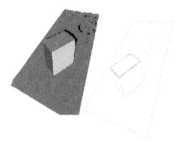

Fig. 1. Plane model segmentation. The left picture is the segmented plane of target (using different colors for visualization) and the right one is the contour of these plane.

When it comes to the plane selection, i.e. determine whether it is an object part or not, it is similar to the semantic segmentation task in RGB or RGB-D scenarios. The study offers some important insights into a fast plane selection method, sort the segmented plane by its area. According to our situation, a piece of prior knowledge is taken into consideration that the supported plane $P_{removal}$ is always the biggest one among the planes set U, and the other remaining three planes which are denoted as P_a, P_b, P_c to construct the main body of the carton T.

$$U = \{P_1, P_2, P_3, P_4\}$$
$$P_{removal} = \{x | x = max(P_1, P_2, P_3, P_4)\} \quad (1)$$
$$P_{removal}{}^c = \{P_a, P_b, P_c\} \in T$$

where the target three planes is the set complement after our filtering process as shown in above Eq. 1.

2.2   Extraction of Intersection Line Using Threshold Method

In this section, we will talk about the extraction of intersection lines, as we know the line in 3D space has different intersection situations and may not intersect with each other at all. Firstly, we talk about the intersection of the line in 3D space. Below we have two spaceplane T_1 and T_2 described as below:

$$\begin{cases} A_1x + B_1y + C_1z + D_1 = 0 \ (T_1, TargetPlane1) \\ A_2x + B_2y + C_2z + D_2 = 0 \ (T_2, TargetPlane2) \end{cases} \quad (2)$$

and the normal vector of them is

$$\vec{n}_1 = \{A_1, B_1, C_1\}$$

and

$$\vec{n}_2 = \{A_2, B_2, C_2\}$$

the direction vector of the intersection line $\vec{n}_3$ is the cross product of the two-plane normal vector.

$$\vec{n}_3 = \vec{n}_1 \times \vec{n}_2 = \{m, n, p\}$$

Then we can use any point (x_0, y_0, z_0) on the line combined with direction vector to get the parameter of space line which is our final target. The mathematical parameter of the line is denoted as Eq. 3. The m, n, p is the direction vector parameters of line.

$$\frac{(x - x_0)}{m} = \frac{(y - y_0)}{n} = \frac{(z - z_0)}{p} \tag{3}$$

Secondly, there is an unavoidable problem is that the point cloud in real-time is not steady all the time, maybe there is a corner point this time but vanished in the next frame. In order to get the length of the target line, we truly need to know which points in the point cloud belong to this line so there is a threshold between infinite line in space and the captured point cloud to get the steady points inliers which lie on the line model. Here, a threshold Γ is imported. If the distance from the point to the line is less than this predefined threshold (for our instance, $\Gamma = 8$ mm), the point cloud data belonging to this spatial line will be extracted and the number of points varies when the threshold is different which is shown in Fig. 2. The image shows the different results of threshold vary from 3 mm to 10 mm, the thickness of point mask with RGB on spaceline is different. As shown in Fig. 3 box-plot, here we take the length measurement data as an example, the ground truth is highlighted in the green dash line (0.155 m) and when the threshold getting bigger, the average length of the box is getting bigger too, but as it using $\Gamma = 10$ millimeter, the measured length exceeds the ground-truth and a little thick in the point cloud as shown in Fig. 2. So here we use $\Gamma = 8$ mm.

Threshold = 3mm   Threshold = 6mm   Threshold = 8mm   Threshold = 10mm

Fig. 2. A proposed extraction of intersection line using different threshold.

In this section, the intersection line between the three planes is obtained (every line L_1, L_2, L_3 is consist of a cluster of points $(p_{10}, p_{12}, \ldots) \in L_1\_point$) and then the length of each line will be calculated using the 3D information of point in the point cloud.

$$\begin{aligned}
L_1\_point &= \{p_{10}, p_{12}, p_{13}, p_{14}, \ldots\} \\
L_2\_point &= \{p_{20}, p_{21}, p_{22}, p_{23}, \ldots\} \\
L_3\_point &= \{p_{30}, p_{31}, p_{32}, p_{33}, \ldots\}
\end{aligned} \tag{4}$$

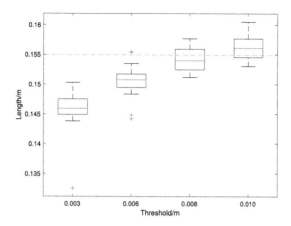

Fig. 3. The comparison of calculated length under different thresholds.

$$L_1\_point = \{p \mid (p \text{ to } L_1) \leq \Gamma, p \in (T_1 \cup T_2)\} \tag{5}$$

L_1_point is the set of points whose distance to the line equation L_1 less than a predefined threshold Γ, and they belong to the union of plane T_1 and T_2.

2.3 Length Computation

Followed with the above section, here we will talk about the length computation of the output point cloud line cluster. A length computation method was proposed by calculating all the distances between points in these lines, the maximum is the target length. Here suppose we have 2 two points in $L1$, denoted as p_{10} and p_{11}, and the distance d between them is as described as Eq. 6

$$
\begin{aligned}
p_{10} &= (x_0, y_0, z_0) \\
p_{12} &= (x_1, y_1, z_1) \\
d &= \sqrt{(x_0 - x_1)^2 + (y_0 - y_1)^2 + (z_0 - z_1)^2} \\
L_{1\_len} &= \{x \mid x = max(d_1, d_2, d_3, \ldots)\}
\end{aligned}
\tag{6}
$$

Here we iterate the distance of the points in L_1, and find the max of them as the final result, the same operation on L_2 and L_3.

2.4 Volume Measurement of Deformed Cartons

Deformed cartons are a common condition that has a considerable impact on volume measurement and quality assurance. In this section, we will expand our aforementioned method for addressing the problem of deformation measurement. The determination of the carton's size is technically challenging. It is hard to get the size or scale of random deformed cartons, by using the point cloud segmentation and bounding box strategy, the maximum size of a carton's bounding box could be obtained when searching in the target point cloud.

As for the difference of deformation, it is hard to get a universal solution for the RGB-D camera to get a neatly segmented point cloud of our target, so we have test two different strategies to handle this problem. When the carton is partially deformed and have a strong plane or line feature, we could use this information to extract what we want, as shown in Fig. 4, here we get the segmented plane and size of the target by performing a bounding box on each of them. The bounding box plays a critical role in the maintenance of the measurement task under the situation that the carton has severe deformation. Firstly, the covariance matrix of the point cloud is calculated and its eigenvalues and vectors are computed (the major eigenvector represents X-axis and the minor vector represents Z-axis). In the next step, the major eigenvector is rotated On each iteration. Rotation order is always the same and performed around the other eigenvectors, this provides the invariance to the rotation of the point cloud. Henceforth, we will refer to this rotated major vector as the current axis and the bounding box is along this axis which is as shown in Fig. 5. The first column is the RGB image of the scene, the second and third rows have shown the segmented target carton and bounding box using our methods respectively.

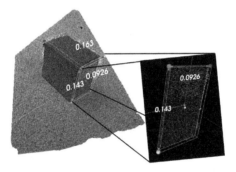

Fig. 4. Using bounding box to get target's size.

Fig. 5. Using bounding box to get target's size. The left picture is the scene of target and the right one is the result of proposed bounding box measurement.

3   Experimental Verification

The RGB-D point cloud of logistics carton is obtained by ASUS Xtion Pro Live mounted outside of conveyor-belt as shown in Fig. 6, and the camera to gather most reliable depth data at distances of 0.5–1.7 m with the suggestion in [7]. The system is on a laptop with Ubuntu 16.04 and ROS kinetic, which has a 12G RAM and Intel Core i5-4200H CPU (2.8 GHz). The software is based on the PCL library [11]. Because we want to measure the length, width, and height of the logistics cartons, suppose that in every frame of the captured point cloud, all three planes of the target carton cloud be got.

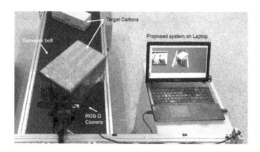

Fig. 6. A proposed extraction of intersection line using different threshold

The 3D camera is mounted on the conveyor belt and looks down for dynamic point cloud recording and size measurement. Because of the inner active lightning system of the 3D camera, there is no need for specific light conditions to work appropriately. The system consists of four main phases: 1. Point cloud acquisition; 2. Region of interest (ROI) and plane segmentation; 3. The extraction of intersection line; 4. Length computation. Usually, the input point cloud data is tremendous and the noise is inevitable, in the ROI segmentation part, the data followed with the voxel filter and pass-through filer which will down-sampling the point cloud to reduce the number of points and exclude noise data (NaN or infinite point) to accelerate process phase. As for the plane segmentation part, the Random sample consensus (RANSAC) plane extraction method is introduced which finds all the points within a point cloud that support a plane model (in $ax + by + cz + d = 0$ form). 3D camera sensor captures images and generates point clouds for the objects. A voting-scheme allows the pose estimation system to estimate the type of the different objects in the bin and their 6-DoF poses. The target selection system selects the best target to pick up from all of the recognized objects and determines the pose that is most suitable to allow the robot gripper to pick up the target.

3.1   Precision and Efficiency

The basic result of the method is evaluated by experiments on several typical carton samples. Several error distribution experiments with different algorithm parameters are set to verify the validity and stability of our method. In this section, 6 different types of cartons were tested in our system which is shown in Fig. 7. Carton E and Carton F are the smallest and biggest ones in our experiment. The first row is the RGB picture of cartons, the second row is the segmented plane (denoted with a different color) and the final extracted line between them (denoted with Red, Green, and Blue line for visual purpose). As for the last row, we use the extracted line to compute the length of our cartons' size which is shown in RGB-D image.

Table 1. The results of volume measurement

Item name description	Plane points	Line points	Length (mm)		Width (mm)		Height (mm)		Times (ms)
			GT	Estimated (mean ± std)	GT	Estimated (mean ± std)	GT	Estimated (mean ± std)	
A	15544	724	200.5	195.08 ± 3.08	90.2	91.38 ± 1.98	225.2	223.16 ± 1.27	96
B	12905	384	150.4	145.00 ± 1.48	150.1	146.97 ± 1.42	150.4	141.34 ± 6.24	87
C	17342	1073	350.4	342.93 ± 4.18	120.5	120.80 ± 0.94	110.3	103.01 ± 3.21	101
D	17743	380	180.6	180.63 ± 4.10	190.4	187.12 ± 1.80	95.4	90.78 ± 4.8	75
E (Smallest carton)	5909	368	100.1	100.08 ± 3.09	95.6	92.49 ± 3.18	80.3	75.01 ± 7.56	39
F (Biggest carton)	43699	1328	390.5	383.84 ± 2.1	260.2	253.40 ± 4.84	225.4	220.36 ± 6.6	216

As for the measurement accuracy, in general, the higher the frame rate of the RGB-D camera, and the lower speed of the conveyor, the faster the update rate and greater density of the point cloud which is more conductive to reduce the measurement error. However, cameras with higher frame rates are expansive, while lower conveyor speed will extend the logistics transportation time. Considering this, we choose the RGB-D camera with 15 fps and set the speed of the conveyor as 12 cm/s. We have tested on 6 different types of logistics cartons every 50 times respectively and use our methods to get the size parameters. As shown in the Table 1, the size measurement max error data we get from the table vary from 5 mm to 16 mm using the affordable 3D camera, this value is computed using ground truth minus min estimated value in table. Besides, the consuming time value differs from 96ms to 216 ms with the plane points from 5909 to 43699, the plane size has a significant impact on the time. In Fig. 8, the length, width, and height typical error vary from 2.98–4.87%, and the maximum error is 6.36%. While as the Fig. 9 shows, the volume of our test samples is mainly under 0.005 m^3 cartons, the smallest and the biggest volumes vary from 0.00076 m^3 to 0.0228 m^3, and the maximum error in volume is 5.92%.

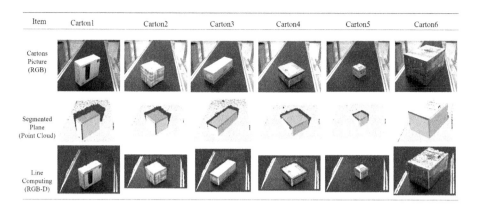

Fig. 7. Different types of carton to be measured.

4 Discussions and Conclusion

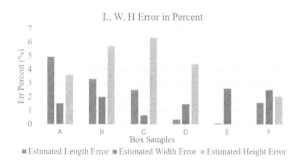

Fig. 8. Length, width, height error compared with the ground truth

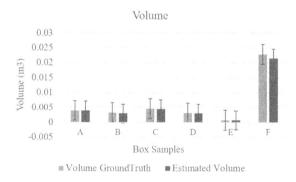

Fig. 9. Estimated volume compared with the ground truth

As yet, volumes of similar objects (parcels, etc.) are still measured manually with a ruler in many places. We expect an error percentage for manual measurements between 1.6–7.9% [3], which is in a similar range as the error of the proposed method. For a commercial volume measurement system, Intel has released their compact active stereo camera RealSense series, and a prototype measurement system integrated into the tablet for hand-hold use in 2017 [8]. SICK has released several track and trace systems VMS420/520 with Line scan laser on the conveyor belt which has a length error ±5 mm, corresponding to an error percentage for the shoe-box of 8%. Hence, in a small warehouse scenario, consumer depth cameras as the Kinect or Xtion could be used to measure objects with similar performance. The precision of the method could be improved by using more views, improving the merging procedure itself, or by altering the sensor baseline and depth of field. So far, we only measured the volumes of objects having fairly cubic shapes. In the future, we aim to apply the proposed procedure to objects with more complex or irregular shapes.

Given the obtained results, it can be stated that a fast and robust system has been designed, which is able to estimate the volume of the logistics cartons on a conveyor belt even with the deformed targets. By using a point cloud segmentation algorithm, our method could estimate the size and volume occupation for multiple objects fast and accurately. Within the speed range of 12 cm/s, and about 1.5 m installation distance, we can achieve accuracy within 5–16 using a consumer RGB-D camera. But there is room to improve the quality of the predicted size information in clustered scenes, as well as the other deformed parts. This will be the topic of our future research.

References

1. Al Muallim, M.T., Küçük, H., Yılmaz, F., Kahraman, M.: Development of a dimensions measurement system based on depth camera for logistic applications. In: Eleventh International Conference on Machine Vision (ICMV 2018), vol. 11041, p. 110410Z. International Society for Optics and Photonics (2019)
2. Chen, W., Jia, X., Chang, H.J., Duan, J., Shen, L., Leonardis, A.: FS-net: fast shape-based network for category-level 6d object pose estimation with decoupled rotation mechanism. arXiv preprint arXiv:2103.07054 (2021)
3. Dellen, B., Rojas Jofre, I.A.: Volume measurement with a consumer depth camera based on structured infrared light. In: Proceedings of the 16th Catalan Conference on Artificial Intelligence, Poster Session, pp. 1–10 (2013)
4. Ferreira, B.Q., Griné, M., Gameiro, D., Costeira, J.P., Santos, B.S.: VOLUMNECT: measuring volumes with kinect. In: Three-Dimensional Image Processing, Measurement (3DIPM), and Applications 2014, vol. 9013, p. 901304. International Society for Optics and Photonics (2014)
5. Fojtík, D.: Measurement of the volume of material on the conveyor belt measuring of the volume of wood chips during transport on the conveyor belt using a laser scanning. In: Proceedings of the 2014 15th International Carpathian Control Conference (ICCC), pp. 121–124. IEEE (2014)
6. Gao, Q., Yin, D., Luo, Q., Liu, J.: Minimum elastic bounding box algorithm for dimension detection of 3D objects: a case of airline baggage measurement. IET Image Proc. **12**(8), 1313–1321 (2018)

7. Halmetschlager-Funek, G., Suchi, M., Kampel, M., Vincze, M.: An empirical evaluation of ten depth cameras: bias, precision, lateral noise, different lighting conditions and materials, and multiple sensor setups in indoor environments. IEEE Robot. Autom. Mag. **26**(1), 67–77 (2018)

8. Keselman, L., Iselin Woodfill, J., Grunnet-Jepsen, A., Bhowmik, A.: Intel realsense stereoscopic depth cameras. In: Proceedings of the IEEE Conference on Computer Vision and Pattern Recognition Workshops, pp. 1–10 (2017)

9. Lo, F.P.W., Sun, Y., Qiu, J., Lo, B.P.: Point2volume: a vision-based dietary assessment approach using view synthesis. IEEE Trans. Industr. Inf. **16**(1), 577–586 (2019)

10. Peng, T., Zhang, Z., Song, Y., Chen, F., Zeng, D.: Portable system for box volume measurement based on line-structured light vision and deep learning. Sensors **19**(18), 3921 (2019)

11. Rusu, R.B., Cousins, S.: 3D is here: point cloud library (PCL). In: 2011 IEEE International Conference on Robotics and Automation, pp. 1–4. IEEE (2011)

12. Yang, B., et al.: Learning object bounding boxes for 3D instance segmentation on point clouds. In: NeurIPS, pp. 6737–6746 (2019)

13. Zewei, X., Jieru, P., Xianqiao, C.: A method for vehicle three-dimensional size measurement based on laser ranging. In: 2015 International Conference on Transportation Information and Safety (ICTIS), pp. 34–37. IEEE (2015)

Study on High-Efficient Derusting Method for Vision-Based Derusting Robot

Shanwei Liao[1,2(✉)], Haitao Fang[1,2], and Kai He[1,2,3,4]

[1] Shenzhen Institute of Advanced Technology, Chinese Academy of Sciences, Shenzhen, Guangdong, China
sw.liao@siat.ac.cn
[2] Shenzhen Key Laboratory of Precision Engineering, Shenzhen, Guangdong, China
[3] Guangdong-Hong Kong-Macao Joint Laboratory of Human-Machine Intelligence-Synergy Systems, Shenzhen Institute of Advanced Technology, Chinese Academy of Sciences, Shenzhen, Guangdong, China
[4] Shenzhen Institute of Artificial Intelligence and Robotics for Society, Shenzhen, China

Abstract. In this paper, a new type of high-efficient derusting method for wall-climbing-cleaning robot is proposed in order to surmount the shortcomings of current wall-climbing-cleaning robots. It takes advantage of Open Source Computer Vision Library (OpenCV) to establish a detection system, and uses a development framework called QT to do the experimental analysis. The experimental results show that the system can complete real-time image recognition in the working environment of the wall-climbing cleaning robot, which makes the foundation for the intelligent trajectory planning of the wall-climbing-cleaning robot.

Keywords: Wall-climbing robot · Image processing · Real-time control

1 Introduction

Firstly, as shown in Fig. 1, the manual remote control method currently used by the wall-climbing-cleaning robot [1], so there are subjective influences of manual operation, and its precision is low and reliability is weak [2]. Secondly, the large ships of several hundred thousand tons have exceeded the scope of human visual observation. As a kind of high-altitude operation, the wall-climbing-cleaning robot requires workers to use high-altitude vehicles to observe the rust removal [3], which is very troublesome, costly and inefficient. In many cases, human vision is increasingly unable to meet the requirements of macro-distance visual range, objective high precision, and long-term fatigue-free [4].

In this case, because the dock is not suitable for installing UWB base stations, and the surface of the hull is prone to slippage and is disturbed by water stains, the effects of the meter counter and laser rangefinder are not satisfactory. Therefore, it is proposed to replace the current manual operation through the real-time image processing of the camera, which can improve the efficiency of the robot and reduce errors and risks [5]. By developing the vision system of the wall-climbing cleaning robot, the above-mentioned

X.-J. Liu et al. (Eds.): ICIRA 2021, LNAI 13015, pp. 336–344, 2021.
https://doi.org/10.1007/978-3-030-89134-3_31

Fig. 1. Shortcomings of manual remote wall-climbing-cleaning robot.

problems can be easily solved, and the vision system of the wall-climbing cleaning robot with high degree of automation, convenient control and high efficiency can be realized [6].The automatic detection effect is stable and reliable, it can stop work for 24 h, the information integration is also very convenient, and the visibility is good [7].

2   Data Preparation and Analysis

2.1   Data Collection

As shown in Fig. 2, this is some pictures of cleaning walls collected in actual working conditions. It can be seen that the image of the wall surface before cleaning is complicated and difficult to define. The color and texture of the image after cleaning on the wall are also different. But there are obvious differences before and after cleaning. Because the wall image will be different every time the cleaning work is done. Therefore, a fixed image classification method cannot be used alone to perform image segmentation on an image.

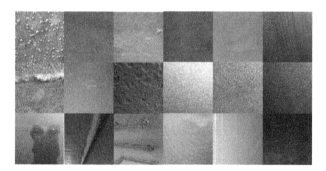

Fig. 2. Collection of rusty paint surface and image after cleaning.

In the previous experiment [8], a clustering color segmentation method was proposed for image segmentation, and the effect is shown in Fig. 3. The partitioning effect of the wall before cleaning may not be good due to factors such as paint peeling and moss. However, the segmentation effect of the wall surface after cleaning is good.

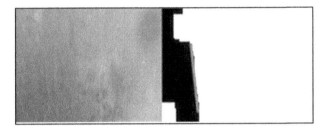

Fig. 3. Image segmentation effect

2.2 The Evaluation of Image Contains Information

As shown in Fig. 4, the image information and the pose relationship of the robot satisfy the rigid body relationship. The schematic diagram of the cleaning path is shown in Fig. 5. Two important parameters can be derived from the image information: one is the current direction of the robot relative to the cleaning boundary, that is, the deflection angle of the cleaning structure. The second is the current position of the robot relative to the cleaning boundary, that is, the deflection distance of the cleaning structure.

Fig. 4. Schematic diagram of camera field of view.

Fig. 5. Schematic diagram of cleaning path.

3 Numerical Analysis and Post-processing

As shown in Fig. 6, the camera is simplified to a triangular symbol, and the light source is simplified to a rectangular symbol. The robot moves in a zigzag pattern. Therefore, the camera in the forward direction is used as the information to read the offset angle and offset distance, and the rear camera is used as an auxiliary verification.

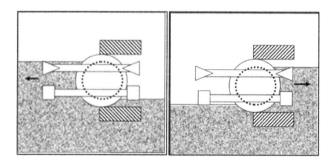

Fig. 6. Schematic diagram of camera

As shown in Fig. 7.1, during normal operation, the camera in the forward direction can adjust its current position according to the last cleaning boundary, so as to achieve the effect of efficient cleaning. Set in the forward direction, the upper left corner is the origin, and the picture is divided into 128 pixels in the horizontal direction and 96 pixels in the vertical direction. Since the camera's field of view width is 0.4 m, the static accuracy is 3 mm.

As shown in Fig. 7.2, there is a rigid relationship between the robot and the visual field. The dotted line in the visual field represents the expected cleaning path, and the solid line represents the current cleaning boundary. Through coordinate conversion, the distance and angle difference between the cleaning plate and the cleaning boundary can be obtained. Therefore, as long as the solid line information in the field of view is obtained, the robot can be controlled to achieve efficient cleaning. Through the Hough line transformation method of the binary graph, or the simple traversal counting method of the binary graph, the two endpoints of the boundary line segment or the center of gravity coordinates of the black block can be obtained. At this time, the X-axis difference of the coordinate value can be approximately regarded as the offset distance of the robot. The difference of the Y-axis can be approximately regarded as the offset angle of the robot.

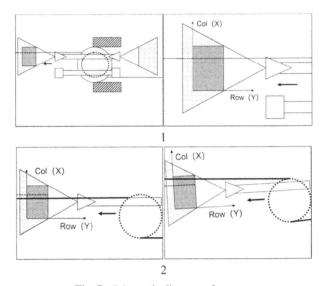

Fig. 7. Schematic diagram of camera.

As shown in Fig. 8, Fig. 8.1 is the acquired original image information. Figure 8.2 is the region of interest after affine transformation and preprocessing of the original image. The rectangular top view is obtained after the aforementioned image segmentation, as shown in Fig. 8.3. So far, the extraction of image information is completed [9].

Fig. 8. Image preprocessing.

It can be seen that because of the uncertainty of the robot's working environment and whether there is interference on the wall after derusting, the processed image is not perfect. Although the image still contains the robot's posture information, there are still various interferences. Therefore, some abnormal detection method settings are needed to detect whether the image segmentation is correct and confirm where the segmentation line is located [10].

A detection method based on prior knowledge is adopted here, that is, according to the installation position of the camera and the path characteristics of the robot cleaning, the perfect image should have a center of gravity value of 48 on the y-axis, and a full range within twice the center of gravity on the x-axis. They are black pixels, and all white pixels outside the double size. The center of gravity value of the x-axis is 18 at this time, then calculate the number of white points less than 36 and the number of black points greater than 36 on the x-axis to obtain the noise value. If the total number of noise values is less than the set value, whether the current image is reliable, otherwise, a second verification is required based on the line segment obtained by the Hough line change. If it still cannot be verified, the boundary detection is performed.

The principle of reaching the boundary detection is that the value of the y axis has changed. As shown in Fig. 9. At this time, the number of black points under $y < 20$ is calculated, and the boundary is confirmed if it is less than or exceeding the expected value, and the boundary reached signal is sent [11].

If the noise value is greater than a certain value, and the image cannot achieve the feature of reaching the boundary, the current image is discarded and a new frame of image is taken until the recognition is completed again, or a long-term unrecognition warning is triggered.

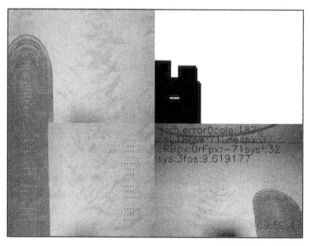

Fig. 9. Features of reaching the boundary image.

The visualization of image information is shown in Fig. 10. The lower left picture is the original picture, showing the ROI area. The upper right picture is the image after binarization, in which the red line segment represents the currently recognized path, and the green line segment represents the reference path. The pink line segment and the blue line segment form an offset curve, which represents the output value of the visual recognition system during this period. When the blue value is higher, it means the robot is shifted to the right.

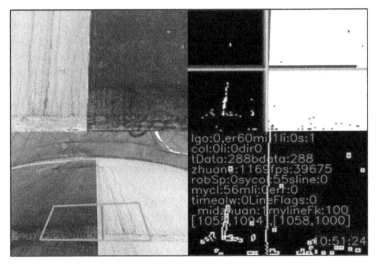

Fig. 10. Visualization of image processing results.

4   Experimental Results and Discussion

Suppose that when the cleaning robot is cleaning, the number of overlapping pixels between the cleaning plate and the cleaning boundary is X, where a negative number represents no overlap, which is a state that is not allowed to occur. When this happens, it means that the robot cannot continue to perform effective cleaning operations and needs to go back a distance and adjust its posture to clean again.

The method to test whether the robot can clean efficiently is to simulate the method of manually operating the robot to clean the wall, and use the vision system to guide the robot to complete the entire cleaning work. Through many cleaning experiments with different initializations and different wall conditions. After reaching the boundary, the robot uses a fixed action with errors to replace the cleaning road, and adjusts the pose in real time during the subsequent cleaning process to determine the amount of overlap. As shown in Fig. 11. In the last cleaning process, the overlap is too large after changing lanes, and the robot gradually adjusts back to the original cleaning overlap.

Through the above experiments, it can be found that although the robot has completed the posture adjustment of high-efficient cleaning, the cleaning trajectory has also

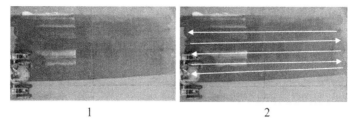

Fig. 11. Schematic diagram of robot motion path.

changed. It can be seen that there will be accumulated errors after cleaning a section of the path, which will cause the path to change. As shown in Fig. 12. But all in all, the robot does not need to use humans to judge the degree of overlap and whether it reaches the boundary and needs to change lanes. Realize the intelligent cleaning function.

Fig. 12. Effect picture of robot cleaning operation on site.

5   Conclusion

By judging and processing the feature values extracted from the preprocessed image, the wheeled cleaning robot can fit the cleaning boundary to the greatest extent, and the offset prompt as shown in the figure basically coincides with the actual path. The horizontal error does not exceed 3 mm, and the response time is 100 ms, so as to complete the cleaning work with the greatest efficiency.

It can be seen that the region of interest in this method is too small, and the relative coordinate system is established. This causes the robot to perform high-efficient cleaning, but without an absolute coordinate system, there will be accumulated errors after cleaning a section of the path, which causes the path to change to an arc shape. Multi-sensor fusion can be added in the future, UWB or tilt sensor can be added for horizontal direction verification and attitude correction.

Acknowledgment. This paper is partially supported by Science and Technology Planning Project of Guangdong Province (2017B090914004), CAS-HK Joint Laboratory of Precision Engineering, and NSFC-Shenzhen Robot Basic Research Center project (U1713224).

References

1. Hu, S., Peng, R., Kai, H., Li, J., Wei, Z.: Structural design and magnetic force analysis of a new crawler-type permanent magnetic adsorption wall—climbing. In: IEEE International Conference on Information & Automation (2017)
2. Guan, X., Huang, J., Tang, T.: Robot vision application on embedded vision implementation with digital signal processor. Int. J. Adv. Robot. Syst. **17**(1) (2020)
3. Xie, M., Liu, J., Luo, X.: The innovation design of the magnetic adsorption climbing-wall flaw detection robot. In: Control & Decision Conference (2015)
4. Guo, Y., Sun, F.-C.: Vision-based lawn boundary recognition for mowing robot. In: 2016 International Conference on Computer Engineering and Information Systems (2016)
5. Sahu, U.K., Patra, D., Subudhi, B.: Vision-based tip position tracking control of two-link flexible manipulator. IET Cyber-Syst. Robot. **2**(2), 53–66 (2020)
6. Zhang, L., et al.: A cross structured light sensor for weld line detection on wall-climbing robot (2013)
7. Duan, T., Kinsner, W.: A rough-fuzzy perception-based computing for a vision-based wall-following robot. In: 2014 IEEE 13th International Conference on Cognitive Informatics & Cognitive Computing (ICCI*CC) (2014)
8. Liao, S., et al.: A study on vision-based rust boundary recognition for derusting robot. In: Proceedings of 2019 International Conference on Computer Science, Communications and Multimedia Engineering (2019)
9. OPENCV Homepage. https://opencv.org/. Accessed 25 Sept 2020
10. Sun, L.: A real-time collision-free path planning of a rust removal robot using an improved neural network. J. Shanghai Jiaotong Univ. (Sci.) **22**(5), 633–640 (2017)
11. QT Homepage. https://www.qt.io/. Accessed 21 Apr 2021

An MRF-Based Intention Recognition Framework for WMRA with Selected Objects as Contextual Clues

Yan Liu, Yufeng Yao, Haoqi Peng, and Yaxin Liu$^{(\boxtimes)}$

Industrial Research Institute of Robotics and Intelligent Equipment, Harbin Institute of
Technology (Weihai), Shandong 264209, China
liuyaxin@hit.edu.cn

Abstract. To mitigate the physical burden of disabled people, we propose an approach that a robot could perceive the implied action intentions of disabled people
by their selected objects. This article presents a framework for recognizing and
learning human intentions based on selected household objects and interaction history. First, the intention network is modeled based on Markov random field (MRF)
to connect the selected objects and daily activities. Second, the q-learning algorithm is added to provide the intention network with the function of adapting to the
user's intention preference. Then, we build the wheelchair-mounted robotic arms
(WMRA) with a green laser pointer as human-robot interaction (HRI). Finally, we
demonstrate the feasibility of the intention recognition framework by evaluating a
scene comprised of objects from 11 categories, along with 7 possible actions, 36
single-object intentions, and 24 multiple-object intentions. We achieve approximately 70% reduction in fewer sessions than the Recursive Bayesian Incremental
Learning and achieve approximately 87.5% and 86.2% reduction in interactions
overall on recognizing multiple-object intention, respectively.

Keywords: Markov random field · Wheel mounted robotic arms · Intention
recognition · Human-robot interaction

1 Introduction

The WMRA [1, 2] could enhance the manipulation functions of disabled people and
relieve the stress on social care. Due to limited physical ability of disabled people,
WMRA needs to effectively perceive disabled people's intentions and autonomously
complete intents-related ADL. Existing works commonly use people's posture as contextual information to infer people's intentions [2–5]. Ashesh Jain et al. [6] proposed a
structural-RNN on spatiotemporal graphs to recognize human intentions by analyzing
human movement posture records. Liu et al. [7] proposed a model that combines ST-
GCN-LSTM and YOLO to recognize human intentions based on the sequence flow of
human joint changes and hand-held objects. Steffen Muller et al. [8] proposed a modular
detection and tracking system to recognize patient intention by modeling the position
and additional properties of persons in the surroundings of a mobile robot. Je-Min Kim

© Springer Nature Switzerland AG 2021
X.-J. Liu et al. (Eds.): ICIRA 2021, LNAI 13015, pp. 345–356, 2021.
https://doi.org/10.1007/978-3-030-89134-3_32

et al. [9] proposed an approach that combines intention ontology and event calculus to recognize human's daily living patterns by their actions and nearby objects as a contextual clue. Although the above methods have higher accuracy of intention recognition, robots may impose additional physical burdens on disabled people. Robots should assist the disabled without accidentally harming their bodies [10]. To reduce the physical burden on disabled people, Kester Duncan et al. [11] proposed an object-action intention network to model household objects and actions to enhance the understanding of the scene. However, their framework only considered the intention recognition of a single object, which was not considering the relationship among objects and actions. To recognize the implied action intention of multiple objects and make objects as contextual information, this paper proposes a framework that combines Markov random field [12, 13] and Q-learning algorithm [14, 15] with selected objects as a contextual clue to model the object-action intention network. Disabled people can use a green laser pointer [16] to select multiple objects that will be executed. We evaluate our intention recognition framework on the WMRA at the end.

2   Object-Action Intention Network

To infer disabled people's intention based on the selected objects in the RGB picture is a challenge. Visual affordance [17] provides a concept to solve this problem, which aims to further understand the implied functions information of objects from images. Before constructing the object-action intention network, we extract people ADL from the International Classification of Functioning, Disability, and Health (ICF) [18]. ICF divided ADL into basic human self-care activities and advanced household tasks. Finally, the objects and actions are trained through MRF, and the generated visual object-action intention network is shown in Fig. 1.

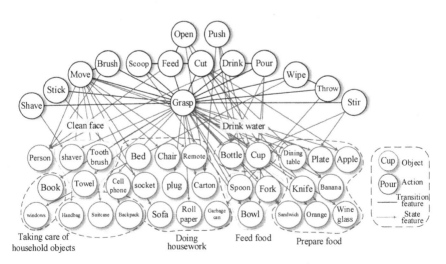

Fig. 1. Object-action intention network

In Fig. 1, the objects of each task are wired through actions to represent that the contextual relationship has existed among them. The red object such as "Spoon", the spoon can stir the liquid in the bottle or cup in "Drink water" and can scoop food in "Feed food". The black circles are the implied operation mapping of each object. One object may contain multiple implied operation mapping due to the object's affordance. It is worth mentioning that the establishment of the training set are described in a sequential way, such as "Grasp-Cup-Drink-People" instead of "people drink water from the grasped cup."

The intention recognition is based on the highest-probability $P(action|object)$, which is established in the form of an exponential function:

$$P(a|o) = \frac{1}{Z(x)} exp\left(\sum_{i,k} \lambda_k t_k(a_{i-1}, a_i, o, i) + \sum_{i,l} \mu_l s_l(a_i, o, i)\right) \qquad (1)$$

Where $P(action|object)$ is represented by $P(a|o)$, and:

$$Z(o) = \sum_a exp\left(\sum_{i,k} \lambda_k t_k(a_{i-1}, a_i, o, i) + \sum_{i,l} \mu_l s_l(a_i, o, i)\right) \qquad (2)$$

The $t_k(a_{i-1}, a_i, o, i)$ represents the transition feature function defined on edge, which depends on the current and previous position; $s_l(a_i, o, i)$ represents the state feature function defined on the node, which depends on the current position; λ_k and μ_l are the weight parameter of the object-action intention network. i represents the sequence number of the object's node. Then we simplify Z and make:

$$f_k(a_{i-1}, a_i, o, i) = \begin{cases} t_k(a_{i-1}, a_i, o, i), & k = 1, 2, ..., K_1 \\ s_l(a_i, o, i), & k = K_1 + l; \ l = 1, 2, ..., K_2 \end{cases} \qquad (3)$$

$$w_k = \begin{cases} \lambda_k, & k = 1, 2, ..., K_1 \\ \mu_l, & k = K_1 + l; l = 1, 2, ..., K_2 \end{cases} \qquad (4)$$

Then (1) and (2) can be expressed as:

$$P(a|o) = \frac{1}{Z(o)} exp \sum_{k=1}^{K} w_k f_k(a, o) \qquad (5)$$

$$Z(o) = \sum_a exp \sum_{k=1}^{K} w_k f_k(a, o) \qquad (6)$$

Next, constructing the loss function $L(w)$ of the probabilistic inference model and solve w_k:

$$L(w) = log \prod_{o, a} P_w(a|o)^{\tilde{P}(o,a)} \qquad (7)$$

Where $\tilde{P}(o, a)$ is experience distribution, and the problem of solving the actual intention network is equivalent to:

$$w_k^* = arg \min_{w_k} L(w) = arg \min_{w_k} \left(\sum_{j=1}^{N} \left(logZ_w(o_j) - \sum_{k=1}^{K} w_k f_k(a_j, o_j) \right) \right) \quad (8)$$

Then, gradient function and gradient update formula as follows:

$$g(w^t) = \sum_{j=1}^{N} \left(P_{w^t}(a_j|o_j) - 1 \right) F(a_j, o_j) \quad (9)$$

$$w^{t+1} = w^t - \eta g(w^t) \quad (10)$$

Where η is learning rate and $F(a_j, o_j) = [f_1(a_j, o_j), f_2(a_j, o_j), ..., f_K(a_j, o_j)]^T$.

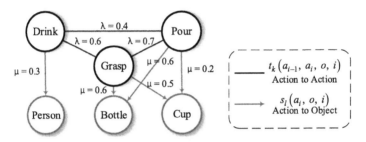

Fig. 2. Example of a small object-action intention network

Figure 2 is an example of a probabilistic inference model (object-action intention network). Each edge of the object-action intention network is given a weight value after the training of the MRF algorithm, where μ.

After solving the optimal w, the mapping relationship of the object-action intention network is established. Then, the Viterbi algorithm will solve the implied action sequence with the highest probability according to the selected visible objects by a user.

$$a^* = arg \max_a w^T F(a, o) \quad (11)$$

Where a^* is the highest-probability implied action intention (hidden sequence).

The object-action intention network has been established, and users can input the "object" (visible sequence) by a laser pointer. Then the intention network will output the implied highest-probability action intention through the Viterbi algorithm. This action intention is identified as the ADL that disabled people want to perform. The Viterbi algorithm will also store lower-probability action intentions because the disabled people may have other action intentions for the same object.

3 Strategies for Learning People Preferences

As above, the object-action intention network can intuitively reflect the connection among objects and actions intention and infer the current highest-probability action intention, but the preset intention network will not correctly recognize intentions when user preferences change. With the gradual use of the intention network by disabled people, the network should gradually grow to adapt to the users' intentions change and preferences. Q-learning algorithm can achieve this goal.

The Q learning algorithm belongs to the reinforcement learning algorithm and is based on the value iteration algorithm in the Markov decision process. It consists of a four-element tuple $< S, A, T, R >$, which are state, action, transfer function, and reward. The reward iterated through the Bellman equation.

To apply Q-Learning to our framework. First, we take the WMRA as the agent and use the "action intention" as the "state". The transition feature function of intention network corresponds to the transition function $T(s_1, a_1)$. If we select two objects continuously, the corresponding state is $T((s_1, a_1), (s_2, a_2))$. The Q-learning algorithm will output the reward score according to whether the action is the optimal strategy (people intention). Finally, we take the Bellman equation to iterate the Q value because the Bellman equation will consider the influence of historical decisions.

$$Q^*(s, a) = \sum_{s'} T(s, a, s') \left(R(s, a, s') + \gamma \max_{a'} Q^*(s', a') \right) \qquad (12)$$

Where γ is the discount coefficient and discounts the rewards received by the agent in the future. When $\gamma = 1$, there is no discount. When $\gamma < 1$, the subsequent discount is greater over time:

$$r_t = \gamma r_{t+1} + \gamma^2 r_{t+2} + \gamma^3 r_{t+3} \cdots \qquad (13)$$

In our system, the iteration of Bellman's formula won't find the optimal strategy like common reinforcement learning algorithms because people will always have new ideas. We place the Bellman equation in the intention recognition framework in our way and as follows:

$$q(s, a) = r(s, a) + \gamma q'(s, a) \qquad (14)$$

Where $q'(s, a)$ represents the original value of action intention a for the state s. $r(s, a)$ represents the reward and punishment for $q'(s, a)$. $r(s, a)$ will equal "1" or "0" when the action was agreed or refused. $q(s, a)$ represents the new value after plus the reward. The new value will be used to improve the object-action intention networks, and it will gradually adapt to the user's preference.

As shown in Fig. 3, the signal of reward or punishment for Intent Network will be published by HRI (a green laser pointer). For example, the Viterbi algorithm outputs the highest-probability selection {grasp, scoop} after the user continuously selects "spoon bowl" by a green laser pointer. If the user doesn't need a "spoon" to execute the "scoop" the user will output a "refuse" signal to the robot by a laser pointer. Then, the intention network will output the second-highest probability intention {grasp, mix}. If the user

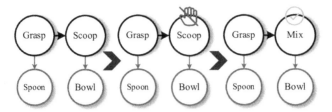

Fig. 3. The process of learning strategy

inputs an "agree" signal through a laser pointer, the learning mechanism will give a reward score to the second action intention and update the Q table.

The Q table is the statistics of the Q value of action. The Q value in the table will be normalized in the implied actions related to {spoon, bowl}. And we can change the discount coefficient to adjust the speed of the intention network to adapt to user preferences. And The Q table update process for the example in Fig. 3 is shown in Fig. 4.

Q	grasp, scoop	grasp, mix	grasp, move
spoon, bowl	2	1	1

↓ After the first confirmation

Q	grasp, scoop	grasp, mix	grasp, move
spoon, bowl	2	2	1

↓ Second confirmation,
...... third confirmation, ...

Fig. 4. The Q table of states {*spoon, bowl*}

After embedding the learning mechanism into the object-action intention network, the user can continuously send "refuse" instructions to the robot through a laser pointer. the robot will extract the action intention with decreasing probability value cached in the Viterbi algorithm and provide the user with a choice until the user is satisfied.

4   Experiment and Discussion

To assist disabled people in manipulating objects without the assistance of other people, we build a wheelchair-mounted 6 degree of freedom robotic arms system known as the WMRA. The WMRA and overview of our intention recognition system are shown in Fig. 5. First, the image identification of object categories and laser points in the scene by the RGB-D camera is based on the YOLO_V4 [19] model. Then, the label of the object selected by the laser pointer and the point clouds information of the scene is sent to the intention network and point cloud processing, respectively. Next, Dynamic movement primitives (DMP) [20–22] get the action intention and the centroid coordinate information of the selected object, which are used to select the trajectory of learning from demonstrate (LfD) [23] from the action library and generalize it. Finally, Jaco's arm gets the coordinate of the trajectory point and performs the task.

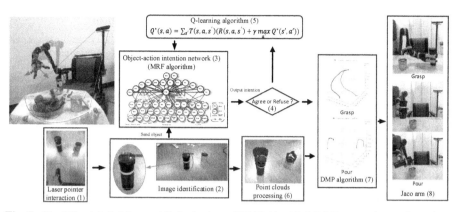

Fig. 5. The Wheelchair-Mounted Robotic Arms (WMRA) with 6-DOF arm and overview of our framework

4.1 Intention Recognition Evaluation

The quantity of implied action intentions that the robot can recognize by the category of an object is one of the evaluation criteria of the intention recognition. Table 1 lists 11 possible object categories, 7 possible actions and demonstrates the intentions that we can recognize under these objects.

Table 2 further lists that our approach has better performance in intention recognition compared with Kester's approach because we have the same quantity of single-object intentions with Kester that can recognize, and only our approach can recognize multi-object intention.

4.2 Learning Strategy Evaluation

Learning Strategy Evaluation of Single-object Intention. It is common for the user's intention of the same objects to change in household environments. The robot's recognition result of the object-action intention may adapt to people over time. In this section, we'll compare the performance between our learning strategy and the one of Kester (their approach was based on the Recursive Bayesian Incremental Learning). We define the process from the "laser pointer interaction" to "Jaco's arm" as a session and define the number of "learning Loop" required to correctly output the people's intention as the number of interactions. Table 3 lists that the scenes evaluated are composed of 8 randomly positioned household objects: Can, Cup, Carton, Mug, Tub, Box, Bowl, Bottle, and 4 groups of desired intentions in this experiment. The average number of interactions required to communicate each intention will be plotted in a column chart along with their standard deviations as error bars.

The baseline in Fig. 6 is that the probabilities for each object-action intention are simply the reciprocal of the total number of object-action intentions possible in the scene. We can see from Fig. 6 that over the span of 20 sessions, the average number of interactions in our framework decreases monotonically, and convergence requires 70% fewer sessions than Kester.

Table 1. Some objects, actions, and object-action intentions

Objects (11)	Bottle, Bowl, Box, Can, Carton, Cup, Mug, Spray-can, Tin, Tube, Tub
Actions (7)	Drink, Grasp, Move, Open, Pour, Push, Squeeze
Object-action intention (36)	Drink-Bottle, Grasp-Bottle, Move-Bottle, Open-Bottle, Pour-Bottle, Grasp-Bowl, Move-Bowl, Push-Bowl, Grasp-Box, Move-Box, Open-Box, Push-Box, Drink-Can, Grasp-Can, Move-Can, Pour-Can, Grasp-Carton, Move-Carton, Open-Carton, Pour-Carton, Drink-Cup, Grasp-Cup, Move-Cup, Drink-Mug, Grasp-Mug, Move-Mug, Grasp-Spray-can, Grasp-Tin, Move-Tin, Open-Tin, Pour-Tin, Grasp-Tube, Squeeze-Tube, Grasp-Tub, Open-Tub, Push-Tub
Objects-actions intention (19)	Grasp-Carton-Move-Box, Grasp-Can-Move-Box, Grasp-Bottle-Move-Box, Grasp-Box-Move-Box, Grasp-Cup-Move-Box, Grasp-Can-Pour-Bowl, Grasp-Can-Pour-Cup, Grasp-Bottle-Pour-Bowl, Grasp-Bottle-Pour-Cup, Grasp-Cup-Pour-Bowl, Grasp-Cup-Pour-Cup, Grasp-Cup-Pour-Bowl-Drink-Person, Grasp-Bowl-Pour-Cup-Drink-Person, Grasp-Can-Pour-Bowl-Drink-Person, Open-Bottle-Pour-Bowl, Open-Bottle-Pour-Cup, Open-Can-Pour-Bowl, Open-Bottle-Pour-Cup-Drink-Person, Grasp-Can-Pour-Cup-Drink-Person

Table 2. Quantity of intentions

	Object quantity	Single-object intention quantity	Multi-object intention quantity
Our approach	11	36	19
Kester Duncan	11	36	0

Table 3. Groups of object-action intentions evaluated in this work

Objects	Can, Cup, Carton, Box, Bowl, Bottle, Mug, Tub
Group 1	Grasp-Box, Open-Box, Grasp-Carton, Open-Carton, Pour-from-Carton
Group 2	Grasp-Can, Move-Can, Pour-from-Can, Drink-from-Cup
Group 3	Grasp-Carton, Move-Carton, Pour-from-Carton, Drink-from-Cup
Group 4	Grasp-Bottle, Move-Bottle, Pour-from-Bottle, Drink-from-Cup

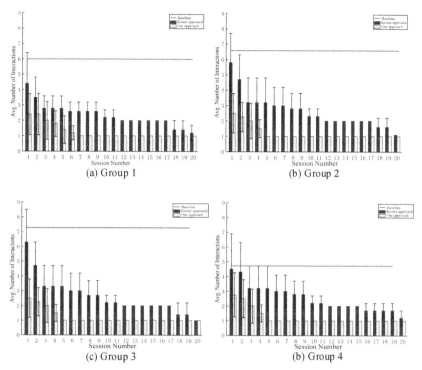

Fig. 6. Intention recognition results compared with Kester [11] on the object-action groups listed in Table 3

Learning Strategy Evaluation of Multi-object Intention. To the best of our knowledge, multi-object action intention recognition is a new capability whereby we didn't have any other approach to perform a direct comparison. We selected intentions related to the "Cup Can Bowl Box Bottle Carton" in object-actions intentions in Table 4, and the experimental procedure is similar to the one presented in the previous section.

Table 4. Groups of objects-actions intentions evaluated in this work

Objects	Can, Cup, Carton, Box, Bowl, Bottle
Group 1	Grasp-Cup-Move-Box, Grasp-Can-Pour-Bowl, open-can-Pour-Bowl, Open-Bottle-Pour-Bowl
Group 2	Grasp-Can-Pour-Cup-Drink-Person, Grasp-Cup-Pour-Bowl-Drink-Person, open-bottle-Pour-cup-drink-Person

Figure 7 (a) shows that it needs more interaction times to recognize the intention involve two objects correctly. However, by constantly selecting the correct intention, the interaction times will monotonously decrease and converge in the 12th session.

Figure 7(b) shows that the number of interactions to recognize the intention involve three objects is more than that of two objects. However, the number of interactions will suddenly decrease in the 8th session and directly adjust to the correct intention. Finally, by observing the interaction times of Fig. 6 and Fig. 7 to get the correct intention for the first time, we found that they have an exponential relationship. After analysis, we thought that this relationship is related to the way of the Viterbi algorithm and the number of implied actions.

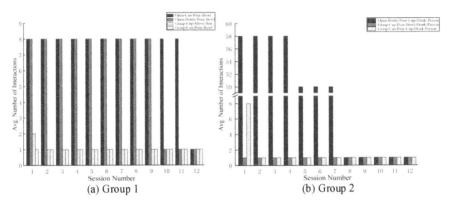

(a) Group 1   (b) Group 2

Fig. 7. Intention recognition results in Table 4

5   Conclusion

This paper develops an intention recognition framework for disabled people by using MRF and Q-learning algorithms. Object-action intention network used the objects selected by disabled people to infer the highest-probability action intention. Q-learning algorithm was used to learn the intention selected by users to adapt to user preferences. Finally, experiments were carried on the WMRA with a laser selection interface and showed that framework could infer the intention and adapt to their preference faster.

Acknowledgment. This work is supported by the National Key R&D Program of China (Grant No. 2018YFB1309400), the Key R&D Program of Shandong Province (Grant No. 2016GGX101013), and the University Common Construction Project of Weihai (Grant No. 2016DXGJMS04).

References

1. Alqasemi, R.M., McCaffrey, E.J., Edwards, K.D., et al.: Analysis, evaluation and development of wheelchair-mounted robotic arms. In: proceedings of the 9th International Conference on Rehabilitation Robotics, 2005 ICORR 2005, pp. 469–472 (2005)

2. Jiang, H., Zhang, T., Wachs, J.P., et al.: Enhanced control of a wheelchair-mounted robotic manipulator using 3-D vision and multimodal interaction. Comput. Vision Image Understand. **149**, 21–31 (2016)
3. Graser, A., Heyer, T., Fotoohi, L., et al.: A supportive friend at work: robotic workplace assistance for the disabled. IEEE Rob. Autom. Mag. **20**(4), 148–159 (2013)
4. Bien, Z., Chung, M.-J., Chang, P.-H., et al.: Integration of a rehabilitation robotic system (KARES II) with human-friendly man-machine interaction units. Auton. Robot. **16**(2), 165–191 (2004)
5. Shishehgar, M., Kerr, D., Blake, J.: The effectiveness of various robotic technologies in assisting older adults. Health Inf. J. **25**(3), 892–918 (2019)
6. Jain, A., Zamir, A.R., Savarese, S, et al.: Structural-rnn: deep learning on spatio-temporal graphs. In: Proceedings of the IEEE Conference on Computer Vision and Pattern Recognition, pp. 5308–5317 (2016)
7. Liu, C., Li, X., Li, Q., et al.: Robot recognizing humans intention and interacting with humans based on a multi-task model combining ST-GCN-LSTM model and YOLO model. Neurocomputing **430**, 174–184 (2021)
8. Müller, S., Wengefeld, T., Trinh, T.Q., et al.: A multi-modal person perception framework for socially interactive mobile service robots. Sensors **20**(3), 722 (2020)
9. Kim, J.-M., Jeon, M.-J., Park, H.-K., et al.: An approach for recognition of human's daily living patterns using intention ontology and event calculus. Expert Syst. Appl. **132**, 256–270 (2019)
10. Melkas, H., Hennala, L., Pekkarinen, S., et al.: Impacts of robot implementation on care personnel and clients in elderly-care institutions. Int. J. Med. Inform. **134**, 104041 (2020)
11. Duncan, K.: Scene-dependent human intention recognition for an assistive robotic system. Org. Agric. **4**(1), 25–42 (2014)
12. Kindermann, R.: Markov random fields and their applications. Am. Math. Soc. (1980)
13. Richardson, M., Domingos, P.: Markov logic networks. Mach. Learn. **62**(1–2), 107–136 (2006)
14. Kallus, N., Uehara, M.: Double reinforcement learning for efficient off-policy evaluation in markov decision processes. J. Mach. Learn. Res. **21**(167), 1–63 (2020)
15. Kumar Shastha, T., Kyrarini, M., Gräser, A.: Application of reinforcement learning to a robotic drinking assistant. Robotics **9**(1), 1 (2020)
16. Gualtieri, M., Kuczynski, J., Shultz, A.M., et al.: Open world assistive grasping using laser selection. In: proceedings of the 2017 IEEE International Conference on Robotics and Automation (ICRA), pp. 4052–4057 (2017)
17. Hassanin, M., Khan, S., Tahtali, M.: Visual affordance and function understanding: a survey. ACM Comput. Surv. **54**(3), 1–35 (2021)
18. Kuhlmann, T.: ICF (International Classification of Functioning, Disability and Health). Suchttherapie **12**(01), 7–7 (2011)
19. Bochkovskiy, A., Wang, C.-Y., Liao, H.-Y.M.: Yolov4: Optimal speed and accuracy of object detection. arXiv preprint arXiv:200410934 (2020)
20. Schaal, S.: Dynamic movement primitives – a framework for motor control in humans and humanoid robotics. In: Kimura, H., Tsuchiya, K., Ishiguro, A., Witte, H. (eds.) Adaptive Motion of Animals and Machines. Springer, Tokyo (2006)
21. Hoffmann, H., Pastor, P., Park, D.-H., et al.: Biologically-inspired dynamical systems for movement generation: automatic real-time goal adaptation and obstacle avoidance. In: Proceedings of the 2009 IEEE International Conference on Robotics and Automation, pp. 2587–2592 (2009)

22. Chi, M., Yao, Y., Liu, Y., et al.: Learning, generalization, and obstacle avoidance with dynamic movement primitives and dynamic potential fields. Appl. Sci. **9**(8), 1535 (2019)
23. Ravichandar, H., Polydoros, A.S., Chernova, S., et al.: Recent Advances in Robot Learning from Demonstration. Annu. Rev. Control Robot. Auton. Syst. **3**(1), 297–330 (2020)

Research on Mobile Robot Platform to Assist Laboratory Management

Yueming Bi, Huan Hu$^{(\boxtimes)}$, Yunfei Luo, Bo Li, Chengxi Wang, and Min Huang

School of Electromechanical Engineering, Beijing Information Science and Technology
University, Beijing 100192, China
huanhu@bistu.edu.cn

Abstract. A laboratory service robot that significantly improves work efficiency, is presented. This solves the problem of inefficient management of laboratory equipment in universities. The robot has the ability to move around the lab freely, responding to voice commands and controlling the appliances. This helps the laboratory manager to record information that will improve laboratory management. This paper discusses innovations in the scope of application of the service robot.

Keywords: Robot · SLAM · ROS · Mapping · Navigation · Voice interaction

1 Introduction

With the rapid development of education, the state and universities have invested more and more resources in the construction and renovation of laboratories. However there have been significant problems in the management of instruments and equipment in traditional laboratories, which makes the utilization rate of laboratory equipment very low. Therefore, the research, design and construction of intelligent laboratories have greater practical application value and broad development prospects [1]. Meanwhile, the emergence of indoor service robots and the rapid development of simultaneous localization and mapping technology (SLAM) [2] has made it possible to introduce service robots to manage laboratories. On the basis of mapping, the use of service robots to manage laboratory equipment including grabbing and storing laboratory equipment, assisting in organizing the environment, and making rounds of the laboratory, achieves the purpose of service robot management in the laboratory. The development of smart home control systems with voice recognition technology is becoming increasingly mature. In the application of these systems to the laboratory service robot, the true value of the intelligent service robot can be realized.

The research object of this paper is a laboratory service robot, which has the following functions: 1) interacting with the human by voice, 2) mapping and performing autonomous navigation, 3) recording the information of laboratory environment while mapping, 4) controlling the appliance such as the air conditioner and lights, etc. in the laboratory. This mobile robot platform, shown in Fig. 1, is based on the Turtlebot2 mobile platform with an Industrial Personal Computer (IPC) as the upper computer, equipped

X.-J. Liu et al. (Eds.): ICIRA 2021, LNAI 13015, pp. 357–366, 2021.
https://doi.org/10.1007/978-3-030-89134-3_33

with LIDAR for mapping and navigation, an external display and microphone for real-time display and voice interaction. More specifically, the control of the robot is based on the open-source robot operating system (ROS) [3], which is a practical platform integrating simulation, control and technology development. SLAM is the key technology for robot localization and navigation, and the basis for the robot to achieve autonomous motion. In this paper, laser SLAM technology is used to accomplish robot localization and navigation. The voice control of the robot is based on the platform of iFLYTEK, which is an open platform of artificial intelligence with voice interaction as the core. The control of home appliances mentioned above is based on the LifeSmart intelligent home control system and Xiao AI, which is the medium for the robot to control lighting and air conditioning and other devices.

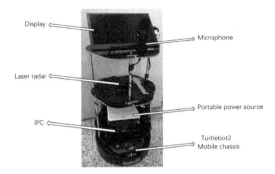

Fig. 1. Mobile robotics platform

2   Overall System Structure

In this paper, the overall system architecture is designed according to the architecture and communication mode of ROS, as shown in Fig. 2. It is divided into four parts: hardware execution layer, hardware driver layer, application function layer, and human-computer interaction layer.

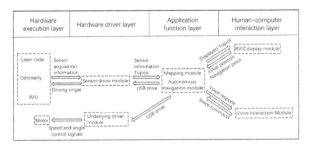

Fig. 2. Overall structure of the robot system

(1) Hardware execution layer: This layer can be divided into two parts: sensor perception and driver execution. The LIDAR sensor in sensor perception collects the laser point cloud information of the surrounding environment and sends it to the LIDAR driver module, the Inertial Measurement Unit (IMU) sensor collects the angular velocity (Turtlebot2's IMU only has gyroscope, no accelerometer) and sends it to the IMU driver module, and the odometry collects the odometry information and sends it to the odometry driver module. The drive execution is the underlying drive module sends control commands to the drive board, which are converted into electrical signals to control the motor.

(2) Hardware driver layer: Including driver modules of various sensors such as LIDAR, IMU and odometry and underlying driver module. The sensor driver module is used to drive the sensors and receive the data collected by the sensors in real time, and the underlying driver module is used to send commands for motion control.

(3) Application function layer: The application function module is divided into two parts: mapping and autonomous navigation, using an IPC as the hardware platform and running ROS in the Ubuntu system. The mapping module is used to build a map of the environment, and the autonomous navigation module is used for path planning, localization and navigation.

(4) Human-robot interaction layer: Includes RVIZ display module and voice interaction module, RVIZ display module is used for real-time display of the robot during mapping and autonomous navigation. The voice interaction module is used for voice interaction between the robot and the experimenter, receiving and executing the experimenter's voice commands and giving responses.

3   ROS-Based Software Platform

In this paper, the software platform of the robot is designed and built on the ROS platform according to the specific functions to be realized. As shown in Fig. 3, the software platform has three main functional modules: the mapping module, the autonomous navigation module and the voice interaction module.

Fig. 3. ROS-based software platform

3.1   Mapping Module

The mapping module is mainly used to build a map of the surrounding environment. There are many kinds of SLAM algorithms for LIDAR in ROS [4], in which the filter-based laser SLAM mainly applies the Gmapping algorithm [5], which is suitable for localization and mapping in small indoor scenes and low-feature environments with high accuracy and low computation, therefore the algorithm is suitable for the laboratory environment. The input of the SLAM system based on the Gmapping algorithm is LIDAR and odometry data, and the output is the robot's own pose and map.

3.2 Autonomous Navigation Module

The autonomous navigation module is specifically used for the robot to obtain information about the target point, derive a rough forward route after global planning, and then derive a specific action strategy for the robot in real-time motion through local planning and cost map information, while performing its own localization. The localization algorithm uses Adaptive Mentcarto Localization (AMCL), which achieves localization by comparing detected obstacles with a known map. The adaptive nature of the AMCL algorithm is reflected in that it can solve the robot abduction problem and the particle number fixation problem. Global planning uses the A* (A-star) algorithm [6], whose basic idea is to use the grid map to calculate the squares that can be moved from the starting point to the target point to form a path. The A* algorithm is a global path planning algorithm with heuristic features, which searches for the least cost path among the possible paths. Local planning uses the Dynamic Window Approach (DWA) algorithm [7], whose main idea is to sample multiple sets of velocities in the velocity space and simulate the trajectories of these velocities in a certain time, and then score these trajectories by the evaluation function, with the highest score corresponding to the optimal velocity.

In ROS, the autonomous navigation function is performed by the move based navigation package. The move_base navigation framework contains the map server node for map loading, the AMCL node for localization, and the move base node for global and local planning.

3.3 Voice Interaction Module

The voice interaction module is used for voice interaction between the robot and the experimenter, receiving and executing the voice commands of the experimenter and giving a response. After receiving the "turn on the light" or "turn off the light" command, the robot navigates to the location of Xiao AI, and then interacts with Xiao AI to turn on or off the light.

- Voice interaction between robot and experimenter
  The experiment is based on the robot voice interaction module developed by the iFLYTEK voice technology platform. In ROS, the voice function package of iFLYTEK includes three nodes, namely, the voice recognition node, the voice synthesis node and the voice interaction node. Figure 4 shows the three nodes of voice control. This interaction function simply improves on the above voice recognition and speech synthesis functions. The '/xf_tts' node is a simple direct speech synthesis output after receiving the text of the speech recognition. The dialogue corresponding to the speech recognition text is selected for synthesis and output, which achieves the purpose of human-computer interaction.

Fig. 4. Voice control node

After constructing the voice interaction module, the motion of the robot can be controlled by voice commands, such as forward, backward, turn, etc. The experiment also combines the mapping system, the autonomous navigation system and the voice control system. During the mapping process, it can control the movement of the robot with voice commands as well as using them during the navigation process to make the robot reach the pre-recorded target point.

- Voice interaction between robot and Xiao AI

The existing smart home control system controls all household appliances through the control center in the local area network, and users can manage the household appliances through the mobile phone app. With the development of Natural Language Processing (NLP), more and more smart homes are equipped with smart speakers, allowing people to control smart devices through voice interaction [8]. For example, in the LifeSmart smart home control system, the smart center connects all smart and smart sensing devices to Xiao AI at the same time, and then uses Xiao AI to voice control various smart devices, as shown in Fig. 5. Based on the above, this experiment uses the voice interaction between the mobile robot and Xiao AI to control the smart device, so as to achieve the purpose of the robot to control the electrical appliances. Since robots cannot directly control electrical appliances, Xiao AI here is the medium for robots to control electrical appliances.

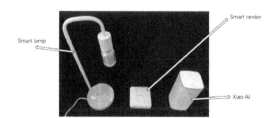

Fig. 5. LifeSmart smart home control system and Xiao AI

4 Experiment and Analysis

This experiment consists of three parts: firstly, mapping, in the process of mapping, the lab table and cabinet location information is marked as the target point during navigation; secondly, autonomous navigation, real-time obstacle avoidance during navigation; finally, voice interaction, including voice interaction between the robot and the experimenter and voice interaction between the robot and Xiao AI.

4.1 Mapping

Figure 6(a) shows the real laboratory environment. Figure 6(b) shows the grid map constructed in the laboratory by the robot equipped with Rplildar A2 using the Gmapping algorithm, the map built in ROS is usually in pgm format. Shown in Fig. 6(c), black in the figure indicates obstacles, white indicates the passable area. This map provides indispensable information for robot positioning and navigation. During the robot mapping process, you can input information by voice to tell the robot that the current locations of the lab table, the cabinet, or the location where the robot is parked when it is not working. The robot will automatically record information about the location of lab equipment. For example, point A in the diagram is the location of the lab table, point B is the location of the cabinet, and point C is the docking position when the robot is not working.

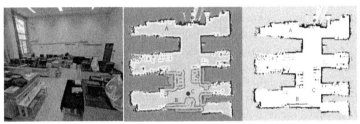

(a) The real environment   (b) The map of the lab (c) The map in pgm format

Fig. 6. Map of the built lab

4.2 Localization and Navigation

To demonstrate the execution process of the AMCL algorithm, as shown in Fig. 7(a), the experiment first breaks up all the particles so that they are evenly distributed throughout the map, and then uses the keyboard to control the robot to move a specific distance, during which the particles will converge as shown in Fig. 7(b) and (c), Finally, all the particles will converge to the robot's position, indicating that the localization has been completed as shown in Fig. 7(d).

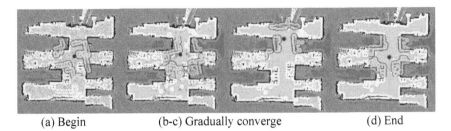

(a) Begin   (b-c) Gradually converge   (d) End

Fig. 7. AMCL localization process

The global planner and local planner use the global costmap shown in Fig. 8(a) and the local costmap shown in Fig. 8(b), respectively. Based on the actual robot size, an inflation layer is formed at the periphery of the obstacle and the mobile robot to form the local cost map, and the inflation layer is considered as an obstacle in the path planning process to ensure that the mobile robot will not collide with the obstacle under normal circumstances.

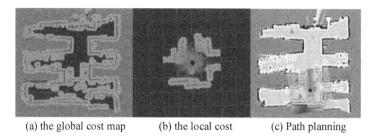

(a) the global cost map   (b) the local cost   (c) Path planning

Fig. 8. Cost map and path planning

Voice input the command for the robot to go to the location of the lab table (point A), then the global planner will automatically plan out a path, as shown in Fig. 8(c). The green line in the figure is the path planned out.

4.3 Dynamic Obstacle Avoidance

In practical situations, it is often necessary to have the robot automatically avoid obstacles. A powerful feature of the move base package is the ability to automatically avoid obstacles during global planning without affecting the global path. Obstacles can be static (e.g., walls, tables) or dynamic (e.g., people walking by). To test this function of dynamic obstacle avoidance, multiple chairs are added to the robot's planned path during the experiment. The initial position of the robot is shown in Fig. 9, and the dynamic obstacle avoidance in multiple cases is shown in Fig. 10.

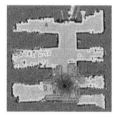

Fig. 9. Initial robot position

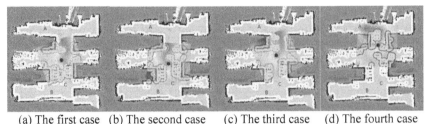

(a) The first case   (b) The second case   (c) The third case   (d) The fourth case

Fig. 10. Dynamic obstacle avoidance (obstacles are chairs in the laboratory, the chairs in the four pictures are in different positions)

4.4 Voice Control and Furniture Control

Start the voice recognition node, then speak the commands out such as "turn the light on" or "turn the light off". The robot recognizes the voice command property as shown in Fig. 11.

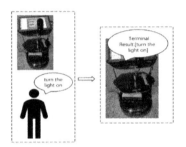

Fig. 11. Recognized

Start the node of voice synthesis, enter the word(s) that the user expects the robot to say in the terminal, such as "Xiao AI, Please turn on the light". After the process of voice synthesis, it will speak "Xiao AI, Please turn on the light", as shown in Fig. 12.

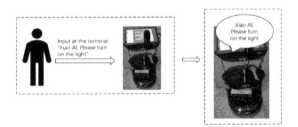

Fig. 12. "Xiao AI, Please turn on the light". Voice synthesized by robot

Start the voice interaction node, then the user can chat with the robot as shown in Fig. 13. For example, voice input "Who Are You?" After recognition, the robot will reply

"I am the lab assistant". If the user asks "What can you do?", the robot will reply "I can help you turn the lights off and on" so as to achieve the purpose of voice interaction.

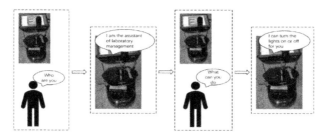

Fig. 13. Voice interaction

Furniture control experiment is based on the LifeSmart smart home control system, XiaoMi and the Xiao AI smart speaker, added to a mobile robot that can be voice controlled. The LifeSmart smart home control system and the Xiao AI smart speaker are placed on a table in the lab, whose location is named as point A. The mobile robot is then placed at its docking position. The navigation and voice control nodes are started by speaking the following words: "turn on the light", the robot will navigate to the previously recorded target point and say "Xiao AI, please turn on the light" to Xiao AI, and the Xiao AI smart speaker will proceed to turn off the light bulb. The flow chart is shown in Fig. 14.

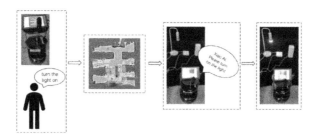

Fig. 14. Flow chart of commanding the robot to turn on the light

5 Conclusion

The hardware platform of the mobile robot is based on Tuttlebot2, and the software is built in ROS. The combination of both this hardware and software complete the task of mapping, autonomous navigation and human voice interaction. The robot can accurately locate itself, map the lab and avoid obstacles in real-time during the navigation to the lab table or cabinet. It can also cooperate with LifeSmart and Xiao AI to take control of the smart furniture such as smart lamp, by the means of human-computer interaction.

Traditional mobile robots can only complete the most basic tasks of mapping and navigation, thus having considerable limitations in practical applications. This paper adds to voice interaction and the smart furniture control module, making controlling the robot by human voice possible. Various complex tasks such as movement controlled by human voice, voice-directed navigation, voice-controlled smart furniture, and human-computer interaction, make the mobile robots more intelligent, and innovate the application scope of service robot, this can be a great help to laboratory personnel who manage the equipment in the lab.

The robot of this study is extendable, by, for example, installing a robotics arm on the top side of the robot for object grabbing. What's more, if combined with autonomous navigation, the robot can store and fetch objects in the lab, making labs managed by mobile robots possible.

Acknowledgments. This work was financially supported by research and development and demonstration application of air-to-land man three-dimensional fire fighting cooperative combat system, Beijing Municipal Science and Technology Project (Z191100001419009) and intelligent management of equipment for smart laboratories, School Research Fund Project (2025001).

References

1. Wu, W., Yang, Q., Shen, X., et al.: The laboratory open management under the intelligent management system. Exp. Technol. Manage. (2011)
2. Khairuddin, A.R., Talib, M.S., Haron, H.: Review on simultaneous localization and mapping (SLAM). In: 2015 IEEE International Conference on Control System, Computing and Engineering (ICCSCE). IEEE (2016)
3. Koubaa, A.: Robot Operating System (ROS). Springer, Cham (2020)
4. Yagfarov, R., Ivanou, M., Afanasyev, I.: Map comparison of LIDAR-based 2D SLAM algorithms using precise ground truth. In: 2018 15th International Conference on Control, Automation, Robotics and Vision (ICARCV). IEEE (2018)
5. Grisetti, G., Stachniss, C., Burgard, W.: Improved techniques for grid mapping with Rao-Blackwellized particle filters. IEEE Trans. Robot. **23**, 34–46 (2007)
6. Hart, P., Nilsson, N., Raphael, B.: A formal basis for the heuristic determination of minimum cost paths. IEEE Trans. Syst. Sci. Cybern. **4**(2), 100–107 (1968). https://doi.org/10.1109/TSSC.1968.300136
7. Fox, D., Burgard, W.: The dynamic window approach to collision avoidance. IEEE Robot. Autom. Mag. **4**(1), 23–33 (1997)
8. Zhang, W., An, Z., Luo, Z., et al.: Development of a voice-control smart home environment. In: IEEE International Conference on Robotics & Biomimetics. IEEE (2017)

A Tracking Method Based on Lightweight Feature Extraction Network for Tracking Robot

Han Hu, Gang Yu$^{(\boxtimes)}$, Geyang Wu, and Tongda Sun

Department of Mechanical Engineering and Automation, Harbin Institute of Technology, Shenzhen, Shenzhen 518055, China
gangyu@hit.edu.cn

Abstract. This paper proposes to use lightweight feature extraction network as backbone of tracking network applied in embeded system of tracking robot, which achieves speed improvement and similar accuracy as compared with other mainstream tracking algorithms. Firstly, since there are unbalance between hard and easy samples on training dataset, data augmentation is proposed to increase hard samples in training phase. Secondly, modified Ghostnet is used as feature extraction network of tracking network, which dramatically decreases the float point operation and model parameters and achives realtime speed to meet the demand of embeded systems. Thirdly, focal loss is used as classification loss function instead of BCE loss, because BCE fuction cannot take unbalance between position and negative samples into consideration, and DIOU loss is taken as regression loss function to train tracking network, which can regress predicted box close to ground truth box. Experimental resutls show that the proposed method has better performance than traditional methods.

Keywords: Target tracking · Tracking robot · Lightweight feature extraction network

1 Instruction

Target tracking algorithms have been developed rapidly in recent years, which mainly can be divided into tracking based on correlation filters and siamese network. In term of tracking algorithm based on correlation filter, David S. Bolme et al. proposed minimum output sum of squared error filter (MOSSE) [1] to track target, which was robust to changes in illumination, scale and non-rigid deformation. However, MOSSE only used grayscale as feature, since its dimension was too low to reflect the characteristics of the target and only estimated the translational movement of the center point of the target area between frames. Henriques proposed kernelized correlation filters (KCF) [2] using the diagonalization property of the circulant matrix in the fourier space to transform matrix operation into Hadamad product of the vector, greatly reducing the amount of

© Springer Nature Switzerland AG 2021
X.-J. Liu et al. (Eds.): ICIRA 2021, LNAI 13015, pp. 367–377, 2021.
https://doi.org/10.1007/978-3-030-89134-3_34

calculation and increasing the speed. However, relying on the circulant matrix affected the performance of target tracking since it was difficult to estimate the scale change of target. Danelljan, M et al. proposed discriminative scale space tracking (DSST) [3], which mainly introduces multi-feature fusion and scale estimation to improve performance based on MOSSE and KCF. In term of tracking algorithm based on siamese network, Siamfc [4] first used siamese network into visual tracking, took target image and search image as input, made correlation calcuration with the output of extracting network after feature extraction network extracting feature. But it only used the last convolution layer of feature extraction network as input to calcurate correlation. Siamrpn [5] improved tracking performance of siamese network, using deeper feature extraction network to classify the background and foreground, and also to regress predicted box close to ground truth box. Siamrpn++ [6] was improved based on Simarpn, using Resnet as feature extraction backbone, which mainly solved the problem that deeper network could not have more higher accuracy compared with shallower network. Siammask [7] unifieds target tracking and target segmentation, through mask to achieving more accurate object tracking. Compared with other tracking algorithms, although it achieves amazing performance, it has more complicated network and difficult to training. As recently anchor-free detection method proposed, using anchor free method for tracking object has become the current tracking developmemt trend, such as Siamfc++ [8]. Siamfc++ mainly modified based on Siamfc. Compared with Simafc, it introduces centerness loss to improve tracking performance, achieving more accuracy than others. While Siamfc++ does not fuse the low level and high level output of feature extraction network to predict the tracking target. The tracking algorithm of correlation filtering has been widely used in the industry since its simplicity, effectiveness and speed. However, with the development of deep learning, tracking based on siamese network have surpassed KCF algorithms in terms of accuracy except speed. In embedded systems application, tracking based on siamese network is still relatively difficult to achieve real-time speed because of embedded systems' poor computing ability. This paper mainly tries to use siamese network to track target through a lightweight feature extraction network on Nvidia Jetson TX2, which improves the speed of the tracking algorithm under the condition of meeting the similar accuracy. The sections of this paper are organized as follows. In Sect. 2, tracking algorithm applied platform and the total system design are introduced. Data augmentation and lightweight extraction network and modified loss function are introduced in Sect. 3. In Sect. 4 and Sect. 5, experiment results and conclusion are reported respectively.

2   System Description

Proposed tracking method mainly applies on tracking robot based on ROS communicating between control board (STM32F407) and embeded computer (Jetson TX2). The system description is shown in Fig. 1. Firstly, the initial bounding box is provided by detection algorithm. Secondly, the tracking algorithm initialized

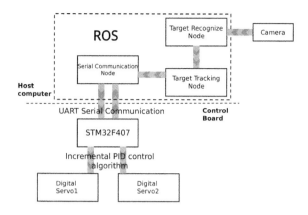

Fig. 1. System control flow chart

by detected bounding box to publish the center position of tracking target in real time. The serial communication node subscribes the center point of the target tracking frame published by the tracking node, and transmits this data to STM32 in real time through the UART serial port. The center point data received by STM32 through the serial port is different from the camera center point position of the known camera parameters. As the control parameter, the incremental PID control algorithm is used to realize the closed-loop control of the rotation angle control of the two steering gears of the camera pan/tilt.

In term of controlling the movement of the robot, the angle of the camera and the robot are collected through three-axis acceleration sensor, one is on the camera and another is on the robot chassis, to calcurate the angle difference between the camera and the robot.

3 Proposed Method

3.1 Data Augmentation Based on Hard Sample

In visual tracking tasks, visual tracking target being occluded has always been a problem. It often makes tracker lose target, which significantly reduces the accuracy and effect of tracking. At present, although the tracked dataset also has various obstacle occlusions and interference by similar target samples, the number of hard samples is still limited as compared to the total number of frames of dataset. In order to better utilize the powerful feature extraction capabilities of deep learning and model generalization ability, it is necessary to increase different occlusion level and similar target interference samples through data augmentation methods.

Random erasing data augmentation [9] was proposed as shown in Fig. 2, which randomly chooses a rectangle region from image and erases its pixels with random value or the dataset mean pixel value. Movitated by this method, data augmentation method is proposed by filling target from similar category from

Fig. 2. Simulation of obstacle occulusion with randomly erasing

Fig. 3. Simulation of occulusion and interference with similar target filling

dataset to randomly erase region from image. Filling similar category target data enhancement method is aimed to simulate the effect of obstacle occlusion and the interference by similar categories of targets, which can increase the number of hard samples in the dataset during training. Except adopting random erasing and random filling similar category, we also adopt random cropping and rotation, channel exchange and so on to expand sample number. In the training phase, random erasing of noise and random filling by similar categories are determined by hyperparameters p_1 and p_2 with a certain probability. The probability p_1 of randomly erasing the noise generated and the probability of filling similar targets is $p_2 - p_1$, and the probability of no processing is $1 - p_2$. In order to achieve the effect of occluding the target, suppose the size of the picture is $w \times h$, the size of the target frame in the picture is $w_{tar} \times h_{tar}$, and the height of the target frame in the picture is offset by $\frac{\beta}{2}$ pixels and the width is offset by $\frac{\alpha}{2}$ pixels. Set the random parameter ratio rates between r_{s1} and r_{s2}, then initialize occluded area is

$$s = (w_{tar} + \alpha) \times (h_{tar} + \beta) \times rates \tag{1}$$

We randomly set the aspect ratio r_{wh} between r_{wh1} and r_{wh2}, then the width and height of the occluded frame are $w_{obs} = \sqrt{\dfrac{s}{r_{wh}}}, h_{obs} = \sqrt{s \times r_{wh}}$. Initialize the upper left corner of the occlusion frame $p_{lt}(x_{lt1}, y_{lt1})$ in the occlusion area randomly, if $x_{lt1} + w_{obs} \leq w$ and $y_{lt1} + h_{obs} \leq h$, set the occlusion area to $(x_{lt1}, y_{lt1}, x_{lt1} + w_{obs}, y_{lt1} + h_{obs})$. Otherwise set the occlusion area to (x_{lt1}, y_{lt1}, w, h). For the simulation of similar category filling simulation occlusion as shown in Fig. 3, the generation of the filled area is the same as that of the obstacle, but the difference is that a similar category pair needs to be generated, which is selected from the similar category and adjusted to the size of the filled area to patch.

3.2   Lightweight Feature Extraction Network Design

Siamfc++ takes Alexnet as the backbone network, which is mainly because the deeper network does not improve the target tracking task. However, as compared with some lightweight network, AlexNet has more float point calculation and model parameters. Ghostnet [10] pointed out that the feature maps obtained after convolution have similar relationships between certain dimensions, and this similar relationship can be approximately replaced by the linear transformation of the feature map as shown in Fig. 4.

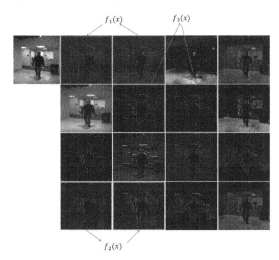

Fig. 4. Feature map visualization

According to Ghostnet's improved convolutional layer calculation, feature maps with fewer channels can be obtained through fewer convolution kernels, and further linear transformations can be used to reduce floating-point operations and model parameters, thereby reducing the weight of the model and accelerating the inference process speed. In this process, the formula (1) can also be used, but the number of output channels N is reduced to M, and $M < N$, that is, the output feature map $Y' \in R^{M \times H' \times W'}$, the convolution kernel $K' \in R^{C \times k \times k \times M}$, the floating point calculation amount is $M \times H' \times W' \times C \times k \times k$, and the model parameter amount $C \times k \times k \times M$. It can be seen that the output of the feature layer with the same number of channels can be obtained through convolution kernel parameters with fewer parameters and floating-point operations. This process can be expressed as:

$$y_{ij} = \Phi(y'_i), \qquad \forall i = 1, ..., M, j = 1, ..., S \tag{2}$$

where y'_i represents the i-th feature map in Y', and Φ_{ij} in the above function uses the $j - th$ linear mapping to generate the $j - th$ feature map y_{ij}. In other words, one feature map y'_i can generate one or more through different linear mappings. For similar feature maps of tradictional convolution, each essential feature map y_i' needs to generate $s - 1$ new features through a convolution operation, because the final output result also retains the original feature map. In the end, the GhostNet convolution output same as traditional convolution's. There are $n = m \times s$ feature maps. Then the complexity of using Ghost convolution is:

$$r_s = \frac{C \times k \times k}{\frac{1}{S} \times C \times k \times k + \frac{S-1}{S} \times d \times d} \approx \frac{S \times C}{S + C - 1} \approx S \qquad (3)$$

The model compression ratio of Ghost convolution is:

$$r_C = \frac{N \times C \times k \times k}{\frac{N}{S} \times C \times k \times k + (S - 1) \times \frac{N}{S} d \times d} \approx \frac{S \times C}{S + C - 1} \approx S \qquad (4)$$

In summary, the use of Ghost convolution can accelerate calculations and achieve model compression compared to traditional convolution. The comparison of the parameters of the backbone network and the AlexNet backbone network is as shown in Table 1.

Table 1. Comparison of improved Ghostnet and Alexnet.

Backbone	Floating-point operation	Model parameters
AlexNet	6.49GFlops	3.75M
Ours	3.787GFlops	0.945M

The modified Ghostnet is used as backbone network of tracking algorithm, and tracking algorithm structure as shown in Fig. 5. After extracting by backbone, the correlation operation on output feature map is:

$$R = \varphi(x) \star \varphi(z) \qquad (5)$$

Among them, $\star$ represents the correlation operation of the channel, R is the response graph output after the cross-correlation, and the number of channels is the same as x and z.

In Siamfc, only the last layer of feature maps is calculated by correlation operation. However, the multi-scale output of the feature network contains rich semantic information. The features of the low-level feature map pay more attention to the extraction of image local information and preserving more fine-grained spatial features, which are more effective for accurate positioning of tracking target. The features extracted from the high-level feature map mainly reflect the semantic characteristics of the target, which are more robust to the apparent changes of the target. Therefore, this paper not only uses the output of the last layer, but also fuses the output of the last three layer feature maps of the backbone network for cross-correlation calculations. After correlation operation, the output of last layer uses 1×1 convolution to fuse in the depth wise, which makes tracking more effective since the semantic information of different layers are fully considered.

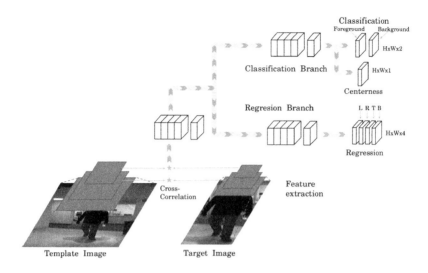

Fig. 5. Tracking network structure

3.3 Improved Loss Function

Compared to tracking based anchor, anchor free has better performance. This paper adopts anchor frame method, which directly returns the offset value of the bounding box according to each point of the response graph.

Classification Branch. The result of classification branch has two channels. Each point maps part of the original image, representing the probability of the foreground and the background. If a specified point on the output response graph falls on the target calibration frame, it is regarded as a positive sample, otherwise it is a negative sample. In the tracking dataset, the tracked target occupies a small area of the overall picture, resulting in a certain imbalance between the positive and negative samples on the response graph. Therefore, this paper improves the BCE classification loss function in traditional target tracking, and uses the focal loss[11] function to solve this problem. Then the classification loss function is:

$$L_{cls}(p_{x,y}^{cls}, C_{x,y}^*) = -\frac{1}{N}\sum_{x,y}\alpha_{x,y}^t(1 - P_{x,y}^t)^\gamma log(P_{x,y}^t) \tag{6}$$

$$P_{x,y}^t = \begin{cases} p, & if c_{x,y}^t = 1, \\ 1-p, & otherwise. \end{cases} \quad \alpha_{x,y}^t = \begin{cases} \alpha, & if c_{x,y}^t = 1, \\ 1-\alpha, & otherwise. \end{cases}$$

among them, α and γ are used to adjust the hyperparameters of positive and negative samples, hard and easy samples respectively.

Regression Branch. The regression loss adopts the distance intersection over union (DIOU) loss [12], since the DIOU loss can consider the relative position relationship between the prediction frame and the target. The DIOU loss is:

$$L_{DIOU} = 1 - \frac{Intersection(B_{pre}, B_{gt})}{Union(B_{pre}, B_{gt})} + \frac{\rho^2(B_{x,y}^{pre} - B_{x,y}^{gt})}{\upsilon^2} \tag{7}$$

Among them, B_{pre} and B_{gt} represent the prediction frame and the real frame respectively, $\rho^2(B_{x,y}^{pre} - B_{x,y}^{gt})$ represents the Euclidean distance between the center of the prediction frame and the true center of the target, and represents the diagonal distance of the smallest rectangle that can cover the prediction frame and the real frame. The regression loss based on DIOU is:

$$L_{reg}(B_{pre}, B_{gt}) = -\frac{1}{N} \sum_{x,y} I_{\{C_{x,y}^* == 1\}} L_{DIOU} \tag{8}$$

In the field of target detection, centerness is proposed by FCOS [13] to improve the performance of the detector. It use centerness to improve the performance of detection, which reduce the weight of the box far away from the center of ground truth box, so that the prediction box closer to the ground truth box has greater weight. In Siamfc++ and SiamCar [14], centerness also is used to improve their performance, so we adds the centerness loss as a part of our loss function. The centerness loss is:

$$L_{ctr} = -\frac{1}{N_{pos}} \sum_{x,y} I_{C_{x,y}^*} \{S_{x,y} log(P_{x,y}^{ctr}) + (1 - S_{x,y}) log(1 - P_{x,y}^{ctr}))\} \tag{9}$$

Among them, $S_{x,y} = I_{x,y}^* \sqrt{\frac{min(\bar{l}, \bar{r})}{max(\bar{l}, \bar{r})} \frac{min(\bar{t}, \bar{b})}{max(\bar{t}, \bar{b})}}$

In summary, the loss function of the lightweight tracking network can be expressed as:

$$L = L_{cls} + \lambda_1 L_{reg} + \lambda_2 L_{ctr} \tag{10}$$

4   Experiment

In order to verify the overall performance of the improved algorithm, this paper compares several algorithm's performance in precision plot and success plot to evaluate the performance of the algorithm on the OTB2015 dataset as shown in Fig. 6.

After using TensorRT to further compress and accelerate the model, the comparision results are shown in Table 2(red represents the best preformance at that column; blue represents the second best performance at that column while yellow represents the third best preformance). Although the improved algorithm in this paper is not the best in precision plot and success plot, it is about twice as fast as other algorithms on the basis that the accuracy and success rate are

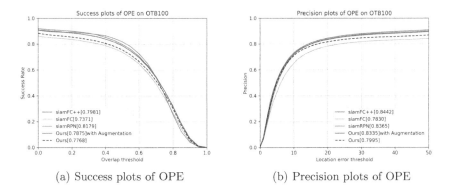

(a) Success plots of OPE   (b) Precision plots of OPE

Fig. 6. Comparison of tracking algorithms on OTB dataset.

(a) Illumination changes

(b) Fast movement frame 1

(c) Fast movement frame 2

Fig. 7. Samples from OTB dataset visualization

Table 2. Comparision with other tracking algorithms in speed and accuracy

Tracker	FPS	Precision plot	Success Plot	Hardware
SiamFc [4]		0.783	0.737	Jetson TX2
SiamRPN [5]	5.23	0.837	0.818	Jetson TX2
SiamFc++ [8]	1.05	0.844	0.798	Jetson TX2
Ours	12.54			Jetson TX2
Ours+TensorRT	15.72	0.802	0.776	Jetson TX2

not too different. The samples of rapid target movement, large-scale changes and illumination changes in the OTB2015 dataset are selected as examples, and the results of different algorithms are visually compared as shown in Fig. 7. In Fig. 8, the blue box show the result of detection algorithm (Yolo detection algorithm), while the red box is the result of our tracking algorithm. It can be seen that the tracking effect of the lightweight tracking network in this paper can meet the tracking requirements, and the two-degree-of-freedom camera platform can achieve continuous tracking of the target.

Fig. 8. Tracking result on the two-degree-of-freedom-platform

5   Conclusion

Data augmentation method is proposed to balance between hard and easy samples. Tracking network feature extraction network adopts lightweight backbone modified from Ghostnet, which achieves less float calculations and fewer model parameters. In addition, modified loss function using focal loss and DIOU loss improve the tracking performance. Experimental results show our method can achieve balance of speed and accuracy on Jetson TX2 than other algorithms and well work on our tracking robot.

References

1. Bolme, D.S., Beveridge, J.R., Draper, B.A., Lui, Y.M.: Visual object tracking using adaptive correlation filters. In: The Twenty-Third IEEE Conference on Computer Vision and Pattern Recognition, CVPR 2010, San Francisco, CA, USA, 13–18 June 2010 (2010)
2. Henriques, J.F., Caseiro, R., Martins, P., Batista, J.: High-speed tracking with kernelized correlation filters. IEEE Trans. Pattern Anal. Mach. Intell. **37**(3), 583–596 (2015)
3. Danelljan, M., Häger, G., Khan, F.S., Felsberg, M.: Accurate scale estimation for robust visual tracking. In: British Machine Vision Conference (2014)
4. Bertinetto, L., Valmadre, J., Henriques, J.F., Vedaldi, A., Torr, P.H.S.: Fully-convolutional siamese networks for object tracking. In: Hua, G., Jégou, H. (eds.) ECCV 2016. LNCS, vol. 9914, pp. 850–865. Springer, Cham (2016). https://doi.org/10.1007/978-3-319-48881-3_56
5. Bo, L., Yan, J., Wei, W., Zheng, Z., Hu, X.: High performance visual tracking with siamese region proposal network. In: 2018 IEEE/CVF Conference on Computer Vision and Pattern Recognition (CVPR) (2018)
6. Li, B., Wei, W., Wang, Q., Zhang, F., Xing, J., Yan, J.: SiamRPN++: evolution of siamese visual tracking with very deep networks. In: 2019 IEEE/CVF Conference on Computer Vision and Pattern Recognition (CVPR) (2020)
7. Wang, Q., Zhang, L., Bertinetto, L., Hu, W., Torr, P.: Fast online object tracking and segmentation: a unifying approach (2018)
8. Xu, Y., Wang, Z., Li, Z., Yuan, Y., Yu, G.: SiamFC++: towards robust and accurate visual tracking with target estimation guidelines. In: Proceedings of the AAAI Conference on Artificial Intelligence, vol. 34, no. 7, pp. 12549–12556 (2020)
9. Zhong, Z., Zheng, L., Kang, G., Li, S., Yang, Y.: Random erasing data augmentation. In: Proceedings of the AAAI Conference on Artificial Intelligence, vol. 34, no. 7 (2017)
10. Han, K., Wang, Y., Tian, Q., Guo, J., Xu, C.: GhostNet: more features from cheap operations. In: 2020 IEEE/CVF Conference on Computer Vision and Pattern Recognition (CVPR) (2020)
11. Lin, T.Y., Goyal, P., Girshick, R., He, K., Dollár, P.: Focal loss for dense object detection. IEEE Trans. Pattern Anal. Mach. Intell. **PP**(99), 2999–3007 (2017)
12. Zheng, Z., Wang, P., Liu, W., Li, J., Ren, D.: Distance-IoU loss: faster and better learning for bounding box regression. In: AAAI Conference on Artificial Intelligence (2020)
13. Tian, Z., Shen, C., Chen, H., He, T.: FCOS: fully convolutional one-stage object detection. In 2019 IEEE/CVF International Conference on Computer Vision (ICCV) (2020)
14. Guo, D., Wang, J., Cui, Y., Wang, Z., Chen, S.: SiamCAR: siamese fully convolutional classification and regression for visual tracking (2019)

Semantic Segmentation and Topological Mapping of Floor Plans

Ke Liu and Ran Huang[(⊠)] [iD]

College of Information Science and Technology, Beijing University of Chemical
Technology, Beijing 100029, China
{2019210437,huangran}@mail.buct.edu.cn

Abstract. When visually impaired people walk in an unknown indoor
environment, it is crucial to build a topological semantic map from the
captured floor plan for navigation purposes. This paper proposes a topological mapping method from the floor plan model based on deep learning semantic segmentation. The topological semantic map can be used
for assistive blind navigation purposes in unknown indoor environments.
A deep learning network is developed for semantic segmentation, and
disturbances such as image rotation, color transformation and Gaussian noises are taken into consideration in the training to enhance the
robustness. With the semantic segmentation result as input, a topological semantic mapping algorithm is then proposed based on the graph
theory. Experiments are presented to demonstrate the effectiveness of
the proposed mapping method.

Keywords: Semantic segmentation · Topological map · Floor plan

1 Introduction

Globally, among 7.79 billion people living in 2020, an estimated 49.1 million were
blind, 221.4 million people had moderate vision impairment(VI), 33.6 million
people had severe VI. The estimated number of blind persons increased from
34.4 million in 1990 to 49.1 million in 2020 [1]. In terms of the current scale
of the blind in China, it is crucial to enhance the ability of the blind to travel
independently in unknown indoor environments.

Normal people can easily walk in an unknown environment without accurate
global environment modeling. The reason lies in that they are able to understand
the semantic signs of the environment and convert the floor plan into a sparse
topological semantic map. So the analysis of the plan can better help the blind to
locate and navigate [2]. Inspired by this, we segment the floorplan and generate
a topological semantic map. The map expresses the connected relation between
rooms, which provides convenience for further path planning.

This work is supported in part by National Natural Science Foundation of China under
Grants U1813220 and 91748102.

X.-J. Liu et al. (Eds.): ICIRA 2021, LNAI 13015, pp. 378–389, 2021.
https://doi.org/10.1007/978-3-030-89134-3_35

The remainder of this paper is organized as follows. Section 2 reviews related work. Section 3 gives the deep learning network for semantic segmentation. The topological semantic mapping algorithm is presented in Sect. 4. To illustrate the effectiveness of the proposed method, experiments performed on various environments are presented in Sect. 5. Finally, Sect. 6 concludes the paper.

2   Related Work

Floor plan analysis and understanding used to apply low-level image processing methods. Low-level features are basic features that can be automatically extracted from an image without any spatial relationship information [3]. Edge types were judged by the thickness of lines in [4]. S. L. Joseph et al. [5] used a heuristic method to detect room number and door shape. D. Sharma et al. [6]got layout segmentation by boundary extraction algorithm and morphological operations. Similarly, morphological closing and the flood-fill technique were used to detect walls and room regions, and scale-invariant features were applied to detect doors in [7] and [8]. B. Li et al. [9] and Z. Fan et al. [10] got semantic information of floor plans from the CAD model.

The above-mentioned heuristic methods and specific detection algorithms for different boundary elements had certain limitations. With complex and variable input, the accuracy would be reduced, and the generalization effect was not desirable when applied to the actual scene.

For a better understanding of floor plans, compound description of environments with semantic information in topological maps has been a popular research topic. In [11] and [12], authors processed spatial relationships and semantic information separately without the integration of measurement information and semantic information. A. K. Krishnan et al. [13] integrated semantic features in topological maps and improved the level of topological maps, however, the application of semantic concepts was still in the primary stage. Graph structure was got from floor plans in [14] but lacked room information.

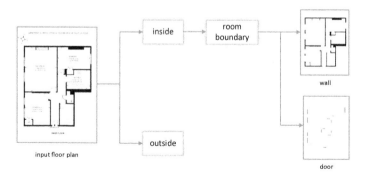

Fig. 1. Floor plan elements

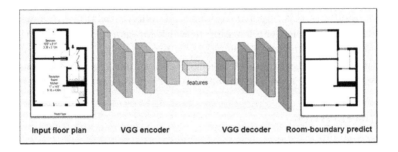

Fig. 2. Network architecture

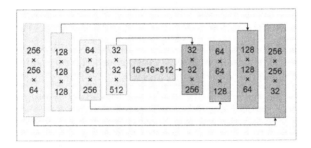

Fig. 3. VGG encoder and decoder

3   Semantic Segmentation

3.1   Goals and Problem Formulation

The goals of our work are as follows. First, we identify room boundary elements in the floor plan to define the room area. Second, some special cases of the plan may appear, such as image rotation, color transformation and Gaussian noises. And we aim to overcome such situations and identify the walls accurately. Motivated by [15], we can identify the elements based on the structure shown in Fig. 1. The pixels in the plan can be identified as inside or outside, and the inside pixels can be further identified as edge elements (doors and walls) of rooms.

3.2   Network Architecture

Our work gets the valuable structure from the overall network architecture in [15]. The VGG (Visual Geometry Group) encoder [16] is retained to extract features and the VGG decoder for predicting room boundary pixels, see Fig. 2 for our network architecture and Fig. 3 for VGG encoder and decoder. It should be noted that the room boundary elements here are not low-level edges or boundaries that separate the background from the content. Instead, the pixels can separate room areas in floor plans, and they are at the same level as the pixels that belong to the room types.

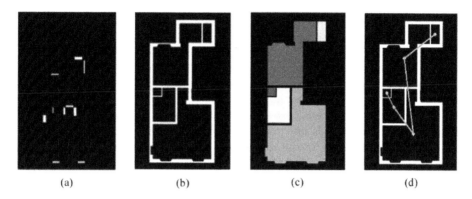

(a)   (b)   (c)   (d)

Fig. 4. Various stages of topological semantic map construction: (a) door image, (b) room image, (c) room image with color, and (d) topological semantic map visualization.

3.3   Network Training

Based on 214 original pictures in [17], 18 circular maps are expanded in R3D dataset, which improves the diversity and complexity of floor plans. Most room shapes in this dataset are non-rectangular, including arc shape, and the wall thickness is nonuniform. Moreover, blurring, light intensity and other situations may occur when we get floor plans from real scene shooting. Taking contrast enhancement, image rotation, color transformation, Gaussian noises into consideration, a new dataset is expanded based on the original one. Through this, the segmentation results are more robust. R3D dataset is randomly divided into 179 images for training and 53 images for testing and ours keeps the same proportion allocation.

We aim to predict room boundary elements (walls and doors) and define the loss function for training as follows:

$$L = w_i \sum_{i=1}^{c} -y_i \log p_i \tag{1}$$

where y_i is the label of the ith floor plan element, c is the number of elements belonging to room boundary, and $p_i \in [0,1]$ is the prediction label of the pixels of the ith floor plan element. In (1), w_i is defined as

$$w_i = \frac{\widehat{N} - \widehat{N}_i}{\sum_{j=1}^{C} \left(\widehat{N} - \widehat{N}_j \right)} \tag{2}$$

where $\widehat{N}_i$ is the total number of ground-truth pixels of the ith floor plan element, $\widehat{N} = \sum_{j=1}^{C} \widehat{N}_i$ which represents the number of ground-truth pixels belonging to room boundary.

4   Topological Semantic Map Construction

After recognizing door pixels and dividing room areas in a floor plan, we construct a topological map that can express the connectivity between rooms, see Fig. 4 for the process. First, we get door and room information including position coordinates, gray value and number. Second, according to the adjacency relation between doors and rooms, we clarify the connected relation between rooms. Third, room information is integrated to visualize the topological map. Finally, we verify the connectivity of the topological map and optimize it.

4.1   Door and Room Information Extraction

Algorithm 1. Information extraction based on the Seed Filling algorithm

---

Input: D, R: door and room image
Output: Rc: room image with color
            d, r: door and room dictionary
1: **procedure** INFORMATION EXTRACTION(D, R)
2:    $d, r \leftarrow$ empty
3:    $dn, rn \leftarrow 1$
4:    $Rc \leftarrow$ image as $BLACK$
5: **for** each pixel in D **do**
6:        $dl \leftarrow$ empty
7:        **if** pixel is door **then**
8:            $dl \leftarrow (i,j)$ ▷ door pixel coordinates
9:            $dl \leftarrow (i_a, j_a)$ ▷ adjacent door pixel coordinates
10:       **end if**
11:       $d[dn] \leftarrow dl$
12:       $dn \leftarrow dn+1$
13: **end for**
14: **for** each pixel in R **do**
15:       **if** pixel is room **then**
16:           $R[i,j] \leftarrow rn$ ▷ label room pixel
17:           $R[i_a, j_a] \leftarrow rn$ ▷ label adjacent room pixel
18:       **end if**
19:       $r[rn] \leftarrow gv$ ▷ random gray value
20:       $rn \leftarrow rn+1$
21: **end for**
22: **for** each pixel in R **do**
23:       **if** pixel is room **then**
24:           $Rc[i,j] \leftarrow R[i,j]$
25:       **end if**
26: **end for**

We process the segmentation results to separate room boundary elements (doors and close walls), see Fig. 4(a) for door image and Fig. 4(b) for room image. For door information extraction, we use the Seed Filling algorithm to label each door and record the coordinates of the pixels contained. In addition, the pixel coordinates of doors are saved to prepare for the elimination of incorrect predictions. For room information extraction, gray value and number are assigned to each room. Then we can get an image filled with different colors for each room as output, see Fig. 4(c).

As shown in Algorithm 1, line 2 to 3 initializes labels and dictionaries of doors and rooms, line 4 initializes the new image all black. Line 5 to 13 uses the Seed Filling algorithm to find each door. Line 14 to 21 expressed a similar process to label the rooms and store their color in the room dictionary. Line 22 to 26 traverses all the pixels in the room image and gets a new room image with color.

4.2   Connected Relation

Algorithm 2. Connected relation between door and room

Input: Rc: room image with color
      d, r: door and room dictionary
Output: c: connected relation dictionary
 1: **procedure** CONNECTED RELATION(Rc, d, r)
 2:   $c \leftarrow$ empty
 3:   **for** dn,dl in d **do** $\triangleright$ dn: door number stored in dictionary d
 4:     $gray \leftarrow$ empty $\triangleright$ gray value of adjacent room
 5:     **for** pixel in dl **do**
 6:       **if** $Rc[i,j]$!=$Rc[i_a,j_a]$ **then** $\triangleright$ $Rc[i,j]$: current pixel value
 7:         $gray \leftarrow Rc[i_a,j_a]$ $\triangleright$ $Rc[i_a,j_a]$: adjacent pixel value
 8:       **end if**
 9:     **end for**
10:     $c[dn] = gray$
11:   **end for**
12:   **for** $dn, gray$ in c **do** $\triangleright$ dn: door number stored in dictionary c
13:     **for** rn, gv in r **do** $\triangleright$ rn: room number stored in dictionary r
14:       **if** $gv == gray$ **then** $\triangleright$ gv: gray value stored in dictionary r
15:         $c[dn] \leftarrow rn$
16:       **end if**
17:     **end for**
18: **end for**

Based on the information obtained in Sect. 4.1, we can judge the adjacency relation between doors and rooms by comparing their gray value. As shown in Algorithm 2, line 2 initializes the connected relation dictionary. Line 3 to 11 traverses door pixels in the door dictionary to check the gray value of adjacent rooms. Line 12 to 18 traverses gray value in room dictionary and stores the relationship between rooms in the connected relation dictionary.

Table 1. Room information.

Room number	Gray value	Contained door number	Room center
1	17	[1, 2, 3, 4]	(190, 284)
2	6	[2]	(263, 233)
3	23	[5]	(149, 357)
4	191	[5, 6, 8]	(166, 387)
5	91	[4, 6, 7, 9, 10]	(212, 443)

4.3   Room Information Summary

We get the door and room information in Sect. 4.1 and the connected relation in Sect. 4.2. And the room image with color in Sect. 4.1 is used to calculate the central coordinates of each room. First, the input image is binarized to find contours. Second, the characteristic moments of contours are calculated by:

$$m_{ji} = \sum_{x,y} \left(\text{array}(x, y) x^j y^i \right) \tag{3}$$

where array (x, y) represents the gray value of the coordinate point (x, y) in the current image. For the binarization image, m_{00} means the area of the contour, and its center position is calculated by:

$$\bar{x} = \frac{m_{10}}{m_{00}}, \quad \bar{y} = \frac{m_{01}}{m_{00}} \tag{4}$$

After the center coordinates are obtained, we summarize all the room information including label, gray value, contained doors and location, see Table 1. Taking each room center as a node, we can visualize the topology map based on the room information summary, see Fig. 4(d).

4.4   Connectivity Verification

After getting the topological map in Fig. 4(d), we need to verify its connectivity. We describe the topology among the nodes by an undirected graph $G = (V, E)$, where V is the vertex set (rooms) and E is the edge set (doors), see Fig. 5.

$$W = \begin{bmatrix} 0 & 1 & 1 & 0 & 0 \\ 1 & 0 & 0 & 0 & 0 \\ 1 & 0 & 0 & 0 & 1 \\ 0 & 0 & 0 & 0 & 1 \\ 0 & 0 & 1 & 1 & 0 \end{bmatrix}, D = \begin{bmatrix} 2 & 0 & 0 & 0 & 0 \\ 0 & 1 & 0 & 0 & 0 \\ 0 & 0 & 2 & 0 & 0 \\ 0 & 0 & 0 & 1 & 0 \\ 0 & 0 & 0 & 0 & 2 \end{bmatrix} \tag{5}$$

$W = [\delta_{ij}] \in R^{N \times N}$ in (5) is the adjacency matrix with elements δ_{ij} and δ_{ji} denoting the same connections such that $\delta_{ij} = \delta_{ji} = 1$ if there is a path between node i and node j. Self edges (i, i) are not allowed, i.e., $\delta_{ii} = 0$ [18]. The degree

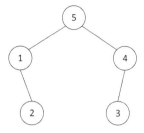

Fig. 5. Undirected graph

matrix D can be calculated by the adjacency matrix. The Laplacian matrix L is defined as:

$$L = D - W = \begin{bmatrix} 2 & -1 & -1 & 0 & 0 \\ -1 & 1 & 0 & 0 & 0 \\ -1 & 0 & 2 & 0 & -1 \\ 0 & 0 & 0 & 1 & -1 \\ 0 & 0 & -1 & -1 & 2 \end{bmatrix} \tag{6}$$

Lemma 1 [19]. *An undirected graph is connected if and only if the rank of its Laplace matrix is $N - 1$.*

According to Lemma 1, the rank of the L matrix verifies that the undirected topological map constructed is connected.

4.5   Optimization

Following the steps above, we get the original topological map. Considering that the segmentation result has certain errors, our algorithm may mistakenly identify several pixels as a door. So we calculate the mean size of doors and delete the wrong door under a proper threshold. This process helps design less impassable routes caused by mistaken door recognition. Taken the new door dictionary as input, we can get the optimized topological map. The connectivity of both topological maps will be verified, if both of them are connected, the optimized topological map will be chosen, which can make route security higher and the actual navigation performance more robust.

5   Experiment

Our work is compared with classical edge detection algorithms such as canny [20]. Each method is evaluated on both R3D dataset and the dataset with complicated situations noted by (n). We employ Precision and F-measure to evaluate boundary detection results. Precision and Recall are the number of correctly-predicted pixels of room boundary divided by the total predicted pixels and divided by the ground-truth pixels, respectively. F-measure combines the performance of Precision and Recall with a certain weight, we set $\beta^2 = 0.3$ here. F-measure is expressed as:

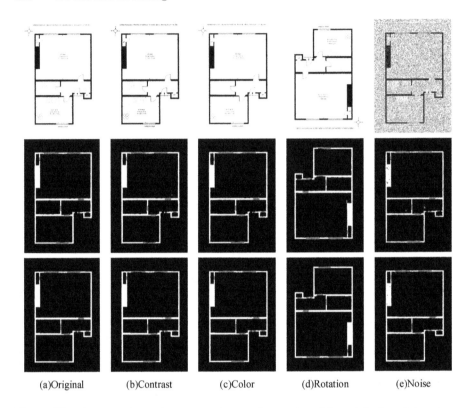

(a)Original   (b)Contrast   (c)Color   (d)Rotation   (e)Noise

Fig. 6. Visual comparison of segmentation results produced by original model and our model. From top to down: input, original model results, and our model results.

Table 2. Comparison with classical edge detection algorithms

Method	Canny	Canny (n)	Sobel	Sobel (n)	Laplacian	Laplacian (n)	Ours	Ours (n)
Precision	0.20	0.23	0.71	0.70	0.74	0.71	**0.93**	**0.92**
F-measure	0.20	0.19	0.40	0.33	0.46	0.34	**0.90**	**0.90**

Table 3. Comparison with original model we trained with R3D dataset

Accuracy	Model	
	Original	Ours
Door	0.72	**0.83**
Wall	0.95	**0.96**
Boundary	0.95	**0.96**

$$\text{F-measure} = \frac{\left(1 + \beta^2\right) \; \text{Precision} \; \times \; \text{Recall}}{\beta^2 \; \text{Precision} \; + \; \text{Recall}} \tag{7}$$

Table 2 reports that our model produces better results.

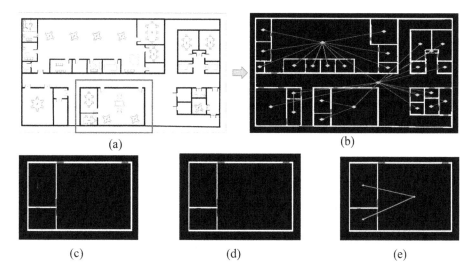

(a) (b)

(c) (d) (e)

Fig. 7. Sample out of dataset.

We compare our model with the one trained with the original dataset, see Fig. 6 for their visual comparison in complicated situations. We use Accuracy to evaluate their performance, which is the ratio of the number of correctly predicted pixels over the total number of ground-truth pixels. Table 3 shows the result that our model adapts to complicated situations with better robustness.

Except for the dataset, we also take an office floor plan as input, see Fig. 7(a) for the overall plan and see Fig. 7(b) for topological semantic map. Here we take part of the floor plan for illustration, see Fig. 7(c) for the original semantic map and Fig. 7(d) for the optimized one. Finally, we get the topological map visualized, see Fig. 7(e). It is verified that the topological map is connected.

6 Conclusion

This paper proposes a topological semantic mapping method from a floor plan model, which can be potentially used to assist the visually impaired to navigate in unknown indoor environments. The mapping method mainly consists of two parts. Based on the public dataset, a deep learning network was trained to realize semantic segmentation of the captured floor map. By integrating semantic and topological information, a mapping algorithm was then developed to build the topological semantic map, and the connectivity can be checked by a rank criterion. Experiments were presented to verify the effectiveness of the proposed mapping method. Localization based on topological semantic maps is a direction for future work.

References

1. Bourne, R.R., Adelson, J., Flaxman, S.: Global prevalence of blindness and distance and near vision impairment in 2020: progress towards the vision 2020 targets and what the future holds. Invest. Ophthalmol. Vis. Sci. **61**(7), 2317 (2020)
2. Watanabe, Y., Amaro, K.R., Ilhan, B., Kinoshita, T., Bock, T., Cheng, G.: Robust localization with architectural floor plans and depth camera. In: 2020 IEEE/SICE International Symposium on System Integration (SII), pp. 133–138 (2020)
3. Name, F., Training, O., Training, P.: Computer Vision Algorithms and Applications. Wiley, New York (2014)
4. Ahmed, S., Liwicki, M., Weber, M., Dengel, A.: Automatic room detection and room labeling from architectural floor plans. In: IAPR International Workshop on Document Analysis Systems (2012)
5. Joseph, S.L., Yi, C., Xiao, J., Tian, Y., Yan, F.: Visual semantic parameterization - to enhance blind user perception for indoor navigation. In: 2013 IEEE International Conference on Multimedia and Expo Workshops (ICMEW), pp. 1–6 (2013)
6. Sharma, D., Chattopadhyay, C., Harit, G.: A unified framework for semantic matching of architectural floorplans. In: 2016 23rd International Conference on Pattern Recognition (ICPR), pp. 2422–2427 (2016)
7. Goyal, S., Chattopadhyay, C., Bhatnagar, G.: Plan2text: a framework for describing building floor plan images from first person perspective. In: 2018 IEEE 14th International Colloquium on Signal Processing Its Applications (CSPA), pp. 35–40 (2018)
8. Goyal, S., Bhavsar, S., Patel, S., Chattopadhyay, C., Bhatnagar, G.: SUGAMAN: describing floor plans for visually impaired by annotation learning and proximity based grammar. IET Image Process. **13**(13), 2623–2635 (2019)
9. Li, B., et al.: Vision-based mobile indoor assistive navigation aid for blind people. IEEE Trans. Mob. Comput. **PP**, 1 (2018)
10. Fan, Z., Zhu, L., Li, H., Chen, X., Zhu, S., Tan, P.: FloorPlanCAD: a large-scale CAD drawing dataset for panoptic symbol spotting. arXiv preprint arXiv:2105.07147 (2021)
11. Galindo, C., Saffiotti, A., Coradeschi, S., Buschka, P., Fernandez-Madrigal, J., Gonzalez, J.: Multi-hierarchical semantic maps for mobile robotics. In: 2005 IEEE/RSJ International Conference on Intelligent Robots and Systems, pp. 2278–2283 (2005)
12. Civera, J., Gálvez-López, D., Riazuelo, L., Tardós, J.D., Montiel, J.M.M.: Towards semantic slam using a monocular camera. In: 2011 IEEE/RSJ International Conference on Intelligent Robots and Systems, pp. 1277–1284 (2011)
13. Krishnan, A.K., Krishna, K.M.: A visual exploration algorithm using semantic cues that constructs image based hybrid maps. In: 2010 IEEE/RSJ International Conference on Intelligent Robots and Systems, pp. 1316–1321 (2010)
14. Yamada, M., Wang, X., Yamasaki, T.: Graph structure extraction from floor plan images and its application to similar property retrieval. In: 2021 IEEE International Conference on Consumer Electronics (ICCE), pp. 1–5 (2021)
15. Zeng, Z., Li, X., Yu, Y.K., Fu, C.W.: Deep floor plan recognition using a multi-task network with room-boundary-guided attention, pp. 9095–9103 (2019)
16. Simonyan, K., Zisserman, A.: Very deep convolutional networks for large-scale image recognition. arXiv preprint arXiv:1409.1556 (2014)
17. Liu, C., Schwing, A.G., Kundu, K., Urtasun, R., Fidler, S.: Rent3D: floor-plan priors for monocular layout estimation. In: 2015 IEEE Conference on Computer Vision and Pattern Recognition (CVPR), pp. 3413–3421 (2015)

18. Huang, R., Ding, Z., Cao, Z.: Distributed output feedback consensus control of networked homogeneous systems with large unknown actuator and sensor delays. Automatica **122**, 109249 (2020)
19. Rota, G.C.: Algebraic Graph Theory. Graduate Texts in Mathematics, vol. 207, no. 3, p. xvi+298 (1994)
20. Canny, J.: A computational approach to edge detection. IEEE Trans. Pattern Anal. Mach. Intell. **PAMI–8**(6), 679–698 (1986)

Novel Mechanisms, Robots
and Applications

An SMA Inchworm-Imitated Robot for Confined Space Inspection

Jung-Che Chang, Nan Ma, Mingfeng Wang, and Xin Dong[✉]

Department of Mechanical, Materials and Manufacturing Engineering,
University of Nottingham, Nottingham NG7 2RD, UK
{jung-che.chang,Nan.Ma,mingfeng.wang,Xin.Dong}@nottingham.ac.uk

Abstract. Machines with complicated inner structures are dominating daily life with its diverse functions and high integration. With the increasing disassembling-assembling difficulty, the in-situ inspection and repairing have become important to low down the cost. This paper provided a simplified Ni-Ti shape memory alloy (SMA) based inchworm-imitated robot, aiming to perform the inspection task in narrow/confined spaces. The experiment showed that the robot marching speed reaches 0.57 mm/s under control of 1.5 A current with a voltage of 7 V. The maximum climbing angle on the metal sheet is 6° and the robot could also walk on the board paper, wood, and painted grounds after adding counterweight. The inchworm-imitated robot shows potential for micro-robot walking inside the confined space to perform the in-situ inspection. This gives the possibility of reducing the inner-structure complexity by decreasing the inspection holes, which leads to better utilization and lower sealing difficulty.

Keywords: In-situ inspection · Shape memory alloy · Inchworm robot

1 Introduction

Due to both the high financial and time cost of replacing or repairing some of the industrial products such as aero-engine [1, 2] and culverts [3], in-situ inspection and repairing show their necessities by reducing the cost through eliminating the disassembling process as well as dealing with the unplanned or emergency tasks.

Micro-robot, regard with its small volume and flexibility, created chances for engineers to remotely accessing to those places conventionally treaded as blind points. However, due to the high complexity and the low robustness, the technical difficulties focus on the mechanism morphology and gait, fabrication, and actuation.

The mechanism morphology should be the most fundamental parts which offers the functionalities for the robot meeting the working condition. Miyashita et al. [4] developed a self-folded polyvinyl chloride (PVC) origami robot which is able to walk and swim in a different environment. Controlling by an alternating external magnetic field, the robot with an asymmetric body balance along the sagittal axis could reach a speed of 3.8 times the robot-length per second. Offering a lower restriction to the environment, Yan et al. [5] came up with a 3° of freedoms (DoFs) novel miniature-step mobile. Driven by a

© Springer Nature Switzerland AG 2021
X.-J. Liu et al. (Eds.): ICIRA 2021, LNAI 13015, pp. 393–403, 2021.
https://doi.org/10.1007/978-3-030-89134-3_36

piezoelectric stack actuator, large stroke translation and rotation with high resolution are achieved through a rhombic flexure hinge mechanism and four electromagnetic legs. The aforementioned mechanisms show a splendid functionality and reach satisfying results to the tasks. However, energy waiste for the weight supporting and the extra controlling load for the balancing makes the engineers started to seek for a simpler solution to reach their goal.

The inchworm-inspired gait allows the robot holding a high energy utilization due its smooth and simple locomotion. Gao et al. [6] proposed a inchworm-like capsule robot which mounted with a lead screw extensor which increased the locomotion efficiency inside the colon by decreasing the marching resistance. Treating two electrodes as robot feet, Cao et al. [7] utilized the electro adhesion to generate the anisotropic friction and controlled the two feet by saddle-like dielectric elastomer actuator (DEA). Such a design offers a simplifier controlling hardware and significantly decreases the size of the robot.

The development of the advanced material shows the potential of designing a highly integrated actuator and also revived the design of smart mechanisms [8–11]. Shape memory alloys (SMA) based actuators, comparing to the dielectric elastomer, allows the robot doing a muscle-like behavior and offering enough stiffness and actuating force. Moreover, the stroke (i.e. deformation) of the SMA actuator could easily amplify without complicated mechanisms such as multi-winding the SMA-string [12]. Driven by symmetrically deployed SMA coiled springs, Koh et al. [13] proposed an "Omegabot" which allows the robot reaching a large deformation locomotion and potentially balanced under any instant posture. Applying the SMA to a soft composite actuation Wang et al. [14] constructed a soft inchworm-inspired robot to offer a higher reliability. Although several successful cases of applying SMA actuators have been found in literature, the complicated configuration rises the difficulty for the analysis and the low accuracy could further set obstacle for a precise thermal controlling. To the author's best knowledge, only few robotics cases have done the analysis to a constitutive level.

In this paper, a simplified inchworm-imitated robot with an SMA actuator was proposed to prove the potential of a analyzable SMA inchworm robot for the in-situ inspection. The folding and unfolding movement of the robot are achieved respectively by the contraction of the SMA and the spring back of the elastic hinge (Sect. 2). Then, the marching speed and the climbing ability of the robot on surfaces of different materials were analyzed (Sect. 3) and tested (Sect. 4). After that, Sect. 5 focused on the discussion of the further improvement in energy efficiency and marching ability from both material and mechanism perspective.

2   Design of SMA Inchworm Robot

2.1   Morphology and Marching Gait

Contacting the ground through the two endpoints (i.e. feet) of the body, the repeating of the pull-push movement and the continuing changing of the foot function between anchor and slider makes the inchworm achieves the marching purpose with characteristics of high stability, small volume and smooth movement (Fig. 1). Imitating the folding movement of the body and the anisotropy of the friction, Fig. 2(a) shows the equivalent mechanism of the inchworm-imitated robot with its marching gait. Two rigid legs (i.e.

links AC and BC) connected by a joint C are able to achieve a folding movement under the control of an SMA actuator (i.e. spring DE) which could be heated by an electric circuit to shorten its length. Each end of the legs (i.e. point A and B) behaves an anisotropic friction coefficient. This allows the endpoints 'slide' on the ground when receiving friction from the forward direction and 'grab' the ground when receiving friction from the other side.

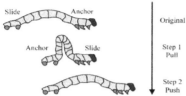
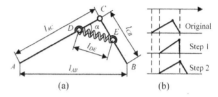

Fig. 1. Marching gait of the inchworm.   **Fig. 2.** Marching gait of the inchworm. (a) Sketch of the proposed inchworm-imitated robot. (b) Marching gait.

As shown in Fig. 2(b), a complete marching period contains two steps: step 1 – the actuator heats up and folds the robot, where the front leg grabs the ground and drags the rear leg which contracts the system; step 2 – the actuator cools down and unfolds the robot while the rear leg grabs the ground and pushes the front leg back and release the body to the initial state to move forward. Repeating the above cycle, the robot could reach a marching purpose.

Defining l as the link length and the subscript as the corresponding link name (e.g. l_{AB} means the length of link AB), the length of the SMA-string after the contraction l_{DEs} could be expressed as follow:

$$l_{DEs} = l_{DE} - \Delta l_{DE} \qquad (1)$$

where Δl_{DE} is the total contraction length of the SMA-string.

Therefore, applying the cosine theorem, the step length of the robot could be estimated as follow:

$$\Delta l_{AB} = l_{AB} - \sqrt{l_{AC}^2 + l_{BC}^2 - \frac{l_{AC} \cdot l_{BC}}{l_{CD} \cdot l_{DEs}} \cdot (l_{CD}^2 + l_{DEs}^2 - l_{CE}^2)} \qquad (2)$$

2.2 Construction of Inchworm-Imitated Robot

The design of the inchworm-imitated robot is shown in Fig. 3. A Ni-Ti SMA-string (from DYNALLOY, Inc.) was linked between a pair of foldable 3D-printed legs which the soft side of the velcro (refer to as brush) was sticked on their endpoint which is expected to utilize the regularly-directed bristles to further enhance the friction anisotropy that mainly created by the unequal leg length. Working as an actuator, the SMA-string applies a pulling force when contracted by heating, which leads to a folding behavior of the legs. The elastic hinge between the front and the rear leg restores the energy generated from

Table 1. Property of the Ni-Ti alloy

Property name	Value
Diameter (mm)	0.31
Resistance (ohms/ meter)	12.2
Heating Pull Gram Force (grams)	1280
Cooling Deformation Force (grams)	512
Approximate Current for 1 s Contraction (mA)	1500
Cooling Time 158° F, 70 °C Wire (seconds)	8.1
Cooling Time 194° F, 90 °C Wire (seconds)	6.8
Contraction rate	4%

the deformation of the SMA-string and causes a 'spring-back' when the SMA-string stops gaining heat. The property of the Ni-Ti SMA-string is shown in Table 1.

Based on the datasheet of SMA material, the contraction rate of the applied SMA-string is about 4%. Directly contact the two legs through the SMA-strings could lead to an unexpected small stroke of the folding considering the small dimension of the legs. To achieve larger deformation of the SMA-string, a 4-pulley set is embedded to the front leg and fixed by glass fiber shafts (Fig. 4). It is worth to note that in the proposed system, the actual contraction rate of the SMA-string would be lower than 4% since the elastic hinge offers an external tension force.

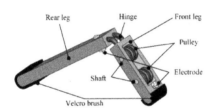  

Fig. 3. Model of the inchworm-imitated robot.   Fig. 4. Deployment of the SMA-string.

3 Modelling of SMA Inchworm Robot

The one-dimension assumption [15] was applied to the SMA-string model based on the ultra-slender configuration of the Ni-Ti string. According to the current experimental setup, the energy inside the string could be decomposed and following the relationship as below:

$$\frac{U^2}{R} + \rho \cdot f' \cdot \Delta H - \alpha \cdot T \cdot \sigma' - \frac{h_a \cdot l}{S}(T - T_a) = q_p \tag{3}$$

where U^2/R – heat gaining from the circuit: U is the applied voltage to the SMA-string and R is the resistance of the SMA-string; $\rho f' \Delta H$ – the heat contributed to the martensite-austenite transformation: ρ is the local density of the SMA-string, f' is the rate of the martensite volumetric fraction f, and ΔH is the latent transformation heat between austenite and martensite; $\alpha T \sigma'$ – the heat contributed to the martensite-austenite transformation: α is the local thermal expansion rate of the SMA-string, T is the local temperature of the SMA-string and σ' is the rate of the local axial stress; $h_s l (T-T_s)/S$ – the losing heat due to the heat exchange with air: h_a is the convection factor, l the total length of the SMA-string, S the cross-section area of the SMA-string and T_a the air temperature. Last, q_p represents the total potential energy restoring inside the SMA-string which could also be defined as follow:

$$q_p = \rho \cdot C_p \cdot T' \tag{4}$$

where C_p is the heat capacity of the SMA-string and T' the time based variation rate of the temperature.

The contact between the SMA-string and the pulley offers the thermal boundary condition as follow:

$$\begin{cases} -\lambda(u_1, t) \cdot \dfrac{\partial T}{\partial x}\bigg|_{u_1} = h_p \cdot \left(T_{p1} - T(u_1, t)\right) \\[2mm] -\lambda(u_2, t) \cdot \dfrac{\partial T}{\partial x}\bigg|_{u_2} = h_p \cdot \left(T_{p2} - T(u_2, t)\right) \end{cases} \tag{5}$$

where λ is the thermal conductivity, u_1 and u_2 the SMA-string length contacting to the two pulleys, h_p the conductance factor between the SMA-string and pulleys, and T_{p1} and T_{p2} the temperature of the pulleys which could be treated as a same value due to the same material of the pulley and their similar mounted environment.

To simplify the calculation, the variation of f was assumed to neglect the R-phase transformation and follow the first order flow rule which was proposed in Ref. which could be expressed as follow:

$$f' = V_b \cdot (f_b - f) \tag{6}$$

where V_b is the maximum transformation rate at the start point of the transformation, f_b is the martensitic fraction when balanced, referring Ref. [16], it could be assumed to follow the lever rule as below:

$$\begin{cases} f_b = 0 & \text{if} \quad \sigma < \sigma_s \\[1mm] f_b = \dfrac{\sigma - \sigma_s}{\sigma_f - \sigma_s} & \text{if } \sigma_s < \sigma < \sigma_f \\[1mm] f_b = 1 & \text{if} \quad \sigma > \sigma_f \end{cases} \tag{7}$$

where σ_s and σ_f are the stress for the start and the end of the austenite-martensite transformation. It should be mentioned that the martensite-austenite transformation also follows a similar relationship but exchange σ_s and σ_f since the numerical high-low relationship are opposite to the austenite-martensite transformation.

Additionally, the intervention of the thermodynamic force F_d should be non-negligible. Ref. [17] pointed out that according to the positive dissipation, F_d follows the bellow condition:

$$\begin{cases} F_d \cdot f' \geq 0 \\ \Delta H = F_d + T \cdot \dfrac{\partial F_d}{\partial T} \end{cases} \tag{8}$$

Then, following the classic strain decomposition which neglected the thermal elasticity [19], the localized total strain ε could be expressed as follow:

$$\varepsilon = \frac{\sigma}{E} + \alpha(T - T_a) + f \cdot \varepsilon_m \tag{9}$$

where the first term on the right-hand side of the equation is the elastic behavior: E is the Youngs modulus. The second term is the thermal expansion, and the third term is the strain contributed by the phase transformation: ε_m is the strain for a complete austenite-matensite transformation.

It should be noted that α, E and λ were dynamic variables. To decrease the calculation load, the simple mixed law and Reuss estimation were suggested and the relationship could be expressed as follow:

$$\begin{cases} \alpha = f \cdot \alpha_M + (1 - f) \cdot \alpha_A \\ E^{-1} = f \cdot E_M^{-1} + (1 - f) \cdot E_A^{-1} \\ \lambda^{-1} = f \cdot \lambda_M^{-1} + (1 - f) \cdot \lambda_A^{-1} \end{cases} \tag{10}$$

where the foot note A and M respectively represents the parameter under the condition of a pure austenite condition and a pure martensite condition.

From a macroscopic perspective, the propose model requires the elastic hinge giving a moment which expands the SMA-string when in the cooling state while still allows the SMA-string shrink when gaining heat. Therefore, the moment of the elastic hinge should comply with the following relationship:

$$M_i < F_i \cdot \sin \alpha \cdot l_{CD} \tag{11}$$

where M_i is the instant moment of the elastic hinge, F_i the instant heating pull force or cooling deformation force of the SMA-string, and α the angle between links CD and DE. Applying the cosine theorem, α could be expressed as follow:

$$\alpha = \arccos \frac{l_{CD}^2 + l_{DEi}^2 - l_{CE}^2}{2 l_{CD} \cdot l_{DEi}} \tag{12}$$

where l_{DEi} is the instant length of the shrinking SMA-string.

The aforementioned equations offer the analysis of the behavior of both inchworm and its SMA-string. The correlation between the two behaviors could be constructed through the force and configuration condition as follow:

$$\begin{cases} \Delta l_{DE} = \displaystyle\int_0^l \varepsilon \, dx \\ F_i = \sigma \cdot S \end{cases} \tag{13}$$

4   Experiment of Inchworm-Imitated Robot

This section focuses on proving the motion of the proposed mechanism and evaluating the marching ability. The experiment was separated into a speed test (Fig. 5) and a climbing ability test (Figs. 6 and 7). The former experiment focuses on the validation of basic marching ability and the latter aims to collect the adaptability of the robot in different environments. Based on the previous analysis, a prototype has been fabricated with the parameters shown in Table 2.

Table 2. Parameters of the inchworm-imitated robot

Property name	Value
l_{AB}	80
l_{BC}	40
l_{AC}	75
l_{DE}	32
l	100

4.1   Speed Test

Placed on a flattened smooth metal sheet, the inchworm-imitated robot was controlled by a 1.5 A direct current and a voltage of 7V (Fig. 5). The switch of the circuit was set to be 'on' at step 1 (0 s to 1 s) and 'off' at step 2 (1 s to 7 s). As shown in the step flow of Fig. 5, the experiment agrees well with the designed marching gait and the marching speed of the inchworm-imitated robot reaches 0.57 mm/s. It is worth to note that there is no unexpected slipping (i.e. front leg slipping in step 1 or rear leg slipping in step 2) been observed during the experiment.

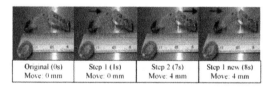

Original (0s)	Step 1 (1s)	Step 2 (7s)	Step 1 new (8s)
Move: 0 mm	Move: 0 mm	Move: 4 mm	Move: 4 mm

Fig. 5.   Marching records in different steps.

4.2   Climbing Ability Test

The low weight of the robot and the low friction coefficient of the velcro could weaken the climbing ability. Since the developed robot could be applied in environments (e.g. aero engine inspection) with different surface materials, in order to guarantee the working performance, the climbing ability of the developed robot was performed in surface with different roughness.

As shown in Fig. 6, the robot was alternatively placed on a board paper, wood sheet and painted ground to test the behavior in different environments. The unexpected slipping was observed in all of the above environments. This phenomenon can be attributed to the low friction coefficient of the velcro, the insufficient total weight of the robot, and the unbalanced weight of the front and rear leg. However, the successful forward movement does achieve to prove the effectiveness of the fundamental mechanism.

Fig. 6. Straight walking test on different materials.

Fig. 7. Marching test on curved metal sheet.

In order to check the implications of the endpoint material for the marching behavior of the developed robot, endpoints with different material were applied by taking off the velcro from the printed legs (i.e. contacting the ground by photosensitive resin). Table 3 shows the result of the robot with different endpoint materials respectively on its front and rear legs marching on different types of surfaces. It should be noted that although the robot successfully marched on three of the surfaces with several kinds of material combination, different severities of slippery behavior was observed which causes demand for further researching. Overall, to maximize the marching effect, the application of the endpoint material might need to be varied according to different types of terrains and surfaces.

To test the performance variation of the robot with different total weight and balancing, counterweights were added on the rear leg of the robot respectively. The result shows that when the weight of the front leg equals to or is slightly bigger than the rear leg, the robot could march on all of the aforementioned materials with velcro mounted on both side of the legs. This shows a more significant effect comparing with the changing of the endpoint material which still unavailable for marching on the wood sheets.

Finally, the robot (without counterweight) was placed on a horizontally placed curved metal sheet and also an inclined metal sheet to test the climbing ability on the inclined surface. The unexpected slipping was observed on the curved sheet, which indicates that current prototype remains further improvements for the environment such as turbine blade (Fig. 7). However, this experiment gives some critical information for how to improve the design in the future work and the experiment on the inclined metal sheet shows that the current design could march on the metal sheet with a 6° inclination.

Table 3. Result of changing the endpoint material

Ground type	Front leg	Rear leg	Succeed	Ground type	Front leg	Rear leg	Succeed
Metal sheet	Y	Y	Y	Wood sheet	Y	Y	N
	Y	N	Y		Y	N	N
	N	Y	Y		N	Y	N
	N	N	Y		N	N	N
Board paper	Y	Y	N	Painted sheet	Y	Y	N
	Y	N	N		Y	N	N
	N	Y	Y		N	Y	Y
	N	N	Y		N	N	Y

4.3 Discussion

The result from the experiment indicates that gaps still exists on the way of reaching the engineering use, but it demonstrates the possibility for using the SMA-string to develop the miniaturized programmable robot marching inside the confined space. Based on the current work, further improvements could be achieved to develop the miniature robot with better crawling ability. This section discussed the possible reasons leading to the current result and pointed out further improvements for better speed, climbing ability, and energy utilization.

The speed test shows a 0.57 mm/s marching speed of the inchworm-imitated robot. The limited speed was mainly caused by the long time cost during the unfolding step (i.e. step 2). Increasing the stiffness of the elastic hinge could fast up the process. However, this also leads to a requirement of higher energy from the circuit during step 1. Neglecting the variation of the rigid-body rotational energy, the simplified energy transmission could be expressed as follow:

$$\begin{cases} E_{\text{kinetic1}} = E_{\text{circuit}} - (E_{\text{SMA1}} + E_{\text{draging1}} + \Delta E_{\text{gravity}} + E_{\text{rod1}} + E_{\text{lose1}}) \\ E_{\text{kinetic2}} = E_{\text{rod2}} + \Delta E_{\text{gravity}} - (E_{\text{SMA2}} + E_{\text{draging2}} + E_{\text{lose2}}) \end{cases} \tag{14}$$

where E_{kinetic1} and E_{kinetic2} are the translation kinetic energy of the robot respectively in step 1 and step 2, E_{circuit} is the output energy from the electric circuit, $\Delta E_{\text{gravity}}$ is the variation of gravity potential energy, E_{draging1} and E_{draging2} are the energy generated by the friction between robot leg and ground respectively in step 1 and step 2, E_{rod1} and E_{rod2} are the potential energy of the elastic hinge respectively in step 1 and step 2, E_{lose1} and E_{lose2} are the losing energy (e.g. heat) respectively in step 1 and step 2, and E_{SMA1} and E_{SMA2} are the contracting energy of the SMA-string without any payload respectively in step 1 and step 2. The sum of E_{kinetic1} and E_{kinetic2} should be the effective energy of the robot translation. Therefore, the efficiency μ could be expressed as follow:

$$\mu = \frac{E_{\text{kinetic1}} + E_{\text{kinetic2}}}{E_{\text{circuit}}} \tag{15}$$

The experiment test of the climbing ability shows that the friction between the robot and the surface should be further improved. As mentioned in Sect. 3, the low friction coefficient of the velcro, the insufficient total weight of the robot, and the unbalanced weight of the front and rear leg should be the reasons that cause the issue. Adding counterweight is the current plan to solve the problem but the trade between weight and speed could be uneconomical. As shown in (13), the increment of the weight affects $E_{draging1}$ and $E_{draging2}$. Additionally, from the transition of kinetic energy perspective, the object weight m shows a linear relationship with the power of the object velocity v^2. Hence, a smaller coefficient (i.e. from $m^{-0.5}$ to $(m + \Delta m)^{-0.5}$) would further decrease the velocity. Therefore, the further optimization of the solution to the low friction issue should be focused on applying better materials instead of the velcro to enhance the coefficient, and fabricating lower weight pulley to decrease the unbalance of the front and rear leg.

5   Conclusion

The inchworm-imitated robot, actuated by the cooperation of the elastic hinge and Ni-Ti SMA-string, is developed in this paper. Pulleys were utilized to increase the contracting length of the SMA-string, which causes a striding motion of the robot and increases the marching speed. The robot with an analyzable structure shows potential for the micro-robot to march inside a confined space for the inspection demand. The versatility and the simplicity of the mechanism offer wide freedom on the selection of materials, give a possibility on further minimizing the dimension, and increase the efficiency.

Controlling by 1.5 A direct current and 7V voltage, the marching speed on a horizontal metal sheet reaches 0.57 mm/s and the maximum passable inclination of the metal sheet is 6°. The endpoint material might need to be varied according to different ground type to maximize the marching effect. However, adding counterweights on the rear leg of the robot more significantly could increase the climbing ability. As a result, the robot holds the ability of marching on metal sheets, wood sheets, painted sheets and board paper.

The future work will focus on proving the effectiveness of the SMA-string analysis, enhancing the climbing ability and optimizing the energy utilization. Utilizing more ideal endpoint material, optimizing the morphology with positioned center gravity and choosing an SMA-string with a higher heating pull force and short cooling time should be the main approach to the above goal.

Acknowledgment. The research leading to these results has received funding from the department of Mechanical, Materials and Manufacturing Engineering of the University of Nottingham, and master student project of the University of Nottingham.

References

1. Wang, M., Dong, X., Ba, W., Mohammad, A., Axinte, D., Norton, A.: Design, modelling and validation of a novel extra slender continuum robot for in-situ inspection and repair in aeroengine. arXiv preprint arXiv:1910.04572 (2019)

2. Alatorre, D., et al.: Teleoperated, in situ repair of an aeroengine: overcoming the internet latency hurdle. IEEE Robot. Autom. Mag. **26**(1), 10–20 (2018)
3. Liu, L.S.: A Smart Tunnel Inspection Robot for the Detection of Pipe Culverts. In: Applied Mechanics and Materials, vol. 614, pp. 184–187. Trans Tech Publ. (2014)
4. Miyashita, S., Guitron, S., Ludersdorfer, M., Sung, C.R., Rus, D.: An untethered miniature origami robot that self-folds, walks, swims, and degrades. In: 2015 IEEE International Conference on Robotics and Automation (ICRA), pp. 1490–1496. IEEE (2015)
5. Yan, S., Zhang, F., Qin, Z., Wen, S.: A 3-DOFs mobile robot driven by a piezoelectric actuator. Smart Mater. Struct. **15**(1), N7 (2005)
6. Gao, J., Yan, G., Shi, Y., Cao, H., Huang, K., Liu, J.: Optimization design of extensor for improving locomotion efficiency of inchworm-like capsule robot. Sci. China Technol. Sci. **62**(11), 1930–1938 (2019). https://doi.org/10.1007/s11431-018-9465-0
7. Cao, J., Liang, W., Wang, Y., Lee, H.P., Zhu, J., Ren, Q.: Control of a soft inchworm robot with environment adaptation. IEEE Trans. Ind. Electron. **67**(5), 3809–3818 (2019)
8. Jingjun, C.B.Z.G.Y., Xin, D.: Dynamic modeling and analysis of 2-DOF quasi-sphere parallel platform. J. Mech. Eng. **2013**(13), 5 (2013)
9. Yu, J., Dong, X., Pei, X., Kong, X.: Mobility and singularity analysis of a class of two degrees of freedom rotational parallel mechanisms using a visual graphic approach. J. Mech. Robot. **4**(4) (2012)
10. Ma, N., et al.: Parametric vibration analysis and validation for a novel portable hexapod machine tool attached to surfaces with unequal stiffness. J. Manuf. Process. **47**, 192–201 (2019)
11. Russo, M., Dong, X.: A calibration procedure for reconfigurable Gough-Stewart manipulators. Mech. Mach. Theory **152**, 103920 (2020)
12. Ma, N., Dong, X., Axinte, D.: Modelling and experimental validation of a compliant underactuated parallel kinematic manipulator. IEEE/ASME Trans. Mechatron. (2020)
13. Koh, J.-S., Cho, K.-J.: Omega-shaped inchworm-inspired crawling robot with large-index-and-pitch (LIP) SMA spring actuators. IEEE/ASME Trans. Mechatron. **18**(2), 419–429 (2012)
14. Wang, W., Lee, J.-Y., Rodrigue, H., Song, S.-H., Chu, W.-S., Ahn, S.-H.: Locomotion of inchworm-inspired robot made of smart soft composite (SSC). Bioinspir. Biomimet. **9**(4), 046006 (2014)
15. Liang, C., Rogers, C.A.: One-dimensional thermomechanical constitutive relations for shape memory materials. J. Intell. Mater. Syst. Struct. **8**(4), 285–302 (1997)
16. Depriester, D., Maynadier, A., Lavernhe-Taillard, K., Hubert, O.: Thermomechanical modelling of a NiTi SMA sample submitted to displacement-controlled tensile test. Int. J. Solids Struct. **51**(10), 1901–1922 (2014)
17. Auricchio, F., Taylor, R.L., Lubliner, J.: Shape-memory alloys: macromodelling and numerical simulations of the superelastic behavior. Comput. Methods Appl. Mech. Eng. **146**(3–4), 281–312 (1997)

A Noncommunicative Transportation Approach for Multiple Physical Connected Objects

Lin Zhang[1]([✉]) [iD], Xianhua Zheng[1] [iD], Qing Han[1], Lingling Su[2] [iD],
and Mingzhou Luo[3]

[1] School of Robot Engineering, Yangtze Normal University, Chongqing 408100, China
[2] College of Science, North China University of Technology, Beijing 100144, China
[3] Jiangsu Key Laboratory of Special Robot Technology, Changzhou, China

Abstract. In this paper, a noncommunicative multi-robot system, which is utilized for heavy equipment transportation on underground longwall mining working face, is discussed. The problem is cooperative transportation of multiple physical connected object (MPO) with limited sensor network and unstable communication. To tackle this problem, pushing-based transportation dynamics of the noncommunicative multi-robot system is derived, and the convergence of the pushing-based transportation dynamics is proven based on leader-follower control strategy. Then simulations considering different transportation ability are carried out. The efficiency and predictability are discussed. Results prove that the transportation time is much reduced, and transportation process is predictable compared to traditional operation. The simulation results show that the potential efficiency of cooperative transportation of MPO.

Keywords: Underground longwall mining working face · Underground robotics · Multi-robot system · Intelligent control

1 Introduction

Research on intelligent equipment control of underground longwall mining face remains great challenge and attracts much research interests in recent years. The intelligent equipment on underground longwall mining face includes a mining machine, a scraper conveyer which is comprised of many interconnected middle troughs (MTs), and corresponding number of mobile support robots (MSRs). Particularly, each MSR relates to a MT, and each MSR is capable of transporting MT through push-pull operation. The transportation system, which is comprised of several MSRs and corresponding number of MTs, can be simplified as a class of multi-robot system that used for transporting multiple physical connected MTs. During the cooperative operation, displacement sensor, which is embedded in the pushing cylinder of MSR, is non-replaceable because of cumbersome mechanical structure and its unmaintainable installation. It will be totally disabled once the sensor is broken, and the replacement process could be extraordinary complex. Additionally, due to the terrible working environment with unstable communication, the sensing information could be unavailable. Consequently, the transportation

X.-J. Liu et al. (Eds.): ICIRA 2021, LNAI 13015, pp. 404–414, 2021.
https://doi.org/10.1007/978-3-030-89134-3_37

result is always out of alignment without considering the sensor-limited characteristics and unstable communication. Thus, the cooperative control method is much needed for such kind of noncommunicative multi-robot system.

Research on multirobot systems has attracted much attention [1]. cooperativity between individuals is the key to multirobot system [2]. To explore the cooperativity between individuals, McCreery [3] and Gelblum [4] research the behavioral mechanisms that led to cooperation in ants. Similarly, Feinerman revisits this problem, and a more detailed research study of the cooperative transportation of ants is published in Nature [5]. Based on the above outstanding research studies, cooperation between individuals is the key to a multirobot system, and the communication between individuals is one of the most essential factors that affect the cooperative performance. For noncommunicative multi-robot system, the cooperative control is much more complicated. Wang [6, 7] et al. propose a method for multi-robot manipulation with only local measurements, which means that communication between individuals was not required. In 2016, Wang applies this method to the cooperative pushing manipulation of an N-robot transport system (ANTS) without communication [8]. The analysis and simulation of two ANTS implementations proves the state-of-the-art method. Considering sensor-limited characteristics and unstable communication conditions, these works inspire us with the idea that noncommunicative cooperative control is essential for the manipulation of MSR.

As to the manipulation of MSR, the push-pull based operation should be discussed further. The manipulation method used for transportation is pushing/pulling, which is researched in 1999 by Rezzoug [9] already. Massive documents recorded the achievements in establishing a model and designing a controller [10, 11]. For example, Ma [12] built an anisotropic friction model to better understand the variability and the predictability of planar friction. Agboh [13] etc. built a task-adaptive model and a corresponding predictive controller were proposed for different accuracy requirements. However, these studies are focused on single object transportation. The transportation of multiple objects by pushing remains great challenge and needs further research. In 2006, Kensuke Harada proposed an edge model for stably pushing a chain of N objects [14]. Both sliding and rotation motion were considered in the final experiment, and the result proved the effectiveness of the proposed method. To study a service robot, the human body was simplified as an object with connected two-links, and the kinematics of the free-ended two-rigid-links were analyzed in Japan [15]. Considering existing affordance models cannot cope with multiple objects that may interact during operation, a relational affordance model was proposed for multiple-object manipulation. The proposed model possessed four advantages compared with the traditional model [16]. Additionally, multiple objects with interlink connections are reviewed. The manipulation planning of multiple interlinked deformable linear objects provides potential application in aerospace and automotive assembly [17]. As a specified application, i.e., aircraft assembly, a mathematical formulation for attaching interlinked deformable linear objects (DLO) to clamping points is proposed, and shape computation and manipulation planning is also tested through this method [18].

Bearing the above observations in mind, to eliminate information uncertainties due to sensor-limited characteristics and unstable communication, we propose an intelligent cooperative transportation approach for multiple physical connected objects (MPO) by utilizing a noncommunicative multi-robot system. The rest of the article is organized as follows. In Sect. 2, cooperative transportation dynamics without communication is derived through push-based operations. In Sect. 2.1, a simple leader-follower control strategy is applied based on the dynamics. Sect. 3 describes simulations with different system configurations to prove the potential effectiveness. Finally, conclusions and future work are summarized in Sect. 4.

2   Pushing-Based Transportation Dynamics

Based on our previous research [19], The physical model of the pushing-based cooperative transportation system, as shown in Fig. 1(a), is composed of MSRs and MTs.

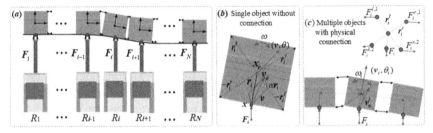

Fig. 1. Pushing-based transportation dynamics for a noncommunicative multi-robot system. (a) The simplified pushing-based transportation model; (b) Mechanical diagram of a single object transportation without a physical connection; (c) Mechanical diagram of multiple objects transportation with physical connections.

To analyze the coupling mechanism of such a multi-robot system, the pushing-based transportation dynamics are considered within a planar region $Q \in \mathbb{R}^2$. The mass of the ith MT is denoted as M_i, and the moment of inertia is J_i. The pose of every MT can be described with three parameters: the position of the mass center $\{x_c, y_c\} \in \mathbb{R}^2$ and the orientation $\theta \in \mathbb{R}^1$. Three kinds of friction need to be considered, including static friction, viscous friction, and kinetic friction. The frictional coefficients are represented as u_s, u_v, and u_k. Since MTs are directly manipulated on ground, both the static friction and the kinetic friction are considered. The acceleration of gravity is g. Then, our problem is that N robots, which were denoted as R_i, $i\epsilon\{1, 2, \ldots, N\}$, try to transport multiple physical connected objects in Q. All robots cannot communicate with each other, and only the first moving robot knew the next destination of the pushing manipulation. The first moving robot is not fixed, and it can either be specified by programming or guided by a human. The objective is to take the first moving robot's force as the input and to generate a sequence of forces corresponding to each robot, and to align in the same direction.

For a single object, as shown in Fig. 1(b), the movement of pushing-based transportation is described as translational velocity v and angular velocity $\omega = \dot{\theta}$ under the forces output from the robots. According to Newton's second law, the translational dynamics can be written and discrete approximated by Euler's method as follows:

$$M_i \frac{v_i^{t+1} - v_i^t}{\Delta t} = F_i - \mu_k M_i g \frac{v_t}{||v_t||} \tag{1}$$

Since the object has a geometric extension around the mass center, two types of torque are studied to characterize the rotational dynamics. One type is associated with friction, and another type is associated with the robot's force. Similar to Wang's solution [8], the frictional torque is derived via the calculus method. The velocity on an arbitrary point of the object can be written as $v_\alpha = v + \omega r_i$, where v_α is the absolute velocity, v is the translational velocity at the mass center $\{x_c, y_c\}$, and r_i is the vector pointing from mass center to the current point. If the density of the object is denoted as ρ, then the kinetic frictional force can be calculated as follows:

$$F_v = -\mu_k M_i g \frac{v_a}{||v_a||} \tag{2}$$

The kinetic frictional torque can then be derived as follows:

$$\begin{aligned} T_f &= -\int_S \mu_k \rho g r_i \frac{v_a}{||v_a||} dx \\ &= -\frac{\mu_k g}{||v_a||} M x_c \times v + \frac{\mu_k M g x_c}{||v_a||} \times v - \left(\frac{\mu_k g}{||v_a||} \int_S \rho r_i^2 dr\right)\omega \end{aligned} \tag{3}$$

Finally, we obtain the frictional torque: $T_f = -\left(\frac{\mu_k g}{||v_a||} \int_S \rho r_i^2 dr\right)\omega = -\frac{\mu_k g}{||v_a||} J_i \omega$.

The robot's torque is much easier to calculate in this case because each object was centrosymmetric around the mass center. The overall rotational dynamics can be written as follows:

$$J_i \dot{\omega} = T_i - T_f = F_i \times r_i - \frac{\mu_k g}{||v_a||} J_i \omega \tag{4}$$

Compared to dynamics of single object transportation, the transportation dynamics of multiple physical connected objects is much more complicated, because both the translational movement and the rotational movement are affected by neighboring forces, as shown in Fig. 1(c). MPO's translational dynamics can be written as follows:

$$M_i \dot{v}_i = F_i - \mu_k M g \frac{v}{||v||} - \sum_{k=1}^{K} \sum_{j=1}^{2} F_i^{k,j} \tag{5}$$

where K denotes the number of neighboring objects that affected the current stage of transportation, and $K \le \lceil F_i / u_k M g \rceil$ must be satisfied. If only two neighbors on both sides are considered, then the equation can be simplified as follows:

$$M_i \dot{v}_i = F_i - \mu_k M g \frac{v}{||v||} - \sum_{j=1}^{2} \left(F_i^{l,j} + F_i^{r,j}\right) \tag{6}$$

where $F_i^{l,1}$ and $F_i^{l,2}$ are the coupling forces at the left-top and left-bottom corners of the neighboring object on the left side. $F_i^{r,1}$ and $F_i^{r,2}$ are the coupling forces at the top-right and bottom-right corners of the neighboring object on the right side. Compared to single object transportation, three types of torque are studied in this case, namely, the kinetic frictional torque, the robot's torque, and the torques that are affected by the neighboring objects T_{ne}. Thus, the overall rotational dynamics can be written as follows:

$$J_i \dot{\omega} = T_i - T_f - T_{ne} = F_i \times r_i - \frac{\mu_k g}{||v_a||} J_i \omega - \sum_{j=1}^{2} \left(F_i^{l,j} \times r_i^{l,j} + F_i^{r,j} \times r_i^{r,j} \right) \quad (7)$$

where $r_i^{l,1}$ and $r_i^{l,2}$ are the position vectors of the top–left corner and the bottom-left corner relative to the mass center. $r_i^{r,1}$ and $r_i^{r,2}$ are the position vectors of the top-right corner and the bottom-right corner relative to the mass center.

2.1 Leader-Follower Control Strategy

Considering the noncommunicative situation of such multi-robot system, a leader-follower control strategy is proposed through above pushing-based transportation dynamics. Convergency of the cooperative transportation dynamics is proven as well.

2.2 Translational Controller

Since the transportation leader can obtain the destination either by programmatic determination or manual guidance, the transportation leader's controller is designed to push its corresponding object along the desired trajectory by applying a force and reducing the error between the object's actual velocity and the desired velocity. The controller is described as follows:

$$F_i^{leader} = K_p max \left\{ ||v_i^d|| - ||v_i||, 0 \right\} \frac{v_i^d}{||v_i^d||} \quad (8)$$

where v_i^d is the desired velocity, and K_p is the proportional factor of the controller. Based on the above equation, F_i^{leader} has the same direction as the desired velocity. The magnitude of the pushing force was adjusted by the difference between v_i^d and v_i.

2.3 Rotational Controller

Because objects are physically connected to each other, the rotational motion is governed by two neighboring objects. The transportation follower's force needs to overcome the frictional forces corresponding to transportation leader and transportation followers. Then transportation follower's controller can be derived as follows:

$$F_i^{follower} = \frac{1}{2} \left(\sum_{j=0}^{2} \mu_k M_i g \frac{v_{i+j-1}}{||v_{i+j-1}||} \right) \quad (9)$$

Based on this equation, we know that the rotational motion of the ith object is affected by two neighbors because their velocity is required for the transportation follower's controller, which means that the communication is necessary. This solution totally depends on communication with neighbors, and it may have led to control uncertainties when using unstable communication, especially in a harsh environment. Because all connected objects are pushed to align with the same direction and velocity in the final state, we can eliminate the reliance on communication by letting $v_{i+j-1}^t \to v_i^t$ ($j = 0,2$) when the final steady state is achieved, i.e., $t \to +\infty$.

2.4 Convergency Proof

As proven in Wang's solution, given a constant vector w, a vector v can be updated using the following discrete formula $v_{t+1} = \alpha_t \omega + \beta_t v_t$, where α_t is a series of non-negative constants, and $\{\beta_t | 0 < \beta_t < 1\}$. Thus, the direction of v_t will converge to the direction of w at $t \to +\infty$, i.e., $v_t \to \gamma \omega$, where $\gamma = \alpha_{t-1} + \beta_{t-1}\alpha_{t-2} + \beta_{t-1}\beta_{t-2}\alpha_{t-3} + \ldots + \beta_{t-1}\beta_{t-2}\beta_{t-3} \ldots \beta_1\alpha_0$ is a positive scalar. For the MPO system described in Eq. (9) and (10), Eq. (6) can be rewritten as follows:

$$M_i \frac{v_i^{t+1} - v_i^t}{\Delta t} = K_p max\left\{||v_i^d|| - ||v_i||, 0\right\} \frac{v_i^d}{||v_i^d||} - \mu_k M_i g \frac{v_i^t}{||v_i^t||} - F_i^{follower} \quad (10)$$

$$F_i^{follower} = \frac{1}{2}\left(\sum_{j=0}^{2} \mu_k M_i g \frac{v_{i+j-1}}{||v_{i+j-1}||}\right) \quad (11)$$

For simplification, the above equation can be rewritten as follows:

$$M_i \frac{v_i^{t+1} - v_i^t}{\Delta t} = \frac{K_p max\left\{||v_i^d|| - ||v_i||, 0\right\}v_i^d}{||v_i^d||} - \frac{1}{2}\mu_k M_i g\left(\frac{3v_i^t}{||v_i^t||} + \frac{v_{i-1}^t}{||v_{i-1}^t||} + \frac{v_{i+1}^t}{||v_{i+1}^t||}\right) \quad (12)$$

Since the objective is to push all objects with a specified formation to align with the same direction, the velocity difference must be minimized to zero, which means that velocity of the neighboring object must be the same at $t \to +\infty$, i.e.,

$$v_i^{t+1} = \frac{\Delta t K_p max\left\{||v_i^d|| - ||v_i||, 0\right\}}{M_i ||v_i^d||} v_i^d + \left(1 - \frac{5\Delta t \mu_k g}{2||v_i^t||}\right)v_i^t \quad (13)$$

Then we can use above conclusion by letting

$$\alpha_t = \frac{\Delta t K_p max\left\{||v_i^d|| - ||v_i||, 0\right\}}{M_i ||v_i^d||}, \beta_t = \left(1 - \frac{5\Delta t \mu_k g}{2||v_i^t||}\right) \quad (14)$$

which is true when the time step satisfied $0 < \Delta t < 0.4||v_i^t||/\mu_k g$. Therefore v_i^t will converge to v_i^d as well. The dynamics can be propagated further to the initial velocity v_i^0. Thus, $||v_i^t - \gamma v_i^d|| \le \beta_m^t ||v_i^0||$ is true, where $\gamma = \alpha_{t-1} + \beta_{t-1}\alpha_{t-2} + \beta_{t-1}\beta_{t-2}\alpha_{t-3} + \ldots + \beta_{t-1}\beta_{t-2}\beta_{t-3} \ldots \beta_1\alpha_0$, and $\beta_m^t = max\{\beta_0, \beta_1, \ldots, \beta_{t-1}\}$. It can be concluded that v_i^t converges to γv_i^d exponentially quickly, and transportation followers' force converge to transportation leader's force exponentially quickly as well.

3   Simulation and Discussion

To verify the efficiency and predictability of this approach, a prototype system based on the pushing-based transportation dynamics considering noncommunicative situation is constructed. The prototype system is established with three-layer architecture, i.e., virtual monitoring layer, virtual simulation layer, and virtual equipment layer. All three layers are synchronized through LabStreamingLayer (LSL), which is a message-oriented data synchronization tool that was used in the lab network.

The virtual monitoring layer is developed with Unity 3D on Windows platform. All actions of the virtual models are driven by simulated data that are synchronized via LSL. The virtual monitoring layer provides a GUI interface for data visualization that can be applied for the data analysis of industrial control. The virtual simulation layer is implemented using Matlab Simulink and Adams Control. the simplified dynamic system is established by using the geometrical model of the MSRs and MTs. The virtual equipment layer is implemented via multi-agent technology. The agent is a quadruple structure, i.e., Agent= <C, ActS, AttS, E>. where, C is the control center that manages all the function modules of the agent. ActS is the action set that toke charge of the pushing-based transportation operations. AttS is the attribute set that is responsible for the attributes such as the current transportation displacement of the ith agent. E is the external interface that can perceive the external environment. The external interface is also capable of communicating with the others that exchanged information among neighbors and makes it possible to transmit the information from the ecosystem to every agent. However, the communication is only used for system initialization and human interaction.

3.1   Efficiency and Predictability

This section describes how an underground longwall mining working face with 122 MSRs was selected as the test sample. To demonstrate the process of pushing-based transportation, we only chose the most undulating segment of the curve.

Firstly, we conduct the simulation by setting a moderate number for K, i.e., K = 8. The results are shown in Fig. 2. In the first stage of transportation, as shown in Fig. 2(a), 10th, 35th, and 58th MSRs are programmatically assigned with destinations according to the sum of the transportation displacement that still needs to be pushed. Because the driven capability of the hydraulic pump is limited, pushing-based transportation are separated into several sequences in a specified transportation stage. Additionally, we assume that the hydraulic pump can provide enough pressure for at least K = 8 MSRs at the same time. Then the first pushing sequence in the first transportation stage needs five steps of pushing, 18.7 s in total. The second and third sequences needs five steps (11.4 s) and three steps (11.3 s), respectively.

In the second stage of transportation, there are more pushing sequences that are needed to be pushed. The most complex transportation process was the second pushing sequence, which needs seven pushing steps, as shown in Fig. 2(b). Only 12 s are needed to complete the process, while it costs 13.3 s to push the first sequence. These simulation results fit with our thinking about pushing-based transportation. The more the transportation displacement left, the longer the transportation time costs. However, this is not absolutely right, because the proposed system is totally autonomous and noncommunicative, which means that the cooperation between the MSRs also affects the final transportation result. This is verified by the transportation results of the 5th and 6th pushing sequences. Theoretically, there should have been more transportation displacement left for the 5th pushing sequences. Then more transportation time should have been occupied. The 5th pushing sequence only costs 2.6 s, while the 6th pushing sequence costs 3.2 s. Thus, if the cooperation between MSRs is good enough, much less transportation time will be occupied. The details for the results and corresponding time of the entire transportation process are shown in Table 1.

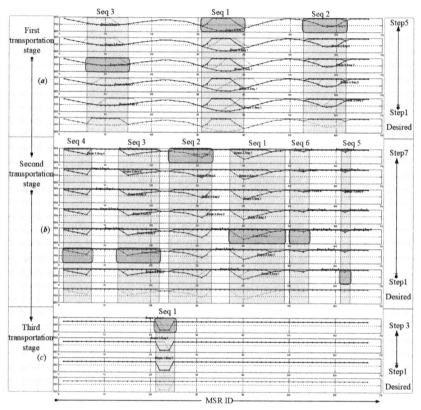

Fig. 2. Simulation results; (a) The result of the first transportation stage, with three sequences presented; (b)The result of the second transportation stage, with six sequences presented; (c) The result of the third transportation stage, with only one sequence presented. The bottom subplot in each transportation stage shows the desired and the current status of transportation.

The traditional human-guided transportation needs to push MTs repeatedly, which may have cost half an hour or even longer. Even worse, the transportation time and steps are not predictable due to uncertainties caused by physical connections and limitations as well as the operational uncertainties of the human-guided process. In contrast, the entire transportation process using the proposed system only costs 32 steps (91.6 s), which dramatically improves the efficiency of pushing-based transportation.

Table 1. Transportation result of the simulation ($K = 8$)

Sequences		Steps	Time (/s)		Sequences	Steps	Time (/s)
Stage1	1	5	18.7	Stage2	6	25	8.8
	2	10	11.4		7	27	7.7
	3	13	11.3		8	28	2.6
Stage2	4	16	13.3		9	31	3.2
	5	23	12	Stage3	10	32	2.6

3.2 Transportation Ability

As can be seen, the parameter K in Eq. (6) affects the number of neighboring MTs within the range of pushing-based transportation. The reason why we have to limit the number of K is that the transportation ability of each MSR depends on hydraulic pressure, which means that the maximum affordable pushing load is limited. Considering this problem, several other simulations are conducted according to different values of K, i.e., K = 4, 12. Results of these simulations are shown in Fig. 3(a) and (b).

Based on the above analysis, the simulation is extended by letting $K \in [1, 16]$. The results are presented in Fig. 4. For the three typical values of K, i.e., K = 4, 8, and 12, the corresponding pushing steps and the count of the manipulation stage are shown in Fig. 4(a), (b), and (c), respectively. More interestingly, we find that the pushing manipulation is completed in only one stage if K is larger than 16, as shown in Fig. 4(d). Theoretically, the transportation process can be completed with the greedy control method if the transportation ability is large enough. In contrast, the entire process needs 93 steps if K is set to 1, which means that the maximum of the steps is 93 for

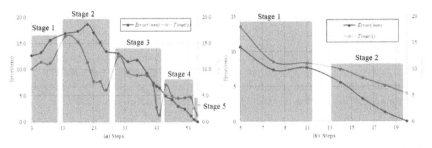

Fig. 3. Transportation errors and time with different transportation abilities; (a) Result of the simulation with $K = 4$. Five transportation stages are needed in total; (b) Result of the simulation with $K = 12$. Only two transportation stages are needed. The blue box in this figure indicates a specified pushing stage. (Color figure online)

the current configuration. All results are consistent with our existing knowledge, which provide valuable basis for practical application.

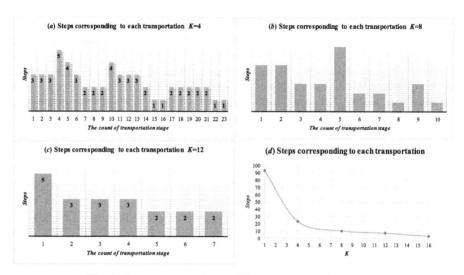

Fig. 4. Steps corresponding to different transportation abilities

4 Conclusion

To explore the dynamics for transportation of MPO, and to overcome the noncommunicative problem during the cooperative control process, in this research, the problem of the cooperative transportation for multirobot transportation system was studied. The pushing-based transportation dynamics of the system were derived and the convergence of the transportation dynamics was proven based on leader-follower control strategy without communication. To verify the efficiency, the derived transportation dynamics were integrated into a prototype system through Adams control-based virtual environment. Simulations were carried out and analyzed with different transportation abilities. Results showed that the derived transportation dynamics were efficient for expressing the dynamic mechanisms for pushing-based transportation. This may provide a theoretical basis for the further control of the noncommunicative planar pushing manipulation of a multi-robot system.

Acknowledgments. The supports of National Natural Science Foundation of China (No. 52004034), and Science and Technology Research Program of Chongqing Municipal Education Commission (No. KJQN202101413) in carrying out this research are gratefully acknowledged.

References

1. Sitti, M.: Bio-inspired robotic collectives fighting cystic fibrosis with small molecules. Nature **567**, 314–315 (2019)

2. Li, S., et al.: Particle robotics based on statistical mechanics of loosely coupled components. Nature **567**(7748), 361–365 (2019)
3. McCreery, H.F., Breed, M.D.: Cooperative transport in ants: a review of proximate mechanisms. Insect. Soc. **61**(2), 99–110 (2014)
4. Gelblum, A., Pinkoviezky, I., Fonio, E., Ghosh, A., Gov, N., Feinerman, O.: Ant groups optimally amplify the effect of transiently informed individuals. Nat. Commun. **6**(1), 7729 (2015)
5. Feinerman, O., Pinkoviezky, I., Gelblum, A., Fonio, E., Gov, N.S.: The physics of cooperative transport in groups of ants. Nat. Phys. **14**(7), 683–693 (2018)
6. Wang, Z., Schwager, M.: Multi-robot manipulation without communication. Distributed Autonomous Robotic Systems, vol. 112, pp. 135–149 (2016)
7. Wang, Z., Schwager, M.: Multi-robot manipulation with no communication using only local measurements. In: Proceedings of the IEEE Conference on Decision and Control, pp. 380–385 (2015)
8. Wang, Z., Schwager, M.: Force-amplifying N-robot transport system (Force-ANTS) for cooperative planar manipulation without communication. Int. J. Robot. Res. **35**(13), 1564–1586 (2016)
9. Rezzoug, N., Gorce, P.: Dynamic control of pushing operations. Robotica **17**(6), 613–620 (1999)
10. Halm, M., Posa, M.: A quasi-static model and simulation approach for pushing, grasping and jamming. arXiv:1902.03487 (2019)
11. Pliego-Jimenez, J., Arteaga-Perez, M.: On the adaptive control of cooperative robots with time-variant holonomic constraints. Int. J. Adapt. Control. **31**(8), 1217–1231 (2017)
12. Ma, D., Rodriguez, A.: Friction variability in planar pushing data: anisotropic friction and data-collection bias. IEEE Robot. Autom. Lett. **3**(4), 3232–3239 (2018). https://doi.org/10.1109/LRA.2018.2851026
13. Agboh, W.C., Dogar, M.R.: Pushing fast and slow: task-adaptive MPC for pushing manipulation under uncertainty. arXiv: 1805.03005 (2018)
14. Harada, K., Nishiyama, J., Murakami, Y., Kaneko, M.: Pushing manipulation for multiple objects. J. Dyn. Syst.-T ASME **128**(2), 422–427 (2006)
15. Zyada, Z., Hayakawa, Y., Hosose, S.: Kinematic analysis of a two-link object for whole arm manipulation. In: Proceedings of the 9th WSEAS International Conference on Signal Processing, Robotics and Automation, pp. 139–145 (2010)
16. Moldovan, B., Moreno, P., Nitti, D., Santos-Victor, J., De Raedt, L.: Relational affordances for multiple-object manipulation. Auton. Robot. **42**(1), 19–44 (2017). https://doi.org/10.1007/s10514-017-9637-x
17. Shah, A.J., Shah, J.A.: Towards manipulation planning for multiple interlinked deformable linear objects. In: Proceedings of IEEE International Conference on Robotics and Automation, pp. 3908–3915 (2016)
18. Shah, A., Blumberg, L., Shah, J.: Planning for manipulation of interlinked deformable linear objects with applications to aircraft assembly. IEEE Trans. Autom. Sci. Eng. **15**(4), 1823–1838 (2018)
19. Zhang, L., Zheng, X., Feng, S., Su, L.: A noncommunicative memory-pushing fuzzy control strategy for sensorless multirobot systems. Complexity **2020**, 1–15 (2020). https://doi.org/10.1155/2020/7256427

Kinematic and Dynamic Analysis of a Novel 5-DOF Multi-fingered Deployable Robotic Gripper

Changqing Gao[1,2] , Bing Li[1,2,3]($\boxtimes$) , Chonglei Hao[2] , Fujun Peng[2] ,
and Aiguo Wu[2]

[1] State Key Laboratory of Robotics and System, Harbin Institute of Technology, Harbin 150001,
People's Republic of China
`libing.sgs@hit.edu.cn`
[2] School of Mechanical Engineering and Automation, Harbin Institute of Technology,
Shenzhen 518055, People's Republic of China
[3] Peng Cheng Laboratory, Shenzhen 518055, People's Republic of China

Abstract. This paper presents a novel 5-DOF deployable robotic gripper for
grasping large-scale unknown objects. This robotic gripper is composed of four
fingers and a single-mobility base mechanism, and each finger is made up of a
serial of basic modules to conveniently store and transport. First, the mechanism
design of the robotic gripper is briefly introduced. By special revolute joint of
the scissor-shaped element, the fingers can form a certainly grasping angle when
the robotic gripper conducts deployment-motion. Second, kinematic analysis is
conducted to generate a workspace and kinematic simulation for the robotic gripper, the result shows that the robotic gripper has quite large reachable workspace.
Dynamic analysis is then performed based on Lagrange dynamic equation, which
is of great significance for further control and optimization. Third, a group of
grasping simulations are performed with a variety of objects to prove the shape
adaptability, and the results show that the robotic gripper has excellent grasping
performance.

Keywords: Deployable mechanism · Kinematic analysis · Dynamic analysis ·
Grasping simulation

1 Introduction

Currently, robotic grippers have become a popular study topic and aroused the interests of a large of researchers. Based on different grasping patterns, robotic grippers
can be divided into finger-tip robotic grippers and enveloping robotic grippers. Finger-
tip robotic grippers always use one or two points of links to contact with objects, the
most representative of which is serial robotic gripper [1]. The most important advantage
of finger-tip robotic grippers is that they are easy to realize dexterous manipulation.
However, due to rare contacting points between robotic grippers and objects, the stiffness and grasping force are low. Compared with finger-tip robotic grippers, enveloping

© Springer Nature Switzerland AG 2021
X.-J. Liu et al. (Eds.): ICIRA 2021, LNAI 13015, pp. 415–424, 2021.
https://doi.org/10.1007/978-3-030-89134-3_38

robotic grippers are suitable for large-scale unknown objects because there exists multiple distributed contact points, but it is difficult to finish dexterous manipulation. The representatives of this type of robotic grippers include serial-parallel robotic grippers [2, 3] and soft robotic grippers [4, 5]. Serial-parallel robotic grippers are usually constructed by connecting a serial of parallel modules in series, which mean that they have sophisticated drive system and large volume. These obvious disadvantages will cause serious difficulties to the lightweight, storage, and transportation. Furthermore, the design ideas of soft robotic grippers usually come from natural biology, which are always fabricated by some soft materials. Although this kind of soft robotic grippers usually have good shape adaptability, soft material limits their stiffness and grasping force, so they can only achieve good results in grasping small objects and struggle to grasp large-scale unknown objects.

For large-scale unknown objects, the robotic gripper firstly needs to have a compact folded configuration and a large deployed configuration, so a good deploy/fold ratio is of great significance for storage and transportation of the robotic gripper [6–8]. Besides, complex drive system should be avoided to realize lightweight. In addition, truss-shaped structure should be adopted in design to afford good stiffness and large grasping force. Finally, multi-fingered structure should be considered to make sure that the robotic gripper can be used to grasp various spatial objects. To solve above challenges, this paper presents a novel 5-DOF multi-fingered deployable robotic gripper composed of four fingers and a base mechanism, in which each finger is composed of four basic modules. To realize deployment-motion, two group of scissor-shaped elements are applied to design of the basic module. Offset revolute joints are used in scissor-shaped elements to form a grasping angle when the basic module performs deployment-motion. Special connecting mechanism ensures that each finger has only one mobility, which simplifies the driving system of robotic gripper. Besides, kinematic analysis is conducted to afford kinematic simulation and dynamic analysis of the robotic gripper are conducted to further control and optimization. Finally, the grasping simulation is carried out to show the excellent grasping performance of the robotic gripper. The remainder of the paper is arranged as follows. Sect. 2 briefly introduces the mechanism design of the robotic gripper. Sect. 3 kinematic analysis and dynamic analysis of the robotic gripper are carried out. Sect. 4 conducts the grasping simulation. Sect. 5 concludes this paper.

2 Design of the Robotic Gripper

The basic module of the robotic gripper is as shown in Fig. 1(a), which is composed of upper platform, lower platform, and two groups of scissor-shaped elements. Upper platform is made up of link 1 and link 2, which are connected by prismatic joint (P_1); lower platform is made up of link 3 and link 4, which are connected by prismatic joint (P_2); scissor-shaped element 1 is made up of link 5 and link 6, which are connected by revolute joint (R_1). On one side of the scissor-shaped element 1, three revolute joints (R_1, R_3, R_4) and one prismatic joint (P_1) are used to form a closed-loop mechanism, which is a planar single-mobility three-revolute-one-prismatic (3R1P) mechanism. On the other side, three revolute joints (R_1, R_5, R_6) and one prismatic joint (P_2) are used to form another closed-loop 3R1P mechanism. So the basic module is a single-mobility mechanism, which is of great significance for lightweight of the robotic gripper. To further enhance the gasping force and stiffness, truss-shaped structure is adapted. Another group of scissor-shaped element is made up of link 7 and link 8, which are connected by revolute joint (R_2). Due to offset of revolute joints (R_1, R_2) of the scissor-shaped elements, the basic module can form a certainly grasping angle when it performs deployment-motion.

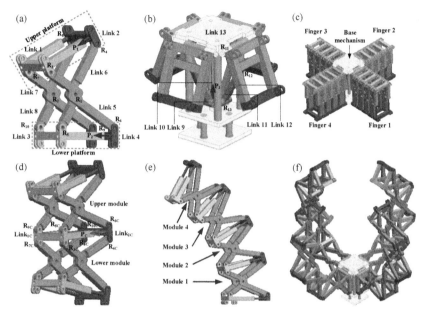

Fig. 1. Design of the robotic gripper. (a) The basic module. (b) The base mechanism. (c) Folded configuration of the robotic gripper. (d) Connection of two basic modules. (e) The finger of the gripper. (f) Grasping configuration of the robotic gripper.

In addition to the basic module, the base mechanism also should be presented. The robotic gripper is composed of four fingers, so the base mechanism must contain four symmetrical positions for installation of fingers. To achieve the lightweight of the robotic gripper, an umbrella-shaped base mechanism is designed as shown in Fig. 1(b). Here, link 9 and link 10 are connected by prismatic joint (P_3). Link 11 is connected with link 12 and link 9 by revolute joints (R_{12}, R_{13}). Link 13 is connected with link 12 by revolute joint (R_{11}). Actually, three revolute joints (R_{11}, R_{12}, R_{13}) and prismatic joint (P_3) are also used to form a 3R1P single-mobility closed-loop mechanism, in which prismatic joint (P_3) can be selected as the driving joint. Similarly, the other three limbs have the same features. With the driving of the prismatic joint (P_3), the link 12 can rotate around the axes of revolute joint (R_{11}). The connection of adjacent two modules is as shown in Fig. 1(d). Two adjacent modules share a few common links and prismatic joint (P_C) such that they can be deployed synchronously. Then the scissor-shaped elements of upper module and lower module are connected with common links (Link 1_C, Link 2_C) by eight revolute joints (R_{3C}, R_{4C}, R_{5C}, R_{6C}, R_{7C}, R_{8C}, R_{9C}, R_{10C}). Using this method, the finger of robotic gripper with four basic modules can be connected, as shown in Fig. 1(e). Finally, the four fingers are connected with the base mechanism and the robotic gripper can be assembled, as shown in Fig. 1(c) and Fig. 1(f), from which one can see that the robotic gripper has a compact folded configuration and large deployed configuration.

3 Kinematics and Dynamics Analysis

To finish the dynamic analysis of the robotic gripper, the kinematic model is firstly established. As there are four identical fingers, only finger 1 is analyzed. The schematic diagram and the coordinate frames $\{O_0\text{-}X_0Y_0Z_0\}$, $\{O_1\text{-}X_1Y_1Z_1\}$, and $\{O_2\text{-}X_2Y_2Z_2\}$ are as shown in Fig. 2. Where R represents the curvature radius of the basic module in deployed configuration; l_i ($i = 1, 2, \ldots, 9$) represents the length of corresponding structure; v_1 represents driving velocity of the base mechanism; d_1 and d_2 will change with motion of the base mechanism and the basic module. Based on geometric relations, the position of point O_1 with respect to the coordinate system $\{O_0\text{-}X_0Y_0Z_0\}$ can be expressed as follows:

$$\boldsymbol{P}_{O_1}^0 = [-l_5 - l_3\cos\beta_1, l_3(1 - \sin\beta_1), 0, 1]^T \tag{1}$$

where β_1 is as shown in Fig. 2(a), which can be obtained by:

$$\begin{cases} d_1 = d_{1\max} - v_1 t_1 = l_3 + l_2\cos\beta_1 + l_1\cos\beta_2 \\ l_5 = l_4 + l_1\sin\beta_2 - l_2\sin\beta_1 \end{cases}, \begin{cases} \beta_1 \in [0, 0.5\pi] \\ \beta_2 \in [0, 0.5\pi] \end{cases} \tag{2}$$

where t_1 represents motion time of the base mechanism; β_2 is as shown in Fig. 2(a); $d_{1\max}$ is the distance between points A and O_0 when the base mechanism is in folded configuration.

Furthermore, end-effector, E, of the finger with respect to the coordinate system $\{O_0\text{-}X_0Y_0Z_0\}$ can be expressed as follows:

$$\boldsymbol{P}_E^0 = \boldsymbol{T}_0^1\boldsymbol{T}_1^2\boldsymbol{P}_E^2 \tag{3}$$

where $\boldsymbol{T}_0^1$ is the transformation matrix between the coordinate frames $\{O_0\text{-}X_0Y_0Z_0\}$ and $\{O_1\text{-}X_1Y_1Z_1\}$; $\boldsymbol{T}_1^2$ is the transformation matrix between the coordinate frames $\{O_1\text{-}X_1Y_1Z_1\}$ and $\{O_2\text{-}X_2Y_2Z_2\}$; $\boldsymbol{P}_E^2$ is the coordinate of end-effector, E, with respect to the coordinate frames $\{O_2\text{-}X_2Y_2Z_2\}$; $\boldsymbol{T}_0^1$, $\boldsymbol{T}_1^2$, and $\boldsymbol{P}_E^2$ can be expressed as:

$$\begin{cases} \boldsymbol{T}_0^1 = \begin{bmatrix} \cos\beta_1 & -\sin\beta_1 & 0 & -l_5 - l_3\cos\beta_1 \\ \sin\beta_1 & \cos\beta_1 & 0 & -l_3 + l_3\sin\beta_1 \\ 0 & 0 & 1 & 0 \\ 0 & 0 & 0 & 1 \end{bmatrix}, \boldsymbol{T}_1^2 = \begin{bmatrix} 1 & 0 & 0 & R \\ 0 & 1 & 0 & 0 \\ 0 & 0 & 1 & 0 \\ 0 & 0 & 0 & 1 \end{bmatrix} \\ \boldsymbol{P}_E^2 = [R\sin(4\theta), -R\cos(4\theta), 0, 1]^T \end{cases} \tag{4}$$

where θ is deployed angle of the basic module, the range of which is determined by scissor-shaped element.

θ and R can be calculated by:

$$\begin{cases} R = \dfrac{l_8\cos\alpha_3 + l_9}{\tan(\frac{\theta}{2})} - l_8\sin\alpha_3 \\ \theta = \pi - 2\alpha_4 - 2\alpha_3 \\ \alpha_4 = 0.5(\pi - \alpha_5) = 0.5(\pi - \arccos(\frac{l_8^2 + l_7^2 - d_2^2}{2l_7 l_8})) \\ \alpha_3 = 0.5\pi - \alpha_1 = 0.5\pi - \arccos(\frac{l_8^2 + d_2^2 - l_7^2}{2l_8 d_2}) \end{cases} \tag{5}$$

where $d_2 = d_{2\max} - v_2 t_2$; v_2 represents driving velocity of the finger 1; t_2 represents motion time of the finger 1; $d_{2\max}$ is the distance between points C_6 and C_5 when finger 1 is in folded configuration.

In this manner, the position of the end-effector, E, can be obtained and the workspace of the finger can be given as shown in Fig. 3. While the position analysis is carried out, the velocity analysis of end-effector, E, can be easily conducted, which can be expressed by taking the derivative of Eq. (3) as:

$$v_E^0 = \frac{\partial T_0^1}{\partial t_1} T_1^2 P_E^2 + T_0^1 \frac{\partial T_1^2}{\partial t_2} P_E^2 + T_0^1 T_1^2 \frac{\partial P_E^2}{\partial t_2} \tag{6}$$

where

$$
\begin{cases}
\frac{\partial T_0^1}{\partial t_1} = \begin{bmatrix} -\omega_{\beta_1} \sin \beta_1 & -\omega_{\beta_1} \cos \beta_1 & 0 & \omega_{\beta_1} l_3 \sin \beta_1 \\ \omega_{\beta_1} \cos \beta_1 & -\omega_{\beta_1} \sin \beta_1 & 0 & \omega_{\beta_1} l_3 \cos \beta_1 \\ 0 & 0 & 0 & 0 \\ 0 & 0 & 0 & 0 \end{bmatrix}, & \frac{\partial T_1^2}{\partial t_2} = \begin{bmatrix} 0 & 0 & 0 & \frac{\partial R}{\partial t_2} \\ 0 & 0 & 0 & 0 \\ 0 & 0 & 0 & 0 \\ 0 & 0 & 0 & 0 \end{bmatrix} \\
\frac{\partial P_E^2}{\partial t_2} = \begin{bmatrix} \frac{\partial R}{\partial t_2} \sin(4\theta) + 4 \frac{\partial \theta}{\partial t_2} R \cos(4\theta), \ 4 \frac{\partial \theta}{\partial t_2} R \sin(4\theta) - \frac{\partial R}{\partial t_2} \cos(4\theta), 0, 0 \end{bmatrix}^T
\end{cases} \tag{7}
$$

where ω_{β_1} is the angular velocity of β_1 and can be obtained by taking the derivative of Eq. (2); $\frac{\partial R}{\partial t_2}$ and $\frac{\partial \theta}{\partial t_2}$ can be obtained by taking the derivative of Eq. (5).

In this way, the velocities of the end-effector, E, can be obtained. Assuming that the driving velocities of base mechanism and the finger 1 are equivalent, we have $v_1 = v_2$, and thus the velocities of the end-effector, E, with different driving velocities can be simulated as shown in Fig. 3(b). Furthermore, the acceleration of the end-effector, E, can also be calculated by taking the derivative of Eq. (6) as:

$$a_E^0 = \begin{cases} \frac{\partial^2 T_0^1}{\partial t_1^2} T_1^2 P_E^2 + \frac{\partial T_0^1}{\partial t_1} \frac{\partial T_1^2}{\partial t_2} P_E^2 + \frac{\partial T_0^1}{\partial t_1} T_1^2 \frac{\partial P_E^2}{\partial t_2} + \frac{\partial T_0^1}{\partial t_1} \frac{\partial T_1^2}{\partial t_2} P_E^2 + T_0^1 \frac{\partial^2 T_1^2}{\partial t_2^2} P_E^2 \\ + T_0^1 \frac{\partial T_1^2}{\partial t_2} \frac{\partial P_E^2}{\partial t_2} + \frac{\partial T_0^1}{\partial t_1} T_1^2 \frac{\partial P_E^2}{\partial t_2} + T_0^1 \frac{\partial T_1^2}{\partial t_2} \frac{\partial P_E^2}{\partial t_2} + T_0^1 T_1^2 \frac{\partial^2 P_E^2}{\partial t_2^2} \end{cases} \tag{8}$$

where

$$
\begin{cases}
\frac{\partial P_E^2}{\partial t_2} = \begin{bmatrix} \frac{\partial^2 R}{\partial t_2^2} \sin(4\theta) + 8 \frac{\partial \theta}{\partial t_2} \frac{\partial R}{\partial t_2} \cos(4\theta) - 16 \frac{\partial^2 \theta}{\partial t_2^2} R \sin(4\theta) \\ -\frac{\partial^2 R}{\partial t_2^2} \cos(4\theta) + 8 \frac{\partial \theta}{\partial t_2} \frac{\partial R}{\partial t_2} \sin(4\theta) + 16 \frac{\partial^2 \theta}{\partial t_2^2} \cos(4\theta) \\ 0 \\ 0 \end{bmatrix}, & \frac{\partial^2 T_1^2}{\partial t_2^2} = \begin{bmatrix} 0 & 0 & 0 & \frac{\partial^2 R}{\partial t_2^2} \\ 0 & 0 & 0 & 0 \\ 0 & 0 & 0 & 0 \\ 0 & 0 & 0 & 0 \end{bmatrix} \\
\frac{\partial^2 T_0^1}{\partial t_1^2} = \alpha_\beta \begin{bmatrix} -\sin \beta_1 & -\cos \beta_1 & 0 & l_3 \sin \beta_1 \\ \cos \beta_1 & -\sin \beta_1 & 0 & l_3 \cos \beta_1 \\ 0 & 0 & 0 & 0 \\ 0 & 0 & 0 & 0 \end{bmatrix} + \omega_{\beta_1}^2 \begin{bmatrix} -\cos \beta_1 & \sin \beta_1 & 0 & l_3 \cos \beta_1 \\ -\sin \beta_1 & -\cos \beta_1 & 0 & -l_3 \sin \beta_1 \\ 0 & 0 & 0 & 0 \\ 0 & 0 & 0 & 0 \end{bmatrix}
\end{cases} \tag{9}
$$

where a_{β_1} is the angular acceleration of β_1 and can be obtained by taking the second derivative of Eq. (2); $\frac{\partial^2 R}{\partial t_2^2}$ and $\frac{\partial^2 \theta}{\partial t_2^2}$ can be obtained by taking the second derivative of Eq. (5).

By this way, the acceleration of the end-effector, E, can also be calculated. Similar to the velocity analysis, the accelerations of end-effector, E, can also be simulated as shown in Fig. 3(c). In addition to kinematic analysis, the dynamic equation of finger 1 based on Lagrange equation can be easily expressed as follows:

$$\begin{cases} L = E_K - P_K \\ F_i = \frac{d}{dt}\left(\frac{\partial L}{\partial \dot{q}}\right) - \frac{\partial L}{\partial q} \end{cases} \tag{10}$$

where L is Lagrange function; E_K is kinetic energy of the system; P_K is potential energy of the system; q and $\dot{q}$ are generalized coordinates and velocities; and F_i is the generalized force corresponding to generalized coordinate q.

The first module of finger 1 is as shown in Fig. 2(b), where C_j ($j = 1, 2, \ldots, 10$) represents rotational center of each revolute joints; $m_{\text{link } i}$ ($i = 1, 2, \ldots, 8$) represents the quality of link i, the Lagrange function of the first module can be expressed as:

$$L_{k1} = \sum_{i=1}^{8}\left(0.5 m_{\text{link } i}\dot{q}_{\text{link } i}^2 - P_{\text{link } i}\right) \tag{11}$$

where $P_{\text{link } i}$ ($i = 1, 2, \ldots, 8$) is ignored.
Kinetic energy of the first module can be expressed as:

$$E_{k1} = \sum_{i=1}^{8} 0.5\left(m_{\text{link } i}v_{\text{link } i}^2 + J_{\text{link } i}\omega_{\text{link } i}^2\right) \tag{12}$$

where $v_{\text{link } i}$ represents translational velocity of the center of mass of link i, ω_i represents rotational velocity of link i, J_i represents rotary inertia of link i.

Based on kinematic analysis, the coordinate of C_j ($j = 3, 4, \ldots, 10$) with respect to the coordinate system $\{O_0\text{-}X_0Y_0Z_0\}$ can be expressed as:

$$P_{C_j}^0 = T_0^1 T_1^2 P_{C_j}^2 \tag{13}$$

where

$$\begin{cases} P_{C_3}^2 = [-R\cos\theta - l_9 sin\theta, R sin\theta - l_9 cos\theta, -0.5l_6, 1]^T \\ P_{C_4}^2 = [-(R+d_2)\cos\theta - l_9 sin\theta, (R+d_2)sin\theta - l_9 cos\theta, -0.5l_6, 1]^T \\ P_{C_5}^2 = [-R, l_9, -0.5l_6, 1]^T \\ P_{C_6}^2 = [-R-d_2, l_9, -0.5l_6, 1]^T \\ P_{C_7}^2 = [-R\cos\theta - l_9 sin\theta, R sin\theta - l_9 cos\theta, 0.5l_6, 1]^T \\ P_{C_8}^2 = [-(R+d_2)\cos\theta - l_9 sin\theta, (R+d_2)sin\theta - l_9 cos\theta, 0.5l_6, 1]^T \\ P_{C_9}^2 = [-R, l_9, 0.5l_6, 1]^T \\ P_{C_{10}}^2 = [-R-d_2, l_9, 0.5l_6, 1]^T \end{cases} \tag{14}$$

For base mechanism, as shown in Fig. 2(a), the kinetic energy can be expressed as:

$$E_{k2} = \sum_{i=9}^{12} 0.5\left(m_{\text{link } i}v_{\text{link } i}^2 + J_{\text{link } i}\omega_{\text{link } i}^2\right) \tag{15}$$

where

$$\begin{cases} \boldsymbol{P}^0_{C_{41}} = [-l_5, -l_3, 0, 1]^T \\ \boldsymbol{P}^0_{C_{42}} = [-l_4 - l_1 sin\beta_2, l_3(sin\beta_1 - 1) - l_2 cos\beta_1, 0, 1]^T \\ \boldsymbol{P}^0_{C_{43}} = [-l_4, v_1 t_1 - d_{1\,max}, 0, 1]^T \\ \boldsymbol{P}^0_{C_{44}} = [0, v_1 t_1 - d_{1\,max}, 0, 1]^T \end{cases} \qquad (16)$$

So the velocity of point C_j can be calculated by:

$$v^0_{C_j} = \frac{\partial \boldsymbol{P}^0_{C_j}}{\partial t_2}, (j = 3, 4, \ldots, 10); v^0_{C_j} = \frac{\partial \boldsymbol{P}^0_{C_j}}{\partial t_1}, (j = 41, 42, 43, 44) \qquad (17)$$

Since finger 1 has four identical modules which move synchronously, the velocities of the corresponding link of each module is equal. As shown in Fig. 2(c), the velocity of each links can thus be summarized as follows:

$$\begin{cases} v^0_{link\,1} = v^0_{c_3}, v^0_{link\,2} = v^0_{c_4}, v^0_{link\,3} = v^0_{c_5}, v^0_{link\,4} = v^0_{c_6}, v^0_{link\,9} = v^0_{c_{44}} \\ v^0_{link\,5} = v^0_{link\,7} = d(\boldsymbol{P}^0_{C_3} - \boldsymbol{P}^0_{C_6})/dt, v^0_{link\,6} = v^0_{link\,8} = d(\boldsymbol{P}^0_{C_4} - \boldsymbol{P}^0_{C_5})/dt \\ v^0_{link\,10} = d(\boldsymbol{P}^0_{C_{42}} - \boldsymbol{P}^0_{C_{43}})/dt, v^0_{link\,11} = 0, v^0_{link\,12} = v^0_{c_{13}}, v^0_{link\,13} = v^0_{c_{14}} \\ v^0_{link\,14} = v^0_{link\,16} = d(\boldsymbol{P}^0_{C_{14}} - \boldsymbol{P}^0_{C_{15}})/dt, v^0_{link\,15} = v^0_{link\,17} = d(\boldsymbol{P}^0_{C_{13}} - \boldsymbol{P}^0_{C_{16}})/dt \\ v^0_{link\,18} = v^0_{c_{23}}, v^0_{link\,19} = v^0_{c_{24}}, v^0_{link\,24} = v^0_{c_{33}}, v^0_{link\,25} = v^0_{c_{34}} \\ v^0_{link\,20} = v^0_{link\,22} = d(\boldsymbol{P}^0_{C_{24}} - \boldsymbol{P}^0_{C_{25}})/dt, v^0_{link\,21} = v^0_{link\,23} = d(\boldsymbol{P}^0_{C_{23}} - \boldsymbol{P}^0_{C_{26}})/dt \\ v^0_{link\,26} = v^0_{link\,28} = d(\boldsymbol{P}^0_{C_{34}} - \boldsymbol{P}^0_{C_{35}})/dt, v^0_{link\,27} = v^0_{link\,29} = d(\boldsymbol{P}^0_{C_{33}} - \boldsymbol{P}^0_{C_{36}})/dt \end{cases} \qquad (18)$$

$$\begin{cases} \omega_{link\,1} = \omega_{link\,2} = \omega_\theta + \omega_{\beta_1}, \omega_{link\,3} = \omega_{link\,4} = \omega_{\beta_1}, \\ \omega_{link\,6} = \omega_{link\,8} = \omega_{\beta_1} + \omega_{\alpha_1}, \omega_{link\,9} = \omega_{link\,11} = 0, \omega_{link\,10} = \omega_{\beta_2} \\ \omega_{link\,12} = \omega_{link\,13} = 2\omega_\theta + \omega_{\beta_1}, \omega_{link\,18} = \omega_{link\,19} = 3\omega_\theta + \omega_{\beta_1}\omega_{\beta_1} \\ \omega_{link\,5} = \omega_{link\,7} = \omega_{\beta_1} - \omega_{\alpha_2}, \omega_{link\,15} = \omega_{link\,17} = \omega_{\beta_1} + \omega_\theta - \omega_{\alpha_2} \\ \omega_{link\,21} = \omega_{link\,23} = \omega_{\beta_1} + 2\omega_\theta - \omega_{\alpha_2}, \omega_{link\,27} = \omega_{link\,29} = \omega_{\beta_1} + 3\omega_\theta - \omega_{\alpha_2} \\ \omega_{link\,6} = \omega_{link\,8} = \omega_{\beta_1} + \omega_{\alpha_1}, \omega_{link\,14} = \omega_{link\,16} = \omega_{\beta_1} + \omega_\theta + \omega_{\alpha_1} \\ \omega_{link\,20} = \omega_{link\,22} = \omega_{\beta_1} + 2\omega_\theta + \omega_{\alpha_1}, \omega_{link\,26} = \omega_{link\,28} = \omega_{\beta_1} + 3\omega_\theta + \omega_{\alpha_1} \end{cases} \qquad (19)$$

In (17), $v^0_{13}, v^0_{14}, v^0_{15}, v^0_{16}, v^0_{23}, v^0_{24}, v^0_{25}, v^0_{26}, v^0_{33}, v^0_{34}, v^0_{35},$ and v^0_{36} can be calculated by $\boldsymbol{P}^2_{13}, \boldsymbol{P}^2_{14}, \boldsymbol{P}^2_{15}, \boldsymbol{P}^2_{16}, \boldsymbol{P}^2_{23}, \boldsymbol{P}^2_{24}, \boldsymbol{P}^2_{25}, \boldsymbol{P}^2_{26}, \boldsymbol{P}^2_{33}, \boldsymbol{P}^2_{34}, \boldsymbol{P}^2_{35},$ and $\boldsymbol{P}^2_{36}$, which can be summarized as:

$$\begin{cases}
\boldsymbol{P}^2_{C_{13}} = [-R\cos(2\theta) - l_9 sin(2\theta), R sin(2\theta) - l_9 cos(2\theta), -0.5l_6, 1]^T \\
\boldsymbol{P}^2_{C_{14}} = [-(R+d_2)\cos(2\theta) - l_9 sin(2\theta), (R+d_2) sin(2\theta) - l_9 cos(2\theta), -0.5l_6, 1]^T \\
\boldsymbol{P}^2_{C_{15}} = [l_9 \sin\theta - R\cos\theta, R\sin\theta + l_9 \cos\theta, -0.5l_6, 1]^T \\
\boldsymbol{P}^2_{C_{16}} = [l_9 \sin\theta - (R+d_2)cos\theta, (R+d_2) \sin\theta + l_9 \cos\theta, -0.5l_6, 1]^T \\
\boldsymbol{P}^2_{C_{23}} = [-R\cos(3\theta) - l_9 sin(3\theta), R sin(3\theta) - l_9 cos(3\theta), -0.5l_6, 1]^T \\
\boldsymbol{P}^2_{C_{24}} = [-(R+d_2)\cos(3\theta) - l_9 sin(3\theta), (R+d_2) sin(3\theta) - l_9 cos(3\theta), -0.5l_6, 1]^T \\
\boldsymbol{P}^2_{C_{25}} = [l_9 \sin(2\theta) - R\cos(2\theta), R\sin(2\theta) + l_9 \cos(2\theta), -0.5l_6, 1]^T \\
\boldsymbol{P}^2_{C_{26}} = [l_9 \sin(2\theta) - (R+d_2)cos(2\theta), (R+d_2) \sin(2\theta) + l_9 \cos(2\theta), -0.5l_6, 1]^T \\
\boldsymbol{P}^2_{C_{33}} = [-R\cos(4\theta) - l_9 sin(4\theta), R sin(4\theta) - l_9 cos(4\theta), -0.5l_6, 1]^T \\
\boldsymbol{P}^2_{C_{34}} = [-(R+d_2)\cos(4\theta) - l_9 sin(4\theta), (R+d_2) sin(4\theta) - l_9 cos(4\theta), -0.5l_6, 1]^T \\
\boldsymbol{P}^2_{C_{35}} = [l_9 \sin(3\theta) - R\cos(3\theta), R\sin(3\theta) + l_9 \cos(3\theta), -0.5l_6, 1]^T \\
\boldsymbol{P}^2_{C_{36}} = [l_9 \sin(3\theta) - (R+d_2)cos(3\theta), (R+d_2) \sin(3\theta) + l_9 \cos(3\theta), -0.5l_6, 1]^T
\end{cases}$$
$$(20)$$

Meanwhile, the following conditions are met:

$$\begin{cases}
J_{\text{link }1} = J_{\text{link }3}, J_{\text{link }2} = J_{\text{link }4}, J_{\text{link }5} = J_{\text{link }6} = J_{\text{link }7} = J_{\text{link }8} \\
m_{\text{link }1} = m_{\text{link }3}, m_{\text{link }2} = m_{\text{link }4}, m_{\text{link }5} = m_{\text{link }6} = m_{\text{link }7} = m_{\text{link }8}
\end{cases} \qquad (21)$$

So the dynamic equation of the finger 1 can be given as:

$$L = \sum_{i=1}^{29} 0.5\left(m_{\text{link }i}v^2_{\text{link }i} + J_{\text{link }i}\omega^2_{\text{link }i}\right) \qquad (22)$$

The driving forces of base mechanism and finger 1 can be calculated by:

$$F_1 = 4\left[\frac{\partial}{dt_1}(\frac{\partial L}{\partial \dot{d}_1}) - \frac{\partial L}{\partial d_1}\right]; \quad F_2 = \frac{\partial}{dt_2}(\frac{\partial L}{\partial \dot{d}_2}) - \frac{\partial L}{\partial d_2} \qquad (23)$$

where F_1 is driving force of base mechanism and F_2 is driving force of finger 1.

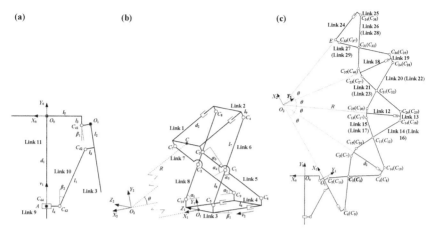

Fig. 2. Kinematic and dynamic diagrams. (a) Schematic diagram of the base mechanism. (b) Schematic diagram of the first module of finger 1. (c) Schematic diagram of finger 1.

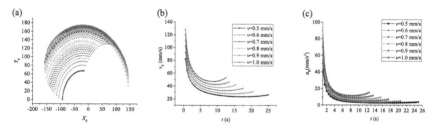

Fig. 3. Kinematic simulation of finger 1. (a) The workspace of finger 1. (b) Velocities of the end-effector, E. (c) Accelerations of end-effector, E.

4 Grasping Simulation

In practice, a good shape adaptability means that the gripper can grasp different-shaped objects. To confirm the shape adaptability of the proposed robotic gripper, a group of grasping simulations are conducted, as shown in Fig. 4.

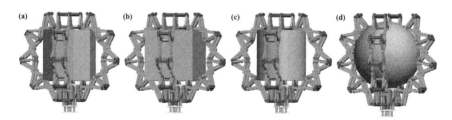

Fig. 4. Shape adaptability during the grasping-motion. (a) Eight prism object grasping. (b) Quadrangular prism object grasping. (c) Cylindrical object grasping. (d) Ball-shaped object grasping.

Unlike the conventional finger-tip robotic grippers and enveloping robotic grippers, the proposed robotic gripper not only has a large reachable workspace but also has a simple drive system. This is also due to the special structure of the robotic gripper.

5   Conclusion

In this paper, a novel 5-DOF deployable robotic gripper is proposed. Then the mechanism design and mobility analysis are performed, from which one can see that the finger of the robotic gripper has only one mobility used to conduct deployment-motion while a grasping angle will be formed with it. Besides, the workspace and kinematic simulation are obtained by kinematic analysis and dynamic analysis are then carried out, which lay a foundation for further optimization and control. Finally, a group of grasping simulations are performed to prove the excellent shape adaptability of the robotic gripper.

Acknowledgment. This work was supported by the Key-Area Research and Development Program of Guangdong Province (Grant No. 2019B090915001), and the Shenzhen Research and Development Program of China (Grant No. JCYJ20200109112818703).

References

1. Ryuta, O., Kenji, T.: Grasp and dexterous manipulation of multi-fingered robotic hands: a review from a control view point. Adv. Robot. **31**(19–20), 1030–1050 (2017). https://doi.org/10.1080/01691864.2017.1365011
2. Romdhane, L.: Design and analysis of a hybrid serial-parallel manipulator. Mech. Mach. Theory **34**(7), 1037–1055 (1999)
3. Bo, H.: Formulation of unified Jacobian for serial-parallel manipulators. Robot. Comput. Integr. Manuf. **30**(5), 460–467 (2014). https://doi.org/10.1016/j.rcim.2014.03.001
4. Zhou, J.S., et al.: SCL-13: a 13-DOF soft robotic hand for dexterous grasping and in-hand manipulation. IEEE Robot. Autom. Lett. **3**(4), 3379–3386 (2018)
5. Li, H.L., et al.: High-force soft pneumatic actuators based on novel casting method for robotic applications. Sens. Actuators A Phys. **306**, 111957 (2020)
6. Gao, C.Q., et al.: Design of the truss-shaped deployable grasping mechanism using mobility bifurcation. Mech. Mach. Theory **139**, 346–358 (2019)
7. Gao, C.Q., et al.: Design and analysis of a novel truss-shaped variable-stiffness deployable robotic gripper. IEEE Access **8**, 112944–112956 (2020)
8. Gao, C.Q., et al.: Design and analysis of a novel deployable robotic gripper. In: Proceedings of the IEEE International Conference on Robotics and Biomimetics (Robio), pp. 481–486. Dali, Yunnan, China (2019 December)

Design and Manufacture of an Origami-Inspired Crawling Mini-robot

Xi Wang, Cuncun Qian, Nan Ma, and Xin Dong[✉]

Department of Mechanical, Materials and Manufacturing Engineering, University of Nottingham, Nottingham NG7 2RD, UK
{Xi.Wang,Cuncun.Qian,Nan.Ma,Xin.Dong}@nottingham.ac.uk

Abstract. The requirement for detection technology in confined space is becoming more diversified with the development of the modern industry. This study aims to design a miniature crawling robot that can perform the inspection and operation tasks in confined environments. To minimize the body structure of the robot for easy transportation and delivery, the origami principle is adopted. As a result, the developed origami-inspired crawling robot can be folded to a spatial structure (length 80 mm, width 80 mm, and height 40 mm) from the initial plate (Length 90 mm and width 80 mm). With the two symmetrical structured PZT actuators, the developed robot can achieve a stable crawling speed of 5 mm/s and a maximum of 9.7 mm/s. It is also demonstrated that the structured robot can climb the slope at 15° and turn with a speed of 0.17 rad/s.

Keywords: Origami-inspired · Mini-robot · Crawling robot

1 Introduction

Industry robot is now widely used in manufacturing [1, 2], measurements [3–6], and aerospace [7]. Meanwhile, the mini robot is also investigated, which are more suitable for the confined space operation [8]. Assembled via micro-scale level parts, this type of robot highly depends on micro-manufacture, material, and the use of a micro-electric device. It can easily assess to small space and provide a new platform for microscale physics/dynamics.

Owns quick fabrication and lower consumption, origami-inspired mini-robots have been developed in recent years; for example, the 3D printed origami-inspired robot [9] tri-bot [10], which shows a quite simple design using the SMA material as the actuator. However, some of these robots are quite large, even though they adopted the folding principle to construct the robot. Some origami-inspired robots were designed for the detection work in pipe environment, like the origami-based earthworm-like locomotion robots [11]. The robot works like an earthworm in the pipe to record the condition of the pipe wall. However, due to the limitation of the actuator, the size of the robot is still quite large, which means it cannot be used in a confined environment with a small access port. Besides, the crawling speed of the robot is also a limitation [12], and the structure

© Springer Nature Switzerland AG 2021
X.-J. Liu et al. (Eds.): ICIRA 2021, LNAI 13015, pp. 425–436, 2021.
https://doi.org/10.1007/978-3-030-89134-3_39

of the robot needs to be assembled part by part, which is time-consuming in the entire operation.

The research process of this paper is the following: based on the principle of origami, designing and prototyping an origami-inspired robot with the miniaturized structure to perform the inspection work in confined space. The robot should have the ability to move and turn in different directions. Also, for easy transportation and delivery, the developed robot should be folded and unfolded easily.

The design of the mini crawling robot is non-conventional, which uses the material deformation to provide the motion of the adjacent links. Also, the piezoelectric actuator provides the potential to increase the crawling speed and decrease the dimension/weight of the robot.

2 Methodology

In this part, the whole design, manufacture, and test process will be demonstrated. First, to provide the power source for the crawling robot, the actuator needs to be determined. Then, based on the motion of the actuator and installation requirement, the structure is built with the considerations of the foldability and stability of the robot. Meanwhile, to achieve high performance of the robot, the suitable material was selected [13] to have high strength and low density.

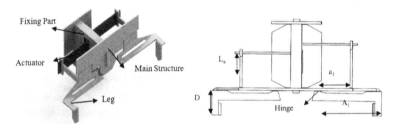

Fig. 1. 3D model of the foldable crawling robot and movable part design

Since the original structure of the robot is a plate, laser cutting is used to complete the first step of processing where the DXF file for laser cutting was provided. Furthermore, the STL file for 3D-printer also will be generated to produce a fixing part for the actuator. The 3D structure will then be assembled. Also, in this part, the control and power supply system was built to drive the robot.

After assembling, the robot performance will be evaluated using three different types of tests where the six different factors of the robot performance in different conditions were measured.

2.1 Actuator and Fixing Part

To meet the requirements of mini-scale, lightweight, easy manufacturing, and good foldability, the amplifying type of piezoelectric actuator is selected to drive the motion of the system. The parameters of the actuator are shown in Table 1. The fixing part is prototyped by 3D printing with a resin material as this material is common, light, and cheap.

Table 1. Data for PL127.10 piezoelectric actuator (pi, 2017)

Parameter	Value
Operating voltage range	0 to 60 V
Displacement	450 μm
Remaining length LF	27 mm
Length L	31 mm
Width W	9.60 mm
Height TH	0.67 mm
Blocking force	1.1 N

Based on the manufacturing recommendations, and to ensure safety, the working frequency should be no more than 1/3 of the resonant frequency, then the max working frequency is:

$$f = \frac{1}{3}f_r \tag{1}$$

where f is the max working frequency, f_r is the resonant frequency (420 Hz).

2.2 Movable Structure and Support Structure

The displacement generated by the bending of the PZT actuator is 0.45 mm, which is relatively small for the locomotion of the robot. Therefore, a new displacement amplifies structure is designed to enlarge the displacement of the actuator. A hinge-like structure is designed to increase the small displacement from the actuators. A foldable leg part needs to be designed with a movable structure to support the robot and output the displacement. It is simple enough to ensure the structure at the 2D level can easily be manufactured by the laser cutter. The 3D model and drawing is shown in Fig. 1.

The displacement L_a given by each actuator is 0.45 mm, the distance between the twist hinge-like part to leg A_1 is 19 mm and to the actuator fixing part a_1 is 7.5 mm, so the output displacement can be calculated:

$$D = L_a\frac{A_1}{a_1} \tag{2}$$

A rectangular plate was cut on the fixing part for the actuators to be assembled to connect the moveable structure and the actuators. To ensure the main structure will not be broken when the hinge-like part twist, the thickness above the movable part was increased, which keeps the robot running stable. Also, the bottom segment has a foldable support leg, which can support the whole structure and ensure the stability of the robot.

2.3 Material

The robot needed to be light, small, and strong due to the requirements of the actual application. Polypropylene was chosen as the main material because of the good performance. The parameters of PP are shown in Table 2.

Table 2. PP datasheet used for the robot

Parameter	Unit	Homopol
Density	kgm^3	905
Price/Tonne	£	680
Tensile Strength	Mpa	33
Tensile Modulus	Gpa	1.4
Elongation at Break	%	150
Oxygen Index	%	17

The main structure volume can be calculated, which is 3125 mm^3. The density of the material PP is 890 kg/m^3. Then the mass of the whole structure is:

$$m = \rho v \tag{3}$$

where m is the mass, ρ is the density of PP, v is the volume of the robot.

By appropriately selecting the material and designing the structure, the robot can achieve the designed requirements (e.g., light, small, and strong). Therefore, the robot can have a good performance for the actual applications.

3 Experimental Results

3.1 Control Design

The control amplifier E650 provided by PI was used to ensure the high motion accuracy of the robot. The type of input analog signal was pulses (Vpp of 10 V, offset of 5 V, the width of half pulse) as the control input. A waveform generator was used to generate the signal for controlling.

The speed of the robot should be linearly improved when the frequency of input signal increases which needs to be proved by tests. There is the possibility that the moveable structure cannot be able to respond to the displacement of actuators in the high operating frequency. So, the highest frequency that the robot still can be controlled needs to be determined.

Table 3. Steps for a main structure fold process

Process	Schematic diagram
Fold from the link between the front support section and bottom section	
Fold from the link between the bottom support section and back section	
Fold the support leg out by folding this part 90 degrees	
Fold the movable parts by 90 degrees	
Fold the movable leg parts until they are all vertical to the ground	
Fold the operated bars until they are all vertical to the front surface	

3.2 Manufacture and Assemble

Two steps are contained in the manufacturing process. The first step is the main structure, which uses laser cutting to obtain the original shape from the PP board. The second step is the actuator fixing part manufactured by 3D printing with resin material.

Laser cutting can make the robot stronger because the laser would not break the main structure away from the cutting area. Moreover, the average time consumed for cutting each robot area is less than 30 s which is quite fast compared to the conventional manufacturing methods. Although laser cutting is a high-precise process, it will not decrease the accuracy of manufacture by the material melting due to the high temperature on the edge of the cutting area. To solve the problem of material melting, two boards will be stacked and cut together. That will ensure the board underneath to be finished with a nice surface condition.

There are two steps for the assembling phase: First, the robot needs to be folded from the 2D state to the 3D state. Then, the actuators need to be assembled with the actuator fixing part. Finally, the two sub-assembly parts can be connected.

The electric devices of the robot need to be connected as well. First, the actuators need to be connected to the PZT connector provided with the amplifier. Then, to get the control signal, the amplifier needs to be connected to the waveform generator. The main steps of the folded process of the main structure are shown in Table 3.

Two finished sub-assembly parts were connected to the main structure by linking the actuators to the operated bars in the main structure. The final assembled robot and control system is shown in Fig. 2.

3.3 Test Stage

Six parameters of the robot were tested: speed, step length, ramp rate, turning speed, the angle of stability. Therefore, the tests were completed with different surface slopes, frequencies, and material surface conditions.

First, the speed of the robot needs to be determined. Here, the table surface was chosen as the standard operating surface. The operating frequency of actuators was selected as 1 Hz, 5 Hz, 10 Hz, 20 Hz, 40 Hz, 80 Hz, and 100 Hz, respectively. To determine the speed of the robot, the time consumed for the robot crawling 50 mm will be measured. A ruler was used to provide the scale of distance. A set of surfaces provides different friction coefficients that the robot may meet in the actual applications. The camera recorded the process.

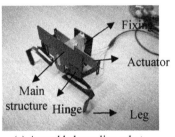
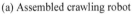
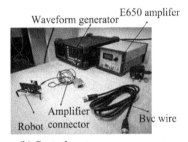

(a) Assembled crawling robot   (b) Control system

Fig. 2. Assembled crawling robot and control system

Then, to determine the crawling performance on different operating surfaces, the robot was performed from table surface to rough plastic surface and foamed plastic surface. The speed and step length tests are repeated on those surfaces.

To test the stability performance on the different slopes, a test paper rig that the angle of the slope can be changed was used. The test rig contains a ramp that can change the angle of slope and a ruler to provide the scale. The angle of slope in this test was changed from 0 to 30°, where the robot will be tested for static stability and the dynamic performance in various frequencies.

Finally, to determine the turning speed, only one actuator was used to make the robot turning around. The time consumed for turning 90° will be measured in different operating frequencies.

3.4 Speed and Step Length on Different Surfaces

The test of speed and step length on the table surface, rough plastic surface, and the foamed plastic surface is shown in Fig. 3.

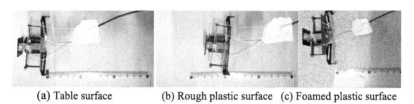

(a) Table surface   (b) Rough plastic surface   (c) Foamed plastic surface

Fig. 3. Speed and step length test on three types of surface

The step length was designed as 1mm in theory, then the other theory values of different frequencies can be calculated based on the theory step length as shown in Table 4:

Table 4. The theoretical value for speed and step length for different operating frequencies

Frequency (Hz)	Step Length (mm)	Speed (mm/s)
1	1.02	1.02
5	1.02	5.1
10	1.02	10.2
20	1.02	20.4
40	1.02	40.8
80	1.02	81.6
100	1.02	102

The friction coefficients between the legs and surfaces used in the tests have the following relationship: foamed plastic > rough plastic surface > table surface. The number of steps for each frequency can be calculated because the frequency of the robot legs changes when the frequency of the input signal is changed. The time consumed for the robot crawling 50 mm was used to calculate the crawling speed.

Then the curves can be plotted to compare the values of theoretical and actual from the result of the test on the table surface, seen in Fig. 4. Similarly, Fig. 5 is on the rough plastic surface.

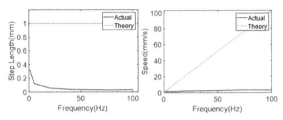

Fig. 4. Step lengths (L) and speeds (R) for the robot with different operating frequencies on the table surface

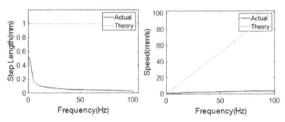

Fig. 5. Step lengths (L) and speeds (R) for the robot with different operating frequencies on the rough plastic surface

It can be found from Fig. 4 and Fig. 5 that the experimental value is different from the theoretical value. The difference is due to the actual resistance factors (e.g., hinge damping, surface friction, and transmission efficiency), reducing the step length and speed.

The robot legs are stocked in the interspace of the foamed plastic Fig. 3(c) no matter how big the operating frequency value is. It was demonstrated that the current design of the robot could not crawl on the foamed plastic surface.

3.5   The Performance of Ramp Speed in Different Angles

To test the performance of ramp speed, the paper rig was used, shown in Fig. 6. The stability of the robot on the ramp can be tested by changing the angle of the paper rig in static conditions and dynamic conditions.

| 0 degree | 5 degrees |
| 10 degrees | 15 degrees |

Fig. 6. Ramp test rig of the crawling robot

In the static test, the angle of the ramp was increased from 0 to the angle that the robot loses stability to measure the largest angle that the robot can keep on the slope. In the dynamic test, the time consumed for the robot crawling 50 mm will be measured with different angles (0–15°) in the frequency of 5 Hz. Then the crawling speed on the slope surface of the robot can be evaluated. The result of the static test is shown in Table 5.

Table 5. Experimental results for robot stability with different angles in static condition and turning performance

Turning angles(degrees)	Status	Frequency (Hz)	Time (s)	Angle (degree)	Speed (rad/s)
0	Stable	1	135	90	0.0114
5	Stable	5	96	90	0.0161
10	Stable	10	77	90	0.02
15	Stable	15	54	90	0.0289
20	Stable	20	30	90	0.0521
21	Stable	40	27	90	0.0579
22	Critical	60	23	90	0.0679
23	unsta-	80	20	90	0.0782
24	unsta-	100	16	90	0.0979
25	unsta-				

In the dynamic test, the angle of slope that the robot cannot move forward was 15°. The experimental results during the test are shown in Fig. 8(a).

3.6 Turning Performance in Different Frequencies

To determine the time consumed for the robot turning 90° within the different frequencies, only one actuator was assembled to actuate the robot turning around. The process

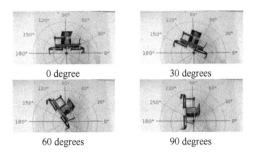

0 degree   30 degrees

60 degrees   90 degrees

Fig. 7. Example test process for robot turn 90°

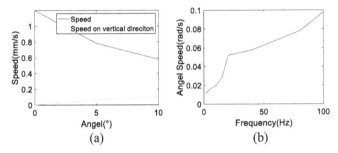

Fig. 8. (a) Speed along the ramp and in the vertical direction for three different angles, (b) The turning speed of the robot under different frequencies

of the test is shown in Fig. 7. The experimental results are shown in Fig. 8(b) and Table 5.

It can be seen from the experimental results that the turning speed of the robot is related to the operating frequency. Especially, it increases rapidly before 20 Hz and then slows down until 100 Hz.

4   Discussion and Significance of the Result

4.1   Discussion

It can be found that the origami-inspired robot does have the ability to walk straight from the test result, which can act as a prototype of the origami-inspired mini-robot used in the detection work of relatively small space (e.g., petrochemical pipes and aircraft engines).

The robot can walk straight on a surface that is not too rough (e.g., table and chair). The maximum speed (2.7 mm/s) can be achieved on the table surface at the operating frequency of 100 Hz, or on the rough plastic surface at the operating frequency of 80 Hz. However, the system is going to losing stability when the operating frequency is over 20Hz. So, to balance the maneuverability and the speed, the recommended operating frequency is 20 Hz when the maximum speed is 1.5 mm/s.

The first test shows the difference of two factors (step length and speed) between actual and theoretical values. Those two factors are not in linear positively correlated with the operating frequency due to the resistance factors (e.g., hinge damping, surface friction, and transmission efficiency).

The second and third parts focus on dynamic performance (e.g., climbing and turning). The robot can keep static stable on the rig when the slope is less than 22°, and it can keep dynamic stable when the slope is less than 15°. The climbing speed is between 1.8 m/h to 3.6 m/h for the ramp slope between zero and 15°. That angle is unfortunately not enough for the practical application. This is mainly caused by the contact surface for each leg is small, which caused the friction is not enough to keep the robot stable. The robot cannot keep stable when the two legs are both in motion that caused less support from the legs. The performance can be improved by increasing the number of legs from 3-legs to 4-legs.

The robot has a good performance on turning in the third test, the time consumed for turn 90° is 30 s in the advised actuator operating frequency of 20 Hz. The turning speed can be stably improved when the operating frequency is increased. So, the operating frequency can be changed to get a different turning speed in the practical application. However, the turning performance is influenced a lot by the wires that may block the motion of the robot and stop the process of turning.

4.2 Conclusion

This paper presents a new origami-inspired mini robot to improve the detection ability in confined spaces. This design provides the possibility to reduce the cost and dimension of the conventional crawling robots, enabling access into environments with confined structures and small entrances.

It can be found from the experimental results based on the current design of the crawling robot. It can achieve the high-speed moving ability (e.g., crawling speed of 2.7 mm/s, turning speed of 0.0979 rad/s) with miniatured dimension (e.g., length 80 mm, width 80 mm, and height 40 mm).

The developed robot can be used in many applications due to the small size and foldable structure. It can also perform in-site repairing or inspecting work with the assembled end-effectors. Based on this concept, more advanced robots can be designed/prototyped to execute the tasks in narrow/confined environments.

Acknowledgment. The research leading to these results has received funding from the Department of Mechanical, Materials, and Manufacturing Engineering of the University of Nottingham and the master student project of the University of Nottingham.

References

1. Dong, X., Palmer, D., Axinte, D., Kell, J.: In-situ repair/maintenance with a continuum robotic machine tool in confined space. J. Manuf. Process. **38**, 313–318 (2019)
2. Ma, N., et al.: Parametric vibration analysis and validation for a novel portable hexapod machine tool attached to surfaces with unequal stiffness. J. Manuf. Process. **47**, 192–201 (2019)

3. Russo, M., Dong, X.: A calibration procedure for reconfigurable Gough-Stewart manipulators. Mech. Mach. Theory **152**, 103920 (2020)
4. Ma, N., Dong, X., Axinte, D.: Modeling and experimental validation of a compliant under-actuated parallel kinematic manipulator. IEEE/ASME Trans. Mechatron. **25**(3), 1409–1421 (2020)
5. Yu, J., Dong, X., Pei, X., Zong, G., Kong, X., Qiu, Q.: Mobility and singularity analysis of a class of 2-DOF rotational parallel mechanisms using a visual graphic approach. In: International Design Engineering Technical Conferences and Computers and Information in Engineering Conference, vol. 54839, pp. 1027–1036 (2011)
6. Chen, B., Zong, G., Yu, J., Dong, X.: Dynamic modeling and analysis of 2-DOF quasi-sphere parallel platform. Chin. J. Mech. Eng.-En **49**(13), 24–31 (2013)
7. Wang, M., Palmer, D., Dong, X., Alatorre, D., Axinte, D., Norton, A.: Design and development of a slender dual-structure continuum robot for in-situ aeroengine repair. In: 2018 IEEE/RSJ International Conference on Intelligent Robots and Systems (IROS), pp. 5648–5653. IEEE (2018)
8. Alatorre, D., et al.: Teleoperated, in situ repair of an aeroengine: overcoming the internet latency hurdle. IEEE Robot. Autom. Mag. **26**(1), 10–20 (2018)
9. Onal, C.D., Tolley, M.T., Wood, R.J., Rus, D.: Origami-inspired printed robots. IEEE/ASME Trans. Mechatron. **20**(5), 2214–2221 (2014)
10. Zhakypov, Z., Falahi, M., Shah, M., Paik, J.: The design and control of the multi-modal locomotion origami robot, Tribot. In: 2015 IEEE/RSJ International Conference on Intelligent Robots and Systems (IROS), pp. 4349–4355. IEEE (2015)
11. Fang, H., Zhang, Y., Wang, K.: Origami-based earthworm-like locomotion robots. Bioinspir. Biomim. **12**(6), 065003 (2017)
12. Goldberg, B., et al.: Power and control autonomy for high-speed locomotion with an insect-scale legged robot. IEEE Robot. Autom. Lett. **3**(2), 987–993 (2018)
13. Tripathi, D.: Practical Guide to Polypropylene. iSmithers Rapra Publishing, Shrewsbury (2002)

Comparison Study on Force/Motion Transmissibility of a Novel 6-DOF Parallel Mechanism and Stewart Platform

Chenglin Dong[1], Haitao Liu[2(✉)], Longqi Cai[1], and Lizhi Liu[1]

[1] Science and Technology on Reactor System Design Technology Laboratory, Nuclear Power Institute of China, Chengdu 610041, China
[2] Key Laboratory of Mechanism Theory and Equipment Design, Ministry of Education, Tianjin University, Tianjin 300072, China
liuht@tju.edu.cn

Abstract. This paper introduces a novel 6-DOF over-constrained parallel mechanism (PM), saving nine 1-DOF joints compared with the well-known Stewart plat-form. To facilitate better use of the proposed 6-DOF PM, a comparison study on the force/motion transmissibility between this PM and the Stewart platform is carried out, provided that they have the same dimensions. The results indicate that the novel 6-DOF PM behaves a better kinematic performance than the Stewart platform. The study provides a theoretical foundation for the industrial application of the novel 6-DOF PM.

Keywords: 6-DOF parallel mechanism · Force/Motion transmissibility

1 Introduction

The existing category of parallel mechanisms (PMs) contains a kind of six degrees of freedom (DOF) multi-closed-loop mechanism, which is known as Stewart platform composed of six $\underline{S}PS$ or $U\underline{P}S$ limbs. Due to its advantages in terms of load carrying capacity, high stiffness, dynamic characteristics and accuracy [1], Stewart platform has drawn a great deal of attentions from researchers, which has been widely applied in industry for the tasks like tire testing [2], flight simulation [3], motion tracking [4], micro positioning and vibration isolation [6–8], and large part manufacturing [9, 10]. More recently, a novel 6-DOF PM (see Fig. 1) has been presented by Luzi [11]. This PM is an evolution of Stewart platform and has several interesting characteristics with respect to Stewart platform: (1) it features a lower number of 1-DOF joints thus improving the stiffness; (2) it is an over-constrained mechanism, giving the opportunity to remove clearance in joints.

In order to facilitate better use of the novel 6-DOF PM, it is necessary and reasonable to firstly obtain a better understanding of its performance in terms of the motion/force transmission capabilities compared with Stewart platform, owing to that the key feature of a PM is to transmit motion/force between its joint space and operational space [12].

© Springer Nature Switzerland AG 2021
X.-J. Liu et al. (Eds.): ICIRA 2021, LNAI 13015, pp. 437–447, 2021.
https://doi.org/10.1007/978-3-030-89134-3_40

Hence, this paper concentrates on the comparison between the novel PM and the Stewart platform with regard to motion/force transmissibility. The rest of this paper is arranged as follows. The structure description and kinematic analysis of the novel PM are given in Sect. 2. In Sect. 3, transmission indices based on screw theory for kinematic performance evaluation are presented. The compared results of the motion/force transmissibility for the novel PM and Stewart platform, provided that they both have same dimensions, are shown in Sect. 4. Finally, conclusions are drawn in Sect. 5.

2   Structure Description and Kinematic Analysis

2.1   Structure Description

Figure 1 shows the CAD model of the novel 6-DOF PM, i.e. 3-R(2-R$\underline{P}$R)U PM, designed by the authors. Different from the well-known Stewart platform (see Fig. 2) supported by six identical U$\underline{P}$S limbs, obviously, 3-R(2-R$\underline{P}$R)U PM consists of a moving platform, a fixed base and three identical R(2-R$\underline{P}$R)U hybrid kinematic chains. The hybrid kinematic chain is essentially composed of a 2-R$\underline{P}$R planar parallel linkage with its base link linked to the base by an R joint and its output link linked the platform by a U joint. Here, R, U, and S represent, respectively, revolute, universal, and spherical joints, and underlined $\underline{P}$ denotes active prismatic joint driven by an actuator. Noted that the 2-R$\underline{P}$R planar parallel linkage has two translations and one rotation (2T1R), the R(2-R$\underline{P}$R)U hybrid kinematic chain can be seen as a 6-DOF limb having two actuated joints. Hence, the 3-R(2-R$\underline{P}$R)U PM can realize 6-DOF motion actuated by six $\underline{P}$ joints. This topological structure leads to that the motions of every two limbs are constrained in a same plane, but the platform is free of constraint wrench. Compared with Stewart platform, the novel 6-DOF PM is an over-constrained mechanism and can save nine 1-DOF joints, thereby theoretically decreasing the joint clearance effectively, and improving the load carrying capacity, stiffness and accuracy.

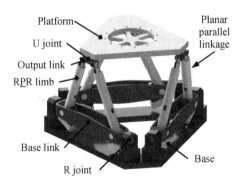

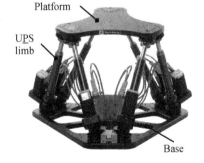

Fig. 1. CAD model of the novel 6-DOF PM   **Fig. 2.** Stewart platform

2.2   Coordinates System and Inverse Position Analysis

The schematic diagram of the 3-R(2-R$\underline{P}$R)U PM is shown in Fig. 3. In order to define the joint and link parameters necessary for modeling, we denote the three identical R(2-R$\underline{P}$R)U kinematic chains as chains 1, 2, and 3, and the two R$\underline{P}$R limbs of the planar parallel linkage in chain i ($i = 1 \sim 3$) as sub-chains 1, i and 2, i. Figure 3 indicates the specific points of interest for the analysis. $B_{j,i}$ and $A_{j,i}$ are where the sub-chain j, i attaches to the base link and output link, respectively; B_i denotes the midpoint of $\overline{B_{1,i}B_{2,i}}$, and A_i represents both the center of the U joint and the midpoint of $\overline{A_{1,i}A_{2,i}}$. Operationally important points at the platform and base, the centroids of $\triangle A_1A_2A_3$ and $\triangle B_1B_2B_3$, are labeled O and P, respectively. To evaluate the vectors involved in the kinematic model, a reference coordinate system $O-xyz$ and a body-fixed coordinate system $P-uvw$ are defined with $y \perp \overline{OB_1}, z \perp \triangle B_1B_2B_3$ and $v \perp \overline{PA_1}, w \perp \triangle A_1A_2A_3$. Meanwhile, a set of body-fixed coordinate systems $A_i-u_iv_iw_i$ ($i = 1 \sim 3$) are also attached at the output links with the u_i axis being perpendicular to the motion plane of the planar parallel linkage and the v_i axis being coincident with $\overline{A_{1,i}A_{2,i}}$ as shown in Fig. 3.

The orientation of the platform with respect to $O-xyz$ can be described using $w-v-w$ Euler angles (ψ, θ, φ) [13] as follow

$$R_P = \text{Rot}(z, \ \psi)\text{Rot}(y', \ \theta)\text{Rot}(z'', \ \varphi) = \begin{bmatrix} u & v & w \end{bmatrix} \tag{1}$$

where u, v and w represent the unit vectors of $P-uvw$. The orientation of $A_i - u_iv_iw_i$ with respect to $O-xyz$ can be expressed by γ_i, α_i and β_i as

$$R_i = \text{Rot}(z, \ \gamma_i)\text{Rot}(y', \ \alpha_i)\text{Rot}(x'', \ \beta_i) = \begin{bmatrix} u_i & v_i & w_i \end{bmatrix} \tag{2}$$

where $\gamma_i = 2(i - 1)\pi/3$ represents the structural angle.

Similarly, by dividing six UPS limb into three groups, the above symbol system of the 3-R(2-RPR)U PM can be followed. The important points and coordinate systems of the Stewart platform are shown in Fig. 4.

In order to evaluate the kinematic performance, it is necessary to carry out the inverse position and velocity analyses. As shown in Fig. 4, given Euler angles (ψ, θ, φ) and r_P (the position vector of the point P), the position vector of the point A_i evaluated in frame $O-xyz$, $r_{A_i} = \left(x_{A_i} \ y_{A_i} \ z_{A_i} \right)^T$, can be solved

$$r_{A_i} = r_P + a_i, \ i = 1, 2, 3 \tag{3}$$

$$r_{A_i} = b_{j,i} + q_{j,i}s_{j,i} - c_{j,i}, \ i = 1, 2, 3, \ j = 1, 2 \tag{4}$$

$$a_i = R_P a_{i,0}, \ c_{j,i} = R_i c_{j,i,0}$$

$$b_{j,i} = \begin{pmatrix} d_b \cos \gamma_i - (-1)^j c_b \sin \gamma_i \\ d_b \sin \gamma_i + (-1)^j c_b \cos \gamma_i \\ 0 \end{pmatrix}, \ a_{i,0} = d_a \begin{pmatrix} \cos \gamma_i \\ \sin \gamma_i \\ 0 \end{pmatrix}, \ c_{j,i,0} = (-1)^j c_a \begin{pmatrix} 0 \\ 1 \\ 0 \end{pmatrix}$$

where $q_{j,i} = \left\| \overrightarrow{B_{j,i}A_{j,i}} \right\|$ and $s_{j,i}$ represent the length and unit vector of the sub-chain j, i, respectively; $d_a = \left\| \overrightarrow{PA_i} \right\|$, $d_b = \left\| \overrightarrow{OB_i} \right\|$, $c_a = \left\| \overrightarrow{A_iA_{j,i}} \right\|$, $c_b = \left\| \overrightarrow{B_iB_{j,i}} \right\|$. Noting that u_i is perpendicular to the motion plane of the planar parallel linkage, and $v_i = s_{u1,i}$,

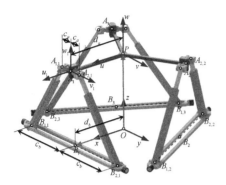
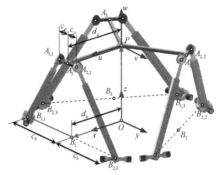

Fig. 3. Schematic diagram of the
3-R(2-RPR)U PM

Fig. 4. Schematic diagram of the Stewart
platform

$v_i \perp s_{u2,i}$, $s_{u2,i} = w$, where $s_{u1,i}$ and $s_{u2,i}$ are unit vectors of the U joint of chain i. Taking
dot products with u_i on both sides of Eq. (4), we can obtain α_i and β_i explicitly via

$$\alpha_i = \arctan \frac{x_{A_i} \cos \gamma_i + y_{A_i} \sin \gamma_i - d_b}{z_{A_i}}, \ \beta_i = \arctan \frac{w_x \sin \gamma_i - w_y \cos \gamma_i}{\left(w_x \cos \gamma_i + w_y \sin \gamma_i\right) \sin \alpha_i - w_z \cos \alpha_i} \tag{5}$$

Hence, R_i is fully defined in terms of α_i and β_i in Eq. (2). Taking norms on both
sides of re-arranged Eq. (4) leads to

$$q_{j,i} = \left\| r_{A_i} - b_{j,i} + c_{j,i} \right\|, \ s_{j,i} = \left(r_{A_i} - b_{j,i} + c_{j,i}\right) / q_{j,i}, \ i = 1, 2, 3, \ j = 1, 2 \tag{6}$$

As for Stewart platform, substituting $c_{j,i} = R_P c_{j,i,0}$ into Eq. (4), $q_{j,i}$ and $s_{j,i}$ can be
obtained via Eq. (6) fairly easily.

2.3 Jacobian Matrix Formulation

Taking the derivatives of Eqs. (3) and (4) with respect to time yields

$$\dot{r}_{A_i} = \dot{r}_P - \omega \times a_i, \ i = 1, 2, 3 \tag{7}$$

$$\dot{r}_{A_i} = \dot{q}_{j,i} s_{j,i} + q_{j,i} \omega_{j,i} \times s_{j,i} - \omega_i \times c_{j,i}, \ i = 1, 2, 3, \ j = 1, 2 \tag{8}$$

where ω (ω_i) and $\dot{r}_P (\dot{r}_{A_i})$ denote the angular velocity of the platform (the output link
in chain i) and the linear velocity of point $P(A_i)$, respectively; $\omega_{j,i}$ and $\dot{q}_{j,i}$ are the angular
velocity of the sub-chain j, i and the joint velocity of $\underline{P}$ joint. Then taking dot products
with $s_{j,i}$ on both sides of Eq. (8) and rewriting in matrix form

$$W_i^T \xi_{A_i} = \dot{q}_i, \ i = 1, 2, 3 \tag{9}$$

$$\xi_{A_i} = \begin{pmatrix} \dot{r}_{A_i} \\ \omega_i \end{pmatrix}, \ \dot{q}_i = \begin{pmatrix} \dot{q}_{1,i} \\ \dot{q}_{2,i} \end{pmatrix}, \ W_i = \begin{bmatrix} \hat{\xi}_{wa,1,i} & \hat{\xi}_{wa,2,i} \end{bmatrix}, \ \hat{\xi}_{wa,j,i} = \begin{pmatrix} s_{j,i} \\ c_{j,i} \times s_{j,i} \end{pmatrix}, \ j = 1, 2$$

where ξ_{A_i} represents the velocity twist of the output link; the physical interpretation of $\hat{\xi}_{wa,j,i}$ is the unit wrench of actuation wrench imposed upon the ith output link by the sub-chain j, i.

Bearing in mind that the relationship between $\omega_{j,i}$ and ω_i satisfies $\omega_{j,i} = \omega_i - \dot{\theta}_{j,i} u_i$, where $\dot{\theta}_{j,i}$ represents the joint velocity of R joint connecting the sub-chain j, i with the ith output link. Besides, since the platform and the ith output link are connected by an integrated U join, it results in $n_{u,i}^T \omega = n_{u,i}^T \omega_i$, $n_{u,i} = s_{u1,i} \times s_{u2,i}$, $i = 1, 2, 3$. Hence, it can be obtained that

$$\xi_{A_i} = X_i^T \xi_P, \quad i = 1, 2, 3 \tag{10}$$

$$\xi_P = \begin{pmatrix} \dot{r}_P \\ \omega \end{pmatrix}, \; X_i = \begin{bmatrix} X_{v,i} \; X_{\omega,i} \end{bmatrix}; \; X_{v,i} = \begin{bmatrix} E_3 \\ -[a_i \times] \end{bmatrix}$$

$$X_{\omega,i} = \begin{bmatrix} u_i & u_i & 0 \\ -a_i \times u_i & -a_i \times u_i & n_{u,i} \end{bmatrix} \begin{bmatrix} q_{1,i} u_i \times s_{1,i} + c_a w_i \; q_{2,i} u_i \times s_{2,i} - c_a w_i \; n_{u,i} \end{bmatrix}^{-1}$$

where ξ_P represents the velocity twist of the output link; E_3 is a unit matrix of order three; X_i denotes the velocity mapping matrix between ξ_{A_i} and ξ_P.

Substituting Eq. (10) into Eq. (9), it leads to the relationship between the input joint rates and the platform output velocity as follows

$$W^T \xi_P = \dot{q} \tag{11}$$

$$W = \begin{bmatrix} X_1 W_1 \; X_2 W_2 \; X_3 W_3 \end{bmatrix}, \; \dot{q} = \begin{pmatrix} \dot{q}_1^T \; \dot{q}_2^T \; \dot{q}_3^T \end{pmatrix}^T$$

where W represents the 6×6 force Jacobian matrix of the 3-R(2-RPR)U PM. As for Stewart platform, W can be directly generated by the observation method [14]

$$W = \begin{bmatrix} W_1 \; W_2 \; W_3 \end{bmatrix} \tag{12}$$

$$W_i = \begin{bmatrix} \hat{\xi}_{wa,1,i} \; \hat{\xi}_{wa,2,i} \end{bmatrix}, \; i = 1, 2, 3; \; \hat{\xi}_{wa,j,i} = \begin{pmatrix} s_{j,i} \\ (a_j + c_{j,i}) \times s_{j,i} \end{pmatrix}, \; j = 1, 2$$

3 Transmission Indices

Force/motion transmissibility is the most used and effective index for the PMs having coupled translational and rotational movement capabilities. On the basic of the 6×6 Jacobian matrix formulated in Sect. 2, the transmission indices for kinematic performance evaluation of 3-R(2-RPR)U PM and Stewart platform will be presented by adopting the approach proposed in Ref. [14].

Letting $T = W^{-T}$ and denoting it by

$$T = \begin{bmatrix} T_1 \; T_2 \; T_3 \end{bmatrix}, \; T_i = \begin{bmatrix} \xi_{ta,1,i}^* \; \xi_{ta,2,i}^* \end{bmatrix} \tag{13}$$

then normalizing $\boldsymbol{\xi}_{ta,j,i}^*$ as unit twist such that $\boldsymbol{\xi}_{ta,j,i}^* = \lambda_{j,i}^{-1}\hat{\boldsymbol{\xi}}_{ta,j,i}^*$, yields

$$T = T^* \Lambda^{-1} \tag{14}$$

$$T^* = \begin{bmatrix} T_1^* & T_2^* & T_3^* \end{bmatrix}, \; \Lambda^{-1} = \mathrm{diag}\begin{bmatrix} \Lambda_i^{-1} \end{bmatrix}; \; T_i^* = \begin{bmatrix} \hat{\boldsymbol{\xi}}_{ta,1,i}^* & \hat{\boldsymbol{\xi}}_{ta,2,i}^* \end{bmatrix}, \; \Lambda_i = \mathrm{diag}\begin{bmatrix} \lambda_{j,i}^{-1} \end{bmatrix}$$

where $\hat{\boldsymbol{\xi}}_{ta,j,i}^*$ represents the unit twist corresponding to $\boldsymbol{\xi}_{ta,j,i}^*$.

Hence, the twist $\boldsymbol{\xi}_P$ of the platform can be expressed as a linear combination of the basis elements of T^*, i.e.

$$\boldsymbol{\xi}_P = T^* \boldsymbol{\rho}^* = W^{-T}\Lambda\boldsymbol{\rho}^*, \; \boldsymbol{\rho}^* = \begin{pmatrix} \rho_1^* \\ \rho_2^* \\ \rho_3^* \end{pmatrix}, \; \boldsymbol{\rho}_i^* = \begin{pmatrix} \rho_{1,i}^* \\ \rho_{2,i}^* \end{pmatrix} \tag{15}$$

where $\boldsymbol{\rho}^*$ can be interpreted as the natural coordinates of $\boldsymbol{\xi}_P$ relative to the basis T^*. Substituting Eq. (15) into Eq. (11), it leads to the map between the joint coordinates $\dot{\boldsymbol{q}}$ and the natural coordinates $\boldsymbol{\rho}^*$ of $\boldsymbol{\xi}_P$ in the operation space

$$\Lambda\boldsymbol{\rho}^* = \dot{\boldsymbol{q}}, \; \Lambda = \mathrm{diag}\begin{bmatrix} \Lambda_i \end{bmatrix} = W^T T^* \tag{16}$$

$$3 - R(2 - RPR)U \; PM: \Lambda_i = \mathrm{diag}\begin{bmatrix} \lambda_{j,i} \end{bmatrix} = \mathrm{diag}\begin{bmatrix} \hat{\boldsymbol{\xi}}_{wa,j,i}^T X_i^T \hat{\boldsymbol{\xi}}_{ta,j,i}^* \end{bmatrix}$$

$$\text{Stewart platform:} \; \Lambda_i = \mathrm{diag}\begin{bmatrix} \lambda_{j,i} \end{bmatrix} = \mathrm{diag}\begin{bmatrix} \hat{\boldsymbol{\xi}}_{wa,j,i}^T \hat{\boldsymbol{\xi}}_{ta,j,i}^* \end{bmatrix}$$

In accordance with definitions appearing in Eq. (16), $\lambda_{j,i}$ is referred to as the motion transmissibility because it represents the ratio of the magnitude of the platform twist along/about the screw axis of $\hat{\boldsymbol{\xi}}_{ta,j,i}^*$ to a unit variation of the actuated joint in the sub-chain j, i. In the light of the dual/reciprocal properties of wrench/twist systems, $\lambda_{j,i}$ may also be referred to as the force transmissibility. Hence, $\lambda_{j,i}$ is called as the force/motion transmissibility, and it is also independent of coordinate system.

With the aid of the procedure to normalize the virtual coefficient, we adopt the following local transmission indices proposed in Ref. [14] to quantitatively measure the kinematic performance of two PMs.

$$\kappa = \min\{\kappa_S, \kappa_P\} \tag{17}$$

$$\kappa_S = \frac{\min\limits_{i=1,2,3}\left\{\min\limits_{j=1,2}\left\{\left|\hat{\boldsymbol{\xi}}_{wa,j,i}^{*T}\hat{\boldsymbol{\xi}}_{ta,j,i}^*\right|\right\}\right\}}{\max\limits_{i=1,2,3}\left\{\max\limits_{j=1,2}\left\{\left|\hat{\boldsymbol{\xi}}_{wa,j,i}^{*T}\hat{\boldsymbol{\xi}}_{ta,j,i}^*\right|_{max}\right\}\right\}}, \; \kappa_P = \frac{\min\limits_{i=1,2,3}\left\{\min\limits_{j=1,2}\left\{\left|\hat{\boldsymbol{\xi}}_{wa,j,i}^{*T}\hat{\boldsymbol{\xi}}_{ta,j,i}^*\right|\right\}\right\}}{\max\limits_{i=1,2,3}\left\{\max\limits_{j=1,2}\left\{\left|\hat{\boldsymbol{\xi}}_{wa,j,i}^{*T}\hat{\boldsymbol{\xi}}_{ta,j,i}^*\right|_{max}\right\}\right\}}$$

where $\hat{\boldsymbol{\xi}}_{ta,j,i} = \left(s_{j,i}^T \; \mathbf{0}\right)^T$ is the unit twist corresponding to the $\underline{P}$ joint in the subchain j, i; for 3-R(2-R$\underline{P}$R)U PM, $\hat{\boldsymbol{\xi}}_{wa,j,i}^*$ represents the unit wrench corresponding to $X_i\hat{\boldsymbol{\xi}}_{wa,j,i}$, while as for Stewart platform, $\hat{\boldsymbol{\xi}}_{wa,j,i}^* = \hat{\boldsymbol{\xi}}_{wa,j,i}$ and $\kappa_S \equiv 1$.

It is easy to find that the above-mentioned indices are homogeneously dimensionless, invariant with respect to the coordinate frame, and taking a value of [0, 1]. Obviously, the larger the value of κ is, the better is the kinematic performance.

4   Comparison Study on Force/Motion Transmissibility

In order to facilitate better use of the novel 6-DOF PM, based on the proposed indices, this section deals with the comparison of its motion/force transmissibility with that of Stewart platform provided that the two PMs both have same dimensions. Without loss of generality, we assume the dimensional parameters for the PMs are: $c_a = 0.07$, $d_a = 0.24$, $c_b = 0.4$ and $d_b = 0.3$.

Figure 5 depicts the distribution of the axes of $\hat{\boldsymbol{\xi}}_{wa,j,i}^{*}$ and $\hat{\boldsymbol{\xi}}_{ta,j,i}^{*}$, i.e. the basis elements of $\boldsymbol{W}$ and $\boldsymbol{T}^{*}$, given that the position vector of the point P is $\boldsymbol{r}_P = \begin{pmatrix} 0\ 0\ 0.75 \end{pmatrix}^{\mathrm{T}}$, and Euler angles $\psi = \varphi = 0°$, $\theta = 0 \sim 40°$. It can be seen that: (1) $\hat{\boldsymbol{\xi}}_{wa,j,i}^{*}$ and $\hat{\boldsymbol{\xi}}_{ta,j,i}^{*}$ of 3-R(2-R$\underline{P}$R)U PM are different from the corresponding $\hat{\boldsymbol{\xi}}_{wa,j,i}^{*}$ and $\hat{\boldsymbol{\xi}}_{ta,j,i}^{*}$ of Stewart platform, leading to that the former has different force/motion transmissibility compared with the latter; (2) for 3-R(2-R$\underline{P}$R)U PM, the distance between the axis of $\hat{\boldsymbol{\xi}}_{wa,j,i}^{*}$ and

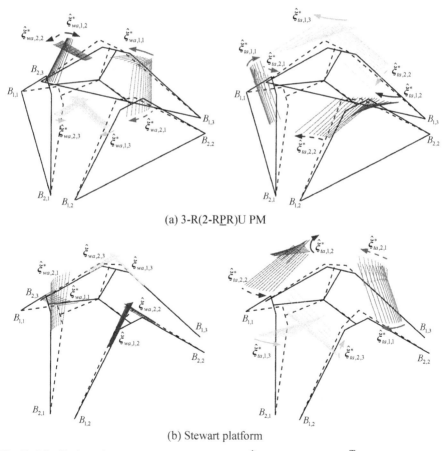

(a) 3-R(2-R$\underline{P}$R)U PM

(b) Stewart platform

Fig. 5. Distribution of the basis elements of $\boldsymbol{W}$ and $\boldsymbol{T}^{*}$ given $\boldsymbol{r}_p = (0\ 0\ 0)^{\mathrm{T}}$, $\Psi = \varphi = 0°$ and $\theta = 0 \sim 40°$

the axis of the sub-chain j, i is larger than the distance between the axis of $\hat{\boldsymbol{\xi}}^*_{ta,j,i}$ and the axis of the sub-chain j, i, while as for Stewart platform, the axes of $\hat{\boldsymbol{\xi}}^*_{wa,j,i}$ and the sub-chain j, i are coincidence, and the distance between the axis of $\hat{\boldsymbol{\xi}}^*_{ta,j,i}$ and the axis of the corresponding sub-chain is much larger; (3) even though the platforms of two PMs are at the same configuration, e.g. $\psi = \varphi = 0°$ and $\theta = 40°$ as shown in Fig. 6 by the dashed lines, the lengths and orientations of the sub-chains having the same number are different.

Figure 6 shows contour distribution of overall transmission index κ throughout an orientation workspace of $\psi = 0 \sim 360°$, $\theta = 0 \sim 40°$ and $\varphi = -\psi$ given $\mathbf{r}_P = \left(0\ 0\ z_P\right)^T$ ($z_P = 0.5, 0.75, 1$). Figure 7 illustrates contour distribution of κ across the $x - y$ plane given $\psi = \theta = \varphi = 0°$. It is easy to see that: (1) for both 3-R(2-R$\underline{P}$R)U PM and Stewart platform, κ is highly pose dependent and axially distributed; (2) given the position vector of the point P, κ takes the maximum values at $\theta = 0°$ and decreases with the increase of θ and z_P, for 3-R(2-R$\underline{P}$R)U PM, $\partial\kappa/\partial\theta$ increases with the increase of θ and decreases with the increase of z_P, while for Stewart platform, $\partial\kappa/\partial\theta$ is independent of θ, but decreases with the increase of z_P; (3) given Euler angles $\psi = \theta = \varphi = 0°$, κ takes the maximum values at the center of $x - y$ plane and decreases with the increase of $r = \sqrt{x_P^2 + y_P^2}$, and $\partial\kappa/\partial r$ also decreases with the increase of r; (4) for the given ranges of position and orientation, when the two PMs are at the same configuration, the kinematic performance of 3-R(2-R$\underline{P}$R)U PM is superior to Stewart platform.

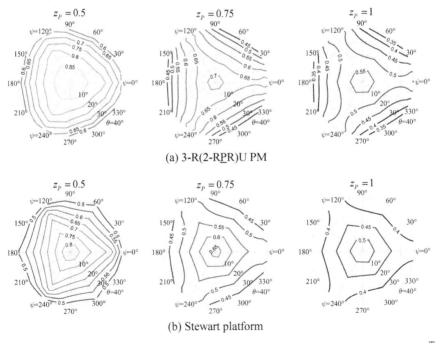

(a) 3-R(2-R$\underline{P}$R)U PM

(b) Stewart platform

Fig. 6. Distribution of κ vs. $\Psi = 0 \sim 360°$, $\theta = 0 \sim 40°$ and $\varphi = -\Psi$ given $\mathbf{r}_p = (0\ 0\ z_p)^T$

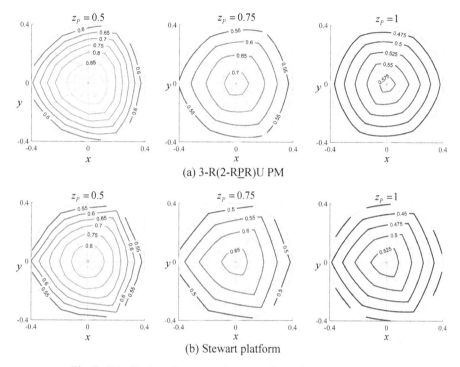

(a) 3-R(2-RPR)U PM

(b) Stewart platform

Fig. 7. Distribution of κ across the $x - y$ plane given $\Psi = \theta = \varphi = 0$

According to Ref. [12], we define the areas which are enclosed by the overall transmission index $\kappa \geq 0.7$ as the respective good transmission workspaces (GTW). With the consideration that 6-DOF PMs have coupled translational and rotational movements, we call the GTW given the position vector of the reference point as good transmission orientation workspace (GTOW), and the GTW given the orientation of platform as good transmission position workspace (GTPW). Figure 8 shows the GTOW of 3-R(2-RPR)U PM and Stewart platform, when the reference point P is on the z-axis. Obviously, the GTOW of 3-R(2-RPR)U PM is much larger than that of Stewart platform. Figure 9 shows the GTPW of two PMs when Euler angles $\psi = \varphi = \theta = 0°$. The results show that the volume of GTPW is 0.1294 for the novel PM, and 0.0739 for Stewart platform. Consequently, the GTPW of the novel PM is about 0.75 times larger than that of Stewart platform.

Based on the above-mentioned studies, it is found, by comparison, that the 3-R(2-RPR)U PM behaves a better kinematic performance in terms of motion/force transmissibility than Stewart platform, providing a theoretical foundation for the industrial application of the novel 6-DOF PM.

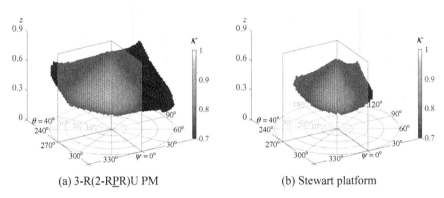

(a) 3-R(2-RPR)U PM   (b) Stewart platform

Fig. 8. Good transmission orientation workspace

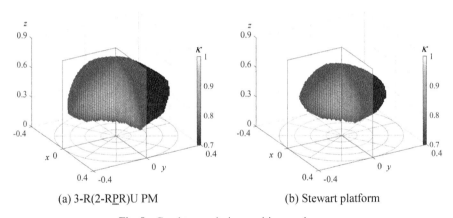

(a) 3-R(2-RPR)U PM   (b) Stewart platform

Fig. 9. Good transmission position workspace

5   Conclusions

Based on screw theory, this paper investigates the comparison of a novel 6-DOF PM with the well-known Stewart platform with regard to motion/force transmissibility. The following conclusions are drawn.

(1) The novel 6-DOF PM, i.e. 3-R(2-RPR)U PM, is an over-constrained mechanism, which can save nine 1-DOF joints compared with Stewart platform, thereby decreasing the joint clearance effectively, and improving the load carrying capacity, stiffness and accuracy.

(2) The comparison study on motion/force transmissibility of the novel PM and Stewart platform provided that they both have same dimensions show that: a) when the two PMs are at the same configuration, the kinematic performance of the novel PM is superior to Stewart platform; b) both the GTPW and GTOW of the novel PM are larger than that of Stewart platform. Hence, the 3-R(2-RPR)U PM behaves a better kinematic performance in terms of motion/force transmissibility than Stewart platform, providing a theoretical foundation for the industrial application of the novel 6-DOF PM.

Acknowledgments. This work is partially supported by National Defense Basic Scientific Research Program of China (grant JCKY2017203B066).

References

1. Dasgupta, B., Mruthyunjaya, T.S.: The Stewart platform manipulator-a review. Mech. Mach. Theory **35**, 15–40 (2000)
2. Gough, V.E., Whitehall, S.G.: Universal type testing machine. In: Proceedings of the 9th International Automobile Technical Congress, London, pp. 117–137 (1962)
3. Liu, G., Qu, Z., Han, J., Liu, X.: Systematic optimal design procedures for the Gough-Stewart platform used as motion simulators. Ind. Robot: Int. J. **40**(6), 550–558 (2013)
4. Kim, Y.S., Shi, H., Dagalakis, N., et al.: Design of a six-DOF motion tracking system based on a Stewart platform and ball-and-socket joints. Mech. Mach. Theory **133**, 84–94 (2019)
5. Dalvand, M.M., Shirinzadeh, B.: Kinematics analysis of 6-DOF parallel micro-manipulators with offset U-joints: a case study. Int. J. Intell. Mechatron. Robot. **2**(1), 28–40 (2012)
6. Hu, F., Jing, X.: A 6-DOF passive vibration isolator based on Stewart structure with X-shaped legs. Nonlinear Dyn. **91**(1), 157–185 (2017). https://doi.org/10.1007/s11071-017-3862-x
7. Zheng, Y., Li, Q., Yan, B., et al.: A Stewart isolator with high-static-low-dynamic stiffness struts based on negative stiffness magnetic springs. J. Sound Vib. **422**, 390–408 (2018)
8. Sun, X., Yang, B., Gao, Y., et al.: Integrated design, fabrication, and experimental study of a parallel micro-nano positioning-vibration isolation stage. Robot. Comput. Integr. Manuf. **66**, 101988 (2020)
9. Axinte, D.A., Allen, J.M., Anderson, R., et al.: Free-leg hexapod: a novel approach of using parallel kinematic platforms for developing miniature machine tools for special purpose operations. CIRP Ann. **60**(1), 395–398 (2011)
10. Tunc, L.T., Shaw, J.: Investigation of the effects of Stewart platform-type industrial robot on stability of robotic milling. Int. J. Adv. Manuf. Technol. **87**(1–4), 189–199 (2016). https://doi.org/10.1007/s00170-016-8420-z
11. Luzi, L., Sancisi, N., Parenti Castelli, V.: A new direct position analysis solution for an over-constrained Gough-Stewart platform. In: Zeghloul, S., Romdhane, L., Laribi, M.A. (eds.) Computational Kinematics. MMS, vol. 50, pp. 585–592. Springer, Cham (2018). https://doi.org/10.1007/978-3-319-60867-9_67
12. Chen, X., Liu, X.J., Xie, F.G., et al.: A comparison study on motion/force transmissibility of two typical 3-DOF parallel manipulators: the sprint Z3 and A3 tool heads. Int. J. Adv. Robot. Syst. **11**(5), 1–10 (2014)
13. Tsai, L.W.: Robot Analysis: The Mechanics of Serial and Parallel Manipulators. Wiley-Interscience Publication, New York (1999)
14. Huang, T., Wang, M.X., Yang, S.F., et al.: Force/motion transmissibility analysis of six degree of freedom parallel mechanisms. J. Mech. Robot. **6**, 031010 (2014)

Follow-the-Leader Deployment of the Interlaced Continuum Robot Based on the Unpowered Lock Mechanism

Peiyi Wang, Sheng Guo$^{(\boxtimes)}$, Fuqun Zhao, Xiangyang Wang, and Majun Song

Beijing Jiaotong University, Beijing, China
{wangpeiyi,shguo}@bjtu.edu.cn

Abstract. Rod-driven continuum robot possessing an elastic structure achieves a curvilinear shape curve, which is beneficial to reach hardly accessible region by avoiding barriers. However, to reach the target position, follow-the-leader (FTL) deployment along the unstructured environment is often required. An interlaced continuum robot with state-lock disks will be capable of such deployment. In this paper, a novel unpowered state-change mechanism is applied to the structure of state-locker disk, which makes the FTL movement of the continuum robot possible. Under the contact force on platform, the state-locker disk exhibits locked, transition and unlocked state. The path deviation and tip position error are used to quantify the accuracy of the FTL strategy. 23 random paths of the three types curve are generated to describe the motion trajectory and three of them are simulated to achieve FTL deployments. One detailed deployment process case is simulated theoretically. Finally, task-based application example shows capability of the FTL movement. The robot has no contact with barriers to reach the target position.

Keywords: Interlaced continuum robot · Lock mechanism · Follow-the-leader deployment

1 Introduction

Continuum robots possessing an elastic structure achieve a curvilinear shape curve of the structure and smooth motions, which extends the use of robots into many new areas where traditional rigid robots cannot be applicable [1, 2]. Especially have the potential use in confined task and unstructured environment such as aero-engine blade [3, 4], deep cavity [5–7] and human body [8, 9], they can perform inspections and other operations with various exchangeable end-effectors.

However, a tradeoff between manipulator dexterity and actuator number should be made. The independent sections of the robot decide their dexterity since every section can be deformed individually. More independent sections mean that the robot needs more actuators. Many researchers pay more attention to design dexterous continuum robots to form complex shape curve.

Continuum robot usually provides three degrees of freedom per segments, such that path-following movement can theoretically be achieved. Palmer et al. [10] designed a

© Springer Nature Switzerland AG 2021
X.-J. Liu et al. (Eds.): ICIRA 2021, LNAI 13015, pp. 448–459, 2021.
https://doi.org/10.1007/978-3-030-89134-3_41

tendon-driven continuum robot with eight segments and 24 DOF for achieving tip following navigation on aerospace turbine. Kang et al. [11] presented the first interlaced continuum robot devised to intrinsically follow the leader. The shape-locker disk consist of piezoelectric actuators enhances the friction between the rod and constraint disks, but a high voltage 125 V should be constantly applied to get a maximum blocking force of 210 N. Tappe et al. [12] achieved the "follow-the-leader (FTL)" movement by combining the binary actuated hyper-redundant manipulator with feed actuation. Amanov et al. [13] proposed a novel three-section tendon-driven continuum robot prototype composed of concentrically arranged tubes, and determined its follow-the-leader deployment theoretically. As far as we know, there does not apply the unpowered lock mechanism to achieve the "follow-the-leader (FTL)" movement and enhanced body stiffness.

The contributions of this paper are presented in the following. An interlaced rod-driven continuum robot is proposed, which can achieve FTL deployment since the structure of the state-locker disk and movement strategy. Simulations and example demonstrate that the robot can multi-curvature bend and reach the target position under no contact with barriers.

The paper is organized as follows. The structure of the interlaced continuum robot and lock mechanism is presented in Sect. 2, while Sect. 3 shows the principle of the lock mechanism and interlaced motion. The trajectory planning during FTL deployment is given in Sect. 4. Section 5 presents the three segments path simulation with the conclusions summarized in Sect. 6.

2   Robot Design

2.1   Structure

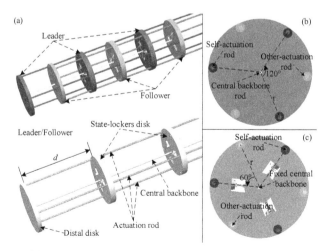

Fig. 1. Structure of the whole robot and constraints disks. (a): structure of the interlaced continuum robot (b): distal disk of LCR and FCR (c): state-locker disk of LCR and FCR

Figure 1 shows the concept of the interlaced continuum robot, which consists of two independent actuated continuum robots named leader continuum robot (LCR) and follower continuum robot (FCR). They are arranged concentrically and angularly shifted and can slide on each other. All disks of the robots are devised to alternatively guide each other except the distal disk of the LCR, which is controlled to incrementally build motion trajectory. During deployment, the distal section of LCR will build the path and FCR is stationary. Then the distal disks of FCR will follow the constructed path and LCR keeps stationary. During retraction, the role of the LCR and FCR will be changed.

Each of the FCR and LCR is composed of distal disks, state-lockers disks, central backbone rod, and three actuation rods. The distal disks and state-lockers are fixed to the central backbone rod which provides constant central backbone constraints between two adjacent disks denoted by d. The actuation rods of FCR which defined as other-actuation rods are fixed to state-locker disks of FCR and the actuation rods of LCR which defined as self-actuation rods can slider freely through the FCR when LCR is deploying the path. When FCR moves along the path, the actuation rod of LCR are fixed to state-lockers disks of LCR. Actuation rods are pulled and pushed to achieve the deployment and retraction of robot under constant rod length constraints between adjacent disks.

2.2 Lock Mechanism

The state-locker disk consists of disk, equivalent 3-PRRP parallel mechanism and clutch mechanism (see Fig. 2). Contact platform is moving platform of the equivalent 3-PRRP parallel mechanism. Each branch has the same structure and is circumferentially evenly arranged. Figure 3 shows the structure of the PRRP branch and clutch mechanism. The platform can move along the axis perpendicular to the disk surface, which is connected with the link by revolute joint. The link can rotate relative to clutch mechanism 1(CM1). CM1 slides along the axis of clutch mechanism 2(CM2). Spring 1 restore the platform to initial position. And Spring 2 provides pushing force to change the state of the clutch mechanism.

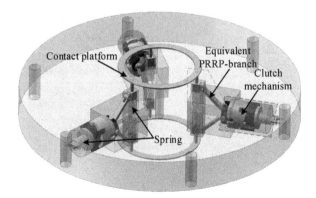

Fig. 2. Structure of the state-locker disk

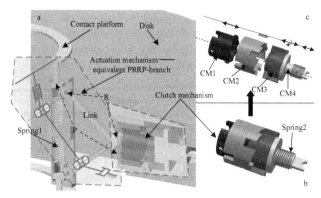

Fig. 3. Structure of equivalent PRRP branch and the clutch mechanism. (a): Structure of equivalent PRRP branch (b)(c): Structure of the clutch mechanism

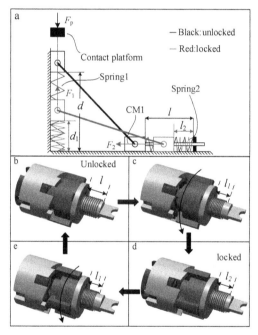

Fig. 4. State change process of the state-lock disk. (a): the motion schematic of the PRRP branch (b): unlocked state of the clutch mechanism (c)(e): transition state of the clutch mechanism (d): locked state of the clutch mechanism

3   Principle of Lock Mechanism and Interlaced Motion

3.1   Principle of State-Locker Disk

Figure 4 gives the state change process of the state-locker disks between the locked and unlocked state. The motion schematic of the equivalent PRRP branch is shown in

Fig. 4(a). Under the contact force F_p, this branch will move from unlocked state (shown as black lines) to locked state (shown as red line). Spring1 push the contact platform to initial position when contact force disappears. Three states of the clutch mechanism named locked state, unlocked state and transition state are shown in Fig. 4(b)–(e). The length of spring 2 is l, l_2 and l_1 respectively satisfied the relationship of $l > l_1 > l_2$.

As shown in Fig. 4(a)(b), the PRRP mechanism and clutch mechanism are in unlocked state. The PRRP mechanism transmits the vertical movement of the platform to the motion of CM1. Thereby CM1 is pushed along CM2. When the end gear of CM1 is in contact with the end gear of CM3, CM1 pushes CM3 to slide forward and rotates about the axis of CM2 (see Fig. 4(c)). When the contact force disappears, spring1 force push the contact platform and CM1 to their initial position, however, CM3 stays static under the blocking effect of the CM2 end gear (see Fig. 4(d)). When another contact force is applied on the platform, the clutch mechanism will be in transition state (see Fig. 4(e)).

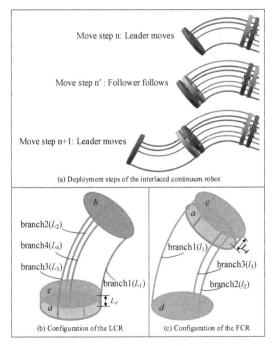

Fig. 5. Move steps of the deployment and actuation configurations (a) move steps for follow-the leader deployment. (b) Actuation configuration of LCR. (c) Actuation configuration of FCR

3.2 Principle of Interlaced Motion

Figure 5(a) shows deployment steps of the interlaced continuum robot. Figure 5(b) is the configuration of the LCR. Figure 5(b) is the configuration of the FCR.

When the whole interlaced continuum robot is on the nth movement step, the LCR will construct moving path and not stop moving until it contacts with the state-locker disks on the FCR and change their disks' state on both parts. After that the FCR will catch up with the LCR along the path and not stop moving until it contacts with the state-locker disks on the leader continuum robot and change their disks' state on both robots. Then the robot will step into the $n + 1^{th}$ step and repeat the above movement. The length of the branch 1, 2, 3 and 4 decides the configuration of the LCR. Since the thickness of the state-locker disks, the final configuration of the leader continuum robot will be determined by the following branch length:

$$L = [L_1 - L_d, L_2 - L_d, L_3 - L_d, L_4 - L_d] \tag{1}$$

The branch4 connect platform a and b and has constant length during movement. Branch1, 2, and 3, actuated by motor, will change the position and orientation of the platform b. The actuator configuration of the follower continuum robot can be solved by the inverse kinematics to achieve the follow-the-leader deployment.

$$l = [l_1, l_2, l_3] \tag{2}$$

4 Motion Planning of FTL Deployment

In the confined and unknown environment, the path of the robot motion is unpredictable. We can get the environment information by using sensors and tools such as attitude sensor, radar, and camera. Once get information around the robot, we can give the best desired path for the current space, which is represented as a general curve $t(s) \in SE(3)$. Supposed that the general curve consists of several constant curvature arcs. The local coordinates corresponding to the point on the curve describe the desired position and orientation. $h(s)$ describe the backbone shape curve and its origin $h(0)$ is coincides with the origin $t(0)$. Without loss of generality, three segments (seg1, seg2, and seg$i$) of the desired path are discussed to analysis the motion planning strategy, which can be generally adapted to n segments.

4.1 Strategy

The FTL motion requires the LCR and FCR extending their segments sequentially and alternatively as shown in Fig. 6, and starts moving from segment1 (seg1). During move step n, the LCR moves along the desired n-path as accurate as possible, and finally form the n-shape of the backbone. During move step n', the FCR will follow the n'-path and form n'-shape since the thickness of the shape locker disks. Therefore, in order to follow the n-path and form the n-shape constructed by the LCR, the whole interlaced continuum robot will move distance L_d along the positive direction of z_n. The above movement strategy is applied to the motion of LCR and FCR during next step n + 1.

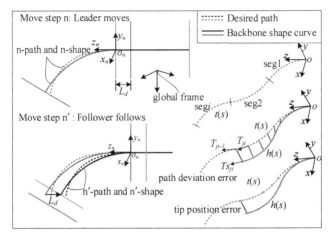

Fig. 6. FTL deployment planning and error metrics

4.2 Error Metric

The accuracy of the above motion planning strategy can be quantified with the path deviation error and tip position error (see Fig. 6). The former, controls the whole robot shape, is the average of the overall Euclidean distances between the backbone shape curve and desired path. The latter is constrained equations to insure the movement of the robot along the desired path. At the same time, the continuum robot should move along the desired path smoothly and continuously. In order to keep this movement feature, the curvature of the end of the backbone curve changes continuously and approaches the curvature of the desired path. The tangent vector of the end shape should lie between the last and current tangent vector of desired path during each moving forward step i. We discretize the desired path $t(s)$ and backbone shape curve $h(s)$ into n intervals for $s \in [0, l]$ with the backbone length l of $h(s)$. Ts_{ji} is the curvature of the end of the backbone curve during forward step i on the j-th segment. T_{ji} and T_{ji-1} are the last and current curvature of desired path during forward step i and i-1 on the j-th segment. We give the path deviation error to establish an objective function.

$$e_p = \frac{\sum\limits_{m=1}^{n} |p_t(m) - p_h(m)|}{n}$$

The tip position error is given as:

$$e_{tip} = |p_t(l) - p_h(l)|$$

The curvature should satisfy:

$$T_{ji-1} \le Ts_{ji} \le T_{ji} \, i = 1 \ldots n$$

For each move step, we use e_{tip} and curvature relationship as constraint equations and e_p as objective formulation to optimize actuation parameters L_1, L_2, L_3, and L_4 or l_1, l_2, and l_3.

4.3 Shape Curve and Bend Type

Each segment bending shape can be expressed by bending plane angle φ, segment arc s and bending angle θ. Different motion trajectory needs different backbone shape of the interlaced continuum robot. According to the bending angle and direction, the shape curve can be classified by the following three types:

- In-plane C-shape satisfies: $\varphi_i = 0$ for all φ except φ_1 and $\theta_i > 0$ for all θ.
- In-plane S-shape satisfies: $\varphi_i = 0$ for all φ except φ_1, and $\theta_j\theta_i < 0$ for all i except $j \neq i$
- Out-plane shape satisfies: $\varphi_i \neq 0$ for any one φ except φ_1, and $\theta_i \neq 0$ for all θ

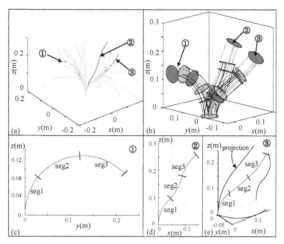

Fig. 7. Random desired path for deployment of the interlaced continuum robot: (a): general moving path (b) interlaced continuum robot moves according to typical path ①, ② and ③ (c): C-shape for in-plane bend (d) S-shape for in-plane bend (e) out-plane bend shape curve

When the interlaced continuum robot is on the moving step n, the end platform of the leader and the shape of the last section is controlled by actuation rod. Since the follower is locked, actuation rod of the follower will give constrains to keep the shape of the robot except the end segment. The shape of the ith segment is decided by the actuation configuration of the LCR. We generate 23 random paths, shown in Fig. 7(a), with parameters the length of backbone $l = 0.1$m, each segment angle $\varphi_{segi} \in [0\ 2\pi]$ for $i = 1, 2, 3$, and each segment bend angle $\theta \in [0, \pi/3]$. As shown in Fig. 7(a)(c)(d)(e), three shape curves of the backbone are simulated according to three type desired paths. The desired path ① and ② is in-plane-bend, which three segment are in one plane. That means the motion of the interlaced continuum robot is planar. But different path on each segment will lead to different whole bend shape including C shape and S shape. General desired C path is shown in Fig. 7(c). One of S path is shown in Fig. 7(d). The desired path ③ is out-plane path, which three segment are not in one plane. One of the out-plane-bend is shown in Fig. 7(e). All of the three segments are not coplanar, which means that the interlaced continuum robot will get space motion.

4.4   Simulation for Three Segment Paths

As shown in Fig. 7(b), the interlaced continuum robot moves according to three typical path ①, ② and ③. According to the desired path curve, we can actuate our robot to achieve it. But they will exist path deviation between robot backbone shape and desired path. Figure 8 gives path deviation for every typical path. The pink curve is the backbone shape curve of the robot. The shadow area is the path deviation between shape curve and desired path. C-shape has the same bending direction of each section, and S-shape in-plane bend and out-plane bend has different bending direction. the coupling effect for the latter is much bigger than that of former. Obviously, the path deviation during in-plane bend is less than that during out-plane motion.

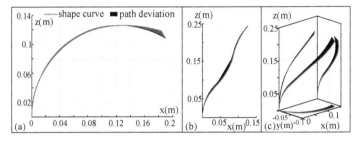

Fig. 8. Path deviation for three typical shape curves. (a): Typical path ① (b): Typical path ② (c): Typical path ③

In order to understand the interlaced motion according to typical path, we take the S shape path for in-plane-bend as an example. As shown in Fig. 9, we give motion process of the LCR according to three segments of path curve ②. When the end disk of the leader move to the end of seg1, the shape locker will be activated to lock actuation rod on leader and release actuation rod on follower. And then the follower will not stop moving until its shape locker disks contact to leader and change the disk state successfully. It is noticed that the follower motion is always the same as the leader. Therefore, Fig. 9 does not give the motion of the follower.

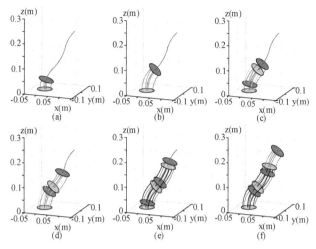

Fig. 9. FTL deployment simulation: (a)-(b): the leader moves according to seg1 of curve ② (c)-(d): the leader moves according to seg2 of curve ② (e)-(f): the leader moves according to seg3 of curve ②

5 Application Example of the Interlaced Continuum Robot

The interlaced continuum robot with two actuation modules will produce more than three segments of backbone shape, which has the potential use in confined task and unstructured environment. Figure 10 gives an application example requiring multi-curvature bend of the interlaced continuum robot on unstructured environment.

The initial position of the robot and environment information are shown in Fig. 10(a1)(a2). The task needs that the robot has no contact with barriers in the environment to reach the target position. It is difficult to get the target directly since the barriers between the robot and target. However, the interlaced continuum robot reaches the target position through three move steps. The move step 1 is that the LCR moves firstly to constructed the path (see Fig. 10(b1)(b2)), and then the FCR follows (see Fig. 10(c1)(c2)).

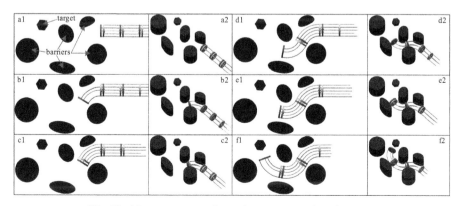

Fig. 10. Movement example on the unstructured environment

The move step 2 (see Fig. 10(d1)(d2)) is the same as move step 1, but the bending direction is opposite. In the last step, the LCR bends opposite to the seg2, and reach the target position. As we can see, the robot backbone has three bending curvature shape.

6 Conclusion

A novel lock mechanism is proposed based on the equivalent 3-PRRP parallel mechanism and clutch mechanism, which is used to change the state between the actuation rod and constraint disks. Under the contact force on platform, the clutch mechanism will 'lock' the rod and make the interlaced motion of the continuum robot possible. The motion planning strategy of FTL deployment requires the LCR and FCR extending their segments sequentially and alternatively. The path deviation error and tip position error are used to quantify the accuracy of motion planning strategy. Three shape curves of the backbone are simulated according to three type desired paths by quantifying the error metric. One of these typical curves was given to enhance the understanding of the FTL deployment motion. Movement on the unstructured environment validates the flexibility and feasibility of the interlaced continuum robot, which shows the huge potential application on the confined task and unstructured environment such as aero-engine blade, deep cavity, and human body.

Acknowledgments. This work was supported by the National Natural Science Foundation of China (Grant no. 51875033).

References

1. Webster, R.J., Jones, B.A.: Design and kinematic modeling of constant curvature continuum robots: a review. Int. J. Robot. Res. **29**(13), 1661–1683 (2010)
2. Walker, I.D.: Continuous backbone "continuum" robot manipulators. ISRN Robot. **2013**, 1–19 (2013)
3. Ma, N., Yu, J.J., Dong, X., Axinte, D.: Design and stiffness analysis of a class of 2-dof tendon driven parallel kinematics mechanism. Mech. Mach. Theory **129**, 202–217 (2018)
4. Barrientos-Diez, J., Dong, X., Axinte, D., Kell, J.: Real-time kinematics of continuum robots: modelling and validation. Robot. Comput.-Integr. Manuf. **67**, 102019 (2021)
5. Tang, L., Huang, J., Zhu, L.M., Zhu, X., Gu, G.: Path tracking of a cable-driven snake robot with a two-level motion planning method. IEEE/ASME Trans. Mechatron. **24**(3), 935–946 (2019)
6. Tang, L., Wang, J., Zheng, Y., Gu, G., Zhu, L., Zhu, X.: Design of a cable-driven hyper-redundant robot with experimental validation. Int. J. Adv. Rob. Syst. **14**(5), 1–12 (2017)
7. Liu, S.T., Yang, Z.X., Zhu, Z.J., Han, L.L., Zhu, X.Y., Xu, K.: Development of a dexterous continuum manipulator for exploration and inspection in confined spaces. Ind. Robot Int. J. **43**(3), 284–295 (2016)
8. Xu, K., Zhao, J.R., Fu, M.X.: Development of the sjtu unfoldable robotic system (SURS) for single port laparoscopy. IEEE/ASME Trans. Mechatron. **20**(5), 2133–2145 (2015)
9. Gilbert, H.B., Neimat, J., Webster, R.J., III.: Concentric tube robots as steerable needles: achieving follow-the-leader deployment. IEEE Trans. Rob. **31**(2), 246–258 (2015)

10. Palmer, D., Cobos-Guzman, S., Axinte, D.: Real-time method for tip following navigation of continuum snake arm robots. Robot. Auton. Syst. **62**(10), 1478–1485 (2014)
11. Kang, B., Kojcev, R., Sinibaldi, E.: The first interlaced continuum robot, devised to intrinsically follow the leader. Plos One **11**(2), e0150278 (2016)
12. Tappe, S., Pohlmann, J., Kotlarski, J., Ortmaier, T.: Towards a follow-the-leader control for a binary actuated hyper-redundant manipulator. In: Proceedings of the 2015 IEEE/RSJ International Conference on Intelligent Robots and Systems (IROS), pp. 3195–3201. IEEE, Hamburg (2015)
13. Amanov, E., Nguyen, T.D., Burgner-Kahrs, J.: Tendon-driven continuum robots with extensible sections-a model-based evaluation of path-following motions. Int. J. Robot. Res. **40**(1), 7–23 (2019)

Design and Motion/Force Transmissibility Analysis of Two Motion-Decoupled 3T1R Parallel Robots with Full Rotational Capability

Xin Yuan[1], Qizhi Meng[1,2]([✉]), Fugui Xie[1,2], Zhenguo Nie[1,2], and Xin-Jun Liu[1,2]

[1] The State Key Laboratory of Tribology and Institute of Manufacturing Engineering, Department of Mechanical Engineering, Tsinghua University, Beijing 100084, China
qizhimeng@mail.tsinghua.edu.cn
[2] Beijing Key Lab of Precision/Ultra-precision Manufacturing Equipments and Control, Tsinghua University, Beijing 100084, China

Abstract. The high-speed parallel robots with 3T1R (3T: three translations; 1R: one rotation) motions have been widely utilized in pick-and-place applications such as packaging, sorting, and assembling in light industries. However, most high-speed 3T1R parallel robots have highly coupled motions, which lead to highly nonlinear control models and complex control processes. Besides, some of these robots don't have the rotational capability to well meet the requirements of full-circle rotation operation on the production line. In this paper, two novel motion-decoupled high-speed 3T1R parallel robots with full rotational capability are proposed to address the above challenges. Each robot has four identical limbs, in which the three translations are realized by the first three limbs, and the rotation is realized by the fourth limb plus a rack-and-pinion or screw-and-nut mechanism. The motion/force transmissibilities of the two robots are analyzed and compared by using several well-defined indices. The results show that each robot has its strengths and weaknesses compared with the other.

Keywords: Motion-decoupled 3T1R parallel robots · Full rotational capability · Mechanism design · Motion/Force transmissibility

1 Introduction

The high-speed parallel robots with 3T1R motions have been widely used in many light industries, including plastics, electronics, medicine, and food. Their function is to carry out pick-and-place tasks such as packaging, sorting, and assembling on the production line [1]. As the counterparts of the well-known serial SCARA (Selective Compliance Assembly Robot Arm) robots, the 3T1R parallel robots have the advantages of high speed, high acceleration, and compact structure [2].

The first and also the most famous 3T1R parallel robot is the Delta robot with a central UPU (U: universal joint; P: prismatic joint) limb [3]. At present, the Delta robot has been successfully applied to many production lines in the field of high-speed pick-and-place. However, the central telescopic limb usually generates severe wear and

© Springer Nature Switzerland AG 2021
X.-J. Liu et al. (Eds.): ICIRA 2021, LNAI 13015, pp. 460–469, 2021.
https://doi.org/10.1007/978-3-030-89134-3_42

possesses low stiffness at the workspace boundary, thus resulting in short service life [4]. After that, the past two decades have witnessed a huge growth in the number of new 3T1R parallel robots. In particular, several articulated-platform parallel robots have attracted much attention, among which the most representative is the H4 parallel robot proposed by Pierrot et al. [5]. This robot innovatively adopts four identical limbs and a double-platform structure. In this design, the rotational motion is generated by the relative motion of the two platforms. Inspired by this, other articulated-platform robots such as I4 [6], Par4 [7], and C4 [4] were developed. The main difference among these robots is the structure of the mobile platform. Moreover, Yi et al. [8] presented several 3T1R parallel robots with asymmetric four limbs to minimize the effect of the architectural singularity problem. These robots have high potential in multi-task oriented industrial applications. Li et al. [9] proposed a class of 3T1R parallel robots with the simplest topology. Wu et al. [10] introduced a 3T1R parallel robot that can generate a rectangular workspace for better pick-and-place operations. There have been several 3T1R parallel robots with specific advantages so far, and it is still of great significance and broad prospect to develop novel 3T1R parallel robots with different characteristics for various industrial applications.

It is well known that decoupled motions lead to simple kinematics, thus providing a series of advantages for robots, such as linearized control models and easier calibration processes. Especially for the high-speed 3T1R parallel robots, simple kinematics are more conducive to achieve high-speed and high-acceleration operations. Besides, due to the sorting needs for personalized scattered incoming materials in industrial applications, the 3T1R parallel robots with full rotational capability are desirable. There are already some 3T1R parallel robots that can realize decoupled motions or full rotational capability. For example, Xu et al. [11] presented a partially decoupled 3T1R parallel robot. Briot et al. [12] proposed a fully decoupled 3T1R parallel robot. Furthermore, Tu et al. [13] proposed a 3T1R parallel robot with full rotational capability. It can be inferred that the 3T1R parallel robots with both decoupled motions and full rotational capability may have better comprehensive performance and are expected to better adapt to scattered incoming materials on the production line. Such robots have good application prospects and need further study.

In this paper, two novel motion-decoupled high-speed 3T1R parallel robots with full rotational capability are proposed. The remainder of this paper is organized as follows. Sect. 2 introduces the design and inverse kinematics of the two robots. In Sect. 3, the motion/force transmissibilities of the two robots are analyzed and compared by using three motion/force transmission indices. Conclusions are given in Sect. 4.

2 Mechanism Design and Inverse Kinematics

2.1 Mechanism Design

Two motion-decoupled high-speed 3T1R parallel robots with full rotational capability are designed and shown in Figs. 1 and 2. Each robot has four identical limbs and a mobile platform fitted with a transmission mechanism.

For the robot in Fig. 1(a), its mobile platform consists of a sub-platform, an end-effector, and a rack-and-pinion mechanism, as shown in Fig. 1(b). The sub-platform is

462   X. Yuan et al.

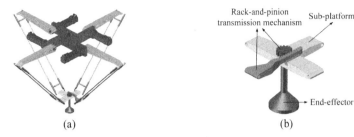

Fig. 1. Robot with a rack-and-pinion mechanism: (a) conceptual model; (b) mobile platform.

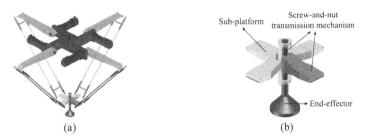

Fig. 2. Robot with a screw-and-nut mechanism: (a) conceptual model; (b) mobile platform.

connected to the base through the first three RPa (R: active revolute joint; Pa: parallelogram mechanism with four spherical joints) limbs. The rack is connected to the base through the fourth RPa limb. The end-effector is fixed to the pinion which is rotatably arranged in the sub-platform. The sub-platform and end-effector together realize three translational motions (3T) by driving the first three limbs. Moreover, by driving the fourth limb, the rack moves along the guide groove on the sub-platform in the horizontal plane, so that the relative motion between the rack and pinion generates the end-effector's one rotational motion (1R) about the vertical axis.

For the robot in Fig. 2(a), its mobile platform consists of a sub-platform, an end-effector, and a screw-and-nut mechanism, as shown in Fig. 2(b). The difference between it and the robot in Fig. 1(a) is the transmission mode between the fourth limb and the end-effector, which is as follows: By driving the fourth limb, the nut moves along the anticollision groove which is fixed vertically on the sub-platform, so that the relative motion between the nut and screw generates the end-effector's one rotational motion (1R) about the vertical axis. The transmission modes of the rack-and-pinion and screw-and-nut mechanisms have the characteristics of high transmission accuracy and constant instantaneous transmission ratio, which are good for accurate and stable transmission between the fourth limb and the end-effector. Moreover, by changing the transmission ratio and moving range of the rack-and-pinion or screw-and-nut mechanism, the configuration of the fourth limb at the workspace boundary of the robot can be adjusted to make the performance of the limb relatively good.

The proposed robots both achieve 3T1R motions, and the translations and rotation are decoupled. Moreover, the end-effectors of both robots realize full-circle rotation.

2.2 Inverse Kinematics

As shown in Fig. 3, the global frame $\{o\}$: $o\text{-}xyz$ is set up in the center of the base plane across the active joints (A_1, A_2, A_3, A_4), where the x-axis and y-axis are along $\boldsymbol{o}A_2$ and $\boldsymbol{o}A_1$, respectively. The input angles between $\boldsymbol{o}A_i$ and A_iB_i are θ_i ($i = 1, 2, 3, 4$), and the position of the center point o' of the sub-platform is (x, y, z). To make the structures of the two robots symmetrical, the angle η between $\boldsymbol{o}A_2$ and $\boldsymbol{o}A_1$ (or between $\boldsymbol{o}A_2$ and $\boldsymbol{o}A_3$) is set as $90°$, and $\boldsymbol{o}A_2$ is collinear with $\boldsymbol{o}A_4$. If (x, y, z) is given, the position vectors of points A_i, B_i, and C_i ($i = 1, 2, 3$) in the frame $o\text{-}xyz$ can be written as

$$\begin{cases} \boldsymbol{o}A_1 = [0, R, 0]^T, \ \boldsymbol{o}B_1 = [0, R - L_1\cos\theta_1, L_1\sin\theta_1]^T, \ \boldsymbol{o}C_1 = \left[x, y+r, z\right]^T \\ \boldsymbol{o}A_2 = [R, 0, 0]^T, \ \boldsymbol{o}B_2 = [R - L_1\cos\theta_2, 0, L_1\sin\theta_2]^T, \ \boldsymbol{o}C_2 = \left[x+r, y, z\right]^T \\ \boldsymbol{o}A_3 = [0, -R, 0]^T, \ \boldsymbol{o}B_3 = [0, L_1\cos\theta_3 - R, L_1\sin\theta_3]^T, \ \boldsymbol{o}C_3 = \left[x, y-r, z\right]^T \end{cases}$$

$$(1)$$

where R represents the radius of the base, r represents the radius of the sub-platform, L_1 is the length of A_iB_i. The inverse kinematics related to the first three limbs can be solved according to the geometric relations $|B_1C_1|^2 = |B_2C_2|^2 = |B_3C_3|^2 = L_2^2$, where L_2 is the length of B_iC_i. The solution can be expressed as

$$\theta_i = 2\arctan\left[\left(-c_i + \sqrt{c_i^2 - a_i^2 + b_i^2}\right) \Big/ (a_i - b_i)\right], (i = 1, 2, 3), \qquad (2)$$

where
$$\begin{cases} a_1 = x^2 + (y+r-R)^2 + z^2 + L_1^2 - L_2^2, \ b_1 = 2L_1(y+r-R), \ c_1 = -2L_1z \\ a_2 = (x+r-R)^2 + y^2 + z^2 + L_1^2 - L_2^2, \ b_2 = 2L_1(x+r-R), \ c_2 = -2L_1z \\ a_3 = x^2 + (y-r+R)^2 + z^2 + L_1^2 - L_2^2, \ b_3 = 2L_1(r-R-y), \ c_3 = -2L_1z \end{cases}$$
The inverse kinematics related to the fourth limb is solved by the motion of the rack or nut. For the robot in Fig. 1, if the distance l the rack moves along the x-axis from point o' is given, the position vectors of points A_4, B_4, and C_4 in the frame $o\text{-}xyz$ is

$$\boldsymbol{o}A_4 = [-R, 0, 0]^T, \ \boldsymbol{o}B_4 = [-R + L_1\cos\theta_4, 0, L_1\sin\theta_4]^T, \ \boldsymbol{o}C_4 = \left[x-r+l, y, z\right]^T.$$
$$(3)$$

Then the solution of the inverse kinematics related to the fourth limb is expressed as

$$\theta_4 = 2\arctan\left[\left(-c_4 + \sqrt{c_4^2 - a_4^2 + b_4^2}\right) \Big/ (a_4 - b_4)\right], \qquad (4)$$

where $a_4 = (x-r+R+l)^2 + y^2 + z^2 + L_1^2 - L_2^2$, $b_4 = -2L_1(x-r+R+l)$, $c_4 = -2L_1z$. Similarly, for the robot in Fig. 2, if the distance h the nut moves along the z-axis from point o' is given, the position vectors of points A_4, B_4, and C_4 in the frame $o\text{-}xyz$ is

$$\boldsymbol{o}A_4 = [-R, 0, 0]^T, \ \boldsymbol{o}B_4 = [-R + L_1\cos\theta_4, 0, L_1\sin\theta_4]^T, \ \boldsymbol{o}C_4 = \left[x-r, y, z+h\right]^T.$$
$$(5)$$

The solution of the inverse kinematics related to the fourth limb is

$$\theta_4 = 2 \arctan\left[\left(-n_4 + \sqrt{n_4^2 - d_4^2 + m_4^2}\right)\Big/ (d_4 - m_4)\right], \tag{6}$$

where $d_4 = (x - r + R)^2 + y^2 + (z + h)^2 + L_1^2 - L_2^2$, $m_4 = 2L_1(r - R - x)$, $n_4 = -2L_1(z + h)$.

For comparison, the transmission ratios of the rack-and-pinion and screw-and-nut mechanisms are set to be equal. In other words, when the pinion or screw rotates at the same angle, the rack or nut moves the same distance. Moreover, the maximum distances the rack and nut allowed to move are the same, i.e. $l_{max} = h_{max}$.

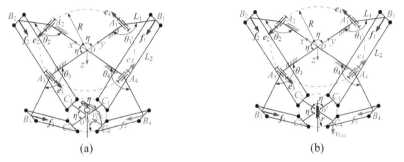

(a)   (b)

Fig. 3. Schematic diagrams of the two robots: (a) robot with a rack-and-pinion mechanism; (b) robot with a screw-and-nut mechanism.

3   Motion/Force Transmissibility Analysis

3.1   Motion/Force Transmission Indices

Performance evaluation is one of the most important problems in the analysis and design of robots. For parallel robots with closed-loop characteristics, good motion/force transmission performance is desired. In this section, the motion/force transmissibilities of the two proposed robots are evaluated by using several transmission indices proposed in Ref. [14], including the input transmission index (ITI), the output transmission index (OTI), and the local transmission index (LTI).

For an n-DOF parallel robot, each limb has its actuator. Therefore, the ITI of each limb can be solved separately. As shown in Figs. 3(a) and 3(b), the transmission wrench screw $\$_{Ti}$ and the input twist screw $\$_{Ii}$ of the ith limb can be expressed as

$$\$_{Ti} = (f_i; oB_i \times f_i), \ \$_{Ii} = (e_i; oA_i \times e_i), \ (i = 1, 2, 3, 4), \tag{7}$$

where $f_i = B_iC_i/L_2$, $e_1 = [1, 0, 0]^T$, $e_2 = [0, -1, 0]^T$, $e_3 = [-1, 0, 0]^T$, $e_4 = [0, 1, 0]^T$. According to the index definition, the ITI of the ith limb is

$$\text{ITI}_i = \frac{\left|\$_{Ti} \circ \$_{Ii}\right|}{\left|\$_{Ti} \circ \$_{Ii}\right|_{max}} = \frac{|B_iC_i \cdot (e_i \times A_iB_i)|}{L_1L_2}, \ (i = 1, 2, 3, 4). \tag{8}$$

Since all limbs make their contribution to the output motion of the end-effector, the output twist screw $\$_{Oi}$ corresponding to the $\$_{Ti}$ is obtained by the method of blocking all the inputs except the ith, and hereby the OTI of the ith limb is obtained.

For the first three limbs, by blocking the other two inputs except for the ith, the sub-platform performs a translational motion, which can be expressed as

$$\$_{Oi} = (\mathbf{0}_3; v_{Oi}), (i = 1, 2, 3). \tag{9}$$

In this case, only the transmission wrench screw represented by $\$_{Ti}$ contributes to the sub-platform, while the other two transmission wrench screws apply no work. Hereby, the output twist screw $\$_{Oi}$ can be derived by the reciprocal condition

$$\$_{Tj} \circ \$_{Oi} = 0, (j = 1, 2, 3, j \neq i). \tag{10}$$

Substituting Eqs. (7) and (9) into Eq. (10), the following equations can be obtained:
$f_2 \cdot v_{O1} = 0, f_3 \cdot v_{O1} = 0; f_1 \cdot v_{O2} = 0, f_3 \cdot v_{O2} = 0; f_1 \cdot v_{O3} = 0, f_2 \cdot v_{O3} = 0.$
Therefore, $\$_{Oi}$ can be obtained as

$$\$_{O1} = (\mathbf{0}_3; \frac{f_3 \times f_2}{\|f_3 \times f_2\|}), \$_{O2} = (\mathbf{0}_3; \frac{f_1 \times f_3}{\|f_1 \times f_3\|}), \$_{O3} = (\mathbf{0}_3; \frac{f_2 \times f_1}{\|f_2 \times f_1\|}). \tag{11}$$

The OTI of the ith ($i = 1, 2, 3$) limb is $OTI_i = \frac{|\$_{Ti} \circ \$_{Oi}|}{|\$_{Ti} \circ \$_{Oi}|_{max}}$, and the result is

$$OTI_1 = \frac{|f_1 \cdot (f_3 \times f_2)|}{\|f_3 \times f_2\|}, \quad OTI_2 = \frac{|f_2 \cdot (f_1 \times f_3)|}{\|f_1 \times f_3\|}, \quad OTI_3 = \frac{|f_3 \cdot (f_2 \times f_1)|}{\|f_2 \times f_1\|}. \tag{12}$$

For the fourth limb in Fig. 3(a), the output motion of the rack is the translational motion along the x-axis, which is expressed as $\$_{O4} = (\mathbf{0}_3; v_{O4}) = (\mathbf{0}_3; 1, 0, 0)$. Hereby, the OTI of the fourth limb can be written as

$$OTI_4 = \frac{|\$_{T4} \circ \$_{O4}|}{|\$_{T4} \circ \$_{O4}|_{max}} = \frac{|f_4 \cdot v_{O4}|}{|f_4 \cdot v_{O4}|_{max}} = |f_4 \cdot (1, 0, 0)| = \left| \frac{x - r + R + l - L_1 \cos\theta_4}{L_2} \right|. \tag{13}$$

Similarly, for the fourth limb in Fig. 3(b), the output motion of the nut is the translational motion along the z-axis, which is represented as $\$_{O4} = (\mathbf{0}_3; v_{O4}) = (\mathbf{0}_3; 0, 0, 1)$. Then the OTI of the fourth limb can be written as

$$OTI_4 = \frac{|\$_{T4} \circ \$_{O4}|}{|\$_{T4} \circ \$_{O4}|_{max}} = \frac{|f_4 \cdot v_{O4}|}{|f_4 \cdot v_{O4}|_{max}} = |f_4 \cdot (0, 0, 1)| = \left| \frac{z + h - L_1 \sin\theta_4}{L_2} \right|. \tag{14}$$

As can be seen from Eqs. (3), (5), (8), (13), and (14), the values of ITI_4 and OTI_4 change with l or h. To evaluate the motion/force transmissibility of the fourth limb during the end-effector's full rotation, the minimums of ITI_4 and OTI_4 are defined as

$$ITI_{4\,min} = \min_{l \text{ or } h} ITI_4, \quad (-l_{max}/2 \le l \le l_{max}/2, -h_{max}/2 \le h \le h_{max}/2), \tag{15}$$

$$\text{OTI}_{4\,\text{min}} = \min_{l\,\text{or}\,h} \text{OTI}_4, \ (-l_{\text{max}}/2 \le l \le l_{\text{max}}/2, -h_{\text{max}}/2 \le h \le h_{\text{max}}/2). \tag{16}$$

For the integrated parallel robot, the ITI and OTI are defined as

$$\text{ITI} = \min_i\{\text{ITI}_i, \text{ITI}_{4\,\text{min}}\}, \text{OTI} = \min_i\{\text{OTI}_i, \text{OTI}_{4\,\text{min}}\}, \ (i = 1, 2, 3). \tag{17}$$

As a result, the LTI of the parallel robot can be defined as

$$\text{LTI} = \min\{\text{ITI}, \text{OTI}\}. \tag{18}$$

3.2 Performance Analysis of the Two Robots

Giving the parameters as $R = 255$ mm, $r = 170$ mm, $L_1 = 325$ mm, $L_2 = 650$ mm, $l_{\text{max}} = h_{\text{max}} = r/2$, the distributions of LTI on several horizontal planes are plotted as follows. It should be noted that the given parameters are not optimized.

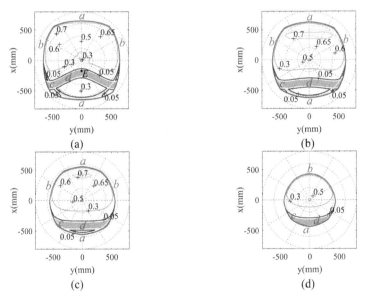

Fig. 4. LTI distributions of the robot with a rack-and-pinion mechanism in different planes: (a) $z = 350$ mm; (b) $z = 500$ mm; (c) $z = 650$ mm; (d) $z = 800$ mm.

In Figs. 4 and 5, the locus marked by a and b represent the input transmission singular loci of the first three limbs and the fourth limb, respectively. The locus marked by c is the output transmission singular locus of the first three limbs. The zone marked by d is the output transmission singular zone of the fourth limb. As seen from Eq. (16), the $\text{OTI}_{4\text{min}}$ is the minimum value of OTI_4 within the entire moving range of the rack or nut. This indicates that the fourth limb can reach the output transmission singularity within a zone of the workspace, which is the zone marked by d mentioned above.

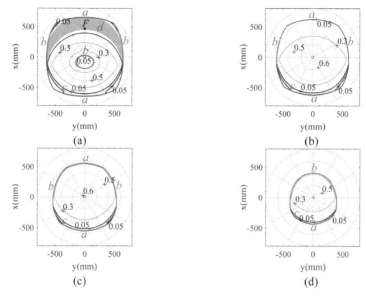

Fig. 5. LTI distributions of the robot with a screw-and-nut mechanism in different planes: (a) $z = 350$ mm; (b) $z = 500$ mm; (c) $z = 650$ mm; (d) $z = 800$ mm.

The loci marked by a and b together form the boundary of the workspace. The locus marked by c and the zone marked by d divide the workspace into several continuous non-singular regions, and a relatively large region is selected as the useful workspace. In the useful workspace, a continuous region where the LTI is greater than 0.5 is defined as the good transmission workspace in this paper. The three-dimensional good transmission workspace of the two robots is shown in Fig. 6.

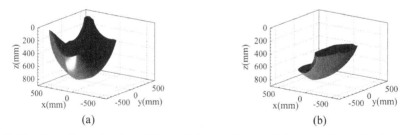

Fig. 6. The three-dimensional good transmission workspace of the two robots: (a) robot with a rack-and-pinion mechanism; (b) robot with a screw-and-nut mechanism.

The following conclusions can be drawn:

(1) For the two robots, the LTI distributions are symmetric about $y = 0$, which are in accord with their configurational characteristics. Moreover, the LTI values first increase and then decrease along the z-axis. This indicates that the motion/force

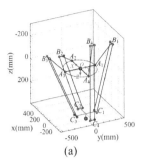
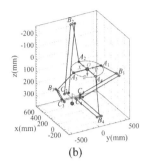

(a)   (b)

Fig. 7. Output transmission singularities of the two robots at: (a) point E; (b) point F.

transmissibilities become better at first, and then decrease when they reach the optimums.

(2) For the robot in Fig. 1, there are output transmission singular zones of the fourth limb on all selected planes, which reduce its useful workspace. Whereas for the robot in Fig. 2, there are no these zones on the selected planes except the plane $z = 350$ mm. As a result, the useful workspace of the robot in Fig. 2 is larger than that of the robot in Fig. 1. Analyzing the reason, it is known that for the robot in Fig. 1, the output transmission singularity of the fourth limb occurs when f_4 and v_{O4} are perpendicular, that is, when B_4C_4 is vertical. For example, the output transmission singularity occurs at point E in Fig. 4(a), and its corresponding configuration is shown in Fig. 7(a). For the robot in Fig. 2, f_4 is perpendicular to v_{O4} only when B_4C_4 is horizontal, then the output transmission singularity of the fourth limb occurs, such as point F in Fig. 5(a). Its corresponding configuration is shown in Fig. 7(b). According to the characteristics of the structure of the two robots, it can be inferred that B_4C_4 is more likely to be vertical than horizontal. As a consequence, the output transmission singularity is easier to occur for the robot in Fig. 1, so its useful workspace is smaller.

(3) The LTI values on the selected planes of the robot in Fig. 2 are smaller than those of the robot in Fig. 1. Moreover, as seen from Fig. 6, the 3D good transmission workspace of the robot in Fig. 2 is smaller than that of the robot in Fig. 1.

4 Conclusion

In this paper, two novel motion-decoupled high-speed 3T1R parallel robots with full rotational capability are proposed. Through the motion/force transmissibility analysis of the two robots with given parameters, it can be seen that each robot has its strengths and weaknesses compared with the other. Specifically, the useful workspace of the robot with a screw-and-nut mechanism is larger than that of the robot with a rack-and-pinion mechanism, while the LTI values on the selected horizontal planes and the 3D good transmission workspace of the robot with a screw-and-nut mechanism are smaller than that of the robot with a rack-and-pinion mechanism.

Acknowledgements. This work was supported by the National Natural Science Foundation of China (Grant No. 52105026) and the China Postdoctoral Science Foundation (Grant No. 2021TQ0176), as well as the Shuimu Tsinghua Scholar Program (Grant No. 2020SM081).

References

1. Meng, Q.Z., Xie, F.G., Liu, X.-J., et al.: Screw theory-based motion/force transmissibility analysis of high-speed parallel robots with articulated platforms. J. Mech. Robot.-Trans. ASME **12**(4), 041011 (2020)
2. Xie, F.G., Liu, X.-J.: Design and development of a high-speed and high-rotation robot with four identical arms and a single platform. J. Mech. Robot.-Trans. ASME **7**(4), 041015 (2015)
3. Clavel, R.: Device for the movement and positioning of an element in space. U.S. Patent No. 4976582 (1990)
4. Liu, S.T., Huang, T., Mei, J.P., et al.: Optimal design of a 4-DOF SCARA type parallel robot using dynamic performance indices and angular constraints. J. Mech. Robot.-Trans. ASME **4**(3), 031005 (2012)
5. Pierrot, F., Company, O.: H4: a new family of 4-DOF parallel robots. In: 1999 IEEE/ASME International Conference on Advanced Intelligent Mechatronics, Atlanta, GA, USA, pp. 508–513 (1999)
6. Krut, S., Company, O., Benoit, M., et al.: I4: a new parallel mechanism for SCARA motions. In: 20th IEEE International Conference on Robotics and Automation (ICRA), Taipei, Taiwan, pp. 1875–1880 (2003)
7. Nabat, V., de la O Rodriguez, M., Company, O., et al.: Par4: very high speed parallel robot for pick-and-place. In: 2005 IEEE/RSJ International Conference on Intelligent Robots and Systems, Edmonton, Alberta, Canada, pp. 553–558 (2005)
8. Yi, B.J., Kim, S.M., Kwak, H.K., et al.: Multi-task oriented design of an asymmetric 3T1R type 4-DOF parallel mechanism. Proc. Inst. Mech. Eng. Part C-J. Mech. Eng. Sci. **227**(10), 2236–2255 (2013)
9. Li, Z.B., Lou, Y.J., Zhang, Y.S., et al.: Type synthesis, kinematic analysis, and optimal design of a novel class of Schonflies-motion parallel manipulators. IEEE Trans. Autom. Sci. Eng. **10**(3), 674–686 (2013)
10. Wu, G., Bai, S., Hjørnet, P.: Design analysis and dynamic modeling of a high-speed 3T1R pick-and-place parallel robot. In: Bai, S., Ceccarelli, M. (eds.) Recent Advances in Mechanism Design for Robotics. MMS, vol. 33, pp. 285–295. Springer, Cham (2015). https://doi.org/10.1007/978-3-319-18126-4_27
11. Xu, K., Liu, H., Shen, H., Yang, T.: Structure design and kinematic analysis of a partially-decoupled 3T1R parallel manipulator. In: Yu, H., Liu, J., Liu, L., Ju, Z., Liu, Y., Zhou, D. (eds.) ICIRA 2019. LNCS (LNAI), vol. 11742, pp. 415–424. Springer, Cham (2019). https://doi.org/10.1007/978-3-030-27535-8_37
12. Briot, S., Bonev, I.A.: Pantopteron-4: a new 3T1R decoupled parallel manipulator for pick-and-place applications. Mech. Mach. Theory **45**(5), 707–721 (2010)
13. Tu, Y., Chen, Q., Ye, W., Li, Q.: Kinematics, singularity, and optimal design of a novel 3T1R parallel manipulator with full rotational capability. J. Mech. Sci. Technol. **32**(6), 2877–2887 (2018). https://doi.org/10.1007/s12206-018-0543-8
14. Wang, J.S., Wu, C., Liu, X.-J.: Performance evaluation of parallel manipulators: motion/force transmissibility and its index. Mech. Mach. Theory **45**, 1462–1476 (2010)

Motion/Force Transmissibility and Constrainability of a Double-Platform Parallel Manipulator

Qizhi Meng[1,2]($\boxtimes$), Xin Yuan[1], Xinchen Zhuang[1,2], Fugui Xie[1,2], and Xin-Jun Liu[1,2]

[1] The State Key Laboratory of Tribology & Institute of Manufacturing Engineering, Department of Mechanical Engineering, Tsinghua University, Beijing 100084, China
qizhimeng@mail.tsinghua.edu.cn
[2] Beijing Key Lab of Precision/Ultra-Precision Manufacturing Equipments and Control, Tsinghua University, Beijing 100084, China

Abstract. In this paper, a spatial double-platform parallel manipulator with closed joints (compared to open cup-and-ball joints in the Delta robot) is proposed to generate the Schönflies motion. A description of its architecture is presented. The mobility analysis of the end-effector and the sub-platforms are carried out by resorting to the screw theory. To investigate the characteristics of motion/force transmissibility and constrainability of the double-platform manipulator, an equivalent transmission wrench analysis is presented by considering that the transmission wrench should be applied to the end-effector but not the sub-platforms from active arms. Then, the motion/force performance indices which consider the input transmissibility, output transmissibility, and constraint transmissibility are extended to evaluating the performance of the proposed double-platform parallel manipulator. As a result, the good transmission and constraint workspace is identified under the given parameters.

Keywords: Schönflies motion · Parallel manipulator · Double-platform · Transmissibility · Constrainability

1 Introduction

Due to their advantages on the compact structure, high stiffness and good dynamic response, parallel manipulators (PMs) have attracted widespread attention from academia to industry and also achieved great success, i.e. the Sprint Z3 head, Tricept, Exechon, and Metrom, in the field of machine tool and robot, etc. PMs with Schönflies motions [1, 2] are the parallel counterparts of the well-known SCARA robots [3], which are qualified for pick-and-place operations. As the most significant and representative motion form, pick-and-place operation [4] is essential in many light industries, whose function is to move an object from one position to another and adjust its posture on the horizontal plane.

The design and development of different working conditions-oriented high-performance PMs with Schönflies motions are challenging but have important practical

© Springer Nature Switzerland AG 2021
X.-J. Liu et al. (Eds.): ICIRA 2021, LNAI 13015, pp. 470–481, 2021.
https://doi.org/10.1007/978-3-030-89134-3_43

significance. The first and also the most famous Delta robot with three identical $\underline{R}$Pa limbs and a $\underline{R}$UPUR telescope limb has been proposed by Clavel [5, 6]. This PM is the milepost in the high-speed pick-and-place parallel robots and achieves great commercial success. However, the fourthly added telescope limb becomes a weak point with short service life [7]. To overcome this shortcoming, the Quattro robot based on a new family of 4-DOF PMs called H4 with four identical $\underline{R}$Pa limbs and a general mobile platform is proposed [8]. Due to their good dynamic performance benefited from lightweight and easy-assembly design (i.e., the parallelogram passive arms with open cup-and-ball joints, slender carbon rod, and spring system structure features), the above robots have been widely used and achieved lots of approvals in the process of automation of light industry.

Performance evaluation is one of the most important issues in the analysis and design of PMs. Establishing an effective and univocal performance index is of crucial significance in the singularity analysis and dimensional optimization of PMs outputting mixed degrees of freedom, i.e., rotations and translations. Based on the concept of transmission angle or pressure angle, a transmission index as a performance index of motion and force transmission characteristics of the single-platform fully PMs is proposed by Takeda and Funabashi [9]. After this, following the concept of the virtual coefficient introduced by Ball [10], the performance evaluation of PMs whose main contributions are motion/force transmissibility and its index is presented by Wang et al. [11]. Further, the more complete motion/force performance indices which include the ITI, OTI, and CTI are proposed for singularity analysis and closeness measurement to singularities of PMs by Liu et al. [12]. In fact, with the continuous invention of double-platform PMs, the traditional performance evaluation indices are confronted with challenges and the double-platform related evaluation system is under urgent demand and needs to be established.

In this paper, inspired by the Par4 and Heli4 robots, two double-platform PMs with closed joints are proposed to generate the Schönflies motion. The remainder of this paper is organized as follows. Section 2 presents the description of the architecture and geometry constraints of the proposed PMs. Then, the inverse kinematics are briefly introduced. Choosing one of the proposed PMs, the mobility and the equivalent transmission wrench analysis are carried out using screw theory in Sect. 3. After this, the motion/force performance indices are extended to evaluating the motion/force transmissibility and constrainability of the proposed double-platform PM in Sect. 4, where the good motion/force transmission and constraint workspace (GTCW) is also identified. The conclusion is given in the last section.

2   Architecture Description and Inverse Kinematics

Two parallel manipulators with four identical limbs $\underline{R}$UU and a general mobile platform are presented in Fig. 1. The general mobile platform which consists of two sub-platform and an end-effector is connected to the base through four identical $\underline{R}$UU kinematic chains. The inputs of the mechanism are provided by four revolute actuators attached to the base. The difference between the two proposed PMs is that *type I* is based on the 2$\underline{R}$UU-R/2$\underline{R}$UU-R topology while *type II* is based on the 2$\underline{R}$UU-H/2$\underline{R}$UU-R topology.

Of note is that the rotation axle of the active R joint should be parallel to one of the rotation axles of the U joint, and two corresponding rotation axles of each U joint need to be parallel to each other. The joint-and-loop graphs of the proposed PMs are shown in Fig. 2.

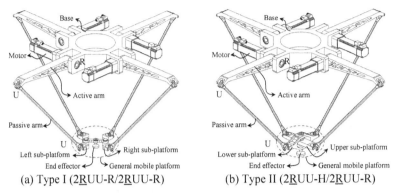

(a) Type I (2$\underline{R}$UU-R/2$\underline{R}$UU-R)   (b) Type II (2$\underline{R}$UU-H/2$\underline{R}$UU-R)

Fig. 1. Concept models of the proposed parallel manipulators.

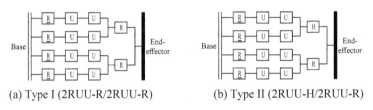

(a) Type I (2RUU-R/2RUU-R)   (b) Type II (2RUU-H/2RUU-R)

Fig. 2. Joint-and-loop graphs for the basic principles.

The kinematic schematic diagrams of the manipulators are illustrated in Fig. 3, where the global coordinate frame $\mathfrak{R}$: O-XYZ is built with the origin located at the geometric center of the base, the X-axis and Y-axis being parallel to segment A_3A_1 and A_4A_2 respectively. The four actuated R joints are equally distributed at a normal angle of 90° on a circle whose radius is r_1. r_2 represents the distance from the center (O') of the mobile platform to the point C_i at the initial state. The lengths of active and passive limbs are l_1 and l_2, respectively. Under this frame, the position vectors of points A_i and B_i in the frame $\mathfrak{R}$ are expressed by

$$a_i = r_1[cos\,\beta_i \; sin\,\beta_i \; 0]^T, \; \beta_i = (i-1)\pi/2; b_i = a_i + l_1u_i, u_i = R_Z(\beta_i)R_Y(\theta_i)i, \quad (1)$$

where $\theta_i = \pi - \alpha_i$ is the input angle of the ith active arm as shown in Fig. 3. Let the coordinate of the end-effector be denoted by $[x, y, z, \varphi]$, where $\boldsymbol{p} = [x, y, z]^T$ is the position and φ is the pose. The connection points C_i between the limbs and general mobile platform can be expressed as

$$\begin{cases} c_i = sgn(cos\,\alpha_i)r_2R_Z(\varphi)i + sgn(sin\,\alpha_i)l_3j + p, \; \textbf{type I} \\ c_i = r_2R_Z(\alpha_i)i + mod(i+1,2)^h\varphi/_{2\pi}k + p, \; \textbf{type II} \end{cases}, \quad (2)$$

where sgn($\odot$) and mod($\odot$) are the sign and modulo function of ($\odot$), respectively, h is the helical pitch of the screw joint of the *type II* PM.

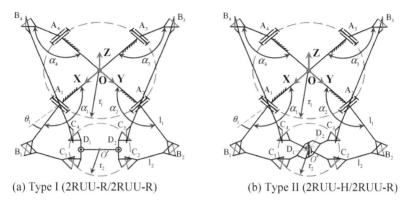

(a) Type I (2RUU-R/2RUU-R)   (b) Type II (2RUU-H/2RUU-R)

Fig. 3. Schematic diagrams of the proposed parallel manipulators.

This kind of inverse kinematic problem has been well solved, it can be calculated by the following kinematic constraint equations:

$$B_i C_i = \sqrt{(c_i - b_i)^T (c_i - b_i)} = l_2. \tag{3}$$

The substitution of Eq. (1) and Eq. (2) into the Eq. (3), one simplified trigonometric function is obtained

$$L_i \sin \theta_i + M_i \cos \theta_i + N_i = 0, \tag{4}$$

where $L_i = -2l_1 (c_i - a_i)^T k$, $M_i = -2l_1 (c_i - a_i)^T (\cos \alpha_i \, i + \sin \alpha_i j)$, and $N_i = (c_i - a_i)^T (c_i - a_i) + l_1^2 - l_2^2$. The i, j, k above are the unit vectors of X, Y, Z and the solution of Eq. (4), i.e., the trigonometric function, leads to

$$\theta_i = 2 \arctan \frac{-L_i - \sqrt{L_i^2 - M_i^2 + N_i^2}}{M_i^2 - N_i^2}. \tag{5}$$

3   Mobility and Equivalent Transmission Wrench Analysis

Mobility is the most fundamental structural information which essentially reflects the kinematic features of a mechanism. The equivalent transmission wrench is important to analyze the motion/force performance [13]. In this section, the mobility and equivalent transmission wrench analysis are carried out based on the screw theory.

As shown in Fig. 4, corresponding to five one-DOF joints, the twist screw system of the ith limb with respect to the local coordinate $\mathfrak{R}'$: o'-$x'y'z'$ can be given as

$$\$_i^{\omega 1} = \begin{pmatrix} 0 \; 1 \; 0; & -l_1 cos \zeta_1 \; 0 \; -l_1 sin \zeta_1 \end{pmatrix} \tag{6}$$

$$\$_i^{\omega 2} = \left(0\ 1\ 0;\ 0\ 0\ 0 \right) \tag{7}$$

$$\$_i^{\omega 3} = \left(cos\zeta_3\ 0\ -sin\zeta_3;\ 0\ 0\ 0 \right) \tag{8}$$

$$\$_i^{\omega 4} = \left(0\ 1\ 0;\ l_2 sin\zeta_2 cos\zeta_3\ 0\ -l_2 sin\zeta_2 sin\zeta_3 \right) \tag{9}$$

$$\$_i^{\omega 5} = \left(cos\zeta_3\ 0\ -sin\zeta_3;\ -l_2 cos\zeta_2 sin\zeta_3\ -l_2 sin\zeta_2\ -l_2 cos\zeta_2\ cos\ \zeta_3 \right) \tag{10}$$

Using reciprocal screw theory, the constraint wrench screw system of the ith limb can be defined as

$$\$_i^{\tau 1} = \left(0\ 0\ 0;\ sin\zeta_3\ 0\ cos\ \zeta_3 \right) = \left(\mathbf{0};\ \boldsymbol{\tau}_i \right), \tag{11}$$

where $\boldsymbol{\tau}_i$ represents a constraint moment in physics. The axis of $\$_i^{\tau 1}$ is perpendicular to the two rotation axles of the U joint in each limb. Therefore, the constraint wrench screw of the lower sub-platform suffered from the 1st and 3rd limb as shown in Fig. 5(b) can be written as

$$\$_1^{\tau 1} = \left(\mathbf{0};\ \boldsymbol{\tau}_1 \right) \text{ and } \$_3^{\tau 1} = \left(\mathbf{0};\ \boldsymbol{\tau}_3 \right). \tag{12}$$

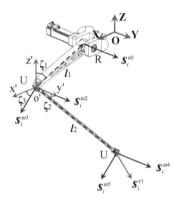

Fig. 4. Twist and wrench analysis of the ith limb.

Using reciprocal screw theory, up to now, the twist screw system of the lower sub-platform can be obtained

$$span\left\{ \$_L^{v1},\ \$_L^{v2},\ \$_L^{v3},\ \$_L^{\omega 4} \right\}, \tag{13}$$

where $\$_L^{v1} = \left(\mathbf{0};\ \boldsymbol{i} \right)$, $\$_L^{v2} = \left(\mathbf{0};\ \boldsymbol{j} \right)$, $\$_L^{v3} = \left(\mathbf{0};\ \boldsymbol{k} \right)$, $\$_L^{\omega 4} = \left(\boldsymbol{\tau}_1 \times \boldsymbol{\tau}_3;\ \boldsymbol{r}_P \times (\boldsymbol{\tau}_1 \times \boldsymbol{\tau}_3) \right)$. As shown in Fig. 2, there is an R joint between the end-effector and the lower sub-platform. The twist screw system of the end-effector can be derived as

$$span\left\{ \$_L^{v1},\ \$_L^{v2},\ \$_L^{v3},\ \$_L^{\omega 4},\ \$_L^{\omega 5} \right\}, \tag{14}$$

where $\$_L^{\omega 5} = (k; r_P \times k)$. Using reciprocal screw theory, the constraint wrench screw system of the end-effector suffered from the lower sub-platform as shown in Fig. 5(d) can be defined as

$$\$_L^{\tau 1} = (0; (\tau_1 \times \tau_3) \times k). \tag{15}$$

Similarly, the constraint wrench screw of the upper sub-platform suffered from the 2nd and 4th limb as shown in Fig. 5(f) can be written as

$$\$_2^{\tau 1} = (0; \tau_2) \text{ and } \$_4^{\tau 1} = (0; \tau_4). \tag{16}$$

Using reciprocal screw theory, up to now, the twist screw system of the upper sub-platform can be obtained

$$span\left\{ \$_U^{v1}, \$_U^{v2}, \$_U^{v3}, \$_U^{\omega 4} \right\}, \tag{17}$$

where $\$_U^{v1} = (0; i)$, $\$_U^{v2} = (0; j)$, $\$_U^{v3} = (0; k)$, $\$_U^{\omega 4} = (\tau_2 \times \tau_4; r_Q \times (\tau_2 \times \tau_4))$. As shown in Fig. 2, there is an H joint between the end-effector and the upper sub-platform. The twist screw system of the end-effector can be also derived as

$$span\left\{ \$_U^{v1}, \$_U^{v2}, \$_U^{v3}, \$_U^{\omega 4}, \$_U^{s5} \right\}, \tag{18}$$

where $\$_U^{s5} = (k; r_Q \times k + hk)$. As mentioned in Sect. 2, here h is the helical pitch of the H joint. P and Q are the two points on the end-effector.

Using reciprocal screw theory, the constraint wrench screw system of the end-effector suffer from the upper sub-platform as shown in Fig. 5(h) can be defined as

$$\$_U^{\tau 1} = (0; (\tau_2 \times \tau_4) \times k). \tag{19}$$

Until now, the constraint wrench screw system of the end-effector as shown in Fig. 5(i) can be defined as

$$span\left\{ \$_L^{\tau 1}, \$_U^{\tau 1} \right\}, \tag{20}$$

Using reciprocal screw theory, the twist screw system of the end-effector can be derived by

$$span\left\{ \$_E^{v1} \$_E^{v2} \$_E^{v3} \$_E^{\omega 4} \right\}, \tag{21}$$

where $\$_E^{v1} = (0; i), \$_E^{v2} = (0; j), \$_E^{v3} = (0; k), \$_E^{\omega 4} = (k; r_P \times k). \$_E^{v1}, \$_E^{v2}$, and $\$_E^{v3}$ denote three translations along the x-, y-, and z-direction, $\$_E^{\omega 4}$ denotes a revolution around the z-axis. Therefore, the proposed PM can generate the Schönflies motions and is qualified for the pick-and-place operations.

For the lower sub-platform, according to Eq. (12) and Eq. (15), the constraint wrench screw of the lower sub-platform suffer from the 1st, the 3rd limb and the end-effector. Therefore, the constraint wrench screw system of the lower sub-platform is

$$span\left\{ \$_1^{\tau 1}, \$_3^{\tau 2}, \$_{L'}^{\tau 1} \right\}, \tag{22}$$

where $\$_{L'}^{\tau 1}$ is the counterforce of $\$_L^{\tau 1}$ as shown in Fig. 5(j). Similarly, for the upper sub-platform, according to Eq. (16) and Eq. (19), the constraint wrench screw system of the upper sub-platform is

$$span\left\{ \$_2^{\tau 1}, \$_4^{\tau 2}, \$_{U'}^{\tau 1} \right\}, \tag{23}$$

where $\$_{U'}^{\tau 1}$ is the counterforce of $\$_U^{\tau 1}$ as shown in Fig. 5(k).

Using reciprocal screw theory, the twist screw system of the two sub-platforms can be derived by

$$span\left\{ \$_S^{v1}, \$_S^{v2}, \$_S^{v3} \right\}, \tag{24}$$

where $\$_S^{v1} = \left(\mathbf{0}; \mathbf{i}\right)$, $\$_S^{v2} = \left(\mathbf{0}; \mathbf{j}\right)$, $\$_S^{v3} = \left(\mathbf{0}; \mathbf{k}\right)$. $\$_S^{v1}$, $\$_S^{v2}$, and $\$_S^{v3}$ denote three translations along the x-, y-, and z-direction, Therefore, the two sub-platforms can generate the three translational motions.

Let $\$_{j,i}$ be the unit twist screw of the jth joint in the ith limb. The instantaneous twist of the end-effector can be expressed by

$$\$_p = \sum_{j=1}^{5} \dot{\theta}_{j,i}\$_{j,i} + \dot{\theta}_{D_k}\$_{D_k} \ (i = 1, 3; k = 1 \ or \ i = 2, 4; k = 2), \tag{25}$$

where D_k is the connection points between the sub-platforms and the end-effector, and $\$_{1,i} = \left(\mathbf{s}_{1,i}; \mathbf{a}_i \times \mathbf{s}_{1,i}\right)$, $\$_{2,i} = \left(\mathbf{s}_{2,i}; \mathbf{b}_i \times \mathbf{s}_{2,i}\right)$, $\$_{3,i} = \left(\mathbf{s}_{3,i}; \mathbf{b}_i \times \mathbf{s}_{3,i}\right)$, $\$_{4,i} = \left(\mathbf{s}_{4,i}; \mathbf{c}_i \times \mathbf{s}_{4,i}\right)$, $\$_{5,i} = \left(\mathbf{s}_{5,i}; \mathbf{c}_i \times \mathbf{s}_{5,i}\right)$, $\$_{D_1} = \left(\mathbf{k}; \mathbf{r}_F \times \mathbf{k}\right)$ when $i = 1, 3$; $\$_{D_2} = \left(\mathbf{k}; \mathbf{r}_F \times \mathbf{k} + h\mathbf{k}\right)$ when $i = 2, 4$. Note that the joint axes are arranged to satisfy the conditions $\mathbf{s}_{1,i} = \mathbf{s}_{2,i} = \mathbf{s}_{4,i}$ and $\mathbf{s}_{3,i} = \mathbf{s}_{5,i}$. Taking the mobility analysis result into consideration, two limited equations can be obtained

$$\$_L = \sum_{j=1}^{5} \dot{\theta}_{j,1}\$_{j,1} = \sum_{j=1}^{5} \dot{\theta}_{j,3}\$_{j,3} = \left(\mathbf{0}; \mathbf{v}_{D_1}\right), \tag{26}$$

$$\$_U = \sum_{j=1}^{5} \dot{\theta}_{j,2}\$_{j,2} = \sum_{j=1}^{5} \dot{\theta}_{j,4}\$_{j,4} = \left(\mathbf{0}; \mathbf{v}_{D_2}\right). \tag{27}$$

By substituting $\$_{j,i}$ into Eq. (26) and Eq. (27), one obtains

$$\sum_{j=1}^{5} \dot{\theta}_{j,i}\mathbf{s}_{j,i} = \mathbf{0} \ (i = 1, \cdots, 4). \tag{28}$$

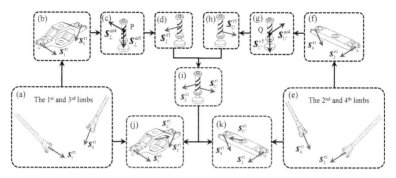

Fig. 5. Wrench analysis of the end-effector.

Let $D_k (i = 1, 2)$ be the equivalent points because they are the points on which the end-effector suffers the wrench from. The following equation should be satisfied

$$\sum_{j=1}^{5} \dot{\theta}_{j,i} \cdot \left(\overrightarrow{C_i D_k} \times s_{j,i} \right) = \mathbf{0} \ (i = 1, 3; k = 1 \ \text{or} \ i = 2, 4; k = 2). \quad (29)$$

The instantaneous twist of the end-effector can be equivalently expressed by

$$\$_p = \sum_{j=1}^{6} \dot{\theta}_{j,i} \$_{j,i}^* (i = 1, \cdots, 4), \quad (30)$$

where $\$_{1,i}^* = \left(s_{1,i}; \left(a_i + \overrightarrow{C_i D_k} \right) \times s_{1,i} \right), \ \$_{2,i}^* = \left(s_{2,i}; \left(b_i + \overrightarrow{C_i D_k} \right) \times s_{2,i} \right),$ $\$_{3,i}^* = \left(s_{3,i}; \left(b_i + \overrightarrow{C_i D_k} \right) \times s_{3,i} \right), \ \$_{4,i}^* = \left(s_{4,i}; d_k \times s_{4,i} \right), \ \$_{5,i}^* = \left(s_{5,i}; d_k \times s_{5,i} \right),$ $\$_{6,i}^* = \$_{D_1}$ when $i = 1, 3; \ \$_{6,i}^* = \$_{D_2}$ when $i = 2, 4$.

According to the method in Ref. [13], the equivalent transmission wrenches of the proposed double-platform PM are obtained as

$$\hat{\$}_{r,2,i}^* = \left(\overrightarrow{B_i C_i}; \ \overrightarrow{O D_k} \times \overrightarrow{B_i C_i} \right) = \left(n_i; d_i \times n_i \right), (i = 1, 3), \quad (31)$$

$$\hat{\$}_{r,2,i}^* = \left(\overrightarrow{B_i C_i}; \ \overrightarrow{O D_k} \times \overrightarrow{B_i C_i} \right) = \left(n_i; d_i \times n_i - \mathsf{h} n_i \right), (i = 2, 4). \quad (32)$$

4   Motion/ Force Performance Analysis

A detailed introduction to the ITI, OTI, and CTI based on screw theory is given in Refs. [11] and [12]. Here, these indices are extended to evaluate the kinematic performance of the proposed double-platform PM.

4.1 Input Transmission Index

The input twist screws are the active twist screws in each limb which can be represented by

$$\$^i_{ITS} = \$^{\omega 1}_i. \tag{33}$$

The transmission wrench $\$^i_{TWS}$ is a linear force along the passive limb of the manipulator. Then, the ITI can be derived by

$$\gamma_I = \min_i\{\lambda_i\} = \min_i \left\{ \frac{\left|\$^i_{ITS} \circ \$^i_{TWS}\right|}{\left|\$^i_{ITS} \circ \$^i_{TWS}\right|_{max}} \right\} \quad (i = 1, 2, \cdots, n). \tag{34}$$

4.2 Output Transmission Index

According to Eq. (15) and Eq. (19), the end-effector suffers a two-dimensional constraint wrench screw system

$$span\left(\$^1_{CWS}, \$^2_{CWS}\right), \tag{35}$$

where $\$^1_{CWS} = \$^L_C = (0; (\tau_1 \times \tau_3) \times k)$, $\$^2_{CWS} = \$^U_C = (0; (\tau_2 \times \tau_4) \times k)$.
Provided that the output twist screws of the mechanism can be expressed by

$$\$^i_{OTS} = \left(s_i; r_i \times s_i\right) = \left(L_i\ M_i\ N_i;\ P_i\ Q_i\ R_i\right), i = 1, \cdots, 4 \tag{36}$$

where $\$^i_{OTS}$ can be identified by the following equations

$$\begin{cases} \$^i_{OTS} \circ \$^j_{ETWS} = 0, i \neq j \\ \$^i_{OTS} \circ \$^k_{CWS} = 0, \\ |s_i| = 1 \end{cases} \quad \begin{pmatrix} i, j = 1, 2, 3, 4 \\ k = 1, 2 \end{pmatrix} \tag{37}$$

Thus, the OTI can be derived by

$$\gamma_O = \min_i\{\eta_i\} = \min_i \left\{ \frac{\left|\$^i_{ETWS} \circ \$^i_{OTS}\right|}{\left|\$^i_{ETWS} \circ \$^i_{OTS}\right|_{max}} \right\} \quad (i = 1, 2, \cdots, n). \tag{38}$$

4.3 Constraint Transmission Index

Provided that the output twist screws of the manipulator can be expressed by

$$\$^j_{OTS} = \left(s_j; r_j \times s_j\right) = \left(L_j\ M_j\ N_j;\ P_j\ Q_j\ R_j\right), j = 1, 2, \tag{39}$$

where the $\boldsymbol{\$}^j_{\text{OTS}}$ can be identified by the following equations

$$\begin{cases} \boldsymbol{\$}^j_{\text{OTS}} \circ \boldsymbol{\$}^k_{\text{CWS}} = 0, j \neq k \\ \boldsymbol{\$}^j_{\text{OTS}} \circ \boldsymbol{\$}^i_{\text{ETWS}} = 0, \\ \left| s_j \right| = 1 \end{cases} , \begin{pmatrix} i, j = 1, 2, 3, 4 \\ k = 1, 2 \end{pmatrix}. \tag{40}$$

Thus, the CTI can be derived by

$$\gamma_C = \min_j \{ \kappa_j \} = \min_j \left\{ \frac{\left| \boldsymbol{\$}^j_{\text{CWS}} \circ \boldsymbol{\$}^j_{\text{OTS}} \right|}{\left| \boldsymbol{\$}^j_{\text{CWS}} \circ \boldsymbol{\$}^j_{\text{OTS}} \right|_{\max}} \right\} \ (j = 1, 2). \tag{41}$$

4.4 Local Singularity Index

Furthermore, for the overall evaluation of the above performance, an index is defined as

$$\gamma_L = \min \{ \gamma_I, \ \gamma_O, \ \gamma_C \}. \tag{42}$$

where γ_L is be referred to as the local singularity index. The higher LSI is, the better the motion/force transmissibility and constrainability of the PM.

5 Workspace Identification

Let the geometric parameters of the proposed PM be $l_1 = 375$ mm; $l_2 = 825$ mm; $r_1 = 275$ mm; $r_2 = 210$ mm, then the distributions of the ITI, OTI, CTI and LSI can be illustrated in Fig. 6 when fixing the rotation of the end-effector as $\theta = 0°$. In the atlas, the area enveloped by $\gamma_L = 0.7$ shown in Fig. 5(d), in which the manipulator is good at both transmissibility and constrainability, is defined as the good motion/force transmission and constraint workspace (GTCW)

$$GTCW = \int_W \gamma_L \geq 0.7 \mathrm{d}W. \tag{43}$$

Distributions of LSI values are presented in Fig. 7. Figure 7(a) shows the outline of the GTCW. Figure 7(b) ~ (j) shows the distributions of LSI values on different horizontal planes while Fig. 7(k) shows the distribution LSI values when Y = 0 mm. Figure 7(l) shows the boundary feature points of the GCTW on the plane Y = 0 mm, which are provided in Table 1. These points outline a regular cylinder and a truncated cone-shaped workspaces, in which the proposed manipulator can achieve a high-performance operation.

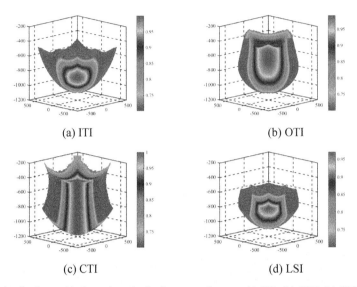

(a) ITI

(b) OTI

(c) CTI

(d) LSI

Fig. 6. Distributions of index values in the linear workspace: (a) ITI; (b) OTI; (c) CTI; (d) LSI.

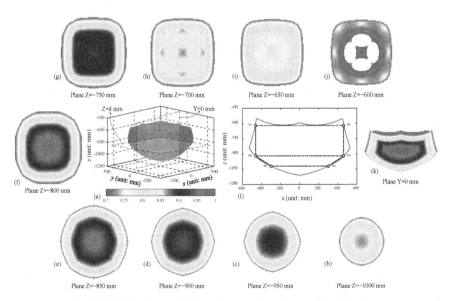

Fig. 7. Distributions of index values and workspace identification.

Table 1. Boundary feature points of GTCW on the plane Y = 0 mm.

W_1/mm	W_2/mm	W_3/mm	W_4/mm	W_5/mm	W_6/mm
(0, − 460, − 600)	(0, 460, − 600)	(0, 460, − 730)	(0, 350, − 830)	(0, − 350, − 830)	(0, − 460, − 730)

6 Conclusion

In this paper, two double-platform PMs which can generate the Schönflies motion with closed joints are proposed. Choosing one of them, the mobility and equivalent transmission wrench analysis are carried out based on screw theory. Then, the motion/force performance of the proposed double-platform PM is analyzed to identify the GTCW. This work offers an alternative parallel robot solution for pick-and-place operations. More importantly, the performance evaluation approach considering the motion/force transmission and constraint characteristics is extended from single-platform PMs to the field of double-platform PMs.

Acknowledgements. This work was supported by the National Natural Science Foundation of China (Grant No. 52105026) and the China Postdoctoral Science Foundation (Grant No. 2021TQ0176), as well as the Shuimu Tsinghua Scholar Program (Grant No. 2020SM081).

References

1. Isaksson, M., Gosselin, C., Marlow, K.: Singularity analysis of a class of kinematically redundant parallel Schönflies motion generators. Mech. Mach. Theory **112**, 172–191 (2017)
2. Eskandary, P.K., Angeles, J.: The dynamics of a parallel Schönflies-motion generator. Mech. Mach. Theory **119**, 119–129 (2018)
3. Visioli, A., Legnani, G.: On the trajectory tracking control of industrial SCARA robot manipulators. IEEE Trans. Ind. Electron. **49**(1), 224–232 (2002)
4. Altuzarra, O., Pinto, C., Petuya, V.: A symmetric parallel Schönflies-motion manipulator for pick-and-place operations. Robotica **29**(6), 853–862 (2011)
5. Clavel, R.: Device for the movement and positioning of an element in space. U.S. Patent No. 4,976,582 (1990)
6. Rey, L., Clavel, R.: The delta parallel robot. In: Boër, C.R., Molinari-Tosatti, L., Smith, K.S. (eds.) Parallel Kinematic Machines, pp. 401–417. Springer London, London (1999). https://doi.org/10.1007/978-1-4471-0885-6_29
7. Huang, T., Liu, S., Mei, J., et al.: Optimal design of a 4-DOF SCARA type parallel robot using dynamic performance indices and angular constraints. Mech. Mach. Theory **70**(3), 246–253 (2012)
8. Pierrot, F., Company, O.: H4: a new family of 4-DOF parallel robots. In: IEEE/ASME International Conference on Advanced Intelligent Mechatronics, pp. 508–513 (1999)
9. Takeda, Y., Funabashi, H.: Motion transmissibility of in-parallel actuated manipulators. JSME Int J., Ser. C **38**(4), 749–755 (1995)
10. Ball, R.S.: A Treatise on the Theory of Screws. Cambridge University Press, Cambridge (1900)
11. Wang, J.S., Wu, C., Liu, X.-J.: Performance evaluation of parallel robots: motion/force transmissibility and its index. Mech. Mach. Theory **45**(10), 1462–1476 (2010)
12. Liu, X.-J., Wu, C., Wang, J.S.: A new approach for singularity analysis and closeness measurement to singularities of parallel manipulators. J. Mech. Robot. **4**(4), 041001 (2012)
13. Meng, Q.Z., Xie, F.G., Liu, X.-J., et al.: Screw theory-based motion/force transmissibility analysis of high-speed parallel robots with articulated platforms. J. Mech. Robot. **12**(4), 041011 (2020)

Modeling of Passive Dynamic Walking Behavior of the Asymmetric Spatial Rimless Wheel on Slope

Jiacheng Yu[1], Wenchuan Jia[1(✉)], Yi Sun[1], Shugen Ma[1,2], Jianjun Yuan[1], and Quan Zhan[1]

[1] School of Mechatronic Engineering and Automation, Shanghai Key Laboratory of Intelligent Manufacturing and Robotics, Shanghai University, Shanghai 200444, China
lovvchris@shu.edu.cn
[2] Department of Robotics, Ritsumeikan Universitny, Shiga 525-8577, Japan

Abstract. The rimless wheel mechanism is an important basic model for studying passive dynamic walking, which provides a direct reference for the realization of a stable and efficient anthropomorphic gait. However, the simplification of model parameters such as motion dimensions has weakened this reference. This paper specifically studies the motion behavior of an Asymmetric Spatial Rimless Wheel (ASRW) on a spatial slope. For different motion phases of the ASRW in the periodic motion process, the dynamic model is established in Cartesian space. And the Poincare map method is used to numerically solve the fixed points of the stride function. The dynamic model obtained in this paper can more realistically reflect the similarity of motion behavior and gait characteristics between the rimless wheel and the human body. The correctness of modeling and calculation is verified by simulation. Moreover, the limit analysis also shows that the ASRW provides a bridge connecting the biped walking model and the rolling motion model.

Keywords: Passive walking · Dynamics · Wheeled robots

1 Introduction

The technology of legged robots is advancing rapidly. The combination of stronger driving ability and better dynamic control methods provide the engine for realizing high dynamics and high balance of bionic motion. While the classic passive walking theory provides another way to improve the inherent stability and energy efficiency of the mechanism.

McGeer firstly proposed the concept of passive dynamic walking and the basic model of the rimless wheel [1]. The rimless wheel mechanism can achieve intermittent collision contact between the ends of its spokes and the slope without an internal power source, so as to imitate the rhythmic contact characteristics of the stable walking gait. Furthermore, McGeer successfully developed a classic passive biped robot with knee joints [2], which can show a gait similar to human walking. On this basis, other passive walking robots have also been studied by Cornell University [3], MIT [4] and Delft University [5], etc.

© Springer Nature Switzerland AG 2021
X.-J. Liu et al. (Eds.): ICIRA 2021, LNAI 13015, pp. 482–493, 2021.
https://doi.org/10.1007/978-3-030-89134-3_44

The motion state of the completely passive rimless mechanism only depends on its own geometric and physical properties, initial state, and terrain.

Therefore, the research focuses on analyzing and effectively using the interaction between the physical properties of the mechanism and the environment.

In 2010, Jian et al. analyzed the gait of the rimless wheel mechanism with flat feet, which has faster walking speed and better energy efficiency [6]. In 2019, Smyrli et al. designed a series of rimless wheel with feet which have different curvature of the shape, and proved that gait and energy efficiency can be optimized by changing the shape of the feet [7]. Asano et al. studied the effects of double-support phase and swing-leg retraction phase on gait efficiency by adding viscous friction at the rotation axis of the passive dynamic walker, and analyzed the basic characteristics of rigid legs and viscoelastic legs in these two phases [8, 9]. In addition, he introduced a novel underactuated rimless wheel models with reaction wheel on the hip joint [10, 11], and proposed a method to generate collisionless gait that adapted to rough terrain [12]. Rasouli et al. introduced two asymmetric passive dynamic walker models to study the gait stability with different mass distribution, mass ratio, and slope angle, and showed that the stability is more sensitive to the mass ratio of the legs [13]. Znegui et al. developed and verified the explicit analytical expression of Poincare map of the passive compass-gait, by linearizing differential-algebraic equations [14]. In recent years, some scholars have also studied the compass-gait biped robots that include active hip joints and active ankle joints [15, 16], and theoretically proved that the robot uses hip and ankle joints to walk on a flat surface is similar to walk on a slope passively, and further realize the stable walking gait of the semi-passive dynamic walker on the slope [17]. Moon et al. found that a compass-gait biped robot has a stable focus of energy, which corresponding to the stable limit cycle in the phase plane, and is formed by balanced interactions between energy loss and gain in ground collision [18].

In addition, the actively powered rimless wheel can achieve level ground walking, by leaning forward to provide extra gravitation moment to the rimless wheel [19], or by driving the rimless wheel directly [20].

Although many passive walking robots based on rimless wheel mechanisms have been developed [21, 22], how to construct the rimless wheel mechanism and its inter-action model to accurately describe the anthropomorphic gait is still the key problem to research. And this is the essential meaning of the existence of the rimless wheel mechanism as the basic principle model of passive biped walking. As shown in Fig. 1, the bipedal gait of a man walking on flat ground is generated by the musculoskeletal system accompanied by the highly intelligent clock-tick of the body, which shows stable rhythmic motion in all dimensions. During the entire gait process, every lift and fall of the foot is a direct excitation to adjust the trajectory and motion rhythm of different parts of the body, and this is the theoretical basis of the CPG model [23]. Therefore, how to achieve similar motion behavior characteristics to humans in terms of motion rhythm and motion stability, and to achieve similar gait characteristics to humans in terms of physical spatial posture and stride are the specific objectives of the construction of the rimless wheel mechanism model.

The goal of this paper is to fully simulate the motion behavior and gait characteristics of biped walking, specifically to construct and calculate the model of the rimless wheel mechanism in three-dimensional space. In our previous work, we have proposed two rimless wheel mechanisms [24, 25], which can directly simulate the biped gait and analyze the system stability. In this paper, we will fully analyze the spatial motion process of the rimless mechanism on the spatial slope in detail and derive its dynamic equations in different phases of motion by the Newton-Euler method. Then, we analyze its motion characteristics to provide a more adequate and accurate reference for passive walking research.

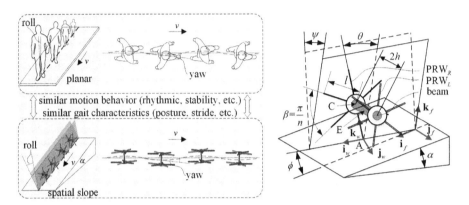

Fig. 1. The similarity of motion behavior between ASRW walking on a spatial slope and human walking (left). The ASRW model and its coordinate system (right).

2   Modeling

2.1   The ASRW Model and Coordinate System

The ASRW model and its coordinate system is shown in Fig. 1. The model is composed of two identical crossed planar rimless wheels (PRW) and a beam. Where the single solid line represents PRW_R, and the double solid line represents PRW_L. The total mass of the model is m and the number of legs is n. The mass of the beam is neglectable and its length is $2h$. The width-length ratio ρ is set to h/l and the adjacent angle β between PRW_L and PRW_R is set to $2\pi/n$.

The geometric center of PRW_R is marked by C and the midpoint of the beam is marked by E, where point E is also the geometric center of the model. The yaw angle is represented by ϕ, the roll angle is represented by ψ, and the rotation angle is represented by θ. The fixed coordinate system on the slope is represented by $\{F\}$, and the motion coordinate system that linked on the model is represented by $\{W\}$. The relationship between the two coordinate systems can be given by 3–1-2 Euler angle as

$$\{W\} = R_2(\theta) \cdot R_1(\psi) \cdot R_3(\phi)\{F\} \tag{1}$$

Thus, the angular velocity of $\{W\}$ relative to $\{F\}$ is

$$^F\omega_W = \dot{\phi}R_2(\theta)R_1(\psi)k_w + \dot{\psi}R_2(\theta)i_w + \dot{\theta}j_w$$

$$= \dot{\phi} \begin{bmatrix} \cos\theta & 0 & -\sin\theta \\ 0 & 1 & 0 \\ \sin\theta & 0 & \cos\theta \end{bmatrix} \begin{bmatrix} 1 & 0 & 0 \\ 0 & \cos\psi & \sin\psi \\ 0 & -\sin\psi & \cos\psi \end{bmatrix} \mathbf{k}_w + \dot{\psi} \begin{bmatrix} \cos\theta & 0 & -\sin\theta \\ 0 & 1 & 0 \\ \sin\theta & 0 & \cos\theta \end{bmatrix} \mathbf{i}_w + \dot{\theta}\mathbf{j}_w$$

$$(2)$$

2.2 Inertia Tensor

Assuming that the mass of PRW_R is distributed in its longitudinal plane and is symmetric with respect to point C, the inertia tensor of PRW_R at point C is obtained

$$\mathbf{I}_C = \begin{bmatrix} D + 2mh^2 & 0 & 0 \\ 0 & 2D & 0 \\ 0 & 0 & D + 2mh^2 \end{bmatrix} \tag{3}$$

In the same way, the inertia tensor of the contact point A between PRW_R and the slope can be obtained. Where $2D$ is correspond to the central-axis moment of inertia of ASRW and is a constant greater than 0.

3 Dynamic Modeling

3.1 Motion Phases and Assumptions

The motion process of the ASRW on the spatial slope is shown in Fig. 2. The two rotation phases and two collision phases are defined as a gait cycle. During the walk movement, the legs in PRW_L and PRW_R collide with the ground alternately.

- Rotation phase I: The ASRW rotates around the contact point between PRW_R and slope. Let contact point A be the origin of $\{\mathbf{W}\}$. There may be a state in which one leg or two legs are in contact with the slope. Therefore, it can be divided into single-support phase and double-support phase.
- Collision phase I: This phase occurs at the moment when PRW_L collides with the ground.
- Rotation phase II: This phase is similar to the rotation phase I. Let point B'' be the origin of $\{\mathbf{W}\}$, which is the projection of contact point B on the longitudinal plane of PRW_R.

- Collision phase II: This phase occurs at the moment when PRW_R collides with ground.

Let $\mathbf{q} = \begin{bmatrix} \phi, \psi, \theta, \dot{\phi}, \dot{\psi}, \dot{\theta} \end{bmatrix}^{\mathrm{T}}$ be the state space. The angle θ in the rotation phase is strictly limited to the range of $[-\pi/n, \pi/n]$. The angle θ before the collision phase is π/n, marked by θ^-, and it is reset to $-\pi/n$ after the collision phase, marked by θ^+, where '$-$' and '$+$' represent the state before and after collision respectively.

The following are the assumptions:

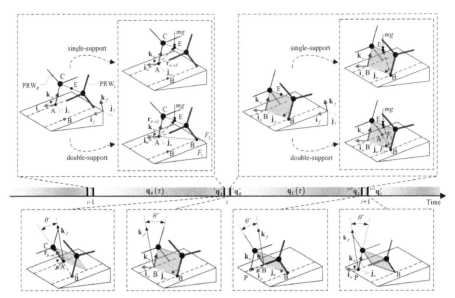

Fig. 2. Two rotation phases and two collision phases in a gait cycle. Where i represents the number of collisions, $^i\mathbf{q}_R^-$ and $^i\mathbf{q}_R^+$ represent the state before and after the ith collision, $^{i+1}\mathbf{q}_L^-$ and $^{i+1}\mathbf{q}_L^+$ represent the state before and after the $i+1$th collision, rotation phase I with right leg is represented as $\mathbf{q}_R(\tau)$, rotation phase II with left leg is represented as $\mathbf{q}_L(\tau)$.

- The ASRW will not deform during the walk movement.
- The supporting leg will not slide relative to the spatial slope during the walk movement.
- The collision phase is a completely inelastic collision, and when the supporting leg collides with the slope, the previous supporting leg immediately leaves the slope.

3.2   Rotation Phase

The Rotation phase of ASRW includes Single-support phase and Double-support phase. The Single-support phase is shown in Fig. 2, the ASRW has only one leg in contact with the slope, and the system has three degrees of freedom. The dynamic equation can be derived from the angular momentum theorem at the rotating contact point. The rotating contact point of $\mathbf{q}_R(\tau)$ is contact point A, and the rotating contact point of $\mathbf{q}_L(\tau)$ is contact point B. We take the analysis of $\mathbf{q}_R(\tau)$ as an example and get

$$\sum \mathbf{M}_A = {}^F\dot{\mathbf{H}}_A \tag{4}$$

$$\sum \mathbf{M}_A = \mathbf{r}_{A \to E} \times mg\left(\sin\alpha \cdot \mathbf{i}_f - \cos\alpha \cdot \mathbf{k}_f\right) \tag{5}$$

$$^F\dot{\mathbf{H}}_A = {}^W\dot{\mathbf{H}}_A + {}^F\boldsymbol{\omega}_W \times \mathbf{H}_A \tag{6}$$

$$\mathbf{H}_A = \mathbf{I}_A \cdot {}^F\boldsymbol{\omega}_W \tag{7}$$

$$^W\dot{\mathbf{H}}_A = \mathbf{I}_A \cdot {}^F\dot{\&}_W \tag{8}$$

where $\mathbf{M}$ is the moment of force and $\mathbf{H}$ is the moment of momentum. The moment of inertia D and time t have been nondimensionalized by the rescaling of $J = D/(ml^2)$ and $\tau = \sqrt{g/l} \cdot t$.

The difference between $\mathbf{q}_L(\tau)$ and $\mathbf{q}_R(\tau)$ is that the moment of gravity on the rotating contact point is opposite. The dynamic equations of $\mathbf{q}_R(\tau)$ and $\mathbf{q}_L(\tau)$ can be expressed by $\mathbf{q}$ and then become

$$\dot{\mathbf{q}} = \mathbf{S}_{1R}\left(\mathbf{q}, \lambda^2, \alpha\right) \tag{9}$$

$$\dot{\mathbf{q}} = \mathbf{S}_{1L}\left(\mathbf{q}, \lambda^2, \alpha\right) \tag{10}$$

The Double-support phase is shown in Fig. 2, the ASRW has two legs in contact with the slope, and the system has three degrees of freedom. The dynamic equation can be derived from the angular momentum theorem of the rotation axis. The rotation axis of $\mathbf{q}_R(\tau)$ is AB', and the rotation axis of $\mathbf{q}_L(\tau)$ is AB. This subsection takes the analysis of $\mathbf{q}_R(\tau)$ as an example. Assuming that the contact point B' is separated from the slope, the force components F_1 and F_2 at contact point B' are additionally taken into account in the equation. Therefore, the dynamic equation of the double-support phase is still derived from the angular momentum theorem at the rotating contact point.

3.3 Collision Phase

As shown in Fig. 2, the collision phase of the system occurs at the end of each rotation phase. Due to the extremely short collision time, the angle ϕ and ψ of the system are unchanged in the collision phase. The motion coordinate system $\{W\}$ rotates by $-2\pi/n$ around the axis $\mathbf{j}_w$, so the angle θ changes from π/n to $-\pi/n$. It has

$$\begin{bmatrix} \phi^+ \\ \psi^+ \\ \theta^+ \end{bmatrix} = \begin{bmatrix} 1 & 0 & 0 \\ 0 & 1 & 0 \\ 0 & 0 & -1 \end{bmatrix} \begin{bmatrix} \phi^- \\ \psi^- \\ \theta^- \end{bmatrix} \tag{11}$$

In this phase, the angular velocity relationship of the system can be derived from the angular momentum theorem at the contact point B. We get

$$\mathbf{H}_B^- = \mathbf{H}_B^+ \tag{12}$$

$$\mathbf{H}_B^- = \mathbf{H}_C^- + \mathbf{r}_{B \to C} \times m\mathbf{v}_C^- \tag{13}$$

$$\mathbf{H}_B^+ = \mathbf{I}_B \boldsymbol{\omega}_W^+ = \mathbf{I}_A \boldsymbol{\omega}_W^+ \tag{14}$$

where $\mathbf{H}_B^-$ is the moment of momentum for the contact point B before the collision phase, and the ASRW rotates around the contact point A at this moment. $\mathbf{H}_B^+$ is the moment of momentum for the contact point B after the collision phase, and the ASRW rotates around the contact point B at this moment.

As shown in Fig. 2, the ith collision phase is defined as ${}^i\mathbf{q}_R$, and the $i + 1$th collision phase is defined as ${}^{i+1}\mathbf{q}_L$. The difference between ${}^i\mathbf{q}_R$ and ${}^{i+1}\mathbf{q}_L$ is the position of the contact point relative to $\{\mathbf{W}\}$ is opposite. After dimensionless, the dynamic equations of ${}^i\mathbf{q}_R$ and ${}^{i+1}\mathbf{q}_L$ can be expressed by $\mathbf{q}$ and then become

$$\mathbf{q}^+ = \mathbf{T}_R\left(\mathbf{q}^-, \lambda^2\right) \cdot \mathbf{q}^- \tag{15}$$

$$\mathbf{q}^+ = \mathbf{T}_L\left(\mathbf{q}^-, \lambda^2\right) \cdot \mathbf{q}^- \tag{16}$$

4 Analysis and Simulation

This subsection calculates the fixed point during the motion of the ASRW, where the system initial state point $\mathbf{q}_0$ is set to $[0.6284, -0.0400, -0.1900, 0, 0, 0.7420]$, and the system parameter $2J = 0.5$, $\alpha = \pi/10$ [rad]. We adopt the Poincare map method to numerically solve the fixed points of the stride function. Then we use ADAMS to simulate and analyze the correctness of theoretical calculation.

4.1 Fixed Point

The fixed point $\mathbf{q}^*$ of the system is the state space when the ASRW walks stably on the slope. The moment at the beginning of the rotation phase is defined as the Poincare section, and the system state at the moment after the ith collision is marked by ${}^i\mathbf{q}^+$, in the same way, ${}^{i+1}\mathbf{q}^+$ and ${}^{i+2}\mathbf{q}^+$ are obtained. Let $\mathbf{F}$ be the stride function, then the expression from the moment after the ith collision to the moment after the $i + 1$th collision is given by

$$^{i+1}\mathbf{q}^+ = \mathbf{F}\left({}^i\mathbf{q}^+\right) \tag{17}$$

Therefore, the input and output of the stride function are only related to the system state space of the Poincare section. The stride function can be expressed as a combination of two functions, denoted as $\mathbf{F} = \mathbf{N} \circ \mathbf{C}$. The function $\mathbf{N}$ is derived from the integral result of the dynamic equation in the rotation phase, the function $\mathbf{C}$ is derived from the dynamic equation in the collision phase, and '$\circ$' is a certain combination of relationships.

The complete stride function of the ASRW walking on the slope for a cycle then becomes

$$^{i+2}\mathbf{q}^+ = \mathbf{F}^2\left({}^i\mathbf{q}^+\right) = \mathbf{F}_L\left(\mathbf{F}_R\left({}^i\mathbf{q}^+\right)\right) \tag{18}$$

Since the Eq. (18) cannot be expressed as an explicit function, we adopt the numerical iteration method (Newton-Raphson) to find the fixed point $\mathbf{q}^*$ of this equation. Assuming that $\mathbf{q}_k$ is the kth iteration value of the fixed point $\mathbf{q}^*$, then the $k + 1$th iteration value is given by Eq. (19), where $D\mathbf{F}^2(\mathbf{q}_k)$ is the Jacobian of $\mathbf{F}^2$ in $\mathbf{q}_k$, and the iteration cut-off condition is defined by Eq. (20), where $\mathbf{q}_{accuracy}$ is the calculation accuracy. When the difference of the state space values is less than the calculation accuracy, $\mathbf{q}_{k+1} \approx \mathbf{q}_k \approx \mathbf{q}^*$.

$$\mathbf{q}_{k+1} = \mathbf{q}_k - \left[\frac{D\left(\mathbf{F}^2(\mathbf{q}) - \mathbf{q}\right)}{D\mathbf{q}} \Bigg|_{\mathbf{q}=\mathbf{q}_k} \right]^{-1} \cdot \left(\mathbf{F}^2(\mathbf{q}_k) - \mathbf{q}_k\right) \tag{19}$$

$$\mathbf{F}^2(\mathbf{q}_k) - \mathbf{q}_k = \mathbf{q}_{k+1} - \mathbf{q}_k \leq \mathbf{q}_{accuracy} \tag{20}$$

Taking the single-support walk as an example, the relationship between the state space $\mathbf{q}$ and the number of iterations is shown in Fig. 3. After about 14 iterations, the system state space $\mathbf{q}$ is almost constant. The fixed point $\mathbf{q}^* = [-0.3050, 0.0943, -0.1981, -0.1033, 0.0411, 1.2880]$.

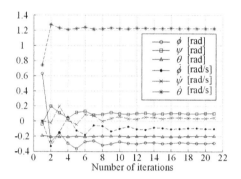

Fig. 3. The change of state space $\mathbf{q}$ in the single-support walk, where $n = 16$ and $\rho = 0.1$.

4.2 Simulation Analysis

The theoretical simplified model is constructed in ADAMS, where $n = 10$ and $\rho = 0.1$, and other system parameters are constant. Then the simulation experiment of the model walking on the slope is shown in Fig. 4(a), which shows the position and posture of the model at different moments.

Taking the single-support walk as an example. The calculation results of the angular velocity $\dot{\phi}$ and $\dot{\psi}$ are shown in Fig. 4(b), which are within the tolerance of error. The simulation result verifies the correctness of the theoretical calculation results. The angular velocity change gradually decreases after several cycles of motion, and the two angular velocity curves converge, which indicates that the system will reach to a stable state. The motion state is also stable in double-support walk, as shown in Fig. 4(c).

4.3 Comparison

This subsection investigates the geometry and motion relationship of the ASRW and the PRW on the slope, and the motion behavior of the ASRW and human. The PRW is

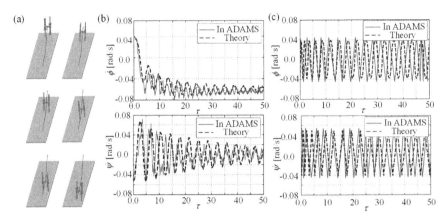

Fig. 4. (a) ASRW's walking simulation experiment. The red line is the trajectory of the model's center of mass. (b) Simulation results when walking with single leg support. (c) Simulation results when walking with two legs support. (Color figure online)

a special case of the ASRW, and its physical parameters $h = 0$. From the perspective of geometric relations, the projection of the ASRW to the longitudinal plane forms the PRW, e.g. PRW_R, as shown in Fig. 5(a). With the increase of n, the double-support walk of ASRW can be equivalent to a cylinder rolling on the slope.

The relationship between the state space value and the system parameter value when the ASRW moves stably with double-support walk is shown in Fig. 5(b). We can find that the amplitude of angle ϕ and ψ decreases with the increase of parameter ρ, and the final stable amplitude of angle ϕ and ψ gradually decrease and approach 0 when $n \to \infty$, which is consistent with the result of the cylindrical motion model.

As shown in Fig. 5(b), the system rotation velocity approaches a straight line with the increase of system parameter n. It is calculated that the angular acceleration of the system with $n = 50$ and the dimensionless angular acceleration of the ideal cylindrical motion model moving on the slope are within the tolerance of error.

$$\ddot{\theta}_{n\to\infty} = \sqrt{1/(2J)} \sin \alpha = 0.4370 \tag{21}$$

$$\ddot{\theta}_{n\to50} = 0.4333 \approx \ddot{\theta}_{n\to\infty} \tag{22}$$

5 Experiments

A simple experiment of the ASRW model dynamically walking on an inclined treadmill, as shown in Fig. 6(a), was carried out to further explore the dynamic behavior. An IMU sensor is installed at the geometric center of the ASRW to measure posture and acceleration in real time. The experimental results when the original speed is almost 0 are shown in Fig. 6(b), which also corresponds to the image shown in Fig. 6(a). The actual structure parameters of the ASRW for the experiments and other measurement parameters are also showed. When the ASRW model changes to a stable state in the

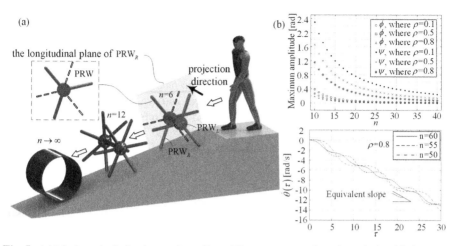

Fig. 5. (a) Limit analysis for the number of legs. The geometry and motion relationship between the ASRW and the PRW is also showed. (b) The relationship between the state space value and the system parameter n where $2J = 0.5$ and $\alpha = \pi/10$.

motion process, the angular velocity $\dot{\psi}$ and $\dot{\phi}$ fluctuates around 0 and the angle ψ and ϕ converges, the trend of which is similar to the simulation.

The experiment clearly reflects that the robot mixes different dynamic behaviors during walking. Note that the ASRW is mainly supported by two legs during rolling, while the support for single legs has not been clearly observed. Perhaps this is related to the low initial velocity of ASRW and the low average velocity during movement. The motion state of the system is closely related to the initial value, which is also specifically analyzed in our previous work [24, 25].

6 Conclusion

In this manuscript, a spatial two-wheeled rimless wheel mechanism named ASRW is proposed. This mechanism is composed of two planar rimless wheels with the same structure. which is used to directly simulate the human legs alternately advancing during walking. We decompose the movement process of ASRW into rotation phase and collision phase. Furthermore, we subdivide rotation phase into single-leg support stage and double-legs support stage. We constructed a unified coordinate system to simplify modeling and calculation, and used the Newton Euler method to model the dynamic behavior of ASRW in each stage, which contains the motion parameters of ASRW in three-dimensional space.

Based on the derived dynamic model, we use Newton-Raphson method to obtain the calculation equation of the fixed point in the Poincare map of the stride function, which can then be used in the theoretical analysis of system stability. The simulation results in ADAMS show that the dynamic model derived in this paper is correct. In addition, the limit analysis results of the number of legs in the model show that ASRW with a small number of legs can simulate human walking, while an ASRW with a large number of legs is equivalent to the rolling of the wheel, which is interesting. In the experiment, we tried to show all the movement process. However, due to the inability to accurately set the initial motion state of ASRW in the experiment, we only use the static placement method, and this makes the initial motion velocity close to zero. In this case, ASRW mainly exhibits as double-support during the rotation phase.

Nevertheless, we believe that the physical devices and dynamics models proposed in this manuscript can provide a more accurate and effective reference for passive walking research than the simplified planar models and behaviors. The hyperlink of one summary video is https://v.youku.com/v_show/id_XNTE0NTAxMzAwOA==.html, with the access password *2021*.

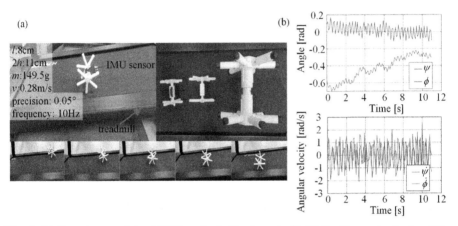

Fig. 6. (a) Experiments of the ASRW on the inclined treadmill. (b) Position and velocity of the angle that measured in experiments.

References

1. McGeer, T.: Passive dynamic walking. Int. J. Robot. Res. **9**(2), 62–82 (1990)
2. McGeer, T.: Passive walking with knees. In: IEEE International Conference on Robotics and Automation, pp. 1640–1645 (1990)
3. Collins, S.H., Ruina, A.: A bipedal walking robot with efficient and human-like gait. In: IEEE International Conference on Robotics and Automation, pp. 1983–1988 (2005)
4. Tedrake, R., Zhang, T.W., Fong, M., Seung, H.S.: Actuating a simple 3D passive dynamic walker. In: IEEE International Conference on Robotics and Automation, pp. 4656–4661 (2004)
5. Hobbelen, D.G.E., Wisse, M.: A disturbance rejection measure for limit cycle walkers: the gait sensitivity norm. IEEE Trans. **23**(6), 1213–1224 (2007)
6. Jiao, J., Zhao, M., Mu, C.: Rimless wheel with asymmetric flat feet. In: IEEE International Conference on Robotics and Biomimetics, pp. 288–293 (2010)
7. Smyrli, A., Ghiassi, M., Kecskeméthy, A., Papadopoulos, E.: On the effect of semielliptical foot shape on the energetic efficiency of passive bipedal gait*. In: IEEE/RSJ International Conference on Intelligent Robots and Systems, pp. 6302–6307 (2019)

8. Asano, F.: Simulation and experimental studies on passive-dynamic walker that consists of two identical crossed frames. In: IEEE International Conference on Robotics and Automation, pp. 1703–1708 (2010)
9. Asano, F., Kawamoto, J.: Passive dynamic walking of viscoelastic-legged rimless wheel. In: IEEE International Conference on Robotics and Automation, pp. 2331–2336 (2012)
10. Asano, F.: Underactuated rimless wheel with small passive rollers aiming at verification experiment for sliding limit cycle walking. In: IEEE/RSJ International Conference on Intelligent Robots and Systems, pp. 6312–6317 (2015)
11. Asano, F., Nakamura, R., Wu, M., Seino, T., Zheng, Y.: Modeling and control of underactuated rimless wheel for walking over quagmire. In: Australian Control Conference, pp. 364–369 (2016)
12. Asano, F., Kikuchi, Y., Xiao, X.: Control of underactuated rimless wheel that walks on steep slope. In: IEEE/RSJ International Conference on Intelligent Robots and Systems, pp. 335–340 (2017)
13. Rasouli, F., Naraghi, M., Safa, A.T.: Asymmetric gait analysis based on passive dynamic walking theory. In: 4th International Conference on Robotics and Mechatronics, pp. 361–366 (2016)
14. Znegui, W., Gritli, H., Belghith, S.: An explicit analytical expression of the poincaré map for analyzing passive dynamic walking of the compass-gait biped model. In: International Conference on Advanced Systems and Emergent Technologies, pp.388–394 (2019)
15. Vargas, A.M., González-Hernández, H.G.: Dynamic passive biped robot simulation based on virtual gravity using Matlab®. In: 23rd International Conference on Electronics, Communications and Computing, pp. 207–211 (2013)
16. Mizani, A., Bejnordi, V.E., Safa, A.T., Naraghi, M.: From passive dynamic walking to ankle push-off actuation: an MSC ADAMS approach to design. In: 6th RSI International Conference on Robotics and Mechatronics, pp. 400–405 (2018)
17. Suzuki, K., Naruse, K.: Robustness of semi-passive dynamic walking models for steep slopes. In: 3rd International Conference on Awareness Science and Technology, pp. 303–308 (2011)
18. Moon, J., Spong, M.W.: Energy plane analysis for passive dynamic walking. In: IEEE-RAS International Conference on Humanoid Robots, pp. 580–585 (2012)
19. Bhounsule, P.A., Ameperosa, E., Miller, S., Seay, K., Ulep, R.: Dead-beat control of walking for a torso-actuated rimless wheel using an event-based, discrete, linear controller. In: Proceedings of the 40th Mechanisms and Robotics Conference, ASME (2016)
20. Robotics Unlimited: Meet outrunner: The world's first remotely controlled running robot. https://youtu.be/LTIpdtv_AK8. Accessed 2015
21. Osuka, K., Fujitani, T., Ono, T.: Passive walking robot quartet. In: IEEE International Conference on Control Applications, pp. 478–483 (1999)
22. Jeans, J.B., Hong, D.: IMPASS: intelligent mobility platform with active spoke system. In: IEEE International Conference on Robotics and Automation, pp. 1605–1606 (2009)
23. Delcomyn, F.: Neural basis of rhythmic behavior in animals. Am. Assoc. Adv. Sci. **210**(4469), 492–498 (1980)
24. Zhang, Q., Jia, W., Pu, H., Li, L.: The analysis and control method about the stop motion of symmetric planar rimless wheel on slope. In: IEEE International Conference on Robotics and Biomimetics, pp. 434–439 (2015)
25. Jia, W., et al.: Modelling and analysis of the passive planar rimless wheel mechanism in universal domain. In: IEEE/RSJ International Conference on Intelligent Robots and Systems, pp. 4969–4975 (2017)

MF-SLAM: Multi-focal SLAM

Mingchi Feng[✉], Jinglin Liu, Xin Wang, and Chengnan Li

School of Advanced Manufacturing Engineering, Chongqing University of Posts and
Telecommunications, Chongqing 400065, China
fengmc@cqupt.edu.cn

Abstract. SLAM has achieved excellent achievement in the development of the
past two decades and it has been extensively developed in robotics communities.
The present binocular SLAM is based on the standard binocular camera to obtain
images, and they have good positioning accuracy. However, it is necessary to
detect and locate objects in the scene. In this article, we propose MF-SLAM
that combines two different focal lengths into binocular vision, which overcome
the shortcoming that standard binocular cameras cannot detect objects on long
distance. Specifically, we improve the OpenCV stereo correction method and use
stereo correction parameters to correct just ORB feature points, not to correct
stereo images. Because of the difference of multi-focal length visual field, we also
propose a feature extraction method that increases the same field of view and a
feature matching method for multi-focal binocular camera to increase the number
of feature matching. Experiments on the KITTI dataset show compatibility of
MF-SLAM, and the RMSE of MF-SLAM decreases 5.17%. In our dataset, the
RMSE of MF-SLAM is 18.58% lower than ORB-SLAM3, and the experimental
results proved the accuracy of MF-SLAM.

Keywords: Visual SLAM · Stereo SLAM · Multi-focal stereo · Stereo
Calibration

1 Introduction

Simultaneous localization and mapping (SLAM) has been a research hotspot in the field
of computer vision and robotics in the past two decades [1]. It has been extensively
developed in universities and robotics communities around the world, many excellent
SLAM systems have appeared in this field, such as MonoSLAM [2], S-PTAM [3],
ORB-SLAM [4–6], LSD-SLAM [7], SVO [8], DSO [9]. These systems use single or
binocular cameras to obtain satisfactory performance, but only using a single camera is
unobservable. The binocular camera uses the parallax to calculate the depth of the scene
and obtain the true map scale. The existing stereo vision frameworks include ProSLAM
[10], ORB-SLAM and OpenVSLAM [11]. They are all typical open-source indirect
VSLAM frameworks with different functional applications and excellent performance.

ProSLAM (Programmers SLAM) is a simple stereo vision framework that uses stereo
images as the sole input of the system and four-loop modules: Triangulation, Incremental

© Springer Nature Switzerland AG 2021
X.-J. Liu et al. (Eds.): ICIRA 2021, LNAI 13015, pp. 494–502, 2021.
https://doi.org/10.1007/978-3-030-89134-3_45

Motion Estimation, Map Management, and Relocalization. It can execute the framework in a single thread to avoid the complexity of multi-thread synchronization.

ORB-SLAM2 is an open-source complete indirect VSLAM framework for monocular, stereo and RGB-D cameras. ORB-SLAM2 has three main parallel threads: tracking, local mapping and loop closing, and then the global BA thread as a global optimization. ORB-SLAM3 is an improvement over ORB-SLAM2 with the addition of multiple map threads, and added multiple map threads in it. When the visual tracking is lost, it will start a new map. When the area is remapped, it will seamlessly merge with the previous map.

Sumikura et al. [11]. proposed a high usable and extensible visual SLAM framework, OpenVSLAM. It is appropriately designed as open-source callable libraries from third-party programs. OpenVSLAM is compatible with various types of cameras, even with fisheye and equirectangular cameras. Besides, the built maps can be stored and loaded for future localization applications with interfaces that are provided for convenience.

These binocular vision frames are based on the same focal length combination, and their advantage is that it can obtain rich close-range environment information. As shown in Fig. 1, the picture on the left is an image taken by a camera with a focal length of 12.5 mm, and the picture on the right is an image taken by a camera with a focal length of 16 mm. We can see that the distant target can be detected in the 16 mm focal length image, it will fail in the 12.5 mm focal length image. They are all used YOLOv3 [12] to detect. To improve the detection accuracy of distant objects in the car driving scene, one solution is to use two long focal cameras to form stereo vision, but it is not conducive to visual positioning and mapping. Another solution is to add a third camera as a long focal camera, but this kind of scheme increases the cost. Therefore, we propose a multi-focal binocular vision SLAM, which can be combined into stereo vision by two cameras with different focal lengths and it can obtain robust positioning.

Fig. 1. Detection results of YOLOv3 network (Left: 12.5 mm focal camera. Right: 16 mm focal camera)

2   MF-SLAM

As shown in the left figure of Fig. 2, the left image is a standard binocular ranging principle, which can determine the depth of the point P in space, so the spatial position of the point P can be calculated. The binocular cameras are placed horizontally on the left and right, and the optical centers of the two cameras are on the x axis. o_L, o_R stand for left and right camera aperture center, f stands for focal length, u_L, u_R stand for pixel coordinates of the imaging plane, b is the baseline of the binocular camera. The pixel coordinates of the point P in the imaging plane of the left camera is P_L, the right camera is P_R. The two imaging positions of the spatial point P are different, so the disparity is written as $d = u_L - u_R$. According to the similar triangle relationship between $\triangle PP_LP_R$ and $\triangle PO_LO_R$, the depth $z = fb/d$ of point P can be determined.

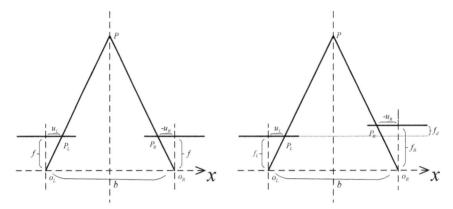

Fig. 2. Principle of Binocular Ranging (Left: Standard binocular distance measurement. Right: Multi-focal distance measurement principle)

The parallax calculation of multi-focal binocular cameras is different from that of a standard binocular camera. As shown in the right figure of Fig. 2, f_L stands for the focal length of the left camera, and f_R stands for the focal length of the right camera, but the focal lengths of f_L and f_R are not equal. Therefore, the same parallax formula $d = u_L - u_R$ cannot be used to calculate the depth z of the feature point.

2.1 Improved Calibration of the Multi-focal Stereo Camera

Based on the standard OpenCV dual-target calibration procedure, we propose an improved OpenCV calibration method for multi-focal cameras in SLAM systems, which can calibrate multi-focal combined binocular cameras. This calibration result will be used in MF-SLAM.

We also use the OpenCV single-camera calibration program to calibrate the intrinsic parameters K_l, K_r and distortion coefficient D_l, D_r, which in the left image and the right image, as shown in Eq. 1 and Eq. 2. For reference, ORB-SLAM3 uses the left camera as the main tracking image frame strategy. The left camera uses a short focal camera, and the right camera uses a long focal camera, so $f_{xl} < f_{xr}, f_{yl} < f_{yr}$.

$$K_l = \begin{Bmatrix} f_{xl} & 0 & c_{xl} \\ 0 & f_{yl} & c_{yl} \\ 0 & 0 & 1 \end{Bmatrix} \quad K_r = \begin{Bmatrix} f_{xr} & 0 & c_{xr} \\ 0 & f_{yr} & c_{yr} \\ 0 & 0 & 1 \end{Bmatrix}, \tag{1}$$

$$P_l = \begin{Bmatrix} f_x & 0 & c_x & 0 \\ 0 & f_y & c_y & 0 \\ 0 & 0 & 1 & 0 \end{Bmatrix} P_r = \begin{Bmatrix} f_x & 0 & c_x & bf_x \\ 0 & f_y & c_y & 0 \\ 0 & 0 & 1 & 0 \end{Bmatrix}, \tag{2}$$

In order to obtain the projection matrices P_l and P_r of the stereo calibration camera, its parameters are written as:

$$f_x = f_{xl} \tag{3}$$

$$c_x = (c_{xl} + c_{xr})/2 \tag{4}$$

$$c_y = (c_{yl} + c_{yr})/2 \tag{5}$$

Where f_x, f_y stand for the focal length of the camera, c_x, c_y stand for the optical center for the camera, b is the baseline distance of the binocular camera. We use the combination of 12.5 mm focal camera and 16 mm focal camera to form binocular vision, and use the improved stereo calibration algorithm to obtain the projection matrix P_l and P_r, which is:

$$P_l = \begin{bmatrix} 1.21641e+03 & 0 & 6.00788e+02 & 0 \\ 0 & 1.21641e+03 & 4.69419e+02 & 0 \\ 0 & 0 & 1 & 0 \end{bmatrix} \tag{6}$$

$$P_r = \begin{bmatrix} 1.21641e+03 & 0 & 6.00788e+02 & -5.63120e+02 \\ 0 & 1.21641e+03 & 4.69419e+02 & 0 \\ 0 & 0 & 1 & 0 \end{bmatrix} \tag{7}$$

2.2 Extract Feature Points

The feature points with depth information will be used for tracking, so the number of extracted feature points is increased in the ROI which located on each layer of the image pyramid of the left image, and the number of feature points extracted outside the ROI is reduced. Set the number of feature points needed to be extracted from the layer α of the left image to be extracted as N_α. The number of feature points in the ROI is increased without increasing the total number of feature points, the formula can be written as:

$$N'_\alpha = \left(N_\alpha \frac{s^2_{roi}}{s^2_{img}} (1+p) \right)_{inner} + \left(N_\alpha \left(1 - \frac{s^2_{roi}}{s^2_{img}} \right)(1-p) \right)_{outer} \tag{8}$$

$$N_\alpha = \frac{N\{1-s\}}{\{1 - s^{n-L_{dis}+1}\}} s^\alpha \tag{9}$$

Where $N'_\alpha = N_\alpha$, s^2_{img} stands for the area of the entire image, s^2_{roi} represents the area within the ROI, p represents the percentage to increase the number of points extracted. We take p as 0.4 in MF-SLAM. By improving the image pyramid feature point extraction strategy and increasing the feature points in the ROI, the number of stereo matching can be effectively increased, so that the MF-SLAM is more robust.

2.3 Stereo Matching

The image features with different focal lengths are different. The matched feature points are not within the same line range, which in the left image and the right image. Therefore, the line matching stereo feature points cannot be used directly. MF-SLAM stereo matching feature points use the calibration parameters obtained by the improved calibration method to stereo correct the multi-focal distance binocular feature points. The advantage of this method is that it does not correct the image distortion, instead corrects the distortion of the feature points extracted from the image, and then uses the epipolar matching the stereo feature point method to match feature points. Another advantage is that it can increase the speed of stereo matching. Besides, image block matching is used in stereo matching to improve the accuracy of feature point matching. This image block matching method needs to obtain image gray information. Since MF-SLAM only performs stereo correction on the feature points, the obtained image block still uses the position image area before the feature point stereo correction.

3 Experiments and Discussion

We evaluated MF-SLAM in the KITTI dataset [13] and our multi-focal dataset and compared them with ORB-SLAM3. All experiments are performed on a computer with Intel i7-8700 CPU, NVIDIA GeForce RTX 2060, and 16G memory. In order to account for the non-deterministic nature of the multithreading system, we run each sequence five times and show median results for the accuracy of the estimated trajectory.

3.1 KITTI Dataset

The KITTI dataset contains stereo sequences recorded from a car in urban and highway environments. The stereo sensor has a ∼54-cm baseline and works at 10 Hz with a resolution after rectification of 1240 * 376 pixels, and the number of extracted feature points is 2000. Table 1 shows results in the 11 training sequences, with ground truth compared to the Stereo ORB-SLAM3. We use two indicators for evaluation, one is mean tracking time and the other is root-mean-square error (RMSE), and we also record the time when NCC obtains the ROI corner point, which is processed once at the beginning of the system. The mean tracking time of MF-SLAM is 5.56% longer than ORB-SLAM, but RMSE is reduced 5.17%. What's more, it shows that MF-SLAM is also capable of the same focal length binocular, and has good accuracy. Figure 3 shows the comparison between MF-SLAM trajectory and ground truth.

3.2 Our Dataset

Because the existing public data does not have a multi-focal length binocular image dataset, we collected a multi-focal length binocular image dataset. We use three cameras with a 10 Hz trigger signal to collect at the same time. Figure 4 shows the layout of our cameras, and Fig. 5 shows images of our dataset. Cam0 and Cam1 cameras are 12.5 mm lenses, Cam2 is 16 mm lenses, and the stereo sensor has a ∼45-cm or a ∼90-cm

Table 1. Comparison of accuracy in the KITTI dataset.

| Sequence | ORB-SLAM3 | | MF-SLAM | | |
	Mean Tracking Time (s)	RMSE (m)	NCC Time (ms)	Mean Tracking Time (s)	RMSE (m)
00	0.065154	1.259229	0.470224	0.070750	1.042626
01	0.086784	10.15592	0.582408	0.087613	8.664446
02	0.065327	4.588812	0.564447	0.069680	4.067885
03	0.067732	1.332730	0.776397	0.070011	1.206471
04	0.067519	0.211317	0.611926	0.071245	0.596054
05	0.066091	0.855843	0.553984	0.071692	1.151716
06	0.073282	0.677790	0.567520	0.077142	1.189313
07	0.062962	0.503142	0.340521	0.067142	0.480690
08	0.061791	3.858526	0.460573	0.066761	3.186968
09	0.061563	1.967049	0.405772	0.065148	2.343033
10	0.060442	1.097377	0.555654	0.062532	1.207852
Mean	0.067150	2.409794	0.535402	0.0708837	2.285186

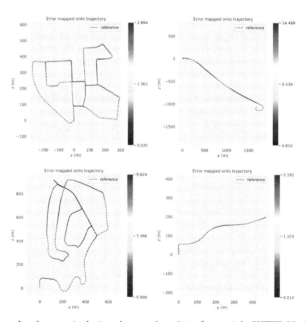

Fig. 3. Estimated trajectory (color) and ground truth (reference) in KITTI 00, 01,02, and 03.

baseline and provides gray images at 10 Hz. Besides, all image sizes are 1218 * 962. We use a satellite positioning measurement system with a GPS/IMU system with RTK to simultaneously record the longitude and latitude information at 10 Hz as ground truth for SLAM evaluation accuracy.

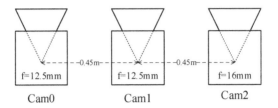

Fig. 4. Camera layout (The baseline distance between Cam0 and Cam1 is about 0.45 m, the baseline distance between Cam1 and Cam2 is about 0.45 m, and the three cameras are arranged horizontally).

Fig. 5. Images of our dataset (Left: image of Cam0. Center: image of Cam1. Right: image of Cam2).

Table 2. Comparison of accuracy in our dataset (Cam1&Cam2).

	ORB-SLAM3 (Cam0&Cam1)		MF-SLAM (Cam1&Cam2)		
	Mean Tracking Time (s)	RMSE (m)	NCC Time (s)	Mean Tracking Time (s)	RMSE (m)
Sq00	0.104145	1.960408	3.10020	0.0999838	1.254723
Sq01	0.109128	3.976883	3.08743	0.1056800	3.579467

We collected two sets of data sets with different lengths. There are 1353 images in Sq00, 503.072 m long, and 2667 images in Sq01, 1372.931m long. The extracted feature points are the same 2000. Table 2 and Table 3 show the experimental results of MF and ORB-SLAM3 in our dataset. The results of the combined experiment of Cam1 and Cam2 are shown in Table 2, where the baseline distance between the cameras is about 45 cm, and the results of the combined experiment of Cam0 and Cam2 are shown in Table 3, where the baseline distance between the cameras is about 90 cm. Figure 6 shows the comparison between MF-SLAM trajectory and ground truth.

Table 3. Comparison of accuracy in our dataset (Cam0&Cam2).

	ORB-SLAM3 (Cam0&Cam1)		MF-SLAM (Cam0&Cam2)		
	Mean Tracking Time (s)	RMSE (m)	NCC Time (s)	Mean Tracking Time (s)	RMSE (m)
Sq00	0.104145	1.960408	3.06102	0.0937426	1.086545
Sq01	0.109128	3.976883	3.07062	0.0967661	2.063896

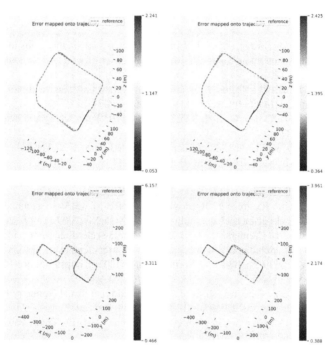

Fig. 6. Estimated trajectory (color) and ground truth (reference) in our dataset 00 and 01 (Left: Cam1&Cam2. Right: Cam0&Cam2).

4 Conclusions

In this paper, we propose a multi-focal length combination of binocular vision SLAM, which can be combined with different focal cameras to complete localization and mapping, and we also support standard binocular cameras with better accuracy. The improved method based on OpenCV stereo calibration is used to calibrate multi-focal camera, and the obtained camera parameters are used for MF-SLAM stereo correction of feature points. The feature positions obtained by the improved stereo matching method are used for tracking. It has the same robustness and accuracy as ORB-SLAM3 with the same focal binocular camera. Besides, MF-SLAM can obtain more in-depth scene information with the same field of view. What's more, its positioning accuracy is more accurate than ORB-SLAM3.

Acknowledgment. This work was supported by the Chongqing Science and Technology Bureau (cstc2019jscx-zdztzxX0050), the National Natural Science Foundation of China (51505054).

References

1. Wang, F.R., Lu, E.L., Wang, Y., et al.: Efficient stereo visual simultaneous localization and mapping for an autonomous unmanned forklift in an unstructured warehouse. Appl. Sci. **10**(2), 2292–2295 (2016)
2. Davison, A.J., Reid, I.D., Molton, N.D.: MonoSLAM: real-time single camera SLAM. IEEE Trans. Pattern Anal. Mach. Intell. **29**(6), 1052–1067 (2007)
3. Pire, T., Fischer, T., Castro, G, et al. S-PTAM: stereo parallel tracking and mapping. Robot. Auton. Syst. **93**, 27–42 (2017)
4. Mur-Artal, R., Montiel, J.M.M., Tardos, J.D.: ORB-SLAM: a Versatile and accurate monocular SLAM system IEEE Trans. Robot. **31**, 1147–1163 (2015)
5. Mur-Artal, R., Tardos, J.D.: ORB-SLAM2: an open-source SLAM system for monocular, stereo and RGB-D Cameras. IEEE Trans. Robot. 33, 1255–1262 (2017)
6. Campos, C.., Elvira, R., Juan, J., Rrodríguez, G.: ORB-SLAM3: an accurate open-source library for visual, visual-inertial and multi-map SLAM. arXiv:2007.1189-8 (2020)
7. Engel, J., Schöps, T., Cremers, D.: LSD-SLAM: Large-scale direct monocular SLAM. In: Fleet, D., Pajdla, T., Schiele, B., Tuytelaars, T. (eds.) Computer Vision – ECCV 2014. ECCV 2014, LNCS, vol. 8690, pp. 834–849. Springer, Cham (2014). https://doi.org/10.1007/978-3-319-10605-2_54
8. Forster, C., Zhang, Z., Gassner, M., et al.: SVO: Semidirect visual odometry for monocular and multicamera systems. IEEE Trans. Robot. **33**, 249–265 (2017)
9. Engel, J., Koltun, V., Cremers, D.: Direct sparse odometry. IEEE Trans. Patt. Anal. Mach. Intell. J. **40**, 611–625 (2017)
10. Schlegel, D., Colosi, M., Grisetti, G.: ProSLAM: graph SLAM from a programmer's perspective. In: 2018 IEEE International Conference on Robotics and Automation (ICRA), Brisbane, QLD, Australia, 21–25 May 2018, pp. 3833–3840. IEEE, Brisbane (2018)
11. Sumikura, S., Shibuya, M., Sakurada, K.: OpenVSLAM: a versatile visual SLAM framework. In: Proceedings of the 27th Acm International Conference on Multimedia, 21–25 October 2019, pp. 2292–2295. Assoc Computing Machinery, New York (2019)
12. Redmon, J., Farhadi, A.: YOLOv3: An Incremental Improvement. arXiv:1804.02767 (2018)
13. Geiger, A., Lenz, P., Stiller, C., et al.: Vision meets robotics: the KITTI dataset. Int. J. Robot. Res. **32**(11), 1231–1237 (2013)

Neural Network-Based Method for Solving Inverse Kinematics of Hyper-redundant Cable-Driven Manipulators

Chi Zhang[1] and Jianqing Peng[1,2(✉)]

[1] Sun Yat-Sen University, Shenzhen 518107, China
pengjq7@mail.sysu.edu.cn
[2] Guangdong Provincial Key Laboratory of Fire Science and Technology,
Guangzhou 510006, China

Abstract. Compared with traditional manipulator (TM), hyper-redundant cable-driven manipulators (HRCDMs) has superior performance, especially its great bendability and flexibility, which can avoid obstacles in narrow and confined workspaces. However, as the degrees of freedom (DOFs) increase, inverse kinematics (IK) of the HRCDM becomes more challenging. The traditional method consists of two steps: from operational space (OS) to joint space (JS) and from JS to cable-driven space (CDS). It is particularly time-consuming to solve joint angle based on Jacobian iteratively, and it is of great difficulty to meet the real-time requirement of HRCDM operations. Besides, it is not easy to obtain cable lengths and pulling forces of HRCDMs. Based on this, this paper proposes two inverse kinematics solving methods based on neural network (NN) modeling, which incorporates the feedback information of joint angles. These methods do not need to calculate the intermediate variable of joint angle, but directly establishes BPNN and RBFNN from pose to cable length, which improves the convenience of modeling and computation efficiency. Finally, a tracking experiment of three different trajectories is designed on an HRCDM with 12-DOFs. In terms of trajectory tracking error and computational efficiency, the presented BPNN and RBFNN modeling methods are compared with the traditional Jacobian-based iterative approach. Simulation results show that, in the case of comparable end-effector tracking accuracy, the computational efficiency of the NN-based method is significantly higher than that of the traditional approach, and RBFNN is better than BPNN in performance.

Keywords: Cable-driven robots · Inverse kinematics · BPNN · RBFNN

1 Introduction

With the deepening application of robotics in complex scenarios such as space stations [1], medical assistance [2], disaster rescue [3], underwater detection [4] or other fields, higher performance is required for robots. Because of the limitation of low DOFs, TM is poor at obstacle avoidance in confined workspaces [5]. Benefiting from multiple DOFs

© Springer Nature Switzerland AG 2021
X.-J. Liu et al. (Eds.): ICIRA 2021, LNAI 13015, pp. 503–514, 2021.
https://doi.org/10.1007/978-3-030-89134-3_46

and unique mechanical structure (i.e.: slender body and electromechanical separation), the HRCDM is suitable for the above environment [6].

Kinematic analysis lays the foundation for trajectory planning, control [7, 8] and so on. The methods of forward kinematics (FK) modeling of redundant manipulator (RM) have attracted great attention of many researchers. Liu *et al.* [9, 10] adopted D-H modeling method to establish FK model for HRCDMs, which is the most classic modeling method for discrete model. Li *et al.* [11] used POE-based method, which applies the concept of motion screw to establish kinematics model (KM). The constant curvature modeling approach, which fits snake-like manipulator [12, 13], essentially discretizes continuous manipulator into finite sections and then uses Frenet-Serret method [14] to deduces the coordinate transformation matrix.

RM has excellent performance because of increasing DOFs; however, the difficulty of IK also intensifies. Jacobian-based iterative method, which is a general approach for RM [15–17], requires complicated calculations to obtain the pseudo-inverse of the Jacobian matrix (JM), whose increasing dimensionality greatly slow down the calculation speed. Kolpashchikov *et al.* applied geometry-based method and FABRIK algorithm [18], and Zhang *et al.* introduced heuristic iteration [19]. Actually, IK of RM is a nonlinear problem, and NN has a solid ability to fit nonlinear functions. NN have been proven to provide high computational efficiency and great fitting effects in IK of TM [20–23]. However, TM is driven by actuators on each joint, while HRCDM is indirectly driven by cables, which are pulled by actuators on the base. The IK output of the former is joint angle, but the latter is cable length. In addition, it is difficult to measure lengths and tension forces of cables on HRCDM. However, it is a feasible approach to measure the joint angle by installing encoders at each modular joint (MJ). Therefore, two NN-based methods for solving IK of HRCDM is proposed, which combines the feedback information of joint encoders, the traditional two-layer calculation model is simplified and the computation efficiency is improved.

The remaining sections are organized as follows: Sect. 2 establishes the traditional KM of the HRCDM. Section 3 proposes the BPNN-based and RBFNN-based IK solving methods of the HRCDM, which establish the mapping from the pose to cable lengths. Section 4 sets up a comparative simulation experiment to verify above models. The last section gives a conclusion and future research directions.

2   Traditional Kinematics Modeling Method of HRCDM

In this paper, the HRCDM is connected by M MJs, each of which has two orthogonal DOFs (yaw and pitch) and is driven by three cables. For HRCDM, KM needs to be analyzed in two parts: one is between JS and OS, another is between CDS and JS.

2.1   Kinematics Analysis Between JS and OS

As shown in Fig. 1, the HRCDM are connected by MJs, and the KM between the joint and the end-effector is similar to that of TM. Therefore, the kinematics analysis of TM can be applied in this part. D-H method is generally applied to build FK model. In general,

Jacobian-based iterative method is used to calculate joint angles from the end-effector pose:

$$T_e = \text{fkine}(\theta_1, \theta_2, \cdots, \theta_{2M-1}, \theta_{2M}) \tag{1}$$

where, fkine() represents FK equation of the HRCDM.

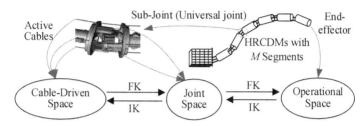

Fig. 1. Schematic diagram of traditional two-layer kinematics conversion modeling

2.2 Kinematics Analysis Between CDS and JS

The mth ($m = 1, 2,..., M$) MJ is controlled by its corresponding three cables (cable lengths are respectively denoted as $l_{m,3m-2}$, $l_{m,3m-1}$ and $l_{m,3m}$), and three cable lengths are described as:

$$\begin{cases} l_{m,3m-2} = f_{m,3m-2}(\theta_{2m-1}, \theta_{2m}) \\ l_{m,3m-1} = f_{m,3m-1}(\theta_{2m-1}, \theta_{2m}) \\ l_{m,3m} = f_{m,3m}(\theta_{2m-1}, \theta_{2m}) \end{cases} \tag{2}$$

where, $f_{m,k}(\theta_{2m-1}, \theta_{2m})$ represents mapping relationship from two joint angles (θ_{2m-1} and θ_{2m}) corresponding to the MJ to cable length $l_{m,k}$ of the kth ($k = 1, 2, ..., 3M$) cable.

Since the system is close-coupled and nonlinear, it is extremely difficult to get a solution numerically. Jacobian-based iteration is one of the effective methods for obtaining joint angles. JM of the above equations can be expressed as:

$$J_{\text{L}} = \begin{bmatrix} \frac{\partial f_{m,3m-2}}{\partial \theta_{2m-1}} & \frac{\partial f_{m,3m-1}}{\partial \theta_{2m-1}} & \frac{\partial f_{m,3m}}{\partial \theta_{2m-1}} \\ \frac{\partial f_{m,3m-2}}{\partial \theta_{2m}} & \frac{\partial f_{m,3m-1}}{\partial \theta_{2m}} & \frac{\partial f_{m,3m}}{\partial \theta_{2m}} \end{bmatrix}^{\text{T}} \tag{3}$$

Therefore, function between cable length deviation and joint angle deviation can be expressed as:

$$\begin{bmatrix} d\theta_{2m-1} \\ d\theta_{2m} \end{bmatrix} = J_{\text{L}}^{+} \begin{bmatrix} dl_{m,3m-2} & dl_{m,3m-1} & dl_{m,3m} \end{bmatrix}^{\text{T}} \tag{4}$$

where, J_L^{+} donates the pseudo-inverse of JM (i.e.: J_L). Thus, the numerical iteration can be used to obtain the optimal joint angles.

3   NN-Based IK Method for HRCDM

The HRCDM is driven by cables, the NN for the TM (network output is joint angle) cannot directly apply to the IK problem of the HRCDM. It is necessary to establish an optimized NN structure suitable for the HRCDM. Though cable lengths and tensile forces of the HRCDM are difficult to measure, joint angles can be obtained through encoders at each MJ and then inputted into the NN to improve the accuracy. Here, the overall structure of the optimized NN is proposed: the input is the acquired joint angle θ and the desired end-effector pose p, while the output is the cable length.

3.1   BPNN-Based Method

The BPNN is a sample training-based network, which has a solid ability to fit the nonlinear function. As shown in Fig. 2, the designed BPNN has two parts of input: the desired end-effector pose p represented by 12 variables (the first three rows of pose transformation matrix T_e) and $2M$ feedback variables. The output layer is linear, containing $3M$ nodes (correspond to $3M$ cable lengths). The number of hidden layers and nodes in each layer are designed according to the number of MJs of the HRCDM.

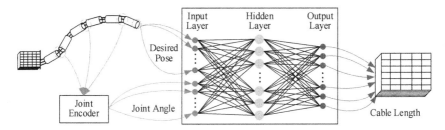

Fig. 2. The NN structure considering feedback from joint encoders

The tansig function, which is a non-linear function, is selected as the activation function of hidden layers. The input-output function of the kth node is described as:

$$y_k = \sum_{i=1}^{n} w_{i,k} x_i + b_k \tag{5}$$

$$f(y_k) = \frac{2}{1 + e^{-2y_k}} - 1 \tag{6}$$

where, n is the number of nodes of the previous layer; x_i represents ith output of the previous layer; $x_{i,k}$ represents weight of connection between ith node of the previous layer and kth node, while b_k represents bias.

In addition, the mean square error (MSE) is used to measure fitting effect of BPNN, namely:

$$MSE = \frac{1}{S} \sum_{j=1}^{S} \left\| (l_j - \hat{l}_j) \right\|^2 \tag{7}$$

where, S is the number of samples; l represents the cable length, which is the output of BPNN; $\hat{l}_j$ represents the actual cable length.

3.2 RBFNN-Based Method

The RBFNN not only has the ability of non-linear fitting as BPNN, but also has more advantages in convergence speed than the latter, and it is easier to obtain the global optimal solution. The RBFNN has stronger ability of IK modeling for HRCDM with complex parameters.

The overall architecture of RBFNN is similar to BPNN (see Fig. 2), which also consists of $2M + 12$ input nodes, including desired end-effector pose and joint angle feedback, and $3M$ output nodes. The advantage of RBFNN for solving IK problem is mainly reflected in the setting of hidden layer. The Gaussian function is selected as activation function, and the function between input y_k and output of the kth node is described as:

$$f(y_k) = \exp(-\frac{1}{2\sigma_k^2}\|y_k - c_k\|^2) \tag{8}$$

where, c_k and σ_k respectively represent center and variance of activation function. Unlike BPNN, training RBFNN needs to update not only the weight and bias of each layer, but also c_k and σ_k.

4 Simulation

The simulation was based on an HRCDM with six MJs (12-DOFs). The length of each link is 90 mm. The distance of two disks in each MJ is 25 mm in the initial state. The distribute diameter of cables in each disk is 50 mm.

The KM established in Sect. 2 is used to generate dataset. Then, build and train BPNN and RBFNN described in Sect. 3. The trained models can be also applied in the real scene. Finally, two trained NN are used to solve IK problem of three trajectories (circle, triangle, and square), and FK analysis method introduced in Sect. 2 is applied to verify.

4.1 Circle Trajectory

The equation of the designed circle trajectory is described as (the unit is mm): $x = 450$ and $y^2 + z^2 = 150^2$. The start point of the circle trajectory is (450, 0, 150) mm.

The BPNN and the RBFNN are respectively applied to solve the IK of the generated expected trajectory. The cable lengths predicted by the NN is substituted into the mathematical model to obtain each T_e of the actual trajectory. The attitude disturbance is used to measure the attitude error:

$$\delta C = R_{actual}^{T} \cdot R_{ed} \tag{9}$$

where, R_{actual} represents the actual rotation matrix of the end-effector, while R_{ed} represents the desired rotation matrix. Furthermore, the attitude disturbance is converted into the three-axis rotation angle error:

$$\delta o = \frac{1}{2} \begin{bmatrix} \delta C(2, 3) - \delta C(3, 2) \\ \delta C(3, 1) - \delta C(1, 3) \\ \delta C(1, 2) - \delta C(2, 1) \end{bmatrix} \tag{10}$$

Based on the initial condition of the circle trajectory and simulation results, absolute errors (AEs) of 18 cable lengths are shown in Fig. 3. The AE curves in attitude of the circle trajectory are shown in Fig. 4. Actual and desired trajectories are shown in Fig. 5. Three-axis AEs are used to measure position error, and the deviation is shown in Fig. 6.

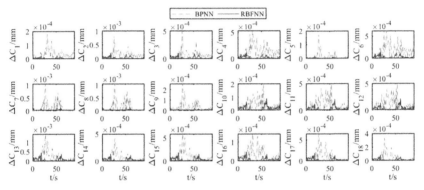

Fig. 3. The cable length error of circle trajectory

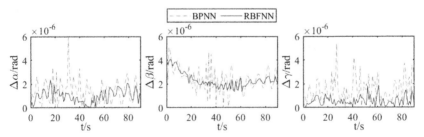

Fig. 4. The attitude error of circle trajectory

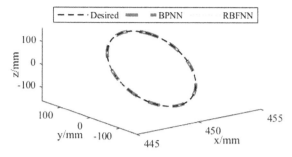

Fig. 5. The desired and actual circle trajectory

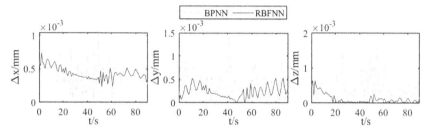

Fig. 6. The position error of circle trajectory

4.2 Triangle Trajectory

Three vertices of the designed triangle trajectory are: A (520, 0, 69.28) mm, B (520, 60, −34.64) mm, C (520, −60, −34.64) mm, and the start point is point A. The trained BPNN and RBFNN are respectively used to solve the IK of the generated triangle trajectory.

Based on the initial condition of the triangle trajectory and simulation results, AEs of cable lengths are shown in Fig. 7. AE curves in attitude of the triangle trajectory are shown in Fig. 8. Actual and desired trajectories are shown in Fig. 9. Three-axis AEs in position are shown in Fig. 10.

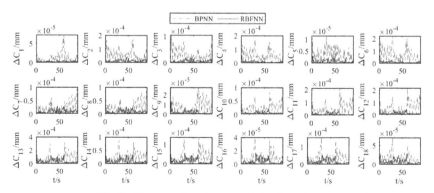

Fig. 7. The cable length error of triangle trajectory

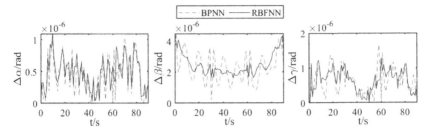

Fig. 8. The attitude error of triangle trajectory

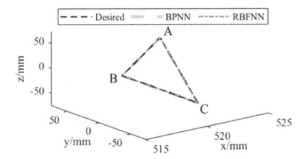

Fig. 9. The desired and actual triangle trajectory

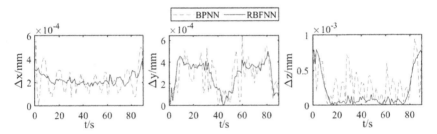

Fig. 10. The position error of triangle trajectory

4.3 Square Trajectory

Four vertices of the designed square trajectory are: A (480, −40, 40), B (480, 40, 40), C (480, 40, −40), D (480, −40, −40), and the start point is A. Based on the initial condition of the square trajectory and simulation results, AEs of cable lengths are shown in Fig. 11. AE curves in attitude of the square trajectory are shown in Fig. 12. Actual and desired trajectories are shown in Fig. 13. Three-axis AEs in position are shown in Fig. 14.

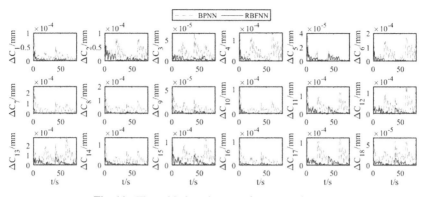

Fig. 11. The cable length error of square trajectory

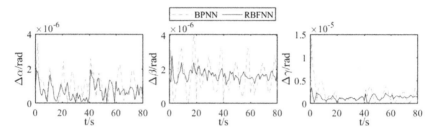

Fig. 12. The attitude error of square trajectory

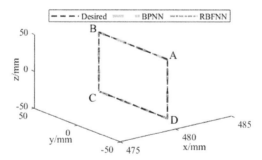

Fig. 13. The desired and actual square trajectory

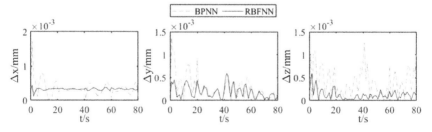

Fig. 14. The position error of triangle trajectory

4.4 Simulation Result

For three trajectories, average absolute error (MAE), root MSE (RMSE) and calculation time of traditional method, BPNN and RBFNN are counted.

$$MAE = \frac{1}{M} \sum_{i=1}^{M} \left| x_i - \hat{x}_i \right| \tag{11}$$

$$RMSE = \sqrt{\frac{1}{M} \sum_{j=1}^{M} (x_i - \hat{x}_i)^2} \tag{12}$$

where, M represents the number of interpolation points of a trajectory; x represents actual value, while $\hat{x}$ represents desired value.

Attitude error ($\sqrt{\Delta\alpha^2 + \Delta\beta^2 + \Delta\gamma^2}$ rad) and position error ($\sqrt{\Delta x^2 + \Delta y^2 + \Delta z^2}$ mm) shown in Table 1, and the calculation time is shown in Table 2.

Table 1. The attitude and position error of three trajectories.

Method		Circle		Triangle		Square	
		Attitude	Position	Attitude	Position	Attitude	Position
Traditional	MAE	2.5718e−6	4.9873e−4	2.6172e−6	4.0000e−4	2.1316e−6	3.5301e−4
	RMSE	2.7053e−6	5.3562e−4	2.7319e−6	4.9204e−4	2.1823e−6	3.6132e−4
RBFNN	MAE	2.5853e−6	5.0675e−4	2.5999e−6	4.0672e−4	2.2145e−6	3.9320e−4
	RMSE	2.7512e−6	5.4975e−4	2.7175e−6	4.9437e−4	2.3437e−6	4.2942e−4
BPNN	MAE	3.1384e−6	7.1100e−4	2.4454e−6	4.6574e−4	2.7150e−6	6.0023e−4
	RMSE	3.6130e−6	8.5221e−4	2.6622e−6	5.5082e−4	3.5448e−6	7.5359e−4

Table 2. The calculation time.

Method	Circle	Triangle	Square
Traditional	36.862	12.694	11.517
BPNN	0.341	0.330	0.325
RBFNN	0.329	0.338	0.327

Comparative analysis indicates that, in the case of comparable end-effector accuracy, the calculation speed of the NN-based method for solving IK is much higher than that of the traditional method. In addition, the fitting effect of RBFNN is better than that of the BPNN in terms of accuracy and stability.

5 Conclusion

With the increasing of DOFs, it is more troublesome to solve IK of the HRCDM, and the traditional Jacobian-based iterative method is difficult to meet the real-time requirement. In this paper, the NN-based modeling method has been proposed, which incorporates feedback variables of joint encoders, simplifies the original two-layer IK conversion operation and improves the computational efficiency. An HRCDM simulation system with 12-DOFs is designed. Through training two NNs (BPNN and RBFNN), the IK simulation of three trajectories is carried out. The computational efficiency of two NN-based methods is much higher. In addition, the fitting effect, accuracy and stability of RBFNN are better than those of BPNN. The analysis results will lay the foundation for future research on NN-based intelligent control.

Acknowledgment. This work was supported by the Key Area Research and Development Program of Guangdong Province (Grant No. 2020B1111010001), the Shenzhen Municipal Basic Research Project for Natural Science Foundation (Grant No. JCYJ20190806143408992), Guangdong Basic and Applied Basic Research Foundation (Grant No. 2019A1515110680), and the Fundamental Research Funds for the Central Universities (Grant No. 2021qntd08), Sun Yat-sen University.

References

1. Weber, B., et al.: Teleoperating robots from the international space station: microgravity effects on performance with force feedback. In: IEEE/RSJ International Conference on Intelligent Robots and Systems (IROS), Macau, China, pp. 8144–8150 (2019)
2. Burgner-Kahrs, J., et al.: Continuum robots for medical applications: a survey. IEEE Trans. Robot. **31**(6), 1261–1280 (2015)
3. Whitman, J., et al.: Snake robot urban search after the 2017 Mexico City earthquake. In: IEEE International Symposium on Safety, Security, and Rescue Robotics (SSRR), Philadelphia, PA, USA, pp. 1–6 (2018)
4. Renda, F., et al.: Dynamic model of a multibending soft robot arm driven by cables. IEEE Trans. Robot. **30**(5), 1109–1122 (2014)
5. Li, J., et al.: Can a continuum manipulator fetch an object in an unknown cluttered space? IEEE Robot. Autom. Lett. **2**(1), 2–9 (2017)
6. Xu, W., et al.: Kinematics, dynamics, and control of a cable-driven hyper-redundant manipulator. IEEE/ASME Trans. Mechatron. **23**(4), 1693–1704 (2018)
7. Peng, J., Xu, W., Yang, T., Hu, Z., Liang, B.: Dynamic modeling and trajectory tracking control method of segmented linkage cable-driven hyper-redundant robot. Nonlinear Dyn. **101**(1), 233–253 (2020). https://doi.org/10.1007/s11071-020-05764-7
8. Peng, J., et al.: End-effector pose and arm shape synchronous planning methods of a hyper-redundant manipulator for spacecraft repairing. Mech. Mach. Theory. **155**, 1–25 (2021)
9. Liu, T., et al.: A cable-driven redundant spatial manipulator with improved stiffness and load capacity. In: IEEE/RSJ International Conference on Intelligent Robots and Systems (IROS), Madrid, Spain, pp. 6628–6633 (2018)
10. Liu, T., et al.: Improved mechanical design and simplified motion planning of hybrid active and passive cable-driven segmented manipulator with coupled motion. In: IEEE/RSJ International Conference on Intelligent Robots and Systems (IROS), Macau, China, pp. 5978–5983 (2019)

11. Li, C., et al.: POE-based robot kinematic calibration using axis configuration space and the adjoint error model. IEEE Trans. Robot. **32**(5), 1264–1279 (2016)

12. Rolf, M., Steil, J.J.: Constant curvature continuum kinematics as fast approximate model for the Bionic Handling Assistant. In: Proceedings of IEEE/RSJ International Conference on Intelligent Robots and Systems, Vilamoura-Algarve, Portugal, pp. 3440–3446 (2012)

13. Hassan, T., et al.: Active-braid, a bioinspired continuum manipulator. IEEE Robot. Autom. Lett. **2**(4), 2104–2110 (2017)

14. Chirikjian, G.S., Burdick, J.W.: Kinematically optimal hyper-redundant manipulator configurations. In: 1992 IEEE International Conference on Robotics and Automation, Nice, France, pp. 415–420 (1992)

15. Colomé, A., Torras, C.: Closed-loop inverse kinematics for redundant robots: comparative assessment and two enhancements. IEEE/ASME Trans. Mechatron. **20**(2), 944–955 (2015)

16. Xu, W., et al.: Singularity analysis and avoidance for robot manipulators with nonspherical wrists. IEEE Trans. Ind. Electron. **63**(1), 277–290 (2016)

17. Liu, T., et al.: A hybrid active and passive cable-driven segmented redundant manipulator: design, kinematics, and planning. IEEE/ASME Trans. Mechatron. **26**(2), 930–942 (2021)

18. Kolpashchikov, D.Y., et al.: FABRIK-based inverse kinematics for multi-section continuum robots. In: The 2018 18th International Conference on Mechatronics - Mechatronika (ME), Brno, Czech Republic, pp. 1–8 (2018)

19. Zhang, W., et al.: FABRIKc: an efficient iterative inverse kinematics solver for continuum robots. In: IEEE/ASME International Conference on Advanced Intelligent Mechatronics (AIM), Auckland, New Zealand, pp. 346–352 (2018)

20. Grassmann, R., et al.: Learning the forward and inverse kinematics of a 6-DOF concentric tube continuum robot in SE(3). In: Proceedings of IEEE/RSJ International Conference on Intelligent Robots and Systems (IROS), Madrid, Spain, pp. 5125–5132 (2018)

21. Sun, C., et al.: Adaptive neural network control of biped robots. IEEE Trans. Syst. Man Cybern. Syst. **47**(2), 315–326 (2017)

22. Li, S., et al.: Kinematic control of redundant manipulators using neural networks. IEEE Trans. Neural Netw. Learn. Syst. **28**(10), 2243–2254 (2017)

23. Peng, J., et al.: A hybrid hand-eye calibration method for multilink cable-driven hyper-redundant manipulators. IEEE Trans. Instrum. Meas. **70**(5010413), 1–13 (2021)

A Thermal Analysis Method for Integrated Joints of Collaborative Robots

Xing Kefan, Gong HaoQin, Chen Diansheng$^{(\boxtimes)}$, Wang Diwen, and Xue Ruilong

Institute of Robotics, Beihang University, Beijing, China
chends@buaa.edu.cn

Abstract. The integrated joint has a broad application prospect in the field of cooperative robots. In this paper, aiming at the problem of joint temperature rising under universal joint rating, a series of research on joint temperature distribution and improvement measures are carried out, and a three-dimensional finite element analysis model of joint based on AnsysWorkbench is established, the steady-state thermal analysis was carried out, and the temperature distribution of the whole joint was obtained. The analysis results show that the temperature of the joint is stable below 50 °C when the rated power of the joint is stable, which indicates that the configuration has good heat dissipation property. In this paper, a method to reduce the joint temperature is proposed based on the simulation model. An integrated joint thermal analysis method for cooperative robots is presented in this paper, which will provide theoretical guidance for the design of integrated joint of cooperative robots.

Keywords: Collaborative robots · Joints · Thermal models

1 Introduction

The integrated joint is an important core component of the collaborative robot, and its characteristics play an important decisive role in the performance of the collaborative robot [1–3]. In recent years, some well-known robot component companies in the world have also introduced integrated joint products, such as the RGM series integrated joints of Kollmorgen of the United States, which is based on frameless torque servo motors, and the world's largest harmonic reducer company, Harmonic Drive Systems Inc. whose SHA series integrated joints, etc. The integrated joint is a direct execution component that realizes various motions, and it is mainly composed of brakes, motors, encoders, harmonic reducers, joint drivers, bearings and other components. Collaborative robot manipulators are affected by the comprehensive effects of the environment in industrial applications. Among the components of the joints, the motors, brakes, harmonic reducers, and joint drives produce relatively large amounts of heat. The modular design ensures that the internal components are compact, but it also leads to problems such as the concentration of heat sources inside the modules and heat dissipation problems.

Due to the requirements of lightweight design, harmonic reducers are generally used for joints, but the transmission efficiency of harmonic reducers is relatively low, and part

© Springer Nature Switzerland AG 2021
X.-J. Liu et al. (Eds.): ICIRA 2021, LNAI 13015, pp. 515–523, 2021.
https://doi.org/10.1007/978-3-030-89134-3_47

of the transferred energy will be lost in the form of heat energy, which will cause the temperature of the joints to rise. In addition, the iron loss and copper loss during the use of the joint motor will also generate a lot of heat, which will cause the temperature of the joint motor to rise, and the increase in temperature affects the stiffness of the joint and the electromagnetic performance of the motor [4]. Therefore, it is particularly important to establish a joint heat dissipation model to analyze the heat dissipation performance of the joint, study the influence of the temperature rise of the joint on the joint performance, and provide a basis for the optimal design of the joint.

2 Cooperative Manipulator Joint Structure and Loss Analysis

As the main drive transmission mechanism of the cooperative manipulator, the joint is a complex mechatronics system composed of a reducer, a motor, a controller, and a sensor. It has the function of outputting speed and torque as required. The joint deceleration mechanism of the collaborative robot generally uses a harmonic reducer. The joints are highly integrated and modularized harmonic deceleration transmission joints, which are mainly composed of harmonic reducers, motor components, joint torque sensors, encoders, and drivers. Affected by the working principle of the joint and the output torque requirement, the internal heat source of the joint consumes a lot of power.

The integrated joint analyzed in this paper uses a 500 W, 3000 r/min hollow motor, and the outer diameter of the motor stator is 80 mm (Fig. 1).

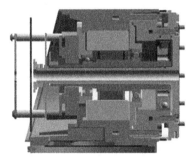

Fig. 1. Integrated joint structure diagram

First of all, to calculate the temperature field of the driving joint module, it is necessary to analyze the heat loss of the joint module. Among them, the harmonic reducer and the motor are the main parts of the loss, and these losses become the heat source of the driving joint module. When the motor is working, there will always be some losses. These losses are unavoidable. The losses are basically dissipated in the form of heat, resulting in the motor temperature will increase, This is the main reason for the increase in the temperature of the whole joint. In the analysis of the temperature field in this paper, the loss is regarded as the heat source driving the joint module. This paper divides the heat loss into three categories, namely mechanical loss, core loss and winding loss. The three types of loss are calculated and analyzed below.

(1) Motor core loss

The loss of the iron core in the motor can be mainly divided into eddy current loss and hysteresis loss [5]. When both appear in the core at the same time, by considering the actual situation, it is not necessary to calculate the two separately. The expression of basic iron loss [6] can be calculated by the following formula:

$$P_F = p_F K_a G_F \tag{1}$$

In the formula: p_F is the loss per unit mass of the iron core; G_F is the weight of the iron core; K_a is the empirical coefficient of the increase in the loss of the silicon steel sheet iron core; p_F can be calculated by the following formula:

$$p_F = p_{10/50} B_t^2 \left(\frac{f}{50}\right)^{1.3} \tag{2}$$

In the formula: $p_{10/50}$ is the loss per unit weight; B_t is the magnetic flux density; f is the alternating frequency of the armature magnetic field, $f = np/60$, n is the motor speed, and p is the number of pole pairs.

(2) Winding copper loss

Copper loss can be calculated according to the basic Joule-Lenz law. The loss of a single-phase winding is equal to the product of the square of the current through the winding and the winding resistance. The working frequency of the motor in this paper is 1 kHz, and the influence of the winding skin effect can be ignored [7]. When the motor has multiple phases, the losses of each winding should be calculated separately and then added, as shown in the following formula:

$$P_c = \Sigma\left(I_x^2 R_x\right) \tag{3}$$

In the formula, I_x—current in the single-phase winding; R_x—winding resistance.

For the motor used in this paper, the rated current resistance of each phase is the same. Assuming that the current is evenly distributed across the section [8], the loss of the m-phase winding can be written as:

$$P_c = mI^2 R \tag{4}$$

(3) Mechanical loss

The mechanical loss of the joint includes the friction loss of the reducer and the air friction loss. Air friction loss is difficult to calculate accurately in most cases and accounts for a relatively small proportion. Therefore, this paper only calculates the friction loss of the reducer.

The friction between the internal components of the harmonic reducer is the root cause of the initial reduction in efficiency. In order to better calculate the loss of the harmonic reducer, the following formula is used in this paper, the calculation of this formula strips the influence of factors other than friction on the transmission efficiency of the reducer [9].

$$\eta = \frac{T_o}{\left(\frac{T_o}{\eta_{teeth}} + T_N\right) \times i} \tag{5}$$

In the formula, T_o: output torque; T_N: no-load running torque; η_{teeth}: meshing efficiency of gear teeth.

3 Theoretical Analysis of Joint Heat Transfer

3.1 Basic Equations of Heat Transfer

The formula for temperature rise analysis is based on the heat conduction equation. According to Fourier's law and the law of conservation of energy, a general differential equation for the temperature inside the object can be obtained [10–13]:

$$\text{div}(\lambda gradT) + q_v = \rho c \frac{\partial T}{\partial \tau} \tag{6}$$

Therefore, for anisotropic media, the thermal conductivity differential equation in the Cartesian coordinate system is:

$$\frac{\partial}{\partial x}\left(\lambda_x \frac{\partial T}{\partial x}\right) + \frac{\partial}{\partial y}\left(\lambda_y \frac{\partial T}{\partial y}\right) + \frac{\partial}{\partial z}\left(\lambda_z \frac{\partial T}{\partial z}\right) + q_v = \rho c \frac{\partial T}{\partial \tau} \tag{7}$$

For the steady-state temperature field, the temperature T does not change with time τ, that is $\frac{\partial T}{\partial \tau} = 0$:

$$\frac{\partial}{\partial x}\left(\lambda_x \frac{\partial T}{\partial x}\right) + \frac{\partial}{\partial y}\left(\lambda_y \frac{\partial T}{\partial y}\right) + \frac{\partial}{\partial z}\left(\lambda_z \frac{\partial T}{\partial z}\right) = -q_v \tag{8}$$

After considering the conduction and convection inside the motor and the convection on the external surface, the mixed boundary value problem of the three-dimensional steady-state temperature field in the anisotropic medium is

$$\frac{\partial}{\partial x}\left(\lambda_x \frac{\partial T}{\partial x}\right) + \frac{\partial}{\partial y}\left(\lambda_y \frac{\partial T}{\partial y}\right) + \frac{\partial}{\partial z}\left(\lambda_z \frac{\partial T}{\partial z}\right) = -q_v \tag{9}$$

$$T|_{S_1} = T_0 \tag{10}$$

$$\lambda \frac{\partial T}{\partial n}\bigg|_{S_2} = q_0 \tag{11}$$

$$\lambda \frac{\partial T}{\partial n}\bigg|_{S_3} = -\alpha(T - T_f) \tag{12}$$

3.2 Convection Boundary Conditions

Convection heat transfer is a very complicated process, which depends on many factors, mainly the nature of the fluid itself, the velocity of the fluid, the shape and size of the heat transfer surface, etc. The heat lost and dissipated in the integrated joint module is mainly dissipated into the air through convection heat exchange.

There are two types of convection boundary conditions [14]. The convection between the joint housing and the air belongs to natural convection; the convection between the motor stator, rotor and the air inside the drive joint module belongs to forced convection.

The convective heat transfer coefficient [15] of each surface of the joint is shown in Table 1 below.

Table 1. Convective heat transfer coefficient of each surface of the joint

Joint surfaces	Convection heat transfer coefficient $(W/m^2 \cdot K)$
External surface of joint	14.2
Motor air gap surface	53.1
Stator end face	33.4
Rotor end face	94.6

3.3 Thermal Analysis Parameters Acquisition of Joints

The thermal analysis parameters of the joint are mainly the materials and thermal conductivity of the parts that make up the joint, the loss value of the heating source and the heat transfer coefficient of each surface. Table 2 shows the materials of each part of the joint and their respective thermal conductivity.

Table 2. Materials and thermal conductivity of main parts of joints

Part name	Material	Thermal Conductivity (W/m * K)
Harmonic reducer	45# steel	50.2
Motor shaft	40Cr	32.6
Shell	7075-T6	130
Rear end of motor cover	7075-T6	130

The main heat sources of the joints: the iron loss of the stator core, the basic copper loss and the mechanical loss of the harmonic reducer. The calculated results are shown in Table 3.

Table 3. Loss of joint heat source

Part name	Loss value (W)
Stator core loss	21.8
Basic copper loss under rated conditions	11.7
Mechanical loss	59.9

The heat generation rate is the heating power per unit volume of the part. The heat generation rate of each heat source of the joint is shown in Table 4.

Table 4. Heat generation rate of joint heating source

Part name	Heat generation rate (W/m^3)
Motor stator under rated conditions	2.51×10^5
Harmonic reducer	3.19×10^5

4   Finite Element Simulation Analysis of Joints

Perform thermal simulation analysis on the integrated joints analyzed in the previous article.This chapter uses the three-dimensional modeling software Catia to virtually model the integrated joints, and uses the finite element simulation analysis software Ansys to establish a virtual prototype, perform simulation and analysis, and provide a theoretical basis for the development of the physical prototype.

4.1   Establishment of Finite Element Model

The structure of the drive joint module is relatively complicated. When performing finite element analysis directly, it will consume a lot of time in meshing and calculation. Therefore, the structure in the model that has little effect on the result should be simplified. Mainly simplify the screws, reducers, bearings, etc.; delete the screws on the parts of the drive joint module; simplify the wave generator of the harmonic reducer; simplify the bearings, etc. (Fig. 2).

Fig. 2.   Simplified integrated joint diagram

Import the model built in Catia into the "Geometry" module of Ansys Workbench, as shown in the figure. In the module to each component to add materials, mainly thermal conductivity parameters of the corresponding.After importing the model, select the "Steady-State Thermal" module of Ansys Workbench, then perform mesh division, select the mesh parameters, and then generate the mesh, as shown in the figure below (Fig. 3).

For steady-state thermal analysis simulation, boundary conditions and loads are also required. First, set the ambient temperature to 22 °C, then set the heat generation rate of the heat source inside the joint model, and finally set the convective heat transfer coefficient of each part surface.

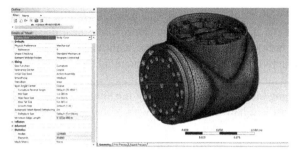

Fig. 3. Meshed joint diagram

4.2 Simulation of Steady State Thermal Analysis

Under rated working conditions, the finite element analysis is performed on the state of the joint when it reaches thermal equilibrium, and the temperature field distribution results obtained by the simulation are shown in the following figure.The maximum temperature of the joint model surface is about 49.18 °C. The surface temperature of the joint is still decreasing from the harmonic reducer to the motor direction, which has good heat dissipation properties, and the maximum temperature meets the requirements of the rated working conditions.Due to the lightweight requirements of collaborative robots, and they are mainly used in human-machine collaboration, the maximum temperature obtained by simulation analysis is safe for short-term contact with humans (Fig. 4).

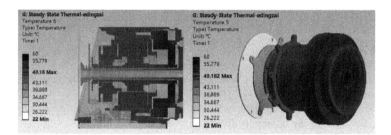

Fig. 4. Integrated joint simulation temperature field cloud map

From the previous theoretical analysis, it can be known that the highest heating power and heat generation rate in the integrated joint are the mechanical losses of the harmonic reducer, so improving the transmission efficiency of the harmonic reducer is also a key part of solving the joint heating.

4.3 Measures to Reduce Temperature

The ways of heat conduction in joints are: convective heat transfer, heat conduction, and radiation heat transfer. The most important ones are convective heat transfer and heat conduction, while radiative heat transfer has little effect on the loss of joint temperature. It can be seen that there are three main ways to reduce the temperature rise of joints under natural convection conditions under the general working conditions of joints: the first is improving the module structure to improve the heat dissipation performance, such as the use of hollow shafts or perforations on the shaft. The second is by improving the thermal conductivity of each component material, speed up the heat loss, such as replacing the shell and other component materials with higher thermal c to reduce the heat loss by reducing the internal heat source of the joint, such as the use of conductivity materials. The third is a harmonic reducer with higher transmission efficiency. These three methods can be used to optimize the design of the heat dissipation performance of the drive joint module.

5 Conclusion

The temperature analysis and calculation in this paper are the key steps in the design of integrated joints. This paper takes a universal joint as the object and uses ANSYS Workbench software to conduct loss analysis, thermal modeling and temperature field simulation research, which breaks through the integrated joint key technologies such as thermal loss analysis, three-dimensional thermal modeling and temperature field simulation, and the resulting temperature field simulation results play an important role in supporting the design of integrated joints, and also provide a way to reduce joint temperature.

Acknowledgements. This work is supported by National Key R&D Program Project (2019YFB1309900).

References

1. Zhao, J., Zhang, Z.Q., Zheng, Q., Chen, D.S., Gui, S.: Research status and development trend of robot safety. J. Beihang Univ. **44**(07), 1347–1358 (2018)
2. Chu, M.M.: Research and Implementation of Integrated Joint Light Brake for Cooperative Robot. Beijing Jiaotong University (2018)
3. Zhou, P.Y.: AUBO: strengthening China's collaborative robot. Zhong Guan Cun **4**, 58–59 (2021)
4. Song, J.Q., Wang, H.W., Zhang, D.N., et al.: Performance analysis of electric joint integrated permanent magnet motor based on ANSYS. Small Spec. Electr. Mach. **48**(4), 43–45, 59
5. Deng, J.G.: Analysis and calculation of armature transient temperature field of single-phase series motor. J. Hunan Univ. (Nat. Sci. Edn.) **06**, 61–66 (1998)
6. Xu, L.K.: Loss and Thermal Analysis of Drum-type Brushless DC Motor, pp. 39–40. Northeastern University, Shenyang (2008)
7. Aglen, O.: Loss calculation and thermal analysis of a high-speed generator. In: 2003 IEEE International Electric Machines and Drives Conference, vol. 2, pp. 1117–1123. IEEE, Madison (2003)
8. Wang, Y., Chau, K.T., Gan, J., et al.: Design and analysis of a new multiphase polygonal-winding permanent-magnet brushless DC machine. IEEE Trans. Magn. **38**, 3258–3260 (2002)
9. Li, J.Y.: Study on Failure Mechanism and Accelerated Life Test Method of Space Lubrication Harmonic Reducer, pp. 87–88. Chongqing University, Chongqing (2012)

10. Huang, D.: Numerical Calculation of Electromagnetic Field and Temperature Field of Large and Medium Asynchronous Motor, pp. 27–29. Harbin University of Science and Technology (2004)
11. Li, K.T., Huang, A.X., Huang, Q.H.: Finite Element Method and Its Application, pp. 15–17. Science Press, Nevada (2006)
12. Weng, R.Z.: Finite Element Method for Heat Transfer. Jinan University Press (2000)
13. Wang, X.H.: Permanent Magnet Motor, 2nd edn. China Electric Power Press, Beijing (2011)
14. Xue, D.Y., Chen, Y.Q.: System Simulation Technology and Application Based on MAT-LAB/Simulink. Tsinghua University Press, Beijing (2011)
15. Liu, W.: Temperature Rise Modeling and Cooling Performance Analysis of Permanent Magnet Synchronous Motor

Inverse Determination of B340LA Material Parameters in Bending Springback Process by Dynamic Optimization Approach

Zhefeng Guo, Li Liang$^{(\boxtimes)}$, Tianyue Zhou, Huixian Zhang, and Limin Ma

Department of Mechanical Engineering,
Luoyang Institute of Science and Technology, Luoyang 471023, China

Abstract. In order to obtain the accurate B340LA material parameter, in this paper, a dynamic optimization approach was proposed to inverse determine the material parameters in bending springback process. After the inverse determination for material parameters, the finite element simulation result indicates a close agreement with actual experiment, and the relative errors between inverse determined and actual material parameters are also very small. It can be concluded that proposed optimization approach to inverse determine the material parameters is efficient and accurate.

Keywords: Inverse determination · Material parameters · Bending springback · Dynamic optimization

1 Introduction

The sheet metal bending is an essential metalworking process in many industries [1], and the research of V-die bending is always a hot issue in the stamping field. The flat sheet is bent to a curved sheet by the pressing on the bending machine. Because of the existence of elastic deformation in curved sheet, some springback will be occurred when the curved sheet is relaxed from the bending machine. Then, the final bending angle of curved sheet will be obtained.

It is a popular research method that the actual experiment is token the place of finite element (FE) simulation [2], which costs less time and can achieve the experimental data of difficult operation in reality. For the bending process, material parameters are sensitive for FE simulation. If the value of material parameters is unknown, the user must to make a reasonable set for it. As we all known, there are many parameters in the material, it is difficult that the material parameters are adjusted to the best directly by user, and it greatly depends on the user's experience and skill level. Therefore, it is necessary to develop a reasonable and efficient calculation method to obtain accurate material parameters. It is generally known that when other process parameters in FE model are set accurately, the more accurate the material parameters are, the more accurate FE simulation result is, and the smaller the deviation between FE simulation and corresponding experiment

© Springer Nature Switzerland AG 2021
X.-J. Liu et al. (Eds.): ICIRA 2021, LNAI 13015, pp. 524–535, 2021.
https://doi.org/10.1007/978-3-030-89134-3_48

is. Thus, the material parameters can be inverse determined according to this common phenomenon.

As an efficient and reasonable method, accurate material constitutive parameters can be obtained from the inverse determination by the optimization algorithm. In general, for the optimization algorithm, intelligent optimization algorithms such as genetic algorithm (GA) [3–5], simulated annealing algorithm [6] and particle swarm optimization algorithm (PSO) [7–10] are not easy to fall into the local optimization. Although they have better global optimization capability, the amount of calculation often is enormous. In order to reduce the amount of FE simulation when using the intelligent optimization algorithms, the surrogate approximate model can be developed to replace FE simulation. Then, using the optimization algorithm to optimize the surrogate approximate model, the approximate global optimization solution will be obtained.

It needs a lot of samples that the surrogate approximate model is developed, higher efficient experimental design methods such as Orthogonal experiment [11] and Latin hypercube design (LHD) [12] can obviously reduce the number of samples in the same calculation accuracy of surrogate approximate model. Using FE to calculate the response of samples after the finishing of experimental design, then, the surrogate approximate model can be obtained by mathematical model procedure. Many kinds of surrogate model can achieve the approximation of bending springback process, such as artificial neural network [13–16], radial basis function (RBF) [17] and response surface method [18, 19], etc. RBF was adopted in this work due to its fine performance on computational efficiency, numerical stability and capacity of capturing nonlinear behavior [20]. Surrogate approximate model is divided into static and dynamic model based on the construction process in optimization. It is the static model that constructs the model with sufficient samples which are obtained at a single time, the sample numbers will be not changed in the subsequent optimization process [6]. In order to enhance the accuracy of static approximate model, sufficient samples are necessary. It will increase FE simulation times. Thus, the optimization efficiency will be cut down. Dynamic model can update the sample set and variable space to reconstruct the approximate model in the optimization process, its optimization efficiency is higher in comparison with static approximate model. In recent years, many scholars arouse great interest in the research of dynamic approximate model [21, 22]. Adaptive response surface method is a representative dynamic approximate model [23], it has great advantages on global convergence and optimization efficiency.

Zhang, et al. [20] proposed an inverse procedure to identify the viscoplastic material properties of polymer Nafion, by minimizing differences in the force-displacement responses of uniaxial tension test between experimental and simulation results. In the procedure, the radial basis function response surface was used to replace the complicated FE simulation. Intergeneration projection genetic algorithm was employed as the inverse operator on the response surface to determine the unknown material parameters. The inverse result is satisfied when the optimization stopping. Liu, et al. [24] proposed a method to inverse determine the material performance parameters in sheet metal forming, which is combined with the FE and the genetic algorithm. Through the comparison of actual stamping results and inverse determined simulation results, authors concluded that this inverse determination method is effective, reliable and accurate. Yan, et al. [25]

determined the parameters of Hill48 yield criterion by an inverse identification method. The press bending and roll forming processes were selected to verify this parameter identification method, the compared results between experiment and simulation show that the inverse identified parameters of Hill48 yield criterion is better than Mises criterion. To observe above articles, it can be found that the comparison of FE simulation and actual experiment is a necessary section in inverse determination process of material parameters. Using the optimization procedure to minimize the difference between FE simulation and experiment, when the difference tends to the minimum value, the optimal material parameters will be obtained.

At present, a cooperative company has some steel sheets used in bending, due to the limitation of realistic conditions, the material parameters can't be obtained in time through traditional tensile test. In this case, the company entrusts us to provide a novel method to determine the material parameters. This method not only needs to avoid the tensile test, but also needs to have the characteristic of simplicity and convenience for implementation on engineering. Under this background, in this paper, take B340LA steel sheet as the research material, an optimization approach based on dynamic RBF was proposed to determine the material parameters. The inverse determination method was used to minimize the deviation between experimental and FE simulated results. The accurate material parameters will be obtained when the optimization was completed. The optimized result shows a good agreement with the material parameters which were obtained by tensile test. Therefore, it can be concluded that the method of inverse determination material parameters in this paper has the characteristic of simplicity and convenience on the one hand, and on the other hand, the method also has accurate calculation result. In this paper, a convenient method was provided to obtain the material parameter. This method doesn't need to do the tensile test which is easy to be restricted by production conditions. It is very suitable for extension and application in engineering field.

2   Optimization Approach of Dynamic RBF

The optimization flowchart of dynamic RBF in this paper is shown as Fig. 1.

In this optimization approach, beginning a new iteration is based on the accuracy examination of optimal solution. It will ensure every approximate optimal solution as the center of new variable space is credible. This characteristic feature is major difference of RBF-PSO dynamic optimization approach between this paper and others. To sample nearby the sub-variable space will reduce unnecessary sample at some unimportant variable space, it can cut down the labor consumption greatly and is more helpful to find out actual global optimal solution.

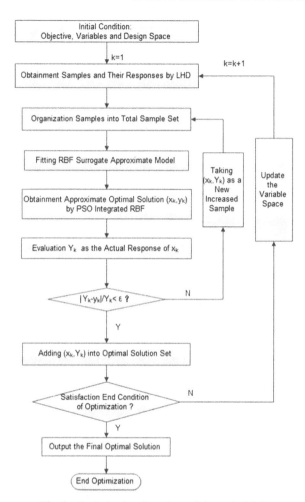

Fig. 1. Optimization flowchart of dynamic RBF.

3   The Experiment and Simulation on Bending Springback Process

3.1   Introduction of Bending Springback Process

The sheet bending springback process was shown as Fig. 2. The flat metal sheet in the state of Fig. 2(a) is bent to a curved sheet, due to the elastic of material, if bending tools are relaxed, the curved sheet will be springback as the state of Fig. 2(b), the angle of sheet becomes α from α_0. In Fig. 2, D is the punch displacement, H is the depth of punch pressed in die, it is obvious that $D = H + t$. To bending springback process, a certain D will be corresponding to a certain bending angle α.

R, r, t, V and β in Fig. 2 are die radius, punch radius, thickness of metal sheet, nominal width of die notch and die angle respectively.

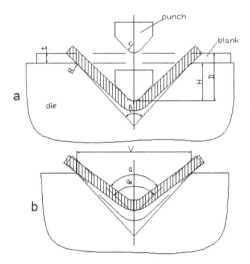

Fig. 2. Schematic diagram of bending springback process.

3.2 Experiments of Bending Springback Process

The sheet of steel material B340LA with 30-mm width was used to bend, D was observed directly from number control system named Delem of bending machine. The sheet was relaxed directly after bending, it will undergo springback immediately. After springback, using angle measurement instrument to measure the final bending angle α, the α is the mean value of three bending angles which were measured from three same D. The experiment moulds were shown as Fig. 3.

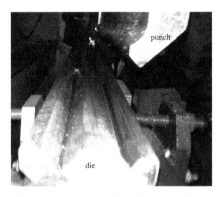

Fig. 3. The moulds of bending experiment.

The mould and steel sheet parameters as following:
$V = 12$ mm, $\beta = 86°$, $R = 1$ mm, $r = 1$ mm, $t = 1.4$ mm.
The results of bending experiment were shown as Table 1.

Table 1. Results of bending experiment

D (mm)	$\alpha_1(°)$	$\alpha_2(°)$	$\alpha_3(°)$	$\alpha(°)$
4.975	89.7	90.1	90.3	90.03333
4.848	92.5	92.7	92.7	92.63333
4.723	93.4	94.2	93.8	93.8
4.601	95.5	96	96	95.83333
4.481	97.7	97.8	97.8	97.76667
4.364	99.4	99.3	99.4	99.3667
4.135	103.5	102.4	103.2	103.0333
4.042	105	105	105.2	105.0667
3.805	108.8	109	109	108.9333
3.698	109.9	110	109.9	109.9333
3.487	113.5	114.6	114.5	114.2
3.28	117	116.8	116.8	116.8667
3.177	118	118.3	118.2	118.1667
3.076	121.6	121.3	120.9	121.2667
2.874	125.5	125	125.2	125.2333
2.575	131	130.8	131	130.9333

It can be find that when the punch displacement D is reduced from 4.975 mm to 2.575 mm, the bending angle α is increased from 90° to 130.9°, the increase of α is a gradual process based on the reduction of D. the change of D on 0.1 mm order of magnitude will lead to the modification of α about 1°~3°, the D is a sensitive parameter for α.

In the following FE model, the material parameters of B340LA will be assumed to be unknown, and needs to be inverse determined by optimization. From the Table 1, it can be found that every stage of bending is almost involved. Therefore, the statistics of bending experiment is more comprehensive, it is very beneficial for accurate inverse determination of material parameters.

3.3 FE Simulation of Bending Springback Process

In this paper, FE software named ABAQUS was used to simulate the bending and springback process. The huge deformation of bending process is suitable to be simulated with explicit module, whose calculation speed is faster. The springback process is suitable to be simulated with implicit module, whose calculation accuracy is higher. Through the combination of explicit and implicit module, the FE software not only has accurate simulation result, but also has faster calculation speed at the same time. Thus, in this paper, this combined FE model was used to simulation the bending and springback process.

In the bending and springback process, sheet width direction sectional deformation is almost the same. Thus, the 2D element was used to simulate in FE model, it will reduce the time consumption than 3D element in the simulation process. In the FE, the surface to surface contact model was adopted in which the coulomb friction law has been considered. Two contact pairs, namely, punch-sheet and die-sheet, were created. The degrees of die freedom were all restricted, the punch was restricted to only can move on the Y direction (direction of punch displacement), and the degree of sheet freedom have not any restriction. The friction coefficient was set to 0.1 as an ordinary scale of metal contact in bending process. The punch and die were considered as rigid body. The sheet mesh size in die notch width direction was increase gradually in the order of 0.03 to 0.2 from middle to both ends. The mesh size of sheet thickness was set up to 0.05. This mesh will decrease the mesh density with the reduction of sheet deformation scale. Thus, the FE model would have a fast calculation speed, and the calculation accuracy would not be reduced obviously. Element type of parts was chosen as the four node bilinear plane stress quadrilateral element (CPS4R), The mesh division figure was shown as Fig. 4. The remaining parameters were set to the default of the software.

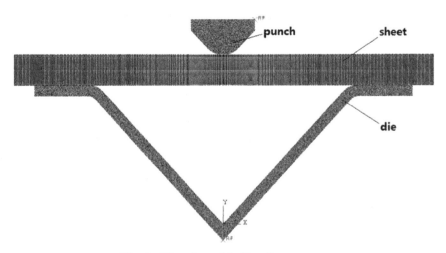

Fig. 4. FE mesh model of bending process.

In general, the relation between stress and strain on material plasticity can be obtained from tensile test. Then, through a series of transformation and fitting, the exponential form relation curve between true stress and true strain can be considered as the Eq. (1). This function style is very convenient for appliance on FE software and other field.

$$\begin{cases} \sigma = E\varepsilon, & (\varepsilon \leq \varepsilon_0) \\ \sigma = K\varepsilon^n, & (\varepsilon > \varepsilon_0) \end{cases} \tag{1}$$

where E, K, n and ε_0 are elastic modulus, hardening coefficient, hardening exponent and yield strain respectively. The Poisson's ratio v was set to 0.28 in FE.

The stress distribution contours of a bending before and after springback were shown as Fig. 5(a) and Fig. 5(b) respectively. Before springback, the stress from the double surfaces to the interior of the curved sheet section is decreased gradually. After springback, the stress was reduced greatly. The biggest stress is not on the sheet surfaces anymore, but in the interior. Because different sheet sections need different strains when the stress rebounds to the balance, it will lead to the interaction between different sheet sections, the complex stress state leads to the stress distribution as shown in Fig. 5(b).

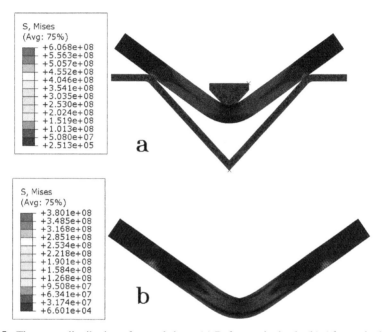

Fig. 5. The stress distribution of curved sheet: (a) Before springback; (b) After springback.

Because it is a wide range about the bending experiment samples, when the inaccurate material parameters were used to simulate in FE, the comparison between FE simulation and bending experiment, a part of samples may be the same, but, the most of samples will have bigger deviation. Only the accurate material parameters were used to simulate in FE, the most of samples between FE and experiment will have a close agreement. In other word, the deviation between FE simulation and experiment is the minimum at this time. It is the basis of the inverse determination in this paper.

4   Inverse Determination of Material Parameter

4.1   Objective Function and Parameter Effect

In order to save calculation consumption and select representational points, the references were selected by several experiment points of Table 1 whose bending angles are distributed uniformly, these experiment points are that D are 4.975, 4.364, 3.698, 3.076 and 2.575 respectively. Objective function as following:

$$\text{OBJ:} \quad y = \sum_{i=1}^{5} \frac{(\alpha_i - \tilde{\alpha}_i)^2}{2} \tag{2}$$

In the Eq. (2), α_i is the corresponding experiment bending angle of each D, $\tilde{\alpha}_i$ is the corresponding FE simulation bending angle of each D.

In this paper, only E was omitted in the next research, it was set to 207 GPa which is a common value of the B340LA. Take K, n and ε_0 as variables to inverse determine the material parameters.

4.2 Inverse Determination of Material Parameters

The optimization model of material parameters inverse determination was shown as the Eq. (3).

$$\begin{cases} \text{OBJ:} \quad y = \sum_{i=1}^{5} \frac{(\alpha_i - \tilde{\alpha}_i)^2}{2} \\ \quad\quad 500 < K < 1000 \\ \text{st:} \quad 0.1 < n < 0.2 \\ \quad\quad 0.001 < \varepsilon_0 < 0.002 \end{cases} \tag{3}$$

Using proposed optimization approach to optimize the Eq. (3). In this optimization process, set $\zeta = 0.25$, $\xi = 0.02$, initial sample numbers and subsample numbers are set to 21 and 9 respectively. The variable spaces and optimized solutions were shown as Table 2.

Table 2. Variable spaces and optimization solutions

k	$x^l\left(K^l, n^l, \varepsilon_0^l\right)$	$x^u\left(K^u, n^u, \varepsilon_0^u\right)$	$x(K, n, \varepsilon_0)$	OBJ
1	600, 0.15, 0.0015	1000, 0.2, 0.002	792.7, 0.16, 0.001948	0.2935
2	692.7, 0.1475, 0.001823	892.7, 0.1725, 0.002073	771.3, 0.1593, 0.001918	0.284
3	721.3, 0.15305, 0.001856	821.3, 0.16555, 0.001981	767.7, 0.16, 0.001917	0.2756
4	742.7, 0.15688, 0.001886	792.7, 0.16313, 0.001948	742.65, 0.16167, 0.001905	0.2651
5	730.15, 0.16011, 0.001889	755.15, 0.16323, 0.001921	742.65, 0.16167, 0.001905	0.2651

It was observed that the objective is gradually reduced to 0.2651 from 0.2935 through five iterations. The amount of reduction is close to 10% of first iteration. The first iteration has an approximate model which can be treated as a static model consisting of the initial samples. By the increase of iteration, the sample number nearby the objective is gradually increased, and the local accuracy of approximate model nearby the objective is higher and higher until the objective can't be reduced at the fifth iteration. Then, the iteration was stopped, the ultimate variables value can be treated as the optimized solution.

4.3 Comparison and Discussion

The inverse determined material parameters were used to simulate in FE, the simulated results in comparison with the bending experiments of Table 1 were shown as Fig. 6.

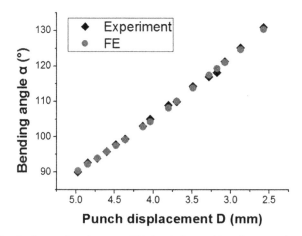

Fig. 6. Comparison between FE simulation and bending experiment.

From the Fig. 6, it can be observed that all the bending angle deviations are very smaller. The maximum bending angle deviation is only $1.17°$ which is corresponding to punch displacement D = 3.177. The FE simulation result indicates in a good agreement with actual experiment.

In order to verify the material parameters of inverse determination is accurate from other field, they were compared with the actual B340LA material parameters which were obtained by transformation and fitting after tensile test [26], as shown in Table 3.

Table 3. Comparison between actual and optimized material parameters

B340LA	K (MPa)	n	ε_0
Actual	678	0.16	0.00193
Optimized	742.65	0.16167	0.001905
Error	8.7%	1%	1.3%

From the Table 3, it can be observed that the material parameters of inverse determination is in close agreement with the actual B340LA, the relative errors of K, n and

ε_0 are only 8.7%, 1% and 1.3% respectively. Thus, it can be concluded that proposed optimization approach not only has the characteristic of simplicity and efficiency, but also has enough calculation accuracy. It is a reliable approach to inverse determinate the material parameters, and also can be used to inverse determine other material parameters as the approach of this paper.

5   Conclusions

In this paper, in order to obtain accurate material parameters from other aspect which don't need to do the tensile test, an optimization approach based on dynamic RBF was proposed to inverse determine the material parameters of B340LA in bending springback process. After the inverse determination of material parameters, the FE simulation result is in a good agreement with the bending experiment, and the inverse determined material parameters is also consistent with the actual B340LA material parameters. It can be concluded that proposed optimization approach is an efficient and accurate tool to inverse determine the material parameters. It also can be used in other fields as the approach of this paper. It is very suitable for extension and application in engineering field.

Funding. This work was supported by National Key Research and Development Program of China (2019YFB1312101).

References

1. Leu, D.-K.: Position deviation and springback in V-die bending process with asymmetric dies. Int. J. Adv. Manuf. Technol. **79**(5–8), 1095–1108 (2015). https://doi.org/10.1007/s00 170-014-6532-x
2. Zong, Y., Liu, P., Guo, B., Shan, D.: Springback evaluation in hot v-bending of Ti-6Al-4V alloy sheets. Int. J. Adv. Manuf. Technol. **76**, 1–9 (2014). https://doi.org/10.1007/s00170-014-6190-z
3. Zhou, J., Zhuo, F., Huang, L., Luo, Y.: Multi-objective optimization of stamping forming process of head using Pareto-based genetic algorithm. J. Central South Univ. **22**(9), 3287–3295 (2015). https://doi.org/10.1007/s11771-015-2868-0
4. Barathwaj, N., Raja, P., Gokulraj, S.: Optimization of assembly line balancing using genetic algorithm. J. Central South Univ. **22**(10), 3957–3969 (2015). https://doi.org/10.1007/s11771-015-2940-9
5. Ghorbani, H., et al.: Performance comparison of bubble point pressure from oil PVT data: several neurocomputing techniques compared. Experimental Comput. Multiphase Flow **2**(4), 225–246 (2019). https://doi.org/10.1007/s42757-019-0047-5
6. Manoochehri, M., Kolahan, F.: Integration of artificial neural network and simulated annealing algorithm to optimize deep drawing process. Int. J. Adv. Manuf. Technol. **73**(1–4), 241–249 (2014). https://doi.org/10.1007/s00170-014-5788-5
7. Vitorino, L.N., Ribeiro, S.F., Bastos, C.J.A.: A mechanism based on artificial Bee colony to generate diversity in particle swarm optimization. Neurocomputing **148**, 39–45 (2015)
8. Eberhart, R., Kennedy, J.: New optimizer using particle swarm theory. In: Proceedings of the 1995 6th International Symposium on Micro Machine and Human Science, Nagoya, Japan, pp. 39–43 (1995)

9. Bonyadi, M.R. A theoretical guideline for designing an effective adaptive particle swarm. IEEE Trans. Evol. Comput. **2019** (2019)
10. Chen, D.-D., Lin, Y.-C., Chen, X.-M.: A strategy to control microstructures of a Ni-based superalloy during hot forging based on particle swarm optimization algorithm. Adv. Manuf. **2019**, 238–247 (2019)
11. Winnicki, M., Małachowska, A., Ambroziak, A.: Taguchi optimization of the thickness of a coating deposited by LPCS. Arch. Civ. Mech. Eng. **14**(4), 561–568 (2014). https://doi.org/10.1016/j.acme.2014.04.006
12. Piffl, M., Stadlober, E.: The depth-design: an efficient generation of high dimensional computer experiments. J. Stat. Plan. Infer. **164**, 10–26 (2015)
13. Milivojevic, M., Stopic, S., Friedrich, B., Stojanovic, B., Drndarevic, D.: Computer modeling of high-pressure leaching process of nickel laterite by design of experiments and neural networks. Int. J. Min. Met. Mater. **19**, 584–594 (2012)
14. Hasanzadehshooiili, H., Lakirouhani, A., Šapalas, A.: Neural network prediction of buckling load of steel arch-shells. Arch. Civ. Mech. Eng. **12**(4), 477–484 (2012). https://doi.org/10.1016/j.acme.2012.07.005
15. Haddadzadeh, M., Razfar, M.R., Mamaghani, M.R.M.: Novel approach to initial blank design in deep drawing using artificial neural network. P I Mech. Eng. B-J Eng. **223**, 1323–1330 (2009)
16. Song, Y., Yu, Z.: Springback prediction in T-section beam bending process using neural networks and finite element method. Arch. Civ. Mech. Eng. **13**(2), 229–241 (2013). https://doi.org/10.1016/j.acme.2012.11.004
17. Kitayama, S., Huang, S.S., Yamazaki, K.: Optimization of variable blank holder force trajectory for springback reduction via sequential approximate optimization with radial basis function network. Struct. Multidiscip. O **47**, 289–300 (2013)
18. Song, J.H., Huh, H., Kim, S.H.: Stress-based springback reduction of a channel shaped autobody part with high-strength steel using response surface methodology. J. Eng. Mater-T ASME **129**, 397–406 (2007)
19. Guo, X., Li, D., Wu, Z., Tian, Q.-H.: Application of response surface methodology in optimizaing the sulfationoastingeaching process of nickel laterite. Int. J. Miner. Metall. Mater. **19**(3), 199–204 (2012). https://doi.org/10.1007/s12613-012-0538
20. Zhang, W., Cho, C., Xiao, Y.: An effective inverse procedure for identifying viscoplastic material properties of polymer Nafion. Comp. Mater. Sci. **95**, 159–165 (2014)
21. Wang, L.Q., Shan, S.Q., Wang, G.G.: Mode-pursuing sampling method for global optimization on expensive black-box functions. Eng. Optimiz. **36**, 419–438 (2004)
22. Duan, X., Wang, G.G., Kang, X., Niu, Q., Naterer, G., Peng, Q.: Performance study of mode-pursuing sampling method. Eng. Optimiz. **41**, 1–21 (2009)
23. Wang, G.G.: Adaptive response surface method using inherited Latin hypercube design points. J. Mech. Design. **125**, 210–220 (2003)
24. Liu, H., Jiang, K.Y., Li, B., Lu, P.: A rapid inverse determination of material performance parameters in sheet metal forming. In: 2nd International Conference on Advanced Engineering Materials and Technology, Zhuhai, China, pp. 1035–1040, 06–08 July 2012
25. Yan, Y., Wang, H.B., Li, Q.: The inverse parameter identification of Hill 48 yield criterion and its verification in press bending and roll forming process simulations. J. Manuf. Process. **20**, 46–53 (2015)
26. Zhu, Q.C.: Research on the Drawing Process and Spring Back Control of the B-pillar Reinforced Panel. master. Thesis, Hefei University of Technology, Hefei, China (2013) (in Chinese)

Compact Multispectral Camera Using RGB LED and Optimization

Cui Ma[1]([✉]), Ming Yu[1,2], Fokui Chen[1], Hui Zhu[1], and Haitao Fang[1,2]

[1] Shenzhen Institute of Advanced Technology, Chinese Academy of Sciences, Shenzhen, China
cui.ma@siat.ac.cn
[2] Shenzhen Key Laboratory of Precision Engineering, Shenzhen, China

Abstract. Multispectral camera gets the three-dimensional spatial information and spectral reflection of natural objects. It is useful to exploit the shape or color difference, even the material variation. This paper introduces a compact multispectral camera. It is composed by a gray camera and RGB LED. The multispectral images are recovered using quadratic optimization and known eigenvector of Mussel color chips. It is an active illumination method and the spectral response of LED and detector are calibrated to obtain the actual spectral reflection. We analyze the accuracy of recovered spectrum using simulation and build a prototype to validate it. The experiment shows that it can distinguish the close colors effectively. This multispectral camera can be an enhanced camera for intelligent detection.

Keywords: Multispectral camera · Optimization · LED

1 Introduction

Comparing the ordinary RGB camera's three channels, multispectral camera obtains several or dozens of channels with different wavebands. It can get the spectral reflectance to distinguish or segment the objects which have close colors or different material. Multispectral camera can be an enhanced camera for the intelligent inspection.

Many methods have been developed to obtain multispectral images [1], including the wavelength-scan method, spatial-scan method, time-scan method and snapshot method. For simplicity, it can be divided into spectral scanner and spectral camera. Spectral scanner has higher spectral resolution, but it usually has moving parts for scanning. Comparing to spectral scanner, the spectral camera has simple structure with lower spectral resolution. There are already some spectral cameras on the market. It mainly includes two types. One is the multi-lens spectral camera. It has several lens and every lens has a different light filter, such as the SEQUOIA of Parrot, the RedEdge-MX and ALTUM of MicaSense. These spectral cameras are often used for remote sensing. It is not suitable for close inspection due to the different view field of multi-lens. The other type is the Mosaic camera which has a thin filter with different wavebands on the detector, such as the 9-channel camera of SILIOS Technologies, the xiSpec camera of XIMEA Company. These cameras often have limited spatial resolution because of the pixel binning of multi- channels. Besides, some researchers have developed other

© Springer Nature Switzerland AG 2021
X.-J. Liu et al. (Eds.): ICIRA 2021, LNAI 13015, pp. 536–544, 2021.
https://doi.org/10.1007/978-3-030-89134-3_49

methods for spectral camera. Park, et al. [2] use five LEDs and RGB camera to establish a multispectral imaging system. The optimal algorithm is applied to find the best combination of multiplexed illumination and recover the multispectral images. Kamshilin [3, 4] use 17 LEDs to generate mutually orthogonal spectral functions to recover the multispectral images. Tschannerl, et al. [5] use LED ring and a deep Multi-layer perceptron to reconstruct spectral image. With the development of deep learning, multispectral images can be recovered directly from a single RGB image. The sparse representation method [6, 7], manifold based mapping [8], convolutional neural network based method [9] are developed to reconstruct spectral images from a RGB image. These systems only use a simple RGB camera, but the deep learning method needs numerous training data and complex computation.

In this paper, we introduce a compact multispectral camera. It is composed by RGB LED and a gray camera. The multispectral images are recovered by using simple optimization. The spectral camera can provide more information than ordinary camera and distinguish similar colors effectively. The following part 2 presents the system principle. Part 3 gives the simulation and experiment in detail. And part 4 is the conclusion.

2 Principle

2.1 System Structure

This multispectral camera includes RGB LED for illumination and a gray camera for detection, shown as the Fig. 1. The R/G/B LED are lighted respectively and three gray images are detected.

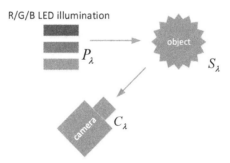

Fig. 1. Illustration of multispectral camera

$$I = \sum_{\lambda=1}^{L} S_\lambda C_\lambda P_\lambda \tag{1}$$

Where, I is the intensity of detected gray image. S_λ is the spectral reflection of detected object. $\lambda = 1, 2\ldots L$ is the wavebands. C_λ is the spectral response of detector. P_λ is the spectral response of LEDs.

The objective is to recover the spectrum S_λ from the Eq. (1). In this system, R/G/B LED are lighted respectively and the detector I has 3 images. In order to recover the visible spectrum between 400 nm and 700 nm which is more than 3 wavebands, the convex optimization algorithm is used to solve the underdetermined equation.

2.2 Recovery Algorithm

Owing to the smoothness of spectral reflectance for most real-world surfaces, the spectral reflection can be compressed to several feature vectors using PCA (Principal Component Analysis). Parkkinen, et al. [10] proposed a linear model using the set of orthogonal basic functions $b_k(\lambda)$. The spectral reflectance can be written as:

$$S_\lambda = \sum_{k=1}^{K} \sigma_k b_k(\lambda) \tag{2}$$

Where, σ_k are scalar coefficients, $k = 1, 2, \ldots K$ indicates the number of coefficients. $b_k(\lambda)$ are the orthogonal basis functions. They are eigenvectors derived from the spectral reflectance of 1257 Munsell color chips and the $K \geq 5$ is better [10]. Here the $K = 8$ is used. By substituting Eq. (2) in Eq. (1), we get the expression of Eq. (3).

$$I = \sum_{k=1}^{K} \sigma_k \sum_{\lambda=1}^{L} b_k(\lambda) C_\lambda P_\lambda \tag{3}$$

Where, $C_\lambda P_\lambda$ are the spectral response of LED and camera detector. They are determined via calibration using a spectrometer and white board. $b_k(\lambda)$ are known values in the paper [10]. Using the matrix form, Eq. (3) is rewritten as:

$$\mathbf{I} = \mathbf{F}\sigma \tag{4}$$

Where, $\mathbf{F}$ includes the known quantities $b_k(\lambda) C_\lambda P_\lambda$. σ is the matrix form of coefficients σ_k. Then, the coefficients σ can be solved using optimization.

$$\arg \min_{\sigma} \|\mathbf{F}\sigma - \mathbf{I}\|_2^2 \tag{5}$$

Since the spectral reflectance must be positive, we add the constraint, $S_\lambda = \sum_{k=1}^{K} \sigma_k b_k(\lambda) > 0$. That is, $\mathbf{A}\sigma > \mathbf{0}$, where $\mathbf{A}$ is the matrix form of $b_k(\lambda)$. In addition, the spectral reflectance of real-world is smooth, a smooth constraint is also imposed using the second derivative of spectral reflectance, $\left|\frac{\partial^2 S_\lambda}{\partial \lambda^2}\right| = |\mathbf{P}\sigma|$. Adding the two constraints, the Eq. (5) is written as:

$$\arg \min_{\sigma} \left[\|\mathbf{F}\sigma - \mathbf{I}\|_2^2 + \|\mathbf{P}\sigma\|^2 \right], \quad \mathbf{A}\sigma > \mathbf{0} \tag{6}$$

This regularized minimization can be solved using quadratic programming. After obtaining the optimal values of coefficients σ_k^{opt}, the spectral reflectance can be calculated using Eq. (7).

$$S'_\lambda = \sum_{k=1}^{K=8} \sigma_k^{opt} \cdot b_k(\lambda) \tag{7}$$

3   Simulation and Experiments

Given the detected intensity I and the corresponding spectral response of LED and detector, reflection spectrum S_λ can be recovered based on the above algorithm. In the following simulation and experiment, the parameter $K = 8, L = 31$ (31 wavebands, from 400 nm to 700 nm and interval 10 nm) are used. The spectral response of $C_\lambda \cdot P_\lambda$ are shown as Fig. 2.

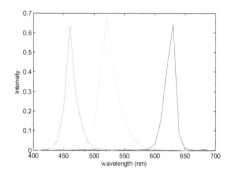

Fig. 2.   Spectral response of RGB LED and detector

3.1   Simulation

For spectral reflection, the peak position and spectral resolution are two important features. They indicate the spectral accuracy. The Gauss function is used as reference for

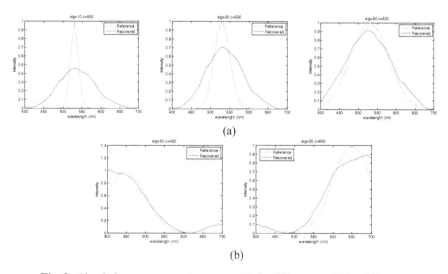

Fig. 3.   Simulation on recovered spectrum (a) for different σ; (b) for different c

simulation, that is, $S(\lambda) = e^{\frac{-(\lambda-c)^2}{2\sigma^2}}$. Simulate the ideal detected values I firstly, and then recover spectral reflection using optimization. The reference and recovered curves are compared for different parameter c and σ. From the Fig. 3, it can be seen that the peak position is quite accurate when $c = 530$, but it has some deviation at both ends, for example the $c = 450$ and 650. The deviation is relevant with the spectral response of light source greatly. It increases when the c is away the spectral peak of LED. The FWHM (Full Width at Half Maximum) is used to represent the spectral resolution. The FWHM of recovered spectrum is over 100 nm for different σ. One reason of the limited resolution is that we have assumed the spectrum is smooth in the Eq. (6). The other reason is that there are certain errors recovering 31 spectral values from only 3 detected values. Although the spectral resolution is limited, the recovered spectrum has similar trend with reference.

In addition to the spectral curve, multispectral image dataset [11] is used for simulation. It consists of 31 images from 400 nm to 700 nm. Calculate the ideal detected three images using Eq. (1) firstly. And then, recover spectral images using optimization. Figure 4 is the original color image of reference. Figure 5 shows the reference multispectral images and recovered images. There is no obvious difference for human eyes.

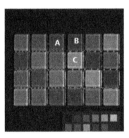

Fig. 4. Original color image for simulation

The PSNR (Peak Single Noise Rate) is calculated to compare the difference quantitatively. The higher PSNR is, the more similar between the reference and recovered image. In Fig. 6(a), the average PSNR is 31.2 dB which means good spatial quality. But at both ends the PSNR is a little low. The Fig. 6(b) shows three pairs of spectrum for the region 'A', 'B' and 'C' labelled in Fig. 4. Although there are some deviation, the recovered spectrum has similar trends with reference.

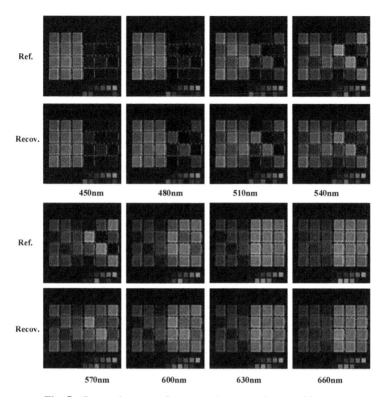

Fig. 5. Comparison on reference and recovered spectral images

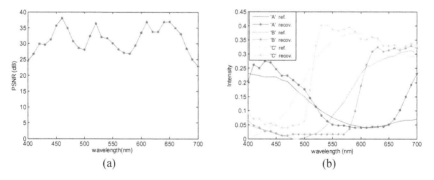

Fig. 6. (a) PSNRs for recovered images; (b) Spectrum comparison for points 'A' 'B' and 'C'

3.2 Experiment

To further test the performance of this compact spectral camera, we build a prototype shown in Fig. 7. It is composed by a USB camera and a LED circuit board.

The PH test paper is tested. There are some close color in the PH standard card, for example the PH 4, 5 and 6. In experiment, the ordinary water and alkaline nature

Fig. 7. Prototype of compact spectral camera

water are dropped on the test paper. In Fig. 8, the right region 'A' is wet using alkaline nature water and the left region 'B' 'C' are ordinary water. The 'B' and 'C' have slight difference for the different amount of water. The RGB image can define the general area of PH value, but it is a little hard to determine the exact value.

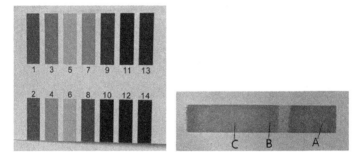

Fig. 8. PH standard card and the under-test paper

The spectral camera has higher ability to distinguish color than ordinary camera. We use the compact spectral camera to test the PH paper. Figure 9 shows several wavebands of the recovered multispectral images. The first row is gray image and the next row is the pseudo-color image changing with intensity. The pseudo-color image can see the intensity variation clearly. To determine the PH value of test paper, we calculate the spectral similarity between test paper and PH standard card. The Eq. (8) is used for similarity mainly considering the spectral direction.

$$sim(S_1, S_2) = \cos^{-1}\left(\frac{(S_1 - \overline{s_1})^{\mathrm{T}} \cdot (S_2 - \overline{s_2})}{\|S_1 - \overline{s_1}\| \cdot \|S_2 - \overline{s_2}\|} \right) \tag{8}$$

Where, S_1 is the spectral of test paper. S_2 is the spectral of PH standard cards. $\overline{s_1}, \overline{s_2}$ are the mean values.

Figure 10 is the *sim* value of test paper. The smaller value means the more similarity. It can be seen that the 'A' region is close to PH 8, the 'B' and 'C' are both small among PH 5 and 7. The 'B' region is more close to PH 7 and the 'C' region is more close to PH 5.

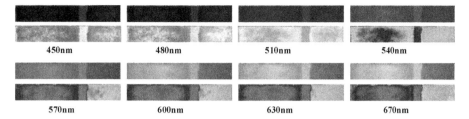

450nm 480nm 510nm 540nm

570nm 600nm 630nm 670nm

Fig. 9. Reconstructed spectral images (gray and pseudo-color images)

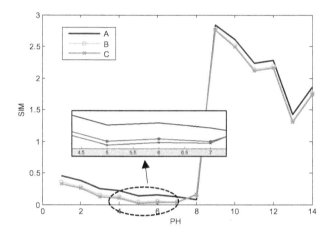

Fig. 10. *sim* value for PH test

4 Conclusion

This paper presents a compact multispectral camera which composed by a gray camera and RGB LEDs. The quadratic optimization are applied to recover multispectral images. The spectral information of multispectral images can distinguish similar color. It is proved to be effective by simulation and experiment.

This multispectral camera is small and low-cost. It can be an enhanced camera for visual inspection. To exploit more applications, better algorithms are being researched to improve the spectral resolution further.

Acknowledgment. This paper is partially supported by NSFC-Shenzhen Robot Basic Research Center project (U1713224) and Shenzhen Fundamental Research Program (JCYJ20170818163928953).

References

1. Garini, Y., Young, I.T., McNamara, G.: Spectral imaging: principles and applications. Cytometry **69A**, 735–747 (2006)

2. Park, J.I., Lee, M.H., Grossberg, M.D., Nayar, S.K.: Multispectral imaging using multiplexed illumination. IEEE (2007)
3. Kamshilin, A.A., Nippolainen, E.: Chromatic discrimination by use of computer controlled set of light-emitting diodes. Opt. Express **15**(23), 15093–15100 (2007)
4. Fauch, L., Nippolainen, E., Teplov, V., Kamshilin, A.A.: Recovery of reflection spectra in a multispectral imaging system with light emitting diodes. Opt. Express **18**(22), 23394–23405 (2010)
5. Tschannerl, J., Ren, J., Zhao, H., Kao, F., Marshall, S., Yuen, P.: Hyperspectral image reconstruction using multi-color and time-multiplexed LED illumination. Opt. Lasers Eng. **121**, 352–357 (2019)
6. Arad, B., Ben-Shahar, O.: Sparse recovery of hyperspectral signal from natural RGB images. In: Leibe, B., Matas, J., Sebe, N., Welling, M. (eds.) ECCV 2016. LNCS, vol. 9911, pp. 19–34. Springer, Cham (2016). https://doi.org/10.1007/978-3-319-46478-7_2
7. Fu, Y., Zheng, Y., Zhang, L., Huang, H.: Spectral reflectance recovery from a single RGB image. IEEE Trans. Comput. Imaging **4**(3), 382–394 (2018)
8. Jia, Y., et al.: From RGB to spectrum for natural scenes via manifold-based mapping. In: IEEE International Conference on Computer Vision, pp. 4715–4723 (2017)
9. Zhao, Y., Guo, H., Ma, Z., Cao, X., Yue, T., Hu, X.: Hyperspectral imaging with random printed mask. In: CVPR, pp. 10149–10157. IEEE (2018)
10. Parkkinen, J.P.S., Hallikainen, J., Jaaskelainen, T.: Characteristic spectra of Munsell colors. J. Opt. Soc. Am. A **6**(2), 318–322 (1989)
11. Multispectral database. http://www.cs.columbia.edu/CAVE/databases/multispectral/

A Memory Module Assembly System Using Parallel Robots

Fang Zhang, Feng Gao$^{(\boxtimes)}$, Qingshan Zeng, and Hao Zheng

School of Mechanical Engineering, Shanghai Jiao Tong
University, Shanghai 200240, People's Republic of China
{zhangfzhuif,fengg}@sjtu.edu.cn

Abstract. In this paper, a memory module assembly system is designed, and the mechanical composition and control method of the system are introduced in detail. In order to achieve accurate motion control and force control, the assembly system uses a combination of a 6PUS 6-DOF parallel robot and a 2PP 2-DOF parallel robot. The kinematics models of two kinds of parallel robots are analyzed afterwards. In addition, a 6 dimensions (6D) force sensor, which can measure the force and torque of the gripper in all directions, is attached to the end effector. In this paper, the requirements of the assembly system for position control and force control under different contact states between memory module and memory slot during the assembly process is analyzed, and a series of control strategies and a complete set of control processes based on these requirements is designed. Using the parallel robots and control method designed in this paper, experiments are carried out, and the assembly of memory module is finally realized successfully. The experimental results are analyzed at the end of this paper.

Keywords: Memory module assembly · Automatic assembly · Parallel robot · Kinematics analysis

1 Introduction

With the rapid development of computer technology, computer has gradually become an indispensable tool for human beings [1]. According to the statistical data [2], from 2005 to 2019, the proportion of households with computers in the world has been on the rise. Even if there are huge demand and shipments [3], motherboard, as the core of the computer, is still assembled manually. This is mainly because the components involved in the motherboard assembly are too precise and expensive, and manual assembly can ensure the success rate of assembly [4].

This paper focuses on memory module assembly, which is part of the motherboard assembly, and aims to design and manufacture an automatic assembly system for memory module. The common type of memory modules and memory-module slots are shown in the Fig. 1. Although automatic assembly technology is widely used nowadays, to be applied to the motherboard assembly, the assembly system must have higher accuracy, faster response speed, higher rigidity, and smaller inertia, which can be met by the

© Springer Nature Switzerland AG 2021
X.-J. Liu et al. (Eds.): ICIRA 2021, LNAI 13015, pp. 545–555, 2021.
https://doi.org/10.1007/978-3-030-89134-3_50

usage of parallel robots [5]. In this paper, a combined mechanism (as shown in Fig. 2) is proposed. Based on the combination of parallel robots, a memory module assembly system is designed. This paper will introduce the composition, working principle and control method of the memory module assembly system, as well as the experiments and results analysis.

(a)   (b)

Fig. 1. (a) Memory module; (b) Memory-module slots.

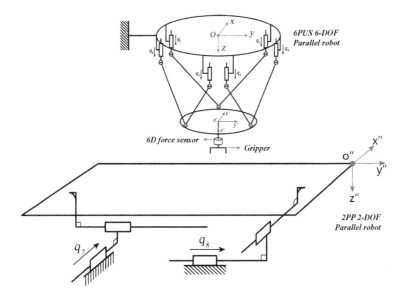

Fig. 2. Schematic diagram of the combination of parallel robots.

2 Design and Configuration

The memory module assembly system is composed of mechanical system and control system.

2.1 Mechanical System

The mechanical part is divided into upper platform and lower platform. The upper platform is mainly responsible for the assembly of memory modules, while the lower

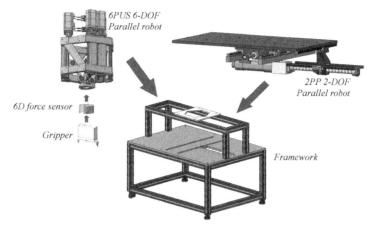

Fig. 3. Schematic diagram of the mechanical system.

platform is mainly used to coordinate the assembly of the upper platform through the plane movement. The composition of the mechanical system is shown in Fig. 3.

The main part of the upper platform is a 6PUS 6-DOF parallel robot. The 6PUS parallel robot is responsible for complex operations such as inserting or pulling the memory modules, which require high response speed and precision. The mechanism is composed of a base, six branch chains and a platform, each branch chain is composed of a prismatic pair, a universal joint and a spherical joint. The mechanism can realize three-dimensional movement and three-dimensional rotation. Compared with 6-DOF series manipulators, the parallel mechanism can provide higher accuracy, faster speed, higher rigidity and smaller inertia when using the same specification motors [5]. Moreover, the driving motors of the parallel mechanism are fixed on the base, so the repeated bending and the fatigue damage of the wires can be avoided. Compared with the mechanisms introduced in Refs. [6–8], the 6PUS parallel robot in this paper uses three compound spherical joints instead of six spherical joints (as shown in Fig. 2), this scheme can effectively reduce the radius of the end platform, thus reducing the mass and inertia of the end, improve the response speed of the mechanism, and can increase the workspace of the mechanism to a certain extent.

The lower platform is a 2PP 2-DOF parallel robot [9]. It is responsible for the horizontal movement of the motherboard and memory module box, which can make up for the small working space of 6PUS parallel robot. The 2PP parallel robot consists of a base, four prismatic pairs, and a platform. Among them, two mutually perpendicular prismatic pairs fixed to the base provide drive to enable the platform to achieve a 2-DOF plane motion.

A six dimensions (6D) force sensor is installed on the end of the 6PUS parallel robot, and a gripper is installed on the other end of the 6D force sensor. The 6D force sensor is used to collect the three-dimensional force and three-dimensional torque signal of the memory module during the assembly process [10].

The gripper is used to clamp the memory module and has three modes of motion: relative motion, absolute motion, and push motion. The push motion allows the gripper to push with a given force. One of the motion modes can be selected according to the demands.

2.2 Control System

The control system block diagram of the assembly system is shown in Fig. 4. It is composed of controllers, servo motors and their drivers, sensors and their drivers, and some other parts.

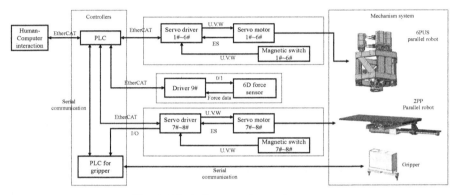

Fig. 4. Block diagram of control system.

In the control system, the functions of the main programmable logic controller (PLC) are: running the human-computer interaction system, controlling the servo motors of two parallel robots, collecting and processing the forces and torques data of the 6D force sensor, as well as the level signal of the magnetic switches.

In addition, the main PLC can be used to program the PLC of gripper as well. After programmed, the gripper movement can be controlled by I/O signal.

The 6D force sensor can provide data of three-dimensional forces and torques of the gripper in real time for force control. Magnetic switches act as reset sensors for prismatic pairs. When prismatic pairs reach their zero position, the magnetic switches transmit the falling edge signal to the controller through the drivers.

3 Mechanism Analysis

In order to control the memory module assembly system, the kinematics models of the two parallel robots should be analyzed first. Then the kinematics models should be taken as the theoretical basis of motion control.

3.1 Kinematics Analysis of 6PUS 6-DOF Parallel Robot

To establish the kinematics model of 6PUS 6-DOF parallel robot, coordinate systems, as shown in Fig. 2, should be established on the base and the end of the mechanism. First, solve the inverse kinematics of the mechanism. As shown in Fig. 5, establish a closed loop of a branch chain of the 6PUS parallel robot:

The vector equation can be obtained from the closed loop:

$$p + R \cdot a_i' = c_i + q_i \cdot e_i + l_i \tag{1}$$

In Eq. (1), a_i' is the position vector of spherical hinge in the connected coordinate system of the end of the mechanism; R is the rotation matrix of the connected coordinate system of the end in the base coordinate system. e_i is the unit vector of motion direction of the prismatic pair.

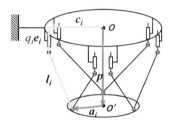

Fig. 5. The vector closed-loop of a branch chain of 6PUS parallel robot.

Set $H_i = p + Ra_i' - c_i$, and q_i can be solved:

$$q_i = H_i \cdot e_i \pm \sqrt{(H_i \cdot e_i)^2 - H_i^2 + l_i^2} \tag{2}$$

It can be seen from Eq. (2) that when the spatial pose of the end of the mechanism is determined, there are two solutions for the displacement of the prismatic pair of each branch chain. Substitute $\sqrt{(H_i \cdot e_i)^2 - H_i^2 + l_i^2} = 0$ into Eq. (1), $l_i \cdot e_i = 0$ is obtained, which means that the branch chain is at a singular position when the connecting rod vector is perpendicular to e_i. No branch chain can reach or move through the singular position in general because of physical restrictions, so the only solution can be determined by the initial state of the mechanism:

$$q_i = H_i \cdot e_i - \sqrt{(H_i \cdot e_i)^2 - H_i^2 + l_i^2} \tag{3}$$

Next, shift Eq. (1) and take the derivative:

$$\dot{q}_i \cdot e_i = v + \omega \times (Ra_i') - \omega_{li} \times l_i \tag{4}$$

In Eq. (4), ω_{li} is the angular velocity of the connecting rod. Calculate the dot product of l_i and both sides of the equation and simplify the equation:

$$\dot{q}_i = \begin{bmatrix} \dfrac{l_i}{l_i e_i} \\ Ra_i' \times \dfrac{l_i}{l_i e_i} \end{bmatrix}^T \begin{bmatrix} v \\ \omega \end{bmatrix} = G_i \cdot \begin{bmatrix} v \\ \omega \end{bmatrix} \tag{5}$$

Set $\dot{q} = [q_1 \, q_2 \cdots q_6]^T$, $G = [G_1 \, G_2 \cdots G_6]^T$, $\dot{X} = [v \, \omega]^T$, the solution of inverse velocity is:·

$$\dot{q} = G^T \dot{X} \tag{6}$$

Next, analyze the forward kinematics of the mechanism, where the iterative method is used. First, express the functional relationship between the displacement of the prismatic pairs and the pose of the end, then construct the function used for iteration:

$$q = F(X) \tag{7}$$

$$f(X) = F(X) - q = 0 \tag{8}$$

Newton iteration method is used to obtain Eq. (9):

$$X_n = X_{n-1} - \frac{f(X_{n-1})}{f'(X_{n-1})} = X_{n-1} - \frac{F(X_{n-1}) - q_n}{F'(X_{n-1})} \tag{9}$$

Take the derivative of Eq. (7): $\dot{q} = F'(X)\dot{X}$, compared with Eq. (6), it is found that $F'(X) = G^T$, considering the relationship between the Jacobian matrix of velocity and the Jacobian matrix of force [11]: $J = (G^T)^{-1}$, Eq. (9) can be rewritten as:

$$X_n = X_{n-1} - J_{X_{n-1}} \cdot (q_{n-1} - q_n) \tag{10}$$

To solve the kinematics under a certain input, $X = [0 \, 0 \, h \, 0 \, 0 \, 0]^T$ can be taken as the initial iteration value of Eq. (10). To solve the forward solutions under a series of continuous inputs, the pose calculated under the previous inputs can be taken as the initial iteration value of the next inputs, so as to reduce the number of iterations and improve the calculation accuracy.

3.2 Kinematics Analysis of 2PP 2-DOF Parallel Robot

As shown in Fig. 2, the base coordinate system and the connected body coordinate system of the 2PP 2-DOF parallel robot are established. To achieve unity with the motion analysis of 6PUS, the base coordinate system is established on the base of the 6PUS parallel robot. The 2PP parallel robot has only two inputs and two outputs in x and y directions, so the kinematic model is simple. The relationship between inputs and outputs is: $X = q$, $\dot{X} = \dot{q}$, $\ddot{X} = \ddot{q}$.

The content above is the kinematics models of two parallel robots. Next, the force control design of the assembly system will be introduced.

4 Design of Force Control Method

In order to enable the assembly system to adjust the motion of 6PUS parallel robots based on the actual force of memory module in the assembly process, it is necessary to design a reasonable force control method for the assembly system.

The most commonly used methods of force control methods are impedance control and admittance control, which share a same dynamic model. Compared with admittance control, impedance control requires a precise dynamic model, which is difficult to establish. Therefore, admittance model is selected as the active compliance control method in this paper.

Memory module assembly involves several steps, and force control is required in the following steps.

4.1   Force Control Strategy for Memory Module Insertion

During the process of memory module insertion, admittance control is needed to correct the pose of memory module to ensure that the memory module can be inserted into the memory module slot accurately. The force control strategy for this step needs to be adjusted according to the contact state between the memory module and the slot.

For ease of analysis, the directions mentioned below are directions in the body-fixed coordinate system of memory module (as shown in Fig. 6).

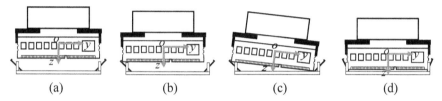

| (a) | (b) | (c) | (d) |

Fig. 6. The process of inserting the memory module into the slot. (a) Before contact; (b) One side contact; (c) The result of one side contact; (d) After entering the slot.

Before Contact. As shown in Fig. 6(a), there is no contact between the memory module and the slot. The gripper holds the memory module and walks a predetermined trajectory, which is along the direction of z-axis in this state. That means only the position in the z direction needs to be artificially constrained.

One Side Contact. As shown in Fig. 6(b), only one side of the memory module is in contact with the slot. If a normal admittance control strategy is used, the memory module will rotate under the action of the torque generated by the contact (as shown in Fig. 6(c)), which is inconsistent with the expected action and may lead to assembly failure. In this case, a specifically step is designed to find the correct location of the slot: before the memory module reaches a preset position in z direction, if there is a large torque in y (or x) direction, it is determined as a one side contact. At this time, the position of the memory module in x (or y) direction instead of the attitude angle is to be adjusted according to the torque until the torque is less than a specified threshold. Continue to insert the memory module and repeat the action if a larger torque occurs again before the memory module reaches the preset position in z direction.

After Entering the Slot. As shown in Fig. 6(d), the memory module will contact the clips, bottom and sides of the slot as enters the slot slowly. At this point, it is necessary to control the following status parameters of the memory module: the forces and the torques in x and y directions, the torque in z direction, and the position in z direction. During the execution of the control strategy, the force in z direction is to be monitored. When the force in z direction reaches the preset threshold, it is considered that the memory module has been inserted into the bottom of the slot, and the insertion action is completed.

In addition, it should be noted that in the actual production and assembly process, there will be differences in tightness and roughness on both sides of the slot. Such errors will result in the difference between the friction forces of the two sides of the memory module. Even if the memory module is inserted into the slot with an accurate posse, this friction error will still cause a large torque in y direction of the memory module. The friction error should be taken into account when design the control parameters and analyze the experimental results.

4.2   Other Steps that Require Force Control

Take the Memory Module Out from the Memory Module Box. It is necessary to control the force of the gripper within a certain range, so as to prevent an unsuitable force of the gripper from destroying the memory module or causing the memory module to slide down. Restricted by the hardware of the gripper, this step of force control is achieved through a current loop.

After the Insertion is Complete. It is necessary to use the gripper to press the memory module quickly for several times after the insertion is complete. This step is to eliminate the bad contact between the memory module and the slot. This step can also adjust the uneven stress between the memory module and the slot. The control method of this step is to make the gripper move down from 1 cm above the assembled memory module, and use admittance control for the movement and rotation of the gripper in x and y directions after touching the memory module. At the same time, monitor the force of gripper in z direction, raise the gripper to prepare for the next press or to stop operation once the force in z direction reached the preset threshold.

5   Experiments and Analysis

5.1   Experimental Process

The picture of the assembly system is shown in Fig. 7.

The memory module box and the motherboard are fixed on the lower platform. In the experiment, two memory modules should be taken out from the memory module box and then be inserted into the memory-module slots. Before inserting the memory module, clips on both sides of the slots must be opened in case that the memory module collide with it and squeeze it. According to the shape and structural characteristics of the memory modules and the slots (Fig. 1), the experimental process is designed, and the flow chart is shown in Fig. 8.

Fig. 7. Picture of the memory module assembly system.

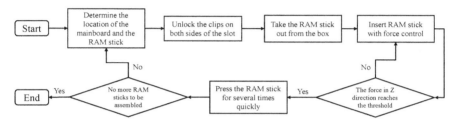

Fig. 8. Flow chart of assembly process.

5.2   Results and Analysis

Using the force control strategy and experimental flow designed in this paper, the memory modules are successfully assembled.

The force curves of the memory module in the assembly process are shown in Fig. 9. It can be seen from the figures that the force in z direction changes the most, this is because the forces in x and y directions are mainly generated by the extrusion deformation between the memory module and the inner wall of the slot, and the extrusion deformation is generated by position deviations of the memory module in x and y directions, which become small after the position correction.

The torque curves of memory modules during assembly are shown in Fig. 10. It can be seen that the torque in y direction changes the most. This is because the tightness and friction coefficient of the left and right sides of the slots are different, and that leads to the inconsistency of the dynamic friction forces of the left and right sides. The error of the dynamic friction force produces the greatest torque in the y direction, because the force arm corresponding to y axis is the longest.

From Figs. 9 and 10, it can be found that only the force in y direction and the torque in x direction converge to 0 at the last stage of memory module assembly, while the absolute value of the other four curves begin to increase rapidly. This is because when the memory module touches the groove at the bottom of the slot, a large force is applied in the z direction to press the memory module into the slot until the clips on two sides of the slots lock automatically. Due to the impact of the processing error of the slots and the clips, the gripper's pose error and other factors, the force between the memory module and the slot is not completely parallel to the z axis, there must be component forces in other directions. The greater the force applied to press the memory module, the greater the component forces generated in other directions, and the greater the torques produced by these forces. The memory module and the groove at the bottom of the card slot are in interference fit in y direction of the memory module, and the contact surface grows with the insertion of the memory module. The interference fit of the memory module and the groove allows the memory module to adjust itself quickly with a small attitude angle adjustment in x direction and a small position adjustment in y direction. The rapid pose adjustment results in the rapid decrease of the component force in y direction and the torque generated in x direction.

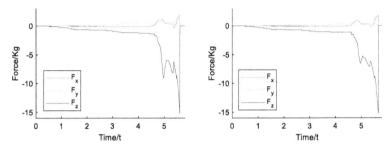

Fig. 9. The force curve of two memory modules.

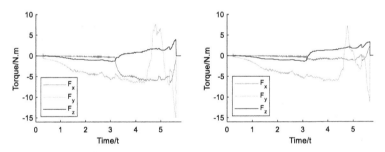

Fig. 10. The torque curve of two memory modules.

The reasons above make the curves of forces and torques in the final stage of the assembly showing the trends in Figs. 9 and 10.

6   Conclusions

In this paper, a memory module assembly system based on 6PUS 6-DOF parallel robot and 2PP 2-DOF parallel robot is designed and manufactured. A series of control strategies are designed to meet the requirements of position control and force control in memory module assembly process. The parallel robots can guarantee the position control effect of the assembly system. In this paper, a 6D force sensor is used in the assembly system, which can measure the force and torque of the memory modules in all directions of space, so as to realize the force control of the spatial movement and rotation of the gripper. Using the mechanism and control method designed in this paper, the assembly of memory module is successfully realized.

In order to ensure the safety of the experiment, the assembly system is still assembled at a slower speed currently. In the future, the execution speed and safety of the assembly system can be improved by optimizing the size of the parallel robots, optimizing the control algorithm, and improving the control of the gripper.

References

1. Du, J.: Research on the development trend of computer science and technology in the "Internet+" Era. J. Phys.: Conf. Ser. **1682**, 012070 (2020)
2. Share of households with a computer at home worldwide from 2005 to 2019. https://www.statista.com/statistics/748551/worldwide-households-with-computer. Accessed box and the motherboard 09 2020
3. Total unit shipments of personal computers (PCs) worldwide from 2006 to 2020. https://www.statista.com/statistics/273495/global-shipments-of-personal-computers-since-2006. Accessed 01 2021
4. Di Pasquale, V., Miranda, S., Neumann, W.P., et al: Human reliability in manual assembly systems: a systematic literature review. IFAC-PapersOnLine **51**(11), 675–680 (2018)
5. Pandilov, Z., Dukovski, V.: Comparison of the characteristics between serial and parallel robots. Acta Technica Corviniensis-Bull. Eng. **7**(1), 143–160 (2014)
6. Cao, R., Gao, F., Zhang, Y., et al: A new parameter design method of a 6-DOF parallel motion simulator for a given workspace. Mech. Based Des. Struct. Mach. **43**(1), 1–18 (2015)
7. Hou, F., Luo, M., Zhang, Z.: An inverse kinematic analysis modeling on a 6-PSS compliant parallel platform for optoelectronic packaging. CES Trans. Electr. Mach. Syst. **3**(1), 81–87 (2019)
8. Cao, X., Zhao, W., Zhao, H., et al.: 6-PSS Precision Positioning Stewart platform for the space telescope adjustment mechanism. In: 2018 IEEE International Conference on Mechatronics and Automation (ICMA), pp. 487–492 (2018)
9. Li, Y., Xu, Q.: Design and analysis of a totally decoupled flexure-based XY parallel micromanipulator. IEEE Trans. Robot. **25**(3) 645–657 (2009)
10. Zhou, S.L., Sun, J., Gao, F.: Influence of flexible spherical joints parameters on accuracy of the six-axis force/torque sensor with three-three orthogonal parallel mechanism. Mech. Mach. Theory **145**, 103697 (2020)
11. Huang, Z., Zhao, Y.S., Zhao, T.S.: Advanced Spatial Mechanism, 2nd edn. Higher Education Press, Beijing (2004)

Terrain Attribute Recognition System for CPG-Based Legged Robot

Hongjin Chen[1], Xi Zhu[1], Siting Zhu[1], Haoyao Chen[1(✉)], Shiwu Zhang[2], and Yunjiang Lou[1]

[1] School of Mechanical Engineering and Automation, Harbin Institute of Technology Shenzhen, Shenzhen 518055, China
hychen5@hit.edu.cn
[2] Department of Precision Machinery and Precision Instrumentation, University of Science and Technology of China, Hefei 230026, China

Abstract. In this paper, we develop a terrain attribute recognition system for CPG-based legged robots. First, a low-cost sensing hardware device is designed to be integrated into the robot, including a tactile sensor array and RGB camera. Second, for the tactile modality, a novel terrain attribute recognition framework is proposed. A data generation strategy that adapts to the motion characteristics is presented, which transforms the original tactile signal into a structured representation, and extract meaningful features. Based on unsupervised and supervised machine learning classifiers, the recognition rates reach 94.0% and 95.5%, and the switching time is 1 to 3 steps. Third, for the recognition of terrain attributes in the visual modality, a lightweight real-time mobile attention coding network (MACNet) is proposed as an end-to-end model, which shows an exhibiting an accuracy of 88.5% on the improved GTOS mobile data set, 169FPS inference speed and 6.6 MB model parameter occupancy. Finally, these two methods are simultaneously applied to the AmphiHex-II robot for outdoor experiments. Experimental results show that each modality has its own advantages and disadvantages, and the complementary relationship between multiple modalities plays an irreplaceable role in a broader scene.

Keywords: Terrain attribute recognition · Tactile and visual sensing · CPG-based legged robot · Deep neural network

1 Introduction

Unlike artificial or structured terrain, mobile robots often face unexpected accidents on unstructured terrain. Reliable terrain recognition is a key technology for autonomous and safe decision-making by robots. However, this problem is extremely challenging because of external disturbances such as weather and light.

Video of this work: https://v.youku.com/v_show/id_XNTE3NTM0NjE1Mg==.html.
H. Chen and X. Zhu—contribute equally to this work.

Previous works can be divided into two sensing methods: exteroceptive [1] and proprioceptive [2]. Visual-based terrain recognition with a DNN is an active area of the former. Xue et al. [3] designed a DEPNet to classify top-down terrain images taken by mobile phones with the highest accuracy of 82.18%. Among proprioceptive modalities, the features extracted by tactile sensors are closely related to the physical attributes behind the terrain, thereby further achieve fine-grained terrain attribute recognition. Bednarek et al. [4] provided a machine learning approach for the quadruped and hexapod robots based on raw force-torque signals, achieving 80% accuracy in most instances. Wu et al. [5] designed a capacitive tactile sensor system and mounted them on the small hexapod robot, achieving 82.5% accuracy through the SVM classifier. More recently, Wellhausen et al. [6] defined the ground reaction score as an empirical terrain property to summarizes the terrain properties when the robot collides with terrains.

It can be seen that previous works can neither complete the identification in real-time and lightweight, nor explicitly represent the physical attributes of the terrain to adapt to reality. Recently, CPG-based legged robots have shown superior terrain traversal capabilities especially in unstructured environments [7]. Due to the rhythmic movement of the rotating legs, the body of the robot usually vibrates violently, which makes the IMU-based method infeasible [8]. Until now there is no reliable and low-cost terrain attribute recognition system for such robot. To this end, we make several contributions to the terrain attribute recognition problem of CPG-based legged robots:

- A low-cost terrain attribute recognition sensing hardware device is designed, mainly composed of a tactile sensor array and RGB camera.
- A tactile-based terrain attribute recognition framework is presented, composed of a data preprocessing module, a peak window segmentation module, a tactile feature extractor, and a machine learning classifier.
- A real-time lightweight deep neural network, the mobile attention coding network (MACNet), is proposed for terrain attribute recognition in the visual modality.

2 Tactile Sensing

The developed tactile-based terrain attribute recognition framework is illustrated in Fig. 1, which mainly consists of five parts: array tactile sensing hardware device, data preprocessing module, peak window segmentation module, tactile feature extractor, and machine learning classifier.

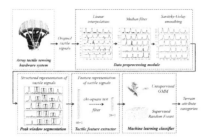

Fig. 1. Tactile-based terrain attribute recognition framework.

2.1 Array Tactile Sensing Hardware System

Mounting the tactile sensor array on the bottom of the robot leg is beneficial for the robot to acquire ground information. Five fully flexible elastic capacitive pressure sensors (RH-ESPB-02, Elastech Inc.) are chosen to form an array as the sensing front end. The parameters of this sensor are: volume of $15 \times 40 \times 2$ (mm^3), resolution of $(95\,\mu m)$, load range of $(0\text{--}400\,N)$, fast response speed $(\geq 50\,Hz)$, linearity of (99.1%) and waterproof surface.

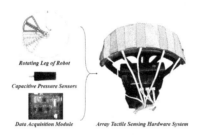

Fig. 2. Integration of the tactile sensing hardware system.

Subsequently, the detection, processing and transmission of pressure signals are completed by the data acquisition module, which mainly contains a microcontroller (STM32F103), a capacitance-to-digital converter (CDC, AD7147), a Bluetooth communication module (HC-05), and a display screen. Figure 2 illustrates the integration of the array tactile sensing system.

2.2 Data Preprocessing Module

To process the raw signal which is transmitted through wireless Bluetooth, two modules are designed to reduce the influence of outliers in the signal as well as segment it. A software-level signal preprocessing module, including linear interpolation, median filtering, and Savitzky-Golay smoothing, is designed to process the signal. Linear interpolation is used to fill the missing values at the head and tail with nearest neighbour. Then, a median filter eliminates the impulse noise that deviates from the initial value. Finally, a Savitzky-Golay filter is used to smooth the signal. After preprocessing, the tactile signal becomes smoother, while still retains its original trend.

2.3   Peak Window Segmentation Module

Previous works often used the rectangular window to segment the time series. By sliding the window on the time axis, each segment is extracted independently, and then fed into the subsequent modules for analysis. As the length of the window increases, the information of each segment will become richer. However, since most of the accumulated data in the window are still past data, the contribution of new information is insufficient. Secondly, the fixed-length rectangular window segmentation does not consider the robot's variable-frequency gait. Besides, it is not conducive to transfer the model of one gait to other gaits.

Therefore, we introduce a peak window segmentation (PWS) strategy to adapt to the situation of legged amphibious robots. Based on the rectangular window, PWS further extracts the data at the moment of interaction between the robot and the terrain and then aligns the peaks of different channels to generate soft-synchronized samples. In practice, we utilize the numerical calculation library SciPy to set up constraints. Specifically, we restrict the height of the peak to be greater than the median of the sequence, the horizontal distance between adjacent peaks greater than 300 points and set the minimum value of the prominence and width of the peak to 0.1 and 1. Then, through a simple strategy of comparing adjacent values in the sequence, we successfully capture the positions of the peaks in the time series.

After signal preprocessing, there are still abnormalities when the robot is walking on real terrain. For example, some channels cannot detect any peaks at a certain moment, while other channels output normally. The strategy we adopted mainly consists of three steps. Remove the first and the last peak, leaving the intermediate peaks. Second, traverse the positions of all peaks in each channel, and check whether the peaks of its adjacent channels are within $\pm 20\%$. If yes, keep all peaks at that moment. Otherwise take the peak position in the channel at the next moment as a substitute. Third, check whether the number of peaks in each channel is the same. Otherwise use the first peak in the first channel as the starting point and the least number of peaks in all five channels as the length, and adjust each channel to the same size. If yes, the PWS procedure is completed. Thus a structured representation of the tactile signal is generated, called peak window matrix denoted as $P_{C \times N}$, C represents the number of channels while N is the number of peaks in a rectangular window. As shown in Fig. 3, even though the tactile signals present irregular shapes in the dimensions of time and channel, PWS successfully achieves soft synchronization of data between different channels.

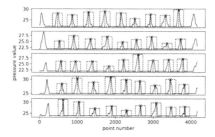

Fig. 3. Structured representation of peak window matrix $P_{5\times9}$ for tactile signals.

2.4 Tactile Feature Extractor

We designed the feature calculator and selector to further obtain the latent representation of the original data. Specifically, for each peak window sample $p_{ij}(i = 1\ldots5, j = 1\ldots N)$ in $P_{5\times N}$, we first calculated 12-dimensional tactile features for the five sensor channels, as shown in Table 1. The orginal tactile features can be denoted as $F = \{F_1, \ldots, F_{60}\}$. Afterwards, the chi-square test was utilized as a feature selector to measure the correlation between each feature and terrain attribute categories. The original features with $p - value > 0.05$ are filtered out because they have a 95% probability of accepting the hypothesis. In this way, a series of refined 26-dimensional tactile features are obtained, denoted as $F^* = \{F_1^*, \ldots, F_{26}^*\}$.

Table 1. 12-dimensional tactile features designed for terrain attribute recognition.

Feature	Description and Calculation
Absolute energy	The sum of squared peak data
Auto correlation	The autocorrelation coefficient of the specified lag value, characterizing the correlation degree within a peak window
Complexity-invariant distance	The estimation of the complexity degree within a peak window
Kurtosis	The kurtosis of the peak by Fisher-Pearson standardized moment coefficient G_2
Maximum	The maximum value of the peak
Mean	The mean value of the peak
Median	The median value of the peak
Minimum	The minimum value of the peak
Sample entropy	The probability of generating a new pattern in a peak window to measure the complexity of the time series
Skewness	The skewness of the peak by Fisher-Pearson standardized moment coefficient G_1
Standard deviation	The standard deviation of the peak
Variance	The variance of the peak

2.5   Machine Learning Classifier

We use multi-class classification to complete the exploration of terrain attributes to meet the needs of CPG-based legged robots. Gaussian mixture model (GMM) is used as the unsupervised classifier. Even if there is no prior information about the terrain, the data samples can be mapped into separable clusters by the designed feature extractor, which can demonstrate the extracted features have a beneficial effect on distinguishing terrain with different attributes. Besides, the supervised Random forest (RF) classifier, which is not easy to over-fit, is also used because of its fast training and testing to achieve better performance than unsupervised.

3   Visual Sensing

For visual modality, the robot perceives surface features of terrains. This section describes our deep neural network for terrain attribute recognition, called Mobile Attention Coding Network (MACNet) shown in Fig. 4, which consists of attention-feature extraction network, texture encoding network, and classification network.

3.1   Attention-Feature Extraction Network

Taking advantage of the combination of point-wise and depth-wise convolution in MobileNetV2 [9], an input RGB image with a size of $224 \times 224 \times 3$ is filtered by a 3×3 convolutional kernel to obtain an initial feature map. Then, the feature map is fed to an Inverted Residual block. In its first half, a 1×1 point-wise convolution expands the feature map channels first, a 3×3 depth-wise convolution with the stride of 2 samples the feature map, and then a 1×1 point-wise convolution shrinks the channels back. As for the second, the convolution processing flow is the same, only the stride in the depth-wise convolution is changed to 1. This is to keep the spatial size unchanged because the feature map is refined through a shortcut branch of the attention mechanism module, and then added to the output of the last point-wise convolution. We choose CBAM [10] as the attention mechanism module to improve the problem of poor information circulation in spatial and channel dimensions. In practice, most convolution layers are followed by a Batch Normalization layer and a *ReLU* activation function, except that the last point-wise convolution in the Inverted Residual block is linear. In this way, the size of the output feature map of attention-feature extraction network is $14 \times 14 \times 256$.

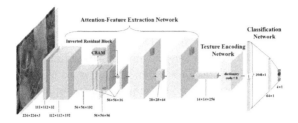

Fig. 4. The structure of Mobile Attention Coding Network (MACNet).

3.2 Texture Encoding Network

Then, the feature map is represented as a smaller size, followed by the texture encoding network. The texture representation depicts the disorder degree of materials, and the dictionary encoding retains visual details to the greatest extent. Therefore, we also use this texture layer, which is the most advanced module for terrain visual classification tasks. We set the number of dictionary codes to 8, combined with 256-dimensional input channels to form a 2048-dimensional texture encoding vector.

3.3 Fully Connected Network

Finally, the classification network is composed of two linearly connected layers with sizes of 2048×64 and 64×4 to map the texture encoding vector into four terrain attribute categories.

4 Experiments and Results

4.1 CPG-Based Legged Robot Platform: AmphiHex-II

We use a CPG-based legged robot named AmphiHex-II [11] to test our methods, shown in Fig. 5. As CPG neural network is usually used in the rhythmic movement of animals, we chose it as the control strategy to achieve smooth gait control and fast gait transition. A Hoof oscillator is adopted at each driving module to generate a stable self-oscillation signal. In this way, the complex gait adjustment and speed control of the CPG-based robot can be simplified by only managing parameters such as frequency ω, phase difference θ, and offset angle Φ.

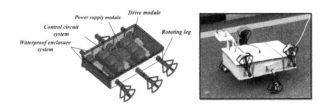

Fig. 5. The structure of AmphiHex-II robot.

4.2   Data Collection

We collected four common terrain data in the HITsz campus to represent stiffness levels: Very Hard, Hard, Soft, and Very Soft. The control commands were sent to drive the robot to move on terrains in the tripod gait with a fixed frequency. When the robot is moving, array tactile sensing system transmits tactile signals to the laptop by the Bluetooth module, and the equipped camera (Intel RealSense D435i) records the RGB image of the terrain (640×480) from the top view.

For tactile modality, we collected 169 peaks as the training samples and 109 peaks as the test samples. For visual modality, we combined the GTOS-mobile dataset [3] with the terrain images we collected to form four corresponding stiffness levels, which can be used as the benchmark for evaluating the visual-based models. As a result, 61222 training samples and 4939 test samples were obtained, covering different conditions (Figs. 6 and 7).

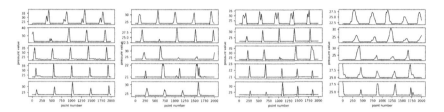

Fig. 6. Samples of array tactile signals (left to right: Very Hard, Hard, Soft, Very Soft).

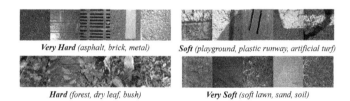

Very Hard (asphalt, brick, metal)   *Soft (playground, plastic runway, artificial turf)*

Hard (forest, dry leaf, bush)   *Very Soft (soft lawn, sand, soil)*

Fig. 7. Samples of terrain images (combination of GTOS-mobile [3] and our dataset).

4.3   Training Procedure

We use the scikit-learn machine learning library with the number of decision trees to 5 and criteria to the information gain. As for visual modality, we use Pytorch to construct MACNet's architecture and train the deep neural network. The Data argument is adopted to improve the generalization ability of the model, which includes random scaling, cropping, inversion, brightness, and contrast jitter ($\pm 40\%$). Adam is chosen as optimization algorithm, and cross entropy as the evaluation criterion. The learning rate is 0.01, reduced by 10 times every 10 epochs. The batch size of the training set is set to 256, and the test set is 128.

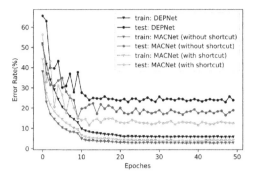

Fig. 8. The error rates of visual-based models in the training process.

Figure 8 shows the error rates of MACNet and DEPNet [3] in the training process of 50 epochs. The testing error rate of DEPNet is around 25% while MACNet without CBAM shortcut is around 17%, which indicates that MACNet better fits the relationship between the RGB image and the terrain attribute category by mining deeper features related to the terrain. When the CBAM shortcut is added to MACNet, error rate drops to the lowest 11.5%, which means that the performance of the deep neural network model has been further improved.

4.4   Terrain Attribute Recognition Results

Tactile Modality. For tactile modality, PCA was utilized, obtaining two dominant features, pca_1 and pca_2. Then, the Pearson correlation coefficients of pca_1 and pca_2 were calculated to obtain the Gaussian ellipse of each category's samples. Therefore, GMM was utilized to perform unsupervised classification. As shown in Fig. 9(a), different stiffness levels' ground truths are located in different positions in the two-dimensional feature plane. Meanwhile, in Fig. 9(b), it can be seen that the clusters divided by GMM have good consistency with the distribution of ground truth indeed. From a quantitative point of view, the recognition accuracy of GMM reaches 94% (classification labels are artificially assigned after clustering), with the confusion matrix shown in Fig. 10(c).

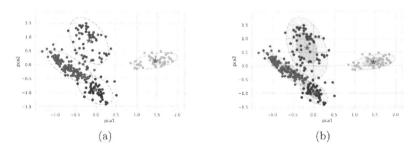

(a)   (b)

Fig. 9. Two-dimensional feature distribution of different stiffness levels (a) ground truth (b) GMM clustering result (yellow-Very Soft, green-Soft, blue-Hard, red-Very Hard). (Color figure online)

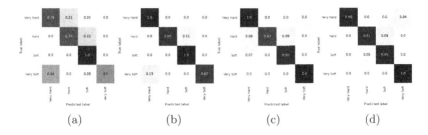

Fig. 10. Confusion matrix of (a) 300-points rectangular window (b) 2000-points rectangular window (c) 300-points peak window (unsupervised GMM) (d) 300-points peak window (supervised RF).

AmphiHex-II generates about 300 data points in one step, which is the length of a peak window. Therefore, we introduced the traditional rectangular window segmentation with lengths of 300 and 2000 to compare with the peak window segmentation method we proposed. Figure 10(a) shows that the recognition accuracy of a 300-points rectangular window is 76.5%. Figure 10(b) shows that when the length increases to 2000, the accuracy rises 94.0%. Although the recognition accuracy is improved with the expansion of the rectangular window, these methods sacrifice the critical real-time performance for robots. For example, in the case of 2000-points, the robot needs to walk about 8–10 steps to predict the latest terrain attributes once. However, if the terrain changes quickly, the robot will not be able to make correct recognition in time. Figure 10(c) and Fig. 10(d) show the results based on peak window segmentation with unsupervised GMM classifier and supervised RF classifier. As their accuracy reaches 94.0% and 95.5% respectively, it can be concluded that for CPG-based legged robots, the method of peak window segmentation is much better than traditional rectangular windows. Although fewer data points are used, our method can identify the correct terrain with faster inference time (0.003 s) and higher accuracy, which shows that the accurate capture of the robot-terrain collision process is effective for the terrain recognition task.

Table 2. Performance comparison of tactile-based methods

Methods	Evaluation metrics	
	Recognition accuracy (%)	Switching time (step)
300-points rectangular window (RF)	76.5	1–3
1000-points rectangular window (RF)	86.5	4–5
2000-points rectangular window (RF)	94.0	8–10
300-points peak window (GMM)	94.0	1–3
300-points peak window (RF)	95.5	1–3

Visual Modality. As shown in Fig. 11 and Table 2, DEPNet has an average accuracy of 76.3%, inference speed of 222 FPS, and model parameter occupancy of 150.3 MB. However, for the Hard, Soft, and Very Soft terrains, it respectively has 32%, 14%, and 36% probability to misclassify them into other categories. MACNet has an average accuracy of 88.50%, inference speed of 169 FPS, and model parameter occupancy of 6.6 MB. Only a few classification errors occur between the Very Soft and Hard terrains, which may be due to the existence of similar green vegetation and branches on forests and lawns (Table 3).

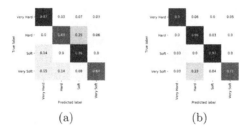

(a)   (b)

Fig. 11. Onfusion matrix of (a) DEPNet (b) MACNet.

Table 3. Performance comparison of visual-based models

Models	Evaluation metrics		
	Recognition accuracy (%)	Inference speed (fps)	Model parameter occupancy (MB)
DEPNet	76.3	222	150.3
MACNet	88.5	169	6.6

Discussion of Two Modality. Visual-based method has a satisfactory accuracy with a superior generalization ability. However, when robot walking on scene with insufficient light, the visual sensor will completely lose its effectiveness. In this situation, the terrain attribute recognition module of the tactile modality can still operate normally. Besides, the tactile-based solution also has the disadvantage of poor real-time performance. Compared to the inference speed of 169 FPS in the visual-based method, it must take the robot 1–3 steps at least to obtain correct results. Secondly, the tactile sensors mounted on the robot's legs can only recognize the terrain at the current moment, without predicting the terrain ahead. Because different modalities have complementary effects, it can be concluded that developing a terrain attribute recognition architecture under the fusion of multiple sensors is an inevitable trend, which also proves that our work in this paper has laid an important foundation for this research field in the future.

5 Conclusion

In this work, we develop a terrain attribute recognition method based on the tactile and visual modality of CPG-based legged robots. The designed tactile sensor array hardware device measures the interactions between the robot and the terrain. For the tactile modality, the maximum accuracy is 95.5% and the switching time is 1 to 3 steps. In terms of the visual modality, MACNet is superior to other models on the benchmark data set, with an accuracy rate of 88.5%, an inference speed of 169FPS, and a model parameter occupancy of 6.6 MB. Taking the AmphiHex-II as test, the feasibility of this method is verified. We believe that the methods can be flexibly applied to other robots, especially CPG-based legged robots. Also the semantic tags obtained from the terrain attributes can be applied to other operational tasks such as navigation, planning, and anomaly detection for mobile robots.

References

1. Belter, D., Wietrzykowski, J., Skrzypczyński, P.: Employing natural terrain semantics in motion planning for a multi-legged robot. J. Intell. Robot. Syst. **93**(3), 723–743 (2019)
2. Bhattacharya, S., et al.: Surface-property recognition with force sensors for stable walking of humanoid robot. IEEE Access **7**, 146443–146456 (2019)
3. Xue, J., Zhang, H., Dana, K.: Deep texture manifold for ground terrain recognition. In: Proceedings of the IEEE Conference on Computer Vision and Pattern Recognition, pp. 558–567 (2018)
4. Bednarek, J., Bednarek, M., Wellhausen, L., Hutter, M., Walas, K.: What am i touching? learning to classify terrain via haptic sensing. In: 2019 International Conference on Robotics and Automation (ICRA), pp. 7187–7193. IEEE (2019)
5. Wu, X.A., Huh, T.M., Sabin, A., Suresh, S.A., Cutkosky, M.R.: Tactile sensing and terrain-based gait control for small legged robots. IEEE Trans. Robot. **36**(1), 15–27 (2019)
6. Wellhausen, L., Dosovitskiy, A., Ranftl, R., Walas, K., Cadena, C., Hutter, M.: Where should i walk? Predicting terrain properties from images via self-supervised learning. IEEE Robot. Autom. Lett. **4**(2), 1509–1516 (2019)
7. Zhang, S., Zhou, Y., Xu, M., Liang, X., Liu, J., Yang, J.: Amphihex-i: locomotory performance in amphibious environments with specially designed transformable flipper legs. IEEE/ASME Trans. Mechatron. **21**(3), 1720–1731 (2015)
8. Manjanna, S., Dudek, G.: Autonomous gait selection for energy efficient walking. In: 2015 IEEE International Conference on Robotics and Automation (ICRA), pp. 5155–5162. IEEE (2015)
9. Sandler, M., Howard, A., Zhu, M., Zhmoginov, A., Chen, L.C.: MobileNetV 2: inverted residuals and linear bottlenecks. In: Proceedings of the IEEE Conference on Computer Vision and Pattern Recognition, pp. 4510–4520 (2018)
10. Woo, S., Park, J., Lee, J.Y., Kweon, I.S.: CBAM: convolutional block attention module. In: Proceedings of the European Conference on Computer Vision (ECCV), pp. 3–19 (2018)
11. Zhong, B., Zhang, S., Xu, M., Zhou, Y., Fang, T., Li, W.: On a CPG-based hexapod robot: Amphihex-II with variable stiffness legs. IEEE/ASME Trans. Mechatron. **23**(2), 542–551 (2018)

Kinematic Reliability Evaluation of Planar Mechanisms with Time-Varying Correlation of Wear in Multiple Joints

Xinchen Zhuang[1,2]([✉]), Qizhi Meng[1,2], and Xin-Jun Liu[1,2]

[1] The State Key Laboratory of Tribology and Institute of Manufacturing Engineering, Department of Mechanical Engineering, Tsinghua University, Beijing 100084, China
[2] Beijing Key Lab of Precision/Ultra-Precision Manufacturing Equipments and Control, Tsinghua University, Beijing 100084, China

Abstract. The wear in joints is a critical factor influencing the service life of the mechanism. Unlike existing researches that focus on wear prediction of joints, the correlation of wear among multiple joints in a mechanism is investigated in this study. The wear correlation of multiple joints in a mechanism is analyzed firstly. Then, a kinematic reliability evaluation method of planar mechanisms considering the wear correlation of joints is proposed. In the method, the wear depth in joints is modeled by Gamma process to take the stochastic characteristic into account. Vine copula functions and two correlation evolution equations are introduced to capture the time-varying and pairwise correlation of wear in the joints. At last, a numerical procedure is presented based on the Monte Carlo simulation. A four-bar mechanism is used to illustrate the proposed method. The results show that the wear of joints in a mechanism correlates with each other strongly, and the correlation varied with time. The correlation differs with one another in different pairs of joints. Besides, the time-varying correlation of wear has a significant influence on the kinematic reliability of the mechanism.

Keywords: Wear · Clearance joint · Correlation · Kinematic reliability

1 Introduction

Wear is inevitable in the joints due to the relative motion between the components and eventually causes failure of the mechanism. As a critical factor influencing the service life of mechanical systems, it is important to investigate the wear behavior of joints and its influence on the kinematic outputs [1].

Over the last few decades, a significant number of researchers have theoretically and experimentally studied the wear of revolute joints. At the early stage, the research mainly focused on uniform wear in joints [2, 3]. With the increase of requirement for accurate joints clearance modeling, the non-uniform wear in the joints has attracted considerable attention [4]. A large number of methods were proposed from different aspects to obtain the accurate prediction of joints wear, for instance, the method based on Winkler model [5], the method integrating multi-body kinematics with a finite element model [6], the

© Springer Nature Switzerland AG 2021
X.-J. Liu et al. (Eds.): ICIRA 2021, LNAI 13015, pp. 568–580, 2021.
https://doi.org/10.1007/978-3-030-89134-3_52

method combining monitoring data with Bayesian theory [7], the method based on multi-body dynamic models [4]. With these models, the effects of different factors on wear of joints were studied. Li et al. found that the clearance sizes nonlinearly influenced the wear depths of the two joints with clearance in a slider-crank mechanism [8]. Jiang et al. presented the initial clearance sizes and driving speeds had a strong influence on wear phenomenon in the joints [9]. These researches on wear behavior of joints have played a positive role in the dynamic design, optimization analysis, and performance improvement of mechanisms considering joints wear.

In engineering, the kinematic accuracy of a mechanism is also the main concern. The accuracy decrease due to the progress of wear is gaining more and more attention in recent years. The kinematic reliability of a mechanism with joints clearance has been extensively studied [10]. Based on these studies, some researchers further investigated the kinematic reliability of mechanisms involving joints wear. Wu et al. proposed an indirect probability model for mechanism reliability evaluation of multi-body mechanisms considering the wear of joints [3]. Geng et al. presented an integrated non-probabilistic kinematic analysis of precision mechanisms with non-uniform wear in joints by combining multi-body dynamic analysis, wear prediction, and kinematic reliability analysis [11]. However, these researches ignore the wear correlation among multiple clearances. For a mechanism with multiple clearance joints, the joints interact with each other [12]. And hence there is correlation of wear among joints. The existing studies concerning wear correlation are limited to wear of two joints in a mechanism [8, 9]. A real mechanism normally has multiple joints. The wear correlation is much more complex due to the unpredictable interaction among the joints, compared with the correlation between two joints. Besides, these researches just studied the correlation from one or two aspects. Comprehensive research is required, for example, how does the wear of one joint influence the other one? What are the factors contributing to the correlation? To what degree the correlation is and how is the correlation varied with time?

To fill the gap, the correlation effects of wear in multiple joints are studied. Then, a dynamic reliability evaluation method for planar mechanisms considering joints wear is proposed. In the method, the distinct correlation between different pairs of joints is considered by a vine copula function. Two correlation evolution equations are introduced to describe the time-varying correlation among the joints wear. A four-bar mechanism is used to illustrate our proposed method. Finally, some conclusions are made.

2 Wear Correlation of Multiple Joints in a Mechanism

The correlation of wear is analyzed firstly. As is shown in Fig. 1, there are three clearance joints (C_1, C_2 and C_3) and three linkages (L_1, L_2, and L_3). Joint C_1 includes a journal (J_1) and a bearing (B_1) while Joint C_1 includes a journal (J_2) and a bearing (B_2). When the mechanism operates, J_1 contacts with B_1, which produces the force F_1 (include the normal force and tangential force). F_1 not only depends on the clearance size of Joint C_1, but also is influenced by the clearance size of Joint C_2 [13]. In a similar way, Joint C_2 affects the contact force in Joint C_1. The contact forces are also influenced by other factors, such as the dimensions L of the linkages, mass M of the linkages, operation velocity V of the mechanism, and the load P applied to the mechanism. We have

$$
\begin{cases}
F_1 = G_{F,1}(c_1, c_2, L, M, P, V) \\
F_2 = G_{F,2}(c_1, c_2, L, M, P, V)
\end{cases}
\tag{1}
$$

where, $G_{F,1}$ and $G_{F,2}$ represent functions reflecting the relationship between the contact forces and their influencing factors, respectively.

Similar to the contact force, The relative sliding distance between the journal center and bearing center of the two joints can be written as

$$
\begin{cases}
S_1 = G_{S,1}(c_1, c_2, L, M, P, V) \\
S_2 = G_{S,2}(c_1, c_2, L, M, P, V)
\end{cases}
\tag{2}
$$

where, S_1 and S_2 denote the relative sliding distance between the journal center and bearing center of Joints C_1 and C_2, respectively. $G_{S,1}$ and $G_{S,2}$ are functions reflecting the relationship between the relative sliding distance and their influencing factors, respectively.

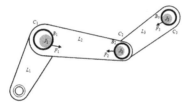

Fig. 1. Two joints in a mechanism

According to Archard's wear model [14], the wear depth of a joint is determined by the contact force and relative sliding distance between the journal and bearing. Both the contact forces and relative sliding distances of the two joints are influenced by the same factors. Thus wear of Joints C_1 and C_2 is correlated. As the joints size enlarges during the progress of wear and there exists randomness in the load, the correlation of wear may be time-varying with the operation of the mechanism.

In Fig. 1, the interaction of Joint C_1 with Joint C_3 is transmitted through linkages L_2 and L_3 while the interaction of Joint C_2 with Joint C_3 is transmitted by linkage L_3. It is obvious the interaction between Joints C_1 and C_3 differs from that between Joints C_2 and C_3. In addition, the effects of the load and other influencing factors on the joints are different due to the configuration of the mechanism. It means the correlation of wear between different pairs of joints is different in a mechanism.

3   Reliability Evaluation Considering Time-Varying Correlation of Wear in Multiple Joints

A kinematic reliability evaluation method considering the time-varying correlation of wear is proposed. The developed method aims to obtain the dynamic reliability of the mechanism while the joints experiencing wear. This requires to: (1) model the wear process of the joints; (2) characterize the time-varying correlation of wear in multiple joints; (3) perform reliability evaluation of the mechanism.

3.1 Wear Modeling of a Single Joint

The cumulative wear depth of a joint is stochastic due to the variation of material properties and dimensions in processing and manufacturing. We treat the wear of joints as a stochastic process. In engineering, the hardness of the journal is usually much larger than that of the bearing, and hence the wear in the journal can be ignored. The wear depth is assumed to be uniform along the circumference of the bearing. Gamma process is used to govern the wear depth of the bearing in individual joints. Gamma process with shape parameter v and scale parameter u is a continuous-time stochastic process $\{Y(t), t \geq 0\}$ with the following properties [15]: (1) $Y(0) = 0$ with probability one; (2) $Y(t)$ has independent increments; (3) $Y(t + \Delta t) - Y(t) \sim G(v\Delta t, u)$, for $t \geq 0$. where $G(y|v, u)$ is the probability density function of a random variable $Y(Y \geq 0)$ having Gamma distribution with shape parameter v and scale parameter u given by

$$G(y|v, u) = \frac{u^v}{\Gamma(v)} y^{v-1} \exp(-uy), \quad \Gamma(v) = \int_0^\infty y^{v-1} e^{-y} dy \qquad (3)$$

The wear depth increment $\Delta y_i^j = y_i(t_j) - y_i(t_{j-1}), j = 2, \ldots, m$ denotes the degradation increment of the ith components at the time interval $[t_{j-1}, t_j]$. The corresponding CDF and PDF are $F(\Delta y_i^j)$ and $f(\Delta y_i^j)$, respectively.

3.2 Time-Varying Correlation of Wear in Multiple Joints

From the conclusions in Sect. 2, the wear of multiple joints in a mechanism is correlated. It is important to model the correlation of joints wear to obtain accurate reliability evaluation results. Vine copulas are developed in recent years to solve the complex correlation among multiple variables [16]. It converts the joint probability density distributinon PDF into a product of the marginal distributions and multiple bivariate copula functions. Then, it can describe the correlation of each pair of variables accurately. Therefore, the vine copula function is adopted to model the correlation of wear in multiple joints.

In a mechanism with n clearance joints, at the time point t_{j-1}, the cumulative wear depth of each joint is represented by y_i^{j-1} ($i = 1, 2, \ldots n$). The wear of each joint at the time interval $[t_{j-1}, t_j]$ is represented by $\Delta y_i^j (i = 1, 2, \ldots n)$. The wear depth increments of each joint at the same time interval are correlated and the correlation differs for different pairs of joints. The joint PDF of wear depth increment for the joints at time interval $[t_{j-1}, t_j]$ is written as [17]

$$f(\Delta y_1^j, \Delta y_2^j, \ldots, \Delta y_n^j) = \prod_{k=1}^n f(\Delta y_k^j) \prod_{q=1}^{n-1} \prod_{p=1}^{n-q} c_{p,p+q|p+1,\ldots,p+q-1} \left(F_{p|p+1,\ldots,p+q-1} \left(\Delta y_p^j | \Delta y_{p+1}^j, \ldots, \Delta y_{p+q-1}^j \right), \right.$$

$$\left. F_{p+q|p+1,\ldots,p+q-1} \left(\Delta y_{p+q}^j | \Delta y_{p+1}^j, \ldots, \Delta y_{p+q-1}^j \right), \theta_{p,p+q|p+1,\ldots,p+q-1} (t_{j-1}) \right. \qquad (4)$$

where $c_{X_s, V_s | V_{-s}}(\cdot | \cdot)$ denotes the bivariate conditional copula density, and it is shown as follows,

$$
\begin{aligned}
&c_{X_s, V_s | V_{-s}}\left(F_{X_s, | V_{-s}}(X_s | V_{-s}), F_{V_s, | V_{-s}}(V_s | V_{-s}), \theta_{p,p+q|p+1,\ldots,p+q-1}(t_{j-1})\right) \\
&= \frac{\partial C\left(F_{X_s, | V_{-s}}(X_s | V_{-s}), F_{V_s, | V_{-s}}(V_s | V_{-s})\right) \theta_{p,p+q|p+1,\ldots,p+q-1}(t_{j-1})}{\partial F_{X_s, | V_{-s}}(X_s | V_{-s}) \partial F_{V_s, | V_{-s}}(V_s | V_{-s})}
\end{aligned}
\tag{5}
$$

where $C(.)$ is a bivariate copula function. $\theta_{p,p+q|p+1,\ldots,p+q-1}(t_{j-1})$ is the parameter of the copula function, reflecting the correlation relationship of the variables at the time point t_{j-1}. Copula function is a function combining the marginal distribution with the joint distribution of the variables:

$$
H(x_1, x_2) = C(F_1(x_1), F_2(x_2), \theta)
\tag{6}
$$

where $H(x_1, x_2)$ represents the joint distribution of variables (x_1, x_2). $F_1(x_1)$ and $F_2(x_2)$ denote the marginal distributions of the variables x_1 and x_2, respectively. θ is the parameter of the copula function.

The conditional distributions of the form $F_{X|V}(.|.)$ in Eq. (5) can be calculated by

$$
F_{X|V}(X|V) = \frac{\partial C_{X, V_s | V_{-s}}(F(X | V_{-s}), F_{V_s, | V_{-s}}(V_s | V_{-s}))}{\partial F_{V_s, | V_{-s}}(V_s | V_{-s})}
\tag{7}
$$

For the special case of binary conditional distribution, X is represented by x_r and V is represented by x_s. The conditional distribution can be expressed by an h function:

$$
F_{r|s}(x_r | x_s) = h_{rs}(u_r, u_s) = \frac{\partial C_{r,s}(u_r, u_s)}{\partial u_s}
\tag{8}
$$

According to the research in Sect. 2, the correlation of wear varies with the increasing of time. Wear is a slow process, and the correlation of wear between different joints also changes slowly. Hence, only the parameter of the Copula function varies, and the copula function form remains fixed over time. For the slowly changing correlation in engineering, there are two models of Kendall's tau $\tau(t)$ presented in reference [18]: Time-varying Stable Model and Time-varying Unstable Model.

1) Time-varying stable model (TSM):

$$
\tau(t) = L \cdot [\sin(2\pi \cdot (1 + \gamma \cdot e^{-\zeta t}))]^\kappa + \psi
\tag{9}
$$

where L refers to the saturation level. γ represents the minitrim factor. ζ denotes the changing rate factor. κ depicts the shape factor and ψ denotes a stable value. When t is large enough, $\tau(t) \to \psi$.

2) Time-varying unstable model (TUM):

$$
\tau(t) = \sum_{q=1}^{m} (a_q \cos(q \cdot w \cdot t) + b_q \cos(q \cdot w \cdot t)) + a_0
\tag{10}
$$

where $a_q, b_q (q = 1, 2, ..., m)$, a_0 and ω represent undetermined parameters without special meanings for them.

When Kendall's tau tends to be constant with the increasing time, TSM can be used. In contrast, TUM is suitable in the case where Kendall's tau changes irregularly and will not eventually approach to be a constant.

In Eq. (4), the parameter $\theta_{p,p+q|p+1,...,p+q-1}$ has the following relationship with the rank correlation coefficient Kendall's tau τ: For arbitrary copula function $C(u, v, \theta)$ with its integrable partial derivatives $\partial C(u, v, \theta)/\partial u$, $\partial C(u, v, \theta)/\partial v$ in $I^2 = [1, 2]^2$,

$$\tau_\theta = 1 - \iint_{I^2} \frac{\partial C(u, v, \theta)}{\partial u} \frac{\partial C(u, v, \theta)}{\partial v} du dv = \varphi(\theta) \tag{11}$$

When the evolution equation of Kendall's tau is obtained with Eqs. (9) or (10), the parameter in the copula function can be calculated according to Eq. (12):

$$\theta(t) = \varphi^{-1}(\tau) \tag{12}$$

After the joint PDF is built, the next step is parameter estimation, which consists of two steps. The first step is to select the suitable bivariate copula functions in Eq. (4), and the second step is to perform parameter estimation.

There are many classes of copula functions, and the commonly used copulas that aim to describe the dependence of variables in engineering are Clayton, Gumbel, Frank, and Gaussian copula. They can almost cover the common correlation relationship between variables in engineering. Hence, they are selected as candidate Copula functions in this paper. When the candidate copula functions are chosen, the bivariate copula functions can be selected based on the maximum likelihood method (MLE) and Akaike information criterion (AIC) [19].

The second step is parameter estimation. A joint parameter estimation method based on Bayesian inference is used to facilitate parameter estimation. The parameters include two parts: parameters of the Gamma processes θ_g and parameters of the vine copula function θ_c (parameters of the TSM model or the TUM model). Using the Bayesian method, the posterior distribution of the parameters can be obtained:

$$p(\theta_g, \theta_c | \Delta y_1, \Delta y_2, ..., \Delta y_n) \propto \pi(\theta_g, \theta_c) \times \prod_{k=1}^{q} \prod_{j=1}^{p} \left[f(\Delta y_{1j}^k, \Delta y_{2j}^k, ..., \Delta y_{nj}^k) \right] \tag{13}$$

where p is the number of time intervals; q is the number of samples for wear data of the joints in a mechanism; Δy_{ij}^k is the wear depth increment of the ith joint in the kth sample at the time interval $[t_{j-1}, t_j]$.

It is quite complicated to perform parameter estimation in Eq. (13) with a large amount of data. Hence, the Bayesian Markov chain Monte Carlo (MCMC) method is used to estimate the parameters. In this paper, the prior distributions in Eq. (13) of all the unknown parameters are non-informative.

3.3 Dynamic Reliability Evaluation

For a mechanism, the kinematic reliability with a given input angle θ_{in} is the probability that the kinematic error is less than the allowable value ε.

$$R(\theta_{in}) = \Pr\{|S(\theta_{in}, \boldsymbol{L}, \boldsymbol{r})| \leq \varepsilon\} \tag{14}$$

where $\boldsymbol{L}$ represent the dimensions of the linkages. The symbol $\boldsymbol{r}$ denotes the clearance of the joints, which equals the sum of the wear depth and initial joint clearance. As the kinematic error is uncertain due to the clearance of the joints and the randomness of the linkage dimensions, we use the upper limit of the kinematic error $\left|\overline{\overline{S}}(\theta_{in}, \boldsymbol{L}, \boldsymbol{r})\right|$ obtained from the method in reference [20] to replace the kinematic error $|S(\theta_{in}, \boldsymbol{L}, \boldsymbol{r})|$ in Eq. (14). The reliability of the mechanism can be represented as

$$\hat{R}(\theta_{in}) = \Pr\left\{\left|\overline{\overline{S}}(\theta_{in}, \boldsymbol{L}, \boldsymbol{r})\right| \leq \varepsilon\right\} \tag{15}$$

As the upper limit of the kinematic error is used, the result from Eq. (15) is conservative.

It is difficult to obtain the reliability in Eq. (15) analytically. A Monte Carlo-based method is proposed. The flowchart of the method is shown in Fig. 2.

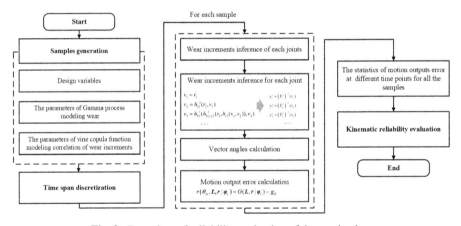

Fig. 2. Procedure of reliability evaluation of the mechanism

The detailed procedures are given as follows.

Step1: Determine the distribution of random variables X in the mechanism, including the linkage length X_L, initial joint clearance X_C. Then, according to the posterior distribution of the parameters of Gamma processes, the parameters of the vine copula functions in Eq. (13), and the distributions of the random variables X, draw N samples $Z = [\theta_g, \theta_c, x]$.

Step2: Divide the operation time-span of the mechanism into m discrete time intervals $[t_0, t_1]$, $[t_1, t_2]$, …, $[t_{m-1}, t_m]$. The time-span is the time length, in which the reliability of the mechanism is concerned.

Step 3: Set $k = 1$ and start the evaluation. We aim to calculate the kinematic error for the N samples at the time points $t_1, t_2, ..., t_m$.

Step 4: For the kth sample, generate the wear depth increments of all the joints at the time intervals $[t_0, t_1], [t_1, t_2], ..., [t_{m-1}, t_m]$. For the jth ($1 \leq j \leq m$) time interval, the wear depth increments can be obtained by conducting the following operations by using Rosenblatt transformation [21]:

1) Generate multidimensional independent uniform distribution random variables $r = (r_1, r_2, ..., r_n)$ on the interval $[0, 1]$.

2) According to the TSM model in Eq. (9) or the TUM model in Eq. (10), calculate the values of Kendall's tau for each pair of variables for the corresponding bivariate copula functions in Eq. (4) at the time point t_{j-1}. Then obtain the parameter values of these bivariate copula functions by Eq. (12) at the time point t_{j-1}.

3) Let $v_1 = r_1$. The wear depth increment of the first joint at the time interval $[t_{j-1}, t_j]$ can be represented as $\Delta y_1^j = \left(F_1^j\right)^{-1}(v_1)$, where $\left(F_1^j\right)^{-1}(\cdot)$ represents the inverse function of the CDF of the wear depth increment in the first joint at the time interval $[t_{j-1}, t_j]$.

4) Let $F_{2|1}(\Delta y_2^j|\Delta y_2^j) = \partial C_{12}(F_1^j(\Delta y_1^j), F_2^j(\Delta y_2^j), \theta_j)\big/\partial F_2^j(\Delta y_2^j) = h_{21}(v_1, v_2) = r_2$ We can obtain $v_2 = h_{21}^{-1}(r_2, v_1)$ and $\Delta y_2^j = \left(F_2^j\right)^{-1}(v_2)$, where $\left(F_2^j\right)^{-1}(\cdot)$ represents the inverse function of the CDF of the wear depth increment in the second joint at the time interval $[t_{j-1}, t_j]$.

5)   Let $F_{3|12}(\Delta y_3^j|\Delta y_1^j, \Delta y_2^j)$ $=$
$\partial C_{13|2}(F_{3|2}(\Delta y_3^j|\Delta y_2^j), F_{1|2}(\Delta y_1^j|\Delta y_2^j), \theta_j)\big/\partial F_{1|2}(\Delta y_1^j|\Delta y_2^j)$ $=$
$h_{3|2,1|2}(h_{32}(v_3, v_2), h_{12}(v_1, v_2)) = v_3v_2), h_{12}(v_1, v_2)) = v_3$. We can obtain $v_3 =$
$h_{32}^{-1}(h_{3|2,1|2}^{-1}(r_3, h_{12}(v_1, v_2)), v_2)$, and $\Delta y_3^j = \left(F_3^j\right)^{-1}(v_3)$, where $\left(F_3^j\right)^{-1}(\cdot)$ represents the inverse function of the CDF of the wear depth increment in the third joint at the time interval $[t_{j-1}, t_j]$.

6) A group of wear depth increments $\left(\Delta y_1^j, \Delta y_2^j, ..., \Delta y_n^j\right)$ of the joints following the joint PDF in Eq. (4) at the time interval $[t_{j-1}, t_j]$ are obtained. For the details about sampling on multidimensional random variables based on a vine copula function, please refer to reference [18].

Step 5: Calculate the kinematic error of the mechanism. The cumulative wear depth of the ith $((1 \leq i \leq n))$ joint at the time point t_j is $y_i^j = y_i^{j-1} + \Delta y_i^j$. Then, the upper limit of the kinematic error $\overline{\overline{S}}(\theta_{in}, L, r)$ are calculated. Compare the upper limit of the kinematic error with threshold ε. The failure occurs if the absolute kinematic error is greater than the threshold.

Step 6: Set $j = j + 1$ and repeat Steps 4 to 5 until $j > m$ to obtain the kinematic error and the state (failure or working) of the mechanism of the kth sample at different time points.

Step 7: Set $k = k + 1$ and repeat Steps 4 to 6 until $k > N$ to obtain the state (failure or working) of the mechanism at different time points for the N samples.

Step 8: The reliability can be estimated based on the statistics of all the samples.

4 Case Study

Take a four-bar mechanism in Fig. 3 to illustrate the proposed method. The wear prediction of each joint is based on the method in reference [2]. Three clearance joints are
considered: Joint B, Joint C, and Joint D. The initial clearance size of the three joints
is 0.01 mm. The radii of the bearings are 10 mm, and the journal-bearing width equals
10 mm. Joint A is modeled as an ideal joint.

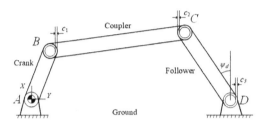

Fig. 3. Four-bar mechanism

Due to the variation of material properties and dimensions in processing and manufacturing, uncertainties exist in the mechanism. The distributions of the parameters in
the four-bar mechanism are listed in Table 1. In the table, the symbols l_{AB}, l_{BC}, l_{CD}, and
l_{AD} represent the length of the linkages. The symbols m_{AB}, m_{BC}, and m_{CD} denote the
mass of the linkages. The symbols c_B, c_C, and c_D are the clearance of the three joints.
The symbols k represents the wear coefficient. The symbol 'SD' represent the standard
deviation.

Other parameters of the mechanism are listed in Table 2.

Table 1. Variables and distributions

No.	Variables	Type	Mean	SD
1	l_{AB}	Normal	90 mm	0.15 mm
2	l_{BC}	Normal	190 mm	0.20 mm
3	l_{CD}	Normal	140 mm	0.17 mm
4	l_{AD}	Normal	220 mm	0.20 mm
5	m_{AB}	Normal	0.315 kg	0.03 kg
6	m_{BC}	Normal	0.462 kg	0.03 kg
7	m_{CD}	Normal	0.477 kg	0.03 kg
7	c_D	Normal	0.01 mm	0.0005 mm
8	k	Normal	6.205×10^{-11} Pa^{-1}	3.103×10^{-12} Pa^{-1}

Based on the parameter distributions in Table 1, with the Latin hypercube sampling
(LHS) method, 50 groups of parameters are generated. Then each group of parameters

Table 2. Properties of the mechanism

Young's modulus	207 GPa
Restitution coefficient	0.2
Dynamic friction coefficient	0.1
Static friction coefficient	0.15
Input speed of the crank	120 r/min

is substituted into the dynamic model of the four-bar mechanism to predict the wear of Joints B, C, and D with 100,000 cycles. The wear prediction results corresponding to a group of parameters is treated as a sample. In this way, 50 samples can be obtained. 15 samples are shown in Fig. 4. It can be observed that the cumulative wear depth is varied in different samples due to the uncertainties of the parameters.

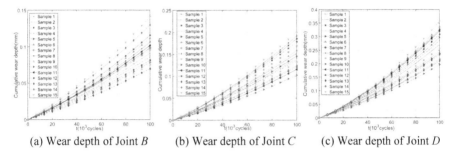

(a) Wear depth of Joint B (b) Wear depth of Joint C (c) Wear depth of Joint D

Fig. 4. Samples of three joints

The dependence measure Kendall's tau for wear depth increments of the three pairs of joints at different time intervals is calculated. The time interval is set as 25,000 cycles. The results are shown in Fig. 5. It can be observed that the correlation relationships are strong. The correlation relationship between joints B and D is stronger than the correlation relationship between Joint B and Joint C. Besides, the correlation becomes stronger with the increasing of time.

The desired kinematic output ψ_d in Fig. 3 is the nominal angle without clearances. The threshold $\varepsilon = 0.2°$. The joint PDF for the wear increments at the time interval $[t_j\ t_{j-1}]$ is constructed based on Eq. (4):

$$f(\Delta y_B^j, \Delta y_C^j, \Delta y_D^j) = f(\Delta y_B^j)f(\Delta y_C^j)f(\Delta y_D^j)c_{BC}(F(\Delta y_B^j), F(\Delta y_C^j), \theta_{12}(t_j))$$
$$c_{CD}(F(\Delta y_C^j), F(\Delta y_D^j), \theta_{CD}(t_j))c_{BD|C}(F(\Delta y_{B|C}^j), F(\Delta y_{D|B}^j), \theta_{BD|C}(t_j))$$
$$(16)$$

We first determine the time-varying correlation model between the variables. Based on the Kendall's tau between Joints B and C, and the Kendall's tau between Joints C and D, as well as the Kendall's tau between the conditional variables $\Delta y_{B|C}^j$ and $\Delta y_{D|C}^j$, TSM model is chosen to model the correlation.

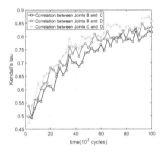

Fig. 5. Kendall's tau between wear depth increments in the same time intervals

The corresponding copula functions are Clayton, Clayton and Frank copula for C_{BC}, C_{CD} and $C_{BD|C}$ in Eq. (16). The reliability evaluation results with two input angles (30° and 60°) are shown in Fig. 6. For comparison, the reliability evaluation results of the other two cases are also presented. In Fig. 6, Case 1 plots the results by our proposed method. The case where the correlation of the wear depth increments is assumed to be constant are represented by Case 2. It means the degree of correlation for the wear depth increments in the joints keeps constant. For Case 3, The wear depth increments of the joints are independent (meaning that there is no correlation among wear of the joints).

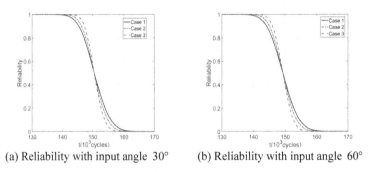

(a) Reliability with input angle 30°   (b) Reliability with input angle 60°

Fig. 6. Reliability evaluation results with different input angles

From Fig. 6, it can be observed that the reliability under Case 3 is departed significantly from the other two cases. The reliability is superior under independence up to a specific time point, and after this time point, the reliability is larger under correlation. Similarly, the reliability value under Case 2 is superior at the beginning and after a specific time point, the value is lower to the reliability value of Case 1. There is a large difference when the correlation is not considered. The difference is also considerable when the time-varying correlation is not taken into account. As a result, for the reliability evaluation of a mechanism, the time-varying correlation of the wear among multiple joints cannot be ignored. It is important to model the correlation among the wear increments properly to obtain accurate reliability evaluation results.

5 Conclusion

Wear correlation among multiple joints is investigated in this study. Results show wear of the joints in a mechanism has a positive correlation with each other. Each joint has different effects on the wear of other joints. Besides, the correlation becomes stronger with the operation of the mechanism. These conclusions can give a more comprehensive understanding of wear behavior of joints. The analysis results can provide an important reference for the mechanical design considering joints wear.

References

1. Li, Y., Chen, G., Sun, D., Gao, Y., Wang, K.: Dynamic analysis and optimization design of a planar slider-crank mechanism with flexible components and two clearance joints. Mech. Mach. Theory **99**, 37–57 (2016)
2. Lai, X., et al.: Computational prediction and experimental validation of revolute joint clearance wear in the low-velocity planar mechanism. Mech. Syst. Sig. Process. **85**, 963–976 (2017)
3. Wu, J., Yan, S., Zuo, M.J.: Evaluating the reliability of multi-body mechanisms: a method considering the uncertainties of dynamic performance. Reliab. Eng. Syst. Saf. **149**, 96–106 (2016)
4. Bai, Z.F., Zhao, Y., Chen, J.: Dynamics analysis of planar mechanical system considering revolute clearance joint wear. Tribol. Int. **64**, 85–95 (2013)
5. Zhu, A., He, S., Zhao, J., Luo, W.: A nonlinear contact pressure distribution model for wear calculation of planar revolute joint with clearance. Nonlinear Dyn. **88**(1), 315–328 (2016). https://doi.org/10.1007/s11071-016-3244-9
6. Su, Y., Chen, W., Tong, Y., Xie, Y.: Wear prediction of clearance joint by integrating multi-body kinematics with finite-element method. Proc. Inst. Mech. Eng. Part J J. Eng. Tribol. **224**(8), 815–823 (2010)
7. An, D., Choi, J.-H., Schmitz, T.L., Kim, N.H.: In situ monitoring and prediction of progressive joint wear using Bayesian statistics. Wear **270**(11–12), 828–838 (2011)
8. Li, P., Chen, W., Li, D., Yu, R., Zhang, W.: Wear analysis of two revolute joints with clearance in multibody systems. J. Comput. Nonlinear Dyn. **11**(1), 011009–7 (2016)
9. Jiang, S., Chen, X., Deng, Y.: Dynamic response analysis of planar multilink mechanism considering wear in clearances. Shock Vib. **2019**, 5389732 (2019)
10. Wang, W., Gao, H., Zhou, C., Zhang, Z.: Reliability analysis of motion mechanism under three types of hybrid uncertainties. Mech. Mach. Theory **121**, 769–784 (2018)
11. Geng, X., Li, M., Liu, Y., Zheng, W., Zhao, Z.: Non-probabilistic kinematic reliability analysis of planar mechanisms with non-uniform revolute clearance joints. Mech. Mach. Theory **140**, 413–433 (2019)
12. Bai, Z.F., Sun, Y.: A study on dynamics of planar multibody mechanical systems with multiple revolute clearance joints. Eur. J. Mech. - A Solids **60**, 95–111 (2016)
13. Flores, P., Lankarani, H.M.: Dynamic response of multibody systems with multiple clearance joints. J. Comput. Nonlinear Dyn. **7**(3), 031003 (2012)
14. Archard, J.: Wear Theory and Mechanisms. Wear Control Handbook, New York (1980)
15. Pan, Z., Balakrishnan, N.: Reliability modeling of degradation of products with multiple performance characteristics based on gamma processes. Reliab. Eng. Syst. Saf. **96**(8), 949–957 (2011)
16. Bedford, T., Cooke, R.M.: Probability density decomposition for conditionally dependent random variables modeled by vines. Ann. Math. Artif. Intell. **32**(1), 245–268 (2001)

17. Aas, K., Czado, C., Frigessi, A., Bakken, H.: Pair-copula constructions of multiple dependence. Insur. Math. Econ. **44**(2), 182–198 (2009)
18. Jiang, C., Zhang, W., Han, B., Ni, Y., Song, L.J.: A vine-copula-based reliability analysis method for structures with multidimensional correlation. J. Mech. Des. **137**(6), 061405–061413 (2015)
19. Akaike, H.: Information Theory and An Extension of the Maximum Likelihood Principle. Springer, Berlin (1998)
20. Jawale, H.P., Thorat, H.T.: Investigation of positional error in two degree of freedom mechanism with joint clearance. J. Mech. Robot. **4**, 011002 (2012)
21. Rosenblatt, M.: Remarks on a multivariate transformation. Ann. Math. Stat. **23**(3), 470–472 (1952)

Abnormal Rotation Analysis of 6-PUS Robot's Compound Spherical Joint

Qingshan Zeng, Feng Gao[✉], Jimu Liu, Fang Zhang, and Hao Zheng

School of Mechanical Engineering, Shanghai Jiao Tong University, No. 800 Dongchuan Road,
Minhang District, Shanghai 200240, China
{qingshanzeng,fengg}@sjtu.edu.cn

Abstract. Parallel robots are increasingly used in many applications where the positioning accuracy is of great importance. Compound spherical joints (CSJ) are commonly used in lightweight and miniaturized parallel robots. The study of CSJ's motion principle is important for the accuracy analysis of the parallel robot. In this paper, the static and dynamic geometric models of the CSJ's structure of the 6-PUS robot are proposed, in order to explain the problem of abnormal rotation of CSJ. Analyses of the principle and influence factors of CSJ's abnormal rotation are conducted based on models. Through analyses, the conclusion that the abnormal rotation can be weakened by increasing the angle θ, increasing the rigidity of the mechanism and working at a larger β is obtained. The orthogonal simulation study demonstrates that the proposed model can explain the cause of abnormal rotation and the analysis of influence factors is correct.

Keywords: Compound spherical joint · Kinematic analysis · Parallel mechanism

1 Introduction

Parallel robots are increasingly used in light industrial fields such as electronics and medical due to their high rigidity and high control accuracy [1, 2]. In applications such as force control polishing and micro-nano operation, not only the robot operation accuracy requirements are very strict, but also the operation end is required to be small enough [3]. It is very important to ensure the high precision of the parallel robot while being lightweight and miniaturized.

The relationship between the sources of errors that influence the motion accuracy of parallel robots is complex and unpredictable, which make it almost impossible to calibrate and compensate the error. Most of the studies focused only on certain error factors. In response to joint clearance, input uncertainty, and manufacturing imperfection, Qingqiang Zhao proposed a generalized approach to error space calculation for parallel/hybrid manipulators, which linearize the relationship between the local pose error caused by the disturbance of the passive joint and that by other error sources [4]. Genliang Chen proposed a unified approach to predict the accuracy performance of the parallel manipulators, considering the coupling relationship between errors, but it is only suitable for general planar mechanism [5]. Masory Q comprehensively considered

© Springer Nature Switzerland AG 2021
X.-J. Liu et al. (Eds.): ICIRA 2021, LNAI 13015, pp. 581–591, 2021.
https://doi.org/10.1007/978-3-030-89134-3_53

the hinge's assembly and adjustment errors, machining errors, and end pose measurement errors to analyze the end accuracy of the 6-DOF parallel adjustment mechanism
[6, 7]. Different from the approaches used in the above researches, Yao Rui not only
studied the error of six-degree-of-freedom precision positioning platforms with various
configurations, but also optimally allocated the errors to each sub-structure [8]. The
structure of the mechanism also determines the influence of the error on the accuracy
of the mechanism. Based on the error model of a 6-DOF parallel platform, Yunfeng Li
analyzed the influence of structural parameters on the accuracy and sensitivity of the
moving platform [9]. In terms of geometric parameter error model modeling, in order
to simplify the difficulties of kinematic calibration and error modeling, usually only the
node installation positions of universal joints and spherical joints are considered, and
other defects such as processing errors, assembly errors and joint stiffness are ignored
[10, 11]. In actual situations, the error caused by these factors can't be ignored.

At certain moments in the movement of the 6PUS robot, the CSJ of the robot will
suddenly and rapidly rotate. In this paper, the static and dynamic geometric models of
the CSJ are established to explain the abnormal rotation. Models are built by abstracting
the geometrical structure of the CSJ, which overcomes the complexity of the dual matrix
method or Spinor approach. Theoretical analyses of the principle and influence factors
of CSJ's abnormal rotation are conducted based on models.

2   Compound Spherical Joint Model

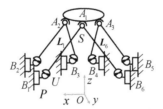

Fig. 1. Structure diagram of 6-PUS parallel mechanism

The model of CSJ is built based on a 6-PUS parallel robot. The structure of the
6-PUS parallel robot is shown in Fig. 1. A_iB_j is the PUS branch chain. The prismatic
pairs move on six parallel and regularly distributed linear guides. The branch chains are
grouped in pairs and connected with the robot's end through the CSJ. According to the
subscript of A_i, each branch chain group is represented as G_i. The coordinate system
shown in Fig. 1 is established.

In order to realize the function of the CSJ, the structure of the CSJ is designed as
shown in Fig. 2. L_1 and L_6 are linkages (from the universal joint to spherical joint). v,
a and n are the rotation axis of revolute joints, intersecting at point A_1 in the space. θ
represent the angle between L_i and v, and α represent the angle between L_1 and L_6. L_1
and L_6 can be obtained from the 6-PUS mechanism's kinematics model [12], n can be
obtained according to the posture of 6-PUS mechanism's end, and θ is a known structural
parameter. The mathematical model of the CSJ is established below.

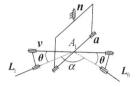

Fig. 2. Structure diagram of compound spherical joint

2.1 Branch Chain Group Model

Branch chain group G_1's physical model and geometric model are shown in Fig. 3. Noted that Fig. 3 is a three-dimensional diagram. A_1 is the center of the CSJ. B_1 and B_6 represent the center of the universal joints. Δh is the distance of B_1 and B_6 in the direction of the axis Z. L_1 and L_6 are vectors of Linkages B_1A_1 and B_6A_1. d represent the distance between the first and sixth linear guides.

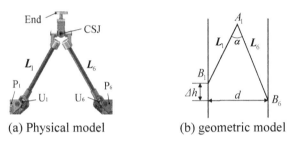

(a) Physical model   (b) geometric model

Fig. 3. Branch chain group G_1's model

The relationship between α and other parameters is shown in Eq. (1):

$$\alpha = \arccos(\frac{L_1^2 + L_2^2 - (d^2 + \Delta h^2)}{2|L_1||L_2|}) \tag{1}$$

$$\Delta h = q_1 - q_6 \tag{2}$$

In Eq. (1), $|L_1|$, $|L_6|$ and d are inherent parameters of the mechanism, and Δh is obtained by Eq. (2). q_1 and q_6 are positions of P_1 and P_6, which are calculated from the inverse kinematic model of the 6-PUS mechanism [11].

The CSJ's parameter α in different motion states are determined by the branch chain group's model, and can be calculated according to Eq. (1).

2.2 Static Geometric Model

When the pose of the 6-PUS mechanism is determined, the position of all components of the entire mechanism are fixed, that is, n, L_1, L_6, θ, and α are all known. In order to establish the CSJ's model in a static state, it is necessary to obtain a mathematical model

Fig. 4. Static geometric model of CSJ

of the CSJ based on the known parameters of the mechanism. Under static conditions, the model can be built as shown in Fig. 4.

According to the geometric relationship between the vectors, the model in Fig. 4 can be described by formula (3). In formula (3), $L_1 = [a_1 \ a_2 \ a_3]^T$, $L_6 = [b_1 \ b_2 \ b_3]^T$.

$$\begin{cases} L_1 \cdot v = |L_1| \cdot |v| \cdot \cos(\theta) \\ L_6 \cdot v = -|L_6| \cdot |v| \cdot \cos(\theta) \\ |v| = 1 \end{cases} \tag{3}$$

The solutions of v are expressed in formula (4).

$$\begin{cases} v_3 = (-b \pm \sqrt{b^2 - 4ac})/(2a) \\ v_2 = F - Gv_3 \\ v_1 = D - Ev_3 \end{cases} \tag{4}$$

In formula (4), D, E, F, G, a, b and c are parameters about L_1, L_6 and θ.

v has two solutions in Formula (4). If and only if $b^2 - 4ac = 0$, v has two same solutions, corresponding to the case where L_1, L_6 and v are coplanar.

a can be derived from v and n, as show in Eq. (5).

$$a = \frac{n \times v}{|n \times v|} \tag{5}$$

2.3 Dynamic Geometric Model

The CSJ rotates within a certain range when an external force is applied to it, even if the input of the mechanism is fixed. The static model cannot describe the dynamic process of the CSJ well. A dynamic geometric model needs to be established.

When mechanism's input and output are determined, according to Sect. 2.2, the motion of v describes the motion of CSJ. The solution of v is a geometric problem: three vectors L_1, L_6 and v intersect at a point in space, where L_1, L_6 and θ are known and fixed. Figure 5(a) is the description of this geometric problem. The rotation axes of the cones 1 and 6 are respectively L_1 and L_6, and the cone $1'$ is obtained by the cone 1 symmetrically about the center A_1. The three cones have the same parameters of size. The generatrix of the cone is the possible position of v. The collinear generatrix between cone 1 and cone 6 is the solution of v, which corresponds to the intersection of the cone surface $1'$ and the cone surface 6. Through the above analysis, the CSJ's dynamic geometric model is described in Fig. 5(b). v and v' correspond to the two solutions in the static model, γ is the angle between v and v', and β is the angle between the overlapping parts of the two cones. When β changes, v also changes accordingly.

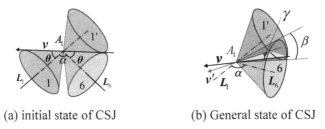

(a) initial state of CSJ   (b) General state of CSJ

Fig. 5. Dynamic geometric model of CSJ

Figures 6(a) and (b) are the front cross-sectional view and top view of Fig. 5(b) respectively. In front view, l is the height of the cone and h is the distance from A_1 to the intersection line of the bottom of the cones. PRelationship between β and θ is shown in Eq. (6). h can be calculated by Eq. (7).

$$\beta = 2\theta - (\pi - \alpha) \tag{6}$$

$$h = \frac{h'}{\cos(\theta - \beta/2)} \tag{7}$$

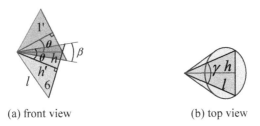

(a) front view   (b) top view

Fig. 6. Different view of the dynamic geometric model

In top view, the yellow area is the geometric model enclosed by the intersection of the cones $1'$ and cone 6. Equations (8) and (9) are obtained according to the triangle relationship.

$$l = h'/\cos\theta \tag{8}$$

$$\gamma = 2 \cdot \arccos(h/l) \tag{9}$$

Bring Eqs. (7) and (8) into Eqs. (9), (10) is obtained.

$$\gamma = 2\arccos\left(\frac{1}{\cos(\beta/2) + \tan\theta \cdot \sin(\beta/2)}\right) \tag{10}$$

From Eqs. (6) and (10), we know that the change of α will affect β and thus the angle γ.

3 Analysis of Abnormal Rotation

The analysis of rotation aims to reveal the reason for the abnormal rotation of CSJ according to the mathematical model of CSJ when the input of 6-PUS mechanism is determined, and to obtain the influence of parameters on the rotation.

The parameters of the CSJ's mathematical model come from the actual physical prototype. The length of L_i is 160 mm, d is 158.536 mm and θ is 60.3023°. In the initial state, L_1, L_6 and v are coplanar, as show in Fig. 5(a).

3.1 Rotation Process

The rotation process of CSJ is a dynamic process and can be obtained according to the dynamic geometric model in Sect. 2.3. In order to realize the rotation, v needs to continuously rotate around the point A_1, and at the same time satisfy the condition that v is the intersection of the cone surface $1'$ and the cone surface 6. When β changes continuously, v can move continuously around the point A_1 and along the conical surface. Note that the two ends of rods L_1 and L_6 are respectively connected with a universal joint and a spherical joint, and both rods are slender rods. Because of the combined effects of assembly clearance and deformation, the branch chain group's geometric properties are easily changed, which makes the affected equivalent rods inconsistent with the ideal situation analyzed in Sect. 2.3. As shown in Fig. 7, the red lines are the affected equivalent rods and the black dotted lines are ideal rods L_1 and L_6. The error caused by the actual physical structure is reflected in the dynamic geometric model of the CSJ as a change in angle α, and it is known from Eq. (6) that the change of α will lead to a change in β.

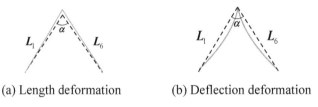

(a) Length deformation   (b) Deflection deformation

Fig. 7. Schematic diagram of equivalent linkages (Color figure online)

Figure 8 is a graph of the mutual influence between β and γ obtained by Eq. (10). In the initial state, β is 0, and the state of the CSJ is shown in Fig. 5(a). When β changes from 0° to 0.5°, the angle between the two solutions of v changes from 0° to 14°. If v is one of the solutions of the static model, when the 6-PUS mechanism applies a single-directional torque to the CSJ, v moves in one direction. Due to the continuous change of β caused by the deformation, the CSJ realizes the continuous rotation.

If the initial value of β is small, the deformation range of rods is large enough and the direction of the torque is such that v moves from the current solution to the other solution, then v can move from one solution to another solution along the surface of cone 6. When the initial value of β is 0.5° and the variable range of β caused by deformation is larger than 0.5°, v can achieve a spatial rotation greater than 14°. The rotation process is shown in Fig. 9.

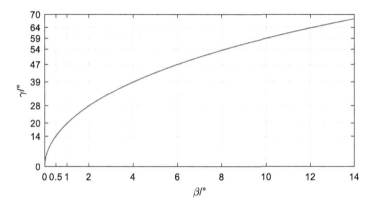

Fig. 8. Relationship between β and CSJ's rotation Angle γ

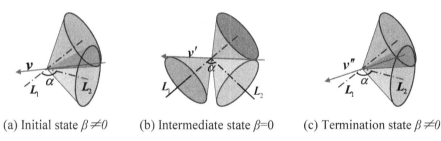

(a) Initial state $\beta \neq 0$ (b) Intermediate state $\beta=0$ (c) Termination state $\beta \neq 0$

Fig. 9. The rotation process of the CSJ

Figure 8 reveals the dramatic influence of change of β on the state of the CSJ. The size of the rotation angle is related to the degree of the deformation. When the variable range of β caused by the deformation cannot cross the zero point (the state in Fig. 9(b)), v can only rotate near one solution of static model. For example, if β is larger than 4° and the variable range of β is $-1°$–$1°$, the variable range of γ is about 9°, and v can only rotate about 4.5° around one solution of static model.

Equation (11) is obtained by combining Eqs. (2) and (6), which reveal the relationship between β and branch chain group model.

$$\beta = 2\theta + \arccos(\frac{L_1^2 + L_2^2 - (d^2 + \Delta h^2)}{2|L_1||L_2|}) - \pi \tag{11}$$

The relationship between β and Δh is shown in Fig. 10. β and Δh are positively correlated and the slope of the curve is small at the beginning. When Δh changes in the range of 0–40 mm, β changes in the range of 0–2°. In this situation, the CSJ is in the state of easy to be rotated even if the deformation of rods is small. When Δh is greater than 40 mm, β is large, and the deformation of rods can no longer make β cross the zero point.

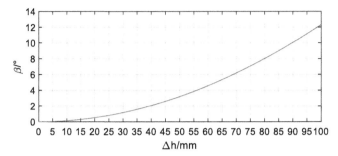

Fig. 10. Relationship between Δh and β

3.2 Influencing Factors

The curve in Fig. 8 reveals the principle of abnormal rotation of the CSJ. According to Eq. (10), the curve is affected by θ. From the analysis in Sect. 3.1, it is known that the rotation range of the CSJ is related to the variation range of β ($\Delta\beta$) caused by deformation and the initial value of β. Thus, θ, $\Delta\beta$, and β's initial value are three factors that affect the rotation of the CSJ.

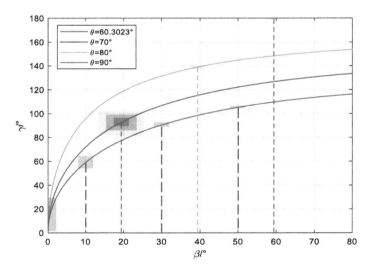

Fig. 11. β-γ relationship curve under different θ (Color figure online)

According to the actual physical prototype, under the initial state, α is 59.3954°, and θ is 60.3023°. α is only related to the motion state of the mechanism, and its minimum value is its initial value. θ can be artificially designed. Figure 11 is the β-γ relationship curve under different θ. In Fig. 11, the width of the semi-transparent box represents $\Delta\beta$ (the blue box on the left has a range of $0°$–$2°$ because of β's nonnegative, and others are $-2°$–$2°$), and the height represents the variation range of the γ.

When θ equals to $60.3023°$, $70°$, $80°$, and $90°$, the minimum and initial value of β is $0°$, $19.3954°$, $39.3954°$ and $59.3954°$, corresponding to the blue, red, green and purple dotted line in Fig. 11. It can be seen from the height of the semi-transparent box in Fig. 11 that as θ increases, under the same α and the same $\Delta\beta$, the variation range of γ becomes smaller. When θ is set to $90°$, the rotation of the CSJ will no longer be affected by changes of β.

The red area in Fig. 11 is a comparison chart of the variation range of γ under different $\Delta\beta$. The value of β is $19.3954°$, θ is $70°$, and the value of $\Delta\beta$ are -2–$2°$, $-4°$–$4°$ and $-6°$–$6°$ respectively. As $\Delta\beta$ decreases, the variation range of γ decreases. $\Delta\beta$ is affected by the stiffness and assembly accuracy of the machine. Increasing the rigidity of the rods and improving the assembly accuracy of the machine will help reduce $\Delta\beta$, thereby reducing the abnormal rotation range of the CSJ.

The blue semi-transparent box along the blue curve in Fig. 11 is a comparison chart of the variation range of γ under different β. $\Delta\beta$ is $-2°$–$2°$, and θ is $60.3023°$. When β increases, within the same $\Delta\beta$, the rotation range of the CSJ becomes smaller. Combining Figs. 10 and 11, it can be found that the rotation range of the CSJ becomes smaller with same $\Delta\beta$ when Δh increase.

Considering the influence of three factors on the rotation of the CSJ, in order to reduce the uncontrollable rotation of the CSJ during the movement of the mechanism, it should be considered in the design to increase the angle θ, reduce $\Delta\beta$, and increase the initial value of angle β.

4   Simulation

In this section, we simulate the CSJ in simulation software ADAMS to verify the analysis in Sect. 3. The simulation model is the branch chain group G_1 of the 6-PUS parallel mechanism. The connection and position arrangement of each part conform to the 6-PUS model. Although a single branch chain group is used, its input and output are calculated by the complete 6-PUS mechanism model. The branch chain group's prismatic pairs and the end of mechanism are fixed. Rods L_1 and L_2 are flexible rods with a length of 130 mm, a diameter of 8 mm, and the shape of a long cylinder. The other parts are set as rigid bodies. The deformation in the rotation analysis is equivalent to the flexible rods' deformation, and the force applied to the CSJ by the machine motion is equivalent to the torque applied to CSJ around n-axis.

The simulation comparison experiment is designed by the orthogonal experiment method. The control variables are the value of torque (the equivalent of $\Delta\beta$), θ, and the end pose (the equivalent of initial value of β). Parameters of the four groups of simulation experiments are shown in Table 1. The parameters are derived from the actual physical structure. The Young's modulus and Poisson's ratio of carbon fiber material are 330 GPa and 0.29.

Figure 12 is a diagram showing the rotation angle of the CSJ around the n-axis in Fig. 2 under the influence of the deformation of rods. Positive rotation angle corresponds

Table 1. Orthogonal simulation parameters

NO.	Torque (N • m)	$\theta(°)$	End pose (mm, °)	Initial $\beta(°)$	Material of L_i
1	±5	60.3023	[0 0 0 0 0 0]	0	Carbon fiber
2	±0.5	60.3023	[0 0 0 0 0 0]	0	Carbon fiber
3	±5	60.3023	[20 0 0 0 0 0]	0.7258	Carbon fiber
4	±5	90	[0 0 0 0 0 0]	59.3594	Carbon fiber

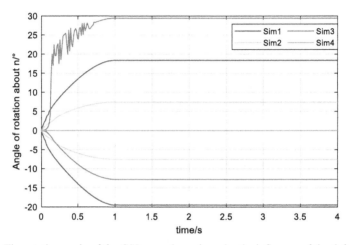

Fig. 12. The rotation angle of the CSJ around n-axis under the influence of the deformation.

to a positive torque, and negative rotation angle corresponds to a negative torque. When the 6-PUS mechanism is in the same posture, we found from simulation 1 and 4 that when θ is 90°, the rotation angle is reduced from 13.2° to 0.17°, which significantly reduce the rotation caused by the deformation of rods. Note that when θ is 90°, the rotation angle is not equal to 0°. This is because the torque causes the entire CSJ to rotate around the n-axis. Comparing simulation 1 and 2, the reduction of the deformation of rods also reduces the rotation of the CSJ. Comparing the curve of simulation 1 and 3 when receiving negative torque, increasing the initial value of β can reduce the rotation angle. In simulation 3, when the torque is positive, the rotation range is large, and there is a sudden rotation at 0.14 s. This is because the variable range of β caused by $\Delta\beta$ has crossed the zero position of β. CSJ realizes the process of rotating from the current steady state to another steady state, corresponding to two solutions of static model of CSJ. The process is consistent with the process revealed in Fig. 9, and is also an observable phenomenon that easily occurs when the machine is actually running. The above results verify the correctness of the analysis of rotation in this paper.

5 Conclusion

In this paper, we established the mathematical models of the CSJ based on a 6-PUS parallel mechanism to reveal the principle and the influencing factors of abnormal rotation of CSJ. The static geometric model describes two possible states of the CSJ in static state, and the dynamic geometric model describes the motion process of the CSJ under the influence of factors such as an external force and deformation. The premise of the model establishment is that the CSJ is a spherical joint in the sense of ideal geometry, and its rotation is only affected by the equivalent rod. The simulation results verify the correctness of the proposed mathematical model and the correctness of the analysis of the influencing factors. It is concluded that increasing the angle θ, increasing the rigidity of the mechanism and working at a larger angle β can reduce the abnormal rotation. The mathematical model and analysis method can be widely used in the design of the similar CSJ structure in the parallel mechanism and the accuracy design and error analysis of the parallel robot using this kind of CSJ.

References

1. Cai, G.Q., et al.: Development of a robotized grinding machine with tripod linkage. Manuf. Technol. and Machi. Tool. **435**(10), 4–6 (1998)
2. Kucuk, S., Gungor, B.D.: Inverse kinematics solution of a new hybrid robot manipulator proposed for medical purposes. In: 2016 Medical Technologies National Congress (TIPTEKNO), pp. 1–4 (2016)
3. Dong, Y., Gao, F., Yue, Y.: Modeling and prototype experiment of a six-DOF parallel micromanipulator with nano-scale accuracy. Proc. Inst. Mech. Eng. Part C J. Mech. Eng. Sci. **229**(14), 2611–2625 (2015)
4. Zhao, Q., Guo, J., Hong, J.: Closed-form error space calculation for parallel/hybrid manipulators considering joint clearance, input uncertainty, and manufacturing imperfection. Mech. Mach. Theory. **142**, 103608 (2019)
5. Chen, G., Hao, W., Lin, Z.: A unified approach to the accuracy analysis of planar parallel manipulators both with input uncertainties and joint clearance. Mech. Mach. Theory. **64**(6), 1–17 (2013)
6. Masory, O., Wang, J., Zhuang, H.: On the accuracy of a Stewart platform-part II: kinematic calibration and compensation. In: IEEE International Conference on Robotics and Automation, pp. 725–731. IEEE (1993)
7. Wang, J., Masory, O.: On the accuracy of a Stewart platform part I: the effect of manufacturing tolerances. In: IEEE International Conference on Robotics and Automation, pp. 114–120. IEEE (1993)
8. Yao, R., Zhu, W., Huang, P.: Accuracy analysis of Stewart platform based on interval analysis method. Chin. J. Mech. Eng. **26**(1), 29–34 (2013)
9. Li, Y., Li, C., Qu, D., et al.: Errors modeling and sensitivity analysis for a novel parallel manipulator. In: International Conference on Mechatronics and Automation. IEEE (2012)
10. Tian, W., Yin, F., Liu, H., et al.: Kinematic calibration of a 3-DOF spindle head using a double ball bar. Mech. Mach. Theory. **102**, 167–178 (2016)
11. Jiang, Y., Li, T., Wang, L., et al.: Kinematic error modeling and identification of the overconstrained parallel kinematic machine. Robot. Comput.-Integr. Manuf. **49**, 105–119 (2018)
12. Cao, R., Gao, F., Zhang, Y., et al.: A new parameter design method of a 6-DOF parallel motion simulator for a given workspace. Mech. Based Des. Struct. Mach. **43**(1), 1–18 (2015)

Kinematic Modeling and Analysis of Support Mechanism for Folding Rib Deployable Antenna

Dake Tian[1] , Xiaodong Fan[1] , Lu Jin[2(✉)] , Rongqiang Liu[3] ,
and Hongwei Guo[3]

[1] School of Mechanical Engineering, Shenyang Jianzhu University, Shenyang 110168, China
[2] School of Civil Engineering, Shenyang Jianzhu University, Shenyang 110168, China
jinlu@sjzu.edu.cn
[3] State Key Laboratory of Robotics and System, Harbin Institute
of Technology, Harbin 150001, China

Abstract. To meet the requirement of large aperture development trend of space deployable antenna, a space deployable antenna with high folding ratio and light weight is researched. A folding rib deployable antenna mechanism configuration is proposed and the structure analysis of deployable antenna mechanism is carried out based on modular design idea. Based on the basic theory of robotics, the forward kinematics model of the mechanism is established, and the inverse kinematics analysis is carried out from two aspects: identification of deployment state and research on driving law. The mechanism principle, forward kinematics model and inverse kinematics analysis are verified by numerical simulation software. The numerical simulation results show that the folded rib deployable antenna mechanism can realize the movement change from fully stowed to fully deployed without singularity. The movement law of key points at the end of mechanism is closely related to the development law of each corner in mechanism. The configuration scheme of folding rib deployable antenna mechanism proposed in this paper is reasonable and feasible. The established forward/reverse kinematic model can provide reference and help for kinematic characteristics analysis of mechanism and driving law research of mechanism.

Keywords: Deployable antenna · Folding rib · Modular structure · Kinematic modeling · Numerical simulation

1 Introduction

The average orbital height of navigation satellites is about 20,000 km, the moon is about 380,000 km from the Earth, and the closest distance between Mars and Earth is about 55 million km. From satellite navigation to lunar exploration to Mars exploration, with the increasing complexity of space missions, communication capability is required more and more, such as ultra-long distance, ultra-high resolution, ultra-low delay and so on. Space deployable antenna is an indispensable core equipment in spacecraft communication system, and has been applied in meteorological monitoring, military reconnaissance,

© Springer Nature Switzerland AG 2021
X.-J. Liu et al. (Eds.): ICIRA 2021, LNAI 13015, pp. 592–601, 2021.
https://doi.org/10.1007/978-3-030-89134-3_54

satellite navigation, deep space exploration and other fields. With the complexity of space mission, space deployable antenna with large aperture, high accuracy and high folding ratio characteristics is in urgent need [1–3]. It is of great theoretical significance and scientific research value to carry out relevant basic research.

The space deployable antenna stowed in the load compartment of the carrier rocket when it is launched and deployed on the rail when it works. Because the volume of the load compartment of the carrier rocket is limited and the stowed volume of the antenna increases with the aperture, the space deployable antenna must have a high folding ratio while achieving a large aperture. The AstroMesh ring deployable antenna [4] has the advantages of light weight and high folding ratio, but it has the problems of insufficient rigidity as the aperture increases. Reference [5] proposed a double-layer ring deployable antenna mechanism, which can further improve the rigidity of the deployable antenna mechanism. Japan Aerospace Exploration Agency developed a modular deployable antenna (ETS-VIII) consisting of 14 hexagonal prism modules [6, 7], which was successfully deployed in orbit in 2006. The modular deployable antenna has flexible topology and high rigidity. Reference [8, 9] developed a modular deployable antenna prototype, and carried out experimental research on the surface accuracy of the deployable antenna by means of digital close-range photogrammetry, and analyzed the influence of the support structure of the deployable antenna on the surface accuracy of the reflector. Reference [10] proposed a design scheme of cable-rib tension folding antenna mechanism, which has higher rigidity and lighter mass than traditional truss articulated deployable mechanism. Reference [11] designed an umbrella-shaped deployable antenna mechanism, which has the advantages of high accuracy, high rigidity and high reliability, but its aperture is generally small.

From the above analysis, the existing deployable antenna cannot meet both large aperture and high stiffness. A deployable antenna mechanism with high stiffness, large aperture and flexible topology is proposed in this paper. The forward/inverse kinematics model of the mechanism is established. The deployment function of the mechanism is verified by numerical simulation method and the driving law is studied. This configuration is of great significance and research value for enriching the types of deployable antenna mechanism and expanding the design method and theoretical research of deployable antenna mechanism.

2   Composition and Deployment Principle of Antenna Structure

The basic unit structure is shown in Fig. 1. In this basic unit, the power source is provided by both the main spring and the auxiliary spring. The two ends of the control cable are connected with slider and motor respectively and are mainly used to control the deployment speed of the mechanism. When the basic unit is in the stowed state, the main/auxiliary springs are compressed to store the elastic potential energy and the slider is at the bottom of the center bar. When the mechanism is deployed, the motor slowly releases the control cable, the main spring drives the slider upward, the auxiliary spring drives the lower chord clockwise, and the whole mechanism slowly deploy. When the mechanism is extended to the end limit position, the axis of the small diagonal bar and the large diagonal bar coincide and the whole mechanism is locked, thus the basic unit becomes a stable structure.

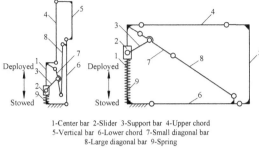

1-Center bar 2-Slider 3-Support bar 4-Upper chord
5-Vertical bar 6-Lower chord 7-Small diagonal bar
8-Large diagonal bar 9-Spring

Fig. 1. Basic unit structure and development principle

The folding rib deployable antenna support structure is shown in Fig. 2. The basic unit is the smallest unit of the folding rib deployable antenna support structure. Each triple-ribbed unit consists of three basic units, and the whole mechanism consists of eight triple-ribbed units with the same structure and uniform circumferential distribution along the center.

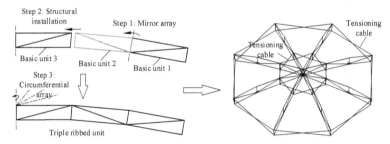

Fig. 2. Composition of support structure for folding rib deployable antenna

3 Forward Kinematics Modeling

Kinematic analysis is a very important research content in the research of deployable antenna mechanism, and is the basis of mechanism design and dynamic characteristics research. Kinematics analysis usually includes forward kinematics analysis and inverse kinematics analysis. In this section, firstly, forward kinematics modeling of folded rib deployable antenna mechanism is carried out. From the analysis of the folding rib deployable antenna support mechanism, the basic unit is the smallest deployable unit of the whole mechanism. Therefore, the kinematic model of the basic unit is established first, and then the kinematic model of the three folding rib unit is established by means of coordinate transformation. Finally, the kinematic model of the entire folding rib deployable antenna support structure is established.

3.1 Kinematic Modeling of Basic Units

The space rectangular coordinate system $\{O\}$ of the basic unit is established by taking O point as the origin of the coordinate, JI direction as the x-axis positive direction, JC direction as the z-axis positive direction and y-axis as determined by the right-hand method, as shown in Fig. 3(a).

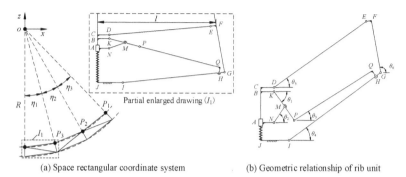

(a) Space rectangular coordinate system   (b) Geometric relationship of rib unit

Fig. 3. Space rectangular coordinate system

Each angle in the basic unit is marked as shown in Fig. 3(b). According to the geometric relationship in the figure, the kinematic equation of the basic unit can be obtained:

$$
\begin{cases}
L_{BK} + L_{KM}\cos\theta_1 - L_{NM}\cos\theta_2 - L_{AN} = 0 \\
L_{AB} - L_{KM}\sin\theta_1 - L_{NM}\sin\theta_2 = 0 \\
L_{BK} + L_{KP}\cos\theta_1 + L_{PH}\cos(\theta_3 - \arctan(L_{QH}/L_{PQ})) - L_{IH}\cos\theta_4 - L_{JI} = 0 \\
L_{JB} - L_{KP}\sin\theta_1 + L_{PH}\sin(\theta_3 - \arctan(L_{QH}/L_{PQ})) - L_{IH}\sin\theta_4 = 0 \\
L_{CD} + L_{DE}\cos\theta_5 + L_{EG}\cos(\theta_6 + \arctan(L_{EF}/L_{GF})) - L_{GI}\cos\theta_4 - L_{JI} = 0 \\
L_{JC} + L_{DE}\sin\theta_5 - L_{EG}\sin(\theta_6 + \arctan(L_{EF}/L_{GF})) - L_{GI}\sin\theta_4 = 0
\end{cases}
\tag{1}
$$

The relationship between the angle $\theta_1 \sim \theta_6$ and the displacement of the slider L_{AB} can be obtained by solving Eq. (1).

The coordinates of all points in Fig. 3(b) can be expressed in the form of column vectors. Take point F as an example

$$
\begin{bmatrix} x_F \\ y_F \\ z_F \end{bmatrix} =
\begin{bmatrix} L_{JI} + L_{IG}\cos\theta_4 + L_{GF}\cos\theta_6 \\ 0 \\ -(R + L_{JC} - L_{IG}\sin\theta_4 - L_{GF}\sin\theta_6) \end{bmatrix}
\tag{2}
$$

The coordinates of all points on the basic unit are expressed in the form of column vectors, and the column vectors of the above points are combined into a matrix L_1

$$
L_1 = \begin{bmatrix} x_A & x_B & \cdots & x_Q \\ y_A & y_B & \cdots & y_Q \\ z_A & z_B & \cdots & z_Q \end{bmatrix}
\tag{3}
$$

The matrix L_1 is the set of coordinates of all points on the basic unit, and the coordinates of these points change with the change of slider displacement L_{AB}.

3.2 Kinematic Modeling of Triple-Folded Rib Unit

According to the topological relationship from the basic unit to the supporting mechanism in Fig. 2, the topological process from the basic unit to the triple rib unit is represented by coordinate transformation. Equation (3) is the matrix of the basic unit, then the coordinate transformation process from the basic unit to the triple rib unit can be expressed as follows:

Rotate the matrix L_1 180° counterclockwise about the z-axis to get the matrix L_2

$$L_2 = \text{Rot}(z, \pi)L_1 \tag{4}$$

Combine matrix L_1 and L_2 to get the matrix L_3

$$L_3 = \begin{bmatrix} L_1 \ L_2 \end{bmatrix} \tag{5}$$

Rotate matrix L_3 around y axis to get matrix L_4

$$L_4 = \text{Rot}(y, 2\arctan\frac{x_{P_3}}{|z_{P_3}|})L_3 \tag{6}$$

Combine matrices L_1 and L_4 to get the matrix U_1

$$U_1 = \begin{bmatrix} L_1 \ L_4 \end{bmatrix} \tag{7}$$

Equation (7) is the process of coordinate transformation from basic unit to triple rib unit.

3.3 Kinematic Modeling of Supporting Mechanism

The deployable antenna mechanism composed of eight triple rib units can be regarded as a single triple rib unit through a 45° ring array. The matrix $U_2 \sim U_8$ can be obtained by rotating the matrix U_1 around the z-axis

$$U_i = \text{Rot}(z, \frac{(i-1)\pi}{4})U_1 \ i = 2, 3, \cdots, 8 \tag{8}$$

The matrix M_8 can be obtained by combining matrix $U_1 \sim U_8$

$$M_8 = \begin{bmatrix} U_1 \ U_2 \ U_3 \cdots U_8 \end{bmatrix} \tag{9}$$

Equation (9) is the coordinate transformation process from the triple rib unit to the supporting structure.

4 Inverse Kinematics Analysis

The inverse kinematics analysis is mainly based on the coordinates of the key points at the end of the deployable antenna mechanism to determine whether the deployment state of the antenna is normal at a certain time, and according to the motion curve of the end point of the deployable antenna mechanism to determine the motion law of the driving source, to provide theoretical reference for the selection and design of the driving system of the space deployable antenna. In this part, the support mechanism is analyzed from two aspects of inverse kinematics.

4.1 Development State Discrimination

Deployable antenna support mechanism is a complex mechanical system composed of multiple components and motion pairs. In order to better understand whether the components of the support mechanism move according to the normal law in the deployment process, it is necessary to judge the deployment state of the support mechanism, to ensure the smooth completion of the deployment process. Suppose that the coordinates of a key point at the end of each triple rib unit are known, such as point P_1 in Fig. 3(a), so the coordinates of eight points on the deployable antenna mechanism composed of eight triple rib unit are known. Because the eight ribs of the deployable antenna mechanism are deployed synchronously, the above eight points are always on the same space circle during the deployment process of the deployable antenna. Assuming that points P_1, Q_1, V_1 and T_1 are any four of the above eight points, then these four points will satisfy the following equations

$$\begin{cases} (x_{P_1} - x_S)^2 + (y_{P_1} - y_S)^2 + (z_{P_1} - z_S)^2 = r^2 \\ (x_{Q_1} - x_S)^2 + (y_{Q_1} - y_S)^2 + (z_{Q_1} - z_S)^2 = r^2 \\ (x_{V_1} - x_S)^2 + (y_{V_1} - y_S)^2 + (z_{V_1} - z_S)^2 = r^2 \\ (x_{T_1} - x_S)^2 + (y_{T_1} - y_S)^2 + (z_{T_1} - z_S)^2 = r^2 \end{cases} \tag{10}$$

Where S is the center of the circle and r is the radius of the circle.

The center coordinate S and radius r of the circle can be obtained from Eq. (10). Taking any four of the eight points, there are 70 combinations, that is, 70 R values can be solved by Eq. (10). If all 70 R values are equal, the deployment state is normal at this time; If it is not equal, it indicates that there is a fault at that time in the deployment.

4.2 Research on Driving Law

The deployment of basic unit is realized by spring drive. During deployment, the greater the acceleration of motion, the greater the possibility of mechanism vibration. Therefore, it has certain research value to design the movement curve of slider according to the ideal movement law of mechanism.

In inverse kinematics modeling, it is assumed that the coordinates of point P_1 in Fig. 3(a) are known, and that the triple rib unit consists of several basic units of equal size.

$$\eta_1 = \eta_2 = \eta_3 = \left(\arctan\left(x_{P_1} / |z_{P_1}|\right)\right)/3 \tag{11}$$

Point P_3 in Fig. 3(a) has the same position relationship as point F in Fig. 3(b). According to the geometric relationship in Fig. 3(b), there is

$$\theta_6 = \eta_1 + \pi/2 \tag{12}$$

There are 7 variables in Eq. (1). Determining one can solve the remaining 6 variables. By substituting Eq. (12) into Eq. (1), the relationship between end point P_1 of the triple rib unit and the displacement of the slider can be established. Therefore, the driving curve of the slider can be determined by selecting the motion law of point P_1.

5   Model Validation and Analysis

In order to verify the correctness of the kinematics model of the folding rib deployable antenna mechanism, the numerical simulation software MATLAB is used to verify the deployment function and driving law of the model, and the simulation results are analyzed.

5.1   Deployment Function Verification

The main parameters of the basic unit are shown in Table 1. Set the speed of the slider as 1 mm/s and the stroke of the slider as 55 mm. Use the numerical simulation software MATLAB to simulate the kinematics of the model represented by Eq. (9). The deployment states of the space deployable antenna support mechanism are shown in Fig. 4. During the deployment process, the motion trajectory of the end point of the mechanism and the displacement, and velocity curves of P_1, P_2 and P_3 relative to the z-axis are shown in Fig. 5.

Table 1. Main parameters of basic unit/mm

R	L_{JC}	L_{JI}	L_{IG}	L_{GF}	L_{DE}
4701	150	50	563	150	554

It can be seen from Fig. 4 that the smallest volume of deployable antenna mechanism is in the fully stowed state; When fully deployed, the envelope volume of the mechanism is the largest; During the process of folding to deployment, the triple rib unit of the mechanism realize synchronous motion and simultaneous deployment without connection deviation and motion interference. The numerical simulation shows that the structure design, kinematics model of the mechanism are correct.

It can be seen from Fig. 5 that the deployable antenna mechanism has completed most of the displacement in the first 20 s. After 20 s, the movement tends to be uniform, and the whole deployment process is relatively stable. In addition, when the main structural parameters of each basic unit are taken as listed in Table 1, the aperture of the deployable antenna mechanism with folded ribs is about 3.6 m after it is fully deployed.

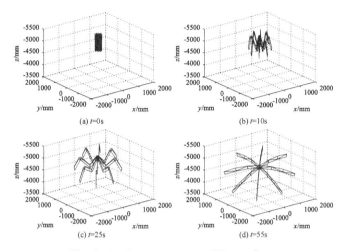

Fig. 4. Deployment status at different times

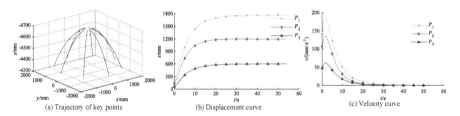

Fig. 5. Motion law

5.2 Driving Law Verification

During the deployment, the three basic units constituting the triple rib unit are synchronized. In Fig. 3(b), there are six angles ($\theta_1 \sim \theta_6$), of which angle $\theta_1 \sim \theta_3$ is inside the mechanism. Because of the relationship of rod length, the motion laws of angle θ_4 and angle θ_5 are close. Therefore, this paper takes angle θ_5 and angle θ_6 as research objects to study the influence of the motion laws of these two angles on the motion of the whole mechanism. Assuming that angle θ_5 and angle θ_6 are driven uniformly, the acceleration curves of points $P_1 \sim P_3$ are shown in Fig. 6(a) and (b) and the displacement curves of sliders are shown in Fig. 6(c).

The original moving part of the mechanism is the slider, but in the simulation, it can be assumed that the angle θ_5 or θ_6 is active, and the corresponding slider motion curve can be derived by comparing the motion curves of the key points. It can be seen from Fig. 6(a) and (b) that when angle θ_5 is driven at a constant speed, the acceleration of P_1, P_2 and P_3 in the deployment process is small, and the motion is relatively stable. Therefore, when the angle θ_5 in Fig. 6(c) is uniformly driven, the corresponding slider motion curve is the ideal driving curve of the slider. The fitting equation of the curve is

$$L_{AB}(t) = -0.3657e^{0.086t} + 71.74 \tag{13}$$

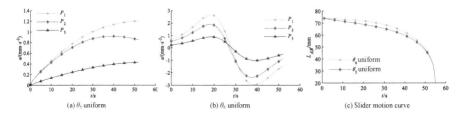

Fig. 6. Theoretical motion curve of slider

6 Conclusion

In order to meet the requirements of large-scale development trend of space deployable antenna, a folding rib space deployable antenna mechanism with high folding ratio and flexible topology is proposed. The forward/inverse kinematics modeling and analysis are carried out, and the numerical simulation and verification are carried out.

(1) It is feasible to obtain the support mechanism of folded rib space deployable antenna by using the idea of modularization and topological transformation of the smallest deployable unit. The support mechanism has the advantages of flexible topology and high folding ratio, and has the potential to develop into a large aperture deployable antenna.

(2) By using the numerical simulation software to analyze the mechanism, triple rib unit can realize synchronous deployment and smooth deployment in the process of mechanism deployment, which indicates that the established forward kinematics model is correct.

(3) In the inverse kinematics analysis, the functional relationship between the key points at the end of the mechanism and the rotation angles in the mechanism is established, and the angle θ_5 or θ_6 is selected as the input to analyze the influence law between the input and output. This research provides a theoretical basis for further research on the driving law of the folding rib deployable antenna support mechanism.

Acknowledgment. This project is supported by Key Program of National Natural Science Foundation of China (No. 51835002), China Postdoctoral Science Foundation (No. 2019M661126), the program for "Xing liao talent" of Liaoning province, China (No. XLYC1807188), and Natural Foundation Guidance Program of Liaoning Province (No. 2019-ZD-0655, No. 2019-ZD-0678).

References

1. Liu, R.Q., Shi, C., Guo, H.W., et al.: Review of space deployable antenna mechanisms. J. Mech. Eng. **56**(5), 1–12 (2020). (in Chinese)
2. Liu, R.W., Guo, H.W., Liu, R.Q., et al.: Structural design and optimization of large cable-rib tension deployable antenna structure with dynamic constraint. Acta Astronaut. **151**, 160–172 (2018)

3. Qi, X. Z., Huang, H. L., Miao, Z. H., et al.: Design and mobility analysis of large deployable mechanisms based on plane-symmetric bricard linkage. ASME J. Mech. Des. 139(2), 022302 (2017)
4. Thomson, M.: AstroMesh deployable reflectors for Ku and Ka band commercial satellites. In: 20th AIAA International Communication Satellite Systems Conference and Exhibit, 12–15 May 2002, Montreal, Quebec, Canada (2002)
5. Shi, C., Guo, H.W., Zheng, Z., et al.: Conceptual configuration synthesis and topology structure analysis of double-layer hoop deployable antenna unit. Mech. Mach. Theory 129, 232–260 (2018)
6. Meguro, A., Shintate, K., Usui, M., et al.: In-orbit deployment characteristics of large deployable antenna reflector onboard Engineering Testing Satellite VIII. Acta Astronaut. 65(9), 1306–1316 (2009)
7. Mitsugi, J., Ando, K., Senbokuya, Y., et al.: Deployment analysis of large space antenna using flexible multibody dynamics simulation. Acta Astronaut. 47(1), 19–26 (2000)
8. Tian, D. K., Liu, R. Q., Jin, L., et al.: Experimental research on dynamic characteristics of truss structure for modular space deployable truss antenna. In: 12th International Conference Intelligent Robotics and Applications, Shenyang, China, pp. 273–282 (2019)
9. Tian, D.K., Liu, R.Q., Yang, X.L., et al.: Deployment accuracy measurement and analysis of truss structure for modular space deployable truss antenna. J. Mech. Eng. 56(5), 63–71 (2020). (in Chinese)
10. Liu, R.W., Guo, H.W., Liu, R.Q., et al.: Shape accuracy optimization for cable-rib tension deployable antenna structure with tensioned cables. Acta Astronaut. 140, 66–77 (2017)
11. Chen, G., Hua, Y., Wang, B., et al.: Design and verification for umbrella-type deployable antenna of Chang'e-4 lunar relay satellite. J. Deep Space Explor. 5(6), 524–530 (2018). (in Chinese)
12. Tian, D.K., Fan, X.D., Zheng, X.J., et al.: Research status and prospect of micro-gravity environment simulation for space deployable antenna. J. Mech. Eng. 57(3), 11–25 (2021). (in Chinese)

Dynamics Modeling and Multi-condition Analysis for 6-DOF Industrial Manipulator

Yang Jing, Weifan Gao, Zejie Han, and Ming Hu$^{(\boxtimes)}$

Faculty of Mechanical Engineering & Automation, Zhejiang Sci-Tech
University, Hangzhou 310018, China
huming@zstu.edu.cn

Abstract. For the flexible control problem of industrial manipulator, the dynamic model of its manipulator is established. Firstly, according to the D-H kinematics model modeling method, the kinematics coordinate system of the 6-DOF manipulator is established. On the basis of obtaining the D-H parameters, the forward kinematics model of the manipulator is established, and the correctness of the kinematics model is verified by Simulink program. Secondly, the dynamic model of the manipulator is derived by using the Newton-Euler equation and the kinematic model of the manipulator obtained previously. The virtual prototype of the manipulator is established by Adams, and the correctness of the established dynamic model is verified by dynamic simulation. The established dynamic model of the manipulator will provide a theoretical basis for its flexible control.

Keywords: Manipulator · Kinematics · Dynamics · Newton-Euler equation · Virtual prototype

1 Introduction

With the development of intelligent manufacturing, the requirement of manipulator in modern manufacturing process is higher and higher, and the cooperation and safety between operator and manipulator are also put forward. The control performance of the manipulator is also put forward higher requirements. The basis of solving these problems is the dynamic model of the manipulator [1].

For the dynamics of manipulator, many scholars at home and abroad have also carried out related research, and achieved certain results. Su Huayong et al. deduced the accurate dynamic model by Lagrange method and Rayleigh-Ritz method to analyze the influence of elastic deformation on the motion of manipulator [2]. Based on Lagrangian dynamic equation, Li Mengfei established the dynamic model of work-related manipulator and verified its correctness by simulation [3]. Xiao Shuang et al. simplified the dynamic equation expansion of the five-degree-of-freedom industrial manipulator by using the Pieper criterion and proposed a simplified model using open source engine ODE to complete the dynamic calculation of the manipulator [4]. Tian Bo et al. obtained the dynamic model of series rope driven manipulator by Newton Euler method and verified the correctness in the Adams [5]. Xue Shuai and others established the common

© Springer Nature Switzerland AG 2021
X.-J. Liu et al. (Eds.): ICIRA 2021, LNAI 13015, pp. 602–610, 2021.
https://doi.org/10.1007/978-3-030-89134-3_55

coordinate system and the conjoined coordinate system on the manipulator to deduce the Jacobian matrix of the manipulator, and simulated the motion of the manipulator under the condition of uniform speed and variable acceleration [6]. Ma Shuguang and others derived the dynamic equation of the manipulator by using the algebraic method of space operator and analyzed the numerical simulation efficiency of the dynamic model [7]. Liu Jia gives a kind of constraint relation which has broad significance by using the two-arm coordinated moving object Wei object [8]. Based on Lagrangian equation, Liu Qiang and others established the dynamic model of flexible load system with limited manipulator operation, and deduced the inverse dynamic model and the positive dynamic model of the system [9]. Liang Yuhang, Taiyuan University of Technology, established the dynamic equation of human lower limbs by Newton-Euler equation, and verified the correctness of the dynamic model of limbs by simulation [10]. Liu Peng et al. established the dynamic model of the two-degree-of-freedom manipulator through Lagrange, and summarized and analyzed the dynamic control problem of the manipulator by simulation [11]. Based on Lagrangian equation, the dynamic model of space manipulator is established and simulated [12]. Based on Newton Euler method, Zhang Tie et al. of South China University of Technology established the dynamic model of SCARA robot, and identified the dynamic parameters of the manipulator by practical experiments [13]. By establishing the three-dimensional model of the manipulator and using the Adams simulation software for dynamic analysis, Liu Zeyu and others have studied the control of the manipulator [14].

In this paper, the dynamic problem of industrial manipulator is studied. On the basis of establishing the accurate kinematics model of the six-degree-of-freedom manipulator, the dynamic model is established by Newton-Euler equation, and the accuracy of the model is verified by simulation.

2   Kinematics Model and Verification of Manipulator

Aiming at the dynamic model of the industrial manipulator, the kinematics model of the manipulator should be solved first. The manipulator includes six rotational degrees of freedom. The standard D-H modeling method is adopted to establish the kinematics coordinate system of the 6-DOF manipulator, as shown in Fig. 1 (Table 1).

Using the coordinate system pre-modeling method, the transformation matrix between joint coordinate systems is shown in Eq. 1. By using the kinematics parameters of the six degree of freedom manipulator obtained by the standard D-H modeling method, the transformation matrix between each joint coordinate system can be obtained by substituting formula 1 in turn, and finally the kinematics model of the end of the manipulator relative to its base coordinate system is obtained.

$$
{}^{i-1}T_i = \begin{bmatrix} \cos\theta_i & -\sin\theta_i \cdot \cos\alpha_i & \sin\theta_i \cdot \sin\alpha_i & a_i \cdot \cos\theta_i \\ \sin\theta_i & \cos\theta_i \cdot \cos\alpha_i & -\cos\theta_i \cdot \sin\alpha_i & a_i \cdot \sin\theta_i \\ 0 & \sin\alpha_i & \cos\alpha_i & d_i \\ 0 & 0 & 0 & 1 \end{bmatrix} \tag{1}
$$

To verify the correctness of the kinematics model, the kinematics model is used as the theoretical model, and the mechanism model of the manipulator is built by using the

Fig. 1. Structure and kinematics coordinate system of free manipulator

Table 1. D-H parameters of the robot

Joint i	$\theta_i(°)$	d_i(mm)	a_i(mm)	$\alpha_i(°)$
1	$\theta 1(0)$	330	40	90
2	$\theta 2(-90)$	0	−315	0
3	$\theta 3(0)$	0	−70	−90
4	$\theta 4(180)$	310	0	−90
5	$\theta 5(180)$	0	0	−90
6	$\theta 6(0)$	0	0	0

Matlab simechanics toolbox as the simulation model. Finally, the kinematics model verification Simulink program of the manipulator is shown in Fig. 2, in which the manipulator mechanism model is shown in Fig. 3.

The error between the output position and attitude of the two models can be obtained by giving the same angle input of the theoretical model and the mechanism model, as shown in Fig. 4. It can be seen from the simulation results that the numerical solution errors of the two models are very small and negligible, which proves that the kinematics model of the manipulator is correct.

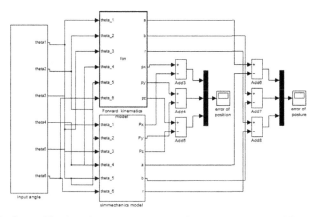

Fig. 2. Verification simulink procedure of kinematics model of free arm

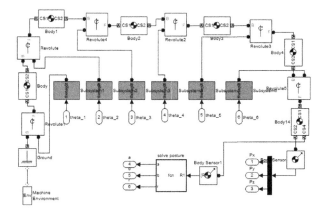

Fig. 3. Simmechanics model of six free manipulator

3   Establishment and Verification of Mechanical Arm Dynamics Model

Before establishing the dynamic model of the manipulator, the velocity and acceleration of each member are analyzed first.

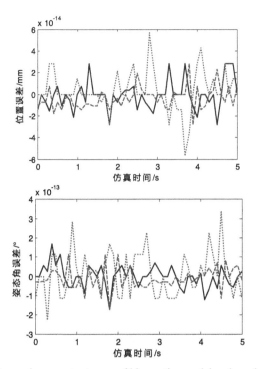

Fig. 4. Position and pose output error of kinematics model and mechanism model

(1) Motion velocity and acceleration of the member.

The velocity of the connecting rod is divided into linear velocity and angular velocity. For the angular velocity of the connecting rod relative to the base system, the calculation results are shown in the following formula 1.

$$
\begin{cases}
\omega_1 = R_{01} \cdot (Z_0 \cdot \dot{\theta}_1) \\
\omega_2 = R_{12} \cdot (\omega_1 + Z_0 \cdot \dot{\theta}_2) \\
\omega_3 = R_{23} \cdot (\omega_2 + Z_0 \cdot \dot{\theta}_3) \\
\omega_4 = R_{34} \cdot (\omega_3 + Z_0 \cdot \dot{\theta}_4) \\
\omega_5 = R_{45} \cdot (\omega_4 + Z_0 \cdot \dot{\theta}_5) \\
\omega_6 = R_{56} \cdot (\omega_5 + Z_0 \cdot \dot{\theta}_6)
\end{cases}
\tag{2}
$$

Where R_{01}, R_{12}, R_{23}, R_{34}, R_{45}, is the rotation matrix of the connecting rod i-1 relative to the I; $Z_0 = [\,0;0;1]$. $\dot{\theta}_i$ is the joint rotation speed. The angular acceleration of the connecting rod is calculated as shown in formula 2.

$$
\begin{cases}
\alpha_1 = R_{01} \cdot (\alpha_0 + Z_0 \cdot \ddot{\theta}_1 + \omega_0 \times (Z_0 \cdot \dot{\theta}_1)) \\
\alpha_2 = R_{12} \cdot (\alpha_1 + Z_0 \cdot \ddot{\theta}_2 + \omega_1 \times (Z_0 \cdot \dot{\theta}_2)) \\
\alpha_3 = R_{23} \cdot (\alpha_2 + Z_0 \cdot \ddot{\theta}_3 + \omega_2 \times (Z_0 \cdot \dot{\theta}_3)) \\
\alpha_4 = R_{34} \cdot (\alpha_3 + Z_0 \cdot \ddot{\theta}_4 + \omega_3 \times (Z_0 \cdot \dot{\theta}_4)) \\
\alpha_5 = R_{45} \cdot (\alpha_4 + Z_0 \cdot \ddot{\theta}_5 + \omega_4 \times (Z_0 \cdot \dot{\theta}_5)) \\
\alpha_6 = R_{56} \cdot (\alpha_5 + Z_0 \cdot \ddot{\theta}_6 + \omega_5 \times (Z_0 \cdot \dot{\theta}_6))
\end{cases}
\tag{3}
$$

For the linear acceleration of the connecting rod coordinate system relative to the basic coordinate system dvi the calculation results are shown in formula 3. Where p_i is the position of the vector from the origin of coordinate system $x_{i-1}y_{i-1}z_{i-1}$ to the origin of coordinate system $x_i y_i i_i$

$$
\begin{cases}
dv1 = \alpha_1 \times p_1 + \omega_1 \times (\omega_1 \times p_1) + R_{01} \cdot dv0 \\
dv2 = \alpha_2 \times p_2 + \omega_2 \times (\omega_2 \times p_2) + R_{12} \cdot dv1 \\
dv3 = \alpha_3 \times p_3 + \omega_3 \times (\omega_3 \times p_3) + R_{23} \cdot dv2 \\
dv4 = \alpha_4 \times p_4 + \omega_4 \times (\omega_4 \times p_4) + R_{34} \cdot dv3 \\
dv5 = \alpha_5 \times p_5 + \omega_5 \times (\omega_5 \times p_5) + R_{45} \cdot dv4 \\
dv6 = \alpha_6 \times p_6 + \omega_6 \times (\omega_6 \times p_6) + R_{56} \cdot dv5
\end{cases}
\tag{4}
$$

The calculated results of centroid acceleration are shown in formula 4, in which the s_i is the position of the centroid of the connecting rod under the $x_i y_i z_i$ of its own connecting rod coordinate system.

$$
\begin{cases}
a\_c1 = \alpha_1 \times s_1 + \omega_1 \times (\omega_1 \times s_1) + dv1 \\
a\_c2 = \alpha_2 \times s_2 + \omega_2 \times (\omega_2 \times s_2) + dv2 \\
a\_c3 = \alpha_3 \times s_3 + \omega_3 \times (\omega_3 \times s_3) + dv3 \\
a\_c4 = \alpha_4 \times s_4 + \omega_4 \times (\omega_4 \times s_4) + dv4 \\
a\_c5 = \alpha_5 \times s_5 + \omega_5 \times (\omega_5 \times s_5) + dv5 \\
a\_c6 = \alpha_6 \times s_6 + \omega_6 \times (\omega_6 \times s_6) + dv6
\end{cases}
\tag{5}
$$

The calculation result of the moment ni of member $i - 1$ acting on member i in the coordinate system $i - 1$ is shown in Eq. 5. Where n_i is the moment of member $i - 1$ acting on member i in the coordinate system $i - 1$. f_i is the force of member $i - 1$ acting on member i in the coordinate system $i - 1$. II is the inertia matrix of connecting rod i.

$$
\begin{cases}
\text{n6} = p_6 \times f_6 + s_6 \times (\text{m}_6 \cdot \text{a\_c6}) + I_6 \cdot \alpha_6 + \omega_6 \times (I_6 \cdot \omega_6) \\
\text{n5} = R_{65} \cdot \text{n6} + p_5 \times f_5 + s_5 \times (\text{m}_5 \cdot \text{a\_c5}) + I_5 \cdot \alpha_5 + \omega_5 \times (I_5 \cdot \omega_5) \\
\text{n4} = R_{54} \cdot \text{n5} + p_4 \times f_4 + s_4 \times (\text{m}_4 \cdot \text{a\_c4}) + I_4 \cdot \alpha_4 + \omega_4 \times (I_4 \cdot \omega_4) \\
\text{n3} = R_{43} \cdot \text{n4} + p_3 \times f_3 + s_3 \times (\text{m}_3 \cdot \text{a\_c3}) + I_3 \cdot \alpha_3 + \omega_3 \times (I_3 \cdot \omega_3) \\
\text{n2} = R_{32} \cdot \text{n3} + p_2 \times f_2 + s_2 \times (\text{m}_2 \cdot \text{a\_c2}) + I_2 \cdot \alpha_2 + \omega_2 \times (I_2 \cdot \omega_2) \\
\text{n1} = R_{21} \cdot \text{n2} + p_1 \times f_1 + s_1 \times (\text{m}_1 \cdot \text{a\_c1}) + I_1 \cdot \alpha_1 + \omega_1 \times (I_1 \cdot \omega_1)
\end{cases} \tag{6}
$$

The calculation results of driving torque of each joint are shown in formula 6.

$$
\begin{cases}
\tau_1 = \text{n1}' \cdot (R_{01} \cdot Z_0) \\
\tau_2 = \text{n2}' \cdot (R_{12} \cdot Z_0) \\
\tau_3 = \text{n3}' \cdot (R_{23} \cdot Z_0) \\
\tau_4 = \text{n4}' \cdot (R_{34} \cdot Z_0) \\
\tau_5 = \text{n5}' \cdot (R_{45} \cdot Z_0) \\
\tau_6 = \text{n6}' \cdot (R_{56} \cdot Z_0)
\end{cases} \tag{7}
$$

Based on the three-dimensional model of manipulator, a virtual prototype model of six-degree-of-freedom manipulator is built by dynamic simulation software Adams in order to verify the accuracy of the established dynamic model. The physical parameters of the model are measured by the three-dimensional model. The rotation pair constraint and joint motion function are added to the model.

Taking the dynamic simulation results of the virtual prototype model as the actual joint torque results, the mechanical arm dynamics model is compiled into a M file by Matlab as the theoretical joint torque results of the manipulator. By giving the same joint motion parameters as the virtual prototype model and the theoretical model, the theoretical and practical results of the joint driving torque are obtained by running the

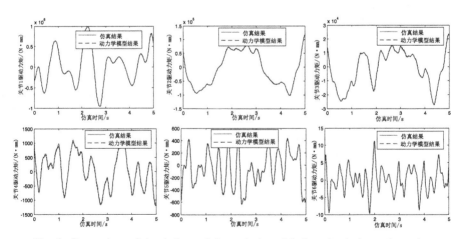

Fig. 5. Comparison of simulation and theoretical model of mechanical arm dynamics

simulation. It can be seen from the comparison results that the results obtained by the theoretical model are close to the dynamic simulation results and prove that the established dynamic model is correct (Fig. 5).

4 Multi-condition Dynamic Simulation of 6-DOF Industrial Manipulator

Since industrial robots are commonly used in welding, spraying, polishing, grinding, handling and other industrial operations, the working conditions are divided into no-load conditions, intermittent load conditions and heavy load conditions. No-load conditions correspond to the installation of welding guns or spray guns at the end of the manipulator and other execution tools that do not contact with the workpiece. Intermittent load conditions correspond to intermittent contact with the workpiece such as polishing or grinding. Heavy load conditions are mainly aimed at the operation of the manipulator to carry heavy load workpieces.

4.1 No-Load Dynamic Simulation

The flexibility requirement of the end of the manipulator is relatively high. Given the complex trajectory of the end and no-load, the joint driving torque is obtained for analysis.

4.2 Dynamic Simulation of Intermittent

Loading Given the end of the complex trajectory, intermittent load, joint drive torque analysis.

4.3 Dynamic Simulation of Heavy Haul Condition

Given a simple trajectory, large load (10 kg), the joint driving torque is analyzed.

5 Conclusions

In this paper, the kinematics model of six-DOF manipulator is established based on D-H modeling method, and the kinematics model is verified by the mechanism model built by matlab. On the basis of establishing its kinematic model, the dynamic model of the manipulator is established by using Newton-Euler equation, and the established model is verified by virtual prototype technology. The established dynamic model will provide the basis for the compliant control of the manipulator.

Acknowledgements. The authors gratefully acknowledge the financial supports for this research from National key research and development plan project (2018YFB1308100). This work is supported by Zhejiang Provincial Natural Science Foundation under Grant LQ21F020026, Science Foundation of Zhejiang Sci-Tech University(ZSTU) under Grant No.19022104-Y. General Scientific Research Project of Zhejiang Provincial Department of Education Grant No.19020038-F,19020033-F.

References

1. Wang, X.L., Zhao, D.J., Zhang, B., et al.: Kinematics analysis and optimization design of Noval 4-DOF parallel mechanism. J. Northeastern Univ. (Nat. Sci.) **39**(04), 532–537 (2018)
2. Shi, Z., Luo, Y., Chen, H., et al.: On global performance indices of robotic mechanisms. Robot **27**(5), 420–422 (2005)
3. Tian, H.B., Ma, H.W., Wei, J.: Workspace and structural parameters analysis for manipulator of serial robot. Trans. Chin. Soc. Agric. Mach. **44**(4), 196–201 (2013)
4. Ding, Y., Wang, X.: Optimization method of serial manipulator structure. J. Zhejiang Univ. Eng. Sci. **44**(12), 2360–2364 (2010)
5. Sun, W., Li, G.: Multiobjective optimization for the forging manipulator based on the comprehensive manipulation performance indices. J. Mech. Eng. **50**(17), 52–60 (2014)
6. Xiao, Y.F., Wang, X.L., Zhang, F.H., et al.: A global-parameter optimal design method for Seroal manipulators. China Mech. Eng. **25**(16), 2235–2239 (2014)
7. Chen, X.L., Jiang, D.Y., Chen, L.L., et al.: Kinematics performance analysis and optimal design of redundant actuation parallel mechanism. Trans. Chin. Soc. Agric. Mach. **47**(06), 340–347 (2016)
8. Dong, C., Liu, H., Huang, T.: Kinematic performance analysis of redundantly actuated 4-UPS&UP parallel manipulator. J. Mech. Eng. **50**(17), 52–60 (2014)
9. Yang, H., Fang, H., Li, D., et al.: Kinematics analysis and multi-objective optimization of a novel parallel perfusion robot. J. Beijing Univ. Aeronaut. Astronaut. **44**(03), 568–575 (2018)

Autonomous Landing Allocation of Multiple Unmanned Aerial Vehicles on Multiple Unmanned Surface Vessels Subject to Energy Consumption

Jingtian Ye[2], Bin-Bin Hu[1], Zhecheng Xu[1], Bin Liu[1], and Hai-Tao Zhang[1(✉)]

[1] School of Artificial Intelligence and Automation, The Key Laboratory of Image Processing and Intelligent Control, and the State Key Lab of Digital Manufacturing Equipment and Technology, Huazhong University of Science and Technology, Wuhan 430074, People's Republic of China
zht@mail.hust.edu.cn

[2] China-EU Insititute for Clean and Renewable Energy, Huazhong University of Science and Technology, Wuhan 430074, People's Republic of China

Abstract. This paper proposes a distributed energy-based landing allocation method of multiple unmanned aerial vehicles (UAVs) on multiple unmanned surface vessels (USVs). First, an optimization function is established, which consists of the limited energy battery, the flight distance and the flight speed. Then, a distributed landing allocation scheme is designed to minimize the energy consumption difference. Finally, real lake experiments of multiple M-100UAVs and HUSTER-30 USVs are conducted to verify the effectiveness of the proposed method.

Keywords: Autonomous landing allocation · Unmanned aerial vehicles (UAVs) · Unmanned surface vessels (USVs) · Energy consumption

1 Introduction

Recent years have witnessed the rapid development of the unmanned systems. The initial explorations of the unmanned systems mainly focused on the coordination of unmanned surface vehicles and the unmanned aerial vehicles [1–6], which could expand the maneuverability and application scenarios of unmanned systems. However, due to the limitations of current battery technology, the flight

This work was supported by in part by the National Natural Science Foundation of China (NNSFC) under Grants U1713203, 51729501, 61673330, 62003145 in part by the Natural Science Foundation of Hubei Province under Grant 2019CFA005, in part by the Program for Core Technology Tackling Key Problems of Dongguan City under Grant 2019622101007, and in part by the Fundamental Research Funds for Central Universities, HUST: 2020JYCXJJ070.

© Springer Nature Switzerland AG 2021
X.-J. Liu et al. (Eds.): ICIRA 2021, LNAI 13015, pp. 611–621, 2021.
https://doi.org/10.1007/978-3-030-89134-3_56

time of multi-rotor drones is relatively short and the flight range is always limited, which is even more difficult for the UAVs to independently perform tasks on a wide surface of the water with installed loads. In contrast, USVs consist of better carrying performance, longer endurance, and wider mission coverage, whose sailing speed and maneuverability are however limited. To this end, it becomes a future tendency to cooperate UAVs and USVs together to expand the application scenarios of unmanned systems.

In the coordination of multi-UAV multi-USV system, the landing control is a necessary premise for the further application. In this pursuit, Xu *et al.* [7] proposed the method of landing the UAV on a moving USV through visual guidance. However, different from the single UAV-USV system, landing allocation is important in the multi-UAV multi-USV system, which implies the USV needs to choose a proper landing USV platform from multiple USVs. Additionally, it is necessary to reduce energy consumption and the energy consumption difference as much as possible during the landing process. In this way, the integrity of the UAV system is stronger. It will not happen that some drones have insufficient power while others have sufficient power. To this end, it becomes an urgent task to establish a UAV energy consumption model, and then design a reasonable task allocation plan subject to the energy constraints.

Among the construction of the UAV energy consumption model, Modares *et al.* [8] designed an experimental method to approximate the relationship between energy consumption and speed, flight distance, and turning radius. Franco *et al.* [9] further considered the impact of acceleration and deceleration on the energy consumption of the UAV in a experiment, and fitted the energy consumption curve through experiment. A similar method was also studied in [10], and the polynomial relationship between energy consumption and speed is further given. Marins *et al.* [11] analyzes the forces on the drone during the flight by means of physical modeling, and derives the power consumed by the drone during the hovering process. Uehara *et al.* [12] discussed the endurance of drones on Titan, and also obtained an energy consumption model similar to ACE by means of physical modeling.

Notably, the task distribution methods are generally divided into centralized and distributed ones [13], where the centralized task distribution method performs calculations on the designated platform, and then assigns tasks to the designated nodes. Jia *et al.* [14] proposed a genetic algorithm with multi-layer coding for the task assignment of heterogeneous UAVs under time-varying conditions. Although the heuristic algorithm fails to guarantee the global optimal solution, it can give a better allocation method within the required task window time, which is used to solve the task assignment problem of large formation and high real-time requirements. However, the distributed algorithm uses the communication negotiation method to solve each problem by sharing data with each node. Zhang *et al.* [15] designed the auction method in a task allocation process. Brunet *et al.* [16] proposed the adjust bidding strategies through the revenue function to auction the task, which has high requirements for communication and needs to share auction process information among various nodes in real time.

To this end, this paper improves a distributed auction algorithm for the mission point allocation problem of UAV based on energy consumption, making the UAV group have the smallest energy consumption while meeting the smallest difference. Meanwhile, experiments are conducted on a group of UAVs and USVs to verify the effectiveness of the proposed method.

The remainder of this paper is organized as below: Sect. 2 introduces modeling and problem statement; Sect. 3 presents the landing allocation method of the multi-UAV multi-USV system; simulation and real lake experiment are conducted in Sect. 4; finally the conclusion is drawn in Sect. 5.

2   Modeling and Problem Statement

The selection of mission points for UAVs based on energy consumption is a multi-constrained task assignment problem. First, it is necessary to analyze the energy consumption of the UAV during the flight.

2.1   UAV and Energy Consumption Modeling

Generally, multi-rotor UAVs have two layout forms, which are cross-shaped and x-shaped, and have four motors. We analyze the dynamics of the x-shaped UAV, and its structure is shown in the Fig. 1:

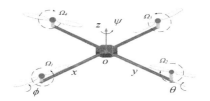

Fig. 1. Illustration of the UAV's model.

The dynamic model [17] of this structure can be written as the Eq. (1):

$$
\begin{cases}
\ddot{\phi} = \dot{\theta}\dot{\psi}\left(\dfrac{I_y - I_z}{I_x}\right) - \dfrac{J_r}{I_x}\dot{\theta}\Omega + \dfrac{l}{I_x}U_2 - \dfrac{l}{m}\dot{\phi} \\[2mm]
\ddot{\theta} = \dot{\phi}\dot{\psi}\left(\dfrac{I_z - I_x}{I_y}\right) + \dfrac{J_r}{I_y}\dot{\phi}\Omega + \dfrac{l}{I_y}U_3 - \dfrac{l}{m}\dot{\theta} \\[2mm]
\ddot{\psi} = \dot{\phi}\dot{\theta}\left(\dfrac{I_x - I_y}{I_z}\right) + \dfrac{l}{I_z}U_4 - \dfrac{1}{m}\dot{\psi} \\[2mm]
\ddot{x} = (\cos\phi\sin\theta\cos\psi + \sin\phi\sin\psi)\dfrac{1}{m}U_1 - \dfrac{1}{m}\dot{x} \\[2mm]
\ddot{y} = (\cos\phi\sin\theta\sin\psi - \sin\phi\cos\psi)\dfrac{1}{m}U_1 - \dfrac{1}{m}\dot{y} \\[2mm]
\dot{z} = (\cos\phi\cos\theta)\dfrac{1}{m}U_1 - g - \dfrac{1}{m}\dot{z}
\end{cases}
\tag{1}
$$

Among them, ϕ, θ, and ψ respectively represent the angle of counterclockwise rotation around the x, y, and z axes; I_x, I_y, and I_z respectively represent the moment of inertia of the UAV on the three coordinate axes. The moment of inertia is represented by J_r. The distance from the center of the motor to the center of mass is l; the mass of the aircraft is m; g is the acceleration of gravity.

The UAV studied in this article is the x configuration. For this type of UAV, the parameters U_1, U_2, U_3, U_4, Ω are given by the Eq. (2):

$$\begin{cases} U_1 = b\left(\Omega_1^2 + \Omega_2^2 + \Omega_3^2 + \Omega_4^2\right) \\ U_2 = b\left(\Omega_4^2 - \Omega_2^2\right) \\ U_3 = b\left(\Omega_3^2 - \Omega_1^2\right) \\ U_4 = d\left(\Omega_2^2 + \Omega_4^2 - \Omega_1^2 - \Omega_4^3\right) \\ \Omega = \Omega_2 + \Omega_4 - \Omega_1 - \Omega_3 \end{cases} \tag{2}$$

where b is the lift coefficient, and Ω_1 to Ω_4 are the speeds of motors 1 to 4 respectively.

The energy consumption of a quadrotor during flight can be divided into two parts: 1) the energy consumed during hovering, and 2) the energy consumed during forwarding. Since the energy consumption of the electronic components that control the UAV flight is small, the energy consumption of the electronic components is not considered in this article. The power of the UAV during the hovering process can be obtained by Bernoulli equation [11] and momentum theorem, and it is expressed in Eq. (3):

$$P_{\text{hov}} = \frac{(mg)^{\frac{3}{2}}}{\eta_{\text{tot}}\sqrt{2\rho A}} \tag{3}$$

where η_{tot} is the overall efficiency of the motor and the propeller, ρ is the air density, and A is the total area swept by the blades.

The process of the aircraft flying forward can be divided into acceleration, uniform motion, and deceleration phases. Assuming that the initial speed and final speed of the UAV are zero, the UAV accelerates from stationary to speed v during the acceleration phase. During the uniform movement stage, the UAV moves at a speed v. During the deceleration phase, the UAV decelerates from speed v to zero. The total energy consumption of the UAV in this case is expressed by the Eq. (4):

$$E_{\text{tot}} = \frac{1}{\eta}[(\frac{s}{v} + \frac{v}{s})P_{\text{hov}} + mv^2 + \frac{\rho}{2}sC_D A_e v^2] \tag{4}$$

where s is the flight distance, C_D is the coefficient of air resistance, and A_e is the effective windward area of the UAV.

2.2 Problem Statement

Suppose that a group of stationary UAVs on a lake are ready to return to USVs for landing. There are multiple USVs on the lake that can be selected by UAVs as landing points. But they can only choose one-to-one correspondence with each other. We assume that at the beginning of the selection, all UAVs know all the locations of all USVs that can be selected.

In this scenario, the drone needs to use the known information to select a reasonable location and ensure that the energy consumption during the flight is as small as possible by using an proper flying velocity. Since unmanned systems have high integrity demands, it is hoped that in the planning process, the difference in energy consumption of each UAV is as small as possible. This problem is essentially a task planning problem with multiple constraints, and its expression is as follows:

$$\min\{E_{\text{diff}}\} \tag{5}$$

subject to:

$$
\begin{cases}
\sum_{j=1}^{N_{\text{usv}}} x_{ij} \leq 1 \quad \forall i \in I \\
\sum_{i=1}^{N_{\text{uav}}} x_{ij} \leq 1 \quad \forall j \in J \\
\sum_{i=1}^{N_{\text{uav}}} (\sum_{j=1}^{N_{\text{usv}}} (x_{ij})) = \min\{N_{\text{usv}}, N_{\text{uav}}\} \\
E_{ij} = \frac{1}{\eta}[(\frac{s_{ij}}{v_i} + \frac{v_i}{s_{ij}})P_{\text{hov}} + mv_i^2 + \frac{\rho}{2}s_{ij}C_D A_e v_i^2 \\
E_{\text{diff}} = \sum_{i=1}^{N_{\text{uav}}} (\sum_{j=1}^{N_{\text{usv}}} (E_{ij}x_{ij} - \text{mean}(E_{ij}x_{ij})))
\end{cases}
$$

where x_{ij} is the selection relationship between the UAV i and the USV j. $x_{ij} = 1$ means that the UAV i selects the USV j, and $x_{ij} = 0$ means it is not selected. I and J are the number sets of UAVs and USVs respectively; N_{uav} and N_{usv} represent the number of UAVs and USVs respectively; s_{ij} represents the distance from the UAV i to the USV j.

3   Allocation Algorithm Design

The distributed auction algorithm combines the characteristics of the auction algorithm and the consensus algorithm, and can complete task assignment under the condition of limited communication. This paper improves the distributed auction algorithm by introducing a new method of generating bid list of each individual. The improved algorithm makes the energy consumption difference of each individuals smaller when the lowest energy consumption constraint of the unmanned system is considered.

Before starting the algorithm, we must first preprocess the problem. In this problem, each UAV knows the location of all USVs. In the following, the position of the USV is regarded as the mission point of UAV planning. In the research, it is found that optimizing energy consumption and meeting the limit of small energy consumption difference at the same time will make the problem very complicated. In order to simplify the analysis, the optimization progress is decoupled here [11]. First, analyze the Eq. (4) and find that when the distance is constant, the velocity corresponding to the optimal energy consumption can be obtained by solving the Eq. (6):

$$(2m + s\rho C_D A)v^3 + (\frac{P_0}{a})v^2 - sP_0 = 0 \tag{6}$$

Each individual drone i can calculate the Eq. (6) to obtain the minimum energy consumption E_{ij} to reach different mission point j. This value can be used to generate the energy consumption matrix of each UAV. Assuming that the profit matrix is c, the smaller the energy consumption difference, the greater the profit. In order to achieve the average energy consumption of different UAVs in the system, the Eq. (7) is used to generate the profit matrix:

$$\begin{cases} avg = \text{mean}(E_{ij}) \\ c_{ij} = \dfrac{1}{\text{abs}(E_{ij} - avg)} \end{cases} \tag{7}$$

where avg represents the average value, abs calculates the absolute value.

In the distributed auction algorithm, all UAVs do not have any mission point in the initial state. Each individual i has its own profit list c_{ij}, a bid list y_i and a mission vector x_i. The position j of the vector x_i indicates the selection status of the task, $x_i(j) = 0$ means not selected, and $x_i(j) = 1$ means selected. For example, $x_i = [0,0,0,0,1,0]$ means individual i has selected mission point 5. The bid list y_i indicates the desire degree of each node i for mission point j. The higher the value of its position j, the higher its bid for mission point j. In the process of each auction, first find mission point that can still be profitable by comparing the profit list c_{ij} and bid list y_i. Then calculate the optimal profit t_{ij^*}, and suboptimal profit $t_{ij'}$, where j^* and j' respectively represent the optimal and suboptimal mission points. Finally calculate the new bid list $y_{ij_{new}}$ and new profit list $c_{ij_{new}}$. Equations can be expressed as the following [18]:

$$\begin{cases} H_{ij} = f(c_{ij} > y_{ij}) \\ t_{ij^*} = \max\{H_{ij}\} \\ t_{ij'} = \max_{k \neq j^*}\{H_{ij}\} \\ y_{ij_{new}} = y_{ij^*} + t_{ij^*} - t_{ij'} + \varepsilon \\ c_{ij_{new}} = c_{ij^*} - (t_{ij^*} - t_{ij'} - \varepsilon) \end{cases} \tag{8}$$

where the $f(c,y)$ function can find the profitable mission points collection H_{ij} and ε is the update range of each auction, usually taken as $\varepsilon < \frac{1}{N_{uav}}$.

The second stage of the algorithm is the consensus process [19]. First define the undirected graph g to represent the connectivity of the communication network. Assume that the matrix is a symmetric matrix, and there is a communication relationship between two connected points. If two points are connected to each other, then $g_{mn} = g_{nm} = 1$; if there is no interconnection between two points, then $g_{mn} = g_{nm} = 0$. In g, each node is considered to be self-connected, that is, $g_{nn} = 1$.

In the process of consensus, each individual i and the connected individual i' in this iteration will share their bid list information y_i and $y_{i'}$. Individual i compares y_i with $y_{i'}$, and updates the highest bid into all y_i and $y_{i'}$. At the same time, if it is found that there is a higher bid in $y_{i'}$ than the task selected by itself, individual i will lose the task selected in this iteration [16].

4   Simulation and Experiment

In order to test the robustness and effectiveness of the algorithm, methods of simulation and experiment are used for verification in this section. More UAVs are set up in the simulation to increase the intensity of competition in the allocation process; finally, the usability of the algorithm is tested in actual experiments.

50 UAVs and 50 USVs are set up in the simulation. The UAVs are numbered 1 to 50. Adjacent UAVs will exchange the current bid list y_{ij} with each other. Take the mass of the UAV as $m = 2.5\,\text{kg}$. Acceleration $a = 1\,\text{m/s}^2$. $C_D \times A_e = 0.01547\,\text{m}$. Hovering power $P_{\text{hov}} = 572.7\,\text{W}$. Efficiency $\eta = 0.9$. The positions of UAVs and USVs are randomly initialized in the range of 0 to 50 and 50 to 100 on the x and y axes, and the limit of simulation iterations is set to 10,000.

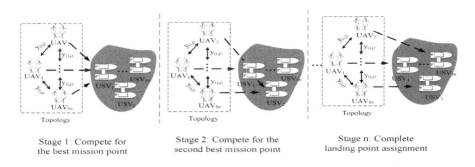

Fig. 2. Competition progress in the algorithm.

In the simulation, since the UAV knows the position of all mission points at the beginning, the optimal speed to reach each mission point can be solved by Eq. (6). In the unimproved algorithm, each UAV brings the optimal speed into Eq. (4) to obtain the optimal energy consumption to reach each mission point. Then the algorithm will make each UAV preferentially select the mission point with the lowest energy consumption. Under normal circumstances, the shorter the flight distance, the lower the energy consumption, so the drone group will give priority to the closest point, which will cause fierce competition. The process is shown in Fig. 2. Figure 3 (a) shows the competitive process at a certain mission point in the unimproved algorithm. It can be seen that the number of UAVs participating in the competition is large, and it takes multiple rounds of iterations to end the competition. From the perspective of system energy consumption, the energy consumed by each UAV is quite different, as shown in Fig. 4 (a).

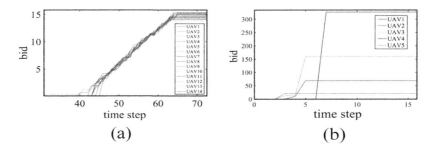

(a)   (b)

Fig. 3. (a) UAVs compete for a certain mission point in the unimproved algorithm. 14 drones participated in the bidding process, and finally UAV4 obtained the mission point; (b)UAVs compete for a certain mission point in the improved algorithm. The number of UAVs participating in the competition has decreased significantly. The UAV that most want to get this mission point will give a higher bid, and the mission point will be selected after fewer iterations.

Using Eq. (7) to improve the algorithm can make the optimal mission points of each UAV more dispersed and reduce the number of UAVs participating in the competition. Figure 3 (b) shows the competitive process at a certain mission point after the algorithm is improved. It can be seen that the number of UAVs participating in the competition for this point has decreased significantly. At the same time, this improved method can also make the energy consumption of each UAV more even, as shown in Fig. 4 (b). This can improve the integrity of the whole unmanned system.

In order to test this algorithm, an UAV experimental platform is built, and actual experiments are completed on a lake in Dongguan, Guangdong, China as shown in Fig. 5.

In this experiment, dji M100 series unmanned aerial (wheelbase 650mm) vehicles and huster30 (300 cm in length) and huster12 (120 cm in length) series USVs are used as the experimental platform. The M100 is equipped with a manifold onboard computer for control, and uses vonets 5G module for communication. The position of the unmanned boat is forwarded to the drone through the base station, so that the drone can obtain the positions of all mission points. The architecture of the experimental platform is shown in the Fig. 6.

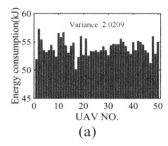 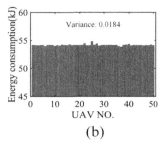

(a)   (b)

Fig. 4. (a) UAV energy consumption in the unimproved algorithm. (b) UAV energy consumption int the improved algorithm.

 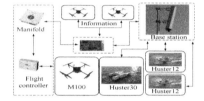

Fig. 5. Experiment on lake.   **Fig. 6.** Structure of the multi-UAV multi-USV system.

Three UAVs and three USVs are deployed scattered on the lake in this experiment. After the experiment starts, the UAVs will compete with each other for three USVs, which is regarded as the mission point, and then fly to them. The algorithm first initializes the minimum energy consumption and corresponding velocity of each UAV to each mission point through the model in Eq. (4) and Eq. (6). The energy consumption and corresponding velocity of the UAV arriving at different mission points is shown in Fig. 7. Then, through experiment, the task allocation of the algorithm before and after the improvement is compared.

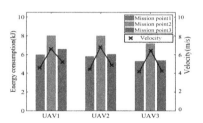 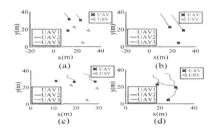

Fig. 7. Energy consumption and velocities of UAVs to various points.

Fig. 8. (a)–(b) are experimental routes of the unimproved algorithm; (c)–(d) are improved algorithm.

Figure 8 are the results of the assignment of task points by the two algorithms. Figure 9 shows the velocity changes of the two algorithms in the process which corresponds to the velocity data in the Fig. 7. What needs to be pointed out is that since the flight path may cross, we have added a collision avoidance item to the control algorithm. When the distance between two aircraft is less than the safety limit, evasive action will be taken, so the speed in the Fig. 9 (b) fluctuates. Figure 10 shows the distribution result of the final energy consumption of the UAVs. It can be seen that when the algorithm is improved, the energy consumption of the unmanned system is more even.

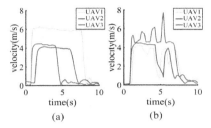
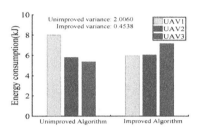

Fig. 9. (a)Velocities of UAVs in the unimproved algorithm; (b) Velocities of UAVs in the improved algorithm.

Fig. 10. Experimental results.

5   Conclusion

In this paper, a distributed allocation method of multiple unmanned aerial vehicles (UAVs) on multiple unmanned surface vessels (USVs) is proposed for the UAVs landing allocation with minimum energy consumption. With such a proposed method, the multiple UAVs land on the multiple USVs with the minimized energy consumption difference. Finally, experiments based on our multi-UAV multi-USV system are conducted to substantiate the proposed method. It is viable that the presented allocation protocol would be applicable in the further cooperation of multi-UAV multi-USV systems.

References

1. Zhang, H.T., Chen, M.Z.Q., Zhou, T.: Improve consensus via decentralized predictive mechanisms. EPL **86**(4), 40011 (2009)
2. Hu, B., Liu, B., Zhang, H.-T.: Cooperative hunting control for multi-underactuated surface vehicles. In: 2018 37th Chinese Control Conference (CCC), pp. 6602–6607. IEEE (2018)

3. Liu, B., Zhang, H.-T., Meng, H., Fu, D., Su, H.: Scanning-chain formation control for multiple unmanned surface vessels to pass through water channels. IEEE Trans. Cybern. (in press). https://doi.org/10.1109/TCYB.2020.2997833

4. Hu, B.-B., Zhang, H.-T., Wang, J.: Multiple-target surrounding and collision avoidance with second-order nonlinear multi-agent systems. IEEE Trans. Ind. Electron. (in press). https://doi.org/10.1109/TIE.2020.3000092

5. Hu, B.-B., Zhang, H.-T.: Bearing-only motional target-surrounding control for multiple unmanned surface vessels. IEEE Trans. Ind. Electron. (in press). https://doi.org/10.1109/TIE.2021.3076719

6. Hu, B.-B., Zhang, H.-T., Liu, B., Meng, H., Chen, G.: Distributed surrounding control of multiple unmanned surface vessels with varying interconnection topologies. IEEE Trans. Control Syst. Technol. (in press). https://doi.org/10.1109/TCST.2021.3057640

7. Xu, Z.C., Hu, B.B., Liu, B., Wang, X.D., Zhang, H.T.: Vision-based autonomous landing of unmanned aerial vehicle on a motional unmanned surface vessel. In: 2020 39th Chinese Control Conference (CCC), pp. 6845–6850 (2020)

8. Modares, J., Ghanei, F., Mastronarde, N., Dantu, K.: UB-ANC planner: energy efficient coverage path planning with multiple drones. In: 2017 IEEE International Conference on Robotics and Automation (ICRA), pp. 6182–6189 (2017)

9. Di Franco, C., Buttazzo, G.: Energy-aware coverage path planning of UAVs. In: 2015 IEEE International Conference on Autonomous Robot Systems and Competitions, pp. 111–117 (2015)

10. Abeywickrama, H.V., Jayawickrama, B.A., He, Y., Dutkiewicz, E.: Empirical power consumption model for UAVs. In: 2018 IEEE 88th Vehicular Technology Conference (VTC-Fall), pp. 1–5 (2018)

11. Marins, J.L., Cabreira, T.M., Kappel, K.S., Ferreira, P.R.: A closed-form energy model for multi-rotors based on the dynamic of the movement. In: 2018 VIII Brazilian Symposium on Computing Systems Engineering (SBESC), pp. 256–261 (2018)

12. Uehara, D., Matthies, L.: Energy modeling of VTOL aircraft for Titan Aerial Daughtercraft (TAD)concepts. In: 2019 IEEE Aerospace Conference, pp. 1–19 (2019)

13. Gaowei, J., Jianfeng, W.: Research status and development of UAV swarms mission planning. In: 2020 Systems Engineering and Electronics, pp. 1–19 (2020)

14. Gaowei, J., Jianfeng, W., Peng, W., Qingyang, C., Yujie, W.: Using multi-layer coding genetic algorithm to solve time-critical task assignment of heterogeneous UAV teaming. In: 2019 International Conference on Control, Automation and Diagnosis (ICCAD), pp. 1–5 (2019)

15. Zhang, Z., Wang, J., Xu, D., Meng, Y.: Task allocation of multi-AUVs based on innovative auction algorithm. In: 2017 10th International Symposium on Computational Intelligence and Design (ISCID), vol. 2, pp. 83–88 (2017)

16. Brunet, L., Choi, H.L., How, J.P.: Consensus-based auction approaches for decentralized task assignment (2013)

17. Salih, A.L., Moghavvemi, M., Mohamed, H.A.F., Gaeid, K.S.: Modelling and PID controller design for a quadrotor unmanned air vehicle. In: 2010 IEEE International Conference on Automation, Quality and Testing, Robotics (AQTR), vol. 1, pp. 1–5 (2010)

18. Bertsekas, D.P.: The auction algorithm: a distributed relaxation method for the assignment problem. Ann. Oper. Res. **14**(1), 105–123 (1988)

19. Choi, H., Brunet, L., How, J.P.: Consensus-based decentralized auctions for robust task allocation. IEEE Trans. Rob. **25**(4), 912–926 (2009)

Design of a Compliant Joint Based on Antagonistic-Driven Torsion Springs

Yifan Liu[1,2], Yinghao Ning[1,2], Hailin Huang[1,2(✉)], Xiaojun Yang[1,2], Zhisen Li[1,2], Bing Li[1,2,3(✉)], Fujun Peng[2], and Aiguo Wu[2]

[1] State Key Laboratory of Robotics and System (HIT), Harbin 150001, China
{huanghailin,libing.sgs}@hit.edu.cn
[2] Harbin Institute of Technology, Shenzhen 518055, China
[3] Peng Cheng Laboratory, Shenzhen 518055, China

Abstract. This paper proposes a novel series elastic actuator (SEA) based on torsion springs with antagonistic structure intended for human-robot interaction. Different from the traditional compliant joints constructed with torsion spring, the proposed novel SEA utilizes two torsion spring modules to construct the antagonistic structure for alleviating the empty return journey. The expression that depicts the relationship between the design parameters and stiffness of torsion spring is derived, which is conducive to designing proper torsion spring for a desired stiffness. Finally, experiments are conducted to verify the effectiveness of the proposed SEA for a friendly human-robot interaction.

Keywords: Series elastic actuator · Torsion spring · Antagonistic structure

1 Introduction

Safety is of great concern in occasions involving physical human-robot interaction. Leveraging the flexible actuators is a popular solution to improve the safety performance, since they bear several dramatic properties such as low output impedance, back drivability and shock tolerance [1].

Flexible actuators can be grouped into series elastic actuator (SEA) and variable stiffness actuator (VSA), depending on whether the stiffness could be changed actively. For SEA, the stiffness is constant [2] or changeable passively [3] based on the different compliant mechanisms. While, the stiffness of VSA could be regulated actively using one additional motor to drive the stiffness regulation mechanism [4]. This paper proposes a torsion-spring based SEA for safe human-robot interaction.

A lot of SEAs based on torsion spring have been explored in literature. One deficiency of these SEAs is the empty return journey [3]. The term "empty return journey" refers that, the actuator is required to return back to equilibrium point firstly before exerting force to the opposite direction. Antagonistic structure is a proper solution for alleviating the empty return journey. However, little attention has been paid to such area. Besides, the stiffness of the torsion spring with plane spiral structure is usually inconsistent in two-direction. The stiffness of the torsion spring is usually obtained through simulation.

© Springer Nature Switzerland AG 2021
X.-J. Liu et al. (Eds.): ICIRA 2021, LNAI 13015, pp. 622–630, 2021.
https://doi.org/10.1007/978-3-030-89134-3_57

The relationship between the parameters of structure and stiffness is still unexplored systematically.

In this paper, the SEA based on torsion springs with antagonistic structure is developed for safety human-robot interaction. Two torsion springs are placed antagonistically to alleviate the empty return journey, each of which is only responsible for the torque in one direction. The relationship between the design parameters and stiffness of torsion spring is analyzed, and the expression is derived which is beneficial for designing proper torsion spring for a desired stiffness. Finally, experiments are conducted to verify the effectiveness of the proposed SEA.

The rest words are organized as follows. In Sect. 2, the structure of the proposed SEA is introduced. In Sect. 3, the design of torsion spring is described in detail. Section 4 gives the experimental results. Concluding remarks are given in Sect. 5.

2 Mechanical Design of the Proposed SEA

For a torsion spring, it should return back to the equilibrium point firstly before exerting the force in the opposite direction, as shown in Fig. 1. In order to alleviate the empty return journey, two torsion spring modules are integrated into the proposed SEA to construct the antagonistic structure. Each torsion spring is only responsible for one-direction transmission. To achieve this target, the inner and outer ring of the torsion spring should be decoupled from the joint. The one-way bearing and the sprag freewheels clutch in one torsion spring module have the same locking direction. Only in this way can they be in locking state to transmit torque. While the two torsion spring modules' locking directions should be opposite, the joint can transmit bidirectional torque. Figure 2 describes the structure of the proposed SEA.

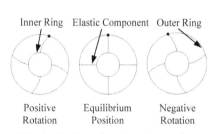
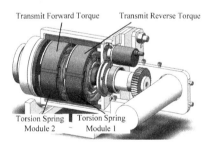

Inner Ring   Elastic Component   Outer Ring

Positive   Equilibrium   Negative
Rotation   Position   Rotation

Fig. 1. Deformation of torsion spring.

Transmit Forward Torque   Transmit Reverse Torque

Torsion Spring   Torsion Spring
Module 2   Module 1

Fig. 2. Principle of proposed SEA.

The structure of the torsion spring module is shown in Fig. 3. One-way bearing and sprag clutch make the inner and outer rings of torsion spring decoupled from the joint. The bearing sleeve and the inner ring of the torsion spring are connected by 6 keys which are evenly distributed. Similarly, the connecting ring and the output housing are also connected by 4 keys with even distribution.

Figure 4 presents the design of the proposed SEA, which is mainly made up with two spring modules, a shaft, a motor, an encoder and a pair of worm gear. A DC motor (Maxon motor RE35, 24V, 90W) is utilized to provide the power of the actuator. The power is strengthened by a gear pair and is further augmented by a pair of worm gear. The total reduction ratio of the joint is 746.7.

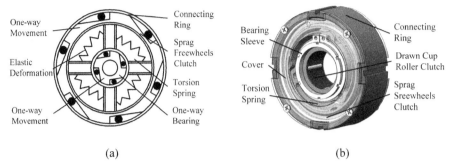

(a)   (b)

Fig. 3. Torsion Spring Module. (a) Principle of Transmission. (b) Structure

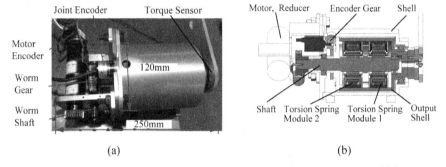

(a)   (b)

Fig. 4. Structure of the joint. (a) Prototype of the joint. (b)Section view of joint.

The internal deflection of the spring modules can be calculated from the positions of motor and joint, and the torque can be estimated by multiplying the internal deflection of spring modules and the stiffness of the joint.

3 Stiffness Analysis of Torsion Spring

3.1 Structure of Torsion Spring

A typical torsion spring with plane spiral structure is shown in Fig. 5. Three groups of plane spirals exist starting from the base circle on the inner ring and extending outward to the outer ring. To limit the maximum rotation angle of the torsion spring and avoid fatal stress, several blocks are placed both on inner ring and outer ring of torsion spring. Besides, the block can make the flexible beam protrude from the inner and outer rings of the torsion spring, avoid forming small sharp corner, and reduce the mechanical properties of the torsion spring. The holes on the blocks can reduce the weight of the torsion spring without weakening structural strength.

The main design parameters of the torsion spring are the thickness of the torsion spring b, the average radius of the flexible beam R, and the continuation angle h.

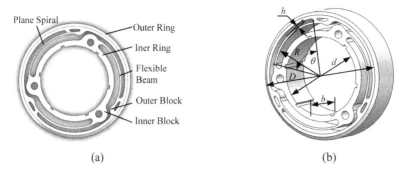

Fig. 5. Torsion spring. (a) Structure of the torsion spring. (b) Design parameters.

3.2 Stiffness Modeling of Torsion Spring

The stiffness of torsion spring analyzed by the ANSYS workbench can be seen in Fig. 6 (b). The deformation model of the flexible beam is presented in Fig. 6 (a). The AB and CD segments are hinged on the inner and outer rings of the torsion spring. The BC section can be regarded as a telescopic link with spring. During the deformation, the angles between the start section of the flexible beam and inner ring approximately keep constant. Similarly, the angle between the end section and outer ring is also approximately constant. Figure 6 (b) presents the results of finite element analysis for the torsion spring. Pseudo-rigid-body model is adopted in the simulation.

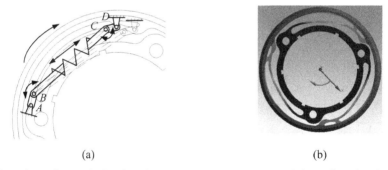

Fig. 6. Deformation analysis of torsion spring. (a) Flexible beam deformation. (b) Simulation results.

The established pseudo-rigid-body models are shown in Fig. 7. Due to the hinged joints at A and D, the ends of the flexible beam are only subjected to horizontal force F_x. Figure 7 (a) presents the pseudo-rigid-body model of the pined segment [5]. Flexible beam is divided into two identical sections from the midpoint for further analysis and the deformation of the flexible beam is approximately symmetrical. In each segment, the angle between the flexible beam and the inner ring or outer ring can be regarded as approximately unchanged in the case of small deformation. Therefore, we can apply the fixed-guided pseudo-rigid-body model to analyze the flexible segment [6] as shown in

Fig. 7 (b). Combining the two pseudo-rigid body-models, the overall pseudo-rigid-body model shown in Fig. 7 (c) can be obtained, where l_t is the length of the flexible rod.

Figure 7 (a) presents the force diagram of flexible beam. F is the simplified force applied to the flexible beam in the tangential direction, calculated as $F = T/(N \times R)$, where T is the torque applied to the outer ring of the torsion spring, N is the number of flexible beams in the plane torsion spring. The force alone x direction is $F_x = F \times \sin(\pi/2 - \theta/2)$, where R is the average radius of the flexible beam, and θ is the angle of the flexible beam. The length a is calculated as $a = 2 \times R \sin(\theta/2)$, and b is calculated as $b = R(1 - \cos(\theta/2))$. In the half of the flexible beam, the stiffness of each characteristic pivot is $K_t = 2\gamma K_\theta EI/l_t = 4\gamma K_\theta EI/l$. In the entire flexible beam, there are two such flexible segments in series configuration, so that the overall stiffness of the flexible beam is half of a single segment which is $K = 2\gamma K_\theta EI/l$. In the stiffness expression, γ is the characteristic radius coefficient, K_θ is the stiffness coefficient, E is the elastic modulus of the material, I is the inertia of the section, and l is the length of the flexible beam. The characteristic radius coefficient γ and stiffness coefficient K_θ of the pseudo-rigid-body model are determined by coefficient n, and the calculation method can be found in the literature [7]. Fig. 8 (a) presents the pseudo-rigid body-model. The characteristic pivot O_2 and C deform under the force F_x. The deformation of the characteristic pivot C is relatively small.

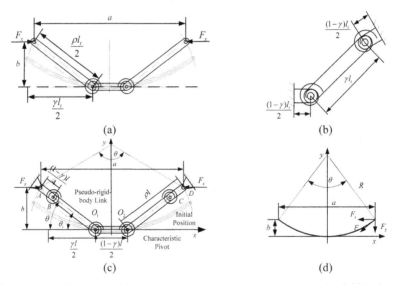

(a)

(b)

(c)

(d)

Fig. 7. Pseudo-rigid-body model. (a) Articulated-articulated segment pseudo-rigid-body model. (b) Fixed-guided flexible segment pseudo-rigid-body model. (c)Pseudo-rigid-body model of flexible beam. (d) Force diagram of flexible beam

Therefore, only the deformation of the characteristic pivot O_2 is considered. The torque acting on the characteristic hinge O_2 is $M_{O2} = F_x b$.

Under the action of the torque M_{O2}, the angle of the pseudo-rigid body link changes $\Delta\Theta = \Theta - \Theta_i = M_{O2}/K$. The displacement along x direction of the link's end is Δx.

When the deformation of the torsional spring is small, $\Delta\Theta$ is relatively small. There are $BC \approx BC = \rho l/2 \cdot \Delta\Theta$ and $\angle DBC \approx \angle EAF = \Theta_i$, as shown in Fig. 8 (b). There is $\Delta x/\rho l \cdot \Delta\Theta_i = \sin\Theta_i$ in $\triangle BDC$, where ρ is the characteristic radius coefficient of the initial bending flexible segment and expressed as $\rho = \sqrt{[a/(2l) - (1-\gamma)/4]^2}$.$\Theta$ is the pseudo-rigid-body angle. Because the flexible segment is initially curved, there is also an initial pseudo-rigid body angle $\Theta_i = \arctan\{b/[a/2 - (1-\gamma)/4 \times l]\}$ [8].

For the entire flexible beam, the deformation alone x direction is $2\Delta x$, which corresponds to the displacement of the telescopic link described above. The flexible beam can only move alone circumference due to the constraint of outer ring. The rotation angle corresponding to the deformation of flexible beam is $\Delta\theta = 2\Delta x/R$.Therefore, the stiffness of the plane torsion spring can be expressed as $K_{ts} = T/\Delta\theta$.

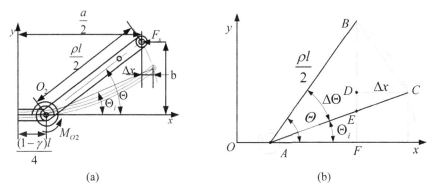

Fig. 8. Analysis of pseudo-rigid-body model. (a) Flexible segment deformation. (b) Geometrical relationship between $\Delta\Theta$ and Δx

By organizing the formulas above, the expression for stiffness calculation of the torsion spring can be expressed as

$$K_{ts} = \frac{2NR \times \gamma K_\theta EI}{\rho l^2 \times \cos\frac{\theta}{2}(1 - \cos\frac{\theta}{2}) \times \sin\Theta_i} \tag{1}$$

3.3 Analysis of Stiffness Model

In order to verify the accuracy of the stiffness formula derived above, several torsion springs with different design parameters are modeled. In the simulation, the material is assumed to be PA12, whose elastic modulus is 1700 Mpa. The fixed displacement constraint is applied to the inner ring, and the displacement constraint is applied to the outer ring to restrict the outer ring to move only in the circumferential direction. Torque is applied to the outer ring of the torsion spring. Table 1 shows the results.

One possible reason for the modeling error is that the simulation model is not exactly consistent with the actual one. Fillets are used in the modeling to reduce stress concentration and the direction of force and the deformation of the flexible beam are simplified.

The assumption of small deformation is also used in the derivation of the geometric relationship, which will also affect the accuracy of stiffness modeling.

Figure 9 shows how the design parameters affect stiffness of torsion spring. K_{ts}(N · m/rad) presents the theoretical results, while K_{ac}(N · m/rad) presents the simulation results. Figure 9(a) depicts the influence of R and θ of torsion spring on the stiffness, when the width of flexible beam b is 20 mm, the thickness of flexible beam h is 0.9 mm, and N is 3. Figure 9 (b) illustrates the effects of changing b and h on the stiffness, where R is 26 mm, θ is 69° and N is 3. When the average radius of flexible beam R and angle of the flexible beam θ are reduced, the torque of inertia of the flexible beam increases which makes the flexible beam short and thick, thus leading to the increase of stiffness. In addition, with the increase of b and h, the torque of inertia of the cross-section of the flexible beam becomes larger, which lead to a greater stiffness of the torsion spring.

Table 1. Accuracy of stiffness modeling

R (mm)	θ (°)	b (mm)	h (mm)	N	K_{ts}	K_{ac}	e
25.7	69.2901	10	0.9	3	2254.4212	2455.4942	-8.19%
23.7	62.1875	20	0.9	3	4850.1145	4972.2795	– 2.46%
21.7	65.6005	20	0.9	3	6864.3484	7213.8361	– 4.84%
25.68	62.1875	20	0.9	3	7443.7841	8111.4513	– 8.23%
25.75	69.0534	20	1	3	6267.2119	6771.0537	– 7.44%
25.75	69.0534	20	1	2	4178.1413	4638.1651	– 9.92%

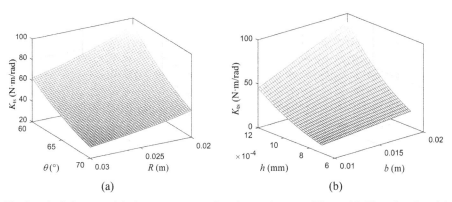

(a)   (b)

Fig. 9. The influence of design parameters of torsion spring on stiffness. (a) Changing R and θ of torsion spring. (b) Changing b and h of torsion spring.

4 Experiments and Results

4.1 Stiffness Calibration

Figure 10 (a) shows the stiffness of the SEA, different kinds of loads with different masses are utilized to calibrate the stiffness. One additional torque sensor is utilized to measure the torque applied to the joint by the load. Different loads usually lead to different internal deformation of joint. The relationship between the torque exerted onto the joint and the internal deformation of SEA could be obtained through utilizing proper loads. The slope of the curve in Fig. 10 (b) is the stiffness value of the joint which is 470.8 N · m/rad.

4.2 Collision Safety Experiment

The collision safety is an important property for human-robot interaction SEA. Figure 11 shows the experiment and result of collision safety. When the joint collides with obstacle and the contact torque exceeds the safety threshold, the internal deflection of torsion spring increases to certain value, which means the collision occurs, the joint rotates in the opposite direction to be away from the obstacle. The changes of torque exerted on the SEA from the obstacle can be seen in Fig. 11 (a) and the detail of experiments is illustrated in Fig. 11 (b). It can be found that the proposed SEA bears a better performance of collision safety for occasions of human-robot interaction.

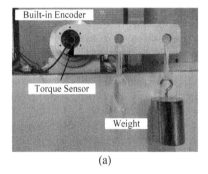 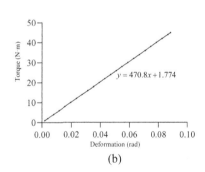

(a)   (b)

Fig. 10. Stiffness calibration. (a) Experimental setup. (b) Results of stiffness calibration

(a)   (b)

Fig. 11. Collision Safety Experiment. (a) Changes of torque exerted on the SEA. (b) Movement of the SEA when colliding obstacle.

5 Conclusion

This paper describes a SEA based on torsion springs with antagonistic structure for a friendly human-robot interaction. Two torsion springs are placed antagonistically to alleviate the empty return journey, each of which is only responsible for the torque in one direction. The expression that depicts the relationship between the design parameters and stiffness of torsion spring is derived, which is conducive to designing proper torsion spring for a desired stiffness. The experiment of stiffness calibration is conducted to verify the accuracy of stiffness modeling and the collision safety experiment is managed to verify the effectiveness of the proposed SEA for a friendly human-robot interaction. In the future, the proposed SEA could be used to construct a robot for upper-limb rehabilitation in order to improve the performance of safety.

Acknowledgement. This work was supported by the Key-Area Research and Development Program of Guangdong Province (Grant No. 2019B090915001), and the Shenzhen Research and Development Program of China (Grant No. JCYJ20200109112818703).

References

1. Vanderborght, B., et al.: Variable impedance actuators: a review. Robot. Auton. Syst. **61**(12), 1601–1614 (2013)
2. Yu, H., Huang, S., Chen, G., Pan, Y., Guo, Z.: Human-robot interaction control of rehabilitation robots with series elastic actuators. IEEE Trans. Robot. **31**, 1089–1100 (2015)
3. Ning, Y., Xu, W., Huang, H., Li, B., Liu, F.: Design methodology of a novel variable stiffness actuator based on antagonistic-driven mechanism. Proc. Inst. Mech. Eng. C J. Mech. Eng. Sci. **233**(19–20), 6967–6984 (2019)
4. Ning, Y., Huang, H., Xu, W., Zhang, W., Li, B.: Design and implementation of a novel variable stiffness actuator with cam-based relocation mechanism. J. Mech. Robot. **13**(2), 021009 (2021)
5. Edwards, B.T., Jensen, B.D., Howell, L.L.: A pseudo-rigid-body model for initially-curved pinned-pinned segments used in compliant mechanisms. J. Mech. Des. **123**(3), 464–468 (2001)
6. Howell, L.L., Midha, A.: Parametric deflection approximations for end-loaded, large-deflection beams in compliant mechanisms. J. Mech. Des. **117**(1), 156–165 (1995)
7. Howell, L.L.: Compliant Mechanisms 21st Century Kinematics. Springer, London (2013)
8. Howell, L.L., Ashok Midha, A.: Parametric deflection approximations for initially curved, large-deflection beams in compliant mechanisms. In: ASME Design Engineering Technical Conferences, pp. 12–15 (1996)

Design and Control of a Quadruped Robot with Changeable Configuration

Zhongkai Sun, Zhengguo Zhu, Guoteng Zhang$^{(\boxtimes)}$, Yibin Li, and Xuewen Rong

School of Control Science and Engineering, Shandong University, Jinan, China
zhanggt@sdu.edu.cn

Abstract. This paper introduces a quadruped robot with a wide range of motion for joints, which provides a basis for the robot to change its configuration. Two basic configurations are defined for the robot, including mammal-like configuration, which the front and hind knees point to each other and one reptile-like configuration with sprawling legs. Different control modes are configured to make the robot can switch between different configuration, which gives it ability to face different environments. For the mammal-like configuration, a parametric trotting gait is designed to traverse structural terrain level ground. For the reptile-like configuration, a turtle gait is designed to achieve robust locomotion on uneven terrain. Simulations and experiments show that the robot is capable to move on multiple terrains, including doorsills, slopes, stones. This paper demonstrates that through the design of leg foot configuration, some difficult tasks can be achieved in a rather simple way without using complicated control algorithms, which shows the potential of multi configuration in the application of quadruped robot.

Keywords: Quadruped robot · Kinematics · Multi-configuration

1 Introduction

Common mobile robots have crawler, wheeled and leg-footed movement methods, among which leg-footed robots have more advantages than crawler or wheeled robots in terms of flexibility and versatility, and leg-footed robots can be more well adapted to uneven and harsh terrain environment [1]. However, the manufacturing and control of quadruped robots is more complicated. But with the current control theory, computer system and hardware platform improvement, more and more legged robots are put into experimental development and even practical applications [2]. Legged robots have become a research hotspot.

Many leg foot robots are currently in laboratory research, Some use mammalian configurations, such as BigDog [3], HyQ [4], Anymal [2], StarlETH [5]

This work was supported by the National Natural Science Foundation of China (62003190), the China Postdoctoral Science Foundation (2019M662359), the fellowship of China Postdoctoral Science Foundation (2020T130369), and the Natural Science Foundation of Shandong Province (ZR201911040226).

X.-J. Liu et al. (Eds.): ICIRA 2021, LNAI 13015, pp. 631–641, 2021.
https://doi.org/10.1007/978-3-030-89134-3_58

RHex [6], MIT's directly electrically actuated cheetah [7], or ETH's serial elastic robot StarlETH [8]. Center for Robotics of Shandong University has been developing the hydraulically actuated quadruped robot SCalf [1]. All these robots have demonstrated dynamic running on different grounds or to dynamically overcome obstacles - however, none of these machines has been used in a real world application. There are also legged robots that use the configuration of reptiles, such as SILO4 [9], TITANXIII [10]. Lu et al. [14] proposed a novel multi-configuration quadruped robot with redundant DOF and analyzed its application scenarios. The quadruped robot in mammalian-like configuration can move at a faster speed, while the quadruped robot in reptile-like configuration can walk stably in a simple way with good load performance.

In order to deal with the more complex and special environment, it is necessary for robots to be able to cope with various terrain. Considering the advantages of both mammal-like and reptile-like quadruped robots, it is naturally to think about integrating them into one robot with changeable leg configuration. Based on the existing platform, a small quadruped robot with two configurations can be designed. This paper introduces a multi-configuration quadruped robot which can be used as a platform for studying gait switching and configurations of quadruped robot. The quadruped robot with multi-configuration can adapt to more environment (Figs. 1 and 2).

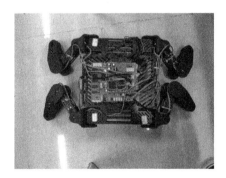

Fig. 1. Reptile-like configuration   Fig. 2. Mammal-like configuration

2   System Description

2.1   Mechanism Design

Compared with the quadruped robot of mammal configuration, first, we study the body shape and movement law of quadruped reptiles (such as gecko) with stable movement ability. By retaining the main skeleton frame and the main joint topology, the quadruped movement configuration suitable for the ground movement is concluded, just like an enlarged gecko, as shown in Fig. 6. The robot under this configuration can achieve stable ground movement in relatively simple control mode, and can move on the ground through rough terrain and steep slope.

Each leg of the robot has a hip joint for abduction/adduction, a hip joint for flexion/extension and a knee joint for flexion/extension, which is the minimum requirement to allow the foot to locate in the three-dimensional workspace around the hip, and also reduces the complexity of the quadruped machine. For lightweight design, the main body and legs of the robot are made of carbon fiber. The leg joints are driven by custom-made motors, and the robot is equipped with a battery to provide power. In order to provide a certain buffer, an elastic fiber ball is installed at the foot of the robot.

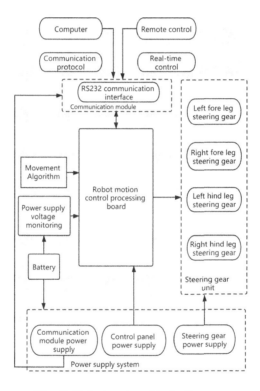

Fig. 3. Robot system block diagram

2.2   Control System

Integrated power management, CPU, main control board of acquisition module, battery and communication module are integrated in robot main body. The Fig. 3 shows the system block diagram of robot. The control circuit of the robot is designed based on STM32h7 series single-chip microcomputer. Robot main control board is shown in Fig. 4. The minimum system board is responsible for algorithm calculation, processing received information, and sending out control instructions; the control instructions are input to the steering gear through the steering gear interface to realize joint control; the serial port module can realize the signal transmission between the main control board and the upper computer and the remote controller; the power supply of the main control board is connected by the battery input interface, and connected to the minimum system through the sampling module to monitor the battery, and send a signal when the voltage is abnormal; the power supply module in the figure can achieve electrical isolation and avoid interference. The Fig. 5 shows the control flow chart. The steering gear module uses the optocoupler isolation chip to prevent the minimum system transmission PWM control signal from being interfered.

Fig. 4. Robot main control board

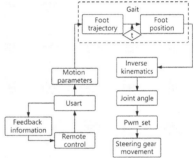

Fig. 5. Robot control flow chart

3 Gait Planning

3.1 Kinematic Equations

As shown in Fig. 6, the origin of the body fixed coordinate frame $\{O_b\}$ locates in the geometric center of the torso, and x_b points to the forward direction, z_b points opposite to the gravity direction, y_b axis is confirmed using right-hand rule. There are four coordinate frames noted as $\{O_{i0}\}$ $(i = 0, 1, 2, 3)$ fixed on the four corners of the torso respectively.

First, the reference coordinate system, namely coordinate system $\{O_{00}\}$, is defined, which is equivalent to fixed on the base. When the first joint variable value is 0, the coordinate system $\{O_{00}\}$ and coordinate system $\{O_{01}\}$ are completely coincident, and the axis of z_0 coincides with the axis of hip joint. Since all joint axes are perpendicular to or in the plane where the link model is located, there is no link offset, and all d_i is 0. All joints are rotating joints, so when the angle is 0, all X-axis must be in a straight line. The parameters of each coordinate system in Fig. 6 can be determined by the above analysis.

Since the four legs of robot have the same D-H coordinate frames and link parameters, they have same forward kinematic equations from $\{O_{i0}\}$ to $\{O_{i4}\}$. the coordinate of $\{x_i, y_i, z_i\}^T$ one foot in $\{O_b\}$ can be gained by

$$
\begin{aligned}
x_i &= -L_{i1} \sin \theta_{i1} - L_i \sin (\theta_{i1} + \theta_{i2}) + \delta l \\
y_i &= L_{i0} \sin \theta_{i0} + L_{i1} \sin \theta_{i0} \cos \theta_{i1} + L_{i2} \sin \theta_{i0} \cos (\theta_{i1} + \theta_{i2}) + \lambda w \quad (1) \\
z_i &= -L_{i0} \cos \theta_{i0} - L_{i1} \cos \theta_{i0} \cos \theta_{i1} - L_{i2} \cos \theta_{i0} \cos (\theta_{i1} + \theta_{i2})
\end{aligned}
$$

δ and λ are sign flags which are defined as below:

$$
\delta \begin{cases} 1, i = 0, 1 \\ -1, i = 2, 3 \end{cases} \quad \lambda \begin{cases} 1, i = 0, 3 \\ -1, i = 1, 2 \end{cases} \quad (2)
$$

The inverse kinematic analysis is necessary for motion planning and controlling. Moreover, its coordinates in other frames can be obtained by forward and inverse homogenous transformation. Reference [12] gives the detailed derivation for inverse kinematic equations of a quadruped robot. This paper gives the results directly as follows:

$$
\begin{aligned}
\theta_{i0} &= \arctan \left(\frac{y_i}{-z_i} \right) \\
\theta_{i1} &= \varphi_i - \arctan \left(\frac{x_i}{-L_{i0} - z_i / \cos \theta_{i0}} \right) \quad (3) \\
\theta_{i2} &= \arccos \left(\frac{L_{i1}^2 + L_{i2}^2 - L_{12}^2}{2 L_{i1} L_{i2}} \right) - \pi
\end{aligned}
$$

Among them

$$
\begin{aligned}
L_{i12} &= \sqrt{(L_{i0} + z_i / \cos \theta_{i0})^2 + x_i^2} \\
\varphi_i &= \arccos \left(\frac{L_1^2 + L_{i12}^2 - L_2^2}{2 L_1 L_{12}} \right)
\end{aligned}
$$

3.2   Workspace of the Foot

Given the mechanical parameters of robot and rotation range of the joints, we could get the foot workspaces of the robot. The workspace can help us in the motion planning of each foot. Take the left front leg as an example, we could get the foot workspace which is shown in Fig. 7. The blue part represents the main working range of the robot, and the red part represents the main working range of the robot in the reptile configuration, it can be seen that the joint offset enables a huge range of motion which provides a basis for the robot to change its configuration. And we could plan the trajectory of left front foot in this workspace. The parameters of the robot are as follows, body length $l = 110\,\text{mm}$, width $w = 50\,\text{mm}$. For leg, $a_0 = 40\,\text{mm}$, $a_1 = 100$, $a_2 = 100\,\text{mm}$. For reptile-like configuration, we choose the point $(110, 20, -20)^T$ as the initial foot position, and for mammal-like configuration, we choose the point $(120, 0, -100)^T$ as the initial foot position, since there are rather big space for the foot to move near this point. Initial position of the other three feet are confirmed similarly.

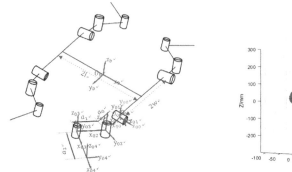 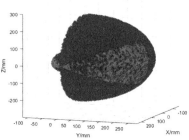

Fig. 6. Topology of robot   **Fig. 7.** Workspace

3.3 Trotting Gait

In nature, several quadruped running gaits can be observed, such as crawling, trotting, pacing, bounding or galloping. It has been generally accepted that quadruped animals choose the gait and preferred forward velocity to minimize energy consumption and to avoid injuries created by excessive musculoskeletal forces at foot touch-down [13]. The trot, which pairs diagonal legs, exhibits good energy efficiency over a wide range of running speed, shows no significant pitch or roll motion during each stride and therefore is often seen in nature.

In order to minimize the contact forces between ground and the foot, it is generally considered that the foot trajectory should meet the demand that velocity and acceleration become zero at the time of touchdown, liftoff and maximum foot height. The composite cycloid foot trajectory meets the demand well [11]. But it also has a serious defect that is the obvious relative slippage between feet and ground at the landing moment. The defect has been verified in experiments with physical robot. To improve this, Xuewen Rong et al. [12] proposed a composite foot trajectory composed of cubic curve for swing phase and straight line for stance phase. This foot trajectory makes their quadruped robot more stable in both simulations and experiments than other trajectories.

So we decided to take the composite foot trajectory in our robot.

$$x_i(t) = \begin{cases} x_{i\_ini} + L \times \left(-\frac{16}{T^3}t^3 + \frac{12}{T^2}t^2 - \frac{1}{T}t - \frac{1}{4}\right), for\ 0 \le t < \frac{T}{2} \\ x_{i\_ini} + L \times \left(-\frac{1}{T}t + \frac{3}{4}\right), for\ \frac{T}{2} \le t < T \end{cases} \quad (4)$$

$$y_i(t) = y_{i\_ini}, for\ 0 \le t < T \quad (5)$$

$$z_i(t) = \begin{cases} z_{i\_ini} + H_f \times \left(-\frac{128}{T^3}t^3 + \frac{48}{T^2}t^2\right), for\ 0 \le t < \frac{T}{4} \\ z_{i\_ini} + H_f \times \left(\frac{128}{T^3}t^3 - \frac{144}{T^2}t^2 + \frac{48}{T}t - 4\right) \\ \qquad, for\ \frac{T}{4} \le t < \frac{T}{2} \\ z_{i\_ini}, for\ \frac{T}{2} \le t < T \end{cases} \quad (6)$$

where L represents stride length, T represents cycle time, t represents the operating time in one cycle time, H_f represents the maximum foot height with reference to the ground respectively. $\{x_{i\_ini}, y_{i\_ini}, x_{z\_ini}\}^T$ is the initial foot position of leg i in $\{O_b\}$. For $0 \leq t \leq T/2$, the foot is in the swing phase while for $T/2 \leq t \leq T$ the foot is in the support phase.

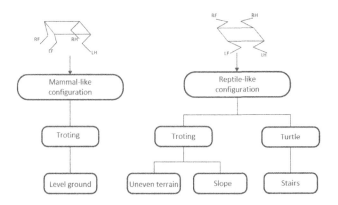

Fig. 8. Match between different gaits and tasks

3.4   Change of Configuration

By controlling the joint position of the robot, we can make the conversion between the mammal-like configuration and reptile-like configuration. The two configurations of robot can adapt to different environments, when the robot is in the form of a mammal-like configuration, it can pass through the level ground, and it can get faster movement speed by setting the gait parameters of the robot. When the robot encounters uneven terrain or slope, the center of gravity of the robot can be reduced, and the robot can be transformed into a reptile-like configuration. The match between different gaits and environments is shown in Fig. 8.

In this paper, we defined a turtle gait. The phase diagram of trot gait and turtle gait is shown in the Fig. 9, the gait cycle includes 4 phases: (1) The robot's four feet are raised up; (2) The feet move forward for distance d; (3) The feet move down from overhead to lift the body from the ground; (4) The body move forward for distance d. The motion sequence of turtle gait in one gait cycle is shown in Fig. 10. The trot gait can be used when the robot is in the mode of mammal-like configuration, which has good effect in level ground. When the robot is transformed into a reptile-like configuration, not only trot gait but also turtle gait can be used. When using this turtle gait, because of the simultaneous movement of the front and rear legs, that can provide a relatively big stability margin. At the same time, the center of the robot is very low, which reduces

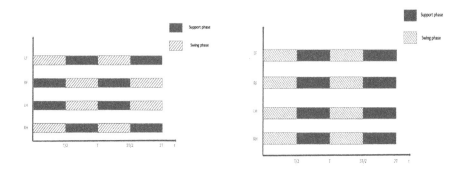

(a) Trotting gait phase diagram   (b) Turtle gait phase diagram

Fig. 9. Phase diagram

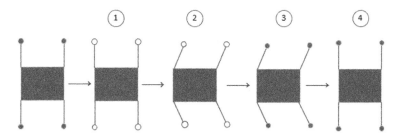

Fig. 10. Gait cycle of the turtle gait

the probability of the robot overturning. Therefore, the mammal-like configuration provides the possibility for the robot to move rapidly, while the reptile-like configuration increases the ability of the robot to overcome the uneven terrain.

4   Simulation and Experiments

For the sake of verifying kinematic equations and the performance of our foot trajectory, and getting some important parameters, simulations are made using the mobile robotics simulate software Webots. Figure 11 shows the virtual prototype of robot in Webots. Figure 12 shows the joint torque and angular velocity of robot.

In the simulation, the ability of the robot to walk stably in the trot gait is verified. When a slope is placed in the direction of the robot, the robot can climb up the slope stably and climb down from the other end. When a platform is placed in front of the robot, we can control the robot to turn into a turtle gait, so that the robot can climb over the obstacles. It is verified that the robot can adapt to different environments and choose the right posture and gait to work. The experimental for the slope and platform task is shown in Fig. 13. It is found that the robot can climb a 20° slope, it can also climb a small platform with a

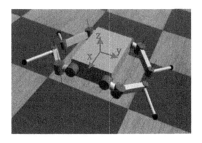

Fig. 11. Match between different gaits and tasks.

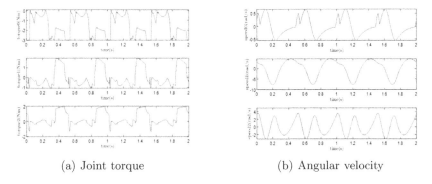

(a) Joint torque   (b) Angular velocity

Fig. 12. Robot simulation experiment data

(a)   (b)   (c)

(d)   (e)   (f)

Fig. 13. Experiment with robot, a ~c: Climbing experiment; d ~f: Obstacle crossing experiment

certain height. Considering the performance of the robot in two configuration, we believe that it has great potential to adapt to different environments.

5   Conclusion

This paper introduces the design and control of a quadruped robot with changeable configuration, the kinematics and gait planning of the robot. The robot adopts a composite foot trajectory composed of cubic curve and straight line while moving forward. By designing different gait and two configuration of the robot, the robot can move stably in reptile-like configuration, which also has stronger load-bearing ability. When the speed needs to be increased, the reptile-like configuration can be switched to the mammal-like configuration. Through the switching of gait and configuration, the robot can adapt to different ground environment.

In the future work, we will add more sensors to the robot and test other more kinds of gaits and foot trajectories on it. At the same time, we can test whether the robot can move as fast as skating on the flat ground by adding a sliding wheel to the trunk of the robot, so as to improve the speed of the robot. And add the hook and claw device to the robot, so that the robot can realize the climbing function. There would be more simulations and experiments.

References

1. Rong, X., Li, Y., Ruan, J., et al.: Design and simulation for a hydraulic actuated quadruped robot. J. Mech. Sci. Technol. **26**, 1171–1177 (2012)
2. Hutter, M., et al.: ANYmal - toward legged robots for harsh environments. Adv. Robot. **31**(17) (2017). https://doi.org/10.1080/01691864.2017.1378591
3. Raibert, M., Blankespoor, K., Nelson, G., Playter, R.: BigDog, the rough-terrain quadruped robot. In: Proceedings of the 17th World Congress, pp. 10823–10825 (2008)
4. Semini, C., Tsagarakis, N.G., Guglielmino, E., Focchi, M., Cannella, F., Caldwell, D.G.: Design of HyQ - a hydraulically and electrically actuated quadruped robot. In: Proceedings of the Institution of Mechanical Engineers, Part I: Journal of Systems and Control Engineering, vol. 225, no. 6, pp. 831–849 (2011)
5. Wang, H., Zheng, Y.F., Jun, Y., Oh, P.: DRC-hubo walking on rough terrains. In: IEEE International Conference on Technologies for Practical Robot Applications (TePRA) (2014)
6. Saranli, U., Buehler, M., Koditschek, D.E.: RHex: a simple and highly mobile hexapod robot. Int. J. Robot. Res. **20**(7), 616–631 (2001)
7. Seok, S., Wang, A., Otten, D., Lang, J., Kim, S.: Design principles for highly efficient quadrupeds and implementation on the MIT Cheetah robot. In: IEEE International Conference on Robotics and Automation (ICRA), pp. 3307–3312 (2013)
8. Hutter, M., Gehring, C., Bloesch, M., Hoepflinger, M.H., Remy, C.D., Siegwart, R.: StarlETH: a compliant quadrupedal robot for fast, efficient, and versatile locomotion. In: International Conference on Climbing and Walking Robots (CLAWAR), pp. 483–490 (2012)

9. Tarokh, M., Lee, M.: Kinematics Modeling of Multi-legged Robots walking on Rough Terrain. In: 2008 Second International Conference on Future Generation Communication and Networking Symposia, Sanya, pp. 12–16 (2008)
10. Kitano, S., Hirose, S., Endo, G., Fukushima, E.F.: Development of lightweight sprawling-type quadruped robot TITAN-XIII and its dynamic walking. In: 2013 IEEE/RSJ International Conference on Intelligent Robots and Systems, Tokyo, pp. 6025–6030 (2013)
11. Sakakibara, Y., Kan, K., Hosoda, Y., Hattori, M., Fujie, M.: Foot trajectory for a quadruped walking machine. In: Proceedings of IEEE International Workshop on Intelligent Robots and Systems, Towards a New Frontier of Applications, IROS 1990, pp. 315–322. IEEE (1990)
12. Rong, X.W., Li, Y.B., Ruan, J.H., Song, H.J.: Kinematics analysis and simulation of a quadruped robot. Appl. Mech. Mater. **26**, 517–522 (2010)
13. Farley, C.T., Taylor, C.R.: A mechanical trigger for the trot-gallop transition in horses. Science **253**(5017), 306–308 (1991)
14. Lu, G., et al.: A novel multi-configuration quadruped robot with redundant DOFs and its application scenario analysis. In: 2021 International Conference on Computer, Control and Robotics (ICCCR) (2021)

Configuration Design and Evaluation of Bionic Grinding Manipulator Based on Human Upper Limb

Jinzhu Zhang[1,2,4]([⊠]), Hanqing Shi[1], Tao Wang[1,4], Xinjun Liu[2], Li Jiang[3], and Qingxue Huang[1,4]

[1] College of Mechanical and Vehicle Engineering, Taiyuan
University of Technology, Taiyuan 030024, China
zhangjinzhu@tyut.edu.cn
[2] Department of Mechanical Engineering, The State Key Laboratory of Tribology &,
Institute of Manufacturing Engineering, Tsinghua University, Beijing 100084, China
[3] State Key Laboratory of Robotics and System, Harbin Institute
of Technology, Harbin 150001, China
[4] Engineering Research Center of Advanced Metal Composites Forming
Technology and Equipment, Ministry of Education, Taiyuan 030024, China

Abstract. Manual grinding is still the most common treatment method for rod surface defects in special steel factory. In order to realize the robot to replace the workers to complete this work, this paper proposes a 5-degree-of-freedom parallel driving grinding manipulator based on the process of manual grinding. At first, the topological structure and degree of freedom configuration of the mechanism composed of human arm are analyzed. The motional characteristics of the grinding manipulator are determined based on the requirements of rod grinding technology. Then, a variety of executive mechanisms are synthesized. Based on a typical configuration of these executive mechanisms, a parallel driving grinding manipulator with multi branches coupling similar to human upper limb structure is designed. Final, the motional performance evaluation index of the manipulator is defined and the local motional performance of the manipulator is evaluated. The research contents of this paper lay a theoretical foundation for its prototype design and development.

Keywords: Bionics · Special steel rod · Parallel driving mechanism · Configuration design · Performance evaluation

1 Introduction

The steel industry is one of the process industries with a high level of automation. In many developed countries, a large number of industrial robots have been used in steel production lines. In recent years, some steel factories in China have begun to apply industrial robots in the key processes of steel making and rolling. Special steel rod finishing operation has the characteristics of high transfer frequency, poor working

© Springer Nature Switzerland AG 2021
X.-J. Liu et al. (Eds.): ICIRA 2021, LNAI 13015, pp. 642–652, 2021.
https://doi.org/10.1007/978-3-030-89134-3_59

environment and high safety risk, so it is urgent to replace workers with robots to promote the safe, high quality and efficient production of special steel factory.

As a key process of special steel rod finishing, grinding can eliminate product defects and improve the added value of products. At present, the manufacturing/processing equipment based on series mechanism is the most widely used in the field of grinding operation [1, 2]. However, when a large amount of cutting is used to grind a hard material such as special steel, the series manipulator needs to provide a large grinding force, which is easy to exceed its maximum load limit.

Compared with the traditional series mechanism, the parallel mechanism has the advantages of compact structure, high stiffness, small inertia and good dynamic response because of its multi-closed-loop structure [3–7]. At the same time, there are many limitations, such as small workspace, limited rotation angle and so on, which limit the application of parallel mechanism in some specific fields. In order to make up for these limitations, many scholars have started to study generalized parallel mechanisms [8]. This mechanism is different from parallel mechanism in structure [9–11], and it is a supplement to the existing parallel mechanism in function. For example, Xie et al. [12] proposed a new type of spatial parallel mechanism, in which two driving branches have a closed-loop structure, which significantly improves the stiffness and bearing capacity of the mechanism. Jin et al. [13–17] proposed the concept of parallel driving mechanism, the composition principle of which is that both the executive mechanism and the driving mechanism are connected to the frame, and they are connected by at least one joint. This kind of mechanism has good dynamic characteristics, large workspace and good bearing capacity. The emergence of these generalized parallel mechanisms not only extends the concept of parallel mechanisms, but also expands the application range of parallel mechanisms. Therefore, the research on generalized parallel mechanism is of great significance.

In this paper, based on the study of the motion mode and structure of two arms in the process of manual grinding, a parallel driving grinding manipulator with multi branches coupling is designed, which have three-dimensional movement and two-dimensional rotation. The driving mechanism of the parallel driving grinding manipulator is composed of multi branches chains in parallel. The executive mechanism of the parallel driving grinding manipulator has a spatial closed-loop kinematic chain. Firstly, the relationship between upper limb structure and artificial both arms grinding is analyzed, and the topological relationship among upper limb bones, joints and muscle group is studied. Then, the executive mechanism of the parallel driving grinding manipulator is determined according to the manual grinding process and technology requirements, and the driving mechanism of the parallel driving grinding manipulator is determined by the principle of bionics. Finally, the local motional performance of the parallel driving grinding manipulator is evaluated, which provides a theoretical basis for the whole machine design of the parallel driving grinding manipulator.

2   Structure of Manual Grinding with Both Arms

The hardness of special steel rod is high (HV $\leq$ 260), and the grinding force is large. During manual grinding on site, workers usually maintain the posture shown in Fig. 1(a) in order to increase the stiffness of the arm and maintain the stability of the angle grinder. In this posture, the bones and joints of the human arms work together to form a polygonal closed-loop structure. The arms take the torso as the base, which are driven to complete the movements of flexion, extension, abduction and adduction under the joint action of different muscle groups. Muscle groups play the role of position limit and configuration protection in this process so as to cooperate with the arms to complete different movements. As shown in Fig. 1(b), in the human upper limb, the clavicle, scapula, humerus, radial bone and ulna bone are connected in series through the shoulder joint, elbow joint and wrist joint to form a single open chain unit. As shown in Table 1, each joint can be equivalent to the revolute joint, the hook hinge and the spherical joint respectively according to the motion form of each joint.

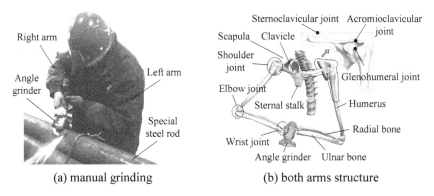

(a) manual grinding   (b) both arms structure

Fig. 1. Schematic diagram of artificial both arms grinding and upper limb structure

Table 1. Equivalent kinematic joint of human joints

Human joint	Equivalent kinematic joint
Sternoclavicular joint	Hook hinge
Acromioclavicular joint	Revolute joint
Glenohumeral joint	Spherical joint
Elbow joint	Hook hinge
Wrist joint	Spherical joint

Muscle groups provide driving forces in each movement of the upper limb, as shown in Fig. 2. Muscle groups are distributed in parallel, connecting each bone and joint. This parallel driving structure ensures that the upper limb has large stiffness and strong pose adjustment ability.

Figure 3 is a schematic diagram of the composition of the bionic grinding mechanism. The bones and joints of the both arms are equivalent to passive executive mechanism, which do not contain driving joints. The muscle groups are equivalent to a driving

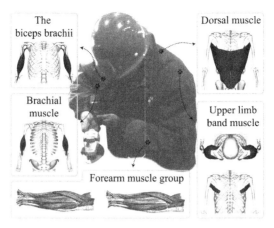

Fig. 2. Schematic diagram of muscle groups of upper limb

mechanism composed of multi branched chains in parallel, which is directly connected to the body (frame). Motional characteristics provided by driving mechanism are input to executive mechanism through connecting joints.

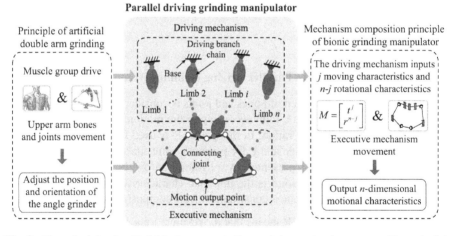

Fig. 3. The principle of artificial both arms grinding and the mechanism composition principle of bionic grinding manipulator

3 Design of Parallel Driving Grinding Manipulator

3.1 Motional Characteristics Configuration of Grinding Manipulator

From the point of view of on-site manual grinding, the general distribution of defect on the surface of rod is shown in Fig. 4. It can be seen from the figure that the defect parameters have components in the direction of the three axes, and the both arms of the human body need to provide three moving characteristics during the grinding operation. In addition, based on the rod grinding technology (the smooth transition between the grinding area and the surface of the rod after grinding without the appearance of table angle, end face and other characteristics), the both arms need to provide three rotational characteristics. Due to the rotational characteristics of the grinding wheel, the rotation of the grinding wheel has the same effect as the rotation of the both arms around the grinding wheel axis, so the position and orientation set dimension of the both arms are 5, that is, three-dimensional movement and two-dimensional rotation. The three moving characteristics are along the x-axis, y-axis and z-axis direction respectively, and the two rotational characteristics are parallel to the x-axis and y-axis direction respectively, which can be expressed as $G_F^I(T_x, T_y, T_z, T_\alpha, T_\beta, 0)$.

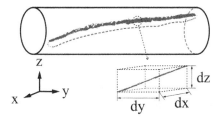

Fig. 4. Schematic diagram of defect distribution of rod

3.2   Configuration Design of Parallel Driving Grinding Manipulator

The closed-loop chain composed of bones and joints is considered separately, and each joint is equivalent to a kinematic joint according to the motional characteristics of the upper limb in the grinding operation. In this paper, R is used for revolute joint, S for spherical joint, U for hook hinge and P for prismatic joint. In order to express clearly, when the kinematic joint is represented by a symbol, an overline is marked above it to indicate that the kinematic joint is the motional characteristic input point, and the corresponding input characteristic is consistent with the composition characteristic of the kinematic joint. For example, $^x \overline{R}$ means that the revolute joint needs to input rotational characteristic parallel to the x-axis, $^{xy} \overline{S}$ means that the spherical joint needs to input rotational characteristics parallel to the x-axis and y-axis, and $\overline{P}$ means that the prismatic joint needs to input moving characteristic.

Because the position and orientation characteristic set of R joint motional member includes a rotational characteristic and an accompanying moving characteristic, the position and orientation characteristic set of U motional member includes two rotational characteristics and two accompanying moving characteristics, the position and orientation characteristic set of S motional member includes three rotational characteristics and two accompanying moving characteristics, and the position and orientation characteristic set of P motional member contains only one moving characteristic. The equivalent kinematic joints of each joint are configured, and the configuration of the manipulator executive mechanism that meets the requirements of the rod grinding technology is shown in Fig. 5 (a) ~ (f), and the scheme of (a) ~ (f) is analyzed, one can see that:

- In terms of the complexity of the mechanism topology, (a) and (e) require the most joints (the number is 9), (b) and (c) take second place (the number is 7), and (d) and (f) require the least (the number is 5).
- In terms of the sum of the number of motional characteristics need to input, the scheme (a) needs to input the largest number of motional characteristics (the number is 9), (b) ~ (f) schemes require the least (the number is 7).
- In addition, the scheme (d) has a semi-stable topological structure and is sensitive to a variety of errors. In the scheme (e), the moving characteristic $\overline{P}$ needs more than one revolute joint to provide accompanying moving characteristics, which requires higher requirements for the manufacturing of the driving branch chain. The end of the scheme (e) is composed of revolute joint, and the rotational characteristic parallel to the y-axis is coupled with the moving characteristic parallel to the x-axis, which is not conducive to the position and orientation adjustment of the angle grinder. On the other hand, the scheme (f) has the characteristic of partial decoupling, which can provide a larger working space for the angle grinder. Therefore, scheme (f) is the preferred scheme for the executive mechanism configuration of the grinding manipulator.

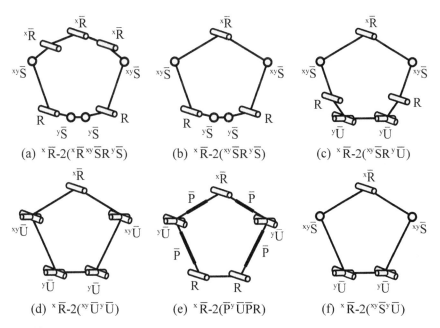

Fig. 5. Configuration synthesis of executive mechanism of grinding manipulator

The muscle groups (driving mechanism) provide the driving force for the movement of both arms (executive mechanism). In the myofibril of muscle, thick myofilament and fine myofilament combine in a certain way, and the fine myofilament can slide between thick filament through the allosteric action of protein which can produce muscle contraction activity. It is consistent with the function of prismatic joint in the mechanism. In addition, in the process of manual grinding, the muscle group near the sternoclavicular joint drives the clavicle movement through in situ contraction, which is consistent with the function of the revolute joint in the mechanism. Therefore, on the basis of the topological structure of the scheme (f) in Fig. 5, the rotational input characteristics of the upper ($^x\bar{R}$-$2^x\bar{S}$) parallel to the x-axis can be combined, and the corresponding motional input point is equivalent to the revolute joint. As shown in Fig. 6, the configuration of the first driving branch can be determined:

1. Configuration: RR-2RPR
2. Basic scale constraints: $R_1\|R_2\|R_6$, $R_2\|R_3$, $R_3\|R_4\|R_5$, $R_2\perp P_2$, $R_6\perp P_4$

Among them, "∥" means that the axis of the kinematic joint is parallel, and "⊥" means that the axis of the kinematic joint is vertical.

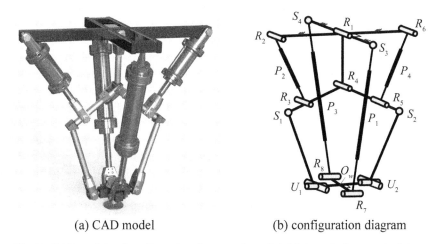

(a) CAD model   (b) configuration diagram

Fig. 6. CAD model and configuration diagram of parallel driving grinding manipulator

On the basis of receiving the upper motional characteristics ($G_{F1}(0, T_y, T_z, T\alpha, 0, 0)$), the lower ($2^y\bar{S}$ $^y\bar{U}$) of the executive mechanism inputs the rotational characteristic parallel to the y-axis, so that the executive mechanism can have independent moving characteristic along the x-axis and rotational characteristic parallel to the y-axis. Therefore, the lower motional input point of the executive mechanism is equivalent to the revolute joint, as shown in Fig. 6. The SPR branch chain which is consistent with the motional characteristics of the end of the executive mechanism is selected based on the principle of simple manufacturing process, and the configuration of the second driving branch can be determined:

1. Configuration: 2SPR
2. Basic scale constraints: $R_7 \| R_8$, $R_3 \perp R_7$, $R_7 \perp P_1$, $R_8 \perp P_3$, $S_3 S_4 \perp R_2 R_6$

   The first and second driving branches are crossed, and the scale constraint is $\diamond S_3 R_7 R_8 S_4 \perp \diamond R_2 R_3 R_5 R_6$. The axes and central points of R_1, R_2, R_6, S_3 and S_4 was fixed to form a static platform. The end of the executive mechanism crosses with the end of the second driving branch to form a moving platform. R_3, R_4, R_5, R_7 and R_8 are selected as the motional input points of the executive mechanism, so the terminal O_w of the executive mechanism can complete three-dimensional moving output and two-dimensional rotational output.

4 Evaluation of Local Motion Performance of Parallel Driving Grinding Manipulator

The main geometric parameters of the parallel driving grinding manipulator are: $R_1 R_4 = l_1$, $R_3 R_4 = R_4 R_5 = l_2$, $R_5 S_2 = R_3 S_1 = l_3$, $S_1 U_1 = S_2 U_2 = l_4$, $U_1 U_2 = 2b_1$, $R_7 R_8 = 2b_2$, $R_1 R_2 = R_1 R_6 = a_1$, $R_1 S_3 = R_1 S_4 = a_2$. The establishment of the coordinate system is shown in Fig. 7. The fixed coordinate system $\{J\}$: $O_0 \text{-} x_0 y_0 z_0$ is established with the midpoint of $R_2 R_6$ as the origin. The reference coordinate system $\{C\}$: $O_c \text{-} x_c y_c z_c$ and the moving reference coordinate system $\{DC\}$: $O_{dc} \text{-} x_{dc} y_{dc} z_{dc}$ are established with the midpoint of $S_1 S_2$ as the origin. The tool coordinate system $\{W\}$: $O_w \text{-} x_w y_w z_w$ is established with the midpoint of $R_9 R_{10}$ as the origin. Among them, $x_0 \| R_2 R_6$, $y_0 \| S_3 S_4$, $x_c \| S_1 S_2$, $z_c \perp S_1 S_2$, $x_{dc} \| S_1 S_2$, $z_{dc} \| O_c O_w$, $x_w \| R_9 R_{10}$, $y_w \| R_7 R_8$, z_0, y_c, y_{dc} and z_w are identified by right hand screw rule. θ_1 is the angle between $S_1 R_4$ and x_0 negative direction, θ_2 is an angle between $S_2 R_4$ and x_0 positive direction, θ_3 and θ_4 are the angle between $R_7 S_3$ and $R_8 S_4$ and $S_3 S_4$ respectively, θ_5 and θ_6 are the angle between $R_3 R_2$ and $R_5 R_6$ and $R_2 R_6$ respectively, θ_7 is the angle between $S_1 S_2$ and $S_1 R_9$, θ_8 is an angle of rotation of $\{DC\}$ in x_c, β_1 is an angle of rotation of $R_1 R_4$ in y_0. It is also stipulated that the counterclockwise needle rotates to a positive value and clockwise to a negative value.

The velocity of the parallel driving grinding manipulator is analyzed by using the position and orientation transformation relationship of O_w in $\{J\}$, $\{C\}$, $\{DC\}$ and $\{W\}$, and the relationship between the velocity vector $\dot{\chi}$ of the moving platform and the change rate of each driver ($\dot{q} = (\dot{\beta}_1 \, \dot{P}_2 \, \dot{P}_4 \, \dot{P}_1 \, \dot{P}_3)^\mathrm{T}$) can be obtained.

$$\dot{q} = J \dot{\chi} \tag{1}$$

In the formula, J represents the Jacobian matrix represented by $l_1, l_2, l_3, l_4, a_1, a_2, b_1, b_2, \beta, \theta_1, \theta_2, \theta_3, \theta_4, \theta_5, \theta_6, \theta_7$ and θ_8. Because of the three-dimensional movement and two-dimensional rotation at the end of the manipulator, the dimensionally consistent Jacobian matrix J_{norm} can be expressed as

$$J_{norm} = J \cdot \mathrm{diag}[1, \ 1, \ 1, \ 1/b, \ 1/b] \tag{2}$$

In the formula, diag represents the diagonal matrix and b represents the radius of the moving platform.

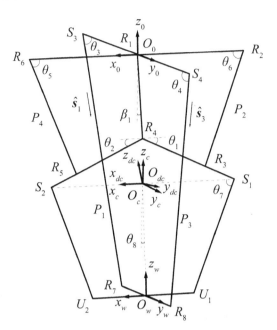

Fig. 7. Geometric structure of parallel driving grinding manipulator

In this section, the local motional performance of the parallel driving grinding manipulator is measured by using the reciprocal of the condition number of J_{norm}, and its expression is

$$\frac{1}{\kappa} = \frac{\sigma_{\min}}{\sigma_{\max}} \tag{3}$$

In the formula, $\sigma_{\max}$ and $\sigma_{\min}$ denote the maximum singular value and the minimum singular value of J_{norm} respectively.

The main geometric parameters of the parallel driving grinding manipulator are set up (unit: mm): $a_1 = 645$, $a_2 = 455$, $b_1 = 165$, $b_2 = 85$, $l_1 = 370$, $l_2 = 300$, $l_3 = 110$, $l_4 = 525$. Figure 8 show the distribution of $1/\kappa$ under different z values in the working space.

The distribution diagram of the local motion performance of the parallel driving grinding manipulator is shown in Fig. 8(a) ~ (c), which shows that the local motional performance is related to the configuration of the mechanism. On the whole, the peak value of the local motional performance increases with the increase of the z value, but the index of the local motional performance is not close to 1, that is, the parallel driving grinding manipulator is not isotropic. The closer the value of the local motional performance is to 1, the better the conversion characteristic of the velocity and force between the joint space and the operation space of the mechanism, on the contrary, the smaller the value of the local motional performance is, the worse the conversion characteristic is. When the z value is -1000 mm, the local motional performance on both sides of the near center position along the y direction is symmetrically distributed, and is proportional to the absolute value of y. When the z value is -1050 mm, the local motional performance distribution is more uniform, and reaches the maximum near the boundary along the y-axis. When the z value is -1100 mm, the motional performance is better near the center.

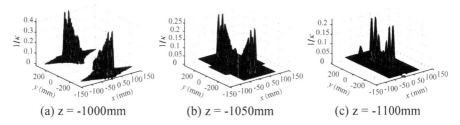

(a) z = -1000mm   (b) z = -1050mm   (c) z = -1100mm

Fig. 8. Distribution atlas of local motional performance in different z value

5 Conclusion

In this paper, a new type of grinding manipulator imitating human upper limb structure is proposed combined with the configuration design problem of surface defects grinding equipment in the process of special steel rod grinding. The conclusions are as follows:

(1) Based on the grinding technology of defects on the surface of special steel rod, the degree of freedom characteristics of the grinding manipulator is determined, that is, three-dimensional movement and two-dimensional rotation.
(2) The parallel driving grinding manipulator is composed by coupling the executive mechanism and multi driving branches, in which the executive mechanism is a R-2SU closed-chain mechanism, and the driving mechanism is composed of two driving branches with configurations of RR-2RPR and 2SPR respectively.
(3) The evaluation index of the local motional performance of the parallel driving grinding manipulator is defined. The evaluation results show that the motional performance of the mechanism in the central area of the workspace is good and can meet the requirements of the grinding operation. The research content of this paper can lay a foundation for the optimal design and dimension synthesis of the grinding manipulator.

Acknowledgment. The authors would like to acknowledge: (1) Project (51905367) supported by The National Nature Science Foundation of China, (2) Project (2018YFB1308702) supported by The National Key Research and Development Program of China, (3) Project (SKLRS-2020-KF-17) supported by The Open Foundation of the State key Laboratory, (4) Project (201901D211011) supported by The Foundation of Applied Basic Research General Youth Program of Shanxi, (5) Project (2019L0176) supported by The Scientific and Technological Innovation Programs of Higher Education Institutions of Shanxi, (6) Project (20181102016, 20181102015) supported by The Major Special Program of Science and Technology of Shanxi, (7) Project (YDZX20191400002149) supported by The Central Government Guides Special Funds for Local Science and Technology Development.

References

1. Feng, F., Yan, S.J., Ding, H.: Design and research of multi-robot collaborative polishing system for large wind turbine blades. Robot. Techn. App. **2018**(5), 16–24 (2018)
2. Xie, F.G., et al.: Novel mode and equipment for machining large complex components. J. Mech. Eng. **56**(19), 70–78 (2020)
3. Xu, Y.D., et al.: Application of 2RPU-UPR parallel mechanism in antenna support. China Mech. Eng. **30**(14), 1748–1755 (2019)
4. Chen, Z.M., et al.: Dynamics analysis of a symmetrical 2R1T 3-UPU parallel mechanism. J. Mech. Eng. **53**(21), 46–53 (2017)
5. Chen, Z.M., et al.: Kinematics analysis of a 3-DOF symmetrical rotational parallel mechanism without intersecting axes. China Mech. Eng. **27**(9), 1215–1222 (2016)
6. Gao, F., Yang, J.L., Ge, Q.D.: GF Set Theory of Parallel Robot Synthesis. Science Press, Beijing (2011)
7. Huang, Z., Zhao, Y.S., Zhao, T.S.: Advanced Spatial Mechanism. Higher Education Press, Beijing (2006)
8. Jin, X.D., et al.: A class of novel 2T2R and 3T2R parallel mechanisms with large decoupled output rotational angles. Mech. Mach. Theory **114**(2017), 156–169 (2017)
9. Zeng, Q., Ehmann, K.F.: Design of parallel hybrid-loop manipulators with kinematotropic property and deployability. Mech. Mach. Theory **71**(2014), 1–26 (2014)
10. Zeng, Q., Fang, Y.F.: Structural synthesis and analysis of serial–parallel hybrid mechanisms with spatial multi-loop kinematic chains. Mech. Mach. Theory **49**(2012), 198–215 (2012)
11. Ding, H.F., et al.: Structural synthesis of two-layer and two-loop spatial mechanisms with coupling chains. Mech. Mach. Theory **92**(2015), 289–313 (2015)
12. Xie, F.G., et al.: Mobility, singularity, and kinematics analyses of a novel spatial parallel mechanism. J. Mech. Robot. **8**(6), 061022 (2016)
13. Jin, Z.L., Zhang, J.Z., Gao, F.: A firefighting six—legged robot and its kinematics analysis of leg mechanisms. China Mech. Eng. **27**(7), 865–871 (2016)
14. Zhang, J., Jin, Z., Zhao, Y.: Dynamics analysis of leg mechanism of six-legged firefighting robot. J. Mech. Sci. Technol. **32**(1), 351–361 (2018). https://doi.org/10.1007/s12206-017-1235-5
15. Zhang, J.Z., Jin, Z.L., Feng, H.B.: Type synthesis of a 3-mixed-DOF protectable leg mechanism of a firefighting multi-legged robot based on GF set theory. Mech. Mach. Theory **130**(2018), 567–584 (2018)
16. Zhang, J.Z., Jin, Z.L., Zhang, T.H.: Kinematic/static performance evaluation and geometric parameter design of parallel-driving leg mechanism. Trans. CSAE **33**(21), 61–69 (2017)
17. Zhang, J.Z., Jin, Z.L., Chen, G.G.: Kinematic analysis of leg mechanism of six-legged walking robot. Trans. CSAE **32**(9), 45–52 (2016)

Workspace Analysis and Stiffness Optimization of Snake-Like Cable-Driven Redundant Robots

Haoxuan Wu[1], Jianqing Peng[1,2(✉)], and Yu Han[1,2]

[1] Sun Yat-Sen University, Shenzhen 518055, China
pengjq7@mail.sysu.edu.cn
[2] Guangdong Provincial Key Laboratory of Fire Science and Technology,
Guangzhou 510006, China

Abstract. Snake-like cable-driven redundant robots (SCDRR) have great application prospects in narrow and complex environments, thus are being widely research in recent years. However, the effect of links length distribution on workspace is rarely studied. Meanwhile, the stiffness optimization of SCDRR is an important issue, due to its relatively poor stiffness performance compared with industrial robots. This paper first analyzes the relationship between workspace area, workspace volume and manipulability to illustrate the effect of links length distribution on workspace. Then stiffness optimization model with and without the variation of the Jacobian matrix can be established by statics and stiffness model. Lastly, simulations show that the optimization result between two models is not much different when cables tension are relatively low, while the simplify one has less computational complexity. The workspace analysis in this paper can provide guidance for SCDRR design. And the comparison of two proposed optimization model can provide a basis for the research of variable stiffness control.

Keywords: Cable-driven · Snake-link Redundant Robots · Workspace Analysis · Stiffness Optimization

1 Introduction

Snake-like cable-driven redundant robots (SCDRR) are being widely researched due to its potential for operating in narrow and complex environments. Owning to the characteristics of the cable driving, SCDRR have the advantages of lightweight and slender body, which enable them to add more movable joints and, thus, have better flexibility, compared to traditional robots [1]. Many researchers and companies have designed and apply them in many different fields. Simaan designed a continuum robot for throat surgery, whose body is only 4 mm in diameter [2, 3]. The Cleveland Medical Center also developed a SCDRR for single-port urologic surgery [4]. OC Robotics developed snake-arm robots mounted on industry robot to conduct aircraft assembly tasks [5]. Peng researched the application of SCDRR in spacecraft repairing [6].

Due to the relatively low stiffness of cable, SCDRR suffer from low stiffness. Many researches are done to solve this problem. One solution is to improve the stiffness of the

© Springer Nature Switzerland AG 2021
X.-J. Liu et al. (Eds.): ICIRA 2021, LNAI 13015, pp. 653–665, 2021.
https://doi.org/10.1007/978-3-030-89134-3_60

mechanical mechanism. Liu designed a cable-driven hyper-redundant manipulator with active and passive joints, which can maintain stiffness of manipulator while increasing flexibility [7]. Another solution is to enhance the cable stiffness. By adopting variable stiffness devices, the stiffness of cable can be improved as cables tension increase, and thus improve the robot's stiffness performance [8, 9]. However, those methods involve complex mechanical designs, which increase system's complexity. Exploiting the redundancy of SCDRR to improving its stiffness performance is a simpler and lower cost solution. Meanwhile the workspace analysis of SCDRR is rather complicate because of its high degree of freedom. Most of researches on SCDRR are done under the assumption that all links have the same length, few studies consider the effect of different link length combinations on workspace. Thus, in this paper, stiffness optimization methods of SCDRR will be studied by considering kinematics redundancy, and the SCDRR's workspace with different links length distribution will also be analyzed.

In this paper, a typical SCDRR model and its kinematics are discussed in Sect. 2, and the workspace with variable links length is analyzed in Sect. 3. The statics and stiffness model are studied in Sect. 4. Optimization methods are proposed in Sect. 5 and simulations are then conducted to verify the effectiveness of those methods.

2   Kinematic Model of SCDRR

2.1   A Typical SCDRR Model

For generality, a typical SCDRR is studied in this paper. The SCDRR can be divided into two parts: 1) the driving box,2) the arm, which is composed of universal joints and rigid links. The adjacent rigid links are connected by one universal joint, and each link is driven by three cables which are arranged at equal angles on the disk. The cables are pulled by the driving box at the bottom of the body. SCDRR with n links have n universal joints and $3n$ driving cables, therefore have $2n$ DOFs and $3n$ actuators.

2.2   Kinematics Modeling

Joint to End Kinematics. A D-H coordinate is established to better describe the SCDRR's joint-to-end kinematic relationship (REF _Ref70406587 \h * MERGEFORMAT Fig. 1). The pose of SCDRR's end-effector with respect to the base frame can be obtained by transformation matrix:

$$^0T_{2n} = \prod_{k=1}^{2n} {}^{k-1}T_k = \prod_{k=1}^{2n} \begin{bmatrix} {}^{k-1}R_k & {}^{k-1}P_k \\ O_{1\times3} & 1 \end{bmatrix} = f_x(q) \tag{1}$$

where ${}^{k-1}T_k$ is the homogeneous transformation matrix between k-1-th and k-th frame and q represents the vector of joints angle, which is a column vector with $2n$ components. Then the joint-to-end differential kinematics can be expressed as:

$$\dot{x}_e = \begin{bmatrix} \dot{p}_e \\ \dot{\varphi}_e \end{bmatrix} = J_x(q)\dot{q} \tag{2}$$

where $\dot{p}_e$ and $\dot{\varphi}_e$ denote the linear and angular velocity of end-effector in cartesian space. $J_x(q)$ is a $6 \times 2n$ joint-to-end Jacobian matrix.

Cable to Joint Kinematics. According to the cable distribution model, the cable-to-joint differential kinematics can also be determined by:

$$\dot{l} = J_l(q)\dot{q} \tag{3}$$

where $\dot{l}$ is a $3n \times 1$ cables velocity vector, and $J_l(q)$ is a $3n \times 2n$ cable-to-joint Jacobian matrix.

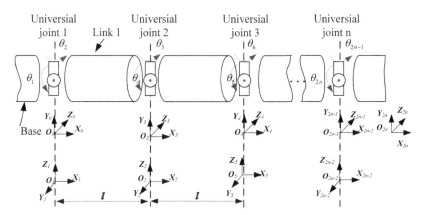

Fig. 1. D-H coordinate of SCDRR

3   Workspace Analysis with Variable Link Length

Since most of existing SCDRR are designed with equal link length, and the effect of link length on manipulator's workspace is lack of research. Thus, the effect of link length on SCDRR's workspace is studied in this chapter.

3.1   Effect of Link Length on Workspace Area

The pose of end-effector can be determined by (1), we have:

$$x_e(q, L) = \begin{bmatrix} p_e \\ \varphi_e \end{bmatrix} = \begin{bmatrix} \sum_{k=1}^{2n} \left(\prod_{j=1}^{k-1} {}^{j-1}R_j \right) {}^{k-1}P_k \\ E_{ZYX} \left(\prod_{k=1}^{2n} {}^{k-1}R_k \right) \end{bmatrix} \tag{4}$$

The workspace area can be defined as the projected area of the workspace on the xy, xz and yz plane, and the value of each area is, respectively.

The workspace of SCDRR is obtained by Monte Carlo Method. By dividing the projection area into a finite number of rectangular areas whose height is the coordinate difference of boundary point and width is δ, then the area of workspace can be expressed as:

$$
\begin{cases}
S_{xy} = \sum_{i=1}^{m} S_m = \delta \cdot \sum_{i=1}^{m} \sum_{k=1}^{a/2} (y_{2k} - y_{2k-1}) \\[2mm]
S_{xz} = \sum_{i=1}^{m} S_m = \delta \cdot \sum_{i=1}^{m} \sum_{k=1}^{a/2} (z_{2k} - z_{2k-1}) \\[2mm]
S_{yz} = \sum_{i=1}^{m} S_m = \delta \cdot \sum_{i=1}^{m} \sum_{k=1}^{a/2} (y_{2k} - y_{2k-1})
\end{cases} \tag{5}
$$

where, m is the number of rectangular areas, x_k, y_k, z_k are the corresponding coordinates of boundary points. S_{xy}, S_{xz}, S_{yz} are the projected area of the workspace on the xy, xz and yz plane, respectively.

A three-link SCDRR is used to demonstrate the problem. Let the sum of links length be a constant, $L1 + L2 + L3 = 270\,\text{mm}$ (Li is the length of i-th link), the length range of each link $10\,\text{mm} \leq L1 \leq 250\,\text{mm}$, $10\,\text{mm} \leq L2 \leq 250\,\text{mm}$ and $q \in [-25°, 25°]$. By iterate through every combination of links length, the contour map of workspace area of each plane can be obtained. And the projected area of the workspace on xy plane with three different link length combinations is shown in Fig. 2.

3.2 Effect of Link Length on Workspace Volume

In the same way, workspace is divided into infinite layers with h in height, through the infinitesimal method, the volume of workspace can be expressed as:

$$
V = h \cdot \sum_{i=1}^{c} S_{yz}(x_i) \tag{6}
$$

where, c is the number of layers. Then the contour map of workspace volume with variable links length can be obtained (Fig. 3(d)).

3.3 Effect of Link Length on Dexterity

Dexterity reflects the overall movement transformation ability of the robotic system, that is, the manipulator's ability to move in any direction. Many methods are used to quantify the dexterity of manipulators, manipulability is one of them. The manipulability of manipulator can be defined as $\omega = \sqrt{\det(JJ^T)}$.

Substituting $J_p = \dot{p}_e/\dot{q}$ and $J_o = \dot{\varphi}_e/\dot{q}$ into the equation, we have the manipulability in position and orientation, which are ω_p, ω_o, respectively. The manipulability parameters of manipulator with three different configurations are shown in Table 1.

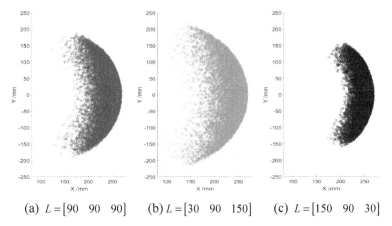

(a) $L = \begin{bmatrix} 90 & 90 & 90 \end{bmatrix}$ (b) $L = \begin{bmatrix} 30 & 90 & 150 \end{bmatrix}$ (c) $L = \begin{bmatrix} 150 & 90 & 30 \end{bmatrix}$

Fig. 2. The projected area of the workspace on xy plane with three different link length combinations

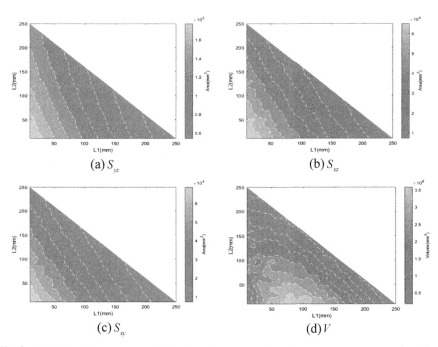

(a) S_{yz} (b) S_{xz}

(c) S_{xy} (d) V

Fig. 3. (a), (b) and (c) are respectively the contour map of workspace area on yz, xz and xy plane and (d) is the contour map of workspace volume

Table 1. The manipulability parameters of three different links configurations

Links length (mm)	Average ω_p(mm/°)	Max ω_p(mm/°)	Average ω_o	Max ω_o
$L = \begin{bmatrix} 30 & 90 & 150 \end{bmatrix}$	2.754×10^6	4.812×10^6	56.021	115.974
$L = \begin{bmatrix} 90 & 90 & 90 \end{bmatrix}$	2.583×10^6	4.652×10^6	95.077	185.670
$L = \begin{bmatrix} 150 & 90 & 30 \end{bmatrix}$	1.800×10^6	3.300×10^6	138.431	268.854

3.4 Workspace Simulation Analysis

From the three simulations that are conducted above, the following analysis conclusions can be drawn:

1. For the workspace projection area on each plane, they have the same trend as links length change. As the sum of $L1$ and $L2$ decreases, projected area in three directions all increase, and close to highest value when both $L1$ and $L2$ are around their lower bound while the lowest level value is obtained when $L1$ is close to its upper bound and $L2$ is close to its lower one.
2. As for the volume of workspace, it has a peak-like contour map. The maximum volume is obtained around $L = \begin{bmatrix} 90 & 10 & 170 \end{bmatrix}$, and gradually decreases outward.
3. The link-length distribution has a significant impact on both position and orientation manipulability. As $L1$ shortens, the both average and max value of position manipulability get larger, however, the orientation manipulability improve significantly, compared to the evenly distributed model. As $L3$ shortens, a contrary conclusion can be drawn.

To sum up, the overall position manipulability of SCDRR improve as the sum of $L1$ and $L2$ decreases, and therefore SCDRR has larger workspace projection, at the same time, orientation manipulability is weakened. By increasing the sum of $L1$ and $L2$, although the translation ability is weakened, orientation manipulability is improved significantly. It can be generalized to SCDRR with more than three links.

4   Statics Model and Stiffness Analysis for SCDRR

In this paper, SCDRR's stiffness is discussed under following assumption:

1. The manipulator is in static equilibrium and totally unloaded.
2. Each driving cable is identical and the stiffness of cable is a constant value.

To derive SCDRR's stiffness model, the statics model of the manipulators has to be studied first. The SCDRR at rest is mainly subject to following forces: 1) gravity, 2) tensions of driving cables, 3) external forces acting on the end-effector,4) fictions between driving cables and disks. It's worth noting that the fictions caused by cable-disk contact can be reduce significantly by properly adopting lubrication and control compensation techniques. Thus, for simplicity, the fiction will not be taken into account in this paper.

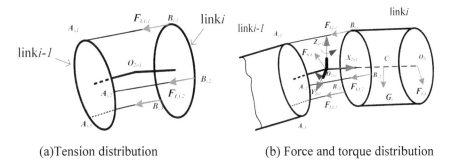

(a)Tension distribution   (b) Force and torque distribution

Fig. 4. Schematic diagram of force of each link

4.1   Cable Tension Analysis

According to Fig. 4(a), the position vector of points $B_{i,k}$ with respect to O_{2i} and points $A_{i,k}$ with respect to O_{2i-1} can be defined as:
When i = odd number,

$$\begin{cases} ^{2(i-1)}A_{i,k} = [-d\ r\cos\beta_{i,k}\ r\sin\beta_{i,k}\ 1]^T \\ ^{2i}B_{i,k} = [d-l\ r\sin\beta_{i,k}\ -r\cos\beta_{i,k}\ 1]^T \end{cases} \quad (7)$$

When i = even number,

$$\begin{cases} ^{2(i-1)}A_{i,k} = [-d\ r\sin\beta_{i,k}\ -r\cos\beta_{i,k}\ 1]^T \\ ^{2i}B_{i,k} = [d-l\ r\cos\beta_{i,k}\ -r\sin\beta_{i,k}\ 1]^T \end{cases} \quad (8)$$

Therefore, cable direction vector with respective to world frame (i.e., $A_{n,k}B_{n,k}$) can be determined as follow:

$$A_{i,k}B_{i,k} = \begin{cases} ^{0}T_{2i}{}^{2i}B_{i,k} - [-d\ r\cos\beta_{1,k}\ r\sin\beta_{1,k}\ 1]^T & i = 1 \\ ^{0}T_{2i}{}^{2i}B_{i,k} - {}^{0}T_{2(i-1)}{}^{2(i-1)}A_{i,k} & i > 1 \end{cases} \quad (9)$$

Then the vector of driving cables tension can be written as:

$$F_{t,i,k} = F_{t,i,k}\frac{A_{i,k}B_{i,k}}{\|A_{i,k}B_{i,k}\|} = F_{t,i,k}e_{t,i,k} \quad (10)$$

where $F_{t,i,k}$ and $e_{t,i,k}$ are, respectively, the tension magnitude and unit direction vector of k-th driving cable of i-th link.

4.2 Statics Equilibrium

As shown in Fig. 4(b), each link is subjected to six forces:1) supporting force from the previous joint,2) reaction force from the supporting force of next joint,3) gravity acting on the center of mass,4) tension from 3 driving cables. For the last link, reaction force is from the external force acting on the end-effector. According to the force balance, for i-th link:

$$\begin{cases} \boldsymbol{F}_{s,i} + \boldsymbol{F}_{r,i} + \boldsymbol{G}_i + \sum_{k=1}^{3} \boldsymbol{F}_{t,i,k} = 0 \\ \boldsymbol{F}_{s,i+1} = -\boldsymbol{F}_{r,i} \end{cases} \tag{11}$$

where $\boldsymbol{F}_{s,i}$, $\boldsymbol{F}_{r,i}$ and $\boldsymbol{G}_i$ represent the supporting force vector, reaction force vector, and gravity vector respectively. Force equilibrium of the whole arm can be derived through inward force iteration from n-th to 1-th link.

Each link of manipulator also has to achieve torque balance to keep still. For i-th link, the sum of the torques about X_{2i-1}, Y_{2i-1} and Z_{2i-1} axis is zero:

$$\sum T^{2i-1} = \sum_{k=1}^{3} O_{2i-1} \boldsymbol{B}_{i,k} \times \boldsymbol{F}_{t,i,k} + O_{2i-1} \boldsymbol{C}_i \times \boldsymbol{G}_i + O_{2i-1} O_{2i} \times \boldsymbol{F}_{r,i} = 0 \tag{12}$$

Since the universal joint rotate around Y_{2i-1} and Z_{2i-1} axis, torque balance about X_{2i-1} axis is achieved by the internal force of joints and links. Therefore, the torque balance equation of i-th link can be described as:

$$\begin{cases} T_y^{2i-1} = [0\ 1\ 0] \cdot {}^{2i-1}R_0 \cdot \sum T^{2i-1} = 0 \\ T_z^{2i-1} = [0\ 0\ 1] \cdot {}^{2i-1}R_0 \cdot \sum T^{2i-1} = 0 \end{cases} \tag{13}$$

where T_y^{2i-1}, T_y^{2i-1} denote total torque about Y_{2i-1} and Z_{2i-1} axis. For every link, equation must be satisfied due to statics equilibrium. Therefore, if external force $\boldsymbol{F}_e$ and gravity $\boldsymbol{G}_i$ are given, supporting force $\boldsymbol{F}_{s,i}$ and cables tension $\boldsymbol{F}_{t,i,k}$ can be solved.

4.3 End-Effector Stiffness Matrix

The stiffness of manipulator's end-effector can be described as small displacement of end-effector due to small changes in external force:

$$K_q = \frac{dF_e}{dx_e} \tag{14}$$

where F_e and x_e is a 6×1 vector, representing external force acting on end-effector and end-effector pose in cartesian space respectively. According to the principle of virtual work, the following equation can be obtained:

$$F_e^T \delta x_e = F_t^T \delta l \tag{15}$$

Specifically, $F_t = [F_{t,1,1}\ F_{t,1,2}\ ...\ F_{t,n,3}]^T$ which contains all cables' tension, δx_e and δl denote the variation of end-effector and cables length. Combine (2) and (3):

$$F_e^T J_x = F_t^T J_l \tag{16}$$

Taking transpose of both side of (16), then differentiating, we can get:

$$J_x^T \cdot \frac{dF_e}{dq} = -\frac{\partial J_x^T}{\partial q} F_e + J_l^T K_C J_l + \frac{\partial J_l^T}{\partial q} F_t \tag{17}$$

where $K_C = diag[k_1 \ldots k_{3i}] = diag[k \ldots k]_{3i \times 3i}$, since all driving cables are assumed to be identical and their stiffness coefficient are k. Meanwhile the manipulator is unloaded, which means $F_e = 0$. Then can also be written as:

$$J_x^T \cdot \frac{dF_e}{dq} = J_l^T K_C J_l + \frac{\partial J_l^T}{\partial q} F_t \tag{18}$$

Substituting $J_x^T \cdot \frac{dF_e}{dq} = J_l^T K_C J_l + \frac{\partial J_l^T}{\partial q} F_t$ (18) into (16), the stiffness matrix can be expressed as:

$$K_q = \frac{\delta F_e}{\delta x_e} = (J_x K_J^{-1} J_x^T)^{-1} \tag{19}$$

where $K_J = J_l^T K_C J_l + \frac{\partial J_l^T}{\partial \theta} F_t$.

5 Stiffness Optimization

The SCDRR is kinematics redundant, that is to say fixed end-effector pose can have many different solutions of joint configurations. Moreover, it also has redundancy in actuation, which means there are infinite combinations of cables tension for a given joint torque. The redundancy can be exploited to enhance its stiffness performance.

5.1 Optimization Through Joints Configuration and Cables Tension

From (19) we can see the stiffness of end-effector could be optimized by adjusting joints configuration and cables tension. Many methods were employed to evaluate robots' stiffness performance. The trace of stiffness matrix is used as a matric of manipulator's stiffness performance, the following optimization model can be obtained:

$$(q^*, F_t^*) = arg \max_{q, F_t} trace \, K_q(q, F_t)$$

$$s.t. \begin{cases} \sum T^{2i-1} = 0 \\ F_{t\min} \le F_t \le F_{t\max} \\ q_{\min} \le q \le q_{\max} \\ \left\| {}^0 p_{2n} - p_{desird} \right\| \le \delta \end{cases} \tag{20}$$

where $\sum T^{2i-1} = 0$ represent the torque balance equation of i-th joint ($i = 1,2\ldots n$), $q_{\min}$ and $q_{\max}$ are the upper and lower bound of joints angle, respectively. δ is the pose error threshold of end-effector, ensuring the end-effector pose is within allowable error range. $F_{t\max}$ and $F_{t\min}$ is the minimum and maximum value of F_t.

5.2 Optimization Through Joints Configuration

A simplified stiffness model can be used to calculate the stiffness matrix to reduce computational complexity, which neglecting the variation of the Jacobian matrices. And it has been verified that the simplified model used to calculating the stiffness matrix of cable-driven serial robot only causes less 1% relative difference compared to the proposed one, when the cables tension is relatively small [15]. Therefore, we can neglect the variation of the Jacobian matrices in (20). The simplified optimization model which only considering joints configuration can be formulated:

$$q^* = arg \max_{q} \; trace \, K_q(q)$$

$$s.t. \begin{cases} q_{min} \leq q \leq q_{max} \\ \left\| {}^0p_{2n} - p_{desird} \right\| \leq \delta \end{cases} \tag{21}$$

From the perspective of energy saving and protecting actuators, a minimum-tension scheme can be employed to deal with the actuation redundancy:

$$F_t^* = arg \max_{F_t} \sum_{i=1}^{9} \sum_{k=1}^{3} F_{t,i,k}$$

$$s.t. \begin{cases} \sum T^{2i-1} = 0 \\ F_{t\,min} \leq F_t \leq F_{t\,max} \end{cases} \tag{22}$$

6 Simulation for Stiffness Optimization

CASE 1. The parameter of the SCDRR for this simulation is given in Table 2. The initial joints angle are the minimum norm solution calculated by inverse kinematics, and the corresponding cable tension are the minimum tension solution. By solving (20), the optimized stiffness matrix of end-effector in cartesian space can be obtained:

$$K_p = \begin{bmatrix} 533.189 & 111.590 & 4.230 \\ 111.590 & 23.993 & 1.147 \\ 4.230 & 1.147 & 0.839 \end{bmatrix}$$

The comparison of parameters before and after optimization is shown in Table 3.

CASE 2. The initial state is same as last case. By applying different model and objective function (21) (22), following result is obtained (Table 4). It can be observed that in both cases the trace of K_q increases significantly compared to the initial state, and the end-effector stay around the target position. The results of are not much different, which only have 0.5% relative difference. However, the cables tension drops dramatically in the second case compared to the first one.

Table 2. The parameter of the SCDRR

Parameter	Value	Parameter	Value
Number of links	3	Stiffness of each cable	100 (N/mm)
Link length	$\begin{bmatrix} 90\ 90\ 90 \end{bmatrix}$ (mm)	Gravity of each link	$\begin{bmatrix} -2\ 0\ 0 \end{bmatrix}$ (N)
Joint angle limit	$q \in [-25, 25](^{\circ})$	Target position	$\begin{bmatrix} 250\ 60\ 0 \end{bmatrix}$ (mm)
Cables tension range	$F_t \in [1, 100](N)$		

Table 3. Joints configuration and cables tension optimization result.

End-effector pose	Joints configuration ($^{\circ}$)	Cables tension (N)	Trace of K_q(N/mm)
Initial state $p_0 =$ [260 50 0]	$q_0 = [-3.930\ 0.000\ 16.751;$ $0.000\ 10.830\ 0.000]$	$F_{t0} =$ [18.934 5.805 1.031; 1.102 2.534 4.617; 1.007 1.332 4.456]	127.468
After optimization $p_{end} =$ [260.8 50.2 0.0]	$q^* =$ [3.248 8.394 15.789; $-19.221\ \ -8.565\ \ 12.734]$	$F_t^* =$ [98.891 1.030 52.209; 1.107 28.286 23.092; 11.826 14.495 16.063]	558.021

Table 4. Joints configuration optimization result.

End-effector pose	Joints configuration ($^{\circ}$)	Cables tension (N)	Trace of K_q(N/mm)
Initial state $p_0 =$ [260 50 0]	$q_0 =$ [-3.930 0.000 16.751; 0.000 10.830 0.000]	$F_{t0} =$ [18.934 5.805 1.031; 1.102 2.534 4.617; 1.007 1.332 4.456]	127.468
After optimization $p_{end} =$s [260.6 50.1 0.0]	$q^* =$ [3.140 8.651 15.820; − 19.420 −8.340 12.308]	$F_t^* =$ [30.481 1.050 17.540; 1.004 10.406 12.378; 1.132 1.260 ss 2.894]	551.579

7 Conclusion

In this paper the different links length effect on SCDRR's workspace area, workspace volume and manipulability are studied and draw the conclusion that when the sum of decreases, the position manipulability increases and so does workspace area. And for orientation manipulability, there is the opposite trend. Meanwhile two stiffness optimization model is proposed. Simulation shows that the optimization result of two models has not much difference, and a much smaller tension solution can be obtained through the model neglecting the variation of the Jacobian matrix. It shows that the simplified model is more suitable for practical engineering applications.

References

1. Thuruthel, T.G., Ansari, Y., Falotico, E., Laschi, C.: Control strategies for soft robotic manipulators: a survey. Soft Rob. **5**(2), 149–163 (2018). https://doi.org/10.1089/soro.2017.0007
2. Simaan, N.: Snake-like units using flexible backbones and actuation redundancy for enhanced miniaturization. In: Proceedings of the 2005 IEEE International Conference on Robotics and Automation, pp. 3012–3017. IEEE (2005)
3. Kai, X., Simaan, N.: An investigation of the intrinsic force sensing capabilities of continuum robots. IEEE Trans. Rob. **24**(3), 576–587 (2008). https://doi.org/10.1109/TRO.2008.924266
4. Kaouk, J.H., et al.: A novel robotic system for single-port urologic surgery: first clinical investigation. Eur. Urol. **66**(6), 1033–1043 (2014). https://doi.org/10.1016/j.eururo.2014.06.039
5. Anscombe, R., et al.: Snake-arm robots: a new approach to aircraft assembly. SAE Technical Paper No. 2006-01-3141(2006)
6. Peng, J., Xu, W., Liu, T., Yuan, H., Liang, B.: End-effector pose and arm shape synchronous planning methods of a hyper-redundant manipulator for spacecraft repairing. Mech. Mach. Theory. **155**, 1–25 (2021)
7. Liu, T., Mu, Z., Wang, H., Xu, W., Li, Y.: A cable-driven redundant spatial manipulator with improved stiffness and load capacity. In: 2018 IEEE/RSJ International Conference on Intelligent Robots and Systems (IROS), pp. 6628–6633. IEEE (2018)
8. Wang, Y., Yang, G., Yang, K., Zheng, T.: The kinematic analysis and stiffness optimization for an 8-DOF cable-driven manipulator. In: 2017 IEEE International Conference on Cybernetics and Intelligent Systems (CIS) and IEEE Conference on Robotics, Automation and Mechatronics (RAM), pp. 682–687. IEEE (2017)
9. Yeo, S.H., Yang, G., Lim, W.B.: Design and analysis of cable-driven manipulators with variable stiffness. Mech. Mach. Theory **69**, 230–244 (2013). https://doi.org/10.1016/j.mechmachtheory.2013.06.005
10. Peng, J., Xu, W., Yang, T., Hu, Z., Liang, B.: Dynamic modeling and trajectory tracking control method of segmented linkage cable-driven hyper-redundant robot. Nonlinear Dyn. **101**(1), 233–253 (2020). https://doi.org/10.1007/s11071-020-05764-7
11. Xu, W., Liu, T., Li, Y.: Kinematics, dynamics, and control of a cable-driven hyper-redundant manipulator. IEEE/ASME Trans. Mechatron. **23**(4), 1693–1704 (2018). https://doi.org/10.1109/TMECH.2018.2842141
12. Chen, S.F., Kao, I., Hollerbach, J.H., Koditschek, D.E.: The conservative congruence transformation of stiffness control in robotic grasping and manipulation. In: Proceedings of the 9th International Symposium of Robotics Research, pp. 7–14 (1999)

13. Chen, S.-F., Kao, I.: Conservative congruence transformation for joint and Cartesian stiffness matrices of robotic hands and fingers. Int. J. Rob. Res. **19**(9), 835–847 (2000). https://doi.org/10.1177/02783640022067201
14. Xu, D., Li, E., Liang, Z.: Kinematics and statics analysis of a novel cable-driven snake arm robot. In: 2017 Chinese Automation Congress (CAC), pp. 439–444. IEEE (2017)
15. Yuan, H., Zhang, W., Dai, Y., Xu, W.: Analytical and numerical methods for the stiffness modeling of cable-driven serpentinse manipulators. Mech. Mach. Theor. **156**, 104179 (2021)

Inverse Kinematics of a 7-DOF Spray-Painting Robot with a Telescopic Forearm

Yutian Wang[1,2], Jiahao Qiu[1,2], Jun Wu[2,1(✉)], and Jinsong Wang[1,2]

[1] State Key Laboratory of Tribology and Institute of Manufacturing Engineering,
Department of Mechanical Engineering, Tsinghua University, Beijing 100084, China
[2] Beijing Key Lab of Precision/Ultra-Precision Manufacturing Equipment
and Control, Beijing 100084, China
jhwu@mail.tsinghua.edu.cn

Abstract. Inverse kinematics is an important issue for redundant robot. This paper studies the inverse kinematics of a 7 degree of freedom (7-DOF) spray-painting robot with a telescopic forearm. The mapping relationship between the joint and the end-effector is studied and a method to find the solution of the inverse solution is proposed. The position of the end point of the painting gun are affected by five joints and the position of the two joints from the five joints are taken as independent variables. Except the two joints with their position taken as independent variables, the analytical solutions of other five joints are written as function of the two independent variables. An objective function that considers the joint limit is presented to optimize the two independent variables. The proposed method is compared with the direct Jacobian iteration method.

Keywords: Redundant robot · Inverse kinematics · Analytical solution · Jacobian

1 Introduction

The inverse kinematics of a 7-DOF redundant robots is an important issue in robot field. The inverse kinematics of a robot is to determine the joint parameters based on the kinematic equations and specified position and orientation of the end-effector [1, 2]. For many robots with 6 or less DOFs, the inverse kinematics generally can be analytically solved to obtain the exact solution with low computational cost. For the 7-DOF robot, the inverse kinematic problem has many solutions, and the system of equations is indeterminate. Some researchers concluded that there are no analytical inverse kinematic solution for the 7-DOF robot like the Barrett whole arm manipulator [3]. Berenson et al. [4] reported that no analytical algorithm can be used to find the solution of inverse kinematics for redundant robots such as the 7-DOF whole arm manipulator.

Methods for solve the inverse kinematics of a 7-DOF robot can be approximately divided into two kinds. The first kind is to impose an additional constraint and then the analytical solution is found [5, 6]. Dahm et al. [7] provided a closed-form solution of the inverse kinematics for a 7-DOF robot by taking the successive roll and pitch

© Springer Nature Switzerland AG 2021
X.-J. Liu et al. (Eds.): ICIRA 2021, LNAI 13015, pp. 666–679, 2021.
https://doi.org/10.1007/978-3-030-89134-3_61

joints together as a spherical joint. Based on this solution, Moradi et al. [8] addressed the joint limits for the redundancy angle parameter of a 7-DOF robot. The second kind is the numerical method that generally depend on the iterative optimization to find an approximate solution [9–11]. Zhao et al. [12] reported a synthetic inverse kinematic approach to find the numerical solution of a 7-DOF robot based on a combination of the damped least-squares method and the Newton-Raphson method. Dubery et al. [13] solves the inverse kinematic solution of a 7-DOF robot by using a gradient projection optimization method and it doesnot need to compute the generalized inverse of the Jacobian. However, to the best knowledge of the authors, these works focus on the robot with one redundant DOF and there is less work on the robot with 2 redundant DOFs.

In this paper, the inverse kinematics of a 7-DOF spray-painting robot with a telescopic forearm is investigated. The mapping relationship between the joint and the end-effector is studied and a method to find the solution of the inverse solution is proposed. The position of the end point of the painting gun are affected by five joints and it is assumed that the solution of arbitrary two joints from the five joints are known. The analytical solutions of other five joints are found by writing as the position function of two known joints. Then, the solution of the two joints that their solutions are supposed to be known are optimized by taking the joint limit into account. Based on the optimized results, the solution of other joints is determined. The proposed method is compared with the direct Jacobian iteration method.

2 Structure Description and D-H Parameters

The 3-D model of a 7-DOF spray-painting robot for completing complex painting task is shown Fig. 1. The robot has two translational degrees of freedom (DOF) and five rotational DOFs. In the figure, part 1 is the translational DOF, and the robot can move along a guideway. The other translational motion is realized by a four-side deployable link which consists of many scissor-form structures that can stretch outside and retract back. To realize the rotational DOF in part 4, a parallelogram structure with high rigidity is used.

The coordinate systems are established by the principle of Denavit-Hartenaarg (D-H) convention, as shown in Fig. 2. The coordinate system $O_0-X_0Y_0Z_0$ is the base coordinate system and $O_i-X_iY_iZ_i$ is the coordinate system fixed on the joint. The forward kinematics for the manipulator is easily expressed in the D-H convention, which find the position and orientation of the end-effector with the given seven joint variables $[d_1, \theta_2, \theta_3, \theta_4, \theta_5, d_6, \theta_7]$. Let α_{i-1} be the angle from Z_{i-1} axis to Z_{i-1} axis about X_{i-1} axis, a_{i-1} be the distance from Z_{i-1} axis to Z_i axis along X_{i-1} axis, d_i be the distance from X_{i-1} axis to X_i axis along Z_i axis, and θ_i be the angle from X_{i-1} axis to X_i axis about Z_i axis. The transformation matrix from coordinate system $O_{i-1} - X_{i-1}Y_{i-1}Z_{i-1}$ to $O_i - X_iY_iZ_i$ can be written as

$$
^{i-1}T_i = \begin{bmatrix}
\cos\theta_i & -\sin\theta_i & 0 & a_{i-1} \\
\sin\theta_i\cos\alpha_{i-1} & \cos\theta_i\cos\alpha_{i-1} & -\sin\alpha_{i-1} & -d_i\sin\alpha_{i-1} \\
\sin\theta_i\sin\alpha_{i-1} & \cos\theta_i\sin\alpha_{i-1} & \cos\alpha_{i-1} & d_i\cos\alpha_{i-1} \\
0 & 0 & 0 & 1
\end{bmatrix} \tag{1}
$$

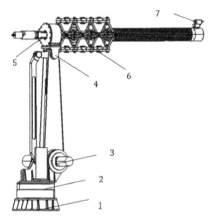

Fig. 1. 3-D model of the spray-painting robot. 1-mobile platform, 2-rotational DOF around the vertical direction, 3-rotational DOF, 4-rotational DOF, 5-rotational DOF around the horizontal axis, 6-translational DOF, 7-rotational DOF

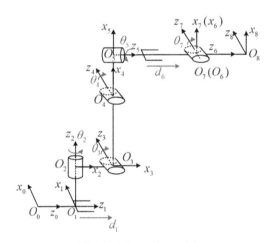

Fig. 2. Kinematic model

where $^{i-1}T_i$ is a 4×4 matrix, with the first 3×3 rotation sub matrix representing the orientation of the coordinate system attached to the link and the three entries in the fourth column of $^{i-1}T_i$ representing the position. The D-H parameters of the robot is given in Table 1. Based on Eq. (1), the transformation matrix between adjacent coordinate system $^0T_1$ $^6T_7$ can be determined. Let $[p_x, p_y, p_z]^T$ and $n = \begin{bmatrix} n_x & n_y & n_z \end{bmatrix}^T$ be the position and orientation of the end-effector. The complete transformation matrix from the base to the end-effector can be written as

$$^0T_7 = {}^0T_1 T_2^2 T_3^3 T_4^4 T_5^5 T_6^6 T_7 = \begin{bmatrix} n_x & o_x & a_x & p_x \\ n_y & o_y & a_y & p_y \\ n_z & o_z & a_z & p_z \\ 0 & 0 & 0 & 1 \end{bmatrix} \tag{2}$$

where

$$\begin{cases} n_x = s_2s_5c_7 - c_2s_{34}s_7 + c_2c_{34}c_5c_7 \\ n_y = -s_{34}c_5c_7 - c_{34}s_7 \\ n_z = c_2s_5c_7 + s_2s_{34}s_7 - s_2c_{34}c_5c_7 \\ o_x = -s_2s_5s_7 - c_2s_{34}c_7 - c_2c_{34}c_5s_7 \\ o_y = s_{34}c_5s_7 - c_{34}c_7 \\ o_z = -c_2s_5s_7 + s_2s_{34}c_7 + s_2c_{34}c_5s_7 \\ a_x = -s_2c_5 + c_2c_{34}s_5 \\ a_y = -s_{34}s_5 \\ a_z = -s_2c_{34}s_5 - c_2c_5 \\ p_x = a_2c_2 + a_3c_2c_3 + a_4c_2c_{34} - d_6c_2s_{34} \\ p_y = d_2 - a_3s_3 - a_4s_{34} - d_6c_{34} \\ p_z = d_1 - a_2s_2 - a_3s_2c_3 - a_4s_2c_{34} + d_6s_2s_{34} \end{cases} \qquad (3)$$

where $s_i = \sin(\theta_i)$, $c_i = \cos(\theta_i)$, $s_{34} = \sin(\theta_3 + \theta_4)$, $c_{34} = \cos(\theta_3 + \theta_4)$, d_1, θ_2, θ_3, θ_4, θ_5, d_6 and θ_7 are seven joint variables.

Table 1. D-H parameters of the 7-DOF robot

Joint	a_{i-1}/mm	α_{i-1}/°	d_i/mm	θ_i/°
1	0	0	d_1	0
2	0	-90	d_2	θ_2
3	a_2	-90	0	θ_3
4	a_3	0	0	θ_4
5	a_4	-90	0	θ_5
6	0	0	d_6	0
7	0	90	0	θ_7

3   Analytical Solution for Joints 2,3,4, 5 and 7

3.1   Kinematic Analysis Method

The spray-paint robot has 7 DOFs in the joint space and 5 DOFs in the task space. Thus, the robot has two redundant DOFs. Based on Fig. 2, it can be concluded that the motion of joints 5 and 7 has the characteristics: 1) the position of the end-effector isnot affected by joints 5 and 7 and is determined by other 5 joints. 2) the orientation of the end-effector can be determined by joints 5 and 7 since the rotational axes of joints 5 and 7 intersect at right angle. Thus, there is a mapping relationship between the position of joints 1,2,3,4 and 6 and the position of the end effector. It is a mapping from 5-dimensional joint space to 3-dimensional task space and the 5-dimensional joint space with joints 1,2,3,4 and 6 has two redundant DOFs.

Therefore, a method to find the solution of the inverse kinematics is proposed: 1) It is assumed that the joint variables of arbitrary two undetermined joints in joints 1,2,3,4 and 6 are known and the analytical solutions of the other 5 joints that are the function of two undetermined joint variables can be determined. 2) The solution of the two undetermined joints are optimized based on numerical method.

3.2 Solution for Joints 2,3,4 5 and 7

For convenience, it is assumed that joint variables d_1 and d_6 for joints 1 and 6 are undetermined variables. This section will find the analytical solution of joints 2,3,4,5 and 7 that are the function of d_1 and d_6. Based on the position of then end point of the painting gun $[p_x, p_y, p_z]^T$, θ_2, θ_3 and θ_4 can be determined and then θ_5 and θ_7 can be found according to the orientation of the painting gun $n = [n_x \, n_y \, n_z]^T$.

Based on $p_x = a_2c_2 + a_3c_2c_3 + a_4c_2c_{34} - d_6c_2s_{34}$ and $p_z = d_1 - a_2s_2 - a_3s_2c_3 - a_4s_2c_{34} + d_6s_2s_{34}$, the following equations can be obtained

$$c_2 = \frac{p_x}{a_2 + a_3c_3 + a_4c_{34} - d_6s_{34}} \tag{4}$$

$$s_2 = \frac{d_1 - p_z}{a_2 + a_3c_3 + a_4c_{34} - d_6s_{34}} \tag{5}$$

Based on Eqs. (3) and (4), θ_2 can be written as

$$\theta_2 = \text{atan2}\left(\frac{d_1 - p_z}{a_2 + a_3c_3 + a_4c_{34} - d_6s_{34}}, \frac{p_x}{a_2 + a_3c_3 + a_4c_{34} - d_6s_{34}}\right)$$
$$= \text{atan2}(d_1 - p_z, p_x) \tag{6}$$

Taking the square sum of Eqs. (3) and (4) leads to

$$\pm\sqrt{p_x^2 + (d_1 - p_z)^2} = a_2 + a_3c_3 + a_4c_{34} - d_6s_{34} \tag{7}$$

For the configuration shown in Fig. 2, the " $\pm$ " in Eq. (6) should be only " $+$ ".

$$a_3c_3 + a_4c_{34} - d_6s_{34} = -a_2 + \sqrt{p_x^2 + (d_1 - p_z)^2} \tag{8}$$

In Eq. (2), $p_y = d_2 - a_3s_3 - a_4s_{34} - d_6c_{34}$ can be rewritten as

$$a_3s_3 + a_4s_{34} + d_6c_{34} = d_2 - p_y \tag{9}$$

According to Eqs. (7) and (8), we can get

$$\left(-a_2 + \sqrt{p_x^2 + (d_1 - p_z)^2} - a_3c_3\right)^2 + (d_2 - p_y - a_3s_3)^2 = a_4^2 + d_6^2 \tag{10}$$

Let $A = -a_2 + \sqrt{p_x^2 + (d_1 - p_z)^2}$ and $B = d_2 - p_y$. Equation (9) can be rewritten as

$$Ac_3 + Bs_3 = \frac{A^2 + B^2 + a_3^2 - a_4^2 - d_6^2}{2a_3} \tag{11}$$

Thus, θ_3 can be determined by

$$\theta_3 = \arccos \frac{A^2 + B^2 + a_3^2 - a_4^2 - d_6^2}{2a_3\sqrt{A^2 + B^2}} + \text{atan2}(B, A) \tag{12}$$

Equations (7) and (8) can be rewritten as

$$\begin{bmatrix} a_4 & -d_6 \\ d_6 & a_4 \end{bmatrix} \begin{bmatrix} c_{34} \\ s_{34} \end{bmatrix} = \begin{bmatrix} A - a_3c_3 \\ B - A_3s_3 \end{bmatrix} \tag{13}$$

Namely

$$\begin{bmatrix} c_{34} \\ s_{34} \end{bmatrix} = \begin{bmatrix} \frac{a_4(A-a_3c_3)+d_6(B-a_3s_3)}{a_4^2+d_6^2} \\ \frac{a_4(B-a_3s_3)-d_6(A-a_3c_3)}{a_4^2+d_6^2} \end{bmatrix} \tag{14}$$

Thus, θ_4 can be determined by

$$\theta_4 = \text{atan2}(s_{34}, c_{34}) - \theta_3 \tag{15}$$

Therefore, θ_2, θ_3 and θ_4 in Eqs. (5), (11) and (14) are determined by taking d_1, d_6 as the undetermined variables. The following is to find the solution of θ_5 and θ_7.

Based on Eq. (2), the following equations can be obtained

$$n_x c_2 = s_2 c_2 s_5 c_7 - c_2^2 s_{34} s_7 + c_2^2 c_{34} c_5 c_7 \tag{16}$$

$$n_z s_2 = s_2 c_2 s_5 c_7 + s_2^2 s_{34} s_7 - s_2^2 c_{34} c_5 c_7 \tag{17}$$

Equation (15) minus Eq. (16) yields

$$n_z s_2 - n_x c_2 = s_{34} s_7 - c_{34} c_5 c_7 \tag{18}$$

Based on $n_y = -s_{34} c_5 c_7 - c_{34} s_7$ and Eq. (17), the following equations can be obtained

$$\begin{bmatrix} s_{34} & -c_{34} \\ c_{34} & s_{34} \end{bmatrix} \begin{bmatrix} s_7 \\ c_5 c_7 \end{bmatrix} = \begin{bmatrix} n_z s_2 - n_x c_2 \\ -n_y \end{bmatrix} \tag{19}$$

s_7 and $c_5 c_7$ can be written as

$$\begin{bmatrix} s_7 \\ c_5 c_7 \end{bmatrix} = \begin{bmatrix} (n_z s_2 - n_x c_2)s_{34} - n_y c_{34} \\ (n_x c_2 - n_z s_2)c_{34} - n_y s_{34} \end{bmatrix} \tag{20}$$

Thus,

$$\theta_7 = \operatorname{asin}\big((n_z s_2 - n_x c_2)s_{34} - n_y c_{34}\big) \tag{21}$$

In Eq. (2), $n_x = s_2 s_5 c_7 - c_2 s_{34} s_7 + c_2 c_{34} c_5 c_7$ and $n_z = c_2 s_5 c_7 + s_2 s_{34} s_7 - s_2 c_{34} c_5 c_7$. The two equations can be rewritten as

$$n_x s_2 = s_2^2 s_5 c_7 - s_2 c_2 s_{34} s_7 + s_2 c_2 c_{34} c_5 c_7 \tag{22}$$

$$n_z c_2 = c_2^2 s_5 c_7 + s_2 c_2 s_{34} s_7 - s_2 c_2 c_{34} c_5 c_7 \tag{23}$$

The sum of Eqs. (21) and (22) can be expressed as

$$n_x s_2 + n_z c_2 = s_5 c_7 \tag{24}$$

In Eq. (2), $n_y = -s_{34} c_5 c_7 - c_{34} s_7$. Thus, c_5 can be expressed as

$$c_5 = \frac{-n_y - c_{34} s_7}{s_{34} c_7} \tag{25}$$

Based on Eqs. (23) and (24), θ_5 can be determined by

$$\theta_5 = \operatorname{atan2}\left(\frac{n_x s_2 + n_z c_2}{c_7}, \frac{-n_y - c_{34} s_7}{s_{34} c_7}\right) \tag{26}$$

Therefore, based on the given position and orientation, θ_2, θ_3 and θ_4, θ_5, θ_7 are determined.

4   Numerical Solution for Joints 1 and 6

4.1   Objective Function

For convenience, q_i is used to represent the joint variable. Namely,

$$q = \begin{bmatrix} q_1 & q_2 & \cdots & q_7 \end{bmatrix}^T = \begin{bmatrix} d_1 & \theta_2 & \theta_3 & \theta_4 & \theta_5 & d_6 & \theta_7 \end{bmatrix}^T \tag{27}$$

When the robot moves in its workspace, each joint is constrained by the joint limit. In order to ensure the smooth and safe movement, each joint should be as far away from its joint limit as possible.

For a given trajectory of the end-effector, the trajectory is discretized into a sequence of end-effector pose with time information by trajectory planning. Let p_i and n_i be the coordinate of discretized trajectory point and the direction of the spray gun at time t_i, respectively. q_j^i represents the joint coordinate of the j-th joint at time t_i.

According to the solution strategy described above, for a given end pose of the end-effector, q_1 and q_6 are properly selected so that all seven joints are as far away from the corresponding joint limits as possible. In fact, when all the joints are far away from their limits, it is not necessary to consider joint limits. When a joint is close to its joint limit, it is necessary to choose appropriate q_1 and q_6 to keep the joint from approaching its limit [14].

Since the joints have different dimensions, each joint value is firstly normalized by considering the relative distance between its current position and its limit position. Namely,

$$x_i = \frac{2}{q_i^u - q_i^l}\left(q_i - \frac{q_i^u + q_i^l}{2}\right) \tag{28}$$

where the superscripts u and l indicate the upper and lower limits of the joint, respectively. It is obvious that $x_i = 1$ and $x_i = -1$ when the joint reaches its upper limit and lower limit, respectively. x_i varies evenly from -1 to 1 as the joint value increases from the lower limit to the upper limit.

In order to make each joint as far away from the joint limit as possible, the objective function is defined as

$$f_1 = \sum_{j=1}^{7} w_j(x_j^i)\left[q_j^{i+1} - q_j^i\right]^2 \tag{29}$$

where $w_j(x_j^i)$ is the weight function of the j th joint. The weight function has the following characteristics:

1) When the joint j is far away from its joint limit, the value of w_j is very small. When the joint j approaches its joint limit and reaches its joint limit, the value of w_j is large and tends to be positive infinity, respectively.
2) When the joint j is far away from its joint limit, w_j increases slowly; when the joint j is close to its joint limit, w_j increases rapidly until it reaches positive infinity.
3) When all joints are far from their limits, the weights of all joints are similar. When one of the joints is close to its joint limit, its weight is far greater than other joints.

Based on the above characteristics, the weight function is defined as

$$w(x) = \begin{cases} \frac{bx}{e^{a(1-x)}-1}, & 0 \le x < 1; \\ \frac{-bx}{e^{a(1+x)}-1}, & -1 < x < 0; \end{cases} \quad a > 0, \ b > 0 \tag{30}$$

4.2 Smoothing Treatment of q_1 and q_6

Since the movement of joints 1and 6 may be not continuous. Thus, the smoothing treatment of q_1 and q_6 is necessary and then the analytical solutions of other joints are determined. In this paper, the moving average filter is used for the smoothing treatment of q_1 and q_6. Let the span for the smoothing treatment of $X = [x_1, x_2, \cdots, x_n]$ be k.

The following equations can be obtained

$$
\begin{cases}
\tilde{x}_1 = x_1 \\
\tilde{x}_2 = (x_1 + x_2 + x_3)/3 \\
\tilde{x}_3 = (x_1 + x_2 + x_3 + x_4 + x_5)/5 \\
\vdots \\
\tilde{x}_i = \frac{1}{k}\left(\sum_{j=i-k/2}^{i+k/2} x_j\right)
\end{cases}
\tag{31}
$$

where $\tilde{X} = \left[\tilde{x}_1, \tilde{x}_2, \cdots, \tilde{x}_n\right]$ are the results after smoothing treatment of $X = [x_1, x_2, \cdots, x_n]$.

From Eqs. (5), (11), (14), (20) and (25), one may see that the motion of joints 2, 3, 4, 5 and 7 will be continuous as long as the motion of joints 1 and 6 are continuous.

5 Numerical Simulation

5.1 Motion Trajectory of the Robot

In order to validate the inverse solution of the kinematics, a complex motion trajectory of the end-effector is designed. A trajectory of the end-effector is given as

$$
\begin{cases}
\tilde{x} = r\sin\left(\frac{\pi}{8}\left(1 + \sin 2\pi\frac{\tilde{z}}{l}\right)\right) \\
\tilde{y} = r\cos\left(\frac{\pi}{8}\left(1 + \sin 2\pi\frac{\tilde{z}}{l}\right)\right)
\end{cases} \quad \text{(m)}
\tag{32}
$$

The trajectory shown in Eq. (31) is not complex. Furthermore, Let the trajectory rotate around the Y_0 axis by $\gamma = 10°$ and then move 2.8 m in the negative direction of the X_0 axis and 1.8 m in the negative direction of the Y_0 axis. The matrix of the above rotational and translational operations can be written as

$$
T_{traj} = \begin{bmatrix}
\cos\gamma & 0 & \sin\gamma & -2.8 \\
0 & 1 & 0 & -1.8 \\
-\sin\gamma & 0 & \cos\gamma & 0 \\
0 & 0 & 0 & 1
\end{bmatrix}
\tag{33}
$$

Let $\left[x, y, z\right]^T$ be the coordinate of end point of the painting gun. The motion trajectory of end point of the painting gun in the simulation can be expressed as

$$
\begin{bmatrix} x \\ y \\ z \\ 1 \end{bmatrix} = T_{traj} \begin{bmatrix} \tilde{x} \\ \tilde{y} \\ \tilde{z} \\ 1 \end{bmatrix}
\tag{34}
$$

Based on Eq. (33), the motion trajectory is shown in Fig. 3. The direction of the painting gun can be written as

$$
n = \frac{1}{r}\begin{bmatrix}
\cos\gamma & 0 & \sin\gamma \\
0 & 1 & 0 \\
-\sin\gamma & 0 & \cos\gamma
\end{bmatrix}\begin{bmatrix} -\tilde{x} \\ -\tilde{y} \\ 0 \end{bmatrix}
\tag{35}
$$

In the simulation, the end point of the painting gun moves along the motion trajectory at a uniform speed $v_0 = 0.04$ m/s. The geometrical parameters are shown in Table 2.

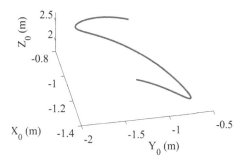

Fig. 3. Motion trajectory

Table 2. Geometrical parameters of the robot

Parameters	d_2	a_2	a_3	a_4
Values/m	0.626	0.250	1.350	0.246

5.2 Simulation Results

When the robot moves along the trajectory shown in Fig. 3, the joint position and velocity are shown in Fig. 4. The normalized value of each joint shown in Eq. (27) and the calculation error of the inverse kinematic solution are also simulated. One may see that the joint velocity changes smoothly except the first joint due to the mechanism. The calculation error is about 1×10^{-15} m and the error is very small.

As a comparison, the direct Jacobian iteration method is also used to find its kinematic inverse solution when the robot moves along the trajectory shown in Fig. 3, and the corresponding results are shown in Fig. 5. From Fig. 4, one may see that all joints keep a safe distance from their limit position when the proposed method in this paper is used to find the solution of the kinematics. The joint displacement shown in Fig. 5 exceeds its limit when the direct Jacobian iteration method is used. The velocity obtained by the proposed method is more smooth than that obtained by the direct Jacobian iteration method. The calculation error of the inverse solution is close to zero. Therefore, the proposed method to find the inverse kinematic solution of the 7-DOF robot is effective.

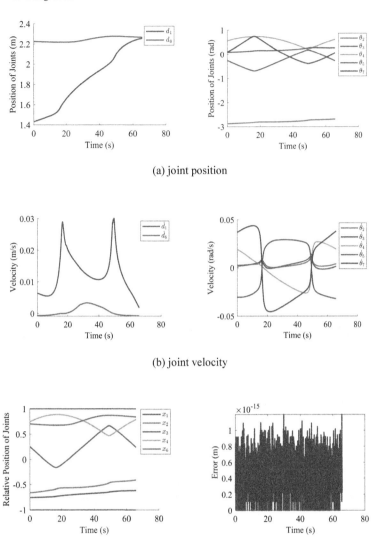

(a) joint position

(b) joint velocity

(c) joint position relative to limit position   (d) calculation error of the inverse kinematic solution

Fig. 4. Joint position and velocity

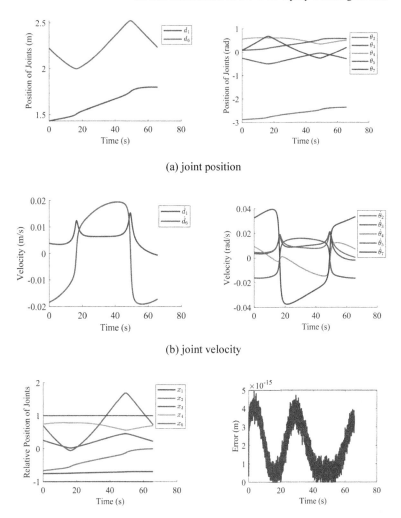

(a) joint position

(b) joint velocity

(c) joint position relative to limit position   (d) calculation error of the inverse kinematic solution

Fig. 5. Joint position and velocity obtained by Jacobian iteration method

6 Conclusions

The inverse kinematics of a 7-DOF spray-painting robot with a telescopic forearm is investigated and a method to find the solution of the inverse solution is proposed. The position of joints 1 and 6 are supposed to be known and the analytical solutions of other joints are found by writing as the position function of joints 1 and 6. Then, the solution of joints 1 and 6 are optimized by taking the joint limit into account. Based on the solution of joints 1 and 6, the solution of other joints is determined. The proposed method is compared with the direct Jacobian iteration method. Based on the proposed method in this paper, all joints donot exceed their limit position and the joint velocity changes smoothly. The calculation error of the inverse kinematic solution is about 1×10^{-15} m. It is very small. When the direct Jacobian iteration method is used, the joint exceeds its limit position. This work is important for the trajectory planning and motion control of redundant robots.

Acknowledgments. This work was supported by the National Natural Science Foundation of China (Grant No. 51975321).

References

1. Wu, J., Gao, Y., Zhang, B., Wang, L.: Workspace and dynamic performance evaluation of the parallel manipulators in a spray-painting equipment. Robot. Comput. Integr. Manuf. **44**, 199–207 (2017)
2. Wu, J., Wang, J., You, Z.: An overview of dynamic parameter identification of robots. Robot. Comput. Integr. Manuf. **26**(5), 414–419 (2010)
3. Singh, G.K., Claassens, J.: An analytical solution for the inverse kinematics of a redundant 7DoF manipulator with link offsets. In: IEEE/RSJ 2010 International Conference on Intelligent Robots and Systems (IROS 2010), pp. 2976–2982 (2010)
4. Berenson, D., Srinivasa, S.S., Ferguson, D., Collet, A., Kuffner, J.J.: Manipulation planning with workspace goal regions. In: ICRA: 2009 IEEE International Conference on Robotics and Automation, pp. 1–7, 1397–1403 (2009)
5. Crenganis, M., Tera, M., Biris, C., Girjob, C.: Dynamic analysis of a 7 DOF robot using fuzzy logic for inverse kinematics problem. In: 7th International Conference on Information Technology and Quantitative Management (ITQM 2019): Information Technology and Quantitative Management Based on Artificial Intelligence, vol. 162, pp. 298–306 (2019)
6. Faria, C., Ferreira, F., Erlhagen, W., Monteiro, S., Bicho, E.: Position-based kinematics for 7-DoF serial manipulators with global configuration control, joint limit and singularity avoidance. Mech. Mach. Theor. **121**, 317–334 (2018). https://doi.org/10.1016/j.mechmachtheory.2017.10.025
7. Dahm, P., Joublin, F.: Closed form solution for the inverse kinematics of a redundant robot arm. Comput. Aided Geom. Des. 163–171 (2016)
8. Moradi, H., Lee, S.: Joint limit analysis and elbow movement minimization for redundant manipulators using closed form method. In: Huang, D.-S., Zhang, X.-P., Huang, G.-B. (eds.) Advances in Intelligent Computing, pp. 423–432. Springer, Berlin, Heidelberg (2005). https://doi.org/10.1007/11538356_44
9. Wang, J., Li, Y., Zhao, X.: Inverse kinematics and control of a 7-DOF redundant manipulator based on the closed-loop algorithm. Int. J. Adv. Rob. Syst. **7**(4), 1–9 (2010)

10. Gan, W.W., Pellegrino, S.: Numerical approach to the kinematic analysis of deployable structures forming a closed loop. Proc. Inst. Mech. Eng. Part C-J. Mech. Eng. Sci. **220**(7), 1045–1056 (2006)
11. Kucuk, S., Bingul, Z.: The inverse kinematics solutions of fundamental robot manipulators with offset wrist. IEEE Int. Conf. Mechatron. (ICM) **2005**, 197–202 (2005)
12. Zhao, J., Xu, T., Fang, Q., Xie, Y., Zhu, Y.: A synthetic inverse kinematic algorithm for 7-DOF redundant manipulator. In: Proceedings of 2018 IEEE International Conference on Real-Time Computing and Robotics (IEEE RCAR), pp. 112–117 (2018)
13. Dubey, R.V., Euler, J.A., Babcock, S.M.: An efficient gradient projection optimization scheme for a seven-degree-of-freedom redundant robot with spherical wrist. In: Proceedings of the 1988 IEEE International Conference on Robotics and Automation (CAT. No.88CH2555–1), pp. 1, 28–36 (1988)
14. Hu, K., Zhang, J., Dong, Y., Wu, D.: Inverse kinematic optimization for 7-DoF serial manipulators with joint limits. J. Tsinghua Univ. (Sci. Technol.) **60**(12), 1007–1015 (2020)

Electric Vehicle Charging Robot Charging Port Identification Method Based on Multi-algorithm Fusion

Jia Zhang[1], Tao Geng[1(✉)], Jun Xu[2], Yang Li[2], and Chen Zhang[3]

[1] Shaanxi Key Laboratory of Intelligent Robots, Xi'an Jiaotong
University, Xi'an, People's Republic of China
ttgeng@xjtu.edu.cn
[2] School of Mechanical Engineering, Xi'an Jiaotong
University, Xi'an, People's Republic of China
[3] Mechanical Engineering, Xi'an Jiaotong University City College, Xi'an 710018,
Shaanxi, People's Republic of China

Abstract. Aiming at the problem of plugging and positioning identification in the process of automatic charging of electric vehicles, especially the difficult problem of low efficiency and accuracy of identification in complex operation environment, this article proposes a multi-algorithm fusion of electric vehicle charging port identification method, which can effectively obtain the characteristic information of the round hole of charging port and realize the purpose of automatic identification of charging port by robot. Firstly, an electric vehicle charging port in a complex environment is analyzed and simulated, and camera selection and calibration are explained; on this basis, algorithms based on image smoothing filtering, feature detection segmentation of ROI region, improved Canny edge detection and combined mathematical morphology are proposed to correlate the charging port image respectively, and the features of the target charging port jack are extracted. Finally, the experimental verification of the charging port identification method was conducted for different illumination intensities and different shooting distances. The experimental results show that the identification success rate is 93.3% under the weak illumination and 97.8% under the normal illumination intensity of 4000lx. This shows that the method can effectively improve the robustness and accuracy of the charging port identification.

Keywords: Charging port · Identification algorithm · Charging robot

1 Introduction

The emergence of electric vehicles has led to more diversified transportation choices. As the increasing popularity of electric vehicles, the problems of frequent charging and difficulty in plugging and unplugging guns of electric vehicles need to be solved urgently. Since machine vision has the advantages of higher fault tolerance and safety, stronger real-time, high accuracy and high speed, locating the charging port of electric vehicles

© Springer Nature Switzerland AG 2021
X.-J. Liu et al. (Eds.): ICIRA 2021, LNAI 13015, pp. 680–693, 2021.
https://doi.org/10.1007/978-3-030-89134-3_62

based on visual identification is one of the important research methods to solve this problem at present.

In recent years, scholars from various countries have also conducted relevant studies on this subject. In 2018, Austrian scholars developed a robot-controlled fast-charging system for electric vehicles [1], where the vehicle enters the area to be charged, the charging station is stationary, the vehicle's charging socket is identified by a camera mounted above the robot, and a charging gun is installed below the robot to charge the vehicle directly. The Volkswagen Group and KUKA have jointly developed a charging robot for future vehicles [2], which can move autonomously after parking an electric vehicle in a designated parking space. The camera on the robot scans the area near the vehicle's charging socket and then charges the vehicle via a KUKA robot manipulator. Wang [3] used a laser ranging method to scan the electric vehicle charging port, fixing the camera and laser on the robot end-effector, and completing the identification of the charging port by two steps of coarse positioning and fine positioning.

To effectively identify the charging port in a complex environment, it is necessary to obtain an image of target using a camera. During the image acquisition process, the environment of the target is difficult to predict and may show scattered distribution, unclear texture, uneven lighting, and occlusion. Meanwhile, it is difficult to avoid the interference of factors such as noise. Therefore, effective noise suppression, noise removal and provision of the light source, to preserve the original fine structure of the image, plays a critical role in identifying the charging port. Yu et al. [4] used an RGB-D depth camera for identification of litchi fruits and proposed a method based on multiscale detection and non-maximum suppression, and the experimental results showed that the identification rate of red litchi and green litchi was 89.92% and 94.50%, respectively, which has implications for the identification of charging ports in similar environments of type. Yin [5] proposed a combined high and low exposure identification method based on texture features to achieve the identification of charging ports by using a monocular camera. Miseikis et al. [6] proposed a shape matching method based on binocular stereo vision to identify the charging port, and by comparing the difference of displacement and deformation between the original image and the template image, the bit pose of the charging port can be better obtained.

In this article, we propose a multi-algorithm fusion method to identify the charging port image, and simulate the effect of different illumination intensities (i.e., day and night) and different distances on the identification of electric vehicle charging ports, and obtain the identification success rate under different circumstances, to verify the accuracy and feasibility of the method.

2 Prototype Description

2.1 Charging Port Structure and Environmental Analysis

At present, the charging operation of electric vehicle charging port is mainly completed by manual. The DC charging port of electric vehicle is shown in Fig. 1, and the automatic charging transformation of charging station is realized without drastically changing the existing charging station environment facilities, also there are strong light changes and complex strong electromagnetic interference in the field environment, which will bring noise pollution to the image acquisition data in the automatic charging process. The success of automatic identification of charging port mainly depends on the following three points:

- Affected by the complex background structure of the charging port and the uneven illumination of the site environment, reflective metal screws, protruding printed letters, shading of the charging port cover, etc. (see Fig. 1c).
- Affected by the noise introduced by electromagnetic interference in the charging station area, it adds additional difficulty to the charging port image identification.
- Affected by the lack of charging port feature information, the charging port can only be identified by grayscale, and the feature extraction algorithm based on texture features will fail.

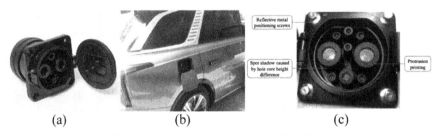

(a)   (b)   (c)

Fig. 1. DC charging port for electric vehicles, **a** Standard DC charging port appearance structure; **b** Hong Qi EHS9 DC charging port; **c** Charging port internal structure interference items

In summary, the charging port can be divided into interference area and to be identified area, interference area contains 4 metal screws, to be identified area contains significant characteristics of 9 round holes, these 9 round holes have protruding printed letters on the surface, easy to cause unavoidable visual identification error. In addition, if the ambient light is dark, it is difficult to accurately and effectively identify the edge, the middle diameter of the two largest holes has better recognition information.

2.2 Charging Port Identification System Construction

In the vision-based electric vehicle charging port identification method, the selection of vision sensors must adapt to both normal natural light during the day and weak natural light at night.

According to the uncertainty and complexity of realistic light intensity, the RGB-D depth camera Framos D435 with active stereo vision technology is selected in this paper. Through the depth image acquisition and processing of this camera, the approximate location information of the charging port outline located in the vehicle body can be obtained to realize the rough positioning function of the charging port, and then through the monocular image acquisition and processing of this camera, the charging port can be precise positioning.

In this article, the fine positioning method of electric vehicle charging port based on stereo vision coarse positioning is investigated. Taking the electric SUV vehicle Hong Qi E-HS9 as an example, the DC charging port of this model is simulated, and the identification process of charging port is realized by the robot (see Fig. 2). In this study, a 6-axis collaborative robot was used, which has a repeatable positioning accuracy of ± 0.03 mm.

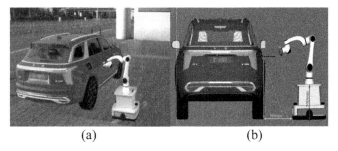

(a)   (b)

Fig. 2. Robot identification of electric vehicle charging port process, **a** Visualization model for robot identification of charging port; **b** Robot identification of charging port range

The electric vehicle charging port identification system (see Fig. 3a), the robot is controlled by the host computer to move to a suitable position near the charging port area for identification, and the position can collect clear charging port images from the host computer. The Ubuntu system is installed on the host computer, and the charging port image processing and identification algorithms are run on this host computer. The illuminance meter detects the change of illumination intensity in real-time, and the environment simulation light simulates the illumination intensity of the environment for the charging port. The framework of the electric vehicle charging port identification system (see Fig. 3b), which is divided into hardware layer, software layer, and application layer.

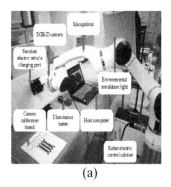
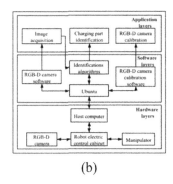

(a)   (b)

Fig. 3. Built electric vehicle charging port identification system, **a** Electric vehicle charging port identification system; **b** Electric vehicle charging port identification system framework

3 Calibration Procedure

The camera maps coordinate points in 3D space to the 2D image plane, a process that can be described by a linear pinhole imaging model [7], Due to the influence of the lens, the camera needs to be calibrated before use, which can effectively correct the aberration. The internal parameter matrix M_1 and external parameters R and t of the color camera in RGB-D camera can be obtained using the calibration software that comes with the RGB-D camera as follows:

$$M_1 = \begin{bmatrix} 1383.2916 & 0 & 959.5447 \\ 0 & 1381.8622 & 541.5519 \\ 0 & 0 & 1 \end{bmatrix} \tag{1}$$

$$R = \begin{bmatrix} 0.999997 & -0.002368 & 0.000870 \\ 0.002371 & 0.999994 & -0.002702 \\ -0.000864 & 0.002704 & 0.999996 \end{bmatrix} \tag{2}$$

$$t = \begin{bmatrix} 14.892988 & 0.049739 & -0.170782 \end{bmatrix} \tag{3}$$

4 Method

The charging port identification process described in this paper is shown in Fig. 4, which mainly includes: filtering algorithm based on image smoothing, feature detection segmentation algorithm based on ROI region, algorithm based on improved Canny edge detection algorithm and algorithm based on combined morphology for effective identification of charging port location, and the specific methods and processes are as follows.

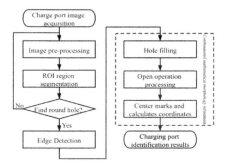

Fig. 4. Charging port identification process flow diagram

4.1 Image Smoothing Based Filtering Algorithm

After the stereo vision camera calibration is completed, the charging port image is collected through RGB-D camera software, and the complete charging port image is collected. Aiming at the noise caused by the strong electromagnetic field in the charging port area and the interference of natural light on the charging port image, the noise caused by the strong electromagnetic field mainly includes salt and pepper noise [8].

In order to prevent noise from producing phenomena such as blurred images and serious loss of edge information, it is necessary to preserve as much as possible the important characteristics of the edges of the charging port images for subsequent recognition work. Therefore, this paper adopts median filtering for noise reduction of charging port images. Median filtering is a kind of nonlinear filtering and convolution filtering, and its principle is to change the replacement value of image element from the average value of image element in the neighborhood to the middle value of image element in the neighborhood [9]. At the coordinate point (x, y), the window of size $m \times n$ is denoted as S_{xy}, and the median filtering is to select the median of the disturbed image $g(x, y)$ in the window S_{xy} as the output of the coordinate point (x, y), which can be defined as:

$$f(x, y) = \text{Median}\big[g(s, t)\big](s, t) \in S_{xy} \tag{4}$$

In Eq. 4, where $g(s, t)$ is the original image; $f(x, y)$ is the filtered image; S_{xy} denotes the filter template.

Median filtering uses suitable points to replace the noise, and it is effective in removing the pretzel noise, and Fig. 5 shows the noise reduction results of median filtering.

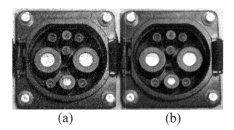

(a)   (b)

Fig. 5. Median filtering noise reduction results, **a** Before noise reduction; **b** After noise reduction

4.2 Segmentation Algorithm Based on ROI Region Feature Detection

A region of interest (ROI) of an image is a region that can mimic human vision and reflect the important content of the whole image [10]. This region is a collection composed of one or more fixed divided subgraphs, which is also the key region of the image. According to the previous analysis, the prominent feature information of the charging port is the 9 round holes and the adjacent areas. The 9 round holes are the target regions of the charging port image, and the segmentation algorithm based on the ROI can effectively and accurately utilize the important regions of the image while eliminating the interference of the secondary regions (i.e., the reflective 4 metal locating screws and the edge text).

In order to facilitate the robot to identify the information of the region within the charging port and reduce the false identification and missed identification in the feature identification and detection process, this paper adopts the ROI -based to complete the segmentation of the charging port image. Firstly, the shape of the ROI needs to be selected, and since the ROI is presented as a middle axis-symmetric arrangement with a certain regularity, we defined the range frame as a rectangle, and secondly, by finding the smallest rectangle covering the area where the 9 round holes are located. By performing ROI segmentation on the previous images, the results are shown in Fig. 6 below:

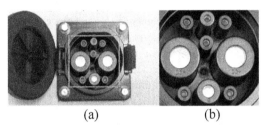

(a)   (b)

Fig. 6. Results of feature detection segmentation based on ROI, **a** Before ROI processing; **b** After ROI processing

4.3   Based on an Improved Canny Edge Detection Algorithm

Edge is an important feature of the image, in order to accurately identify the 9 round holes in the charging port image, it is necessary to distinguish the round hole and background in the charging port image, and make use of the difference of image characteristics between the two to achieve edge detection and extract the edge information of the round hole. Commonly used edge detection operators such as Sobel and Prewitt [11] can perform edge extraction for simpler images, while it is difficult to perform effective edge extraction for complex images such as charging ports. The Canny operator [12] is divided into the following main steps:

(1) To reduce the effect of noise on the edges, image smoothing is performed by using a two-dimensional Gaussian filter $g(x, y)$. Let the original image be $I(x, y)$, then the image obtained after Gaussian smoothing is $H(x, y)$, the latter noise will be much reduced compared to the former, and the smoothed image $H(x, y)$ can be expressed as:

$$H(x, y) = G(x, y) * I(x, y) \tag{5}$$

$$G(x, y) = \frac{1}{2\pi\sigma^2} \exp\left(-\frac{x^2 + y^2}{2\sigma^2}\right) \tag{6}$$

In Eq. 5, where $G(x, y)$ is a two-dimensional Gaussian function; "$*$"denotes the convolution, σ is the standard deviation, the value is related to the smoothing effect, the larger σ, the better the smoothing effect.

(2) Find the location in the image where the intensity changes significantly, as shown in Fig. 7 c for the gradient amplitude map of the charging port, and calculate the gradient amplitude $A(x, y)$ and direction $\theta(x, y)$ of the image using the Gaussian first-order differential equation, which can be expressed as:

$$\begin{cases} M_x(x, y) = \frac{\partial G}{\partial x} * I(x, y) \\ M_y(x, y) = \frac{\partial G}{\partial y} * I(x, y) \end{cases} \tag{7}$$

$$\begin{cases} A(x, y) = \sqrt{[M_x(x, y)]^2 + [M_y(x, y)]^2} \\ \theta(x, y) = arctan\frac{M_y(x, y)}{M_x(x, y)} \end{cases} \tag{8}$$

In Eq. 8, where $[M_x(x, y)]^2$ is the horizontal direction difference, and $[M_y(x, y)]^2$ is the vertical direction difference; where $\theta \varepsilon (-\pi, \pi)$.

(3) Non-maximum suppression is used to remove missed and false detections in the gradient direction to ensure that the edge boundaries become clear and reduce the probability of false detection of edge blurring. If the gradient value of a pixel point is smaller than the gradient value in the neighboring gradient direction, then the point is a non-edge point and needs to be removed, and vice versa, to ensure that the edge is refined. Figure 7 shows the non-maximum suppression proximity pixel relationship, and Fig. 7d shows the non-maximum suppression of the charging port.

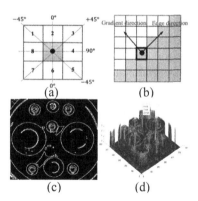

Fig. 7. Non-maximum suppression adjacent pixel relationship graph, **a** Pixel edge 4 directions; **b** Pixel and edge pixel positions to be examined; **c** Gradient directions graph of charging port; **d** Non-maximum suppression graph of charging port

(4) The gradient is thresholded twice to determine the potential boundary, and these two thresholds are divided into high and low thresholds. If the gradient value of the edge pixel point is greater than the high threshold, the point is an edge point, and vice versa, it is not an edge point, and if it is in between, it is a weak edge point.

(5) Edge tracking uses a hysteresis technique, which is mainly used to detect the 8-connected neighborhood pixels of weak edge points and determine whether they are larger than the high threshold, and if they are, they need to be retained.

Since the conventional Canny edge detection algorithm is only sensitive to Gaussian noise and can extract better edge information, but it is difficult to effectively identify and detect the local region in practical situations. In order to better identify the charging port region, this paper calculates the gradient amplitude and gradient direction in $-45°$ and $45°$ directions respectively based on the conventional Canny algorithm, and the local region of the charging port is non-maximum suppression processing. The conventional Canny algorithm can only calculate the gradient amplitude and direction by Sobel algorithm in 2×2 neighborhood, but not analyze other edge directions [13], this paper adopts the gradient amplitude and direction in $-45°$ and $45°$ directions by Sobel operator in 3×3 neighborhood, respectively, and the obtained gradient amplitude $A(x, y)$ and direction angle $\theta(x, y)$:

$$A(x, y) = \sqrt{\left[M_x(x, y)\right]^2 + \left[M_y(x, y)\right]^2 + \left[M_{45°}(x, y)\right]^2 + \left[M_{-45°}(x, y)\right]^2} \quad (9)$$

$$\theta(x, y) = \arctan\left(\frac{\left[M_x(x, y)\right]^2}{\left[M_y(x, y)\right]^2}\right) \quad (10)$$

In order to verify the effectiveness of the algorithm in this paper, the results are shown in Fig. 8 by comparing the improved Canny edge detection algorithm with the conventional Canny edge detection algorithm based on the improved Canny edge detection algorithm. The conventional Canny edge detection algorithm for the identification of the round hole of the charging port has a fault phenomenon, while the information of the identified round hole edge is less, and the identified edge line is thin, which is easy to produce edge contour gap, which is not conducive to the later hole filling processing. And this paper based on the improved Canny algorithm for edge identification is very effective, compared to the conventional algorithm for edge refinement, the extracted edge lines are thicker, to ensure the integrity of the closed edge. At the same time, the edges that cannot be detected by the conventional Canny edge detection algorithm are detected, while the edges that are detected incorrectly are eliminated.

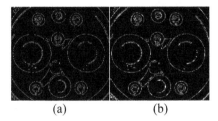

(a)   (b)

Fig. 8. Comparison of two Canny edge detection algorithms, **a** Conventional canny edge detection; **b** Improved canny edge detection

By identifying the local boundary region of the charging port and using non-maximum suppression to remove misidentification in the gradient direction (see Fig. 9).

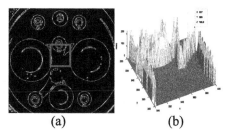

(a)   (b)

Fig. 9. Local edge detection analysis, **a** Local boundary region identification of charging port; **b** Non-maximum suppression graph of local boundaries

4.4 Algorithms Based on Mathematical Combinatorial Morphology

Hole Filling: Holes are produced in some regions of the charging port, and these holes seriously affect the detection effect and image integrity of the charging port. In order to better highlight the target charging port foreground, the binary images of these charging ports need to be hole-filled. The premise of hole filling is to close the region surrounded by complete edges, and the edges should not be broken, notched, etc. The filled round hole can be connected naturally and smoothly with other regions of the charging port, and the hole filling is defined as follows:

$$X_k = (X_{k-1} \oplus B) \cap A^c \quad K = 1, 2, 3 \tag{11}$$

In Eq. 11, where X_k is the region block of the region to be filled partitioned; X_0 is the array of zeros and the initial position of the boundary; B is the structure element with known symmetry; A^c is the complement of A.

When the algorithm runs until $X_k = X_{k-1}$, the holes finish filling, and the concatenation of the set X_k and A contains the set of filled as well as the set of boundary elements. Since the internal hole core and the external column in the identified nine circular holes can be approximated as a whole, the holes can be filled (see Fig. 10a).

Open Operation and Center Mark: The open operation is a mathematical morphological operator, through the process of first erosion and then expansion, and the closed operation is its dual operation, the open operation processing of the charging port [14] can eliminate the fine protrusions and narrow interruptions in the background, so that the contour of the target charging port becomes smooth, which can effectively remove edge objects other than the target's 9 circular holes, which is beneficial to highlight important information such as the target round holes and improve the accuracy of identification, and finally the center of the round holes of the charging port is marked, while the edges are auxiliary marked, and the two-dimenonal coordinate points of the center of the round holes can be obtained, which helps the robot to carry out the subsequent grasping work. The definition of open operation is as follows:

$$A \circ B = (A \ominus B) \oplus B \tag{12}$$

In Eq. 12, where $A \circ B$ is the structural element B to open the binary image charging port A; $\ominus$. and $\oplus$ represent corrosion and expansion respectively;

The final identification result of the charging port is shown in Fig. 10, which can be seen from the figure, the method used herein can be well identified as the charging port of the electric vehicle.

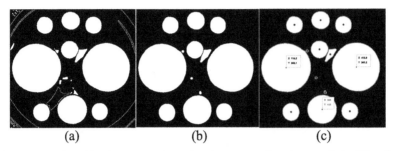

(a)   (b)   (c)

Fig. 10. The final identification result of the charging port, **a** Charging port hole filling; **b** Open operation processing; **c** Two-dimensional coordinates acquired by the center mark

5   Experiment and Discussion

In order to verify the feasibility of the above algorithm, we simulate the detection experiment of a real environment to identify the charging port of electric vehicles by different illumination intensity and different shooting distance based on coarse positioning to ensure the complete and clear appearance of the charging port in the field of view. The luminance of the light source is divided into two ranges: normal light and weak light, and the illuminance meter detects the illumination intensity of the two ranges in real-time. In the case of weak light, the camera is converted to the left and right infrared camera mode of RGB-D camera to complete the acquisition of grayscale images, and in the case of detecting normal light, the camera is converted to an individual color camera mode to complete the acquisition of color images of charging ports.

In the case of two different illumination intensities and different shooting distance ranges of the camera, the experiments were collected 270 times each for the charging port images, and the identification of the charging port was accomplished in the normal light phase of the experiment by illumination intensities of 3000 lx, 4000 lx and 5000 lx and shooting distances of 200 mm, 250 mm and 300 mm, respectively. In the low light stage, the illumination intensity is 0 lx, 500 lx and 1000 lx, and the shooting distance is 100 mm, 150 mm and 200 mm to complete the image acquisition and identification of the charging port. The results of the two ranges of charging port identification in the experiment are shown in Table 1 and Table 2 respectively.

It can be seen from Table 1 that the illumination intensity and shooting distance have a great influence on the identification result of the charging port. In the normal light range, the identification success takes the lead in increasing and then decreasing when the illumination intensity is from 3000 lx to 5000 lx, at this time, the light is from dark to light, and when the illumination intensity is at 4000 lx, the identification success rate of the charging port is the highest, reaching 97.8%, and at a distance of

Table 1. Charging port identification results under different illumination intensities and different shooting distances in the normal light range.

Illumination intensity(lux)	200 mm (30 images)	250 mm (30 images)	300 mm (30 images)	Success rate (%)
3000	29	29	28	95.6%
4000	29	30	29	97.8%
5000	27	28	26	90.0%

Table 2. Charging port identification results under different illumination intensities and different shooting distances in the weak light range

Illumination intensity(lux)	100 mm (30 images)	150 mm (30 images)	200 mm (30 images)	Success rate (%)
0	28	29	27	93.3%
500	29	27	26	91.1%
1000	27	26	26	87.8%

250 mm, it can identify a higher number of images of the charging port. In the faint light range, the resolution of the grayscale map obtained by the left and right infrared cameras decreases, which will have some influence on the identification results and is not as good as the identification in the normal light range. In the weak light range (see Table 2), the illumination intensity and shooting distance will have an impact on the identification results, shooting distance 100 mm compared with shooting distance 200 mm, the former the better the charging port identification results. With the increase of illumination intensity, the infrared component of natural light gradually increases the interference to the image captured by the camera, and the identification success rate gradually decreases, and the identification success rate of the charging port is 93.3% at 0 lx. Under the condition that the existing camera resolution is not improved, the identification success rate of the charging port can be effectively improved by real-time detection of illumination intensity and strict control of the shooting distance of the infrared camera.

6   Conclusion

In this article, we propose a multi-algorithm fusion method adapted to electric vehicle charging port identification. This method includes a novel ROI region segmentation algorithm that can reduce the false identification in the complex background of the charging port image and highlight the important regions of the charging port. In addition, an improved Canny edge detection algorithm that can adaptively detect the local boundary region lines of the charging port to ensure the integrity of the boundary region and eliminate the false identification. Finally, using the combined morphology of hole filling, opening operation and center marker to further refine the charging port, which can effectively highlight the round hole information of the charging port and obtain the center two-dimensional coordinates. The accurate identification information is beneficial to the subsequent automatic charging of the robot. Experimental verification of the charging port identification method using manipulator under different illumination intensity and shooting distance. The experimental results show that when the illumination intensity is in 3000–5000 lx, the identification success rate increases first and then decreases. When the illumination intensity is in 4000 lx, the highest identification success rate of the charging port is 97.8%. The success rate of identification is 93.3% in the weak light range when the illumination intensity is 0 lx. The identification method can have good robustness and accuracy for the identification of charging ports in complex environments such as within a certain range illumination intensity and identification distance.

Future research work will further optimize the errors influence generated by this method, and improve the real-time performance of this method without affecting the identification results.

Acknowledgments. The authors gratefully acknowledge the financial support provided by The National Natural Science Foundation of China (No. 51775424).

References

1. Hirz, M., et al.: Automated Robot Charging of Electric Cars (2018)
2. Fondahl, K., et al. Automation beyond self-driving-the role of automotive service robots for automated mobility systems. In: AmE 2017-Automotive meets Electronics; 8th GMM-Symposium. VDE, Dortmund, Germany, pp. 1–6 (2017)
3. Wang, C.: Research on laser scanning and positioning technology of electric vehicle charging port position. Harbin Institute of Technology, People's Republic of China (2019)
4. Yu, L., Xiong, J., et al.: A litchi fruit recognition method in a natural environment using RGB-D images. Biosys. Eng. **204**, 50–63 (2021)
5. Yin, K.: Research on the visual positioning technology of electric vehicle charging port position. Harbin Institute of Technology, People's Republic of China (2020)
6. Miseikis, J., et al.: 3D vision guided robotic charging station for electric and plug-in hybrid vehicles. arXiv preprint arXiv:1703.05381 (2017)
7. Grossberg, M.D., Nayar, S.K.: A general imaging model and a method for finding its parameters. In: Proceedings Eighth IEEE International Conference on Computer Vision. ICCV 2001, vol. 2, pp. 108–115. IEEE. Vancouver, BC, Canada (2001)
8. Chan, R.H., Ho, C.W., et al.: Salt-and-pepper noise removal by median-type noise detectors and detail-preserving regularization. IEEE Trans. Image Process. **14**(10), 1479–1485 (2005)
9. Gilboa, G., Sochen, N., et al.: Image enhancement and denoising by complex diffusion processes. IEEE Trans. Pattern Anal. Mach. Intell. **26**(8), 1020–1036 (2004)
10. Eswaraiah, R., Reddy, E.S.: Robust medical image watermarking technique for accurate detection of tampers inside region of interest and recovering original region of interest. IET Image Proc. **9**(8), 615–625 (2015)
11. Gonzalez, R.C., Woods, R.E.: Digital Image Processing. 4th edn. Pearson, New York (2018)
12. Canny, J.: A computational approach to edge detection. IEEE Trans. Pattern Anal. Mach. Intell. **6**, 679–698 (1986)

13. Nikolic, M., et al.: Edge detection in medical ultrasound images using adjusted Canny edge detection algorithm. In: 2016 24th Telecommunications Forum (TELFOR), pp. 1–4. IEEE. Belgrade, Serbia (2016)
14. Haralick, R.M., et al.: Image analysis using mathematical morphology. IEEE Trans. Pattern Anal. Mach. Intell. **4**, 532–550 (1987)

Efficient Power Grid Topology Control
via Two-Stage Action Search

Yuecheng Liu[ID], Yanjie Li[(✉)][ID], Qi Liu[ID], Yunhong Xu[ID], Shaohua Lv[ID],
and Meiling Chen[ID]

Harbin Institute of Technology, Shenzhen, China
{19S153206,19B953036,19S053099,19S053101,
19S153214}@stu.hit.edu.cn, autolyj@hit.edu.cn

Abstract. Topology control in large-scale power grid system is a challenging problem because of the enormous state and action space. This paper proposes an efficient two-stage topology control framework to make a trade off between speed and accuracy. The framework consists of two components: a fast *nominator* for candidate actions generation and a slower but more accurate *ranker* for final action selection. Differing from previous works, this paper formulates candidates generation as a *sequential* decision making process, so as to take full advantage of information feedback from the *ranker* to guide the subsequent candidates generation process. To achieve this, the *nominator* is built as a GRU-based agent and is trained via reinforcement learning (RL). Experiment results show that the *nominator* is able to capture valuable information from historical feedback from *ranker*, and our method outperforms traditional methods on *L2RPN NeurIPS 2020 Adaptability Track* benchmark.

Keywords: Topology control · Two-stage · Reinforcement learning · Smart grid

1 Introduction

Over the past century, power grid has played a central role in the economy and society by providing reliable power to industries, services, and consumers. The power system will encounter various problems in the operation process. First of all, the high popularity of renewable energy (such as wind and solar energy and other intermittent energy) has brought greater uncertainty to the power system. In addition, some unexpected events (such as thunderstorms, emergency line maintenance, etc.) may cause disconnection of some transmission lines, which have a great impact on the operating state of the power grid. In order to maintain the performance of the power grid, past researchers have explored two kind of methods: power generation control and topology control. Power

This work was supported by the Shenzhen basic research program [JCYJ20180507183837726] and the National Natural Science Foundation [U1813206, 61977019].

generation control has been well studied in the past research [3,9,14,16], but topology control is not fully studied yet. Some works try to apply reinforcement learning for power grid topology control [11,17]. These methods have achieved certain results in small grid scenarios. However, when it comes to larger scale grid scenarios (such as IEEE 118), these methods do not work well due to the enormous state space and discrete action space.

In order to obtain the best solution, the most direct way is to enumerate the entire action space and select the best action. To give a score for each action, a numerical solver can be used to solve the state transition equation of the power grid, and the action is scored according to the state transition result. In spite of the high accuracy, this method suffers from low time-efficiency especially when the action space is large. On the other hand, some works try to approximate the transition model via a neural network [5]. This method is faster compared with numerical solver. However, experiment results show that neural networks are difficult to learn an accurate transition model in large scale scenarios.

Inspired by some recent works in the field of recommender systems [8,12], we construct a two-stage topology control method consisting of a *nominator* for fast and efficient candidate actions generation in the first stage and a more accurate *ranker* in the second stage for final action selection. Differing from previous works in recommender systems where all candidates are generated independently [1,12], we formulate the candidates generation stage as a sequential decision making process to take advantage of information feedback from the *ranker* and train the *nominator* via reinforcement learning. We show that with these extra information from the *ranker*, it is easier for the *nominator* to understand the current state and generate better candidate actions in the subsequent process.

2   Related Work

The topology control of the power is a relatively less researched direction in the field of power grid dispatching. Since the number of possible topologies increases exponentially with the number of substations, the enormous state space and action space greatly increase the complexity of the problem. Therefore, it is still a great challenge to make appropriate topology control in large-scale grid scenarios. Mixed integer programming was used to solve the optimal transmission switching problem of the power grid [6,10]. However, this type of method requires huge time expenditure and cannot meet the real-time requirements of complex power grid scenarios. Some heuristic methods were used to reduce the time expenditure of the algorithm [7]. Recently, Marot et al. investigated the use of substation bus configuration to adjust the grid topology [13], which is a more complicated situation than line switching. The author used an algorithm based on an expert system to demonstrate the feasibility of this topology adjustment method. Recently, deep reinforcement learning based methods were introduced for topology control. A RL method was built based on Dueling-DQN algorithm [11], and imitation learning and guided exploration are used to accelerate the training process. Yoon et al. [17] considered the power grid topology

control problem as a two-level decision-making problem, and built an SAC based
agent for top-level control.

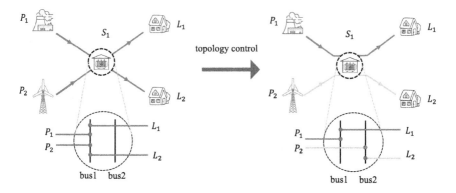

Fig. 1. Illustration of power grid topology control via substation bus assignment. (Left)
All plants and loads are connected to the same busbar on S_1. (Right) P_1 and L_1 are
connected to busbar 1 and P_2 and L_2 are connected the other busbar. In this case, the
power grid is splitted into two separate subsystems.

On the other hand, in the field of recommander system, to tackle the enormous action space, two-stage recommender systems are widely adopted in industry due to their scalability and maintainability [8,12]. In these works, a set of
computationally efficient *nominators* narrows down the search from millions to
only hundreds of items. The slower but more accurate *ranker* selects and reorders
a few items which are eventually served to the user. Based on this idea, we consider a two-stage method for power grid topology control problem. However,
differing from the above methods, we consider candidates generation as a *step-
by-step* process rather than generate all candidates independently [1,12] in order
to take advantage of valuable information feedback from the *ranker* to guide the
subsequent candidates generating process.

3   Preliminary

3.1   Power Grid Emergency Control via Topology Configuration

In the power grid management problem, a power grid system consists of three
kind of elements: power plants P (indexed by $P_1, P_2, ..., P_{N_P}$), loads L (indexed
by $L_1, L_2, ..., L_{N_L}$) and substations S (indexed by $S_1, S_2, ..., S_{N_S}$). All of these
elements are connected together with power lines. Thus the whole power grid
system can be concluded as an undirected graph $G = (V, E)$, where $V = P \cup L \cup
S$ is the node set consisting of all plants, loads and substations, and E consists
of all power lines which connect the nodes together. For each substation, there
are 2 busbars, and elements connected to the substation can only be connected

to one of the them or neither of them (as shown in Fig. 1). Power thus can only travels over elements on the same busbar. To maintain electrical flows of power lines within acceptable range, people are required to appropriately adjust the power grid topology by switching elements to different busbars on substations in emergency circumstances.

To illustrate the topology configuration method by bus assignment, we provide a toy example in Fig. 1. In this example, there are 5 elements: plants P_1, P_2, loads L_1, L_2 and substation S_1, and P_1, P_2, L_1, L_2 are connected to substation S_1. In the left figure, P_1, P_2, L_1, L_2 are all connected to the same busbar of S_1. In this case, the substation can be considered as a single intersection point which connects all the other elements together, and plants P_1, P_2 provide electricity to two loads L_1 and L_2 simultaneously. In the right figure, we change the topology configuration on substation S_1 by switching P_2 and L_2 to another busbar. In this case the whole power grid system can be considered to be splitted into two separate subsystems. Plant P_1 only provides electricity for load L_1 and plant P_2 only provides electricity for load L_2. The current value on power lines and some other electrical variables are thus changed under the new topology configuration.

3.2   Problem Definition

In this section, we present a model to formulate the topology control problem, including the state space, action space and final goal.

State. Here we introduce the features of power grid state: Time information t, including the current year, month, day, hour, minute and week; Active power p, a float vector of length $N_P + N_L + N_{line}$, denoting the active power magnitude of all plants, loads and power lines (MW); Reactive power q, a float vector of length $N_P + N_L + N_{line}$, denoting the reactive power magnitude of all elements $(MVar)$; Voltage v, a float vector of length $N_P + N_L + N_{line}$, the voltage magnitude of all elements (kV); Capacity ratio ρ, a float vector of length N_{line}, defined as the ratio between current flow (magnitude) and thermal limit of power lines; Topology configuration vector s_{topo}, an int vector of length $N_P + N_L + 2 \times N_{line}$ ($2 \times N_{line}$ represents the both ends of power lines), every value in the vector should be "0", "1" or "2", where "0" indicates that the element is connected to neither of two busbars and "1" and "2" indicates that the element is connected to busbar 1 and busbar 2 respectively; Line status s_l, a boolean value vector of length N_{line}, indicating whether the power lines are connected or disconnected; t_o, a vector of length N_{line}, indicating the number of time steps each line is overflowed. t_{line}, a vector of length N_{line}, denoting how much time for each line is left until it can be operated; t_{sub}, a vector of length N_S, denoting how much time for each substation is left until it can be operated; t_n, a vector of length N_{line}, the time of planned maintenance, an agent can not operate on the lines with maintenance. t_d, a vector of length N_{line}, the number of time steps that the maintenance will last. Particularly, $t_{line}, t_{sub}, t_n, t_d$ indicate that some of the actions are illegal in some cases, and we will describe this fact in the following subsection.

Y. Liu et al.

In conclusion, denote $\mathcal{S}_p$ as the state space of power grid system, it can be written as $\mathcal{S}_p = (t, p, q, v, \rho, s_{topo}, s_l, t_o, t_{line}, t_{sub}, t_n, t_d)$. In the later part of this paper, we will call S_p as "power grid state" to distinguish from the "MDP state" which will be introduced in Sect. 4.3.

Action. As described in Sect. 3.1, the topology control of power grid is realized by bus assignment (see Fig. 1). Without loss of generality, assume that we can only change the topology configuration over one substation at each time step. Define the number of elements (power lines, plants and loads) connected to ith substation as $Sub(i)$, so the total number of actions is $M = |\mathcal{A}| = \sum_{i=0}^{N_S} 3^{Sub(i)}$. For example, in Fig. 1, there are 4 elements connected to substation S_1, i.e., $Sub(1) = 4$, so there are $M = 3^4 = 81$ possible actions in this case.

Subject to some constraints ($t_{line}, t_{sub}, t_n, t_d$, which have been introduced above), actions in $\mathcal{A}$ are not always available under different cases. Here we define the legal action space under power grid state S_p as $\mathcal{A}^{S_p}$, and only actions in $\mathcal{A}^{S_p}$ can be selected under power grid state S_p.

Goal. To maintain the performance of the power grid in emergency circumstances, we should avoid overloads of all power lines. Define ρ_i as the current capacity ratio (ratio between current flow and thermal limit) of power line l_i, and $\rho_{\max}$ as the maximum value in all ρ_is, $\rho_{\max} = \max_i\{\rho_i | i = 1, 2, ..., N_{\text{line}}\}$, i.e., the worst case of all power lines. The goal of this work is to reduce $\rho_{\max}$ by the proper adjustment of power grid topology, as described in Sect. 3 and Fig. 1.

4 Two-Stage Topology Control

4.1 Methodology

Our method consists of two components: (i) a fast *nominator* responsible for generating N ($N << M$) candidate actions from legal action space $\mathcal{A}^{S_p}$ in the first stage given the power grid state S_p, (ii) a slower but more accurate *ranker* to select the final action from N candidate actions (see Fig. 2). More details of *ranker* and *nominator* are described in Sect. 4.2 and 4.3 respectively.

4.2 Ranker

In our method, a numerical solver (which uses Newton-Raphson algorithm as the backend) works as the *ranker* to give a score r for each candidate action a, given current power grid state S_p. More exactly, the ranker will predict S_p^a (next state after taking action a under power grid state S_p) by using the numerical solver to solve the system transition function f. Denote $\rho_{\max}(S_p)$ and $\rho_{\max}(S_p^a)$ as the maximum capacity ratio of all power lines under S_p and S_p^a respectively. The score of a is then obtained based on $\rho_{\max}(S_p^a)$. In this work, we define r as

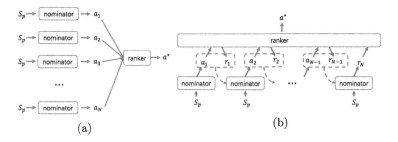

(a)   (b)

Fig. 2. Comparison of different candidates generation methods. (a) Traditional candidates generation process in recommender systems, in which all candidates are generated independently. (b) Our method, candidates are generated in a *step-by-step* manner, which can take advantage of information feedback from the *ranker* to guide the subsequent action search process.

$\rho_{\max}(S_p) - \rho_{\max}(S_p^a)$, i.e., the decrement of maximum capacity ratio of all power lines after taking action a. $\rho_{\max}(S_p)$ works as a baseline to reduce the variance of the algorithm during the training process. The maximum capacity ratio can thus be reduced most by selecting the action a^* with the largest reward r^*.

$$(S_p, a) \xrightarrow{f} S_p^a \longrightarrow \rho_{\max}(S_p^a) \tag{1}$$

$$r = \rho_{\max}(S_p) - \rho_{\max}(S_p^a) \tag{2}$$

4.3   Nominator

In large scale power grid control problem, traditional machine learning based topology control method usually failed to get satisfying results because of the difficulty of effective feature extraction in high-dimensional feature cases. This work tries to alleviate the problem by taking advantage of extra information feedback from the *ranker*. We illustrate our motivation in Fig. 3. In this case, an agent takes original power grid state S_p as input and obtains hidden state representation h for S_p. However, the hidden state h is not effective enough because of the difficulty of feature extraction. Based on this awful hidden state representation, the agent outputs a Q value vector and an action a is selected based on Q. The agent should have expect a high reward under (S_p, a). However, a bad reward (unexpected) is obtained from the environment (since the hidden state representation h is awful and thus Q values are wrongly estimated). The agent should then notice the inappropriateness of current hidden state representation and try to improve it based on these information feedback and get a better representation h' for next time step. We will show that with these extra information, it is easier for agent (nominator) to understand the current state and generate more effective candidate actions.

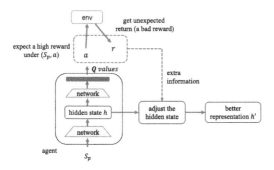

Fig. 3. Motivation of our method.

In our method, the candidate generation process is formulated as a sequential decision making problem. We define a Markov decision process, where S_t is the MDP state at step t for decision making. Define $S_1 = \{S_p\}$, $S_2 = \{S_p, a_1, r_1\}$, $S_3 = \{S_p, a_1, r_1, a_2, r_2\}$, ..., until $S_N = \{S_p, a_1, r_1, a_2, r_2, ..., a_{N-1}, r_{N-1}\}$, where a_t is the tth generated candidate action and r_t denote the reward from the *ranker* for action a_t as defined in Sect. 4.2. The agent (*nominator*) generate tth candidate action a_t from legal action space $\mathcal{A}^{S_p}$ (make a decision) based on S_t at time step t, i.e., $a_t \sim \pi(S_t)$.

The agent seeks to maximize the expected discounted return, so as to generate more effective candidate actions to minimize the maximum capacity ratio of all power lines. We define the discounted return as $R = \sum_{t=1}^{T}[\gamma^{t-1}r_t]$, and $\gamma \in [0, 1]$ is a discount factor that trades-off the importance of immediate and future rewards.

In this work, we adopt Double-DQN [15] algorithm to train the *nominator*. Given a policy π, the action-value function is defined as $Q(s, a) = \mathbb{E}[r_1 + \gamma r_2 + ... \gamma^{N-1} r_N | S_0 = s, A_0 = a]$. Double-DQN alleviates the *overestimation* problem in Q-learning by decoupling the critic and action using a *target network*. Formally, the update equation can be written as,

$$\boldsymbol{\theta}_{\text{new}} = \boldsymbol{\theta} + \alpha(y_t - Q(s_t, a_t; \boldsymbol{\theta}))\nabla_{\boldsymbol{\theta}}Q(s_t, a_t; \boldsymbol{\theta}) \tag{3}$$

where

$$y_t = r_{t+1} + \gamma Q(s_{t+1}, \arg\max_{a \in \mathcal{A}^{S_p}} Q(s_{t+1}, a; \boldsymbol{\theta}); \boldsymbol{\theta}') \tag{4}$$

To deal with the continuous changing history information $\{a_1, r_1, ..., a_{t-1}, r_{t-1}\}$ together with power grid state S_p, we build a novel architecture for the *nominator* based on GRU [2] (shown in Fig. 4). The total process can be concluded as two phases: power grid state embedding phase and candidate actions generating phase. In phase 1, the power grid state information S_p is embedded into the initial hidden state h_0 of GRU using feedforward neural networks; In phase 2, at each time step t, the agent (nominator) takes last generated action a_{t-1} and corresponding reward r_{t-1} as input and then output a Q vector based on these inputs for action sampling. Note that only actions from legal action

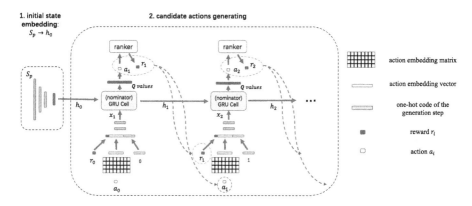

Fig. 4. Architecture of the nominator. (i) In phase 1, the state of power grid S_p is embedded into the initial hidden states h_0 of GRU using feedforward neural network. (ii) In phase 2, the nominator recurrently takes action a_{t-1} and corresponding reward r_{t-1} from last time step as input. A embedding matrix is also used for action representation. Then, the candidate action is sampled according to the Q values outputted from the nominator.

space $\mathcal{A}^{S_p}$ can be sampled, so we will mask the Q values of all illegal actions with $-\infty$ to make sure that these illegal actions will not be sampled. We also introduce an embedding matrix for action representation (which has been widely used in natural language processing), each action is mapped to a particular vector representation in a high dimensional space. We hope that with this framework, model can implicitly capture the relationship between different actions under the new representation space. All of the components are trained end-to-end.

5   Experiments

Experiment Setup. We train and evaluate our method on *L2RPN NeurIPS 2020 Adaptability Track* benchmark using Grid2op [4] environment. It is a large-scale power grid environment consisting of 118 substations, 186 lines, 62 plants and 99 loads. The problem is particularly challenging because of the unexpected attack on power lines (disconnect some of the power lines randomly). In our experiment, we set $N = 10$ (number of generated candidate actions) and $M = 1000$ ($|\mathcal{A}|$) for simplification, but people can make appropriate adjustments according to their own needs.

Nominator Training Results. We train our nominator on a pre-collected dataset, and the training results are shown in Fig. 5(a). To illustrate the effectiveness of our method, we add an additional experiment where historical information from *ranker* are removed, shown as the green curve. Experimental results show that the average return of our method (red curve) significantly outperforms the green curve, which indicates that the *nominator* is able to capture valuable

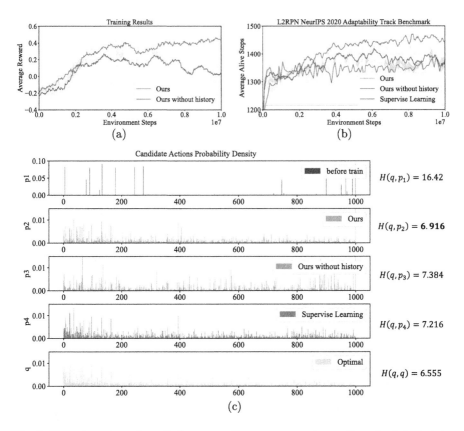

Fig. 5. Experiment results, all shown results are averaged over 3 seeds. (a) Training results of the *nominator* on a pre-collected dataset. The shown results are evaluated on an individual validation set. (b) Evaluation results on *L2RPN NeurIPS 2020 Adaptability Track* benchmark. (c) Comparison of learnt candidate actions distribution and optimal candidate actions distribution. $H(q, p_i)$ denote the *cross-entropy* of distributions q and p_i. (Color figure online)

information from history to guide subsequent candidate actions generating process. And our method has better generalization property during the training process, as is shown in Fig. 5(a),(b).

Evaluation Results. After training of the *nominator*, our two-stage topology control method is evaluated on *L2RPN NeurIPS Adaptability Track* benchmark, shown in Fig. 5(b). We build a supervise learning based nominator as the baseline for comparison (shown as the blue curve). In the supervise learning method, we construct a neural network to predict the reward r for each action a under power grid state S_p. In other words, this supervise learning method tries to approximate the reward function $\mathcal{R}(S_p, a)$ directly. And the candidate actions are selected based on the predicted reward of each action. Results show that our method (red curve) outperforms supervise learning method on the benchmark.

We further analyse the learnt candidate actions distribution generated by the nominators, shown in Fig. 5(c). p_1, p_2, p_3, p_4 denote the learnt distributions under different methods and q denote the distribution under optimal policy (acquired by traversing the entire action space). $H(q, p_i)$ denote the *cross-entropy* of distributions q and p_i. It is showed in result that our method (p_2, red) get the smallest cross-entropy, indicating that the learnt distribution is closest to the optimal result in these methods.

6   Conclusion

In this paper, we propose a two-stage topology control method for efficient power grid emergency control. The approach built a novel GRU-based *nominator* for sequential candidates generation and train it via reinforcement learning. The method alleviate the difficult feature extraction problem by taking advantage of extra information from the *ranker*, so as to make it easier for nominator to understand the current state. Experimental results show that our *nominator* is able to capture valuable information from the *ranker*, and the proposed method outperforms traditional methods on *L2RPN NeurIPS 2020 Adaptability Track* benchmark.

References

1. Chen, M., Beutel, A., Covington, P., Jain, S., Belletti, F., Chi, E.H.: Top-k off-policy correction for a reinforce recommender system. In: Proceedings of the Twelfth ACM International Conference on Web Search and Data Mining, pp. 456–464 (2019)
2. Chung, J., Gulcehre, C., Cho, K., Bengio, Y.: Empirical evaluation of gated recurrent neural networks on sequence modeling. arXiv preprint arXiv:1412.3555 (2014)
3. Diao, R., Wang, Z., Shi, D., Chang, Q., Duan, J., Zhang, X.: Autonomous voltage control for grid operation using deep reinforcement learning. In: 2019 IEEE Power & Energy Society General Meeting (PESGM), pp. 1–5. IEEE (2019)
4. Donnot, B.: Grid2op documentation. https://grid2op.readthedocs.io/en/latest/
5. Donon, B., Donnot, B., Guyon, I., Marot, A.: Graph neural solver for power systems. In: 2019 International Joint Conference on Neural Networks (IJCNN), pp. 1–8. IEEE (2019)
6. Fisher, E.B., O'Neill, R.P., Ferris, M.C.: Optimal transmission switching. IEEE Trans. Power Syst. **23**(3), 1346–1355 (2008)
7. Fuller, J.D., Ramasra, R., Cha, A.: Fast heuristics for transmission-line switching. IEEE Trans. Power Syst. **27**(3), 1377–1386 (2012)
8. Hron, J., Krauth, K., Jordan, M.I., Kilbertus, N.: Exploration in two-stage recommender systems. arXiv preprint arXiv:2009.08956 (2020)
9. Hua, H., Qin, Y., Hao, C., Cao, J.: Optimal energy management strategies for energy internet via deep reinforcement learning approach. Appl. Energy **239**, 598–609 (2019)

10. Khodaei, A., Shahidehpour, M.: Transmission switching in security-constrained unit commitment. IEEE Trans. Power Syst. **25**(4), 1937–1945 (2010)
11. Lan, T., et al.: AI-based autonomous line flow control via topology adjustment for maximizing time-series ATCs. In: 2020 IEEE Power & Energy Society General Meeting (PESGM), pp. 1–5. IEEE (2020)
12. Ma, J., et al.: Off-policy learning in two-stage recommender systems. In: Proceedings of The Web Conference 2020, pp. 463–473 (2020)
13. Marot, A., Donnot, B., Tazi, S., Panciatici, P.: Expert system for topological remedial action discovery in smart grids (2018)
14. Srikakulapu, R., Vinatha, U.: Optimized design of collector topology for offshore wind farm based on ant colony optimization with multiple travelling salesman problem. J. Mod. Power Syst. Clean Energy **6**(6), 1181–1192 (2018)
15. Van Hasselt, H., Guez, A., Silver, D.: Deep reinforcement learning with double Q-learning. In: Proceedings of the AAAI Conference on Artificial Intelligence, vol. 30 (2016)
16. Wang, W., Yu, N., Gao, Y., Shi, J.: Safe off-policy deep reinforcement learning algorithm for Volt-VAR control in power distribution systems. IEEE Trans. Smart Grid **11**(4), 3008–3018 (2019)
17. Yoon, D., Hong, S., Lee, B.J., Kim, K.E.: Winning the L2RPN challenge: power grid management via semi-Markov afterstate actor-critic. In: International Conference on Learning Representations (ICLR), vol. 5 (2021)

Research on Robot Classifiable Grasp Detection Method Based on Convolutional Neural Network

Lin Yang, Guohua Cui, Saixuan Chen$^{(\boxtimes)}$, and Xinlong Zhu

Institute of Intelligent Cooperative Robot Application Technology, Shanghai University of Engineering Science, Shanghai 201620, China

Abstract. Aiming at the problem that FC-GQ-CNNs cannot classify the object of grasp detection, we propose a new method of classifiable grasp detection combining object detection and grasp detection based on FC-GQ-CNNs and YOLOv4. First, using FC-GQ-CNNs to detect various types of parts to obtain the highest quality grasp of the robot (grasp point 3D coordinates and grasp plane angle); secondly, using YOLOv4 trained on the parts dataset detect various types of parts to obtain the classification and positioning bounding boxes; thirdly, by adding Canny edge detection, Sklansky algorithm and other image processing methods, the positioning bounding box have been improved to the minimum bounding rectangle frame; finally, the left-ray method is used to match the grasp point 2D coordinates with the improved positioning bounding box - the minimum bounding rectangle frame, and the classified grasp detection result are obtained according to the minimum bounding rectangle frame that the grasp point coordinates fall into. Experimental results show that the proposed method can identify the classification of the object, and the improved positioning bounding box can solve the problem of classification errors caused by matching the grasp point coordinates to multiple positioning bounding boxes, and improve the accuracy of grasp detection classification rate.

Keywords: Grasp detection · FC-GQ-CNNs · YOLOv4

1 Introduction

In recent years, as an important step in the robot grasp task, grasp detection has become one of the popular research directions of the robot grasp technology. Grabbing pose detection can be divided into the traditional analysis method and the data-driven method. The data-driven method can also be divided into three methods according to the detection object, there are positioning and posture methods, such as 6D grasp detection using multi-view RGB-D data [1] and SilhoNet [2] which predicts the posture of 6D objects based on monocular images, etc.; there are positioning and no posture methods, such as shape primitives Grasp detection [3], suitable for similar object, partial-based grasp detection [4], depth-based Grasp Quality convolutional neural networks (GQ-CNNs) [5], six-DOF grasp method proposed by Ten et al. [6] and multi-level spatial transformation network to

Foundation: National Natural Science Foundation of China (Grant No. 51775165).

X.-J. Liu et al. (Eds.): ICIRA 2021, LNAI 13015, pp. 705–715, 2021.
https://doi.org/10.1007/978-3-030-89134-3_64

predict grasp candidates proposed by Park et al. [7]; and mainly based on deep learning no positioning and no posture methods, such as grasp detection method using shared convolutional neural networks [8], two-step cascade system using two deep networks grasp detection [9] and the grasp and recognize object in a chaotic environment [10].

Dex-Net (Dexterity Network) [11] is a robot grasp detection project of the University of California, Berkeley's AI Laboratory. In July 2017, Jeff Mahler and others proposed the new version dataset Dex-Net 1.0 extended from the original Dex-Net 1.0 dataset. Dex-Net 2.0 dataset contains 6.7 million parallel gripping robust grasp point cloud data generated from thousands of 3D models, which increases the sampling complexity of robust grasp planning. The trained GQ-CNNs Grasp Detection is used to process the depth image of rigid grasping object, and it only takes about 0.8 s to predict the highest quality grasp, which is 3 times faster than the known method through 3D point cloud matching dataset. FC-GQ-CNNs (Fully Convolutional Grasp Quality Neural Networks) [12] improved by Fully Convolutional Networks (FCN) [13], using the FCN architecture instead of the cross-entropy Method (CEM), and effectively improved in computational efficiency from GQ-CNNs, and MPPH (mean picks per hour) has increased from 250 to 296.

Aiming at the limitation that the FC-GQ-CNNS grasp detection cannot classify the detected object, propose a new classifiable grasp detection method, which is based on the FC-GQ-CNNs grasp detection and the Yolov4 object detection [14], then the ray method [15] is used to match the coordinates of the grasp point and the coordinates of the positioning bounding box. At the same time, Canny edge detection [16] and Sklansky algorithm [17] were used to improve the results of positioning bounding box. Experimental results show that the improvement can effectively solve the classification error problem caused by directly using the YOLOv4 normal rectangle prediction bounding box for coordinate matching, and improve the classification accuracy of the classifiable grasp detection method.

2 Grasp Detection and Object Detection Methods

2.1 FC-GQ-CNNs Grasp Detection

FC-GQ-CNNs grasp detection is the latest research results of the Dex-Net robot grasp detection project. Due to the cross-entropy evolution strategy used in GQCNNs need to repeatedly search the action space in the calculation process to obtain the highest quality grasp, it has problems such as complex calculation process and difficult adjustment of parameters. while FC-GQ-CNNs use an FCN to overcome these shortcomings, and FC-GQ-CNNs can perform intensive and efficient evaluation based on the entire action space in the calculation process.

As shown in Fig. 1, the execution process of FC-GQ-CNNs grasp detection includes: 1) Input the depth map and mask map of the detected object; 2) Use FCGQ-CNNS grasp quality policy reason out the highest quality grasp; 3) Output the highest quality grasp (3D coordinates of grasp point and plane Angle). Among them, the grasp quality policy function in FC-GQ-CNNS is:

$$\pi_\theta(x) = argmax Q_\theta(y, u)$$
$$u \in U(y)$$

(1)

Where, $\pi_\theta(x)$ is the grasp quality policy function with parameters θ, and the *argmax* function to obtain the maximum value; Q_θ represents the mass function with parameters θ, where y represents the observed value of point cloud, $U(y)$ represents the action space, and u belongs to $U(y)$.

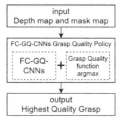

Fig. 1. FC-GQ-CNNS grasp detection policy execution flow chart.

2.2 YOLOv4 Object Detection

In 2020, Alexey et al. added a variety of effective convolutional neural network optimization techniques in YOLOV3 [18] proposed by Joseph the founder of YOLO. Optimization techniques such as enhancement of Mosaic data to improve detection robustness and avoid overfitting; Label smoothing, smoothing the traditional category one-hot vector, enhance the generalization ability; and Cross MiniBatch Normalization (CMBN) to accelerate the training speed, etc. The network architecture is still a one-stage method, which can directly carry out object detection through the convolutional neural network, and use CSP Dark-Net53 as the backbone to improve the accuracy, receptive field and speed. Finally, according to the optimal balance of speed and Precision, YOLOV4 object detection was proposed, which can be trained quickly by ordinary computer graphics card. Compared with YOLOv3, the AP (Average Precision) on COCO dataset improves by 10% and 12% FPS (Frames Per Second).

3 The Establishment of the Classifiable Grasp Detection

Due to the FC-GQ-CNNs grasp detection has no classification function, in other words, the grasp detection result of the output of the network is only have the highest quality grasp includes 3D coordinates of grasp point and plane angle, which is suitable for the robot equipped with parallel grasping clamp to grasp 2D plane task.

Aiming at the problem that the FC-GQ-CNNs grasp detection cannot classify the object, a new method based on FC-GQ-CNNs grasp detection is proposed. As shown in Fig. 2, the classification function can be achieved by adding YOLOv4 object detection, the coordinates of the grasp point are matched with the positioning Boundary Box coordinates, and the classification of the object is judged by the location boundary frame that the grasp point falls into. In addition, the location boundary frame of the object detection is optimized and improved, and the minimum bounding rectangle frame is used to replace the original location rectangular frame to improve the accuracy of the classification.

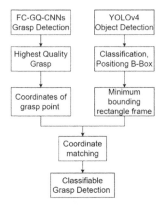

Fig. 2. Classifiable grasp detection method flow chart.

3.1 Improvement of Positioning Bounding Box

The specific formula of YOLOv4 object detection and prediction positioning is as follows:

$$
\begin{cases}
b_x = \sigma(t_x) * k + c_x \\
b_y = \sigma(t_y) * k + c_y \\
b_w = p_w e^{t_w} \\
b_h = p_h e^{t_h} \\
\sigma(t_0) = P_r(\text{object}) * IoU(b, \text{object})
\end{cases}
\tag{2}
$$

Where, t_x, t_y, t_w and t_h represent the offset value of the prediction coordinate, c_x and c_y represent the grid coordinates in the upper left corner, p_w and p_h represent the width and height of the prior box, t_o represent the prediction confidence, $\sigma(t_0)$ represent the logical regression of the confidence by using the S function (Sigmoid). In addition, a scale factor $k(k \geq 1)$ is added after the function. Make sure b_x, b_y, b_w and b_h not be restricted by the Sigmoid range (0, 1) to eliminate grid sensitivity. Finally, according to the pre-set IOU threshold (IOU is generally set at 0.5), the Boundary Box is screened to get the coordinates of the upper left (x1, y1) and lower right (x2, y2) points of the Boundary Box in the entire image coordinate system. Because of the final output is a straight rectangular box, when there is a distance between irregular shape parts or components is too close or even have overlap will cause positioning bounding box with large areas of overlap, if directly use YOLOv4 output for subsequent grasp point matching to determine the object's classification, classification failure may occur because the grasp point coordinates fall into multiple positioning bounding boxes.

To solve the above problem, we add some image processing methods such as Canny edge detection and Sklansky algorithm to improve the positioning bounding box of YOLOv4. As shown in Fig. 3, the original rectangular box is improved into a minimum bounding rectangle frame, that can be better represent the true shape of the part.

Figure 4 show the improvement flow chart of the positioning bounding box. The specific improvement methods are as follows: 1) Crop the image according to the part

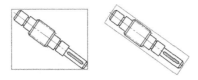

Fig. 3. Comparison diagram of positioning bounding box before and after improvement.

image by the positioning bounding box, and pre-process the image with Gaussian blur; 2) Use Canny edge detection to separate the parts from the background and get the contour map; 3) The contour image is treated with image expansion and corrosion to eliminate the boundary effect caused by Canny edge detection and solve the problem of contour discontinuity; 4) Select the main contour of the part according to the number of contour's coordinate, and use Sklansky algorithm to calculate the convex hull of the main contour; 4) Calculate the minimum area of the outer rectangle according to the convex hull, that is the minimum bounding rectangle frame.

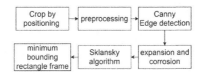

Fig. 4. Positioning bounding box improvement flow chart.

Figure 5 is an example of using the improved method to deal with various types of parts, in which there is an example of the specific improvement process of the gear shaft, and the contrast between original YOLOv4 object detection result and the improved minimum bounding rectangle frame.

3.2 Coordinate Matching of Grasp Point

As shown in Fig. 6, grasp point coordinate and positioning boundary box coordinate matching process mainly includes: 1) input the 2D coordinates of the grasp point from the highest quality grasp output from the grasp detection and the object detection improved positioning bounding box--minimum bounding rectangle frame into coordinate matching system; 2) Use X-axis left-ray method to determine which positioning boundary box the grasp point coordinate fall into; 3) Output the classification result to get the grasp detection results with classification information.

The X-axis left-ray method is used to determine whether the coordinate of grasp point fall into minimum bounding rectangle frame as follows: take the x-axis coordinate of the grasp point as the starting point, make the parallel to the x-axis negative ray, calculate the number of intersections between the ray and the minimum bounding rectangle frame, if the point number is 1 (odd intersection number), it means that the grasp point coordinate fall into the minimum bounding rectangle frame, conversely is not, at last, according to the classification of the minimum bounding rectangle frame's classification output the classification of the object.

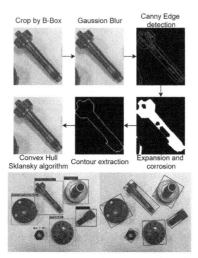

Fig. 5. An example diagram of positioning bounding box improvement.

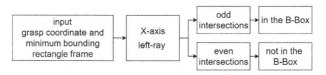

Fig. 6. Flow chart of coordinate matching.

Figure 7 is a diagram of how to use the X-axis left-ray method to match the coordinate of the grasp point with the minimum bounding rectangle frame. The number of intersections of the ray and the rectangle box in the diagram is 1, represents that the coordinate of the grasp point within the minimum bounding rectangle frame, the object classification of the grasp detection can be obtained.

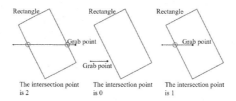

Fig. 7. Schematic diagram of coordinate matching of left ray method of X axis.

4   Experiment

The designed experimental procedure of classifiable grasp detection is shown in Fig. 8. The main experimental content based on FC-GQ-CNNs and YOLOv4 mainly include the three parts: 1) The production of parts dataset in the early stage; 2) The YOLOv4 object detection part, which mainly includes the steps of training on the parts dataset in the early stage, using the trained network for object detection in the experiment, and improving the positioning Boundary Box to the minimum bounding rectangle frame, etc. 3) FC-GQ-CNNs grasp detection part, using FCGQ-CNNs to detect the depth map and mask map of the parts; 4) Match the coordinates of the minimum bounding rectangle frame in step 2 with the coordinate of the grasp point in step 3, and finally get the grasp detection result with classification.

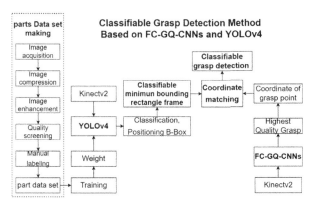

Fig. 8. Flow chart of experimental steps.

4.1 Experimental Environment

In the experiment, the YOLOv4 training environment and the classifiable grasp detection environment are all carried out in the same workstation, as shown in Table 1:

Table 1. Experimental environment.

	Version
System	Ubuntu 18.04.1 LTS
CPU	Intel Core i7-9800X @ 3.80 GHz * 16
GPU	RTX2080, 16 GB
Frame	Pytorch 1.2
Camera	Kinect v2

4.2 Experimental Dataset

The YOLOV4 weight file used in the object detection in the experiment was trained on the produced parts dataset, and the FC-GQ-CNNs network weight file used in the grasp detection was trained on the Dex-Net 2.0 dataset by the authorities. The depth map and mask map of the parts collected by Kinectv2 camera in the grasp detection experiment are consistent with the parts collected when making the dataset of the parts.

The main process of making parts dataset includes: 1) Use the camera collects images of common parts, including nut, screw, gear shaft, planet carrier and 2 different types of gears, a total of 6 kinds, and 1224 images are collected; 2) Use OpenCV to perform image processing, such as rotation, translation and mirroring, after that, 2448 part images were finally screened; 3) Use the image manual labeling tool " labelImg" to manually label 2448 part images, and finally make them into parts dataset. The specific information of parts dataset is shown in Table 2:

Table 2. Parts dataset.

	Nut	Screw	Gear1	Gear2	Gear-shaft	Planet-carrier
Number	746	864	1423	1568	1758	1782

4.3   Experimental Results and Analysis

In the classifiable grasp detection experiment, firstly, using a Kincetv2 camera to collect 100 images of multiple parts. Secondly, using the unimproved positioning bounding box (use the original positioning bounding box of Yolov4's during coordinate matching with grasp point) to carry out classifiable grasp detection experiment on those 100 images, then those 100 images were detected again, but use the pro-posed improve the positioning Boundary Box to the minimum bounding rectangle frame method; finally, compare the results of the two experiments above.

The first experimental result of classifiable grasp detection using the unimproved positioning bounding box were as follows: there were classification errors in 7 grasp detections, 2 of them were object detection errors, and 5 of them could not be determined because the grasp points were fall into two positioning bounding boxes, Fig. 9 is the wrong grasp detection result maps, from the depth map with the grasp point can be seen that 5-classification concentrated in the part of screw.

As shown in Fig. 10 (a), due to the close distance between the screw and the gear shaft in the experiment, the positioning Boundary Box area of the screw is smaller, while the positioning boundary box area of the right-inclined gear shaft is larger, resulting in a large overlap between the two positioning Boundary Boxes, the rays emitted towards the negative direction of the X-axis intersect with the detection boxes both of the gear shaft and the screw once, so that the grasp point P is matched to both the wrong gear shaft positioning bounding box and the correct screw positioning bounding box at the same time.

Re-experiment on those 100 images using the classifiable grasp detection method with the improved YOLOv4 positioning bounding box to the minimum bounding rectangle frame. The experimental results are: 5 classification errors caused by the above positioning bounding box problem are all achieved the correct matching of the grasp

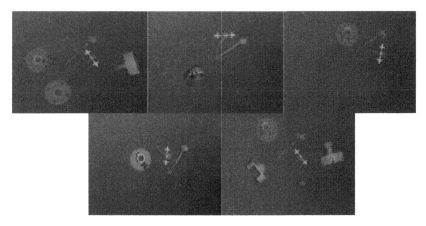

Fig. 9. Misclassified grasp detection result.

point coordinate, and the correct classification result have been obtained. In Fig. 10 (b), after using the improved method of the minimum bounding rectangle frame, the minimum bounding rectangle frames of gear shaft and screw no longer overlap, grasp point P of screw felled into the correct the minimum bounding rectangle frame, the launch of the ray in the direction of X-axis negative only have one intersection with it, which can get the correct classification result by coordinate matching.

Finally, the experimental results show that improving the Yolov4 positioning Boundary Box to the minimum bounding rectangle frame, the proposed method achieved a classification success rate of 98%, which is 5% higher than 93% before the improvement.

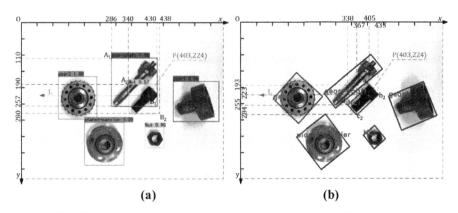

Fig. 10. Comparison of coordinate matching before and after improvement.

5   Conclusion

The classifiable robot grasp detection method combines YOLOv4 on the basis of FC-GQ-CNNs, and improves the positioning bounding box of YOLOv4: 1)aiming at the problem that there have no classification function in FC-GQ-CNNs, use the X-axis left-ray to match the coordinates of the grasp point with the positioning bounding box, determine the location bounding box of the grasp point and get the classification of the object; 2)aiming at the problem that because of the shape and position angle of the parts, the positioning bounding box overlap, so that the coordinate of the grasp point may fall into several positioning bounding boxes during the matching process, which causes the failure of classification, use Canny edge detection and others to improve the positioning bounding box to the minimum bounding rectangle frame, and input it into the coordinate matching system which can better represent the shape of the part, so as to improve the accuracy of object classification. In addition, instance segmentation may have better classification results, but most instance segmentation methods have disadvantages such as complex calculations and heavy workload, these problems can be further studied in the future.

Acknowledgement. This paper was funded by the National Natural Science Foundation of China (Grant No. 51775165).

References

1. Zeng, A., et al.: Multi-view self-supervised deep learning for 6D pose estimation in the amazon picking challenge. In: 2017 IEEE International Conference on Robotics and Automation (ICRA) (2017)
2. Billings, G., Johnson-Roberson, M.: SilhoNet: an RGB method for 3D object pose estimation and grasp planning (2018)
3. Miller, A.T., Knoop, S., Christensen, H.I., Allen, P.K.: Automatic grasp planning using shape primitives. In: 2003 IEEE International Conference on Robotics and Automation (Cat. No.03CH37422), vol. 2, pp. 1824–1829 (2003)
4. Vahrenkamp, N., Westkamp, L., Yamanobe, N.: Part-based grasp planning for familiar objects. In IEEE-RAS International Conference on Humanoid Robots, pp. 919–925 (2016)
5. Mahler, J., et al.: Dex-Net 2.0: deep learning to plan robust grasps with synthetic point clouds and analytic grasp metrics. In Robotics: Science and Systems 2017, vol. 13 (2017)
6. Ten Pas, A., Gualtieri, M., Saenko, K.: Grasp pose detection in point clouds. Int. J. Robot. Res. 36(13/14), 1455–1473 (2017)
7. Park, D., Chun, S.Y.: Classification based Grasp Detection using Spatial Transformer Network. arXiv Preprint https://arxiv.org/abs/1803.01356 (2018)
8. Guo, D., Kong, T., Sun, F., Liu, H.: Object discovery and grasp detection with a shared convolutional neural network. In 2016 IEEE International Conference on Robotics and Automation (ICRA), pp. 2038–2043 (2016)
9. Lenz, I., Lee, H., Saxena, A.: Deep learning for detecting robotic grasps. Int. J. Robot. Res. 34(4), 705–724 (2015)
10. Zeng, A., et al.: Robotic pick-and-place of novel objects in clutter with multi-affordance grasping and cross-domain image matching. In: 2018 IEEE International Conference on Robotics and Automation (ICRA), pp. 3750–3757 (2018)
11. Mahler, J., et al.: Dex-Net 1.0: A cloud-based network of 3D objects for robust grasp planning using a multi-armed bandit model with correlated rewards. In: 2016 IEEE International Conference on Robotics and Automation (ICRA), pp. 1957–1964 (2016)

12. Satish, V., Mahler, J., Goldberg, K.: On-policy dataset synthesis for learning robot grasping policies using fully convolutional deep networks. IEEE Robot. Autom. Lett. **4**(2), 1 (2019)
13. Long, J., Shelhamer, E., Darrell, T.: Fully convolutional networks for semantic segmentation. In: 2015 IEEE Conference on Computer Vision and Pattern Recognition (CVPR), pp. 3431–3440 (2015)
14. Bochkovskiy, A., Wang, C.-Y., Liao, H.-Y.M.: YOLOv4: Optimal Speed and Accuracy of Object Detection. arXiv Preprint https://arxiv.org/abs/2004.10934 (2020)
15. Yanpin, W., Yonghe, L.: The algorithm of using the method of radial to judge the points in flat in and out of the polygon. Shanxi Archit. **33**, 364–365 (2007)
16. Canny, J.: A computational approach to edge detection. IEEE Trans. Pattern Anal. Mach. Intell. **8**(6), 679–698 (1986)
17. Sklansky, J.: Finding the convex hull of a simple polygon. Pattern Recogn. Lett. **1**(2), 79–83 (1982)
18. Redmon, J., Farhadi, A.: YOLOv3: An Incremental Improvement. arXiv Preprint https://arxiv.org/abs/1804.02767 (2018)

Workspace Analysis of a Mobile Robot System for the Ship Section Painting

Shan Zhang[1] , Jinbo Qie[2], Zhufeng Shao[3,4(✉)], and Zheng Sun[1]

[1] Zaozhuang University, Zaozhuang 277160, China
[2] Shanghai Ship Technology Research Institute, Shanghai 200032, China
[3] State Key Laboratory of Tribology and, Institute of Manufacturing Engineering, Tsinghua University, Beijing 100084, China
shaozf@tsinghua.edu.cn
[4] Beijing Key Lab of Precision/Ultra-Precision Manufacturing Equipments and Control, Tsinghua University, Beijing 100084, China

Abstract. In order to implement the painting of large unstructured surface in the ship section, the mobile robot system consisting of an automatic guided vehicle (AGV), a scissors elevator, and a 6R industrial painting robot is proposed. To ensure the terminal accuracy and reduce the requirements on cooperative control, the intermittent operation mode will be adopted with the station planning. In order to facilitate the station planning, this paper carried out the analysis of the regular manipulating workspace for the system. Firstly, the reachable workspace is established with the homogeneous transformation matrix and the kinematic analysis. The singularity and accuracy is analyzed considering the distribution of the condition number. Based the projection, the interference is analyzed between the robot and other parts. Finally, boundaries of the regular workspace are formulated for the mobile robot system, which provides a solid foundation for the station planning and efficient painting.

Keywords: Mobile robot system · Kinematics · Interference · Manipulating workspace

1 Introduction

Industrial robots have been widely used in painting automobiles. However, for the huge ship surface, it is impossible for a industrial painting robot to cover all the area due to the limited workspace. A general solution is adopting a mobile platform to transport the robot to different locations [1]. Several automatic painting systems have been designed for large surface painting, such as MMPS [2] and RAFS [3]. Inspired by the above painting systems, to meet the unstructured surface painting requirements of huge ship sections, this paper proposed a mobile robot system consisting of an automatic guided vehicle (AGV), a scissors elevator, and a 6R industrial painting robot, which breaks through the limit of horizontal motion and takes into account the painting surface of ship bottom.

© Springer Nature Switzerland AG 2021
X.-J. Liu et al. (Eds.): ICIRA 2021, LNAI 13015, pp. 716–727, 2021.
https://doi.org/10.1007/978-3-030-89134-3_65

For the painting of large parts, the mobile platform is set to discrete locations in series [2, 5], and the robot paints the corresponding areas in sequence. The robot positions (stations) need to be planned to make full use of the workspace and paint the whole surface efficiently, and the process is usually called the station planning. Before the planning, it is necessary to establish the mapping between the robot base position and the terminal reachable pose of the robot, therefore, the system workspace analysis is the foundation [1, 6].

Workspace analysis of the industrial robot has been carried out considered positioning, orientation, and singularity [1]. Positioning constraints determine the reachable workspace, while the dexterous workspace is determined considering the orientation. Klein et al. [7] studied the relationship of the determinant, the condition number and the smallest singular value [8], and recommended the condition number in prevention of singularities [9].

The proposed mobile robot system is an integrated application of mature industrial products with good industrial foundation. This paper focused on its workspace analysis. AGV and the scissors elevator expand the reachable workspace of the industrial painting robot. At the same time, the painting robot may interfere with the AGV and other parts, so the interference need to be considered in the system workspace analysis. The common way to solve this problem is to transform the collision detection into the interference of 3D geometric model. Most of collision detection methods require the calculation of the minimum distance between robot and surrounding environment [10]. However, due to modeling in 3D space, the modeling process is complex, the derivation process of the minimum distance model is cumbersome, and the amount of calculation is large. To alleviate computational burden, methods to reduce dimensions like the projection method are employed to solve complicated problems [11]. In this paper, for the interference between the robot and the system, based the projection the 3D space interference is transformed into 2D plane interference by graphic transformation. The proposed method does not need to establish 3D geometric equations representing the robot link and obstacles. The modeling process is simple and the amount of calculation is greatly reduced.

This paper is organized as follows. Section 2 introduces the mobile robot system and illustrates the kinematic analysis. Section 3 studied the boundaries of the regular manipulating workspace. The conclusion is given in Sect. 4.

2   System Description and Kinematics

2.1   System Description

According to the requirements of the large unstructured surface painting in ship section, the mobile robot system is designed, as shown in Fig. 1. The system consists of an AGV, a scissors elevator, and a 6R industrial painting robot. The electrical control cabinet of the system is placed at the tail of AGV. The physical prototype of the mobile painting system is established as shown in Fig. 1(b). The AGV is a four-wheeled mobile platform to realize omnidirectional movement which has two steering wheels and two castor wheels. The two steering wheels are arranged diagonally. The scissors elevator is driven by two electric cylinders to realize vertical lifting with the range of 400 mm–2100 mm.

The EFORT GR680ST painting robot is adopted. The robot consists of 6 rotational joints to enable the 6 DOFs motion. The offset wrist is adopted and three rotational axes do not intersect in a point.

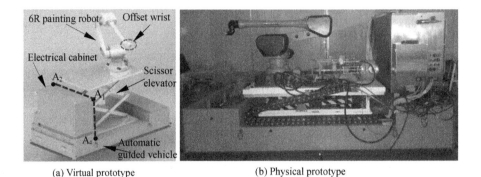

(a) Virtual prototype   (b) Physical prototype

Fig. 1. The mobile robot system for ship section painting.

2.2 Kinematic Analysis

The GR680ST robot was mounted on the mobile base composed of an AGV and an elevator. The base has three translational and one rotational DOFs. After the station planning, the AGV carries the industrial robot to the designated station, the elevator will raise the industrial robot up to the goal height, and the robot carry out the painting operation. This intermittent operation mode shows that the AGV and the scissors elevator just make the position and orientation change of the robot base according to the task requirements. The focus of the kinematic analysis is the 6R painting robot. The coordinate frame of the robot base is shown in Fig. 2(a). The Cartesian coordinate system O_0-$X_0Y_0Z_0$ is the global coordinate system, the O_r-$X_rY_rZ_r$ is the AGV centroid coordinate system. θ is the rotation angle of the robot base around the Z_0-axis, h is the distance between the base center and O_r point along Y_r-axis. Since the AGV moves on the horizontal plane, the transformation matrix of the 6R painting robot with respect to the global coordinate system can be derived:

$$
{}^b_0\mathbf{T} = \begin{bmatrix} c\theta & -s\theta & 0 & x_r - hs\theta \\ s\theta & c\theta & 0 & y_r + hc\theta \\ 0 & 0 & 1 & z_r \\ 0 & 0 & 0 & 0 \end{bmatrix}
\tag{1}
$$

where (x_r, y_r, z_r) is the position of O_r point, $s\theta = \sin\theta$, $c\theta = \cos\theta$.

Figure 2(b) shows the kinematic model of the GR680ST robot consisting of a 6R serial chain. Coordinate frames are assigned as in Fig. 2(b). They are established by the principle of Denavit-Hartenbarg (D-H) convention where Z_i is the direction of the motion for the corresponding joint. The D-H parameters are listed in Table 1. The forward kinematic equation can be expressed as

$$_0^6T = {}_0^bT\,_b^1T\,_1^2T\,_2^3T\,_3^4T\,_4^5T\,_5^6T \tag{2}$$

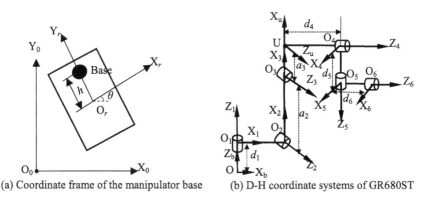

(a) Coordinate frame of the manipulator base   (b) D-H coordinate systems of GR680ST

Fig. 2. Kinematic model of the mobile robot system.

3 Workspace Analysis

Singularities should be avoided in painting tasks. Besides, due to the existence of electrical cabinet at the tail of AGV and other parts, the robot needs to avoid interference in the process of operation.

When the AGV and the scissors elevator keep the robot base at a certain position and posture, there are four factors that determine the manipulating workspace: (1) *Reachable workspace*: This mainly refers to the joint angle ranges of the first three axes; (2) *Orientation requirement*: This refers to the notion that the specified orientation must be achieved, which mainly depends on the manipulability of the wrist; (3) *Singularity and accuracy*: All the areas near the singularity should be avoided in the manipulating workspace; (4) *Interference*: The interference between the robot and other parts of the system is mainly considered.

According to Table 1, each joint of the offset wrist can rotate forward and backward 360°. In addition, the AGV can also rotate around the Z_0 axis, it can infer that the end effector has sufficiently motion ranges. Therefore, reachable workspace, singularity, and interference are considered in this section.

Table 1. D-H parameters of the 6-DOF painting robot.

Link (i)	a_{i-1}(mm)	$\alpha_{i-1}(°)$	d_i(mm)	θ_i	Joint rotation angle limitation(°)
1	0	0	598.6	θ_1	$-175° - 175°$
2	210	90	0	θ_2	$-60° - 170°$
3	1000	0	0	θ_3	$-80° - 125°$
4	115	90	1501	θ_4	$-360° - 360°$
5	0	-90	136.5	θ_5	$-360° - 360°$
6	0	90	88.5	θ_6	$-360° - 360°$

3.1 Reachable Workspace

Taking the point O_4 as the reference point, we can obtain the reachable workspace by using the geometry method. According to Subsect. 2.2, Eq. (1) can be transformed into $^b_0\mathbf{T} = Trans(x_b, y_b, z_b)Rot(z, \theta)$, where $x_b = x_r - hs\theta$, $y_b = y_r + hc\theta$, $z_b = z_r$. Equation (2) becomes $^6_0\mathbf{T} = Trans(x_b, y_b, z_b)Rot(z, \theta)^6_b\mathbf{T}$. Figure 3 shows the cross section of the reachable workspace for the mobile robot system in X- and Z-directions with respect to different z_b and θ.

Considering the motion range of the scissors elevator, the height variation range of the industrial robot base is [753 mm, 2453 mm]. Consequently, in Fig. 3(a), the curve 1, 2, and 3 are the workspace boundaries when the lifting height z_b is 753 mm, 1752 mm, and 2453 mm respectively, and $x_r = 0$, $y_r = 0$ and $\theta = 90°$. The curve 4 and 5 is the workspace boundary at $x_r = 500$ mm, -500 mm respectively, and $y_r = 0$, $z_b = 2453$ mm and $\theta = 90°$. In Fig. 3(b), the curve 6–11 are the workspace boundaries when $\theta = 0°, 30°, -30°, 60°, 90°$, and $-90°$ respectively, and $x_r = 0$, $y_r = 0$, $z_b = 2453$ mm.

From Fig. 3, the followings can be obtained: (1) From the curves 3–5, by using the AGV to move the robot base, the system workspace can reach 16m in X- and Y-directions; (2) From the curves 1–3, the system workspace can reach about 5.5 m in Z- direction, by using the scissors elevator to move the robot base; (3) Since the initial installation position and posture of the robot base are shown in Fig. 1(b), when θ_1 and θ are $0°$, the workspace is projected as a straight line 6 on the X-Z plane. In fact, the workspace boundary curve on this section is similar to curve 11; (4) From the curves 6–11, the rotation of AGV expands the system workspace and can effectively avoid interference with the environment.

3.2 Singularity and Accuracy Analysis

All the singularities and nearby areas should be avoided in the manipulating workspace. Klein et al. [7] recommended the condition number in prevention of singularities [8]. Define $k_s = 1/k(\mathbf{J})$ $(0 \leq k_s \leq 1)$, where $k(\mathbf{J}) = \sigma_{max}/\sigma_{min}$ is the condition number, σ_{min}, σ_{max} are the minimum and maximum singular values of the Jacobian matrix. k_s represents the distance from the position and posture point to the singular point. Meanwhile, $k(\mathbf{J})$ can be used as a practical measure of kinematic accuracy of a manipulator over its whole workspace. The robot is in a singular pose when k_s goes to 0, the greater the k_s, the farther

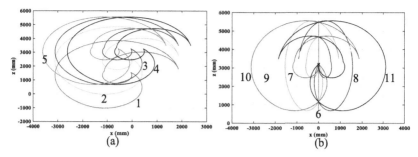

Fig. 3. Reachable workspace of the mobile robot system.

away from the singular pose, the better the robot terminal accuracy. Figure 4 shows k_s in the reachable workspace of the industrial robot. The region with better performance can be selected as the regular manipulating workspace to avoid singularity and improve terminal accuracy.

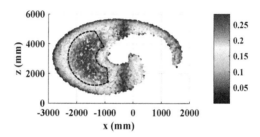

Fig. 4. k_s in the reachable workspace of the 6R industrial robot.

3.3 Interference Analysis

From Fig. 1, due to the limitation of the structure size, the 6R industrial robot may interfere with the AGV and the scissors elevator, which needs to be analyzed. To alleviate computational burden, based the projection the 3D space interference is transformed into 2D plane interference by graphic transformation. The interference analysis is carried out separately as follows:

(1) Interference between the robot end-effector and the system.

During the lifting of the elevator, the robot end effector may interfere with the electrical cabinet and other parts. The interference analysis between the 6R robot end effector and the system is to identify whether the reachable workspace of the robot overlap with the system. Figure 5 shows this kind of interference. The curves 1−3 are the workspace boundaries at the XOZ plane when the lifting height is 753 mm, 1752 mm and 2453 mm respectively, and $x_r = 0$, $y_r = 0$, $\theta = 0°$ and $\theta_1 = 90°$. The projection of electrical cabinet is rectangle 4; the projection of front end of the AGV is straight line segment 5; the projection of scissors elevator platform from 753 mm to 2453 mm is rectangle 6. This interference could be avoided by defining an unusable region as the area on the right of dotted line segment 7 in the Fig. 5.

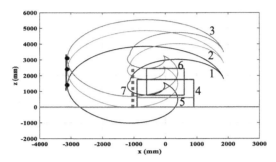

Fig. 5. Interference analysis of the robot system considering the end effector.

(2) Interference between the robot links and the system.

This kind of interference mainly analyzes the interference between the forearm and the electrical cabinet. The forearm is simplified as a cylindrical rod, and the length of the rod is from U to O_4. Electrical cabinet can be simplified into a cuboid, as shown in Fig. 1. Hence, this kind of interference is to analyze the interference between the cylindrical rod and the edge A_1A_2, A_1A_4, A_2A_3.

First of all, the interference between the cylindrical rod and the edge A_1A_2 is as follows. Project the cylindrical rod and the edge A_1A_2 on the XOY plane, YOZ plane and XOZ plane, separately, as shown in Fig. 6(a)–6(c). Only when the interference conditions of projection on three planes are satisfied, the interference between the cylindrical rod and the edge A_1A_2 occurs. The other two cases is the same.

From Fig. 6(a), if UO_4 in the XOY plane intersects with M_2M_1, the forearm may interfere with electrical cabinet. The interference condition is as follows:

$$-600 \leq \frac{1011\sin(\theta_1 + \theta) + h\sin\theta_1}{\cos(\theta_1 + \theta)} \leq 900 \tag{3}$$

When $\theta = 0°$, θ_1 satisfying inequality (3) is $[-175°, -169°]$, $[-23°, 32°]$, and $[157°, 175°]$.

From Fig. 6(b), if UO_4 in YOZ plane passes through M_3, the forearm may interfere with electrical cabinet. The interference condition can be simplified as $O_{4y} \leq -1011$, when θ_1 is $[-175°, -169°]$ and $[157°, 175°]$, θ_3 is $[-80°, 125°]$, and θ_2 is $[8.59°, 108.86°]$, the forearm may interfere with electrical cabinet.

From Fig. 6(c), if UO_4 in XOZ plane intersects with M_5M_4, the forearm may interfere with electrical cabinet. The interference condition is as follows:

$$-200 \leq s1[-\tan23z_r + g_1 \leq 900] \tag{4}$$

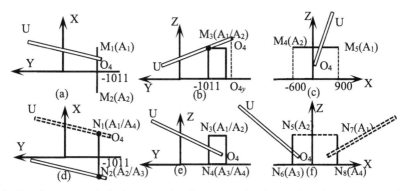

Fig. 6. Interference analysis between the forearm and edge A_1A_2, the forearm and edge A_1A_4/A_2A_3.

where $g_1 = -a_1 - a_3c23 - a_2c2 - tan23(a_3s23 + a_2s2 - 1153.4)$ $si = \sin\theta i$, $ci = \cos\theta i$, $sij = \sin(\theta i + \theta j)$, $cij = \cos(\theta i + \theta j)$. Combined with the above interference analysis results, this situation is analyzed as follows:

θ_1 is $[157°, 175°]$, inequality (4) can be changed to $-200/\sin\theta_1 \leq -tan23z_r + g_1 \leq 1300/\sin\theta_1$, then calculate $-tan23z_r + g_1$ as in Fig. 7(a)–(c) −. After traversing θ_2 and θ_3, the blank area is that does not meet the inequality (4). From Fig. 7(a)–(c) −, as the robot is raised, θ_3 decreases, which makes the forearm interfere with A_1A_2.

θ_1 is $[-175°, -169°]$, inequality (4) can be changed to $1300/\sin\theta_1 \leq -tan23z_r + g_1 \leq -200/\sin\theta_1$, then calculate $-tan23z_r + g_1$ as in Fig. 7(d)–(f). After traversing θ_2 and θ_3, the blank area is that does not meet the inequality (4). As the robot is raised, θ_3 decreases, which makes the forearm interfere with the edge A_1A_2.

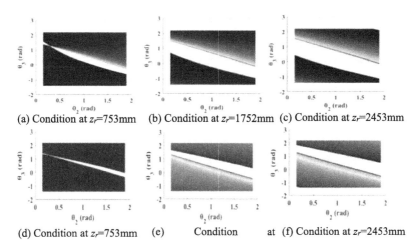

(a) Condition at z_r=753mm   (b) Condition at z_r=1752mm   (c) Condition at z_r=2453mm

(d) Condition at z_r=753mm   (e)   Condition   at   (f) Condition at z_r=2453mm

Fig. 7. The judging condition of inequality (4) when θ_1 is $[157°, 175°]$ and $[-175°, -169°]$.

Summing up the three cases in Fig. 6(a)–(c), θ_1 is $[-175°, -169°]$ and $[157°, 175°]$, the forearm may interfere with A_1A_2. Therefore, this kind of interference can be effectively avoided by establishing θ_1 as $[-150°, 150°]$.

Secondly, the interference between the cylindrical rod and A_1A_4, A_2A_3 is as follows. Such interference is projected onto XOY, YOZ and XOZ plane, as in Fig. 6(d)–(f).

From Fig. 6(d), if UO_4 passes through N_2 or N_1 in XOY plane, the forearm may interfere with electrical cabinet. The interference conditions can be simplified as

$$-1011 = \frac{600c1 + hs1}{s1} \tag{5}$$

$$-1011 = \frac{-900c1 + hs1}{s1} \tag{6}$$

From Fig. 6(e), if UO_4 in YOZ plane intersects with N_3N_4, the forearm may interfere with electrical cabinet. The interference condition is as follows:

$$373 \leq g_3 + \frac{(1011 + h)\cot 23}{c1} \leq 1752 \tag{7}$$

where $g_3 = z_r + a_2 s2 + a_3 s23 + \cot 23(a_3 c23 + a_2 c2 + 210) + d_1$. From Fig. 6(f), if UO_4 intersects with N_5N_6, or N_7N_8, the forearm may interfere the electrical cabinet, and the conditions are as follows:

$$373 \leq g_3 - \frac{600\cot 23}{s1} \leq 1752 \tag{8}$$

$$373 \leq g_3 + \frac{900\cot 23}{s1} \leq 1752 \tag{9}$$

For the interference between A_1A_4 and forearm, θ_2 and θ_3 satisfying inequality (7) and (8) can be obtained through simulation, as in Fig. 8. Figure 8(a)–(c) are at $\theta_1 = 156.96°$, Fig. 8(d)–(f) are at $\theta_1 = -23.04°$. The green area is where A_1A_4 interferes with forearm. As the robot is raised, the interference between A_1A_4 and forearm becomes smaller.

For the interference between A_2A_3 and the forearm, θ_2 and θ_3 satisfying inequality (7) and (9) can be obtained through simulation as in Fig. 9. Figure 9(a)–(c) are at $\theta_1 = 32.53°$, Fig. 9(d)–(f) are at $\theta_1 = -147.47°$. The green area is θ_2 and θ_3 at which A_2A_3 interferes with forearm. Summing up the three cases in Fig. 6(d)–(f), θ_1 are equal to $156.96°/-23.04°$, $32.53°/-147.47°$, the forearm may interfere with A_1A_4 and A_2A_3.

In summary, the interference between forearm and electrical cabinet can be effectively avoided by establishing θ_1 as $[-140°, 140°]$, but when θ_1 is $-23.04°/32.53°$, θ_2 and θ_3 should be checked. Actually, the interference between forearm and the front end of the AGV also needs to considered, but by using the above analysis method, the interference will not occur when θ_1 is $[-140°, 140°]$.

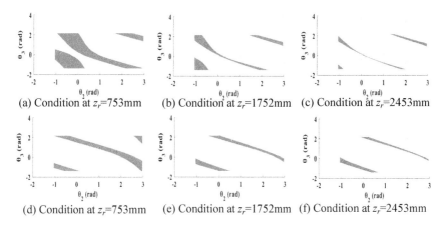

(a) Condition at z_r=753mm   (b) Condition at z_r=1752mm   (c) Condition at z_r=2453mm

(d) Condition at z_r=753mm   (e) Condition at z_r=1752mm   (f) Condition at z_r=2453mm

Fig. 8. Interference analysis between the forearm and edge A_1A_4 at $\theta_1 = 156.96°/-23.04°$.

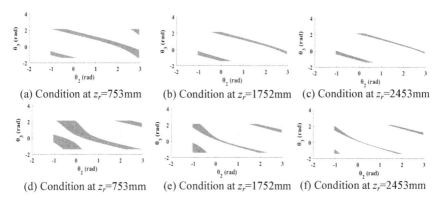

(a) Condition at z_r=753mm   (b) Condition at z_r=1752mm   (c) Condition at z_r=2453mm

(d) Condition at z_r=753mm   (e) Condition at z_r=1752mm   (f) Condition at z_r=2453mm

Fig. 9. Interference analysis between the forearm and edge A_2A_3 at $\theta_1 = 32.53°/-147.47°$.

3.4 Manipulating Workspace

By synthesizing the above conditions, the cross section of the system regular manipulating workspace in X- and Z-directions is shown in Fig. 10. According to the rotation range of joint 1([−140°, 140°]), the regular manipulating workspace can be established. Curves 1–3 are the manipulating workspace boundaries when the lifting height is 753 mm, 1752 mm and 2453 mm respectively, and $x_r = 0$, $y_r = 0$ and $\theta = 90°$. The shape of the manipulating workspace formed by different positions of the robot base is similar, so just list the boundary equation of curve 1. Curve 1–c and 1-d are parts of a circle, their centers are (−550 mm, 1351 mm), (−1200 mm, 1351 mm), their radii are 1000 mm, and 1450 mm, the boundary equation of outer circle curve 1-d is

$$\begin{cases} x = -1200 + 1450\,cos\theta_{10} \\ z = 1351 + 1450\,sin\theta_{10} \end{cases} \tag{10}$$

726   S. Zhang et al.

The boundary equation of inner circle curve 1–c is

$$\begin{cases} x = -550 + 1000\,cos\theta_{20} \\ z = 1351 + 1000\,sin\theta_{20} \end{cases} \tag{11}$$

where θ_{10} is from $[90°, 270°]$, θ_{20} is from $[130°, 240°]$.
The line segment 1-a equation is

$$\begin{cases} z = -94083x + 1.11e5 \\ x \in (-1200mm, -1192.8mm) \end{cases} \tag{12}$$

The line segment 1-b equation is

$$\begin{cases} z = 3.07x + 3769.6 \\ x \in (-1260.3mm, -1067.1mm) \end{cases} \tag{13}$$

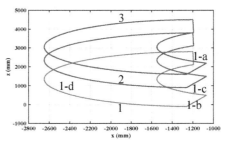

Fig. 10. Manipulating workspace of the mobile robot system.

4 Conclusions

This paper presents a visualization method to determine a regular manipulating workspace of the mobile robot system for ship section painting. Based on the homogeneous transformation matrix of the kinematics, the system reachable workspace is obtained. Based on the condition number distribution, the regular manipulating workspace is determined considering singularity and accuracy. Through the interference analysis between the 6R robot and other parts, θ_1 is determined as $[-140°, 140°]$. Finally, the regular manipulating workspace are formulated, which makes the boundary position clear, and provides great convenience for station planning.

Acknowledgment. This work was financially supported by the Joint Funds of the National Natural Science Foundation of China (Grant No. U19A20101) and High-tech Ship Project of the Ministry of Industry and Information Technology of China (Grant No. MC-201906-Z01).

References

1. Wang, G., Yu, Q., Ren, T., Hua, X., Chen, K.: Task planning for mobile painting manipulators based on manipulating space. Assembly. Autom. **38**(1), 57–66 (2017)
2. Ren, S., Yang, X., Xu, J., Wang, G., Xie, Y., Chen, K.: Determination of the base position and working area for mobile manipulators. Assembly. Autom. **36**(1), 80–88 (2016)
3. Seegmiller, N., Bailiff, J., Franks, R.: Precision robotic coating application and thickness control optimization for F-35 final finishes. SAE Int. J. Aerosp. **2**(1), 284–290 (2010)
4. Ren, S., Xie, Y., Yang, X., Xu, J., Wang, G., Chen, K.: A method for optimizing the base position of mobile painting manipulators. IEEE Autom. Sci. Eng. **14**(1), 370–375 (2017)
5. Yu, Q., Wang, G., Hua, X., Chen, K.: Base position optimization for mobile painting robot manipulators with multiple constraints. Robot. Cim-int. Manuf. **54**, 56–64 (2018)
6. Ceccarelli, M.: Workspace analysis and design of open-chain manipulator. In: Proceedings of AIP Conference, pp. 388–405. MD, USA (1998)
7. Klein, C.A., Blaho, B.E.: Dexterity measures for the design and control of kinematically redundant manipulators. Int. J. Robot. Res. **6**(2), 72–83 (1987)
8. Zacharias, F., Borst, C., Hirzinger, G.: Capturing robot workspace structure: representing robot capabilities. In: IEEE/RSJ International Conference on Intelligent Robots & Systems, pp.3229–3236. IEEE, San Diego (2007)
9. Pamanes, G., Zeghloul, S.: Optimal placement of robotic manipulators using multiple kinematic criteria. In: 1991 IEEE International Conference on Robotics and Automation, pp.933–938. IEEE, Sacramento (1991)
10. Safeea, M., Neto, P., Bearee, R.: Efficient calculation of minimum distance between capsules and its use in robotics. IEEE Access. **7**, 5368–5373 (2019)
11. Xing, D., Liu, F., Liu, S., Xu, D.: Motion control for cylindrical objects in microscope's view using a projection method—II: collision avoidance with reduced dimensional guidance. Ieee. T. Ind. Electron. **64**(7), 5534–5544 (2017)

Kinematics of a One-DOF Four-Finger Gripper Constructed with Two-Fold Symmetric Bricard Linkages

Kunjing Chen, Fufu Yang[✉], and Jun Zhang

School of Mechanical Engineering and Automation, Fuzhou University, Fuzhou 350100, China
yangfufu@fzu.edu.cn

Abstract. Gripper, contacting with the workpiece directly, is one of most important parts in robot, has thus attracted the attention of many scholars. The function and working efficiency are always determined by its structure to a great extent. However, the existed grippers either are composed with many parts or requires a complicated process to produce, which renders the grippers be not easy to use and always with high-cost. In this paper, we proposed a one-DOF network with four Bricard 6R linkages. The mobility-, singularity-, and kinematics- analysis shows that the mechanism has great potential to realize the function of a simple gripper by the compliant mechanism technique, and a physical prototype with 3D printing also verified the design and analysis. This work gives an idea for simplifying the manufacture of grippers, and will reduce the cost greatly.

Keywords: Gripper · Mobility analysis · Singularity · Kinematic analysis

1 Introduction

As a typical form of end effector for manipulators or robots, there is a diverse development trend of grippers due to the diversity of functional requirements, which has attracted widespread attention of scholars [1–3].

In order to adapt to various objects with different rigidity, many adaptive control algorithms are introduced into the manipulator. Yang et al. [4] presented an extreme learning machine (ELM)-based control scheme for uncertain robot manipulate or stop perform haptic identification. Cao and Liu [5] consider a boundary control problem for a constrained two-link rigid-flexible manipulator. Zhou et al. [6] developed an observer-based adaptive boundary iterative learning control method. In recent years, in order to adapt to various target objects, scholars have turned their attention to flexible manipulators with foldable and bionic structures. Shintake et al. [7] summarized most soft robotic grippers. Jeong and Lee [8] introduced a new three-finger manipulator based on origami twisted tower design. Shang et al. [9] proposed a new type of adjustable stiffness

Financial supports from the National Natural Science Foundation of China (Project No. 51905101) and the Natural Science Foundation of Fujian Province, China (Project No. 2019J01209) are acknowledged.

X.-J. Liu et al. (Eds.): ICIRA 2021, LNAI 13015, pp. 728–738, 2021.
https://doi.org/10.1007/978-3-030-89134-3_66

and foldable manipulator for minimally invasive surgery. Zhang et al. [10] introduced a design and manufacturing method of a pneumatic flexible manipulator arm based on a 3D printed origami skeleton. Laschi et al. [11] proposed a soft robotic arm. Meng et al. [12] proposed a bionic exoskeleton manipulator based on flexible hinges.

However, the above-mentioned manipulators are either assembled of many rigid parts, or require a complicated process to produce, which will affect the manufacturing cost, reliability and stability. As we know, spatial single freedom over-constraint mechanisms [13] have the advantages of simple structure and good rigidity. If introducing the compliant mechanism technique to the network of overconstrained linkages to realize the grasping function, the design and manufacture will be greatly simplified. Therefore, we choose a typical overconstrained linkage with great symmetries, two-fold symmetric Bricard 6R linkage [14], to construct a one-DOF gripper.

This paper will study its feasibility from the perspective of mechanism kinematics. The layout of this paper is as follows. Section 2 introduces the geometric conditions and characteristics of the two-fold symmetric Bricard 6R linkage. In Sect. 3, a network with four two-fold symmetric Bricard 6R linkages is designed for the potential use of the gripper by the compliant mechanism technique. Mobility of the mechanism is analyzed in Sect. 4. Singularity and kinematics are carried out in Sects. 5, and 6, respectively, to show the folding properties, and a physical prototype is fabricated to demonstrated the design. Final conclusions are drawn in Sect. 7.

2 Two-Fold Symmetric Bricard Linkage

2.1 Geometric Conditions

The two-fold symmetric Bricard linkage, see Fig. 1, is a one-DOF single-loop overconstrained mechanism composed of six links and six revolute joints (R-joints), in which there are two symmetric planes for these R-joints. The geometric conditions are

$$\alpha_{12} = \alpha_{45} = \alpha, \alpha_{34} = \alpha_{61} = \beta = 2\pi - \alpha, \ \alpha_{23} = -\alpha_{56} = \gamma. \tag{1a}$$

$$a_{12} = a_{34} = a_{45} = a_{61} = a, \ a_{23} = a_{56} = 0. \tag{1b}$$

$$R_1 = R_4 = 0, \ R_2 = R_5 = -r, R_3 = R_6 = r.(|BP| = |CP| = |EQ| = |FQ| = r) \tag{1c}$$

The coordinate frames are set up by the D-H notation [15]. Here, a, r, α, γ are the geometrical parameters of the linkage.

2.2 Kinematic Equation

According to [14], two-fold symmetric Bricard linkage usually has three motion modes, i.e., twofold symmetric 6R motion mode, plane symmetric 6R motion mode and spherical 4R motion mode. The kinematic equations are:
(1) two-fold symmetric 6R motion mode

$$\theta_5 = \theta_3, \ \theta_6 = \theta_2, \ \theta_4 = \theta_1, \ \theta_3 = \theta_2 + \pi, \ \tan(\theta_1/2) = D/E. \tag{2}$$

(2) plane symmetric 6R motion mode

$$\theta_5 = \theta_3, \ \theta_6 = \theta_2, \ \tan(\theta_3/2) = C/F, \ \tan(\theta_1/2) = G/H, \ \tan(\theta_4/2) = I/J. \quad (3)$$

(3) spherical 4R motion mode

$$\sin\phi_{23}\sin\phi_{35}\cos\phi_{35}\cos(\theta_2 - \psi) - \left(\begin{array}{l}\sin\phi_{23}\cos\phi_{35} \\ + \cos\phi_{23}\sin\phi_{35}\cos(\theta_2 - \psi)\end{array}\right)L_1 . \quad (4a)$$
$$- \sin\phi_{35}\sin(\theta_2 - \psi)L_2 - \cos\phi_{23}\cos^2\phi_{35} + \cos\phi_{23} = 0$$

$$\theta_5 = \theta_2 + \pi \text{ or } \theta_5 = 2\psi - \theta_2 + p, \quad (4b)$$

$$\sin\phi_{35}\sin\phi_{23}\cos\phi_{23}\cos(\theta_2 - \psi) + \left(\begin{array}{l}\sin\phi_{23}\cos\phi_{23} \\ \sin^2\phi_{23}\cot\phi_{35}\cos(\theta_2 - \psi)\end{array}\right)M_1 . \quad (4c)$$
$$+ \frac{\sin^2\phi_{23}}{\sin\phi_{35}}\sin(\theta_2 - \psi)M_2 - \cos\phi_{35}\cos^2\phi_{23} + \cos\phi_{35} = 0$$

in which $C, D, E, F, G, H, I, J, \phi_{23}, \phi_{35}, \psi, L_1, L_2, M_1$, and M_2 can be found in [14].

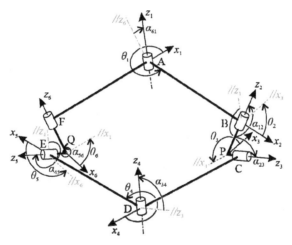

Fig. 1. The two-fold symmetric Bricard linkage

3   The Network of Four Two-Fold Symmetric Bricard Linkages

Since the final target is to construct a one-DOF gripper by a network of two-fold symmetric Bricard linkages using the technique of flexible mechanism [16], the facilitation of fabrication will be considered. One of the most common ways is to mill in propene polymer panels, in which the thick slices are links and the thin ones are to realise the function of R-joints. Therefore, the axes of R-joints are eighter parallel to the panel or perpendicular to it. A design for the milling model is given in Fig. 2(a), where dotted lines represent the revolute axes paralleling to the panel and a dot in a circle represents the one perpendicular to the panel. It is easy to find that the model is a network of four two-fold symmetric Bricard linkages, please see Fig. 2(c) for the linkage, in the form of 2×2 arrays and there are 17 links (divided by R-joints) whose schematic diagram unit is shown in Fig. 2(b). According to the definition of parameters in the previous section, $\alpha = 3\pi/2$ and $\gamma = \pi/2$ here.

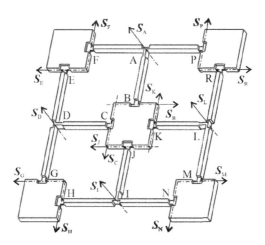

(a) The model for the flexible mechanism

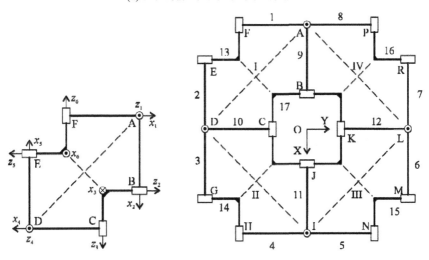

(b) Single two-fold symmetric Bricard linkage unit   (c) Structure diagram

Fig. 2. Four-fingers gripper

In this mechanism, links 13, 14, 15, and 16 can be viewed as four fingers and link 17 is the palm of the gripper. Mobility and kinematics will be studied as follows to evaluate the property of the mechanism showing the potential as a gripper.

4 Degree of Freedom Analysis

According to the theory of topology, each loop of the mechanism can be described by a plane polygon, where the vertices represent the links of the mechanism, and the edges represent the joints. By making the same vertices and edges coincide, the polygons of the loop can be merged into a plane graph [17]. The mechanism contains 17 links, 16 R-joints, and there are 4 basic loops I, II, III, and IV, please see Fig. 3. Among them, the links are labeled with numbers, and the joints with capital letters.

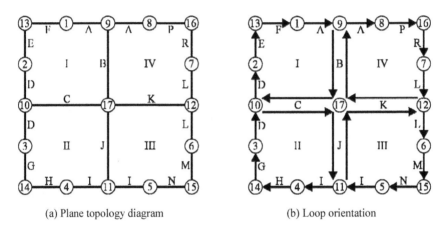

(a) Plane topology diagram   (b) Loop orientation

Fig. 3. Plane topology and loop orientation of the four-finger gripper

Take the center of the member 17 as the origin O, the $\overrightarrow{BJ}$ direction as the X axis, and the $\overrightarrow{CK}$ direction as the Y axis, the global coordinate system O-XYZ is established, as shown in Fig. 2(b). Here, $a = 15$ mm and $r = 5$ mm are adopted. Therefore, the coordinate values of each point of the mechanism are,

$$A = (-20, 0, 0)^T, \ B = (-5, 0, 0)^T, \ C = (0, -5, 0)^T, \ D = (0, -20, 0)^T, \quad (5a)$$

$$E = (-15, -20, 0)^T, \ F = (-20, -15, 0)^T, \ G = (15, -20, 0)^T, \ H = (20, -15, 0)^T, \quad (5b)$$

$$I = (20, 0, 0)^T, \ J = (5, 0, 0)^T, \ K = (0, 5, 0)^T, \ L = (0, 20, 0)^T, \quad (5c)$$

$$M = (15, 20, 0)^T, \ N = (20, 15, 0)^T, \ R = (-15, 20, 0)^T, \ P = (-20, 15, 0)^T. \quad (5d)$$

Then, the screws [18] of the R-joints are,

$$S_A = (0, 0, 1, 0, 20, 0)^T, \ S_B = (0, 1, 0, 0, 0, -5)^T, \ S_C = (1, 0, 0, 0, 0, 5)^T, \quad (6a)$$

$$S_D = (0, 0, 1, -20, 0, 0)^T, \; S_E = (0, -1, 0, 0, 0, 15)^T, \; S_F = (-1, 0, 0, 0, 0, -15)^T,$$
(6b)

$$S_G = (0, -1, 0, 0, 0, -15)^T, \; S_H = (1, 0, 0, 0, 0, 15)^T, \; S_I = (0, 0, 1, 0, -20, 0)^T,$$
(6c)

$$S_J = (0, -1, 0, 0, 0, -5)^T, \; S_K = (-1, 0, 0, 0, 0, 5)^T, \; S_L = (0, 0, 1, 20, 0, 0)^T,$$
(6d)

$$S_M = (0, 1, 0, 0, 0, 15)^T, \; S_N = (1, 0, 0, 0, 0, -15)^T, \; S_R = (0, 1, 0, 0, 0, -15)^T,$$
(6e)

$$S_P = (-1, 0, 0, 0, 0, 15)^T.$$
(6f)

According to [17], the kinematic constraint equations are,

$$\omega_A S_A + \omega_B S_B + \omega_C S_C + \omega_D S_D + \omega_E S_E + \omega_F S_F = 0,$$
(7a)

$$-\omega_C S_C + \omega_D S_D + \omega_G S_G + \omega_H S_H + \omega_I S_I - \omega_J S_J = 0,$$
(7b)

$$\omega_I S_I + \omega_J S_J + \omega_K S_K + \omega_L S_L + \omega_M S_M + \omega_N S_N = 0,$$
(7c)

$$\omega_A S_A - \omega_B S_B - \omega_K S_K + \omega_L S_L + \omega_R S_R + \omega_P S_P = 0.$$
(7d)

where ω_i represents the angular velocity of R-joint i, and it can be written as

$$H_{24 \times 16} \cdot \omega_{16 \times 1} = 0.$$
(8)

By the calculation in MATLAB,

$$rank(\omega) = 16 - rank(H_{24 \times 16}) = 16 - 15 = 1.$$
(9)

Therefore, the degree of freedom of the mechanism at this position is one.

5 Singularity Analysis

Since the mobility obtained above is instantaneous at the planar configuration while the two-fold symmetric Bricard 6R linkage has three motion modes, it is difficult to determine the motion path directly. Here, the truss-transformation method [19] will be employed to analyze the motion numerically, namely, the mechanism will be transformed to a mobile truss which is kinematically equivalent to the original mechanism, numerical approaches will then be carried out to the equivalent matrix to predict the next configuration, and an algorithm is required to modify the predict configurations, please see refs. [19–21] for details.

By the truss transformation, the mechanism is equivalently transformed into the truss form shown in Fig. 4. Among them, the model contains three types of bar-shaped truss

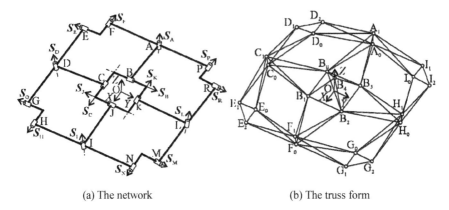

(a) The network   (b) The truss form

Fig. 4. The mechanism and its truss form

transformations, namely tetrahedron, triangle and pentahedron. For example, link AB is equivalent to tetrahedron $A_0A_1B_0B_3$, link EF is equivalent to triangle $D_0D_1D_2$, and link BCJK is equivalent to pentahedron $B_0B_1B_2B_3B_4$. Since coordinate values of all vertices and all joint axes are known, the equivalent matrix [20] could be established. Then, the motion animation is simulated by dealing with the equivalent matrix. Meanwhile, the singular value decomposition (SVD) method is also carried out to the equivalent matrix to reflect the singularity, and the last three singular values are recorded in Fig. 5.

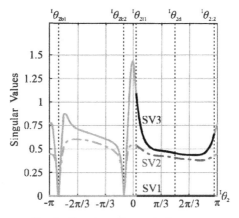

Fig. 5. Singular value analysis curves

It can be seen that the first singular value SV1 is always zero, indicating that the mechanism is mobile. At the same time, when the mechanism moves on the motion trajectory, the second singular value SV2 and the third singular value SV3 trend to zero twice, $^1\theta_{2b1} = -2.80$ and $^1\theta_{2b2} = -0.34$, indicating that the mobility uncertainty increases with motion singularity.

However, according to the result of simulation, there is no bifurcation path at both of these two configurations, namely, the folding process is determined one. Meanwhile, the range of the effective gripping area for the input parameter $^I\theta_2$ is $[^I\theta_{2f1},\,^I\theta_{2f2}]$ considering physical interference, where $^I\theta_{2f1}$ and $^I\theta_{2f2}$ indicate the folding configurations and are determined by physical models, $^I\theta_{2f2}$ is close but smaller than π while $^I\theta_{2f1}$ is close but larger than zero. $^I\theta_{2d} = \pi/2$ represents the deploying configuration, namely, the planar one, see Fig. 2. Therefore, the singular points $^I\theta_{2b1}$ and $^I\theta_{2b2}$ belong to the interference zone of the mechanism.

6 Kinematic Analysis

In order to further analyze the overall motion law of the four-finger gripper analytically, the coordinate system i-xyz is established according to the D-H method [15] in each Bricard mechanism unit, as shown in Fig. 6. Among them, the design parameters of units I and III are $\alpha^{I(III)} = 3\pi/2$ and $\gamma^{I(III)} = \pi/2$, respectively, and are $\alpha^{II(IV)} = \pi/2$ and $\gamma^{I(III)} = \pi/2$ for II and IV, respectively. At the same time, define $^j\theta_i$ to represent the i-th joint variable of the j-th unit, $i = 1, 2, 3, 4, 5, 6, j = $ I, II, III, IV. For example, $^I\theta_2$ represents the second joint variable of the first unit.

According to the simulation and the singularity analysis in the above section, all Bricard linkages moves in the two-fold symmetric $6R$ motion mode, and no movement bifurcation occurs. Therefore, according to the two-fold symmetry $6R$ mode equation of the two-fold symmetric Bricard linkage,

$$^I\theta_2 =\,^I\theta_6,\ ^I\theta_3 =\,^I\theta_5 =\,^I\theta_2 + \pi,\ ^I\theta_1 =\,^I\theta_4 = -2\arctan\left(\sin\,^I\theta_2\right). \tag{10a}$$

$$^{II}\theta_2 =\,^{II}\theta_6,\ ^{II}\theta_3 =\,^{II}\theta_5 =\,^{II}\theta_2 + \pi,\ ^{II}\theta_1 =\,^{II}\theta_4 = 2\arctan\left(\sin\,^{II}\theta_2\right). \tag{10b}$$

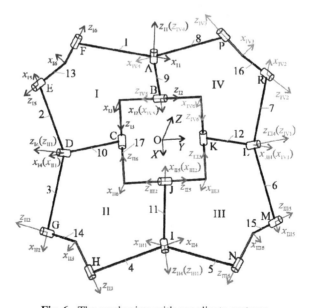

Fig. 6. The mechanism with coordinate systems.

$$^{III}\theta_2 = {}^{III}\theta_6, \ ^{III}\theta_3 = {}^{III}\theta_5 = {}^{III}\theta_2 + \pi, \ ^{III}\theta_1 = {}^{III}\theta_4 = -2\arctan\left(\sin^{III}\theta_2\right). \quad (10c)$$

$$^{IV}\theta_2 = {}^{IV}\theta_6, \ ^{IV}\theta_3 = {}^{IV}\theta_5 = {}^{IV}\theta_2 + \pi, \ ^{IV}\theta_1 = {}^{IV}\theta_4 = 2\arctan\left(\sin^{IV}\theta_2\right). \quad (10d)$$

(1) (1) Since the coordinate system 4 of unit I and the coordinate system 1 of unit II belong to the same coordinate system, so

$$^{I}T_{40} = {}^{I}T_{30} \cdot {}^{I}T_{43} = {}^{II}T_{60} \cdot {}^{II}T_{16}. \quad (11)$$

Therefore, $^{II}\theta_2 = \pi - {}^{I}\theta_2$. In the same way, we can also get $^{IV}\theta_2 = \pi - {}^{III}\theta_2$.

(2) Due to

$$^{III}T_{20} = {}^{II}T_{60} \cdot {}^{II}T_{56} \cdot T(0, 0, 0, \pi) = {}^{III}T_{30} \cdot {}^{III}T_{23}, \quad (12)$$

Therefore, $^{II}\theta_2 = \pi - {}^{III}\theta_2$. Similarly, we can also get $^{IV}\theta_2 = \pi - {}^{I}\theta_2$.

(3) In summary, we can get

$$^{I}\theta_2 = {}^{III}\theta_2 = \pi - {}^{II}\theta_2 = \pi - {}^{IV}\theta_2. \quad (13)$$

Therefore, the motion characteristics of the four-finger gripper can be determined by Eqs. (10a)–(10d) and (13). In addition, each kinematic joint variable of the mechanism is uniquely determined by $^{I}\theta_2$, and has nothing to do with the linkage parameters a and r.

According to result above and the conclusion of the previous section, the kinematic curve of the four-finger gripper can both be obtained, as shown in Fig. 7. It can be seen that the I and III units of the four-finger gripper have the same movement laws, while the II and IV units have the same movement laws.

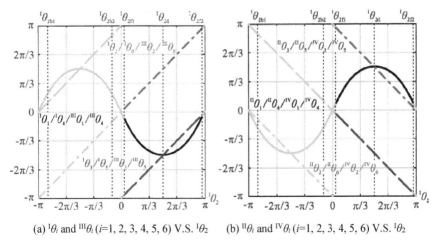

(a) $^{I}\theta_i$ and $^{III}\theta_i$ (i=1, 2, 3, 4, 5, 6) V.S. $^{I}\theta_2$ (b) $^{II}\theta_i$ and $^{IV}\theta_i$ (i=1, 2, 3, 4, 5, 6) V.S. $^{I}\theta_2$

Fig. 7. Kinematic curves of four-finger gripper.

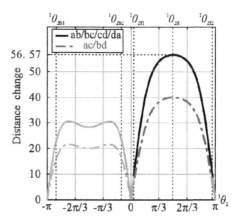

Fig. 8. The distances among fingers

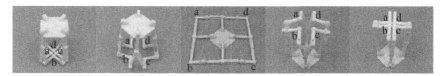

Fig. 9. The prototype with parameters $\alpha = 3\pi/2$, $\gamma = \pi/2$, $a = 54$ mm, $r = 35$ mm

In order to evaluate the potential of grasping of the mechanism, the distances among four fingers, ab, bc, cd, da, ac, and bd are calculated, as shown in Fig. 8. It can be found that when $^1\theta_2$ approaches $^1\theta_{2f1}$ and $^1\theta_{2f2}$, the distances are both close to zero, which indicates that the gripper is grasping the target object tightly. When $^1\theta_2$ approaches $^1\theta_{2d}$, the gripping point distance is the maximum, which indicates that the gripper returns to the released state, please see Fig. 8 for details. Finally, a prototype is fabricated to show the folding process, where the design parameters are $\alpha = 3\pi/2$, $\gamma = \pi/2$, $a = 54$ mm, $r = 35$ mm, see Fig. 9.

7   Conclusions

In this paper, a network is constructed with four two-fold symmetric Bricard $6R$ linkages. By mobility analysis, singularity analysis, kinematic derivation, and physical prototype, we found that the network exhibits excellent grasping properties. Therefore, the network has the potential to realize a one-DOF gripper, especially using flexible mechanism. In the future, we will design and fabricate a gripper by the compliant mechanism technique based on the proposed mechanism.

References

1. Kocabas, H.: Gripper design with spherical parallelogram mechanism. J Mech. Des. **131**(7), 075001-1-075001–9 (2009)
2. Lu, Y., Zhang, C.G., Cao, C.J., et al.: Kinematics and dynamics of a novel hybrid manipulator. Proc. Inst. Mech. Eng., Part C: J. Mech. Eng. Sci. **230**(10), 1644–1657 (2016)

3. Xu, D., Li, E., Liang, Z., Gao, Z.: Design and tension modeling of a novel cable-driven rigid snake-like manipulator. J. Intell. Rob. Syst. **99**(2), 211–228 (2020). https://doi.org/10.1007/s10846-019-01115-w

4. Yang, C.G., Huang, K.X., Cheng, H., et al.: Haptic identification by ELM-controlled uncertain manipulator. IEEE **47**(8), 2398–2409 (2017)

5. Cao, F.F., Liu, J.K.: Boundary control for a constrained two-link rigid-flexible manipulator with prescribed performance. Int. J. Control **91**(5), 1091–1103 (2018).

6. Zhou, X.Y., Wang, H.P., Tian, Y., et al.: Disturbance observer-based adaptive boundary iterative learning control for a rigid-flexible manipulator with input backlash and endpoint constraint. Int. J. Adapt. Control, **34**(9), 1–22 (2020)

7. Shintake, J., Cacucciolo, V., Floreano, D., et al.: Soft robotic grippers. Adv. Mater. **30**(29), 1–33 (2018)

8. Jeong, D., Lee, K.: Design and analysis of an origami-based three-finger manipulator. Robotica 1–14 (2017)

9. Shang, Z.F., Ma, J.Y., You, Z., et al.: A foldable manipulator with tunable stiffness based on braided structure. J. Biomed. Mater. Res. Part B **000B**, 1–10 (2019)

10. Zhang, K., Zhu, Y., Lou, C., et al.: A design and fabrication approach for pneumatic soft robotic arms using 3D printed origami skeletons. In: 2019 2nd IEEE International Conference on Soft Robotics (RoboSoft), pp. 821–827. IEEE, New York (2019)

11. Laschi, C., Cianchetti, M., Mazzolai, B., et al.: Soft robot arm inspired by the octopus. Adv. Rob. **26**(7), 709–727 (2012)

12. Meng, Q.L., Shen, Z.J., Chen, Z.Z., et al.: Design and research of bionic hand exoskeleton based on flexible hinge. Chin. J. Biomed. Eng. **39**(5), 557–565 (2020). (in Chinese)

13. Mavroidis, C., Roth, B.: New and revised overconstrained mechanisms. J. Mech. Des. **117**(1), 75–82 (1995)

14. Yang, F.F., Chen, K.J.: General kinematics of twofold-symmetric Bricard 6R linkage. J. Tianjin Univ. **54**(11), 1168–1178 (2021). (in Chinese)

15. Denavit, J., Hartenberg, R.S.: A kinematic notation for lower-pair mechanisms. J. Appl. Mech. **22**, 215–221 (1955)

16. Yu, J.J., Hao, G.B., Chen, G.M., et al.: State-of-art of compliant mechanisms and their applications. J. Mech. Eng. **51**(13), 53–68 (2015). (in Chinese)

17. Wohlhart, K.: Screw spaces and connectivities in multiloop linkages. In: On Advances in Robot Kinematics, pp. 97–104 (2004). https://doi.org/10.1007/978-1-4020-2249-4_11

18. Dai, J.S.: Historical relation between mechanisms and screw theory and the development of finite displacement screws. J. Mech. Eng. **51**(13), 13–26 (2015). (in Chinese)

19. Yang, F.F., Chen, Y., Kang, R., et al.: Truss transformation method to obtain the non-overconstrained forms of 3D overconstrained linkages. Mech. Mach. Theor. **102**, 149–166 (2016)

20. Pellegrino, S., Calladine, C.R.: Matrix analysis of statically and kinematically indeterminate frameworks. Int. J. Solids Struct. **22**(4), 409–428 (1986)

21. Kumar, P., Pellegrino, S.: Computation of kinematic paths and bifurcation points. Int. J. Solids Struct. **37**(46–47), 7003–7027 (2000)

A Micro Bionic Flapping Wing Robot on Water Surface

Rila Nai, Xin Zhang, Jihong Yan$^{(\boxtimes)}$, and Jie Zhao

State Key Laboratory of Robotics and System, Harbin Institute of Technology, Harbin 150001, Heilongjiang, China
jhyan@hit.edu.cn

Abstract. Sliding and jumping are the two main motion modes of micro water sports robots, flying motion can further expand the range of motion in near-water space and improve the maneuverability and flexibility of robots, it has become an inevitable trend in the development of micro-robots. Surface flying involves two media, water and air. Limited by the complexity of water supporting force and lift resistance, it is difficult for a robot to take off on the water surface. In this paper, a micro flapping wing flying robot that can take off on the water surface is developed by combining the floating principle of water strider and the flying motion of hummingbirds. The weight and wingspan of the robot are 13 g and 21 cm respectively, and the flapping amplitude is 180°. The water surface flying experiments verifies that the flying height is 25 cm, the take-off response time is 0.1 s, and the average vertical take-off speed is 1 m/s.

Keywords: Micro robot · Bionic robot · Flapping wing · Water surface flying

1 Introduction

The water strider can slide and jump flexibly on the water surface because of the hydrophobic bristles on the supporting and driving legs. The superiority of this movement has attracted the research interest of scholars at home and abroad [1–3]. In 2003, Professor Bush of the Massachusetts Institute of Technology developed the world's first bionic water strider robot Robostrider [4]. The robot is 13 cm long and weighs 0.35 g, and four hydrophobic treated steel wires ware used as the supporting legs. The maximum sliding speed of the robot can reach 20 cm/s. In 2015, Professor Jihong Yan of HIT developed the world's first bionic water strider robot that can continuously jump on the surface [5]. Hydrophobic nickel foam was used as the supporting legs, and the jumping height and distance of the robot were 140 mm and 350 mm respectively. In the same year, Je-Sungkoh et al. designed a micro water jumping robot driven by SMA [6], which weights only 68 mg. The robot floats on the water surface by surface tension, and its jumping height is 14.2 cm. These micro-robots can move in the space near water surface, while flying motion can effectively expand the robot's motion space

Research supported by Natural Science Foundation of China (NSFC, Grant 51775133) and National Defense Science and Technology Innovation Special Zone Project.

X.-J. Liu et al. (Eds.): ICIRA 2021, LNAI 13015, pp. 739–749, 2021.
https://doi.org/10.1007/978-3-030-89134-3_67

and improve the practical level of robot. Flying robots are mainly divided into flapping wing, fixed wing and rotary wing according to the movement mode of flying wings. For micro-scale robots, the flapping-wing has higher maneuverability and flexibility than other motion modes. As a typical representative of the flapping-wing flying mode, the hummingbird has become the main imitation object of the flapping-wing flying robot [7–9]. In 2011, the American AeroVironment team developed the Nano Hummingbird, a bionic hummingbird robot with a weight of 19 g and a wingspan of 16.5 cm [10]. By controlling the distortion of the wing surface, the robot can fly in any posture. In 2018, Matěj Karásek at Delft University of Technology developed the Delfly Nimble, a robot that can accurately mimic the rapid escape movements of a fly, with four flapping wings, a weight of 28.2 g and a wingspan of 33 cm [11]. In 2019, Professor Xinyan Deng of Purdue University successfully simulated the movements of a hummingbird by using a pair of electric motors to control the flapping wings. The robot weighed 17 g and had a wingspan of 22 cm [12].

In summary, the two main motion modes of the micro water sports robot, sliding and jumping, are limited to the space close to the water surface. The flight movement can expand the robot's movement space. However, the flying robots developed by scholars are mainly used in the land environment, and no specific research on the water environment has been carried out. The water surface is fluid and soft, making it difficult to provide stable support for the robot. The disturbance caused by the high-frequency flapping of the wings can cause the robot's attitude to tilt or even sink. In addition, the lift generated by the flapping wing movement also limits the size and weight of the entire robot. These factors make the research of surface micro flying robots more challenging. In 2019, Professor Wood of Harvard University designed a flapping-wing robot Robobee that can fly from underwater to the surface [13]. The robot weighs 500 mg and achieves instantaneous huge thrust by igniting explosive gas in a gas cavity. However, due to its small weight and volume, the robot needs external high-voltage power to ignite the gas cavity, so there is a big hidden danger in safety.

In this paper, a micro flying robot that can take off on the water surface is developed by combining the floating principle of water strider and the flying characteristics of hummingbirds. By optimizing the shape and size of the flapping wings and supporting mechanism, the stability of the robot's take-off attitude is improved. Finally, the land and water flying experiments were carried out. The experiments show that the robot's water surface flying height is 25 cm, the take-off response time is 0.1 s, and the vertical take-off speed is 1 m/s.

2   Robot Design

The prototype of the robot is shown in Fig. 1. Its height and wingspan are 5 cm and 21 cm respectively. The robot is mainly composed of supporting structure, wings and flapping mechanism. Figure 2a shows the schematic of the flapping mechanism. The motor outputs power to the eccentric wheel through a reduction gear (reduction ratio of 21), drives the four-bar mechanism to swing, and then drives the rocker to swing at a high frequency, so that the flapping wings generate lift. Figure 2b shows the exploded view of the flapping mechanism, which is composed of mechanism linkage, fixing rivets, leading edge bar, tapping screws, gears, bearings and DC motor. In order to achieve the stable and fast flying performance, it is necessary to optimize the structure parameters of flapping wings and supporting structure of the robot.

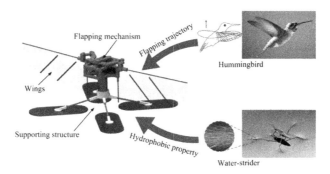

Fig. 1. Robot prototype inspired by hummingbirds and water striders.

2.1 Flapping Mechanism

The hummingbird's motion mode has the advantages of small vibration and large lift force. In 2013, Professor Matej Karásek designed a micro flying robot according to the flapping principle of flying birds [14]. The flapping mechanism schematic is shown in Fig. 2a. The input angle of the motor is θ, and the output angle of the leading edge rod is Φ. The flapping mechanism can ensure the synchronization of the flapping wings on both sides. Inspired by the driving principle, this paper optimized the structure parameters of the four-bar linkage to reduce the inertial force of the mechanism during high-speed flapping. The main frame of the robot is made of POM material through 3D printing method. The leading edge bar of the flapping wing is made of CFRP with a diameter of 0.7 mm. In order to improve the stability and compactness of the robot, the motor is arranged directly below the flapping-wing drive mechanism, the transmission mechanism is supported on both ends, and ceramic bearings are used to reduce the friction caused by high-frequency flapping.

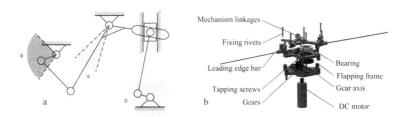

Fig. 2. Flapping mechanism. a: driving schematic. b: exploded view of the mechanism.

2.2 Supporting Structure

Floating on the water surface stably is the basis for the robot to take off from the water surface. Water striders can move flexibly and quickly on the water surface, mainly due to the hydrophobic bristle structure of its legs, which brings a large supporting force and effectively reduce the dragging force when skating on water surface. Inspired by this, the supporting legs of the robot is made of foamed nickel sheet and coated with hydrophobic material (EverDryTM, UltraTech International Inc.). Compared with the cylindrical support leg, hydrophobic sheet can provide a larger supporting force. In order to reduce the influence of flapping wing vibration on the robot's attitude and improve the stability of the robot during the take-off process, the four supporting legs are evenly arranged around the body.

3 Force Analysis of the Robot and Optimization

3.1 Analysis of Robot Take-Off Process on Water Surface

There are two stages in which the robot goes from floating on the water to being completely out of the water, as Fig. 3. (i) The supporting legs on one side squeeze the water surface and are supported by the water surface, the supporting legs on the other side begin to leave the water surface and are dragged by the water surface. (ii) The supporting legs on one side completely out of the water, the supporting legs on the other side begin to leave the water surface and are dragged by the water surface. In order to analyze the influence of supporting legs and flapping wings on the water surface flight and optimize the flight performance, we establish a force analysis model for the whole take-off process of the robot.

In the stage 1, While the flapping wings generate lift F_L, it also generate a lifting moment T_L that tilts the robot to one side, therefore, the side needs to provide sufficient support to prevent the robot from overturning. In the mean time, The other side is affected by the dragging force F_T, which will raise the water surface to a certain height, and the detachment height h should be higher than the maximum detachment height h_0 of the supporting legs. There is a minimum inclination angle θ, which will makes the take-off attitude of the robot in the stage 1 is the most stable. Combine with the relevant size of the supporting structure, the θ can be obtained by formula (1).

$$\theta = \arcsin(\frac{h_0}{L_3}) \tag{1}$$

$$\begin{cases} F_L L_1 + F_D L_2 = F_N L_3 + F_T L_3 \\ F_L + F_N > G + F_T \end{cases} \tag{2}$$

In the stage 2, one side of the supporting legs of the robot have been completely out of the water, and the robot is simply affected by gravity, lift and resistance of the flapping wings and the dragging force of one side of the supporting legs. In order to achieve water surface take-off, the lifting force must be higher than the other two forces, as formula (3).

$$\begin{cases} F_L L_1 = F_T L_3 \\ F_L > G + F_T \end{cases} \tag{3}$$

In summary, the optimal design principles of the supporting legs and flapping wings of the robot are obtained as follow:

- The supporting force of the supporting legs should be satisfied that the robot could not puncture the water surface when the robot takes off, and the drag force and detachment height should be as small as possible to improve the stability of the robot when it completely leaves the water surface.
- The lift force should meet the conditions for the robot to take off on the water surface, and at the same time, the lifting moment and the resisting moment should not exceed the limit of the supporting torque, so as to prevent the robot from leaning too much and even puncture the water surface.

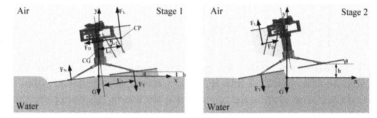

Fig. 3. The process of the robot taking off on the water surface

3.2 Force Analysis and Optimization of the Supporting Leg

The supporting force produced by supporting leg mainly includes hydrostatic pressure and surface tension, the hydrostatic pressure is a function of the depth of supporting leg into the water, and the vertical component of the surface tension is obtained by solving the volume of water discharged by the free surface deformation. The profile curve of water air interface can be obtained by solving young Laplace equation, as formula (4).

$$
x = \begin{cases} \sqrt{4k - h_0^2} - \sqrt{4k - h^2} + \sqrt{k}\lg \dfrac{|h_0|(2\sqrt{k} + \sqrt{4k - h^2})}{|h|(2\sqrt{k} + \sqrt{4k - h_0^2})} & 0 \leq |\varphi_0| \leq 90° \\[4mm] \sqrt{2k} - \sqrt{4k - h^2} + \sqrt{k}\lg \dfrac{2\sqrt{k} + \sqrt{4k - h^2}}{(1 + \sqrt{2})|h|} & 90° < |\varphi_0| \leq 180° \end{cases}
\tag{4}
$$

The process that the supporting legs into water is shown in Fig. 4, which is mainly divided into three stages: (a) The three-phase contact line intersect at the lower edge of the rectangular section, and the water entry depth of the section is h1. (b) the three-phase contact line slides along both sides of the section, and the water entry depth of the section is h2. (c) the three-phase contact line intersect at the top edge of the section, and the water entry depth of the section is h3. As the supporting leg continues to enter the water, the angle between the surface tension and the horizontal direction gradually increases to the contact angle, it will not be able to maintain the water air profile section, and the supporting leg will sink completely. At this time, the maximum water entry depth is h4. The water entry depth h of supporting leg at each stage and the supporting force are shown in formula 5 and 6.

$$
\begin{cases}
h_1 = -2\sqrt{k}\sin\frac{(\theta_c-90°)}{2} \\
h_2 = -2\sqrt{k}\sin\frac{(\theta_c-90°)}{2} - T \\
h_3 = -2\sqrt{k}\sin 45° - T \\
h_4 = -2\sqrt{k}\sin\frac{\theta_c}{2}
\end{cases}
\tag{5}
$$

$$
\begin{cases}
-\rho g l W h + 2\gamma(l+W)\sin\varphi & h_1 < h \le 0 \\
-\rho g l W h + 2\gamma(l+W)\sin\left(\theta_c - \dfrac{\pi}{2}\right) & h_2 < h \le h_1 \\
-\rho g l W h + 2\gamma(l+W)\sin\varphi & h_3 < h \le h_2 \\
\rho g l W T - 2\gamma(l+W)\displaystyle\int_{h-T}^{0} h(z)dz & h_4 \le h \le h_3
\end{cases}
\tag{6}
$$

The process of the supporting leg leaving water surface is shown in Fig. 4d. As shown in Fig. 4d, two points A and B are the intersection points of robot water air three-phase contact line. During the process of robot leaving the water, the three-phase contact line is always on the lower surface of the rectangular supporting leg, and the hydrostatic pressure and surface tension gradually increase. When the angle between the surface tension and the horizontal direction reaches the material contact angle, the supporting leg will completely leave the water, at this time, the ultimate height of water surface h_c and the dragging force on supporting leg are shown in formula 7 and formula 8 respectively.

$$
h_c = -2\sqrt{k}\sin\frac{(\theta_c - 180°)}{2}
\tag{7}
$$

$$
F_d = -\rho g W h_0 + 2\gamma l \sin\varphi
\tag{8}
$$

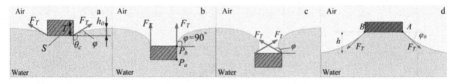

Fig. 4. a b c show the process of the supporting leg into water; d shows the process of supporting leg out of water

The supporting leg should avoid puncturing the water surface at the moment of take-off, at the same time, the dragging force should be as small as possible to reduce the impact on the robot take-off attitude. This paper is based on the force model of supporting leg, the shape and size of the supporting leg are optimized analysis. As shown in Fig. 5, as the volume increases, the ratio of the dragging force to supporting force increases gradually. And under the same volume condition, the ratio of the dragging force and the supporting force of circular and rectangular combined supporting leg is the smallest, it's good for robot to take off on the water surface, so the robot uses this shape as supporting legs.

The size ratio is another important factor affecting the dragging force and supporting force, Fig. 5 shows the changes of supporting force and dragging force of the supporting leg with different length to width ratios. With the increase of length-width ratio, the dragging force and supporting force are increased, the ratio of drag force to support force decreases slightly. Therefore, choosing appropriate volume of circular and rectangular combined supporting leg is important.

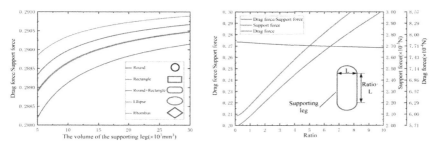

Fig. 5. The supporting leg optimization. Left: Plane shape and volume. Right: Length-width ratio

3.3 Aerodynamics Analysis of Flapping Wings and Optimization

Since flapping wing flight involves unsteady aerodynamics, it is difficult to accurately calculate the lift and resistance during flight. The quasi steady modelling approach can be used to calculate the estimated value of the flapping wing lift and resistance, which has sufficient accuracy compared with CFD and can be used for the establishment of lift and resistance model and optimization analysis [15]. The quasi-static method needs to consider that the flapping wings will be affected by the normal F_{Ntr} and tangential force F_{Ttr} caused by the delayed stall effect, the normal force F_{RN} caused by the pitch rotation effect, and the normal force FAN caused by the additional mass effect, as formula 9.

$$
\begin{cases}
F_{Ntr} = \frac{1}{2}\rho C_N(\alpha)SU_{CP}^2 \\
F_{Ttr} = \frac{1}{2}\rho C_T(\alpha)SU_{CP}^2 \\
F_{RN} = \rho\pi(\frac{3}{4} - \hat{x}_0)\dot{\alpha}U_{CP}\frac{R\bar{c}^2}{\hat{r}_2}\int_0^1 \hat{c}^2(r)\hat{r}d\hat{r} \\
C_N(\alpha) = 3.4\sin(\alpha) \\
C_T(\alpha) = \begin{cases} 0.4\cos^2(2\alpha) & 0 \le |\alpha| < \frac{\pi}{4} \\ 0 & \frac{\pi}{4} \le |\alpha| < \frac{3\pi}{4} \end{cases}
\end{cases}
\tag{9}
$$

Both the normal force and tangential force calculated by the quasi steady modelling approach can be equivalently acted on the pressure center of the flapping wing. As shown in the Fig. 6, according to the stroke angle and attack angle of the flapping wing in motion, the normal force and tangential force of the flapping wing calculated by the quasi-static method can be equivalent to the lift F_L, resistance F_D and side force F_Y of the robot.

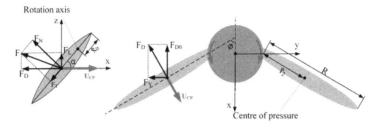

Fig. 6. Aerodynamics analysis of flapping wings. Left: Airfoil section.Right: Top view of flapping wing movement

In the meantime, the lifting moment T_L will be caused by the lift force, due to the reciprocating flapping of the flapping wing, as formula 10: To facilitate the optimization of wing parameters, the aspect ratio was defined as $AR = 2R^2/S$, as well as the taper ratio C_T/C_R was defined as the ratio of wing-tip length to wing-root length.

$$\begin{cases} F_L = \rho S^2 \dot{\phi}\{\frac{1}{4}\zeta AR\dot{\phi}[C_N(\alpha)\cos(|\alpha|) - C_T(\alpha)\sin(|\alpha|)] + \pi(\frac{3}{4} - \hat{x}_0)\dot{\alpha}\eta\} \\ F_D = \rho S^2 \dot{\phi}\cos\phi\{\frac{1}{4}\zeta AR\dot{\phi}[C_N(\alpha)\sin(|\alpha|) + C_T(\alpha)\cos(|\alpha|)] + \pi(\frac{3}{4} - \hat{x}_0)\dot{\alpha}\eta\sin(|\alpha|)\} \\ F_Y = \rho S^2 \dot{\phi}\sin\phi\{\frac{1}{4}\zeta AR\dot{\phi}[C_N(\alpha)\sin(\alpha) + C_T(\alpha)\sin(\alpha)] + \pi(\frac{3}{4} - \hat{x}_0)\dot{\alpha}\eta\cos(\alpha)\} \\ T_L = F_L \tan(|\phi|)\hat{r}_2 R \\ \zeta = \frac{3^{CT}/CR+1}{6^{CT}/CR+6} \\ \eta = \frac{3^{CT}/CR^2 + 2^{CT}/CR + 1}{3^{CT}/CR^2 + 6^{CT}/CR + 3} \end{cases}$$

$$(10)$$

In order to make the robot take off from the water, and the lift torque won't be too large, according to the aerodynamic model of flapping wing established above, the wing parameters of flapping wing are optimized and analyzed. The area of the flapping wing S, the aspect ratio AR, and the taper ratio CT/CR are important factors that affect the lift force and lift torque of the robot, as shown in Fig. 7.

With the increase of S, AR and CT/CR, both lift and lift torque show an increasing trend, but the increase of lift torque is greater than lift. Excessive lift moment will cause the robot to overturn, while too little lift will prevent it from leaving the water. Therefore, when the lift meets the minimum lift, the lift moment cannot exceed the maximum support moment provided by the support legs to prevent the robot from overturning. The wing area should be selected within the range of 1300 mm^2–1950 mm^2. The final selected wing parameters: S = 1650 mm^2 as the median value of the range, AR = 9.0, CT/CR = 0.49.

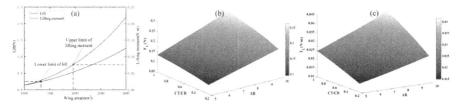

Fig. 7. Optimization of wing area, aspect ratio and taper ratio. a: Influence of wing area. b: Influence of AR and CT/CR on lift. c: Influence of AR and CT/CR on lift moment

4 Experiment and Discussion

4.1 Robot Fabrication and Experiment Platform

The robot and water flying robot experiment platform are shown in the Fig. 8. The weight, height and wingspan of the robot are 13 g, 5 cm and 21 cm respectively. In order to reduce the weight of the robot, the main body frame and gears are made by 3D printing method with POM as material. The flapping wing is made of 12 um thick polyester film. And the leading-edge bar, the wing root bar and the connecting bar of the supporting legs are made of CFRP bar with a diameter of 0.7 mm. The rib of flapping wing is made of 0.1 mm thick CFRP stiffeners, to prevent the coefficient of lift decreases caused by the curl of flapping wing in high frequency flapping. The supporting leg is made of 1 mm thick plate type nickel foam material, which is hydrophobically treated by hydrophobic material, to enhance the supporting force of the robot. The wing root adjusting plate, which is introduced to prevent errors in production and assembly from making the robot unable to fly vertically, can adjust the angle direction of the wing root so as to change the lift and resistance direction. Finally, a water flight experiment was carried out to verify the flight performance in the water environment.

Water flying robot experiment platform consists of robot prototype, phototron high-speed camera, light source, PC, experimental water tank and scale lable. The high-speed camera was set to record the robot's flight at 2,000 fps, and the geometric center point of the robot is set as the mark point. The Open CV video processing module was used to record the motion trajectory of the robot, remove the deviation point and perform the fitting of the flight trajectory. This method was used to obtain the flight trajectory of the robot in subsequent experiments.

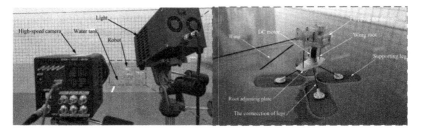

Fig. 8. The assembled prototype

4.2 Robot Flight Experiment on Land and Water Surface

Point A and B are the starting and end position of the flying trajectory, respectively. The robot performs a take-off response time of 0.05 s, on land, the maximum attitude change is 29° and the vertical flying speed is 1.3 m/s. On water surface, the take-off time is 0.1 s. The two support legs in the front of the robot are separated from the water surface at 0.05 s, while all the legs are completely detached at 0.1 s. The maximum attitude change angle is 74° and the vertical flying speed is up to 1 m/s. This experiment shows that the robot has the ability to take off from water surface (Fig. 9).

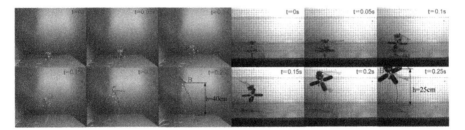

Fig. 9. Land and Water surface flight experiment

4.3 Discussion

Experiments have proved that the robot can take off from the surface. The deviation of the robot's flight trajectory in the water environment is mainly caused by the following reasons: (i) The non-vertical lift caused by the production and assembly errors; (ii) The external power cord has a drag effect on the robot, causing the flight posture to tilt.

It is more severe of the attitude change compared with the land flying environment, when the robot takes off on the water surface. The main reason may be the following: the vibration of the robot during the take-off process, insufficient force of the supporting legs to achieve stability, and the dragging force generated by the water surface during the take-off process. To sum up, it can be seen that the robot takes off on the water surface is more challenging.

5 Conclusion

By combining the floating mechanism of the water strider with the flying characteristics of hummingbirds, the article develops the world's first micro flapping wing flying robot that can take off from the water surface. The weight and wingspan of the robot are 13 g and 21 cm respectively, and the flapping amplitude is 180°. The robot is mainly composed of supporting structure, wings, and flapping mechanism. The supporting structure provide sufficient support and reduce the drag force on the water surface. The flapping mechanism generates high flapping to drive the robot to take off. The force model of supporting legs and flapping wings ware established to analyze the flying performance of the robot on the water surface. By optimizing the shape and size of the supporting legs and flapping wings, the robot's take-off attitude is improved. Finally, the land and water flying experiments were carried out. The robot's water surface flying height is 25 cm, the take-off response time is 0.1 s, and the vertical take-off speed is 1 m/s. In the following research work, the influence of the shake of the flapping wings will be analyzed to improve the take-off attitude of the robot, and introducing active control system to improve flight performance.

References

1. Yan, J., Zhang, X., Yang, K., et al.: A single driven bionic water strider sliding robot mimicking the spatial elliptical trajectory. In: 2019 IEEE International Conference on Robotics and Biomimetics (ROBIO), pp. 142–147 (2019)
2. Shin, B., Kim, H.Y., Cho, K.J.: Towards a biologically inspired small-scale water jumping robot. In: 2nd IEEE RAS & EMBS International Conference on Biomedical Robotics and Biomechatronics, BioRob 2008, pp. 127–131. IEEE (2008)
3. Yan, J., Zhang, X., Zhao, J., et al.: A miniature surface tension-driven robot using spatially elliptical moving legs to mimic a water strider's locomotion. Bioinspiration Biomimetics **10**(4), 046016 (2015)
4. Hu, D.L., Bush, J.W.M., et al.: The hydrodynamics of water-walking arthropods. J. Fluid Mech. **644**, 5–33 (2010)
5. Jiang, F., Zhao, J., Kota, A.K., et al.: A miniature water surface jumping robot. IEEE Robot. Autom. Lett. **2**(3), 1272–1279 (2017)
6. Koh, J.S., Yang, E., Jung, G.P., et al.: Jumping on water: Surface tension–dominated jumping of water striders and robotic insects. Science **349**(6247), 517 (2015)
7. Phan, H.V., Kang, T., Park, H.C., et al.: Design and stable flight of a 21 g insect-like tailless flapping wing micro air vehicle with angular rates feedback control. Bioinspiration Biomimetics **12**(3), Article no. 036006 (2017)
8. Roshanbin, A., Altartouri, H., et al.: COLIBRI: a hovering flapping twin-wing robot. Int. J. Mirco Air Veh. **9**(4), 270–282 (2017)
9. Nguyen, Q.V., Chan, W.-L., et al.: Performance tests of a hovering flapping wing micro air vehicle with double wing clap-and-fling mechanism. In: Proceedings of International Micro Air Vehicles Conference on Flight Competition, pp. 1–8 (2015)
10. Keennon, M.T., Klingebiel, K., et al.: Development of the nano hummingbird: a tailless flapping wing micro air vehicle. In: Proceedings of the AIAA, p. 588 (2012)
11. Karásek, M., Muijres, F.T., et al.: A tailless aerial robotic flapper reveals that flies use torque coupling in rapid banked turns. Science **361**(6407), 1089–1094 (2018)
12. Zhang, J., Fei, F., Tu, Z., Deng, X., et al.: Design optimization and system integration of robotic hummingbird. In: Proceedings of the IEEE International Conference on Robotics and Automation (ICRA), May/June 2017, pp. 5422–5428 (2017)
13. Chen, Y., Wang, H., Wood, R.J., et al.: A biologically inspired, flapping-wing, hybrid aerial-aquatic microrobot. Sci. Robot. (2017)
14. Karásek, M., Nan, Y.H., et al.: Pitch moment generation and measurement in a robotic hummingbird. Int. J. Micro Air Veh. **5**, 299–310 (2013)
15. Karásek, M.: Robotic hummingbird: design of a control mechanism for a hovering flapping wing micro air vehicle. Ph.D. thesis, Université Libre de Bruxelles, Active Structures Laboratory (2014)

Design of a De-Tumbling Robot for Space Noncooperative Targets

Xuecong Kang, Zhenjie Huang, Hengyuan Yan, Tieniu Chen,
and Yunjiang Lou[✉]

Harbin Institute of Technology Shenzhen, Shenzhen, China
louyj@hit.edu.cn

Abstract. The aerospace industry continues to progress and develop. The waste left in space by human beings in space activities has lost its attitude adjustment ability and been turned into space junk. This not only causes a waste of orbital resources, but also spacecraft collisions, which could cause the mission to fail. In this paper, the problem of detumbling in the process of capturing noncooperative targets is studied, a set of multi-wheel arm test platform is designed, and a model is built, aiming to complete detumbling for low-speed rotating targets to recycle. Finally, the experimental results show that the performance and function test of the platform have a good effect on the problem of detumbling. This multi-wheel arm test platform is an effective and feasible method for the detumbling of noncooperative targets.

Keywords: Space noncooperative targets · De-tumbling robot · Multi-wheel arm platform

1 Introduction

With the development of space technology, the number of space exploration missions has increased year by year. The waste left by human beings, including the final stage of the rocket, failed satellites and so on, has become a noncooperative target due to its loss of attitude adjustment ability, also called space junk [1–3]. A schematic diagram of the distribution of space junk in the Earth orbit is shown in Fig. 1. If they are not recycled and processed, a large number of them will be stranded in space, which will not only cause a waste of orbital resources, but also spacecraft collisions in orbit. In view of the importance of space activities, the recycling of space junk is of great significance [4]. The noncooperative target refers to the target with free floating orbit, unstable slow rotation or rolling attitude, no cooperative attitude control and information interaction support ability, uncontrolled and not equipped with the capture device used for spacecraft capture. For the on-orbit capture of targets, the key is to reduce the spin speed of targets to a reasonable range, that is, to detumble [5,6].

This work was supported partially by the NSFC-Shenzhen Robotics Basic Research Center Program (No. U1713202) and partially by the Shenzhen Science and Technology Program (No. JSGG20191129114035610).

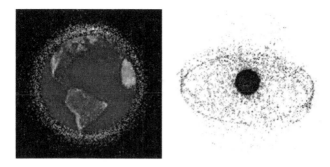

Fig. 1. Distribution of space junk in Earth orbit.

Contact-type detumbling is to use the end effector of the manipulator to apply force to the free-rolling target surface to achieve the purpose of detumbling [7]. Daneshjou [8] et al. proposed a spring-damper buffering device, which performed a certain detumbling through the collision during the docking process; Nishid [9] et al. designed a detumbling device in which the end effector uses a retarder brush to utilize elastic force with target. Huang [10] et al. proposed a attitude control method based on a tether terminal, which used a viscous tether to attach to the roll target, and stabilized its attitude by controlling the tether tension and damping force; Matunaga et al. [11] designed soft cushion damper detumbling method; Literature [12–14] studied the detumbling control of noncooperative targets using the manipulator. The advantage of this method is that it can provide a large control torque, the detumbling effect is obvious, and it is realized that the operation of detumbling, capture and drag off-orbit can be completed at the same time with one device. In this paper, in order to design the detumbling platform for noncooperative targets, we provided a contact-type detumbling method, designed and assembled a set of multi-wheel arm test platform, and built a software test platform to eliminate the rotation angular velocity of the target in space through the coordinated movement of three multi-wheel arms. Finally, the overall function debugging was completed through experiments, which verified the correctness, effectiveness and feasibility.

2   Design of Hardware Platform

A good electromechanical configuration is the basis for the success of a complex automatic control system. The purpose of this part is to design a multi-wheel arm test platform based on the contact-type detumbling strategy, which has a good effect on the low-speed rotating target while ensuring the safety and stability of the robotic arm and the space noncooperative target.

2.1   Mechanics

The schematic diagram of the designed multi-wheel arm hardware system is shown in Fig. 2. The uppermost layer is the target object; the second layer is the three sets of wheel hand movement mechanisms, which are the driving devices; the third layer is the connecting flange and the bottom plate, which have a fixed support for the wheel hand movement mechanism; the bottom layer is the electrical hardware system and the main control system, including a DC stabilized power supply, nine motor drivers, a STM32 microcontrollers, some connection lines, etc.

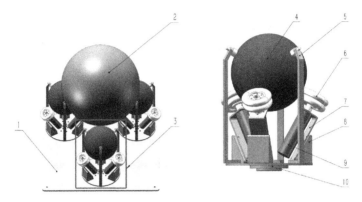

Fig. 2. Overall configuration of Ballbot. In the figure, 1 represents the bottom plate; 2 represents the target object; 3 represents the wheel arm movement mechanism assembly; 4 represents the 150 mm diameter wheel arm; 5 represents the fixed beam; 6 represents the omni-wheel; 7 represents the motor bracket; 8 represents the triangle block; 9 represents the RMSD-109 motor combination; 10 represents the robot arm connecting flange.

The wheel-hand movement mechanism is a key component of the platform, and it adopts the driving method of the omni-wheel directly driven by the motors. The omni-wheel can make the driving ball move in all directions and rotate at the same time. Compared with other driving methods, this method has more degrees of freedom and reduces the structural difficulty. In the structure, the projections of the three omni-wheels on the horizontal plane form an angle of 120° with each other, and the tangent point between the driving ball and the omni-wheel is located at the zenith angle of 45° under the ball. The driving ball is fixed by three beams to ensure that no displacement occurs during movement. The wheel arm is connected to the end robot arm through a connecting flange, and finally the robot arm can be operated to ensure that the wheel arm can always contact with the space noncooperative target.

2.2   Kinematics

The control form of the platform is 9 motors driving 9 omni-wheels. Every three omni-wheels drive a driving ball. The three driving small balls act on a target ball. We can divide it into two parts for analysis: (1) Three motors drive three omni-wheels, which in turn drive a driving ball. (2) Three driving balls act as power devices to drive the target ball.

Omni-Wheel Drive Ball

The omni-wheel is shown in Fig. 3(a). The outer ring drives the ball when the big wheel rotates, and the small wheel reduces the friction force between the ball and the big wheel to zero in the vertical direction, and the omni-wheel only provides the ball with tangential force. Assuming that there is no relative sliding between the ball and each tangent omni-wheel, the tangential velocity of the contact between the wheel and the ball is the same.

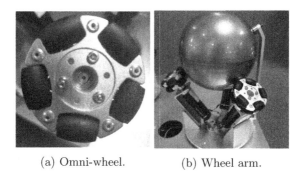

(a) Omni-wheel.   (b) Wheel arm.

Fig. 3. Driving device of the test platform.

- Define the reference coordinate system and give the linear velocity of the contact point and the omni-wheel in the direction of rotation. The reference coordinate system is a rectangular coordinate system which the origin is located at the center of the sphere, the plane of the x and y axes is parallel to the horizontal plane, and the z axis is vertically upward.

  Suppose p_i is the position vector and ω is the angular velocity of a driving ball, then the linear velocity at the contact point P_i can be written as:

  $$\nu_i = \omega \times p_i \tag{1}$$

  where $i = 1, 2, 3$.

  The velocity v is decomposed into v_c and v_s. v_c is generated by the rotation of the wheel, and v_s represents the linear velocity of the wheel. Assuming that the unit vector in the rotating direction of the wheel is s, and the linear velocity can be obtained according to the vector correlation theorem:

  $$\nu \cdot \mathbf{s} = (\nu_c + \nu_s) \cdot \mathbf{s} = |\nu_s| \tag{2}$$

- According to the definition of the coordinate system, the position vector p_i and the unit vector in the rotating direction s of each wheel are represented. Three omni-wheels are placed at equal intervals on the ball where the zenith angle is ϕ, then the position vector of the contact point can be written as:

$$\begin{cases} p_1 = (r \sin \varphi \ \ 0 \ \ r \cos \varphi) \\ p_2 = \left(\left(-\frac{1}{2} \right) r \sin \varphi \ \ \left(\frac{\sqrt{3}}{2} \right) \sin \varphi \ \ r \cos \varphi \right) \\ p_3 = \left(\left(-\frac{1}{2} \right) r \sin \varphi \ \ \left(-\frac{\sqrt{3}}{2} \right) \sin \varphi \ \ r \cos \varphi \right) \end{cases} \tag{3}$$

Among them, r is the radius of the driving ball.

The unit vectors in the direction of rotation of the omni-wheel are respectively written as: $s_1 = (0 \ -1 \ 0)$, $s_2 = \left(\frac{\sqrt{3}}{2} \ \frac{1}{2} \ 0 \right)$, $s_3 = \left(-\frac{\sqrt{3}}{2} \ \frac{1}{2} \ 0 \right)$

- We respectively show the corresponding speed vectors of each omni-wheel when the ball rotates around the three axes.

$$v_i = (\omega_x \ 0 \ 0) \times (p_{ix} \ p_{iy} \ p_{iz}) = (0 \ -p_{iz}\omega_x \ p_{iy}\omega_x) \tag{4}$$

$$v_i = (0 \ \omega_y \ 0) \times (p_{ix} \ p_{iy} \ p_{iz}) = (p_{iz}\omega_y \ 0 \ -p_{ix}\omega_y) \tag{5}$$

$$v_i = (0 \ 0 \ \omega_z) \times (p_{ix} \ p_{iy} \ p_{iz}) = (-p_{iy}\omega_z \ p_{ix}\omega_z \ 0) \tag{6}$$

- According to the speed vector, the linear velocity of each wheel is calculated and then the speed of each omni-wheel can be obtained through the superimposition of equation when the ball moves in any direction.

$$\begin{bmatrix} |v_{s1}| \\ |v_{s2}| \\ |v_{s3}| \end{bmatrix} = \begin{bmatrix} r \cos \varphi & 0 & -r \sin \varphi \\ -\frac{1}{2} r \cos \varphi & \frac{\sqrt{3}}{2} r \cos \varphi & -r \sin \varphi \\ -\frac{1}{2} r \cos \varphi & -\frac{\sqrt{3}}{2} r \cos \varphi & -r \sin \varphi \end{bmatrix} \cdot \begin{bmatrix} \omega_x \\ \omega_y \\ \omega_z \end{bmatrix} \tag{7}$$

Driving Balls Drive Target

- Define the reference rectangular coordinate system.
  As shown in Fig. 4, with each sphere center as the origin of the respective coordinate system, four rectangular coordinate systems are established with the same axis directions. Among them, L_1, L_2, and L_3 are three small spherical coordinate systems, B_1 is the coordinate system of the target. The Z axis and X, Y axis constitute the right hand system.

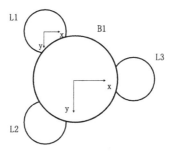

Fig. 4. Definition of coordinate system.

- Establish the kinematic relationship between the driving ball and the target ball.

Taking the driving ball L_1 as an example, its angular velocity is marked as $\Omega_1 = \begin{bmatrix} w_x & w_y & w_z \end{bmatrix}^T$, the angular velocity of the target ball B_1 is Ω. Suppose the tangent point of L_1 and B_1 is Q_1, and the position vector of Q_1 in the L_1 coordinate system is $R_{q1} = \begin{bmatrix} q_{11} & q_{21} & q_{31} \end{bmatrix}^T$. The position vector of the tangent point Q_1 in the coordinate system of the target ball B_1 is $R_{Q1} = \begin{bmatrix} Q_{11} & Q_{21} & Q_{31} \end{bmatrix}^T$.

We can obtain $v_i = w \times p_i$. Then in the body coordinate system of L_1, the velocity vector of the ball at the tangent point Q_1 can be written as

$$V_{q1} = \Omega_1 \times R_{q1} = -R_{q1}{}^\times \Omega_1 \tag{8}$$

Similarly, in the body coordinate system of B_1, the velocity vector of the big ball at the tangent point Q_1 can be written as

$$V_{Q1} = \Omega \times R_{Q1} = -R_{Q1}{}^\times \Omega \tag{9}$$

At the tangent point Q_1, assuming that there is no relative sliding, the speeds of the target ball and the driving ball are in the same direction, and the axes of the rectangular coordinate system L_1 and B_1 are parallel and have the same positive direction, so we can obtain

$$V_{q1} = V_{Q1} = -R_{q1}{}^\times \Omega_1 = -R_{Q1}{}^\times \Omega \tag{10}$$

The same can be obtained:

$$V_{qi} = V_{Qi} = -R_{qi}{}^\times \Omega_i = -R_{Qi}{}^\times \Omega \tag{11}$$

among them, $R^\times = \begin{bmatrix} 0 & -q_3 & q_2 \\ q_3 & 0 & -q_1 \\ -q_2 & q_1 & 0 \end{bmatrix}$, $i = 1, 2, 3$.

- Solve the system of equations.

Let $\Omega = \begin{bmatrix} 0 & 0 & 1 \end{bmatrix}^T$, $R_{qi}{}^\times$, $-R_{Qi}{}^\times$ are all known, and Ω_1, Ω_2, Ω_3 can be obtained by Eq. (11). Similarly, we can respectively find a set of angular velocity relations of three driving balls in $\Omega = \begin{bmatrix} 0 & 1 & 0 \end{bmatrix}^T$, $\Omega = \begin{bmatrix} 1 & 0 & 0 \end{bmatrix}^T$. From this we obtain the angular velocity of the driving ball when the target ball rotates around the Y axis or the X axis respectively.

Knowing the angular velocity relationship of the driving ball when the target ball rotates around the X-axis, Y-axis, or Z-axis, we can obtain the angular velocity of the driving ball relationship that can make the target ball rotate around any axis.

3   Electronics

The purpose of this part is mainly to introduce the control framework and the development of drivers and communication programs designed for the test platform above.

The software system of the multi-wheel arm experiment platform is mainly composed of STM32 NUCLED development board, MAX485 chip, and 9 RMDS-109 drivers, as shown in Fig. 5. The development board is mainly used to control the driver and exchange information with the host computer, and it integrates STM32F303RET6, which has a lot of scalability. MAX485 is an RS-485 chip used to send and receive information between the controller and the driver. The 485 communication mode is half-duplex, and can only use the one-main communication mode. And the information sending and receiving requires the controller software switching, and the sequence in time should be strict. In the communication circuit, we have connected 120 Ω resistor to increase the stability of information transmission. The drivers accurately control the motor of wheel hand according to the instructions sent by the controller, and the RMDS-109 driver has a variety of motion modes, including open loop mode, current mode, speed mode, etc. The main driving method we finally adopt is speed-position mode, which performs closed-loop control for the position and controls the speed of the motor. The accuracy of the position is extremely high, which meets our requirements. The control algorithm of the test platform is designed and written on the software platform of the PC section, and downloaded directly to the controller of the robot hardware platform through code generation to run. The performance of the algorithm on the hardware platform can be evaluated through real-time debugging.

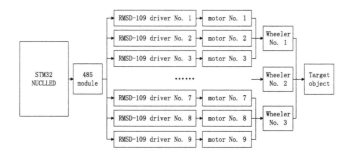

Fig. 5. Frame of software platform.

4   Experiment

The purpose of this paper is to eliminate the rotation angular velocity of the target object through the coordinated movement of three multi-wheel arms. In view of the difficulty of simulating the experimental effect of "detumbling" in a gravity environment, this experiment verifies the feasibility of the scheme by driving the target object to rotate along the axis.

According to the previous design, we built the test platform shown in Fig. 6. The size of target object is 350 mm, and the size of driving ball is 150 mm. Taking

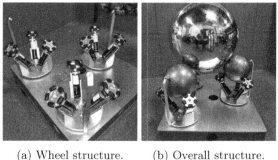

(a) Wheel structure.   (b) Overall structure.

Fig. 6. Main structure of the test platform.

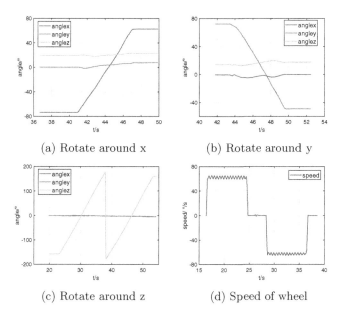

(a) Rotate around x   (b) Rotate around y

(c) Rotate around z   (d) Speed of wheel

Fig. 7. Test results of multi-wheel arms.

into account factors such as quality, surface stiffness, friction, and cost, we finally use the hard plastic ball in the picture as the driving ball.

During the test, we use the STM Studio to observe and adjust the variables to facilitate the debugging of the program. At the same time, the inertial measurement unit (IMU) fixed on the driving ball and the target object is used to obtain the rotation angular velocity, rotation angle, and rotation accuracy and other motion parameter information.

It can be seen from Fig. 7 that when the driving ball rotates around the X axis, the angles of the Y-axis and Z-axis remain unchanged, while the angle of X-axis is approximately linear with time. Similarly, the driving ball around

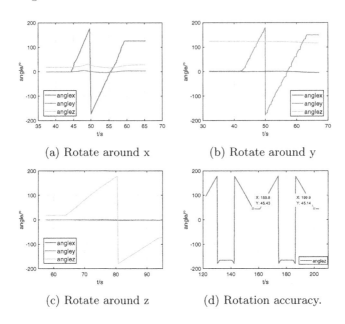

(a) Rotate around x   (b) Rotate around y

(c) Rotate around z   (d) Rotation accuracy.

Fig. 8. Test results of target object.

the Y axis or Z axis both meet requirements. Because the range of the IMU is
$-180°$ to $180°$, a periodic curve is obtained. In the same way, it can be seen
from Fig. 8 that we have realized the control of the target ball around the X-
axis, Y-axis and Z-axis. Finally, the three axes are synthesized, and the target
ball can be controlled to rotate around any axis, so as to realize the detumbling
of the target object. In the wheel hand speed test experiment, a wheel hand
is controlled to rotate positively and negatively around a fixed axis at a fixed
speed, and the data is obtained by the IMU and displayed by drawing. It can be
seen from Fig. 7(d) that this method can make the speed reach $60°$ per second.
In addition, in the accuracy test experiment, we control wheel to rotate to a
certain position around the Z axis at a fixed speed, and after the end, it returns
back to the same position as a rotation cycle. The data is also obtained and
displayed, as shown in Fig. 8(d). It can be seen that the accuracy in one rotation
cycle is $0.29°$, which meets the requirements of rotation accuracy within $0.5°$.

5   Conclusion

In this paper, we researched the problem of detumbling in the process of capturing noncooperative targets in space. We designed a multi-wheel arm test platform
and built a physical model. On the basis of the physical model, the electrical
hardware system is developed on the PC side based on STM32 NUCLED, and
the joint control of multiple groups of single-axis motors is realized. Furthermore, the speed and pose control of the wheel hand and the target object are

realized according to the kinematic analysis. The experimental results show that the platform performance and function test have a good effect on eliminating the rotation problems at low speed. This multi-wheel arm test platform is an effective and feasible method for the elimination of spherical targets in space. For noncooperative targets in real space, due to their randomness, we plan to conduct research on other special-shaped target objects in the future to improve the adaptability of the design.

References

1. Sgobba, T., Rongier, I.: Space Safety is No Accident. Springer, Heidelberg (2015). https://doi.org/10.1007/978-3-319-15982-9
2. Lu, Y., Liu, X.G., Zhou, Y., et al.: Review of detumbling technologies for active removal of uncooperative targets. Acta Aeronautica et Astronautica Sinica **39**(1), 21302–021302 (2018). (in Chinese)
3. Esmiller, B., Jacquelard, C., Eckel, H.-A., Wnuk, E., Gouy, Y.: Space debris removal by ground based laser main conclusions of the European project CLEANSPACE. In: Sgobba, T., Rongier, I. (eds.) Space Safety is No Accident, pp. 13–22. Springer, Cham (2015). https://doi.org/10.1007/978-3-319-15982-9_2
4. Silha, J., Pittet, J.N., Hamara, M., et al.: Apparent rotation properties of space debris extracted from photometric measurements. Adv. Space Res. **61**(3), 884–861 (2018)
5. Cai, H.L., Gao, Y.M., et al.: The research status and key technology analysis of foreign non-cooperative target in space capture system. J. Acad. Equip. Command Technol. **21**(6), 71–77 (2010)
6. Geng, Y.H., Lu, W., Chen, X.Q.: Attitude synchronization control of on-orbit servicing spacecraft with respect to out-of-control target. J. Harbin Inst. Technol. **44**(1), 1–6 (2012). (in Chinese)
7. Gomez, N.O., Walker, S.J.I.: Earth's gravity gradient and eddy currents effects on the rotational dynamics of space debris objects: envisat case study: a new validation approach. Adv. Space Res. **56**(3), 494–508 (2015)
8. Daneshjou, K., Alibakhshi, R.: Multibody dynamical modeling for spacecraft docking process with spring-damper buffering device: a new validation approach. Adv. Space Res. **61**(1), 497–512 (2017)
9. Nishida, S.I., Kawamoto, S.: Strategy for capturing of a tumbling space debris. Acta Astronaut. **68**(1–2), 113–120 (2011)
10. Huang, P., Wang, M., et al.: Reconfigurable spacecraft attitude takeover control in post-capture of target by space manipulators. J. Franklin Inst. **353**(9), 1985–2008 (2016)
11. Matunaga, S., Kanzawa, T., Ohkami, Y.: Rotational motion-damper for the capture of an uncontrolled floating satellite. Control. Eng. Pract. **9**(2), 199–205 (2001)
12. Nagamatsu H, Kubota T, Nakatani I.: Capture strategy for retrieval of a tumbling satellite by a space robotic manipulator. In: IEEE International Conference on Robotics & Automation, pp. 70–75. IEEE (1996)
13. Nakasuka S, Fujiwara T.: New method of capturing tumbling object in space and its control aspects. In: IEEE International Conference on Control Applications, pp. 973–978. IEEE (1999)
14. Flores-Abad, A., Crespo, L.G.: A robotic concept for the NASA asteroid-capture mission. In: AIAA Space Conference & Exposition (2015)

Design and Control of Penta-Jet Aerial Vehicle

Yankai Yin[1], Feng Duan[1(✉)], and Fei Kang[2]

[1] Department of Artificial Intelligence, Nankai University, Tianjin 300350, China
`duanf@nankai.edu.cn`
[2] Department of Systems Life Engineering, Maebashi Institute of Technology,
Maebashi 371-0816, Japan

Abstract. As a new type of aircraft, the unmanned aerial vehicle (UAV) industry has been strongly supported by various countries and has been widely used in civil fields. By combining the advantages of small rotor aircraft and large fixed wing aircraft, we developed a new aircraft named "penta-jet", which has higher power and more flexible flight conditions. The aircraft uses different types of turbojet engines as the power source and uses a thrust vectoring system to control the aircraft's movement. For this new design, we established a mathematical model of penta-jet through dynamic analysis. In order to realize the trajectory tracking ability of the aircraft, we propose a PID-back stepping controller considering the control accuracy and control complexity. Simulations are demonstrate the effectiveness of the designed nonlinear controller.

Keywords: Penta-jet · Mathematical model · PID-back stepping controller

1 Introduction

Unmanned aerial vehicle (UAV), as a new type of aircraft equipment, has become a hot topic for researchers and scholars due to its wide application in several essential application fields such as smart transportation [1], disaster monitoring [2], agricultural mapping [3] and earthquake rescue [4]. UAV can be simply divided into small rotor aircraft and large fixed wing aircraft. Small rotor aircraft use brushless motors as a power source, which has the advantages of low take-off and landing conditions and flexible flight attitude. However, the small size of rotor craft also limits its flight time and load, and is always used in short-distance, lightweight tasks. The power source of the large fixed-wing aircraft is the fuel-based engine. Its more extensive volume and more substantial power

This work was supported by the National Key R&D Program of China (No. 2017YFE0129700), the National Natural Science Foundation of China (Key Program) (No. 11932013), the Tianjin Natural Science Foundation for Distinguished Young Scholars (No. 18JCJQJC46100), and the Tianjin Science and Technology Plan Project (No. 18ZXJMTG00260).

X.-J. Liu et al. (Eds.): ICIRA 2021, LNAI 13015, pp. 760–770, 2021.
https://doi.org/10.1007/978-3-030-89134-3_69

make it have a stronger capacity and longer endurance. However, this also leads to higher landing requirements and greater control difficulty. How to take into account the advantages of small rotor craft and large fixed-wing aircraft, provide better flight performance and lower usage restrictions, is the current focus of aircraft research.

The advent of micro turbojet engines provides new ideas for aircraft research [5]. A new type of small jet aircraft with a structure similar to that of a quadrotor was unveiled for the first time in 2017 [6]. Four turbojet engines are fixed at the corners of the aircraft. A similar study was proposed by Türkmen et al. in 2020 [7]. Although the above research solves the VTOL problem of traditional fixed-wing aircraft, it has the disadvantages of complicated control and poor resistance to environmental interference. In order to reduce the control difficulty of the aircraft, we proposed a new type of jet aircraft design called "penta-jet", using two different types of engines to provide power, and designed a thrust vectoring system to reduce the control difficulty. Penta-jet system has strong nonlinear characteristics and significant hysteresis characteristics, which lead traditional control methods unable to achieve better results. Designing the controller to make the aircraft move according to the desired trajectory is the critical step in aircraft design. In the past few years, researchers have been paying attention to the application of control algorithms in the field of aircraft and have conducted a large number of simulation studies [7–11], such as PID control [12], sliding-mode control [13–16] and fuzzy logic control [17]. In this paper, the penta-jet control structure based on PID-back stepping method is proposed considering the feasibility and control effect of the controller.

This paper are structured as follows: Sect. 2 proposed a new design of the small aircraft vehicle and the translational and rotational model is established; Section 3 provided a controller based on the PID-back stepping method, and the effectiveness of the controller is proved based on Lyapunov's second method for stability; Section 4 shows the control performance of PID-back stepping controller; Conclusion are given in the Sect. 5.

2   Design and Modeling of the Penta-Jet

2.1   Mechanical Design

In order to ensure the structural stability of the aircraft, the proposed jet aircraft uses a rectangle as the main frame. To make the aircraft have sufficient flight power at full load, we use a large turbojet engine as the main power source of the aircraft. The large turbojet engine is located in the center of the aircraft body and provides the main longitudinal thrust for the aircraft. The thrust of the large turbojet engine used in this article is 300 N, and the thrust of the small turbojet engine is 60 N, both of which are purchased from SWIWIN®Turbojet Power Equipment R&D Co., Ltd. The overall structure of the aircraft is shown in Fig. 1(a). The thrust vectoring system of the aircraft is composed of a turbojet engine and a vectoring nozzle as shown in Fig. 1(b). The range of rotation angle α in Fig. 1(b) is within $[-90°, 90°]$.

2.2   Dynamic Modeling

In this section, a mathematical model of the penta-jet aerial vehicle is presented. We uniformly use the superscript b to indicate that the variable belongs to the body fixed frame and e to indicate that it belongs to the inertia frame. First, define the inertia frame $\mathscr{F}^e = \{O^e; X^e, Y^e, Z^e\}$ and the body fixed frame $\mathscr{F}^b = \{O^b; X^b, Y^b, Z^b\}$, as shown in Fig. 1(a). The four small turbojet engines are arranged counterclockwise and numbered, and the distance from the center of the aircraft to the corners are represented by L_x and L_y.

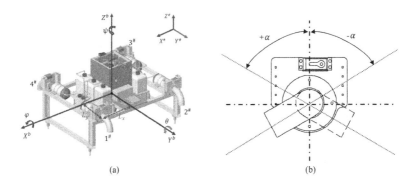

(a)   (b)

Fig. 1. (a) Penta-jet configuration frame scheme with body fixed and the inertia frames; (b) Diagram of thrust vector system.

Define $\xi^e = [\varphi, \ \theta, \ \psi]^T \in \mathbb{R}^3$, where φ, θ and ψ denote the roll angle, pitch angle and yaw angle. The $w^b = [p, \ q, \ r]^T$, where p, q and r represent angular rate with respect to the body fixed frame. By defining the coordinate system as shown in Fig. 1(a) and combining the Euler angles rotation order "φ-θ-ψ", the rotation matrix between $\mathscr{F}^e$ and $\mathscr{F}^b$ is given as:

$$R_b^e = \begin{bmatrix} C_\psi C_\theta & C_\psi S_\theta S_\varphi - S_\psi C_\varphi & C_\psi S_\theta C_\varphi + S_\psi S_\varphi \\ S_\psi C_\theta & S_\psi S_\theta S_\varphi - S_\psi C_\varphi & S_\psi S_\theta C_\varphi - C_\psi S_\varphi \\ S_\theta & C_\theta S_\varphi & C_\theta C_\varphi \end{bmatrix}, \tag{1}$$

where $S_{(\cdot)}$ denotes $\sin(\cdot)$ and $C_{(\cdot)}$ represents $\cos(\cdot)$. The conversion relationship between Euler angles ξ^e and the angular velocity w^b can be expressed as:

$$\begin{bmatrix} p \\ q \\ r \end{bmatrix} = \begin{bmatrix} 1 & 0 & -\sin(\theta) \\ 0 & \cos(\varphi) & \cos(\theta)\sin(\varphi) \\ 0 & -\sin(\varphi) & \cos(\theta)\cos(\varphi) \end{bmatrix} \begin{bmatrix} \dot{\varphi} \\ \dot{\theta} \\ \dot{\psi} \end{bmatrix}. \tag{2}$$

Assuming that the aircraft rotates at a small angle, the above equation can be rewritten as:

$$[p, q, r]^T = \left[\dot{\varphi}, \dot{\theta}, \dot{\psi} \right]^T. \tag{3}$$

Similar to quadrotor, the following assumptions are defined to make the modeling process more concise and controller design more rigorous [18]:

(i) The penta-jet aerial vehicle system is considered a rigid body system symmetrical on the X, Y, and Z axes, and the structure is rigid without internal force and deformation [19].
(ii) The torque generated by the turbine rotation in the turbojet engine to the system is ignored.
(iii) The origin in the body fixed frame coincides with the center of gravity.
(iv) Assuming that the turbojet engine system has no time lag and can quickly reach the desired control value.

Translational Dynamic Model. To decrease the difficulty of control and reduce the influence of the differences between turbojet engines on the model, the thrust of large turbojet engines is set to be constant, and the thrust of small turbojet engines can only changing at the same time. Use F_0 to represents the constant thrust generated by the central turbojet, and use F to represent the thrust generated by the small turbojets, respectively. The subscript i was used to represent the number of turbojets and the corresponding vector nozzles in Fig. 1(a), and the thrust in body fixed frame is defined as:

$$F_i^b = \begin{bmatrix} F\sin(\alpha_i) \\ 0 \\ F\cos(\alpha_i) \end{bmatrix}. \tag{4}$$

The total thrust produced by turbojet engine is given as:

$$F_T^b = \sum_{i=1}^{4} F_i^b + \begin{bmatrix} 0 \\ 0 \\ F_0 \end{bmatrix}. \tag{5}$$

The total force of the aerial vehicle in the inertia frame can be expressed as:

$$F_T^e = R_b^e \cdot F_T^b + F_g^e, \tag{6}$$

where F_g^e represents the gravity of penta-jet. It is worth noting that the inner and cross product is defined as symbols $\cdot$ and $\times$, respectively.

According to the Newton's laws of motion, the translational dynamic model can be expressed as:

$$m\ddot{P}^e = F_T^e. \tag{7}$$

where $P^e = [x, y, z]^T$ is the position with respect to the inertia frame.

Rotational Dynamic Model. The torque produced by i-th jet engine with respect to the body-fixed frame is given as follows:

$$M_i^b = L_i^b \times F_i^b, \tag{8}$$

where L_i denotes the distance between turbojet engine and the center of gravity can be obtained from Fig. 1(a) and given as:

$$\begin{cases} L_1 = [L_x, L_y, 0]^T \\ L_2 = [-L_x, L_y, 0]^T \\ L_3 = [-L_x, -L_y, 0]^T \\ L_4 = [L_x, -L_y, 0]^T \end{cases}. \tag{9}$$

The total torque produced by turbojet engine can be be expressed as:

$$M_T^b = \sum_{i=1}^{4} L_i^b \times F_i^b. \tag{10}$$

Assuming that the system is symmetric about X, Y, Z axis, and J denotes diagonal inertia matrix, which can be described as:

$$J = \begin{bmatrix} J_{xx} & 0 & 0 \\ 0 & J_{yy} & 0 \\ 0 & 0 & J_{zz} \end{bmatrix}. \tag{11}$$

According to the Newton–Euler equations, the rotational equation of the penta-jet's motion can be written as:

$$M_T^b = J\dot{\omega}^b + (\omega^b \times J\omega^b). \tag{12}$$

Through the analysis of the translational and rotational dynamic model, the input variables are F, α_1, α_2, α_3 and α_4. In order to simplify the model, five virtual control variables are set as control inputs defined as follows:

$$\begin{cases} U_0 = F_{Tx}^b = F[\sin(\alpha_1) + \sin(\alpha_2) + \sin(\alpha_3) + \sin(\alpha_4)] \\ U_1 = F_{Tz}^b = F[\cos(\alpha_1) + \cos(\alpha_2) + \cos(\alpha_3) + \cos(\alpha_4)] + F_0 \\ U_2 = M_{Tx}^b = L_y F[\cos(\alpha_1) + \cos(\alpha_2) - \cos(\alpha_3) - \cos(\alpha_4)] \\ U_3 = M_{Ty}^b = L_x F[-\cos(\alpha_1) + \cos(\alpha_2) + \cos(\alpha_3) - \cos(\alpha_4)] \\ U_4 = M_{Tz}^b = L_y F[-\cos(\alpha_1) - \cos(\alpha_2) + \cos(\alpha_3) + \cos(\alpha_4)] \end{cases}, \tag{13}$$

where F_{Tx}^b and F_{Tz}^b are the forces on the X and Z axis of the aircraft with respect to the body-fixed frame, respectively. M_{Tx}^b, M_{Ty}^b and M_{Tz}^b are the torques on the X, Y and Z axes of the aircraft, respectively.

Combine Eq. (7), Eq. (12) and Eq. (13), and convert the obtained penta-jet mathematical model into a state space model is given by:

$$\begin{cases} \ddot{x} = \frac{U_0}{m}(C_\psi C_\theta) + \frac{U_1}{m}(S_\psi S_\varphi + C_\psi S_\theta C_\varphi) \\ \ddot{y} = \frac{U_0}{m}(S_\psi C_\theta) + \frac{U_1}{m}(-C_\psi S_\varphi + S_\psi S_\theta C_\varphi) \\ \ddot{z} = \frac{U_0}{m}(-S_\theta) + \frac{U_1}{m}(C_\theta C_\varphi) - g \end{cases} \quad \begin{cases} \ddot{\varphi} = \frac{J_{yy}-J_{zz}}{J_{xx}}\dot{\theta}\dot{\psi} + \frac{U_2}{J_{xx}} \\ \ddot{\theta} = \frac{J_{zz}-J_{xx}}{J_{yy}}\dot{\varphi}\dot{\psi} + \frac{U_3}{J_{yy}} \\ \ddot{\psi} = \frac{J_{xx}-J_{yy}}{J_{zz}}\dot{\varphi}\dot{\theta} + \frac{U_4}{J_{zz}}) \end{cases}. \tag{14}$$

The parameters for the penta-jet aerial vehicle proposed in this study are described in Table 1.

Table 1. Penta-jet physical parameters.

Symbol	Value	Units	Symbol	Value	Units
m	25	kg	J_{xx}	9	N s^2 rad^{-2}
g	9.8	m/s^2	J_{yy}	10	N s^2 rad^{-2}
L_x	0.3775	m	J_{zz}	17	N s^2 rad^{-2}
L_y	0.275	m			

3 Controller Design

The unique design of penta-jet aerial vehicle system makes it has the character-istics of highly nonlinear and strong coupling. The properties of under-actuated also make the controller design more difficult. The traditional PID controller has a simple structure and easy parameter adjustment characteristics, but the control accuracy is low, and the control effect for nonlinear systems is not ideal. Back stepping controller is a controller design method based on the reverse design. It combines the selection of the Lyapunov function with the design of the controller. It has the ability to control the nonlinear nth-order differential systems, which has received more and more attention in the aircraft field. In this section, a PID-back stepping controller is proposed, and the effectiveness of the controller is proved based on Lyapunov's second method for stability.

By optimizing the dynamic model of the aircraft system, Eq. (14) can be rewritten as:

$$
\begin{cases}
\dot{x}_1 = \dot{\varphi} = x_2 \\
\dot{x}_2 = a_1 x_4 x_6 + b_1 U_2 \\
\dot{x}_3 = \dot{\theta} = x_4 \\
\dot{x}_4 = a_2 x_2 x_6 + b_2 U_3 \\
\dot{x}_5 = \dot{\psi} = x_6 \\
\dot{x}_6 = a_3 x_2 x_4 + b_3 U_4
\end{cases}
\qquad
\begin{cases}
\dot{x}_7 = \dot{z} = x_8 \\
\dot{x}_8 = \frac{U_0}{m}\left(-S_\theta\right) + \frac{U_1}{m}\left(C_\theta C_\varphi\right) - g \\
\dot{x}_9 = \dot{x} = x_{10} \\
\dot{x}_{10} = \frac{U_0}{m}\left(C_\psi C_\theta\right) + \frac{U_1}{m}\left(S_\psi S_\varphi + C_\psi S_\theta C_\varphi\right) \\
\dot{x}_{11} = \dot{y} = x_{12} \\
\dot{x}_{12} = \frac{U_0}{m}\left(S_\psi C_\theta\right) + \frac{U_1}{m}\left(-C_\psi S_\varphi + S_\psi S_\theta C_\varphi\right)
\end{cases}
\tag{15}
$$

where $a_1 = \frac{J_{yy} - J_{zz}}{J_{xx}}$, $a_2 = \frac{J_{zz} - J_{xx}}{J_{yy}}$, $a_3 = \frac{J_{xx} - J_{yy}}{J_{zz}}$, $b_1 = \frac{1}{J_{xx}}$, $b_2 = \frac{1}{J_{yy}}$ and $b_3 = \frac{1}{J_{zz}}$.

The PID-backstepping controller adopts a cascade control structure, and the output of the outer loop system is used as the desired input of the inner loop system. The block diagram of the PID-back stepping control structure is shown in Fig. 2. The reference trajectory of the system are $\{x_d, y_d, z_d, \theta_d, \psi_d\}$, and the output of the PID controller is used to obtained the desired ψ trajectory in the inner loop of the system.

First, the PID algorithm was used to obtain the virtual control variables U_y, which can described as

$$
U_y = k_{py}\left(y - y_d\right) + k_{iy}\int\left(y - y_d\right)\mathrm{d}t + k_{dy}\left(\dot{y} - \dot{y}_d\right),
\tag{16}
$$

where k_{py} is the proportional gain, k_{dy} represents the derivative gain, k_{iy} is the integral gain. Substituting Eq. (16) into the 12th equation of Eq. (15) can obtained:

$$U_y = \frac{U_0}{m}\left(S_\psi C_\theta\right) + \frac{U_1}{m}\left(-C_\psi S_\varphi + S_\psi S_\theta C\varphi\right). \tag{17}$$

Remark: We design the controller for aircraft at and small angle hovering station, and linearize the dynamics at the hover state, where we have $U_0 \approx 0$, $U_1 \approx mg$, $\sin(\varphi_d) \approx \varphi_d$, $\sin(\theta_d) \approx \theta_d$, $\cos(\varphi_d) = \cos(\theta_d) \approx 1$.

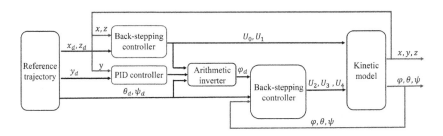

Fig. 2. Block diagram of the PID-backstepping control structure

The φ_d can be obtained by transforming Eq. (17):

$$\varphi_d = \frac{U_y - g\left(S_{\varphi_d}\theta_d\right)}{g\left(-C_{\psi_d}\right)}. \tag{18}$$

The controller design for the desired position $\{x_d, z_d\}$ and the desired rotation angles $\{\varphi_d, \theta_d, \psi_d\}$ will adopt the back stepping method. The tracking error between reference altitude z_d and actual system output z can be defined as

$$e_{z1} = z_d - z = x_{7d} - x_7, \tag{19}$$

and the derivative of e_{z1} can obtained:

$$\dot{e}_{z1} = \dot{z}_d - \dot{z} = \dot{x}_{7d} - \dot{x}_7 = \dot{x}_{7d} - x_8. \tag{20}$$

The Lyapunov candidate is designed as

$$V_{z1} = \frac{1}{2}e_{z1}{}^2. \tag{21}$$

The derivative of Eq. (21) with respect to the time can be expressed as:

$$\dot{V}_{z1} = e_{z1}\dot{e}_{z1} = e_{z1}\left(\dot{x}_{7d} - x_{7d}\right). \tag{22}$$

For Eq. (21) to be stable, $\dot{x}_7$ is adopted as virtual control, and $(\dot{x}_7)_d$ should satisfy the following condition:

$$(\dot{x}_7)_d = c_{z1}e_{z1} + \dot{x}_{7d}, \tag{23}$$

where c_{z1} is a positive constant, which satisfy $\dot{V}_1 \leq 0$.

By substituting Eq. (23) to Eq. (20), we can obtained:

$$\dot{e}_{z1} = \dot{x}_{7d} - \dot{x}_7 = (\dot{x}_7)_d - c_{z1}e_{z1} - \dot{x}_7. \tag{24}$$

The designed error between the virtual control $\dot{x}_7$ and the desired value $(\dot{x}_7)_d$ is shown as

$$e_{z2} = (\dot{x}_7)_d - \dot{x}_7 = c_{z1}e_{z1} + \dot{x}_{7d} - \dot{x}_7. \tag{25}$$

The derivation of Eq. (25) with substitute Eq. (24) is obtained as follows:

$$\begin{aligned}
\dot{e}_{z2} &= c_{z1}\dot{e}_{z1} + \ddot{x}_{7d} - \ddot{x}_7 = c_{z1}\dot{e}_{z1} + \ddot{x}_{7d} - \dot{x}_8 \\
&= c_{z1}(-c_{z1}e_{z1} + e_{z2}) + \ddot{x}_{7d} - [\frac{U_0}{m}(-S_\theta) + \frac{U_1}{m}(C_\theta C_\varphi) - g]
\end{aligned} \tag{26}$$

The second Lyapunov candidate for altitude is chosen as

$$V_{z2} = \frac{1}{2}e_{z1}{}^2 + \frac{1}{2}e_{z2}{}^2. \tag{27}$$

The derivative of Eq. (27) with respect to the time can be described by substituting Eq. (24) as

$$\dot{V}_{z2} = e_{z1}\dot{e}_{z1} + e_{z2}\dot{e}_{z2} = e_{z1}(-c_{z1}e_{z1} + e_{z2}) + e_{z2}\dot{e}_{z2}. \tag{28}$$

To stabilize V_{z2}, the $\dot{e}_{z2}$ can be defined as

$$\dot{e}_{z2} = -c_{z2}e_{z2} - e_{z1}, \tag{29}$$

where c_{z2} is a positive constant, and the following equation can be obtained:

$$\begin{aligned}
\dot{V}_{z2} &= e_{z1}(-c_{z1}e_{z1} + e_{z2}) - c_{z2}e_{z2}{}^2 - e_{z1}e_{z2} \\
&= -c_{z1}e_{z1}{}^2 - c_{z2}e_{z2}{}^2 \le 0
\end{aligned} \tag{30}$$

By combined Eq. (26) with Eq. (29), the back stepping controller is given as

$$U_1 = \frac{m}{C_\theta C_\varphi}\left[(-c_{z1}{}^2 + 1)e_{z1} + (c_{z1} + c_{z2})e_{z2} + \ddot{x}_{7d} + \frac{U_0}{m}S_\theta + g\right]. \tag{31}$$

Combining the dynamic model described in Eq. (15), the backstepping controller for $\{x, \varphi, \theta, \psi\}$ can be obtained by using same method are given as:

$$U_0 = \frac{m}{C_\psi C_\theta}\left[(-c_{x1}{}^2 + 1)e_{x1} + (c_{x1} + c_{x2})e_{x2} + \ddot{x}_{9d} - \frac{U_1}{m}(S_\psi S_\varphi + C_\psi S_\theta C_\varphi)\right], \tag{32}$$

$$U_2 = \frac{1}{b_1}\left[(-c_{\varphi1}{}^2 + 1)e_{\varphi1} + (c_{\varphi1} + c_{\varphi2})e_{\varphi2} + \ddot{x}_{1d} - a_1 x_4 x_6\right], \tag{33}$$

$$U_3 = \frac{1}{b_2}\left[(-c_{\theta1}{}^2 + 1)e_{\theta1} + (c_{\theta1} + c_{\theta2})e_{\theta2} + \ddot{x}_{3d} - a_2 x_2 x_6\right], \tag{34}$$

$$U_4 = \frac{1}{b_3}\left[(-c_{\psi1}{}^2 + 1)e_{\psi1} + (c_{\psi1} + c_{\psi2})e_{\psi2} + \ddot{x}_{5d} - a_3 x_2 x_4\right]. \tag{35}$$

4 Simulation

In this section, the method proposed in Sect. 3 is used for simulation to verify the effectiveness of the proposed PID-back stepping controller. The desired trajectory of the aircraft is set as:

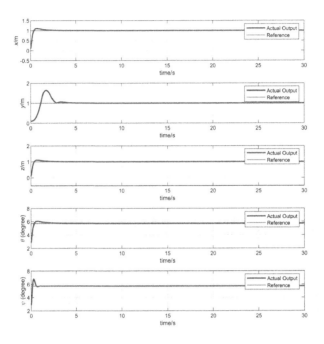

Fig. 3. Control performance by using PID-back stepping controller.

$$x_d = 1, y_d = 1, z_d = 2, \theta_d = 0.2, \psi_d = 0.2. \tag{36}$$

The parameter used in the PID controller in this study is $k_{py} = 0.9$, $k_{dy} = 0.3$, $k_{iy} = 0.8$, and the tracking performance of the PID-back stepping controller to the desired position and attitude is shown in Fig. 3. The adjustment time of x, y, z, θ and ψ are 3 s, 5 s, 2 s, 2 s and 1 s, respectively. It can be seen from the Fig. 3 that the PID-back stepping controller proposed in this paper has a better performance in the penta-jet model. The result of Fig. 4 indicate that compared to using PID controller to direct control y-position, the tracking error is much larger than that of x-position and z-position controlled by back stepping controller. This is because the back stepping method is a model-based control method, which is more powerful for complex nonlinear model control. However, if the back stepping method is used for both x-position, y-position, and z-position, it will lead to the computational complexity greatly increased when calculate φ_d by using arithmetic inverse.

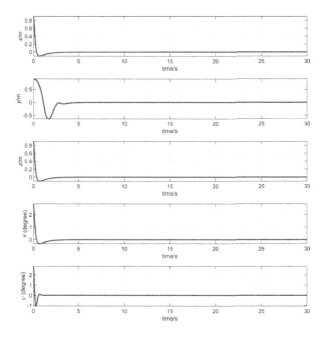

Fig. 4. Trajectory tracking errors vs. time.

5   Conclusion

By combining the advantages of rotor aircraft and fixed-wing aircraft, this paper proposes a new type of turbojet aircraft design called "penta-jet", which has lower take-off and landing conditions and easier to control. This paper describes the structure design of penta-jet in detail and establishes a nonlinear mathematical model through the dynamic analysis of the aircraft. By comprehensively considering the complexity and accuracy of the controller design, a robust controller combining PID control and back stepping control methods are proposed. The performance of the proposed PID-back stepping controller is tested through the expected motion trajectory tracking, and the simulation results prove the effectiveness of the proposed method. The series of aircraft design and control methods proposed in this paper have guiding significance for the research and development of new jet aircraft. Our future work includes iterating the penta-jet design and developing more robust controllers.

References

1. Menouar, H., Guvenc, I., Akkaya, K., et al.: UAV-enabled intelligent transportation systems for the smart city: applications and challenges. IEEE Commun. Mag. **55**(3), 22–28 (2017)
2. Panda, K.G., Das, S., Sen, D., et al.: Design and deployment of UAV-aided postdisaster emergency network. IEEE Access **7**, 102985–102999 (2019)

3. Sun, F., Wang, X., Zhang, R.: Task scheduling system for UAV operations in agricultural plant protection environment. J. Ambient Intell. Hum. Comput. 1–15 (2020)

4. Martin, P.G., Payton, O.D., Fardoulis, J.S., et al.: Low altitude unmanned aerial vehicle for characterising remediation effectiveness following the FDNPP accident. J. Environ. Radioact. **151**, 58–63 (2016)

5. Jafari, S., Miran Fashandi, S.A., Nikolaidis, T.: Control requirements for future gas turbine-powered unmanned drones: JetQuads. Appl. Sci. **8**(12), 2675 (2018)

6. Fashandi, S.A.M., Montazeri-gh, M.: Modeling and simulation of JetQuad aerial robot. In: 2017 IEEE 4th International Conference on Knowledge-Based Engineering and Innovation (KBEI), pp. 753–762. IEEE (2017)

7. Tayebi, A., McGilvray, S.: Attitude stabilization of a VTOL quadrotor aircraft. IEEE Trans. Control Syst. Technol. **14**(3), 562–571 (2006)

8. Bertrand, S., Guénard, N., Hamel, T., et al.: A hierarchical controller for miniature VTOL UAVs: design and stability analysis using singular perturbation theory. Control. Eng. Pract. **19**(10), 1099–1108 (2011)

9. Zhang, Y., Chen, Z., Zhang, X., et al.: A novel control scheme for quadrotor UAV based upon active disturbance rejection control. Aerosp. Sci. Technol. **79**, 601–609 (2018)

10. Alexis, K., Nikolakopoulos, G., Tzes, A.: Switching model predictive attitude control for a quadrotor helicopter subject to atmospheric disturbances. Control. Eng. Pract. **19**(10), 1195–1207 (2011)

11. Taeyoung, L.: Robust adaptive attitude tracking on with an application to a quadrotor UAV. IEEE Trans. Control Syst. Technol.: Publ. IEEE Control Syst. Soc. **21**(5), 1924–1930 (2013)

12. Pounds, P.E.I., Bersak, D.R., Dollar, A.M.: Stability of small-scale UAV helicopters and quadrotors with added payload mass under PID control. Auton. Robot. **33**(1), 129–142 (2012)

13. Mokhtari, A., Benallegue, A., Orlov, Y.: Exact linearization and sliding mode observer for a quadrotor unmanned aerial vehicle. Int. J. Robot. Autom. **21**(1), 39–49 (2006)

14. Merheb A R, Noura H, Bateman F.: Design of passive fault-tolerant controllers of a quadrotor based on sliding mode theory. Int. J. Appl. Math. Comput. Sci. **25** (2015)

15. Wang, T., Xie, W., Zhang, Y.: Sliding mode reconfigurable control using information on the control effectiveness of actuators. J. Aerosp. Eng. **27**(3), 587–596 (2014)

16. Besnard, L., Shtessel, Y.B., Landrum, B.: Quadrotor vehicle control via sliding mode controller driven by sliding mode disturbance observer. J. Franklin Inst. **349**(2), 658–684 (2012)

17. Fu, C., Sarabakha, A., Kayacan, E., et al.: Input uncertainty sensitivity enhanced nonsingleton fuzzy logic controllers for long-term navigation of quadrotor UAVs. IEEE/ASME Trans. Mechatron. **23**(2), 725–734 (2018)

18. Alkamachi, A., Erçelebi, E.: Modelling and genetic algorithm based-PID control of H-shaped racing quadcopter. Arab. J. Sci. Eng. **42**(7), 2777–2786 (2017)

19. Hua, M.D., Hamel, T., Morin, P., et al.: Introduction to feedback control of underactuated VTOL vehicles: a review of basic control design ideas and principles. IEEE Control Syst. Mag. **33**(1), 61–75 (2013)

Leg Design for Delivery Quadruped Robots Based on EMA and Energy Optimization

Haoyuan Yi[1], Zhenyu Xu[1,2], Liming Zhou[2], and Xin Luo[1(✉)]

[1] School of Mechanical Science and Engineering, Huazhong University of Science and Technology, Wuhan, China
mexinluo@hust.edu.cn

[2] Research Institute, Inner Mongolia First Machinery Group Co. Ltd, Baotou, China

Abstract. In biomechanics and robotics, the effective mechanical advantage (EMA) is a characteristic quantity representing the relationship between the joint driving force and environmental contact force. EMA and energy consumption are particularly critical for the delivery legged robot because an optimized EMA can reduce the demand for joint actuation forces, thus reduce energy consumption. This paper proposes a leg design approach based on EMA and energy cost optimization for developing a delivery legged robot which optimizes the leg dimensions and hinge point locations. An electrically actuated tri-segmented leg prototype has been developed following the optimal leg structure. The hinge points of each joint are close to the main support line to achieve the effect of dead-lock support. The design load capacity of the leg is 3 tons with a load-to-weight ratio of 15:1. It can realize a swing frequency of 0.65 Hz at a stride length of 0.8 m.

Keywords: Legged robot · EMA · Energy consumption · Dead-lock support

1 Introduction

Legged robots have good adaptability and fault tolerance in complex terrain [1]. Thus they have potential applications in the fields of mountain materials delivery, urban logistics distribution. The load capacity and energy consumption are crucial indicators for delivery legged robots. But high load capacity poses a challenge to the design of the robot's legs. Current designs for legged robots often use solutions with ultra-high drive requirements to enhance the mobility of robots. However, such design ideas are unsuitable for heavy-duty legged robots due to the existing drive system power-to-weight ratio. Biomechanical studies have shown that EMA is an essential indicator of the force generation mechanism of terrestrial mammals [2]. The effective mechanical advantage (EMA) is an essential characteristic quantity of the input and output of the legged force generation system. As the size of terrestrial mammals increases, their posture becomes more upright, and the EMA increases [3]. Mammals can use structural dead-end support to enhance the load-bearing capacity and reduce the muscle force requirements during walking. Such a legged force-generating mechanism can provide design ideas for the legs of heavy-duty legged robots.

© Springer Nature Switzerland AG 2021
X.-J. Liu et al. (Eds.): ICIRA 2021, LNAI 13015, pp. 771–780, 2021.
https://doi.org/10.1007/978-3-030-89134-3_70

The leg design of current legged robots is mainly bio-inspired, based on geometrical similarity to the terrestrial mammals. Researchers often choose a mammal's leg as the template and design the leg structure reference to each part of the mammal's leg length ratio. Garcia used the horse's leg structure as a bionic template and developed the HADE2 leg prototype based on the horse's leg length ratio [4]. Alexander Spröwitz designed the Cheetah-cup prototype based on the length ratio of the cat's legs [5]. However, there are also a few robots introduce modified mammal leg structure, such as ASV. The ASV leg adopts a parallelogram mechanism, which simplifies the movement of the leg [6]. But the leg components still bear a large bending moment as the leg's knee joint is severely bent during walking.

Much research has been done on the legged force germination mechanism. Andrew A. Biewener analyzed different types of mammals and found that a more upright posture could potentially increase the EMA of an animal's muscles by aligning the limb's joints more closely with the ground reaction force's vector and an increased EMA allows a decrease in muscle force without loss of torque [7]. M. Reilly found that the small mammal's leg is often crouched to complete most motion, and the large mammal's leg is much more upright to complete the motion [3]. He also found that the EMA of the leg increase as the size of the mammal increase. Michael Gunther conducted a mathematical analysis on optimizing the leg component layout based on EMA [8]. Duncan W. Haldane designed a robotic galago considering the MA (mechanical advantage) to achieve outstanding jumping ability [9].

This paper focuses on the mechanical design of legs for heavy-duty leg robots and proposes an EMA-based leg design method. We construct an analysis model of the robot's leg based on the EMA and energy consumption and optimize the limb length and actuator hinge position. A real leg prototype has been developed following the proposed leg structure. The motion test experiment has been conducted, and the leg prototype shows good motion capacity.

2 Model Analysis of Legged System

2.1 EMA Analysis of the Robot Leg

Biomechanical studies have shown that small mammals move in a curled limb posture, while large mammals are much more upright. This change in the limb configuration is necessary because it affects the muscles' forces to support the limb during contact with the ground.

Limb muscles support and move the mammals by exerting moments about the muscles must exert is determined by the equation for the balance of moments acting about the joint:

$$f \times r = F_r \times R \tag{1}$$

where r is the moment arm of the muscle and R is the moment arm of the ground reaction force (F_r). The effective mechanical advantage (EMA) of muscle as the moment arm ratio, r/R, which determines the relative magnitude of muscle force needed to counteract the external force acting about the joint. An increased EMA permits a decrease in muscle force without loss of torque. According to Eq. (1), when F_r and R are certain, the decrease of r can reduce the demand of leg joint driving force f.

The current legged robots mainly adopt two kinds of configurations, two-segmented and tri-segmented. When the max effective lengths of the legs are equal, the tri-segmented leg allows the leg drive joints to be closer to the main support line at the same walking height and stride length. This characteristic can reduce joint drive force requirements achieving the effect of "dead point" support. On the other hand, suppose the two-segment leg want to achieve the same effect. In that case, it needs to remain nearly straight in the movement process, which would cause fluctuations in the body's center of gravity during walking, reducing the smoothness of movement. Thus the tri-segmented leg configuration can reduce the drive requirement while ensuring the smooth motion of the robot.

As for the specific structure of the tri-segmented leg, we assume that the shape of each limb is polygons, and the specific structure of the leg can be determined based on the dimensional parameters of each polygon. And the leg adopts the linear actuator. The assumed tri-segmented leg is as shown in Fig. 1. According to the definition of EMA, the EMA of each driving joint is as follows.

$$\begin{aligned} \text{EMA}_{hip} &= \tfrac{r_1}{R_1} = \tfrac{r_1}{|P_{x3}|} \\ \text{EMA}_{knee} &= \tfrac{r_2}{R_2} = \tfrac{r_2}{|P_{x3}-P_{x1}|} \\ \text{EMA}_{ankle} &= \tfrac{r_3}{R_3} = \tfrac{r_3}{|P_{x3}-P_{x2}|} \end{aligned} \qquad (2)$$

For the hip joint, the position of the linear actuator hinge can be determined by four length parameters, l_{uv0}, l_{uh0}, l_{uv1}, l_{uh1}. We can set the coefficients of these parameters with the length of the first limb so that the location of the actuator hinge point can be determined from the limb length and these coefficients. The coefficients are as follow, $p_{uv0} = l_{uv0}/L_1$, $p_{uh0} = l_{uh0}/L_1$, $p_{uv1} = l_{uv1}/L_1$, $p_{uh1} = l_{uh1}/L_1$. Similarly, we can define the knee joint and ankle joint parameters, and each includes five parameters. The knee joint parameters are $(L_2, p_{mv0}, p_{mh0}, p_{mv1}, p_{mh1})$, where $p_{mv0} = l_{mv0}/L_1$, $p_{mh0} = l_{mh0}/L_1$, $p_{mv1} = l_{mv1}/L_2$, $p_{mh1} = l_{mh1}/L_2$. The ankle joint parameters are $(L_3, p_{dv0}, p_{dh0}, p_{dv1}, p_{dh1})$, where $p_{dv0} = l_{dv0}/L_2$, $p_{dh0} = l_{dh0}/L_2$, $p_{dv1} = l_{dv1}/L_3$, $p_{dh1} = l_{dh1}/L_3$. Thus, there are fifteen parameters of the leg structure, and these parameters can be divided into two groups. One group is the limb length parameters (L_1, L_2, L_3), and one group is the actuator hinge position parameters $(p_{uv0}, p_{uh0}, p_{uv1}, p_{uh1}, p_{mv0}, p_{mh0}, p_{mv1}, p_{mh1}, p_{dv0}, p_{dh0}, p_{dv1}, p_{dh1})$. We will analyze the kinematics, dynamics, and energy consumption models of the tri-segmented leg, which will be used to optimize the leg structure parameters.

2.2 Kinematics, Dynamics and Energy Cost Analysis

The kinematics parameters of the tri-segmented leg are defined as shown in Fig. 2.
The direct kinematics is

$$\begin{cases} x = L_1 \cos(q_1) + L_2 \cos(q_1 + q_2) + L_3 \cos(q_1 + q_2 + q_3) \\ z = -(L_1 \sin(q_1) + L_2 \sin(q_1 + q_2) + L_3 \sin(q_1 + q_2 + q_3)) \end{cases} \qquad (3)$$

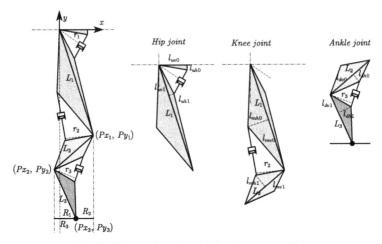

Fig. 1. The configuration of the tri-segmented leg

Fig. 2. Kinematics parameters of the leg

The jacobian matrix of the leg is

$$\mathbf{J} = \begin{bmatrix} -L_1\sin(q_1) - L_2\sin(q_1+q_2) - L_3\sin(q_1+q_2+q_3) & -L_2\sin(q_1+q_2) - L_3\sin(q_1+q_2+q_3) & -L_3\sin(q_1+q_2+q_3) \\ -L_1\cos(q_1) - L_2\cos(q_1+q_2) - L_3\cos(q_1+q_2+q_3) & -L_2\cos(q_1+q_2) - L_3\cos(q_1+q_2+q_3) & -L_3\cos(q_1+q_2+q_3) \end{bmatrix}$$

When the mobile robot moves its leg, the driving force should overcome the inertia force of the leg. This part of dynamics can be derived through the Lagrangian equation.

$$\begin{cases} \frac{\mathrm{d}}{\mathrm{dt}}\left(\frac{\partial L}{\partial \dot{q}}\right) - \frac{\partial L}{\partial q} = 0 \\ L = T - V \end{cases} \tag{4}$$

In the equation, L is Lagrange quantity, T is system kinetic energy, V is system potential. The final dynamics equation is as follow

$$\tau = \mathrm{M}(q)\ddot{q} + \mathrm{C}(q,\dot{q})\dot{q} + \mathrm{G}(q) \tag{5}$$

When the robot walks at a constant horizontal speed v, the foot of the standing leg will get the reaction force of the ground. The foot reaction force should make sure the foot does not slip and support the body's motion. The support foot has two degrees of freedom along the ground and the ground's normal direction. These two directions need to be constrained to keep the support foot stationary. The friction between the support foot and the ground prevents the support foot from sliding along the ground, and the ground support force ensures that the support foot is always on the ground during walking.

Suppose the angle between the leg support line and the ground normal line is θ. Then, the body's motion can be decomposed into a circular motion with linear velocity $v \cos \theta$ and motion radius $R = H / \cos \theta$, and a motion along the leg support line with a velocity of $v \sin \theta$. The decomposition of motion is shown in Fig. 3.

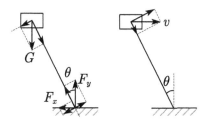

Fig. 3. Motion decomposition

Combined with the above analysis, the system motion needs to satisfy the following constraint equations:

$$
\begin{aligned}
G \cos \theta - F_y \cos \theta - F_x \sin \theta &= m_0 \left(\frac{v^2 \cos^2 \theta}{R} + \dot{v} \sin \theta \right) \\
F_y \sin \theta - F_x \cos \theta - G \sin \theta &= -m_0 \dot{v} \cos \theta
\end{aligned}
\tag{6}
$$

Since the body is moving at a constant horizontal velocity v, $\dot{v} = 0$. The relationship between driving joint torque and foot reaction force is $\tau = \mathbf{J}^T \mathbf{F}$.

The energy consumption depends on the torque and speed of every joint, which is related to physical parameters, such as the robot's weight, body speed, and gait parameters. We assume the weight (G) does not change, and the body speed is constant. Then we choose the specific resistance ε as our energy consumption analysis index [10], which is defined as

$$
\varepsilon = \frac{E}{GL} = \frac{P}{Gv}
\tag{7}
$$

where E is the energy required to travel a distance, L, by a robot with weight G. P is the power consumed and v is the robot's speed. It is a relative comparison that considers the power consumed per unit of mass and unit of speed.

3   Mechanic Design of the Leg Based on EMA and Energy

According to the previous definition of the leg, there are two groups of structural parameters, limb length parameters and actuator hinge position parameters. We optimize these parameters in groups to obtain the optimal leg structure. For limb length parameters (L_1, L_2, L_3), the energy consumption and joint torque are considered together. The optimizations of actuator hinge position parameters are based on each drive joint's EMA. As the leg design method is mainly developed for large delivery legged robots, thus we set some basic compute conditions for the leg structure optimization. The total length of the leg is 2 m, ie. $L_1 + L_2 + L_3 = 2m$. The robot's walking speed is 1.4 m/s, the walking height is 1.8 m, and the leg walking cycle is 1 s. Based on the set conditions and the constructed model, we carry out the optimization of structural parameters.

3.1 Limb Length Optimization Based on Energy Consumption Analysis

As the total length of the leg is determined, the limb length ratio of the leg affects the energy cost when robot walking. It is necessary to optimize the limb length ratio of the leg to reduce the energy consumption when robot walking. The first limb length ratio is $\lambda_1 = \frac{L_1}{L_1 + L_2 + L_3}$, the second limb length ratio is $\lambda_2 = \frac{L_2}{L_1 + L_2 + L_3}$, the third limb length ratio is $\lambda_3 = \frac{L_3}{L_1 + L_2 + L_3}$ and $\lambda_1 + \lambda_2 + \lambda_3 = 1$.

The peak power and peak joint torque of the legs during one gait cycle can guide the design of the leg's drive system. Reducing peak power and peak power is beneficial to the optimal design of the drive system. In this paper, we assume that the robot legs use an electric drive system. The negative power generated by the process of leg movement will be consumed in the form of heat energy. So the negative power of the drive joint will be recorded as zero.

Based on the constructed model, we compute a set of calculations. To ensure the foot's workspace during walking, the variation of λ_1 is set from 0.2 to 0.5, and the variation of λ_2 is set from 0.2 to 0.4. The result is shown in Fig. 4. From the s pecific resistance and max leg power variation, we find that the energy consumption becomes better as the λ_1 and λ_2 increase, but the max joint torque increases as λ_2 increases. When λ_2 is greater than 0.25, the system's energy consumption decreases very slowly, but the maximum joint torque increases sharply. Thus we chose $\lambda_1 = 0.5$ and $\lambda_2 = 0.25$ as limb length ratio. The limb length parameters are as follows, $L_1 = 1$ m, $L_2 = 0.5$ m , $L_3 = 0.5$ m.

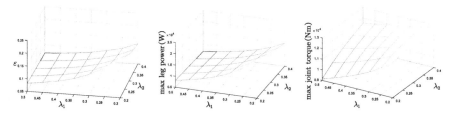

Fig. 4. Compute results as λ_1 and λ_2 change

3.2 Actuator Hinge Position Optimization Based on EMA

Based on the limb length, we can optimize the actuator hinge position to get better EMA. The motion of the legs consists of a swing phase and a supporting phase when the robot moves. The force on the leg during the transition between the swing phase and the support phase can reflect the limit of the force exerted by the driving joint. According to the definition of EMA, "R" reaches the max at the phase transition. Thus we chose the EMA of the leg when the foot strokes the floor as the criterion.

The optimization has fifteen parameters. Those parameters can be divided into three groups to be analyzed separately. The first parameter group is for the hip driving joint, $(p_{uv0}, p_{uh0}, p_{uv1}, p_{uh1})$. Considering the assembling relation of the leg and robot body in practical application, we chose $p_{uv0} = 0.2$ and $p_{uh0} = 0.0$. Then, we use the model conducted to compute and analyze the relationship between EMA_{hip} and (p_{uv1}, p_{uh1}). The computed result is shown in Fig. 5, and we can find that the EMA_{hip} increases as the p_{uv1} and p_{uh1} increase. But when p_{uv1} is greater than 0.3 and p_{uh1} is greater than 0.1, the increase of EMA_{hip} is tiny. The larger the values of p_{uv1} and p_{uh1}, the larger space and mass occupied by the drive system on the hip joint will be. Thus we $p_{uv1} = 0.3$ and $p_{uh1} = 0.1$ as the optimal results.

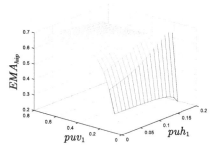

Fig. 5. EMA of hip joint

As for the knee joint, there are also four parameters $(p_{mv0}, p_{mh0}, p_{mv1}, p_{mh1})$. We also separate the parameter into two groups to compute and analyze. The computed results are shown in Fig. 6. From Fig. 9(a) we can find that the EMA_{knee} increases as the p_{mv0} increases. However, when p_{mv0} is greater than 0.5, the increase of EMA_{knee} is tiny. When $p_{mv0} = 0$, the value of EMA_{knee} does almost not change. The larger the values of p_{mv0} and p_{mh0}, the larger space and mass occupied by the drive system on the knee joint will be. Thus we $p_{mv0} = 0.5$ and $p_{mh0} = 0.0$ as the optimal results. From Fig. 9(b) we can find that the EMA_{knee} increases as the p_{mv1} and p_{mh1} increase. Thus we $p_{mv1} = 0.5$ and $p_{mh1} = 0.3$ as the optimal results.

As for the ankle joint, there are also four parameters $(p_{dv0}, p_{dh0}, p_{dv1}, p_{dh1})$. We also separate the parameter into two groups to compute and analyze. The computed results are shown in Fig. 7. From Fig. 10(a), we can find that the EMA_{ankle} increases as the p_{dv0} and p_{dh0} increase. However, when p_{dv0} is greater than 0.4 and p_{dh0} is greater than 0.15, the increase of EMA_{knee} is tiny. The larger the values of p_{dv0} and p_{dh0}, the larger space and mass occupied by the drive system on the ankle joint will be. Thus we $p_{dv0} = 0.4$ and $p_{dh0} = 0.15$ as the optimal results. From Fig. 10(b), we can find that the EMA_{ankle} increases as the p_{dv1} and p_{dh1} increase. However, when p_{dv1} is greater than 0.4 and p_{dh1} is greater than 0.3, the increase of EMA_{knee} is tiny. The larger the values of p_{dv1} and

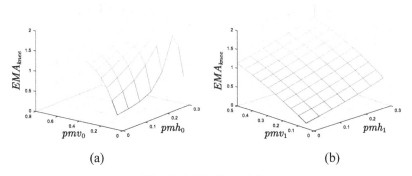

Fig. 6. EMA of knee joint

p_{dh1}, the larger space and mass occupied by the drive system on the ankle joint will be. Thus we $p_{dv1} = 0.4$ and $p_{dh1} = 0.3$ as the optimal results.

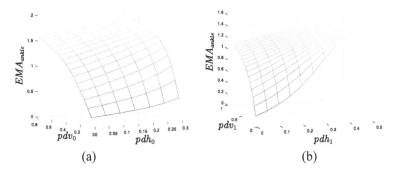

Fig. 7. EMA of ankle joint

4   Experiments on the Leg

Based on the optimized designed leg structure parameters, we constructed a single-leg prototype for a large delivery legged robot. The experimental platform is shown in Fig. 8. The length of the first limb is 1 m, the length of the second limb is 0.48 m, and the length of the third limb is 0.48 m. The joint drive system is a motor-driven planetary roller screw, which can achieve high responsiveness and accuracy. Positions of the hinge point for each joint drive are design as the optimized parameters above. The total mass of the leg prototype is 220 kg, and the design load capacity of the leg is 3 tons.

Based on the leg prototype structure, the EMA of each joint during the leg stance phase in the walking cycle is shown in Fig. 9. For the hip joint, the value of EMA is increasing and then decreasing. When the foot moves just under the hip joint, the EMA of the hip joint converges to infinity. The trend of EMA-ankle is similar to the EMA-hip. For the knee joint, the value of EMA keeps decreasing.

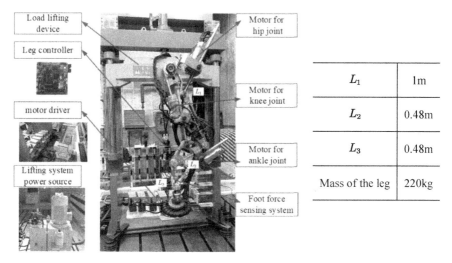

L_1	1m
L_2	0.48m
L_3	0.48m
Mass of the leg	220kg

Fig. 8. Experimental platform

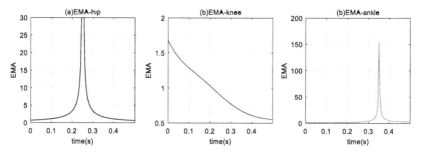

Fig. 9. The EMA data during the leg stance phase

We conducted the leg stepping exercise experiment. The leg prototype can realize a swing frequency of 0.65 Hz at a stride length of 0.8 m. The tracking error is less than 2%, and the data of each joint is shown in Fig. 10.

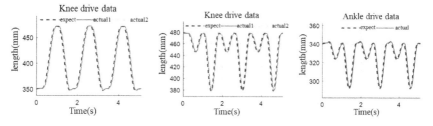

Fig. 10. Drive data of each joint

5 Conclusion

This paper proposes a bio-inspired approach to the leg design of delivery legged robots based on EMA and energy analysis. The analysis model based on EMA energy consumption of the robot's leg is constructed to optimize the limb length and driver layout position. Based on the optimized structure parameters, we propose a real mechanical leg design solution for the electrical driving legged robot. The leg uses mechanism compressive stress not structural bending stress to bear the load, and shows high motion precision.

Future research mainly focuses on leg motion control experiment study with different walking parameters and control strategies. Both simulation and experiment of force analysis will be tested, and the mechanism and control strategy will be studied.

Acknowledgment. This research was supported by the National Key R&D Program of China under grant numbers 2019YFB1309502.

References

1. Raibert, M.H.: Legged Robots that Balance. MIT Press, Cambridge (1985)
2. Biewener, A.A.: Mammalian terrestrial locomotion and size. Bioscience **39**(11), 776–783 (1989)
3. Reilly, S.M., McElroy, E.J., Biknevicius, A.R.: Posture, gait and the ecological relevance of locomotor costs and energy-saving mechanisms in tetrapods. Zoology **110**(4), 271–289 (2007). https://doi.org/10.1016/j.zool.2007.01.003
4. Garcia, E., Arevalo, J.C., Muñoz, G., Gonzalez-de-Santos, P.: On the biomimetic design of agile-robot legs. Sensors **11**(12), 11305–11334 (2011)
5. Sprowitz, A., Tuleu, A., Vespignani, M., Ajallooeian, M., Badri, E., Ijspeert, A.J.: Towards dynamic trot gait locomotion: design, control, and experiments with Cheetah-cub, a compliant quadruped robot. Int. J. Robot. Res. **32**(8), 932–950 (2013)
6. Waldron, K., Vohnout, V.: Configuration design of the adaptive suspension vehicle. Intl. J. Robot. Res. **3**, 37–48 (1984)
7. Biewener, A.A.: Biomechanics of mammalian terrestrial locomotion. Sci. Wash. **250**(4984), 1097 (1990)
8. Gunther, M., Keppler, V., Seyfarth, A., Blickhan, R.: Human leg design: optimal axial alignment under constraints. J. Math. Biol. **48**(6), 623–646 (2004)
9. Haldane, D.W., Plecnik, M.M., Yim, J.K., Fearing, R.S.: Robotic vertical jumping agility via series-elastic power modulation, Sci. Robot. **1**(1), 2048–2048 (2016)
10. de Santos, P.G., Garcia, E., Ponticelli, R., Armada, M.: Minimizing energy consumption in hexapod robots. Adv. Robot. **23**(6), 681–704 (2009)

Research on Damping Control of Cable-Climbing Robot Based on Spring-Magnetorheological Damping Coupling Mechanism

Wei Shi[1,2] , Kaiwei Ma[1,2] , Jialei Lu[1,2] , and Fengyu Xu[1,2(✉)]

[1] College of Automation and College of Artificial Intelligence, Nanjing University of Posts and Telecommunications, Nanjiang 210023, China
[2] Jiangsu Engineering Lab for IOT Intelligent Robots (IOTRobot), Nanjing 210023, China

Abstract. The cable detection robot is of great significance to the automatic maintenance of Bridges. In order to ensure the climbing stability of the detection robot, a spring - magnetorheological damping coupling loading mechanism was proposed. Firstly, aiming at the influence of vibration and disturbance on cable safety performance of heavy-duty climbing robot, a robot-cable coupling dynamic model was established. Secondly, the vibration suppression mechanism of the robot with variable damping was studied, and a variable damping coupling loading mechanism was proposed for the climbing robot. Thirdly, an adaptive controller for cable-climbing robot acting on multiple coupling loading mechanisms under random disturbance is designed. Finally, experiments were carried out to verify the vibration suppression effect of the coupling loading mechanism and improve the safety and detection performance of the robot-stay cable system.

Keywords: Cable detection robot · Variable damping · Coupling loading mechanism · Adaptive control · Experimental research

1 Introduction

As the main component of cable-stayed bridge, the cables need to be inspected and maintained regularly. This method is not only inefficient, costly and difficult to ensure the safety of inspectors, but also only applicable to small cable-stayed Bridges. Therefore, the application of safe, stable and efficient robot system to solve the industry demand of bridge cable automatic inspection has become an inevitable requirement. Research has been carried out on cable detection robots or magnetorheological dampers, as follows:

In terms of the structure and control of the high-altitude cable detection robot, Kim et al. [1] proposed a suspension bridge cable climbing robot, which adopted the three-side compression method to obtain the adhesion of the robot on the cable. Xu et al. designed a kind of bilateral wheeled cable testing robot [2] and helical cable testing robot [3, 4], which can overcome the influence of wind load at high altitude. Vaughan et al. [5] studied the rocking vibration phenomenon of the suspended line patrolling

© Springer Nature Switzerland AG 2021
X.-J. Liu et al. (Eds.): ICIRA 2021, LNAI 13015, pp. 781–792, 2021.
https://doi.org/10.1007/978-3-030-89134-3_71

robot under wind load, established the robot's rocking dynamic model, and designed the input shaping controller to suppress the rocking vibration. Yang et al. [6] proposed a state-feedback controller to suppress the coupling vibration of robot-cable system. Chen et al. [7] proposed an adaptive gain scheduling back-pushing control method and established a nonlinear dynamics model of the patrolling robot.

In terms of the structure and control of magnetorheological damper, Parlak et al. [8] proposed a single coil magnetorheological damper. Peng et al. [9] proposed MRD with parallel connecting holes and established the damping force calculation model of the new damper. Bai et al. [10] proposed a magnetorheological damper hysteresis model based on resistor-capacitance (RC) operator. Hu et al. [11] designed a target tracking sliding mode controller with magnetorheological shock absorber as the object. Hu et al. [12] designed a target tracking sliding mode controller with magnetorheological shock absorber as the object. Yoon [13] proposed a new magnetorheological damper and its robust sliding mode controller to realize vibration reduction control of suspension system. ASW et al. [14] proposed a modeling method of indirect magnetorheological damper. Shiao et al. [15] designed a self-adjusting fuzzy logic controller for magnetorheological damper.

Wheeled cable detection robot generally uses a spring to make the roller clamp on the cable surface. The influence of vibration makes the clamping force of the robot roller change, and then affects the stability of the robot climbing, resulting in the detection image jitter is not clear and other problems. Therefore, it is a key problem in the research of cable detection robot to solve the vibration caused by the robot itself by designing vibration damping mechanism and adaptive control algorithm. In this paper, a spring-magnetorheological damping coupling mechanism is proposed and its dynamic characteristics are analyzed. The coupling dynamics model of the climbing robot-stay cable system under the condition of random disturbance is established. A fuzzy PID adaptive control method for climbing robot subjected to random disturbance is proposed. Experiments were carried out to verify the damping performance of the damping coupling mechanism and the influence of the damping mechanism on the climbing stability of the robot under vibration conditions.

2   Based on the Dynamic Characteristics of Spring and Magnetor-Heological Damping Coupling Loading Mechanism and Robot-Cable System

2.1   Dynamic Characteristics of Robot-Cable Coupling

The system coordinate system was established $\{O\}$, to establish the coupling relationship between the climbing robot and the cable system (Fig. 1). The lower anchor end of the cable is set as the origin, along the horizontal direction is set as the axis, and the vertical direction is set as the Y-axis. The system coordinate system $\{O\}$, is the same as the origin of the cable system coordinate system $\{O_l\}$,. Suppose the robot is at the point of the cable. Since the climbing robot moves along with the point k, the base coordinate system $\{O_r\}$, of the robot is a moving coordinate system. Considering the influence of cable vibration, the auxiliary coordinate system $\{O_k\}$, is set at the point k, and the direction of each axis is the same as that of the cable system coordinate system. Assuming that the Angle between the coordinate system $\{O\}$ of the system and the coordinate system $\{O_l\}$ of the cable system is. Combined with the transformation relationship between the coordinate system of the auxiliary coordinate system $\{O_k\}$ and the coordinate system of the cable system $\{O_l\}$, the coupling dynamic equation of the robot-stay cable in the system coordinate system is:

$$\begin{bmatrix} \ddot{x} \\ \ddot{y} \end{bmatrix} = \begin{bmatrix} \sin\alpha & \cos\alpha \\ -\cos\alpha & \sin\alpha \end{bmatrix} \begin{bmatrix} \ddot{x}_r \\ \ddot{y}(x_r, t) \end{bmatrix} \tag{1}$$

Where, $\ddot{y}(x_r, t)$ is the vibration response acceleration of the cable at point, $\ddot{x}_r$ is the climbing acceleration of the robot.

2.2 Analysis of Dynamic Characteristics of Coupling Loading Mechanism with Spring and Magnetorheological Damping

An integrated loading mechanism coupled with spring and magnetorheological damper was installed on a three-wheel fully driven climbing robot (Fig. 11). One end of the coupling loading mechanism is fixed on the upper frame and the other end is fixed on the cross bar of the lower frame. The damping force generated by the coupling loading mechanism is adjusted by adjusting the input current of the magnetorheological damper, and the damping force generated by the coupling loading mechanism absorbs the vibration response under external interference, so as to reduce the clamping force change caused by vibration.

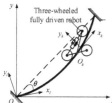

Fig. 1. Coupling dynamics model analysis

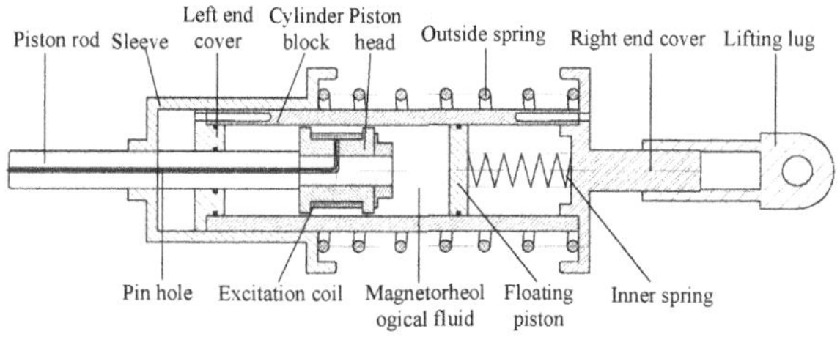

Fig. 2. Structure diagram of magnetorheological damper.

The designed spring magnetorheological coupling loading mechanism structure is shown in Fig. 2. Its structure mainly includes piston rod, sleeve, left end cover, right end cover, magnetorheological fluid, cylinder block, piston head, floating piston, inner spring, outside spring, excitation coil and lifting lug, etc. When the outside world produces random disturbance, it will cause the vibration of the climbing robot-cable system, the clamping force will change, and the robot will climb unstably. When the excitation coil is fed into the current, the piston head can reciprocate in the damper cylinder. Under the joint action of the outer spiral spring and the magnetorheological damper, the coupling loading mechanism outputs continuous, stable and controllable damping force. The coupling loading mechanism can reduce the vibration of the robot-cable coupling system under random disturbance, so that the robot can climb stably on the stay cable.

2.3   Analysis of Dynamic Characteristics of Coupling Loading Mechanism with Spring and Magnetorheological Damping

Bingham model can effectively describe the relationship between input and damping force under random external disturbance. The Bingham viscoplastic model is adopted to establish the mechanical model of magnetorheological damper under the flow shear mixed working mode, as follows:

(1) The damping force models of magnetorheological damper (MRD) in flow mode and shear mode were established.

The working process of the magnetorheological fluid was simplified as a flow model between two mutually moving plates. The flow situation and velocity distribution were shown in Fig. 3. Set the gap between two plates as h, the length is l, the width is v, the flow velocity is u, the flow velocity direction is the direction x, and there is no displacement on y. According to Bingham model, MRD damping force in flow mode can be deduced as follows:

$$F_1 = \frac{12\eta l}{bh^3}A_p^2 v + \frac{3l\tau_y}{h} \tag{2}$$

Similarly, the output damping force in the shear mode can be obtained as follow:

$$F_2 = \frac{\eta bl}{h}v + bl\tau_y \tag{3}$$

A_p is the cross-sectional area of the MR damper, τ_y and η is the yield stress and viscosity of the MRF.

(2) Establish the MRD damping force model in the mixed mode.

The MR damper in the mixed working mode is the superposition of the damping force in the flow mode and the shear mode, the following can be obtained:

$$F = \left(\frac{12\eta l A_p^2}{bh^3} + \frac{\eta bl}{h}\right)v + \left(\frac{3l A_p}{h} + bl\right)\tau_y sgn(v) \tag{4}$$

In the formula, the first term is viscous damping force, and the second term is Coulomb damping force, which is determined by the magnetic field strength, and reflects the controllable characteristics of the magnetorheological damper.

(3) Mathematical models of excitation current, robot vibration acceleration and damping force are established.

When the cable vibrates, the coupling mechanism of helical spring and magnetorheological damper can reduce the vibration of the robot-cable system under random disturbance. The spiral spring can not only provide stable clamping force for the robot to climb, but also adjust the natural frequency of the robot to avoid the system vibration point. The variable damping of the MR damper can be realized by adjusting the input current, which can effectively reduce the vibration peak of the robot-stay cable system. The coupling loading force can be described as:

$$F = \left(\frac{12\eta l A_p^2}{bh^3} + \frac{\eta bl}{h}\right)v + \left(\frac{3lA_p}{h} + bl\right)\tau_y(v, I)sgn(v) + xk \tag{5}$$

In the formula, x- displacement of piston motion, k- elastic coefficient of spring.

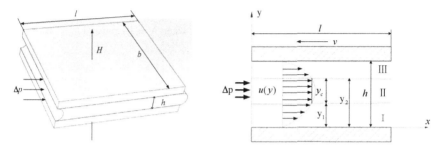

Fig. 3. Flow and velocity distribution of magnetorheological fluid in a plate

(4) Matlab/Simulink modeling and simulation of coupling loading mechanism.

The simulation mathematical model of MR damper used is Bingham model, which can truly describe the mechanical properties of MR damper.MRF-132LD, a MRF fluid produced by Lord Company, was used, and the MR damper was simulated, and its performance and basic requirements were analyzed. Substituting all parameters into the loading force formula of the coupling mechanism, we can get:

$$F = 74.73\dot{x} + 0.018\left(-38580e^{-I} + 14193\ln(I + e) + 1925I\right)sgn(\dot{x}) + 2.5x \tag{6}$$

Relevant studies show that the vibration frequency of the robot is generally in the range of 0–100 Hz when various random disturbances are generated to the cable - robot coupling system. Coupling loading mechanism stroke is 0–15 mm. The Bingham model of magnetorheological damper was established by SIMULINK modeling. The model is loaded with sinusoidal vibration excitation $x = A sin(2\pi ft)$, and the corresponding frequency and amplitude are set according to the vibration frequency of the robot and the travel of the coupling loading mechanism, and different current values are input to obtain the relation curve of the damping force of the coupling loading mechanism with the change of displacement and velocity under different conditions, as shown in Figs. 4, 5 and 6.

It can be seen from Figs. 4, 5 and 6 that the established force model can well reflect the basic characteristics of magnetorheological damper. Among them, the F-x curve is

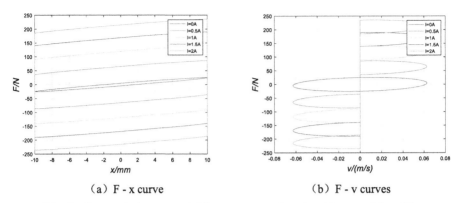

(a) F - x curve   (b) F - v curves

Fig. 4. Characteristic curves of different current when A = 10 mm and f = 1 Hz

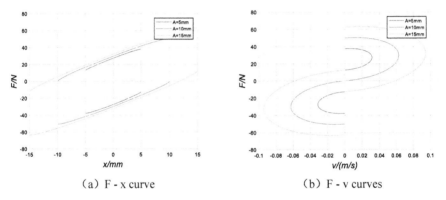

(a) F - x curve   (b) F - v curves

Fig. 5. Characteristic curves at different amplitudes when f = 1 Hz and I = 0.2 A

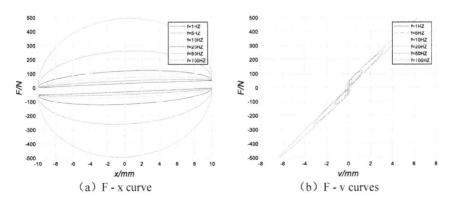

(a) F - x curve   (b) F - v curves

Fig. 6. Characteristic curves at different frequencies when A = 10 mm and I = 0.2 A

full, indicating that the floating piston type volume compensation device can effectively compensate the volume difference caused by the stretching and compression of piston rod. The damping force increases with the increase of the loading current, and the area surrounded by the curve also increases, indicating that the power consumption capacity of MRD is constantly increasing. In the F-v curve, when the loading current is the same, the damping force increases linearly with the increase of velocity, and this part of damping force is mainly generated by viscous damping force. When the velocity is constant, the damping force increases with the increase of the loading current. This part is provided by the adjustable damping force, which is consistent with the variation characteristics of Bingham model. The hysteresis characteristics are better and more obvious with the increase of frequency. In general, the damping force is greatly affected by the control current and vibration frequency, but is less affected by the amplitude.

3   Control Method Analysis of Coupling Loading Mechanism with Helical Spring and Magnetorheological Damping

Compared with other control algorithms, the fuzzy PID control has the advantages of simple modeling, high control precision, strong nonlinear adaptability and good dynamic performance. In this paper, fuzzy PID algorithm is used to control the coupling loading mechanism of spring and magnetorheological damper.

3.1   Fuzzy PID Controller Design

Through the acceleration sensor, the acceleration deviation of the magnetorheological damper in axial vibration and the change of the current deviation and the last deviation are determined. Fuzzy reasoning is carried out according to the given fuzzy rules. Finally, the fuzzy parameters are de-fuzzy and the PID control parameters are output (Fig. 7).

The main design process of fuzzy controller includes: variable fuzzification, membership function, establishment of fuzzy control rule table and unfuzziness, and then add coefficients, and parameters of the fuzzy controller to the PID controller respectively, and then complete the connection with the PID controller, so as to form the required fuzzy PID controller.

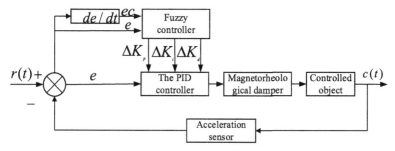

Fig. 7. Schematic diagram of fuzzy PID controller

3.2 Fuzzy PID Simulation and Analysis

In the MATLAB /Simulink simulation environment, a Simulink simulation block diagram of the single degree of freedom active and passive fuzzy PID control system is established, which takes the vibration acceleration of the damper as the control object and the input current of the magnetorheological damper as the output of the fuzzy PID controller. The input amplituresare 10 mm, and the frequencies are sinusoidal excitation signals of 1 Hz, 10 Hz and 50 Hz respectively. After repeated debugging and selection, $K_p = 11, K_i = 7, K_d = 0.5$.the vibration acceleration curve is obtained, as shown in Fig. 8. Using fuzzy PID control strategy to reduce vibration effect is very good.

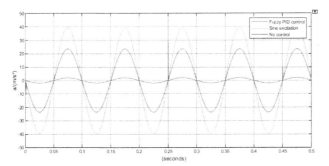

(a) Response curve with amplitude of 10mm and frequency of 10Hz

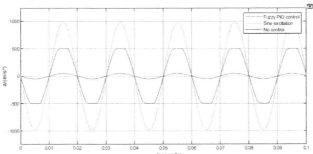

(b) Response curve with amplitude of 10mm and frequency of 50Hz

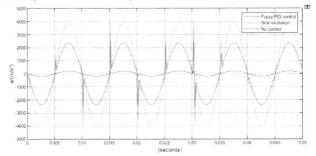

(c) Response curve with amplitude of 10mm and frequency of 100Hz

Fig. 8. Response curves at different vibration frequencies

4   Experimental Scheme of Cable Climbing Robot

4.1   Experimental Study on Loading Performance of Coupling Mechanism of Spring and Magnetorheological Damping

A universal experimental machine platform (Fig. 9) was built to conduct tensile and compression experiments on the coupling loading mechanism. The universal experimental machine loads sinusoidal vibration excitation to the coupling loading mechanism, the amplitude is A = 10 mm, the frequency is 1 Hz, and different current values are input to obtain the corresponding damping force.

Figure 10(a) and Fig. 10(b) are the displacement-damping force relationship curve and velocity damping force curve measured by the test respectively, and are compared with the simulation curve of Eq. (6). It can be seen from Fig. 10 that the damping force fitted by Eq. (6) is close to the measured value and relatively accurate.

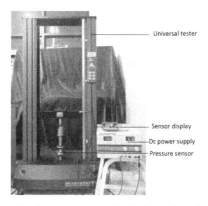

Fig. 9. Experiment of spring-magnetorheological coupling damping mechanism

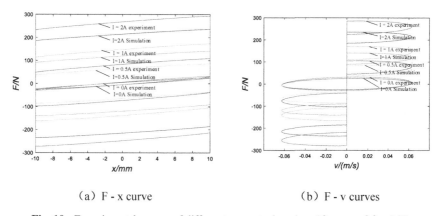

(a) F - x curve   (b) F - v curves

Fig. 10. Experimental curves of different current when A = 10 mm and f = 1 Hz

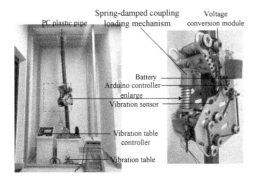

Fig. 11. Experiment of spring magnetorheological damping coupling mechanism

4.2 Robot Climbing Experiment Under Cable Vibration Condition

The vibration platform of the climbing robot-cable coupling system is built, and a coupling loading mechanism is installed on the climbing robot, and the corresponding controller is connected (Fig. 11). The robot climbs on A PC tube with an inclination Angle of 75° with the ground. At the same time, the vibration table system input amplitude A = 10 mm and sinusoidal excitation frequencies of 10 Hz, 50Hz and 100 Hz respectively, so as to obtain the climbing speed of the robot under different conditions.

It can be seen from Table 1 that the climbing stability of the robot with coupling loading mechanism is significantly improved compared with that without coupling loading mechanism. When the fuzzy PID control algorithm is added, the climbing stability of the robot is further improved.

Table 1. The climbing speed of the robot under different conditions.

Excitation frequency	Not using a coupling loading mechanism average climbing speed v/ (m/s)	Climb speed using coupling loading mechanism average climbing speed v/(m/s)	
		No control algorithm	Add fuzzy PID control algorithm
f = 0 Hz	0.27	0.27	0.27
f = 10 Hz	0.24	0.26	0.27
f = 50 Hz	0.18	0.24	0.25
f = 100 Hz	0.15	0.18	0.21

5 The Conclusion

In this paper, a spring-magnetorheological coupling loading mechanism is designed for the vibration system of cable-climbing robot under random disturbance. The coupling dynamics model of robot-stay cable system is established. The dynamic characteristics and nonlinear hysteresis effect of the coupling loading mechanism were analyzed to accurately predict the vibration state of the cable, and an adaptive control method for the climbing robot under random disturbance was proposed. Experiments were carried out to verify the vibration suppression effect of the coupling loading mechanism and the climbing performance of the robot under vibration conditions.

Simulation and experiment results show that the damping force generated by the spring-magnetorheological coupling loading mechanism is in the range of 0–250 N, and the maximum stroke of the coupling loading mechanism is 15 mm. The coupling loading mechanism with fuzzy PID adaptive control strategy can reduce the vibration of the cable-robot vibration system, which greatly improves the safety and detection performance of the system.

Acknowledgements. This project is supported by the National Natural Foundation of China (52175100), the Primary Research & Development Plan of Jiangsu Province (BE2018734), the Natural Science Foundation of Jiangsu Province (BK20201379), and Six Talent Peaks Project in Jiangsu Province (JY-081).

References

1. Cho, K.H., Kim, H.M., Jin, Y.H., Liu, F.: Inspection robot for hanger cable of suspension bridge: mechanism design and analysis. IEEE/ASME Trans. Mechatron. **18**(6), 1665–1674 (2013)
2. Xu, F., Wang, X., Wang, L., et al.: Cable inspection robot for cable-stayed bridges: design, analysis, and application. J. Field Robot. **28**(3), 441–459 (2011)
3. Xu, F., Hu, J., Wang, X., et al.: Helix cable-detecting robot for cable-stayed bridge: design and analysis. Int. J. Robot. Autom. **29**(4), 406–414 (2014)
4. Xu, F., Jiang, Q.: Dynamic obstacle-surmounting analysis of a bilateral-wheeled cable-climbing robot for cable-stayed bridges. Ind. Robot. **46**(3), 431–443 (2019)
5. Vaughan, J., Guarnieri, M., Debenest, P.: 3C15 limiting rocking oscillation of cable-riding robots subject to wind disturbances. In: The 12th International Conference on Motion and Vibration, pp.1–8 (2014)
6. Yang, D., Feng, Z., Ren, X., Lu, N.: A novel power line inspection robot with dual-parallelogram architecture and its vibration suppression control. Adv. Robot. **28**(12), 807–819 (2014)
7. Dian, S.Y., Chen, L., Hoang, S., et al.: Dynamic balance control based on an adaptive gain-scheduled backstepping scheme for power-line inspection robots. IEEE/CAA J. Autom. Sin. **6**(1), 198–208 (2019)
8. Parlak, Z., Engin, T., Calli I.: Optimal design of MR damper via finite element analyses of fluid dynamic and magnetic field. Mechatronics **22**(6), 890–903 (2012)
9. Zhizhao, P., Zhang, J., Yue, J., Zhang, L., Huang, D.: Design and analysis of a magnetorheological damper with parallel normal hole. J. Mech. Eng. **51**(08),172–177 (2015)
10. Bai, X.X., Li, C.: Precise real-time hysteretic force tracking of magnetorheological damper. Smart Mater. Struct. **29**(10) (2020).
11. Hongsheng, H., Jiong, W., Suxiang, Q., Yancheng, L., Na, S., Gongbiao, Y.: Dynamic modeling and sliding mode control of magnetorheological damper under impact loading. J. Mech. Eng. **47**(13), 84–91 (2011)

12. Pohoryles, D.A., Duffour, P.: Adaptive control of structures under dynamic excitation using magnetorheological dampers: an improved clipped-optimal control algorithm. J. Vib. Control **21**(13), 2569–2582 (2013)
13. Yoon, D.S., Kim, G.W., Choi, S.B.: Response time of magnetorheological dampers to current inputs in a semi-active suspension system: modeling, control and sensitivity analysis – ScienceDirect. Mech. Syst. Sig. Process. **146**, 106999 (2021)
14. ASW, CJWB, CJOAB.: Method for improving the neural network model of the magnetorheological damper-ScienceDirect. Mech. Syst. Sign. Process. **149** (2021)
15. Shiao, Y.J., Nguyen, Q.A., Lai, C.C.: Application of Magneto rheological damper on semi-active suspension system. Appl. Mech. Materials, **284**, 1754–1758 (2013)

The Metamorphic Variable-Axis Revolute Hinge and Its Induced Reconfiguration of Robotic Legged Lander

Youcheng Han⬤, Caizhi Zhou⬤, and Weizhong Guo(✉)⬤

State Key Laboratory of Mechanical Systems and Vibration, School of Mechanical Engineering,
Shanghai Jiao Tong University, Shanghai, China
{youcheng,ajth132,wzguo}@sjtu.edu.cn

Abstract. The robotic legged lander has three operation modes from adjusting, landing, to roving. To facilitate its reconfiguration reliably, this paper firstly introduces the design of a novel metamorphic variable-axis revolute hinge utilizing clutch and gripper together with dead-point properties. It owns three alternative phases, containing the rigid body phase and two independent rotation phases by switching between two orthogonal topological axes. Hence, the robotic legged lander can reconfigure from the adjusting mode (active mechanism) with rotation axis 1 phase, to the landing mode (truss structure) with rigid body phase, then to the roving mode (active mechanism) with rotation axis 2 phase. To further reveal the principles of mode switch, the unified differential kinematics throughout all operation modes is established according to screw theory, and the distribution principles of singularity loci and workspace are identified next. Finally, two bifurcation evolution routes of the robotic legged lander from adjusting, soft/propulsive landing, to roving are demonstrated for the future application scenario.

Keywords: Metamorphic hinge · Robotic legged lander · Reconfigurable mechanism · Legged robot · Singularity loci · Bifurcated evolution

1 Introduction

Future development for extraterrestrial exploration demands the novel detection probe with multi-functional integration, as seen in autonomous robot [1], reconfigurable mechanism [2], aerospace engineering [3], etc. Complex task requirements have been put forward for the close-distance investigation of hostile extraterrestrial environment that never be visited. Given the robotized consideration of the current legged lander [4], a novel type of *robotic legged lander* (RLL) has been proposed with adjusting, landing, and roving modes [5, 6]. The adjusting mode is targeted for the unreachable area by matching four footpads according to the irregular landform topography (rock, slope, canyon, crater, gully, etc.); the landing mode utilizes the mature landing technology of current legged lander [7] to facilitate the technical promotion, so the landing after adjusting possesses a good adaptability for extreme landforms intelligently; finally, the roving mode is designed for the broad-range locomotion detection.

© Springer Nature Switzerland AG 2021
X.-J. Liu et al. (Eds.): ICIRA 2021, LNAI 13015, pp. 793–802, 2021.
https://doi.org/10.1007/978-3-030-89134-3_72

However, there are still some tough problems for practical purposes on how to construct feasible structures for RLL utilizing reliable reconfiguration principles, and most importantly, how to utilize an effective reconfigurable hinge to switch among three modes. Given the field of reconfigurable mechanism, Dai and Jones [8] proposed the metamorphic mechanism and introduced a new mechanism topic with variable mobility and topology. Some well-renowned reconfigurable hinges were also invented for supporting the metamorphosis, such as the reconfigurable Hooke hinge (rT) and reconfigurable revolute hinge (rR) by Gan [9, 10], the variable-axis hinge (vA) invented by Zhang [11], etc. However, these results still cannot be employed directly for this study, the desirable reconfigurable hinge must be designed tailoredly.

2   Missions and Operation Modes of RLL

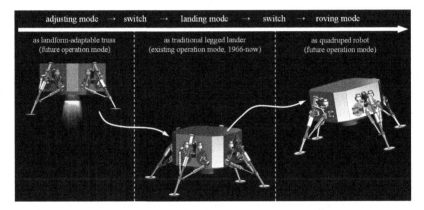

Fig. 1. Sketch of operation mode and functional implementation of the RLL

As shown in Fig. 1, the RLL is a novel reconfigurable detection probe targeted for exploring the hostile extraterrestrial landform. It has three operation modes following practical implementation sequences: (1) adjusting mode: to expand more vast area from flat terrain to severe terrain (rock, slope, crater, canyon, gulley, etc.), the RLL is designed with adjusting mode to enhance the environmental suitability and touchdown at irregular landform. It can match the position of the footpad according to the geometrical morphology of terrain surface, and then result in a stable and adaptive landing posture of the single leg and overall lander; (2) landing mode: to guarantee the technical feasibility for the sake of engineering practice, the landing mode takes the identical topology with Chang'E 3–5 lunar landers [12, 13] to absorb the buffering impact energy and land securely on the extraterrestrial surface; (3) roving mode: it changes the RLL into a quadruped robot, and conducts the legged locomotion to expand the detection range on the extraterrestrial surface. The mobile detection merit can enhance the survivability and reachability in hostile topography utilizing abundant gaits (walking, crawling, trotting, pacing, etc.).

3   Reconfigurable Mechanism System Design of RLL

The RLL can reconfigure from adjusting, landing, to roving owing it possesses a complete reconfigurable mechanism system—three portions constructed in Fig. 2.

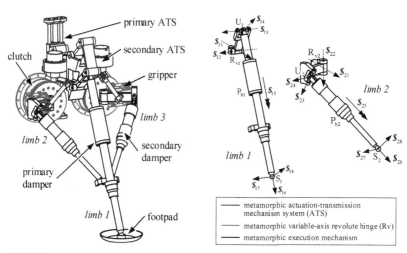

Fig. 2. Sketch of reconfigurable mechanism system and twist screws of single leg

Firstly, the metamorphic execution mechanism is a 3-DOF and 3-limb topology to interact with extraterrestrial environment. The primary limb (limb 1) is composed of a metamorphic variable-axis revolute hinge R_v, a universal hinge U, a buffering damper P_b, and a spherical hinge S. Two secondary limbs (2 and 3) are symmetrical with the same hinge sequences as primary limb. Hence, the metamorphic execution mechanism has the integrated topology $(^mR_vU\&2\ ^mR_vU^mP_bS) - {}^mP_bS$, where "m" is the symbol to denote adjusting mode as "a", landing mode as "l", roving mode as "r", and $^aR_{vj}$ has the axis $\$_{j1}$ ($j = 1$–3, represents the jth limb), $^lR_{vj}$ is a rigid connection, $^rR_{vj}$ has the axis $\$_{j2}$, ^aP_b and ^rP_b are rigid connections, ^lP_b is equivalent to a passive prismatic hinge with spring & damping factors; next, the metamorphic actuation-transmission mechanism system (ATS) [14] is designed to correspond to execution limbs. It powers and controls the adjusting and roving motions. The metamorphic ATS is composed of a revolute hinge R, two spherical hinges S, and one R_v (common connection and kernel device between execution limb and ATS for switching modes).

As aforementioned, the design demands and motivations for R_v are elicited: as the adjusting mode is designed for landing on the hostile topography stably and reliably, the universal hinge of the damper should lean on the sidewall during the adjusting process to guarantee a good transfer path of buffering energy flow. Furthermore, the roving mode requires changing the configurations of dampers to achieve good locomotion capabilities. These are the reasons that R_v is designed with three alternative phases, i.e., two rotation phases with orthogonal axes and one rigid phase. Actually, the reconfigurability of RLL results from the axis direction and existence of R_v, and the state of damper P_b (plasticity in landing mode and rigidity in other modes).

4   Design of Metamorphic Variable-Axis Revolute Hinge R_v

Figure 3 shows the construction of R_v, which is constituted by a clutch-gripper mechanism system to switch among two rotations phases and one rigid phase.

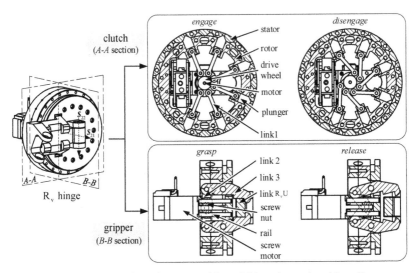

clutch
(*A-A* section)

engage   stator
                            rotor
                            drive
                            wheel
                            motor
                            plunger
                            link1
disengage

R_v hinge

grasp   link 2
           link 3
           link R_vU
           screw
           nut
           rail
           screw
           motor
release

gripper
(*B-B* section)

Fig. 3. Construction of metamorphic variable-axis revolute hinge R_v

Thereinto, the clutch is one-input and six-output with six planar RRRP mechanisms in a circular arrangement. Its engaging state is when the plunger comes into the stator bore and three axes of R hinges are in a common plane (i.e. the dead-point phenomenon with force-amplifier property), and the disengaging state is when the plunger comes back that the rotor cab rotate around $\$_{j1}$. Furthermore, the gripper is one-input and two-output with two planar PRRR mechanisms in a symmetrical arrangement. Its grasping state is when two links 3 grasp the link R_vU and link 2 is vertical to the axis of screw motor (i.e. dead point to amplify force), and the releasing state is when two links 3 cannot touch link R_vU so the link can rotate around $\$_{j2}$. In the following, the R_v-induced reconfiguration to switch mode and change topology is explained.

Step 1: The metamorphic execution mechanism in adjusting mode has the topology of $(^aR_vU\&2\,{}^aR_vUS) - S$. The clutch disengages the stator and rotor, while the gripper grasps the link $^aR_{vj}U_j$. So the clutch rotor can be actuated by ATS so that the execution mechanism can be controlled optimally to match the landform topography;

Step 2: Switching from adjusting to landing: after turning into the optimal landing configuration, the clutch is engaging and the gripper is grasping, and all motors of ATS are stopped;

Step 3: The metamorphic execution mechanism in landing mode has the topology of $(U\&2U\,{}^lP_bS) - {}^lP_bS$—a truss structure regarded as a special passive mechanism with 3 buffering DOF and 2R1T buffering motion characteristics (driven by the touchdown impact force). This mode has an identical topology with the Chang'E lunar lander to facilitate the technical upgrade;

Step 4: Switching from landing to roving: after landing on the extraterrestrial terrain, the clutch is engaging and gripper is releasing, all motors of ATS are actuated;

Step 5: The metamorphic execution mechanism in roving mode has the topology of $('R_vU\&2\,'R_vUS) - S$. After actuating three ATS motors, the single leg becomes active for the legged locomotion.

5 Unified Differential Kinematics Modeling

Figure 4 illustrates the single leg in three modes, where $\{C\}$ is a static frame; $\{R_{vj}\}$ is located at R_{vj}, z-axis is perpendicular to the base, x-axis concides with the initial pose of $R_{vj}U_j$. Moreover, $\{A\}$ is located at the moving platform, z-axis is in line with U_1S_1, y-axis is parallel to S_3S_2. φ_j is the adjusting actuation angle, α_j is the roving actuation angle, $l_1 + l_4$ is primary damper length, l_2, l_3 are secondary dampers lengths.

Firstly, the reconfigurable twist screw system ^mS_j (containing ^mR_v and ^mP_b) for the jth limb of the metamorphic execution mechanism has a unified formulation

$$^mS_j = span\{c_1\$_{j1}, c_2\$_{j2}, \$_{j3}, \$_{j4}, c_5\$_{j5}, \$_{j6}, \$_{j7}, \$_{j8}\}$$

$$[c_1, c_2, c_5] = \begin{cases} [1, 0, 0] \; m = a \\ [0, 0, 1] \; m = l \\ [0, 1, 0] \; m = r \end{cases} \tag{1}$$

where $\$_{ji}$ ($i = 1 - 8$, is the ith hinge axis) are twist screws of all hinges of the jth limb in Fig. 2; and c_1, c_2, c_5 denote the corresponding coefficiences.

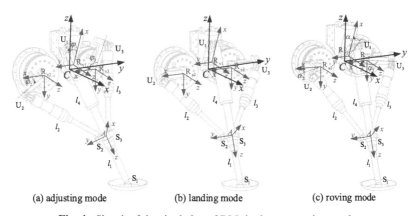

(a) adjusting mode   (b) landing mode   (c) roving mode

Fig. 4. Sketch of the single leg of RLL in three operation modes

We let $^m\$_M$ denote the twist of the point in moving platform coincident with C instantaneously. Given the linear combination operation of joints' twists in each limb, we can obtain

$$^m\$_M =$$
$$\begin{cases} c_1\dot{\varphi}_j\$_{j1} + c_2\dot{\alpha}_j\$_{j2} + \dot{\beta}_j\$_{j3} + \dot{\gamma}_j\$_{j4} + c_5\dot{l}_j\$_{j5} & j = 1 \\ c_1\dot{\varphi}_j\$_{j1} + c_2\dot{\alpha}_j\$_{j2} + \dot{\beta}_j\$_{j3} + \dot{\gamma}_j\$_{j4} + c_5\dot{l}_j\$_{j5} + \dot{\theta}_{j6}\$_{j6} + \dot{\theta}_{j7}\$_{j7} + \dot{\theta}_{j8}\$_{j8} & j = 2, 3 \end{cases} \quad (2)$$

where $\$_{j1}$ and $\dot{\varphi}_j$ are the unit line vector and angular rate of the jth actuated adjusting joint, $\$_{j2}$ and $\dot{\alpha}_j$ are those of the jth actuated roving joint, $\$_{j3}$, $\$_{j4}$ and $\dot{\beta}_j$, $\dot{\gamma}_j$ are those of the first and second axes of U_j, $\$_{j5}$ and $\dot{l}_j$ are unit couple vectors and buffering speeds of the jth damper, and $\$_{j6}$, $\$_{j7}$, $\$_{j8}$ and $\dot{\theta}_{j6}$, $\dot{\theta}_{j7}$, $\dot{\theta}_{j8}$ are three orthogonal line vectors and Euler angular rates of S_j.

To reveal the relationships between motion and constraint for the RLL throughout all three modes: one can see the constraint wrenches exerted on the moving platform are all supplied by the primary limb, because the secondary limbs in each mode are all full mobility. Therefore, the unified constraint equations for three modes are identified

$$^m\$_{Ck} \circ {}^m\$_M = 0$$

$$\begin{cases} {}^a\$_{Ck} = \begin{cases} \left[e_{R1U1}^T, (CU_1 \times e_{R1U1})^T \right]^T & k = 1 \\ \left[e_{11}^T, (CU_1 \times e_{11})^T \right]^T & k = 2 \\ \left[e_{13}^T, (CP \times e_{13})^T \right]^T & k = 3 \end{cases} \\ {}^l\$_{Ck} = \begin{cases} \left[e_{14}^T, (CU_1 \times e_{14})^T \right]^T & k = 1 \\ \left[n_{11}^T, (CU_1 \times n_{11})^T \right]^T & k = 2 \\ \left[0_{3\times 1}^T, n_{12}^T \right]^T & k = 3 \end{cases} \\ {}^r\$_{Ck} = \begin{cases} \left[e_{R1U1}^T, (CU_1 \times e_{R1U1})^T \right] & k = 1 \\ \left[e_{13}^T, (CU_1 \times e_{13})^T \right]^T & k = 2 \\ \left[0_{3\times 1}^T, (e_{13} \times e_{14})^T \right]^T & k = 3 \end{cases} \end{cases} \quad (3)$$

where $^m\$_{Ck}$ is the k th $(k = 1, 2, 3)$ constraint wrench screw, $e_{R1U1} = R_1U_1/\|R_1U_1\|$, e_{ji} is the unit directional vector of $\$_{ji}$, P is the intersection point of $\$_{11}$ and $\$_{14}$, $n_{11} = e_{14} \times e_{15}$, $n_{12} = e_{13} \times e_{14}$.

To reveal the relationships between motion and transmission for the RLL throughout all three modes: one can see the transmission wrenches exerted on the moving platform are provided by both primary and secondary limbs in each mode. By locking the actuation joint in each limb respectively, the newly added constraint wrench is exactly the transmission wrench, denoted as $^m\$_{Tj}$, implementing the motion and force transmission from actuated joint to moving platform. As the reciprocity between the transmission wrench screw and twist screw system (except the input twist screw), the unified transmission equations for three modes can be yielded by taking the reciprocal product for both sides of Eq. (2) with $^m\$_{Tj}$, given by

$$
^m\$_{Tj} \circ {}^m\$_M = {}^m\dot{q}_j{}^m\$_{Tj} \circ {}^m\$_{qj}
$$

$$
\begin{cases}
{}^a\$_{Tj} = \begin{cases}
\left[e_{13}^T, (CU_1 \times e_{13})^T\right]^T & j = 1 \\
\left[e_{25}^T, (CU_2 \times e_{25})^T\right]^T & j = 2 \\
\left[e_{35}^T, (CU_3 \times e_{35})^T\right]^T & j = 3
\end{cases} \\[2mm]
{}^l\$_{Tj} = \begin{cases}
\left[e_{15}^T, (CU_1 \times e_{15})^T\right]^T & j = 1 \\
\left[e_{25}^T, (CU_2 \times e_{25})^T\right]^T & j = 2 \\
\left[e_{35}^T, (CU_3 \times e_{35})^T\right]^T & j = 3
\end{cases} \\[2mm]
{}^r\$_{Tj} = \begin{cases}
\left[m_1^T, (CU_1 \times m_1)^T\right]^T & j = 1 \\
\left[e_{25}^T, (CU_2 \times e_{25})^T\right]^T & j = 2 \\
\left[e_{35}^T, (CU_3 \times e_{35})^T\right]^T & j = 3
\end{cases} \\[2mm]
{}^m\$_{qj} = \begin{cases}
c_1\$_{j1} + c_2\$_{j2} + c_5\$_{j5} & j = 1 \\
c_1\$_{j1} + c_2\$_{j2} + c_5\$_{j5} + c_5\$_{15} & j = 2, 3
\end{cases}
\end{cases}
\tag{4}
$$

Combining Eqs. (3)–(4) into matrix form yield the complete velocity mapping between input and output unifying all three modes, given by

$$
^mJ_x{}^m\$_M = {}^mJ_q{}^m\dot{q}
\tag{5}
$$

where ^mJ_x is a 6×6 matrix representing the six-order screw system of constraint and transmission wrenches exerted on the moving platform, and ^mJ_q is a 6×6 diagonal matrix representing the input power coefficients of three actuated limbs, and $^m\dot{q}$ is the velocities of the actuation joints.

6   Singularity and Bifurcated Evolution of RLL

The distribution property of singularity loci and workspace in each mode determines the basic operational capability and survivability in extraterrestrial environments.

The forward singularities occur when $|^mJ_x| = 0$. At this time, the end of the single leg will gain one or more uncontrollable mobilities. Hence, they will lead to unexpected adjusting, landing, roving configurations. They also add dangerousness for the landing and roving security. The inverse singularities occur when $|^mJ_q(1:3, 1:3)| = 0$. At this time, the single leg will lose one or more mobilities, and locate at dead-point positions. The combined singularities are $|^mJ_x| = 0$ and $|^mJ_q(1:3, 1:3)| = 0$.

In Fig. 5(a), the yellow loci denote the forward singularity, blue and red loci are two kinds of inverse singularities, and the purple and green are workspace calculated by two practicable solutions; in (b), the red and blue surfaces are forward singularities, and the purple is the buffering workspace. One can conclude that the singularity loci do not exist in the practicable buffering workspace. Hence, the landing leg will possess good buffering speed, impact-resistance payload, stiffness, etc. during the touchdown process. This conclusion also verifies the theoretical rationality and technical reliability for the landing leg of the conventional cantilever-type legged lander (like Apollo and Chang'E lunar landers); (c) illustrates the forward singularity in yellow, inverse singularity in blue & red, and workspace in pink.

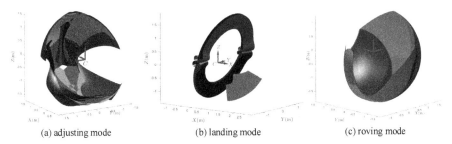

(a) adjusting mode   (b) landing mode   (c) roving mode

Fig. 5. Distribution of singularity loci with respect to the workspaces in three modes (Color figure online)

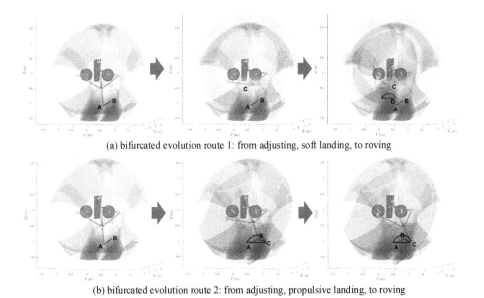

(a) bifurcated evolution route 1: from adjusting, soft landing, to roving

(b) bifurcated evolution route 2: from adjusting, propulsive landing, to roving

Fig. 6. Process shots of two bifurcated evolution routes using soft and propulsive landings

As illustrated in Fig. 6, two bifurcated evolution routes are compared according to if the thrust engine is applied for landing for the future application scenario.

Upon route 1 (adjusting → soft landing → roving): initially, to match with the touchdown landform topography, the RLL adjusts the pose of single leg and overall lander by changing the footpad position from A to B; next, the RLL switches the operation modes from adjusting to landing—the landing mode relying only upon buffering dampers without thrust engine is called as the soft landing. The process from B to C describes the buffering process to absorb the touchdown impact energy according to the dynamic principle; at last, the RLL switches modes from landing to roving—the quadruped locomotion like crawling, walking, trotting, etc. One can see the operation modes are implemented sequentially, in which the distribution properties of workspace and singularity loci for the latter mode are affected by the former mode.

Upon route 2 (adjusting → propulsive landing → roving): distinguished from route 1, it consumes the kinetic and potential energies before touchdown utilizing the work of thrust engine (the dampers are of no use). It is called the propulsive landing here. Hence, the landing mode just owns a point-like workspace, indicating the terminal configuration of adjusting mode is exactly the initial configuration of roving mode.

7 Conclusion

The R_v hinge is invented as a kernel device for robotic legged lander. It utilizes clutch and gripper together with dead-point properties, to support the RLL for switching among three operation modes and two actuation states (passive mechanism in landing mode, while active mechanisms in other modes). Then, unified differential kinematics modeling and distributions of singularity loci and workspace in each mode are analyzed. Results show that the robotic legged lander has good operation capabilities far away from the singularity. Finally, two bifurcated evolution routes are compared with their differences from soft landing to propulsive landing.

References

1. Zhang, K., Chermprayong, P., et al.: Bioinspired design of a landing system with soft shock absorbers for autonomous aerial robots. J. Field Robot. **36**(1), 230–251 (2019)
2. Ibarreche, J.I., Hernández, A., Petuya, V., Urízar, M.: A methodology to achieve the set of operation modes of reconfigurable parallel manipulators. Meccanica **54**(15), 2507–2520 (2019). https://doi.org/10.1007/s11012-019-01081-5
3. Wan, W.X., Wang, C., et al.: China's first mission to mars. Nat. Astron **4**(7), 721 (2020)
4. Li, C., Zuo, W., et al.: Overview of the chang'e-4 mission: opening the frontier of scientific exploration of the lunar far side. Space Sci. Rev. **217**(2), 1–32 (2021)
5. Han, Y., Guo, W., et al.: Dimensional synthesis of the reconfigurable legged mobile lander with multi-mode and complex mechanism topology. Mech. Mach. Theory **155**(1), 104097 (2021)
6. Han, Y., Zhou, C., et al.: Singularity loci, bifurcated evolution routes, and configuration transitions of reconfigurable legged mobile lander from adjusting, landing, to roving. J. Mech. Robot. **13**(4), 1–11 (2021)
7. Yang, J., Zeng, F., et al.: Design and verification of the landing impact attenuation system for chang'e-3 lander. SCIENTIA SINICA Technol. **44**(05), 440–449 (2014)
8. Dai, J.S., Jones, J.R.: Mobility in metamorphic mechanisms of foldable/erectable kinds. In: The Proceedings of 25th ASME Biennial Mechanisms Conference (1998), Atlanta, USA (1988)
9. Gan, D., Dai, J.S., Liao, Q.: Mobility change in two types of metamorphic parallel mechanisms. J. Mech. Robot. **1**(4), 41007 (2009)

10. Gan, D., Dias, J., Seneviratne, L.: Unified kinematics and optimal design of a 3RRPS meta-morphic parallel mechanism with a reconfigurable revolute joint. Mech. Mach. Theory **96**(2), 239–254 (2016)
11. Zhang, K., Dai, J.S., Fang, Y.: Topology and constraint analysis of phase change in the metamorphic chain and its evolved mechanism. J. Mech. Design **132**(12) (2010)
12. Yang, J.: Spacecraft Landing Buffer Mechanism. China Aerospace Publishing House, China (2015)
13. Han, Y., Guo, W., Gao, F., Yang, J.: A new dimension design method for the cantilever-type legged lander based on truss-mechanism transformation. Mech. Mach. Theory **142**(12), 103611 (2019)
14. Han, Y., Guo, W.: Novel design of the actuation-transmission system for legged mobile lander considering large impact. In: Uhl, T. (ed.) Advances in Mechanism and Machine Science. IFToMM WC 2019. Mechanisms and Machine Science, vol. 73, pp. 1859–1868. Springer, Cham (2019). https://doi.org/10.1007/978-3-030-20131-9_184

Design of a Reconfigurable Planar Parallel Continuum Manipulator with Variable Stiffness

Wei Yan[1], Genliang Chen[1,2(✉)], Shujie Tang[1], Zhuang Zhang[1], Xuyang Duan[1], and Hao Wang[1,2]

[1] State Key Laboratory of Mechanical Systems and Vibration, Shanghai Jiao Tong University, Shanghai 200240, China
{ywgump,leungchan,sjtang,z.zhang,clf,wanghao}@sjtu.edu.cn
[2] Shanghai Key Laboratory of Digital Manufacturing for Thin-Walled Structures, Shanghai Jiao Tong University, Shanghai 200240, China

Abstract. This paper presents the design and analysis of a novel planar parallel continuum manipulator, in which slender flexible links are used as kinematic limbs to connect the moving platform and the fixed one. Different from its rigid-body counterparts, the studied flexible manipulator is articulated by large deflections of the coupled flexible links, rather than relative displacements of rigid joints. Using two-DOF compound drives, the presented parallel manipulator is of actuation redundancy. As a result, its Cartesian stiffness is capable of varying for different circumstances, even when the pose of end-effector is prescribed for specific tasks. Moreover, the sequence of the compound drives is switchable to each other, such that the presented manipulator can be reconfigured to increase the workspace for orientation. A prototype of the studied parallel continuum manipulator is developed, on which preliminary validation experiments have been conducted. And the results demonstrate the feasibility of the proposed idea for developing reconfigurable flexible parallel manipulators with variable Cartesian stiffness.

Keywords: Parallel continuum manipulator · Reconfigurable mechanism · Actuation redundancy · Variable stiffness

1 Introduction

Concerning on the human-robot interaction [1], Cartesian compliance can significantly improve the safety and reliability of robot manipulators when performing pick-and-place tasks where large contact force will arise from small position misalignment. Hence, parallel continuum manipulators (PCMs) [2,3] have been increasingly attracted attentions because of their intrinsic advantages, such as reduction of backlash and simplicity to implement. Comparing to their rigid-body counterparts, this new kind of manipulators has intrinsic structural compliance, which is particularly suitable for human-robot interaction [4]. Furthermore, additional properties, such as variable stiffness and reconfigurable working mode, can also be acquired to enrich the potential applications.

© Springer Nature Switzerland AG 2021
X.-J. Liu et al. (Eds.): ICIRA 2021, LNAI 13015, pp. 803–813, 2021.
https://doi.org/10.1007/978-3-030-89134-3_73

With the diversity of working environment, the demands of reconfiguration to the robot are increasing. How to use one robot to solve multiple conditions becomes a popular direction. Research on reconfigurable mechanisms dates back to the 1990s. Dai proposed a kind of mechanism [5] which can change structure if it was folded based on the research to the decorative gifts. Wohlhart found another kind of mechanism [6] which called kinematotropic mechanism. At present, the reconfigurable mechanism is widely applied in many areas. Carroll from Brigham Young University applied the metamorphic method to the manufacture to simplified manufacturing process [7]. Cui enlarges the working space and flexibility of multifingered hand with reconfigurable palm [8].

Furthermore, variable stiffness is another important characteristic of mechanism because of its advantages in processing and manufacturing, such as shaft-hole assembly [9]. The types of variable stiffness mechanisms (VSMs) can be divided into passive one and active one. Different shapes of spring were applied in the design of passive VSMs [10]. The structure of passive VSMs is simple, but its stiffness is different in the case of different external forces. By contrast, active VSMs provided the adjustment of stiffness which have more application. To realize the active control of stiffness, additional actuators like pneumatic actuators [11] and motors [12] are necessary. Most of existing studies devoted to the combination of variable stiffness unit and rigid body. Thus, the range of compliance is limited by the size of variable stiffness unit.

To combine the stiffness varying and reconfiguration capabilities together, a planar parallel continuum manipulator with the structure of 3-$\underline{PR}F_{lex}$ is proposed in this paper. 2-DOF compound drives are introduced to this manipulator to drive three flexible branch limbs. Three redundant actuators give the ability of variable stiffness at the end-effector. Compared with the current active variable stiffness device, the characteristics of variable stiffness were integrated into the body of manipulator which made the structure more compact. Meanwhile, the manipulator is reconfigurable. Through switching the sequence of the compound PR drives, the workspace for orientation of manipulator can be increased. Based on the approach to large deflection problems using principal axes decomposition [13,14], the kinematics of the manipulator were analyzed.

2   Mechanism Design

As shown in Fig. 1, the planar parallel continuum manipulator (PPCM) studied in this paper, consists of three identical kinematic limbs, with the structure of '$\underline{PR}F_{lex}$'. Here, 'P' and 'R' represent the conventional prismatic and revolute joints, respectively. 'F_{lex}' denotes a slender flexible link undergoing nonlinear large deflection. And the underlined '$\underline{PR}$' indicates that both the prismatic and revolute joints in the limbs are actively actuated.

In each limb, the slender flexible link is fixedly mounted to the corresponding $\underline{PR}$ joints (which are termed as *compound $\underline{PR}$ drives* hereafter in this paper) and the manipulator's moving platform at its proximal and distal ends, respectively. Different from its rigid-body counterparts, the mobility of the studied PPCM is

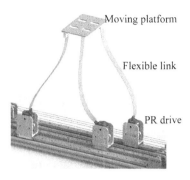

Fig. 1. The structure of the 3-$\underline{\text{PR}}\text{F}_{lex}$ parallel continuum manipulator.

realized by means of coupling the large deflections of the flexible limbs, rather than the relative motion of rigid joints. Since the compound $\underline{\text{PR}}$ drives are actuated actively, the position and orientation of the flexible limbs can be controlled accordingly at their proximal ends. As a result, the pose of the manipulator's end-effector can then be articulated precisely for prescribed tasks, by means of properly actuating the limbs' compound $\underline{\text{PR}}$ drives simultaneously.

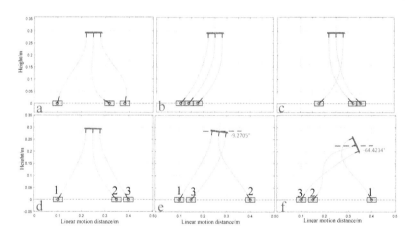

Fig. 2. (a–c) Redundancy in actuation for prescribed end-effector poses. (d–f) Reconfiguration of limb structure for the studied PPCM.

Note that each compound $\underline{\text{PR}}$ drive has two controlling variables. On the contrary, the moving platform of the manipulator is only capable of generating 3-DOF planar displacements. Consequently, there totally exist six independent input variables to control a 3-DOF output motion. In other words, the studied PPCM possesses redundancy in actuation, which results in multiple solutions to the inverse problems of kinetostatics. As demonstrated in Fig. 2(a–c), given a specific pose for the end-effector, different combinations of inputs can be assigned to the PR drives to articulate the manipulator for the prescribed task. In this paper, the capability of varying the Cartesian stiffness is exhibited through a developed manipulator. In Sect. 4, preliminary experiments are conducted on the prototype to verify this characteristics.

Further, a compact tendon-driven differential-motion mechanism is particularly designed in this paper to actuate the 2-DOF compound PR drives in the manipulator's flexible limbs. Moreover, the three -$\underline{PR}F_{lex}$ limbs of the studied PPCM are arranged parallel within different planes. Hence, the sequence of the flexible limbs is switchable to each other, such that the structure of limbs in the parallel continuum manipulator can be reconfigured to enlarge the workspace, especially the orientation one, for the end-effector.

As exhibited in Fig. 2(d–f), given three pairs of specific inputs for the compound PR drives, the static equilibrium configuration of the redundant PPCM will be quite different, in the case that the flexible limbs are arranged in variant orders. Therefore, by means of changing the sequence of the limbs, the proposed PPCM can work from one configuration to another. Moreover, owing to the structural compliance of flexible links, the working mode of this redundant PPCM can be reconfigured from one to the other, through a continuous path without causing singularity.

3   Kinetostatics Modeling and Analysis

This section presents the kinetostatics modeling and analysis of the synthesized PPCM, as exhibited in Sect. 2. A discretization-based approach, developed in our prior work [14], is then employed as the framework for elastostatics modeling of flexible links undergoing nonlinear large deflections. Using the proposed method, the kinetostatics analysis of the developed flexible parallel manipulator can be implemented in the categories of kinematics/statics of rigid multi-body systems. Moreover, using the product-of-exponentials (POE) formulation [15], gradient-based searching algorithms can be adopted to identify the corresponding static equilibrium configurations of the studied redundant PPCM efficiently.

3.1   Kinetostatics Modeling of the Flexible Links

Based on the principal-axes decomposition of structural compliance matrix [13], a general approach to the nonlinear large deflection problems of slender flexible links is established in our prior work [14], and has been successfully applied to the kinetostatics modeling, analysis, and control of several PCMs [2,3,16].

To some extent, the proposed approach can be regarded as a special kind of finite-element method. As shown in Fig. 3, using this method, a slender flexible link will be discretized into a number of small segments with elasticity. By applying the principal-axes decomposition to the structural compliance matrices of these segments, spatial six-DOF serial mechanisms with rigid bodies and passive elastic joints can then be synthesized to characterize the elasticity. Moreover, for the links with uniform cross-section, the corresponding approximation mechanisms can be reconstructed by two sets of orthogonal joints, which are concurrent at a common point. The geometric distribution of the elastic joints and the corresponding mechanical properties, namely the joint twist t_i and the stiffness constants k_i, can be uniquely determined according to the decomposition of the segments' structural compliance. Please refer to [14] for details.

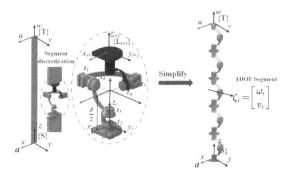

Fig. 3. Mechanism approximation of slender flexible links.

Furthermore, these elastic joints could be related to particular effects of the segments' deflections. First, the three revolute joints correspond to the bending about the section plane, and the torsion along the axis, respectively. Meanwhile, the prismatic joints are associated with the shearing and extension/compression deformations. Particularly, as for slender flexible links, the effects of shearing and elongation can be neglected comparing to the bending and torsion. Thus, in the case of planar mechanisms, only the revolute joint corresponding to bending needs to be taken into account. As a result, a planar n-R hyper-redundant linkage can be obtained to approximate the elastostatics of the slender flexible links. Here, n denotes the number of segments discretized from the link.

Using POE formulation, the forward kinematics of the link's approximation mechanism can be represented as

$$\mathbf{g}_{st}(\boldsymbol{\theta}) = \exp(\hat{\boldsymbol{\zeta}}_1 \theta_1) \cdots \exp(\hat{\boldsymbol{\zeta}}_n \theta_n)\, \mathbf{g}_{st,0} \tag{1}$$

where $\hat{\boldsymbol{\zeta}}_i \in se(3)$, $i = 1, \cdots, n$, represent the twists of the elastic joints in the approximation mechanism. $\boldsymbol{\theta} = [\theta_1, \cdots, \theta_n]^T \in \mathbb{R}^{n \times 1}$ is the corresponding vector of joint variables. $\mathbf{g}_{st} \in SE(3)$ is the relative pose of the tip frame $\{T\}$ with respect to the spatial one $\{S\}$. And $\mathbf{g}_{st,0} = \mathbf{g}_{st}(\boldsymbol{0})$ relates to the initial position.

Using such a representation, the kinetostatics model can be established by a combination of the geometric constraint to the tip frame in Cartesian space and the static equilibrium condition of the elastic joints in joint space, as

$$\boldsymbol{f}(\boldsymbol{\theta}, \boldsymbol{F}) = \begin{bmatrix} \boldsymbol{y} \\ \boldsymbol{\tau} \end{bmatrix} = \begin{bmatrix} (\mathbf{g}_{st}\mathbf{g}_t^{-1})^{\vee} \\ \mathbf{K}_\theta \boldsymbol{\theta} - \mathbf{J}^T \boldsymbol{F} \end{bmatrix} = \boldsymbol{0} \tag{2}$$

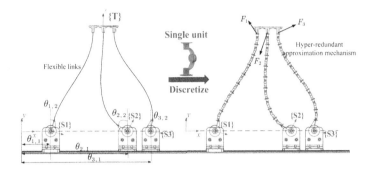

Fig. 4. Mechanism approximation of the 3-PRF$_{lex}$ PPCM.

where $\mathbf{g}_t$ denotes the target pose for $\{\mathrm{T}\}$. $\mathbf{K}_\theta = \mathrm{diag}(k_1, \cdots, k_n) \in \mathbb{R}^{n\times n}$ is the diagonal matrix of joint stiffness. $\mathbf{F} \in \mathbb{R}^{6\times 1}$ represents the external wrench applied at $\{\mathrm{T}\}$. And $\mathbf{J}$ is the Jocobian matrix of the approximation mechanism, which can be written in a concise form as

$$(\dot{\mathbf{g}}_{st}\mathbf{g}_{st}^{-1})^\vee = \mathbf{J}\dot{\boldsymbol{\theta}} \ \Rightarrow \ \mathbf{J} = [\boldsymbol{\xi}_1, \cdots, \boldsymbol{\xi}_n] \in \mathbb{R}^{6\times n} \tag{3}$$

where $\boldsymbol{\xi}_i = \mathrm{Ad}(\exp(\hat{\boldsymbol{\zeta}}_1\theta_1)\cdots\exp(\hat{\boldsymbol{\zeta}}_{i-1}\theta_{i-1}))\boldsymbol{\zeta}_i$ represent the joint twists, in 6×1 vector form with respect to $\{\mathrm{S}\}$, in current configuration.

According to the reciprocity between motion/force transmission, it is known that the transpose of the Jacobian matrix $\mathbf{J}$ simply corresponds to the inverse force Jacobian. Thus, the second equation in (2) relates to the torque deviations between the motion-induced resistance and those transmitted from the tip frame. Further, a closed-form solution to the gradient of (2) can be derived as

$$\nabla = \begin{bmatrix} \frac{\partial y}{\partial \theta} & \frac{\partial y}{\partial F} \\ \frac{\partial \tau}{\partial \theta} & \frac{\partial \tau}{\partial F} \end{bmatrix} = \begin{bmatrix} \mathbf{J} & \mathbf{0} \\ \mathbf{K}_\theta - \mathbf{K_J} & -\mathbf{J}^T \end{bmatrix} \tag{4}$$

where $\mathbf{K_J} = \frac{\partial}{\partial \theta}(\mathbf{J}^T\mathbf{F})$ is the configuration-dependent item of the system's overall stiffness. The details can be found in [14].

3.2 Kinetostatics Models of the 3-PRF$_{lex}$ PPCM

As indicated in Sect. 2, the PPCM consists of three limbs with the structure of 'PRF$_{lex}$'. Applying the mechanism approximation to each link, a planar hyper-redundant link with two rigid active joints and n passive elastic ones can be constructed. The kinetostatics models of the flexible limbs can be represented as

$$\begin{cases} \mathbf{g}_{j,st}(\boldsymbol{\theta}_j) = \exp(\hat{\boldsymbol{\zeta}}_{j,1}\theta_{j,1})\cdots\exp(\hat{\boldsymbol{\zeta}}_{j,n+2}\theta_{j,n+2})\,\mathbf{g}_{j,0} \\ \boldsymbol{\tau}_j = \mathbf{K}_{j,p}\boldsymbol{\theta}_{j,p} - \mathbf{J}_{j,p}^T\mathbf{F}_j \end{cases}, \ j = 1,2,3 \tag{5}$$

where $\boldsymbol{\theta}_j = [\theta_{j,1}, \cdots, \theta_{j,n+2}]^T \in \mathbb{R}^{(n+2)\times 1}$ is the limb's vector of joint variables, including the compound PR drive. So $\theta_{j,1}$ and $\theta_{j,2}$ correspond to the translation and rotation of the active prismatic and revolute joints, respectively, as shown in Fig. 4. Accordingly, $\hat{\zeta}_{j,1}$ and $\hat{\zeta}_{j,2}$ relate to the corresponding joint twists. While $\hat{\zeta}_{j,k}, k \geq 3$, are those discretized from the flexible link. $\theta_{j,p} = [\theta_{j,3}, \cdots, \theta_{j,n+2}]^T \in \mathbb{R}^{n \times 1}$ and $\mathbf{K}_{j,p} = \text{diag}(k_{j,3}, \cdots, k_{j,n+2}) \in \mathbb{R}^{n \times n}$ are the variables and stiffness of the passive joints. Similarly, $\mathbf{J}_{j,p} = [\boldsymbol{\xi}_{j,3}, \cdots, \boldsymbol{\xi}_{j,n+2}] \in \mathbb{R}^{6 \times n}$ is the Jacobian matrix relating the passive joints to the tip frame. Here, $\mathbf{g}_{j,0}$ denotes the initial pose of {T} with respect to {S} in limb j and $\mathbf{F}_j$ is the wrench reacted between the moving platform and the corresponding limb.

In the kinetostatics analysis of the whole manipulator, the target poses $\mathbf{g}_{j,st}$ and the reaction wrenches $\mathbf{F}_j$ need to be identified simultaneously for all limbs. So, extra constraints should be introduced to make the problem deterministic.

In parallel manipulators, the kinematic limbs are geometrically compatible to each others at the moving platform, meanwhile, the end-effector should be in static equilibrium undergoing the external loads and the reaction forces from the limbs. Accordingly, the coupling of the manipulator's limbs can be represented in light of the geometric constraints and static equilibrium conditions as

$$\begin{cases} \mathbf{g}_{1,st} = \mathbf{g}_{2,st} = \mathbf{g}_{3,st} = \mathbf{g}_{st} \\ \mathbf{F}_e - \mathbf{F}_1 - \mathbf{F}_2 - \mathbf{F}_3 = \mathbf{0} \end{cases} \tag{6}$$

where $\mathbf{g}_{st}$ is the target pose for the tool frame. $\mathbf{F}_e$ is the external wrench.

Combining (5) and (6), the system kinetostatics model can be obtained as

$$\boldsymbol{f}(\boldsymbol{\theta}, \boldsymbol{F}, \mathbf{g}_{st}) = \begin{bmatrix} \boldsymbol{X}_j \\ \boldsymbol{\tau}_0 \\ \boldsymbol{\tau}_j \end{bmatrix} = \begin{bmatrix} \left(\ln(\mathbf{g}_{j,st} \, \mathbf{g}_{st}^{-1}) \right)^{\vee} \\ \boldsymbol{F}_e - \boldsymbol{F}_1 - \boldsymbol{F}_2 - \boldsymbol{F}_3 \\ \mathbf{K}_{j,p} \, \boldsymbol{\theta}_{j,p} - \mathbf{J}_{j,p}^T \, \boldsymbol{F}_j \end{bmatrix} = \mathbf{0}, \quad j = 1, 2, 3 \tag{7}$$

where $\boldsymbol{X}_j = (\ln(\mathbf{g}_{j,st} \, \mathbf{g}_{st}^{-1}))^{\vee} \in \mathbb{R}^{6 \times 1}$ denotes the pose deviation of the tip frame. $\boldsymbol{\theta} = [\boldsymbol{\theta}_1^T, \boldsymbol{\theta}_2^T, \boldsymbol{\theta}_3^T]^T \in \mathbb{R}^{(3n+6) \times 1}$ and $\boldsymbol{F} = [\boldsymbol{F}_1^T, \boldsymbol{F}_2^T, \boldsymbol{F}_3^T]^T \in \mathbb{R}^{18 \times 1}$ are the system vector of joint variables and reaction wrenches.

In the system kinetostatics model (7), there are totally $3n + 12$ equations in terms of $3n + 18$ unknown variables. It is worth noting that, in the studied planar case, the geometric constraints $\boldsymbol{X}_j$ and the equilibrium condition $\boldsymbol{\tau}_0$ degenerate to 3-dimensional components. As well, the reaction wrenches $\boldsymbol{F}_j$ and the target pose $\mathbf{g}_{st}$ yield to 3-dimensional variables. Consequently, in order to make the model solvable, some of the unknown variables should be specified in advance.

In the forward kinetostatics problem, the inputs of the compound PR drives are given. Thus, the number of unknown variables decreases to $3n + 12$, which is as same as that of the equations. Then, the corresponding forward model can be directly inherited from (7), by replacing the joint variable $\boldsymbol{\theta}$ with the passive one $\boldsymbol{\theta}_p = [\boldsymbol{\theta}_{1,p}^T, \boldsymbol{\theta}_{2,p}^T, \boldsymbol{\theta}_{3,p}^T]^T$. Further, the corresponding gradient can be derived in closed-form using the same strategy to (4), given by

$$\nabla_{fwd} = \begin{bmatrix} \dfrac{\partial \boldsymbol{f}_{fwd}}{\partial \boldsymbol{\theta}_p}, & \dfrac{\partial \boldsymbol{f}_{fwd}}{\partial \boldsymbol{F}}, & \dfrac{\partial \boldsymbol{f}_{fwd}}{\partial \boldsymbol{\xi}_{st}} \end{bmatrix} = \begin{bmatrix} \mathbf{J}_p & \mathbf{0} & \mathbf{J}_{\boldsymbol{\xi}_{st}} \\ \mathbf{0} & \mathbf{J}_F & \mathbf{0} \\ \mathbf{K}_p & -\mathbf{J}_p^T & \mathbf{0} \end{bmatrix} \tag{8}$$

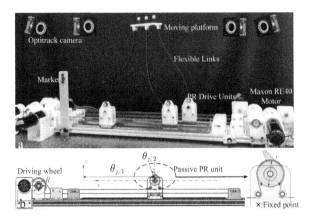

Fig. 5. Prototype of the studied PPCM with actuation redundancy.

where $\boldsymbol{\xi}_{st} = (\log(\mathbf{g}_{st}))^\vee \in \mathbb{R}^{6\times 1}$ is the twist coordinates of $\mathbf{g}_{st}$. The components can be derived readily by referring to (4), as $\mathbf{J}_p = \frac{\partial \mathbf{X}}{\partial \boldsymbol{\theta}_p}$, $\mathbf{J}_{\boldsymbol{\xi}_{st}} = \frac{\partial \mathbf{X}}{\partial \boldsymbol{\xi}_{st}}$, $\mathbf{J}_{\boldsymbol{F}} = \frac{\partial \boldsymbol{\tau}_0}{\partial \boldsymbol{F}}$, and $\mathbf{K}_p = \frac{\partial \boldsymbol{\tau}}{\partial \boldsymbol{\theta}_p}$. The details are not given in the paper due to space limitation.

Then, the forward problem of kinetostatics analysis can be solved efficiently using gradient-based searching algorithms, following the update theme as

$$\boldsymbol{x}_{fwd}^{(k+1)} = \boldsymbol{x}_{fwd}^{(k)} - (\boldsymbol{\nabla}_{fwd}^{(k)})^{-1} \boldsymbol{f}_{fwd}^{(k)} \tag{9}$$

where $\boldsymbol{x}_{fwd} = [\boldsymbol{\theta}_p^T, \boldsymbol{F}^T, \boldsymbol{\xi}_{st}^T]^T$ are the unknown variables to be identified.

Similarly, the inverse kinetostatics model can also be derived directly from (7). In this case, the target pose $\mathbf{g}_{st}$ is prescribed and the corresponding inputs of the active joints require to be determined. The number of unknown variables becomes $n + 15$, which is still greater the number of equations. As indicated in Sect. 2, this property is caused by the actuation redundancy. Due to space limitation, the details of derivation is not provided in the paper.

4 Experimental Validation

To validate the feasibility of the proposed idea, a prototype of the studied PPCM is developed using easy-to-access materials and simple fabrication methods. Preliminary experiments are conducted and the results demonstrate the manipulator's capability of variable stiffness and reconfiguration.

4.1 Prototyping and Experimental Setup

As illustrated in Fig. 5, a prototype of the studied PPCM is developed in this section. Slender spring-steel strips are employed as the flexible links. A compact cable-driven differential-motion mechanism, as shown in the figure, is particularly designed to actuate the compound PR drives. To make the limb sequence switchable, the three $\underline{PRF}_{lex}$ limbs are arranged parallel on different planes. The Optitrack motion capture system is employed to measure the end pose.

Two sets of differential-motion cables are arranged parallel. When the two driving wheels rotate in the same direction, it generates a translational motion. Otherwise, it produces a rotation. The geometric parameters of the $\underline{PR}$ drive are as follows: radius of driving wheel - R, radius of passive unit- r, input angle of two driving wheels - ϕ_1 and ϕ_2. Then, the relationship between the input and output prismatic joint $\theta_{1,j}$ and revolute joint $\theta_{2,j}$ can be written as

$$\begin{bmatrix} \theta_{2,j} \\ \theta_{1,j} \end{bmatrix} = \begin{bmatrix} \frac{R}{2r} & \frac{-R}{2r} \\ \frac{R}{2} & \frac{R}{2} \end{bmatrix} \begin{bmatrix} \phi_1 \\ \phi_2 \end{bmatrix} \tag{10}$$

4.2 Validation of Variable Stiffness

As introduced in Sect. 2, the Cartesian stiffness can be adjusted in the case that the pose of end-effector is prescribed. To verify the characteristics of variable stiffness, a preliminary force compliant experiment was conducted in the section. Based on three different combination of inputs with the same end pose shown in Fig. 2, their longitudinal and lateral force compliant characteristics were analyzed. Horizontal right and vertical downward external forces were respectively applied to the end-effector corresponding to three different combinations of inputs. Then, the displacement in the direction of the force was recorded.

To keep the load direction precise, the external force is applied via a rope traction. The proximal end of rope is fixed on the mid-point of the end-effector, and the distal end is connected to the load. When the horizontal force is applied, the gravity of load is converted to the horizontal force through the fixed pulley, as shown in Fig. 6. The external force is ranged from 0 to $6N$ with the increment of $1N$. The results are shown in Fig. 6.

Among three different inputs in Fig. 2(a–c), the first has high stiffness in both lateral and longitudinal directions. The third has relatively high longitudinal

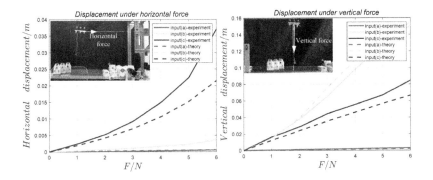

Fig. 6. Load-induced deflections in horizontal vertical directions.

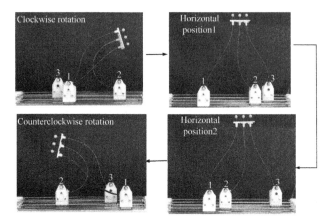

Fig. 7. Reconfiguration of different working modes.

stiffness, but low lateral stiffness. While in the second case, the manipulator is of lowest stiffness in both lateral and longitudinal directions.

4.3 Validation of Reconfiguration

As indicated in Sect. 2, the sequence of the compound PR drives is switchable to each other, such that the developed prototype of studied PPCM can reconfigure its working mode to increase the workspace, especially for orientation. To validate this characteristics, different sequence of the PR drives was actuated and the corresponding configurations are measured. As shown in Fig. 7, several key positions are illustrated. First, the moving platform can reach a large rotation to the right when three PR drives are arranged in the order of 3-1-2. Then the pose becomes horizontal with adjusting the order to 1-2-3, but the bending direction of flexible links is not changed. In addition, the pose is kept the same, but the bending direction of middle link is changed. Finally, the pose reached a large rotation to the left by adjusting the order to 2-3-1.

5   Conclusion

In this paper, a novel planar parallel continuum manipulator with actuation redundancy is proposed. Different from the traditional rigid mechanism which driven by the motion of rigid joint, the studied manipulator was articulated by large deflection of the coupled flexible links. Through adding redundant actuators and switching the sequence of three PR drives, the variable stiffness and reconfiguration can be respectively realized. Based on the above concept, the prototype was designed. Combining the experiments and Theoretical analysis, the characteristics of variable stiffness and reconfiguration were validated. The proposed manipulator can meet the demands of diversity working scene.

Acknowledgement. This work was jointly supported by the National Key R&D Program of China (Grant No. 2017YFE0111300) and National Science Foundation of China (Grant No. 52022056 and No. 51875334).

References

1. Bicchi, A., Tonietti, G.: Fast and "soft-arm" tactics robot arm design. IEEE Robot. Autom. Mag. **11**(2), 22–33 (2004)
2. Du, C., Chen, G., Zhang, Z., Tang, L., Wang, H.: Design and experimental analysis of a planar compliant parallel manipulator. In: Yu, H., Liu, J., Liu, L., Ju, Z., Liu, Y., Zhou, D. (eds.) ICIRA 2019. LNCS (LNAI), vol. 11744, pp. 637–647. Springer, Cham (2019). https://doi.org/10.1007/978-3-030-27541-9_52
3. Chen, G., Zhang, Z., Kong, L., et al.: Analysis and validation of a flexible planar two degrees-of-freedom parallel manipulator with structural passive compliance. ASME J. Mech. Robot. **12**(1), 011011 (2020)
4. Ham, R., Sugar, T., Vanderborght, B., et al.: Compliant actuator designs. IEEE Robot. Autom. Mag. **3**(16), 81–94 (2009)
5. Dai, J., Rees, J.: Mobility in metamorphic mechanisms of foldable/erectable kinds. ASME J. Mech. Des. **121**(3), 375–382 (1999)
6. Wohlhart, K.: Kinematotropic Linkages. In: Lenarčič, J., Parenti-Castelli, V. (eds.) Recent Advances in Robot Kinematics, pp. 359–368. Springer, Dordrecht (1996). https://doi.org/10.1007/978-94-009-1718-7_36
7. Carroll, D., Magleby, S., Howell, L., et al.: Simplified manufacturing through a metamorphic process for compliant ortho-planar mechanisms. In: 2005 ASME International Mechanical Engineering Congress and Exposition, Orlando, Florida, USA, vol. 42150, pp. 389–399 (2005)
8. Cui, L., Dai, J.: Posture, workspace, and manipulability of the metamorphic multifingered hand with an articulated palm. ASME J. Mech. Robot. **3**(2), 021001 (2011)
9. Jaura, A., Osman, M., Krouglicof, N.: Hybrid compliance control for intelligent assembly in a robot work cell. Int. J. Prod. Res. **36**(9), 2573–2583 (1998)
10. Accoto, D., Tagliamonte, N., Carpino G, et al.: pVEJ: a modular passive viscoelastic joint for assistive wearable robots. In: 2012 IEEE International Conference on Robotics and Automation, Saint Paul, MN, USA, pp. 3361–3366 (2012)
11. Kajikawa, S., Abe, K.: Robot finger module with multidirectional adjustable joint stiffness. IEEE/ASME Trans. Mechatron. **17**(1), 128–135 (2012)
12. Wolf, S., Hirzinger, G.,: A new variable stiffness design: matching requirements of the next robot generation. In: 2008 IEEE International Conference on Robotics and Automation, Pasadena, CA, USA, pp. 1741–1746 (2008)
13. Chen, G., Wang, H., Lin, Z., et al.: The principal axes decomposition of spatial stiffness matrices. IEEE Trans. Rob. **31**(1), 191–207 (2015)
14. Chen, G., Zhang, Z., Wang, H.: A general approach to the large deflection problems of spatial flexible rods using principal axes decomposition of compliance matrices. ASME J. Mech. Robot. **10**(3), 031012 (2018)
15. Chen, G., Wang, H., Lin, Z.: Determination of the identifiable parameters in robot calibration based on the POE formula. IEEE Trans. Rob. **30**(5), 1066–1077 (2014)
16. Pan, H., Chen, G., Kang, Y., et al.: Design and kinematic analysis of a flexible-link parallel mechanism with a spatially translational end-effector. ASME J. Mech. Robot. **12**(1), 011022 (2021)

Parameter Optimization and Vibration Isolation Control of a Mobile Parallel Robot

Shuzhan Shentu[1], Xin-Jun Liu[1,2(✉)], Fugui Xie[1,2], Zhao Gong[1], Fuqiang Yu[3], and Hongxi Cui[3]

[1] The State Key Laboratory of Tribology, Department of Mechanical Engineering (DME), Tsinghua University, Beijing 100084, China
xinjunliu@mail.tsinghua.edu.cn
[2] Beijing Key Lab of Precision/Ultra-Precision Manufacturing Equipments and Control, Tsinghua University, Beijing 100084, China
[3] Yantai Tsingke+ Robot Joint Research Institute Co., Ltd., Yantai 264006, China

Abstract. YRob is a mobile parallel robot with 6 degrees of freedom. Previous works mainly focus on the control of this robot, and the parallel module is passive. In this paper, three wheeled chassis and attitude-adjustment mechanism (AM) with the 6-SPU configuration are employed as driving units. YRob can achieve redundancy control of 6 degrees of freedom movement to realize wide-range movement and vibration isolation. The scheme of the mechanism and two inverse kinematic solutions are given. The dimensional parameters of the AM are optimized to enlarge the workspace and improve the motion/force transmissibility. The driving modules of the AM are selected through joint simulations and static analysis. Then the multistage shock absorption system of the wheeled chassis and the AM is established. This work provides a new approach to achieve dynamic stability of the mobile parallel robot whether it works on a flat or rough road.

Keywords: Mobile parallel robot · Parameter optimization · Vibration isolation control

1 Introduction

In the past decades, parallel robots have been widely studied and used in various fields [1]. Parallel robots are generally composed of end-effects, multiple limbs, driving units and fixed basement [2]. Compared to serial robots, the parallel robot has the performance of flexible attitude adjustment and fast dynamic response [3]. However, due to the limitations of the joint angles, limbs, and the fixed basement, parallel robots have the disadvantage of a small workspace [4].

To solve the problem, many researchers designed mobile parallel robots (MPR) by substituting the driving unit with planar drives or mobile robots [5]. MPR combines the advantages of two kinds of robots, including good flexibility, high stiffness, increased workspace, etc. [6]. Tahmasebi designed a 3-PPSR mechanism driven by a five-bar linkage mechanism and analyzed the direct and inverse kinematic solutions [7]. Ben-Horin

© Springer Nature Switzerland AG 2021
X.-J. Liu et al. (Eds.): ICIRA 2021, LNAI 13015, pp. 814–824, 2021.
https://doi.org/10.1007/978-3-030-89134-3_74

proposed a 3-PPRS mechanism and improved the workspace [8]. To further improve the working volume of the MPR on rough terrain or sand-gravel surface, Gong employed three tracked vehicles with the 3-PPSR configuration named VicRoB [9]. Gong also proposed a motion planning method to solve the coordinate motion of three tracked vehicles [10].

However, the limbs of parallel mechanisms in the above-mentioned robots are all with fixed length, which means the parallel mechanism can only be adjusted passively. And the tracked vehicles satisfy the non-holonomic constraints and the center point has only one degree of freedom instantly, so it is difficult to adjust the attitude quickly. The vibration generated in the field will have an impact on the end-effector and cause many unexpected problems. Therefore, linear motors are elected as the driving modules of the parallel robots into the parallel mobile robot (named YRob) to isolate the shocks and vibrations.

Of note is that, the motion control method of mobile robots has been proposed in the previous works [9, 10], it will be no longer elaborated here. In order to improve the property of vibration isolation, the rest of the paper is organized as follows. The inverse solution of YRob is given in Sect. 2. In Sect. 3, the parameters of YRob is optimized and the structure is designed. Finally, the driving module is selected and a series of simulation experiments is carried out to test the performance of vibration isolation.

2   Kinematics Analysis of the Mechanism

YRob includes three wheeled chassis and an attitude-adjustment mechanism(AM), as shown in Fig. 1. Both of them can achieve the 6-DoF movement. The AM adopts Stewart mechanism configuration(6-SPU), consisting of a bearing platform, universal joints, driving modules, and spherical joints. The lower ends of six driving modules are connected to the wheeled chassis through three composite spherical joints(points A_1, A_2, and A_3), respectively. The upper ends of the driving modules are connected to the bearing platform through six universal joints (points B_i, $i = 1, 2, 3, 4, 5, 6$). The length of each driving module is l_i. The distance from the center of the bearing platform, point o', to each side of the platform is represented by k.

The global frame $(o - xyz, \{N\})$ and the bearing platform reference frame $(o' - x'y'z', \{M\})$ are defined as shown in Fig. 1. The relationship of the frame can be expressed by two transform matrices. $^N T_M$ means the transform matrix from $\{N\}$ to $\{M\}$ and $^M T_N$ means the transform matrix from $\{M\}$ to $\{N\}$:

$$^N T_M = \begin{pmatrix} \mathbf{R} & \mathbf{t} \\ 0 & 1 \end{pmatrix}, ^M T_N = \begin{pmatrix} \mathbf{R}^T & -\mathbf{R}^T\mathbf{t} \\ 0 & 1 \end{pmatrix} \tag{1}$$

where $\mathbf{R}$ is the rotation matrix between two frames and $\mathbf{t}$ denotes the position coordinate of the point o' in the frame $\{N\}$. Points f_i and d_i ($i = 1, 2, 3$) are the foot of perpendiculars from o' and A_i to the sides of the bearing platform respectively.

Firstly, consider the situation that the driving modules are locked and the motion of the bearing platform is realized by three wheeled chassis. The current length l_i is obtained from the encoder data. Based on the geometrical conditions and mechanical structural parameters, the coordinates of the center of the spherical joints are expressed in frame $\{M\}$:

$$
{}^{M}A_1 = \begin{cases} -(k + T_1 \cdot l \cos \theta_1) \\ l/2 - T_1 \cdot l/\tan \alpha_1 \\ -T \cdot l \sin \theta_1 \end{cases}
$$

$$
{}^{M}A_2 = \begin{cases} (k + T_2 \cdot l \cos \theta_2)/2 - \sqrt{3}(l/2 - x_2)/2 \\ (k + T_2 \cdot l \cos \theta_2)\sqrt{3}/2 - (l/2 - x_2)/2 \\ -T \cdot l \sin \theta_2 \end{cases} \tag{2}
$$

$$
{}^{M}A_3 = \begin{cases} (k + T_3 \cdot l \cos \theta_2)/2 - \sqrt{3}(l/2 - x_3)/2 \\ -(k + T_3 \cdot l \cos \theta_3)\sqrt{3}/2 + (l/2 - x_3)/2 \\ -T \cdot l \sin \theta_3 \end{cases}
$$

where

$T_i = \tan \alpha_i \cdot \tan \beta_i/(\tan \alpha_i + \tan \beta_i), x_i = b_{2i-1}d_i,$
$\alpha_i = \arccos(l^2 + l_{2i-1}^2 - l_{2i}^2)/2l \cdot l_{2i-1}$ and $\beta_i = \arccos(l^2 + l_{2i}^2 - l_{2i-1}^2)/2l \cdot l_{2i}$.

Using the transform matrix ${}^{M}T_N$, the coordinates of ${}^{N}A_i$ in the global reference frame can be obtained by the homogeneous transformation. Considering that all three driving units are on the ground, the z coordinate values of ${}^{N}A_i$ are zero. By definition, the values of θ_i range from 0 to 90°, so there is only one solution of θ_i, which can be represented by the given parameters:

$$
\theta_1 = sin^{-1}\frac{|\mathbf{P}| - k \cdot x_k + y_k (l/2 - l \cdot T_1/\tan \alpha_1)}{T_1 \cdot l \cdot \sqrt{x_k^2 + z_k^2}} - sin^{-1}\frac{x_k}{\sqrt{x_k^2 + z_k^2}}
$$

$$
\theta_2 = sin^{-1}\frac{|\mathbf{P}| + k\left(x_k - \sqrt{3}y_k\right)/2 - (l/4 - x_2/2)\left(\sqrt{3}x_k - y_k\right)}{T_2 \cdot l\sqrt{z_k^2 + \left(x_k - \sqrt{3}y_k\right)^2/4}} + sin^{-1}\frac{\left(x_k - \sqrt{3}y_k\right)/2}{\sqrt{z_k^2 + \left(x_k - \sqrt{3}y_k\right)^2/4}} \tag{3}
$$

$$
\theta_3 = sin^{-1}\frac{|\mathbf{P}| + k\left(x_k + \sqrt{3}y_k\right)/2 - (l/4 - x_3/2)\left(\sqrt{3}x_k + y_k\right)}{T_2 \cdot l\sqrt{z_k^2 + \left(x_k + \sqrt{3}y_k\right)^2/4}} + sin^{-1}\frac{\left(x_k + \sqrt{3}y_k\right)/2}{\sqrt{z_k^2 + \left(x_k + \sqrt{3}y_k\right)^2/4}}
$$

With Eq. (2) and Eq. (3), finally ${}^{N}A_i$ is given by the formula:

$$
{}^{N}A_i = {}^{N}T_M {}^{M}A_i \tag{4}
$$

Secondly, keep the wheeled chassis fixed and the bearing platform only controlled by the driving modules. The inverse kinematics solution can be expressed as

$$l_i = \sqrt{\left(\mathbf{R} \cdot {}^M \mathbf{B_i} + \mathbf{t} - {}^N \mathbf{A_i}\right)^T \left(\mathbf{R} \cdot {}^M \mathbf{B_i} + \mathbf{t} - {}^N \mathbf{A_i}\right)} \tag{5}$$

According to Eqs. (4) and (5), given the target position and attitude, the target position of the wheeled chassis and the length of the six motors can be calculated. It is possible to achieve the desired path of the bearing platform.

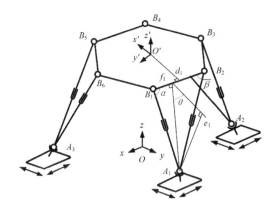

Fig. 1. Parameters description of the kinematic scheme.

3 Parameter Optimization of the AM

The AM adopts 6-SPU parallel configuration. Three composite spherical joints connect with 6 driving modules, and they are evenly distributed around a circumference considering symmetry. The dimensional parameters to be optimized are shown in Fig. 2. k_1 represents the distance from point o' to the side of the bearing platform, k_2 is the radius of the circumference, k_3 is the length between the two universal joints, and the height of the bearing platform from the basement is denoted by Zc.

The optimization objectives of this study mainly consider the workspace and motion/force transmissibility. The performance desires of the AM include that the attitude adjustment capacity of the bearing platform should reach 25°, the height adjustment capacity should be more than 300 mm, and the mechanism has better motion/force transfer performance in the heavy-load situation. Input transmission index and output transmission index are introduced as the optimization performance evaluation indices and defined by

$$\gamma_1 = \min_i \left\{ \frac{\left|\hat{\boldsymbol{S}}_{TWS} \circ \hat{\boldsymbol{S}}_{ITS}\right|}{\left|\hat{\boldsymbol{S}}_{TWS} \circ \hat{\boldsymbol{S}}_{ITS}\right|_{max}} \right\}, \gamma_O = \min_i \left\{ \frac{\left|\hat{\boldsymbol{S}}_{TWS} \circ \hat{\boldsymbol{S}}_{OTS}\right|}{\left|\hat{\boldsymbol{S}}_{TWS} \circ \hat{\boldsymbol{S}}_{OTS}\right|_{max}} \right\} (i = 1, 2, \ ,n). \tag{6}$$

then the motion/force transmission index (LTI) is given

$$\gamma = \min_i\{\gamma_1, \gamma_O\}(i = 1, 2, \ldots, n).\tag{7}$$

More detailed information about LTI is in Ref. [11]. The optimal dimensional parameters are obtained as follows:

$$k_1 = 400\,\text{mm}, k_2 = 900\,\text{mm}, k_3 = 460\,\text{mm}, Z_c = 850\,\text{mm}$$

And the motion/force transmission index of the AM represented by the T&T angle [12] is demonstrated in Fig. 3. Notice that LTI is larger than 0.7 within the whole rotating workspace, therefore, this set of parameters shows satisfactory motion/force transfer performance. Meanwhile, the range of Z_c is from 700 mm to 1000 mm. Then the static analysis of the AM is carried out.

Table 1 displays the results of the force, stroke, and rotation angles of the six driving modules at three limit positions, including the maximum angle, minimum and maximum positions. The force calculation of the driving module includes self-weight and 150 kg load. We can come to the conclusion that the force variation of the drive module is about 303 N, and the stroke is within 300 mm, which provides a basis for the subsequent selection of drive modules. Then the structure of the AM is designed as shown in Fig. 4.

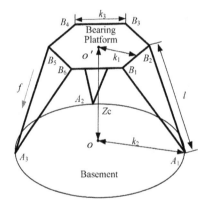

Fig. 2. Description of the parameters

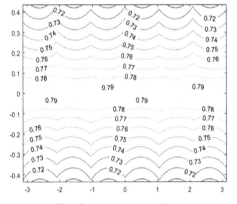

Fig. 3. Distribution of LTI

Table 1. Statics analysis of the AM

Z_c/mm	$\varphi/^\circ$	f_{max}/N	f_{min}/N	l_{max}/mm	l_{min}/mm	$\theta_{max}/^\circ$	$\theta_{min}/^\circ$
850	25	570	267	1175	878	87	41
700	0	424	424	890	890	54	54
1000	0	380	380	1141	1141	63	63

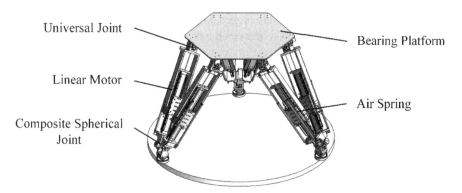

Universal Joint

Linear Motor

Composite Spherical
Joint

Bearing Platform

Air Spring

Fig. 4. Schematic diagram of the AM

4   Vibration Isolation Control

In Sect. 2, the AM is designed and optimized. The next step is to select the driving module to ensure the stability property when moving on the uneven road. The wheeled chassis have a suspension system, which is the assembly of all the connecting devices, used to slow down the impact of the bumpy road on the body. Both the wheeled chassis and the AM constitute a multistage shock absorption system. Since there are six driving modules, the one sixth simplified model is first established, as shown in Fig. 5.

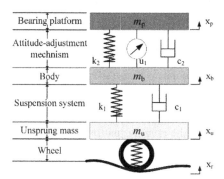

Fig. 5. The multistage shock absorption system consists of a wheel, the suspension system, and the driving module of the AM.

Based on the model, the dynamic equation of multistage shock absorption system is established in Eq. (8). Since the road input signal is not easy to measure and the stiffness of the wheel is large, the unsprung mass is used as the input of the model.

$$\begin{pmatrix} m_p & 0 \\ 0 & m_b \end{pmatrix}\begin{pmatrix} \ddot{x}_p \\ \ddot{x}_b \end{pmatrix} + \begin{pmatrix} c_2 & -c_2 \\ -c_2 & c_1 + c_2 \end{pmatrix}\begin{pmatrix} \dot{x}_p \\ \dot{x}_b \end{pmatrix} + \begin{pmatrix} k_2 & -k_2 \\ -k_2 & k_1 + k_2 \end{pmatrix}\begin{pmatrix} x_p \\ x_b \end{pmatrix} = \begin{pmatrix} -u \\ u + c_1\dot{x}_u + k_1 x_u \end{pmatrix}$$

(8)

Assuming that the initial condition is zero, take the Laplace transform of the above expression, and the transfer function between the platform and the disturbance input can be expressed as

$$G(s) = \frac{x_p(s)}{x_u(s)} = \frac{(k_1 + c_1 s)(k_2 + c_2 s)}{(k_1 + c_1 s + m_b s^2)(k_2 + c_2 s + m_p + P) + m_p s^2(k_2 + c_2 s)} \tag{9}$$

where $u(s)$ is the feedback of the bearing platform position, which can be written as $u(s) = Px_p(s)$, and P is a rational function of s.

The multistage shock absorption system is modeled in Adams as shown in Fig. 6. There are several obstacles and a step of 100 mm in the model. The dimensions of deceleration belts are 300×60 mm and 350×50 mm, and the length of the side of the square obstacle is 40 mm and 60 mm.

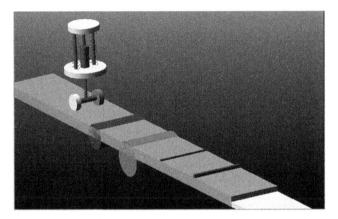

Fig. 6. Adams model of the multistage shock absorption system with obstacle

The closed-loop feedback controller is constructed by Simulink in Fig. 7. Input parameters are the height of the bearing platform off the ground and the speed of the wheel. The objective is to maintain the height of the bearing platform from the ground stable through dynamic adjustment of the driving module.

A PID controller is designed and optimized as the control parameter P in Eq. (9). The speed of the wheel is 5 m/s and the target height of the bearing platform is 1.5 m. The detection cycle of the system is 0.005 s.

The simulation results are shown in Fig. 8. When the maximum position error of bearing platform is 0.013 m, the driver module should have the following performance:$v_{max} \geq 1.1$ m/s, $a_{max} \geq 19$ m/s^2, $F_{max} \geq 1267$ N. Combined with the static analysis results, the load of the driving module changes no more than 400 N within the workspace. Therefore, in order to achieve the velocity and acceleration, the linear motor with air springs as auxiliary support equipment is selected as the driving module. The rated thrust of the linear motor is 500 N, peak motor thrust is 1500 N, and each air spring thrust is 250 N.

Using linear motor direct driving can eliminate the disadvantages of the conventional rotary-to-linear conversion mechanism, improve greatly the rapid response and control precision. To verify the effectiveness of the selected motor, the signal obtained by Gaussian white noise filtering is introduced as the random road excitation signal $x_r(t)$, its time domain expression is:

$$\dot{x}_r(t) = -2\pi f_0 x_r(t) + 2\pi n_0 \sqrt{G_0 v} w_t \quad (10)$$

where $n_0 = 0.1 \, \text{m}^{-1}$ means spatial reference frequency; w_t is white Gaussian noise; G_0 is road roughness coefficient; v is the speed of the wheel (m/s); f_0 represents the lower cutoff frequency of the filter.

The signal used in the simulation is B class road, that is, $G_0 = 64 \times 10^{-6} \, \text{m}^3$ and $u = 5$ m/s. Figure 9 is the excitation signal of B class road. And the simulation result is shown in Fig. 10. It is obvious that when the road disturbance is nearly 4 cm, the position error of the bearing platform is only 5 mm after vibration isolation control. Finally, we establish the whole model of YRob in Adams to test the dynamic property as shown in Fig. 11. The step height is 100 mm, the bearing platform weighs 150 kg, each linear motor weighs 20 kg, and the speed of the wheeled chassis is from 0 to 5 m/s in 2 s.

Since the linear motors are installed in different directions, in order to avoid exceeding the threshold, the force of the linear motors in motion is analyzed. The numbers of the linear motors are shown in the Fig. 12, and the calculation result is in Eq. (11). The effect coefficient of acceleration is significantly larger than that of gravity and is related to the dimensional parameters. The simulation result is satisfactory and verifies the effectiveness of the multistage shock absorption system to isolate the vibration.

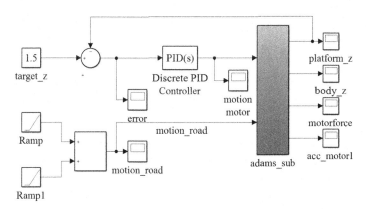

Fig. 7. The closed-loop feedback controller in Simulation

$$\begin{bmatrix} f_1 \\ f_2 \\ f_3 \\ f_4 \\ f_5 \\ f_6 \end{bmatrix} = \begin{bmatrix} 0.2mg - 0.36mx - 0.62my \\ 0.2mg - 0.36mx + 0.62my \\ 0.2mg + 0.72mx \\ 0.2mg - 0.36mx - 0.62my \\ 0.2mg - 0.36mx + 0.62my \\ 0.2mg + 0.72mx \end{bmatrix} \quad (11)$$

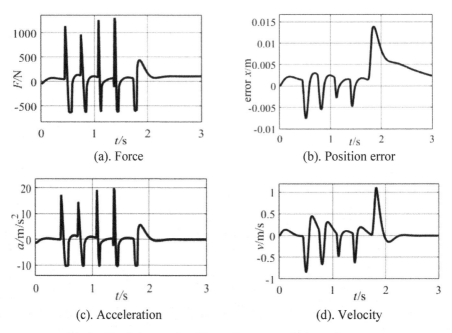

(a). Force

(b). Position error

(c). Acceleration

(d). Velocity

Fig. 8. Simulation results of the multistage shock absorption system

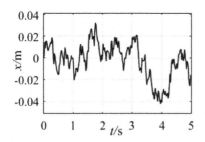

Fig. 9. Excitation signal of B class road

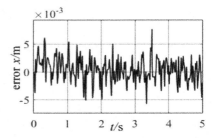

Fig. 10. Excitation signal response error

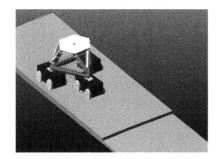

Fig. 11. The whole modle of YRob

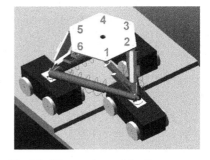

Fig. 12. The numbers of the linear motors

5   Conclusion

This paper presents a new mobile parallel robot named YRob with dynamic stability property. The robot employs three wheeled chassis and the attitude-adjustment mechanism as the driving units. The AM adopts the 6-SPU configuration and the dimensional parameters are optimized by using the motion/force transmission performance index. Both the AM and the wheeled chassis constitute a multistage shock absorption system, which can achieve wide range movement and vibration isolation. The two inverse kinematic solutions of the robot are calculated and the PID controller is designed to reduce position error. The linear motor is selected as the driving module to achieve the ability of quick response. Finally, through the random pavement response simulation and the whole robot simulation, the effectiveness of the structure design and the control method is verified.

In the future, the redundant motion assignment scheme and adaptive robust controller will be investigated to improve the response ability of the robot.

Acknowledgments. . This work was supported by the National Key R&D Program of China under Grant 2019YFA0706701 and by the National Natural Science Foundation of China under Grants 91948301 and 51922057.

References

1. Xie, F.G., Liu, X.-J., Wu, C., Zhang, P.: A novel spray painting robotic device for the coating process in automotive industry. Proc. Inst. Mech. Eng. Part C: J. Mech. Eng. Sci. **229**(11), 2081–2093 (2015)
2. Chen, X., Liu, X.-J., Xie, F.G.: Screw theory based singularity analysis of lower-mobility parallel robots considering the motion/force transmissibility and constrainability. Math. Probl. Eng. **2015**, 1–11 (2015)
3. Xie, Z.H., Xie, F.G., Liu, X.J., Wang, J.S., Mei, B.: Tracking error prediction informed motion control of a parallel machine tool for high-performance machining. Int. J. Mach. Tools. Manuf. **164**, 103714 (2021)
4. Wang, J.S., Liu, X.-J., Wu, C.: Optimal design of a new spatial 3-DOF parallel robot with respect to a frame-free index. Sci. China. Ser. E. Technol. Sci. **52**(4), 986–999 (2009)
5. Hu, Y., Zhang, J., Wan, Z., Lin, J.: Design and analysis of a 6-DOF mobile parallel robot with 3 limbs. J. Mech. Sci. Technol. **25**(12), 3215–3222 (2011)
6. Horin, P.B., Djerassi, S., Shoham, M., et al.: Dynamics of a six degrees-of-freedom parallel robot actuated by three two-wheel carts. Multibody Syst. Dyn. **16**(2), 105–121 (2006)
7. Tahmasebi, F., Tsai, L.W.: Closed-form direct kinematics solution of a new parallel minimanipulator. J. Mech. Des. **116**(4), 1141–1147 (1994)
8. Ben-Horin, R., Shoham, M., Djerassi, S.: Kinematics, dynamics and construction of a planarly actuated parallel robot. Robot. Comput. Integr. Manuf. **14**(2), 163–172 (1998)
9. Liu, X.-J., Gong, Z., Xie, F.G., Shentu, S.Z.: Kinematics analysis and motion control of a mobile robot driven by three tracked vehicles. In: ASME 2018 International Design Engineering Technical Conferences and Computers and Information in Engineering Conference, pp. V05AT07A068-V05AT07A068 (2018)
10. Shentu, S.Z., Xie, F.G., Liu, X.-J., Gong, Z.: Motion Control and Trajectory Planning for Obstacle Avoidance of the Mobile Parallel Robot Driven by Three Tracked Vehicles. Robotica. **39**, 1–14 (2020)

11. Wang, J.S., Wu, C., Liu, X.-J.: Performance evaluation of parallel manipulators: Motion/force transmissibility and its index. Mech. Mach. Theory **45**(10), 1462–1476 (2010)
12. Bonev, I.A.: Geometric Analysis of Parallel Mechanisms. Université Laval, Canada (2002)

Gait Design and Foot Trajectory Planning for a Wall-Climbing Robot with Spiny Toes

Shuyuan Shi[1,2] 📷, Shengchang Fang[1,2] 📷, Xuan Wu[1(✉)] 📷, and Xiaojie Wang[1] 📷

[1] Institute of Intelligent Machines, Hefei Institutes of Physical Science, Chinese Academy of Sciences, Hefei 230031, China
xwu@iamt.ac.cn
[2] University of Science and Technology of China, Hefei 230026, China

Abstract. This paper proposes a foot trajectory planning strategy for a wall-climbing robot (WCR) by introducing a detaching angle, a pause and a backswing movement of spiny toes into the locomotion, allowing easy detachment of the spines and the surface. Foot placement positions are found and optimized via an off-line search algorithm which yields the most body motion for per period with stable locomotion. Relevant coordinates and joint angles are obtained from the forward and the inverse kinematics through the screw theory. Furthermore, the gait is designed for the forward motion and the backward motion based on a quadrupedal trot, with a phase difference to assure a full contact of the feet with the wall. Results of the experiments reveal that the prototype WCR implemented with the planning of the gait and the foot trajectories can achieve speeds up to 125 mm/s on a vertical rough wall with stable forward and backward locomotion.

Keywords: Foot trajectory · Gait design · Climbing robot · Spiny toe

1 Introduction

WCRs developed for accomplishing tasks on steep slopes or cliffs have shown specific applications in search-and-rescue, space exploration, and reconnaissance, etc. Since most natural and man-made surfaces are rough and dusty, WCRs employing spiny toes with attachment mechanisms inspired by animals such as insects and squirrels have been investigated extensively [1–6]. WCRs based on spine adhesion mechanism are different from regular WCRs because they need efficient gait design and foot trajectory planning for the spiny toepads in order to climb steadily on the rough and uneven walls. In general, there are two types of gaits designed for spiny climbing robots: the quasi-static gait and the dynamic gait. The quasi-static gait, which was designed to maintain the mass center of the devices within the convex hull of a tripod of legs [7], was operated on early WCRs with spiny toes such as RiSE V1 and RiSE V2 [1, 2]. However, in these cases the stability was achieved at the cost of slow speed maneuvering. Later, RiSE V3 was built incorporated with a dynamic gait called half-bound-half-crawl gait to gain a faster movement speed than previous designs [3]. With this gait panning strategy the quadruped WCR was capable of climbing dynamically without pitching back [3]. Zhu et al. [4] developed

© Springer Nature Switzerland AG 2021
X.-J. Liu et al. (Eds.): ICIRA 2021, LNAI 13015, pp. 825–835, 2021.
https://doi.org/10.1007/978-3-030-89134-3_75

a diagonal symmetric gait (a trot) for a gecko-inspired WCR on the basis of the GPL (gecko-inspired mechanism with a pendular waist and linear legs) model. As for this gait planning, the legs on the same diagonal of the WCR move in synchrony while the waist joints move along a trajectory planned through Hermite interpolation method. Later, the same research group performed a sinusoidal waist trajectory based on the GPL model on a newly developed WCR called DracoBot, which had lower energy consumption [5]. However, their research work mainly focused on the trajectory planning of the waist joint rather than the foot. Ji et al. [6], on the other hand, developed a WCR utilizing flexible pads with claws and planned two foot trajectories with detaching angles (angles formed by wall surfaces and tangents of foot trajectories during the detachment) of 68° and 20° respectively. The robot was able to climb on rough vertical surfaces with a stable speed in a dynamic diagonal gait or a quasi-static triangle gait.

In this study, we proposed a gait design and foot trajectory planning for a quadruped WCR with spiny toes to achieve fast and stable locomotion on vertical walls with various roughness surfaces. The diagonal gaits were designed for the forward and the backward motions of the WCR which had three-freedom legs and a flexible tail. A detaching angle, a pause phase and a backswing phase were introduced to the gaits to help the detachment of the feet with the wall surfaces. Corresponding foot trajectories which were adaptive to the attachment and the detachment mechanisms were proposed utilizing piecewise cubic polynomials. According to the kinematic modeling results derived from the screw theory, the optimal foot placement positions were examined in the simulation workspace and the obtained key parameters were implemented into a prototype WCR to verify the feasibility of the foot trajectories and the gait planning.

2   Kinematic Analysis

2.1   Forward Kinematics

The topology of the WCR model is presented (see Fig. 1 (a)). Here, l_b, w_b, l_t denote the body length, the body width, and the tail length, while a_i ($i = 0, 1, 2, 3$) represents the lengths of the connecting rods. θ_i ($i = 0, 1, 2$) defines the joint angles, and γ is the angle of the ankle. The reference coordinate system O-XYZ is fixed on O, the geometric center of the robot body.

The initiative posture of the left front leg, $g_{st}(\mathbf{0})$ is defined as an example (see Fig. 1 (b)), where the dash line depict an auxiliary, hypothetically active ankle joint. Here, d_c denotes the vertical distance between the knee joint and the ankle joint, while h_c represents the vertical distance from the ankle joint to the foot. Initiative values of θ_0, θ_1, θ_2, and γ are defined as 0.5π, 0, 0, and π. The position of the end-effector is treated as the position of the reference point C.

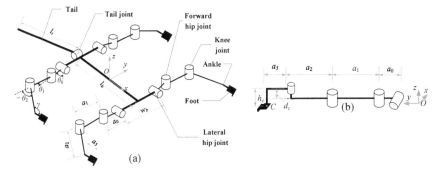

Fig. 1. WCR model. (a) Topology of the WCR. (b) Initiative posture of the left front leg.

The screw system [8] of the left front leg in the coordinate frame $\{O\}$ is

$$
\begin{cases}
S_0 = (1, 0, 0, 0, 0, -\frac{w_b}{2})^{\mathrm{T}} \\
S_1 = (0, 0, 1, a_0 + \frac{w_b}{2}, -\frac{l_b}{2}, 0)^{\mathrm{T}} \\
S_2 = (0, 0, 1, a_0 + a_1 + \frac{w_b}{2}, -\frac{l_b}{2}, 0)^{\mathrm{T}} \\
S_3 = (0, 0, -1, -a_0 - a_1 - a_2 - \frac{w_b}{2}, \frac{l_b}{2}, 0)^{\mathrm{T}} \\
S_4 = (0, 0, 0, 0, 1, 0)^{\mathrm{T}} \\
S_5 = (0, 0, 0, 0, 0, 1)^{\mathrm{T}}
\end{cases}
\tag{1}
$$

where $S_0 \sim S_3$ are screws of the lateral hip, the forward hip, the knee and the hypothetical ankle joint, while S_4 and S_5 are end effector screws.

The posture of the leg can be obtained from

$$
g_{st}(\boldsymbol{\theta}) = (\prod_{i=0}^{5} e^{\hat{S}_i q_i}) g_{st}(\mathbf{0}) = (\prod_{i=0}^{5} \boldsymbol{T}_i) g_{st}(\mathbf{0})
\tag{2}
$$

where θ represents the joint angles, while q_i represents the quantity of the rotational or the translational motion, with a value of $\theta_0 - 0.5\pi$, θ_1, θ_2, $\pi - \gamma$, a_3 or $d_c - h_c$ when i ranges from 0 to 5.

2.2 Inverse Kinematics

It is necessary to calculate joint angles when the coordinate figures of the end-effectors are given. Let (x, y, z) be the coordinate figures of the end effector in the Cartesian space. Equation (2) can be written in the form of

$$
\begin{cases}
\boldsymbol{T}_0^{-1} g_{st}(\boldsymbol{\theta}) = (\prod_{i=1}^{5} \boldsymbol{T}_i) g_{st}(\mathbf{0}) \\
\boldsymbol{T}_1^{-1} \boldsymbol{T}_0^{-1} g_{st}(\boldsymbol{\theta}) = (\prod_{i=2}^{5} \boldsymbol{T}_i) g_{st}(\mathbf{0})
\end{cases}
\tag{3}
$$

Thus the joint angles can be calculated as

$$
\begin{cases}
\theta_0 = \arcsin(\dfrac{h_c - d_c}{\sqrt{(y - \frac{w_b}{2})^2 + z^2}}) - \arctan(\dfrac{y - \frac{w_b}{2}}{z}) + \pi \\[2ex]
\theta_1 = \arccos(\dfrac{a_1 + a_2 c_2 - a_3 c_{2\gamma}}{r}) - \arctan(\dfrac{x - \frac{l_b}{2}}{-[a_0 - (y - \frac{w_b}{2}) s_0 + z c_0]}) \quad , \\[2ex]
\theta_2 = \arccos(\dfrac{A}{2a_1\sqrt{a_2^2 + a_3^2 - 2a_2 a_3 c_\gamma}}) - \arcsin(\dfrac{a_3 \sin\gamma}{\sqrt{a_2^2 + a_3^2 - 2a_2 a_3 c_\gamma}})
\end{cases}
\tag{4}
$$

where

$$
\begin{cases}
r = \sqrt{(x - \dfrac{l_b}{2})^2 + [a_0 - (y - \dfrac{w_b}{2}) s_0 + z c_0]^2} \\[2ex]
A = a_1^2 + a_2^2 + a_3^2 - 2a_2 a_3 c_\gamma - (x - \dfrac{l_b}{2})^2 - [a_0 - (y - \dfrac{w_b}{2}) s_0 + z c_0]^2
\end{cases}
\tag{5}
$$

with $s_0 = \sin\theta_0$; $c_0 = \cos\theta_0$; $c_\gamma = \cos\gamma$; $c_{2\gamma} = \cos(\theta_2 + \gamma)$.

3   Foot Trajectory Planning and Optimization

3.1   Foot Trajectory Planning

Foot trajectories are planned for the forward motion and the backward motion respectively. The foot trajectory of the forward motion can be divided into four sections: the attachment, the stance, the detachment and the swing (see Fig. 2 (a)), and a backswing is added to the foot trajectory of the backward motion (see Fig. 2 (b)). Here, β_{app} and β_{detach} denote the attaching and the detaching angle respectively. When a foot is in full contact with a wall surface, the spines are assumed to be embedded in the wall (see Fig. 3). Therefore, there is a strong resistance when the foot tries to pull the spines out of the wall. Theoretically, the end of the detachment foot trajectory should be along the spines (Trajectory A) to reduce the resistance. However, since the spines are in very small sizes, the bend can be neglected and a straight detachment foot trajectory (Trajectory B) is adopted. The trajectory forms a detaching angle β_{detach} of 30° and an attachment angle β_{app} of 90°.

Foot trajectories of the attachment section (see Fig. 2 (c)) and the detachment section (see Fig. 2 (d)) are planned via the interpolation of cubic polynomials [9] with respect to the coordinate system O_c-$X_c Y_c Z_c$ on the plane Π, which is formed by the middle section of the ankle and the central axis of the spine array. Define the start and the termination time of each phase as t_s and t_t, and the detachment foot trajectory (from B to B_p) can be obtained from

$$
\begin{cases}
[z_c(t_s), z_c'(t_s)]^T = [0, 0]^T \\
[z_c(t_t), z_c'(t_t)]^T = [h_d, v_d]^T \\
x_c(t) = z_c(t) \cot \beta_{detach} \\
y_c(t) = 0
\end{cases}
\tag{6}
$$

Here, h_a and h_d denote the vertical distance traveled by the foot during the attachment and the detachment respectively, while v_d represents the detaching speed. To lower the impact, velocities are set to be zero when the foot starts to touch or leave the wall [10].

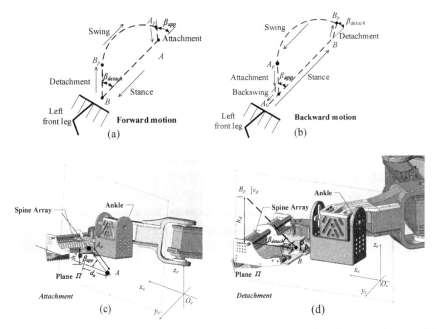

Fig. 2. Foot trajectory panning. (a) Foot trajectory of the forward motion. (b) Foot trajectory of the backward motion. (c) Planning for the attachment foot trajectory. (d) Planning for the detachment foot trajectory.

Let (x, y, z) be a point in the body frame $\{O\}$ with a coordinate figure (x_c, y_c, z_c) related to the local frame $\{O_c\}$. The conversion of the coordinate figures is as follows:

$$[x, y, z]^T = \boldsymbol{R}_{co}[x_c, y_c, z_c]^T + \boldsymbol{r}_{co}, \tag{7}$$

with $\boldsymbol{R}_{co}$ being the rotation matrix; $\boldsymbol{r}_{co}$ being the position vector from the point O_c to the point O. Thus the detachment foot trajectory with respect to $\{O\}$ can be derived from (6) and (7), while the attachment foot trajectory can be obtained in the same way.

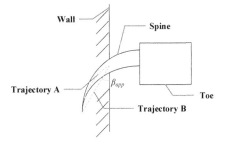

Fig. 3. A spine in full contact with the wall.

Foot trajectories of the other phases are planned directly in the body frame $\{O\}$ instead of $\{O_c\}$ via the interpolation of cubic polynomials in a similar way. However, the velocity v_d thus needs to be translated into the coordinate system $\{O\}$.

3.2 Trajectory Optimization

The foot trajectory needs to be optimized to satisfy the speed and the stability requirements. Thus the starting and the termination points of the stance foot trajectory, which determine the stride of a step, have to be chosen appropriately. Set θ_0 to be 0.5π. With θ_1 ranging from -0.5π to 0.5π and θ_2 from -0.7π to 0, the planar workspace containing all the possible foot placement positions on the plane xOy is given by (2) and is shown as the blue shaded region (see Fig. 4 (a)). Here, (x_{upper}, y_A) and (x_{lower}, y_A) are intersections of the shaded region and the vertical line, respectively denote the highest and the lowest positions the foot can reach.

Define (x_{max}, y_A) and (x_{min}, y_A) as the start point and the termination point of the foot trajectory of the stance phase, and $(x_{max}-x_{min})$ as the stride length of a step. We need to find out $[x_{min}, x_{max}]$ in $[x_{lower}, x_{upper}]$ and a corresponding y_A which yield the most body motion for per period, generating a motion speed as high as possible. Furthermore, the spine arrays of two feet on the diagonal of the body pierce into the wall at the start of the stance phase and remain at rest in the world frame but move in the body frame $\{O\}$ during the phase. Define λ as the angle formed by the spines and the x-axis. λ remains unchanged during the stance phase and is always equal to the angle formed by the middle section of the ankle (plane Π) and the x-axis at the start point (x_{max}, y_A) (see Fig. 5(b)). Therefore during the stance phase there exists

$$2F\cos\lambda - mg = ma, \tag{8}$$

where F is the force provided by a spine array, m is the mass of the robot and a is the acceleration of the body. Here, the value of λ needs to be as small as possible ($\lambda < 10°$) to prevent the spines from exerting excessive forces. In addition, a strip of flexible material is placed at the junction of the foot and the spine array, leading to the foot rotating around the reference point C during the stance phase while the array remains still. The angle formed by the foot and the spine array is defined as ξ. We need to reduce $\Delta\xi$ (the angle change of ξ during the stance phase, see in Fig. 4 (b)) to a value smaller than $20°$ to avoid the overmuch torsion of the flexible material at the foot. Thus y_A is chosen by

$$\underset{x_{max}-x_{min}}{Maximize} \rightarrow y_A$$
$$subject\ to \begin{cases} \lambda \leq 10 \\ \Delta\xi \leq 20 \end{cases}. \tag{9}$$

Here,

$$\lambda = \frac{\pi}{2} - \gamma - (\theta_1 + \theta_2), \tag{10}$$

$$\Delta\xi = \Delta(\theta_1 + \theta_2). \tag{11}$$

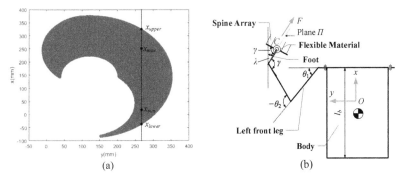

Fig. 4. Foot Trajectory Analysis. (a) Planar workspace. (b) Definitions of relevant parameters.

To find y_A, the shaded region is searched for a value y_B assigning a value as big as possible to $(x_{upper} - x_{lower})$. The algorithm starts at $y = y_B$, cycles through each value of y in the adjacent area, and through each potential value of x, calculating the joint angles according to (4) and obtaining λ and ξ. Finally, the y_A that satisfies (7) is determined.

4   Gait Design

The present gait design for the forward and the backward motion of a quadruped climbing WCR with spiny toes is based on a diagonal trot [11]. However, in a trot gait, there are only two phases and the legs change the phases simultaneously. Therefore, the robot would fall off the wall if a trot gait was directly applied on a climbing robot since all of the feet would be in the air during the phase changes. In addition, the gait should be adaptive to the structure of the spiny toes. Thus the gait needs to be improved.

4.1   Forward Motion

A gait is designed for the forward motion, where legs in the stance phase are represented as solid lines and legs in the attachment, the detachment or the swing phases are indicated by dashed lines (see Fig. 5 (a)). The schematic diagram of the forward climbing gait is also presented (see Fig. 5 (b)).

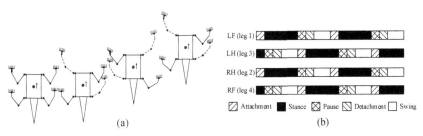

Fig. 5. Forward Gait. (a) Conceptual graph of the forward motion gait. (b) Schematic diagram of the forward climbing gait.

It can be found that the gait keeps at least two feet in contact with the wall at every moment by introducing a phase difference to ensure the stability of the locomotion since there is a transition stage before the phase change. The foot pauses on the wall surface right after the stance phase and remain at rest in the body frame $\{O\}$. On one hand, when leg 1 and leg 2 are at pause, the other two legs are in the attachment phase, and leg 1 and leg 2 will not start the detachment and leave the wall until the other two legs finish the attachment and enter the stance phase. Thus leg 1 and leg 2 in the detachment phase are driven forward together with the body by the other two legs. On the other hand, when leg 3 and leg 4 are at pause, the other two legs are at the start of their stance phases and provide support, therefore leg 3 and leg 4 move forward together with the body in the world frame. In these two cases, the movement of the legs provides an extra or an initial upward speed for the current or the following detachment, making it easier for the leg to pull the spines out. This also prevents the robot from pitching back to a certain extent since the front leg left at the wall surface hold the body in position. In addition, when leg 1 and leg 2 are in the attachment phase, the other two legs are at the final stage of the stance phase. Leg 3 and leg 4 drive the body upward altogether with the other two legs. Theoretically the upward speed generates a tendency to pull the spines out of the wall and resists the attachment of leg 1 and leg 2. However, the speed of the foot at the end of the stance phase is close to zero, therefore the upward speed brought by leg 3 and leg 4 is also close to zero and the movement has little effect on the attachment phase of leg 1 and leg 2.

4.2 Backward Motion

The conceptual graph (see Fig. 6 (a)) and the schematic diagram (see Fig. 6 (b)) of the backward motion gait is also presented here. Similar to the forward gait, a phase difference is also introduced here. Moreover, a backswing phase is added, which generates an upward burst of the body and brings the feet experiencing the other phases upward. When leg 3 and leg 4 are in the detachment phase, the other two legs are in the backswing phase. Theoretically leg 3 and leg 4 have fully left the wall surface when the swing phase starts. However in practice it is possible that leg 3 and leg 4 are still in contact with the wall at the initial stage of the swing phase. In this case the backswing of leg 1 and leg 2 helps leg 3 and leg 4 pull their spines out of the wall by providing an extra upward detaching speed since the backswing takes more time than the detachment. On the other hand, when leg 3 and leg 4 are in the backswing phase, the other two legs are at the end of the stance phase, remaining at rest on the wall in the world frame but moving upward in the body frame. Since the stance phase is followed by the detachment phase, the backswing of leg 3 and leg 4 provides an initial upward speed for the detachment of leg 1 and leg 2. Additionally, when two legs are in the attachment phase, the other two legs are in the stance phase. Thus the legs in the attachment phase are driven downward altogether with the body by the legs at stance, and the movement provides a downward speed for the attachment and helps the spines pierce into the wall since the tips of the spines are down bent.

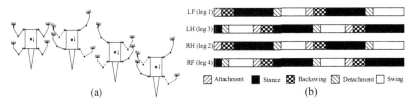

LF (leg 1)

LH (leg 3)

RH (leg 2)

RF (leg 4)

☑ Attachment ■ Stance ⊠ Backswing ◻ Detachment ☐ Swing

(a)   (b)

Fig. 6. Backward Gait. (a) Conceptual graph of the backward motion gait. (b) Schematic diagram of the backward climbing gait.

5 Experiment and Discussion

The optimized trajectory and the improved gait are operated on our prototype (see Fig. 7, and the parameters of the prototype are shown in Table 1.

(a)   (b)

Fig. 7. Experimental robot. (a) 3D structure of the robot. (b) Prototype.

Table 1. Parameters of the prototype.

Parameters	Symbols	Values	Parameters	Symbols	Values
Body length	l_b (mm)	288.4	Shin length	a_2 (mm)	100
Body width	w_b (mm)	136.54	Foot length	a_3 (mm)	41.62
Body height	h_b (mm)	30	Foot height	h_c (mm)	34.7
Tail length	l_t (mm)	300	Knee-ankle distance	d_c (mm)	29.9
Hip length	a_0 (mm)	53	Ankle angle	γ (°)	130
Thigh length	a_1 (mm)	100	Weight	(kg)	3

The experiments are carried out on a vertical rough sandstone wall to test the forward and the backward climbing ability of the prototype. In the forward gait (see Fig. 8 (a)), we set the detaching speed v_d to be 10 mm/s and the step height to be 10 mm to generate a relatively gentle movement since a violent movement would increase the overturning moment and may result in the robot pitching back and falling off the wall. However, in the experiment we find that the same parameters would not work for the backward gait (see Fig. 8 (b)) since the detachment could not be completed. Therefore, we gradually increase the detaching speed and the step height and it turns out that a v_d of 50 mm/s and a step height of 30 mm is appropriate. The values are big enough for the spiny toes to complete the detachment while the pitching back can be overcome by the prototype. During the climbing, the gravity helps the WCR hang on the wall via the down bent spines during the attachment of the feet and the wall surface. However, during the detachment the spines need to generate an upward speed to be pulled out of the wall and the gravity becomes resistance. Therefore, it is more difficult to complete the detachment than the attachment.

The step length of the forward climbing is 130 mm. As for the backward gait, in the backswing phase the foot travels a distance of 10 mm, and the backward step length is set to be 50 mm. Experiments of the forward climbing and the backward climbing are carried out respectively, where the prototype covers the distance of one meter. The average forward speed is about 125 mm/s and the average backward speed is about 22.7 mm/s, which is much slower.

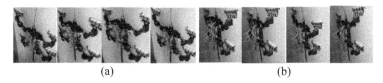

(a)   (b)

Fig. 8. Photographs of experiments. (a) Forward gait. (b) Backward gait.

6   Conclusion and Future Work

This paper proposed optimized foot trajectories and gait planning for a WCR with spiny toes which can achieve a trade-off performance between the speed and the stability of locomotion on vertical rough walls. The kinematics analysis was put forward and provided reference for the trajectory planning, where the stride length was maximized and the deflections of the ankle and the foot were limited to low values. Additionally, a detaching angle of 60° and a backswing phase were introduced to overcome the detachment difficulty caused by the foot structure. Moreover, the gait staggered the attachment and the detachment phases of different legs, maintaining at least two legs at the wall every moment and preventing the body from pitching back. Results of the experiments validated the feasibility of the proposed foot trajectories and the gait planning for the WCR, with evidence of a stable climbing with a faster speed up to 0.1 m/s.

Corresponding foot trajectory will be explored in the future for the WCR to realize a transition from the ground to the vertical wall. Further work will be carried out by including a feedback control strategy for the system.

Acknowledgment. This research was supported by the Key Research and Development Plan of Jiangsu Province (No. BE2020082-3) and Provincial Natural Science Foundation of Anhui (No. 2008085QE253).

References

1. Haynes, G.C., Rizzi, A.A.: Gait regulation and feedback on a robotic climbing hexapod. In: Robotics: Science and Systems II, pp. 97–104. Philadelphia, Pennsylvania, USA (2006)
2. Spenko, M.J., et al.: Biologically inspired climbing with a hexapedal robot. J. Field Robot. **25**(4–5), 223–242 (2008)
3. Haynes, G.C., et al.: Rapid pole climbing with a quadrupedal robot. In: IEEE International Conference on Robotics & Automation, pp. 2767–2772. Kobe, Japan (2009)
4. Zhu, P., Wang, W., Wu, S., Li, X., Meng, F.: Configuration and trajectory optimization for a Gecko Inspired climbing robot with a Pendular waist. In: IEEE International Conference on Robotics & Biomimetics, pp. 1870–1875. Qingdao, China (2017)
5. Wang, W., Li, X., Wu, S., Zhu, P., Zhao, F.: Effects of pendular waist on gecko's climbing: dynamic gait, analytical model and bio-inspired robot. J. Bionic Eng. **14**(2), 191–201 (2017)
6. Ji, A., Zhao, Z., Manoonpong, P., Wang, W., Chen, G., Dai, Z.: A bio-inspired climbing robot with flexible pads and claws. J. Bionic Eng. **15**(2), 368–378 (2018)
7. Holmes, R., Full, J., Koditschek, D., Guckenheime, J.: The dynamics of legged locomotion: models, analyses, and challenges. SIAM Rev. **48**(2), 207–304 (2006)
8. Man, C., Fan, X., Li, C., Zhao, Z.: Kinematics analysis based on screw theory of a humanoid robot. J. China Univ. Min. Technol. **17**(1), 49–52 (2007)
9. Shih, C.L.: Gait synthesis for a biped robot Gait. Robotica **15**(6), 599–608 (1997)
10. Zhang, F., Teng, S., Wang, Y., Guo, Z., Wang, J., Xu, R.: Design of bionic goat quadruped robot mechanism and walking gait planning. Int. J. Agri. Biol. Eng. **13**(5), 32–39 (2020)
11. Li, X., Wang, W., Wu, S., Zhu, P., Zhao, F.: The gait design and trajectory planning of a gecko-inspired climbing robot. Appl. Bionics Biomech. **2018**, 1–13 (2018)

Author Index

Printed in the United States
by Baker & Taylor Publisher Services